Federal Tax Handbook Quick Reference Card
2018 Tax Rates and Key Figures

D0568349

Single Taxpayers

Taxable Income	Amount of tax
Not over $ 9,525	10% of taxable income
Over $ 9,525 but not over $ 38,700	$ 952.50 plus 12% of the excess over $ 9,525
Over $ 38,700 but not over $ 82,500	$ 4,453.50 plus 22% of the excess over $ 38,700
Over $ 82,500 but not over $ 157,500	$ 14,089.50 plus 24% of the excess over $ 82,500
Over $ 157,500 but not over $ 200,000	$ 32,089.50 plus 32% of the excess over $ 157,500
Over $ 200,000 but not over $ 500,000	$ 45,689.50 plus 35% of the excess over $ 200,000
Over $ 500,000	$ 150,689.50 plus 37% of the excess over $ 500,000

Married Taxpayers and Qualifying

Taxable Income	Amount of tax
Not over $19,050	10% of taxable income
Over $19,050 but not over $ 77,400	$1,905 plus 12% of the excess over $19,050
Over $ 77,400 but not over $165,000	$ 8,907 plus 22% of the excess over $ 77,400
Over $165,000 but not over $ 315,000	$ 28,179 plus 24% of the excess over $165,000
Over $ 315,000 but not over $ 400,000	$ 64,179 plus 32% of the excess over $ 315,000
Over $ 400,000 but not over $ 600,000	$ 91,379 plus 35% of the excess over $ 400,000
Over $ 600,000	$161,379 plus 37% of the excess over $600,000

Married Taxpayers Filing Separate Returns

Taxable Income	Amount of tax
Not over $ 9,525	10% of taxable income
Over $ 9,525 but not over $ 38,700	$ 952.50 plus 12% of the excess over $ 9,525
Over $ 38,700 but not over $ 82,500	$ 4,453.50 plus 22% of the excess over $38,700
Over $ 82,500 but not over $157,500	$14,089.50 plus 24% of the excess over $ 82,500
Over $157,500 but not over $200,000	$ 32,089.50 plus 32% of the excess over $157,500
Over $ 200,000 but not over $ 300,000	$ 45,689.50 plus 35% of the excess over $ 200,000
Over $ 300,000	$ 80,689.50 plus 37% of the excess over $ 300,000

Heads of Household

Taxable Income	Amount of tax
Not over $ 13,600	10% of taxable income
Over $ 13,600 but not over $ 51,800	$1,360 plus 12% of the excess over $13,600
Over $ 51,800 but not over $ 82,500	$ 5,944 plus 22% of the excess over $51,800
Over $82,500 but not over $157,500	$12,698 plus 24% of the excess over $82,500
Over $157,500 but not over $ 200,000	$ 30,698 plus 32% of the excess over $157,500
Over $ 200,000 but not over $ 500,000	$ 44,298 plus 35% of the excess over $200,000
Over $ 500,000	$ 149,298 plus 37% of the excess over $ 500,000

Estates and Trusts

Taxable Income	Amount of tax
Not over $ 2,550	10% of taxable income
Over $ 2,550 but not over $ 9,150	$ 255 plus 24% of the excess over $2,550
Over $ 9,150 but not over $12,500	$1,839 plus 35% of the excess over $9,150
Over $ 12,500	$ 3,011.50 plus 37% of the excess over $12,500

2018 Unified Gift and Estate Tax Rates

Amount subject to tax	Amount of tax	Rate on excess
Up to $ 10,000	18% of amount transferred	
$ 10,000	$1,800	20%
$ 20,000	$3,800	22%
$ 40,000	$8,200	24%
$ 60,000	$13,000	26%
$ 80,000	$18,200	28%
$ 100,000	$ 23,800	30%
$ 150,000	$ 38,800	32%
$ 250,000	$ 70,800	34%
$ 500,000	$ 155,800	37%
$ 750,000	$ 248,300	39%
$ 1,000,000	$ 345,800	40%

Subject to the applicable exclusion amount for US citizens and residents.

Standard Deductions

Basic*

Single or married filing separate	$ 12,000
Married filing joint and surviving spouses	$ 24,000
Head of household	$ 18,000

Additional (for 65 or over and/or blind)

Unmarried (including head of household)	$ 1,600
Married or surviving spouse (whether or not joint return)	$ 1,300

* Limited to greater than $1,050 or the sum of $350 – plus earned income for individuals who can be claimed as a dependent by another taxpayer.

Standard Mileage Rates

Business use of auto	54.5¢ a mile
Charitable	14¢ a mile
Medical	18¢ a mile
Moving expenses	18¢ a mile*

* For tax years 2018-2025, the moving expense deduction is limited to members of the U.S. Armed Forces on active duty who meet certain criteria

Federal Tax Handbook Quick Reference Card
2018 Tax Rates and Key Figures

Itemized Deductions
Percentage Limitations

Medical expenses	7.5% of adjusted gross income (AGI)—floor
Personal interest	0%
Net nonbusiness casualty losses	10%* of AGI (after $100 per casualty limitation) — floor
Charitable contributions	60%** of AGI—ceiling on deductible amount
Miscellaneous itemized deductions	Suspended through 2025

* Only if attributable to a federally declared disaster
** Other limits apply depending on type of gift and/or recipient

Personal Exemption

Personal exemption is suspended for 2018-2025.

Alternative Minimum Tax

AMT rates on taxable excess (i.e., on alternative minimum taxable income (AMTI), less AMT exemption amount):

	AMTI threshhold	AMT rate
Individual, estate, trust*	$0 – $191,100	26%
	over $191,100	28%
Married filing separately*	$0 – $95,550	26%
	over $95,550	28%

* Tax rate on net capital gain and qualified dividend income is the same as for regular tax.

AMT Exemption Amounts		Phaseout range
Single or head of household	$70,300	$500,000–781,200
Married filing separately**	$54,700	$500,000–718,800
Joint filers or surviving spouse	$109,400	$1,000,000–1,437,600
Estate, trust	$24,600	$81,900–180,300

** Must also add the lesser of the following to AMTI: (1) 25% of the excess of AMTI over $718,800, or (2) $54,700

Corporations

Flat rate of 21%

Social Security Tax

FICA	Tax base	Rate	Maximum tax
Social Security	$128,400	6.2%	$ 7,960.80
Medicare			
Married filing jointly	$250,000 over $250,000	1.45% 2.35%	$3,625 no limit
Married filing separate	$125,000 over $125,000	1.45% 2.35%	$1,812.50 no limit
All other individuals	$200,000 over $200,000	1.45% 2.35%	$2,900 no limit

Capital gains and
qualified dividend income*—
Individuals, Estates & Trusts

Net short-term (held one year or less) **capital gain** is taxed at: ordinary income rates

Adjusted net capital gain (i.e., net capital gain plus qualified dividend income, minus certain specified types of long-term capital gain taxed at 28% or 25%; see below) is taxed as follows:

. . . the 0% tax rate applies to adjusted net **capital gain** up to $77,200 for joint filers and surviving spouses, $51,700 for heads of household, $38,600 for single filers, $38,600 for married taxpayers filing separately, and $2,600 for estates and trusts;

. . . the 15% tax rate applies to adjusted net **capital gain** over the amount subject to the 0% rate, and up to $479,000 for joint filers and surviving spouses, $452,400 for heads of household, $425,800 for single filers, $239,500 for married taxpayers filing separately, and $12,700 for estates and trusts; and

. . . the 20% tax rate applies to adjusted net **capital gain** over $479,000 for joint filers and surviving spouses, $452,400 for heads of household, $425,800 for single filers, $239,500 for married taxpayers filing separately, and $12,700 for estates and trusts.

Except the maximum tax on:

Unrecaptured section 1250 gain (attributable to real estate depreciation) is:	25%
Collectibles gain (on works of art, rugs, antiques, etc.) is	28%
Section 1202 gain (from the sale of small business stock eligible for partial exclusion from gross income) is:	28%

* Equals dividends from domestic corporations and qualified foreign corporations that meet specified holding period requirements. Exclusions may apply.

3.8% net investment income tax may also apply.

Self-Employment Tax

FICA	Tax base	Rate	Maximum tax
Social Security	$128,400	12.4%	$15,921.60
Medicare			
Married filing jointly	$250,000 over $250,000	2.9% 3.8%	$7,250 no limit
Married filing separate	$125,000 over $125,000	2.9% 3.8%	$3,625 no limit
All other individuals	$200,000 over $200,000	2.9% 3.8%	$5,800 no limit

3.8% Tax on Individuals'
Net Investment Income

Individuals with modified AGI (MAGI) over $200,000 ($250,000 for joint filers or surviving spouses; $125,000 for married separate filers) must pay the Net Investment Income Tax, which is 3.8% of the lesser of: (1) "net investment income" (interest, dividends, etc.), or (2) MAGI over these thresholds.

Get more out of your Federal Tax Handbook

The **Federal Tax Handbook** continues to be the premier source for today's federal tax law. This year's edition provides you with precise explanations of significant tax changes affecting you and your business, including the latest guidance on the Tax Cuts and Jobs Act.

But it's more than just a comprehensive tax resource.

Use it as a valued resource for your staff

Put this insightful advice and guidance on the latest tax topics and changes right at your employees' fingertips.

The Federal Tax Handbook offers:

- Detailed coverage of the latest tax legislation
- Income tax rates, estate, gift and excise tax rates, and Social Security tax thresholds
- Guidance on which forms to use to report transactions
- Extensive professional guidance based on the experience of our expert editorial team

Use it as a high quality premium for your clients

Did you know that you can customize the Federal Tax Handbook for your business? Start planning today to build your company's prestige by providing customized Federal Tax Handbooks to your employees or clients. You can add your logo, your contact information and office locations, or customize the entire cover with your organization's branding element.

Whether it's used as a resource for your employees or a quality premium for your clients, the Federal Tax Handbook is the best tax resource for all of your day-to-day tax questions.

Available in print and eBook.

Call **800.950.1216** or visit **tax.tr.com/fth2019** for multi-copy pricing.

Federal Depreciation Handbook

The **Federal Depreciation Handbook** from Thomson Reuters provides expert guidance on tax depreciation and other cost recovery issues to help tax practitioners make tax-efficient decisions and elections when an asset is placed in service. The Handbook also explains how to structure business property transactions to optimize federal income tax results when performing general tax planning or transactional consulting services.

Featured in the 2019 Handbook are the Tax Cuts and Jobs Act (TCJA) provisions that impact tax depreciation and related issues. The many new law provisions that are thoroughly addressed in this year's Handbook include:

- 100% first year bonus deprecation—which property qualifies, effective date and phaseout rules, and how to take maximum advantage.

- Section 179 increased deduction limits and expanded definition of qualified property.

- New advantageous depreciation rules for farm property.

- Revised depreciation rules for qualified improvement property and other real estate depreciation changes.

- Like-kind exchange rules that are now more restrictive.

The Federal Depreciation Handbook's TCJA coverage is integrated with its numerous quick-reference tables and charts, real life examples, and detailed tax compliance guidance to make it your all-in-one federal depreciation resource.

CHECKPOINT LEARNING

800.231.1860 | cl.tr.com

RIA® Federal Tax Review Self-Study CPE

Expert coverage of tax and accounting issues from Thomson Reuters

For more than 70 years, RIA has delivered accurate, insightful and accessible research and productivity-enhancing solutions to tax, accounting and corporate finance professionals.

Rely on RIA's must-have Federal Tax Review

RIA Federal Tax Review Course 2019

The RIA *Federal Tax Review 2019* CPE Course is comprised of three modules: Individual Taxes (8 CPE), Business Taxes (10 CPE), and Special Situations (9 CPE). A general refresher in federal taxation, this course will reinforce basic tax law interpretations to keep you up to date on the latest and most important changes for both the 2018 and 2019 tax years.

Grading fee of $95 for each module, with discounts available if you complete two or all three modules — see website for details.

Immediate RIA course access plus Online Grading

Download PDF version of this course at no charge

At cl.tr.com, click on the "Search Courses" link in the top menu and type "RIA" under Keywords.

> **Grading fees for these courses are included with the Premier and Premier Plus CPE Packages! Details on reverse.**

Online Grading for immediate results

The Checkpoint Learning Online Grading Center provides convenient access to self-study course exams, with real-time test results as soon as you complete your courses. Print CPE certificates with a simple mouse click—the Online Grading Center retains all of your certificates and exam results for retrieval at any time!

For more CPE information and to access the PDF download of this course or the online grading tool for this course, visit cl.tr.com.

RFBB038

The intelligence, technology
and human expertise you need
to find trusted answers.

the answer company™
THOMSON REUTERS®

CHECKPOINT LEARNING

800.231.1860 | cl.tr.com

Available for independent professionals and for firms!

Checkpoint Learning provides reporting, learning reminders and prompts, CPE compliance tracking, interactive online courses, downloadable self-study courses, online grading and much more!

ONLINE LEARNING

Checkpoint Learning CPE Packages

Our single-price comprehensive subscriptions are an industry first, bringing all of your CPE needs together: online and print-based self-study courses, webinars, CPE tracking and compliance monitoring, plus huge discounts on live seminars and conferences! Visit website for details on the Premier, Premier Plus, and Professional CPE Packages.

Checkpoint Learning Online Courses

More than 560 interactive online courses (2,500 credits of CPE training) are available exclusively on the Checkpoint Learning platform. Online course content meets the CPE requirements for CPAs in all 50 states with more than 30 ethics courses to meet mandatory CPA and EA ethics requirements.

Checkpoint Learning Webinars

Webinars cover the latest developments in tax, accounting, auditing, finance and more — all you need is a high-speed internet connection! Over 40 events to choose from each month — including full-day webinars offering 8 CPE credits.

CERTIFICATE PROGRAMS

Checkpoint Learning Certificate Programs are blended-learning programs that offer a new level of assurance in core knowledge or specialty knowledge, leading to an earned certificate that represents proven expertise in the key areas.

- Small Business Start-Up Certificate Program
- Compilation and Review Certificate Program
- Forensic Accounting Certificate Program
- Tax Fundamentals Certificate Program
- Tax Research Certificate Program
- Retirement Planning Certificate Program

Each program can be completed in three months to a year and is a great way to earn CPE and specialized technical expertise in key subject areas. Find out more at cl.tr.com/getcertificate.

IN-HOUSE TRAINING

In-House Seminars

On-site customized training on over 50 topics related to accounting and tax professions. This learning experience is custom-tailored to meet your needs, taught by highly rated instructors, and features current, relevant course content. For more information call 800.387.1120.

AuditWatch

AuditWatch has an intense focus on serving the audit and accounting profession with leading experts to train and consult with firms that provide auditing services. Call 800.775.9866 for more information.

LearnLive

LearnLive automates the creation, delivery, management and certification of accredited eLearning programs for professionals including accounting, legal and finance. LearnLive allows firms to record their own webinars and replay them for in-house training and customer viewing. Find out more at learnlive.com.

CPE Network®

CPE Network is a 90-minute video news-style format subscription featuring in-depth interviews with today's foremost industry experts delivering timely updates. You can opt to receive reports 11 times per year or quarterly. Learn more at cl.tr.com/getnetwork.

LIVE SEMINARS AND CONFERENCES

Gear Up Live Seminars and Conferences

A leading provider of tax and accounting education nationwide for more than 45 years, combining seminars and exciting conferences! Week-long conferences with great speakers are available in Las Vegas and Orlando.

AuditWatch Live Seminars

Staff level training programs available on-site or at public locations nationwide through AuditWatch University and TaxWatch University.

For more CPE information on all of these solutions and products, visit cl.tr.com.

To order additional copies of this publication, please call Toll Free 1-800-950-1216, ext. 1, or visit our Product Store at tax.tr.com/store.

2019 Federal Tax Handbook

The 2019 edition of the Thomson Reuters Federal Tax Handbook is designed to answer the tax questions and resolve the tax problems that arise in everyday business and personal transactions. It helps in preparing 2018 federal income tax returns and provides specific guidance about the tax consequences of transactions occurring in 2019. It is prepared by the professional staff that prepares Thomson Reuters' comprehensive federal tax service on Checkpoint, the Federal Tax Coordinator 2d, and is derived from that tax service.

The 2019 Federal Tax Handbook reflects all federal tax legislation passed by Congress to date of publication, including the Tax Cuts and Jobs Act (TCJA; P.L. 115-97, 12/22/2017), the sweeping tax reform law that entirely changed the tax landscape, and the Bipartisan Budget Act of 2018 (P.L. 115-123, 2/9/2018). It also reflects other key developments (such as new regulations, rulings, and revenue procedures) affecting 2018 returns and the 2019 tax year. The Handbook also includes Thomson Reuters' projections, based on inflation data, of what many inflation-adjusted 2019 tax figures will be, as IRS had not officially released these figures as of the date the book went to press.

caution: For highlights of later-enacted tax laws that affect the 2019 edition, consult the homepage dedicated to handbook users (tax.thomsonreuters.com/federaltaxhandbookupdates). The final 2019 tax figures, upon IRS's release, will be posted to the homepage as well.

The Handbook discusses and explains common tax problems in clear, concise, nontechnical language. And, where appropriate, the Handbook includes:

illustration: To clarify the tax rules and problems discussed, with simple, easy-to-follow examples.

caution: To warn of dangers that arise in particular tax situations and, where appropriate, to indicate what should be done.

recommendation: To provide specific, carefully studied guides to action which will keep taxes at a legal minimum.

observation: For professional analysis or commentary that is not part of cited authorities.

Forms to use: The Handbook explains which IRS forms to use to report transactions, pay taxes, make elections, etc. For a complete list of all official forms discussed, with references to the paragraph where they are discussed, see the "Forms" entry in the Topic Index.

References: The Handbook uses the following references:

. . . "Code Sec." references are to sections of the Internal Revenue Code.

. . . "Reg § " references are to sections of the federal tax regulations. "Prop Reg § " references are to proposed regulations, which are only cited in the text where IRS has indicated that "Taxpayers may rely" on them.

. . . Footnote references beginning with a single letter are to paragraphs in the Federal Tax Coordinator 2d and RIA's Analysis of Federal Taxes: Income. However, RIA's Analysis of Federal Taxes: Income doesn't include coverage of estate, gift and excise taxes. Accordingly, references to ¶Q-1000 *et seq.* (gift tax), ¶R-1000 *et seq.* (estate tax), and ¶W-1000 *et seq.* (excise taxes) are only to paragraphs in the Federal Tax Coordinator 2d. References beginning with numbers are to paragraphs in the United States Tax Reporter.

¶ 101. Highlights of the 2019 Edition.

The 2019 Thomson Reuters Checkpoint Federal Tax Handbook reflects federal tax laws enacted since publication of the 2018 edition in November of 2017, including the Tax Cuts and Jobs Act (TCJA; P.L. 115-97, 12/22/2017), as well as other key developments (such as new regulations, rulings, revenue procedures, and significant case law) affecting 2018 returns and the 2019 tax year.

Many of the 2019 figures listed below are projections by Thomson Reuters based on inflation data, as IRS had not released the official numbers at the time of publication. The TCJA, which changed the way in which these figures are calculated, contains a number of errors and ambiguities that have not yet been subject to a technical corrections bill. Where these issues arose in the context of inflation adjustments, we construed provisions in the way that seemed the most consistent with Congressional intent, reflecting our assumption that these ambiguities will eventually be resolved accordingly. While these projections reflect our best judgment, it is nonetheless worth noting that there are instances where the statute could be interpreted in a contrary manner. The final figures, when available, will be posted at tax.thomsonreuters.com/federaltaxhandbookupdates.

What's new in the 2019 Edition. The 2019 Federal Tax Handbook reflects the new tax developments listed below.

Chapter 1. Tax Rates and Tables.

• Changes and new items reflected on the 2018 IRS Form 1040 and related forms are noted. (¶105)

• The 2018 and 2019 income tax rates for individuals, trusts and estates are provided. (¶1100 *et seq.*)

• The 2018 and 2019 wage bases and rates for Social Security and Medicare taxes, for employers, employees (¶1108) and self-employed taxpayers are provided. (¶1109)

• The 2018 draft tax tables for individuals are provided. (¶1111 *et seq.*)

• The 2018 draft earned income tax credit table is provided. (¶1112)

• For tax years beginning after 2017, the corporate income tax rate is 21%, and the corporate alternative minimum tax (AMT) is repealed. (¶1113)

• For tax years beginning after 2017, tax bracket amounts and certain other tax parameters under the Code that are adjusted for inflation under Code Sec. 1(f)(3) will be adjusted in reference to chained CPI-U (Consumer Price Index for "all urban customers"). (¶1115)

• The 2.3% medical device excise tax doesn't apply to sales during 2018 or 2019. (¶1116)

• The annual fee on health insurance providers remains in effect for 2018 (but is suspended for calendar year 2019). (¶1117)

Chapter 2. Income—Taxable and Exempt.

• Generally effective for stock attributable to options exercised or restricted stock units settled after 2017, a qualified employee can elect under Code Sec. 83(i) to defer, for income tax purposes, recognition of the amount of income attributable to qualified stock transferred to the employee by the employer, for up to five years after vesting. (¶1216)

• Special "combat zone" benefits (such as the exclusion from income of certain combat pay) are extended retroactively to members of the armed forces performing services in the Sinai Peninsula of Egypt. (¶1222)

• For 2018, the optional standard mileage rate for valuing an employee's use of an employer-provided auto is 54.5¢ per mile. (¶1234)

• For 2018, an employee can exclude up to $260 a month ($265 in 2019) of employer-provided qualified parking benefits and the same amount for the combined value of transit passes and transportation in a commuter highway vehicle. (¶1245)

- The exclusion for qualified bicycle commuting reimbursements is suspended from 2018 through 2025. (¶1245)

- The exclusion for qualified moving expense reimbursements (except for certain members of the Armed Forces) is suspended from 2018 through 2025. (¶1246)

- For 2018, the maximum exclusion for employer-provided adoption assistance is $13,810 ($14,080 for 2019). AGI phase-out amounts for the two years are provided. (¶1252)

- For 2018, an employee's contribution to a health flexible spending account (FSA) through salary reduction contributions can't exceed $2,650 ($2,700 for 2019). (¶1267)

- Statutory breakpoints (as adjusted for inflation) are provided for the imposition of 15% and 20% capital gains/qualified dividend rates for 2018 and 2019. (¶1294)

- Certain exceptions to the life insurance transfer-for-value rule don't apply to life settlement transactions for transfers after 2017. (¶1348)

- For 2018, the income threshold for the definition of a "highly compensated employee" under the employer-owned life insurance rules is $120,000 ($125,000 for 2019). (¶1349)

- For 2018, the per-diem dollar threshold in computing the limits for the exclusion of benefits from long-term care insurance is $360 ($370 for 2019). (¶1368)

- Certain student loans that are discharged on account of death or total and permanent disability of the student during 2018 through 2025 are excluded from gross income. (¶1378)

- The exception from cancellation of debt (COD) income for certain discharges of qualified principal residence indebtedness was retroactively extended through 2017. Absent future legislation, this provision does not apply to 2018 and later years. (¶1388)

Chapter 3. Deductions — Expenses of a Business.

- New definitions of "publicly held corporation," "covered employee," and "applicable employee remuneration" apply to the rules governing the deduction limit for compensation paid to top officers. (¶1518)

- For amounts incurred or paid after 2017, employers may not deduct the expense of a qualified transportation fringe provided to an employee, and deductions are generally not allowed for transportation expenses to an employee for travel between the employee's residence and place of employment. (¶1523)

- For 2018, a high deductible health plan (HDHP) for medical savings account (MSA) purposes is one with an annual deductible of at least $2,300 and not more than $3,450 for individual coverage ($4,550 and not more than $6,850 for family coverage); in addition, the maximum out-of-pocket expenses can't exceed $4,550 for individual coverage ($8,400 for family coverage). (¶1527)

- For 2018 (and 2019), an HDHP is a health plan with an annual deductible that is not less than $1,350 for individual coverage and $2,700 for family coverage. Maximum out-of-pocket expenses for 2018 can't exceed $6,650 for individual coverage and $13,300 for family coverage (for 2019, $6,750 and $13,500, respectively). (¶1528)

- The maximum annual health saving account (HSA) deductible contribution is the sum of the monthly contribution limits, based on eligibility and health plan coverage on the first day of the month. The monthly limit is 1/12 of the indexed amount for self-only coverage ($3,450 for 2018; $3,500 for 2019) and for family coverage ($6,900 for 2018; $7,000 for 2019). (¶1528)

- For 2018, the standard mileage rate for business travel is 54.5¢. (¶1554)

- Business deductions for entertainment expenses are generally disallowed. (¶1555)

- The simplified per diem rates for post-Sept. 30, 2018 travel are $287 for high-cost areas and $195 for all other localities. For pre-Oct. 1, 2018 travel, these amounts were $284 and $191, respectively. (¶1566)

- For amounts paid or incurred after 2017, cash, gift cards, and other intangible personal property specifically don't qualify as employee achievement awards. (¶1575)

- For amounts paid or incurred after 2017, no deduction is allowed for attorney fees paid in connection with a sexual harassment suit subject to a nondisclosure agreement. (¶1586)

- Generally for amounts paid or incurred on or after Dec. 22, 2017, no deduction is allowed for: (i) any otherwise deductible amount paid or incurred to, or at the direction of, a government or specified nongovernmental entity in relation to the violation of any law or the investigation or inquiry by such government or entity into the potential violation of any law; or (ii) any settlement, payout, or attorneys fees related to sexual harassment or sexual abuse if such payments are subject to a nondisclosure agreement. (¶1594)

- For tax years beginning after 2017, taxpayers may deduct 20% of "qualified business income" (i.e., the "pass-through" deduction) from a partnership, S corporation, or sole proprietorship. (¶1595)

- Proposed reliance regs explain the operation and calculation of the Code Sec. 199A qualified business income (QBI) passthrough deduction. (¶1595)

- Proposed reliance regs define a specified service trade or business and the trade or business of an employee for purposes of the QBI passthrough deduction. (¶1597)

- Proposed reliance regs define the combined qualified business income amount for purposes of the QBI passthrough deduction. (¶1598)

- Proposed reliance regs explain "trade or business" aggregation rules for purposes of the QBI passthrough deduction. (¶1599)

- For tax years beginning after 2017, specified agricultural or horticultural cooperatives may claim a deduction for a percentage of the cooperative's qualified production activities income (QPAI), similar to the pre-2018 domestic production activities deduction (DPAD). (¶1601)

- The business expense deduction for lobbying local governments is repealed. (¶1614)

- The moving expense deduction is suspended from 2018 through 2025, except for certain moves by members of the Armed Forces. (¶1627)

- For tax years beginning after 2017, "small resellers" for purposes of the Code Sec. 263A uniform capitalization rules includes taxpayers with annual gross receipts of up to $25 million. (¶1640)

Chapter 4. Interest Expense—Taxes—Losses—Bad Debts.

- The documentary requirements under the earnings-stripping regs will apply only to interest issued or deemed issued on or after Jan. 1, 2019. (¶1709)

- For tax years beginning after 2017, subject to limited exceptions, a taxpayer's deduction for business interest is limited to the sum of: (i) the taxpayer's business interest income for the year, (ii) 30% of the taxpayer's adjusted taxable income for the year (but not less than zero), plus (iii) the taxpayer's floor plan financing interest (i.e., certain interest paid by vehicle dealers) for the tax year. (¶1710)

- For tax years beginning after 2017, taxpayers can't deduct any "disqualified related party amount" (certain interest or royalties) paid or accrued under a hybrid transaction or by, or to, a "hybrid entity." (¶1712)

- The aggregate amount of debt that can be treated as "acquisition indebtedness" is generally limited to $750,000 ($375,000 for a married individual filing a separate return) for each tax year from 2018 through 2025. (¶1730)

- The deduction for interest on "home equity debt" has been suspended from 2018 through 2025, but interest on a home equity loan used to buy, build or improve a home may be deductible. (¶1731)

- The treatment of mortgage insurance premiums as qualified residence interest was retroactively extended through 2017. Absent future legislation, this provision does not apply to 2018 and later years. (¶1733)

- The safe harbor for governmental homeowner assistance payments has been extended through 2021. (¶1747)

- From 2018 through 2025, the annual deduction for state and local property, income, etc. taxes is limited to $10,000. (¶1747)

- From 2018 through 2025, foreign real property tax may not be deducted, other than taxes paid or accrued in carrying on a trade or business or in an activity for the production or collection of income. (¶1747)

- From 2018 through 2025, a noncorporate taxpayer's "excess business" loss is disallowed and carried forward and treated as part of the taxpayer's net operating loss (NOL) carryforward in subsequent tax years. (¶1774)

- For 2018 through 2025, all deductions for expenses incurred in carrying out wagering transactions, and not just gambling losses, are limited to the amount of gambling winnings. (¶1778)

- The deduction for personal casualty and theft losses is generally suspended from 2018 through 2025, except for: a) personal casualty losses incurred in a Federally declared disaster; and b) nondisaster personal casualty losses to the extent of personal casualty gains. (¶1782)

- Special rules apply for designated personal casualty losses. (¶1783)

- For 2018 through 2025, theft losses are deductible only when attributable to a federally declared disaster. (¶1787)

- For losses arising in tax years beginning after 2017, the NOL deduction is limited to 80% of taxable income, and it generally cannot be carried back but can be carried forward indefinitely. (¶1819)

Chapter 5. Depreciation, Amortization, Property Expensing and Depletion.

- 3-year MACRS depreciation for all racehorses was retroactively extended through 2017. Absent future legislation, this provision does not apply to 2018 and later years. (¶1914)

- For property placed in service after 2017, machinery and equipment used in agriculture is part of the 5-year MACRS class. (¶1915)

- 7-year MACRS depreciation for motorsports entertainment complexes was retroactively extended through 2017. Absent future legislation, this provision does not apply to 2018 and later years. (¶1916)

- For property placed in service after 2017, the categories of qualified leasehold improvement property, qualified restaurant property, and qualified retail improvement property are no longer eligible for 15-year MACRS depreciation (39-year MACRS applies instead). (¶1918, ¶1920)

- For property placed in service after 2017, depreciation under the alternate depreciation system (ADS) is required for any nonresidential real property, residential rental property and qualified improvement property held by an electing real property trade or business. Depreciation under the ADS is also required of any MACRS property with a recovery period of 10 years or more that is held by a farm business that makes a similar election. (¶1930)

- For property placed in service after 2017, the ADS recovery period for residential rental property is 30 years. (¶1931)

- Generally for property that is both (1) acquired and placed in service after Sept. 27, 2017, and (2) placed in service before 2027, bonus depreciation is increased to 100% (full expensing), with the phasedown generally deferred from 2018 to 2023. (¶1932)

- Proposed regs, on which taxpayers can rely, clarify the post-Sept. 27, 2018 placed-in-service-and-acquisition requirement that applies to 100% bonus depreciation and to other changes in the bonus depreciation rules. (¶1932)
- For property placed in service after Sept. 27, 2017 and before 2027, qualified film, television, and live theatrical productions are "qualified property." (¶1933)
- Proposed regs, on which taxpayers can rely, provide guidance as to how used property can qualify for bonus depreciation. (¶1934)
- For tax years beginning after 2017, the election trading bonus and accelerated depreciation for otherwise-deferred AMT credits is repealed. (¶1938)
- Bonus depreciation for certain property used in biofuel production was retroactively extended through 2017. Absent future legislation, this provision does not apply to 2018 and later years. (¶1939)
- For tax years beginning in 2018, the Code Sec. 179 expensing limit is $1 million ($1,020,000 for 2019). (¶1940)
- For tax years beginning in 2018, the investment-based phase-out level for Code Sec. 179 expensing is $2.5 million ($2,550,000 for tax years beginning in 2019). (¶1940)
- More generous Code Sec. 179 expensing election for qualified zone property generally was retroactively extended to property placed in service through 2017. (¶1941)
- The Code Sec. 179 expensing limit for heavy SUVs is $25,000 for tax years beginning in 2018 ($25,500 for 2019). (¶1942)
- For property placed in service after 2017, any computer or peripheral equipment except those owned or leased by the taxpayer, and used exclusively at the taxpayer's regular business establishment, is no longer "listed property." (¶1946)
- Regular (as opposed to bonus first-year) depreciation and expensing limits for autos, trucks and vans placed in service in 2018 are provided. (¶1951)
- The $8,000 increase for "qualified property" in the first-year depreciation cap for passenger autos is extended, effective for property both acquired and placed in service after Sept. 27, 2017 and before 2027. (¶1952)
- Autos, trucks and vans leased in 2018 are subject to revised income inclusion amounts. (¶1954)
- Expensing for certain film, TV, and qualified theater production costs was retroactively extended through 2017. For 100% bonus depreciation, see ¶1933. (¶1961)
- The energy efficient commercial building property deduction was retroactively extended through 2017. Absent future legislation, this provision does not apply to 2018 and later years. (¶1961)

Chapter 6. Charitable Contributions—Medical Expenses—Alimony—Other Nonbusiness Deductions.

- For cash contributions made in 2018 through 2025, the 50% limitation under Code Sec. 170(b) for an individual's cash contributions to public charities and certain private foundations is increased to 60%. (¶2100)
- The amounts of benefits received by charitable donors that are considered to be inconsequential have increased for 2018 and 2019. (¶2104)
- For contributions made in tax years beginning after 2017, no charitable deduction is allowed for any payment to an institution of higher education in exchange for which the taxpayer receives the right to buy tickets or seating at an athletic event. (¶2104)
- The Tax Court held that a long-term lessee of buildings couldn't contribute a facade conservation easement. (¶2114)
- Certain charitable deduction limitations are suspended for individuals making "qualifying charitable contributions" for relief efforts in the Hurricane Harvey, Irma, and

Maria disaster areas, and for relief efforts in the California wildfire disaster area. (¶2123)

• Certain charitable deduction limitations are suspended, and special carryover rules are provided, for corporations making "qualifying charitable contributions" for relief efforts in the Hurricane Harvey, Irma, and Maria disaster areas, as well as the California wildfire disaster area. (¶2131)

• Final charitable contribution substantiation/reporting regs include variety of new rules. (¶2135 et seq)

• For 2018, the "floor" on medical expense deductions is 7.5% (10% after 2018). (¶2140)

• The maximum premiums paid for a qualified long-term care insurance contract, deductible as a medical expense, have increased for 2018 and 2019. (¶2145)

• For 2018, the mileage rate for use of a car for qualified medical transportation is 18¢ per mile. (¶2148)

• For any divorce or separation agreement that's executed after 2018, or executed on or before that date but modified thereafter, the alimony-paying spouse won't be able to deduct the payments, and the alimony-receiving spouse won't include them in gross income. (¶2152)

• IRS has said that it will issue regs clarifying that Code Sec. 682, which was repealed by the Tax Cuts and Jobs Act, will generally continue to apply with regard to trust income payable to a former spouse who was divorced or legally separated under a divorce or separation instrument executed before 2019. (¶2152)

Chapter 7. Education—Tax Credits, Exclusions, Deductions—ABLE Accounts.

• The Lifetime Learning credit phases out over higher levels of modified AGI for 2019 as compared to 2018. (¶2203)

• Beginning in 2018, "qualified higher education expenses" for qualified tuition program (QTP) purposes include up to $10,000 per beneficiary per tax year for expenses for tuition in connection with enrollment or attendance at an elementary or secondary public, private, or religious school. (¶2210)

• The higher education exclusion for savings bond income phases out over higher levels of modified AGI for 2019 as compared to 2018. (¶2218)

• The deduction for interest paid on qualified higher education loans phases out at higher levels of modified AGI for 2019 as compared to 2018. (¶2220)

• For 2018 and 2019, the maximum teachers' out-of-pocket classroom-related expenses is $250. (¶2224)

• The deduction for higher education expenses was retroactively extended through 2017. Absent future legislation, this provision does not apply to 2018 and later years. (¶2225)

• For 2018 and 2019, the amount of aggregate contributions from all taxpayers that a qualified ABLE account may receive is $15,000. (¶2226)

• For 2018 through 2025, after the general dollar limit for ABLE account contributions is reached, an ABLE account's designated beneficiary may contribute, subject to a number of limitations, an additional amount, up to the lesser of (a) the beneficiary's compensation for the tax year, or (b) the federal poverty line for a one-person household. (¶2226)

Chapter 8. Tax Credits.

• The railroad track maintenance credit was retroactively extended through 2017. Absent future legislation, this provision does not apply to 2018 and later years. (¶2301)

• The general business credit limitation for a corporation is applied by treating the corporation as having a minimum tax of zero, negating the corporate AMT (repealed after 2017) as a limit on allowable business credits for corporations. (¶2302)

• For amounts paid or incurred after 2017, the rehabilitation credit is no longer two-tiered. A single 20% credit is allowed over a 5-year period. (¶2307)

- Each component of the business energy credit for which a 30% energy percentage can be claimed (i.e. fiber optic solar energy property, non-fiber optic solar energy property, qualified fuel cell property, and qualified small wind property) is subject to a phaseout for property the construction of which begins after 2019. Notwithstanding the phaseouts, each type of property must be placed in service before 2024. (¶2310)

- The carbon sequestration credit has been restructured to account for both carbon dioxide and carbon oxide with the amount of credit based, in part, on whether carbon oxide was captured before or after Feb. 9, 2018. (¶2314)

- The second generation biofuel producer credit was retroactively extended through 2017. Absent future legislation, this provision does not apply to 2018 and later years. (¶2318)

- For 2018, a credit for rehabilitation expenditures is allowed only if, during any 24-month period, the expenditures are the greater of: (i) 20% of the building's adjusted basis, or (ii) $6,800 ($7,000 for 2019). (¶2320)

- For 2018, the refined coal credit is $7.03 per ton of refined credit coal, with no phaseout. (¶2324)

- The empowerment zone employment credit was retroactively extended through 2017. Absent future legislation, this provision does not apply to 2018 and later years. (¶2325)

- The Indian employment tax credit was retroactively extended through 2017. Absent future legislation, this provision does not apply to 2018 and later years. (¶2326)

- The orphan drug credit is reduced to 25% of qualified clinical expenses, and taxpayers may elect to take a reduced credit in lieu of reducing otherwise allowable deductions. (¶2328)

- For 2018, the small employer health insurance credit is reduced if the average annual full-time wages per employee were more than $26,800 ($27,100 for 2019). (¶2332)

- The credit for biodiesel and renewable diesel was retroactively extended through 2017. Absent future legislation, this provision does not apply to 2018 and later years. (¶2333)

- The credit for energy-efficient new homes was retroactively extended through 2017. Absent future legislation, this provision does not apply to 2018 and later years. (¶2334)

- The new employer-paid family and medical leave credit for 2018 and 2019 is up to 12.5% of the amount of wages paid to qualifying employees during any period they're on family and medical leave if the rate of payment is at least 50% of the wages normally paid to an employee, up to maximum of 12 weeks of leave for any employee during the tax year. (¶2336)

- The maximum amount of the earned income tax credit (EITC) and the credit's AGI-based phaseout thresholds have increased for 2018 and 2019. (¶2338)

- Certain individuals affected by Hurricane Harvey, Irma, or Maria, and by California wildfires, may be able to use the amount of the preceding tax year's earned income in computing the EITC. (¶2339)

- For 2018, the maximum amount of investment income that can be received for EITC purposes is $3,500 ($3,600 for 2019). (¶2341)

- For the premium tax credit, an eligible employer-sponsored plan is "affordable" if the part of the annual premium that an employee must pay for self-only coverage is 9.56% or less of the taxpayer's household income for the 2018 plan year (9.86% or less for the 2019 plan year). (¶2344)

- For 2018, the adoption expense credit is $13,810 ($14,080 for 2019). (¶2349)

- For 2018 through 2025, a "partial" $500 credit is available for each dependent of the taxpayer who is a U.S. citizen, national or resident, other than a qualifying child. (¶2350)

- For 2018 through 2025, the child tax credit is increased to $2,000, and the credit phaseout thresholds are increased. (¶2350)

- For 2018 through 2025, the refundable portion of the child tax credit for any qualifying child is limited to $1,400. (¶2351)

- The nonbusiness energy property credit was retroactively extended through 2017. Absent future legislation, this provision does not apply to 2018 and later years. (¶2353)

- The new qualified fuel cell motor credit was retroactively extended through 2017. Absent future legislation, this provision does not apply to 2018 and later years. (¶2355)

- The alternative fuel vehicle refueling property credit was retroactively extended through 2017. Absent future legislation, this provision does not apply to 2018 and later years. (¶2356)

- The credit for 2-wheeled electric plug-in vehicles was retroactively extended through 2017. Absent future legislation, this provision does not apply to 2018 and later years. (¶2357)

- The AGI amounts used in computing the "saver's" credit for elective deferrals and IRA contributions have increased for 2018 and 2019. (¶2358)

- For amounts contributed in tax years beginning after Dec. 22, 2017 and before 2026, amounts contributed to an ABLE account by the account's designated beneficiary are eligible for the saver's credit. (¶2359)

- For tax years beginning after 2017 and before 2022, a corporation's minimum tax credit (MTC) (1) may offset regular tax liability for any tax year, and (2) is refundable for any tax year beginning after 2017 and before 2022 in an amount equal to 50% (100% for tax years beginning in 2021) of the excess MTC for the tax year, over the amount of the credit allowable for the year against regular tax liability. (¶2360)

- The authority to issue various tax-credit and direct pay bonds is repealed. (¶2361)

- The possessions tax credit for American Samoa was retroactively extended through 2017. Absent future legislation, this provision does not apply to 2018 and later years. (¶2362)

- For purposes of the foreign tax credit limitation, there are now additional separate categories for "global intangible low-taxed income" and "foreign branch income." (¶2366)

- For purposes of the foreign tax credit, an 80% "deemed paid" foreign tax credit is available for amounts included in the U.S. shareholder's income as global intangible low-taxed income (GILTI). (¶2369)

- For tax years beginning after 2017 and before 2028, a taxpayer may, with respect to pre-2018 unused overall domestic loss, elect to recapture up to 100% of its U.S. source income for the tax year. (¶2367)

- A 10% corporate U.S. shareholder of a "specified 10% owned foreign corporation" may generally deduct 100% of the foreign-source portion of a dividend received from the specified 10% owned foreign corporation, and the deemed-paid credit under Code Sec. 902 no longer applies. A domestic corporation that is a U.S. shareholder of a controlled foreign corporation (CFC) may still claim a deemed-paid credit, but this credit is limited to 80% of foreign taxes paid with respect to global intangible low-taxed income. (¶2369)

Chapter 9. Sales and Exchanges—Tax-Free Exchanges—Basis.

- Generally for tax years beginning after 2017, an accrual basis seller reports gain or loss not later than the year in which the income is taken into account for financial reporting purposes. (¶2407)

- For exchanges completed after 2017 (subject to transition rules), like-kind exchange treatment is limited to exchanges of real property. (¶2417)

- Gains invested in a "Qualified Opportunity Fund" can be temporarily deferred and, if the investment in the Fund is held for 10 years, permanently excluded. (¶2429)

- Each population census tract in Puerto Rico that is a low-income community is considered to be certified and designated as a Qualified Opportunity (QO) Zone. (¶2429)

- IRS issued a complete list of all population census tracts it has designated as QO Zones. (¶2429)
- Retroactively effective for transactions entered into after Aug. 25, 2009, in determining the basis of a life insurance or annuity contract, no adjustment is made for mortality, expense, or other reasonable charges incurred under the contracts. (¶2473)
- For business autos for which the optional business standard mileage rate is used, depreciation is considered to have been allowed at a rate of 25¢ for 2018. (¶2475)
- For distributions after 2017, a deduction is allowed for the foreign-source portion of the dividend, if a corporation that is a "U.S. shareholder" of a 10% owned specified foreign corporation receives a dividend from the foreign corporation. (¶2495)

Chapter 10. Capital Gains and Losses — Section 1231 — Depreciation Recapture.

- For 2018 and 2019, statutory breakpoints (as adjusted for inflation) are provided for the imposition of 15% and 20% capital gains/qualified dividend rates for noncorporate taxpayers. (¶2602)
- For dispositions after 2017, patents, inventions, models or designs (whether or not patented), secret formulas or processes are excluded from the definition of "capital assets." (¶2612 and ¶2615)
- For tax years beginning after 2017, partnership interests ("carried interests") received for the performance of substantial services in certain specified trades or businesses must be held for more than three years to qualify for long-term capital gains rates. (¶2657)

Chapter 11. Tax Accounting — Inventories.

- For 2018, three-year-average gross receipts of a business must be $25 million or less to be excepted from the general limitation on use of the cash method ($26 million for 2019). (¶2818)
- Generally for tax years beginning after 2017, the all-events test for any item of gross income isn't be treated as met any later than when the item is taken into account as revenue in an applicable financial statement (if the taxpayer has one for a tax year) or other financial statement specified by IRS. (¶2823)
- For tax years beginning after 2017, the deferral method of accounting for advance payments for goods and services has been codified. (¶2827)
- Accrual-method taxpayers may rely on prior guidance on deferral of advance payments until guidance on newly codified deferral rules is issued and becomes effective. (¶2827)
- Code Sec. 481 adjustments that are attributable to S elections revoked by certain corporations during the 2-year period beginning Dec. 22, 2017 are taken into account ratably over a 6-tax year period beginning with the year of change. (¶2840)
- IRS has updated automatic consent procedures for accounting method changes, including many occasioned by the Tax Cuts and Jobs Act provisions. (¶2842)
- IRS has updated automatic consent procedures for accounting method changes made to conform with FASB and IASB contract revenue recognition standards. (¶2842)
- For 2018, the three-year-average annual gross receipts of a business must be $25 million or less to be excepted from use of the percentage-of-completion long-term contract method ($26 million for 2019). (¶2845; ¶2849)
- For 2018, three-year-average annual gross receipts of a business must be $25 million or less to be exempt from mandatory inventory accounting ($26 million for 2019). (¶2857)
- Until IRS issues further guidance, it won't assert that construction contractors engaged in certain types of activities must maintain inventory accounts for their supplies. (¶2857)

Chapter 12. Withholding Tax on Wages and Other Income Payments.

• For stock attributable to options exercised, or restricted stock units settled, after 2017, withholding is required at the highest individual rate when stock subject to a Code Sec. 83(i) deferral election is included in income. (¶3005)

• For 2018 through 2025, when the exemption amount is zero, employees are entitled to a "withholding allowance" instead of an "exemption" for each item under Code Sec. 3402(f)(1). (¶3016)

• For 2018, an employee who could have been claimed as a dependent on someone else's return can't claim an exemption from withholding if his or her income exceeded $1,050 ($1,100 for 2019) and includes more than $350 (same for 2019) of unearned income. (¶3018)

• For 2018 and 2019, the threshold amount subjecting cash payments to domestic service employees (e.g., nannies) to FICA is $2,100. (¶3031)

Chapter 13. Individual's Tax Computation—Kiddie Tax—Self-Employment Tax—Net Investment Income Tax—Estimated Tax.

• For tax years beginning after 2017, an above-the-line deduction is allowed (with limits) for attorneys' fees and court costs relating to awards under SEC Act of '34 § 21F, a state law false or fraudulent claim meeting requirements of Social Security Act, §1909(b) or Commodity Exchange Act § 23. (¶3108)

• Miscellaneous itemized deductions subject to the 2%-of-AGI floor are suspended from 2018 to 2025. (¶3109)

• The standard deduction amounts for 2018 and 2019, which are almost double the amounts in prior years, are listed. (¶3110)

• IRS will issue proposed regs providing that the reduction of the exemption amount to zero won't be taken into account in determining whether a person is a qualifying relative. (¶3112)

• Personal exemptions (and personal exemption phaseout (PEP)) are suspended from 2018 through 2025. (¶3112)

• Stepchildren of a U.S. citizen, who haven't been adopted or lawfully placed for adoption, aren't dependents for the dependency exemption. (¶3113)

• From 2018 through 2025, the taxable income of a child attributable to earned income is taxed under the rates for single individuals, and taxable income of a child attributable to net unearned income is taxed according to the brackets applicable to trusts and estates. (¶3129)

• For 2018, the dollar thresholds for the optional methods of computing net earnings from self-employment are $5,717.38 and $7,920 (for 2019, $5,890.63 and $8,160). (¶3141)

Chapter 14. Alternative Minimum Tax.

• For tax years beginning after 2017, the corporate alternative minimum tax (AMT) has been repealed. (¶3200)

• For 2018, the inflation-adjusted amount used to determine the tentative minimum tax is $191,100 ($194,800 for 2019). (¶3201)

• For tax years beginning in 2018, the individual AMT exemption amounts are: $70,300 for unmarried individuals, $109,400 for married individuals filing jointly, and $54,700 (50% of the joint filing amount) for married individuals filing separately. (The corresponding 2019 amounts are $71,700, $111,700, and $55,850). (¶3203)

• For tax years beginning in 2018, the AMT exemption amount for estates and trusts is $24,600 ($25,000 for 2019). (¶3203)

• For 2018, the AMT exemption amount for a child subject to the kiddie tax is the lesser of $7,600 plus the child's earned income, or $70,300 (for 2019, these amounts are $7,750 and $71,700). (¶3204)

Chapter 15. Corporations—Accumulated Earnings Tax—Personal Holding Companies—Consolidated Returns—Estimated Tax—S Corporations.

- Generally for contributions made after 2017, the term "contributions to capital" generally no longer includes: (i) any contribution in aid of construction or any other contribution as a customer or potential customer, or (ii) any contribution by any governmental entity or civic group (other than a contribution made by a shareholder as such). (¶3304)

- For tax years beginning after 2017, the 70% dividends received deduction is reduced to 50%, and the 80% dividends received deductions is reduced to 65%. (¶3306)

- For 2018 through 2025, subject to a limitation based on taxable income, domestic corporations are allowed deductions for foreign-derived intangible income (FDII) and global intangible low-taxed income (GILTI). (¶3312)

- For distributions after 2017, a domestic corporation that is a "U.S. shareholder" of a "specified 10%-owned foreign corporation" can, if certain requirements are met, deduct an amount equal to the foreign-source portion of any dividend from the specified 10%-owned foreign corporation. (¶3315)

- For amounts paid or accrued in tax years beginning after 2017, certain corporate taxpayers are subject to a tax on "base erosion payments" under Code Sec. 59A. (¶3316)

- For tax years beginning after 2017, qualified personal service corporations are subject to a flat 21% tax rate. (¶3330)

- For tax years beginning after 2017, a nonresident alien can now be a potential current beneficiary of an Electing Small Business Trust (ESBT). (¶3354)

- For S elections that are revoked by an "eligible terminated S corporation" during the 2-year period beginning Dec. 22, 2017, special rules govern both: (i) adjustments made under Code Sec. 481 that are attributable to the revocation; and (ii) the treatment of post-revocation distributions under Code Sec. 1371(f). (¶3376)

Chapter 16. Corporate Transactions—Organization—Distributions—Reorganization—Acquisitions—Liquidations.

- Long-term exempt rates for the Code Sec. 382 limitation are updated. (¶3554)

- For transfers after 2017, the "active trade or business exception" to Code Sec. 367 is eliminated. (¶3568)

Chapter 17. Partnerships.

- For partnership tax years beginning after 2017, in determining the amount of the partner's loss, the partner's distributive shares under Code Sec. 702(a) of partnership charitable contributions and taxes paid or accrued to foreign countries or U.S. possessions are taken into account; however, in the case of a charitable contribution of property with a fair market value that exceeds its adjusted basis, the partner's distributive share of the excess is not taken into account. (¶3734)

- IRS issued final regs to prevent corporate partners from avoiding gain in partnership transactions. (¶3744)

- For partnership tax years beginning after 2017, a partnership has a substantial built-in loss with respect to a transfer of a partnership interest if either: (1) the partnership's adjusted basis in the partnership property exceeds by more than $250,000 the fair market value of the property, or (2) the transferee partner would be allocated a loss of more than $250,000 if the partnership assets were sold for cash equal to their fair market value immediately after the transfer. (¶3768)

- For partnership tax years beginning after 2017, the partnership technical termination rule has been repealed. (¶3773)

- IRS privately ruled that the cessation of doing business as a partnership may result from a cessation of the business or from the fact that there is only one continuing partner in the partnership. (¶3773)

Chapter 18. Trusts—Estates—Decedents.

- The threshold amounts of taxable income of trusts and estates to which the 0%, 15% and 20% rates for capital gains and qualified dividends apply for 2018 and 2019 are provided. (¶3900)
- IRS has issued proposed regs regarding the creation of multiple trusts for tax avoidance purposes. (¶3911)
- IRS intends to issue regs clarifying that non-grantor trusts may continue to deduct expenses under Code Sec. 67(e) during tax years when miscellaneous itemized deductions are not available. (¶3919)
- For 2018, the exemption amount for a qualified disability trust is $4,150 ($4,200 for 2019). The beginning phaseout levels are also provided. (¶3926)
- Payments made from a modified trust were not allowed as a charitable deduction where the payments had been made possible only because of the trust modification. (¶3929)
- A charitable deduction for the excess of fair market value over adjusted basis of property contributed to a charity was not allowed. (¶3929)

Chapter 19. Exempt Organizations.

- For tax years beginning after 2017, "applicable tax-exempt organizations" are subject to a 21% excise tax on (i) remuneration exceeding $1 million paid to a covered employee, and (ii) excess parachute payments made to a covered employee. (¶4113)
- For tax years beginning after 2017, certain private colleges and universities with at least 500 tuition paying students, and with assets of at least $500,000 per student, are subject to a 1.4% excise tax on net investment income. (¶4114)
- For 2018, tax-exempt entities that fail to disclose their participation in prohibited tax shelter transactions are subject to a $100 per day penalty, not to exceed $52,000 (for 2019, $105 and $53,500). (¶4116)
- For 2018, agricultural or horticultural organizations may exclude annual dues up to $165 from unrelated taxable income ($169 for 2019). (¶4124)
- For amounts paid or incurred after 2017, unrelated business taxable income of a tax-exempt organization also includes any expenses paid or incurred for "qualified transportation fringe benefits," for a parking facility used in connection with "qualified parking," or for any "on-premises athletic facility," if certain requirements are met. (¶4124)
- Generally for tax years beginning after 2017, tax-exempt organizations with more than one unrelated trade or business generally must calculate their UBTI separately for each trade or business, such that losses from one may not be used to offset income of another. (¶4124)
- For tax years beginning after 2017, an exception to the tax on "excess business holdings" applies if certain requirements are met. (¶4129)

Chapter 20. RICs (Mutual Funds), REITs, REMICs, Banks and Other Special Corporations.

- For tax years beginning after 2017, the small life insurance company deduction has been repealed. (¶4211)

Chapter 21. Pension and Profit-Sharing Plans—401(k) Plans—Roth 401(k) Plans—IRAs—Roth IRAs—SEPs—SIMPLE Plans.

- For 2018, the limit on 401(k) plan elective deferrals is $18,500 ($19,000 for 2019). (¶4306)
- For 2018 and 2019, the catch-up contribution limit for 401(k), Code Sec. 457, and most Code Sec. 403(b) participants is $6,000. (¶4306)
- For plan years beginning after 2018, hardship distributions may be made from contributions to a profit-sharing or stock bonus plan cash or deferred arrangement; certain

employer nonelective contributions; employer matching contributions; and earnings on all of them. Also, failure to take an available plan loan no longer disqualifies an employee from receiving a hardship distribution. (¶4306)

• For 2018, the annual compensation limit on plan benefits and contributions under Code Sec. 401(a)(17) is $275,000 ($280,000 for 2019). (¶4308)

• For 2018, the compensation amount used in determining "highly compensated employee" status under the qualified plan coverage and eligibility rules is $120,000 ($125,000 for 2019). (¶4315)

• For 2018, annual additions under a participant's defined contribution plans cannot exceed $55,000 ($56,000 for 2019). (¶4317)

• For 2018, the annual benefit provided under a defined benefit plan cannot exceed $220,000 ($225,000 for 2019). (¶4317)

• Special increased limitations and relaxed repayment dates apply with regard to loans from qualified plans taken by individuals impacted by certain specified disasters. (¶4332)

• Relief from the 10% early withdrawal penalty tax and other temporary tax relief is provided to individuals impacted by certain specified disasters. (¶4333)

• For 2018, employees and self-employed individuals in an employer-maintained retirement plan may deduct up to $5,500 ($6,000 for 2019). (¶4340)

• For amounts treated as distributed in tax years beginning after 2017, the rollover period for certain "qualified plan loan offsets" is extended from 60 days to the tax return due date. (¶4348)

• For amounts paid in tax years beginning after 2017, wrongfully levied retirement plan account or benefit returned after 2017, and interest on such, is eligible for tax-free 60-day rollover treatment. (¶4349)

• The modified AGI limits for making contributions to Roth IRAs are provided for 2018 and 2019. (¶4357)

• For tax years beginning after 2017, under Code Sec. 408A(d)(6)(B), an IRA-to-Roth-IRA conversion can no longer be recharacterized (i.e., converted back to a regular IRA), and therefore cannot be reconverted. (¶4360)

• Relaxed rules apply to hardship distributions from, and rollovers to, Code Sec. 403(b) plans to victims of certain specified disasters. (¶4376)

Chapter 22. Farmers.

• For net operating losses (NOLs) arising in tax years after 2017, any part of an NOL that's a "farming loss" can be carried back to each of the two tax years preceding the tax year of the loss. (¶4503)

• From 2018 through 2025, the limitation of deduction of farm losses is suspended, and a broader "excess business loss" disallowance rule applies. (¶4504)

• For tax years beginning after 2017, the cash method may be used by farming C corporations (and farming partnerships with a C corporation partner) that satisfy a $25 million gross receipts test. (¶4510)

• For amounts paid or incurred for replanting, etc. after Dec. 22, 2017, and before Dec. 23, 2027 for citrus plants lost or damaged due to casualty, the costs may also be deducted by a person other than the taxpayer if certain requirements are met. (¶4520)

• IRS provided automatic consent for taxpayers to change method of accounting to deduct post-casualty citrus replanting costs. (¶4520)

• Most MACRS farming property placed in service after 2017 may be depreciated under the 200% declining balance method. (¶4523)

Chapter 23. Foreign Income—Foreign Taxpayers—Foreign Currency Transactions.

- Foreign earned income exclusion amounts are provided for 2018 and 2019. (¶4605)

- Limitations in high-cost localities for purposes of the exclusion for foreign housing costs are updated. (¶4606)

- For tax years beginning after 2017, individuals serving in combat zones are now excepted from the rule that an individual does not have a tax home in a foreign country for any period his abode is in the U.S. (¶4608)

- IRS has stated that individuals won't lose their status as bona fide residents of Puerto Rico or the Virgin Islands due to a dislocation of up to 268 days (effective beginning Sept. 6, 2017, and ending May 31, 2018) caused by Hurricane Irma or Hurricane Maria. (¶4603)

- For tax years of foreign corporations beginning after 2017, and tax years of U.S. shareholders with or within which those tax years of foreign corporations end, a "U.S. shareholder" of a CFC is now determined based on either voting power or value of stock owned. (¶4612)

- For tax years of foreign corporations beginning after 2017, and tax years of U.S. shareholders with or within which those tax years of foreign corporations end, U.S. shareholders of CFCs must include in gross income global intangible low-taxed income (GILTI), in a manner generally similar to inclusions of subpart F income. Proposed regs to implement the GILTI regime, including reporting rules, have been issued. (¶4614)

- Generally effective for the last tax year of a "deferred income corporation" beginning before 2018, U.S. shareholder must include in income its pro rata share of the undistributed, non-previously-taxed post-'86 foreign earnings of the corporation (the "deemed repatriation" provision). Proposed regs (that would apply retroactively)have been issued to implement, supplement, and modify prior guidance under the deemed repatriation rules. (¶4615)

- For sales or exchanges after 2017, in the case of the sale or exchange by a domestic corporation of stock in a foreign corporation held for one year or more, any amount received by the domestic corporation which is treated as a dividend by reason of Code Sec. 1248 is now treated as a dividend for purposes of applying the Code Sec. 245A dividend received deduction rules. (¶4616)

- For tax years beginning after 2017, proceeds from the sale of inventory are now generally sourced on the basis of the production activities with respect to the property. (¶4627)

- For sales, exchanges, and dispositions after Nov. 26, 2017, notwithstanding any other tax rules, if a nonresident alien individual or foreign corporation owns, directly or indirectly, an interest in a partnership that is engaged in any trade or business in the U.S., gain or loss on the sale or exchange of all (or any portion of) the interest is treated as effectively connected with the conduct of the trade or business to the extent the gain or loss does not exceed certain limitations. (¶4631)

- For 2018, an individual with "average annual net income tax" of more than $165,000 ($168,000 for 2019) for the five tax years ending before the date of the loss of U.S. citizenship will be a covered expatriate. Under a mark-to-market deemed sale rule, all property of a covered expatriate is treated as sold on the day before the expatriation date for its fair market value. However, for tax years beginning in 2018, the amount that would otherwise be includible in the gross income of any individual under these mark-to-market rules will be reduced by $711,000 ($725,000 for 2019). (¶4640)

- IRS has announced that, until regs are issued implementing the requirement to withhold on amounts realized on dispositions of partnership interests, taxpayers must use the principles applicable to withholding on U.S. real property interests, including the use of Forms 8288 and 8288-A. (¶4659)

Chapter 24. Returns and Payment of Tax.

• Individual return filing thresholds have increased for 2018 and 2019. (¶4701)

• For tax years beginning after Feb. 9, 2018, persons age 65 and older at the end of the tax year can use Form 1040SR, which will be similar to Form 1040EZ, but not restricted based on income, which can include Social Security benefits, distributions from retirement plans, annuities and other deferred pay arrangements, interest and dividends, and adjusted net capital gain. (¶4702)

• The filing deadline for 2018 individual returns is Apr. 15, 2019 (Apr. 17 for individuals living in Maine or Massachusetts). (¶4716)

• The income tax return filing threshold for a bankruptcy estate of an individual is $12,000 for 2018 ($12,200 for 2019). (¶4736)

• After 2017, reporting requirements apply to the acquirer of an existing life insurance contract or interest therein in a reportable policy sale (and to the issuer of the contract) and to the payor of reportable death benefits. IRS has issued draft 2018 Form 1099-LS, which is to be used by acquirers of a life insurance contract. (¶4746)

• Generally for amounts paid or incurred after 2017, government agencies (or entities treated as such agencies) that are complainants or investigators with respect to a violation or potential violation of any law must report to IRS and to the taxpayer the amount of each settlement agreement or order entered into where the aggregate amount required to be paid or incurred to or at the direction of the government is at least $600 (or such other amount as may be specified by IRS). (¶4746)

• For returns due after Dec. 31, 2018, anyone required to file Form W-2 series returns (except Form W-2G) or a form reporting nonemployee compensation will only be allowed to request a single 30-day non-automatic extension. (¶4747)

Chapter 25. Deficiencies—Refunds—Penalties.

• A 6-year assessment period applies in the assessment of the net tax liability due to pre-2018 accumulated foreign income. (¶4801)

• Where a taxpayer fails to notify IRS of an election not to take the paid family and medical leave credit, or the revocation of that election, the assessment period of a deficiency attributable to such an election is suspended until one year after IRS is notified of the election or revocation. (¶4834)

• Generally for returns for partnership tax years beginning after 2017, streamlined unified audit partnership rules replace the TEFRA and electing large partnership rules. Under the new rules, adjustment to items of income, gain, loss, deduction, or credit of a partnership for a partnership tax year, and any partner's distributive share of such adjustment, is generally determined at the partnership level. (¶4846)

• The 2018 interest rates with respect to interest on overpayments (¶4856) and underpayments (¶4868) of tax are provided.

• For a refund claim for overpayment of excludible wrongful incarceration damages, the limitation period is waived until Dec. 18, 2019. (¶4857)

• For 2018, the minimum failure to file penalty on income tax returns filed more than 60 days late, unless due to reasonable cause, is the lesser of $210 or the amount of tax required to be shown on the return ($215 for 2019). (¶4875)

• Certain civil penalties on tax return preparers, and total maximum amounts that can be imposed, increase for 2018 and 2019. (¶4890)

• For 2018, the monthly national average bronze plan premium for purposes of the individual shared responsibility payment is $283 for an individual and $1,415 for a family of 5 or more. (¶4898)

• The penalties for failure to file information returns and provide payee statements have increased for 2019 as compared with 2018. (¶4899)

• For 2018, failure to file a partnership return exposes the partnership to a $200 per-partner, per-month penalty ($205 for 2019). (¶4900)

- For 2018, failure to file an S corporation return exposes the S corporation to a $200 per-shareholder, per-month penalty ($205 for 2019). (¶4900)

- "Seriously delinquent tax debt" for purposes of Code Sec. 7345 is $51,000 for 2018 ($52,000 for 2019). (¶4904)

- The user fee for entering into an installment agreement increases to $225 (but is lowered in the case of certain online agreements and direct debit payments, and waived or refunded for certain low-income taxpayers). (¶4906)

- For wrongful IRS levies made after Dec. 22, 2017 (and those for which the prior-law 9-month period of limitations remained open), an amount equal to the money levied upon or the money received from a sale of the property may be returned within two years from the date of the levy. (¶4908)

Chapter 26. Estate, Gift and Generation-Skipping Transfer Taxes.

- The Tax Court denied summary judgment to an estate which argued that the value of a decedent's rights in three split-dollar life insurance arrangements was not includible in the estate under Code Sec. 2036 and Code Sec. 2038. (¶5004)

- The value of a grantor retained annuity trust (GRAT) was includible in an estate because the right to the annuity was determined to be a right to possess or enjoy the income from the transferred property. (¶5000, ¶5016)

- The total decrease in the value of all real property under the special use valuation election may not exceed $1,140,000 for 2018 deaths ($1,160,000 for 2019 deaths). (¶5017)

- For 2018, the basic exclusion amount for gift and estate tax purposes is $11,180,000 ($11,400,000 for 2019). (¶5000, ¶5041)

- For 2018, the applicable credit amount has increased to $4,417,800 ($4,505,800 for 2019), which is the tax that would otherwise be imposed on $11,180,000 ($11,400,000 for 2019). (¶5028, ¶5053)

- When the second spouse dies, IRS may examine the estate tax return of the predeceased spouse if that spouse elected portability. (¶5029)

- An executor must file an estate tax return if the decedent's gross estate at death exceeds the basic exclusion amount of $11,180,000 for 2018 ($11,400,000 for 2019). (¶5036)

- For 2018 and 2019, the gift tax exclusion is $15,000. (¶5049)

- For 2018, the gift tax annual exclusion for gifts to a noncitizen spouse is $152,000 ($155,000 for 2019). (¶5049)

- For 2018, the generation skipping transfer (GST) exemption is $11,180,000 ($11,400,000 for 2019). (¶5060)

¶ 105. What's New on the 2018 Form 1040?

Here are the changes with the greatest impact on the preparation of 2018 individual returns, cross-referenced to where they are discussed in the Handbook, and referenced to the appropriate lines on the Form 1040 and related Schedules (which, as of when the Handbook went to press, had been released only in draft form).

The draft 2018 Form 1040 has been significantly reduced in size and contains far fewer lines than any of its predecessors. For the most part, the removed lines have been moved to six new accompanying schedules, Schedules 1 through 6. While our discussion below explains each of these six new accompanying schedules in general, it does not make mention of each line that has been moved from 2017 Form 1040 to one of the six new schedules.

Also note that the line numbers mentioned below are the line numbers on the draft 2018 forms; with respect to many of the forms and schedules, particularly Form 1040 and Form 1040, Schedule A, those numbers are often different from the line numbers on 2017 Form 1040. The line numbers on Schedules 1-6 are generally the line numbers for the corresponding item on 2017 Form 1040. Schedules 1-6 have many lines that are labelled "Reserved"; in most cases, these lines are not there in case Congress changes laws but rather to allow IRS to have the Schedule 1-6 lines correspond with the lines on 2017 Form 1040.

And note that the *lettered* Form 1040 Schedules, i.e., Schedule A, Schedule B, etc., continue to exist and function much as they did in earlier years.

FORM 1040—ITEMS THAT ARE NOT TIED TO SPECIFIC LINES ON THE FORM

Due date. Form 1040's due date is Apr. 15, 2019 for most taxpayers. However, calendar year taxpayers in Maine and Massachusetts have until Apr. 17, 2019 to file their 2018 returns. (¶4716)

Elimination of Forms 1040A and 1040-EZ. Forms 1040A and 1040-EZ aren't available to file 2018 taxes. Taxpayers who used one of these forms in the past will file 2018 Form 1040. (¶4702)

FORM 1040 PAGE 1, AND FORM 1040, SCHEDULE 6— MISCELLANEOUS TAXPAYER INFORMATION

General function of Form 1040, page 1. IRS has consolidated most of the non-dollar-amount information that, for prior years, was in various parts of pages 1 and 2 of Form 1040, and put it onto 2018 Form 1040, page 1. Note also that this non-dollar-amount information is in a quite different order, with quite different graphics, as compared to 2017.

Identity Protection Personal Identification Numbers (IP PINs). IRS has changed the instructions regarding IP PINs for taxpayers filing joint returns. For 2018, the instructions provide that taxpayers filing a joint return, where both taxpayers have received an IP PIN, should enter both IP PINs in the spaces provided. For 2018 there are places for both spouses to enter their IP PINs; for 2017, there was only a place for the first spouse's IP PIN.

Foreign address. 2018 Form 1040 eliminates spaces from the 2017 version of the form where a taxpayer with a foreign address would specify the foreign country name, province, and postal code, and instead directs a taxpayer with a foreign address to attach new Schedule 6, "Foreign Address and Third Party Designee," and provide this information on that Schedule.

Third party designee. IRS has changed its instructions regarding third party designees, i.e., parties that a taxpayer chooses to discuss his or her 2018 tax return with IRS. In prior years, there was one line on page 2 of Form 1040 to designate any type of third party designee. For 2018, taxpayers who wish to designate their paid preparer as a third party designee, so indicate in the bottom left-hand corner of page 1 of form 1040. If the taxpayer chooses to have any other party serve as his or her third party designee, the taxpayer so indicates on Schedule 6.

FORM 1040, PAGE 2, AND FORM 1040, SCHEDULE 1—GROSS INCOME

Form 1040, Lines 4a and 4b. IRAs, pensions and annuities. Under the Tax Cuts and Jobs Act (TCJA, P.L. 115-97), Disaster Tax Relief and Airport and Airway Extension Act of 2017 (P.L. 115-63) and the Bipartisan Budget Act of 2018 (P.L. 115-123), special rules may apply to taxpayers that received a qualified distribution from profit-sharing plans or retirement plans during 2018, whose main home was in one of the Presidentially declared disaster areas eligible for these special rules on the specified date. Special rules also may apply to taxpayers that received a distribution on certain dates to buy or construct a main home in one of the Presidentially declared disaster areas eligible for these special rules, but that home wasn't bought or constructed because of the disaster. (¶4333)

Schedule 1, Line 21. Other income. The exclusion from gross income where "qualified principal residence indebtedness" is discharged only applies to discharges that took place before Jan. 1, 2018 or were subject to an arrangement that was entered into and evidenced in writing before Jan. 1, 2018. As a result, unless Congress extends this provision, most discharges of "qualified principal residence indebtedness" in 2018 will not be excluded from gross income. (¶1388)

Taxpayers that own (directly or indirectly) certain foreign corporations may have to include on their return certain deferred foreign income, i.e., the net section 965(a) inclusion. They may pay the entire amount of tax due with respect to this deferred foreign income this year or elect to make payment in eight installments. Taxpayers that have a net section 965(a) inclusion enter "SEC 965" and the net inclusion amount on the dotted line next to Line 21 and include that amount in the entry they make on Line 21. They must also complete and attach Form 965 and Form 965-A to their return. (¶4615)

FORM 1040, PAGE 2, AND FORM 1040, SCHEDULE 1—ADJUSTMENTS TO INCOME

Schedule 1, Line 23. Educator expenses. For 2018, educators can claim an up-to-$250 deduction for qualifying "educator expenses." (¶2224)

Schedule 1, Line 26. Moving expenses for members of the Armed Forces. A taxpayer can deduct moving expenses only if he or she is a member of the Armed Forces on active duty and, due to a military order, moves because of a permanent change of station. (¶1246) The 2018 standard mileage rate for moving expenses is 18¢ per mile. (¶1646)

Schedule 1, Line 32. IRA deduction. In general, an individual who isn't an active participant in certain employer-sponsored retirement plans, and whose spouse isn't an active participant, may make an annual deductible cash contribution to an IRA up to the lesser of: (1) a statutory dollar limit, or (2) 100% of the compensation that's includible in his or her gross income for that year. For 2018, the statutory dollar limit is $5,500, plus an additional $1,000 for those age 50 or older. If the individual (or individual's spouse) is an active plan participant, the deduction phases out over a specified dollar range of modified AGI (MAGI). For 2018, a taxpayer may be able to take an IRA deduction if the taxpayer was covered by a retirement plan and his or her 2018 MAGI is less than $73,000 ($121,000 if married filing jointly or qualifying widow(er)). If the taxpayer's spouse was covered by a retirement plan, but the taxpayer was not, the taxpayer may be able to take an IRA deduction if 2018 MAGI is less than $199,000. (¶4341)

Schedule 1, Line 34. Reserved. In prior years, Line 34 was titled "Tuition and fees." Unless Congress acts to extend it, the tuition and fees deduction has expired. Line 34 is now shown as "Reserved" in case Congress extends the tuition and fees deduction for

Schedule 1, Line 36. Add lines 23 through 35. The domestic production activities deduction (DPAD), for various trade or business activities conducted in the U.S., has been repealed for tax years beginning in 2018 or later. However, partners etc. of fiscal-year pass-through entities that have a DPAD generated in a tax year beginning on or before Dec. 31, 2017 should enter their share of the entity's DPAD on the dotted line next to Line 36, identify it as "DPAD," and include that amount on Line 36.

FORM 1040, PAGE 2— DEDUCTIONS FROM ADJUSTED GROSS INCOME

Form 1040, Line 8. Standard deduction or itemized deductions. For 2018, the standard deduction is $12,000 for single filers and for married persons filing separately, $24,000 for joint filers and qualifying widow(er)s, and $18,000 for heads of household. Additional standard deductions may be claimed by taxpayers who are elderly or blind. (¶3109, (¶3110))

A taxpayer who had a net qualified disaster loss may elect to increase his or her standard deduction by the amount of the taxpayer's net qualified disaster loss. The taxpayer uses Schedule A to figure his or her standard deduction in that case. For additional instructions, see "Line 16" under "Form 1040, Schedule A ... " below.

Form 1040, Line 9. Qualified business income deduction. The qualified business income deduction is a new deduction for 2018 that can be taken in addition to the standard deduction or itemized deductions. It is generally equal to 20% of the taxpayer's net qualified business income plus 20% of qualified real estate investment trust dividends and publicly traded partnership income.

Generally, taxpayers whose 2018 taxable income is less than $157,500 ($315,000 if married filing jointly) compute the deduction using the 2018 Qualified Business Income Deduction—Simplified Worksheet that is contained in the Form 1040 instructions. Other taxpayers must use the worksheet in Publication 535 instead. (¶1605)

Exemptions. The deduction for exemptions for taxpayers, spouses and dependents has been eliminated for 2018. (¶3112)

FORM 1040 PAGE 2, AND FORM 1040, SCHEDULE 2—TAX

Schedule 2, Line 45. Alternative minimum tax. Under Code Sec. 55(d), the alternative minimum tax (AMT) exemption amount for 2018 is $70,300 ($109,400 if married filing jointly or a qualifying widow(er); $54,700 if married filing separately). The AMT exemption amount is reduced if alternative minimum taxable income is above statutorily-defined amounts that depend upon filing status. (¶3203)

FORM 1040, PAGE 2, AND FORM 1040, SCHEDULE 3—NONREFUNDABLE CREDITS

Form 1040, Line 12a. Child tax credit/credit for other dependents. For 2018, the maximum child tax credit has increased to $2,000 per qualifying child, of which $1,400 can be claimed for the additional child tax credit (Form 1040, Line 17b). In addition, the MAGI threshold at which the credit begins to phase out has increased to $200,000 ($400,000 if married filing jointly),

There is also a new credit for other dependents. The credit is a nonrefundable credit of up to $500 for each eligible dependent who can't be claimed for the child tax credit.

The child tax credit and credit for other dependents are both figured using the Child Tax Credit and Credit for Other Dependents Worksheet.

A child must have a Social Security number valid for employment issued before the due date of the parent's 2018 return (including extensions) to be claimed as a qualifying child for the child tax credit. If a child doesn't qualify his or her parent for the child tax credit but has a taxpayer identification number issued on or before the due date of the parent's 2018 return (including extensions), the parent may be able to claim the new credit for other dependents for that child. (¶2350)

Schedule 3, Line 53. Residential energy credit. As of the time the Federal Tax Handbook went to press, one of the credits that in the past had been shown on this line, the nonbusiness energy property credit, had expired and thus, unless legislation is enacted to extend the credit, no entry should be made on this line for that credit. (¶2353)

Schedule 3, Line 54. Other credits. For 2018, the maximum adoption credit is $13,810 per eligible child for both non-special needs adoptions and special needs adoptions. The amount begins to phase out if modified adjusted gross income (MAGI) is in excess of $207,140 and is completely phased out if MAGI is $247,140 or more. (¶2349)

FORM 1040 PAGE 2, AND FORM 1040, SCHEDULE 4—OTHER TAXES

Schedule 4, Line 57. Self-employment tax. For 2018, the maximum amount of self-employment income subject to FICA tax is $128,400; there is no ceiling on the Medicare wage base. (¶1109)

An individual may use the farm optional method only if the individual's (a) gross farm income was not more than $7,920 or (b) net farm profits were less than $5,717. Using this method, farm self-employment earnings equals the smaller of (1) two-thirds of gross farm income, or (2) $5,280. (¶3141)

An individual may use the nonfarm optional method only if (a) the individual's net nonfarm profits were less than $5,717 and also less than 72.189% of his or her gross nonfarm income and (b) the individual had net earnings from self-employment of at least $400 in 2 of the prior 3 years. Individuals may compute their self-employment earnings as the smaller of two-thirds of gross nonfarm income or $5,280. (¶3141)

A self-employed individual with both farm and nonfarm incomes is allowed to use both optional computation methods if the farm income qualifies for the farm optional method and the nonfarm income qualifies for the nonfarm optional method. If both optional methods are used to compute net earnings from self-employment, the maximum combined total net earnings from self-employment for any tax year can't be more than $5,280. (¶3141)

Schedule 4, Line 61. Health care: individual responsibility. For 2018, a taxpayer must either:

• indicate by checking a box on Form 1040, page 1 that the taxpayer, the taxpayer's spouse (if filing jointly) and his or her dependents had health care coverage throughout 2018;

• claim an exemption from the health care coverage requirement for some or all of 2018 and attach Form 8965; or

• make a "shared responsibility payment" if, for any month in 2018, the taxpayer, the taxpayer's spouse (if filing jointly) or his or her dependents did not have coverage and do not qualify for a coverage exemption.

For 2018, the shared responsibility payment amount is the lesser of (i) the sum of the monthly penalty amounts for months in the tax year during which one or more failures occurs, or (ii) the sum of the monthly national average bronze plan premiums for the plan. The monthly penalty amount is equal to $1/12$ of the greater of $695 per family member (up to a ceiling of $2,085) or 2.5% of the amount by which the taxpayer's household income exceeds the filing threshold. (¶4898)

FORM 1040 PAGE 2, AND FORM 1040, SCHEDULE 5—OTHER PAYMENTS AND REFUNDABLE CREDITS

Form 1040, Line 12a. Earned income credit (EIC). The maximum credit, and the AGI-based phaseout figures, increased for 2018. (¶2338)

Form 1040, Line 12b. Additional child tax credit. For 2018, the additional child tax credit can be as much as $1,400 per qualifying child.

A child must have an Social Security number valid for employment issued before the due date of the parent's 2018 return (including extensions) to be claimed as a qualifying child for the additional child tax credit. If a child doesn't qualify his parent for the child tax credit but has a taxpayer identification number issued on or before the due date of his parent's 2018 return (including extensions), the parent may be able to claim the new credit for other dependents (see Form 1040, Line 12a, above) for that child. (¶2351)

Schedule 5, Line 72. Excess social security and RRTA tax withheld. Maximum Social Security (OASDI) tax for 2018 is $7,960.80 (computed on the first $128,400 of wages) for purposes of the credit for excess tax withheld. (¶1108)

Schedule 5, Line 74. Credits. Line 74, box b is labeled as "Reserved." The draft instructions contain no information on this box. The final version of 2017 Form 1040 also had this box labeled as "Reserved."

Taxpayers that have a net section 965(a) inclusion in 2018 (see Schedule 1, Line 21 above) and have elected to pay their 965 net tax liability in installments check box d and enter "TAX" and the amount of net 965 tax liability remaining. (¶4615)

FORM 1040—SCHEDULE A, ITEMIZED DEDUCTIONS

Line 1. Medical and dental expenses. The 2018 standard mileage rate for medically-related use of an auto is 18¢ per mile. (¶2148)

Line 5. State and local taxes. Both 2017 and 2018 Line 5 are entitled "State and local taxes." However, while in 2017, Line 5 only included lines for taxpayers to choose between state and local income taxes and state and local sales taxes, 2018 Line 5 also has lines for state and local real and personal property taxes and for limiting all state and local income, sales and property taxes to $10,000. (¶1747, ¶1748)

Line 6. Other taxes. This line should be used for taxes other than state and local taxes. For 2018, IRS has added the following instructions for this line: 1) Don't include taxes paid to a U.S. possession on this line; instead, include U.S. possession taxes on the appropriate state and local tax line. 2) Don't include federal estate tax on income in respect of a decedent on this line; instead, include it on Line 16, Other itemized deductions. 3) Foreign taxes paid on real estate are not deductible. (¶1747)

Line 8. Home mortgage interest and points. IRS has added a new checkbox to Line 8. Taxpayers should check this box if they had one or more home mortgages in 2018 with an outstanding balance and they didn't use all of the home mortgage proceeds from those loans to buy, build, or substantially improve their home.

As in previous years, Schedule A has four lines that pertain to mortgage interest: mortgage interest and points reported on Form 1098, mortgage interest not reported on Form 1098, points not reported on Form 1098, and mortgage interest insurance. And, as in prior years, the Schedule A instructions provide for limits on the amounts to be reported on those lines. The Schedule A instructions contain the following new limitations: 1) Taxpayers may deduct mortgage interest only on the first $750,000 ($375,000 if married filing separately) of indebtedness. Higher limitations apply for taxpayers that are deducting mortgage interest from indebtedness incurred on or before Dec. 15, 2017. 2) No matter when the indebtedness was incurred, taxpayers can no longer deduct the interest from a loan secured by their home to the extent the loan proceeds weren't used to buy, build, or improve their home. (¶1729)

Line 8d. Reserved. In prior years, amounts paid for premiums for mortgage insurance in connection with acquisition indebtedness with respect to a qualified residence of the taxpayer were deductible as interest, subject to a phaseout based on AGI. As of the time the Federal Tax Handbook went to press, that deduction was scheduled to terminate with respect to amounts paid or accrued after Dec. 31, 2017. IRS has left a line, Line 8d, as "Reserved" in case Congress retroactively extends this provision for 2018. (¶1733)

Line 11. Gifts by cash or check. For most gifts by cash or check, the total amount of such contributions that can be deducted is now limited to 60% of the taxpayer's contribution base, instead of the 50% limit that applied in prior years. (¶2123)

Under the Bipartisan Budget Act of 2018, charitable contributions of money for relief efforts in the 2017 California Wildfire area, that were made during the period beginning on Oct. 8, 2017, and ending on Dec. 31, 2018, are not subject to the 60%, 30% or 20% of AGI limitations that otherwise apply to charitable contributions. (¶2123)

Line 12. Gifts to charity, other than by cash or check. The standard mileage rate is 14¢ per mile for use of an auto in rendering gratuitous services to a charitable organization. (¶2120)

Line 15. Casualty or theft losses. Taxpayers can no longer deduct a personal casualty or theft loss unless the loss is from a federally declared disaster. (¶1783)

And, taxpayers should not enter a "net qualified disaster loss" here; instead, they should enter that amount on Schedule A, Line 16. For additional information about how to treat net qualified disaster losses, see "Line 16" below.

Line 16. Other. Qualified disaster losses are personal casualty losses sustained as a result of a federally declared disaster that occurred in 2016, as well as those sustained from Hurricane Harvey or Tropical Storm Harvey, Hurricane Irma, Hurricane Maria, or the California wildfires. Net qualified disaster losses are the net of qualified disaster losses and gains from qualified disasters.

The Schedule A instructions provide the following detailed instructions for taxpayers who have net qualified disaster losses:

Taxpayers who have a net qualified disaster loss on Form 4684 (Casualties and Thefts), Line 15, and who are not itemizing their deductions, can claim an increased standard deduction using Schedule A by doing the following.

(1) List the amount from Form 4684, Line 15, on the dotted line next to Line 16 as "Net Qualified Disaster Loss," and attach Form 4684.

(2) List the taxpayer's standard deduction amount on the dotted line next to Line 16 as "Standard Deduction Claimed With Qualified Disaster Loss."

(3) Combine the two amounts on Line 16, and enter on Form 1040, Line 8.

Taxpayer who have a net qualified disaster loss on Form 4684, Line 15 and are itemizing deductions should list the amount from Form 4684, Line 15, on the dotted line next to Line 16 as "Net Qualified Disaster Loss" and include it with their other miscellaneous deductions on Line 16.

Lines eliminated from 2018 Schedule A. The section from 2017 Schedule A that was entitled "Job Expenses and Certain Miscellaneous deductions" has been eliminated because all of the deductions that, in prior years, had been subject to the 2%-of-AGI limitation have been eliminated. (¶3109)

There is no longer an overall limitation on itemized deductions based on the taxpayer's AGI; as a result, the line for this, Line 29 on 2017 Schedule A, has been eliminated. (¶3114)

FORM 1040—SCHEDULE B, INTEREST AND ORDINARY DIVIDENDS

Line 1. Interest. Accrued interest on Series EE U.S. savings bonds issued in '88 is taxable. (¶1331)

Line 3. Excludable interest on Series EE or Series I U.S. savings bonds. The exclusion for education-related savings bond interest phases out at higher income levels. For 2018, the phaseout begins at modified AGI above $79,550 ($119,300 on a joint return). (¶2218)

FORM 1040—SCHEDULE C, PROFIT OR LOSS FROM BUSINESS

Part I, Line F. Accounting method. In prior years, unless the taxpayer had small amounts of gross income, the taxpayer had to use an accrual method. For 2018, the term for taxpayers who do not have to use the accrual method is "small business taxpayer," and that term encompasses more taxpayers than in previous years. For 2018, a small business taxpayer is a taxpayer that is not a tax shelter and that has average annual gross receipts of $25 million or less for the three prior tax years. (¶2818)

Line 9. Car and truck expenses. The 2018 standard mileage rate for business travel is 54.5¢ per mile. (¶1555)

Line 16a and 16b. Interest. Except for small business taxpayers (as defined under "Schedule C, Part I, Line F," above), businesses are subject to a disallowance of a deduction for net interest expense in excess of 30% of the business's adjusted taxable income. Taxpayers other than small business taxpayers must file Form 8990, Limitation on Business Interest Expense IRC 163(j), in order to deduct any interest expenses. (¶1710)

Line 13. Depreciation and section 179 expense. See entries for Form 4562, below.

Line 24b. Deductible meals. In previous years, Line 24 was titled "Deductible meals and entertainment." Entertainment expenses are no longer deductible. Taxpayers may still deduct 50% of business meal expenses that are not entertainment expenses. (¶1556)

Line 26. Wages (less employment credits). As of the time the Federal Tax Handbook went to press, the empowerment zone employment credit (¶2325) and the Indian employment credit (¶2326) had expired. If extended for 2018, claiming these credits could affect the amount that should be shown on Line 26.

Line 27a. Other expenses. As of the time the Federal Tax Handbook went to press, the rule under which taxpayers may elect to deduct costs of certain qualified film, television and live theatrical productions was scheduled to terminate with respect to productions that began after Dec. 31, 2017. But, historically, Congress has retroactively extended this provision. (¶1961)

Deduction for qualified business income. The deduction for qualified business income is not taken on Schedule C. See discussion of this deduction under "Form 1040, Page 2... Adjusted Gross Income," above.

Line 31. Net profit or (loss). Taxpayers who report a loss on Line 31 may be subject to a new business loss limitation. The disallowed loss resulting from this new limitation will not be reflected on Line 31 of Schedule C. Instead, taxpayers must use new Form 461 to determine the amount of their excess business loss, which will be included as income on Schedule 1 (Form 1040), Line 21. Any disallowed loss resulting from this limitation will be treated as a net operating loss that may be carried forward and deducted in a subsequent year. (¶1775)

FORM 4562, DEPRECIATION AND AMORTIZATION

Part I. Election to expense certain tangible property under Sec. 179. For tax years beginning in 2018, the maximum section 179 expense deduction is $1 million. This limit is reduced by the amount by which the cost of section 179 property placed in service during the tax year exceeds $2.5 million. (¶1940)

Line 14. Special depreciation allowance. The TCJA provides that 100% bonus depreciation applies to certain depreciable property acquired and placed in service in a taxpayer's 2018 tax year. For such property, the TCJA also eliminates the requirement that the original use of the property start with the taxpayer. The TCJA also expands the definition of qualified property to include qualified film, television, and live theatrical productions released, etc. during a taxpayer's 2018 tax year. (¶1932)

Part V. Listed property. The first-year luxury auto limit for vehicles first placed in service in 2018, that are eligible for bonus first-year depreciation, is $18,000 for autos, light trucks and vans. (¶1952)

Form 1040—SCHEDULE E, SUPPLEMENTAL INCOME AND LOSS

Line 12. Mortgage interest. Line 13. Interest. Except for small business taxpayers (as defined under "Schedule C, Part I, Line F," above), businesses are subject to a disallowance of a deduction for net interest expense in excess of 30% of the business's adjusted taxable income. Taxpayers other than small business taxpayers must file Form 8990, Limitation on Business Interest Expense IRC 163(j), in order to deduct any interest expenses. (¶1710)

Line 41. Total profit or (loss). Taxpayers who report a loss on Line 26, 32, 37, or 39 of Schedule E (Form 1040) may be subject to a new business loss limitation. The disallowed loss resulting from this new limitation will not be reflected on Line 26, 32, 37, or 39 of Schedule E. Instead, taxpayers must use new Form 461 to determine the amount of their excess business loss, which will be included as income on Schedule 1 (Form 1040), Line 21. Any disallowed loss resulting from this limitation will be treated as a net operating loss that may be carried forward and deducted in a subsequent year. (¶1775)

Standard mileage rate. The 2018 standard mileage rate for miles driven in connection with the taxpayer's rental activities is 54.5¢ per mile. (¶1555)

Deduction for qualified business income. The deduction for qualified business income is not taken on Schedule E. See discussion of this deduction under "Form 1040, Page 2... Adjusted Gross Income," above.

FORM 1040—SCHEDULE F, PROFIT OR LOSS FROM FARMING

Line 10. Car and truck expenses. The 2018 standard mileage rate for business travel is 54.5¢ per mile. (¶1555)

Line 34. Farm profit or (loss). Once the taxpayer figures its net profit or loss, it must also consider any excess business loss limitation. (¶2123) For more information, see Schedule C, Line 31, above.

The excess farm loss disallowance rule under Code Sec. 461(j), which, in prior years, limited the amount of farming losses that could be claimed for any tax year in which certain subsidies were received, is not applicable for 2018. (¶4504)

Line 35. Reserved. The instructions for this line provide detail regarding the excess business loss limitation.

Form 1040 Department of the Treasury—Internal Revenue Service (99)
U.S. Individual Income Tax Return **2018** OMB No. 1545-0074 | IRS Use Only—Do not write or staple in this space.

| Filing status: | ☐ Single | ☐ Married filing jointly | ☐ Married filing separately | ☐ Head of household | ☐ Qualifying widow(er) |

Your first name and initial | Last name | **Your social security number**

Your standard deduction: ☐ Someone can claim you as a dependent | ☐ You were born before January 2, 1954 | ☐ You are blind

If joint return, spouse's first name and initial | Last name | **Spouse's social security number**

Spouse standard deduction: ☐ Someone can claim your spouse as a dependent | ☐ Spouse was born before January 2, 1954
☐ Spouse is blind | ☐ Spouse itemizes on a separate return or you were dual-status alien | ☐ Full-year health care coverage or exempt (see inst.)

Home address (number and street). If you have a P.O. box, see instructions. | Apt. no. | **Presidential Election Campaign** (see inst.) ☐ You ☐ Spouse

City, town or post office, state, and ZIP code. If you have a foreign address, attach Schedule 6. | If more than four dependents, see inst. and ✓ here ▶ ☐

Dependents (see instructions):		(2) Social security number	(3) Relationship to you	(4) ✓ if qualifies for (see inst.):
(1) First name	Last name			Child tax credit / Credit for other dependents
				☐ ☐
				☐ ☐
				☐ ☐
				☐ ☐

Sign Here

Under penalties of perjury, I declare that I have examined this return and accompanying schedules and statements, and to the best of my knowledge and belief, they are true, correct, and complete. Declaration of preparer (other than taxpayer) is based on all information of which preparer has any knowledge.

Joint return?
See instructions.
Keep a copy for your records.

Your signature | Date | Your occupation | If the IRS sent you an Identity Protection PIN, enter it here (see inst.)

Spouse's signature. If a joint return, **both** must sign. | Date | Spouse's occupation | If the IRS sent you an Identity Protection PIN, enter it here (see inst.)

Paid Preparer Use Only

Preparer's name | Preparer's signature | PTIN | Firm's EIN | Check if:
☐ 3rd Party Designee
☐ Self-employed

Firm's name ▶ | Phone no.

Firm's address ▶

For Disclosure, Privacy Act, and Paperwork Reduction Act Notice, see separate instructions. | Cat. No. 11320B | Form **1040** (2018)

27

	1	Wages, salaries, tips, etc. Attach Form(s) W-2			**1**
Attach Form(s) W-2. Also attach Form(s) W-2G and 1099-R if tax was withheld.	**2a**	Tax-exempt interest . . .	**2a**	**b** Taxable interest . . .	**2b**
	3a	Qualified dividends . . .	**3a**	**b** Ordinary dividends . . .	**3b**
	4a	IRAs, pensions, and annuities .	**4a**	**b** Taxable amount . . .	**4b**
	5a	Social security benefits .	**5a**	**b** Taxable amount . . .	**5b**
	6	Total income. Add lines 1 through 5. Add any amount from Schedule 1, line 22			**6**
	7	Adjusted gross income. If you have no adjustments to income, enter the amount from line 6; otherwise, subtract Schedule 1, line 36, from line 6			**7**
Standard Deduction for— • Single or married filing separately, $12,000 • Married filing jointly or Qualifying widow(er), $24,000 • Head of household, $18,000 • If you checked any box under Standard deduction, see instructions.	**8**	**Standard deduction or itemized deductions** (from Schedule A)			**8**
	9	Qualified business income deduction (see instructions) . . .			**9**
	10	Taxable income. Subtract lines 8 and 9 from line 7. If zero or less, enter -0-			**10**
	11	**a** Tax (see inst.) (check if any from: 1 ☐ Form(s) 8814 2 ☐ Form 4972 3 ☐) **b Add** any amount from Schedule 2 and check here ▶ ☐			**11**
	12	**a** Child tax credit/credit for other dependents **b Add** any amount from Schedule 3 and check here ▶ ☐			**12**
	13	Subtract line 12 from line 11. If zero or less, enter -0-			**13**
	14	Other taxes. Attach Schedule 4 . . .			**14**
	15	Total tax. Add lines 13 and 14 . . .			**15**
	16	Federal income tax withheld from Forms W-2 and 1099 . . .			**16**
	17	Refundable credits: **a** EIC (see inst.) **b** Sch 8812 **c** Form 8863			
		Add any amount from Schedule 5			**17**
	18	Add lines 16 and 17. These are your total payments . . .			**18**
Refund	**19**	If line 18 is more than line 15, subtract line 15 from line 18. This is the amount you **overpaid**			**19**
Direct deposit? See instructions.	**20a**	Amount of line 19 you want **refunded to you.** If Form 8888 is attached, check here . . ▶ ☐			**20a**
	b	Routing number ▶ **c** Type: ☐ Checking ☐ Savings			
	d	Account number			
	21	Amount of line 19 you want **applied to your 2019 estimated tax** ▶	**21**		
Amount You Owe	**22**	**Amount you owe.** Subtract line 18 from line 15. For details on how to pay, see instructions ▶			**22**
	23	Estimated tax penalty (see instructions) . . . ▶	**23**		

Go to *www.irs.gov/Form1040* for instructions and the latest information.   Form **1040** (2018)

SCHEDULE 1
(Form 1040)

Department of the Treasury
Internal Revenue Service

Additional Income and Adjustments to Income

▶ Attach to Form 1040.
▶ Go to *www.irs.gov/Form1040* for instructions and the latest information.

OMB No. 1545-0074

2018

Attachment
Sequence No. **01**

Name(s) shown on Form 1040

Your social security number

Additional Income	1–9b	Reserved		1–9b	
	10	Taxable refunds, credits, or offsets of state and local income taxes . . .		10	
	11	Alimony received		11	
	12	Business income or (loss). Attach Schedule C or C-EZ		12	
	13	Capital gain or (loss). Attach Schedule D if required. If not required, check here ▶ ☐		13	
	14	Other gains or (losses). Attach Form 4797		14	
	15a	Reserved		15b	
	16a	Reserved		16b	
	17	Rental real estate, royalties, partnerships, S corporations, trusts, etc. Attach Schedule E		17	
	18	Farm income or (loss). Attach Schedule F		18	
	19	Unemployment compensation		19	
	20a	Reserved		20b	
	21	Other income. List type and amount ▶		21	
	22	Combine the amounts in the far right column. If you don't have any adjustments to income, enter here and on Form 1040, line 6. Otherwise, go to line 23 . . .		22	
Adjustments to Income	23	Educator expenses	23		
	24	Certain business expenses of reservists, performing artists, and fee-basis government officials. Attach Form 2106 . .	24		
	25	Health savings account deduction. Attach Form 8889 .	25		
	26	Moving expenses for members of the Armed Forces. Attach Form 3903	26		
	27	Deductible part of self-employment tax. Attach Schedule SE	27		
	28	Self-employed SEP, SIMPLE, and qualified plans . .	28		
	29	Self-employed health insurance deduction	29		
	30	Penalty on early withdrawal of savings	30		
	31a	Alimony paid **b** Recipient's SSN ▶	31a		
	32	IRA deduction	32		
	33	Student loan interest deduction	33		
	34	Reserved	34		
	35	Reserved	35		
	36	Add lines 23 through 35		36	

For Paperwork Reduction Act Notice, see your tax return instructions.

Cat. No. 71479F

Schedule 1 (Form 1040) 2018

29

SCHEDULE 2
(Form 1040)

Department of the Treasury
Internal Revenue Service

Tax

▶ **Attach to Form 1040.**
▶ **Go to** *www.irs.gov/Form1040* **for instructions and the latest information.**

OMB No. 1545-0074

2018

Attachment
Sequence No. **02**

Name(s) shown on Form 1040

Your social security number

Tax	38–44	Reserved	38–44	
	45	Alternative minimum tax. Attach Form 6251	45	
	46	Excess advance premium tax credit repayment. Attach Form 8962	46	
	47	Add the amounts in the far right column. Enter here and include on Form 1040, line 11	47	

SCHEDULE 3 (Form 1040)	**Nonrefundable Credits**	OMB No. 1545-0074
Department of the Treasury Internal Revenue Service	▶ Attach to Form 1040. ▶ Go to *www.irs.gov/Form1040* for instructions and the latest information.	**2018** Attachment Sequence No. **03**
Name(s) shown on Form 1040		Your social security number

Nonrefundable Credits	48	Foreign tax credit. Attach Form 1116 if required	48	
	49	Credit for child and dependent care expenses. Attach Form 2441 . .	49	
	50	Education credits from Form 8863, line 19	50	
	51	Retirement savings contributions credit. Attach Form 8880	51	
	52	Reserved	52	
	53	Residential energy credit. Attach Form 5695	53	
	54	Other credits from Form **a** ☐ 3800 **b** ☐ 8801 **c** ☐	54	
	55	Add the amounts in the far right column. Enter here and include on Form 1040, line 12	55	

For Paperwork Reduction Act Notice, see your tax return instructions.   Cat. No. 71480G   Schedule 3 (Form 1040) 2018

Nonrefundable Credits

▶ Attach to Form 1040.
▶ Go to *www.irs.gov/Form1040* for instructions and the latest information.

OMB No. 1545-0074

2018

Attachment
Sequence No. 03

Name(s) shown on Form 1040

Your social security number

Nonrefundable Credits	48	Foreign tax credit. Attach Form 1116 if required	48	
	49	Credit for child and dependent care expenses. Attach Form 2441 . . .	49	
	50	Education credits from Form 8863, line 19	50	
	51	Retirement savings contributions credit. Attach Form 8880	51	
	52	Reserved	52	
	53	Residential energy credit. Attach Form 5695	53	
	54	Other credits from Form a ☐ 3800 b ☐ 8801 c ☐ _____	54	
	55	Add the amounts in the far right column. Enter here and include on Form 1040, line 12	55	

For Paperwork Reduction Act Notice, see your tax return instructions.   Cat. No. 71480G   Schedule 3 (Form 1040) 2018

SCHEDULE 4
(Form 1040)

Department of the Treasury
Internal Revenue Service

Other Taxes

▶ Attach to Form 1040.
▶ Go to *www.irs.gov/Form1040* for instructions and the latest information.

OMB No. 1545-0074

2018

Attachment
Sequence No. **04**

Name(s) shown on Form 1040

Your social security number

Other Taxes	57	Self-employment tax. Attach Schedule SE	57	
	58	Unreported social security and Medicare tax from: Form **a** ☐ 4137 **b** ☐ 8919	58	
	59	Additional tax on IRAs, other qualified retirement plans, and other tax-favored accounts. Attach Form 5329 if required	59	
	60a	Household employment taxes. Attach Schedule H	60a	
	b	Repayment of first-time homebuyer credit from Form 5405. Attach Form 5405 if required	60b	
	61	Health care: individual responsibility (see instructions)	61	
	62	Taxes from: **a** ☐ Form 8959 **b** ☐ Form 8960 **c** ☐ Instructions; enter code(s)	62	
	63	Section 965 net tax liability installment from Form 965-A 63		
	64	Add the amounts in the far right column. These are your **total other taxes.** Enter here and on Form 1040, line 14	64	

For Paperwork Reduction Act Notice, see your tax return instructions.   Cat. No. 71481R   Schedule 4 (Form 1040) 2018

SCHEDULE 5
(Form 1040)

Department of the Treasury
Internal Revenue Service

Other Payments and Refundable Credits

▶ Attach to Form 1040.
▶ Go to *www.irs.gov/Form1040* for instructions and the latest information.

OMB No. 1545-0074

2018
Attachment
Sequence No. **05**

Name(s) shown on Form 1040

Your social security number

Other Payments and Refundable Credits	65	Reserved	65
	66	2018 estimated tax payments and amount applied from 2017 return . .	66
	67a	Reserved	67a
	b	Reserved	67b
	68–69	Reserved	68–69
	70	Net premium tax credit. Attach Form 8962	70
	71	Amount paid with request for extension to file (see instructions) . .	71
	72	Excess social security and tier 1 RRTA tax withheld	72
	73	Credit for federal tax on fuels. Attach Form 4136	73
	74	Credits from Form: **a** ☐ 2439 **b** ☐ Reserved **c** ☐ 8885 **d** ☐ _____	74
	75	Add the amounts in the far right column. These are your total **other payments and refundable credits.** Enter here and include on Form 1040, line 17 . . .	75

For Paperwork Reduction Act Notice, see your tax return instructions.

Cat. No. 71482C

Schedule 5 (Form 1040) 2018

34

SCHEDULE 6
(Form 1040)

Department of the Treasury
Internal Revenue Service

Foreign Address and Third Party Designee

► Attach to Form 1040.
► Go to *www.irs.gov/Form1040* for instructions and the latest information.

OMB No. 1545-0074

2018

Attachment
Sequence No. **05A**

Name(s) shown on Form 1040

Your social security number

Foreign Address	Foreign country name		Foreign province/county	Foreign postal code

| **Third Party Designee** | Do you want to allow another person to discuss this return with the IRS (see instructions)? ☐ **Yes.** Complete below. ☐ **No** | | | |
| | Designee's name ► | Phone no. ► | Personal identification number (PIN) ► | |

For Paperwork Reduction Act Notice, see your tax return instructions.   Cat. No. 71483N   Schedule 6 (Form 1040) 2018

¶1000. Tax Calendar—2019 Due Dates.

Here are the principal 2019 tax due dates. The effect of Saturdays, Sundays, and federal (but not State) holidays has been taken into account.

January 15, 2019

Individuals.

Make a payment of your estimated tax for 2018 if you didn't pay your 2018 income tax through withholding (or didn't pay in enough tax that way). Use Form 1040-ES, or pay by various electronic means. This is the final installment date for 2018 estimated tax. However, you don't have to make this payment if you file your 2018 return (Form 1040) and pay any tax due by Jan. 31, 2019.

Farmers and fishermen.

Pay your estimated tax for 2018 by using Form 1040-ES or by paying by various electronic means. You can then file your 2018 income tax return (Form 1040) by Apr. 15. If you don't make this estimated payment this time, file your 2018 return and pay any tax due by Mar. 1, 2019, to avoid an estimated tax penalty.

January 31, 2019

Individuals.

File your income tax return (Form 1040) for 2018 if you didn't pay your last installment of estimated tax by Jan. 15. Filing your return now prevents any penalty for late payment of the last installment.

Employers.

Give your employees their copies of Form W-2 for 2018.

File Form W-3 along with Copy A of all the Form W-2s you issued for 2018.

Applicable Large Employers under the affordable Care Act provide Forms 1095-C to full time employees. All other providers of Minimum Essential Coverage, provide Forms 1095-B to responsible individuals.

All businesses.

Give an annual information statement to recipients of certain payments you made during 2018. (You can use a copy of the appropriate Form 1099.)

File Form 1099-MISC if reporting nonemployee compensation payments in box 7 (otherwise, by Feb. 28, 2019 if on paper, Apr. 1, 2019 if electronically).

February 15, 2019

Individuals.

If you claimed exemption from income tax withholding for 2018 on the Form W-4 you gave your employer, you must file a new Form W-4 by this date to continue your exemption for another year.

All businesses.

Give an annual information statement to recipients of certain payments (e.g., proceeds from broker and barter transactions) you made during 2018. (You can use a copy of the appropriate Form 1099.)

February 28, 2019

All businesses.

File an information return (Form 1099) with IRS for certain payments you made during 2018. There are different versions of Form 1099 for different types of payments. For a

30-day extension of time to file, use Form 8809. The due date for electronic filers is Apr. 1, 2019.

Large food and beverage establishment employers.

File Form 8027 to report tip income and allocated tips. Use Form 8027-T to summarize and transmit Form 8027 if you have more than one establishment. The due date for electronic filers is Apr. 1, 2019.

March 1, 2019

Farmers and fishermen.

File your 2018 income tax return (Form 1040) and pay any tax due. However, you have until Apr. 15 (Apr. 17 for taxpayers in Maine and Massachusetts) if you paid your 2018 estimated tax by Jan. 15, 2019.

March 15, 2019

Partnerships.

File a 2018 calendar year return (Form 1065), and provide each partner with a copy of Schedule K-1. If you want an automatic 6-month extension to file the return and provide Schedule K-1 or a substitute Schedule K-1, file Form 7004. Then file Form 1065 by Sept. 16.

S corporations.

File a 2018 calendar year income tax return (Form 1120S), pay any tax still due, and provide each shareholder with a copy of Schedule K-1. If you want an automatic 6-month extension, file Form 7004 and deposit what you estimate you owe.

S elections.

File Form 2553 to choose to be treated as an S corporation for calendar year 2019 and thereafter. If Form 2553 is filed late, S treatment will begin with calendar year 2020 (unless the taxpayer qualifies for late election relief).

April 1, 2019

Electronic filers of information returns.

Electronically file those information returns listed under Feb. 28 above (e.g., Form 1099s, Form W-2s, etc.). (Feb. 28 is the due date for non-electronic filers.)

April 15, 2019

Individuals.

Individual taxpayers (except those living in Maine or Massachusetts, who have until Apr. 17) file an income tax return for 2018 (Form 1040), and pay any tax due. Taxpayers who can't make payments should request (on Form 9465) an agreement to pay in installments. If you want an automatic 6-month extension to file, file Form 4868 or make an electronic payment by Apr. 15. Then file Form 1040 by Oct. 15.

U.S. citizens and resident aliens living and working (or on military duty) outside the U.S. and Puerto Rico are allowed an automatic 2-month extension of time (to June 17) to file their returns and pay any tax due.

If you aren't paying your 2019 income tax through withholding (or won't pay in enough tax during the year that way), pay the first installment of your 2019 estimated tax by this date. Use Form 1040-ES, or pay by various electronic means.

Contributions to an IRA for 2018 must be made by Apr. 15.

C corporations.

File a 2018 *calendar year* income tax return (Form 1120), and pay any tax still due. If you want an automatic 6-month extension, file Form 7004 and deposit what you estimate you owe.

Corporations.

Calendar year corporations must deposit the first installment of estimated income tax for 2019.

June 17, 2019

Individuals.

Make the second installment payment of your 2019 estimated tax, if you aren't paying your income tax for the year through withholding (or won't pay in enough tax that way). Use Form 1040-ES, or pay by various electronic means.

If you are a U.S. citizen or resident alien living and working (or on military duty) outside the U.S. and Puerto Rico, file your 2018 Form 1040 and pay any tax, interest and penalties due. For a 4-month filing extension to Oct. 15, file Form 4868 and check the box on line 8 If you are a participant in a combat zone, you may be able to further extend the filing deadline.

Corporations.

Calendar year corporations must deposit the second installment of estimated income tax for 2019.

July 31, 2019

All employers.

If you maintain an employee benefit plan, such as a pension, profit-sharing, or stock bonus plan, file Form 5500 or Form 5500-EZ for calendar year 2018. If you use a fiscal year as your plan year, file the form by the last day of the seventh month after the plan year ends.

September 16, 2019

Individuals.

Make the third installment payment of your 2019 estimated tax, if you aren't paying your income tax for the year through withholding (or won't pay in enough tax that way). Use Form 1040-ES, or pay by various electronic means.

S corporations.

File a 2018 calendar year income tax return (Form 1120S), and pay any tax due if you were given an automatic 6-month extension.

Corporations.

Calendar year corporations must deposit the third installment of estimated income tax for 2019.

Partnerships.

File a 2018 calendar year return (Form 1065) if you were given an automatic 6-month extension.

October 15, 2019

Individuals.

If you have an automatic 4-month or 6-month extension to file your income tax return for 2018, file Form 1040 and pay any tax, interest, and penalties due.

C corporations.

File a 2018 calendar year income tax return (Form 1120), and pay any tax due if you were given an automatic 6-month extension.

During November, 2019

All employers.

Request that employees whose withholding exemptions will be different in 2020 fill out a new Form W-4.

December 16, 2019

Corporations.

Calendar year corporation must deposit the fourth installment of estimated income tax for 2019.

2019 FEDERAL TAX HANDBOOK

Contents

Table of Contents—Main Topics

Chapter 1 Tax Rates and Tables

¶ 1100   **Tax Rates and Tables.** ▬▬▬▬▬▬▬

Different rates apply for federal income (¶1101 *et seq.*), gift (¶1114), excise (¶1117), and other taxes. The income tax tables are reflected at ¶1111.

¶ 1101   **Income tax rates for individuals.**

Different rates apply to:

. . . single taxpayers (¶1102);

. . . married persons filing joint returns (see ¶4705) and qualified widows and widowers (¶1103);

. . . married persons filing separate returns (¶1104); and

. . . heads of households (¶1105).

Bankruptcy estates of individuals compute their tax using the same rate schedule as married individuals filing separate tax returns.

Individuals with taxable income under a ceiling amount ($100,000) may compute their tax using tax tables (Code Sec. 3); see ¶1111.

For the 3.8% surtax on "unearned income," see ¶1107.

For capital gains rates, see ¶2600 *et seq.*

¶ 1102   **Single individuals.**

Taxpayers who aren't married *at year's end* and who don't qualify as surviving spouses or heads of household, and certain married taxpayers living apart compute their tax under the following tax rates for single persons if they can't use the tax tables.

The rates for 2018 are:

If taxable income is:	The tax is:
Not over $9,525	10% of taxable income
Over $9,525 but not over $38,700	$952.50 plus 12% of the excess over $9,525
Over $38,700 but not over $82,500	$4,453.50 plus 22% of the excess over $38,700
Over $82,500 but not over $157,500	$14,089.50 plus 24% of the excess over $82,500
Over $157,500 but not over $200,000	$32,089.50 plus 32% of the excess over $157,500
Over $200,000 but not over $500,000	$45,689.50 plus 35% of the excess over $200,000
Over $500,000	$150,689.50 plus 37% of the excess over $500,000

The rates for 2019 are, as calculated by Thomson Reuters based on inflation data:

If taxable income is:	The tax is:
Not over $9,700	10% of taxable income
Over $9,700 but not over $39,475	$970 plus 12% of the excess over $9,700
Over $39,475 but not over $84,200	$4,543 plus 22% of the excess over $39,475
Over $84,200 but not over $160,725	$14,382.50 plus 24% of the excess over $84,200

Over $160,725 but not over $204,100	$32,748.50 plus 32% of the excess over $160,725
Over $204,100 but not over $510,300	$46,628.50 plus 35% of the excess over $204,100
Over $510,300	$153,798.50 plus 37% of the excess over $510,300

¶ 1103   Married filing joint returns and surviving spouses.

Married taxpayers filing joint returns and surviving spouses who can't use the tax tables compute their tax on the basis of the rates indicated below.

The rates for 2018 are:

If taxable income is:	The tax is:
Not over $19,050	10% of taxable income
Over $19,050 but not over $77,400	$1,905 plus 12% of the excess over $19,050
Over $77,400 but not over $165,000	$8,907 plus 22% of the excess over $77,400
Over $165,000 but not over $315,000	$28,179 plus 24% of the excess over $165,000
Over $315,000 but not over $400,000	$64,179 plus 32% of the excess over $315,000
Over $400,000 but not over $600,000	$91,379 plus 35% of the excess over $400,000
Over $600,000	$161,379 plus 37% of the excess over $600,000

The rates for 2019 are, as calculated by Thomson Reuters based on inflation data:

If taxable income is:	The tax is:
Not over $19,400	10% of taxable income
Over $19,400 but not over $78,950	$1,940 plus 12% of the excess over $19,400
Over $78,950 but not over $168,400	$9,086 plus 22% of the excess over $78,950
Over $168,400 but not over $321,450	$28,765 plus 24% of the excess over $168,400
Over $321,450 but not over $408,200	$65,497 plus 32% of the excess over $321,450
Over $408,200 but not over $612,350	$93,257 plus 35% of the excess over $408,200
Over $612,350	$164,709.50 plus 37% of the excess over $612,350

¶ 1104   Married filing separate returns.

Married taxpayers filing separate returns who can't use the tax tables compute their tax on the basis of the rates indicated below.

The rates for 2018 are:

If taxable income is:	The tax is:
Not over $9,525	10% of taxable income
Over $9,525 but not over $38,700	$952.50 plus 12% of the excess over $9,525
Over $38,700 but not over $82,500	$4,453.50 plus 22% of the excess over $38,700
Over $82,500 but not over $157,500	$14,089.50 plus 24% of the excess over $82,500
Over $157,500 but not over $200,000	$32,089.50 plus 32% of the excess over $157,500
Over $200,000 but not over $300,000	$45,689.50 plus 35% of the excess over $200,000
Over $300,000	$80,689.50 plus 37% of the excess over $300,000

The rates for 2019 are, as calculated by Thomson Reuters based on inflation data:

If taxable income is:	The tax is:
Not over $9,700	10% of taxable income
Over $9,700 but not over $39,475	$970 plus 12% of the excess over $9,700
Over $39,475 but not over $84,200	$4,543 plus 22% of the excess over $39,475
Over $84,200 but not over $160,725	$14,382.50 plus 24% of the excess over $84,200
Over $160,725 but not over $204,100	$32,748.50 plus 32% of the excess over $160,725
Over $204,100 but not over $306,175	$46,628.50 plus 35% of the excess over $204,100
Over $306,175	$82,354.75 plus 37% of the excess over $306,175

¶ 1105   Head of household.

Unmarried persons maintaining households who can't use the tax tables compute their tax on the basis of the rates indicated below.

The rates for 2018 are:

If taxable income is:	The tax is:
Not over $13,600	10% of taxable income
Over $13,600 but not over $51,800	$1,360 plus 12% of the excess over $13,600
Over $51,800 but not over $82,500	$5,944 plus 22% of the excess over $51,800
Over $82,500 but not over $157,500	$12,698 plus 24% of the excess over $82,500
Over $157,500 but not over $200,000	$30,698 plus 32% of the excess over $157,500
Over $200,000 but not over $500,000	$44,298 plus 35% of the excess over $200,000
Over $500,000	$149,298 plus 37% of the excess over $500,000

The rates for 2019 are, as calculated by Thomson Reuters based on inflation data:

If taxable income is:	The tax is:
Not over $13,850	10% of taxable income
Over $13,850 but not over $52,850	$1,385 plus 12% of the excess over $13,850
Over $52,850 but not over $84,200	$6,065 plus 22% of the excess over $52,850
Over $84,200 but not over $160,700	$12,962 plus 24% of the excess over $84,200
Over $160,700 but not over $204,100	$31,322 plus 32% of the excess over $160,700
Over $204,100 but not over $510,300	$45,210 plus 35% of the excess over $204,100
Over $510,300	$152,380 plus 37% of the excess over $510,300

¶ 1106   Income tax rates for trusts and estates.

The income tax on trusts and decedent's estates is imposed at graduated rates on their taxable income. (Code Sec. 1(e)) For capital gains rates, see ¶2600.

The rates for 2018 are:

If taxable income is:	The tax is:
Not over $2,550	10% of taxable income
Over $2,550 but not over $9,150	$255 plus 24% of the excess over $2,550
Over $9,150 but not over $12,500	$1,839 plus 35% of the excess over $9,150
Over $12,500	$3,011.50 plus 37% of the excess over $12,500

The rates for 2019 are, as calculated by Thomson Reuters based on inflation data:

If taxable income is:	The tax is:
Not over $2,600	10% of taxable income
Over $2,600 but not over $9,300	$260 plus 24% of the excess over $2,600
Over $9,300 but not over $12,750	$1,868 plus 35% of the excess over $9,300
Over $12,750	$3,075.50 plus 37% of the excess over $12,750

¶ 1107   3.8% surtax on "unearned income."

Certain unearned income of individuals, trusts, and estates is subject to a surtax (i.e., it's payable on top of any other tax payable on that income). For individuals, the surtax is 3.8% of the lesser of (1) "net investment income" or (2) the excess of modified adjusted gross income (MAGI) over the threshold amount ($250,000 for joint filers or surviving spouses, $125,000 for a married individual filing a separate return, and $200,000 in any other case). Special computations apply to estates and trusts. (Code Sec. 1411(a)(1), Code Sec. 1411(b))[1] For details, see ¶3142 *et seq.*

¶ 1108   FICA (Social Security and Medicare) tax.

For 2018, an employer pays a 7.65% FICA tax, consisting of:

(a) 6.20% Social Security tax on the first $128,400 of an employee's wages (maximum tax is $7,960.80 [6.20% of $128,400]), plus

(b) 1.45% Medicare tax on the employee's total wages (no ceiling).

For 2018, an employee pays:

(a) 6.20% Social Security tax on the first $128,400 of wages (maximum tax is $7,960.80 [6.20% of $128,400]), plus

(b) 1.45% Medicare tax on the first $200,000 of wages ($250,000 for joint returns; $125,000 for married taxpayers filing a separate return), plus

(c) 2.35% Medicare tax (regular 1.45% Medicare tax + 0.9% additional Medicare tax) on all wages in excess of $200,000 ($250,000 for joint returns; $125,000 for married taxpayers filing a separate return). (Code Sec. 3101(b)(2))

For 2019, an employer pays a 7.65% FICA tax, consisting of:

(a) 6.20% Social Security tax on the first $132,900 of an employee's wages (maximum tax is $8,239.80 [6.20% of $132,900]), plus

(b) 1.45% Medicare tax on the employee's total wages (no ceiling).

For 2019, an employee pays:

(a) 6.20% Social Security tax on the first $132,900 of wages (maximum tax is $8,239.80 [6.20% of $132,900]), plus

(b) 1.45% Medicare tax on the first $200,000 of wages ($250,000 for joint returns; $125,000 for married taxpayers filing a separate return), plus

(c) 2.35% Medicare tax (regular 1.45% Medicare tax + 0.9% additional Medicare tax) on all wages in excess of $200,000 ($250,000 for joint returns; $125,000 for married taxpayers filing a separate return). (Code Sec. 3101(b)(2))

The 0.9% additional Medicare tax applies only to employees, not employers. Employers

---

1. ¶A-6361; ¶14,114.01

must begin withholding the additional Medicare tax once an employee's wages exceed $200,000, even if the employee may not ultimately be liable for the additional tax (e.g., employee earns $210,000, his or her spouse earns $25,000, and they file a joint return). Any excess additional Medicare tax withheld will be credited against the total tax liability shown on the employee's income tax return. Conversely, the 0.9% additional Medicare tax may be owed on the employee's income tax return where there was no withholding for it (e.g., employee earns $175,000 and her spouse earns $150,000). [2]

¶ 1109   Self-employment tax.

For 2018, the self-employment tax imposed on self-employed people is:

- 12.40% OASDI on the first $128,400 of self-employment income, for a maximum tax of $15,921.60 (12.40% of $128,400); plus

- 2.90% Medicare tax on the first $200,000 of self-employment income ($250,000 of combined self-employment income on a joint return, $125,000 on a separate return), (Code Sec. 1401(a), Code Sec. 1401(b)), plus

- 3.8% (2.90% regular Medicare tax + 0.9% additional Medicare tax) on all self-employment income in excess of $200,000 ($250,000 of combined self-employment income on a joint return, $125,000 for married taxpayers filing a separate return). (Code Sec. 1401(b)(2))

For 2019, the self-employment tax imposed on self-employed people is:

- 12.40% OASDI on the first $132,900 of self-employment income, for a maximum tax of $16,479.00 (12.40% of $132,900); plus

- 2.90% Medicare tax on the first $200,000 of self-employment income ($250,000 of combined self-employment income on a joint return, $125,000 on a separate return), (Code Sec. 1401(a), Code Sec. 1401(b)); plus

- 3.8% (2.90% regular Medicare tax + 0.9% additional Medicare tax) on all self-employment income in excess of $200,000 ($250,000 of combined self-employment income on a joint return, $125,000 for married taxpayers filing a separate return). (Code Sec. 1401(b)(2))

The above $250,000, $125,000, and $200,000 thresholds are reduced (but not below zero) by the amount of wages taken into account in determining the additional 0.9% HI tax on wages (i.e., the taxpayer's FICA tax, see ¶1108). (Code Sec. 1401(b)(2)(B))[3]

illustration: A single taxpayer has $150,000 in self-employment income and $120,000 in wages. The taxpayer's wages didn't exceed $200,000, so the taxpayer's employer didn't withhold the 0.9% tax. However, the $120,000 in wages reduces the $200,000 threshold for the 0.9% additional Medicare tax to $80,000, so the taxpayer owes the 0.9% tax on $70,000 of self-employment income (i.e., the extent to which the taxpayer's $150,000 in self-employment income exceeds the $80,000 threshold). (Reg § 1.1401-1(d)(2), 3)

observation: Sole proprietors and partners are subject to Medicare tax on their entire self-employment income even if the income isn't distributed (unlike shareholders in an S corporation, who aren't subject to the self-employment tax on their share of the corporation's net income whether distributed or not, see ¶3135).

observation: Amounts subject to self-employment tax are excluded from "investment income" for purposes of the 3.8% net investment income tax (¶1107).

---

2. ¶H-4687; ¶35,014.07   3. ¶A-6001.2; ¶14,014

¶ 1110   Federal unemployment tax (FUTA).

Employers pay a 6.0% (Code Sec. 3301) tax on the first $7,000 paid each employee as wages during the calendar year. (Code Sec. 3306(b)) This tax may be offset by a credit of up to 5.4% for contributions paid into state unemployment funds, effectively reducing the net FUTA tax rate for the majority of employers to 0.6% (i.e., 6.0% − 5.4%). However, the amount of the 5.4% credit can be reduced for employers in states that borrowed funds from the federal government to pay unemployment benefits and defaulted on repayment of the loan.

¶ 1111   Tax Table for Individuals.

2018 Tax Table

⚠ CAUTION

See the instructions for line 11a to see if you must use the Tax Table below to figure your tax.

Example. Mr. and Mrs. Brown are filing a joint return. Their taxable income on Form 1040, line 10, is $25,300. First, they find the $25,300-25,350 taxable income line. Next, they find the column for married filing jointly and read down the column. The amount shown where the taxable income line and filing status column meet is $2,658. This is the tax amount they should enter in the entry space on Form 1040, line 11a.

Sample Table

At Least	But Less Than	Single	Married filing jointly*	Married filing separately	Head of a household
			Your tax is—		
25,200	25,250	2,837	2,646	2,837	2,755
25,250	25,300	2,843	2,652	2,843	2,761
25,300	25,350	2,849	(2,658)	2,849	2,767
25,350	25,400	2,855	2,664	2,855	2,773

DRAFT AS OF September 26, 2018

If line 10 (taxable income) is— At least	But less than	Single	Married filing jointly*	Married filing separately	Head of a household
			Your tax is—		
0	5	0	0	0	0
5	15	1	1	1	1
15	25	2	2	2	2
25	50	4	4	4	4
50	75	6	6	6	6
75	100	9	9	9	9
100	125	11	11	11	11
125	150	14	14	14	14
150	175	16	16	16	16
175	200	19	19	19	19
200	225	21	21	21	21
225	250	24	24	24	24
250	275	26	26	26	26
275	300	29	29	29	29
300	325	31	31	31	31
325	350	34	34	34	34
350	375	36	36	36	36
375	400	39	39	39	39
400	425	41	41	41	41
425	450	44	44	44	44
450	475	46	46	46	46
475	500	49	49	49	49
500	525	51	51	51	51
525	550	54	54	54	54
550	575	56	56	56	56
575	600	59	59	59	59
600	625	61	61	61	61
625	650	64	64	64	64
650	675	66	66	66	66
675	700	69	69	69	69
700	725	71	71	71	71
725	750	74	74	74	74
750	775	76	76	76	76
775	800	79	79	79	79
800	825	81	81	81	81
825	850	84	84	84	84
850	875	86	86	86	86
875	900	89	89	89	89
900	925	91	91	91	91
925	950	94	94	94	94
950	975	96	96	96	96
975	1,000	99	99	99	99

1,000

At least	But less than	Single	Married filing jointly*	Married filing separately	Head of a household
1,000	1,025	101	101	101	101
1,025	1,050	104	104	104	104
1,050	1,075	106	106	106	106
1,075	1,100	109	109	109	109
1,100	1,125	111	111	111	111
1,125	1,150	114	114	114	114
1,150	1,175	116	116	116	116
1,175	1,200	119	119	119	119
1,200	1,225	121	121	121	121
1,225	1,250	124	124	124	124
1,250	1,275	126	126	126	126
1,275	1,300	129	129	129	129
1,300	1,325	131	131	131	131
1,325	1,350	134	134	134	134
1,350	1,375	136	136	136	136
1,375	1,400	139	139	139	139
1,400	1,425	141	141	141	141
1,425	1,450	144	144	144	144
1,450	1,475	146	146	146	146
1,475	1,500	149	149	149	149
1,500	1,525	151	151	151	151
1,525	1,550	154	154	154	154
1,550	1,575	156	156	156	156
1,575	1,600	159	159	159	159
1,600	1,625	161	161	161	161
1,625	1,650	164	164	164	164
1,650	1,675	166	166	166	166
1,675	1,700	169	169	169	169
1,700	1,725	171	171	171	171
1,725	1,750	174	174	174	174
1,750	1,775	176	176	176	176
1,775	1,800	179	179	179	179
1,800	1,825	181	181	181	181
1,825	1,850	184	184	184	184
1,850	1,875	186	186	186	186
1,875	1,900	189	189	189	189
1,900	1,925	191	191	191	191
1,925	1,950	194	194	194	194
1,950	1,975	196	196	196	196
1,975	2,000	199	199	199	199

2,000

At least	But less than	Single	Married filing jointly*	Married filing separately	Head of a household
2,000	2,025	201	201	201	201
2,025	2,050	204	204	204	204
2,050	2,075	206	206	206	206
2,075	2,100	209	209	209	209
2,100	2,125	211	211	211	211
2,125	2,150	214	214	214	214
2,150	2,175	216	216	216	216
2,175	2,200	219	219	219	219
2,200	2,225	221	221	221	221
2,225	2,250	224	224	224	224
2,250	2,275	226	226	226	226
2,275	2,300	229	229	229	229
2,300	2,325	231	231	231	231
2,325	2,350	234	234	234	234
2,350	2,375	236	236	236	236
2,375	2,400	239	239	239	239
2,400	2,425	241	241	241	241
2,425	2,450	244	244	244	244
2,450	2,475	246	246	246	246
2,475	2,500	249	249	249	249
2,500	2,525	251	251	251	251
2,525	2,550	254	254	254	254
2,550	2,575	256	256	256	256
2,575	2,600	259	259	259	259
2,600	2,625	261	261	261	261
2,625	2,650	264	264	264	264
2,650	2,675	266	266	266	266
2,675	2,700	269	269	269	269
2,700	2,725	271	271	271	271
2,725	2,750	274	274	274	274
2,750	2,775	276	276	276	276
2,775	2,800	279	279	279	279
2,800	2,825	281	281	281	281
2,825	2,850	284	284	284	284
2,850	2,875	286	286	286	286
2,875	2,900	289	289	289	289
2,900	2,925	291	291	291	291
2,925	2,950	294	294	294	294
2,950	2,975	296	296	296	296
2,975	3,000	299	299	299	299

(Continued)

* This column must also be used by a qualifying widow(er).

Draft As of September 26, 2018.

2018 Tax Table — *Continued*

3,000

At least	But less than	Single	Married filing jointly *	Married filing separately	Head of a household
3,000	3,050	303	303	303	303
3,050	3,100	308	308	308	308
3,100	3,150	313	313	313	313
3,150	3,200	318	318	318	318
3,200	3,250	323	323	323	323
3,250	3,300	328	328	328	328
3,300	3,350	333	333	333	333
3,350	3,400	338	338	338	338
3,400	3,450	343	343	343	343
3,450	3,500	348	348	348	348
3,500	3,550	353	353	353	353
3,550	3,600	358	358	358	358
3,600	3,650	363	363	363	363
3,650	3,700	368	368	368	368
3,700	3,750	373	373	373	373
3,750	3,800	378	378	378	378
3,800	3,850	383	383	383	383
3,850	3,900	388	388	388	388
3,900	3,950	393	393	393	393
3,950	4,000	398	398	398	398

4,000

At least	But less than	Single	Married filing jointly *	Married filing separately	Head of a household
4,000	4,050	403	403	403	403
4,050	4,100	408	408	408	408
4,100	4,150	413	413	413	413
4,150	4,200	418	418	418	418
4,200	4,250	423	423	423	423
4,250	4,300	428	428	428	428
4,300	4,350	433	433	433	433
4,350	4,400	438	438	438	438
4,400	4,450	443	443	443	443
4,450	4,500	448	448	448	448
4,500	4,550	453	453	453	453
4,550	4,600	458	458	458	458
4,600	4,650	463	463	463	463
4,650	4,700	468	468	468	468
4,700	4,750	473	473	473	473
4,750	4,800	478	478	478	478
4,800	4,850	483	483	483	483
4,850	4,900	488	488	488	488
4,900	4,950	493	493	493	493
4,950	5,000	498	498	498	498

5,000

At least	But less than	Single	Married filing jointly *	Married filing separately	Head of a household
5,000	5,050	503	503	503	503
5,050	5,100	508	508	508	508
5,100	5,150	513	513	513	513
5,150	5,200	518	518	518	518
5,200	5,250	523	523	523	523
5,250	5,300	528	528	528	528
5,300	5,350	533	533	533	533
5,350	5,400	538	538	538	538
5,400	5,450	543	543	543	543
5,450	5,500	548	548	548	548
5,500	5,550	553	553	553	553
5,550	5,600	558	558	558	558
5,600	5,650	563	563	563	563
5,650	5,700	568	568	568	568
5,700	5,750	573	573	573	573
5,750	5,800	578	578	578	578
5,800	5,850	583	583	583	583
5,850	5,900	588	588	588	588
5,900	5,950	593	593	593	593
5,950	6,000	598	598	598	598

6,000

At least	But less than	Single	Married filing jointly *	Married filing separately	Head of a household
6,000	6,050	603	603	603	603
6,050	6,100	608	608	608	608
6,100	6,150	613	613	613	613
6,150	6,200	618	618	618	618
6,200	6,250	623	623	623	623
6,250	6,300	628	628	628	628
6,300	6,350	633	633	633	633
6,350	6,400	638	638	638	638
6,400	6,450	643	643	643	643
6,450	6,500	648	648	648	648
6,500	6,550	653	653	653	653
6,550	6,600	658	658	658	658
6,600	6,650	663	663	663	663
6,650	6,700	668	668	668	668
6,700	6,750	673	673	673	673
6,750	6,800	678	678	678	678
6,800	6,850	683	683	683	683
6,850	6,900	688	688	688	688
6,900	6,950	693	693	693	693
6,950	7,000	698	698	698	698

7,000

At least	But less than	Single	Married filing jointly *	Married filing separately	Head of a household
7,000	7,050	703	703	703	703
7,050	7,100	708	708	708	708
7,100	7,150	713	713	713	713
7,150	7,200	718	718	718	718
7,200	7,250	723	723	723	723
7,250	7,300	728	728	728	728
7,300	7,350	733	733	733	733
7,350	7,400	738	738	738	738
7,400	7,450	743	743	743	743
7,450	7,500	748	748	748	748
7,500	7,550	753	753	753	753
7,550	7,600	758	758	758	758
7,600	7,650	763	763	763	763
7,650	7,700	768	768	768	768
7,700	7,750	773	773	773	773
7,750	7,800	778	778	778	778
7,800	7,850	783	783	783	783
7,850	7,900	788	788	788	788
7,900	7,950	793	793	793	793
7,950	8,000	798	798	798	798

8,000

At least	But less than	Single	Married filing jointly *	Married filing separately	Head of a household
8,000	8,050	803	803	803	803
8,050	8,100	808	808	808	808
8,100	8,150	813	813	813	813
8,150	8,200	818	818	818	818
8,200	8,250	823	823	823	823
8,250	8,300	828	828	828	828
8,300	8,350	833	833	833	833
8,350	8,400	838	838	838	838
8,400	8,450	843	843	843	843
8,450	8,500	848	848	848	848
8,500	8,550	853	853	853	853
8,550	8,600	858	858	858	858
8,600	8,650	863	863	863	863
8,650	8,700	868	868	868	868
8,700	8,750	873	873	873	873
8,750	8,800	878	878	878	878
8,800	8,850	883	883	883	883
8,850	8,900	888	888	888	888
8,900	8,950	893	893	893	893
8,950	9,000	898	898	898	898

9,000

At least	But less than	Single	Married filing jointly *	Married filing separately	Head of a household
9,000	9,050	903	903	903	903
9,050	9,100	908	908	908	908
9,100	9,150	913	913	913	913
9,150	9,200	918	918	918	918
9,200	9,250	923	923	923	923
9,250	9,300	928	928	928	928
9,300	9,350	933	933	933	933
9,350	9,400	938	938	938	938
9,400	9,450	943	943	943	943
9,450	9,500	948	948	948	948
9,500	9,550	953	953	953	953
9,550	9,600	959	958	959	958
9,600	9,650	965	963	965	963
9,650	9,700	971	968	971	968
9,700	9,750	977	973	977	973
9,750	9,800	983	978	983	978
9,800	9,850	989	983	989	983
9,850	9,900	995	988	995	988
9,900	9,950	1,001	993	1,001	993
9,950	10,000	1,007	998	1,007	998

10,000

At least	But less than	Single	Married filing jointly *	Married filing separately	Head of a household
10,000	10,050	1,013	1,003	1,013	1,003
10,050	10,100	1,019	1,008	1,019	1,008
10,100	10,150	1,025	1,013	1,025	1,013
10,150	10,200	1,031	1,018	1,031	1,018
10,200	10,250	1,037	1,023	1,037	1,023
10,250	10,300	1,043	1,028	1,043	1,028
10,300	10,350	1,049	1,033	1,049	1,033
10,350	10,400	1,055	1,038	1,055	1,038
10,400	10,450	1,061	1,043	1,061	1,043
10,450	10,500	1,067	1,048	1,067	1,048
10,500	10,550	1,073	1,053	1,073	1,053
10,550	10,600	1,079	1,058	1,079	1,058
10,600	10,650	1,085	1,063	1,085	1,063
10,650	10,700	1,091	1,068	1,091	1,068
10,700	10,750	1,097	1,073	1,097	1,073
10,750	10,800	1,103	1,078	1,103	1,078
10,800	10,850	1,109	1,083	1,109	1,083
10,850	10,900	1,115	1,088	1,115	1,088
10,900	10,950	1,121	1,093	1,121	1,093
10,950	11,000	1,127	1,098	1,127	1,098

11,000

At least	But less than	Single	Married filing jointly *	Married filing separately	Head of a household
11,000	11,050	1,133	1,103	1,133	1,103
11,050	11,100	1,139	1,108	1,139	1,108
11,100	11,150	1,145	1,113	1,145	1,113
11,150	11,200	1,151	1,118	1,151	1,118
11,200	11,250	1,157	1,123	1,157	1,123
11,250	11,300	1,163	1,128	1,163	1,128
11,300	11,350	1,169	1,133	1,169	1,133
11,350	11,400	1,175	1,138	1,175	1,138
11,400	11,450	1,181	1,143	1,181	1,143
11,450	11,500	1,187	1,148	1,187	1,148
11,500	11,550	1,193	1,153	1,193	1,155
11,550	11,600	1,199	1,158	1,199	1,158
11,600	11,650	1,205	1,163	1,205	1,163
11,650	11,700	1,211	1,168	1,211	1,168
11,700	11,750	1,217	1,173	1,217	1,173
11,750	11,800	1,223	1,178	1,223	1,178
11,800	11,850	1,229	1,183	1,229	1,183
11,850	11,900	1,235	1,188	1,235	1,188
11,900	11,950	1,241	1,193	1,241	1,193
11,950	12,000	1,247	1,198	1,247	1,198

(Continued)

* This column must also be used by a qualifying widow(er).

Draft As of September 26, 2018.

2018 Tax Table — *Continued*

DRAFT AS OF September 26, 2018

Left panel (12,000 – 14,999)

If line 10 (taxable income) is— At least	But less than	Single	Married filing jointly *	Married filing separately	Head of a household
			Your tax is—		
12,000					
12,000	12,050	1,253	1,203	1,253	1,203
12,050	12,100	1,259	1,208	1,259	1,208
12,100	12,150	1,265	1,213	1,265	1,213
12,150	12,200	1,271	1,218	1,271	1,218
12,200	12,250	1,277	1,223	1,277	1,223
12,250	12,300	1,283	1,228	1,283	1,228
12,300	12,350	1,289	1,233	1,289	1,233
12,350	12,400	1,295	1,238	1,295	1,238
12,400	12,450	1,301	1,243	1,301	1,243
12,450	12,500	1,307	1,248	1,307	1,248
12,500	12,550	1,313	1,253	1,313	1,253
12,550	12,600	1,319	1,258	1,319	1,258
12,600	12,650	1,325	1,263	1,325	1,263
12,650	12,700	1,331	1,268	1,331	1,268
12,700	12,750	1,337	1,273	1,337	1,273
12,750	12,800	1,343	1,278	1,343	1,278
12,800	12,850	1,349	1,283	1,349	1,283
12,850	12,900	1,355	1,288	1,355	1,288
12,900	12,950	1,361	1,293	1,361	1,293
12,950	13,000	1,367	1,298	1,367	1,298
13,000					
13,000	13,050	1,373	1,303	1,373	1,303
13,050	13,100	1,379	1,308	1,379	1,308
13,100	13,150	1,385	1,313	1,385	1,313
13,150	13,200	1,391	1,318	1,391	1,318
13,200	13,250	1,397	1,323	1,397	1,323
13,250	13,300	1,403	1,328	1,403	1,328
13,300	13,350	1,409	1,333	1,409	1,333
13,350	13,400	1,415	1,338	1,415	1,338
13,400	13,450	1,421	1,343	1,421	1,343
13,450	13,500	1,427	1,348	1,427	1,348
13,500	13,550	1,433	1,353	1,433	1,353
13,550	13,600	1,439	1,358	1,439	1,358
13,600	13,650	1,445	1,363	1,445	1,363
13,650	13,700	1,451	1,368	1,451	1,368
13,700	13,750	1,457	1,373	1,457	1,373
13,750	13,800	1,463	1,378	1,463	1,381
13,800	13,850	1,469	1,383	1,469	1,387
13,850	13,900	1,475	1,388	1,475	1,393
13,900	13,950	1,481	1,393	1,481	1,399
13,950	14,000	1,487	1,398	1,487	1,405
14,000					
14,000	14,050	1,493	1,403	1,493	1,411
14,050	14,100	1,499	1,408	1,499	1,417
14,100	14,150	1,505	1,413	1,505	1,423
14,150	14,200	1,511	1,418	1,511	1,429
14,200	14,250	1,517	1,423	1,517	1,435
14,250	14,300	1,523	1,428	1,523	1,441
14,300	14,350	1,529	1,433	1,529	1,447
14,350	14,400	1,535	1,438	1,535	1,453
14,400	14,450	1,541	1,443	1,541	1,459
14,450	14,500	1,547	1,448	1,547	1,465
14,500	14,550	1,553	1,453	1,553	1,471
14,550	14,600	1,559	1,458	1,559	1,477
14,600	14,650	1,565	1,463	1,565	1,483
14,650	14,700	1,571	1,468	1,571	1,489
14,700	14,750	1,577	1,473	1,577	1,495
14,750	14,800	1,583	1,478	1,583	1,501
14,800	14,850	1,589	1,483	1,589	1,507
14,850	14,900	1,595	1,488	1,595	1,513
14,900	14,950	1,601	1,493	1,601	1,519
14,950	15,000	1,607	1,498	1,607	1,525

Middle panel (15,000 – 17,999)

At least	But less than	Single	Married filing jointly *	Married filing separately	Head of a household
			Your tax is—		
15,000					
15,000	15,050	1,613	1,503	1,613	1,531
15,050	15,100	1,619	1,508	1,619	1,537
15,100	15,150	1,625	1,513	1,625	1,543
15,150	15,200	1,631	1,518	1,631	1,549
15,200	15,250	1,637	1,523	1,637	1,555
15,250	15,300	1,643	1,528	1,643	1,561
15,300	15,350	1,649	1,533	1,649	1,567
15,350	15,400	1,655	1,538	1,655	1,573
15,400	15,450	1,661	1,543	1,661	1,579
15,450	15,500	1,667	1,548	1,667	1,585
15,500	15,550	1,673	1,553	1,673	1,591
15,550	15,600	1,679	1,558	1,679	1,597
15,600	15,650	1,685	1,563	1,685	1,603
15,650	15,700	1,691	1,568	1,691	1,609
15,700	15,750	1,697	1,573	1,697	1,615
15,750	15,800	1,703	1,578	1,703	1,621
15,800	15,850	1,709	1,583	1,709	1,627
15,850	15,900	1,715	1,588	1,715	1,633
15,900	15,950	1,721	1,593	1,721	1,639
15,950	16,000	1,727	1,598	1,727	1,645
16,000					
16,000	16,050	1,733	1,603	1,733	1,651
16,050	16,100	1,739	1,608	1,739	1,657
16,100	16,150	1,745	1,613	1,745	1,663
16,150	16,200	1,751	1,618	1,751	1,669
16,200	16,250	1,757	1,623	1,757	1,675
16,250	16,300	1,763	1,628	1,763	1,681
16,300	16,350	1,769	1,633	1,769	1,687
16,350	16,400	1,775	1,638	1,775	1,693
16,400	16,450	1,781	1,643	1,781	1,699
16,450	16,500	1,787	1,648	1,787	1,705
16,500	16,550	1,793	1,653	1,793	1,711
16,550	16,600	1,799	1,658	1,799	1,717
16,600	16,650	1,805	1,663	1,805	1,723
16,650	16,700	1,811	1,668	1,811	1,729
16,700	16,750	1,817	1,673	1,817	1,735
16,750	16,800	1,823	1,678	1,823	1,741
16,800	16,850	1,829	1,683	1,829	1,747
16,850	16,900	1,835	1,688	1,835	1,753
16,900	16,950	1,841	1,693	1,841	1,759
16,950	17,000	1,847	1,698	1,847	1,765
17,000					
17,000	17,050	1,853	1,703	1,853	1,771
17,050	17,100	1,859	1,708	1,859	1,777
17,100	17,150	1,865	1,713	1,865	1,783
17,150	17,200	1,871	1,718	1,871	1,789
17,200	17,250	1,877	1,723	1,877	1,795
17,250	17,300	1,883	1,728	1,883	1,801
17,300	17,350	1,889	1,733	1,889	1,807
17,350	17,400	1,895	1,738	1,895	1,813
17,400	17,450	1,901	1,743	1,901	1,819
17,450	17,500	1,907	1,748	1,907	1,825
17,500	17,550	1,913	1,753	1,913	1,831
17,550	17,600	1,919	1,758	1,919	1,837
17,600	17,650	1,925	1,763	1,925	1,843
17,650	17,700	1,931	1,768	1,931	1,849
17,700	17,750	1,937	1,773	1,937	1,855
17,750	17,800	1,943	1,778	1,943	1,861
17,800	17,850	1,949	1,783	1,949	1,867
17,850	17,900	1,955	1,788	1,955	1,873
17,900	17,950	1,961	1,793	1,961	1,879
17,950	18,000	1,967	1,798	1,967	1,885

Right panel (18,000 – 20,999)

At least	But less than	Single	Married filing jointly *	Married filing separately	Head of a household
			Your tax is—		
18,000					
18,000	18,050	1,973	1,803	1,973	1,891
18,050	18,100	1,979	1,808	1,979	1,897
18,100	18,150	1,985	1,813	1,985	1,903
18,150	18,200	1,991	1,818	1,991	1,909
18,200	18,250	1,997	1,823	1,997	1,915
18,250	18,300	2,003	1,828	2,003	1,921
18,300	18,350	2,009	1,833	2,009	1,927
18,350	18,400	2,015	1,838	2,015	1,933
18,400	18,450	2,021	1,843	2,021	1,939
18,450	18,500	2,027	1,848	2,027	1,945
18,500	18,550	2,033	1,853	2,033	1,951
18,550	18,600	2,039	1,858	2,039	1,957
18,600	18,650	2,045	1,863	2,045	1,963
18,650	18,700	2,051	1,868	2,051	1,969
18,700	18,750	2,057	1,873	2,057	1,975
18,750	18,800	2,063	1,878	2,063	1,981
18,800	18,850	2,069	1,883	2,069	1,987
18,850	18,900	2,075	1,888	2,075	1,993
18,900	18,950	2,081	1,893	2,081	1,999
18,950	19,000	2,087	1,898	2,087	2,005
19,000					
19,000	19,050	2,093	1,903	2,093	2,011
19,050	19,100	2,099	1,908	2,099	2,017
19,100	19,150	2,105	1,914	2,105	2,023
19,150	19,200	2,111	1,920	2,111	2,029
19,200	19,250	2,117	1,926	2,117	2,035
19,250	19,300	2,123	1,932	2,123	2,041
19,300	19,350	2,129	1,938	2,129	2,047
19,350	19,400	2,135	1,944	2,135	2,053
19,400	19,450	2,141	1,950	2,141	2,059
19,450	19,500	2,147	1,956	2,147	2,065
19,500	19,550	2,153	1,962	2,153	2,071
19,550	19,600	2,159	1,968	2,159	2,077
19,600	19,650	2,165	1,974	2,165	2,083
19,650	19,700	2,171	1,980	2,171	2,089
19,700	19,750	2,177	1,986	2,177	2,095
19,750	19,800	2,183	1,992	2,183	2,101
19,800	19,850	2,189	1,998	2,189	2,107
19,850	19,900	2,195	2,004	2,195	2,113
19,900	19,950	2,201	2,010	2,201	2,119
19,950	20,000	2,207	2,016	2,207	2,125
20,000					
20,000	20,050	2,213	2,022	2,213	2,131
20,050	20,100	2,219	2,028	2,219	2,137
20,100	20,150	2,225	2,034	2,225	2,143
20,150	20,200	2,231	2,040	2,231	2,149
20,200	20,250	2,237	2,046	2,237	2,155
20,250	20,300	2,243	2,052	2,243	2,161
20,300	20,350	2,249	2,058	2,249	2,167
20,350	20,400	2,255	2,064	2,255	2,173
20,400	20,450	2,261	2,070	2,261	2,179
20,450	20,500	2,267	2,076	2,267	2,185
20,500	20,550	2,273	2,082	2,273	2,191
20,550	20,600	2,279	2,088	2,279	2,197
20,600	20,650	2,285	2,094	2,285	2,203
20,650	20,700	2,291	2,100	2,291	2,209
20,700	20,750	2,297	2,106	2,297	2,215
20,750	20,800	2,303	2,112	2,303	2,221
20,800	20,850	2,309	2,118	2,309	2,227
20,850	20,900	2,315	2,124	2,315	2,233
20,900	20,950	2,321	2,130	2,321	2,239
20,950	21,000	2,327	2,136	2,327	2,245

* This column must also be used by a qualifying widow(er).

(Continued)

Draft As of September 26, 2018.

2018 Tax Table — *Continued*

DRAFT AS OF September 26, 2018

If line 10 (taxable income) is—		And you are—			
At least	But less than	Single	Married filing jointly *	Married filing separately	Head of a household
		Your tax is—			
21,000					
21,000	21,050	2,333	2,142	2,333	2,251
21,050	21,100	2,339	2,148	2,339	2,257
21,100	21,150	2,345	2,154	2,345	2,263
21,150	21,200	2,351	2,160	2,351	2,269
21,200	21,250	2,357	2,166	2,357	2,275
21,250	21,300	2,363	2,172	2,363	2,281
21,300	21,350	2,369	2,178	2,369	2,287
21,350	21,400	2,375	2,184	2,375	2,293
21,400	21,450	2,381	2,190	2,381	2,299
21,450	21,500	2,387	2,196	2,387	2,305
21,500	21,550	2,393	2,202	2,393	2,311
21,550	21,600	2,399	2,208	2,399	2,317
21,600	21,650	2,405	2,214	2,405	2,323
21,650	21,700	2,411	2,220	2,411	2,329
21,700	21,750	2,417	2,226	2,417	2,335
21,750	21,800	2,423	2,232	2,423	2,341
21,800	21,850	2,429	2,238	2,429	2,347
21,850	21,900	2,435	2,244	2,435	2,353
21,900	21,950	2,441	2,250	2,441	2,359
21,950	22,000	2,447	2,256	2,447	2,365
22,000					
22,000	22,050	2,453	2,262	2,453	2,371
22,050	22,100	2,459	2,268	2,459	2,377
22,100	22,150	2,465	2,274	2,465	2,383
22,150	22,200	2,471	2,280	2,471	2,389
22,200	22,250	2,477	2,286	2,477	2,395
22,250	22,300	2,483	2,292	2,483	2,401
22,300	22,350	2,489	2,298	2,489	2,407
22,350	22,400	2,495	2,304	2,495	2,413
22,400	22,450	2,501	2,310	2,501	2,419
22,450	22,500	2,507	2,316	2,507	2,425
22,500	22,550	2,513	2,322	2,513	2,431
22,550	22,600	2,519	2,328	2,519	2,437
22,600	22,650	2,525	2,334	2,525	2,443
22,650	22,700	2,531	2,340	2,531	2,449
22,700	22,750	2,537	2,346	2,537	2,455
22,750	22,800	2,543	2,352	2,543	2,461
22,800	22,850	2,549	2,358	2,549	2,467
22,850	22,900	2,555	2,364	2,555	2,473
22,900	22,950	2,561	2,370	2,561	2,479
22,950	23,000	2,567	2,376	2,567	2,485
23,000					
23,000	23,050	2,573	2,382	2,573	2,491
23,050	23,100	2,579	2,388	2,579	2,497
23,100	23,150	2,585	2,394	2,585	2,503
23,150	23,200	2,591	2,400	2,591	2,509
23,200	23,250	2,597	2,406	2,597	2,515
23,250	23,300	2,603	2,412	2,603	2,521
23,300	23,350	2,609	2,418	2,609	2,527
23,350	23,400	2,615	2,424	2,615	2,533
23,400	23,450	2,621	2,430	2,621	2,539
23,450	23,500	2,627	2,436	2,627	2,545
23,500	23,550	2,633	2,442	2,633	2,551
23,550	23,600	2,639	2,448	2,639	2,557
23,600	23,650	2,645	2,454	2,645	2,563
23,650	23,700	2,651	2,460	2,651	2,569
23,700	23,750	2,657	2,466	2,657	2,575
23,750	23,800	2,663	2,472	2,663	2,581
23,800	23,850	2,669	2,478	2,669	2,587
23,850	23,900	2,675	2,484	2,675	2,593
23,900	23,950	2,681	2,490	2,681	2,599
23,950	24,000	2,687	2,496	2,687	2,605

If line 10 (taxable income) is—		And you are—			
At least	But less than	Single	Married filing jointly *	Married filing separately	Head of a household
		Your tax is—			
24,000					
24,000	24,050	2,693	2,502	2,693	2,611
24,050	24,100	2,699	2,508	2,699	2,617
24,100	24,150	2,705	2,514	2,705	2,623
24,150	24,200	2,711	2,520	2,711	2,629
24,200	24,250	2,717	2,526	2,717	2,635
24,250	24,300	2,723	2,532	2,723	2,641
24,300	24,350	2,729	2,538	2,729	2,647
24,350	24,400	2,735	2,544	2,735	2,653
24,400	24,450	2,741	2,550	2,741	2,659
24,450	24,500	2,747	2,556	2,747	2,665
24,500	24,550	2,753	2,562	2,753	2,671
24,550	24,600	2,759	2,568	2,759	2,677
24,600	24,650	2,765	2,574	2,765	2,683
24,650	24,700	2,771	2,580	2,771	2,689
24,700	24,750	2,777	2,586	2,777	2,695
24,750	24,800	2,783	2,592	2,783	2,701
24,800	24,850	2,789	2,598	2,789	2,707
24,850	24,900	2,795	2,604	2,795	2,713
24,900	24,950	2,801	2,610	2,801	2,719
24,950	25,000	2,807	2,616	2,807	2,725
25,000					
25,000	25,050	2,813	2,622	2,813	2,731
25,050	25,100	2,819	2,628	2,819	2,737
25,100	25,150	2,825	2,634	2,825	2,743
25,150	25,200	2,831	2,640	2,831	2,749
25,200	25,250	2,837	2,646	2,837	2,755
25,250	25,300	2,843	2,652	2,843	2,761
25,300	25,350	2,849	2,658	2,849	2,767
25,350	25,400	2,855	2,664	2,855	2,773
25,400	25,450	2,861	2,670	2,861	2,779
25,450	25,500	2,867	2,676	2,867	2,785
25,500	25,550	2,873	2,682	2,873	2,791
25,550	25,600	2,879	2,688	2,879	2,797
25,600	25,650	2,885	2,694	2,885	2,803
25,650	25,700	2,891	2,700	2,891	2,809
25,700	25,750	2,897	2,706	2,897	2,815
25,750	25,800	2,903	2,712	2,903	2,821
25,800	25,850	2,909	2,718	2,909	2,827
25,850	25,900	2,915	2,724	2,915	2,833
25,900	25,950	2,921	2,730	2,921	2,839
25,950	26,000	2,927	2,736	2,927	2,845
26,000					
26,000	26,050	2,933	2,742	2,933	2,851
26,050	26,100	2,939	2,748	2,939	2,857
26,100	26,150	2,945	2,754	2,945	2,863
26,150	26,200	2,951	2,760	2,951	2,869
26,200	26,250	2,957	2,766	2,957	2,875
26,250	26,300	2,963	2,772	2,963	2,881
26,300	26,350	2,969	2,778	2,969	2,887
26,350	26,400	2,975	2,784	2,975	2,893
26,400	26,450	2,981	2,790	2,981	2,899
26,450	26,500	2,987	2,796	2,987	2,905
26,500	26,550	2,993	2,802	2,993	2,911
26,550	26,600	2,999	2,808	2,999	2,917
26,600	26,650	3,005	2,814	3,005	2,923
26,650	26,700	3,011	2,820	3,011	2,929
26,700	26,750	3,017	2,826	3,017	2,935
26,750	26,800	3,023	2,832	3,023	2,941
26,800	26,850	3,029	2,838	3,029	2,947
26,850	26,900	3,035	2,844	3,035	2,953
26,900	26,950	3,041	2,850	3,041	2,959
26,950	27,000	3,047	2,856	3,047	2,965

If line 10 (taxable income) is—		And you are—			
At least	But less than	Single	Married filing jointly *	Married filing separately	Head of a household
		Your tax is—			
27,000					
27,000	27,050	3,053	2,862	3,053	2,971
27,050	27,100	3,059	2,868	3,059	2,977
27,100	27,150	3,065	2,874	3,065	2,983
27,150	27,200	3,071	2,880	3,071	2,989
27,200	27,250	3,077	2,886	3,077	2,995
27,250	27,300	3,083	2,892	3,083	3,001
27,300	27,350	3,089	2,898	3,089	3,007
27,350	27,400	3,095	2,904	3,095	3,013
27,400	27,450	3,101	2,910	3,101	3,019
27,450	27,500	3,107	2,916	3,107	3,025
27,500	27,550	3,113	2,922	3,113	3,031
27,550	27,600	3,119	2,928	3,119	3,037
27,600	27,650	3,125	2,934	3,125	3,043
27,650	27,700	3,131	2,940	3,131	3,049
27,700	27,750	3,137	2,946	3,137	3,055
27,750	27,800	3,143	2,952	3,143	3,061
27,800	27,850	3,149	2,958	3,149	3,067
27,850	27,900	3,155	2,964	3,155	3,073
27,900	27,950	3,161	2,970	3,161	3,079
27,950	28,000	3,167	2,976	3,167	3,085
28,000					
28,000	28,050	3,173	2,982	3,173	3,091
28,050	28,100	3,179	2,988	3,179	3,097
28,100	28,150	3,185	2,994	3,185	3,103
28,150	28,200	3,191	3,000	3,191	3,109
28,200	28,250	3,197	3,006	3,197	3,115
28,250	28,300	3,203	3,012	3,203	3,121
28,300	28,350	3,209	3,018	3,209	3,127
28,350	28,400	3,215	3,024	3,215	3,133
28,400	28,450	3,221	3,030	3,221	3,139
28,450	28,500	3,227	3,036	3,227	3,145
28,500	28,550	3,233	3,042	3,233	3,151
28,550	28,600	3,239	3,048	3,239	3,157
28,600	28,650	3,245	3,054	3,245	3,163
28,650	28,700	3,251	3,060	3,251	3,169
28,700	28,750	3,257	3,066	3,257	3,175
28,750	28,800	3,263	3,072	3,263	3,181
28,800	28,850	3,269	3,078	3,269	3,187
28,850	28,900	3,275	3,084	3,275	3,193
28,900	28,950	3,281	3,090	3,281	3,199
28,950	29,000	3,287	3,096	3,287	3,205
29,000					
29,000	29,050	3,293	3,102	3,293	3,211
29,050	29,100	3,299	3,108	3,299	3,217
29,100	29,150	3,305	3,114	3,305	3,223
29,150	29,200	3,311	3,120	3,311	3,229
29,200	29,250	3,317	3,126	3,317	3,235
29,250	29,300	3,323	3,132	3,323	3,241
29,300	29,350	3,329	3,138	3,329	3,247
29,350	29,400	3,335	3,144	3,335	3,253
29,400	29,450	3,341	3,150	3,341	3,259
29,450	29,500	3,347	3,156	3,347	3,265
29,500	29,550	3,353	3,162	3,353	3,271
29,550	29,600	3,359	3,168	3,359	3,277
29,600	29,650	3,365	3,174	3,365	3,283
29,650	29,700	3,371	3,180	3,371	3,289
29,700	29,750	3,377	3,186	3,377	3,295
29,750	29,800	3,383	3,192	3,383	3,301
29,800	29,850	3,389	3,198	3,389	3,307
29,850	29,900	3,395	3,204	3,395	3,313
29,900	29,950	3,401	3,210	3,401	3,319
29,950	30,000	3,407	3,216	3,407	3,325

(Continued)

* This column must also be used by a qualifying widow(er).

Draft As of September 26, 2018.

2018 Tax Table — *Continued*

DRAFT AS OF September 26, 2018

If line 10 (taxable income) is—		And you are—				If line 10 (taxable income) is—		And you are—				If line 10 (taxable income) is—		And you are—			
At least	But less than	Single	Married filing jointly *	Married filing separately	Head of a house-hold	At least	But less than	Single	Married filing jointly *	Married filing separately	Head of a house-hold	At least	But less than	Single	Married filing jointly *	Married filing separately	Head of a house-hold
		Your tax is—						Your tax is—						Your tax is—			
30,000						**33,000**						**36,000**					
30,000	30,050	3,413	3,222	3,413	3,331	33,000	33,050	3,773	3,582	3,773	3,691	36,000	36,050	4,133	3,942	4,133	4,051
30,050	30,100	3,419	3,228	3,419	3,337	33,050	33,100	3,779	3,588	3,779	3,697	36,050	36,100	4,139	3,948	4,139	4,057
30,100	30,150	3,425	3,234	3,425	3,343	33,100	33,150	3,785	3,594	3,785	3,703	36,100	36,150	4,145	3,954	4,145	4,063
30,150	30,200	3,431	3,240	3,431	3,349	33,150	33,200	3,791	3,600	3,791	3,709	36,150	36,200	4,151	3,960	4,151	4,069
30,200	30,250	3,437	3,246	3,437	3,355	33,200	33,250	3,797	3,606	3,797	3,715	36,200	36,250	4,157	3,966	4,157	4,075
30,250	30,300	3,443	3,252	3,443	3,361	33,250	33,300	3,803	3,612	3,803	3,721	36,250	36,300	4,163	3,972	4,163	4,081
30,300	30,350	3,449	3,258	3,449	3,367	33,300	33,350	3,809	3,618	3,809	3,727	36,300	36,350	4,169	3,978	4,169	4,087
30,350	30,400	3,455	3,264	3,455	3,373	33,350	33,400	3,815	3,624	3,815	3,733	36,350	36,400	4,175	3,984	4,175	4,093
30,400	30,450	3,461	3,270	3,461	3,379	33,400	33,450	3,821	3,630	3,821	3,739	36,400	36,450	4,181	3,990	4,181	4,099
30,450	30,500	3,467	3,276	3,467	3,385	33,450	33,500	3,827	3,636	3,827	3,745	36,450	36,500	4,187	3,996	4,187	4,105
30,500	30,550	3,473	3,282	3,473	3,391	33,500	33,550	3,833	3,642	3,833	3,751	36,500	36,550	4,193	4,002	4,193	4,111
30,550	30,600	3,479	3,288	3,479	3,397	33,550	33,600	3,839	3,648	3,839	3,757	36,550	36,600	4,199	4,008	4,199	4,117
30,600	30,650	3,485	3,294	3,485	3,403	33,600	33,650	3,845	3,654	3,845	3,763	36,600	36,650	4,205	4,014	4,205	4,123
30,650	30,700	3,491	3,300	3,491	3,409	33,650	33,700	3,851	3,660	3,851	3,769	36,650	36,700	4,211	4,020	4,211	4,129
30,700	30,750	3,497	3,306	3,497	3,415	33,700	33,750	3,857	3,666	3,857	3,775	36,700	36,750	4,217	4,026	4,217	4,135
30,750	30,800	3,503	3,312	3,503	3,421	33,750	33,800	3,863	3,672	3,863	3,781	36,750	36,800	4,223	4,032	4,223	4,141
30,800	30,850	3,509	3,318	3,509	3,427	33,800	33,850	3,869	3,678	3,869	3,787	36,800	36,850	4,229	4,038	4,229	4,147
30,850	30,900	3,515	3,324	3,515	3,433	33,850	33,900	3,875	3,684	3,875	3,793	36,850	36,900	4,235	4,044	4,235	4,153
30,900	30,950	3,521	3,330	3,521	3,439	33,900	33,950	3,881	3,690	3,881	3,799	36,900	36,950	4,241	4,050	4,241	4,159
30,950	31,000	3,527	3,336	3,527	3,445	33,950	34,000	3,887	3,696	3,887	3,805	36,950	37,000	4,247	4,056	4,247	4,165
31,000						**34,000**						**37,000**					
31,000	31,050	3,533	3,342	3,533	3,451	34,000	34,050	3,893	3,702	3,893	3,811	37,000	37,050	4,253	4,062	4,253	4,171
31,050	31,100	3,539	3,348	3,539	3,457	34,050	34,100	3,899	3,708	3,899	3,817	37,050	37,100	4,259	4,068	4,259	4,177
31,100	31,150	3,545	3,354	3,545	3,463	34,100	34,150	3,905	3,714	3,905	3,823	37,100	37,150	4,265	4,074	4,265	4,183
31,150	31,200	3,551	3,360	3,551	3,469	34,150	34,200	3,911	3,720	3,911	3,829	37,150	37,200	4,271	4,080	4,271	4,189
31,200	31,250	3,557	3,366	3,557	3,475	34,200	34,250	3,917	3,726	3,917	3,835	37,200	37,250	4,277	4,086	4,277	4,195
31,250	31,300	3,563	3,372	3,563	3,481	34,250	34,300	3,923	3,732	3,923	3,841	37,250	37,300	4,283	4,092	4,283	4,201
31,300	31,350	3,569	3,378	3,569	3,487	34,300	34,350	3,929	3,738	3,929	3,847	37,300	37,350	4,289	4,098	4,289	4,207
31,350	31,400	3,575	3,384	3,575	3,493	34,350	34,400	3,935	3,744	3,935	3,853	37,350	37,400	4,295	4,104	4,295	4,213
31,400	31,450	3,581	3,390	3,581	3,499	34,400	34,450	3,941	3,750	3,941	3,859	37,400	37,450	4,301	4,110	4,301	4,219
31,450	31,500	3,587	3,396	3,587	3,505	34,450	34,500	3,947	3,756	3,947	3,865	37,450	37,500	4,307	4,116	4,307	4,225
31,500	31,550	3,593	3,402	3,593	3,511	34,500	34,550	3,953	3,762	3,953	3,871	37,500	37,550	4,313	4,122	4,313	4,231
31,550	31,600	3,599	3,408	3,599	3,517	34,550	34,600	3,959	3,768	3,959	3,877	37,550	37,600	4,319	4,128	4,319	4,237
31,600	31,650	3,605	3,414	3,605	3,523	34,600	34,650	3,965	3,774	3,965	3,883	37,600	37,650	4,325	4,134	4,325	4,243
31,650	31,700	3,611	3,420	3,611	3,529	34,650	34,700	3,971	3,780	3,971	3,889	37,650	37,700	4,331	4,140	4,331	4,249
31,700	31,750	3,617	3,426	3,617	3,535	34,700	34,750	3,977	3,786	3,977	3,895	37,700	37,750	4,337	4,146	4,337	4,255
31,750	31,800	3,623	3,432	3,623	3,541	34,750	34,800	3,983	3,792	3,983	3,901	37,750	37,800	4,343	4,152	4,343	4,261
31,800	31,850	3,629	3,438	3,629	3,547	34,800	34,850	3,989	3,798	3,989	3,907	37,800	37,850	4,349	4,158	4,349	4,267
31,850	31,900	3,635	3,444	3,635	3,553	34,850	34,900	3,995	3,804	3,995	3,913	37,850	37,900	4,355	4,164	4,355	4,273
31,900	31,950	3,641	3,450	3,641	3,559	34,900	34,950	4,001	3,810	4,001	3,919	37,900	37,950	4,361	4,170	4,361	4,279
31,950	32,000	3,647	3,456	3,647	3,565	34,950	35,000	4,007	3,816	4,007	3,925	37,950	38,000	4,367	4,176	4,367	4,285
32,000						**35,000**						**38,000**					
32,000	32,050	3,653	3,462	3,653	3,571	35,000	35,050	4,013	3,822	4,013	3,931	38,000	38,050	4,373	4,182	4,373	4,291
32,050	32,100	3,659	3,468	3,659	3,577	35,050	35,100	4,019	3,828	4,019	3,937	38,050	38,100	4,379	4,188	4,379	4,297
32,100	32,150	3,665	3,474	3,665	3,583	35,100	35,150	4,025	3,834	4,025	3,943	38,100	38,150	4,385	4,194	4,385	4,303
32,150	32,200	3,671	3,480	3,671	3,589	35,150	35,200	4,031	3,840	4,031	3,949	38,150	38,200	4,391	4,200	4,391	4,309
32,200	32,250	3,677	3,486	3,677	3,595	35,200	35,250	4,037	3,846	4,037	3,955	38,200	38,250	4,397	4,206	4,397	4,315
32,250	32,300	3,683	3,492	3,683	3,601	35,250	35,300	4,043	3,852	4,043	3,961	38,250	38,300	4,403	4,212	4,403	4,321
32,300	32,350	3,689	3,498	3,689	3,607	35,300	35,350	4,049	3,858	4,049	3,967	38,300	38,350	4,409	4,218	4,409	4,327
32,350	32,400	3,695	3,504	3,695	3,613	35,350	35,400	4,055	3,864	4,055	3,973	38,350	38,400	4,415	4,224	4,415	4,333
32,400	32,450	3,701	3,510	3,701	3,619	35,400	35,450	4,061	3,870	4,061	3,979	38,400	38,450	4,421	4,230	4,421	4,339
32,450	32,500	3,707	3,516	3,707	3,625	35,450	35,500	4,067	3,876	4,067	3,985	38,450	38,500	4,427	4,236	4,427	4,345
32,500	32,550	3,713	3,522	3,713	3,631	35,500	35,550	4,073	3,882	4,073	3,991	38,500	38,550	4,433	4,242	4,433	4,351
32,550	32,600	3,719	3,528	3,719	3,637	35,550	35,600	4,079	3,888	4,079	3,997	38,550	38,600	4,439	4,248	4,439	4,357
32,600	32,650	3,725	3,534	3,725	3,643	35,600	35,650	4,085	3,894	4,085	4,003	38,600	38,650	4,445	4,254	4,445	4,363
32,650	32,700	3,731	3,540	3,731	3,649	35,650	35,700	4,091	3,900	4,091	4,009	38,650	38,700	4,451	4,260	4,451	4,369
32,700	32,750	3,737	3,546	3,737	3,655	35,700	35,750	4,097	3,906	4,097	4,015	38,700	38,750	4,457	4,266	4,457	4,375
32,750	32,800	3,743	3,552	3,743	3,661	35,750	35,800	4,103	3,912	4,103	4,021	38,750	38,800	4,470	4,272	4,470	4,381
32,800	32,850	3,749	3,558	3,749	3,667	35,800	35,850	4,109	3,918	4,109	4,027	38,800	38,850	4,481	4,278	4,481	4,387
32,850	32,900	3,755	3,564	3,755	3,673	35,850	35,900	4,115	3,924	4,115	4,033	38,850	38,900	4,492	4,284	4,492	4,393
32,900	32,950	3,761	3,570	3,761	3,679	35,900	35,950	4,121	3,930	4,121	4,039	38,900	38,950	4,503	4,290	4,503	4,399
32,950	33,000	3,767	3,576	3,767	3,685	35,950	36,000	4,127	3,936	4,127	4,045	38,950	39,000	4,514	4,296	4,514	4,405

* This column must also be used by a qualifying widow(er).

(Continued)

Draft As of September 26, 2018.

2018 Tax Table — *Continued*

DRAFT AS OF September 26, 2018

If line 10 (taxable income) is—		And you are—			
At least	But less than	Single	Married filing jointly *	Married filing separately	Head of a household
		Your tax is—			

39,000

At least	But less than	Single	MFJ	MFS	HoH
39,000	39,050	4,525	4,302	4,525	4,411
39,050	39,100	4,536	4,308	4,536	4,417
39,100	39,150	4,547	4,314	4,547	4,423
39,150	39,200	4,558	4,320	4,558	4,429
39,200	39,250	4,569	4,326	4,569	4,435
39,250	39,300	4,580	4,332	4,580	4,441
39,300	39,350	4,591	4,338	4,591	4,447
39,350	39,400	4,602	4,344	4,602	4,453
39,400	39,450	4,613	4,350	4,613	4,459
39,450	39,500	4,624	4,356	4,624	4,465
39,500	39,550	4,635	4,362	4,635	4,471
39,550	39,600	4,646	4,368	4,646	4,477
39,600	39,650	4,657	4,374	4,657	4,483
39,650	39,700	4,668	4,380	4,668	4,489
39,700	39,750	4,679	4,386	4,679	4,495
39,750	39,800	4,690	4,392	4,690	4,501
39,800	39,850	4,701	4,398	4,701	4,507
39,850	39,900	4,712	4,404	4,712	4,513
39,900	39,950	4,723	4,410	4,723	4,519
39,950	40,000	4,734	4,416	4,734	4,525

40,000

At least	But less than	Single	MFJ	MFS	HoH
40,000	40,050	4,745	4,422	4,745	4,531
40,050	40,100	4,756	4,428	4,756	4,537
40,100	40,150	4,767	4,434	4,767	4,543
40,150	40,200	4,778	4,440	4,778	4,549
40,200	40,250	4,789	4,446	4,789	4,555
40,250	40,300	4,800	4,452	4,800	4,561
40,300	40,350	4,811	4,458	4,811	4,567
40,350	40,400	4,822	4,464	4,822	4,573
40,400	40,450	4,833	4,470	4,833	4,579
40,450	40,500	4,844	4,476	4,844	4,585
40,500	40,550	4,855	4,482	4,855	4,591
40,550	40,600	4,866	4,488	4,866	4,597
40,600	40,650	4,877	4,494	4,877	4,603
40,650	40,700	4,888	4,500	4,888	4,609
40,700	40,750	4,899	4,506	4,899	4,615
40,750	40,800	4,910	4,512	4,910	4,621
40,800	40,850	4,921	4,518	4,921	4,627
40,850	40,900	4,932	4,524	4,932	4,633
40,900	40,950	4,943	4,530	4,943	4,639
40,950	41,000	4,954	4,536	4,954	4,645

41,000

At least	But less than	Single	MFJ	MFS	HoH
41,000	41,050	4,965	4,542	4,965	4,651
41,050	41,100	4,976	4,548	4,976	4,657
41,100	41,150	4,987	4,554	4,987	4,663
41,150	41,200	4,998	4,560	4,998	4,669
41,200	41,250	5,009	4,566	5,009	4,675
41,250	41,300	5,020	4,572	5,020	4,681
41,300	41,350	5,031	4,578	5,031	4,687
41,350	41,400	5,042	4,584	5,042	4,693
41,400	41,450	5,053	4,590	5,053	4,699
41,450	41,500	5,064	4,596	5,064	4,705
41,500	41,550	5,075	4,602	5,075	4,711
41,550	41,600	5,086	4,608	5,086	4,717
41,600	41,650	5,097	4,614	5,097	4,723
41,650	41,700	5,108	4,620	5,108	4,729
41,700	41,750	5,119	4,626	5,119	4,735
41,750	41,800	5,130	4,632	5,130	4,741
41,800	41,850	5,141	4,638	5,141	4,747
41,850	41,900	5,152	4,644	5,152	4,753
41,900	41,950	5,163	4,650	5,163	4,759
41,950	42,000	5,174	4,656	5,174	4,765

42,000

At least	But less than	Single	MFJ	MFS	HoH
42,000	42,050	5,185	4,662	5,185	4,771
42,050	42,100	5,196	4,668	5,196	4,777
42,100	42,150	5,207	4,674	5,207	4,783
42,150	42,200	5,218	4,680	5,218	4,789
42,200	42,250	5,229	4,686	5,229	4,795
42,250	42,300	5,240	4,692	5,240	4,801
42,300	42,350	5,251	4,698	5,251	4,807
42,350	42,400	5,262	4,704	5,262	4,813
42,400	42,450	5,273	4,710	5,273	4,819
42,450	42,500	5,284	4,716	5,284	4,825
42,500	42,550	5,295	4,722	5,295	4,831
42,550	42,600	5,306	4,728	5,306	4,837
42,600	42,650	5,317	4,734	5,317	4,843
42,650	42,700	5,328	4,740	5,328	4,849
42,700	42,750	5,339	4,746	5,339	4,855
42,750	42,800	5,350	4,752	5,350	4,861
42,800	42,850	5,361	4,758	5,361	4,867
42,850	42,900	5,372	4,764	5,372	4,873
42,900	42,950	5,383	4,770	5,383	4,879
42,950	43,000	5,394	4,776	5,394	4,885

43,000

At least	But less than	Single	MFJ	MFS	HoH
43,000	43,050	5,405	4,782	5,405	4,891
43,050	43,100	5,416	4,788	5,416	4,897
43,100	43,150	5,427	4,794	5,427	4,903
43,150	43,200	5,438	4,800	5,438	4,909
43,200	43,250	5,449	4,806	5,449	4,915
43,250	43,300	5,460	4,812	5,460	4,921
43,300	43,350	5,471	4,818	5,471	4,927
43,350	43,400	5,482	4,824	5,482	4,933
43,400	43,450	5,493	4,830	5,493	4,939
43,450	43,500	5,504	4,836	5,504	4,945
43,500	43,550	5,515	4,842	5,515	4,951
43,550	43,600	5,526	4,848	5,526	4,957
43,600	43,650	5,537	4,854	5,537	4,963
43,650	43,700	5,548	4,860	5,548	4,969
43,700	43,750	5,559	4,866	5,559	4,975
43,750	43,800	5,570	4,872	5,570	4,981
43,800	43,850	5,581	4,878	5,581	4,987
43,850	43,900	5,592	4,884	5,592	4,993
43,900	43,950	5,603	4,890	5,603	4,999
43,950	44,000	5,614	4,896	5,614	5,005

44,000

At least	But less than	Single	MFJ	MFS	HoH
44,000	44,050	5,625	4,902	5,625	5,011
44,050	44,100	5,636	4,908	5,636	5,017
44,100	44,150	5,647	4,914	5,647	5,023
44,150	44,200	5,658	4,920	5,658	5,029
44,200	44,250	5,669	4,926	5,669	5,035
44,250	44,300	5,680	4,932	5,680	5,041
44,300	44,350	5,691	4,938	5,691	5,047
44,350	44,400	5,702	4,944	5,702	5,053
44,400	44,450	5,713	4,950	5,713	5,059
44,450	44,500	5,724	4,956	5,724	5,065
44,500	44,550	5,735	4,962	5,735	5,071
44,550	44,600	5,746	4,968	5,746	5,077
44,600	44,650	5,757	4,974	5,757	5,083
44,650	44,700	5,768	4,980	5,768	5,089
44,700	44,750	5,779	4,986	5,779	5,095
44,750	44,800	5,790	4,992	5,790	5,101
44,800	44,850	5,801	4,998	5,801	5,107
44,850	44,900	5,812	5,004	5,812	5,113
44,900	44,950	5,823	5,010	5,823	5,119
44,950	45,000	5,834	5,016	5,834	5,125

45,000

At least	But less than	Single	MFJ	MFS	HoH
45,000	45,050	5,845	5,022	5,845	5,131
45,050	45,100	5,856	5,028	5,856	5,137
45,100	45,150	5,867	5,034	5,867	5,143
45,150	45,200	5,878	5,040	5,878	5,149
45,200	45,250	5,889	5,046	5,889	5,155
45,250	45,300	5,900	5,052	5,900	5,161
45,300	45,350	5,911	5,058	5,911	5,167
45,350	45,400	5,922	5,064	5,922	5,173
45,400	45,450	5,933	5,070	5,933	5,179
45,450	45,500	5,944	5,076	5,944	5,185
45,500	45,550	5,955	5,082	5,955	5,191
45,550	45,600	5,966	5,088	5,966	5,197
45,600	45,650	5,977	5,094	5,977	5,203
45,650	45,700	5,988	5,100	5,988	5,209
45,700	45,750	5,999	5,106	5,999	5,215
45,750	45,800	6,010	5,112	6,010	5,221
45,800	45,850	6,021	5,118	6,021	5,227
45,850	45,900	6,032	5,124	6,032	5,233
45,900	45,950	6,043	5,130	6,043	5,239
45,950	46,000	6,054	5,136	6,054	5,245

46,000

At least	But less than	Single	MFJ	MFS	HoH
46,000	46,050	6,065	5,142	6,065	5,251
46,050	46,100	6,076	5,148	6,076	5,257
46,100	46,150	6,087	5,154	6,087	5,263
46,150	46,200	6,098	5,160	6,098	5,269
46,200	46,250	6,109	5,166	6,109	5,275
46,250	46,300	6,120	5,172	6,120	5,281
46,300	46,350	6,131	5,178	6,131	5,287
46,350	46,400	6,142	5,184	6,142	5,293
46,400	46,450	6,153	5,190	6,153	5,299
46,450	46,500	6,164	5,196	6,164	5,305
46,500	46,550	6,175	5,202	6,175	5,311
46,550	46,600	6,186	5,208	6,186	5,317
46,600	46,650	6,197	5,214	6,197	5,323
46,650	46,700	6,208	5,220	6,208	5,329
46,700	46,750	6,219	5,226	6,219	5,335
46,750	46,800	6,230	5,232	6,230	5,341
46,800	46,850	6,241	5,238	6,241	5,347
46,850	46,900	6,252	5,244	6,252	5,353
46,900	46,950	6,263	5,250	6,263	5,359
46,950	47,000	6,274	5,256	6,274	5,365

47,000

At least	But less than	Single	MFJ	MFS	HoH
47,000	47,050	6,285	5,262	6,285	5,371
47,050	47,100	6,296	5,268	6,296	5,377
47,100	47,150	6,307	5,274	6,307	5,383
47,150	47,200	6,318	5,280	6,318	5,389
47,200	47,250	6,329	5,286	6,329	5,395
47,250	47,300	6,340	5,292	6,340	5,401
47,300	47,350	6,351	5,298	6,351	5,407
47,350	47,400	6,362	5,304	6,362	5,413
47,400	47,450	6,373	5,310	6,373	5,419
47,450	47,500	6,384	5,316	6,384	5,425
47,500	47,550	6,395	5,322	6,395	5,431
47,550	47,600	6,406	5,328	6,406	5,437
47,600	47,650	6,417	5,334	6,417	5,443
47,650	47,700	6,428	5,340	6,428	5,449
47,700	47,750	6,439	5,346	6,439	5,456
47,750	47,800	6,450	5,352	6,450	5,461
47,800	47,850	6,461	5,358	6,461	5,467
47,850	47,900	6,472	5,364	6,472	5,473
47,900	47,950	6,483	5,370	6,483	5,479
47,950	48,000	6,494	5,378	6,494	5,485

(Continued)

* This column must also be used by a qualifying widow(er).

Draft As of September 26, 2018.

2018 Tax Table — Continued

If line 10 (taxable income) is—		And you are—				If line 10 (taxable income) is—		And you are—				If line 10 (taxable income) is—		And you are—			
At least	But less than	Single	Married filing jointly *	Married filing sepa-rately	Head of a house-hold	At least	But less than	Single	Married filing jointly *	Married filing sepa-rately	Head of a house-hold	At least	But less than	Single	Married filing jointly *	Married filing sepa-rately	Head of a house-hold
		Your tax is—						Your tax is—						Your tax is—			

48,000 | **51,000** | **54,000**

48,000	48,050	6,505	5,382	6,505	5,491	51,000	51,050	7,165	5,742	7,165	5,851	54,000	54,050	7,825	6,102	7,825	6,434
48,050	48,100	6,516	5,388	6,516	5,497	51,050	51,100	7,176	5,748	7,176	5,857	54,050	54,100	7,836	6,108	7,836	6,445
48,100	48,150	6,527	5,394	6,527	5,503	51,100	51,150	7,187	5,754	7,187	5,863	54,100	54,150	7,847	6,114	7,847	6,456
48,150	48,200	6,538	5,400	6,538	5,509	51,150	51,200	7,198	5,760	7,198	5,869	54,150	54,200	7,858	6,120	7,858	6,467
48,200	48,250	6,549	5,406	6,549	5,515	51,200	51,250	7,209	5,766	7,209	5,875	54,200	54,250	7,869	6,126	7,869	6,478
48,250	48,300	6,560	5,412	6,560	5,521	51,250	51,300	7,220	5,772	7,220	5,881	54,250	54,300	7,880	6,132	7,880	6,489
48,300	48,350	6,571	5,418	6,571	5,527	51,300	51,350	7,231	5,778	7,231	5,887	54,300	54,350	7,891	6,138	7,891	6,500
48,350	48,400	6,582	5,424	6,582	5,533	51,350	51,400	7,242	5,784	7,242	5,893	54,350	54,400	7,902	6,144	7,902	6,511
48,400	48,450	6,593	5,430	6,593	5,539	51,400	51,450	7,253	5,790	7,253	5,899	54,400	54,450	7,913	6,150	7,913	6,522
48,450	48,500	6,604	5,436	6,604	5,545	51,450	51,500	7,264	5,796	7,264	5,905	54,450	54,500	7,924	6,156	7,924	6,533
48,500	48,550	6,615	5,442	6,615	5,551	51,500	51,550	7,275	5,802	7,275	5,911	54,500	54,550	7,935	6,162	7,935	6,544
48,550	48,600	6,626	5,448	6,626	5,557	51,550	51,600	7,286	5,808	7,286	5,917	54,550	54,600	7,946	6,168	7,946	6,555
48,600	48,650	6,637	5,454	6,637	5,563	51,600	51,650	7,297	5,814	7,297	5,923	54,600	54,650	7,957	6,174	7,957	6,566
48,650	48,700	6,648	5,460	6,648	5,569	51,650	51,700	7,308	5,820	7,308	5,929	54,650	54,700	7,968	6,180	7,968	6,577
48,700	48,750	6,659	5,466	6,659	5,575	51,700	51,750	7,319	5,826	7,319	5,935	54,700	54,750	7,979	6,186	7,979	6,588
48,750	48,800	6,670	5,472	6,670	5,581	51,750	51,800	7,330	5,832	7,330	5,941	54,750	54,800	7,990	6,192	7,990	6,599
48,800	48,850	6,681	5,478	6,681	5,587	51,800	51,850	7,341	5,838	7,341	5,950	54,800	54,850	8,001	6,198	8,001	6,610
48,850	48,900	6,692	5,484	6,692	5,593	51,850	51,900	7,352	5,844	7,352	5,961	54,850	54,900	8,012	6,204	8,012	6,621
48,900	48,950	6,703	5,490	6,703	5,599	51,900	51,950	7,363	5,850	7,363	5,972	54,900	54,950	8,023	6,210	8,023	6,632
48,950	49,000	6,714	5,496	6,714	5,605	51,950	52,000	7,374	5,856	7,374	5,983	54,950	55,000	8,034	6,216	8,034	6,643

49,000 | **52,000** | **55,000**

49,000	49,050	6,725	5,502	6,725	5,611	52,000	52,050	7,385	5,862	7,385	5,994	55,000	55,050	8,045	6,222	8,045	6,654
49,050	49,100	6,736	5,508	6,736	5,617	52,050	52,100	7,396	5,868	7,396	6,005	55,050	55,100	8,056	6,228	8,056	6,665
49,100	49,150	6,747	5,514	6,747	5,623	52,100	52,150	7,407	5,874	7,407	6,016	55,100	55,150	8,067	6,234	8,067	6,676
49,150	49,200	6,758	5,520	6,758	5,629	52,150	52,200	7,418	5,880	7,418	6,027	55,150	55,200	8,078	6,240	8,078	6,687
49,200	49,250	6,769	5,526	6,769	5,635	52,200	52,250	7,429	5,886	7,429	6,038	55,200	55,250	8,089	6,246	8,089	6,698
49,250	49,300	6,780	5,532	6,780	5,641	52,250	52,300	7,440	5,892	7,440	6,049	55,250	55,300	8,100	6,252	8,100	6,709
49,300	49,350	6,791	5,538	6,791	5,647	52,300	52,350	7,451	5,898	7,451	6,060	55,300	55,350	8,111	6,258	8,111	6,720
49,350	49,400	6,802	5,544	6,802	5,653	52,350	52,400	7,462	5,904	7,462	6,071	55,350	55,400	8,122	6,264	8,122	6,731
49,400	49,450	6,813	5,550	6,813	5,659	52,400	52,450	7,473	5,910	7,473	6,082	55,400	55,450	8,133	6,270	8,133	6,742
49,450	49,500	6,824	5,556	6,824	5,665	52,450	52,500	7,484	5,916	7,484	6,093	55,450	55,500	8,144	6,276	8,144	6,753
49,500	49,550	6,835	5,562	6,835	5,671	52,500	52,550	7,495	5,922	7,495	6,104	55,500	55,550	8,155	6,282	8,155	6,764
49,550	49,600	6,846	5,568	6,846	5,677	52,550	52,600	7,506	5,928	7,506	6,115	55,550	55,600	8,166	6,288	8,166	6,775
49,600	49,650	6,857	5,574	6,857	5,683	52,600	52,650	7,517	5,934	7,517	6,126	55,600	55,650	8,177	6,294	8,177	6,786
49,650	49,700	6,868	5,580	6,868	5,689	52,650	52,700	7,528	5,940	7,528	6,137	55,650	55,700	8,188	6,300	8,188	6,797
49,700	49,750	6,879	5,586	6,879	5,695	52,700	52,750	7,539	5,946	7,539	6,148	55,700	55,750	8,199	6,306	8,199	6,808
49,750	49,800	6,890	5,592	6,890	5,701	52,750	52,800	7,550	5,952	7,550	6,159	55,750	55,800	8,210	6,312	8,210	6,819
49,800	49,850	6,901	5,598	6,901	5,707	52,800	52,850	7,561	5,958	7,561	6,170	55,800	55,850	8,221	6,318	8,221	6,830
49,850	49,900	6,912	5,604	6,912	5,713	52,850	52,900	7,572	5,964	7,572	6,181	55,850	55,900	8,232	6,324	8,232	6,841
49,900	49,950	6,923	5,610	6,923	5,719	52,900	52,950	7,583	5,970	7,583	6,192	55,900	55,950	8,243	6,330	8,243	6,852
49,950	50,000	6,934	5,616	6,934	5,725	52,950	53,000	7,594	5,976	7,594	6,203	55,950	56,000	8,254	6,336	8,254	6,863

50,000 | **53,000** | **56,000**

50,000	50,050	6,945	5,622	6,945	5,731	53,000	53,050	7,605	5,982	7,605	6,214	56,000	56,050	8,265	6,342	8,265	6,874
50,050	50,100	6,956	5,628	6,956	5,737	53,050	53,100	7,616	5,988	7,616	6,225	56,050	56,100	8,276	6,348	8,276	6,885
50,100	50,150	6,967	5,634	6,967	5,743	53,100	53,150	7,627	5,994	7,627	6,236	56,100	56,150	8,287	6,354	8,287	6,896
50,150	50,200	6,978	5,640	6,978	5,749	53,150	53,200	7,638	6,000	7,638	6,247	56,150	56,200	8,298	6,360	8,298	6,907
50,200	50,250	6,989	5,646	6,989	5,755	53,200	53,250	7,649	6,006	7,649	6,258	56,200	56,250	8,309	6,366	8,309	6,918
50,250	50,300	7,000	5,652	7,000	5,761	53,250	53,300	7,660	6,012	7,660	6,269	56,250	56,300	8,320	6,372	8,320	6,929
50,300	50,350	7,011	5,658	7,011	5,767	53,300	53,350	7,671	6,018	7,671	6,280	56,300	56,350	8,331	6,378	8,331	6,940
50,350	50,400	7,022	5,664	7,022	5,773	53,350	53,400	7,682	6,024	7,682	6,291	56,350	56,400	8,342	6,384	8,342	6,951
50,400	50,450	7,033	5,670	7,033	5,779	53,400	53,450	7,693	6,030	7,693	6,302	56,400	56,450	8,353	6,390	8,353	6,962
50,450	50,500	7,044	5,676	7,044	5,785	53,450	53,500	7,704	6,036	7,704	6,313	56,450	56,500	8,364	6,396	8,364	6,973
50,500	50,550	7,055	5,682	7,055	5,791	53,500	53,550	7,715	6,042	7,715	6,324	56,500	56,550	8,375	6,402	8,375	6,984
50,550	50,600	7,066	5,688	7,066	5,797	53,550	53,600	7,726	6,048	7,726	6,335	56,550	56,600	8,386	6,408	8,386	6,995
50,600	50,650	7,077	5,694	7,077	5,803	53,600	53,650	7,737	6,054	7,737	6,346	56,600	56,650	8,397	6,414	8,397	7,006
50,650	50,700	7,088	5,700	7,088	5,809	53,650	53,700	7,748	6,060	7,748	6,357	56,650	56,700	8,408	6,420	8,408	7,017
50,700	50,750	7,099	5,706	7,099	5,815	53,700	53,750	7,759	6,066	7,759	6,368	56,700	56,750	8,419	6,426	8,419	7,028
50,750	50,800	7,110	5,712	7,110	5,821	53,750	53,800	7,770	6,072	7,770	6,379	56,750	56,800	8,430	6,432	8,430	7,039
50,800	50,850	7,121	5,718	7,121	5,827	53,800	53,850	7,781	6,078	7,781	6,390	56,800	56,850	8,441	6,438	8,441	7,050
50,850	50,900	7,132	5,724	7,132	5,833	53,850	53,900	7,792	6,084	7,792	6,401	56,850	56,900	8,452	6,444	8,452	7,061
50,900	50,950	7,143	5,730	7,143	5,839	53,900	53,950	7,803	6,090	7,803	6,412	56,900	56,950	8,463	6,450	8,463	7,072
50,950	51,000	7,154	5,736	7,154	5,845	53,950	54,000	7,814	6,096	7,814	6,423	56,950	57,000	8,474	6,456	8,474	7,083

(Continued)

* This column must also be used by a qualifying widow(er).

Draft As of September 26, 2018.

2018 Tax Table — *Continued*

If line 10 (taxable income) is—		And you are—			
At least	But less than	Single	Married filing jointly *	Married filing separately	Head of a household
		Your tax is—			

57,000

At least	But less than	Single	MFJ *	MFS	HoH
57,000	57,050	8,485	6,462	8,485	7,094
57,050	57,100	8,496	6,468	8,496	7,105
57,100	57,150	8,507	6,474	8,507	7,116
57,150	57,200	8,518	6,480	8,518	7,127
57,200	57,250	8,529	6,486	8,529	7,138
57,250	57,300	8,540	6,492	8,540	7,149
57,300	57,350	8,551	6,498	8,551	7,160
57,350	57,400	8,562	6,504	8,562	7,171
57,400	57,450	8,573	6,510	8,573	7,182
57,450	57,500	8,584	6,516	8,584	7,193
57,500	57,550	8,595	6,522	8,595	7,204
57,550	57,600	8,606	6,528	8,606	7,215
57,600	57,650	8,617	6,534	8,617	7,226
57,650	57,700	8,628	6,540	8,628	7,237
57,700	57,750	8,639	6,546	8,639	7,248
57,750	57,800	8,650	6,552	8,650	7,259
57,800	57,850	8,661	6,558	8,661	7,270
57,850	57,900	8,672	6,564	8,672	7,281
57,900	57,950	8,683	6,570	8,683	7,292
57,950	58,000	8,694	6,576	8,694	7,303

58,000

At least	But less than	Single	MFJ *	MFS	HoH
58,000	58,050	8,705	6,582	8,705	7,314
58,050	58,100	8,716	6,588	8,716	7,325
58,100	58,150	8,727	6,594	8,727	7,336
58,150	58,200	8,738	6,600	8,738	7,347
58,200	58,250	8,749	6,606	8,749	7,358
58,250	58,300	8,760	6,612	8,760	7,369
58,300	58,350	8,771	6,618	8,771	7,380
58,350	58,400	8,782	6,624	8,782	7,391
58,400	58,450	8,793	6,630	8,793	7,402
58,450	58,500	8,804	6,636	8,804	7,413
58,500	58,550	8,815	6,642	8,815	7,424
58,550	58,600	8,826	6,648	8,826	7,435
58,600	58,650	8,837	6,654	8,837	7,446
58,650	58,700	8,848	6,660	8,848	7,457
58,700	58,750	8,859	6,666	8,859	7,468
58,750	58,800	8,870	6,672	8,870	7,479
58,800	58,850	8,881	6,678	8,881	7,490
58,850	58,900	8,892	6,684	8,892	7,501
58,900	58,950	8,903	6,690	8,903	7,512
58,950	59,000	8,914	6,696	8,914	7,523

59,000

At least	But less than	Single	MFJ *	MFS	HoH
59,000	59,050	8,925	6,702	8,925	7,534
59,050	59,100	8,936	6,708	8,936	7,545
59,100	59,150	8,947	6,714	8,947	7,556
59,150	59,200	8,958	6,720	8,958	7,567
59,200	59,250	8,969	6,726	8,969	7,578
59,250	59,300	8,980	6,732	8,980	7,589
59,300	59,350	8,991	6,738	8,991	7,600
59,350	59,400	9,002	6,744	9,002	7,611
59,400	59,450	9,013	6,750	9,013	7,622
59,450	59,500	9,024	6,756	9,024	7,633
59,500	59,550	9,035	6,762	9,035	7,644
59,550	59,600	9,046	6,768	9,046	7,655
59,600	59,650	9,057	6,774	9,057	7,666
59,650	59,700	9,068	6,780	9,068	7,677
59,700	59,750	9,079	6,786	9,079	7,688
59,750	59,800	9,090	6,792	9,090	7,699
59,800	59,850	9,101	6,798	9,101	7,710
59,850	59,900	9,112	6,804	9,112	7,721
59,900	59,950	9,123	6,810	9,123	7,732
59,950	60,000	9,134	6,816	9,134	7,743

60,000

At least	But less than	Single	MFJ *	MFS	HoH
60,000	60,050	9,145	6,822	9,145	7,754
60,050	60,100	9,156	6,828	9,156	7,765
60,100	60,150	9,167	6,834	9,167	7,776
60,150	60,200	9,178	6,840	9,178	7,787
60,200	60,250	9,189	6,846	9,189	7,798
60,250	60,300	9,200	6,852	9,200	7,809
60,300	60,350	9,211	6,858	9,211	7,820
60,350	60,400	9,222	6,864	9,222	7,831
60,400	60,450	9,233	6,870	9,233	7,842
60,450	60,500	9,244	6,876	9,244	7,853
60,500	60,550	9,255	6,882	9,255	7,864
60,550	60,600	9,266	6,888	9,266	7,875
60,600	60,650	9,277	6,894	9,277	7,886
60,650	60,700	9,288	6,900	9,288	7,897
60,700	60,750	9,299	6,906	9,299	7,908
60,750	60,800	9,310	6,912	9,310	7,919
60,800	60,850	9,321	6,918	9,321	7,930
60,850	60,900	9,332	6,924	9,332	7,941
60,900	60,950	9,343	6,930	9,343	7,952
60,950	61,000	9,354	6,936	9,354	7,963

61,000

At least	But less than	Single	MFJ *	MFS	HoH
61,000	61,050	9,365	6,942	9,365	7,974
61,050	61,100	9,376	6,948	9,376	7,985
61,100	61,150	9,387	6,954	9,387	7,996
61,150	61,200	9,398	6,960	9,398	8,007
61,200	61,250	9,409	6,966	9,409	8,018
61,250	61,300	9,420	6,972	9,420	8,029
61,300	61,350	9,431	6,978	9,431	8,040
61,350	61,400	9,442	6,984	9,442	8,051
61,400	61,450	9,453	6,990	9,453	8,062
61,450	61,500	9,464	6,996	9,464	8,073
61,500	61,550	9,475	7,002	9,475	8,084
61,550	61,600	9,486	7,008	9,486	8,095
61,600	61,650	9,497	7,014	9,497	8,106
61,650	61,700	9,508	7,020	9,508	8,117
61,700	61,750	9,519	7,026	9,519	8,128
61,750	61,800	9,530	7,032	9,530	8,139
61,800	61,850	9,541	7,038	9,541	8,150
61,850	61,900	9,552	7,044	9,552	8,161
61,900	61,950	9,563	7,050	9,563	8,172
61,950	62,000	9,574	7,056	9,574	8,183

62,000

At least	But less than	Single	MFJ *	MFS	HoH
62,000	62,050	9,585	7,062	9,585	8,194
62,050	62,100	9,596	7,068	9,596	8,205
62,100	62,150	9,607	7,074	9,607	8,216
62,150	62,200	9,618	7,080	9,618	8,227
62,200	62,250	9,629	7,086	9,629	8,238
62,250	62,300	9,640	7,092	9,640	8,249
62,300	62,350	9,651	7,098	9,651	8,260
62,350	62,400	9,662	7,104	9,662	8,271
62,400	62,450	9,673	7,110	9,673	8,282
62,450	62,500	9,684	7,116	9,684	8,293
62,500	62,550	9,695	7,122	9,695	8,304
62,550	62,600	9,706	7,128	9,706	8,315
62,600	62,650	9,717	7,134	9,717	8,326
62,650	62,700	9,728	7,140	9,728	8,337
62,700	62,750	9,739	7,146	9,739	8,348
62,750	62,800	9,750	7,152	9,750	8,359
62,800	62,850	9,761	7,158	9,761	8,370
62,850	62,900	9,772	7,164	9,772	8,381
62,900	62,950	9,783	7,170	9,783	8,392
62,950	63,000	9,794	7,176	9,794	8,403

63,000

At least	But less than	Single	MFJ *	MFS	HoH
63,000	63,050	9,805	7,182	9,805	8,414
63,050	63,100	9,816	7,188	9,816	8,425
63,100	63,150	9,827	7,194	9,827	8,436
63,150	63,200	9,838	7,200	9,838	8,447
63,200	63,250	9,849	7,206	9,849	8,458
63,250	63,300	9,860	7,212	9,860	8,469
63,300	63,350	9,871	7,218	9,871	8,480
63,350	63,400	9,882	7,224	9,882	8,491
63,400	63,450	9,893	7,230	9,893	8,502
63,450	63,500	9,904	7,236	9,904	8,513
63,500	63,550	9,915	7,242	9,915	8,524
63,550	63,600	9,926	7,248	9,926	8,535
63,600	63,650	9,937	7,254	9,937	8,546
63,650	63,700	9,948	7,260	9,948	8,557
63,700	63,750	9,959	7,266	9,959	8,568
63,750	63,800	9,970	7,272	9,970	8,579
63,800	63,850	9,981	7,278	9,981	8,590
63,850	63,900	9,992	7,284	9,992	8,601
63,900	63,950	10,003	7,290	10,003	8,612
63,950	64,000	10,014	7,296	10,014	8,623

64,000

At least	But less than	Single	MFJ *	MFS	HoH
64,000	64,050	10,025	7,302	10,025	8,634
64,050	64,100	10,036	7,308	10,036	8,645
64,100	64,150	10,047	7,314	10,047	8,656
64,150	64,200	10,058	7,320	10,058	8,667
64,200	64,250	10,069	7,326	10,069	8,678
64,250	64,300	10,080	7,332	10,080	8,689
64,300	64,350	10,091	7,338	10,091	8,700
64,350	64,400	10,102	7,344	10,102	8,711
64,400	64,450	10,113	7,350	10,113	8,722
64,450	64,500	10,124	7,356	10,124	8,733
64,500	64,550	10,135	7,362	10,135	8,744
64,550	64,600	10,146	7,368	10,146	8,755
64,600	64,650	10,157	7,374	10,157	8,766
64,650	64,700	10,168	7,380	10,168	8,777
64,700	64,750	10,179	7,386	10,179	8,788
64,750	64,800	10,190	7,392	10,190	8,799
64,800	64,850	10,201	7,398	10,201	8,810
64,850	64,900	10,212	7,404	10,212	8,821
64,900	64,950	10,223	7,410	10,223	8,832
64,950	65,000	10,234	7,416	10,234	8,843

65,000

At least	But less than	Single	MFJ *	MFS	HoH
65,000	65,050	10,245	7,422	10,245	8,854
65,050	65,100	10,256	7,428	10,256	8,865
65,100	65,150	10,267	7,434	10,267	8,876
65,150	65,200	10,278	7,440	10,278	8,887
65,200	65,250	10,289	7,446	10,289	8,898
65,250	65,300	10,300	7,452	10,300	8,909
65,300	65,350	10,311	7,458	10,311	8,920
65,350	65,400	10,322	7,464	10,322	8,931
65,400	65,450	10,333	7,470	10,333	8,942
65,450	65,500	10,344	7,476	10,344	8,953
65,500	65,550	10,355	7,482	10,355	8,964
65,550	65,600	10,366	7,488	10,366	8,975
65,600	65,650	10,377	7,494	10,377	8,986
65,650	65,700	10,388	7,500	10,388	8,997
65,700	65,750	10,399	7,506	10,399	9,008
65,750	65,800	10,410	7,512	10,410	9,019
65,800	65,850	10,421	7,518	10,421	9,030
65,850	65,900	10,432	7,524	10,432	9,041
65,900	65,950	10,443	7,530	10,443	9,052
65,950	66,000	10,454	7,536	10,454	9,063

* This column must also be used by a qualifying widow(er).

(Continued)

Draft As of September 26, 2018.

2018 Tax Table — Continued

If line 10 (taxable income) is—		And you are—			
At least	But less than	Single	Married filing jointly *	Married filing separately	Head of a household
		Your tax is—			
66,000					
66,000	66,050	10,465	7,542	10,465	9,074
66,050	66,100	10,476	7,548	10,476	9,085
66,100	66,150	10,487	7,554	10,487	9,096
66,150	66,200	10,498	7,560	10,498	9,107
66,200	66,250	10,509	7,566	10,509	9,118
66,250	66,300	10,520	7,572	10,520	9,129
66,300	66,350	10,531	7,578	10,531	9,140
66,350	66,400	10,542	7,584	10,542	9,151
66,400	66,450	10,553	7,590	10,553	9,162
66,450	66,500	10,564	7,596	10,564	9,173
66,500	66,550	10,575	7,602	10,575	9,184
66,550	66,600	10,586	7,608	10,586	9,195
66,600	66,650	10,597	7,614	10,597	9,206
66,650	66,700	10,608	7,620	10,608	9,217
66,700	66,750	10,619	7,626	10,619	9,228
66,750	66,800	10,630	7,632	10,630	9,239
66,800	66,850	10,641	7,638	10,641	9,250
66,850	66,900	10,652	7,644	10,652	9,261
66,900	66,950	10,663	7,650	10,663	9,272
66,950	67,000	10,674	7,656	10,674	9,283
67,000					
67,000	67,050	10,685	7,662	10,685	9,294
67,050	67,100	10,696	7,668	10,696	9,305
67,100	67,150	10,707	7,674	10,707	9,316
67,150	67,200	10,718	7,680	10,718	9,327
67,200	67,250	10,729	7,686	10,729	9,338
67,250	67,300	10,740	7,692	10,740	9,349
67,300	67,350	10,751	7,698	10,751	9,360
67,350	67,400	10,762	7,704	10,762	9,371
67,400	67,450	10,773	7,710	10,773	9,382
67,450	67,500	10,784	7,716	10,784	9,393
67,500	67,550	10,795	7,722	10,795	9,404
67,550	67,600	10,806	7,728	10,806	9,415
67,600	67,650	10,817	7,734	10,817	9,426
67,650	67,700	10,828	7,740	10,828	9,437
67,700	67,750	10,839	7,746	10,839	9,448
67,750	67,800	10,850	7,752	10,850	9,459
67,800	67,850	10,861	7,758	10,861	9,470
67,850	67,900	10,872	7,764	10,872	9,481
67,900	67,950	10,883	7,770	10,883	9,492
67,950	68,000	10,894	7,776	10,894	9,503
68,000					
68,000	68,050	10,905	7,782	10,905	9,514
68,050	68,100	10,916	7,788	10,916	9,525
68,100	68,150	10,927	7,794	10,927	9,536
68,150	68,200	10,938	7,800	10,938	9,547
68,200	68,250	10,949	7,806	10,949	9,558
68,250	68,300	10,960	7,812	10,960	9,569
68,300	68,350	10,971	7,818	10,971	9,580
68,350	68,400	10,982	7,824	10,982	9,591
68,400	68,450	10,993	7,830	10,993	9,602
68,450	68,500	11,004	7,836	11,004	9,613
68,500	68,550	11,015	7,842	11,015	9,624
68,550	68,600	11,026	7,848	11,026	9,635
68,600	68,650	11,037	7,854	11,037	9,646
68,650	68,700	11,048	7,860	11,048	9,657
68,700	68,750	11,059	7,866	11,059	9,668
68,750	68,800	11,070	7,872	11,070	9,679
68,800	68,850	11,081	7,878	11,081	9,690
68,850	68,900	11,092	7,884	11,092	9,701
68,900	68,950	11,103	7,890	11,103	9,712
68,950	69,000	11,114	7,896	11,114	9,723

If line 10 (taxable income) is—		And you are—			
At least	But less than	Single	Married filing jointly *	Married filing separately	Head of a household
		Your tax is—			
69,000					
69,000	69,050	11,125	7,902	11,125	9,734
69,050	69,100	11,136	7,908	11,136	9,745
69,100	69,150	11,147	7,914	11,147	9,756
69,150	69,200	11,158	7,920	11,158	9,767
69,200	69,250	11,169	7,926	11,169	9,778
69,250	69,300	11,180	7,932	11,180	9,789
69,300	69,350	11,191	7,938	11,191	9,800
69,350	69,400	11,202	7,944	11,202	9,811
69,400	69,450	11,213	7,950	11,213	9,822
69,450	69,500	11,224	7,956	11,224	9,833
69,500	69,550	11,235	7,962	11,235	9,844
69,550	69,600	11,246	7,968	11,246	9,855
69,600	69,650	11,257	7,974	11,257	9,866
69,650	69,700	11,268	7,980	11,268	9,877
69,700	69,750	11,279	7,986	11,279	9,888
69,750	69,800	11,290	7,992	11,290	9,899
69,800	69,850	11,301	7,998	11,301	9,910
69,850	69,900	11,312	8,004	11,312	9,921
69,900	69,950	11,323	8,010	11,323	9,932
69,950	70,000	11,334	8,016	11,334	9,943
70,000					
70,000	70,050	11,345	8,022	11,345	9,954
70,050	70,100	11,356	8,028	11,356	9,965
70,100	70,150	11,367	8,034	11,367	9,976
70,150	70,200	11,378	8,040	11,378	9,987
70,200	70,250	11,389	8,046	11,389	9,998
70,250	70,300	11,400	8,052	11,400	10,009
70,300	70,350	11,411	8,058	11,411	10,020
70,350	70,400	11,422	8,064	11,422	10,031
70,400	70,450	11,433	8,070	11,433	10,042
70,450	70,500	11,444	8,076	11,444	10,053
70,500	70,550	11,455	8,082	11,455	10,064
70,550	70,600	11,466	8,088	11,466	10,075
70,600	70,650	11,477	8,094	11,477	10,086
70,650	70,700	11,488	8,100	11,488	10,097
70,700	70,750	11,499	8,106	11,499	10,108
70,750	70,800	11,510	8,112	11,510	10,119
70,800	70,850	11,521	8,118	11,521	10,130
70,850	70,900	11,532	8,124	11,532	10,141
70,900	70,950	11,543	8,130	11,543	10,152
70,950	71,000	11,554	8,136	11,554	10,163
71,000					
71,000	71,050	11,565	8,142	11,565	10,174
71,050	71,100	11,576	8,148	11,576	10,185
71,100	71,150	11,587	8,154	11,587	10,196
71,150	71,200	11,598	8,160	11,598	10,207
71,200	71,250	11,609	8,166	11,609	10,218
71,250	71,300	11,620	8,172	11,620	10,229
71,300	71,350	11,631	8,178	11,631	10,240
71,350	71,400	11,642	8,184	11,642	10,251
71,400	71,450	11,653	8,190	11,653	10,262
71,450	71,500	11,664	8,196	11,664	10,273
71,500	71,550	11,675	8,202	11,675	10,284
71,550	71,600	11,686	8,208	11,686	10,295
71,600	71,650	11,697	8,214	11,697	10,306
71,650	71,700	11,708	8,220	11,708	10,317
71,700	71,750	11,719	8,226	11,719	10,328
71,750	71,800	11,730	8,232	11,730	10,339
71,800	71,850	11,741	8,238	11,741	10,350
71,850	71,900	11,752	8,244	11,752	10,361
71,900	71,950	11,763	8,250	11,763	10,372
71,950	72,000	11,774	8,256	11,774	10,383

If line 10 (taxable income) is—		And you are—			
At least	But less than	Single	Married filing jointly *	Married filing separately	Head of a household
		Your tax is—			
72,000					
72,000	72,050	11,785	8,262	11,785	10,394
72,050	72,100	11,796	8,268	11,796	10,405
72,100	72,150	11,807	8,274	11,807	10,416
72,150	72,200	11,818	8,280	11,818	10,427
72,200	72,250	11,829	8,286	11,829	10,438
72,250	72,300	11,840	8,292	11,840	10,449
72,300	72,350	11,851	8,298	11,851	10,460
72,350	72,400	11,862	8,304	11,862	10,471
72,400	72,450	11,873	8,310	11,873	10,482
72,450	72,500	11,884	8,316	11,884	10,493
72,500	72,550	11,895	8,322	11,895	10,504
72,550	72,600	11,906	8,328	11,906	10,515
72,600	72,650	11,917	8,334	11,917	10,526
72,650	72,700	11,928	8,340	11,928	10,537
72,700	72,750	11,939	8,346	11,939	10,548
72,750	72,800	11,950	8,352	11,950	10,559
72,800	72,850	11,961	8,358	11,961	10,570
72,850	72,900	11,972	8,364	11,972	10,581
72,900	72,950	11,983	8,370	11,983	10,592
72,950	73,000	11,994	8,376	11,994	10,603
73,000					
73,000	73,050	12,005	8,382	12,005	10,614
73,050	73,100	12,016	8,388	12,016	10,625
73,100	73,150	12,027	8,394	12,027	10,636
73,150	73,200	12,038	8,400	12,038	10,647
73,200	73,250	12,049	8,406	12,049	10,658
73,250	73,300	12,060	8,412	12,060	10,669
73,300	73,350	12,071	8,418	12,071	10,680
73,350	73,400	12,082	8,424	12,082	10,691
73,400	73,450	12,093	8,430	12,093	10,702
73,450	73,500	12,104	8,436	12,104	10,713
73,500	73,550	12,115	8,442	12,115	10,724
73,550	73,600	12,126	8,448	12,126	10,735
73,600	73,650	12,137	8,454	12,137	10,746
73,650	73,700	12,148	8,460	12,148	10,757
73,700	73,750	12,159	8,466	12,159	10,768
73,750	73,800	12,170	8,472	12,170	10,779
73,800	73,850	12,181	8,478	12,181	10,790
73,850	73,900	12,192	8,484	12,192	10,801
73,900	73,950	12,203	8,490	12,203	10,812
73,950	74,000	12,214	8,496	12,214	10,823
74,000					
74,000	74,050	12,225	8,502	12,225	10,834
74,050	74,100	12,236	8,508	12,236	10,845
74,100	74,150	12,247	8,514	12,247	10,856
74,150	74,200	12,258	8,520	12,258	10,867
74,200	74,250	12,269	8,526	12,269	10,878
74,250	74,300	12,280	8,532	12,280	10,889
74,300	74,350	12,291	8,538	12,291	10,900
74,350	74,400	12,302	8,544	12,302	10,911
74,400	74,450	12,313	8,550	12,313	10,922
74,450	74,500	12,324	8,556	12,324	10,933
74,500	74,550	12,335	8,562	12,335	10,944
74,550	74,600	12,346	8,568	12,346	10,955
74,600	74,650	12,357	8,574	12,357	10,966
74,650	74,700	12,368	8,580	12,368	10,977
74,700	74,750	12,379	8,586	12,379	10,988
74,750	74,800	12,390	8,592	12,390	10,999
74,800	74,850	12,401	8,598	12,401	11,010
74,850	74,900	12,412	8,604	12,412	11,021
74,900	74,950	12,423	8,610	12,423	11,032
74,950	75,000	12,434	8,616	12,434	11,043

* This column must also be used by a qualifying widow(er).

(Continued)

Draft As of September 26, 2018.

2018 Tax Table — *Continued*

75,000 – 78,000 – 81,000

If line 10 (taxable income) is—		And you are—			
At least	But less than	Single	Married filing jointly *	Married filing separately	Head of a household
		Your tax is—			
75,000					
75,000	75,050	12,145	8,622	12,445	11,054
75,050	75,100	12,456	8,628	12,456	11,065
75,100	75,150	12,467	8,634	12,467	11,076
75,150	75,200	12,478	8,640	12,478	11,087
75,200	75,250	12,489	8,646	12,489	11,098
75,250	75,300	12,500	8,652	12,500	11,109
75,300	75,350	12,511	8,658	12,511	11,120
75,350	75,400	12,522	8,664	12,522	11,131
75,400	75,450	12,533	8,670	12,533	11,142
75,450	75,500	12,544	8,676	12,544	11,153
75,500	75,550	12,555	8,682	12,555	11,164
75,550	75,600	12,566	8,688	12,566	11,175
75,600	75,650	12,577	8,694	12,577	11,186
75,650	75,700	12,588	8,700	12,588	11,197
75,700	75,750	12,599	8,706	12,599	11,208
75,750	75,800	12,610	8,712	12,610	11,219
75,800	75,850	12,621	8,718	12,621	11,230
75,850	75,900	12,632	8,724	12,632	11,241
75,900	75,950	12,643	8,730	12,643	11,252
75,950	76,000	12,654	8,736	12,654	11,263
76,000					
76,000	76,050	12,665	8,742	12,665	11,274
76,050	76,100	12,676	8,748	12,676	11,285
76,100	76,150	12,687	8,754	12,687	11,296
76,150	76,200	12,698	8,760	12,698	11,307
76,200	76,250	12,709	8,766	12,709	11,318
76,250	76,300	12,720	8,772	12,720	11,329
76,300	76,350	12,731	8,778	12,731	11,340
76,350	76,400	12,742	8,784	12,742	11,351
76,400	76,450	12,753	8,790	12,753	11,362
76,450	76,500	12,764	8,796	12,764	11,373
76,500	76,550	12,775	8,802	12,775	11,384
76,550	76,600	12,786	8,808	12,786	11,395
76,600	76,650	12,797	8,814	12,797	11,406
76,650	76,700	12,808	8,820	12,808	11,417
76,700	76,750	12,819	8,826	12,819	11,428
76,750	76,800	12,830	8,832	12,830	11,439
76,800	76,850	12,841	8,838	12,841	11,450
76,850	76,900	12,852	8,844	12,852	11,461
76,900	76,950	12,863	8,850	12,863	11,472
76,950	77,000	12,874	8,856	12,874	11,483
77,000					
77,000	77,050	12,885	8,862	12,885	11,494
77,050	77,100	12,896	8,868	12,896	11,505
77,100	77,150	12,907	8,874	12,907	11,516
77,150	77,200	12,918	8,880	12,918	11,527
77,200	77,250	12,929	8,886	12,929	11,538
77,250	77,300	12,940	8,892	12,940	11,549
77,300	77,350	12,951	8,898	12,951	11,560
77,350	77,400	12,962	8,904	12,962	11,571
77,400	77,450	12,973	8,913	12,973	11,582
77,450	77,500	12,984	8,924	12,984	11,593
77,500	77,550	12,995	8,935	12,995	11,604
77,550	77,600	13,006	8,946	13,006	11,615
77,600	77,650	13,017	8,957	13,017	11,626
77,650	77,700	13,028	8,968	13,028	11,637
77,700	77,750	13,039	8,979	13,039	11,648
77,750	77,800	13,050	8,990	13,050	11,659
77,800	77,850	13,061	9,001	13,061	11,670
77,850	77,900	13,072	9,012	13,072	11,681
77,900	77,950	13,083	9,023	13,083	11,692
77,950	78,000	13,094	9,034	13,094	11,703

If line 10 (taxable income) is—		And you are—			
At least	But less than	Single	Married filing jointly *	Married filing separately	Head of a household
		Your tax is—			
78,000					
78,000	78,050	13,105	9,045	13,105	11,714
78,050	78,100	13,116	9,056	13,116	11,725
78,100	78,150	13,127	9,067	13,127	11,736
78,150	78,200	13,138	9,078	13,138	11,747
78,200	78,250	13,149	9,089	13,149	11,758
78,250	78,300	13,160	9,100	13,160	11,769
78,300	78,350	13,171	9,111	13,171	11,780
78,350	78,400	13,182	9,122	13,182	11,791
78,400	78,450	13,193	9,133	13,193	11,802
78,450	78,500	13,204	9,144	13,204	11,813
78,500	78,550	13,215	9,155	13,215	11,824
78,550	78,600	13,226	9,166	13,226	11,835
78,600	78,650	13,237	9,177	13,237	11,846
78,650	78,700	13,248	9,188	13,248	11,857
78,700	78,750	13,259	9,199	13,259	11,868
78,750	78,800	13,270	9,210	13,270	11,879
78,800	78,850	13,281	9,221	13,281	11,890
78,850	78,900	13,292	9,232	13,292	11,901
78,900	78,950	13,303	9,243	13,303	11,912
78,950	79,000	13,314	9,254	13,314	11,923
79,000					
79,000	79,050	13,325	9,265	13,325	11,934
79,050	79,100	13,336	9,276	13,336	11,945
79,100	79,150	13,347	9,287	13,347	11,956
79,150	79,200	13,358	9,298	13,358	11,967
79,200	79,250	13,369	9,309	13,369	11,978
79,250	79,300	13,380	9,320	13,380	11,989
79,300	79,350	13,391	9,331	13,391	12,000
79,350	79,400	13,402	9,342	13,402	12,011
79,400	79,450	13,413	9,353	13,413	12,022
79,450	79,500	13,424	9,364	13,424	12,033
79,500	79,550	13,435	9,375	13,435	12,044
79,550	79,600	13,446	9,386	13,446	12,055
79,600	79,650	13,457	9,397	13,457	12,066
79,650	79,700	13,468	9,408	13,468	12,077
79,700	79,750	13,479	9,419	13,479	12,088
79,750	79,800	13,490	9,430	13,490	12,099
79,800	79,850	13,501	9,441	13,501	12,110
79,850	79,900	13,512	9,452	13,512	12,121
79,900	79,950	13,523	9,463	13,523	12,132
79,950	80,000	13,534	9,474	13,534	12,143
80,000					
80,000	80,050	13,545	9,485	13,545	12,154
80,050	80,100	13,556	9,496	13,556	12,165
80,100	80,150	13,567	9,507	13,567	12,176
80,150	80,200	13,578	9,518	13,578	12,187
80,200	80,250	13,589	9,529	13,589	12,198
80,250	80,300	13,600	9,540	13,600	12,209
80,300	80,350	13,611	9,551	13,611	12,220
80,350	80,400	13,622	9,562	13,622	12,231
80,400	80,450	13,633	9,573	13,633	12,242
80,450	80,500	13,644	9,584	13,644	12,253
80,500	80,550	13,655	9,595	13,655	12,264
80,550	80,600	13,666	9,606	13,666	12,275
80,600	80,650	13,677	9,617	13,677	12,286
80,650	80,700	13,688	9,628	13,688	12,297
80,700	80,750	13,699	9,639	13,699	12,308
80,750	80,800	13,710	9,650	13,710	12,319
80,800	80,850	13,721	9,661	13,721	12,330
80,850	80,900	13,732	9,672	13,732	12,341
80,900	80,950	13,743	9,683	13,743	12,352
80,950	81,000	13,754	9,694	13,754	12,363

If line 10 (taxable income) is—		And you are—			
At least	But less than	Single	Married filing jointly *	Married filing separately	Head of a household
		Your tax is—			
81,000					
81,000	81,050	13,765	9,705	13,765	12,374
81,050	81,100	13,776	9,716	13,776	12,385
81,100	81,150	13,787	9,727	13,787	12,396
81,150	81,200	13,798	9,738	13,798	12,407
81,200	81,250	13,809	9,749	13,809	12,418
81,250	81,300	13,820	9,760	13,820	12,429
81,300	81,350	13,831	9,771	13,831	12,440
81,350	81,400	13,842	9,782	13,842	12,451
81,400	81,450	13,853	9,793	13,853	12,462
81,450	81,500	13,864	9,804	13,864	12,473
81,500	81,550	13,875	9,815	13,875	12,484
81,550	81,600	13,886	9,826	13,886	12,495
81,600	81,650	13,897	9,837	13,897	12,506
81,650	81,700	13,908	9,848	13,908	12,517
81,700	81,750	13,919	9,859	13,919	12,528
81,750	81,800	13,930	9,870	13,930	12,539
81,800	81,850	13,941	9,881	13,941	12,550
81,850	81,900	13,952	9,892	13,952	12,561
81,900	81,950	13,963	9,903	13,963	12,572
81,950	82,000	13,974	9,914	13,974	12,583
82,000					
82,000	82,050	13,985	9,925	13,985	12,594
82,050	82,100	13,996	9,936	13,996	12,605
82,100	82,150	14,007	9,947	14,007	12,616
82,150	82,200	14,018	9,958	14,018	12,627
82,200	82,250	14,029	9,969	14,029	12,638
82,250	82,300	14,040	9,980	14,040	12,649
82,300	82,350	14,051	9,991	14,051	12,660
82,350	82,400	14,062	10,002	14,062	12,671
82,400	82,450	14,073	10,013	14,073	12,682
82,450	82,500	14,084	10,024	14,084	12,693
82,500	82,550	14,096	10,035	14,096	12,704
82,550	82,600	14,108	10,046	14,108	12,716
82,600	82,650	14,120	10,057	14,120	12,728
82,650	82,700	14,132	10,068	14,132	12,740
82,700	82,750	14,144	10,079	14,144	12,752
82,750	82,800	14,156	10,090	14,156	12,764
82,800	82,850	14,168	10,101	14,168	12,776
82,850	82,900	14,180	10,112	14,180	12,788
82,900	82,950	14,192	10,123	14,192	12,800
82,950	83,000	14,204	10,134	14,204	12,812
83,000					
83,000	83,050	14,216	10,145	14,216	12,824
83,050	83,100	14,228	10,156	14,228	12,836
83,100	83,150	14,240	10,167	14,240	12,848
83,150	83,200	14,252	10,178	14,252	12,860
83,200	83,250	14,264	10,189	14,264	12,872
83,250	83,300	14,276	10,200	14,276	12,884
83,300	83,350	14,288	10,211	14,288	12,896
83,350	83,400	14,300	10,222	14,300	12,908
83,400	83,450	14,312	10,233	14,312	12,920
83,450	83,500	14,324	10,244	14,324	12,932
83,500	83,550	14,336	10,255	14,336	12,944
83,550	83,600	14,348	10,266	14,348	12,956
83,600	83,650	14,360	10,277	14,360	12,968
83,650	83,700	14,372	10,288	14,372	12,980
83,700	83,750	14,384	10,299	14,384	12,992
83,750	83,800	14,396	10,310	14,396	13,004
83,800	83,850	14,408	10,321	14,408	13,016
83,850	83,900	14,420	10,332	14,420	13,028
83,900	83,950	14,432	10,343	14,432	13,040
83,950	84,000	14,444	10,354	14,444	13,052

(Continued)

* This column must also be used by a qualifying widow(er).

Draft As of September 26, 2018.

2018 Tax Table — Continued

If line 10 (taxable income) is—		And you are—				If line 10 (taxable income) is—		And you are—				If line 10 (taxable income) is—		And you are—			
At least	But less than	Single	Married filing jointly *	Married filing separately	Head of a house-hold	At least	But less than	Single	Married filing jointly *	Married filing separately	Head of a house-hold	At least	But less than	Single	Married filing jointly *	Married filing separately	Head of a house-hold
		Your tax is—						Your tax is—						Your tax is—			
84,000						**87,000**						**90,000**					
84,000	84,050	14,456	10,365	14,456	13,064	87,000	87,050	15,176	11,025	15,176	13,784	90,000	90,050	15,896	11,685	15,896	14,504
84,050	84,100	14,468	10,376	14,468	13,076	87,050	87,100	15,188	11,036	15,188	13,796	90,050	90,100	15,908	11,696	15,908	14,516
84,100	84,150	14,480	10,387	14,480	13,088	87,100	87,150	15,200	11,047	15,200	13,808	90,100	90,150	15,920	11,707	15,920	14,528
84,150	84,200	14,492	10,398	14,492	13,100	87,150	87,200	15,212	11,058	15,212	13,820	90,150	90,200	15,932	11,718	15,932	14,540
84,200	84,250	14,504	10,409	14,504	13,112	87,200	87,250	15,224	11,069	15,224	13,832	90,200	90,250	15,944	11,729	15,944	14,552
84,250	84,300	14,516	10,420	14,516	13,124	87,250	87,300	15,236	11,080	15,236	13,844	90,250	90,300	15,956	11,740	15,956	14,564
84,300	84,350	14,528	10,431	14,528	13,136	87,300	87,350	15,248	11,091	15,248	13,856	90,300	90,350	15,968	11,751	15,968	14,576
84,350	84,400	14,540	10,442	14,540	13,148	87,350	87,400	15,260	11,102	15,260	13,868	90,350	90,400	15,980	11,762	15,980	14,588
84,400	84,450	14,552	10,453	14,552	13,160	87,400	87,450	15,272	11,113	15,272	13,880	90,400	90,450	15,992	11,773	15,992	14,600
84,450	84,500	14,564	10,464	14,564	13,172	87,450	87,500	15,284	11,124	15,284	13,892	90,450	90,500	16,004	11,784	16,004	14,612
84,500	84,550	14,576	10,475	14,576	13,184	87,500	87,550	15,296	11,135	15,296	13,904	90,500	90,550	16,016	11,795	16,016	14,624
84,550	84,600	14,588	10,486	14,588	13,196	87,550	87,600	15,308	11,146	15,308	13,916	90,550	90,600	16,028	11,806	16,028	14,636
84,600	84,650	14,600	10,497	14,600	13,208	87,600	87,650	15,320	11,157	15,320	13,928	90,600	90,650	16,040	11,817	16,040	14,648
84,650	84,700	14,612	10,508	14,612	13,220	87,650	87,700	15,332	11,168	15,332	13,940	90,650	90,700	16,052	11,828	16,052	14,660
84,700	84,750	14,624	10,519	14,624	13,232	87,700	87,750	15,344	11,179	15,344	13,952	90,700	90,750	16,064	11,839	16,064	14,672
84,750	84,800	14,636	10,530	14,636	13,244	87,750	87,800	15,356	11,190	15,356	13,964	90,750	90,800	16,076	11,850	16,076	14,684
84,800	84,850	14,648	10,541	14,648	13,256	87,800	87,850	15,368	11,201	15,368	13,976	90,800	90,850	16,088	11,861	16,088	14,696
84,850	84,900	14,660	10,552	14,660	13,268	87,850	87,900	15,380	11,212	15,380	13,988	90,850	90,900	16,100	11,872	16,100	14,708
84,900	84,950	14,672	10,563	14,672	13,280	87,900	87,950	15,392	11,223	15,392	14,000	90,900	90,950	16,112	11,883	16,112	14,720
84,950	85,000	14,684	10,574	14,684	13,292	87,950	88,000	15,404	11,234	15,404	14,012	90,950	91,000	16,124	11,894	16,124	14,732
85,000						**88,000**						**91,000**					
85,000	85,050	14,696	10,585	14,696	13,304	88,000	88,050	15,416	11,245	15,416	14,024	91,000	91,050	16,136	11,905	16,136	14,744
85,050	85,100	14,708	10,596	14,708	13,316	88,050	88,100	15,428	11,256	15,428	14,036	91,050	91,100	16,148	11,916	16,148	14,756
85,100	85,150	14,720	10,607	14,720	13,328	88,100	88,150	15,440	11,267	15,440	14,048	91,100	91,150	16,160	11,927	16,160	14,768
85,150	85,200	14,732	10,618	14,732	13,340	88,150	88,200	15,452	11,278	15,452	14,060	91,150	91,200	16,172	11,938	16,172	14,780
85,200	85,250	14,744	10,629	14,744	13,352	88,200	88,250	15,464	11,289	15,464	14,072	91,200	91,250	16,184	11,949	16,184	14,792
85,250	85,300	14,756	10,640	14,756	13,364	88,250	88,300	15,476	11,300	15,476	14,084	91,250	91,300	16,196	11,960	16,196	14,804
85,300	85,350	14,768	10,651	14,768	13,376	88,300	88,350	15,488	11,311	15,488	14,096	91,300	91,350	16,208	11,971	16,208	14,816
85,350	85,400	14,780	10,662	14,780	13,388	88,350	88,400	15,500	11,322	15,500	14,108	91,350	91,400	16,220	11,982	16,220	14,828
85,400	85,450	14,792	10,673	14,792	13,400	88,400	88,450	15,512	11,333	15,512	14,120	91,400	91,450	16,232	11,993	16,232	14,840
85,450	85,500	14,804	10,684	14,804	13,412	88,450	88,500	15,524	11,344	15,524	14,132	91,450	91,500	16,244	12,004	16,244	14,852
85,500	85,550	14,816	10,695	14,816	13,424	88,500	88,550	15,536	11,355	15,536	14,144	91,500	91,550	16,256	12,015	16,256	14,864
85,550	85,600	14,828	10,706	14,828	13,436	88,550	88,600	15,548	11,366	15,548	14,156	91,550	91,600	16,268	12,026	16,268	14,876
85,600	85,650	14,840	10,717	14,840	13,448	88,600	88,650	15,560	11,377	15,560	14,168	91,600	91,650	16,280	12,037	16,280	14,888
85,650	85,700	14,852	10,728	14,852	13,460	88,650	88,700	15,572	11,388	15,572	14,180	91,650	91,700	16,292	12,048	16,292	14,900
85,700	85,750	14,864	10,739	14,864	13,472	88,700	88,750	15,584	11,399	15,584	14,192	91,700	91,750	16,304	12,059	16,304	14,912
85,750	85,800	14,876	10,750	14,876	13,484	88,750	88,800	15,596	11,410	15,596	14,204	91,750	91,800	16,316	12,070	16,316	14,924
85,800	85,850	14,888	10,761	14,888	13,496	88,800	88,850	15,608	11,421	15,608	14,216	91,800	91,850	16,328	12,081	16,328	14,936
85,850	85,900	14,900	10,772	14,900	13,508	88,850	88,900	15,620	11,432	15,620	14,228	91,850	91,900	16,340	12,092	16,340	14,948
85,900	85,950	14,912	10,783	14,912	13,520	88,900	88,950	15,632	11,443	15,632	14,240	91,900	91,950	16,352	12,103	16,352	14,960
85,950	86,000	14,924	10,794	14,924	13,532	88,950	89,000	15,644	11,454	15,644	14,252	91,950	92,000	16,364	12,114	16,364	14,972
86,000						**89,000**						**92,000**					
86,000	86,050	14,936	10,805	14,936	13,544	89,000	89,050	15,656	11,465	15,656	14,264	92,000	92,050	16,376	12,125	16,376	14,984
86,050	86,100	14,948	10,816	14,948	13,556	89,050	89,100	15,668	11,476	15,668	14,276	92,050	92,100	16,388	12,136	16,388	14,996
86,100	86,150	14,960	10,827	14,960	13,568	89,100	89,150	15,680	11,487	15,680	14,288	92,100	92,150	16,400	12,147	16,400	15,008
86,150	86,200	14,972	10,838	14,972	13,580	89,150	89,200	15,692	11,498	15,692	14,300	92,150	92,200	16,412	12,158	16,412	15,020
86,200	86,250	14,984	10,849	14,984	13,592	89,200	89,250	15,704	11,509	15,704	14,312	92,200	92,250	16,424	12,169	16,424	15,032
86,250	86,300	14,996	10,860	14,996	13,604	89,250	89,300	15,716	11,520	15,716	14,324	92,250	92,300	16,436	12,180	16,436	15,044
86,300	86,350	15,008	10,871	15,008	13,616	89,300	89,350	15,728	11,531	15,728	14,336	92,300	92,350	16,448	12,191	16,448	15,056
86,350	86,400	15,020	10,882	15,020	13,628	89,350	89,400	15,740	11,542	15,740	14,348	92,350	92,400	16,460	12,202	16,460	15,068
86,400	86,450	15,032	10,893	15,032	13,640	89,400	89,450	15,752	11,553	15,752	14,360	92,400	92,450	16,472	12,213	16,472	15,080
86,450	86,500	15,044	10,904	15,044	13,652	89,450	89,500	15,764	11,564	15,764	14,372	92,450	92,500	16,484	12,224	16,484	15,092
86,500	86,550	15,056	10,915	15,056	13,664	89,500	89,550	15,776	11,575	15,776	14,384	92,500	92,550	16,496	12,235	16,496	15,104
86,550	86,600	15,068	10,926	15,068	13,676	89,550	89,600	15,788	11,586	15,788	14,396	92,550	92,600	16,508	12,246	16,508	15,116
86,600	86,650	15,080	10,937	15,080	13,688	89,600	89,650	15,800	11,597	15,800	14,408	92,600	92,650	16,520	12,257	16,520	15,128
86,650	86,700	15,092	10,948	15,092	13,700	89,650	89,700	15,812	11,608	15,812	14,420	92,650	92,700	16,532	12,268	16,532	15,140
86,700	86,750	15,104	10,959	15,104	13,712	89,700	89,750	15,824	11,619	15,824	14,432	92,700	92,750	16,544	12,279	16,544	15,152
86,750	86,800	15,116	10,970	15,116	13,724	89,750	89,800	15,836	11,630	15,836	14,444	92,750	92,800	16,556	12,290	16,556	15,164
86,800	86,850	15,128	10,981	15,128	13,736	89,800	89,850	15,848	11,641	15,848	14,456	92,800	92,850	16,568	12,301	16,568	15,176
86,850	86,900	15,140	10,992	15,140	13,748	89,850	89,900	15,860	11,652	15,860	14,468	92,850	92,900	16,580	12,312	16,580	15,188
86,900	86,950	15,152	11,003	15,152	13,760	89,900	89,950	15,872	11,663	15,872	14,480	92,900	92,950	16,592	12,323	16,592	15,200
86,950	87,000	15,164	11,014	15,164	13,772	89,950	90,000	15,884	11,674	15,884	14,492	92,950	93,000	16,604	12,334	16,604	15,212

(Continued)

* This column must also be used by a qualifying widow(er).

Draft As of September 26, 2018.

2018 Tax Table — *Continued*

93,000

At least	But less than	Single	Married filing jointly *	Married filing separately	Head of a household
93,000	93,050	16,616	12,345	16,616	15,224
93,050	93,100	16,628	12,356	16,628	15,236
93,100	93,150	16,640	12,367	16,640	15,248
93,150	93,200	16,652	12,378	16,652	15,260
93,200	93,250	16,664	12,389	16,664	15,272
93,250	93,300	16,676	12,400	16,676	15,284
93,300	93,350	16,688	12,411	16,688	15,296
93,350	93,400	16,700	12,422	16,700	15,308
93,400	93,450	16,712	12,433	16,712	15,320
93,450	93,500	16,724	12,444	16,724	15,332
93,500	93,550	16,736	12,455	16,736	15,344
93,550	93,600	16,748	12,466	16,748	15,356
93,600	93,650	16,760	12,477	16,760	15,368
93,650	93,700	16,772	12,488	16,772	15,380
93,700	93,750	16,784	12,499	16,784	15,392
93,750	93,800	16,796	12,510	16,796	15,404
93,800	93,850	16,808	12,521	16,808	15,416
93,850	93,900	16,820	12,532	16,820	15,428
93,900	93,950	16,832	12,543	16,832	15,440
93,950	94,000	16,844	12,554	16,844	15,452

94,000

At least	But less than	Single	Married filing jointly *	Married filing separately	Head of a household
94,000	94,050	16,856	12,565	16,856	15,464
94,050	94,100	16,868	12,576	16,868	15,476
94,100	94,150	16,880	12,587	16,880	15,488
94,150	94,200	16,892	12,598	16,892	15,500
94,200	94,250	16,904	12,609	16,904	15,512
94,250	94,300	16,916	12,620	16,916	15,524
94,300	94,350	16,928	12,631	16,928	15,536
94,350	94,400	16,940	12,642	16,940	15,548
94,400	94,450	16,952	12,653	16,952	15,560
94,450	94,500	16,964	12,664	16,964	15,572
94,500	94,550	16,976	12,675	16,976	15,584
94,550	94,600	16,988	12,686	16,988	15,596
94,600	94,650	17,000	12,697	17,000	15,608
94,650	94,700	17,012	12,708	17,012	15,620
94,700	94,750	17,024	12,719	17,024	15,632
94,750	94,800	17,036	12,730	17,036	15,644
94,800	94,850	17,048	12,741	17,048	15,656
94,850	94,900	17,060	12,752	17,060	15,668
94,900	94,950	17,072	12,763	17,072	15,680
94,950	95,000	17,084	12,774	17,084	15,692

95,000

At least	But less than	Single	Married filing jointly *	Married filing separately	Head of a household
95,000	95,050	17,096	12,785	17,096	15,704
95,050	95,100	17,108	12,796	17,108	15,716
95,100	95,150	17,120	12,807	17,120	15,728
95,150	95,200	17,132	12,818	17,132	15,740
95,200	95,250	17,144	12,829	17,144	15,752
95,250	95,300	17,156	12,840	17,156	15,764
95,300	95,350	17,168	12,851	17,168	15,776
95,350	95,400	17,180	12,862	17,180	15,788
95,400	95,450	17,192	12,873	17,192	15,800
95,450	95,500	17,204	12,884	17,204	15,812
95,500	95,550	17,216	12,895	17,216	15,824
95,550	95,600	17,228	12,906	17,228	15,836
95,600	95,650	17,240	12,917	17,240	15,848
95,650	95,700	17,252	12,928	17,252	15,860
95,700	95,750	17,264	12,939	17,264	15,872
95,750	95,800	17,276	12,950	17,276	15,884
95,800	95,850	17,288	12,961	17,288	15,896
95,850	95,900	17,300	12,972	17,300	15,908
95,900	95,950	17,312	12,983	17,312	15,920
95,950	96,000	17,324	12,994	17,324	15,932

96,000

At least	But less than	Single	Married filing jointly *	Married filing separately	Head of a household
96,000	96,050	17,336	13,005	17,336	15,944
96,050	96,100	17,348	13,016	17,348	15,956
96,100	96,150	17,360	13,027	17,360	15,968
96,150	96,200	17,372	13,038	17,372	15,980
96,200	96,250	17,384	13,049	17,384	15,992
96,250	96,300	17,396	13,060	17,396	16,004
96,300	96,350	17,408	13,071	17,408	16,016
96,350	96,400	17,420	13,082	17,420	16,028
96,400	96,450	17,432	13,093	17,432	16,040
96,450	96,500	17,444	13,104	17,444	16,052
96,500	96,550	17,456	13,115	17,456	16,064
96,550	96,600	17,468	13,126	17,468	16,076
96,600	96,650	17,480	13,137	17,480	16,088
96,650	96,700	17,492	13,148	17,492	16,100
96,700	96,750	17,504	13,159	17,504	16,112
96,750	96,800	17,516	13,170	17,516	16,124
96,800	96,850	17,528	13,181	17,528	16,136
96,850	96,900	17,540	13,192	17,540	16,148
96,900	96,950	17,552	13,203	17,552	16,160
96,950	97,000	17,564	13,214	17,564	16,172

97,000

At least	But less than	Single	Married filing jointly *	Married filing separately	Head of a household
97,000	97,050	17,576	13,225	17,576	16,184
97,050	97,100	17,588	13,236	17,588	16,196
97,100	97,150	17,600	13,247	17,600	16,208
97,150	97,200	17,612	13,258	17,612	16,220
97,200	97,250	17,624	13,269	17,624	16,232
97,250	97,300	17,636	13,280	17,636	16,244
97,300	97,350	17,648	13,291	17,648	16,256
97,350	97,400	17,660	13,302	17,660	16,268
97,400	97,450	17,672	13,313	17,672	16,280
97,450	97,500	17,684	13,324	17,684	16,292
97,500	97,550	17,696	13,335	17,696	16,304
97,550	97,600	17,708	13,346	17,708	16,316
97,600	97,650	17,720	13,357	17,720	16,328
97,650	97,700	17,732	13,368	17,732	16,340
97,700	97,750	17,744	13,379	17,744	16,352
97,750	97,800	17,756	13,390	17,756	16,364
97,800	97,850	17,768	13,401	17,768	16,376
97,850	97,900	17,780	13,412	17,780	16,388
97,900	97,950	17,792	13,423	17,792	16,400
97,950	98,000	17,804	13,434	17,804	16,412

98,000

At least	But less than	Single	Married filing jointly *	Married filing separately	Head of a household
98,000	98,050	17,816	13,445	17,816	16,424
98,050	98,100	17,828	13,456	17,828	16,436
98,100	98,150	17,840	13,467	17,840	16,448
98,150	98,200	17,852	13,478	17,852	16,460
98,200	98,250	17,864	13,489	17,864	16,472
98,250	98,300	17,876	13,500	17,876	16,484
98,300	98,350	17,888	13,511	17,888	16,496
98,350	98,400	17,900	13,522	17,900	16,508
98,400	98,450	17,912	13,533	17,912	16,520
98,450	98,500	17,924	13,544	17,924	16,532
98,500	98,550	17,936	13,555	17,936	16,544
98,550	98,600	17,948	13,566	17,948	16,556
98,600	98,650	17,960	13,577	17,960	16,568
98,650	98,700	17,972	13,588	17,972	16,580
98,700	98,750	17,984	13,599	17,984	16,592
98,750	98,800	17,996	13,610	17,996	16,604
98,800	98,850	18,008	13,621	18,008	16,616
98,850	98,900	18,020	13,632	18,020	16,628
98,900	98,950	18,032	13,643	18,032	16,640
98,950	99,000	18,044	13,654	18,044	16,652

99,000

At least	But less than	Single	Married filing jointly *	Married filing separately	Head of a household
99,000	99,050	18,056	13,665	18,056	16,664
99,050	99,100	18,068	13,676	18,068	16,676
99,100	99,150	18,080	13,687	18,080	16,688
99,150	99,200	18,092	13,698	18,092	16,700
99,200	99,250	18,104	13,709	18,104	16,712
99,250	99,300	18,116	13,720	18,116	16,724
99,300	99,350	18,128	13,731	18,128	16,736
99,350	99,400	18,140	13,742	18,140	16,748
99,400	99,450	18,152	13,753	18,152	16,760
99,450	99,500	18,164	13,764	18,164	16,772
99,500	99,550	18,176	13,775	18,176	16,784
99,550	99,600	18,188	13,786	18,188	16,796
99,600	99,650	18,200	13,797	18,200	16,808
99,650	99,700	18,212	13,808	18,212	16,820
99,700	99,750	18,224	13,819	18,224	16,832
99,750	99,800	18,236	13,830	18,236	16,844
99,800	99,850	18,248	13,841	18,248	16,856
99,850	99,900	18,260	13,852	18,260	16,868
99,900	99,950	18,272	13,863	18,272	16,880
99,950	100,000	18,284	13,874	18,284	16,892

$100,000
or over
use the Tax
Computation
Worksheet

* This column must also be used by a qualifying widow(er).

Draft As of September 26, 2018.

¶ 1112   Earned Income Credit Table.

2018 Earned Income Credit (EIC) Table
Caution. This is **not** a tax table.

1. To find your credit, read down the "At least - But less than" columns and find the line that includes the amount you were told to look up from your EIC Worksheet.

2. Then, go to the column that includes your filing status and the number of qualifying children you have. Enter the credit from that column on your EIC Worksheet.

Example. If your filing status is single, you have one qualifying child, and the amount you are looking up from your EIC Worksheet is $2,455, you would enter $842.

If the amount you are looking up from the worksheet is—		And your filing status is— Single, head of household, or qualifying widow(er) and the number of children you have is—			
At least	But less than	0	1	2	3
		Your credit is—			
2,400	2,450	186	825	970	1,091
2,450	2,500	189	842	990	1,114

If the amount you are looking up from the worksheet is—		And your filing status is— Single, head of household, or qualifying widow(er) and the number of children you have is—				Married filing jointly and the number of children you have is—				If the amount you are looking up from the worksheet is—		Single, head of household, or qualifying widow(er) and the number of children you have is—				Married filing jointly and the number of children you have is—			
At least	But less than	0	1	2	3	0	1	2	3	At least	But less than	0	1	2	3	0	1	2	3
		Your credit is—										Your credit is—							
$1	$50	$2	$9	$10	$11	$2	$9	$10	$11	2,800	2,850	216	961	1,130	1,271	216	961	1,130	1,271
50	100	6	26	30	34	6	26	30	34	2,850	2,900	220	978	1,150	1,294	220	978	1,150	1,294
100	150	10	43	50	56	10	43	50	56	2,900	2,950	224	995	1,170	1,316	224	995	1,170	1,316
150	200	13	60	70	79	13	60	70	79	2,950	3,000	228	1,012	1,190	1,339	228	1,012	1,190	1,339
200	250	17	77	90	101	17	77	90	101	3,000	3,050	231	1,029	1,210	1,361	231	1,029	1,210	1,361
250	300	21	94	110	124	21	94	110	124	3,050	3,100	235	1,046	1,230	1,384	235	1,046	1,230	1,384
300	350	25	111	130	146	25	111	130	146	3,100	3,150	239	1,063	1,250	1,406	239	1,063	1,250	1,406
350	400	29	128	150	169	29	128	150	169	3,150	3,200	243	1,080	1,270	1,429	243	1,080	1,270	1,429
400	450	33	145	170	191	33	145	170	191	3,200	3,250	247	1,097	1,290	1,451	247	1,097	1,290	1,451
450	500	36	162	190	214	36	162	190	214	3,250	3,300	251	1,114	1,310	1,474	251	1,114	1,310	1,474
500	550	40	179	210	236	40	179	210	236	3,300	3,350	254	1,131	1,330	1,496	254	1,131	1,330	1,496
550	600	44	196	230	259	44	196	230	259	3,350	3,400	258	1,148	1,350	1,519	258	1,148	1,350	1,519
600	650	48	213	250	281	48	213	250	281	3,400	3,450	262	1,165	1,370	1,541	262	1,165	1,370	1,541
650	700	52	230	270	304	52	230	270	304	3,450	3,500	266	1,182	1,390	1,564	266	1,182	1,390	1,564
700	750	55	247	290	326	55	247	290	326	3,500	3,550	270	1,199	1,410	1,586	270	1,199	1,410	1,586
750	800	59	264	310	349	59	264	310	349	3,550	3,600	273	1,216	1,430	1,609	273	1,216	1,430	1,609
800	850	63	281	330	371	63	281	330	371	3,600	3,650	277	1,233	1,450	1,631	277	1,233	1,450	1,631
850	900	67	298	350	394	67	298	350	394	3,650	3,700	281	1,250	1,470	1,654	281	1,250	1,470	1,654
900	950	71	315	370	416	71	315	370	416	3,700	3,750	285	1,267	1,490	1,676	285	1,267	1,490	1,676
950	1,000	75	332	390	439	75	332	390	439	3,750	3,800	289	1,284	1,510	1,699	289	1,284	1,510	1,699
1,000	1,050	78	349	410	461	78	349	410	461	3,800	3,850	293	1,301	1,530	1,701	889	1,801	1,530	1,721
1,050	1,100	82	366	430	484	82	366	430	484	3,850	3,900	296	1,318	1,550	1,744	296	1,318	1,550	1,744
1,100	1,150	86	383	450	506	86	383	450	506	3,900	3,950	300	1,335	1,570	1,766	300	1,335	1,570	1,766
1,150	1,200	90	400	470	529	90	400	470	529	3,950	4,000	304	1,352	1,590	1,789	304	1,352	1,590	1,780
1,200	1,250	94	417	490	551	94	417	490	551	4,000	4,050	308	1,369	1,610	1,811	308	1,369	1,610	1,811
1,250	1,300	98	434	510	574	98	434	510	574	4,050	4,100	312	1,386	1,630	1,834	312	1,386	1,630	1,834
1,300	1,350	101	451	530	596	101	451	530	596	4,100	4,150	316	1,403	1,650	1,856	316	1,403	1,650	1,856
1,350	1,400	105	468	550	619	105	468	550	619	4,150	4,200	319	1,420	1,670	1,879	319	1,420	1,670	1,879
1,400	1,450	109	485	570	641	109	485	570	641	4,200	4,250	323	1,437	1,690	1,901	323	1,437	1,690	1,901
1,450	1,500	113	502	590	664	113	502	590	664	4,250	4,300	327	1,454	1,710	1,924	327	1,454	1,710	1,924
1,500	1,550	117	519	610	686	117	519	610	686	4,300	4,350	331	1,471	1,730	1,946	331	1,471	1,730	1,946
1,550	1,600	120	536	630	709	120	536	630	709	4,350	4,400	335	1,488	1,750	1,969	335	1,488	1,750	1,969
1,600	1,650	124	553	650	731	124	553	650	731	4,400	4,450	339	1,505	1,770	1,991	339	1,505	1,770	1,991
1,650	1,700	128	570	670	754	128	570	670	754	4,450	4,500	342	1,522	1,790	2,014	342	1,522	1,790	2,014
1,700	1,750	132	587	690	776	132	587	690	776	4,500	4,550	346	1,539	1,810	2,036	346	1,539	1,810	2,036
1,750	1,800	136	604	710	799	136	604	710	799	4,550	4,600	350	1,556	1,830	2,059	350	1,556	1,830	2,059
1,800	1,850	140	621	730	821	140	621	730	821	4,600	4,650	354	1,573	1,850	2,081	354	1,573	1,850	2,081
1,850	1,900	143	638	750	844	143	638	750	844	4,650	4,700	358	1,590	1,870	2,104	358	1,590	1,870	2,104
1,900	1,950	147	655	770	866	147	655	770	866	4,700	4,750	361	1,607	1,890	2,126	361	1,607	1,890	2,126
1,950	2,000	151	672	790	889	151	672	790	889	4,750	4,800	365	1,624	1,910	2,149	365	1,624	1,910	2,149
2,000	2,050	155	689	810	911	155	689	810	911	4,800	4,850	369	1,641	1,930	2,171	369	1,641	1,930	2,171
2,050	2,100	159	706	830	934	159	706	830	934	4,850	4,900	373	1,658	1,950	2,194	373	1,658	1,950	2,194
2,100	2,150	163	723	850	956	163	723	850	956	4,900	4,950	377	1,675	1,970	2,216	377	1,675	1,970	2,216
2,150	2,200	166	740	870	979	166	740	870	979	4,950	5,000	381	1,692	1,990	2,239	381	1,692	1,990	2,239
2,200	2,250	170	757	890	1,001	170	757	890	1,001	5,000	5,050	384	1,709	2,010	2,261	384	1,709	2,010	2,261
2,250	2,300	174	774	910	1,024	174	774	910	1,024	5,050	5,100	388	1,726	2,030	2,284	388	1,726	2,030	2,284
2,300	2,350	178	791	930	1,046	178	791	930	1,046	5,100	5,150	392	1,743	2,050	2,306	392	1,743	2,050	2,306
2,350	2,400	182	808	950	1,069	182	808	950	1,069	5,150	5,200	396	1,760	2,070	2,329	396	1,760	2,070	2,329
2,400	2,450	186	825	970	1,091	186	825	970	1,091	5,200	5,250	400	1,777	2,090	2,351	400	1,777	2,090	2,351
2,450	2,500	189	842	990	1,114	189	842	990	1,114	5,250	5,300	404	1,794	2,110	2,374	404	1,794	2,110	2,374
2,500	2,550	193	859	1,010	1,136	193	859	1,010	1,136	5,300	5,350	407	1,811	2,130	2,396	407	1,811	2,130	2,396
2,550	2,600	197	876	1,030	1,159	197	876	1,030	1,159	5,350	5,400	411	1,828	2,150	2,419	411	1,828	2,150	2,419
2,600	2,650	201	893	1,050	1,181	201	893	1,050	1,181	5,400	5,450	415	1,845	2,170	2,441	415	1,845	2,170	2,441
2,650	2,700	205	910	1,070	1,204	205	910	1,070	1,204	5,450	5,500	419	1,862	2,190	2,464	419	1,862	2,190	2,464
2,700	2,750	208	927	1,090	1,226	208	927	1,090	1,226	5,500	5,550	423	1,879	2,210	2,486	423	1,879	2,210	2,486
2,750	2,800	212	944	1,110	1,249	212	944	1,110	1,249	5,550	5,600	426	1,896	2,230	2,509	426	1,896	2,230	2,509

(Continued)

Draft As of September 26, 2018.

Earned Income Credit (EIC) Table - *Continued*   (**Caution.** This is **not** a tax table.)

If the amount you are looking up from the worksheet is—		Single, head of household, or qualifying widow(er) and the number of children you have is—				Married filing jointly and the number of children you have is—			
At least	But less than	0	1	2	3	0	1	2	3
		Your credit is—				Your credit is—			
5,600	5,650	430	1,913	2,250	2,531	430	1,913	2,250	2,531
5,650	5,700	434	1,930	2,270	2,554	434	1,930	2,270	2,554
5,700	5,750	438	1,947	2,290	2,576	438	1,947	2,290	2,576
5,750	5,800	442	1,964	2,310	2,599	442	1,964	2,310	2,599
5,800	5,850	446	1,981	2,330	2,621	446	1,981	2,330	2,621
5,850	5,900	449	1,998	2,350	2,644	449	1,998	2,350	2,644
5,900	5,950	453	2,015	2,370	2,666	453	2,015	2,370	2,666
5,950	6,000	457	2,032	2,390	2,689	457	2,032	2,390	2,689
6,000	6,050	461	2,049	2,410	2,711	461	2,049	2,410	2,711
6,050	6,100	465	2,066	2,430	2,734	465	2,066	2,430	2,734
6,100	6,150	469	2,083	2,450	2,756	469	2,083	2,450	2,756
6,150	6,200	472	2,100	2,470	2,779	472	2,100	2,470	2,779
6,200	6,250	476	2,117	2,490	2,801	476	2,117	2,490	2,801
6,250	6,300	480	2,134	2,510	2,824	480	2,134	2,510	2,824
6,300	6,350	484	2,151	2,530	2,846	484	2,151	2,530	2,846
6,350	6,400	488	2,168	2,550	2,869	488	2,168	2,550	2,869
6,400	6,450	492	2,185	2,570	2,891	492	2,185	2,570	2,891
6,450	6,500	495	2,202	2,590	2,914	495	2,202	2,590	2,914
6,500	6,550	499	2,219	2,610	2,936	499	2,219	2,610	2,936
6,550	6,600	503	2,236	2,630	2,959	503	2,236	2,630	2,959
6,600	6,650	507	2,253	2,650	2,981	507	2,253	2,650	2,981
6,650	6,700	511	2,270	2,670	3,004	511	2,270	2,670	3,004
6,700	6,750	514	2,287	2,690	3,026	514	2,287	2,690	3,026
6,750	6,800	519	2,304	2,710	3,049	519	2,304	2,710	3,049
6,800	6,850	519	2,321	2,730	3,071	519	2,321	2,730	3,071
6,850	6,900	519	2,338	2,750	3,094	519	2,338	2,750	3,094
6,900	6,950	519	2,355	2,770	3,116	519	2,355	2,770	3,116
6,950	7,000	519	2,372	2,790	3,139	519	2,372	2,790	3,139
7,000	7,050	519	2,389	2,810	3,161	519	2,389	2,810	3,161
7,050	7,100	519	2,406	2,830	3,184	519	2,406	2,830	3,184
7,100	7,150	519	2,423	2,850	3,206	519	2,423	2,850	3,206
7,150	7,200	519	2,440	2,870	3,229	519	2,440	2,870	3,229
7,200	7,250	519	2,457	2,890	3,251	519	2,457	2,890	3,251
7,250	7,300	519	2,474	2,910	3,274	519	2,474	2,910	3,274
7,300	7,350	519	2,491	2,930	3,296	519	2,491	2,930	3,296
7,350	7,400	519	2,508	2,950	3,319	519	2,508	2,950	3,319
7,400	7,450	519	2,525	2,970	3,341	519	2,525	2,970	3,341
7,450	7,500	519	2,542	2,990	3,364	519	2,542	2,990	3,364
7,500	7,550	519	2,559	3,010	3,386	519	2,559	3,010	3,386
7,550	7,600	519	2,576	3,030	3,409	519	2,576	3,030	3,409
7,600	7,650	519	2,593	3,050	3,431	519	2,593	3,050	3,431
7,650	7,700	519	2,610	3,070	3,454	519	2,610	3,070	3,454
7,700	7,750	519	2,627	3,090	3,476	519	2,627	3,090	3,476
7,750	7,800	519	2,644	3,110	3,499	519	2,644	3,110	3,499
7,800	7,850	519	2,661	3,130	3,521	519	2,661	3,130	3,521
7,850	7,900	519	2,678	3,150	3,544	519	2,678	3,150	3,544
7,900	7,950	519	2,695	3,170	3,566	519	2,695	3,170	3,566
7,950	8,000	519	2,712	3,190	3,589	519	2,712	3,190	3,589
8,000	8,050	519	2,729	3,210	3,611	519	2,729	3,210	3,611
8,050	8,100	519	2,746	3,230	3,634	519	2,746	3,230	3,634
8,100	8,150	519	2,763	3,250	3,656	519	2,763	3,250	3,656
8,150	8,200	519	2,780	3,270	3,679	519	2,780	3,270	3,679
8,200	8,250	519	2,797	3,290	3,701	519	2,797	3,290	3,701
8,250	8,300	519	2,814	3,310	3,724	519	2,814	3,310	3,724
8,300	8,350	519	2,831	3,330	3,746	519	2,831	3,330	3,746
8,350	8,400	519	2,848	3,350	3,769	519	2,848	3,350	3,769
8,400	8,450	519	2,865	3,370	3,791	519	2,865	3,370	3,791
8,450	8,500	519	2,882	3,390	3,814	519	2,882	3,390	3,814
8,500	8,550	516	2,899	3,410	3,836	519	2,899	3,410	3,836
8,550	8,600	512	2,916	3,430	3,859	519	2,916	3,430	3,859
8,600	8,650	508	2,933	3,450	3,881	519	2,933	3,450	3,881
8,650	8,700	505	2,950	3,470	3,904	519	2,950	3,470	3,904
8,700	8,750	501	2,967	3,490	3,926	519	2,967	3,490	3,926
8,750	8,800	497	2,984	3,510	3,949	519	2,984	3,510	3,949

If the amount you are looking up from the worksheet is—		Single, head of household, or qualifying widow(er) and the number of children you have is—				Married filing jointly and the number of children you have is—			
At least	But less than	0	1	2	3	0	1	2	3
		Your credit is—				Your credit is—			
8,800	8,850	493	3,001	3,530	3,971	519	3,001	3,530	3,971
8,850	8,900	489	3,018	3,550	3,994	519	3,018	3,550	3,994
8,900	8,950	485	3,035	3,570	4,016	519	3,035	3,570	4,016
8,950	9,000	482	3,052	3,590	4,039	519	3,052	3,590	4,039
9,000	9,050	478	3,069	3,610	4,061	519	3,069	3,610	4,061
9,050	9,100	474	3,086	3,630	4,084	519	3,086	3,630	4,084
9,100	9,150	470	3,103	3,650	4,106	519	3,103	3,650	4,106
9,150	9,200	466	3,120	3,670	4,129	519	3,120	3,670	4,129
9,200	9,250	462	3,137	3,690	4,151	519	3,137	3,690	4,151
9,250	9,300	459	3,154	3,710	4,174	519	3,154	3,710	4,174
9,300	9,350	455	3,171	3,730	4,196	519	3,171	3,730	4,196
9,350	9,400	451	3,188	3,750	4,219	519	3,188	3,750	4,219
9,400	9,450	447	3,205	3,770	4,241	519	3,205	3,770	4,241
9,450	9,500	443	3,222	3,790	4,264	519	3,222	3,790	4,264
9,500	9,550	439	3,239	3,810	4,286	519	3,239	3,810	4,286
9,550	9,600	436	3,256	3,830	4,309	519	3,256	3,830	4,309
9,600	9,650	432	3,273	3,850	4,331	519	3,273	3,850	4,331
9,650	9,700	428	3,290	3,870	4,354	519	3,290	3,870	4,354
9,700	9,750	424	3,307	3,890	4,376	519	3,307	3,890	4,376
9,750	9,800	420	3,324	3,910	4,399	519	3,324	3,910	4,399
9,800	9,850	417	3,341	3,930	4,421	519	3,341	3,930	4,421
9,850	9,900	413	3,358	3,950	4,444	519	3,358	3,950	4,444
9,900	9,950	409	3,375	3,970	4,466	519	3,375	3,970	4,466
9,950	10,000	405	3,392	3,990	4,489	519	3,392	3,990	4,489
10,000	10,050	401	3,409	4,010	4,511	519	3,409	4,010	4,511
10,050	10,100	397	3,426	4,030	4,534	519	3,426	4,030	4,534
10,100	10,150	394	3,443	4,050	4,556	519	3,443	4,050	4,556
10,150	10,200	390	3,461	4,070	4,579	519	3,461	4,070	4,579
10,200	10,250	386	3,461	4,090	4,601	519	3,461	4,090	4,601
10,250	10,300	382	3,461	4,110	4,624	519	3,461	4,110	4,624
10,300	10,350	378	3,461	4,130	4,646	519	3,461	4,130	4,646
10,350	10,400	374	3,461	4,150	4,669	519	3,461	4,150	4,669
10,400	10,450	371	3,461	4,170	4,691	519	3,461	4,170	4,691
10,450	10,500	367	3,461	4,190	4,714	519	3,461	4,190	4,714
10,500	10,550	363	3,461	4,210	4,736	519	3,461	4,210	4,736
10,550	10,600	359	3,461	4,230	4,759	519	3,461	4,230	4,759
10,600	10,650	355	3,461	4,250	4,781	519	3,461	4,250	4,781
10,650	10,700	352	3,461	4,270	4,804	519	3,461	4,270	4,804
10,700	10,750	348	3,461	4,290	4,826	519	3,461	4,290	4,826
10,750	10,800	344	3,461	4,310	4,849	519	3,461	4,310	4,849
10,800	10,850	340	3,461	4,330	4,871	519	3,461	4,330	4,871
10,850	10,900	336	3,461	4,350	4,894	519	3,461	4,350	4,894
10,900	10,950	332	3,461	4,370	4,916	519	3,461	4,370	4,916
10,950	11,000	329	3,461	4,390	4,939	519	3,461	4,390	4,939
11,000	11,050	325	3,461	4,410	4,961	519	3,461	4,410	4,961
11,050	11,100	321	3,461	4,430	4,984	519	3,461	4,430	4,984
11,100	11,150	317	3,461	4,450	5,006	519	3,461	4,450	5,006
11,150	11,200	313	3,461	4,470	5,029	519	3,461	4,470	5,029
11,200	11,250	309	3,461	4,490	5,051	519	3,461	4,490	5,051
11,250	11,300	306	3,461	4,510	5,074	519	3,461	4,510	5,074
11,300	11,350	302	3,461	4,530	5,096	519	3,461	4,530	5,096
11,350	11,400	298	3,461	4,550	5,119	519	3,461	4,550	5,119
11,400	11,450	294	3,461	4,570	5,141	519	3,461	4,570	5,141
11,450	11,500	290	3,461	4,590	5,164	519	3,461	4,590	5,164
11,500	11,550	286	3,461	4,610	5,186	519	3,461	4,610	5,186
11,550	11,600	283	3,461	4,630	5,209	519	3,461	4,630	5,209
11,600	11,650	279	3,461	4,650	5,231	519	3,461	4,650	5,231
11,650	11,700	275	3,461	4,670	5,254	519	3,461	4,670	5,254
11,700	11,750	271	3,461	4,690	5,276	519	3,461	4,690	5,276
11,750	11,800	267	3,461	4,710	5,299	519	3,461	4,710	5,299
11,800	11,850	264	3,461	4,730	5,321	519	3,461	4,730	5,321
11,850	11,900	260	3,461	4,750	5,344	519	3,461	4,750	5,344
11,900	11,950	256	3,461	4,770	5,366	519	3,461	4,770	5,366
11,950	12,000	252	3,461	4,790	5,389	519	3,461	4,790	5,389

(Continued)

Draft As of September 26, 2018.

Earned Income Credit (EIC) Table - *Continued* (**Caution.** This is **not** a tax table.)

If the amount you are looking up from the worksheet is—		Single, head of household, or qualifying widow(er) and the number of children you have is—				Married filing jointly and the number of children you have is—			
At least	But less than	0	1	2	3	0	1	2	3
12,000	12,050	248	3,461	4,810	5,411	519	3,461	4,810	5,411
12,050	12,100	244	3,461	4,830	5,434	519	3,461	4,830	5,434
12,100	12,150	241	3,461	4,850	5,456	519	3,461	4,850	5,456
12,150	12,200	237	3,461	4,870	5,479	519	3,461	4,870	5,479
12,200	12,250	233	3,461	4,890	5,501	519	3,461	4,890	5,501
12,250	12,300	229	3,461	4,910	5,524	519	3,461	4,910	5,524
12,300	12,350	225	3,461	4,930	5,546	519	3,461	4,930	5,546
12,350	12,400	221	3,461	4,950	5,569	519	3,461	4,950	5,569
12,400	12,450	218	3,461	4,970	5,591	519	3,461	4,970	5,591
12,450	12,500	214	3,461	4,990	5,614	519	3,461	4,990	5,614
12,500	12,550	210	3,461	5,010	5,636	519	3,461	5,010	5,636
12,550	12,600	206	3,461	5,030	5,659	519	3,461	5,030	5,659
12,600	12,650	202	3,461	5,050	5,681	519	3,461	5,050	5,681
12,650	12,700	199	3,461	5,070	5,704	519	3,461	5,070	5,704
12,700	12,750	195	3,461	5,090	5,726	519	3,461	5,090	5,726
12,750	12,800	191	3,461	5,110	5,749	519	3,461	5,110	5,749
12,800	12,850	187	3,461	5,130	5,771	519	3,461	5,130	5,771
12,850	12,900	183	3,461	5,150	5,794	519	3,461	5,150	5,794
12,900	12,950	179	3,461	5,170	5,816	519	3,461	5,170	5,816
12,950	13,000	176	3,461	5,190	5,839	519	3,461	5,190	5,839
13,000	13,050	172	3,461	5,210	5,861	519	3,461	5,210	5,861
13,050	13,100	168	3,461	5,230	5,884	519	3,461	5,230	5,884
13,100	13,150	164	3,461	5,250	5,906	519	3,461	5,250	5,906
13,150	13,200	160	3,461	5,270	5,929	519	3,461	5,270	5,929
13,200	13,250	156	3,461	5,290	5,951	519	3,461	5,290	5,951
13,250	13,300	153	3,461	5,310	5,974	519	3,461	5,310	5,974
13,300	13,350	149	3,461	5,330	5,996	519	3,461	5,330	5,996
13,350	13,400	146	3,461	5,350	6,019	519	3,461	5,350	6,019
13,400	13,450	141	3,461	5,370	6,041	519	3,461	5,370	6,041
13,450	13,500	137	3,461	5,390	6,064	519	3,461	5,390	6,064
13,500	13,550	133	3,461	5,410	6,086	519	3,461	5,410	6,086
13,550	13,600	130	3,461	5,430	6,109	519	3,461	5,430	6,109
13,600	13,650	126	3,461	5,450	6,131	519	3,461	5,450	6,131
13,650	13,700	122	3,461	5,470	6,154	519	3,461	5,470	6,154
13,700	13,750	118	3,461	5,490	6,176	519	3,461	5,490	6,176
13,750	13,800	114	3,461	5,510	6,199	519	3,461	5,510	6,199
13,800	13,850	111	3,461	5,530	6,221	519	3,461	5,530	6,221
13,850	13,900	107	3,461	5,550	6,244	519	3,461	5,550	6,244
13,900	13,950	103	3,461	5,570	6,266	519	3,461	5,570	6,266
13,950	14,000	99	3,461	5,590	6,289	519	3,461	5,590	6,289
14,000	14,050	95	3,461	5,610	6,311	519	3,461	5,610	6,311
14,050	14,100	91	3,461	5,630	6,334	519	3,461	5,630	6,334
14,100	14,150	88	3,461	5,650	6,356	519	3,461	5,650	6,356
14,150	14,200	84	3,461	5,670	6,379	519	3,461	5,670	6,379
14,200	14,250	80	3,461	5,690	6,401	514	3,461	5,690	6,401
14,250	14,300	76	3,461	5,716	6,431	511	3,461	5,716	6,431
14,300	14,350	72	3,461	5,716	6,431	507	3,461	5,716	6,431
14,350	14,400	68	3,461	5,716	6,431	503	3,461	5,716	6,431
14,400	14,450	65	3,461	5,716	6,431	499	3,461	5,716	6,431
14,450	14,500	61	3,461	5,716	6,431	495	3,461	5,716	6,431
14,500	14,550	57	3,461	5,716	6,431	492	3,461	5,716	6,431
14,550	14,600	53	3,461	5,716	6,431	488	3,461	5,716	6,431
14,600	14,650	49	3,461	5,716	6,431	484	3,461	5,716	6,431
14,650	14,700	46	3,461	5,716	6,431	480	3,461	5,716	6,431
14,700	14,750	42	3,461	5,716	6,431	476	3,461	5,716	6,431
14,750	14,800	38	3,461	5,716	6,431	472	3,461	5,716	6,431
14,800	14,850	34	3,461	5,716	6,431	469	3,461	5,716	6,431
14,850	14,900	30	3,461	5,716	6,431	465	3,461	5,716	6,431
14,900	14,950	26	3,461	5,716	6,431	461	3,461	5,716	6,431
14,950	15,000	23	3,461	5,716	6,431	457	3,461	5,716	6,431
15,000	15,050	19	3,461	5,716	6,431	453	3,461	5,716	6,431
15,050	15,100	15	3,461	5,716	6,431	449	3,461	5,716	6,431
15,100	15,150	11	3,461	5,716	6,431	446	3,461	5,716	6,431
15,150	15,200	7	3,461	5,716	6,431	442	3,461	5,716	6,431
15,200	15,250	3	3,461	5,716	6,431	438	3,461	5,716	6,431
15,250	15,300	*	3,461	5,716	6,431	434	3,461	5,716	6,431
15,300	15,350	0	3,461	5,716	6,431	430	3,461	5,716	6,431
15,350	15,400	0	3,461	5,716	6,431	426	3,461	5,716	6,431
15,400	15,450	0	3,461	5,716	6,431	423	3,461	5,716	6,431
15,450	15,500	0	3,461	5,716	6,431	419	3,461	5,716	6,431
15,500	15,550	0	3,461	5,716	6,431	415	3,461	5,716	6,431
15,550	15,600	0	3,461	5,716	6,431	411	3,461	5,716	6,431
15,600	15,650	0	3,461	5,716	6,431	407	3,461	5,716	6,431
15,650	15,700	0	3,461	5,716	6,431	404	3,461	5,716	6,431
15,700	15,750	0	3,461	5,716	6,431	400	3,461	5,716	6,431
15,750	15,800	0	3,461	5,716	6,431	396	3,461	5,716	6,431
15,800	15,850	0	3,461	5,716	6,431	392	3,461	5,716	6,431
15,850	15,900	0	3,461	5,716	6,431	388	3,461	5,716	6,431
15,900	15,950	0	3,461	5,716	6,431	384	3,461	5,716	6,431
15,950	16,000	0	3,461	5,716	6,431	381	3,461	5,716	6,431
16,000	16,050	0	3,461	5,716	6,431	377	3,461	5,716	6,431
16,050	16,100	0	3,461	5,716	6,431	373	3,461	5,716	6,431
16,100	16,150	0	3,461	5,716	6,431	369	3,461	5,716	6,431
16,150	16,200	0	3,461	5,716	6,431	365	3,461	5,716	6,431
16,200	16,250	0	3,461	5,716	6,431	361	3,461	5,716	6,431
16,250	16,300	0	3,461	5,716	6,431	358	3,461	5,716	6,431
16,300	16,350	0	3,461	5,716	6,431	354	3,461	5,716	6,431
16,350	16,400	0	3,461	5,716	6,431	350	3,461	5,716	6,431
16,400	16,450	0	3,461	5,716	6,431	346	3,461	5,716	6,431
16,450	16,500	0	3,461	5,716	6,431	342	3,461	5,716	6,431
16,500	16,550	0	3,461	5,716	6,431	339	3,461	5,716	6,431
16,550	16,600	0	3,461	5,716	6,431	335	3,461	5,716	6,431
16,600	16,650	0	3,461	5,716	6,431	331	3,461	5,716	6,431
16,650	16,700	0	3,461	5,716	6,431	327	3,461	5,716	6,431
16,700	16,750	0	3,461	5,716	6,431	323	3,461	5,716	6,431
16,750	16,800	0	3,461	5,716	6,431	319	3,461	5,716	6,431
16,800	16,850	0	3,461	5,716	6,431	316	3,461	5,716	6,431
16,850	16,900	0	3,461	5,716	6,431	312	3,461	5,716	6,431
16,900	16,950	0	3,461	5,716	6,431	308	3,461	5,716	6,431
16,950	17,000	0	3,461	5,716	6,431	304	3,461	5,716	6,431
17,000	17,050	0	3,461	5,716	6,431	300	3,461	5,716	6,431
17,050	17,100	0	3,461	5,716	6,431	296	3,461	5,716	6,431
17,100	17,150	0	3,461	5,716	6,431	293	3,461	5,716	6,431
17,150	17,200	0	3,461	5,716	6,431	289	3,461	5,716	6,431
17,200	17,250	0	3,461	5,716	6,431	285	3,461	5,716	6,431
17,250	17,300	0	3,461	5,716	6,431	281	3,461	5,716	6,431
17,300	17,350	0	3,461	5,716	6,431	277	3,461	5,716	6,431
17,350	17,400	0	3,461	5,716	6,431	273	3,461	5,716	6,431
17,400	17,450	0	3,461	5,716	6,431	270	3,461	5,716	6,431
17,450	17,500	0	3,461	5,716	6,431	266	3,461	5,716	6,431
17,500	17,550	0	3,461	5,716	6,431	262	3,461	5,716	6,431
17,550	17,600	0	3,461	5,716	6,431	258	3,461	5,716	6,431
17,600	17,650	0	3,461	5,716	6,431	254	3,461	5,716	6,431
17,650	17,700	0	3,461	5,716	6,431	251	3,461	5,716	6,431
17,700	17,750	0	3,461	5,716	6,431	247	3,461	5,716	6,431
17,750	17,800	0	3,461	5,716	6,431	243	3,461	5,716	6,431
17,800	17,850	0	3,461	5,716	6,431	239	3,461	5,716	6,431
17,850	17,900	0	3,461	5,716	6,431	235	3,461	5,716	6,431
17,900	17,950	0	3,461	5,716	6,431	231	3,461	5,716	6,431
17,950	18,000	0	3,461	5,716	6,431	228	3,461	5,716	6,431
18,000	18,050	0	3,461	5,716	6,431	224	3,461	5,716	6,431
18,050	18,100	0	3,461	5,716	6,431	220	3,461	5,716	6,431
18,100	18,150	0	3,461	5,716	6,431	216	3,461	5,716	6,431
18,150	18,200	0	3,461	5,716	6,431	212	3,461	5,716	6,431
18,200	18,250	0	3,461	5,716	6,431	208	3,461	5,716	6,431
18,250	18,300	0	3,461	5,716	6,431	205	3,461	5,716	6,431
18,300	18,350	0	3,461	5,716	6,431	201	3,461	5,716	6,431
18,350	18,400	0	3,461	5,716	6,431	197	3,461	5,716	6,431

* If the amount you are looking up from the worksheet is at least $15,250 but less than $15,270, and you have no qualifying children, your credit is $1. If the amount you are looking up from the worksheet is $15,270 or more, and you have no qualifying children, you can't take the credit.

(Continued)

Draft As of September 26, 2018.

Earned Income Credit (EIC) Table - *Continued*   (**Caution.** This is **not** a tax table.)

If the amount you are looking up from the worksheet is— At least	But less than	Single, head of household, or qualifying widow(er) and the number of children you have is— 0	1	2	3	Married filing jointly and the number of children you have is— 0	1	2	3
18,400	18,450	0	3,461	5,716	6,431	193	3,461	5,716	6,431
18,450	18,500	0	3,461	5,716	6,431	189	3,461	5,716	6,431
18,500	18,550	0	3,461	5,716	6,431	186	3,461	5,716	6,431
18,550	18,600	0	3,461	5,716	6,431	182	3,461	5,716	6,431
18,600	18,650	0	3,461	5,716	6,431	178	3,461	5,716	6,431
18,650	18,700	0	3,461	5,716	6,431	174	3,461	5,716	6,431
18,700	18,750	0	3,451	5,702	6,417	170	3,461	5,716	6,431
18,750	18,800	0	3,443	5,692	6,406	166	3,461	5,716	6,431
18,800	18,850	0	3,435	5,681	6,396	163	3,461	5,716	6,431
18,850	18,900	0	3,427	5,671	6,385	159	3,461	5,716	6,431
18,900	18,950	0	3,419	5,660	6,375	155	3,461	5,716	6,431
18,950	19,000	0	3,411	5,650	6,364	151	3,461	5,716	6,431
19,000	19,050	0	3,403	5,639	6,354	147	3,461	5,716	6,431
19,050	19,100	0	3,395	5,629	6,343	143	3,461	5,716	6,431
19,100	19,150	0	3,387	5,618	6,333	140	3,461	5,716	6,431
19,150	19,200	0	3,379	5,608	6,322	136	3,461	5,716	6,431
19,200	19,250	0	3,371	5,597	6,312	132	3,461	5,716	6,431
19,250	19,300	0	3,363	5,586	6,301	128	3,461	5,716	6,431
19,300	19,350	0	3,355	5,576	6,290	124	3,461	5,716	6,431
19,350	19,400	0	3,347	5,565	6,280	120	3,461	5,716	6,431
19,400	19,450	0	3,339	5,555	6,269	117	3,461	5,716	6,431
19,450	19,500	0	3,331	5,544	6,259	113	3,461	5,716	6,431
19,500	19,550	0	3,323	5,534	6,248	109	3,461	5,716	6,431
19,550	19,600	0	3,315	5,523	6,238	105	3,461	5,716	6,431
19,600	19,650	0	3,307	5,513	6,227	101	3,461	5,716	6,431
19,650	19,700	0	3,299	5,502	6,217	98	3,461	5,716	6,431
19,700	19,750	0	3,291	5,492	6,206	94	3,461	5,716	6,431
19,750	19,800	0	3,283	5,481	6,196	90	3,461	5,716	6,431
19,800	19,850	0	3,275	5,471	6,185	86	3,461	5,716	6,431
19,850	19,900	0	3,267	5,460	6,175	82	3,461	5,716	6,431
19,900	19,950	0	3,259	5,450	6,164	78	3,461	5,716	6,431
19,950	20,000	0	3,251	5,439	6,154	75	3,461	5,716	6,431
20,000	20,050	0	3,243	5,429	6,143	71	3,461	5,716	6,431
20,050	20,100	0	3,235	5,418	6,133	67	3,461	5,716	6,431
20,100	20,150	0	3,227	5,407	6,122	63	3,461	5,716	6,431
20,150	20,200	0	3,219	5,397	6,111	59	3,461	5,716	6,431
20,200	20,250	0	3,211	5,386	6,101	55	3,461	5,716	6,431
20,250	20,300	0	3,203	5,376	6,090	52	3,461	5,716	6,431
20,300	20,350	0	3,195	5,365	6,080	48	3,461	5,716	6,431
20,350	20,400	0	3,187	5,355	6,069	44	3,461	5,716	6,431
20,400	20,450	0	3,179	5,344	6,059	40	3,461	5,716	6,431
20,450	20,500	0	3,171	5,334	6,048	36	3,461	5,716	6,431
20,500	20,550	0	3,163	5,323	6,038	33	3,461	5,716	6,431
20,550	20,600	0	3,155	5,313	6,027	29	3,461	5,716	6,431
20,600	20,650	0	3,147	5,302	6,017	25	3,461	5,716	6,431
20,650	20,700	0	3,139	5,292	6,006	21	3,461	5,716	6,431
20,700	20,750	0	3,131	5,281	5,996	17	3,461	5,716	6,431
20,750	20,800	0	3,123	5,271	5,985	13	3,461	5,716	6,431
20,800	20,850	0	3,115	5,260	5,975	10	3,461	5,716	6,431
20,850	20,900	0	3,107	5,250	5,964	6	3,461	5,716	6,431
20,900	20,950	0	3,099	5,239	5,953	*	3,461	5,716	6,431
20,950	21,000	0	3,091	5,228	5,943	0	3,461	5,716	6,431
21,000	21,050	0	3,083	5,218	5,932	0	3,461	5,716	6,431
21,050	21,100	0	3,075	5,207	5,922	0	3,461	5,716	6,431
21,100	21,150	0	3,067	5,197	5,911	0	3,461	5,716	6,431
21,150	21,200	0	3,059	5,186	5,901	0	3,461	5,716	6,431
21,200	21,250	0	3,051	5,176	5,890	0	3,461	5,716	6,431
21,250	21,300	0	3,043	5,165	5,880	0	3,461	5,716	6,431
21,300	21,350	0	3,035	5,155	5,869	0	3,461	5,716	6,431
21,350	21,400	0	3,027	5,144	5,859	0	3,461	5,716	6,431
21,400	21,450	0	3,019	5,134	5,848	0	3,461	5,716	6,431
21,450	21,500	0	3,011	5,123	5,838	0	3,461	5,716	6,431
21,500	21,550	0	3,003	5,113	5,827	0	3,461	5,716	6,431
21,550	21,600	0	2,995	5,102	5,817	0	3,461	5,716	6,431

If the amount you are looking up from the worksheet is— At least	But less than	Single, head of household, or qualifying widow(er) and the number of children you have is— 0	1	2	3	Married filing jointly and the number of children you have is— 0	1	2	3
21,600	21,650	0	2,987	5,092	5,806	0	3,461	5,716	6,431
21,650	21,700	0	2,979	5,081	5,795	0	3,461	5,716	6,431
21,700	21,750	0	2,971	5,071	5,785	0	3,461	5,716	6,431
21,750	21,800	0	2,963	5,060	5,774	0	3,461	5,716	6,431
21,800	21,850	0	2,955	5,049	5,764	0	3,461	5,716	6,431
21,850	21,900	0	2,947	5,039	5,753	0	3,461	5,716	6,431
21,900	21,950	0	2,939	5,028	5,743	0	3,461	5,716	6,431
21,950	22,000	0	2,931	5,018	5,732	0	3,461	5,716	6,431
22,000	22,050	0	2,923	5,007	5,722	0	3,461	5,716	6,431
22,050	22,100	0	2,915	4,997	5,711	0	3,461	5,716	6,431
22,100	22,150	0	2,907	4,986	5,701	0	3,461	5,716	6,431
22,150	22,200	0	2,900	4,976	5,690	0	3,461	5,716	6,431
22,200	22,250	0	2,892	4,965	5,680	0	3,461	5,716	6,431
22,250	22,300	0	2,884	4,955	5,669	0	3,461	5,716	6,431
22,300	22,350	0	2,876	4,944	5,659	0	3,461	5,716	6,431
22,350	22,400	0	2,868	4,934	5,648	0	3,461	5,716	6,431
22,400	22,450	0	2,860	4,923	5,638	0	3,461	5,716	6,431
22,450	22,500	0	2,852	4,913	5,627	0	3,461	5,716	6,431
22,500	22,550	0	2,844	4,902	5,617	0	3,461	5,716	6,431
22,550	22,600	0	2,836	4,892	5,606	0	3,461	5,716	6,431
22,600	22,650	0	2,828	4,881	5,595	0	3,461	5,716	6,431
22,650	22,700	0	2,820	4,870	5,585	0	3,461	5,716	6,431
22,700	22,750	0	2,812	4,860	5,574	0	3,461	5,716	6,431
22,750	22,800	0	2,804	4,849	5,564	0	3,461	5,716	6,431
22,800	22,850	0	2,796	4,839	5,553	0	3,461	5,716	6,431
22,850	22,900	0	2,788	4,828	5,543	0	3,461	5,716	6,431
22,900	22,950	0	2,780	4,818	5,532	0	3,461	5,716	6,431
22,950	23,000	0	2,772	4,807	5,522	0	3,461	5,716	6,431
23,000	23,050	0	2,764	4,797	5,511	0	3,461	5,716	6,431
23,050	23,100	0	2,756	4,786	5,501	0	3,461	5,716	6,431
23,100	23,150	0	2,748	4,776	5,490	0	3,461	5,716	6,431
23,150	23,200	0	2,740	4,765	5,480	0	3,461	5,716	6,431
23,200	23,250	0	2,732	4,755	5,469	0	3,461	5,716	6,431
23,250	23,300	0	2,724	4,744	5,459	0	3,461	5,716	6,431
23,300	23,350	0	2,716	4,734	5,448	0	3,461	5,716	6,431
23,350	23,400	0	2,708	4,723	5,438	0	3,461	5,716	6,431
23,400	23,450	0	2,700	4,712	5,427	0	3,461	5,716	6,431
23,450	23,500	0	2,692	4,702	5,416	0	3,461	5,716	6,431
23,500	23,550	0	2,684	4,691	5,406	0	3,461	5,716	6,431
23,550	23,600	0	2,676	4,681	5,395	0	3,461	5,716	6,431
23,600	23,650	0	2,668	4,670	5,385	0	3,461	5,716	6,431
23,650	23,700	0	2,660	4,660	5,374	0	3,461	5,716	6,431
23,700	23,750	0	2,652	4,649	5,364	0	3,461	5,716	6,431
23,750	23,800	0	2,644	4,639	5,353	0	3,461	5,716	6,431
23,800	23,850	0	2,636	4,628	5,343	0	3,461	5,716	6,431
23,850	23,900	0	2,628	4,618	5,332	0	3,461	5,716	6,431
23,900	23,950	0	2,620	4,607	5,322	0	3,461	5,716	6,431
23,950	24,000	0	2,612	4,597	5,311	0	3,461	5,716	6,431
24,000	24,050	0	2,604	4,586	5,301	0	3,461	5,716	6,431
24,050	24,100	0	2,598	4,576	5,290	0	3,461	5,716	6,431
24,100	24,150	0	2,588	4,565	5,280	0	3,461	5,716	6,431
24,150	24,200	0	2,580	4,555	5,269	0	3,461	5,716	6,431
24,200	24,250	0	2,572	4,544	5,259	0	3,461	5,716	6,431
24,250	24,300	0	2,564	4,533	5,248	0	3,461	5,716	6,431
24,300	24,350	0	2,556	4,523	5,237	0	3,461	5,716	6,431
24,350	24,400	0	2,548	4,512	5,227	0	3,457†	5,711†	6,425†
24,400	24,450	0	2,540	4,502	5,216	0	3,449	5,700	6,415
24,450	24,500	0	2,532	4,491	5,206	0	3,441	5,690	6,404
24,500	24,550	0	2,524	4,481	5,195	0	3,433	5,679	6,394
24,550	24,600	0	2,516	4,470	5,185	0	3,425	5,669	6,383
24,600	24,650	0	2,508	4,460	5,174	0	3,417	5,658	6,373
24,650	24,700	0	2,500	4,449	5,164	0	3,409	5,648	6,362
24,700	24,750	0	2,492	4,439	5,153	0	3,401	5,637	6,352
24,750	24,800	0	2,484	4,428	5,143	0	3,393	5,626	6,341

* If the amount you are looking up from the worksheet is at least $20,900 but less than $20,950, and you have no qualifying children, your credit is $2.
If the amount you are looking up from the worksheet is $20,950 or more, and you have no qualifying children, you can't take the credit.

† If the amount you are looking up from the worksheet is exactly $24,350, and you have one qualifying child, your credit is $3,461, $5,716 if you have two qualifying children, and $6,431 if you have three qualifying children.

(Continued)

Draft As of September 26, 2018.

Earned Income Credit (EIC) Table - *Continued*   **(Caution.** This is **not** a tax table.)

If the amount you are looking up from the worksheet is–		Single, head of household, or qualifying widow(er) and the number of children you have is–				Married filing jointly and the number of children you have is–			
At least	But less than	0	1	2	3	0	1	2	3
		Your credit is–				Your credit is–			
24,800	24,850	0	2,476	4,418	5,132	0	3,385	5,616	6,330
24,850	24,900	0	2,468	4,407	5,122	0	3,377	5,605	6,320
24,900	24,950	0	2,460	4,397	5,111	0	3,369	5,595	6,309
24,950	25,000	0	2,452	4,386	5,101	0	3,361	5,584	6,299
25,000	25,050	0	2,444	4,376	5,090	0	3,353	5,574	6,288
25,050	25,100	0	2,436	4,365	5,080	0	3,345	5,563	6,278
25,100	25,150	0	2,428	4,354	5,069	0	3,337	5,553	6,267
25,150	25,200	0	2,420	4,344	5,058	0	3,329	5,542	6,257
25,200	25,250	0	2,412	4,333	5,048	0	3,321	5,532	6,246
25,250	25,300	0	2,404	4,323	5,037	0	3,313	5,521	6,236
25,300	25,350	0	2,396	4,312	5,027	0	3,305	5,511	6,225
25,350	25,400	0	2,388	4,302	5,016	0	3,297	5,500	6,215
25,400	25,450	0	2,380	4,291	5,006	0	3,289	5,490	6,204
25,450	25,500	0	2,372	4,281	4,995	0	3,281	5,479	6,194
25,500	25,550	0	2,364	4,270	4,985	0	3,273	5,469	6,183
25,550	25,600	0	2,356	4,260	4,974	0	3,265	5,458	6,173
25,600	25,650	0	2,348	4,249	4,964	0	3,257	5,447	6,162
25,650	25,700	0	2,340	4,239	4,953	0	3,249	5,437	6,151
25,700	25,750	0	2,332	4,228	4,943	0	3,241	5,426	6,141
25,750	25,800	0	2,324	4,218	4,932	0	3,233	5,416	6,130
25,800	25,850	0	2,316	4,207	4,921	0	3,225	5,405	6,120
25,850	25,900	0	2,308	4,197	4,911	0	3,218	5,395	6,109
25,900	25,950	0	2,300	4,186	4,900	0	3,210	5,384	6,099
25,950	26,000	0	2,292	4,175	4,890	0	3,202	5,374	6,088
26,000	26,050	0	2,284	4,165	4,879	0	3,194	5,363	6,078
26,050	26,100	0	2,276	4,154	4,869	0	3,186	5,353	6,067
26,100	26,150	0	2,268	4,144	4,858	0	3,178	5,342	6,057
26,150	26,200	0	2,260	4,133	4,848	0	3,170	5,332	6,046
26,200	26,250	0	2,252	4,123	4,837	0	3,162	5,321	6,036
26,250	26,300	0	2,244	4,112	4,827	0	3,154	5,311	6,025
26,300	26,350	0	2,236	4,102	4,816	0	3,146	5,300	6,015
26,350	26,400	0	2,228	4,091	4,806	0	3,138	5,290	6,004
26,400	26,450	0	2,220	4,081	4,795	0	3,130	5,279	5,994
26,450	26,500	0	2,212	4,070	4,785	0	3,122	5,268	5,983
26,500	26,550	0	2,204	4,060	4,774	0	3,114	5,258	5,972
26,550	26,600	0	2,196	4,049	4,764	0	3,106	5,247	5,962
26,600	26,650	0	2,188	4,039	4,753	0	3,098	5,237	5,951
26,650	26,700	0	2,180	4,028	4,743	0	3,090	5,226	5,941
26,700	26,750	0	2,172	4,018	4,732	0	3,082	5,216	5,930
26,750	26,800	0	2,164	4,007	4,721	0	3,074	5,205	5,920
26,800	26,850	0	2,156	3,996	4,711	0	3,066	5,195	5,909
26,850	26,900	0	2,148	3,986	4,700	0	3,058	5,184	5,899
26,900	26,950	0	2,140	3,975	4,690	0	3,050	5,174	5,888
26,950	27,000	0	2,132	3,965	4,679	0	3,042	5,163	5,878
27,000	27,050	0	2,124	3,954	4,669	0	3,034	5,153	5,867
27,050	27,100	0	2,116	3,944	4,658	0	3,026	5,142	5,857
27,100	27,150	0	2,108	3,933	4,648	0	3,018	5,132	5,846
27,150	27,200	0	2,101	3,923	4,637	0	3,010	5,121	5,836
27,200	27,250	0	2,093	3,912	4,627	0	3,002	5,111	5,825
27,250	27,300	0	2,085	3,902	4,616	0	2,994	5,100	5,814
27,300	27,350	0	2,077	3,891	4,606	0	2,986	5,089	5,804
27,350	27,400	0	2,069	3,881	4,595	0	2,978	5,079	5,793
27,400	27,450	0	2,061	3,870	4,585	0	2,970	5,068	5,783
27,450	27,500	0	2,053	3,860	4,574	0	2,962	5,058	5,772
27,500	27,550	0	2,045	3,849	4,564	0	2,954	5,047	5,762
27,550	27,600	0	2,037	3,839	4,553	0	2,946	5,037	5,751
27,600	27,650	0	2,029	3,828	4,542	0	2,938	5,026	5,741
27,650	27,700	0	2,021	3,817	4,532	0	2,930	5,016	5,730
27,700	27,750	0	2,013	3,807	4,521	0	2,922	5,005	5,720
27,750	27,800	0	2,005	3,796	4,511	0	2,914	4,995	5,709
27,800	27,850	0	1,997	3,786	4,500	0	2,906	4,984	5,699
27,850	27,900	0	1,989	3,775	4,490	0	2,898	4,974	5,688
27,900	27,950	0	1,981	3,765	4,479	0	2,890	4,963	5,678
27,950	28,000	0	1,973	3,754	4,469	0	2,882	4,953	5,667

If the amount you are looking up from the worksheet is–		Single, head of household, or qualifying widow(er) and the number of children you have is–				Married filing jointly and the number of children you have is–			
At least	But less than	0	1	2	3	0	1	2	3
		Your credit is–				Your credit is–			
28,000	28,050	0	1,965	3,744	4,458	0	2,874	4,942	5,657
28,050	28,100	0	1,957	3,733	4,448	0	2,866	4,932	5,646
28,100	28,150	0	1,949	3,723	4,437	0	2,858	4,921	5,635
28,150	28,200	0	1,941	3,712	4,427	0	2,850	4,910	5,625
28,200	28,250	0	1,933	3,702	4,416	0	2,842	4,900	5,614
28,250	28,300	0	1,925	3,691	4,406	0	2,834	4,889	5,604
28,300	28,350	0	1,917	3,681	4,395	0	2,826	4,879	5,593
28,350	28,400	0	1,909	3,670	4,385	0	2,818	4,868	5,583
28,400	28,450	0	1,901	3,659	4,374	0	2,810	4,858	5,572
28,450	28,500	0	1,893	3,649	4,363	0	2,802	4,847	5,562
28,500	28,550	0	1,885	3,638	4,353	0	2,794	4,837	5,551
28,550	28,600	0	1,877	3,628	4,342	0	2,786	4,826	5,541
28,600	28,650	0	1,869	3,617	4,332	0	2,778	4,816	5,530
28,650	28,700	0	1,861	3,607	4,321	0	2,770	4,805	5,520
28,700	28,750	0	1,853	3,596	4,311	0	2,762	4,795	5,509
28,750	28,800	0	1,845	3,586	4,300	0	2,754	4,784	5,499
28,800	28,850	0	1,837	3,575	4,290	0	2,746	4,774	5,488
28,850	28,900	0	1,829	3,565	4,279	0	2,738	4,763	5,478
28,900	28,950	0	1,821	3,554	4,269	0	2,730	4,753	5,467
28,950	29,000	0	1,813	3,544	4,258	0	2,722	4,742	5,456
29,000	29,050	0	1,805	3,533	4,248	0	2,714	4,731	5,446
29,050	29,100	0	1,797	3,523	4,237	0	2,706	4,721	5,435
29,100	29,150	0	1,789	3,512	4,226	0	2,698	4,710	5,425
29,150	29,200	0	1,781	3,502	4,216	0	2,690	4,700	5,414
29,200	29,250	0	1,773	3,491	4,205	0	2,682	4,689	5,404
29,250	29,300	0	1,765	3,480	4,195	0	2,674	4,679	5,393
29,300	29,350	0	1,757	3,470	4,184	0	2,666	4,668	5,383
29,350	29,400	0	1,749	3,459	4,174	0	2,658	4,658	5,372
29,400	29,450	0	1,741	3,449	4,163	0	2,650	4,647	5,362
29,450	29,500	0	1,733	3,438	4,153	0	2,642	4,637	5,351
29,500	29,550	0	1,725	3,428	4,142	0	2,634	4,626	5,341
29,550	29,600	0	1,717	3,417	4,132	0	2,626	4,616	5,330
29,600	29,650	0	1,709	3,407	4,121	0	2,618	4,605	5,320
29,650	29,700	0	1,701	3,396	4,111	0	2,610	4,595	5,309
29,700	29,750	0	1,693	3,386	4,100	0	2,602	4,584	5,299
29,750	29,800	0	1,685	3,375	4,090	0	2,594	4,573	5,288
29,800	29,850	0	1,677	3,365	4,079	0	2,586	4,563	5,277
29,850	29,900	0	1,669	3,354	4,069	0	2,578	4,552	5,267
29,900	29,950	0	1,661	3,344	4,058	0	2,570	4,542	5,256
29,950	30,000	0	1,653	3,333	4,048	0	2,562	4,531	5,246
30,000	30,050	0	1,645	3,323	4,037	0	2,554	4,521	5,235
30,050	30,100	0	1,637	3,312	4,027	0	2,546	4,510	5,225
30,100	30,150	0	1,629	3,301	4,016	0	2,538	4,500	5,214
30,150	30,200	0	1,621	3,291	4,005	0	2,530	4,489	5,204
30,200	30,250	0	1,613	3,280	3,995	0	2,522	4,479	5,193
30,250	30,300	0	1,606	3,270	3,984	0	2,514	4,468	5,183
30,300	30,350	0	1,597	3,259	3,974	0	2,506	4,458	5,172
30,350	30,400	0	1,589	3,249	3,963	0	2,498	4,447	5,162
30,400	30,450	0	1,581	3,238	3,953	0	2,490	4,437	5,151
30,450	30,500	0	1,573	3,228	3,942	0	2,482	4,426	5,141
30,500	30,550	0	1,565	3,217	3,932	0	2,474	4,416	5,130
30,550	30,600	0	1,557	3,207	3,921	0	2,466	4,405	5,120
30,600	30,650	0	1,549	3,196	3,911	0	2,458	4,394	5,109
30,650	30,700	0	1,541	3,186	3,900	0	2,450	4,384	5,098
30,700	30,750	0	1,533	3,175	3,890	0	2,442	4,373	5,088
30,750	30,800	0	1,525	3,165	3,879	0	2,434	4,363	5,077
30,800	30,850	0	1,517	3,154	3,869	0	2,426	4,352	5,067
30,850	30,900	0	1,509	3,144	3,858	0	2,419	4,342	5,056
30,900	30,950	0	1,501	3,133	3,847	0	2,411	4,331	5,046
30,950	31,000	0	1,493	3,122	3,837	0	2,403	4,321	5,035
31,000	31,050	0	1,485	3,112	3,826	0	2,395	4,310	5,025
31,050	31,100	0	1,477	3,101	3,816	0	2,387	4,300	5,014
31,100	31,150	0	1,469	3,091	3,805	0	2,379	4,289	5,004
31,150	31,200	0	1,461	3,080	3,795	0	2,371	4,279	4,993

(Continued)

Draft As of September 26, 2018.

Earned Income Credit (EIC) Table - *Continued*

(**Caution.** This is **not** a tax table.)

If the amount you are looking up from the worksheet is—		Single, head of household, or qualifying widow(er) and the number of children you have is—				Married filing jointly and the number of children you have is—			
At least	But less than	0	1	2	3	0	1	2	3
		Your credit is—				Your credit is—			
31,200	31,250	0	1,453	3,070	3,784	0	2,363	4,288	4,983
31,250	31,300	0	1,445	3,059	3,774	0	2,355	4,258	4,972
31,300	31,350	0	1,437	3,049	3,763	0	2,347	4,247	4,962
31,350	31,400	0	1,429	3,038	3,753	0	2,339	4,237	4,951
31,400	31,450	0	1,421	3,028	3,742	0	2,331	4,226	4,941
31,450	31,500	0	1,413	3,017	3,732	0	2,323	4,215	4,930
31,500	31,550	0	1,405	3,007	3,721	0	2,315	4,205	4,919
31,550	31,600	0	1,397	2,996	3,711	0	2,307	4,194	4,909
31,600	31,650	0	1,389	2,988	3,700	0	2,299	4,184	4,898
31,650	31,700	0	1,381	2,975	3,690	0	2,291	4,173	4,888
31,700	31,750	0	1,373	2,965	3,679	0	2,283	4,163	4,877
31,750	31,800	0	1,365	2,954	3,668	0	2,275	4,152	4,867
31,800	31,850	0	1,357	2,943	3,658	0	2,267	4,142	4,856
31,850	31,900	0	1,349	2,933	3,647	0	2,259	4,131	4,846
31,900	31,950	0	1,341	2,922	3,637	0	2,251	4,121	4,835
31,950	32,000	0	1,333	2,912	3,626	0	2,243	4,110	4,825
32,000	32,050	0	1,325	2,901	3,616	0	2,235	4,100	4,814
32,050	32,100	0	1,317	2,891	3,605	0	2,227	4,089	4,804
32,100	32,150	0	1,309	2,880	3,595	0	2,219	4,079	4,793
32,150	32,200	0	1,302	2,870	3,584	0	2,211	4,068	4,783
32,200	32,250	0	1,294	2,859	3,574	0	2,203	4,058	4,772
32,250	32,300	0	1,286	2,849	3,563	0	2,195	4,047	4,761
32,300	32,350	0	1,278	2,838	3,553	0	2,187	4,036	4,751
32,350	32,400	0	1,270	2,828	3,542	0	2,179	4,026	4,740
32,400	32,450	0	1,262	2,817	3,532	0	2,171	4,015	4,730
32,450	32,500	0	1,254	2,807	3,521	0	2,163	4,005	4,719
32,500	32,550	0	1,246	2,796	3,511	0	2,155	3,994	4,709
32,550	32,600	0	1,238	2,786	3,500	0	2,147	3,984	4,698
32,600	32,650	0	1,230	2,775	3,489	0	2,139	3,973	4,688
32,650	32,700	0	1,222	2,764	3,479	0	2,131	3,963	4,677
32,700	32,750	0	1,214	2,754	3,468	0	2,123	3,952	4,667
32,750	32,800	0	1,206	2,743	3,458	0	2,115	3,942	4,656
32,800	32,850	0	1,198	2,733	3,447	0	2,107	3,931	4,646
32,850	32,900	0	1,190	2,722	3,437	0	2,099	3,921	4,635
32,900	32,950	0	1,182	2,712	3,426	0	2,091	3,910	4,625
32,950	33,000	0	1,174	2,701	3,416	0	2,083	3,900	4,614
33,000	33,050	0	1,166	2,691	3,405	0	2,075	3,889	4,604
33,050	33,100	0	1,158	2,680	3,395	0	2,067	3,879	4,593
33,100	33,150	0	1,150	2,670	3,384	0	2,059	3,868	4,582
33,150	33,200	0	1,142	2,659	3,374	0	2,051	3,857	4,572
33,200	33,250	0	1,134	2,649	3,363	0	2,043	3,847	4,561
33,250	33,300	0	1,126	2,638	3,353	0	2,035	3,836	4,551
33,300	33,350	0	1,118	2,628	3,342	0	2,027	3,826	4,540
33,350	33,400	0	1,110	2,617	3,332	0	2,019	3,815	4,530
33,400	33,450	0	1,102	2,606	3,321	0	2,011	3,805	4,519
33,450	33,500	0	1,094	2,596	3,310	0	2,003	3,794	4,509
33,500	33,550	0	1,086	2,585	3,300	0	1,995	3,784	4,498
33,550	33,600	0	1,078	2,575	3,289	0	1,987	3,773	4,488
33,600	33,650	0	1,070	2,564	3,279	0	1,979	3,763	4,477
33,650	33,700	0	1,062	2,554	3,268	0	1,971	3,752	4,467
33,700	33,750	0	1,054	2,543	3,258	0	1,963	3,742	4,456
33,750	33,800	0	1,046	2,533	3,247	0	1,955	3,731	4,446
33,800	33,850	0	1,038	2,522	3,237	0	1,947	3,721	4,435
33,850	33,900	0	1,030	2,512	3,226	0	1,939	3,710	4,425
33,900	33,950	0	1,022	2,501	3,216	0	1,931	3,700	4,414
33,950	34,000	0	1,014	2,491	3,205	0	1,923	3,689	4,403
34,000	34,050	0	1,006	2,480	3,195	0	1,915	3,678	4,393
34,050	34,100	0	998	2,470	3,184	0	1,907	3,668	4,382
34,100	34,150	0	990	2,459	3,174	0	1,899	3,657	4,372
34,150	34,200	0	982	2,449	3,163	0	1,891	3,647	4,361
34,200	34,250	0	974	2,438	3,153	0	1,883	3,636	4,351
34,250	34,300	0	966	2,427	3,142	0	1,875	3,626	4,340
34,300	34,350	0	958	2,417	3,131	0	1,867	3,615	4,330
34,350	34,400	0	950	2,406	3,121	0	1,859	3,605	4,319

If the amount you are looking up from the worksheet is—		Single, head of household, or qualifying widow(er) and the number of children you have is—				Married filing jointly and the number of children you have is—			
At least	But less than	0	1	2	3	0	1	2	3
		Your credit is—				Your credit is—			
34,400	34,450	0	942	2,396	3,110	0	1,851	3,594	4,309
34,450	34,500	0	934	2,385	3,100	0	1,843	3,584	4,298
34,500	34,550	0	926	2,375	3,089	0	1,835	3,573	4,288
34,550	34,600	0	918	2,364	3,079	0	1,827	3,563	4,277
34,600	34,650	0	910	2,354	3,068	0	1,819	3,552	4,267
34,650	34,700	0	902	2,343	3,058	0	1,811	3,542	4,256
34,700	34,750	0	894	2,333	3,047	0	1,803	3,531	4,246
34,750	34,800	0	886	2,322	3,037	0	1,795	3,520	4,235
34,800	34,850	0	878	2,312	3,026	0	1,787	3,510	4,224
34,850	34,900	0	870	2,301	3,016	0	1,779	3,499	4,214
34,900	34,950	0	862	2,291	3,005	0	1,771	3,489	4,203
34,950	35,000	0	854	2,280	2,995	0	1,763	3,478	4,193
35,000	35,050	0	846	2,270	2,984	0	1,755	3,468	4,182
35,050	35,100	0	838	2,259	2,974	0	1,747	3,457	4,172
35,100	35,150	0	830	2,248	2,963	0	1,739	3,447	4,161
35,150	35,200	0	822	2,238	2,952	0	1,731	3,436	4,151
35,200	35,250	0	814	2,227	2,942	0	1,723	3,426	4,140
35,250	35,300	0	806	2,217	2,931	0	1,715	3,415	4,130
35,300	35,350	0	798	2,206	2,921	0	1,707	3,405	4,119
35,350	35,400	0	790	2,196	2,910	0	1,699	3,394	4,109
35,400	35,450	0	782	2,185	2,900	0	1,691	3,384	4,098
35,450	35,500	0	774	2,175	2,889	0	1,683	3,373	4,088
35,500	35,550	0	766	2,164	2,879	0	1,675	3,363	4,077
35,550	35,600	0	758	2,154	2,868	0	1,667	3,352	4,067
35,600	35,650	0	750	2,143	2,858	0	1,659	3,341	4,056
35,650	35,700	0	742	2,133	2,847	0	1,651	3,331	4,045
35,700	35,750	0	734	2,122	2,837	0	1,643	3,320	4,035
35,750	35,800	0	726	2,112	2,826	0	1,635	3,310	4,024
35,800	35,850	0	718	2,101	2,816	0	1,627	3,299	4,014
35,850	35,900	0	710	2,091	2,805	0	1,620	3,289	4,003
35,900	35,950	0	702	2,080	2,794	0	1,612	3,278	3,993
35,950	36,000	0	694	2,069	2,784	0	1,604	3,268	3,982
36,000	36,050	0	686	2,059	2,773	0	1,596	3,257	3,972
36,050	36,100	0	678	2,048	2,763	0	1,588	3,247	3,961
36,100	36,150	0	670	2,038	2,752	0	1,580	3,236	3,951
36,150	36,200	0	662	2,027	2,742	0	1,572	3,226	3,940
36,200	36,250	0	654	2,017	2,731	0	1,564	3,215	3,930
36,250	36,300	0	646	2,006	2,721	0	1,556	3,205	3,919
36,300	36,350	0	638	1,996	2,710	0	1,548	3,194	3,909
36,350	36,400	0	630	1,985	2,700	0	1,540	3,184	3,898
36,400	36,450	0	622	1,975	2,689	0	1,532	3,173	3,888
36,450	36,500	0	614	1,964	2,679	0	1,524	3,162	3,877
36,500	36,550	0	606	1,954	2,668	0	1,516	3,152	3,866
36,550	36,600	0	598	1,943	2,658	0	1,508	3,141	3,856
36,600	36,650	0	590	1,933	2,647	0	1,500	3,131	3,845
36,650	36,700	0	582	1,922	2,637	0	1,492	3,120	3,835
36,700	36,750	0	574	1,912	2,626	0	1,484	3,110	3,824
36,750	36,800	0	566	1,901	2,615	0	1,476	3,099	3,814
36,800	36,850	0	558	1,890	2,605	0	1,468	3,089	3,803
36,850	36,900	0	550	1,880	2,594	0	1,460	3,078	3,793
36,900	36,950	0	542	1,869	2,584	0	1,452	3,068	3,782
36,950	37,000	0	534	1,859	2,573	0	1,444	3,057	3,772
37,000	37,050	0	526	1,848	2,563	0	1,436	3,047	3,761
37,050	37,100	0	518	1,838	2,552	0	1,428	3,036	3,751
37,100	37,150	0	510	1,827	2,542	0	1,420	3,026	3,740
37,150	37,200	0	503	1,817	2,531	0	1,412	3,015	3,730
37,200	37,250	0	495	1,806	2,521	0	1,404	3,005	3,719
37,250	37,300	0	487	1,796	2,510	0	1,396	2,994	3,708
37,300	37,350	0	479	1,785	2,500	0	1,388	2,983	3,698
37,350	37,400	0	471	1,775	2,489	0	1,380	2,973	3,687
37,400	37,450	0	463	1,764	2,479	0	1,372	2,962	3,677
37,450	37,500	0	455	1,754	2,468	0	1,364	2,952	3,666
37,500	37,550	0	447	1,743	2,458	0	1,356	2,941	3,656
37,550	37,600	0	439	1,733	2,447	0	1,348	2,931	3,645

(Continued)

Draft As of September 26, 2018.

Earned Income Credit (EIC) Table - *Continued*   (**Caution.** This is **not** a tax table.)

If the amount you are looking up from the worksheet is–		Single, head of household, or qualifying widow(er) and the number of children you have is–				Married filing jointly and the number of children you have is–			
At least	But less than	0	1	2	3	0	1	2	3
		Your credit is–				Your credit is–			
37,600	37,650	0	431	1,722	2,436	0	1,340	2,920	3,635
37,650	37,700	0	423	1,711	2,426	0	1,332	2,910	3,624
37,700	37,750	0	415	1,701	2,415	0	1,324	2,899	3,614
37,750	37,800	0	407	1,690	2,405	0	1,316	2,889	3,603
37,800	37,850	0	399	1,680	2,394	0	1,308	2,878	3,593
37,850	37,900	0	391	1,669	2,384	0	1,300	2,868	3,582
37,900	37,950	0	383	1,659	2,373	0	1,292	2,857	3,572
37,950	38,000	0	375	1,648	2,363	0	1,284	2,847	3,561
38,000	38,050	0	367	1,638	2,352	0	1,276	2,836	3,551
38,050	38,100	0	359	1,627	2,342	0	1,268	2,826	3,540
38,100	38,150	0	351	1,617	2,331	0	1,260	2,815	3,529
38,150	38,200	0	343	1,606	2,321	0	1,252	2,804	3,519
38,200	38,250	0	335	1,596	2,310	0	1,244	2,794	3,508
38,250	38,300	0	327	1,585	2,300	0	1,236	2,783	3,498
38,300	38,350	0	319	1,575	2,289	0	1,228	2,773	3,487
38,350	38,400	0	311	1,564	2,279	0	1,220	2,762	3,477
38,400	38,450	0	303	1,553	2,268	0	1,212	2,752	3,466
38,450	38,500	0	295	1,543	2,257	0	1,204	2,741	3,456
38,500	38,550	0	287	1,532	2,247	0	1,196	2,731	3,445
38,550	38,600	0	279	1,522	2,236	0	1,188	2,720	3,435
38,600	38,650	0	271	1,511	2,226	0	1,180	2,710	3,424
38,650	38,700	0	263	1,501	2,215	0	1,172	2,699	3,414
38,700	38,750	0	255	1,490	2,205	0	1,164	2,689	3,403
38,750	38,800	0	247	1,480	2,194	0	1,156	2,678	3,393
38,800	38,850	0	239	1,469	2,184	0	1,148	2,668	3,382
38,850	38,900	0	231	1,459	2,173	0	1,140	2,657	3,372
38,900	38,950	0	223	1,448	2,163	0	1,132	2,647	3,361
38,950	39,000	0	215	1,438	2,152	0	1,124	2,636	3,350
39,000	39,050	0	207	1,427	2,142	0	1,116	2,625	3,340
39,050	39,100	0	199	1,417	2,131	0	1,108	2,615	3,329
39,100	39,150	0	191	1,406	2,121	0	1,100	2,604	3,319
39,150	39,200	0	183	1,396	2,110	0	1,092	2,594	3,308
39,200	39,250	0	175	1,385	2,100	0	1,084	2,583	3,298
39,250	39,300	0	167	1,374	2,089	0	1,076	2,573	3,287
39,300	39,350	0	159	1,364	2,078	0	1,068	2,562	3,277
39,350	39,400	0	151	1,353	2,068	0	1,060	2,552	3,266
39,400	39,450	0	143	1,343	2,057	0	1,052	2,541	3,256
39,450	39,500	0	135	1,332	2,047	0	1,044	2,531	3,245
39,500	39,550	0	127	1,322	2,036	0	1,036	2,520	3,235
39,550	39,600	0	119	1,311	2,026	0	1,028	2,510	3,224
39,600	39,650	0	111	1,301	2,015	0	1,020	2,499	3,213
39,650	39,700	0	103	1,290	2,005	0	1,012	2,489	3,203
39,700	39,750	0	95	1,280	1,994	0	1,004	2,478	3,193
39,750	39,800	0	87	1,269	1,984	0	996	2,467	3,182
39,800	39,850	0	79	1,259	1,973	0	988	2,457	3,171
39,850	39,900	0	71	1,248	1,963	0	980	2,446	3,161
39,900	39,950	0	63	1,238	1,952	0	972	2,436	3,150
39,950	40,000	0	55	1,227	1,942	0	964	2,425	3,140
40,000	40,050	0	47	1,217	1,931	0	956	2,415	3,129
40,050	40,100	0	39	1,206	1,921	0	948	2,404	3,119
40,100	40,150	0	31	1,196	1,910	0	940	2,394	3,108
40,150	40,200	0	23	1,185	1,899	0	932	2,383	3,098
40,200	40,250	0	15	1,174	1,889	0	924	2,373	3,087
40,250	40,300	0	7	1,164	1,878	0	916	2,362	3,077
40,300	40,350	0	*	1,153	1,868	0	908	2,352	3,066
40,350	40,400	0	0	1,143	1,857	0	900	2,341	3,056
40,400	40,450	0	0	1,132	1,847	0	892	2,331	3,045
40,450	40,500	0	0	1,122	1,836	0	884	2,320	3,035
40,500	40,550	0	0	1,111	1,826	0	876	2,310	3,024
40,550	40,600	0	0	1,101	1,815	0	868	2,299	3,014
40,600	40,650	0	0	1,090	1,805	0	860	2,289	3,003
40,650	40,700	0	0	1,080	1,794	0	852	2,278	2,992
40,700	40,750	0	0	1,069	1,784	0	844	2,267	2,982
40,750	40,800	0	0	1,059	1,773	0	836	2,257	2,971

If the amount you are looking up from the worksheet is–		Single, head of household, or qualifying widow(er) and the number of children you have is–				Married filing jointly and the number of children you have is–			
At least	But less than	0	1	2	3	0	1	2	3
		Your credit is–				Your credit is–			
40,800	40,850	0	0	1,048	1,763	0	828	2,246	2,961
40,850	40,900	0	0	1,038	1,752	0	821	2,236	2,950
40,900	40,950	0	0	1,027	1,741	0	813	2,225	2,940
40,950	41,000	0	0	1,016	1,731	0	805	2,215	2,929
41,000	41,050	0	0	1,006	1,720	0	797	2,204	2,919
41,050	41,100	0	0	995	1,710	0	789	2,194	2,908
41,100	41,150	0	0	985	1,699	0	781	2,183	2,898
41,150	41,200	0	0	974	1,689	0	773	2,173	2,887
41,200	41,250	0	0	964	1,678	0	765	2,162	2,877
41,250	41,300	0	0	953	1,668	0	757	2,152	2,866
41,300	41,350	0	0	943	1,657	0	749	2,141	2,856
41,350	41,400	0	0	932	1,647	0	741	2,131	2,845
41,400	41,450	0	0	922	1,636	0	733	2,120	2,835
41,450	41,500	0	0	911	1,626	0	725	2,109	2,824
41,500	41,550	0	0	901	1,615	0	717	2,099	2,813
41,550	41,600	0	0	890	1,605	0	709	2,088	2,803
41,600	41,650	0	0	880	1,594	0	701	2,078	2,792
41,650	41,700	0	0	869	1,584	0	693	2,067	2,782
41,700	41,750	0	0	859	1,573	0	685	2,057	2,771
41,750	41,800	0	0	848	1,562	0	677	2,046	2,761
41,800	41,850	0	0	837	1,552	0	669	2,036	2,750
41,850	41,900	0	0	827	1,541	0	661	2,025	2,740
41,900	41,950	0	0	816	1,531	0	653	2,015	2,729
41,950	42,000	0	0	806	1,520	0	645	2,004	2,719
42,000	42,050	0	0	795	1,510	0	637	1,994	2,708
42,050	42,100	0	0	785	1,499	0	629	1,983	2,698
42,100	42,150	0	0	774	1,489	0	621	1,973	2,687
42,150	42,200	0	0	764	1,478	0	613	1,962	2,677
42,200	42,250	0	0	753	1,468	0	605	1,952	2,666
42,250	42,300	0	0	743	1,457	0	597	1,941	2,655
42,300	42,350	0	0	732	1,447	0	589	1,930	2,645
42,350	42,400	0	0	722	1,436	0	581	1,920	2,634
42,400	42,450	0	0	711	1,426	0	573	1,909	2,624
42,450	42,500	0	0	701	1,415	0	565	1,899	2,613
42,500	42,550	0	0	690	1,405	0	557	1,888	2,603
42,550	42,600	0	0	680	1,394	0	549	1,878	2,592
42,600	42,650	0	0	669	1,383	0	541	1,867	2,582
42,650	42,700	0	0	658	1,373	0	533	1,857	2,571
42,700	42,750	0	0	648	1,362	0	525	1,846	2,560
42,750	42,800	0	0	637	1,352	0	517	1,836	2,550
42,800	42,850	0	0	627	1,341	0	509	1,825	2,540
42,850	42,900	0	0	616	1,331	0	501	1,815	2,529
42,900	42,950	0	0	606	1,320	0	493	1,804	2,519
42,950	43,000	0	0	595	1,310	0	485	1,794	2,508
43,000	43,050	0	0	585	1,299	0	477	1,783	2,498
43,050	43,100	0	0	574	1,289	0	469	1,773	2,487
43,100	43,150	0	0	564	1,278	0	461	1,762	2,476
43,150	43,200	0	0	553	1,268	0	453	1,751	2,466
43,200	43,250	0	0	543	1,257	0	445	1,741	2,455
43,250	43,300	0	0	532	1,247	0	437	1,730	2,445
43,300	43,350	0	0	522	1,236	0	429	1,720	2,434
43,350	43,400	0	0	511	1,226	0	421	1,709	2,424
43,400	43,450	0	0	500	1,215	0	413	1,699	2,413
43,450	43,500	0	0	490	1,204	0	405	1,688	2,403
43,500	43,550	0	0	479	1,194	0	397	1,678	2,392
43,550	43,600	0	0	469	1,183	0	389	1,667	2,382
43,600	43,650	0	0	458	1,173	0	381	1,657	2,371
43,650	43,700	0	0	448	1,162	0	373	1,646	2,361
43,700	43,750	0	0	437	1,152	0	365	1,636	2,350
43,750	43,800	0	0	427	1,141	0	357	1,625	2,340
43,800	43,850	0	0	416	1,131	0	349	1,615	2,329
43,850	43,900	0	0	406	1,120	0	341	1,604	2,319
43,900	43,950	0	0	395	1,110	0	333	1,594	2,308
43,950	44,000	0	0	385	1,099	0	325	1,583	2,297

* If the amount you are looking up from the worksheet is at least $40,300 but less than $40,320, and you have one qualifying child, your credit is $2. If the amount you are looking up from the worksheet is $40,320 or more, and you have one qualifying child, you can't take the credit.

(Continued)

Draft As of September 26, 2018.

Earned Income Credit (EIC) Table - *Continued*

(**Caution.** This is **not** a tax table.)

Left panel:

At least	But less than	Single, head of household, or qualifying widow(er) — 0	1	2	3	Married filing jointly — 0	1	2	3
44,000	44,050	0	0	374	1,089	0	317	1,572	2,287
44,050	44,100	0	0	364	1,078	0	309	1,562	2,276
44,100	44,150	0	0	353	1,068	0	301	1,551	2,266
44,150	44,200	0	0	343	1,057	0	293	1,541	2,255
44,200	44,250	0	0	332	1,047	0	285	1,530	2,245
44,250	44,300	0	0	321	1,036	0	277	1,520	2,234
44,300	44,350	0	0	311	1,025	0	269	1,509	2,224
44,350	44,400	0	0	300	1,015	0	261	1,499	2,213
44,400	44,450	0	0	290	1,004	0	253	1,488	2,203
44,450	44,500	0	0	279	994	0	245	1,478	2,192
44,500	44,550	0	0	269	983	0	237	1,467	2,182
44,550	44,600	0	0	258	973	0	229	1,457	2,171
44,600	44,650	0	0	248	962	0	221	1,446	2,161
44,650	44,700	0	0	237	952	0	213	1,436	2,150
44,700	44,750	0	0	227	941	0	205	1,425	2,140
44,750	44,800	0	0	216	931	0	197	1,414	2,129
44,800	44,850	0	0	206	920	0	189	1,404	2,118
44,850	44,900	0	0	195	910	0	181	1,393	2,108
44,900	44,950	0	0	185	899	0	173	1,383	2,097
44,950	45,000	0	0	174	889	0	165	1,372	2,087
45,000	45,050	0	0	164	878	0	157	1,362	2,076
45,050	45,100	0	0	153	868	0	149	1,351	2,066
45,100	45,150	0	0	142	857	0	141	1,341	2,055
45,150	45,200	0	0	132	846	0	133	1,330	2,045
45,200	45,250	0	0	121	836	0	125	1,320	2,034
45,250	45,300	0	0	111	825	0	117	1,309	2,024
45,300	45,350	0	0	100	815	0	109	1,299	2,013
45,350	45,400	0	0	90	804	0	101	1,288	2,003
45,400	45,450	0	0	79	794	0	93	1,278	1,992
45,450	45,500	0	0	69	783	0	85	1,267	1,982
45,500	45,550	0	0	58	773	0	77	1,257	1,971
45,550	45,600	0	0	48	762	0	69	1,246	1,961
45,600	45,650	0	0	37	752	0	61	1,235	1,950
45,650	45,700	0	0	27	741	0	53	1,225	1,939
45,700	45,750	0	0	16	731	0	45	1,214	1,929
45,750	45,800	0	0	6	720	0	37	1,204	1,918
45,800	45,850	0	0	*	710	0	29	1,193	1,908
45,850	45,900	0	0	0	699	0	22	1,183	1,897
45,900	45,950	0	0	0	688	0	14	1,172	1,887
45,950	46,000	0	0	0	678	0	6	1,162	1,876
46,000	46,050	0	0	0	667	0	**	1,151	1,866
46,050	46,100	0	0	0	657	0	0	1,141	1,855
46,100	46,150	0	0	0	646	0	0	1,130	1,845
46,150	46,200	0	0	0	636	0	0	1,120	1,834
46,200	46,250	0	0	0	625	0	0	1,109	1,824
46,250	46,300	0	0	0	615	0	0	1,099	1,813
46,300	46,350	0	0	0	604	0	0	1,088	1,803
46,350	46,400	0	0	0	594	0	0	1,078	1,792
46,400	46,450	0	0	0	583	0	0	1,067	1,782
46,450	46,500	0	0	0	573	0	0	1,056	1,771
46,500	46,550	0	0	0	562	0	0	1,046	1,760
46,550	46,600	0	0	0	552	0	0	1,035	1,750
46,600	46,650	0	0	0	541	0	0	1,025	1,739
46,650	46,700	0	0	0	531	0	0	1,014	1,729
46,700	46,750	0	0	0	520	0	0	1,004	1,718
46,750	46,800	0	0	0	509	0	0	993	1,708
46,800	46,850	0	0	0	499	0	0	983	1,697
46,850	46,900	0	0	0	488	0	0	972	1,687
46,900	46,950	0	0	0	478	0	0	962	1,676
46,950	47,000	0	0	0	467	0	0	951	1,666
47,000	47,050	0	0	0	457	0	0	941	1,655
47,050	47,100	0	0	0	446	0	0	930	1,645
47,100	47,150	0	0	0	436	0	0	920	1,634
47,150	47,200	0	0	0	425	0	0	909	1,624

Right panel:

At least	But less than	Single, head of household, or qualifying widow(er) — 0	1	2	3	Married filing jointly — 0	1	2	3
47,200	47,250	0	0	0	415	0	0	899	1,613
47,250	47,300	0	0	0	404	0	0	888	1,602
47,300	47,350	0	0	0	394	0	0	877	1,592
47,350	47,400	0	0	0	383	0	0	867	1,581
47,400	47,450	0	0	0	373	0	0	856	1,571
47,450	47,500	0	0	0	362	0	0	846	1,560
47,500	47,550	0	0	0	352	0	0	835	1,550
47,550	47,600	0	0	0	341	0	0	825	1,539
47,600	47,650	0	0	0	330	0	0	814	1,529
47,650	47,700	0	0	0	320	0	0	804	1,518
47,700	47,750	0	0	0	309	0	0	793	1,508
47,750	47,800	0	0	0	299	0	0	783	1,497
47,800	47,850	0	0	0	288	0	0	772	1,487
47,850	47,900	0	0	0	278	0	0	762	1,476
47,900	47,950	0	0	0	267	0	0	751	1,466
47,950	48,000	0	0	0	257	0	0	741	1,455
48,000	48,050	0	0	0	246	0	0	730	1,445
48,050	48,100	0	0	0	236	0	0	720	1,434
48,100	48,150	0	0	0	225	0	0	709	1,423
48,150	48,200	0	0	0	215	0	0	698	1,413
48,200	48,250	0	0	0	204	0	0	688	1,402
48,250	48,300	0	0	0	194	0	0	677	1,392
48,300	48,350	0	0	0	183	0	0	667	1,381
48,350	48,400	0	0	0	173	0	0	656	1,371
48,400	48,450	0	0	0	162	0	0	646	1,360
48,450	48,500	0	0	0	151	0	0	635	1,350
48,500	48,550	0	0	0	141	0	0	625	1,339
48,550	48,600	0	0	0	130	0	0	614	1,329
48,600	48,650	0	0	0	120	0	0	604	1,318
48,650	48,700	0	0	0	109	0	0	593	1,308
48,700	48,750	0	0	0	99	0	0	583	1,297
48,750	48,800	0	0	0	88	0	0	572	1,287
48,800	48,850	0	0	0	78	0	0	562	1,276
48,850	48,900	0	0	0	67	0	0	551	1,266
48,900	48,950	0	0	0	57	0	0	541	1,255
48,950	49,000	0	0	0	46	0	0	530	1,244
49,000	49,050	0	0	0	36	0	0	519	1,234
49,050	49,100	0	0	0	25	0	0	509	1,223
49,100	49,150	0	0	0	15	0	0	498	1,213
49,150	49,200	0	0	0	4	0	0	488	1,202
49,200	49,250	0	0	0	0	0	0	477	1,192
49,250	49,300	0	0	0	0	0	0	467	1,181
49,300	49,350	0	0	0	0	0	0	456	1,171
49,350	49,400	0	0	0	0	0	0	446	1,160
49,400	49,450	0	0	0	0	0	0	435	1,150
49,450	49,500	0	0	0	0	0	0	425	1,139
49,500	49,550	0	0	0	0	0	0	414	1,129
49,550	49,600	0	0	0	0	0	0	404	1,118
49,600	49,650	0	0	0	0	0	0	393	1,108
49,650	49,700	0	0	0	0	0	0	383	1,097
49,700	49,750	0	0	0	0	0	0	372	1,087
49,750	49,800	0	0	0	0	0	0	361	1,076
49,800	49,850	0	0	0	0	0	0	351	1,065
49,850	49,900	0	0	0	0	0	0	340	1,055
49,900	49,950	0	0	0	0	0	0	330	1,044
49,950	50,000	0	0	0	0	0	0	319	1,034
50,000	50,050	0	0	0	0	0	0	309	1,023
50,050	50,100	0	0	0	0	0	0	298	1,013
50,100	50,150	0	0	0	0	0	0	288	1,002
50,150	50,200	0	0	0	0	0	0	277	992
50,200	50,250	0	0	0	0	0	0	267	981
50,250	50,300	0	0	0	0	0	0	256	971
50,300	50,350	0	0	0	0	0	0	246	960
50,350	50,400	0	0	0	0	0	0	235	950

* If the amount you are looking up from the worksheet is at least $45,800 but less than $45,802, and you have two qualifying children, your credit is $0. If the amount you are looking up from the worksheet is $45,802 or more, and you have two qualifying children, you can't take the credit.

** If the amount you are looking up from the worksheet is at least $46,000 but less than $46,010, and you have one qualifying child, your credit is $1. If the amount you are looking up from the worksheet is $46,010 or more, and you have one qualifying child, you can't take the credit.

(Continued)

Draft As of September 26, 2018.

Earned Income Credit (EIC) Table - *Continued*　　　　(**Caution.** This is **not** a tax table.)

If the amount you are looking up from the worksheet is—		Single, head of household, or qualifying widow(er) and the number of children you have is—				Married filing jointly and the number of children you have is—			
At least	But less than	0	1	2	3	0	1	2	3
		Your credit is—				Your credit is—			
50,400	50,450	0	0	0	0	0	0	225	839
50,450	50,500	0	0	0	0	0	0	214	929
50,500	50,550	0	0	0	0	0	0	204	918
50,550	50,600	0	0	0	0	0	0	193	908
50,600	50,650	0	0	0	0	0	0	182	897
50,650	50,700	0	0	0	0	0	0	172	886
50,700	50,750	0	0	0	0	0	0	161	876
50,750	50,800	0	0	0	0	0	0	151	865
50,800	50,850	0	0	0	0	0	0	140	855
50,850	50,900	0	0	0	0	0	0	130	844
50,900	50,950	0	0	0	0	0	0	119	834
50,950	51,000	0	0	0	0	0	0	109	823
51,000	51,050	0	0	0	0	0	0	98	813
51,050	51,100	0	0	0	0	0	0	88	802
51,100	51,150	0	0	0	0	0	0	77	792
51,150	51,200	0	0	0	0	0	0	67	781
51,200	51,250	0	0	0	0	0	0	56	771
51,250	51,300	0	0	0	0	0	0	46	760
51,300	51,350	0	0	0	0	0	0	35	750
51,350	51,400	0	0	0	0	0	0	25	739
51,400	51,450	0	0	0	0	0	0	14	729
51,450	51,500	0	0	0	0	0	0	*	718
51,500	51,550	0	0	0	0	0	0	0	707
51,550	51,600	0	0	0	0	0	0	0	697
51,600	51,650	0	0	0	0	0	0	0	686
51,650	51,700	0	0	0	0	0	0	0	676
51,700	51,750	0	0	0	0	0	0	0	665
51,750	51,800	0	0	0	0	0	0	0	655
51,800	51,850	0	0	0	0	0	0	0	644
51,850	51,900	0	0	0	0	0	0	0	634
51,900	51,950	0	0	0	0	0	0	0	623
51,950	52,000	0	0	0	0	0	0	0	613
52,000	52,050	0	0	0	0	0	0	0	602
52,050	52,100	0	0	0	0	0	0	0	592
52,100	52,150	0	0	0	0	0	0	0	581
52,150	52,200	0	0	0	0	0	0	0	571
52,200	52,250	0	0	0	0	0	0	0	560
52,250	52,300	0	0	0	0	0	0	0	549
52,300	52,350	0	0	0	0	0	0	0	539
52,350	52,400	0	0	0	0	0	0	0	528
52,400	52,450	0	0	0	0	0	0	0	518
52,450	52,500	0	0	0	0	0	0	0	507
52,500	52,550	0	0	0	0	0	0	0	497
52,550	52,600	0	0	0	0	0	0	0	486
52,600	52,650	0	0	0	0	0	0	0	476
52,650	52,700	0	0	0	0	0	0	0	465
52,700	52,750	0	0	0	0	0	0	0	455
52,750	52,800	0	0	0	0	0	0	0	444
52,800	52,850	0	0	0	0	0	0	0	434
52,850	52,900	0	0	0	0	0	0	0	423
52,900	52,950	0	0	0	0	0	0	0	413
52,950	53,000	0	0	0	0	0	0	0	402
53,000	53,050	0	0	0	0	0	0	0	392
53,050	53,100	0	0	0	0	0	0	0	381
53,100	53,150	0	0	0	0	0	0	0	370
53,150	53,200	0	0	0	0	0	0	0	360
53,200	53,250	0	0	0	0	0	0	0	349
53,250	53,300	0	0	0	0	0	0	0	339
53,300	53,350	0	0	0	0	0	0	0	328
53,350	53,400	0	0	0	0	0	0	0	318
53,400	53,450	0	0	0	0	0	0	0	307
53,450	53,500	0	0	0	0	0	0	0	297
53,500	53,550	0	0	0	0	0	0	0	286
53,550	53,600	0	0	0	0	0	0	0	276
53,600	53,650	0	0	0	0	0	0	0	265
53,650	53,700	0	0	0	0	0	0	0	255
53,700	53,750	0	0	0	0	0	0	0	244
53,750	53,800	0	0	0	0	0	0	0	234
53,800	53,850	0	0	0	0	0	0	0	223
53,850	53,900	0	0	0	0	0	0	0	213
53,900	53,950	0	0	0	0	0	0	0	202
53,950	54,000	0	0	0	0	0	0	0	191
54,000	54,050	0	0	0	0	0	0	0	181
54,050	54,100	0	0	0	0	0	0	0	170
54,100	54,150	0	0	0	0	0	0	0	160
54,150	54,200	0	0	0	0	0	0	0	149
54,200	54,250	0	0	0	0	0	0	0	139
54,250	54,300	0	0	0	0	0	0	0	128
54,300	54,350	0	0	0	0	0	0	0	118
54,350	54,400	0	0	0	0	0	0	0	107
54,400	54,450	0	0	0	0	0	0	0	97
54,450	54,500	0	0	0	0	0	0	0	86
54,500	54,550	0	0	0	0	0	0	0	76
54,550	54,600	0	0	0	0	0	0	0	65
54,600	54,650	0	0	0	0	0	0	0	55
54,650	54,700	0	0	0	0	0	0	0	44
54,700	54,750	0	0	0	0	0	0	0	34
54,750	54,800	0	0	0	0	0	0	0	23
54,800	54,850	0	0	0	0	0	0	0	12
54,850	54,900	0	0	0	0	0	0	0	4

* If the amount you are looking up from the worksheet is at least $51,450 but less than $51,492, and you have two qualifying children, your credit is $4.
If the amount you are looking up from the worksheet is $51,492 or more, and you have two qualifying children, you can't take the credit.

Draft As of September 26, 2018.

¶ 1113   Corporate income tax rates.

For tax years beginning after 2017, the corporate tax rate is reduced to a flat 21%, (Code Sec. 11(b)) and the corporate AMT is repealed. (Code Sec. 55(a))[4]

A corporation with a fiscal year that includes Jan. 1, 2018 (a so-called "straddle" year) must apply a blended rate to determine the amount of federal income tax imposed for that tax year. (Code Sec. 15(a)) Thus, a tentative tax of a corporation for the tax year that includes Jan. 1, 2018, is computed by applying the rates of tax that applied under prior law (i.e., the 2017 rates shown below), and a tentative tax for a corporation is computed by applying the 21% rate of tax imposed under the corporate income tax rate after change. The tax imposed for the tax year is the sum of that proportion of each tentative tax which the number of days in each period bears to the number of days in the entire tax year. A similar blended computation must be made for corporate AMT purposes (using the 20% prior law AMT rate and the post-2017 zero rate). [5]

For 2017, the rates for domestic corporations (other than qualified personal service corporations) were:

Taxable income over—	But not over—	The tax is:	Of the amount over—
0	$ 50,000	15%	0
$ 50,000	75,000	$ 7,500 + 25%	$ 50,000
75,000	100,000	13,750 + 34%	75,000
100,000	335,000	22,250 + 39%	100,000
335,000	10,000,000	113,900 + 34%	335,000
10,000,000	15,000,000	3,400,000 + 35%	10,000,000
15,000,000	18,333,333	5,150,000 + 38%	15,000,000
18,333,333	—	35%	0

¶ 1114   Gift and estate tax rates (unified rate schedule).

The estate tax is imposed on the decedent's taxable estate (gross estate less deductions). For credits against the estate tax, see ¶5028 *et seq.* The gift tax is based on the cumulative value of current and prior gifts (after a specified exclusion) after specified deductions, see ¶5041 *et seq.* (Code Sec. 2001, Code Sec. 2501)[6]

The unified rate schedule is as follows (Code Sec. 2001(c), Code Sec. 2502(a)(2)):

Unified Rate Schedule

If the amount with respect to which the tentative tax to be computed is:	The tentative tax is:
Not over $10,000.	18% of such amount.
Over $10,000 but not over $20,000.	$1,800, plus 20% of the excess over $10,000.
Over $20,000 but not over $40,000.	$3,800, plus 22% of the excess over $20,000.
Over $40,000 but not over $60,000.	$8,200, plus 24% of the excess over $40,000.
Over $60,000 but not over $80,000.	$13,000, plus 26% of the excess over $60,000.
Over $80,000 but not over $100,000.	$18,200, plus 28% of the excess over $80,000.
Over $100,000 but not over $150,000.	$23,800, plus 30% of the excess over $100,000.
Over $150,000 but not over $250,000.	$38,800, plus 32% of the excess over $150,000.

---

4. ¶D-1003 *et seq.*; ¶154.01
5. ¶1100 *et seq.*; ¶154.01

6. ¶s Q-8003 *et seq.*, R-7000 *et seq.*; ¶20,014 *et seq.*, ¶25,024 *et seq.* (Estate & Gift)

Over $250,000 but not over $500,000.	$70,800, plus 34% of the excess over $250,000.
Over $500,000 but not over $750,000.	$155,800, plus 37% of the excess over $500,000.
Over $750,000 but not over $1,000,000.	$248,300, plus 39% of the excess over $750,000.
Over $1,000,000.	$345,800, plus 40% of the excess over $1,000,000.

The top estate and gift tax rate (and the GST tax rate) is 40%.

For the estate tax on non-income distributions from a qualified domestic trust for a surviving spouse who isn't a U.S. citizen, see ¶5026.

For the applicable exclusion amount and applicable credit amount, see ¶5028. For the credit against estate tax imposed on estates of nonresident aliens, see ¶5040.

¶ 1115   New measure of inflation beginning in 2018.

Generally effective in tax years beginning after 2017, tax bracket amounts and certain other tax parameters under the Code that are adjusted for inflation under Code Sec. 1(f)(3) will be adjusted in reference to chained CPI-U (Consumer Price Index for "all-urban customers").

¶ 1116   Post-2025 sunset provisions.

Unless Congress acts, many provisions in the Tax Cuts and Jobs Act (TCJA, P.L. 115-97; formally designated as "An Act to provide for reconciliation pursuant to titles II and V of the concurrent resolution on the budget for fiscal year 2018"), the comprehensive tax reform legislation signed into law on Dec. 22, 2017, won't apply after 2025. The majority of the provisions subject to the 2025 sunset affect individuals.

Among the more significant provisions subject to the 2025 sunset are:

. . . the income tax rates (¶1102 et seq)

. . . increased standard deduction amounts, (¶3110)

. . . the reduction of personal exemptions to $0 (¶3112)

. . . the increase in the child tax credit (¶2350 et seq)

. . . the limit on the state and local tax (SALT) deduction (¶1747)

. . . the suspension of miscellaneous itemized deductions (¶3109)

. . . increased AMT exemption amounts (¶3201 et seq)

. . . increased estate and gift tax exemption (¶5000 et seq) and

. . . the new deduction for pass-through income. (¶1595 et seq)

Other TCJA provisions with a fixed statutory expiration date include the 7.5% medical expense floor (in effect for 2017 and 2018) and the new credit for employer-paid family and medical leave (in effect for 2018 and 2019).

caution: Check tax.thomsonreuters.com/federaltaxhandbookupdates to see if legislation making these provisions permanent has been enacted.

¶ 1117   Excise tax rates (nonpenalty).

Here are selected "nonpenalty" excise tax rates. For penalty-type excise taxes, see the entries under "Excise taxes" in the Topic Index.

Retail Excise Taxes

Trucks, trailers, etc.

- auto truck chassis and bodies (for vehicles weighing more than 33,000 lbs),
- truck trailer and semi-trailer chassis and bodies (for vehicles weighing more than 26,000 lbs)
- tractors used chiefly for highway transportation in combination with a trailer or semi-trailer (for tractors weighing more than 19,500 lbs and in combination with trailer or semi-trailer weighing more than 33,000 lbs)
- accessories sold with one of the above or installed within 6 months after one of the above is placed in service

12% of first retail sale amount. Tax scheduled to expire after 9/30/2022.

Transportation Fuel Taxes

Gasoline other than aviation gasoline; gasohol

Through 9/30/2022, on removal at terminal: 18.4¢ per gal.; 4.3¢ per gal. thereafter

Aviation gasoline

Through 9/30/2022, on removal at terminal: 19.4¢ per gal.; 10/1/2022-9/30/2023: 19.3¢ per gal.; 4.3¢ per gal. thereafter

Diesel fuel;* diesohol

Through 9/30/2022, on removal at terminal or retail sale: 24.4¢ per gal.; 4.3¢ per gal. thereafter

- Diesel-water fuel emulsion

Through 9/30/2022, on removal at terminal: 19.8¢ per gal. After 9/30/2022, see diesel fuel rate above

- Dyed diesel fuel, other than for export

Through 9/30/2022, on removal at terminal or retail sale: .1¢ per gal.

Kerosene

Through 9/30/2022, on removal at terminal or retail sale, generally: 24.4¢ per gal.; thereafter, 4.3¢ per gal.

- Noncommercial aviation use —on removal directly into noncommercial aircraft's fuel tank

Through 9/30/2022: 21.9¢ per gal.; 10/1/2022-9/30/2023: 21.8¢ per gal.; 4.3¢ per gal. thereafter

- Commercial aviation use —on removal directly into commercial aircraft's fuel tank

Through 9/30/2022: 4.4¢ per gal.; 4.3¢ per gal. thereafter

- Retail sale for aviation use (where fuel not previously taxed)

Through 9/30/2022, for noncommercial aviation: 21.9¢ per gal.; for commercial aviation: 4.4¢ per gal. After 9/30/2022: 21.8¢ per gal. and 4.3¢ per gal., respectively

- Dyed kerosene, other than for export

  Through 9/30/2022, on removal at terminal or retail sale: .1¢ per gal.

Alternative fuels

- Special motor fuels (other than LPG and LNG)

  Through 9/30/2022, on retail sale or use, for motor vehicle or motorboat use: 18.4¢ per gal.; After 9/30/2022: 4.3¢ thereafter

- Liquefied petroleum gas (LPG) (e.g., propane, butane)

  18.3¢ per energy equivalent of a gal. of gasoline; (13.2¢ per gal.)

- Liquefied natural gas (LNG)

  24.3¢ per energy equivalent of a gal. of diesel fuel, (14.1¢ per gal.)

- Liquid fuel (other than ethanol or methanol) derived from coal and any liquid hydrocarbons derived from biomass

  Through 9/30/2022: 24.4¢ per gal.; 24.3¢ per gal. thereafter

- Partially exempt ethanol and methanol

  Through 9/30/2022, for retail sale or use, of: partially exempt ethanol, 11.4¢ per gal.; partially exempt methanol, 9.25¢ per gal. After 9/30/2022, for partially exempt ethanol, 4.3¢ per gal.; for partially exempt methanol, 2.15¢ per gal.

Compressed natural gas (CNG)

18.3¢ per energy equivalent of a gal. of gasoline (126.67 cu. ft.)

Fuel used in commercial transportation on inland waterways

Through 9/30/2022; 29.1¢ per gal.; 29¢ per gal. thereafter.

Fuel used in fractional ownership aircraft

Through 9/30/2023, 14.1¢ per gal. surtax.

Selected Manufacturers and Other Excise Taxes

Coal (except lignite)

- From underground mines

  Lower of $1.10 per ton or 4.4% of selling price

- From surface mines

  Lower of 55¢ per ton or 4.4% of selling price

Tires (of type used in highway vehicles, wholly or in part made of rubber)

9.45¢ (4.725¢ for biasply or super single tires) for each 10 lbs. the tire's maximum rated load capacity exceeds 3,500 lbs. Tax scheduled to expire after 9/30/2022.

Sport fishing equipment

10% of mfrs. price of specified sport fishing equipment (up to max. of $10 on fishing rods and poles); 3% for electric outboard motors and fishing tackle boxes

Gas guzzling passenger autos, as follows:

If the fuel economy of the model type in which the automobile falls is:	*The tax is:*
At least 22.5	0
At least 21.5 but less than 22.5	$1,000
At least 20.5 but less than 21.5	1,300
At least 19.5 but less than 20.5	1,700
At least 18.5 but less than 19.5	2,100
At least 17.5 but less than 18.5	2,600
At least 16.5 but less than 17.5	3,000

At least 15.5 but less than 16.5	3,700
At least 14.5 but less than 15.5	4,500
At least 13.5 but less than 14.5	5,400
At least 12.5 but less than 13.5	6,400
Less than 12.5	7,700

Medical devices	2.3% of sales price of taxable medical devices; tax suspended for sales in 2016-2019**
Indoor tanning	10% of amount paid for services
Branded prescription drugs	Annual fee on "covered entities"
Health insurance policies and self-insured health plans	Annual fee, for policy or plan years before 10/1/2019
Health Insurance providers	Annual fee on "covered entities;" fee suspended for 2017 and 2019 **

* Special rates apply to diesel fuel used in certain buses and trains.
** Check tax.thomsonreuters.com/federaltaxhandbookupdates to see if the above provision has been extended.

¶ 1118   Applicable Federal Rates.

The IRS tables below show the Applicable one-month Federal Rates (AFRs). The tables provide short-term (obligations not exceeding three years), mid-term (over three years but not over nine years) and long-term (over nine years) rates (in percentages) based on annual, semiannual, quarterly and monthly compounding assumptions. [7]

Applicable Federal Rate (AFR)	Annual	Semi-annual	Quarterly	Monthly
November 2018				
Short-Term				
AFR	2.70%	2.68%	2.67%	2.67%
110% AFR	2.97%	2.95%	2.94%	2.93%
120% AFR	3.25%	3.22%	3.21%	3.20%
130% AFR	3.51%	3.48%	3.46%	3.46%
Mid-Term				
AFR	3.04%	3.02%	3.01%	3.00%
110% AFR	3.35%	3.32%	3.31%	3.30%
120% AFR	3.65%	3.62%	3.60%	3.59%
130% AFR	3.97%	3.93%	3.91%	3.90%
150% AFR	4.58%	4.53%	4.50%	4.49%
175% AFR	5.36%	5.29%	5.26%	5.23%
Long-Term				
AFR	3.22%	3.19%	3.18%	3.17%
110% AFR	3.54%	3.51%	3.49%	3.48%
120% AFR	3.87%	3.83%	3.81%	3.80%
130% AFR	4.19%	4.15%	4.13%	4.11%
October 2018				
Short-Term				
AFR	2.55%	2.53%	2.52%	2.52%
110% AFR	2.80%	2.78%	2.77%	2.76%
120% AFR	3.06%	3.04%	3.03%	3.02%
130% AFR	3.32%	3.29%	3.28%	3.27%
Mid-Term				
AFR	2.83%	2.81%	2.80%	2.79%
110% AFR	3.11%	3.09%	3.08%	3.07%

Applicable Federal Rate (AFR)	Annual	Semi-annual	Quarterly	Monthly
120% AFR	3.40%	3.37%	3.36%	3.35%
130% AFR	3.68%	3.65%	3.63%	3.62%
150% AFR	4.26%	4.22%	4.20%	4.18%
175% AFR	4.98%	4.92%	4.89%	4.87%
Long-Term				
AFR	2.99%	2.97%	2.96%	2.95%
110% AFR	3.30%	3.27%	3.26%	3.25%
120% AFR	3.59%	3.56%	3.54%	3.53%
130% AFR	3.90%	3.86%	3.84%	3.83%
September 2018				
Short-Term				
AFR	2.51%	2.49%	2.48%	2.48%
110% AFR	2.76%	2.74%	2.73%	2.72%
120% AFR	3.01%	2.99%	2.98%	2.97%
130% AFR	3.27%	3.24%	3.23%	3.22%
Mid-Term				
AFR	2.86%	2.84%	2.83%	2.82%
110% AFR	3.14%	3.12%	3.11%	3.10%
120% AFR	3.44%	3.41%	3.40%	3.39%
130% AFR	3.72%	3.69%	3.67%	3.66%
150% AFR	4.31%	4.26%	4.24%	4.22%
175% AFR	5.03%	4.97%	4.94%	4.92%
Long-Term				
AFR	3.02%	3.00%	2.99%	2.98%
110% AFR	3.33%	3.30%	3.29%	3.28%
120% AFR	3.63%	3.60%	3.58%	3.57%
130% AFR	3.94%	3.90%	3.88%	3.87%

7. ¶J-4192; ¶12,714.01

Applicable Federal Rate (AFR)	Annual	Semi-annual	Quarterly	Monthly
August 2018 *Short-Term*				
AFR	2.42%	2.41%	2.40%	2.40%
110% AFR	2.67%	2.65%	2.64%	2.64%
120% AFR	2.91%	2.89%	2.88%	2.87%
130% AFR	3.15%	3.13%	3.12%	3.11%
Mid-Term				
AFR	2.80%	2.78%	2.77%	2.76%
110% AFR	3.08%	3.06%	3.05%	3.04%
120% AFR	3.37%	3.34%	3.33%	3.32%
130% AFR	3.64%	3.61%	3.59%	3.58%
150% AFR	4.21%	4.17%	4.15%	4.13%
175% AFR	4.93%	4.87%	4.84%	4.82%
Long-Term				
AFR	2.95%	2.93%	2.92%	2.91%
110% AFR	3.25%	3.22%	3.21%	3.20%
120% AFR	3.55%	3.52%	3.50%	3.49%
130% AFR	3.85%	3.81%	3.79%	3.78%
July 2018 *Short Term*				
AFR	2.38%	2.37%	2.36%	2.36%
110% AFR	2.63%	2.61%	2.60%	2.60%
120% AFR	2.86%	2.84%	2.83%	2.82%
130% AFR	3.10%	3.08%	3.07%	3.06%
Mid-Term				
AFR	2.87%	2.85%	2.84%	2.83%
110% AFR	3.16%	3.14%	3.13%	3.12%
120% AFR	3.45%	3.42%	3.41%	3.40%
130% AFR	3.74%	3.71%	3.69%	3.68%
150% AFR	4.33%	4.28%	4.26%	4.24%
175% AFR	5.05%	4.99%	4.96%	4.94%
Long-Term				
AFR	3.06%	3.04%	3.03%	3.02%
110% AFR	3.37%	3.34%	3.33%	3.32%
120% AFR	3.68%	3.65%	3.63%	3.62%
130% AFR	3.99%	3.95%	3.93%	3.92%
June 2018 *Short Term*				
AFR	2.34%	2.33%	2.32%	2.32%
110% AFR	2.58%	2.56%	2.55%	2.55%
120% AFR	2.81%	2.80%	2.79%	2.78%
130% AFR	3.05%	3.03%	3.02%	3.01%
Mid-Term				
AFR	2.86%	2.84%	2.83%	2.82%
110% AFR	3.14%	3.12%	3.11%	3.10%
120% AFR	3.44%	3.41%	3.40%	3.39%
130% AFR	3.72%	3.69%	3.67%	3.66%
150% AFR	4.31%	4.26%	4.24%	4.22%
175% AFR	5.03%	4.97%	4.94%	4.92%
Long-Term				
AFR	3.05%	3.03%	3.02%	3.01%
110% AFR	3.36%	3.33%	3.32%	3.31%
120% AFR	3.67%	3.64%	3.62%	3.61%
130% AFR	3.98%	3.94%	3.92%	3.91%
May 2018 *Short-Term*				
AFR	2.18%	2.17%	2.16%	2.16%
110% AFR	2.40%	2.39%	2.38%	2.38%
120% AFR	2.62%	2.60%	2.59%	2.59%
130% AFR	2.84%	2.82%	2.81%	2.80%
Mid-Term				
AFR	2.69%	2.67%	2.66%	2.66%
110% AFR	2.96%	2.94%	2.93%	2.92%
120% AFR	3.23%	3.20%	3.19%	3.18%
130% AFR	3.50%	3.47%	3.46%	3.45%
150% AFR	4.05%	4.01%	3.99%	3.98%
175% AFR	4.72%	4.67%	4.64%	4.63%

Applicable Federal Rate (AFR)	Annual	Semi-annual	Quarterly	Monthly
Long-Term				
AFR	2.94%	2.92%	2.91%	2.90%
110% AFR	3.24%	3.21%	3.20%	3.19%
120% AFR	3.53%	3.50%	3.48%	3.47%
130% AFR	3.84%	3.80%	3.78%	3.77%
April 2018 *Short-Term*				
AFR	2.12%	2.11%	2.10%	2.10%
110% AFR	2.33%	2.32%	2.31%	2.31%
120% AFR	2.55%	2.53%	2.52%	2.52%
130% AFR	2.76%	2.74%	2.73%	2.72%
Mid-Term				
AFR	2.72%	2.70%	2.69%	2.68%
110% AFR	2.99%	2.97%	2.96%	2.95%
120% AFR	3.27%	3.24%	3.23%	3.22%
130% AFR	3.54%	3.51%	3.49%	3.48%
150% AFR	4.09%	4.05%	4.03%	4.02%
175% AFR	4.79%	4.73%	4.70%	4.68%
Long-Term				
AFR	3.04%	3.02%	3.01%	3.00%
110% AFR	3.35%	3.32%	3.31%	3.30%
120% AFR	3.65%	3.62%	3.60%	3.59%
130% AFR	3.97%	3.93%	3.91%	3.90%
March 2018 *Short-Term*				
AFR	1.96%	1.95%	1.95%	1.94%
110% AFR	2.16%	2.15%	2.14%	2.14%
120% AFR	2.35%	2.34%	2.33%	2.33%
130% AFR	2.56%	2.54%	2.53%	2.53%
Mid-Term				
AFR	2.57%	2.55%	2.54%	2.54%
110% AFR	2.83%	2.81%	2.80%	2.79%
120% AFR	3.08%	3.06%	3.05%	3.04%
130% AFR	3.35%	3.32%	3.31%	3.30%
150% AFR	3.87%	3.82%	3.81%	3.80%
175% AFR	4.51%	4.46%	4.44%	4.42%
Long-Term				
AFR	2.88%	2.86%	2.85%	2.84%
110% AFR	3.17%	3.15%	3.14%	3.13%
120% AFR	3.46%	3.43%	3.42%	3.41%
130% AFR	3.75%	3.72%	3.70%	3.69%
February 2018 *Short-Term*				
AFR	1.81%	1.80%	1.80%	1.79%
110% AFR	1.99%	1.98%	1.98%	1.97%
120% AFR	2.17%	2.16%	2.15%	2.15%
130% AFR	2.35%	2.34%	2.33%	2.33%
Mid-Term				
AFR	2.31%	2.30%	2.29%	2.29%
110% AFR	2.55%	2.53%	2.52%	2.52%
120% AFR	2.78%	2.76%	2.75%	2.74%
130% AFR	3.01%	2.99%	2.98%	2.97%
150% AFR	3.48%	3.45%	3.44%	3.43%
175% AFR	4.07%	4.03%	4.01%	4.00%
Long-Term				
AFR	2.66%	2.64%	2.63%	2.63%
110% AFR	2.92%	2.90%	2.89%	2.88%
120% AFR	3.20%	3.17%	3.16%	3.15%
130% AFR	3.46%	3.43%	3.42%	3.41%
January 2018 *Short-Term*				
AFR	1.68%	1.67%	1.67%	1.66%
110% AFR	1.85%	1.84%	1.84%	1.83%
120% AFR	2.01%	2.00%	2.00%	1.99%
130% AFR	2.18%	2.17%	2.16%	2.16%

Applicable Federal Rate (AFR)	Annual	Semi-annual	Quarterly	Monthly	Applicable Federal Rate (AFR)	Annual	Semi-annual	Quarterly	Monthly
					110% AFR	1.67%	1.66%	1.66%	1.65%
					120% AFR	1.82%	1.81%	1.81%	1.80%
		Mid-Term			130% AFR	1.97%	1.96%	1.96%	1.95%
AFR	2.18%	2.17%	2.16%	2.16%			*Mid-Term*		
110% AFR	2.40%	2.39%	2.38%	2.38%					
120% AFR	2.62%	2.60%	2.59%	2.59%	AFR	2.11%	2.10%	2.09%	2.09%
130% AFR	2.84%	2.82%	2.81%	2.80%	110% AFR	2.32%	2.31%	2.30%	2.30%
150% AFR	3.29%	3.26%	3.25%	3.24%	120% AFR	2.54%	2.52%	2.51%	2.51%
175% AFR	3.84%	3.80%	3.78%	3.77%	130% AFR	2.75%	2.73%	2.72%	2.71%
					150% AFR	3.17%	3.15%	3.14%	3.13%
		Long-Term			175% AFR	3.71%	3.68%	3.66%	3.65%
AFR	2.59%	2.57%	2.56%	2.56%			*Long-Term*		
110% AFR	2.85%	2.83%	2.82%	2.81%					
120% AFR	3.10%	3.08%	3.07%	3.06%	AFR	2.64%	2.62%	2.61%	2.61%
130% AFR	3.37%	3.34%	3.33%	3.32%	110% AFR	2.90%	2.88%	2.87%	2.86%
					120% AFR	3.16%	3.14%	3.13%	3.12%
		December 2017			130% AFR	3.44%	3.41%	3.40%	3.39%
		Short-Term							
AFR	1.52%	1.51%	1.51%	1.51%					

¶ 1119 MACRS Tables. ▬▬▬▬▬▬

Here are MACRS depreciation (cost recovery) tables.

The tables reproduced are the MACRS tables (general depreciation as well as alternative depreciation system (ADS)), plus the listed property tables used to determine income inclusion amounts by lessees of listed property other than automobiles. The depreciation amounts for automobiles under the luxury auto restrictions are carried at ¶1951; the income inclusion amounts for lessees of automobiles carried at ¶1120 are explained at ¶1954 *et seq.*

Under the general depreciation system (GDS) of MACRS, the table rates are based on: (1) the 200% declining balance method for 3-, 5-, 7-, and 10-year personal property; (2) the 150% declining balance method for 15- and 20-year personal property; and (3) the straight-line method for residential and nonresidential realty. Under the alternative depreciation system (ADS) of MACRS, the table rates for personal and real property are based on the straight-line method. The use of the tables is discussed in ¶1912. (IRS alternative minimum tax tables and the tables for straight line depreciation under the midquarter convention are not reproduced in this Handbook. For those tables, see the Appendix to Federal Tax Coordinator 2d Chapter L-7400.)

Table 1
General Depreciation System
Applicable Depreciation Method: 200 or 150 Percent
Declining Balance Switching to Straight Line
Applicable Recovery Periods: 3, 5, 7, 10, 15, 20 years
Applicable Convention: Half-year

If the Recovery Year is:	and the Recovery Period is:					
	3-year	5-year	7-year	10-year	15-year	20-year
			the Depreciation Rate is:			
1	33.33	20.00	14.29	10.00	5.00	3.750
2	44.45	32.00	24.49	18.00	9.50	7.219
3	14.81	19.20	17.49	14.40	8.55	6.677
4	7.41	11.52	12.49	11.52	7.70	6.177
5		11.52	8.93	9.22	6.93	5.713
6		5.76	8.92	7.37	6.23	5.285
7			8.93	6.55	5.90	4.888
8			4.46	6.55	5.90	4.522
9				6.56	5.91	4.462
10				6.55	5.90	4.461

Table 1

General Depreciation System
Applicable Depreciation Method: 200 or 150 Percent
Declining Balance Switching to Straight Line
Applicable Recovery Periods: 3, 5, 7, 10, 15, 20 years
Applicable Convention: Half-year
(continued)

11	3.28	5.91	4.462
12		5.90	4.461
13		5.91	4.462
14		5.90	4.461
15		5.91	4.462
16		2.95	4.461
17			4.462
18			4.461
19			4.462
20			4.461
21			2.231

Table 2

General Depreciation System
Applicable Depreciation Method: 200 or 150 Percent
Declining Balance Switching to Straight Line
Applicable Recovery Periods: 3, 5, 7, 10, 15, 20 years
Applicable Convention: Mid-quarter
(property placed in service in first quarter)

If the Recovery Year is:	and the Recovery Period is:					
	3-year	5-year	7-year	10-year	15-year	20-year
	the Depreciation Rate is:					
1	58.33	35.00	25.00	17.50	8.75	6.563
2	27.78	26.00	21.43	16.50	9.13	7.000
3	12.35	15.60	15.31	13.20	8.21	6.482
4	1.54	11.01	10.93	10.56	7.39	5.996
5		11.01	8.75	8.45	6.65	5.546
6		1.38	8.74	6.76	5.99	5.130
7			8.75	6.55	5.90	4.746
8			1.09	6.55	5.91	4.459
9				6.56	5.90	4.459
10				6.55	5.91	4.459
11				0.82	5.90	4.459
12					5.91	4.460
13					5.90	4.459
14					5.91	4.460
15					5.90	4.459
16					0.74	4.460
17						4.459
18						4.460
19						4.459
20						4.460
21						0.557

Table 3

General Depreciation System
Applicable Depreciation Method: 200 or 150 Percent
Declining Balance Switching to Straight Line
Applicable Recovery Periods: 3, 5, 7, 10, 15, 20 years
Applicable Convention: Mid-quarter
(property placed in service in second quarter)

If the Recovery Year is:	and the Recovery Period is:					
	3-year	5-year	7-year	10-year	15-year	20-year
			the Depreciation Rate is:			
1	41.67	25.00	17.85	12.50	6.25	4.688
2	38.89	30.00	23.47	17.50	9.38	7.148
3	14.14	18.00	16.76	14.00	8.44	6.612
4	5.30	11.37	11.97	11.20	7.59	6.116
5		11.37	8.87	8.96	6.83	5.658
6		4.26	8.87	7.17	6.15	5.233
7			8.87	6.55	5.91	4.841
8			3.33	6.55	5.90	4.478
9				6.56	5.91	4.463
10				6.55	5.90	4.463
11				2.46	5.91	4.463
12					5.90	4.463
13					5.91	4.463
14					5.90	4.463
15					5.91	4.462
16					2.21	4.463
17						4.462
18						4.463
19						4.462
20						4.463
21						1.673

Table 4
General Depreciation System
**Applicable Depreciation Method: 200 or 150 Percent
Declining Balance Switching to Straight Line
Applicable Recovery Periods: 3, 5, 7, 10, 15, 20 years
Applicable Convention: Mid-quarter
(property placed in service in third quarter)**

If the Recovery Year is:	and the Recovery Period is:					
	3-year	5-year	7-year	10-year	15-year	20-year
			the Depreciation Rate is:			
1	25.00	15.00	10.71	7.50	3.75	2.813
2	50.00	34.00	25.51	18.50	9.63	7.289
3	16.67	20.40	18.22	14.80	8.66	6.742
4	8.33	12.24	13.02	11.84	7.80	6.237
5		11.30	9.30	9.47	7.02	5.769
6		7.06	8.85	7.58	6.31	5.336
7			8.86	6.55	5.90	4.936
8			5.53	6.55	5.90	4.566
9				6.56	5.91	4.460
10				6.55	5.90	4.460
11				4.10	5.91	4.460
12					5.90	4.460
13					5.91	4.461
14					5.90	4.460
15					5.91	4.461
16					3.69	4.460
17						4.461
18						4.460
19						4.461
20						4.460
21						2.788

Table 5

General Depreciation System
Applicable Depreciation Method: 200 or 150 Percent
Declining Balance Switching to Straight Line
Applicable Recovery Periods: 3, 5, 7, 10, 15, 20 years
Applicable Convention: Mid-quarter
(property placed in service in fourth quarter)

If the Recovery Year is:	and the Recovery Period is:					
	3-year	5-year	7-year	10-year	15-year	20-year
			the Depreciation Rate is:			
1	8.33	5.00	3.57	2.50	1.25	0.938
2	61.11	38.00	27.55	19.50	9.88	7.430
3	20.37	22.80	19.68	15.60	8.89	6.872
4	10.19	13.68	14.06	12.48	8.00	6.357
5		10.94	10.04	9.98	7.20	5.880
6		9.58	8.73	7.99	6.48	5.439
7			8.73	6.55	5.90	5.031
8			7.64	6.55	5.90	4.654
9				6.56	5.90	4.458
10				6.55	5.91	4.458
11				5.74	5.90	4.458
12					5.91	4.458
13					5.90	4.458
14					5.91	4.458
15					5.90	4.458
16					5.17	4.458
17						4.458
18						4.459
19						4.458
20						4.459
21						3.901

Table 6

General Depreciation System
Applicable Depreciation Method: Straight Line
Applicable Recovery Period: 27.5 years
Applicable Convention: Mid-month

If the Recovery Year is:	And the Month in the First Recovery Year the Property is Placed in Service is:											
	1	2	3	4	5	6	7	8	9	10	11	12
						the Depreciation Rate is:						
1	3.485	3.182	2.879	2.576	2.273	1.970	1.667	1.364	1.061	0.758	0.455	0.152
2-9	3.636	3.636	3.636	3.636	3.636	3.636	3.636	3.636	3.636	3.636	3.636	3.636
10	3.637	3.637	3.637	3.637	3.637	3.637	3.636	3.636	3.636	3.636	3.636	3.636
11	3.636	3.636	3.636	3.636	3.636	3.636	3.637	3.637	3.637	3.637	3.637	3.637
12	3.637	3.637	3.637	3.637	3.637	3.637	3.636	3.636	3.636	3.636	3.636	3.636
13	3.636	3.636	3.636	3.636	3.636	3.636	3.637	3.637	3.637	3.637	3.637	3.637
14	3.637	3.637	3.637	3.637	3.637	3.637	3.636	3.636	3.636	3.636	3.636	3.636
15	3.636	3.636	3.636	3.636	3.636	3.636	3.637	3.637	3.637	3.637	3.637	3.637
16	3.637	3.637	3.637	3.637	3.637	3.637	3.636	3.636	3.636	3.636	3.636	3.636
17	3.636	3.636	3.636	3.636	3.636	3.636	3.637	3.637	3.637	3.637	3.637	3.637
18	3.637	3.637	3.637	3.637	3.637	3.637	3.636	3.636	3.636	3.636	3.636	3.636
19	3.636	3.636	3.636	3.636	3.636	3.636	3.637	3.637	3.637	3.637	3.637	3.637
20	3.637	3.637	3.637	3.637	3.637	3.637	3.636	3.636	3.636	3.636	3.636	3.636
21	3.636	3.636	3.636	3.636	3.636	3.636	3.637	3.637	3.637	3.637	3.637	3.637
22	3.637	3.637	3.637	3.637	3.637	3.637	3.636	3.636	3.636	3.636	3.636	3.636
23	3.636	3.636	3.636	3.636	3.636	3.636	3.637	3.637	3.637	3.637	3.637	3.637
24	3.637	3.637	3.637	3.637	3.637	3.637	3.636	3.636	3.636	3.636	3.636	3.636
25	3.636	3.636	3.636	3.636	3.636	3.636	3.637	3.637	3.637	3.637	3.637	3.637
26	3.637	3.637	3.637	3.637	3.637	3.637	3.636	3.636	3.636	3.636	3.636	3.636
27	3.636	3.636	3.636	3.636	3.636	3.636	3.637	3.637	3.637	3.637	3.637	3.637
28	1.970	2.273	2.576	2.879	3.182	3.485	3.636	3.636	3.636	3.636	3.636	3.636
29	0.000	0.000	0.000	0.000	0.000	0.000	0.152	0.455	0.758	1.061	1.364	1.667

Table 7

General Depreciation System
Applicable Depreciation Method: Straight Line
Applicable Recovery Period: 31.5 years
Applicable Convention: Mid-month

If the Recovery Year is:	And the Month in the First Recovery Year the Property is Placed in Service is:											
	1	**2**	**3**	**4**	**5**	**6**	**7**	**8**	**9**	**10**	**11**	**12**
	the Depreciation Rate is:											
1	3.042	2.778	2.513	2.249	1.984	1.720	1.455	1.190	0.926	0.661	0.397	0.132
2-7	3.175	3.175	3.175	3.175	3.175	3.175	3.175	3.175	3.175	3.175	3.175	3.175
8	3.175	3.174	3.175	3.174	3.175	3.174	3.175	3.175	3.175	3.175	3.175	3.175
9	3.174	3.175	3.174	3.175	3.174	3.175	3.174	3.175	3.174	3.175	3.174	3.175
10	3.175	3.174	3.175	3.174	3.175	3.174	3.175	3.174	3.175	3.174	3.175	3.174
11	3.174	3.175	3.174	3.175	3.174	3.175	3.174	3.175	3.174	3.175	3.174	3.175
12	3.175	3.174	3.175	3.174	3.175	3.174	3.175	3.174	3.175	3.174	3.175	3.174
13	3.174	3.175	3.174	3.175	3.174	3.175	3.174	3.175	3.174	3.175	3.174	3.175
14	3.175	3.174	3.175	3.174	3.175	3.174	3.175	3.174	3.175	3.174	3.175	3.174
15	3.174	3.175	3.174	3.175	3.174	3.175	3.174	3.175	3.174	3.175	3.174	3.175
16	3.175	3.174	3.175	3.174	3.175	3.174	3.175	3.174	3.175	3.174	3.175	3.175
17	3.174	3.175	3.174	3.175	3.174	3.175	3.174	3.175	3.174	3.175	3.174	3.175
18	3.175	3.174	3.175	3.174	3.175	3.174	3.175	3.174	3.175	3.174	3.175	3.174
19	3.174	3.175	3.174	3.175	3.174	3.175	3.174	3.175	3.174	3.175	3.174	3.175
20	3.175	3.174	3.175	3.174	3.175	3.174	3.175	3.174	3.175	3.174	3.175	3.174
21	3.174	3.175	3.174	3.175	3.174	3.175	3.174	3.175	3.174	3.175	3.174	3.175
22	3.175	3.174	3.175	3.174	3.175	3.174	3.175	3.174	3.175	3.174	3.175	3.174
23	3.174	3.175	3.174	3.175	3.174	3.175	3.174	3.175	3.174	3.175	3.174	3.175
24	3.175	3.174	3.175	3.174	3.175	3.174	3.175	3.174	3.175	3.174	3.175	3.174
25	3.174	3.175	3.174	3.175	3.174	3.175	3.174	3.175	3.174	3.175	3.174	3.175
26	3.175	3.174	3.175	3.174	3.175	3.174	3.175	3.174	3.175	3.174	3.175	3.174
27	3.174	3.175	3.174	3.175	3.174	3.175	3.174	3.175	3.174	3.175	3.174	3.175
28	3.175	3.174	3.175	3.174	3.175	3.174	3.175	3.174	3.175	3.174	3.175	3.174
29	3.174	3.175	3.174	3.175	3.174	3.175	3.174	3.175	3.174	3.175	3.174	3.175
30	3.175	3.174	3.175	3.174	3.175	3.174	3.175	3.174	3.175	3.174	3.175	3.174
31	3.174	3.175	3.174	3.175	3.174	3.175	3.174	3.175	3.174	3.175	3.174	3.175
32	1.720	1.984	2.249	2.513	2.778	3.042	3.175	3.174	3.175	3.174	3.175	3.174
33	0.000	0.000	0.000	0.000	0.000	0.000	0.132	0.397	0.661	0.926	1.190	1.455

Table 7a

General Depreciation System
Applicable Depreciation Method: Straight Line
Applicable Recovery Period: 39 years
Applicable Convention: Mid-month

Year	Month property placed in service											
	1	**2**	**3**	**4**	**5**	**6**	**7**	**8**	**9**	**10**	**11**	**12**
1	2.461%	2.247%	2.033%	1.819%	1.605%	1.391%	1.177%	0.963%	0.749%	0.535%	0.321%	0.107%
2-39	2.564	2.564	2.564	2.564	2.564	2.564	2.564	2.564	2.564	2.564	2.564	2.564
40	0.107	0.321	0.535	0.749	0.963	1.177	1.391	1.605	1.819	2.033	2.247	2.461

Table 8

General and Alternative Depreciation Systems
Applicable Depreciation Method: Straight Line
Applicable Recovery Periods: 2.5-50 years
Applicable Convention: Half-year

If the Recovery Year is:	2.5	3.0	3.5	4.0	4.5	5.0	5.5	6.0	6.5	7.0	7.5	8.0	8.5	9.0	9.5	10.0
							the Depreciation Rate is:									
1	20.00	16.67	14.29	12.50	11.11	10.00	9.09	8.33	7.69	7.14	6.67	6.25	5.88	5.56	5.26	5.00
2	40.00	33.33	28.57	25.00	22.22	20.00	18.18	16.67	15.39	14.29	13.33	12.50	11.77	11.11	10.53	10.00
3	40.00	33.33	28.57	25.00	22.22	20.00	18.18	16.67	15.38	14.29	13.33	12.50	11.76	11.11	10.53	10.00
4		16.67	28.57	25.00	22.23	20.00	18.18	16.67	15.39	14.28	13.33	12.50	11.77	11.11	10.53	10.00
5				12.50	22.22	20.00	18.19	16.66	15.38	14.29	13.34	12.50	11.76	11.11	10.52	10.00
6						10.00	18.18	16.67	15.39	14.28	13.33	12.50	11.77	11.11	10.53	10.00
7								8.33	15.38	14.29	13.34	12.50	11.76	11.11	10.52	10.00
8										7.14	13.33	12.50	11.77	11.11	10.53	10.00
9												6.25	11.76	11.11	10.52	10.00
10														5.56	10.53	10.00
11																5.00

If the Recovery Year is:	10.5	11.0	11.5	12.0	12.5	13.0	13.5	14.0	14.5	15.0	15.5	16.0	16.5	17.0	17.5	18.0
							the Depreciation Rate is:									
1	4.76	4.55	4.35	4.17	4.00	3.85	3.70	3.57	3.45	3.33	3.23	3.13	3.03	2.94	2.86	2.78
2	9.52	9.09	8.70	8.33	8.00	7.69	7.41	7.14	6.90	6.67	6.45	6.25	6.06	5.88	5.71	5.56
3	9.52	9.09	8.70	8.33	8.00	7.69	7.41	7.14	6.90	6.67	6.45	6.25	6.06	5.88	5.71	5.56
4	9.53	9.09	8.69	8.33	8.00	7.69	7.41	7.14	6.90	6.67	6.45	6.25	6.06	5.88	5.71	5.55
5	9.52	9.09	8.70	8.33	8.00	7.69	7.41	7.14	6.90	6.67	6.45	6.25	6.06	5.88	5.72	5.56
6	9.53	9.09	8.69	8.33	8.00	7.69	7.41	7.14	6.89	6.67	6.45	6.25	6.06	5.88	5.71	5.55
7	9.52	9.09	8.70	8.34	8.00	7.69	7.41	7.14	6.90	6.67	6.45	6.25	6.06	5.88	5.72	5.56
8	9.53	9.09	8.69	8.33	8.00	7.69	7.41	7.15	6.89	6.66	6.45	6.25	6.06	5.88	5.71	5.55
9	9.52	9.09	8.70	8.34	8.00	7.69	7.41	7.14	6.90	6.67	6.45	6.25	6.06	5.88	5.72	5.56
10	9.53	9.09	8.69	8.33	8.00	7.70	7.40	7.15	6.89	6.66	6.45	6.25	6.06	5.88	5.71	5.55
11	9.52	9.09	8.70	8.34	8.00	7.69	7.41	7.14	6.90	6.67	6.45	6.25	6.06	5.89	5.72	5.56
12		4.55	8.69	8.33	8.00	7.70	7.40	7.15	6.89	6.66	6.45	6.25	6.06	5.88	5.71	5.55
13				4.17	8.00	7.69	7.41	7.14	6.90	6.67	6.45	6.25	6.06	5.89	5.72	5.56
14						3.85	7.40	7.15	6.89	6.66	6.46	6.25	6.06	5.88	5.71	5.55
15							3.57	6.90	6.67	6.45	6.25	6.06	5.89	5.72	5.56
16									3.33	6.46	6.25	6.06	5.88	5.71	5.55
17										3.12	6.07	5.89	5.72	5.56
18												2.94	5.71	5.55
19														2.78

Table 8

General and Alternative Depreciation Systems
Applicable Depreciation Method: Straight Line
Applicable Recovery Periods: 2.5-50 years
Applicable Convention: Half-year
(continued)

If the Recovery Year is:	18.5	19.0	19.5	20.0	20.5	21.0	21.5	22.0	22.5	23.0	23.5	24.0	24.5	25.0	25.5	26.0
							and the Recovery Period is:									
							the Depreciation Rate is:									
1	2.70	2.63	2.56	2.500	2.439	2.381	2.326	2.273	2.222	2.174	2.128	2.083	2.041	2.000	1.961	1.923
2	5.41	5.26	5.13	5.000	4.878	4.762	4.651	4.545	4.444	4.348	4.255	4.167	4.082	4.000	3.922	3.846
3	5.41	5.26	5.13	5.000	4.878	4.762	4.651	4.545	4.444	4.348	4.255	4.167	4.082	4.000	3.922	3.846
4	5.41	5.26	5.13	5.000	4.878	4.762	4.651	4.545	4.445	4.348	4.255	4.167	4.082	4.000	3.922	3.846
5	5.40	5.26	5.13	5.000	4.878	4.762	4.651	4.546	4.444	4.348	4.255	4.167	4.082	4.000	3.922	3.846
6	5.41	5.26	5.13	5.000	4.878	4.762	4.651	4.545	4.445	4.348	4.255	4.167	4.082	4.000	3.921	3.846
7	5.40	5.26	5.13	5.000	4.878	4.762	4.651	4.546	4.444	4.348	4.255	4.167	4.082	4.000	3.922	3.846
8	5.41	5.26	5.13	5.000	4.878	4.762	4.651	4.545	4.445	4.348	4.255	4.167	4.082	4.000	3.921	3.846
9	5.40	5.27	5.13	5.000	4.878	4.762	4.651	4.546	4.444	4.348	4.255	4.167	4.081	4.000	3.922	3.846
10	5.41	5.26	5.13	5.000	4.878	4.762	4.651	4.545	4.445	4.348	4.255	4.167	4.082	4.000	3.921	3.846
11	5.40	5.27	5.13	5.000	4.878	4.762	4.651	4.546	4.444	4.348	4.256	4.166	4.081	4.000	3.922	3.846
12	5.41	5.26	5.13	5.000	4.878	4.762	4.651	4.545	4.445	4.348	4.255	4.167	4.082	4.000	3.921	3.846
13	5.40	5.27	5.13	5.000	4.878	4.762	4.651	4.546	4.444	4.348	4.256	4.166	4.081	4.000	3.922	3.846
14	5.41	5.26	5.13	5.000	4.878	4.762	4.651	4.510	4.445	4.348	4.255	4.167	4.082	4.000	3.921	3.846
15	5.40	5.27	5.13	5.000	4.878	4.762	4.651	4.510	4.444	4.348	4.256	4.166	4.081	4.000	3.922	3.846
16	5.41	5.26	5.12	5.000	4.878	4.762	4.651	4.545	4.445	4.348	4.255	4.167	4.082	4.000	3.921	3.846
17	5.40	5.27	5.13	5.000	4.878	4.762	4.652	4.546	4.444	4.347	4.256	4.166	4.081	4.000	3.922	3.846
18	5.41	5.26	5.12	5.000	4.878	4.762	4.651	4.545	4.445	4.348	4.255	4.167	4.082	4.000	3.921	3.846
19	5.40	5.27	5.13	5.000	4.878	4.761	4.652	4.546	4.444	4.347	4.256	4.167	4.081	4.000	3.922	3.846
20		2.63	5.12	5.000	4.879	4.762	4.651	4.545	4.445	4.348	4.255	4.167	4.082	4.000	3.921	3.847
21				2.500	4.878	4.761	4.652	4.546	4.444	4.347	4.256	4.166	4.081	4.000	3.922	3.846
22						2.381	4.651	4.545	4.445	4.348	4.255	4.082	4.081	4.000	3.921	3.847
23								2.273	4.444	4.347	4.256	4.166	4.081	4.000	3.922	3.846
24										2.174	4.255	4.167	4.082	4.000	3.921	3.847
25												2.083	4.081	4.000	3.922	3.846
26														2.000	3.921	3.846
27																1.923

Table 8

General and Alternative Depreciation Systems
Applicable Depreciation Method: Straight Line
Applicable Recovery Periods: 2.5-50 years
Applicable Convention: Half-year
(continued)

If the Recovery Year is:	and the Recovery Period is:															
	26.5	27.0	27.5	28.0	28.5	29.0	29.5	30.0	30.5	31.0	31.5	32.0	32.5	33.0	33.5	34.0
	the Depreciation Rate is:															
1	1.887	1.852	1.818	1.786	1.754	1.724	1.695	1.667	1.639	1.613	1.587	1.563	1.538	1.515	1.493	1.471
2-6	3.774	3.704	3.636	3.571	3.509	3.448	3.390	3.333	3.279	3.226	3.175	3.125	3.077	3.030	2.985	2.941
7	3.773	3.704	3.636	3.572	3.509	3.448	3.390	3.333	3.279	3.226	3.175	3.125	3.077	3.030	2.985	2.941
8	3.774	3.704	3.636	3.571	3.509	3.448	3.390	3.333	3.279	3.226	3.175	3.125	3.077	3.030	2.985	2.941
9	3.773	3.704	3.637	3.572	3.509	3.448	3.390	3.333	3.279	3.226	3.175	3.125	3.077	3.030	2.985	2.941
10	3.774	3.704	3.636	3.571	3.509	3.448	3.390	3.333	3.279	3.226	3.174	3.125	3.077	3.030	2.985	2.941
11	3.773	3.704	3.637	3.572	3.509	3.448	3.390	3.333	3.279	3.226	3.175	3.125	3.077	3.030	2.985	2.941
12	3.774	3.704	3.636	3.571	3.509	3.448	3.390	3.333	3.279	3.226	3.174	3.125	3.077	3.030	2.985	2.941
13	3.773	3.703	3.637	3.572	3.509	3.448	3.390	3.334	3.279	3.226	3.175	3.125	3.077	3.030	2.985	2.941
14	3.773	3.704	3.636	3.571	3.509	3.448	3.390	3.333	3.279	3.226	3.174	3.125	3.077	3.030	2.985	2.941
15	3.774	3.703	3.637	3.572	3.509	3.449	3.390	3.334	3.278	3.226	3.175	3.125	3.077	3.031	2.985	2.941
16	3.773	3.704	3.636	3.571	3.509	3.448	3.390	3.333	3.279	3.226	3.174	3.125	3.077	3.030	2.985	2.941
17	3.774	3.703	3.637	3.572	3.509	3.449	3.390	3.334	3.278	3.226	3.175	3.125	3.077	3.031	2.985	2.941
18	3.773	3.704	3.636	3.571	3.508	3.448	3.390	3.333	3.279	3.226	3.174	3.125	3.077	3.030	2.985	2.941
19	3.774	3.703	3.637	3.572	3.509	3.449	3.390	3.334	3.278	3.226	3.175	3.125	3.077	3.031	2.985	2.941
20	3.773	3.704	3.636	3.571	3.508	3.448	3.390	3.333	3.279	3.226	3.174	3.125	3.077	3.030	2.985	2.941
21	3.774	3.703	3.637	3.572	3.509	3.449	3.389	3.334	3.278	3.225	3.175	3.125	3.077	3.031	2.985	2.941
22	3.773	3.704	3.636	3.571	3.508	3.448	3.390	3.333	3.279	3.226	3.174	3.125	3.077	3.030	2.985	2.941
23	3.774	3.703	3.637	3.572	3.509	3.449	3.389	3.334	3.278	3.225	3.175	3.125	3.077	3.031	2.985	2.941
24	3.773	3.704	3.636	3.571	3.508	3.448	3.390	3.333	3.279	3.226	3.174	3.125	3.077	3.030	2.985	2.941
25	3.774	3.703	3.637	3.572	3.509	3.449	3.389	3.334	3.278	3.225	3.175	3.125	3.077	3.031	2.985	2.942
26	3.773	3.704	3.636	3.571	3.508	3.448	3.390	3.333	3.279	3.226	3.174	3.125	3.077	3.030	2.985	2.941
27	3.774	3.703	3.637	3.572	3.509	3.449	3.389	3.334	3.278	3.225	3.175	3.125	3.077	3.031	2.985	2.942
28		1.852	3.636	3.571	3.508	3.448	3.390	3.333	3.279	3.226	3.174	3.125	3.077	3.030	2.985	2.941
29			1.786	3.509	3.449	3.389	3.334	3.278	3.225	3.175	3.125	3.077	3.031	2.985	2.942
30					1.724	3.390	3.333	3.279	3.226	3.174	3.125	3.077	3.030	2.985	2.941
31						1.667	3.278	3.225	3.175	3.125	3.076	3.031	2.986	2.942
32							1.613	3.174	3.125	3.077	3.030	2.985	2.941
33								1.562	3.076	3.031	2.986	2.942
34									1.515	2.985	2.941
35										1.471

Table 8

General and Alternative Depreciation Systems
Applicable Depreciation Method: Straight Line
Applicable Recovery Periods: 2.5-50 years
Applicable Convention: Half-year
(continued)

If the Recovery Year is:	and the Recovery Period is: 34.5	35.0	35.5	36.0	36.5	37.0	37.5	38.0	38.5	39.0	39.5	40.0	40.5	41.0	41.5	42.0
	the Depreciation Rate is:															
1	1.449	1.429	1.408	1.389	1.370	1.351	1.333	1.316	1.299	1.282	1.266	1.250	1.235	1.220	1.205	1.190
2	2.899	2.857	2.817	2.778	2.740	2.703	2.667	2.632	2.597	2.564	2.532	2.500	2.469	2.439	2.410	2.381
3	2.899	2.857	2.817	2.778	2.740	2.703	2.667	2.632	2.597	2.564	2.532	2.500	2.469	2.439	2.410	2.381
4	2.899	2.857	2.817	2.778	2.740	2.703	2.667	2.632	2.597	2.564	2.532	2.500	2.469	2.439	2.410	2.381
5	2.899	2.857	2.817	2.778	2.740	2.703	2.667	2.632	2.597	2.564	2.532	2.500	2.469	2.439	2.410	2.381
6	2.899	2.857	2.817	2.778	2.740	2.703	2.667	2.632	2.597	2.564	2.532	2.500	2.469	2.439	2.410	2.381
7	2.898	2.857	2.817	2.778	2.740	2.703	2.667	2.632	2.597	2.564	2.532	2.500	2.469	2.439	2.410	2.381
8	2.899	2.857	2.817	2.778	2.740	2.703	2.667	2.631	2.597	2.564	2.532	2.500	2.469	2.439	2.410	2.381
9	2.898	2.857	2.817	2.778	2.740	2.703	2.667	2.632	2.597	2.564	2.532	2.500	2.469	2.439	2.410	2.381
10	2.899	2.857	2.817	2.778	2.740	2.703	2.667	2.631	2.598	2.564	2.532	2.500	2.469	2.439	2.410	2.381
11	2.898	2.857	2.817	2.778	2.740	2.703	2.667	2.632	2.597	2.564	2.532	2.500	2.469	2.439	2.410	2.381
12	2.899	2.857	2.817	2.778	2.740	2.703	2.667	2.631	2.598	2.564	2.532	2.500	2.469	2.439	2.410	2.381
13	2.898	2.857	2.817	2.778	2.740	2.703	2.667	2.632	2.597	2.564	2.532	2.500	2.469	2.439	2.410	2.381
14	2.899	2.857	2.817	2.778	2.740	2.703	2.667	2.631	2.598	2.564	2.531	2.500	2.469	2.439	2.409	2.381
15	2.898	2.857	2.817	2.778	2.740	2.703	2.666	2.632	2.597	2.564	2.532	2.500	2.469	2.439	2.410	2.381
16	2.899	2.857	2.817	2.778	2.740	2.703	2.667	2.631	2.598	2.564	2.531	2.500	2.469	2.439	2.409	2.381
17	2.898	2.857	2.817	2.778	2.740	2.703	2.666	2.632	2.597	2.564	2.532	2.500	2.469	2.439	2.410	2.381
18	2.899	2.857	2.817	2.778	2.740	2.702	2.667	2.631	2.598	2.564	2.531	2.500	2.469	2.439	2.409	2.381
19	2.898	2.857	2.817	2.778	2.739	2.703	2.666	2.632	2.597	2.564	2.532	2.500	2.469	2.439	2.410	2.381
20	2.898	2.857	2.817	2.778	2.740	2.702	2.667	2.631	2.598	2.564	2.531	2.500	2.469	2.439	2.409	2.381
21	2.899	2.857	2.817	2.778	2.739	2.703	2.666	2.632	2.597	2.564	2.532	2.500	2.469	2.439	2.410	2.381
22	2.898	2.857	2.817	2.777	2.740	2.702	2.667	2.631	2.598	2.564	2.531	2.500	2.469	2.439	2.409	2.381
23	2.899	2.857	2.817	2.778	2.739	2.703	2.666	2.632	2.597	2.564	2.532	2.500	2.469	2.439	2.410	2.381
24	2.898	2.857	2.817	2.777	2.740	2.702	2.667	2.631	2.598	2.564	2.531	2.500	2.469	2.439	2.409	2.381
25	2.899	2.857	2.817	2.778	2.739	2.703	2.666	2.632	2.597	2.564	2.532	2.500	2.469	2.439	2.410	2.381
26	2.898	2.857	2.817	2.777	2.740	2.702	2.667	2.631	2.598	2.564	2.531	2.500	2.469	2.439	2.409	2.381
27	2.899	2.857	2.817	2.778	2.739	2.703	2.666	2.632	2.597	2.564	2.532	2.500	2.469	2.439	2.410	2.381
28	2.898	2.857	2.817	2.777	2.740	2.702	2.667	2.631	2.598	2.564	2.531	2.500	2.469	2.439	2.409	2.381
29	2.899	2.857	2.817	2.778	2.739	2.703	2.666	2.632	2.597	2.564	2.532	2.500	2.469	2.439	2.410	2.381
30	2.898	2.858	2.817	2.777	2.740	2.702	2.667	2.631	2.598	2.564	2.531	2.500	2.469	2.439	2.409	2.381
31	2.899	2.857	2.817	2.778	2.739	2.703	2.666	2.632	2.597	2.564	2.532	2.500	2.469	2.439	2.410	2.381
32	2.898	2.858	2.816	2.777	2.740	2.702	2.667	2.631	2.598	2.564	2.531	2.500	2.470	2.439	2.409	2.381
33	2.899	2.857	2.817	2.778	2.739	2.703	2.666	2.632	2.597	2.565	2.532	2.500	2.469	2.439	2.410	2.381
34	2.898	2.858	2.816	2.777	2.740	2.702	2.667	2.631	2.598	2.564	2.531	2.500	2.470	2.439	2.409	2.381
35	2.899	2.857	2.817	2.778	2.739	2.703	2.666	2.632	2.597	2.565	2.532	2.500	2.469	2.439	2.410	2.381
36		1.429	2.816	2.777	2.740	2.702	2.667	2.631	2.598	2.564	2.531	2.500	2.470	2.439	2.409	2.381
37			1.389	2.739	2.703	2.666	2.632	2.597	2.565	2.532	2.500	2.469	2.439	2.410	2.381
38					1.351	2.667	2.631	2.598	2.564	2.531	2.500	2.469	2.439	2.410	2.381
39							1.316	2.597	2.565	2.532	2.500	2.469	2.439	2.410	2.381
40									1.282	2.531	2.500	2.470	2.439	2.409	2.381
41											1.250	2.409	2.439	2.410	2.380
42												1.220	2.409	2.410	2.381
43														1.190

Table 8

General and Alternative Depreciation Systems
Applicable Depreciation Method: Straight Line
Applicable Recovery Periods: 2.5-50 years
Applicable Convention: Half-year
(continued)

If the Recovery Year is:	and the Recovery Period is:															
	42.5	43.0	43.5	44.0	44.5	45.0	45.5	46.0	46.5	47.0	47.5	48.0	48.5	49.0	49.5	50.0
	the Depreciation Rate is:															
1	1.176	1.163	1.149	1.136	1.124	1.111	1.099	1.087	1.075	1.064	1.053	1.042	1.031	1.020	1.010	1.000
2	2.353	2.326	2.299	2.273	2.247	2.222	2.198	2.174	2.151	2.128	2.105	2.083	2.062	2.041	2.020	2.000
3	2.353	2.326	2.299	2.273	2.247	2.222	2.198	2.174	2.151	2.128	2.105	2.083	2.062	2.041	2.020	2.000
4	2.353	2.326	2.299	2.273	2.247	2.222	2.198	2.174	2.151	2.128	2.105	2.083	2.062	2.041	2.020	2.000
5	2.353	2.326	2.299	2.273	2.247	2.222	2.198	2.174	2.151	2.128	2.105	2.083	2.062	2.041	2.020	2.000
6	2.353	2.326	2.299	2.273	2.247	2.222	2.198	2.174	2.151	2.128	2.105	2.083	2.062	2.041	2.020	2.000
7	2.353	2.326	2.299	2.273	2.247	2.222	2.198	2.174	2.150	2.128	2.105	2.083	2.062	2.041	2.020	2.000
8	2.353	2.326	2.299	2.273	2.247	2.222	2.198	2.174	2.151	2.128	2.105	2.083	2.062	2.041	2.020	2.000
9	2.353	2.325	2.299	2.273	2.247	2.222	2.198	2.174	2.150	2.128	2.105	2.083	2.062	2.041	2.020	2.000
10	2.353	2.326	2.299	2.273	2.247	2.222	2.198	2.174	2.151	2.128	2.105	2.083	2.062	2.041	2.020	2.000
11	2.353	2.325	2.299	2.273	2.247	2.222	2.198	2.174	2.150	2.128	2.105	2.083	2.062	2.041	2.020	2.000
12	2.353	2.326	2.299	2.273	2.247	2.222	2.198	2.174	2.151	2.128	2.105	2.083	2.062	2.041	2.020	2.000
13	2.353	2.325	2.299	2.273	2.247	2.222	2.198	2.174	2.150	2.128	2.105	2.083	2.062	2.041	2.020	2.000
14	2.353	2.326	2.299	2.273	2.247	2.222	2.198	2.174	2.151	2.128	2.105	2.083	2.062	2.041	2.020	2.000
15	2.353	2.325	2.299	2.273	2.247	2.222	2.198	2.174	2.150	2.128	2.105	2.083	2.062	2.041	2.020	2.000
16	2.353	2.326	2.299	2.273	2.247	2.222	2.198	2.174	2.151	2.128	2.105	2.083	2.062	2.041	2.020	2.000
17	2.353	2.325	2.299	2.273	2.247	2.222	2.198	2.174	2.150	2.127	2.105	2.083	2.062	2.041	2.020	2.000
18	2.353	2.326	2.299	2.273	2.247	2.222	2.198	2.174	2.151	2.128	2.105	2.083	2.062	2.041	2.020	2.000
19	2.353	2.325	2.299	2.273	2.247	2.222	2.198	2.174	2.150	2.127	2.105	2.084	2.062	2.041	2.020	2.000
20	2.353	2.326	2.299	2.273	2.247	2.222	2.198	2.174	2.151	2.128	2.105	2.083	2.062	2.041	2.020	2.000
21	2.353	2.325	2.299	2.273	2.247	2.222	2.198	2.174	2.150	2.127	2.105	2.084	2.062	2.041	2.020	2.000
22	2.353	2.326	2.299	2.273	2.247	2.222	2.198	2.174	2.151	2.128	2.105	2.083	2.062	2.041	2.020	2.000
23	2.353	2.325	2.299	2.272	2.247	2.222	2.198	2.174	2.150	2.127	2.105	2.084	2.062	2.041	2.020	2.000
24	2.353	2.326	2.299	2.273	2.247	2.222	2.198	2.174	2.151	2.128	2.105	2.083	2.062	2.041	2.020	2.000
25	2.353	2.325	2.299	2.272	2.247	2.222	2.198	2.174	2.150	2.127	2.105	2.084	2.062	2.041	2.020	2.000
26	2.353	2.326	2.299	2.273	2.247	2.222	2.198	2.174	2.151	2.128	2.106	2.083	2.062	2.041	2.020	2.000
27	2.353	2.325	2.299	2.272	2.247	2.223	2.198	2.174	2.150	2.127	2.105	2.084	2.062	2.041	2.020	2.000
28	2.353	2.326	2.299	2.273	2.247	2.222	2.198	2.174	2.151	2.128	2.106	2.083	2.062	2.041	2.020	2.000
29	2.353	2.325	2.299	2.272	2.247	2.223	2.198	2.174	2.150	2.127	2.105	2.084	2.062	2.041	2.020	2.000
30	2.353	2.326	2.299	2.273	2.248	2.222	2.197	2.174	2.151	2.128	2.106	2.083	2.062	2.041	2.020	2.000
31	2.353	2.325	2.299	2.272	2.247	2.223	2.198	2.174	2.150	2.127	2.105	2.084	2.062	2.041	2.021	2.000
32	2.353	2.326	2.299	2.273	2.248	2.222	2.197	2.174	2.151	2.128	2.106	2.083	2.062	2.041	2.020	2.000
33	2.353	2.325	2.298	2.272	2.247	2.223	2.198	2.174	2.150	2.127	2.105	2.084	2.062	2.041	2.021	2.000
34	2.353	2.326	2.299	2.273	2.248	2.222	2.197	2.174	2.151	2.128	2.106	2.083	2.062	2.040	2.020	2.000
35	2.353	2.325	2.298	2.272	2.247	2.223	2.198	2.174	2.150	2.127	2.105	2.084	2.062	2.041	2.021	2.000
36	2.353	2.326	2.299	2.273	2.248	2.222	2.197	2.174	2.151	2.128	2.106	2.083	2.062	2.040	2.020	2.000
37	2.353	2.325	2.298	2.272	2.247	2.223	2.198	2.174	2.150	2.127	2.105	2.084	2.061	2.041	2.021	2.000
38	2.353	2.326	2.299	2.273	2.248	2.222	2.197	2.174	2.151	2.128	2.106	2.083	2.062	2.040	2.020	2.000
39	2.353	2.325	2.298	2.272	2.247	2.223	2.198	2.174	2.150	2.127	2.105	2.084	2.061	2.041	2.021	2.000
40	2.353	2.326	2.299	2.273	2.248	2.222	2.197	2.173	2.151	2.128	2.106	2.083	2.062	2.040	2.020	2.000
41	2.352	2.325	2.298	2.272	2.247	2.223	2.198	2.174	2.150	2.127	2.105	2.084	2.061	2.041	2.021	2.000
42	2.353	2.326	2.299	2.273	2.248	2.222	2.197	2.173	2.151	2.128	2.106	2.083	2.062	2.040	2.020	2.000
43	2.352	2.325	2.298	2.272	2.247	2.223	2.198	2.174	2.150	2.127	2.105	2.084	2.061	2.041	2.021	2.000
44		1.163	2.299	2.273	2.248	2.222	2.197	2.173	2.151	2.128	2.106	2.083	2.062	2.040	2.020	2.000
45				1.136	2.247	2.223	2.198	2.174	2.150	2.127	2.105	2.084	2.061	2.041	2.021	2.000
46						1.111	2.197	2.173	2.151	2.128	2.105	2.084	2.061	2.041	2.020	2.000
47								1.087	2.150	2.127	2.105	2.084	2.061	2.041	2.021	2.000
48										1.064	2.106	2.083	2.062	2.041	2.020	2.000
49												1.042	2.061	2.041	2.021	2.000
50														1.020	2.020	2.000
51																1.000

Table 9
Alternative Depreciation System
Applicable Depreciation Method: Straight Line
Applicable Recovery Period: 40 years
Applicable Convention: Mid-month

And the Month in the First Recovery Year the Property is Placed in Service is:

If the Recovery Year is:	1	2	3	4	5	6	7	8	9	10	11	12
						the Depreciation Rate is:						
1	2.396	2.188	1.979	1.771	1.563	1.354	1.146	0.938	0.729	0.521	0.313	0.104
2 to 40	2.500	2.500	2.500	2.500	2.500	2.500	2.500	2.500	2.500	2.500	2.500	2.500
41	0.104	0.312	0.521	0.729	0.937	1.146	1.354	1.562	1.771	1.979	2.187	2.396

Table I
Leased MACRS Business Listed Property

Income Inclusion Amounts — Step (1) Computation Rates — for Business Listed Property (Except Autos) Leased After '86 (Reg §1.280F-7(b)(2)(i)(C))

First Taxable Year During Lease in Which Business Use Percentage is 50% or Less

Type of Property	1	2	3	4	5	6	7	8	9	10	11	12 & Later
Property with a Recovery Period of Less Than 7 Years under the Alternative Depreciation System (Such as Computers, Trucks and Airplanes)	0.0%	10.0%	22.0%	21.2%	12.7%	12.7%	12.7%	12.7%	12.7%	12.7%	12.7%	12.7%
Property with a 7- to 10-Year Recovery Period under the Alternative Depreciation System (Such as Recreation Property)	0.0%	9.3%	23.8%	31.3%	33.8%	32.7%	31.6%	30.5%	25.0%	15.0%	15.0%	15.0%
Property with Recovery Period of more Than 10 Years under the Alternative Depreciation System (Such as Certain Property with No Class Life)	0.0%	10.1%	26.3%	35.4%	39.6%	40.2%	40.8%	41.4%	37.5%	29.2%	20.8%	12.5%

Table II
Leased MACRS Business Listed Property

Income Inclusion Amounts — Step (2) Computation Rates — for
Business Listed Property (Except Autos) Leased After '86
(Reg §1.280F-7(b)(2)(i)(C))

Type of Property	First Taxable Year During Lease in Which Business Use Percentage is 50% or Less											
	1	2	3	4	5	6	7	8	9	10	11	12 & Later
Property with a Recovery Period of Less Than 7 Years under Alternative Depreciation System (Such as Computers, Trucks and Airplanes)	2.1%	−7.2%	−19.8%	−20.1%	−12.4%	−12.4%	−12.4%	−12.4%	−12.4%	−12.4%	−12.4%	−12.4%
Property with a 7- to 10-Year Recovery Period under the Alternative Depreciation System (Such as Recreation Property)	3.9%	−3.8%	−17.7%	−25.1%	−27.8%	−27.2%	−27.1%	−27.6%	−23.7%	−14.7%	−14.7%	−14.7%
Property with a Recovery Period of More Than 10 Years under the Alternative Depreciation System (Such as Certain Property with No Class Life)	6.6%	−1.6%	−16.9%	−25.6%	−29.9%	−31.1%	−32.8%	−35.1%	−33.3%	−26.7%	−19.7%	−12.2%

¶ 1120   Income Inclusion Amounts for Autos, Trucks and Vans. ▰▰▰▰▰

REV. PROC. 2017-29 TABLE 5

DOLLAR AMOUNTS FOR PASSENGER AUTOMOBILES (THAT ARE NOT TRUCKS OR VANS) WITH A LEASE TERM BEGINNING IN CALENDAR YEAR 2017

Fair Market Value of Passenger Automobile		Tax Year During Lease				
Over	Not Over	1st	2nd	3rd	4th	5th & later
$19,000	$19,500	6	14	20	23	27
19,500	20,000	7	16	23	27	31
20,000	20,500	8	18	26	30	35
20,500	21,000	9	20	28	35	39
21,000	21,500	10	21	32	38	44
21,500	22,000	11	23	35	42	47
22,000	23,000	12	27	39	47	53
23,000	24,000	14	31	45	54	62
24,000	25,000	16	34	52	61	70
25,000	26,000	18	38	58	68	78
26,000	27,000	19	43	63	75	87
27,000	28,000	21	47	69	82	95
28,000	29,000	23	51	75	89	103
29,000	30,000	25	55	80	97	112
30,000	31,000	27	58	87	104	120
31,000	32,000	29	62	93	111	128
32,000	33,000	30	67	99	118	136
33,000	34,000	32	71	104	126	144
34,000	35,000	34	75	110	133	152
35,000	36,000	36	79	116	140	160
36,000	37,000	38	82	123	147	169
37,000	38,000	40	86	129	154	177
38,000	39,000	41	91	134	161	186
39,000	40,000	43	95	140	168	194
40,000	41,000	45	99	146	175	202
41,000	42,000	47	103	152	182	210
42,000	43,000	49	106	159	189	218
43,000	44,000	50	111	164	197	226
44,000	45,000	52	115	170	204	234
45,000	46,000	54	119	176	211	243
46,000	47,000	56	123	182	218	251
47,000	48,000	58	127	187	225	260
48,000	49,000	60	130	194	232	268
49,000	50,000	61	135	200	239	276
50,000	51,000	63	139	206	246	284
51,000	52,000	65	143	211	254	292
52,000	53,000	67	147	217	261	301
53,000	54,000	69	151	223	268	309
54,000	55,000	70	155	229	275	318
55,000	56,000	72	159	235	282	326
56,000	57,000	74	163	241	289	334
57,000	58,000	76	167	247	296	342
58,000	59,000	78	171	253	303	350
59,000	60,000	80	174	260	310	359
60,000	62,000	82	181	268	321	371

REV. PROC. 2017-29 TABLE 5

DOLLAR AMOUNTS FOR PASSENGER AUTOMOBILES
(THAT ARE NOT TRUCKS OR VANS)
WITH A LEASE TERM BEGINNING IN CALENDAR YEAR 2017

Fair Market Value of Passenger Automobile		Tax Year During Lease				
Over	Not Over	1st	2nd	3rd	4th	5th & later
62,000	64,000	86	189	280	335	387
64,000	66,000	90	197	292	349	404
66,000	68,000	93	205	304	364	420
68,000	70,000	97	213	315	379	436
70,000	72,000	101	221	327	393	453
72,000	74,000	104	229	339	407	470
74,000	76,000	108	237	351	421	486
76,000	78,000	111	245	363	436	502
78,000	80,000	115	253	375	450	518
80,000	85,000	122	267	396	474	548
85,000	90,000	131	287	425	511	588
90,000	95,000	140	307	455	546	630
95,000	100,000	149	327	485	581	671
100,000	110,000	162	357	530	635	733
110,000	120,000	181	397	589	706	815
120,000	130,000	199	437	649	777	898
130,000	140,000	217	477	708	849	980
140,000	150,000	235	517	768	920	1,062
150,000	160,000	254	557	827	991	1,145
160,000	170,000	272	597	887	1,062	1,227
170,000	180,000	290	637	946	1,134	1,309
180,000	190,000	308	677	1,006	1,205	1,391
190,000	200,000	326	718	1,064	1,277	1,473
200,000	210,000	345	757	1,124	1,348	1,556
210,000	220,000	363	797	1,184	1,419	1,638
220,000	230,000	381	837	1,244	1,490	1,721
230,000	240,000	399	878	1,302	1,562	1,803
240,000	and over	418	917	1,362	1,633	1,885

REV. PROC. 2017-29 TABLE 6

DOLLAR AMOUNTS FOR TRUCKS AND VANS
WITH A LEASE TERM BEGINNING IN CALENDAR YEAR 2017

Fair Market Value of Passenger Automobile		Tax Year During Lease				
Over	Not Over	1st	2nd	3rd	4th	5th & later
$19,500	$20,000	4	8	11	13	16
20,000	20,500	4	10	14	17	20
20,500	21,000	5	12	17	21	23
21,000	21,500	6	14	20	24	28
21,500	22,000	7	16	23	28	32
22,000	23,000	9	19	27	33	38
23,000	24,000	10	23	34	40	46
24,000	25,000	12	27	39	48	54
25,000	26,000	14	31	45	55	62
26,000	27,000	16	35	51	62	71
27,000	28,000	18	39	57	69	79
28,000	29,000	19	43	63	76	88
29,000	30,000	21	47	69	83	96
30,000	31,000	23	51	75	90	104
31,000	32,000	25	55	81	97	112
32,000	33,000	27	59	87	104	120
33,000	34,000	29	63	93	111	129
34,000	35,000	30	67	99	119	136
35,000	36,000	32	71	105	126	145
36,000	37,000	34	75	111	133	153
37,000	38,000	36	79	117	140	161
38,000	39,000	38	83	122	148	169
39,000	40,000	40	87	128	155	177
40,000	41,000	41	91	135	161	186
41,000	42,000	43	95	141	168	194
42,000	43,000	45	99	146	176	203
43,000	44,000	47	103	152	183	211
44,000	45,000	49	107	158	190	219
45,000	46,000	50	111	165	196	228
46,000	47,000	52	115	170	204	236
47,000	48,000	54	119	176	211	244
48,000	49,000	56	123	182	218	252
49,000	50,000	58	127	188	225	261
50,000	51,000	60	131	194	232	269
51,000	52,000	61	135	200	240	277
52,000	53,000	63	139	206	247	285
53,000	54,000	65	143	212	254	293
54,000	55,000	67	147	218	261	301
55,000	56,000	69	151	224	268	309
56,000	57,000	70	155	230	275	318
57,000	58,000	72	159	236	282	326
58,000	59,000	74	163	242	289	335
59,000	60,000	76	167	248	296	343
60,000	62,000	79	173	256	308	355
62,000	64,000	82	181	269	321	372
64,000	66,000	86	189	280	336	388
66,000	68,000	90	197	292	350	404
68,000	70,000	93	205	304	365	420
70,000	72,000	97	213	316	379	437

REV. PROC. 2017-29 TABLE 6

DOLLAR AMOUNTS FOR TRUCKS AND VANS
WITH A LEASE TERM BEGINNING IN CALENDAR YEAR 2017

Fair Market Value of Passenger Automobile		Tax Year During Lease				
Over	Not Over	1st	2nd	3rd	4th	5th & later
72,000	74,000	101	221	328	393	453
74,000	76,000	104	229	340	407	470
76,000	78,000	108	237	352	421	487
78,000	80,000	111	245	364	436	503
80,000	85,000	118	259	384	461	532
85,000	90,000	127	279	414	497	573
90,000	95,000	136	299	444	532	614
95,000	100,000	145	319	474	567	656
100,000	110,000	159	349	518	621	717
110,000	120,000	177	389	578	692	800
120,000	130,000	195	429	637	764	882
130,000	140,000	213	470	696	835	964
140,000	150,000	232	509	756	906	1,047
150,000	160,000	250	549	816	977	1,129
160,000	170,000	268	589	875	1,049	1,211
170,000	180,000	286	630	934	1,120	1,293
180,000	190,000	305	669	994	1,191	1,376
190,000	200,000	323	709	1,054	1,262	1,458
200,000	210,000	341	750	1,112	1,334	1,540
210,000	220,000	359	790	1,172	1,405	1,623
220,000	230,000	377	830	1,231	1,477	1,705
230,000	240,000	396	870	1,290	1,548	1,787
240,000	and over	414	910	1,350	1,619	1,870

Chapter 2 Income—Taxable and Exempt

¶ 1200 Gross Income.

Gross income consists of all income, from all sources, such as compensation for services, business income, interest, rents, dividends and gains from the sale of property. Only items specifically exempt may be excluded.

Gross income also includes illegal gains and income derived from illegal or criminal activities (e.g., from embezzlement, kickbacks, extortion, fraudulent schemes, shareholder misappropriation, and drug dealing). (Reg § 1.61-14(a))[1]

Gross income is the starting point in determining tax liability and is broadly defined. (Code Sec. 61)[2]

¶ 1201 Assignment of income.

The person who earns and is entitled to receive income is taxed on it and can't avoid being taxed by assigning the income to another person. [3] But if a taxpayer assigns or transfers income-producing *property* before the income is earned, the assignee will be taxed on the income. [4]

¶ 1202 Income from co-owned property—joint tenancies, etc.

In a tenancy in common (co-owners without survivorship), each co-owner is taxable on the income attributable to the taxpayer's share. [5] Co-owners who are joint tenants (with survivorship) split income from their property according to their ownership interests. [6]

Similarly, any gain (or loss) from sale of jointly-owned property is divided among the co-owners unless the joint ownership was created to save taxes on the sale, in which case the original owner is taxed on the full amount of the gain. [7]

Co-owners who are spouses and who file joint returns report their combined income, gains and losses from the jointly-owned property. If they file separately, the income, etc., from the property is split according to how it's shared under state law. [8]

¶ 1203 Community property and income.

Federal tax law recognizes the principle of community income in community property states (AZ, CA, ID, LA, NV, NM, TX, WA and WI) or countries, which treats half of community income and expenses as belonging to each spouse. [9] Community income is all the income from community property (including business property) and salaries, etc., for the services of either or both spouses. Income from separate property during marriage is community income only in ID, LA, TX and WI. [10] If one spouse acts entitled to the full amount of the community income and fails to notify the other spouse of the nature and amount of the income before the return due date (with extensions), IRS may deny the first spouse any community property benefit. (Code Sec. 66(b))[11]

Couples who are married under state law are married for federal tax purposes. While IRS has determined that registered domestic partners and those in civil unions aren't married for federal tax purposes, if state law extends full community property treatment to

---

1. ¶J-1600 *et seq.*; ¶614.176
2. ¶s J-1000 *et seq.*; ¶614
3. ¶J-8151 *et seq.*; ¶s 614.185, 614.192
4. ¶J-8172 *et seq.*; ¶s 614.192, 1024
5. ¶J-8103; ¶614.202
6. ¶s J-8101, J-8102; ¶614.202
7. ¶J-8107; ¶614.202
8. ¶J-8100 *et seq.*; ¶614.202
9. ¶A-5001; ¶79,006.51
10. ¶A-5008
11. ¶A-5026; ¶664

References beginning with a single letter are to paragraphs in Federal Tax Coordinator 2d and RIA's Analysis of Federal Taxes: Income. Those beginning with numbers are to paragraphs in United States Tax Reporter.

registered domestic partners, each partner must report one-half of the community property on the partner's federal income tax return, whether received in the form of compensation for personal services or income from property. Thus, registered domestic partners who reside in community property states must each report half the combined community income earned by the partners. A partner who has income that isn't community income must also report that separate income. [12]

Community property income for a calendar year is taxed to the spouse who earned it if in that year the couple lived apart for the entire year, filed separate returns *and* one or both spouses had earned income no part of which was transferred between them. (Code Sec. 66(a), Code Sec. 66(d)(1))[13]

Relief from separate return liability. A spouse who doesn't file a joint return for the tax year for which relief is sought and omits from gross income the spouse's share of community income is relieved from tax liability on that omitted income if the spouse establishes lack of knowledge or reason to know of the omitted item and, under all the facts and circumstances, it's inequitable to include the omitted item in the spouse's gross income ("traditional relief"). (Code Sec. 66(c); Reg § 1.66-4(a)(1))[14] IRS may grant equitable relief to a separately-filing spouse from liability attributable to a community income item for which relief isn't otherwise available ("equitable relief"). (Code Sec. 66(c); Reg § 1.66-4(b))

Traditional relief applies only to deficiencies arising out of items of omitted income but equitable relief includes relief for underpayments of tax or any deficiency, including those arising from disallowed deductions or credits. (Reg § 1.66-4(c))

A spouse requesting relief under the above provisions does so by filing Form 8857. (Reg § 1.66-4(j)(1))[15] For joint filers, see ¶4711.

¶ 1204   Claim of right.

Income received without restriction —income the taxpayer has dominion and control over—must be reported in the year received, even if there's a possibility it may have to be repaid in a later year. [16] For deduction in the repayment year, see ¶2855 *et seq.*

¶ 1205   The "tax benefit rule"—recoveries attributable to an earlier year's deduction or credit.

The recovery of an amount deducted or credited in an earlier tax year is included in a taxpayer's income in the current (recovery) year, except to the extent the deduction or credit *didn't* reduce federal income tax (or alternative minimum tax, but not the accumulated earnings or personal holding company "penalty" taxes (Code Sec. 111(d)(1))[17] imposed in the earlier year. (Code Sec. 111(a))[18]

Similarly, if there's a downward price adjustment (e.g., price reduction) during the tax year that affects an amount paid or incurred on which a credit (other than the investment credit or the foreign tax credit) was allowed in an earlier year, a taxpayer's tax for the adjustment year is increased by the amount of credit attributable to the adjustment, to the extent it reduced tax in the earlier year. (Code Sec. 111(b))[19]

This "tax benefit rule" applies to recoveries of both itemized deductions (i.e., taxes, medical expenses and other items deductible on Form 1040, Schedule A) and non-itemized deductions (e.g., bad debts). The taxable amount is limited to the itemized deduction amount that reduced the tax in the earlier year. A taxpayer who recovers an amount

---

12. ¶A-5017
13. ¶A-5022; ¶664
14. ¶A-5029; ¶664
15. ¶A-5034; ¶664

16. ¶J-8001 *et seq.*; ¶4514.069 *et seq.*
17. ¶J-5526, ¶J-5527; ¶1114
18. ¶J-5500 *et seq.*; ¶1114 *et seq.*
19. ¶J-5511; ¶1114.02

deducted in an earlier year as an itemized deduction is taxed on the *lesser* of the amount recovered, or the amount deducted on Schedule A. A taxpayer who wasn't required to itemize deductions in the earlier year is taxed on the *lesser* of itemized deduction recoveries or the amount by which itemized deductions exceeded the standard deduction. [20]

If a taxpayer had negative taxable income for the year the items were deducted, the otherwise includable amount of the recovery is reduced by the negative amount. [21]

The tax benefit rule applies to state income taxes deducted in an earlier year where there's a refund or credit of taxes paid or the cancellation of taxes accrued. [22] But a refundable credit not based on taxes previously paid isn't protected by the exclusionary effect of the tax benefit rule, even if the state calls it an overpayment. [23]

The increase of a carryover that hasn't expired as of the start of the tax year of the recovery (deduction) or adjustment (credit item) is treated as a reduction of tax imposed. (Code Sec. 111(c))[24]

The tax rates for the recovery (or adjustment) year are used to compute the tax on the portion that isn't excludible. [25] A recovery of amounts, e.g., bad debts, deducted in more than one tax year must be allocated pro rata between those years. (Reg § 1.111-1(a)(3))[26]

To claim any part of a recovery is tax-free, attach a schedule to the return showing the right to the exclusion. (Reg § 1.111-1(b)(1))[27]

¶ 1206 Miscellaneous taxable and exempt income.

Here are selected items not covered elsewhere in this Handbook, followed by whether they're includable in income (Taxable) or not (Excludable):

... Alaska Permanent Fund Dividend. *Taxable.* [28]

... Alcohol fuel credit. *Taxable.* (Code Sec. 87)[29]

... Electronic health record incentive payments to health care professionals and hospitals for using patients electronic health records. *Taxable.* [30]

... Elderly in-home care payments by a state agency to caregiver to help elderly live at home instead of nursing home. *Excludable,* under so-called "general welfare exclusion".[31]

... Employer-provided death benefits of specified victims of terrorism and astronauts who die in the line of duty. *Excludable.* (Code Sec. 101(i)(1))[32]

... Energy conservation subsidies provided (directly or indirectly) by a public utility to customers for buying or installing "energy conservation measures" for dwelling units. *Excludable. (*Code Sec. 136)[33]

... Executor's or administrator's fees or commissions that are waived. *Excludable,* if executor, etc., files a formal waiver within six months after appointment, or if its conduct amounts to an implied waiver. [34]

... Foster care payments by state or licensed/certified placement agency to individual foster care provider for caring for qualified foster individual (child or adult) in care provider's home (where provider resides). *Excludable,* if payments aren't for the care of more than five individuals age 19 or older. "Difficulty-of-care payments." *Excludable,* unless for more than ten individuals under age 19, or for more than five individuals age

20. ¶J-5512; ¶1114.02
21. ¶J-5512
22. ¶J-5701 *et seq.*; ¶1114
23. ¶J-5505
24. ¶J-5524; ¶1114
25. ¶J-5530; ¶1114.02
26. ¶J-5603; ¶1114.02
27. ¶J-5528

28. ¶J-1493
29. ¶L-17505; ¶874
30. ¶J-1430
31. ¶J-1480A
32. ¶C-9674; ¶1014.10
33. ¶J-1401 *et seq.*; ¶1364
34. ¶J-1419; ¶4514.042

19 or older. (Code Sec. 131) See "Medicaid waiver payments," below. [35]

... Frequent flyer miles earned or received in connection with business travel. *Excludable.* [36]

... Grants to homeowners under a city program to preserve old neighborhoods. *Taxable.* [37]

... Grants in lieu of the Code Sec. 48 energy credit or Code Sec. 45 electricity production credit under ARRA §1603. *Excludable* from income and alternative minimum taxable income. (Code Sec. 48(d)(3)(A))

... 25% of qualifying gain from conservation sales of qualifying mineral or geothermal interests. *Excludable.* [38]

... Identity protection services provided at no cost before or after a data security breach. *Excludable,* but not cash received in lieu of identity protection services, or proceeds received under an identity theft insurance policy. [39]

... Insurance reimbursement for living expenses incurred due to the loss of use of (or government's denial of access to) principal residence (owned or rented) resulting from a fire, storm or other casualty. *Excludable,* to extent it covers additional living expenses (but balance of reimbursement is *taxable*). (Code Sec. 123; Reg § 1.123-1)[40]

... Use and occupancy insurance reimbursements for loss of profits if business is suspended. *Taxable.* [41]

... Leave donated and deposited in an employer-sponsored leave bank under a major disaster leave-sharing plan. *Excludable,* if plan treats payments made by the employer to leave recipients as wages. [42]

... Leave received under employer-sponsored leave-sharing plan which allows employees with a medical emergency to receive leave that other employees surrender or deposit into a leave bank. *Taxable,* as compensation. [43]

... Malpractice settlement received from accountants for advising taxpayers to participate in abusive tax shelter. *Excludable* (under a Tax Court decision, but IRS disagrees). [44]

... Medicaid waiver payments (a type of payment from a state to an individual to take care of another individual who would otherwise be institutionalized). *Excludable* (treated as qualified "Foster care payments," above), even if the care provider is related to the eligible individual. [45]

... Medicare (Part A and Part B). *Excludable,* except for Part B amounts attributable to medical deductions taken in an earlier year. [46]

... Mortgage assistance payments by a federal agency to a mortgagee on mortgagor's behalf, e.g., Pay-for-Performance Success Payments that reduce principal balance of taxpayer's home mortgage under Home Affordable Modification Program. *Excludable,* unless *not* made for the general welfare (e.g., interest reduction payments to mortgagee).[47]

... Pell grants. *Excludable,* but if a taxpayer chooses to include in income, can result in an increased education credit (and lower the total tax or increase the taxpayer's refund).[48]

... Property tax rebates. *Taxable,* to extent they exceed the property tax paid. Rebates received after the year of payment are subject to the tax benefit rule (¶1205). Rebates

---

35. ¶J-1500 *et seq.*; ¶s 1314.01, 1314.02
36. ¶J-1393
37. ¶J-1480
38. ¶I-8851
39. ¶J-1434
40. ¶J-1311 *et seq.*; ¶1234
41. ¶J-5830; ¶614.167

42. ¶H-1013.1
43. ¶H-1013
44. ¶J-5827
45. ¶J-1504
46. ¶J-1307
47. ¶J-1489
48. ¶A-4542

received in the year of payment reduce the amount of tax paid for that year. Where the tax was paid over two years, the rebate is apportioned over them. [49] However, state property tax credits are treated as reducing a taxpayer's property tax liability (so are not treated as income) for the year the credit is claimed or carried forward to.

. . . Rate reduction or nonrefundable credit provided by utility to customer for participation in energy conservation program. *Excludable.* [50]

. . . Rebates of part of purchase price to retail customers. *Excludable,* as an adjustment to the purchase price of acquiring the property. [1]

. . . Relocation payments and similar government subsidies for moving expenses and actual direct losses of property due to displacement from personal residences because of urban renewal projects. *Excludable,* to extent made by government to compensate (and actually so used) for these expenses, [2] and *taxable,* to extent made by nongovernmental landlords as part of co-op or condo conversion. [3]

. . . Relocation and cleaning expense reimbursements to those affected by large California natural gas leak. *Excludable,* but not payments made to family and friends for housing them. [4]

. . . Restitution payments to human trafficking victims mandatorily awarded under 18 U.S.C. §1593. *Excludable.* [5]

. . . Security deposits received. If purpose is to guarantee performance of an obligation, *excludable* where repayment is required if the obligation is performed, but *taxable* to the recipient when the recipient becomes entitled to retain them because of a default. [6] If purpose is to protect taxpayer's interest in property and not to secure payment, *excludable.* [7]

. . . Smart Grid Investment Grant made to a corporation. *Excludable;* corporation must properly reduce the basis of its property. [8]

. . . Subsidies received from Social Security by sponsors of qualified retiree prescription drug plans under the Medicare Prescription Drug Act of 2003 for certain covered retiree drug costs. *Excludable.* (Code Sec. 139A)[9]

. . . Whistleblower awards paid by IRS for information about tax law violations. *Taxable.* (Reg § 301.7623-4(d)(5))[10]

. . . Whistleblower's settlement under Federal False Claims Act *qui tam* action against former employer. *Taxable* (as ordinary income and not capital gain). [11]

¶ 1207   Exclusion for qualified disaster relief or mitigation payments.

A qualified disaster relief payment isn't included in gross income. It also isn't earnings for self-employment tax purposes or wages for employment tax purposes. (Code Sec. 139) The exclusion doesn't apply to amounts received for the sale or disposition of property, but the involuntary conversion rules may apply to such amounts, see ¶2430.[12]

A qualified disaster relief payment is any amount (to the extent not compensated by insurance or otherwise) paid to or for the benefit of an individual:

(1) to reimburse or pay reasonable and necessary personal, family, living, or funeral expenses incurred as a result of a qualified disaster (defined below),

---

49. ¶J-1394.1
50. ¶J-1431
1. ¶J-1391
2. ¶J-1492; ¶614.006
3. ¶J-1492
4. ¶J-1298
5. ¶J-1475A

6. ¶J-1371; ¶4514.166
7. ¶G-2490; ¶4514.166
8. ¶F-1914.1
9. ¶J-1480.2; ¶139A4
10. ¶J-1485.2; ¶76,234
11. ¶J-1485.3
12. ¶J-1296; ¶1394

(2) to reimburse or pay reasonable and necessary expenses incurred to repair or rehabilitate a personal residence (including a rented residence) or repair or replace its contents to the extent that the need for the work results from a qualified disaster,

(3) by a person who provides or sells transportation as a common carrier because of the death or personal physical injuries arising from a qualified disaster, or

(4) if the amount is paid by a federal, state, or local government, or an agency or instrumentality of those governments, in connection with a qualified disaster in order to promote the general welfare (but not if payments are made to businesses or for income replacement or unemployment compensation).

A qualified disaster is a disaster that results from a terroristic or military action, a Federally declared disaster, a disaster resulting from an accident involving a common carrier, or from any other event that's determined by IRS to be of a catastrophic nature, or for payments by a federal, state, or local government, or an agency or instrumentality of those governments, a disaster that's determined by the appropriate governmental authority (as determined by IRS) to warrant assistance from the governmental authority. [13]

Qualified disaster mitigation payments are excluded from gross income. (Code Sec. 139(g)) These include payments under the Flood Mitigation Assistance Program, Pre-Disaster Mitigation Program, and Hazard Mitigation Grant Program. [14]

¶ 1208 Compensation Income. ▮▮▮▮▮▮▮▮▮▮▮▮▮▮▮▮

All forms of compensation received for personal services are included in gross income.

This includes wages, salaries, fees, tips (¶1210), salesperson's commissions (including on sales to self or family), percentage of profits paid as compensation, commissions on insurance premiums, bonuses (including Christmas bonuses, see ¶1211), termination or severance pay, golden parachute payments (excess golden parachute payments subject the recipient to a 20% excise tax (Code Sec. 4999(a)),[15] rewards, jury duty fees (Code Sec. 61(a)(1); Reg § 1.61-2(a)(1)),[16] and fringe benefits not excluded by statute (see ¶1227 *et seq.*). (Code Sec. 61(a)(1)) Vacation pay also is taxable. [17]

Pension or retirement allowances to employees (reported to recipients on Form 1099-R) generally are taxable to the recipient, see ¶4327 *et seq.* (Reg § 1.61-11(a))[18] For rules for certain military pensions, see ¶1282.

Amounts withheld from an employee's pay by the employer for income and social security taxes, savings bonds, union dues, etc., represent compensation constructively received by the employee and must be included in income for the year in which withheld. [19] An employee is taxed on compensation even if the employer can't deduct all or part of the amount because it's "unreasonable." (¶1516). (Reg § 1.162-8)[20]

¶ 1209 Reporting compensation and self-employment income.

The amount of wages, salaries, tips, etc., that's includible in income (¶1208), which should be shown on a Form W-2 issued by the employer, is reported on Form 1040. [21]

Income (or loss) subject to self-employment tax (¶3133) from a business operated, or a profession practiced, as a sole proprietor is reported on Form 1040, Schedule C or C-EZ. If an individual operates more than one business as a sole proprietor, a separate Schedule C

13. ¶J-1290 *et seq.*
14. ¶J-1296; ¶1394
15. ¶H-3003; ¶49,994
16. ¶H-1001 *et seq.*; ¶614.007
17. ¶s H-1001, H-1012

18. ¶H-3245; ¶s 614.007, 4014
19. ¶H-2152
20. ¶H-1021; ¶614.014
21. ¶H-1001.1

or C-EZ must be prepared for each business. An individual can't report income on Schedule C or C-EZ if it's earned as an "employee." [22] For farm income, see ¶4501.

¶ 1210 Tips and similar payments.

Tips and similar payments for special services are income. (Reg § 1.61-2(a)(1)) Service charges imposed by the employer on customers (mandatory add-ons to food and drink bills, such as gratuities automatically added to the bills of large parties at restaurants) in lieu of tipping are part of the employee's wages (rather than a tip subject to tip reporting requirements). [23]

¶ 1211 Compensation distinguished from gift.

Although gifts are generally excluded from the recipient's gross income (¶1365), transfer by or for an employer to or for the benefit of an employee can't be excluded as a gift. (Code Sec. 102(c)(1)) Extraordinary transfers to the natural objects of an employer's bounty (e.g., an employee who is the employer's son) aren't transfers to or for the benefit of the employee if the transfer wasn't made in recognition of employment. [24] For de minimis fringe benefits, see ¶1244. For no-additional-cost services, see ¶1241.

If, as a means of promoting goodwill, an employer makes a general distribution to employees of hams, turkeys or other merchandise of nominal value at Christmas or a comparable holiday, the value of the gifts isn't included in the employees' income. But if an employer distributes cash, gift certificates or similar items of readily convertible cash value, the value of the gifts is additional wages or salary, *regardless* of the value. [25]

¶ 1212 Below-market interest rate loans from employer.

An employee or independent contractor who receives a below-market (¶1303) compensation-related loan (except certain de minimis loans), recognizes compensation income (Code Sec. 7872(a)(1), Code Sec. 7872(b)(1)) equal to: (i) for a demand loan, the foregone interest (at the applicable federal rate; ¶1118) over actual interest payment; and (ii) for other loans, the excess of the amount borrowed over the present value of the payments required to be made under the terms of the loan. [26]).

Certain employee-relocation loans are exempt from these rules. (Reg § 1.7872-5T(b)(6))[27]

¶ 1213 Vacation trips for salespersons; other noncash compensation.

If services rendered by the taxpayer are paid for in property or services rather than money, the fair market value (FMV) of the property or services must be included in income. For example, if a vacation trip is awarded to salespersons as a prize, the FMV of the trip is income. Where a price has been specified for the services being rendered, that price is considered the FMV of the property or services received if there's no evidence showing a different value. (Code Sec. 83; Reg § 1.61-2(d))[28]

¶ 1214 Notes receivable as compensation.

Notes and other evidences of indebtedness received in payment for services or in settlement of a claim for compensation are taxable as compensation in the amount of their fair market value when received. When a taxpayer receives as compensation a non-interest-bearing note regarded as good for its face value at maturity, the note's fair discounted

22. ¶H-1001.1
23. ¶H-4341; ¶60,534
24. ¶H-1027.1 *et seq.*; ¶614.016, ¶1024
25. ¶H-1033; ¶1324.06

26. ¶s H-2002, H-2004; ¶78,724.14
27. ¶H-2014; ¶78,724.20
28. ¶H-2500 *et seq.*; ¶s 614.007, 614.027

value (computed at the prevailing rate) is included in income. As note payments are received, the taxpayer's income includes that portion of each payment representing the proportionate part of the discount originally taken on the entire note. (Reg § 1.61-2(d)(4))[29]

¶ 1215   Bargain purchase from employer.

If property, including stock, is transferred by an employer to an employee for less than its fair market value, the difference is compensation. (Code Sec. 83(a); Reg § 1.83-1(a))[30] For stock options and employee stock purchase plans, see ¶1218 *et seq.*

If an employee pays with a recourse note for stock acquired from an employer under a nonqualified stock option, and the employer later reduces the amount due on the note, the debt reduction is treated as compensation income. [31]

¶ 1216   Restricted stock or other property—Section 83 rules.

A person receiving a beneficial interest in stock or other property for performance of services has compensation income equal to the value of that property at the time of receipt. But if the person's interest in the property is subject to substantial risk of forfeiture (is "restricted") and can't be transferred free of that risk, then income is deferred until the interest in the property either: (1) is no longer subject to that risk, *or* (2) becomes transferable free of the risk, whichever occurs earlier. (Code Sec. 83)[32] For election not to defer income, see ¶1217.

But the employee (or other owner of the property) has income from the property if it's sold or disposed of before (1) or (2), above. (Code Sec. 83(a))[33]

The amount included in income (in the year in which (1) or (2) occurs) is the excess of the fair market value (FMV) of the property in that year (figured without regard to restrictions other than those that by their terms will never lapse), over the amount, if any, paid for the property. (Code Sec. 83(a))[34]

A substantial risk of forfeiture exists only if a person's rights in property that's transferred is conditioned, directly or indirectly, (a) on the future performance (or refraining from performance) of substantial services, or (b) upon the occurrence of a condition related to a purpose of the transfer, if the possibility of forfeiture is substantial. Property isn't transferred subject to a substantial risk of forfeiture if the forfeiture condition is unlikely to be enforced; the employer is required to pay the FMV of a portion of the property to the employee upon the return of the property; or there's a risk that the value of property will decline during a certain period of time. (Code Sec. 83(c)(1), Reg § 1.83-3(c)(1)) An example of property subject to a substantial risk of forfeiture is where property is transferred subject to a requirement that the property must be returned to the employer if total earnings don't increase. (Reg § 1.83-3(c)(2)),[35]

Except as specifically provided in Code Sec. 83(c)(3), Reg § 1.83-3(j) (dealing with the SEC "short swing" rule under which insider must pay over profits if stock is sold within six months of receipt), and Reg § 1.83-3(k) (dealing with the SEC "pooling-of-interests accounting" rule under which employees are prevented from selling stock while their company is engaged in a merger or acquisition), transfer restrictions won't create a substantial risk of forfeiture (including ones which carry the potential for forfeiture or disgorgement of some or all of the property, or other penalties). Transfer restrictions that won't result in a substantial risk of forfeiture include restrictions that, if violated, whether by transfer or attempted transfer of the property, would result in the forfeiture of some or

29. ¶H-2513; ¶614.034
30. ¶H-2509; ¶614.030
31. ¶H-2535
32. ¶H-2500, ¶H-2517 *et seq.*; ¶834

33. ¶H-2547 *et seq.*; ¶834.01
34. ¶H-2532 *et seq.*; ¶834.01
35. ¶H-2521; ¶834.02

all of the property, or liability by the employee for any damages, penalties, fees, or other amount. (Reg § 1.83-3(c)(1))[36]

Post-2017 deferral election. Generally effective for stock of an eligible corporation (one with no stock readily tradable on an established securities market and with a written plan under which a least 80% of U.S. employees are granted stock options or "restricted stock units" (RSUs) (Code Sec. 83(i)(2)(C))) attributable to options exercised or RSUs settled after Dec. 31, 2017 (subject to a transition rule), a "qualified employee" can elect (see below) to defer, for income tax purposes, recognition of the amount of income attributable to qualified stock transferred to the employee by the employer for up to five years after vesting. (Code Sec. 83(i)) The election applies only for income tax purposes; the application of FICA and FUTA is not affected. If an employee makes the Code Sec. 83(i) election, then the employer's deduction of the amount of income attributable to the qualified stock is deferred until the employer's tax year in which or with which ends the tax year of the employee for which the amount is included in the employee's income. [37]

A qualified employee is an individual who isn't an "excluded employee" and who agrees, in the Code Sec. 83(i) election, to meet the requirements, to be determined by IRS, that are necessary to ensure the employer corporation's income tax withholding requirements with respect to the qualified stock are met. Excluded employees include: (1) 1% owners under Code Sec. 416(i)(1)(B)(ii) at any time during the current or preceding 10 calendar years; (2) current or former CEOs, CFOs, or individuals acting in either capacity; (3) individuals who bear a relationship described in Code Sec. 318(a)(1) to an individual in (2); or (4) individuals who are, or were for any of the 10 preceding tax years, one of the four highest compensated officers of the corporation. (Code Sec. 83(i)(3)(B))

The election is made in a manner similar to an Code Sec. 83(b) election (¶1217), with the employee filing the election with IRS and providing a copy to the employer. The election must be made no later than 30 days after the first time the employee's right to the stock is substantially vested or is transferable, whichever occurs earlier. (Code Sec. 83(i)(4)(A))[38]

¶ 1217   Election not to defer income from restricted stock or other property.

An employee or other person who receives restricted stock or other property (¶1216) may elect to recognize the income immediately instead of deferring it. (Code Sec. 83(b)(1))[39]

The amount of compensation income included in the year the property is received is the excess of the fair market value of the property at receipt (without regard to restrictions other than those that by their terms will never lapse), over the amount, if any, paid for the property. (Code Sec. 83(b)(1))[40]

recommendation: Elect if the income taxed at grant would be negligible. This defers tax on any post-grant appreciation until sale, makes it eligible for capital gain rates, and may eliminate additional income tax completely if the property is held until death.

If the stock or other property is forfeited after the election is made, the employee can't get a deduction or refund of tax previously paid on income reported. (Code Sec. 83(b)(1))[41] The employee will have capital loss at the time of forfeiture. (Reg § 1.83-2(a))[42]

Elect within 30 days after the property is transferred to the employee (Code Sec. 83(b)(2)) by filing a statement (specified in the regs) with the IRS office where the person who performs the services files the tax return for that year and submitting a copy to the person for whom the services are performed. (Reg § 1.83-2(c); Reg § 1.83-2(d))[43]

36. ¶H-2530 *et seq.*; ¶834.02
37. ¶H-2900 *et seq.*
38. ¶H-2907
39. ¶H-2540; ¶834.03

40. ¶H-2541; ¶834.03
41. ¶M-3503; ¶834.03
42. ¶I-1020; ¶834.03
43. ¶H-2542 *et seq.*; ¶834.03

IRS will consent to a revocation only if the election was filed under a mistake of fact in the underlying transaction and the revocation is requested within 60 days of discovering the mistake. However, requests to revoke the election within the 30-day period for making it generally will be granted. [44]

¶ 1218   Nonstatutory stock options.

An option—other than an option under an employee stock purchase plan (see ¶1219) or an incentive stock option (ISO, see ¶1220)—which is granted in connection with the performance of services, to buy stock at a bargain, results in compensation income to the employee (or independent contractor) grantee. (Code Sec. 83) If the option has a readily ascertainable fair market value (FMV) at grant, it's subject to the restricted property rules of Code Sec. 83 (¶1216 *et seq.*) when the option is granted. (Code Sec. 83; Reg § 1.83-7(a))[45]

An option "ordinarily" has a readily ascertainable FMV only if it (or a substantially identical option) is actively traded on an established market. If not so traded, it has value only if certain conditions specified in the regs exist. (Reg § 1.83-7(b))[46]

If the option doesn't have a readily ascertainable FMV when granted, the employee doesn't realize compensation until the optioned property is transferred at exercise. The amount of compensation is the FMV of the property at transfer less any amount paid for the property. (Reg § 1.83-7(a))[47] (For the employer's compensation deduction, see ¶1524.)

The above treatment for nonstatutory options without a readily ascertainable FMV doesn't apply where the option is transferred before exercise to a "related person." (Reg § 1.83-7(a))[48]

Under an exception, the exercise of an option is treated as the grant of another option, instead of a transfer of shares, where the amount paid for the exercise is a debt secured by the shares on which there's no personal liability. (Reg § 1.83-3(a)(2)) However, this exception doesn't apply simply because options are exercised through a margin loan, and income will be realized on the exercise of options without a readily ascertainable FMV. [49]

¶ 1219   Employee stock purchase plan (ESPP) options.

These are options issued to employees under an employer plan to buy stock in the employer. The employee pays no tax on the option or the stock until the stock is disposed of. If the option price at least equals the stock's fair market value (FMV) at grant, gain is capital gain. But gain is ordinary compensation income (to the extent of the spread between option price and FMV of stock when option is exercised) if the stock is sold within two years after the option was granted or within one year after its exercise. (Code Sec. 423(a), Code Sec. 423(c); Reg § 1.423-1, Reg § 1.423-2)[50]

If the option price is less than 100% (but at least 85%) of the stock's FMV at grant, and the above holding period is met, the amount treated as ordinary income (rather than capital gain) is the *lesser* of: (1) the FMV of the stock when the option was granted, minus the option price, or (2) the excess of the FMV at the time of disposition or optionee's death over the amount paid for the share under the option. (Code Sec. 423(c); Reg § 1.423-2(k))[1]

An executive branch federal employee (or spouse or dependent child) who acquired stock through the exercise of an ESPP option (or ISO, see ¶1220) and sells the stock in order to comply with Code Sec. 1043 federal conflict-of-interest requirements is deemed to satisfy the Code Sec. 423(a)(1) (or Code Sec. 422(a)(1)) holding period requirement. (Code

---

44. ¶H-2545
45. ¶s H-2853, H-2857; ¶s 834.07, 4214.03
46. ¶H-2872; ¶834.07
47. ¶H-2861; ¶834.07

48. ¶H-2864.1; ¶834.07
49. ¶H-2508.1
50. ¶H-2952 *et seq.*; ¶4234.01
1. ¶H-2953; ¶4234.01

Sec. 421(d))

The plan must be nondiscriminatory, i.e., available to all employees (with certain exceptions). (Code Sec. 423(b)(4))[2]

¶ 1220 Incentive stock options (ISOs).

An ISO is granted to an employee by an employer corporation (or its parent or sub) to buy stock or ownership interests in one of those corporations (a term that takes in S corporations, foreign corporations, and limited liability companies treated as corporations for federal tax purposes). (Reg § 1.421-1(d)(3), Reg § 1.421-1(i)(1)) There are no regular income tax consequences when an ISO is granted or exercised; the employee has capital gain when the stock is sold at a gain. (Code Sec. 421(a))[3] To qualify, an ISO must meet various requirements. (Code Sec. 422(b))[4]

Stock acquired through the exercise of an ISO generally can't be disposed of within two years after the option is granted or one year after the stock is transferred to the employee. (Code Sec. 422(a)(1)) Also, for the entire time from the date an ISO is granted until three months (one year in case of total and permanent disability) before its exercise, the option holder must be an employee of the option grantor (or its parent or sub or certain successor corporations). (Code Sec. 422(a)(2), Code Sec. 422(c)(6))[5] For executive branch federal employee holding period rules, see ¶1219.

If there's a disqualifying disposition of a share of stock, Code Sec. 421 doesn't apply to the transfer of the share. Instead, the exercise of the option is governed by Code Sec. 83 and its regs. Thus, in the tax year in which the disqualifying disposition occurs, the individual recognizes compensation income (and gets a basis increase) equal to the FMV of the stock on the date the stock is transferred, less the exercise price (determined without reduction for any brokerage fees or other disposition costs). (Reg § 1.421-2(b)) If the disqualifying disposition would trigger an allowable loss (e.g., not a sale to a related taxpayer), then the amount includible in the employee's income (and deductible by the employer, see ¶1524) as a result of that disqualifying disposition can't be more than the amount realized on the sale, minus the employee's adjusted basis in the stock. (Code Sec. 422(c)(2); Reg § 1.422-1(b)(2)(i))[6]

caution: For alternative minimum tax treatment, see ¶3206.

¶ 1221 Sale or cancellation of employment contract.

Proceeds from an employee's sale of rights under an employment contract to be performed are ordinary income. The same is true of amounts received from an employer in cancellation of an employment contract.[7]

¶ 1222 Members of Armed Forces.

The pay of Armed Forces members is taxable (Reg § 1.61-2(a)(1)), with exceptions.[8]

Gross income doesn't include any "qualified military benefit," which is any allowance or in-kind benefit (other than personal use of an automobile) received by a member or former member of the uniformed services of the U.S., or a dependent, and which was excludable from gross income on Sept. 9, '86 under any provision of law, reg or administrative practice (other than the Code) in effect on that date. (Code Sec. 134(b)) It includes any bonus payment made by a state or political subdivision to any member or former member of the

---

2. ¶H-2972; ¶4234.02
3. ¶H-2750; ¶4224.01
4. ¶H-2767; ¶4224.02
5. ¶H-2795 *et seq.*; ¶4224.01

6. ¶H-2799; ¶4224.01
7. ¶H-1048 *et seq.*
8. ¶H-3101; ¶614.040

U.S. uniformed services, or a dependent, because of service in a combat zone. (Code Sec. 134(b)(6)) Excludable allowances include (within certain limitations) veteran's benefits (¶1223), medical benefits, disability benefits, dependent care assistance program benefits, professional education, moving and storage, group-term life insurance, survivor and retirement protection plan premiums, subsistence, uniform, housing, overseas cost-of-living, evacuation, family separation allowances, death gratuities, interment allowance, various travel allowances and dependent benefits. [9] Specifically, dislocation allowances, temporary lodging allowances and expenses and move-in housing allowances provided in connection with permanent changes of station are excludible from income. (Reg § 1.61-2(b)(2))[10] For treatment of retirement pay, see ¶1282. A "qualified military base realignment and closure" fringe benefit is excluded and isn't subject to FICA. This benefit is a payment (subject to a maximum allowance) received under the Homeowner's Assistance Program (HAP) (as in effect on 2/17/2009, for payments after that date). (Code Sec. 132(a)(8))[11]

The recipient of a tax-free military housing allowance isn't thereby prevented from deducting mortgage interest or real estate taxes on a personal residence. (Code Sec. 265(a)(6)(A))[12]

The Code also excludes combat-zone (and qualified hazardous duty) compensation (limited, for commissioned officers, to the maximum enlisted amount). (Code Sec. 112; Reg § 1.112-1) Areas designated as combat zones include Pakistan; Tajikistan; Jordan; Uzbekistan; Kyrgyzstan; the Afghanistan area; Serbia/Montenegro; Albania; the Adriatic Sea; the Ionian Sea (north of the 39th parallel); the Persian Gulf area; the Red Sea; the Gulf of Oman; parts of the Arabian Sea; the Gulf of Aden; and the total land areas of Iraq, Kuwait, Saudi Arabia, Oman, Bahrain, Qatar, and the United Arab Emirates. [13] Combat-zone tax benefits have also been retroactively extended to members of the armed forces performing services in the Sinai Peninsula of Egypt, generally effective for services provided on or after June 9, 2015 if, as of Dec. 22, 2017, any member of the U.S. Armed Forces is entitled to special pay under section 310 of title 37, USC (relating to special pay; duty subject to hostile fire or imminent danger), for services performed in such location. This benefit lasts only during the period of such entitlement. [14] IRS is accepting retroactive refund claims back to 2015 and has provided instructions on how qualifying members of the Armed Forces can claim the benefit.

For various deadline extensions for a member of the Armed Forces serving in a designated "combat zone," see ¶4719. For tax relief for military and civilian employees of the U.S. dying in combat or terrorist attacks, see ¶4715. For filing retroactive refund claims, see ¶4723.

¶ 1223   VA and state benefits to veterans.

Benefits under any law, regulation, or practice in effect on Sept. 9, '86 and administered by the Department of Veterans' Affairs are excludable from the recipient's gross income, (Code Sec. 140(a)(3)) including interest earned on dividends left on deposit with the VA. Benefits include amounts received under a VA administered work therapy program. [15] State bonuses to veterans for service rendered to the U.S. are also exempt. [16]

---

9. ¶H-3102; ¶1344
10. ¶H-3103
11. ¶H-3104; ¶1324.11
12. ¶K-9009; ¶2654

13. ¶H-3106 *et seq.*; ¶1124.01
14. ¶H-3109.1
15. ¶H-3128; ¶614.041
16. ¶H-3129

¶ 1224   Government employees' compensation.

Federal, state and municipal employees, including federal judges, are taxable on their salary, wages and other compensation the same as other employees. [17] Payments under the Civil Service Retirement System are taxed like annuities, see ¶1350 *et seq.*[18] For relief for U.S. military and civilian employees dying in combat or terrorist attacks, see ¶4715.

¶ 1225   Members of clergy.

Members of the clergy are taxable on the salaries and fees they receive, and on any offerings they receive for marriages, funerals, masses, etc., *but not* on offerings made to the religious institution. (Reg § 1.61-2(a))[19]

A current or retired member of the clergy who is a "minister of the gospel" [20] can exclude:

. . . the rental value of a home (parsonage allowance), including utilities, furnished to the clergyperson as part of compensation; (Code Sec. 107(1); Reg § 1.107-1(a)) or

. . . the rental allowance (parsonage allowance) paid to the clergyperson as compensation, to the extent it's used in the year received to rent or provide a home(s) and to the extent it doesn't exceed the fair rental value of the home, including furnishings and appurtenances such as a garage, plus the cost of utilities. (Code Sec. 107(2)) The employer church or organization must designate the payment as a rental allowance before the payment is made. (Reg § 1.107-1(b))[21] One district court has found parsonage allowances to be unconstitutional. [22]

The rental allowance exclusion doesn't prevent a minister from deducting mortgage interest or real estate taxes on a personal residence. (Code Sec. 265(a)(6)(B))[23]

¶ 1226   Compensation of minors.

The income of a minor from compensation earned or received in respect of the performance of services is income to the minor, even if received by the parent. (Code Sec. 73(a))[24]

¶ 1227   Fringe Benefits. ▬▬▬▬▬

Unless specifically excluded (¶1240), fringe benefits received by an employee in connection with the performance of services are taxable compensation. (Reg § 1.61-21(a)(3))[25]

The benefit is includible in the gross income of the person performing the services, even if it's furnished to someone else. (Code Sec. 61(a)(1); Reg § 1.61-21(a)(4))[26]

¶ 1228   Valuation of taxable fringe benefits—general rule.

An employee who is taxed on a fringe benefit (¶1227) must include in gross income the fair market value (FMV) of the benefit minus: (1) any payment for the benefit, and (2) any amount specifically excluded by a Code provision. (Reg § 1.61-21(b)(1))[27] The FMV of a fringe benefit generally is the amount that an individual would have to pay for the particular benefit in an arm's-length transaction. (Reg § 1.61-21(b)(2))[28]

---

17. ¶H-3130; ¶614.036
18. ¶J-5052; ¶724.26
19. ¶H-3151; ¶614.007
20. ¶H-3163; ¶1074.02
21. ¶H-3153 *et seq.*; ¶1074
22. ¶H-3153

23. ¶H-3160; ¶s 1074.03, 2654
24. ¶H-3180; ¶734.01
25. ¶H-1051; ¶614.027
26. ¶H-1051, ¶H-1053; ¶614.027
27. ¶H-1055; ¶614.027
28. ¶H-1056; ¶614.027

Unless a special valuation rule (¶1230) applies, an employer-provided vehicle is valued at the comparable lease cost (¶1231) (Reg § 1.61-21(b)(4)),[29] and flights on employer-provided aircraft at comparable charter cost. (Reg § 1.61-21(b)(6), Reg § 1.61-21(b)(7))[30]

Chauffeur services are valued separately from vehicle availability, at comparable arm's-length transaction costs or by reference to the chauffeur's compensation (including any nontaxable lodging, see ¶1265). (Reg § 1.61-21(b)(5))[31]

¶ 1229 Transportation furnished because of unsafe conditions.

Transportation or reimbursement for it (e.g., cab fare) furnished by an employer under a written policy solely because of unsafe conditions for an employee commuting is valued at $1.50 per one-way commute (i.e., from home to work, or work to home) for each qualifying employee. (Reg § 1.61-21(k)(3))[32]

¶ 1230 Special valuation rules for autos, other vehicles and airflights.

Special valuation rules may be used under certain circumstances for certain commonly provided fringe benefits (e.g., automobiles, noncommercial flights, commuting). (Reg § 1.61-21(b), Reg § 1.61-21(c)(1), Reg § 1.61-21(c)(3))[33] Where the special rules aren't used, either by choice or because they aren't permitted, or where they're improperly applied, the value of the fringe benefit must be determined under the general valuation principles at ¶1228. (Reg § 1.61-21(c)(5))[34]

An employee can't use a special valuation rule to value a fringe benefit unless the employer uses the same rule to value it. (Reg § 1.61-21(c)(2))[35]

¶ 1231 Annual lease value method for automobiles—use of IRS table.

To compute an auto's annual lease value, first determine fair market value (FMV) as of the first date it's made available to *any* employee for personal use. Under safe harbor rules, where the auto is bought at arm's length by the employer, the FMV is the cost, including sales tax, title fees and other purchase expenses. Where leased, it's the suggested retail price less 8%, the retail value as reported in a nationally recognized publication that regularly reports such values (Reg § 1.61-21(d)(5)), or the manufacturer's invoice price plus 4%.[36] Then, find the dollar range in column (1) of the table below that includes the auto's FMV. The corresponding amount in column (2) is its annual lease value. (Reg § 1.61-21(d)(2)(iii))

Automobile fair market value (1)	Annual lease value (2)	Automobile fair market value (1)	Annual lease value (2)
$0 to 999	$600	9,000 to 9,999	2,850
1,000 to 1,999	850	10,000 to 10,999	3,100
2,000 to 2,999	1,100	11,000 to 11,999	3,350
3,000 to 3,999	1,350	12,000 to 12,999	3,600
4,000 to 4,999	1,600	13,000 to 13,999	3,850
5,000 to 5,999	1,850	14,000 to 14,999	4,100
6,000 to 6,999	2,100	15,000 to 15,999	4,350
7,000 to 7,999	2,350	16,000 to 16,999	4,600
8,000 to 8,999	2,600	17,000 to 17,999	4,850

29. ¶H-2232; ¶614.027
30. ¶H-2302 *et seq.*; ¶614.027
31. ¶H-2289 *et seq.*; ¶614.027
32. ¶H-2201 *et seq.*
33. ¶H-1056, *et seq.*, ¶H-2200 *et seq.*, ¶H-2300 *et seq.*; ¶614.027
34. ¶H-1057; ¶614.027
35. ¶H-1060; ¶614.027
36. ¶H-2240; ¶614.027

Automobile fair market value (1)	Annual lease value (2)	Automobile fair market value (1)	Annual lease value (2)
18,000 to 18,999	5,100	36,000 to 37,999	9,750
19,000 to 19,999	5,350	38,000 to 39,999	10,250
20,000 to 20,999	5,600	40,000 to 41,999	10,750
21,000 to 21,999	5,850	42,000 to 43,999	11,250
22,000 to 22,999	6,100	44,000 to 45,999	11,750
23,000 to 23,999	6,350	46,000 to 47,999	12,250
24,000 to 24,999	6,600	48,000 to 49,999	12,750
25,000 to 25,999	6,850	50,000 to 51,999	13,250
26,000 to 27,999	7,250	52,000 to 53,999	13,750
28,000 to 29,999	7,750	54,000 to 55,999	14,250
30,000 to 31,999	8,250	56,000 to 57,999	14,750
32,000 to 33,999	8,750	58,000 to 59,999	15,250
34,000 to 35,999	9,250		

For autos with a FMV in excess of $59,999, the annual lease value equals (.25 × auto FMV) + $500.[37]

Illustration: On Jan. 1, of Year 1, X Co. provides a car worth $31,000 free to its employee E. None of the fringe benefit exclusions apply. The annual lease value (see chart above) is $8,250. This is the value of E's benefit for Year 1. E must include $8,250 in income.

This method takes into account the value of employer-provided insurance and maintenance but not the value of fuel, which must be valued separately for inclusion in the employee's income. If reimbursed by or charged to the employer at FMV, fuel is generally valued at its actual reimbursed or charged amount; if it's provided in kind it can be valued based on all facts and circumstances or, alternatively, at 5 1/2¢ per mile for all miles driven (in the U.S., Canada or Mexico) by the employee. (Reg § 1.61-21(d)(3))[38]

The annual lease values computed above are determined on the basis of an assumed 4-year lease term (beginning on the first date this method is used and ending on Dec. 31 of the following fourth full calendar year). The annual lease value for each next 4-year period is determined on the basis of the FMV on the Jan. 1 after the preceding period, using the lease valuation table. (Reg § 1.61-21(d)(2)(iv))[39]

Subject to certain restrictions, an employer with a fleet of 20 or more autos may determine the annual lease value of each auto in the fleet as if its FMV were equal to the "fleet-average value." (Reg § 1.61-21(d)(5)) For 2017, this method couldn't be used for autos with FMVs greater than $21,100 ($23,300 for trucks or vans). [40]

observation: The 2018 figures had not been released as of the date the Federal Tax Handbook went to press. Check tax.thomsonreuters.com/federaltaxhandbookupdates to see if they have been subsequently issued.

¶ 1232 Prorated annual lease value.

Where an employer-provided auto is continuously available to the employee for periods of 30 or more days, but less than an entire calendar year, the value of the availability of the auto is the prorated annual lease value, computed by multiplying the annual lease value (¶1232) by a fraction where the numerator is the number of days of availability and

---

37. ¶s H-2238, H-2239
38. ¶H-2253; ¶614.027

39. ¶H-2246; ¶614.027
40. ¶H-2260; ¶614.027

the denominator is 365. (Reg § 1.61-21(d)(4))[41]

¶ 1233 Daily lease value.

Where an employer-provided auto is continuously available to the employee for at least one but less than 30 days, the value of the use of the auto is its daily lease value, calculated by multiplying the auto's annual lease value (¶1232) by a fraction where the numerator is four times the number of days of the auto's availability and the denominator is 365. A 30-day period may be used even if availability is less than 30 days if this produces a lower valuation. (Reg § 1.61-21(d)(4))[42]

¶ 1234 Cents-per-mile valuation method.

Under the cents-per-mile valuation method, the value of an employer-provided auto equals the total number of miles the employee drove it for personal purposes in the tax year times the optional standard mileage rate (54.5¢ for 2018), see ¶1554.[43] This method takes into account the value of insuring and maintaining the vehicle, and the value of fuel provided by the employer. If fuel isn't provided, the cents-per-mile rate may be reduced by no more than 5.5¢ per mile. (Reg § 1.61-21(e)(3))[44] For 2017, the cents-per-mile method couldn't be used if the auto's fair market value, as of the date it's first made available to any employee for personal use, exceeds $15,900 for autos ($17,800 for a truck or van). [45]

observation: The 2018 figures had not been released as of the date the Federal Tax Handbook went to press. Check tax.thomsonreuters.com/federaltaxhandbookupdates to see if they have been subsequently issued.

¶ 1235 Commuting value method—$1.50 per one-way commute.

Under this method, the value of an employee's use of a vehicle for commuting purposes only is computed as $1.50 per one-way commute (e.g., from home to work, or work to home). If there's more than one employee who commutes in a single vehicle, the commuting benefit is still $1.50 per one-way commute for each employee. (Reg § 1.61-21(f)(3))[46] Various requirements must be satisfied, including that the employee must be required to commute in the auto for bona-fide noncompensatory business reasons. The method can't be used for "control employees" (certain owner-employees, higher-paid employees, and directors) (Reg § 1.61-21(f)(1)), or to value the commuting use of any chauffeur-driven vehicle, except for the commuting use by the chauffeur. (Reg § 1.61-21(f)(2))[47]

¶ 1236 Employer-provided airflights.

Airflights provided by an employer for an employee's personal purposes are fringe benefits includible in the employee's gross income. (Reg § 1.61-21(a)(1))[48]

Special valuation methods are available to value noncommercial flights on employer-provided aircraft (¶1237 *et seq.*), and "space available" flights on commercial aircraft (¶1239). Use of a special method is optional. But if an employer uses either special rule, that rule generally must be used to value all flights taken by employees in a calendar year. (Reg § 1.61-21(g)(14)(i), Reg § 1.61-21(h)(5)(i))[49]

If an employee takes a trip on an employer-provided aircraft primarily for the employer's business, but which includes both personal and business flights, the value of the personal

---

41. ¶H-2243; ¶614.027
42. ¶H-2245; ¶614.027
43. ¶H-2268; ¶614.027
44. ¶H-2277 *et seq.*; ¶614.027
45. ¶H-2272; ¶614.027

46. ¶H-2282; ¶614.027
47. ¶H-2283; ¶614.027
48. ¶H-2301; ¶614.027
49. ¶H-2301 *et seq.*; ¶614.027

flights is a taxable fringe benefit. The value of the benefit equals the excess of the value of all the flights comprising the trip, over the value of the flights the employee would have taken if all travel had been for business. If the employee combines personal and business flights on a trip that's primarily personal, the amount includible is the value of the personal flights that would have been taken had there been only personal flights. The value of all these flights may be computed under the special valuation rules (¶1237 *et seq.*). (Reg § 1.61-21(g)(4))[50]

¶ 1237   SIFL formula for valuing noncommercial flights.

Value is determined by multiplying the "base aircraft valuation formula" —also known as the Standard Industry Fair Level (SIFL) formula (cents-per-mile rates that are revised semi-annually) —in effect at the time of the flight by the "aircraft multiple" (based on the takeoff weight of the plane) and adding the applicable "terminal charge." (Reg § 1.61-21(g)(5))[1]

¶ 1238   "Seating capacity" (zero inclusion) rule for noncommercial flights.

The "seating capacity" rule is available for noncommercial flights on employer-provided aircraft where at least half of the aircraft's passenger seating capacity is occupied by employees whose flights are primarily for the employer's business (and whose flights are excludable as a working condition fringe, see ¶1243). In this situation, the includible value of the flight taken by the employee for personal purposes is zero. (Reg § 1.61-21(g)(12))[2]

¶ 1239   "Space-available" rule for commercial flights.

If an employer provides an employee (as specially defined at Reg § 1.132-1(b)(1)) with a flight on a commercial aircraft for the employee's personal purposes, the flight is a taxable fringe benefit whose value must be included in the employee's gross income (¶1236). If the flight is a "space-available flight" on a commercial airline, its value for certain current or former airline employees may be computed under a special rule: 25% of the actual carrier's highest unrestricted coach fare for the flight taken. (Reg § 1.61-21(h)(1))[3]

¶ 1240   Excludable fringe benefits.

A fringe benefit isn't included in gross income if it's excluded under a specific Code section (see below) (Code Sec. 61(a)), or qualifies as one of the following: (Code Sec. 132(a))[4]

... no additional cost service (¶1241);

... qualified employee discount (¶1242);

... working condition fringe (¶1243);

... de minimis fringe (¶1244);

... qualified transportation fringe (¶1245);

... qualified moving expense reimbursement for certain military personnel (¶1246);

... employer-provided retirement advice (¶1248).

For qualified military base realignment and closure fringe benefit, see ¶1222.

A fringe benefit that's expressly provided for in any other Code section can't be excluded from gross income under the Code Sec. 132 rules, except as a de minimis fringe or as a qualified moving expense reimbursement. (Code Sec. 132(l))[5] Fringe benefits excluded

---

50. ¶s H-2314, H-2315; ¶614.027
1. ¶H-2304, ¶H-2307 *et seq.*; ¶614.027
2. ¶H-2319; ¶614.027

3. ¶H-2337; ¶614.027
4. ¶H-1051; ¶1324
5. ¶H-1052; ¶1324

under a specific Code section include holiday and other gifts of nominal value (¶1211); certain stock options (¶1218); clergy member's home ("parsonage allowance," ¶1225); employee achievement awards (¶1249); on-premises athletic facilities (¶1250); adoption assistance (¶1252); educational assistance (¶2214); medical care coverage, including accident and health insurance (¶1253 *et seq.*); group-term life insurance (¶1260); meals and lodging (¶1265); qualified campus lodging (¶1266); cafeteria (flexible benefit) plans (¶1267); dependent care assistance programs (¶1268); scholarships (¶2215); and cost of living allowances to certain U.S. government employees (¶4610).[6]

¶ 1241   No-additional-cost services.

No-additional-cost services are excluded from an employee's gross income (see   ¶1240). (Code Sec. 132(a)(1))[7] These are services provided by an employer to an employee for personal use by the employee —or the employee's spouse or dependent children —if:

(1) the services are ordinarily offered for sale to nonemployee customers in the ordinary course of the line of business in which the employee works,

(2) the employer incurs no substantial additional cost (including foregone revenue) in providing the services to the employee —computed without regard to any amounts paid by the employee for the services (Code Sec. 132(b)),[8] and

(3) special nondiscrimination rules are satisfied. (Code Sec.   132(j)(1))[9]

No-additional-cost services include services that would remain unused if the employees didn't use them, e.g., hotel accommodations, transportation by air, train, bus, subway or cruise line, and telephone services. (Reg §   1.132-2(a)(2))[10]

¶ 1242   Qualified employee discounts.

A qualified employee discount is excluded from an employee's gross income (see   ¶1240). (Code Sec. 132(a)(2))[11] This is an "employee discount" allowed with respect to "qualified property or services" provided by an employer to an employee, the employee's spouse or dependent children, to the extent the discount doesn't exceed the limits described below. (Code Sec. 132(c)(1))[12]

An "employee discount" is the excess of: (a) the price at which property or services are offered by an employer for sale to nonemployee customers, over (b) the price at which the employer offers the same property or services to employees for use by those employees. (Code Sec. 132(c)(3))[13]

"Qualified property or services" means any property (other than real property, or personal property of a kind held for investment) or services that are offered for sale to nonemployee customers in the ordinary course of the employer's line of business in which the employee works. (Code Sec. 132(c)(4), Code Sec. 132(k))[14]

Limitations. The excludable amount of a qualified employee discount with respect to property is limited to the gross profit percentage of the price at which that property is offered by the employer to customers. (Code Sec. 132(c)(1)(A)) Gross profit percentage equals the aggregate sales price of the property sold by the employer to all customers, whether employees or nonemployees (Reg §   1.132-3(c)(1)(i)), over the aggregate cost of the property (Code Sec. 132(c)(2)(A)(i)), divided by the aggregate sales price. (Code Sec. 132(c)(2)(A)(ii))[15]

6. ¶H-1052; ¶614.027
7. ¶H-1871; ¶1324.03
8. ¶H-1871; ¶1324.03
9. ¶H-1930 *et seq.*; ¶1324.01
10. ¶H-1872; ¶1324.03

11. ¶H-1901; ¶1324.04
12. ¶H-1902; ¶1324.04
13. ¶H-1904; ¶1324.04
14. ¶H-1903; ¶1324.04
15. ¶H-1909; ¶1324.04

The excludable amount for discounted services is limited to 20% of the price at which the employer offers the service to nonemployees. (Code Sec. 132(c)(1)(B), Code Sec. 132(k))[16]

¶ 1243 Working condition fringes.

Working condition fringes are excluded from the employee's gross income (see ¶1240). (Code Sec. 132(a)(3))[17] A "working condition fringe" is any property or service provided to an employee by the employer to the extent the cost of the property or service would have been deductible by the employee under either Code Sec. 162 (as trade or business expenses) or Code Sec. 167 (as a depreciation expense) if the employee had paid for the property or service. (Code Sec. 132(d))[18] Examples include employer-paid business travel and the use of employer-provided vehicles for business purposes. [19]

Certain benefits qualify as working condition fringes only if special requirements are satisfied. These include the use of consumer goods manufactured for sale to nonemployee customers and provided to employees for product testing and evaluation outside the employer's work place (Reg § 1.132-5(n)(1));[20] the personal use of vehicles otherwise used in connection with the business of farming (Reg § 1.132-5(g));[21] job placement assistance; [22] employer-paid club dues (Reg § 1.132-5(s));[23] employer-paid expenses of a companion on a business trip (Reg § 1.132-5(t));[24] "qualified automobile demonstration use" by automobile salespersons (Code Sec. 132(j)(3); Reg § 1.132-5(o)),[25] the use of employer-owned aircraft for business travel (Reg § 1.132-5(k));[26] certain forms of transportation and other employer-provided security measures provided because of bona fide business-oriented security concerns (Reg § 1.132-5(m));[27] the use of "qualified nonpersonal use vehicles" (Reg § 1.132-5(h));[28] and the use of a cell phone provided to an employee primarily for noncompensatory business reasons. [29]

¶ 1244 De minimis fringe benefits.

De minimis fringe benefits are excluded from the recipient's gross income (see ¶1240) (Code Sec. 132(a)(4)) A de minimis fringe is any property or service whose value is so small that accounting for it's unreasonable or administratively impracticable, taking into account the frequency with which similar fringe benefits are provided by the employer to its employees. (Code Sec. 132(e)(1))

Examples of de minimis fringes include occasional meals, supper money, or local transportation provided because of overtime work (Reg § 1.132-6(d)(2)); meals at employer-operated eating facilities (see below); transportation (e.g., taxi fare) where other available means of transportation are unsafe, in excess of value over $1.50 per each one-way commute (¶1229) (Reg § 1.132-6(d)(2)); occasional cocktail parties or picnics; traditional holiday gifts of property (not cash) with a low FMV; flowers, fruit, etc., provided under special circumstances, such as sickness or outstanding performance (Reg § 1.132-6(e)(1)); low-value clothing bearing the employer's name, which must be worn by the employee; electronically filing the employee's income tax return (but not paying someone to prepare the return); and an employee's personal use of a cell phone provided by the employer primarily for noncompensatory business reasons. [30]

No qualified transportation fringe benefit (¶1245) (including amounts in excess of the

16. ¶H-1914; ¶1324.04
17. ¶H-1701; ¶1324.05
18. ¶H-1701; ¶1324.05
19. ¶H-1701; ¶1324.05
20. ¶H-1712; ¶1324.05
21. ¶H-2370; ¶1324.05
22. ¶H-1711; ¶1324.05
23. ¶H-2153.1

24. ¶H-2153.2
25. ¶H-2364; ¶1324.05
26. ¶H-2351; ¶1324.05
27. ¶H-2373 *et seq.*; ¶1324.05
28. ¶H-2354; ¶1324.05
29. ¶H-1707.2; ¶1324.05
30. ¶H-1802 *et seq.*; ¶1324.06

dollar limit) may be excluded as a de minimis fringe benefit. (Code Sec. 132(f)(7))[31] However, partners, more-than-2% S corporation shareholders and independent contractors (but not employees) can exclude transit passes, tokens and fare cards if not in excess of $21 per month.[32]

Meals at employer-operated eating facilities are de minimis fringes if the facility's annual revenues normally equal or exceed its direct operating costs and certain nondiscrimination rules are met. Employees who are entitled (under the rules at ¶1265) to exclude the value of a meal provided at the facility are treated as having paid an amount for the meal equal to the direct operating costs of the facility attributable to the meal. (Code Sec. 132(e)(2); Reg § 1.132-7(a)(2), Reg § 1.132-7(c))[33] Direct operating costs are the costs of the food and beverages served and the labor for related services performed primarily on the facility's premises. (Reg § 1.132-7(b)(1))[34]

¶ 1245   Qualified transportation fringe benefits.

An employee (other than a self-employed person) may exclude from income qualified transportation fringe benefits up to specified dollar amounts (below). (Code Sec. 132(a)(5), Code Sec. 132(f)(5)) These benefits include:

(1) Transportation in a commuter highway vehicle (van pool), if in connection with travel between the employee's residence and place of employment. A commuter highway vehicle has a seating capacity of six adults (excluding the driver) for which 80% of the mileage must be reasonably expected to be for employee commuting and to be for trips where the vehicle is at least 50% full, excluding the driver (known as the 80/50 rule). Different qualification and substantiation rules apply depending on whether the van pool arrangement is employer operated, employee operated, or privately or publicly operated.[35]

(2) Transit passes for use on a mass transit facility (e.g., rail, bus or ferry) or a commuter highway vehicle.

(3) Qualified parking at or near the employer's business premises or a location from which the employee commutes to work by mass transit or hired commuter vehicle. Any parking at or near the employee's residence isn't qualified parking. (Code Sec. 132(f)(1), Code Sec. 132(f)(5); Reg § 1.132-9(b))

For 2018, an employee can exclude up to $260 a month of qualified parking, and up to an additional $260 a month for the combined value of transit passes and transportation in a commuter highway vehicle. For 2019, the exclusion amounts are each $265, as calculated by Thomson Reuters based on inflation data. (Code Sec. 132(f)(2))[36]

Cash reimbursements (but *not* cash advances) for transit passes are excludable where vouchers, etc. (which may be exchanged only for transit passes) aren't readily available for direct distribution by the employer to the employee. (Code Sec. 132(f)(3); Reg § 1.132-9(b)) Employers can't provide qualified transportation fringe benefits in the form of cash reimbursements in areas where a terminal-restricted debit card (one that can be used at points of sale where only transit fares may be purchased) is readily available. [37] (Lump-sum cash payments to employees to reflect retroactive legislation increasing the exemption amount for certain qualified transportation fringe benefits are taxable compensation where transit passes were readily available or, where passes aren't readily available, if not made under a bona fide reimbursement arrangement for expenses actually incurred and substantiated. [38]) IRS has provided detailed guidance on the use of smartcards, debit or credit cards, and

31. ¶H-2202; ¶1324.08
32. ¶H-1806
33. ¶H-1821; ¶1324.06
34. ¶H-1823; ¶1324.06

35. ¶H-2210
36. ¶H-2217; ¶1324.08
37. ¶H-2212, H-2216; ¶1324.08
38. ¶H-2212.1

other electronic media to provide qualified transportation fringe benefits. [39]

No amount is included in an employee's gross income solely because a choice is offered between any qualified transportation fringe and otherwise includible compensation. (Code Sec. 132(f)(4)) But if cash is elected instead of a qualified transportation fringe, the employee will be taxed. [40] If fringes are chosen rather than cash, the employee won't be taxed on any exchanged cash if requirements are met. (Reg § 1.132-9(b))[41]

The qualified transportation fringe exclusion doesn't apply to any arrangement that results in the reimbursement of an expense the employee hasn't actually incurred, e.g., where the employee is reimbursed for an item paid for through a tax-free salary reduction.[42]

Partners, 2% S corporation shareholders and independent contractors can't exclude qualified transportation fringes. (Code Sec. 132(f)(5)(E))[43]

¶ 1246   Qualified moving expense reimbursement for armed forces.

For tax years beginning after Dec. 31, 2017 and before Jan. 1, 2026, qualified moving expense reimbursements are excluded from gross income for members of the U.S. Armed Forces on active duty who move pursuant to a military order and incident to a permanent change of station. (Code Sec. 132(a)(6))[44]

A qualified moving expense reimbursement is any amount received (directly or indirectly) from an employer as a payment of (or reimbursement for) moving expenses that would have been deductible had the taxpayer paid them directly (for employee's moving expense deduction, see ¶1627 *et seq.*). Expenses aren't excludable if the taxpayer actually deducted them in an earlier year. (Code Sec. 132(g))[45] Otherwise an employer's payment or reimbursement is income to the employee. (Code Sec. 82)[46] The employer reports moving expense reimbursements (but not qualifying payments to third parties or qualifying services furnished in kind) to the employee on Form W-2. [47]

¶ 1247   Reimbursement of employee in connection with sale of residence.

An employer's reimbursement for an employee's loss on sale of the employee's home is income to the employee.[48] However, if the employer buys the employee's home at its fair market value (FMV), the employee has no income other than gain on the sale. Where, as an alternative to reimbursing an employee for the loss, the employer buys the home for more than its FMV, that *excess* is taxable to the employee. [49]

¶ 1248   Employer-provided retirement advice.

Qualified retirement planning services are excluded from the income of the employee receiving the services. (Code Sec. 132(a)(7)) These are any retirement planning services provided to an employee by an employer maintaining a qualified employer plan (as defined in Code Sec. 219(g)(5)). (Code Sec. 132(m))[50]

¶ 1249   Employee achievement awards.

Employee achievement awards are excludable only to the extent the employer can deduct the cost of the award — generally limited to $400 for any one employee, or $1,600 for a

39. ¶H-2216A
40. ¶H-2216.1; ¶1324.08
41. ¶H-2216.1; ¶1324.08
42. ¶H-2216
43. ¶H-2206; ¶1324.08
44. ¶H-1971; ¶1324.09

45. ¶H-1971; ¶1324.09
46. ¶H-4418; ¶824
47. ¶S-3170; ¶60,514
48. ¶s H-2161, H-2162; ¶824
49. ¶H-2162
50. ¶H-1980; ¶1324.10

"qualified plan award," see ¶1575. (Code Sec. 74(c)(2))[1]

observation: "Employee achievement awards" don't include cash, cash equivalents, gift cards, gift coupons, gift certificates, vacations, meals, lodging, tickets to theater or sporting events, stocks, bonds, other securities, and other similar items. (Code Sec. 274(j)(3)) See ¶1575.

¶ 1250   On-premises athletic facilities.

The value of an on-premises athletic facility provided by an employer is excluded from an employee's gross income. (Code Sec. 132(j)(4)(A))[2]

¶ 1251   Employer payment of employee's personal expenses.

Where an employer pays the debts or personal expenses of an employee, or reimburses the employee's payment, the employee must include the payment or reimbursement in income.[3] For medical expenses, see ¶1253.

An employer's payment of an employee's income taxes (federal or state) or other taxes is income to the employee. Pyramiding of income, and of tax, results where the employer agrees to pay all the employee's tax. (Reg § 1.61-14)[4]

¶ 1252   Employer-provided adoption assistance—Form 8839.

An employee may exclude amounts paid or expenses incurred by the employer for qualified adoption expenses (¶2349) connected with the employee's adoption of a child, if the amounts are furnished under an adoption assistance program in existence (and known to the employee) before the expenses are incurred. For the adoption of a child with special needs, the exclusion applies regardless of whether the employee actually has qualified adoption expenses. (Code Sec. 137(a), Code Sec. 137(b), Code Sec. 137(f))[5]

The maximum exclusion for employer-provided adoption assistance is $13,810 for 2018 ($14,080 for 2019, as calculated by Thomson Reuters based on inflation data) per child (for both non-special needs and special needs adoptions). (Code Sec. 137(a)(2))

For 2018, the excludable amount is phased out for taxpayers with modified adjusted gross income (MAGI—which is adjusted gross income, as specially computed) over $207,140, and is fully eliminated when MAGI reaches $247,140. For 2019, the phaseout starts at $211,170 and is completed at $251,170, as calculated by Thomson Reuters based on inflation data. (Code Sec. 137(b)(2), Code Sec. 137(f)) To compute the excluded employer-provided adoption benefits, use Form 8839. [6]

Amounts are excludable in the year in which the employer pays for qualified adoption expenses of an eligible child who is a U.S. citizen or resident when the adoption commenced. If the eligible child isn't a U.S. citizen or resident, the exclusion is available only for adoptions that become final, and only in the year that they're finalized. Where expenses of a foreign eligible child are paid in a year before the adoption becomes final, the employee includes the employer's assistance in income for that year, and claims the otherwise available exclusion in the year the adoption becomes final. A taxpayer may claim both an adoption expense credit (see ¶2349) and an exclusion for the adoption of an eligible child, but can't claim a credit and an exclusion for the same expense. [7]

---

1. ¶L-2317 et seq.; ¶744.03
2. ¶H-1951; ¶1324.07
3. ¶H-2151; ¶s 614.007, 614.146
4. ¶H-2157; ¶614.147

5. ¶H-1450 et seq.; ¶1374
6. ¶H-1453; ¶1374
7. ¶H-1451 et seq.; ¶1374

¶ 1253 Employee's medical expenses reimbursed or insured by employer.

An employee excludes from gross income reimbursements from an employer, directly or indirectly, for expenses for the medical care of himself, spouse, and dependents. The exclusion also applies to any child of an employee who hasn't attained age 27 as of the end of the year. (Code Sec. 105(b)) However, reimbursement is includible in the employee's income to the extent it exceeds medical expenses or it's attributable to medical expense deductions taken in a previous year. (Code Sec. 105(b); Reg § 1.105-2)[8][9]

An employee also excludes the cost (i.e., premiums paid) of employer-provided *coverage* under an accident or health plan for the employee; the employee's spouse (partners in registered domestic partnerships, civil unions, or other similar formal relationships that aren't marriages under state law aren't spouses for federal tax purposes); the employee's dependents; and the employee's children who haven't reached age 27 as of the end of the employee's tax year. (Code Sec. 106)[10] But insurance premiums paid for partners and more-than-2% S corporation shareholders (who are treated as partners) aren't excludable.[11]

Highly compensated individuals (as defined in Code Sec. 105(h)(5)) who benefit from an employer's "self-insured" medical reimbursement plan that discriminates in their favor must include "excess reimbursements" (reimbursements for benefits not available to other plan participants) in income. (Code Sec. 105(h))[12]

¶ 1254 Employer contributions to Archer medical savings account (Archer MSA).

Small-employer contributions to an employee's Archer MSA are treated as excludable employer-provided coverage for medical expenses under an accident or health plan (¶1253) to the extent the amounts don't exceed the applicable statutory limits (see ¶1527). (Code Sec. 106(b)(1))[13] Generally, small employers are those that employed on average no more than 50 employees during either of the two preceding years. An employer that grows past the 50-employee limit in a succeeding year may continue MSA contributions until the year after the first year in which it has more than 200 employees. (Code Sec. 220(c)(4))[14] For treatment of Archer MSA distributions, see ¶1369. Employer Archer MSA contributions aren't excludable if made at the employee's election under a salary reduction arrangement under a cafeteria plan. (Code Sec. 125(f))

¶ 1255 Employer contributions to health savings accounts (HSAs).

Employer contributions to an employee's HSA are treated as employer-provided coverage for medical expenses under an accident or health plan (¶1253) to the extent they don't exceed the statutory limits (see ¶1528) applicable to the employee for the tax year, and are deductible by the employer in the year they're paid. (Code Sec. 106(d)(2)) Employer contributions to an HSA on behalf of an eligible individual are excludable from income.[15] The contributions must be reported on the employee's Form W-2.[16] For HSA distributions, see ¶1370. However, where contributions exceed the limits and the employer doesn't recoup the amount, the excess must be included in the employee's income and reported on Form W-2.[17]

8. ¶H-1110 *et seq.*;

9. ¶H-1110; ¶1054.01

10. ¶H-1102; ¶1064

11. ¶H-1126; ¶1064

12. ¶H-1138 *et seq.*; ¶1054.05

13. ¶H-1101.1 et seq., ¶1064

14. ¶s H-1333, H-1333.1; ¶2204.01

15. ¶H-1101.5; ¶1064

16. ¶S-3152; ¶60,514

17. ¶H-1350.8D

There's no constructive receipt of income solely because the employee may choose between employer contributions to an HSA and to another health plan. (Code Sec. 106(d)(2)) Employer contributions to an HSA are excludable if made at the employee's salary-reduction election under a cafeteria plan (see ¶1267). (Code Sec. 125(d)(2))

¶ 1256 Employer's payments for employee's loss of limb, disfigurement, etc.

Amounts received under an employer plan as payment for permanent loss or loss of use of a member or function of the body, or permanent disfigurement, of the employee —or the employee's spouse or dependent —are tax-free, but only if the payment is based on the nature of the injury without regard to the period the employee is absent from work. (Code Sec. 105(c))[18]

¶ 1257 Worker's compensation.

Amounts received under a worker's compensation act or similar law for personal injuries or sickness are excludable from the employee's (or survivor's) income. This rule doesn't apply to the extent payments are determined by reference to the employee's age or length of service or prior contributions, even if retirement is occasioned by occupational injury. (Reg § 1.104-1(b)) Worker's compensation is includible in income to the extent it's attributable to medical expense deductions taken in an earlier year. (Code Sec. 104(a)(1); Reg § 1.104-1(b))[19]

¶ 1258 Annuities paid to survivors of public safety officers killed in line of duty.

Survivor annuity benefits paid on account of the death of a public safety officer (including law enforcement officers, firefighters, rescue squad workers and ambulance crew members) killed in the line of duty are excluded: (1) if provided under a governmental plan that meets the requirements of Code Sec. 401(a) to the officer's spouse, former spouse, or child; and (2) to the extent attributable to the officer's service as a public safety officer. (Code Sec. 101(h)(1)) The exclusion doesn't apply under certain circumstances (e.g., if the death was caused by the officer's intentional misconduct). (Code Sec. 101(h)(2))[20]

¶ 1259 Employer-paid individual life insurance policies.

Premiums paid by an employer for policies on the life of an employee are taxable to the employee if the proceeds are payable to the employee's beneficiary (except for group-term insurance, see ¶1260) but not where the employer is the beneficiary. (Reg § 1.61-2(d)(2))[21]

¶ 1260 Group-term life insurance premiums.

An employee isn't taxed on premiums paid by the employer on insurance covering the employee's life under a group-term life insurance policy to the extent that the employee's total coverage provided by all employers doesn't exceed $50,000. If total coverage exceeds $50,000, the employee is taxed on the "cost" (¶1261) of coverage over $50,000 minus the amount paid by the employee. (Code Sec. 79(a))[22] For coverage of employee's spouse and dependents, see ¶1262.

An employee whose total coverage exceeds $50,000 for only part of the year includes the employer's payments for that part of the year's coverage, even if the average coverage for the year is under this ceiling. (Code Sec. 79(a))[23]

---

18. ¶H-1201; ¶1054.02
19. ¶H-1351; ¶1044.01
20. ¶H-1650 *et seq.*; ¶1014.09

21. ¶H-1501 *et seq.*; ¶614.031
22. ¶H-1518; ¶794
23. ¶H-1520; ¶794.01

But a disabled terminated employee isn't taxable on group term coverage even if it exceeds $50,000. (Code Sec. 79(b)(1))[24] Retired employees are generally treated the same as other employees. (Code Sec. 79(e))[25]

The exclusion doesn't apply to any insurance protection in excess of the maximum allowed by state law for employee group insurance. (Reg § 1.79-1(e))[26]

The exclusion is available to a key employee only if the plan doesn't discriminate in favor of key employees (at any time in the key employee's tax year) (Reg § 1.79-4T, Q&A-11) as to eligibility to participate and in the type and amount of benefits available. (Code Sec. 79(d))[27] If the plan is discriminatory, each key employee must include the *greater of* (a) the actual cost of the insurance (determined by apportioning the net premium allocable to the group-term coverage during the key employee's tax year among the covered employees (Reg § 1.79-4T, Q&A-6(b)), *or* (b) the cost determined from IRS's premium table. (Code Sec. 79(d)(1)(B))[28]

¶ 1261 "Cost" of taxable group-term insurance—IRS uniform premium table.

The employer must compute the "cost" of taxable group-term coverage (¶1260) and notify the employee on Form W-2 of the amount included in income. The employee must compute the cost if coverage is provided by two or more employers.

The cost of group-term life insurance is determined on the basis of uniform premiums (computed on the basis of five-year age brackets) prescribed by IRS. (Code Sec. 79(c)) The cost for each month of coverage is the number of thousands of dollars of coverage over $50,000 (to the nearest tenth) times the amount in IRS's table for the employee's attained age on the last day of the employee's tax year. (Reg § 1.79-3(d)(2))[29] If the employee contributes to the plan, all the employee's contributions for the tax year are considered made for that part of coverage over $50,000. (Code Sec. 79(a)(2))[30]

¶ 1262 Group-term coverage of employee's spouse and dependents.

The cost (as determined at ¶1261) of group-term life insurance on the life of an individual other than an employee (e.g., the employee's spouse or dependent) provided in connection with the performance of services by the employee is includible in the employee's gross income. (Reg § 1.61-2(d)(2)(ii)(b)) If, however, the face amount of employer-provided group-term insurance payable on the death of an employee's spouse or dependent doesn't exceed $2,000, it's an excludable de minimis fringe (¶1244).[31]

¶ 1263 Group-permanent insurance premiums.

Group-permanent insurance premiums that an employer pays on an employee's life are included in the employee's income. Where a group term policy provides permanent benefits, the amount included in income for the permanent benefits is computed under a complex formula. (Reg § 1.79-1(d))[32]

¶ 1264 Split-dollar life insurance.

Under a "split-dollar" insurance arrangement, the employer pays part of the premium for a life insurance policy on the life of the employee (to the extent of the annual increase in cash surrender value) and the employee pays the rest. Out of the insurance proceeds,

24. ¶H-1552; ¶794.03
25. ¶s H-1555, H-1556; ¶794.06
26. ¶H-1537
27. ¶H-1564; ¶794.05
28. ¶H-1565; ¶794.05

29. ¶H-1521; ¶794.01
30. ¶H-1522; ¶794.01
31. ¶H-1560 *et seq.*; ¶614.031, ¶1324.06
32. ¶H-1545; ¶794.04

the employer gets either the cash surrender value or the amount it paid; the employee can designate the beneficiary of the balance. [33] For arrangements entered into (or materially modified) after Sept. 17, 2003, there are two mutually exclusive regimes for taxing split-dollar life insurance arrangements.

Under the economic benefit regime, the policy owner is treated as providing economic benefits to the non-owner (as valued in the regs). This regime governs the taxation of what are known as endorsement split-dollar arrangements (e.g., the employer owns the policy and employee's rights are derived from the employer's endorsement in the contract of those rights). This regime automatically applies if the arrangement is (1) entered into in connection with the performance of services, and the employee or other service provider isn't the contract owner, or (2) a gift situation, and the donee isn't the contract owner. (Reg § 1.61-22)

Under the loan regime, the non-owner of the contract is treated as loaning premium payments to the contract owner. Unless specifically excepted, the loan regime applies to any split-dollar loan. The loan regime also governs what are known as collateral assignment split-dollar life insurance arrangements (e.g., employee owns the policy, which is used as collateral for employer's right to recover the premiums it pays). (Reg § 1.7872-15)

The employer (or donor in a gift arrangement) is treated as the owner of a split-dollar life insurance contract if the only economic benefit that the employee (or donee) has under the arrangement is current life insurance protection. (Reg § 1.61-22(c)(1))

Unless the non-owner's payments are made in consideration of economic benefits, general income, employment, and gift tax principles apply to the arrangement. For example, if an employee/contract owner's repayment obligation to an employer were waived or cancelled, both parties must account for the amount as compensation. (Reg § 1.61-22(b)(6))

In a split-dollar life insurance arrangement taxed under the economic benefit regime, the policy owner is treated as providing economic benefits to the non-owner, and those benefits have to be accounted for fully and consistently by both the owner and the non-owner. The value of the economic benefits, less any consideration paid by the non-owner, is treated as transferred from the owner to the non-owner. The tax consequences of that transfer depend on the relationship between the owner and the non-owner. Thus, depending on the circumstances, it might be treated as compensation, a dividend, or a gift. (Reg § 1.61-22(d)(1))

A payment made under a split-dollar arrangement is a split-dollar loan, and the policy owner and non-owner are treated, respectively, as borrower and lender, if the payment is made directly or indirectly by the non-owner to the owner; the payment either is a loan under general tax law principles or if a reasonable person would expect the payment to be repaid in full to the non-owner; and repayment is to be made from, or secured by, the policy's death benefit or cash surrender value, or both. (Reg § 1.7872-15(a)(2))

Because split-dollar life insurance arrangements typically provide for deferred compensation, Code Sec. 409A (¶1273) generally applies. But Code Sec. 409A doesn't apply for earnings on amounts deferred under a split-dollar life insurance arrangement in tax years beginning before 2005 (unless the plan is materially modified after Oct. 3, 2004), including increases in the policy cash value —but not including increases attributable to continued services performed, compensation earned, or premium payments or other contributions made on or after 2005. [34]

Special rules apply to certain split-dollar life insurance arrangements entered into before Sept. 18, 2003 [35] and before Jan. 28, 2002. [36]

---

33. ¶H-1601; ¶614.033
34. ¶H-3200.6; ¶409A4.01

35. ¶H-1647 *et seq.*; ¶614.033
36. ¶H-1647.11

¶ 1265 Meals and lodging furnished by or on behalf of employer.

Meals or lodging (including utilities) furnished to an employee and family (spouse and dependents) is nontaxable to the employee if (Code Sec. 119):

(1) the meals and lodging are furnished by or on behalf of the employer for the convenience of the employer (e.g., meals supplied because eating places near work are scarce, or because employees must for valid business reasons remain on-premises until their shifts end) (Reg § 1.119-1(a)(2)), and

(2) (a) in the case of *meals,* they're furnished on the employer's business premises, or (b) in the case of *lodging,* the employee is required to accept the lodging as a condition of employment (i.e., to properly perform job duties). (Reg § 1.119-1(b))[37] This means the employee's presence must be required from a business standpoint —e.g., ranches, hotels, motels and resorts.[38] For faculty housing, see ¶1266.

The value (not the cost) of meals or lodging that fails to meet these tests generally is income to the employee. (Reg § 1.61-2(d)(3), Reg § 1.119-1(a)(1))[39] However, all meals furnished on the employer's business premises to its employees are treated as furnished for the employer's convenience—and so are excludable from the employees' income —if *more than half* of the employees to whom the meals are furnished on the premises are furnished the meals for the convenience of the employer. (Code Sec. 119(b)(4))[40]

observation: In other words, if the more-than-half test is met, all employees may exclude the value of meals provided on premises, even those who weren't supplied the meals for the convenience of the employer.

Cash allowances for meals are taxable.[41] If the employee can take either cash, or meals or lodging furnished in kind, the value of meals or lodging furnished is income. But occasional "supper money" paid to overtime employees is excludable as a de minimis fringe, see ¶1244.[42]

¶ 1266 Faculty housing—qualified campus lodging.

The value of qualified campus lodging furnished to an employee of an educational institution is excludable (with limits, below) from gross income. (Code Sec. 119(d))[43]

Qualified campus lodging is lodging that isn't eligible for the exclusion at ¶1265, that's located on or near a campus of a tax-exempt educational institution (or a qualifying academic health center) and is furnished by the institution to an employee, spouse, and dependents for use as a residence. (Code Sec. 119(d)(3), Code Sec. 119(d)(4))[44]

The exclusion isn't a total one. The employee must include the excess of: (1) the lesser of (a) 5% of the appraised value (as of the close of the tax year) of the qualified campus lodging, or (b) the average of the rentals paid by individuals other than employees or students for comparable lodging provided by the institution; over (2) the rent paid by the employee. (Code Sec. 119(d)(2))[45]

¶ 1267 Cafeteria plans (including flexible spending accounts).

No amount is included in the gross income of the participant in a cafeteria plan solely because, under the plan, the participant may choose among the benefits of the plan. (Code

---

37. ¶H-1751; ¶1194.01
38. ¶H-1776; ¶1194.02
39. ¶s H-1751, H-1785; ¶614.027, ¶1194 *et seq.*
40. ¶H-1754; ¶1194.02
41. ¶H-1790; ¶1194.03

42. ¶H-1791; ¶1324.06
43. ¶H-1797; ¶1194.06
44. ¶H-1799; ¶1194.06
45. ¶H-1797; ¶1194.06

Sec. 125(a))[46] Cafeteria plans are generally the sole method of employers providing nontaxable benefits where employees can elect between taxable compensation and nontaxable benefits. (Prop Reg. § 1.125-1(b)(1) ["Taxpayers may rely"])

A "cafeteria plan" (also referred to as a flexible benefit plan) is a written plan under which participants (all employees) may choose their own "menu" of benefits consisting of "cash" and "qualified benefits." (Code Sec. 125(d))[47] For this purpose, cash means cash from current compensation (including salary reduction), payment for annual leave, sick leave, or other paid time off, severance pay, property, and certain after-tax employee contributions; distributions from qualified retirement plans aren't cash. (Prop Reg. § 1.125-1(a)(2) ["Taxpayers may rely"]) A qualified benefit, which generally must be excludible from employees' gross income under a specific Code section —and must not defer compensation (with some exceptions) (Code Sec. 125(d)(2))—includes group-term life insurance on an employee's life (up to the excludable $50,000 amount, see ¶1260); employer-provided accident and health plans (¶1253) (including health flexible spending arrangements (FSAs), and accidental death and dismemberment policies); a dependent care assistance program (¶1268); an adoption assistance program (¶1252); contributions to a Code Sec. 401(k) plan (¶4306); contributions to certain plans maintained by educational organizations, contributions to Health Savings Accounts (HSAs, see ¶1255); and long-term and short-term disability coverage. (Code Sec. 125(f); Prop Reg. § 1.125-1(a)(3) ["Taxpayers may rely"])[48]

A qualified health plan purchased on the individual market through a health insurance Exchange isn't a qualified benefit for a cafeteria plan. However, it can be a qualified cafeteria plan benefit if it's offered by a "qualified employer" (generally, a "small employer" with an average of not more than 50 employees during the preceding calendar year (100 employees at a state's election) offering the employee the opportunity to enroll in a qualified health plan through an Exchange in a group market, or, a larger employer in a state that allows Exchange insurers to offer qualified health plans in a large-group market, if the employer elects to make all full-time employees eligible for a qualified Exchange health plan). (Code Sec. 125(f)(3))[49] Cafeteria plans can allow employees to, in certain cases, revoke their election for coverage under the employer's group health plan (other than an FSA) during a period of coverage in order to purchase a qualified health plan through an Exchange.[50]

In the case of a "highly compensated participant," the exclusion won't apply to any benefit attributable to a plan year for which the plan discriminates in favor of highly compensated participants as to contributions, benefits or eligibility to participate. (Code Sec. 125(b)(1))[1] "Highly compensated participants" include both officers and more-than-5% shareholders of the employer, highly compensated employees (¶1349) and spouses and dependents of such individuals. (Code Sec. 125(e)(1))[2]

In the case of a key employee (defined in Code Sec. 416(i)(1)), the exclusion won't apply to any plan year if the qualified benefits provided to key employees under the plan exceed 25% of the total of such benefits provided for all employees under the plan. (Code Sec. 125(b)(2))[3]

Flexible Spending Accounts. A cafeteria plan also can include one or more FSAs. An FSA is a benefit designed to reimburse employees for expenses incurred for certain qualified benefits, up to a maximum amount not substantially in excess of the salary reduction and employer flex-credits allocated for the benefit. The maximum amount of reimbursement reasonably available must be less than five times the value of the coverage. (Prop Reg.

46. ¶H-2401; ¶1254
47. ¶H-2405; ¶1254.01
48. ¶H-2413 *et seq.*; ¶1254.01
49. ¶H-1165; ¶1254.01

50. ¶H-2426.6
1. ¶H-2450; ¶1254.06
2. ¶H-2455; ¶1254.06
3. ¶H-2456; ¶1254.06

§ 1.125-5(a) ["Taxpayers may rely"]) Employer flex-credits are non-elective contributions that an employer makes available for every employee eligible to participate in the cafeteria plan, to be used at the employee's election only for one or more qualified benefits (but not as cash or other taxable benefits). (Prop Reg. § 1.125-5(b) ["Taxpayers may rely"]) The three types of FSAs are dependent care assistance, adoption assistance and medical care reimbursements (health FSA).

A health FSA may be limited to a subset of permitted Code Sec. 213(d) medical expenses, or it may be an HSA compatible limited-purpose health FSA or post-deductible health FSA. (Prop Reg. § 1.125-5(m) ["Taxpayers may rely"]) A health FSA may not reimburse premiums for accident and health insurance or long-term care insurance. (Code Sec. 125(f)) For the 2018 cafeteria plan year, an employee can't contribute to a health FSA through salary reduction contributions in excess of $2,650 ($2,700 for 2019, as calculated by Thomson Reuters based on inflation data). (Code Sec. 125(i)) However, for a married couple, each person may contribute up to this maximum. The health FSA cap doesn't limit the amount permitted for reimbursement under other employer-provided coverage, such as an FSA for dependent care assistance. [4]

Use-it-or-lose-it rule. Unused cafeteria plan amounts left over at the end of a plan year generally have to be forfeited (use-it-or-lose-it rule). But a cafeteria plan can provide an optional grace period immediately following the end of each plan year, extending the period for incurring expenses for qualified benefits to the 15th day of the third month after the end of the plan year. It may apply to one or more qualified benefits but can't apply to paid time off or elective contributions to Code Sec. 401(k) plans. Benefits or contributions not used as of the end of the grace period are forfeited. (Prop Reg. § 1.125-1(e)(1) ["Taxpayers may rely"]) [5] An exception to this rule, at the plan sponsor's option and in lieu of any grace period, allows employees to carry over up to $500 of unused amounts remaining at year-end in a health FSA (rather than forfeit it). A health FSA must be amended to adopt a carryover provision on or before the last day of the plan year from which amounts may be carried over and may be effective retroactively to the first day of that plan year. Another exception allows FSAs to make distributions of all or part of unused health FSA benefits to military reservists who are called to active duty for a period exceeding 179 days (or an indefinite period). (Code Sec. 125(h)) [6]

If a plan provides a grace period, unused salary reduction contributions to the health FSA that are carried over into the grace period won't count against the annual dollar limit for the later plan year. [7]

¶ 1268 Dependent care assistance payments—Form 2441.

Payments incurred by an employer for dependent care assistance under a written plan are excluded from an employee's gross income. (Code Sec. 129(a)(1)) [8]

The amount an employee can exclude (computed on Form 2441 with Form 1040) can't exceed the employee's earned income (excluding employer dependent care assistance payments) or, for married employees, the earned income of the lower earning spouse. (Code Sec. 129(b)) [9] The aggregate exclusion is further limited to $5,000 ($2,500 for a married individual filing separately). (Code Sec. 129(a)(2)(A)) Any excess is includible in the tax year the dependent care services are provided. (Code Sec. 129(a)(2)(B)) [10]

Dependent care assistance is the payment for or provision of services that if paid for by the employee would be considered employment-related expenses under the child care

---

4. ¶H-2461 *et seq.*; ¶1254.05
5. ¶H-2417.1
6. ¶H-2459.2A; ¶1254.05
7. ¶H-2461.4 *et seq.*; ¶1254.05

8. ¶H-1401; ¶1294 *et seq.*
9. ¶H-1402; ¶1294
10. ¶H-1402 *et seq.*; ¶1294

credit rules (see ¶2348). (Code Sec. 129(e)(1))[11] For eligible dependents, see ¶2348. An employee includes a self-employed individual who can be covered under a self-employed retirement plan. An individual who owns the entire interest in an unincorporated trade or business is treated as both employer and employee. A partnership is treated as the employer of each partner who is eligible to be included in a self-employed retirement plan. (Code Sec. 129(e)(3), Code Sec. 129(e)(4))[12]

No amount is excludable unless the name, address and (except for a tax-exempt service-provider) taxpayer identifying number (TIN) of the person providing the dependent care services are included on the employee's return. The employee can use Form W-10 to ask for this information from the service provider. Failure to provide the form is excused if the employee exercised due diligence in trying to do so. (Code Sec. 129(e)(9))[13]

The plan must satisfy specific nondiscrimination rules and certain other requirements. (Code Sec. 129(d))[14] If an otherwise qualified program fails to meet these requirements, the program will be a dependent care assistance program under which expenses are still excludable for nonhighly compensated employees. (Code Sec. 129(d)(1))[15]

For how dependent care assistance affects the dependent care credit, see ¶2348.

¶ 1269   Time for Reporting Compensation.

Compensation income is reported according to the recipient's accounting method (cash (¶1270) or accrual (¶1271) basis), subject to constructive receipt, prepaid income and deferred income rules.

¶ 1270   Cash basis taxpayers.

Cash basis taxpayers report compensation for the tax year they actually receive it. [16]

Compensation paid by check is reported for the year the check is received, even if the check covers past or future services, or isn't cashed until the following year. [17]

Compensation income must be reported for the year it's constructively received (¶2821), even if it's not actually received until a later year. Income is constructively received for the year it's credited to the taxpayer's account, set apart for the taxpayer, or otherwise made available so the taxpayer can draw upon it at any time, or could have drawn upon it by giving notice of intent to withdraw. (Reg § 1.451-2(a))[18] For advances, see ¶1272.

¶ 1271   Accrual basis taxpayers.

Accrual basis taxpayers report compensation for the tax year in which it accrues. Compensation accrues when all events have occurred that fix the right to receive the income and its amount can be determined with reasonable accuracy. (Reg §   1.451-1(a))[19]

If the right to compensation for services or its amount can't be determined until the services are completed, the amount of compensation ordinarily isn't reported until the tax year the services are completed and the determination can be made. (Reg §   1.451-1(a))[20]

¶ 1272   Advances and drawing accounts.

A cash basis taxpayer who receives advances against commissions that haven't been earned reports the advances as income for the year they're received if not required to repay the amounts received in excess of commissions. If excess drawings are required to be

---

11. ¶H-1419; ¶1294.02
12. ¶H-1413 *et seq.*; ¶1294.02
13. ¶H-1406 *et seq.*; ¶1294.03
14. ¶H-1428 *et seq.*; ¶1294.01
15. ¶H-1418; ¶1294.01

16. ¶H-3501; ¶s 614.023, 4514.003
17. ¶H-3502; ¶s 614.023, 4514.004
18. ¶H-3508; ¶4514.036
19. ¶G-2471; ¶4514.011
20. ¶H-3526; ¶4514.011

repaid, they aren't income until offset by a credit for commissions earned. [21]

¶ 1273 Deferred compensation plans.

All amounts deferred under a nonqualified deferred compensation (NQDC) plan for all tax years are currently includible in gross income to the extent not subject to a substantial risk of forfeiture and not previously included in gross income, unless the plan:

... meets specified distribution, acceleration of benefit, and election requirements; and

... is operated in accordance with these requirements. (Code Sec. 409A(a)(1)(A)(i))[22]

If a NQDC plan doesn't comply with the Code Sec. 409A rules, all amounts deferred under the plan for the tax year and all prior tax years, by any participant to whom the failure relates, are included in income for that year to the extent not subject to a substantial risk of forfeiture and not previously included in income. This amount is also subject to: (1) interest (at the underpayment rate plus one percentage point) on the tax underpayments that would have occurred had the amount been included in income for the tax year when first deferred, or if later, when not subject to a substantial risk of forfeiture; and (2) a penalty of 20% of the compensation required to be included in income. (Code Sec. 409A(a)(1)(B))

For inclusion in income of deferred compensation from tax-indifferent corporations and partnerships, see ¶1275. The Code Sec. 409A rules apply to NQDC plans separately and in addition to the Code Sec. 457A rules dealing with deferred compensation from tax-indifferent entities. (Prop Reg. § 1.409A-1(a)(4) ['Taxpayers may rely''])

Compensation is subject to a substantial risk of forfeiture if entitlement to it's conditioned on a person's performance of substantial future services or the occurrence of a condition related to the compensation's purpose (e.g., an amount conditioned on involuntary separation from service without cause), and the possibility of forfeiture is substantial. An amount isn't subject to a substantial risk of forfeiture merely because the right to the amount is conditioned upon the refraining from performance of services, such as a noncompete clause. (Reg § 1.409A-1(d)(1))[23]

A NQDC plan is any plan that provides for the deferral of compensation, other than (1) a qualified employer plan (retirement plan, tax-deferred annuity, simplified employee pension, SIMPLE plan, qualified governmental excess benefit arrangement under Code Sec. 415(m), or eligible deferred compensation plan under Code Sec. 457(b)), and (2) any bona fide vacation leave, sick leave, compensatory time, disability pay, or death benefit plan. (Code Sec. 409A(d)) It doesn't include annual bonuses or other annual compensation amounts paid within 2 ½ months after the later of a service recipient's or service provider's tax year (later if making the payment during this period violates Federal securities laws or other applicable law). (Prop Reg. § 1.409A-1(b)(4) ['Taxpayers may rely'']) Proposed regs provide when a payment has been made for Code Sec. 409A purposes. (Prop Reg. § 1.409A-1(q) ["Taxpayers may rely'']) [24]

Incentive stock options (ISOs) and options granted under an employee stock purchase plan (ESPP) aren't subject to Code Sec. 409A. Nonqualified stock options and stock appreciation rights (SARs) are similarly excepted if the exercise price may never be less than the fair market value (FMV) of the underlying stock when the option or right is granted, the number of shares subject to the option are fixed on the grant date, and there's no other deferral feature; in addition, the receipt, transfer or exercise of the stock option must be subject to tax under Code Sec. 83, and only the service recipient's stock may be delivered

---

21. ¶H-3515; ¶614.023
22. ¶H-3200; ¶409A4.01

23. ¶H-3200.50; ¶409A4.01
24. ¶H-3200.27; ¶409A4.01

upon a SAR's exercise. (Reg § 1.409A-1(b)(5))[25]

The distribution requirement is met if a NQDC plan provides that compensation deferred under the plan can't be distributed earlier than (1) the participant's separation from service; (2) the date the participant becomes disabled; (3) the participant's death; (4) a time specified, or a schedule fixed, under the plan as of the date of the deferral of the compensation (amounts payable on the occurrence of an event aren't treated as payable at a specified time); (5) a change in the ownership or effective control of the corporation, or in the ownership of a substantial portion of the assets of the corporation; or (6) the occurrence of an unforeseeable emergency such as a severe financial hardship resulting from illness, casualty loss, etc. (Code Sec. 409A(a)(2); Reg § 1.409A-3(a))[26]

The acceleration of benefits requirement is met if a NQDC plan doesn't allow the acceleration of the time or schedule of any payment under the plan, except as provided in IRS regs. (Code Sec. 409A(a)(3)) Changes in the form of distribution that accelerate payments generally are subject to this rule. But payments made in accordance with plan provisions for acceleration in the event of a service provider's separation from service, death or disability, or in the event of a change in control don't violate these rules. [27] Nor do payments under a domestic relations order, [28] or to comply with a certificate of divestiture for a conflict-of-interest,[29] or de minimis nonelective payments to terminate a participant's entire interest in the plan (i.e., $18,500 for 2018, $19,000 for 2019). [30] (Reg § 1.409A-3(j))

The election requirements are met if the plan provides that compensation for services performed during a tax year can be deferred at the participant's election only if the initial deferral election is made (1) not later than the close of the preceding tax year; or (2) at another time provided in IRS regs. For performance-based compensation (e.g., bonuses), based on services performed over a period of at least 12 months, the initial deferral election must be made no later than six months before the end of the period. The time and form of distributions have to be specified at the time of initial deferral. An election made after the initial election (a redeferral election) generally must not take effect until at least 12 months after the date on which the election is made and must require deferral for a period of not less than five years from the date on which payment would otherwise have been made. (Code Sec. 409A(a)(4))[31]

Relief provisions. If there's an unintentional operational failure to comply with specified Code Sec. 409A(a) requirements (e.g., incorrect amount treated as deferred compensation) that's corrected within the year, no amount is generally included in income under Code Sec. 409A(a). Relief is conditioned on timely filing and information reporting and taking commercially reasonable steps to avoid a recurrence of the failure. For other specified unintentional operational failures that aren't corrected in the same year, the amount included in income, and the resulting additional tax, is limited. [32]

¶ 1274   Rabbi trusts and funding triggers.

Amounts deferred under nonqualified deferred compensation (NQDC) plans (¶1273) generally aren't includible in income if the compensation is payable from general corporate funds that are subject to the claims of general creditors. Arrangements known as "rabbi trusts" generally are irrevocable and don't permit the employer to use the assets for purposes other than payment of deferred compensation. However, the trust assets are subject to the claims of the employer's creditors in the case of insolvency or bankruptcy. Because of this feature, rabbi trusts aren't considered to be funded and so compensation is deferred.

25. ¶H-3200.28 *et seq.*; ¶409A4.01
26. ¶H-3200.56; ¶409A4.01
27. ¶H-3200.66; ¶409A4.01
28. ¶H-3200.67

29. ¶H-3200.68
30. ¶H-3200.69
31. ¶H-3200.72 *et seq.*; ¶409A4.01
32. ¶H-3200.18 *et seq.*; ¶409A4.01

Assets directly or indirectly set aside in a trust for purposes of paying nonqualified deferred compensation are treated, for Code Sec. 83 purposes, as property transferred in connection with the performance of services (see ¶1216), whether or not the assets are available to satisfy claims of general creditors (1) at the time set aside, if the assets are located outside of the U.S.; or (2) at the time transferred, if the assets are later transferred outside of the U.S. (Code Sec. 409A(b)(1))

There's also a transfer of property, for Code Sec. 83 purposes, as of the earlier of (1) the date on which a NQDC plan first provides that assets will become restricted to the provision of benefits under the plan in connection with a change in the employer's financial health; or (2) the date on which assets are so restricted. (Code Sec. 409A(b)(2))[33]

Interest and a 20% penalty apply with regard to the off-shore rabbi trust and financial trigger rules. (Code Sec. 409A(b)(5))[34]

¶ 1275 Deferred compensation from tax-indifferent corporations and partnerships.

For deferred amounts attributable to services performed after Dec. 31, 2008, any compensation that's deferred under a nonqualified deferred compensation (NQDC) plan of a nonqualified entity is includible in gross income when there's no substantial risk of forfeiture of the rights to the compensation. (Code Sec. 457A(a))[35] A person's rights to compensation are subject to a substantial risk of forfeiture only if those rights are conditioned on the future performance of substantial services by any individual. (Code Sec. 457A(d)(1)) A nonqualified entity is: (1) any foreign corporation unless substantially all of its income is either effectively connected with the conduct of a trade or business in the U.S. or subject to a comprehensive foreign income tax; and (2) any partnership (either domestic or foreign), unless substantially all of its income is allocated to persons other than foreign persons for whom that income isn't subject to a comprehensive foreign income tax (as defined in Code Sec. 457A(d)(2)); or organizations that are exempt from U.S. income tax. (Code Sec. 457A(b))

A NQDC plan for this purpose generally is one described in Code Sec. 409A(d) (see ¶1273), subject to certain exceptions. (Code Sec. 457A(d)(3))[36]

For foreign corporations with income that's effectively connected with the conduct of a U.S. trade or business, Code Sec. 457A doesn't apply to compensation that the corporation could have deducted against its effectively connected income if it had been paid in cash on the date that it ceased to be subject to a substantial risk of forfeiture. (Code Sec. 457A(d)(4)) Code Sec. 457A doesn't apply to a NQDC plan if the compensation is: (a) payable to an employee of a domestic subsidiary of the entity, and (b) reasonably expected to be deductible by that subsidiary under Code Sec. 404(a)(5) (¶1537) when it's includible in the employee's income.[37]

If an amount of compensation isn't determinable when it's otherwise includible in income under Code Sec. 457A, it's taken into account when it becomes determinable, subject to an additional 20% tax and an interest charge at the Code Sec. 6621 underpayment rate plus one percentage point, from the tax year first deferred or, if later, the first tax year not subject to a substantial risk of forfeiture. (Code Sec. 457A(c)) An amount isn't determinable if, at the time it is no longer subject to a substantial risk of forfeiture, it varies depending on the satisfaction of an objective condition.[38]

To the extent provided in regs, if compensation is determined solely by reference to the amount of gain recognized on the disposition of an investment asset, that compensation is

---

33. ¶H-3233; ¶409A4.20
34. ¶H-2535.1; ¶409A4.20
35. ¶H-3401; ¶457A4

36. ¶H-3404; ¶457A4
37. ¶H-3401; ¶457A4
38. ¶H-3421; ¶457A4

treated as subject to a substantial risk of forfeiture until the date of the disposition. (Code Sec. 457A(d)(1))[39]

Inclusion of pre-2009 amounts. For a deferred amount to which Code Sec. 457A doesn't apply solely because it's attributable to services performed before 2009, to the extent not includible in gross income in a tax year beginning before 2018, it's includible in the later of (1) the last tax year beginning before 2018; or (2) the tax year in which there's no substantial risk of forfeiture of the rights to the compensation. Earnings on deferred amounts attributable to services performed before 2009 are subject to Code Sec. 457A only to the extent that the amounts to which the earnings relate are subject to Code Sec. 457A.[40]

¶ 1276   Social Security, Unemployment and Certain Disability Payments. ■■■■■■■

Social security benefits may be partly taxable. Unemployment benefits are fully taxable. Payments under military and government disability pensions may be excludible from income.

For voluntary withholding on social security and certain other federal payments, and on unemployment compensation payments, see ¶3010.

¶ 1277   Social security payments—the Tier I and Tier II taxes.

A taxpayer whose "provisional income" —i.e., modified adjusted gross income (MAGI, see below) plus one half of the social security benefits (including Tier 1 Railroad Retirement benefits) received —for a tax year exceeds either of two threshold amounts is taxed on a portion of social security benefits received that year, as follows:

Tier I: If provisional income exceeds a "base amount," include in gross income the *lesser* of:

. . . 50% of the social security benefits received that year; (Code Sec. 86(a)(1)(A)) or

. . . 50% of the excess of provisional income over the "base amount." (Code Sec. 86(a)(1)(B))[41]

MAGI means adjusted gross income: (1) determined without regard to the social security benefits; the deduction for qualified education loan interest (¶2220); the deduction for higher education expenses; the exclusions for foreign earned income and housing costs (¶4605 *et seq.*), savings bond proceeds for education expenses (¶2219), employer-provided adoption assistance (¶1252), and income from sources within U.S. possessions and Puerto Rico, and (2) increased by the amount of tax-exempt interest received or accrued by taxpayer during the tax year. (Code Sec. 86(b)(2))[42]

The "base amount" is $32,000 for married individuals filing a joint return; zero for a married individual filing a separate return who doesn't live apart from the individual's spouse for the entire tax year; and $25,000 for all other individuals (Code Sec. 86(c)(1)), such as those filing as single, head of household or qualifying widow(er). [43]

◆illustration: Gary's MAGI for the tax year consists of pension income of $15,000 and $3,000 of taxable interest and dividends. His social security benefit is $12,000. He's married and files a joint return. His spouse has no income. The sum of their MAGI ($18,000) plus one-half of his social security benefit ($6,000) is $24,000. This is less than their base amount ($32,000), so no part of his social security benefit is taxable.

Tier II: If provisional income exceeds an "adjusted base amount," include in gross income the *lesser* of:

39. ¶H-3420; ¶457A4
40. ¶H-3401; ¶457A4
41. ¶J-1456; ¶864.04

42. ¶J-1459; ¶864.02
43. ¶J-1457; ¶864.03

. . . 85% of the social security benefits received that year; or

. . . the sum of: (a) the amount included under the above 50% rule or, if less, one-half of the difference between taxpayer's "adjusted base amount" and "base amount," plus (b) 85% of the excess of provisional income over the "adjusted base amount." (Code Sec. 86(a)(2))

The "adjusted base amount" is $44,000 for married individuals filing jointly; zero for a married individual filing separately who doesn't live apart from the individual's spouse for the entire tax year); and $34,000 for all other individuals. (Code Sec. 86(c)(2))

⚠ caution: Any spike in income, e.g., from the sale of stock or a mutual fund, or a retirement plan distribution, may subject a taxpayer to an unexpected tax on social security benefits, if the extra income causes the taxpayer to exceed the base or adjusted base amount.

Benefits a taxpayer repays during a tax year reduce the benefits taxed that year, whether the repayment is for overpayments received that repayment year or any earlier year. (Code Sec. 86(d)(2)(A))[44]

If any portion of a lump-sum social security benefit received during a tax year is attributable to an earlier year, the taxpayer can elect (write "LSE" on the return) to include in gross income with respect to that portion, the sum of the increases in gross income that would have resulted had the portion been paid in the earlier year. (Code Sec. 86(e)(1))[45]

¶ 1278 Railroad Retirement Act benefits other than Tier 1 benefits.

Railroad Retirement Act benefits (other than Tier 1 benefits, see ¶1277) are treated as benefits provided under an employer plan that meets the requirements of Code Sec. 401(a) (a "qualified plan," see ¶4308 *et seq.*). (Code Sec. 72(r)(1), Code Sec. 72(r)(3)) Lump-sum termination (early retirement) payments have been held to be taxable under these rules. [46]

¶ 1279 Unemployment compensation.

Unemployment compensation (reported to recipients on Form 1099-G) is fully taxable. (Code Sec. 85(a)) Unemployment compensation includes any amount received under a law of the U.S. or a state that's in the nature of unemployment compensation. (Code Sec. 85(b)) It also includes disability benefits paid under federal or state law as a substitute for unemployment benefits to those who are ineligible for unemployment benefits because they're disabled. [47]

¶ 1280 Unemployment benefits paid by employers.

Unemployment benefits (not described at ¶1279) paid directly by an employer are includible in the employee's income. Amounts received from an employer under a "guaranteed annual wage plan" during periods of unemployment are taxable as wages. [48]

¶ 1281 Strike and lockout benefits.

Strike and lockout benefits paid to an employee by a union, from union dues, including both cash and the fair market value of goods received, are included in the employee's income unless the facts clearly show they're intended as a gift. [49]

---

44. ¶J-1467; ¶864.05
45. ¶J-1469; ¶864.08
46. ¶J-1471; ¶724.26

47. ¶H-3007 *et seq.*; ¶854.01
48. ¶H-3005; ¶854.01
49. ¶H-3009

¶ 1282   Certain military and government disability pensions.

Eligible members of the armed forces of any country, the National Oceanic and Atmospheric Administration, or the Public Health Service, and recipients of a disability annuity under section 808 of the Foreign Service Act of 1980, exclude from gross income amounts received as pension, annuity or similar allowance for personal injuries or sickness resulting from active service. Those eligible are primarily individuals with combat-related injuries or sickness or entitled to disability compensation from the Department of Veterans Affairs. (Code Sec. 104(a)(4))[50] While armed forces retirement pay based on length of service is taxable, that pay is excludible to the extent it could be received as a disability pension.[1]

¶ 1283   Dividends.

When a corporation distributes its earnings to its shareholders, the distribution is usually a dividend. If the dividend is "qualified" it's taxable at rates that apply to net capital gain; otherwise it's taxable as ordinary income. But not all corporate distributions are dividends. And some transactions that don't appear to be dividends may be taxed as constructive dividends.

For stock redemptions, see ¶3515 *et seq.* For liquidations, see ¶3558 *et seq.*

¶ 1284   How dividends are taxed to shareholders.

Dividends (defined at ¶1285) are taxable to the person who has the present, enforceable right to receive them, whether or not that person is the owner of the underlying stock. [2] Dividends received by an agent are taxable to the principal. [3] If the stock is sold before a dividend is declared and paid, or between the declaration and record (or "ex dividend") dates, the dividends are taxed to the buyer. Dividends on stock sold on or after the record date are taxed to the seller. (Reg § 1.61-9(c))[4]

Dividends are taxable in the year received or unqualifiedly made subject to the shareholder's demand. This applies to both cash and accrual shareholders. Thus, if a corporation pays a dividend on Dec. 30 last year, and the shareholder receives the check on Jan. 2 this year, the shareholder reports it on this year's return. (Reg § 1.301-1(b))[5] For RIC (mutual fund) dividends, see ¶1296. For REIT dividends, see ¶1297.

Dividends are taxed to shareholders at the rates that apply to net capital gain (see ¶2602) if they constitute "qualified dividend income" (¶1286) paid to noncorporate shareholders (Code Sec. 1(h)(11)) and would otherwise be taxed at ordinary income rates to the extent of the distributing corporation's earnings and profits (E&P, ¶3511). (Code Sec. 301(c)(1)) Thus, for dividends received in 2018, the 15% breakpoint is: $77,200 for joint returns and surviving spouses (half this amount for married taxpayers filing separately), $51,700 for heads of household, $38,600 for single filers, and $2,600 for trusts and estates. For 2019, as calculated by Thomson Reuters based on inflation data, these amounts are $78,750, $52,750, $39,350, and $2,650, respectively. For 2018, the 20% breakpoint is $479,000 for joint returns and surviving spouses (half this amount for married taxpayers filing separately), $452,400 for heads of household, $425,800 for single filers, and $12,700 for estates and trusts. (Code Sec. 1(h)(1)) For 2019, as calculated by Thomson Reuters based on inflation data, these amounts are $488,850, $461,700, $434,550, and $12,950, respectively.

The part of a distribution in excess of E&P is treated as a tax-free return of capital and

---

50. ¶H-3120; ¶s 614.041, 1044.04
1. ¶H-3123; ¶s 614.040, 1044.04
2. ¶J-2401; ¶3014.05

3. ¶J-2405; ¶3014.05
4. ¶J-2406; ¶3014.05
5. ¶J-2451; ¶s 3014.07, 4514.036

is applied against (reduces) the shareholder's basis in the stock. (Code Sec. 301(c)(2)) Any remaining excess (once basis is reduced to zero) is treated as payment for the stock, i.e., as capital gain if the stock is a capital asset in the shareholder's hands. (Code Sec. 301(c)(3))[6]

Exclusion for dividends from surrogate foreign corporations. Generally effective for dividends received after Dec. 22, 2017, any dividend received by an individual shareholder from a corporation which is a "surrogate foreign corporation" as defined in Code Sec. 7874(a)(2)(B) (other than a foreign corporation which is treated as a domestic corporation under Code Sec. 7874(b)), and which first became a surrogate foreign corporation after Dec. 22, 2017, is not entitled to the lower rates on qualified dividends provided for in Code Sec. 1(h).[7]

¶ 1285   Dividend defined.

A dividend is a distribution of money or property, other than the corporation's own stock or rights to that stock (¶1293), by a corporation to its shareholders with respect to its stock, out of accumulated or current earnings and profits (E&P, see ¶3511). (Code Sec. 316(a)) "Property" also includes any economic benefit the corporation gives its shareholders, in whatever form (Reg § 1.317-1), e.g., paying their debts (see ¶1287).[8] The distribution must be made in the ordinary course of the corporation's business, but it may be extraordinary in amount. (Reg § 1.316-1(a)(1))[9] A dividend needn't be proportionate and needn't be formally declared. [10]

¶ 1286   Qualified dividend income defined.

Qualified dividend income is dividend income received from domestic corporations and qualified foreign corporations, i.c., U.S. possession corporations and corporations eligible for benefits of a comprehensive income tax treaty with the U.S. that includes an exchange of information program (which can include controlled foreign corporation (CFC) dividends if not required to be included under Code Sec. 951(a)(1) (¶4611), but not passive foreign investment companies). (Code Sec. 1(h)(11)(B)(i)) Dividends paid by other foreign corporations also are qualified if paid on stock or American Depository Receipts (ADRs) readily tradable on an established U.S. securities market. (Code Sec. 1(h)(11)(C))

Qualified dividend income doesn't include: (1) dividends paid on stock unless the stock has been held for more than 60 days during the 121-day period beginning 60 days before the ex-dividend date (more than 90 days during the 181-day period beginning 90 days before the ex-dividend date for preferred stock dividends attributable to a period of more than 366 days) (Code Sec. 1(h)(11)(B)(iii)(I)); (2) dividends on stock to the extent that the taxpayer is under an obligation to make related payments with respect to positions in substantially similar or related property (Code Sec. 1(h)(11)(B)(iii)(II)); (3) any amount that the taxpayer elects to treat as investment income to support an investment interest deduction (Code Sec. 1(h)(11)(D)(i)) (see ¶1728); (4) dividends from corporations that for the distribution year or the preceding year are exempt from tax under Code Sec. 501 (see ¶4100) or Code Sec. 521 (exempt farmers' cooperatives, see ¶4206 *et seq.*) (Code Sec. 1(h)(11)(B)(ii)(I)); (5) dividends deductible under Code Sec. 591 by mutual savings banks (Code Sec. 1(h)(11)(B)(ii)(II)); and (6) dividends paid on employer securities owned by an employee stock ownership plan (ESOP), which are deductible under Code Sec. 404(k). (Code Sec. 1(h)(11)(B)(ii)(III))[11]

Qualified dividend income doesn't include payments in lieu of dividends (typically made to owners of stock that has been lent in connection with a short sale). However, if a

---

6. ¶J-2350 *et seq.*; ¶3014
7. ¶I-5155.5; ¶14.085
8. ¶J-2357; ¶s 3014.01, 3174

9. ¶J-2356; ¶3164 *et seq.*
10. ¶J-2351; ¶3014, 3014.01
11. ¶I-5115; ¶14.085

payment in lieu of dividends is reported as dividend income on a Form 1099-DIV, the recipient may treat the payment as a dividend, and not as a payment in lieu of dividends, unless the recipient knows, or has reason to know, of the actual character of the payment. [12]

If an individual, trust, or estate receives extraordinary dividends (within the meaning of Code Sec. 1059(c)) that are qualified dividend income, any loss on the dividend-paying stock is a long-term capital loss to the extent of the extraordinary dividends. (Code Sec. 1(h)(11)(D)(ii))[13]

For dividends from RICs, see ¶1296. For dividends from REITs, see ¶1297.

¶ 1287   Constructive or disguised dividends.

When a corporation pays excessive or unreasonably large amounts to a shareholder or a member of the shareholder's family as salary (Reg § 1.162-7(b)(1)) or rent,[14] or for a purchase price,[15] the excess is a constructive dividend (assuming sufficient E&P, see ¶3511). Similarly, constructive dividends include a corporation's payments of a shareholder's debts[16] or personal expenses.[17] A dividend may also result without a direct payment to the shareholder, if the corporation makes a payment to a third party that's for the shareholder's benefit and made with respect to stock owned by the shareholder. [18]

¶ 1288   Loan vs. dividend.

A shareholder may borrow money from the corporation with or without interest, and with or without security. If the agreement and the genuine intent (at withdrawal) is that the amount be repaid to the corporation, and there's persuasive evidence of both that intent *and* the shareholder's ability to carry it out, the amount received is treated as a loan (i.e., nontaxable), and not as a dividend [19] (unless a below-market interest rate is involved, see ¶1289).

¶ 1289   Dividends from below-market loans between corporation and shareholder.

For any below-market interest rate loan (¶1303) (directly or indirectly) between a corporation and a shareholder, the corporation/lender is treated as having paid a dividend, equal to the amount of the foregone interest that's includible in the shareholder/borrower's income. De minimis ($10,000 or less) and certain other loans are excepted. (Code Sec. 7872(a))[20]

¶ 1290   Determining the amount of a dividend (cash and in-kind).

The amount of a dividend is the sum of the cash plus the fair market value (FMV), at distribution, of any other property received (Code Sec. 301(b)(1), Code Sec. 301(b)(3)), reduced (but not below zero) by the amount of any liability of the corporation that the shareholder assumes in connection with the distribution, or to which the property is subject. (Code Sec. 301(b)(2))[21] But the amount taxable as a dividend in kind can't exceed the distributing corporation's E&P (¶3511). (Reg § 1.316-1(a)(2))[22]

A dividend consisting of the corporation's obligations equals the FMV of the notes. (Reg § 1.301-1(d)) For stock dividends, see ¶1294.

---

12. ¶I-5115.4
13. ¶I-5104.1; ¶14.087
14. ¶J-2726; ¶3014.09 *et seq.*
15. ¶J-2730; ¶3014.11
16. ¶J-2749; ¶3014.14
17. ¶J-2757; ¶3014.13

18. ¶J-2700 *et seq.*; ¶3014.14
19. ¶J-2707 *et seq.*; ¶3014.14
20. ¶J-2721 *et seq.*; ¶78,724.16
21. ¶J-2354; ¶3014.02
22. ¶J-2356; ¶3164.01

These rules apply to both corporate (U.S. or foreign) and noncorporate shareholders [23] (but a corporate shareholder may get a dividends-received deduction, see ¶3306 *et seq.*), and to dividends from a foreign corporation to its U.S. corporate shareholder. (Code Sec. 301(b)(1))[24]

¶ 1291 Basis of distributed property to shareholder-distributee.

The basis to the shareholder (corporate or individual) for property received as a dividend (¶1285) is the property's fair market value at distribution (Code Sec. 301(d)), i.e., the amount treated as a dividend (see ¶1290), but without the reduction for liabilities. [25]

¶ 1292 Holding period for property received as a taxable dividend.

The shareholder's holding period for property received as a taxable dividend begins on the date of receipt (actual or constructive). (Code Sec. 1223(2))[26]

¶ 1293 Distributions of stock or rights to stock.

With certain exceptions (see ¶1294), a stock dividend —i.e., a corporation's distribution of its *own* stock, or rights (e.g., options or warrants) to buy its stock, that's made to shareholders with respect to their stock (i.e., not as compensation) —isn't taxable to the shareholder. (Code Sec. 305) But a corporation's distribution of stock, or rights to buy stock, in *another* corporation (even if affiliated) is a regular dividend in kind, taxed under the rules at ¶1284 *et seq.*[27]

Stock splits are treated as stock dividends if identical stock is distributed on stock held. [28]

For stock (rights) received in connection with corporate organizations, reorganizations or divisions, see ¶3540.

¶ 1294 Taxable stock (or rights) dividends.

Where a stock (or rights) dividend is taxable, the dividend amount is the fair market value (FMV) at distribution of the stock (rights), under the "regular" dividend-in-kind rules, see ¶1290.[29] Where the dividend is taxable because of a cash election, the "dividend" equals: (1) the cash received, for shareholders electing cash, and (2) the FMV of the stock (rights) at distribution, for those receiving stock (rights). (Reg § 1.305-1(b))[30]

These stock (or rights) dividends are *not* tax-free:

(1) A distribution in which *any* shareholder has the option to take cash or other property instead of the stock (or rights); (Code Sec. 305(b)(1); Reg § 1.305-2)[31]

(2) A "disproportionate" distribution that results in the receipt of property by some shareholders and, for others, an increase in their proportionate interests in the corporation's assets or earnings and profits; (Code Sec. 305(b)(2); Reg § 1.305-3)[32]

(3) A distribution that results in the receipt of preferred stock by some common shareholders and the receipt of common stock by others; (Code Sec. 305(b)(3); Reg § 1.305-4)[33]

(4) Any distributions on preferred stock, including a redemption premium treated as a distribution (for preferred stock issued after Oct. 9, '90, the premium is included as OID, see ¶1311 *et seq.*), *other than* an increase in the conversion ratio of convertible preferred stock made solely to take into account a stock dividend or stock split with respect to the

23. ¶s 3014, 3014.02
24. ¶J-2400 *et seq.*; ¶3014.02
25. ¶P-5401; ¶3014.03
26. ¶s I-8903, I-8918
27. ¶J-2501; ¶3054.01
28. ¶J-2501; ¶3054.02
29. ¶J-2504, J-2506; ¶3054.02
30. ¶J-2507; ¶3054.02
31. ¶s J-2508 *et seq.*, J-2501; ¶3054.02
32. ¶J-2510 *et seq.*; ¶3054.02
33. ¶J-2515; ¶3054.02

stock into which the preferred is convertible; (Code Sec. 305(b)(4); Reg § 1.305-5)[34]

(5) Any distribution of convertible preferred stock unless IRS is satisfied it won't have the result in (2), above; (Code Sec. 305(b)(5); Reg § 1.305-6)[35]

(6) A constructive stock distribution, e.g., a change in conversion ratio or redemption price, or a redemption premium (difference between redemption price and issue price). (Code Sec. 305(c); Reg § 1.305-5(b), Reg § 1.305-7) Proposed regs detail the amount and timing of taxable income from deemed distributions that are, or that result from, adjustments to rights to acquire stock. (Prop Reg. § 1.305-7(c)(4) ["Taxpayers may rely"]) [36]

¶ 1295   Cash for fractional shares.

Where a corporation's purpose in distributing cash (instead of scrip or fractional shares) in a distribution that otherwise qualifies as a nontaxable stock dividend (¶1293) is to save trouble, expense and inconvenience, and not to give any shareholder(s) an increased interest, the distribution is treated as if the fractional shares had been issued and then redeemed by the corporation. (Reg § 1.305-3(c)) The cash received is treated as an amount realized on the sale of a fractional share. Gain or loss is the cash received minus the basis of the share sold. (Reg § 1.305-3(c)(2))[37]

¶ 1296   Dividends from regulated investment companies (RICs, or mutual funds).

Ordinary dividends a RIC (¶4201) distributes to its shareholders generally are taxed to them just like other corporate dividends. (¶1284, ¶1290) (Code Sec. 852; Reg § 1.852-4(a))[38] However, if the amount of dividends eligible for qualified dividend income treatment (i.e., taxable at the capital gain rates) (¶1284) received by a RIC for a tax year is less than 95% of its gross income (as specially computed), then only the amount of qualified dividend income received by the RIC for the tax year may be distributed to its shareholders as qualified dividend income. (Code Sec. 1(h)(11)(D)(iii), Code Sec. 854(b)(1)(B)) But capital gain dividends, which the RIC need not actually distribute, result in capital gain income (see ¶4201) (Code Sec. 852(b)(3)(D)),[39] and exempt-interest dividends are treated as tax-exempt interest (¶1328). (Code Sec. 852(b)(5)(B))[40] Capital gain dividends aren't treated as qualified dividend income (¶1286). (Code Sec. 854(a)) The amount of RIC dividends that are qualifying dividend income must be reported to RIC shareholders within 60 days after the close of the RIC's tax year. (Code Sec. 854(b)(2))

A dividend the RIC pays after the close of its tax year generally is treated as received by the shareholder in the year actually paid, even if the RIC elects to treat it as paid in the preceding year (see ¶4203). (Code Sec. 855(b))[41] But dividends the RIC declares in Oct., Nov. or Dec. are treated as received by the shareholder on Dec. 31 if the RIC actually pays them during the following Jan. (Code Sec. 852(b)(7))[42]

caution: Since dividends paid in Jan. may have to be picked up in the preceding year's income, that year's Form 1099, and not the RIC's monthly statements, should be used to determine the dividends to report for that year.

---

34. ¶J-2501, J-2516 *et seq.*; ¶3054.02
35. ¶s J-2501, J-2526; ¶3054.02
36. ¶J-2501, ¶J-2527 *et seq.*; ¶3054.02
37. ¶J-2514; ¶3054.01
38. ¶E-6150 *et seq.*; ¶8524.02

39. ¶E-6152; ¶8524.02
40. ¶E-6160; ¶8524.02
41. ¶E-6201; ¶8554.01
42. ¶E-6202; ¶8554.01

¶ 1297   Dividends from real estate investment trusts (REITs).

REITs (¶4202) distribute ordinary dividends and capital gain dividends which (as with RICs, see ¶1296) the beneficiaries or shareholders (investors) treat, respectively, as ordinary income (except there's no dividends-received deduction) (Code Sec. 857(c)) and capital gain. (Code Sec. 857(b)(3)(B))[43] The only REIT dividends that are eligible for qualified dividend income treatment (¶1284) are those that the REIT received as qualified dividend income, such as dividends paid to the REIT from a taxable REIT subsidiary. (Code Sec. 1(h)(11)(D)(iii), Code Sec. 857(c)(2)) For undistributed capital gains of REITs, see ¶4202. A deficiency dividend the REIT pays for any year is taxed to the shareholder in the year it's paid, not the year *for which* it's paid. (Reg § 1.860-2(a)(3)(i))[44] But any dividend declared by the REIT in Oct., Nov. or Dec. and payable to shareholders of record on a specified date in that month is considered received by the shareholder on Dec. 31 if the REIT actually pays it the next Jan. (Code Sec. 857(b)(8)(A))[45]

REITs are subject to the same capital gain designation rules as RICs (see ¶1296).[46]

¶ 1298   Dividends to co-op patrons; patronage dividends.

Distributions made by a co-op (¶4206) on its stock or other proprietary interests are taxed under the "regular" dividend rules (see ¶1290), but the dividends-received deduction doesn't apply if the co-op is exempt. (Code Sec. 246(a)(1))[47]

Patronage dividends and per-unit retain allocations (¶4207) received in money are included in income by the patron in the year received. Qualified written notices of allocation and qualified per-unit retain certificates (¶4207) are included in income at their stated dollar amount when received. Other property (but not nonqualified allocations or nonqualified per-unit retain certificates) is included at its fair market value when received. (Code Sec. 1385)[48]

But the amount of any patronage dividend isn't included in income to the extent it's: (1) properly taken into account as an adjustment to basis of property, or (2) attributable to personal, living or family items. (Code Sec. 1385(b))[49]

¶ 1299   Interest Income.

As a general rule, regardless of the name given to the amounts or the form of the transaction, the receipt or accrual of interest (¶1300) is taxable as ordinary income, unless specifically exempt. (Code Sec. 61(a)(4); Reg § 1.61-7(a))[50]

The interest is taxable even if it's usurious, unless applicable state law automatically converts the illegal portion into a payment of principal. (Reg § 1.61-7(a))[1]

¶ 1300   What is interest?

Interest is the price paid for the use of another's money or for the right to defer payment of money owed to another, regardless of the form of the transaction. [2] Interest generally includes the FMV of gifts or services received for opening or adding to accounts in financial institutions, but not if it's a de minimis premium (for a deposit of less than $5,000, the premium costs the bank $10 or less; for a deposit of $5,000 or more, it costs $20 or less). [3]

43. ¶E-6616; ¶8574.02
44. ¶E-6304; ¶8604
45. ¶E-6704; ¶8574.02
46. ¶E-6617.1; ¶8574.02
47. ¶J-2608; ¶2434.04
48. ¶J-2609 *et seq.*; ¶13,814.13

49. ¶J-2612; ¶13,814.13
50. ¶J-2801; ¶614.067
1. ¶J-2814; ¶614.068
2. ¶J-2802 *et seq.*
3. ¶J-2820

To be interest, generally a payment must be made with respect to a bona fide debt. [4] But other "interest" payments imposed by law, e.g., on judgments, tax refunds, installment sales, etc., are also interest. [5] And IRS may use the Code Sec. 482 allocation rules (¶2853) to "create" interest. [6]

¶ 1301   Interest on defaulted mortgage.

Amounts paid to a mortgagee as a result of the sale of property on foreclosure (or voluntary conveyance in lieu of foreclosure) of the mortgage, that represent accrued interest due on the mortgage, are taxable interest. [7] For mortgagee's gain or loss, see ¶1779.

For mortgage interest recipient's reporting requirements, see ¶4744.

¶ 1302   "Points" and other loan-related fees.

Payments made to a bank or other lender to get a loan are interest, to the extent they're made for the use or forbearance of money rather than for services rendered. Thus, "points" (i.e., charges connected with mortgages that the borrower pays in addition to the stated interest) are interest, while commitment and service fees (for escrow, recording, credit inspection, appraisal) aren't. [8] For recipient's reporting requirements, see ¶4744.

¶ 1303   Below-market interest-rate loans.

The forgone interest on a "below-market" loan is taxed to the lender as interest income. (Code Sec. 7872) [9] A "below-market" loan is:

. . . *a demand loan* where interest is payable on the loan at a rate less than the applicable federal rate (AFR, see ¶1307), (Code Sec. 7872(e)(1)(A)) [10] or

. . . *a term loan* where the amount loaned exceeds the present value of all payments due under the loan. (Code Sec. 7872(e)(1)(B)) [11]

For a below-market demand loan, the "interest" for any period is the excess of: (1) the interest that would have been payable on the loan if it accrued annually at the AFR, over (2) any interest payable on the loan and properly allocable to the period. (Code Sec. 7872(e)(2)) For below-market term loans, the "interest" (treated as original issue discount (OID), see ¶1310 *et seq.*) is the excess of: (a) the amount loaned, over (b) the present value of all payments required to be made under the loan. (Code Sec. 7872(b)(2)(B)) [12]

These rules don't apply to certain de minimis ($10,000 or less) loans (Code Sec. 7872(c)(2), Code Sec. 7872(c)(3)), [13] amounts treated as "unstated interest" (see ¶1304) (Code Sec. 7872(f)(8)), [14] or certain loans under a written continuing care contract to a qualified continuing care facility. (Code Sec. 7872(g)) [15]

¶ 1304   Unstated (imputed) interest on deferred payment sales.

For certain deferred payment or installment sales (¶1305) where the sales contract fails to provide for interest at a minimum rate specified by the Code or by IRS, part of the payments received is treated as interest ("unstated interest") that's taxable to the seller despite any contrary intention of the parties. (Code Sec. 483) [16]

4. ¶J-2803; ¶614.068
5. ¶J-2834 *et seq.*; ¶614.068 *et seq.*
6. ¶J-2817; ¶s 4824, 614.148
7. ¶J-2819; ¶614.083
8. ¶J-2818; ¶1634.005
9. ¶J-2900; ¶78,724 *et seq.*
10. ¶J-2939 *et seq.*; ¶78,724.04

11. ¶J-2947 *et seq.*; ¶78,724.06
12. ¶s J-2902, J-2904; ¶s 78,724.04, 78,724.06
13. ¶J-2961; ¶78,724.12 *et seq.*
14. ¶J-2918; ¶78,724.20
15. ¶J-2988; ¶78,724.20
16. ¶J-3750 *et seq.*; ¶4834

¶ 1305   Payments subject to unstated interest rules.

With certain exceptions (¶1309), the unstated interest rules (¶1304) apply to any payment where *all* the following requirements are met:

(1) The payment must be made on account of the sale or exchange of property.

(2) The payment must be part of the sales price under the contract.

(3) The "sales price" (determined at the time of sale) must be more than $3,000. "Sales price" includes the amount of any down payment, any liability encumbering the property and any amount treated as unstated interest under these rules, but not any *stated* interest payments.

(4) The payment must be due (under the contract) more than six months after the date of the sale or exchange.

(5) At least one payment under the contract must be due more than one year after the date of the sale or exchange.

(6) There must be total unstated interest (¶1306) under the contract. (Code Sec. 483(c)(1), Code Sec. 483(d)(2); Reg § 1.483-1(b)(1))[17]

A debt instrument of the buyer given in exchange for property isn't itself treated as a payment. Rather, any payment due under the instrument is treated as due under the sales contract. (Code Sec. 483(c)(2))[18]

¶ 1306   What is "total unstated interest"?

There's "total unstated interest" under the contract (see ¶1305) if the sum of all payments (other than *stated* interest payments) due under it more than six months after the date of the sale or exchange exceeds the sum of: (1) the present value of all those payments, plus (2) the present value of all interest payments due under the contract (regardless of when due). The total unstated interest equals the excess, if any. (Code Sec. 483(b))[19]

The present value of a payment is determined as of the date of the sale, etc., using a "test" rate prescribed by IRS. This test rate, which depends on the type of property sold, is a discount rate equal to the then applicable federal rate (AFR, see ¶1307), compounded semiannually. (Code Sec. 483(b), Code Sec. 1274(b)(2))[20]

These discount rates are used to determine the amount of unstated interest the seller must report as interest income:

(1) For sales or exchanges of property (not described below), the discount rate may not exceed 9% compounded semiannually if the stated principal amount of the debt instrument doesn't exceed a specified amount, as adjusted for inflation ($5,831,500 for sales and exchanges in 2018).

(2) For sales or exchanges of new investment credit property, the discount rate is 100% of the AFR, compounded semiannually. (Code Sec. 483(b))[21]

(3) For sales or exchanges where part of the sold property is leased back to the seller, the discount rate is 110% of the AFR, compounded semiannually. (Code Sec. 1274(e))[22]

(4) For sales, etc., of land between family members where the aggregate sales price for all land sales between those individuals in that calendar year isn't over $500,000, the discount rate can't exceed 6% compounded semiannually. (Code Sec. 483(e))[23]

---

17. ¶J-3800 *et seq.*; ¶s 4834, 4834.01
18. ¶J-3806; ¶4834.01
19. ¶J-3814; ¶4834
20. ¶J-3814 *et seq.*; ¶4834.01

21. ¶J-3818; ¶4834.01.
22. ¶J-3819; ¶12,714.03
23. ¶J-3820; ¶4834.01

¶ 1307   Applicable federal rate (AFR).

IRS issues monthly tables (reproduced at ¶1118 for the most recent 12 months available as we went to press) showing the AFRs to be used in determining whether there's unstated interest (¶1306) (or OID in some cases, see ¶1315) on a sale or exchange of property, and if there is, the amount of that unstated interest. [24] The rate to use on a particular sale or exchange depends on the term over which the payments are to be made. If the term is three years or less, use the short-term rate (from the tables). If it's more than three years but not more than nine years, use the mid-term rate. If it's more than nine years, use the long-term rate. (Code Sec. 1274(d)(1)(A))[25] The rate to use also depends on when the contract was made. (Code Sec. 1274(d)(2))[26]

¶ 1308   Allocating total unstated interest.

For any payment subject to the unstated interest rules (¶1304), that part of the total unstated interest under the contract (¶1306) which is properly allocable to that payment is treated as interest. This "interest" amount is determined in a manner consistent with the method used to compute the amount of currently includible OID (¶1318) (Code Sec. 483(a)) so that unstated interest income must be reported on an economic accrual basis. [27]

¶ 1309   Exceptions to unstated interest rules.

Even if all the requirements listed at ¶1305 are met, there's no unstated interest on:

(1) sales or exchanges where the sales price (¶1305) is $3,000 or less; (Code Sec. 483(d)(2))[28]

(2) any debt instrument (given in connection with a sale or exchange of property) whose issue price is figured under the OID rules (¶1310 *et seq.*); (Code Sec. 483(d)(1))[29]

(3) any amount received on the sale of patent rights described in Code Sec. 1235(a) that's contingent on the productivity, use or disposition of those rights; (Code Sec. 483(d)(4))[30]

(4) amounts received under certain annuity contracts; [31]

(5) lump-sum divorce payments and property settlements payable in installments; [32]

(6) certain acquisitions of amortizable section 197 intangibles (¶1966); (Reg § 1.197-2(f)(3)(iv)(B)(3))[33]

(7) payments under options to buy or sell property; (Reg § 1.483-1(c)(3)(v))[34]

(8) assumptions of debt in connection with sales or exchanges and acquisitions of property subject to debt; (Code Sec. 1274(c)(4))[35] and

(9) below-market interest rate loans (¶1303) (Code Sec. 7872(f)(8)).[36]

¶ 1310   Current inclusion of original issue discount (OID) as interest income.

If a debt instrument is acquired from an issuer for less than the issuer will have to pay the holder at maturity, the difference is OID (see ¶1311). No matter which method of accounting is used, the holder must report part of the OID as interest income in each tax

---

24. ¶J-4181 *et seq.*; ¶4834.01
25. ¶J-4181; ¶4834.01
26. ¶J-4190 *et seq.*; ¶12,714.03
27. ¶J-3951; ¶s 4834.01, 4464.01
28. ¶J-3901; ¶4834.01
29. ¶J-3902; ¶4834.01
30. ¶J-3903; ¶4834.01
31. ¶J-3905; ¶4834.01
32. ¶J-3906; ¶4834.01
33. ¶J-3903.1
34. ¶J-3904; ¶4834.01
35. ¶J-3909; ¶4834.01
36. ¶J-3910; ¶4834.01

year the debt instrument is held (¶1318), even though the OID won't be paid until maturity. (Code Sec. 1272)[37]

The OID current inclusion rules apply to all debt instruments issued with OID (Code Sec. 1272)[38] *other than:*

(1) Tax-exempt obligations (unless stripped). (Code Sec. 1272(a)(2)(A), Code Sec. 1286(d))

(2) U.S. savings bonds. (Code Sec. 1272(a)(2)(B))

(3) Short-term obligations (i.e., with a fixed maturity date not more than one year from the date of issue). (Code Sec. 1272(a)(2)(C))

(4) Debt instruments issued by natural persons before Mar. 2, '84. (Code Sec. 1272(a)(2)(D))

(5) Certain nonbusiness loans of $10,000 or less between natural persons. (Code Sec. 1272(a)(2)(E))[00]

"Debt instruments" are bonds, debentures, notes, certificates or other instruments or contractual arrangements that are "indebtedness" under tax law principles, e.g., certificates of deposit or loans (Code Sec. 1275(a)(1); Reg § 1.1275-1(d)),[40] and REMIC interests and some similar instruments where payment may be accelerated. (Code Sec. 1272(a)(6)(C))[41] A debt instrument doesn't include a life annuity, or certain annuities issued by insurance companies. (Code Sec. 1275(a)(1)(B); Reg § 1.1275-1(j))[42]

A safe harbor accounting method (the proportional method) can be used in calculating OID accrual on a pool of credit card receivables. [40]

The OID current inclusion rules also apply to bonds, and preferred stock bought (after being stripped) after Apr. 30, '93. (Code Sec. 305(e), Code Sec. 1286(a))[44] The OID current inclusion rules don't apply to a holder who buys a debt instrument at a premium (Code Sec. 1272(c)(1))[45] (except as described at ¶1320).

¶ 1311 Original issue discount (OID) defined.

OID (see ¶1310) is the excess (if any) of: (1) a debt instrument's stated redemption price at maturity (¶1313) over (2) its issue price (¶1314). (Code Sec. 1273(a)(1))[46]

But the OID is treated as zero if that excess is less than 0.25% of the stated redemption price at maturity, times the number of years to maturity. (Code Sec. 1273(a)(3)) In this case, all stated interest (including amounts that would otherwise be OID) is treated as "qualified stated interest" (¶1312). (Reg § 1.1273-1(d)(1))[47]

¶ 1312 "Qualified stated interest" defined.

"Qualified stated interest" is stated interest that's unconditionally payable in cash or property (other than the issuer's debt instruments), or will be constructively received under Code Sec. 451 (¶2821) at least annually at a single fixed rate. (Reg § 1.1273-1(c)(1))[48]

---

37. ¶J-4000 *et seq.*; ¶12,714 *et seq.*
38. ¶J-4051; ¶s 12,714, 12,714.01
39. ¶J-4060 *et seq.*; ¶12,714.01
40. ¶s J-4054, J-4055; ¶12,714
41. ¶J-4343; ¶12,714.01
42. ¶J-4057; ¶12,714

43. ¶J-4345.2
44. ¶J-4400 *et seq.*; ¶12,864
45. ¶J-4005; ¶12714.01
46. ¶J-4100 *et seq.*; ¶12,714
47. ¶J-4102; ¶12,714.01
48. ¶J-4112

¶ 1313   Stated redemption price at maturity—original issue discount (OID).

For OID purposes (¶1311), an instrument's *stated redemption price at maturity* is usually its face value. It includes interest payable at maturity *but not* interest payable at a fixed rate at periodic intervals of a year or less during the entire term of the instrument (Code Sec. 1273(a)(2)), or "qualified stated interest" (¶1312). (Reg § 1.1273-1(b))[49]

¶ 1314   Issue price of debt instrument.

A debt instrument's issue price depends on whether it's issued for cash or property, and if issued for property, whether the instrument or property is publicly traded, as follows:

. . . For a *publicly offered debt instrument issued for money,* the issue price is the initial offering price to the public at which a substantial amount of the instruments is sold. (Code Sec. 1273(b)(1); Reg § 1.1232-3(b)(2)(i))[50]

. . . For a *privately offered debt instrument issued for money,* the issue price is the price paid by the first buyer of that instrument (Code Sec. 1273(b)(2)) or the first price at which a substantial amount of instruments in the issue is sold. (Reg § 1.1273-2(a)(1))[1]

. . . For a *debt instrument issued for property where there's public trading,* the issue price is the instrument's fair market value (FMV) as of the issue date, if it's publicly traded. If the instrument itself isn't publicly traded but is issued for property (i.e., stock or securities) that is, its issue price is the FMV of that property. (Code Sec. 1273(b)(3); Reg § 1.1232-3(b)(2)(iii), Reg § 1.1273-2(b)(1))[2]

. . . For a *nonpublicly traded debt instrument issued for nonpublicly traded property,* the issue price is its stated principal amount (total payments due under the instrument, less stated interest payments or payments designated as interest or points) if the instrument pays adequate stated interest (¶1315), or its imputed principal amount (¶1316) if it doesn't. (Code Sec. 1274(a); Reg § 1.1274-2(b)(1))[3] For exceptions, see ¶1317.

. . . For *Treasury securities,* the issue price is the average price of the securities sold (price sold at auction, if sold before Mar. 13, 2001). (Reg § 1.1275-2(d))[4]

. . . For a *debt instrument that provides for one or more contingent payments,* issued after Aug. 12, '96, the issue price is the lesser of the instrument's noncontingent principal payments, or the sum of the present values of the noncontingent payments. (Reg § 1.1274-2(g))[5]

. . . For a *tax-exempt obligation* issued after Aug. 12, '96, the issue price is (a) the greater of the obligation's FMV or its stated principal amount, or (b) for contingent obligations, its FMV. (Reg § 1.1274-2(j))[6]

The issue price of a debt instrument issued in a potentially abusive situation (e.g., a tax shelter) is the FMV of the property received in exchange for the instrument, reduced by the sum of the money plus the FMV of any property or rights (other than the instrument) that are given for the sale or exchange. (Reg § 1.1274-2(b)(3))[7]

¶ 1315   Adequate stated interest of debt instrument.

There's adequate stated interest for a debt instrument if the sum of the present values (using the discount rate at ¶1306) of all payments of principal and interest due under it equals or exceeds its stated principal amount (¶1314) (Code Sec. 1274(c)(2)), or if the

---

49. ¶J-4111
50. ¶J-4130
1. ¶J-4138
2. ¶J-4140
3. ¶J-4151; ¶12,714.03

4. ¶J-4131
5. ¶J-4151.2; ¶12,714.037
6. ¶J-4151.3, J-4151.4
7. ¶J-4151.5

instrument has a single fixed rate of interest that's paid or compounded at least annually and is at least equal to the test rate. (Reg § 1.1274-2(c))[8]

¶ 1316 Imputed principal amount of debt instrument.

The imputed principal amount is the sum of the present values of all payments of principal and interest due under a debt instrument, computed as of the date of the sale or exchange using the discount rates at ¶1306. (Code Sec. 1274(b)(2); Reg § 1.1274-2(c)(1))[9]

The imputed principal amount of a variable rate debt instrument that provides for stated interest at a qualified floating rate(s) generally is determined by assuming that the instrument provides for a fixed rate of interest for each accrual period to which a qualified floating rate applies. (Reg § 1.1274-2(f)(1)(i))[10]

In a potentially abusive situation (e.g., tax shelter), the imputed principal amount of an instrument received in exchange for property is the property's fair market value, adjusted for other considerations in the transaction. (Code Sec. 1274(b)(3)(A); Reg § 1.1274-3(a))[11]

¶ 1317 Exceptions to original issue discount (OID) rules for nonpublicly traded debt instruments.

The issue price of a nonpublicly traded debt instrument issued for nonpublicly traded property is its stated redemption price at maturity (so there's no OID, see ¶1311), instead of the amount determined under the rules at ¶1314, in these cases: (Code Sec. 1273(b)(4))[12]

(1) sales or exchanges involving total payments of $250,000 or less; (Code Sec. 1274(c)(3)(C))[13]

(2) sales or exchanges by an individual of a principal residence; (Code Sec. 1274(c)(3)(B))[14]

(3) sales or exchanges of certain farms where the sales price can't exceed $1,000,000; (Code Sec. 1274(c)(3)(A))[15]

(4) certain sales of patents; (Code Sec. 1274(c)(3)(E))[16]

(5) certain transfers of land between family members where the total price for all land sales between them for the year isn't more than $500,000; (Code Sec. 1274(c)(3)(F))[17]

(6) sales or exchanges where, in exchange for property, a nonaccrual method buyer (other than a dealer) issues a "cash method debt instrument," i.e., a debt instrument whose principal amount doesn't exceed a specified amount ($4,165,300 for sales and exchanges in 2018), if the "regular" issue price rules otherwise would apply *and* buyer and seller jointly elect cash method treatment for the instrument; (Code Sec. 1274A(c))[18]

(7) sales or exchanges of personal use property (to the issuer) that evidence a below-market loan (¶1303); (Reg § 1.1274-1(b)(3)(i))[19]

(8) transactions involving "demand" below-market loans; (Reg § 1.1274-1(b)(3)(ii))[20] or

(9) transfers between spouses or incident to divorce. (Reg § 1.1274-1(b)(3)(iii))[21]

🄡 *observation:* Even if there's no OID, there may be unstated interest (see ¶1304).

---

8. ¶J-4153 *et seq.*; ¶12,714.03
9. ¶J-4154 *et seq.*; ¶12,714.03
10. ¶J-4157
11. ¶J-4173 *et seq.*; ¶12,714.03
12. ¶J-4196; ¶12,714.03
13. ¶J-4198; ¶12,714.03
14. ¶J-4199

15. ¶J-4200; ¶12,714.03
16. ¶J-4205
17. ¶J-4206
18. ¶J-4207 *et seq.*
19. ¶J-4202; ¶12,714.03
20. ¶J-4203; ¶12,714.03
21. ¶J-4204; ¶12,714.03

¶ 1318   **Determining amount of currently includible original issue discount (OID).**

A holder of a debt instrument issued with OID (¶1311) who is required to include part of the OID in gross income currently must include in gross income for the tax year, an amount equal to the sum of the daily portions of the OID for each day the instrument was held during that year. (Code Sec. 1272(a)(1))[22] For accrual under the constant yield method, see ¶1319.

To determine the daily OID portion, allocate to each day in any "accrual period" (below) that day's ratable portion of the increase (during that period) in the instrument's adjusted issue price (below). This increase equals the excess of: (1) the adjusted issue price at the start of the accrual period times the yield to maturity (based on compounding at the end of each accrual period), over (2) the sum of the amounts payable as interest on the instrument during that accrual period. (Code Sec. 1272(a)(3))[23]

The adjusted issue price of a debt instrument at the start of any accrual period is the sum of its issue price (¶1314), plus all adjustments (i.e., OID inclusions) in that issue price for all earlier accrual periods. (Code Sec. 1272(a)(4))[24]

Accrual period generally means a 6-month period (or shorter period from date of issuance) ending on a day in the calendar year corresponding to the debt instrument's maturity date, or a date six months before that date. (Code Sec. 1272(a)(5))[25]

For *inflation-indexed debt instruments,* OID is computed using the coupon bond method or the discount bond method (see ¶1330). (Reg § 1.1275-7(a))[26]

¶ 1319   **Accrual of original issue discount (OID) using constant yield method.**

Under the constant yield method, the amount of OID includible in the holder's income for a tax year (¶1318) is determined as follows:

(1) Determine the instrument's yield to maturity. This is the discount rate that, when used to compute the present value of all payments under the instrument, produces an amount equal to the instrument's issue price. The yield must be constant over the instrument's term and must be calculated to at least two decimal places. (Reg § 1.1272-1(b)(1)(i))

(2) Determine the accrual period, which may be any length (based on any reasonable accounting convention), but can't exceed one year. Each scheduled payment must occur either on the first or last day of an accrual period. The simplest OID computation is where the accrual periods correspond to the intervals between payment dates set forth by the instrument. (Reg § 1.1272-1(b)(1)(ii))

(3) Determine the OID allocable to each accrual period. This is the instrument's adjusted issue price at the start of the accrual period, times the instrument's yield, less the "qualified stated interest" (¶1312) allocable to the period. (Reg § 1.1272-1(b)(1)(iii))

(4) Determine the daily portions of OID, by allocating to each day in an accrual period the ratable portion of the OID allocable to that period. The holder includes in income the daily portions of OID for each day in the tax year on which the instrument was held. (Reg § 1.1272-1(b)(1)(iv))[27]

The constant yield method may not be used for certain interests held by a REMIC (¶4204), certain instruments with payments subject to acceleration or that provide for

22. ¶J-4301; ¶12,714.01
23. ¶J-4301; ¶12,714.01
24. ¶J-4324; ¶12,714.01

25. ¶J-4301
26. ¶J-4379 *et seq.*; ¶12,714.037
27. ¶J-4302; ¶12,714.01

contingent payments, or certain variable rate instruments. (Reg §   1.1272-1(b)(2))[28]

¶ 1320 Original issue discount (OID) inclusion reduced where holder paid acquisition premium.

If the holder of a debt instrument bought it from someone other than the original issuer, paying an acquisition premium (i.e., an amount in excess of the original issue price plus all OID required to be included in the gross income of earlier holders), the holder's current OID inclusion (¶1318) is reduced. This is done by reducing each daily includible OID portion by this constant fraction: the acquisition premium, divided by the total OID (before reduction) allocable to the days after the purchase date and ending on the date of maturity. However, the reduction applies only to the OID inclusion and isn't taken into account in computing the instrument's adjusted issue price at the start of an accrual period. (Code Sec. 1272(a)(7))[29]

¶ 1321 Accrued market discount on disposition of "market discount bonds."

Gain on the disposition of a market discount bond (¶1323) is ordinary income to the extent of the accrued market discount on the bond (Code Sec. 1276(a)(1)) (unless the holder elects to include the discount currently, see ¶1324). This ordinary income is treated as interest income, with exceptions. (Code Sec. 1276(a)(4))[30] For partial principal payments, see ¶1322.

The accrued market discount interest is computed under a ratable accrual method or, at taxpayer's election, a constant interest rate method. (Code Sec. 1276(b))[31]

Dispositions by gift and transfers to controlled corporations also can result in interest income under this rule. (Code Sec. 1276(d)(1)(A))[32] If the disposition is other than by sale, exchange or involuntary conversion, the amount realized is equal to the bond's fair market value. (Code Sec. 1276(a)(2))[33]

Interest treatment applies even if the gain wouldn't otherwise be recognized. Regs may allow nonrecognition in certain nontaxable transactions. (Code Sec. 1276(a)(1), Code Sec. 1276(d)(1))[34]

¶ 1322 Accrued market discount when partial principal payments are made.

If the principal on a market discount bond (¶1323) (acquired after Oct. 22, '86) is paid in more than one installment, any partial principal payment is included as ordinary income to the extent of the accrued market discount on the bond (Code Sec. 1276(a)(3)(A))[35] (unless the holder elects to include the discount currently, see ¶1324).

Any amount that has been included in gross income under this rule reduces the amount of any accrued market discount that's included on any later disposition of (¶1321), or further partial principal payments on, the bond. (Code Sec. 1276(a)(3)(B))[36]

If bond principal can be paid in two or more payments, the accrued market discount is to be determined under regs. (Code Sec. 1276(b)(3))[37]

28. ¶J-4303; ¶12,714.01
29. ¶J-4349; ¶12,714.01
30. ¶J-4551; ¶12,764 *et seq.*
31. ¶J-4560; ¶12,764.01
32. ¶J-4570; ¶12,764.01

33. ¶J-4551; ¶12,764.01
34. ¶s J-4551, J-4569; ¶12,764.01
35. ¶J-4566; ¶12,764.01
36. ¶J-4567; ¶12,764.01
37. ¶J-4568

¶ 1323   What are market discount bonds?

Market discount bonds are any "bonds" having a market discount *other than* short-term obligations (one year or less), tax-exempt obligations bought before May 1, '93, U.S. savings bonds and certain installment obligations. (Code Sec. 1278(a)(1)(A), Code Sec. 1278(a)(1)(B))[38]

Market discount is the excess (if any) of the bond's stated redemption price at maturity (¶1313) over the taxpayer's basis for the bond immediately after acquiring it. (Code Sec. 1278(a)(2))[39] The market discount is zero if it's less than 0.25% of the bond's stated redemption price at maturity times the number of years to maturity after the taxpayer acquires the bond. (Code Sec. 1278(a)(2)(C))[40]

Special rules determine the stated redemption price at maturity for this purpose if the bond was issued with original issue discount (OID). (Code Sec. 1278(a)(4))[41]

¶ 1324   Election to include accrued market discount in income currently.

Instead of including a bond's accrued market discount on disposition (¶1321) or partial payment of principal (¶1322), a taxpayer may elect to include the discount as interest income for the tax years to which it's attributable, i.e., currently. The taxpayer may use either the ratable accrual method or the constant interest rate method. (Code Sec. 1278(b)(1); Code Sec. 1276(b))[42]

Elect by attaching to a timely filed income tax return, a statement that market discount has been included in gross income under Code Sec. 1278(b), describing the method used to determine the amount attributable to that tax year. [43]

¶ 1325   Acquisition discount on short-term obligations—mandatory accrual.

Certain holders of short-term obligations (not more than one year) are currently taxed on their daily portions of the "acquisition discount" (for government obligations, or nongovernment obligations if the holder so elects) or original issue discount (for nongovernment obligations), for each day during the year that they hold the obligation. (Code Sec. 1281(a)(1), Code Sec. 1283(c)) Any other interest payable on the obligation also must be taken into account as it accrues. (Code Sec. 1281(a)(2))[44]

An obligation's "acquisition discount" is the excess of its stated redemption price at maturity (¶1313) over taxpayer's basis in it. (Code Sec. 1283(a)(2))[45]

The daily portion of the acquisition discount is computed using the ratable accrual method or, if taxpayer so elects, the constant interest method. (Code Sec. 1283(b))[46]

This mandatory accrual rule applies only to these holders of short-term obligations:

(1) Accrual basis taxpayers;

(2) Taxpayers who hold the obligations primarily for sale to customers in the ordinary course of their trade or business. (Code Sec. 1281(b)(1))[47] This doesn't include banks that make short-term loans to customers in the ordinary course of business; [48] ;

(3) Regulated investment companies (mutual funds, ¶4201) or common trust funds (¶4210);

---

38. ¶s J-4552, J-4556; ¶12,764.01
38. ¶s J-4552, J-4556; ¶12,764.01
39. ¶J-4553; ¶12,764.01
40. ¶J-4554; ¶12,764.01
41. ¶J-4553; ¶12,764.01
42. ¶J-4573; ¶12,764.02
43. ¶J-4574; ¶12,764.02

44. ¶s J-4501, J-4506; ¶12,814
45. ¶J-4501; ¶12,814.01
46. ¶J-4500; ¶12,814.01
47. ¶J-4502; ¶12,814
48. ¶J-4501

(4) Taxpayers who identify the obligations as part of a Code Sec. 1256 hedging transaction; and

(5) Taxpayers whose short-term obligations are stripped bonds or stripped coupons that taxpayer stripped. (Code Sec. 1281(b)(1))[49]

The mandatory accrual rule doesn't apply to the ordinary investor. [50] Special rules apply to obligations held by pass-through entities. (Code Sec. 1281(b)(2))[1]

observation: The mandatory accrual rule doesn't apply to a cash basis holder who isn't a dealer in these obligations and isn't subject to the Code Sec. 1256 hedging rules.

¶ 1326   Interest on bonds sold between interest dates.

When fixed-interest bonds (not in default) are sold between interest dates, the amount the buyer pays that represents interest accrued as of the sale date is taxable interest to the seller. (Reg § 1.61-7(d)) Interest accrued after the sale date is taxable to the buyer on receipt.[2]

Bonds in default are usually traded "flat" (no part of the selling price is allocated between interest and principal). If there's accrued interest, the part of the selling price that represents interest accrued before the sale isn't taxable to the buyer until it exceeds the buyer's basis. [3]

¶ 1327   Interest credited to frozen deposits.

Interest credited to a frozen deposit (i.e., in a bankrupt or insolvent (actual or threatened) financial institution) during a calendar year, that's includible in the depositor's income for the year, can't exceed the sum of the net withdrawals during the year plus the amount withdrawable at the end of the year. (Code Sec. 451(g)(1))[4]

¶ 1328   Tax-exempt interest.

Interest on state and local bonds (i.e., obligations of a state, the District of Columbia, a U.S. possession, certain Indian tribal governments or any political subdivision of the foregoing) is exempt from federal income tax (Code Sec. 103(a), Code Sec. 103(c), Code Sec. 7871(a)(4))[5] (with certain exceptions, see ¶1329). For "educational expense" exclusion for certain U.S. savings bonds, see ¶2219 *et seq.* For tax credit bonds, see ¶2361.

observation: Even if interest isn't subject to federal income tax, it may have to be taken into account for certain other purposes.

caution: There's also a bar against deducting interest on debt incurred or continued to buy or carry tax-exempt bonds (¶1723).

Every person required to file a return must report on it all tax-exempt interest received or accrued during the tax year. (Code Sec. 6012(d))[6]

¶ 1329   Taxable interest from private activity bonds, hedge bonds, arbitrage bonds.

Private activity bonds aren't eligible for the interest exemption described at ¶1328 unless the bond meets detailed requirements *and* is one of seven specified types of bonds

---

49. ¶J-4502; ¶12,814
50. ¶J-4502
1. ¶J-4502; ¶12,814
2. ¶J-2827; ¶614.080

3. ¶J-2828 *et seq.*; ¶614.081
4. ¶J-3711; ¶4514.185
5. ¶J-3000; ¶1034
6. ¶J-3002; ¶60,124

(exempt facility, mortgage, veterans' mortgage, small issue, scholarship funding, redevelopment, or Code Sec. 501(c)(3) bonds). (Code Sec. 103(b)(1), Code Sec. 141(e))[7] Pre-Aug. 16, '86 industrial development bonds are subject to similar "qualification" rules. [8]

Hedge bonds (i.e., issued to "hedge" another bond) aren't exempt unless 85% of the bond's spendable proceeds (i.e., net of issuance expenses and certain reserves) are reasonably expected to be spent within specified periods, and at least 95% of the issuance costs (which can't be contingent) are paid within 180 days after issuance. (Code Sec. 149(g))[9]

Arbitrage bonds aren't exempt. (Code Sec. 103(b)(2)) This means a bond forming part of an issue any part of whose proceeds is reasonably expected to be used, directly or indirectly, to acquire (or refinance) nontemporary investments with a materially higher yield (more than 1/8 of 1 percentage point) than the bond itself, unless a required rebate is paid. (Code Sec. 148(a), Code Sec. 148(f); Reg § 1.148-2(d)(2)) If an issuer enters a transaction for a principal purpose of getting a material financial advantage based on the difference between tax-exempt and taxable rates, IRS has discretion to clearly reflect the economic substance of the transaction. (Reg § 1.148-10(e)) An issuer can't avoid having a bond treated as an arbitrage bond by giving away the prohibited arbitrage bond profit, e.g., by buying investments at other than fair market value ("yield burning"). [10]

¶ 1330   Inflation-indexed debt instruments; Treasury Inflation-Indexed Securities.

There are two methods of accounting for stated interest and inflation adjustments on inflation-indexed debt instruments (issued after Jan. 1, '97). Inflation-indexed debt instruments are issued for cash, indexed for inflation and deflation using a general price or wage index, and aren't otherwise contingent payment debt instruments. (Reg § 1.1275-7(c)(1), Reg § 1.1275-7(h)) These rules apply to Treasury Inflation-Indexed Securities (TIPS), but not certain debt instruments, e.g., U.S. savings bonds and bonds issued by qualified tuition programs. (Reg § 1.1275-7(b))[11]

(1) The coupon bond method is a simplified method that applies if (a) the debt instrument is issued at par, and (b) all stated interest on it's qualified stated interest (i.e., it's unconditionally payable in cash at least annually, see ¶1312). Under this method, the stated interest is taxable to the holder when received or accrued, in accordance with its accounting method. Any increase in the inflation-adjusted principal amount is treated as OID (¶1311) for the period in which it occurs. (Reg § 1.1275-7(d)) The coupon bond method applies to TIPS that aren't stripped and to TIPS issued with more than a de minimis amount of premiums. (Reg § 1.1275-7(g)(2))[12]

> **⊘ observation:** Assuming there's some inflation and principal continues to be adjusted upward, holders will have to include amounts not yet realized as interest income.

A decrease in a bond's inflation-indexed principal first reduces the interest income attributable to the interest payments for the year of the adjustment. If the decrease exceeds that income, the excess generally is an ordinary deduction to the extent taxpayer previously included interest from the bond in income. Any remaining decrease is carried forward to reduce interest income in future years. A taxpayer generally has a capital loss if the bond is sold, or it matures, before all the decrease has been used. (Reg § 1.1275-7(f)(1), Reg § 1.1275-7(d)(4))[13]

(2) The discount bond method is used if the instrument doesn't qualify for the coupon bond method (e.g., because it's issued at a discount). Under this method, taxpayers make current adjustments to their OID accruals to account for changes in the inflation-adjusted

---

7. ¶s J-3000 *et seq.*, J-3100, J-3252 *et seq.*, J-3600; ¶1414 *et seq.*
8. ¶s J-3153 *et seq.*, J-3227 *et seq.*, J-3251; ¶1034.01
9. ¶J-3667 *et seq.*; ¶1494.06
10. ¶J-3400 *et seq.*; ¶1484 *et seq.*

11. ¶J-4056.1, J-4379.1 *et seq.*; ¶12,714.037
12. ¶J-4379.1 *et seq.*; ¶12,714.037
13. ¶J-4379.1 *et seq.*; ¶12,714.037

principal amount. If the daily portions for an accrual period are positive amounts, they're taken into account under Code Sec. 1272 by the holder (¶1310). If the daily portions are negative, they're taken into account under the rules for deflation adjustments described above. (Reg § 1.1275-7(e)) The discount bond method applies to TIPS that are stripped under the Treasury's STRIPS (Separate Trading of Registered Interest and Principal of Securities) program. (Reg § 1.1286-2)[14]

¶ 1331   Interest on U.S. savings bonds.

Interest on U.S. savings bonds now being issued is earned in three ways. On Series HH "face amount" bonds (not issued after Aug. 31, 2004), it's paid semiannually by check. On Series EE "discount" bonds, it's reflected as an increase in the bond's value over stated periods. On Series I inflation-indexed face amount bonds, it's credited monthly (at a fixed rate for the 30-year life of the bond and a semiannual variable inflation rate) and paid when the bond is redeemed. The interest on these bonds (and on any unmatured or extended Series E and Series H bonds still outstanding) is fully taxable unless the exclusion at ¶2218 applies.[15]

Cash basis taxpayers report the interest on Series HH (or H) bonds in the year received.[16]

A cash basis owner of Series EE bonds (and outstanding Series E bonds) and Series I bonds may either: (1) defer reporting any interest (i.e., the bond's increase in value) until the year of final maturity, redemption, or other disposition, whichever is earlier, or (2) elect to report the annual increase in value in each year's return.[17]

Some Series E bonds can, at the owner's option, be held up to 30 years beyond their original maturity ("final maturity"). A cash basis owner who hasn't elected to report the interest on a Series E bond annually (under (2), above) must report all of the interest on the bond in the year in which the bond is redeemed or disposed of or, if earlier, the year in which it reaches "final maturity." (Code Sec. 454(a); Reg § 1.454-1(a)(1))[18]

⊘*observation:* Series E bonds issued before Dec., '65 reach final maturity 40 years after their issue date. Series E bonds issued after Nov., '65, and before July, '80, and all Series EE bonds, reach final maturity 30 years after their issue dates. (Series E bonds were issued before July, '80, and stopped paying interest in June of 2011.) This means that any accrued interest on Series EE bonds issued in '82 was taxable in 2012. *Accrual basis taxpayers* include the interest on the above bonds as it accrues.[19]

For the exclusion of income earned on qualified U.S. savings bonds by a payor of higher education expenses, see ¶2218 *et seq.*

¶ 1332   When to report interest income (other than original issue discount (OID)).

Cash basis taxpayers report interest in the tax year it's actually or constructively received, regardless of when the interest is accrued on the debtor's books.[20] Generally, interest isn't constructively received if taxpayer's control of its receipt is subject to substantial limits or restrictions. (Reg § 1.451-2(a))[21] Thus, interest on a 6-month certificate that isn't credited or made available before maturity without penalty isn't taxable until the certificate is redeemed or matures.[22]

Savings institution interest, or interest on life insurance dividends left to accumulate, is

14. ¶J-4379.5; ¶12,714.037
15. ¶s J-3014, J-3719 *et seq.*; ¶4544.01
16. ¶s J-3720, J-3721; ¶4544.01
17. ¶J-3719; ¶4544 *et seq.*
18. ¶s J-3721, J-3722; ¶4544 *et seq.*

19. ¶J-3719 *et seq.*; ¶4544.01
20. ¶J-3703; ¶614.067
21. ¶J-3706; ¶s 4514.036, 4514.053
22. ¶J-3710; ¶4514.053

considered received when credited to the depositor's (policyholder's) account and subject to its withdrawal. [23]

Where a bank charges a penalty for premature withdrawals from a time savings account, the gross amount of interest paid or credited during the withdrawal year is reported as interest that year, even if the penalty partially or completely offsets the interest. [24] For deduction of forfeited interest, see ¶2164.

Matured interest coupons are constructively received in the year they mature unless it can be shown that there are no funds available for payment of the interest during the year.[25]

Accrual basis taxpayers report interest in the tax year in which the right to receive the interest becomes fixed, regardless of when it's received. [26] But if it appears reasonably certain the interest won't be paid because the debtor is insolvent, the creditor can delay reporting the interest until its collection appears reasonably certain. [27]

For cash and accrual taxpayers, there are special rules on when to include "interest" on below-market rate loans (¶1303), (Code Sec. 7872(a)(2), Code Sec. 7872(b)(2)(A))[28] "points" (¶1333), and unstated interest (¶1334).

caution: These rules don't apply to debt issued with OID (¶1310).

¶ 1333   When "points" are included in income.

"Points"(¶1302) in the form of discount are taken into account under the "principal-reduction method"—i.e., as stated principal payments on the loan are made. "Points" paid out of funds not from the lender are included on receipt. [29]

¶ 1334   When to report unstated interest income.

A cash method seller includes unstated interest allocated to a payment (¶1304) as interest income in the tax year the payment is received. An accrual method seller includes the unstated interest in the tax year the payment is due. (Reg § 1.483-2(a)(1)(ii))[30]

¶ 1335   Rents and Royalties.

Rent is the payment for the use of real or tangible personal property (¶1336 *et seq.*). Royalties are payments for the use of certain rights, e.g., intangible rights such as patents (¶1342). Both are includible in gross income.

¶ 1336   Rents.

Rents are includible in gross income, whether paid in cash or property. (Code Sec. 61(a)(5); Reg § 1.61-1(a)) If paid in property, the property's fair market value (at receipt) is the amount taxed as rent. [31]

Rents are reported by cash basis taxpayers when received, and by accrual basis taxpayers when due unless they're considered uncollectible. [32] For advance rentals, see ¶1338.

---

23. ¶s J-3709, J-3717; ¶s 4514.036, 4514.053
24. ¶J-2822
25. ¶J-3715; ¶4514.053
26. ¶J-3701; ¶4514.011
27. ¶J-3702; ¶4514.023
28. ¶J-3708; ¶78,724 *et seq.*
29. ¶E-3004 *et seq.*; ¶4614.75
30. ¶J-3758; ¶4834.01
31. ¶J-2200 *et seq.*; ¶614.084 *et seq.*
32. ¶J-2276; ¶s 4514.001, 4514.023

¶ 1337   Bonuses; lease cancellation payments.

A bonus or extra payment by the tenant to the lessor or sublessor on the execution of the lease is taxable as rent to the lessor or sublessor. [33]

If the tenant pays the landlord for permission to cancel the lease, the payments are rent to the landlord (whether cash or accrual basis) in the year received. (Reg § 1.61-8(a)) Payments to the landlord for modifying a lease or consenting to a sublease are also considered rent.[34] Where the lessor pays the tenant to cancel the lease, see ¶1582.

¶ 1338   Advance rentals and security deposits.

An advance rental is currently taxable (Reg § 1.61-8(b)), even if it's refundable or can be applied against the purchase price. [35] But a security deposit (¶1206) isn't taxable rent. [36]

¶ 1339   Deferred rentals.

Where the rules on deferred payment leases over $250,000 apply (¶1584), the lessor has a "constant accrual" of rental income in the same way that rental expenses are deductible by the lessee. (Code Sec. 467)[37]

¶ 1340   Tenant's payment of landlord's expenses.

Where a tenant is required under the lease to pay interest, property taxes, mortgage principal, etc., thus satisfying the *landlord's* own payment obligation, the payments are treated as rent paid by the tenant to the landlord. (Reg § 1.61-8(c))[38]

¶ 1341   Tenant's improvements to the leased property; construction allowances from lessor.

Where a tenant erects a building or makes other improvements to leased property, the resulting increase in the property's value isn't income to the landlord either at the time the improvements are made or at the end of the lease term. (Code Sec. 109) But the landlord does have rental income if the improvements are made as rent substitutes. [39]

A lessee may exclude any amount received in cash (or as a rent reduction) from a lessor under a short-term lease (15 years or less) of retail space, that's for the purpose of the lessee's constructing or improving qualified long-term real property for use in the lessee's trade or business at the leased space. The construction allowance is excludible to the extent the lessee uses it for that purpose, within 8 1/2 months after the end of the tax year it was received. Qualified long-term real property is nonresidential real property that's part of or otherwise present at the retail space and reverts to the lessor at lease termination. The lessor treats any qualified long-term real property that's constructed or improved with an allowance excluded under these rules as its own nonresidential real property (¶1922). (Code Sec. 110; Reg § 1.110-1)[40]

¶ 1342   Royalties.

Royalties (payments received for the use of copyrights, patents, trademarks, secret processes and similar intangibles, and for the right to exploit mineral or other natural resources) are taxable as ordinary income (Code Sec. 61(a)(6)), regardless of the name

---

33. ¶J-2278
34. ¶J-2215 *et seq.*; ¶4514.022
35. ¶J-2218; ¶4514.193
36. ¶J-2277; ¶4514.194

37. ¶L-6800 *et seq.*; ¶4674
38. ¶J-2210 *et seq.*; ¶614.094
39. ¶J-2250 *et seq.*; ¶1094.01 *et seq.*
40. ¶J-2261 *et seq.*; ¶1104

given to them by the parties or the form of payment (e.g., lump sum or property such as stock).[41]

Royalties are included by cash basis taxpayers on receipt (actual or constructive), and by accrual basis taxpayers when their rights to them are fixed. [42]

¶ 1343   **Life Insurance Proceeds.**

In general, life insurance proceeds payable by reason of the insured's death are fully excludable (Code Sec. 101(a)) or, if paid later than death under an interest option (¶1345) or in installments (¶1344), partially excludable, from the recipient's gross income.

To qualify for the full exclusion, the amounts must be received under a "life insurance contract" (see below) and paid by reason of the insured's death. The exclusion applies to lump sum payments made at the time of the insured's death, and to amounts paid later to the extent the payment doesn't exceed the amount payable at death. (Reg § 1.101-1(a)(1))[43] It doesn't apply if the policy was transferred for value (¶1348). For dividends and other lifetime payments, see ¶1346. For accelerated death benefits, see ¶1347.

To qualify as a life insurance contract, a contract must be a life insurance (or endowment) contract under local law *and* satisfy either (a) a cash value accumulation test, or (b) a combined guideline premium requirement/cash value corridor test. (Code Sec. 101(f), Code Sec. 7702(a), Code Sec. 7702(h))[44] Pre-'85 contracts must entail risk shifting and risk distribution.[45]

¶ 1344   **Life insurance proceeds paid in installments.**

If the life insurance proceeds payable on the insured's death are paid in installments or for life, only part of each payment is excluded. Any amount that exceeds the excluded portion is taxable when received. But if the amount of the total anticipated payments can't exceed the total amount payable at the insured's death, then each payment is fully excludable, whenever it's made. (Code Sec. 101(d)(1); Reg § 1.101-4(a)(1)(i))[46]

The excludable portion of each payment is: (1) the excludable amount held by the insurer with respect to the particular beneficiary, divided by (2) the number of payments to be made or, if payments are for life, the number of payments anticipated over the life expectancy of the beneficiary. This same prorated amount of each payment is excludable, regardless of how many payments are made (Reg § 1.101-4) (i.e., even if the beneficiary exceeds anticipated life expectancy). The excludable amount is the present value to the beneficiary (as of the date of death) of the settlement. [47]

¶ 1345   **Life insurance proceeds left at interest.**

Where excludable life insurance proceeds are held by the insurer under an agreement to pay interest, the interest is taxable to the recipient, whether the interest option was chosen by the insured or by the insured's beneficiaries or estate. No part of this interest may be excluded under the proration rules (¶1344). (Code Sec. 101(c); Reg § 1.101-3(a))[48]

¶ 1346   **Proceeds paid before death of insured—loans, refunds, dividends, policy surrenders.**

Payments made under life insurance or endowment contracts before the death of the

41. ¶J-2300 *et seq.*; ¶614.084 *et seq.*
42. ¶s J-2305, J-2306; ¶4514.001
43. ¶J-4700 *et seq.*; ¶1014
44. ¶J-4800 *et seq.*; ¶s 1014, 77,024

45. ¶J-4950 *et seq.*; ¶1014
46. ¶J-4718; ¶1014.04
47. ¶J-4720; ¶1014.04
48. ¶J-4717; ¶1014.03

insured (e.g., loans, refunds, dividends, and amounts received on surrender, redemption or maturity of a contract) generally are treated as amounts "not received" under an annuity contract (¶1361). (Code Sec. 72(a))[49]

Thus, a transferee generally recognizes ordinary income in the amount received on the surrender of a life insurance policy (cash surrender value) less the adjusted basis in the contract (aggregate premiums paid). [50]

For accelerated death benefits received by terminally or chronically ill individuals, see ¶1347.

¶ 1347 Accelerated death benefits—terminally or chronically ill insureds—viatical settlements.

Amounts received under a life insurance contract on the life of individuals who are certified terminally or chronically ill are excluded from gross income as amounts paid by reason of the death of an insured (¶1343). (Code Sec. 101(g)(1)) A similar exclusion applies to amounts received for the sale or assignment of any portion of a death benefit under a life insurance contract to a viatical settlement provider (one that regularly buys or takes assignments of life insurance contracts on the lives of the terminally ill and meets detailed standards) if the insured under the life insurance contract is either terminally or chronically ill. (Code Sec. 101(g)(2)(A))[1] In the case of chronically ill individuals, the exclusions apply only if detailed requirements are met. (Code Sec. 101(g)(3))[2]

¶ 1348 Death benefits exclusion where contract was transferred.

If a life insurance contract is transferred for valuable consideration, e.g., by sale, during the insured's lifetime, the transferee's exclusion for the life insurance proceeds received under the contract by reason of the insured's death (¶1343) is limited to the value of the consideration paid for the contract, plus the net premiums and "other amounts" paid later (Code Sec. 101(a)(2))[3] For contracts issued after June 8, '97, "other amounts" includes interest paid or accrued by the transferee on debt with respect to a life insurance contract (or to an interest in one) that was transferred for valuable consideration, if the interest is disallowed under Code Sec. 264(a)(4) (see ¶1720). (Code Sec. 101(a)(2))

Thus, a transferee generally recognizes income in the amount received over the adjusted basis in contract (i.e., aggregate premiums paid minus cost of insurance already provided). The cost of insurance is determined by the reduction in the contract's cash surrender value at the time of sale. Inside build-up immediately prior to sale (cash surrender value minus aggregate premiums paid) is ordinary income while any remaining amount is capital gain. On the sale of a term life contract with no cash surrender value, a transferee recognizes capital gain on the excess of the amount realized on the sale over the adjusted basis of contract, with the reduction for the cost of insurance that's been provided each month presumed to be equal to monthly premium paid. [4] For the sale or assignment of any portion of the death benefit to a viatical settlement provider, see ¶1347.

If only an interest in the contract is transferred, the limit applies only to the part of the proceeds attributable to the transferred interest. [5]

This limitation doesn't apply if: (a) the transfer is to the insured, a partner or partnership of the insured, or a corporation in which the insured is a shareholder or officer; (Code Sec. 101(a)(2)(B)) or (b) the transferee's basis for the contract (or interest) is determined in

---

49. ¶J-5055 *et seq.*; ¶724 *et seq.*
50. ¶J-5058
1. ¶J-4750 *et seq.*, ¶J-4818; ¶1014.015
2. ¶J-4754 *et seq.*; ¶1014.015

3. ¶J-4729; ¶1014.02
4. ¶J-5307
5. ¶J-4731; ¶1014.02

whole or in part by reference to the transferor's basis (Code Sec. 101(a)(2)(A)),[6] as in a tax-free reorganization. (Reg § 1.101-1(b)(5), Ex 2)[7] However, for transfers after 2017, these two exceptions don't apply to a transfer of a life insurance contract, or any interest in a life insurance contract, in a "reportable policy sale." (Code Sec. 101(a)(3)(A)) In general, a reportable policy sale is the acquisition of an interest in a life insurance contract, directly or indirectly, if the acquirer has no substantial family, business, or financial relationship with the insured apart from the acquirer's interest in the life insurance contract. (Code Sec. 101(a)(3)(B))[8]

Where the transfer is gratuitous, i.e., a gift, the above limitation doesn't apply and the full death benefit exclusion is preserved. (Reg § 1.101-1(b)(2))[9]

¶ 1349　　Employer-owned life insurance—Form 8925.

For contracts issued after Aug. 17, 2006 (except for tax-free Code Sec. 1035 exchanges), an employer in a trade or businesses owning an employer-owned life insurance contract on an employee (reportable annually on Form 8925 (Code Sec. 6039I)) treats proceeds payable to it from such a policy as income, excluding as a death benefit only the premiums and other amounts it paid for the contract. (Code Sec. 101(j)(1))[10] This rule doesn't apply for a contract for which notice and consent requirements are met, if: (1) the insured was an individual who was an employee within 12 months of death; (2) at the time the contract was issued, the insured was a director; a "highly compensated employee," (i.e., a more-than-5% owner or employee who for the preceding year received in excess of $120,000 for 2018, $125,000 for 2019) (¶4315); or a "highly compensated individual," i.e., one of the five highest paid officers, a shareholder owning more than 10%, or anyone else in the top 35% of employees ranked by pay; (3) the amount is paid to a family member of the insured (under Code Sec. 267(c)(4)), an individual who is a designated beneficiary under the contract (other than the policyholder), a trust established for either the family member's or beneficiary's benefit, or the insured's estate; or (4) the amount is used to buy an equity (or partnership capital or profits) interest in the policyholder from the family member, beneficiary, trust or estate. (Code Sec. 101(j)(2)) It's intended that this amount be paid or used by the due date of the tax return for the policyholder's tax year in which the proceeds are received as a death benefit under the insurance contract, so that who is paid and what purchases are made with proceeds are known in the tax year in which the exception from the income inclusion rule is claimed. [11]

¶ 1350　　Taxation of Annuity Payments. ▬▬▬▬▬▬▬▬▬▬▬▬▬

Annuity payments consist generally of two parts: nontaxable return of investment based on an exclusion ratio (¶1351), and taxable interest. Other amounts (e.g., withdrawals, dividends) are taxable to the extent they exceed the contract's cost.

Gross income include any amount received "as an annuity" that's paid under an annuity, life insurance or endowment contract. (Code Sec. 72(a))[12] For exclusion under the "annuity rule," see ¶1351. For "nonannuity" payments under the contract (e.g., loans, dividends), see ¶1361. For private annuities, see ¶1364. For annuities paid to survivors of certain public safety officers, see ¶1258. For the partial annuitization rule, see ¶1359.

---

6. ¶J-4730; ¶1014.02
7. ¶J-4742; ¶1014.02
8. ¶J-4730
9. ¶J-4732; ¶1014.02

10. ¶J-4744; ¶1014.11
11. ¶J-4744; ¶1014.11
12. ¶J-5001; ¶724 *et seq.*

¶ 1351 The annuity rule—"exclusion ratio" for amounts received "as an annuity."

If a payment under an annuity, life insurance or endowment contract is received "as an annuity" (i.e., a sum of money (or property) payable at regular intervals over a period of more than one full year from the starting date (¶1358) (Reg § 1.72-2(b)), all or part of it may be tax-free (for "natural person" holders, see ¶1352). The part of each "annuity" payment that represents return of investment (e.g., premiums paid) is excludable from the recipient's income until the entire investment is recovered. Excess receipts are fully taxable. (Code Sec. 72(b)(1); Reg § 1.72-4(a))[13]

The excludable portion is computed by multiplying each payment received by an "exclusion ratio," determined by dividing the investment in the contract (¶1356) by the contract's expected return (¶1357) as of the annuity starting date, and rounding to the nearest tenth. (Code Sec. 72(b); Reg § 1.72-4(a)) But the excludable portion of any payment can't exceed the amount of investment in the contract that's unrecovered immediately before the payment is received. (Code Sec. 72(b)(2))[14] (For employee annuities, see ¶1360.)

Once computed, the exclusion ratio is applied to each "annuity" payment received under the contract, until the total investment has been recovered tax-free. (Code Sec. 72(b); Reg § 1.72-4(a))[15] But the ratio must be recomputed if the contract is transferred for valuable consideration, matures, is surrendered, or is exchanged. (Reg § 1.72-4(a)(4))[16]

If there was no investment in the contract, all payments are taxable in full. If investment exceeds total expected return, all payments are tax-free. (Reg § 1.72-4(d))[17]

Where the annuitant's death causes the annuity payments (starting after Jan. 1, '86) to stop, the amount of any investment in the contract that the annuitant hasn't yet recovered tax-free may be deducted on the final income tax return. (Code Sec. 72(b)(3)(A))[18] For after-death distribution requirements, see ¶1353.

¶ 1352 Annuity rule exclusion available only to natural persons.

If an annuity contract is held by a person who isn't a natural person, the annuity rule (¶1351) doesn't apply. The income on the contract (for the holder's tax year) must be treated as ordinary income received or accrued by the holder during that year. (Code Sec. 72(u)(1))[19] A natural person doesn't include a trust or corporation. But holding by a trust, etc., *as agent* for a natural person is disregarded. (Code Sec. 72(u)(1))[20]

However, an *employer* that's the nominal owner (agent) of an annuity contract whose beneficial owners are (the employer's) employees is considered to hold the contract. [21]

The natural person rule *doesn't apply* to contracts acquired by an estate by reason of the decedent's death, held by a qualified plan or IRA, that are "qualified funding assets" (¶1373); bought by an employer on termination of a qualified plan and held until all amounts under the contract are distributed to the employee (or a beneficiary) for whom the contract was bought; or that are immediate annuities. (Code Sec. 72(u)(3))[22]

---

13. ¶J-5100 *et seq.*; ¶724
14. ¶J-5105; ¶724.06
15. ¶J-5104; ¶724.06
16. ¶J-5106; ¶724.06
17. ¶J-5104; ¶724.06

18. ¶J-5109; ¶s 724, 724.06
19. ¶s J-5005, J-5006; ¶724.25
20. ¶J-5005; ¶724.25
21. ¶J-5005; ¶724.25
22. ¶J-5007; ¶724.25

¶ 1353 After-death distribution requirements for annuity contracts.

Payments under a contract aren't entitled to the partial exclusion under the annuity rule *unless* the contract provides that: (1) if any holder ("primary annuitant" for contracts not held by an individual) dies on or after the annuity starting date (¶1358) (and before the entire interest in the contract has been distributed), the balance will be distributed at least as rapidly as it was at the date of death, and (2) if any holder dies before the starting date, the entire interest must be distributed within five years of death. (Code Sec. 72(s)(1))[23]

However, distributions that are payable to (or for) a designated beneficiary can be made for the beneficiary's life or a period not ending past the beneficiary's life expectancy. As long as the payments begin within one year of the holder's death, they'll be considered distributed on that starting date. (Code Sec. 72(s)(2)) A beneficiary who is the holder's surviving spouse will be considered the holder. (Code Sec. 72(s)(3))[24]

observation: Treating the surviving spouse/beneficiary as the holder means that the after-death distribution provisions must be satisfied with respect to the *spouse's* death.

The after-death distribution rules *don't apply to* contracts provided under qualified pension, profit-sharing, stock bonus or annuity plans; tax-sheltered annuities; individual retirement annuities (or contracts provided under IRAs); qualified funding assets (¶1373), regardless of any qualified assignment (Code Sec. 72(s)(5));[25] or contracts issued before Jan. 19, '85.[26]

¶ 1354 Variable annuities.

A variable annuity contract is one where the amount paid varies depending on investment experience, cost of living indexes, market fluctuations, etc. The excludable portion of each payment is computed by dividing the investment in the contract (¶1356) by the total number of anticipated payments. (Reg § 1.72-2(b)(3), Reg § 1.72-4(d)(3))[27]

The excludable amount stays the same regardless of changes in the amount received. (Reg § 1.72-2(b)(3))[28] But if the amount received in a tax year is *less* than the excludable amount, taxpayer may elect (attach a specified statement to the return) to recompute the exclusion ratio for later years' payments. (Reg § 1.72-4(d)(3)(ii), Reg § 1.72-4(d)(3)(iv))[29]

¶ 1355 Joint and survivor annuity contracts.

Under a joint and survivor annuity contract, payments are made during the lives of two annuitants and, after the death of one, during the life of the survivor. A single exclusion ratio (¶1351), based on the aggregate expected return to both annuitants, is applied to the payments received by both annuitants. (Reg § 1.72-2(a)(2))[30]

¶ 1356 Investment in the contract.

For annuity rule purposes (¶1351), the "investment in the contract" is, in general, the net cost of the contract as of the annuity starting date (¶1358) or, if later, the date of the first contract payment. It equals the aggregate amount of premiums and other consideration paid (as of that date) for the contract, minus the aggregate amount previously received under the contract that was excluded from income. (Code Sec. 72(c)(1))[31] It must also be reduced to account for any refund feature. (Code Sec. 72(c)(2))[32] Separate computations

23. ¶s J-5014, J-5015; ¶724.01
24. ¶J-5014; ¶724.01
25. ¶J-5016; ¶724.01
26. ¶J-5014; ¶724.01
27. ¶J-5143; ¶724.08

28. ¶J-5143; ¶724.08
29. ¶J-5145; ¶724.08
30. ¶J-5132 *et seq.*; ¶724.15
31. ¶J-5113; ¶724.10
32. ¶J-5122; ¶724.12

may be required for pre-July '86 and post-June '86 investments. (Reg § 1.72-6(d))[33]

For an employee annuity, investment in the contract includes certain employer contributions that were taxable to the owner (employee). (Reg § 1.72-8(a))[34] Where the annuity began after Nov. 18, '96 (¶1360), or the safe-harbor method is elected for annuities beginning before Nov. 19, '96, no refund feature adjustment is required. [35]

For an employee annuity where the decedent died before Aug. 21, '96, the survivor-annuitant's investment in the contract also includes prior law's $5,000 death benefit exclusion, if applicable. (Reg § 1.72-8(b))[36]

¶ 1357 Expected return from the contract.

For annuity rule purposes (¶1351), the "expected return from the contract" is the total amount to be received (or estimated to be received) under the contract. It's computed as of the annuity starting date (¶1358) (Code Sec. 72(b)(1)) and doesn't take into account any amount for dividends or other payments *not* received as an annuity (¶1361). (Code Sec. 72(c)(3); Reg § 1.72-7(a))[37]

If the annuity is for a fixed term and doesn't depend on any life expectancy, the expected return is the amount of the payment specified for each period multiplied by the number of periods. (Reg § 1.72-5(c))[38]

If the annuity is payable for life or joint lives, the expected return is the amount of the *annual* payment multiplied by the number of years of life expectancy using IRS actuarial tables. (Code Sec. 72(c)(3)(A); Reg § 1.72-5(a))[39]

If the annuity is for an amount certain payable in periodic installments, the expected return is the total amount guaranteed. (Reg § 1.72-5(d))[40]

¶ 1358 Annuity starting date.

The "annuity starting date" is the first day of the first period for which an amount is received *as an annuity* (¶1351) under the contract. This is the date the contractual obligation becomes fixed or, if later, the first day of the period (year, quarter, etc., depending on whether the payments are to be made annually, quarterly, etc.) that ends on the date of the first annuity payment. (Code Sec. 72(c)(4); Reg § 1.72-4(b)(1))[41] Special rules apply if the contract is transferred or exchanged. (Code Sec. 72(g)(3))[42]

¶ 1359 Partial annuitization of annuities.

Taxpayers may partially annuitize a nonqualified annuity, endowment, or life insurance contract. (Code Sec. 72(a)(2)) If any amount is received as an annuity for a period of 10 years or more, or during one or more lives, under any portion of an annuity, endowment, or life insurance contract:

(1) that portion will be treated as a separate contract for annuity taxation purposes;

(2) for purposes of applying Code Sec. 72(b) (calculation of the exclusion ratio for annuity distributions, ¶1351), Code Sec. 72(c) (investment in contract, expected return, and annuity starting date, ¶1356– ¶1358), and Code Sec. 72(e) (taxation of distributions from an annuity, endowment, or life insurance contract, that aren't received as an annuity, ¶1361), the investment in the contract is allocated pro rata between each portion of the contract from which amounts are received as an annuity, and the portion of the contract

33. ¶J-5117 *et seq.*; ¶724.10
34. ¶H-11032 *et seq.*; ¶724.11
35. ¶H-11047; ¶4024.02
36. ¶H-11037; ¶724.12
37. ¶J-5124 *et seq.*; ¶724.14
38. ¶J-5130; ¶724.14
39. ¶J-5126 *et seq.*; ¶724.14
40. ¶J-5131; ¶724.14
41. ¶J-5110; ¶724.09
42. ¶J-5112; ¶724.09

from which amounts aren't received as an annuity, and

(3) a separate annuity starting date under Code Sec. 72(c)(4) (annuity starting date) is determined for each portion of the contract from which amounts are received as an annuity. (Code Sec. 72(a)(2))

¶ 1360 Employee annuities—simplified method for computing nontaxable portion.

The nontaxable portion of amounts received as an annuity (¶1351) under a Code Sec. 401(a) qualified employee plan, a Code Sec. 403(a) qualified employee annuity or a Code Sec. 403(b) tax-sheltered annuity is computed under a simplified method, by dividing the investment in the contract (¶1356) as of the annuity starting date (¶1358) by a designated number of monthly payments. (Code Sec. 72(d)(1)(B))

For an annuity payable over the life of a single individual, the number of payments is 360 if the age of the annuitant on the annuity starting date isn't more than 55; 310 payments if the age is more than 55 but not more than 60; 260 payments if more than 60 but not more than 65; 210 payments if more than 65 but not more than 70; and 160 payments if more than 70. (Code Sec. 72(d)(1)(B)(iii))[43]

For an annuity payable over the lives of more than one individual, the number of payments is 410 if the combined age of the annuitants on the annuity starting date isn't more than 110; 360 payments if more than 110 but not more than 120; 310 payments if more than 120 but not more than 130; 260 payments if more than 130 but not more than 140; and 210 payments if more than 140. (Code Sec. 72(d)(1)(B)(iv))[44]

Appropriate adjustments must be made if payments aren't made on a monthly basis. (Code Sec. 72(d)(1)(F))[45]

The simplified method doesn't apply if the primary annuitant is 75 or older on the annuity starting date, unless there are fewer than five years of guaranteed payments under the annuity. (Code Sec. 72(d)(1)(E))[46]

A lump-sum payment received in connection with the start of annuity payments is taxable under Code Sec. 72(e) as if received before the annuity starting date (see ¶1361), and the investment in the contract is determined by taking into consideration the receipt of this lump-sum payment. (Code Sec. 72(d)(1)(D))[47]

For annuity starting dates after Nov. 18, '96 and before Jan. 1, '98, the designated number of payments is based on the age of the primary annuitant, and there's no separate table for annuities based on the life of more than one individual. [48]

For annuity starting dates before Nov. 19, '96, the regular annuity rules apply (¶1350 et seq.) unless the employee elects a simplified safe-harbor method. [49]

For treatment of payments from a qualified plan during phased retirement, see ¶1361.

¶ 1361 Amounts not received as an annuity—cash withdrawals, dividends, etc.

Payments under life insurance, endowment and annuity contracts (other than modified endowment contracts, see ¶1363) that aren't "annuities" (e.g., cash withdrawals, loans, dividends, etc.) are fully taxable if received *on or after* the annuity starting date (¶1358). (Code Sec. 72(e)(2)(A), Code Sec. 72(e)(3)(A))[50]

---

43. ¶H-11012; ¶4024.02
44. ¶H-11012; ¶4024.02
45. ¶H-11012; ¶4024.02
46. ¶H-11012; ¶4024.02

47. ¶H-11012; ¶4024.02
48. ¶H-11012; ¶4024.02
49. ¶H-11012 et seq.; ¶724.07
50. ¶J-5053; ¶724.17

"Nonannuity" amounts received *before* the annuity starting date are: (1) *not taxable,* to the extent that, as of the date of distribution, they don't exceed the cost of the contract (i.e., accumulated net premiums paid) and (2) *taxable,* to the extent allocable to income (i.e., excess of the contract's cash value over the owner's investment) at that time. (Code Sec. 72(e)(2)(B), Code Sec. 72(e)(3)(B))[1] (Veteran's insurance dividends are tax-free, regardless of cost.)[2]

⚠️ *caution:* The pre-annuity starting date withdrawal may be subject to the premature distribution penalty (¶1362).

Receipts less than an insurance or endowment contract's cost don't give rise to a deductible loss.[3]

The contract's cost is reduced by the nontaxable amount of the dividend, etc., for purposes of computing the taxable portion of later payments. (Code Sec. 72(e)(6)(B))[4] For these purposes, all contracts (other than immediate annuities or qualified plan annuities) issued by the same company (or its affiliates) to the same policyholder during any one calendar year are treated as a single contract. (Code Sec. 72(e)(11))[5]

Payments during phased retirement. Payments received by an employee from a qualified retirement plan during phased retirement are "not received as an annuity" if: (i) the employee begins to receive partial retirement benefits when entering phased retirement and beginning part-time employment, and won't begin receiving entire plan benefits until ceasing employment and commencing full retirement at an indeterminate future time (including the possibility that a set date could change); (ii) the plan's obligations to the employee are based in part on the employee's continued part-time employment; and (iii) the employee doesn't have an election under the plan as to the form of the phased retirement benefit, but elects a distribution option at full retirement that applies to the employee's entire retirement benefit, including the portion that commenced as phased benefits. When an employee commences full retirement, the employee's investment in the contract (¶1356) as of the annuity starting date will take into account the investment in the contract recovered during the period of part-time employment and any additional employee contributions made during that period. [6]

¶ 1362 10% penalty on premature distributions from annuity contracts.

A penalty is imposed (except as noted below) on a person who receives any nonannuity distribution (¶1361) before the annuity starting date (¶1358) in the tax year the distribution is received. The penalty equals 10% of the taxable portion of the distribution. (Code Sec. 72(q)(1))[7] Calculate and pay the penalty on Form 5329. [8]

This 10% penalty *doesn't apply* to any distribution:

(1) made on or after the date taxpayer (recipient) reaches age 59 ½;

(2) made on or after the death of the holder (or the primary annuitant, where the holder isn't an individual);

(3) attributable to recipient's total and indefinite disability;

(4) that's part of a series of substantially equal periodic payments (not less frequently than annually) made for the life (or life expectancy) of taxpayer or the joint lives (or joint life expectancies) of taxpayer and a designated beneficiary;

(5) made from a Code Sec. 401(a) qualified employee plan, a Code Sec. 403(a) qualified annuity plan, a Code Sec. 403(b) tax-sheltered annuity plan or a Code Sec. 818(a)(3)

1. ¶724.17
2. ¶J-5055
3. ¶J-5308
4. ¶J-5063; ¶724.10

5. ¶J-5064; ¶724.17
6. ¶H-11030.1
7. ¶J-5017; ¶724.21
8. ¶S-2510

retirement plan for life insurance company employees (but for the separate penalty on premature distributions from these plans, see ¶4333);

(6) made from an individual retirement account or annuity (but for the separate penalty on premature distributions from these plans, see ¶4333);

(7) made under an annuity contract which is purchased by an employer on termination of a qualified plan (bonus, pension, profit-sharing or annuity) and which is held by the employer until the employee separates from service;

(8) under an immediate annuity;

(9) under a "qualified funding asset" (¶1373), regardless of any qualified assignment;

(10) to which the Code Sec. 72(t) tax on premature distributions from qualified plans applies (without regard to the Code Sec. 72(t)(2) exceptions), see ¶4333; or

(11) allocable to pre-Aug. 14, '82 investment in the contract. (Code Sec. 72(q)(2))[9]

¶ 1363   Modified endowment contracts.

A modified endowment contract is a life insurance contract (entered into after June 20, '88) that fails to meet a "7-pay test" (or that's exchanged for such a contract). The test is failed if the accumulated amount paid under the contract during the first seven years exceeds the net level premiums that would have been paid as paid-up future benefits. (Code Sec. 7702A(a), Code Sec. 7702(b))[10]

Payments under a modified endowment contract that are received before the annuity starting date (¶1358) are includible in gross income to the extent allocable to income on the contract, as described at ¶1361. (Code Sec. 72(e)(10)(A)(i))[11] This applies to any amount received as a loan, or assigned or pledged on the value of the contract, unless the loan, etc., is made solely to cover burial expenses or prearranged funeral expenses where the maximum death benefit under the contract doesn't exceed $25,000. (Code Sec. 72(e)(10)(B)) However, taxpayer's investment in the contract (¶1356) is increased by the amount included in income (as a loan or assignment). (Code Sec. 72(e)(4)(A))[12]

Certain amounts received under a modified endowment contract that are includible in income are subject to a 10% penalty tax (Code Sec. 72(v)(1), Code Sec. 72(v)(2))[13] (use Form 5329).[14]

¶ 1364   Private annuities.

A private annuity generally involves the transfer of money or property to an individual or organization in exchange for the transferee's promise to make lifetime payments to the transferor. These transfers typically are made to family members, controlled entities, or unrelated purchasers; to charitable organizations; and in settlement of a will contest. [15]

Transfer of an "unsecured" private annuity arrangement doesn't result in immediate taxable gain (or loss). Instead, any gain is reportable ratably over the lifetime of the transferor (i.e., annuitant). The gain equals the excess of the present value of the annuity (determined under regs) over the transferor's adjusted basis in the transferred property. Any loss may be disallowed if the arrangement is between related parties (¶2446 *et seq.*).[16]

If the arrangement is "secured" (i.e., the property transferred also is collateral for the payments), it's taxed (except for gift tax aspects) under the rules for commercial annuities, (¶1350 *et seq.*).[17] In applying those rules, the annuitant's basis in the property transferred

9. ¶J-5018; ¶724.21
10. ¶J-5066 *et seq.*; ¶s 724.17, 77,02A4
11. ¶J-5065; ¶724.17
12. ¶J-5063; ¶724.17
13. ¶J-5076; ¶724.17

14. ¶S-2510
15. ¶J-5252; ¶724.01
16. ¶J-5256 *et seq.*; ¶724.05
17. ¶J-5257

for the annuity is used as the annuitant's investment in the contract. [18]

The value of annuities issued by charities is determined under IRS tables. [19]

¶ 1365 Gifts and Inheritances.

Property received as a gift, bequest, devise or inheritance is generally exempt from income tax.

A gift of property isn't taxable to a recipient (Code Sec. 102; Reg § 1.102-1)[20] other than an employee, see ¶1211. For gifts, etc. of income, see below. For employee awards, see ¶1249. For gift tax, see ¶5041 *et seq.*

Gifts, devises, bequests, and inheritances (i.e., money and any property that pass on the death of a person by the person's will or under intestacy, including amounts received in settlement of a will contest) are excluded from gross income. (Code Sec. 102; Reg § 1.102-1)[21] However, this exclusion doesn't apply where the source of a devise, bequest or inheritance is income that a decedent had a right to receive at death but hadn't yet actually or constructively received or accrued (known as "income in respect of a decedent," see ¶3965 *et seq.*). For estate tax, see ¶5000 *et seq.*

The above exclusion applies only to the property transferred. Income from the property itself is taxable to the recipient, whether paid periodically or in a lump sum. (Code Sec. 102(b); Reg § 1.102-1(c))[22] For an exception for income paid or credited as a gift or bequest of specific property or money, see ¶3948.

¶ 1366 Prizes and Awards.

In general, prizes and awards are taxable. (Code Sec. 74(a); Reg § 1.74-1(b))

However, qualified scholarships (¶2215) and Olympic prizes (below) may be excludible in full or in part. A prize may also be excludible if it's primarily for religious, charitable, scientific, educational, artistic, literary, etc., achievement; the recipient was selected without any action on the recipient's part, and isn't required to render substantial future services; *and* it's transferred by the payor to a governmental unit or charity the recipient designated (Code Sec. 74(b))[23] before getting any benefit from it. [24] IRS specifies the requirements of the designation (including model language). [25] For employee awards, see ¶1249. The value of medals, and prizes awarded by the United States Olympic Committee, for participation in Olympic and Paralympic games, are excludable from income for athletes with AGI up to $1 million ($500,000 for married separate return filers). (Code Sec. 74(d))

For a prize paid in property or services, the taxable amount is the prize's current fair market (resale) value. (Reg § 1.74-1(a)(2))[26]

¶ 1367 Accident and Health Insurance Benefits.

Benefits received from accident and health insurance (or through an arrangement having the effect of accident or health insurance) are excluded from gross income unless the benefits compensate for medical expense deductions from an earlier year.

However, this exclusion doesn't apply to amounts received by an employee to the extent the amounts are (1) attributable to employer contributions that weren't includible in the employee's gross income, or (2) are paid by the employer. (Code Sec. 104(a)(3))[27]

18. ¶J-5254; ¶724.05
19. ¶P-6615, ¶P-6674 *et seq.*
20. ¶J-6000 *et seq.*; ¶1024
21. ¶J-6000 *et seq.*; ¶1024.02
22. ¶J-6004, ¶J-6005; ¶1024

23. ¶J-1201 *et seq.*; ¶744
24. ¶J-1208; ¶744.01
25. ¶J-1210; ¶744.01
26. ¶J-1223; ¶744.04
27. ¶J-1301; ¶1044.03

Where an employer-provided disability plan allows employees to elect annually to pay for coverage out of pre- or post-tax dollars, disability benefits paid to an employee who elected the post-tax option for the plan year in which the employee became disabled are excludable from gross income. [28]

Benefits from long-term care insurance policies (¶1368) are subject to special rules.

¶ 1368   Exclusion for benefits from long-term care insurance—per diem limit.

Qualified long-term care insurance contracts (see ¶2145) issued after '96 are treated as accident and health insurance contracts. (Code Sec. 7702B(a)(1)) Pre-'97 contracts that met applicable state long-term care insurance requirements also qualify. (Reg § 1.7702B-2) [29] Amounts (other than policyholder dividends, as defined in Code Sec. 808 or premium refunds) received from such contracts are treated as amounts received for personal injury or sickness and as reimbursement for expenses actually incurred for medical care, and are excludable (see ¶1367), subject to a per diem limit, below. [30]

If the total of (1) the periodic payments received for any period under all qualified long-term care insurance contracts treated as made for qualified long-term care services for an insured and (2) the periodic payments received for the period which are treated under Code Sec. 101(g) (see ¶1347) as paid by reason of the death of the insured, exceeds the per diem limit for the period, the excess is includible in gross income. A payment isn't taken into account under (2) if the insured is a terminally ill individual at the time the payment is received. (Code Sec. 7702B(d)(1)) [31]

The per diem limit for any period is the excess (if any) of: (a) the greater of (i) $360 for 2018 ($370 in 2019, as calculated by Thomson Reuters based on inflation data), or the equivalent amount when payments are made on another periodic basis, or (ii) the costs incurred for qualified long-term care services provided for the insured for the period, over (b) the total payments received as reimbursement (by insurance or otherwise) for qualified long-term care services provided for the insured during the period. (Code Sec. 7702B(d)(2)) If payments exceed this limit, the excess is excludible only to the extent of actual costs incurred for long-term care services; amounts with respect to which no such actual costs are incurred are fully includible. [32]

observation: The above projection for 2019 was computed under the assumption that a drafting error in the Tax Cuts and Jobs Act, which would clearly produce results at odds with the apparent intent of the statute, will be fixed.

¶ 1369   Exclusion for Archer medical savings account (MSA) distributions.

Distributions from an Archer MSA (see ¶1527 for limitations) are excludable from gross income if used exclusively to pay the qualified medical expenses of the individual (account holder) or the account holder's spouse or dependents. (Code Sec. 220(f)(1)) [33] Otherwise, they're (1) included in gross income (Code Sec. 220(f)(2)) and (2) subject to an additional tax of 20% for distributions reported on Form 8853 unless made after the individual attains age 65, dies, or becomes disabled. (Code Sec. 220(f)(4)) [34]

Qualified medical expenses are for medical care as defined under the medical expense deduction rules (see ¶2144), but only to the extent not reimbursed by insurance or otherwise. (Code Sec. 220(d)(2)(A)) Medicine or drugs are qualified medical expenses only if

---

28. ¶H-1115 *et seq.*; ¶1044.03
29. ¶K-2141.6; ¶77,02B4
30. ¶J-1308; ¶7702B4.04
31. ¶J-1308; ¶7702B4.04

32. ¶J-1308; ¶7702B4.04
33. ¶H-1337 *et seq.*; ¶2204.01
34. ¶H-1338 *et seq.*; ¶2204.01

prescribed (whether or not over-the-counter) or if insulin. (Code Sec. 220(d)(2)(A)) Qualified medical expenses don't include insurance premiums other than premiums for qualified long-term care insurance (¶2145), health care continuation coverage (COBRA), and coverage while receiving unemployment compensation. (Code Sec. 220(d)(2)(B))[35]

In any year for which an MSA contribution is made, distributions from that MSA to pay medical expenses are included in gross income if, for the month in which the expense was incurred, the individual for whom the expense was incurred wasn't covered under a "high deductible health plan" or had ineligible coverage. (Code Sec. 220(d)(2)(C))[36]

¶ 1370 Exclusion for health savings account (HSA) distributions.

Distributions from an HSA (see ¶1528) that are used exclusively to pay the qualified medical expenses of an eligible individual (account holder) or the account holder's spouse or dependents are excludable from gross income. (Code Sec. 223(f)) For this purpose, an individual may qualify as a dependent without regard to whether the individual: (1) is subject to the general rule that a dependent of a taxpayer shall be treated as himself having no dependents; (2) is married and files a joint return; and (3) has gross income that exceeds an otherwise applicable gross income limitation. (Code Sec. 223(d)(2)(A))

Qualified medical expenses are expenses paid for medical care as defined under the medical expense deduction rules (see ¶2144), but only to the extent they're not reimbursed by insurance or otherwise. (Code Sec. 223(d)(2)) Medicine or drugs are qualified medical expenses only if prescribed (whether or not over-the-counter) or if insulin. (Code Sec. 223(d)(2)(A)) Qualified medical expenses, which must be incurred after the HSA is established, don't include insurance premiums other than premiums for qualified long-term care insurance (¶2145), health care continuation coverage (COBRA) (see ¶1530), and coverage while the eligible individual is receiving unemployment compensation. (Code Sec. 223(d)(2)(B))[37]

Distributions not used for qualified medical expenses are subject to tax, they also are subject to an additional 20% for distributions reported on Form 8853 unless made after the individual attains age 65, dies, or becomes disabled. (Code Sec. 223(f))[38]

Contributions for a year exceeding the deduction limit (see ¶1528) can be withdrawn tax-free if the distribution is: (1) completed by the extended tax return due date; and (2) accompanied by the net income (includible in the individual's income) attributable to the excess contribution. (Code Sec. 223(f)(3)(A))[39]

¶ 1371 Exclusion for benefits received through health reimbursement arrangements (HRAs).

Except as provided below, amounts received by an employee under an HRA are excluded from gross income as amounts received under an accident and health plan (¶1367). This exclusion doesn't apply if *any* person may receive cash or any benefit from the HRA other than a medical care reimbursement. An HRA is a type of employee benefit plan reimbursing employees for medical expenses not covered by other forms of insurance. Medicine or drugs are qualified medical expenses only if prescribed (whether or not available over-the-counter) or if insulin. (Code Sec. 106(f)) Benefits are paid up to a specific dollar amount from funds provided exclusively by the employer (and not through a salary reduction or otherwise under a cafeteria plan (¶1267)). Balances remaining in the employee's account at the end of a coverage period may be carried forward if the plan so provides. An HRA may use debit cards, credit cards, or other electronic media to support and document the

---

35. ¶H-1337.1 *et seq.*; ¶2204.01
36. ¶H-1337.2; ¶2204.01
37. ¶H-1350.1 *et seq.*; ¶2234

38. ¶H-1350.11 *et seq.*; ¶2234.01
39. ¶H-1350.10; ¶2234.04

tax-free reimbursement of an employee's claimed medical or dental expenses if proper safeguards and substantiation methods are used. [40]

Effective for years beginning after Dec. 31, 2016, payments or reimbursements from a "qualified small employer HRA" (as defined in Code Sec. 9831(d)(2)) are excluded if, for the month in which medical care giving rise to the reimbursement is provided, the individual has minimum essential coverage under Code Sec. 5000A(f) (¶4898).[41]

¶ 1372   Damages.

Compensatory nonbusiness damages received on account of personal physical injuries or personal physical sickness are tax-free, but punitive damages generally aren't excludable.

Non-punitive damages to compensate for personal *physical* injury or personal *physical* sickness, whether received by suit or agreement, in a lump sum or as periodic payments, are excluded from income. (Code Sec. 104(a)(2); Reg § 1.104-1) If an action has its origin in a physical injury or physical sickness, then all nonpunitive damages from that injury or sickness are excluded, whether or not the recipient is the injured party. Emotional distress isn't considered a physical injury or physical sickness, but the exclusion does apply to damages received up to the amount paid for medical care attributable to emotional distress. (Code Sec. 104(a)) Thus, the exclusion doesn't apply to damages (other than for medical expenses attributable to emotional distress) based on a claim of employment discrimination or injury to reputation accompanied by a claim of emotional distress and does apply to nonpunitive damages received based on a claim of emotional distress, that are attributable to a physical injury or physical sickness. [42] The exclusion doesn't apply to "delay damages," i.e., damages awarded due to the delay in payment, which have been held to be in the nature of interest. [43]

Punitive damages generally are taxable, regardless of the nature of the claim. (Code Sec. 104(a)(2)) But under an exception, punitive damages received in connection with a physical injury or sickness are tax-free if the are awarded: (i) in a civil wrongful death action, and (ii) under applicable state law (as in effect on Sept. 13, '95, and without regard to later modification) which provides (or has been construed by a court to provide) that only punitive damages may be awarded in the action. (Code Sec. 104(c))[44]

Where a lump-sum award is specifically allocated by the parties between compensatory and punitive damages, or between personal and business injury, that allocation generally controls. But if no allocation is made, the courts look to the nature of the claims (e.g., primary nature of the harm inflicted) and the payor's intent. [45]

¶ 1373   Amounts received for accepting assignment of personal injury liability.

Amounts received by an assignee (e.g., insurance company) for accepting assignment of a liability to make periodic payments as damages for personal injury or sickness (in a case involving *physical* injury or sickness), including a liability to pay workers' compensation, are excludable from the assignee's gross income, up to the aggregate cost of any "qualified funding asset" used to satisfy the liability. A "qualified funding asset" is a commercial annuity contract, or a U.S. obligation, having payment periods corresponding to those of the liability, which the assignee: (1) purchased within 60 days before or after the date of the assignment, and (2) uses to satisfy that liability. (Code Sec. 130(c))[46]

---

40. ¶H-1349 *et seq.*
41. ¶H-1349.18
42. ¶J-5801; ¶1044.02
43. ¶J-5817; ¶1044.02

44. ¶J-5816.1 *et seq.*
45. ¶J-5810; ¶1044.02
46. ¶J-5833 *et seq.*; ¶s 1304, 1304.01

¶ 1374   Business damages.

Damages received for injury to business that represent compensation for lost profits (including business interruption insurance proceeds) are taxable as ordinary income. This applies to awards for breach of a contract of sale and for business slander. Amounts received for injury to capital (e.g., injury to good will, fraudulent stock sale) are tax-free to the extent of basis; any excess is capital gain. [47] Punitive damages (e.g., insiders' profits, treble damages under antitrust laws) are taxable. (Reg § 1.61-14(a))[48]

There's a special deduction for certain expired net operating losses that resulted from the same injury. (Code Sec. 186(d))[49]

¶ 1375   Attorney's fees payable out of judgment.

When a litigant's (taxpayer's) recovery —money judgment or settlement —constitutes income, the taxpayer must include in income the portion of the recovery paid to the attorney as a contingent fee (a fee that's paid to the attorney only in the case of a successful recovery; generally computed as a percentage of the recovery). In general, attorney's fees payable from the award are deductible only as a miscellaneous itemized deduction, regardless of whether the fees are contingent or noncontingent. [50] However, certain attorney's fees related to qualifying civil rights suits and whistleblower awards are deductible from gross income; see ¶3108.

¶ 1376   Damages for wrongful incarceration.

Gross income doesn't include civil damages, restitution, or other monetary awards (including compensatory or statutory damages) that an individual receives as compensation for a wrongful incarceration. A wrongfully incarcerated individual is either: (1) an individual who was convicted of a criminal offense under Federal or state law, who served all or part of a sentence of imprisonment relating to such offense, and who was pardoned, granted clemency, or granted amnesty because of actual innocence of the offense; or (2) an individual for whom the conviction for such offense was reversed or vacated and for whom the indictment, information, or other accusatory instrument for such offense was dismissed or who was found not guilty at a new trial after the conviction was reversed or vacated. (Code Sec. 139F) The exclusion doesn't apply to amounts received by (1) an individual wrongfully incarcerated but released before trial and not convicted of any crime, or (2) anyone other than the incarcerated individual, such as a family member. [1]

For waiver of time limit for filing a refund claim for a tax overpayment on damages for wrongful incarceration, see ¶4857.

¶ 1377   Income Realized on Discharge or Cancellation of Debt (COD). ▬▬▬▬

Gross income includes income from discharge of indebtedness, whether the debt was reduced or cancelled altogether, and whether the debt was recourse or nonrecourse. (Code Sec. 61(a)(12))[2]

COD income thus can result where a creditor accepts less than full payment as a complete discharge of the debt, or where events or circumstances make its collection unlikely.[3] But if the debtor's payment of the liability would have given rise to a deduction, the debtor won't have income from the discharge. (Code Sec. 108(e)(2))[4]

---

47. ¶J-5819 *et seq.*; ¶614.170 *et seq.*
48. ¶J-5829; ¶614.168
49. ¶K-8501 *et seq.*; ¶1864 *et seq.*
50. ¶J-8258

1. ¶J-5850; ¶139F4
2. ¶J-7001; ¶614.114
3. ¶J-7001 *et seq.*; ¶614.114
4. ¶J-7504; ¶1084.04

For information reporting by banks, etc., that discharge indebtedness, see ¶4746.

¶ 1378 Cancellation of debt (COD) under student loan programs.

There's no COD income (¶1377) from the cancellation of all or part of certain government student loans (or certain loans made by tax-exempt educational organizations), or loans made by exempt educational organizations or other exempt organizations to refinance any student loan, if the debtor is required to perform public service work for a period of time in certain professions for any of a broad range of employers. (Code Sec. 108(f)(1))[5]

Nor does gross income include any amount received under: (a) Sec. 338B(g) of the Public Health Service Act (relating to the National Health Service Corps Loan Repayment Program); (b) a state program described in Sec. 338I of that Act; or (c) any State loan repayment or loan forgiveness program intended to provide for the increased availability of health care services in underserved or health professional shortage areas (as determined by the State). (Code Sec. 108(f)(4))[6]

Taxpayers whose federal student loans are discharged under the Department of Education's Defense to Repayment or Closed School process can exclude the discharged amount from gross income.[7]

For discharges of indebtedness after 2017 and before 2026, certain student loans that are discharged on account of death or total and permanent disability of the student are also excluded from gross income. (Code Sec. 108(f)(5))[8]

¶ 1379 Cancellation of debt (COD) of solvent debtors outside bankruptcy.

Any COD of a debtor, other than in a bankruptcy case (¶1381), or where the debtor is insolvent (¶1380), results in the current (i.e., year of discharge) recognition of COD income (¶1377) in the amount of the discharge (Reg § 1.61-12(a))[9] except for certain farm (¶1382) or real property (¶1383) indebtedness.

¶ 1380 Insolvent debtor outside bankruptcy—"insolvency exception"—Form 982.

If the indebtedness is discharged when the debtor is insolvent (but not in a bankruptcy case), the discharge is excluded from the debtor's gross income up to the amount of the insolvency. (Code Sec. 108(a)(1)(B), Code Sec. 108(a)(2)(A), Code Sec. 108(a)(3))[10]

The amount excluded under this "insolvency exception" must be applied to reduce the debtor's tax attributes such as loss or credit carryovers or basis in assets. (Credit carryovers are reduced 33 1/3¢ per dollar of debt discharge amount; other tax attributes are reduced dollar for dollar.) (Code Sec. 108(b)(3)) (Use Form 982 to report the reduction of tax attributes.) Or the debtor can elect (on Form 982) to apply any or all of the excluded amount *first* to reduce basis in *depreciable* assets (or real property held as inventory). (Code Sec. 108(b)(5)(A), Code Sec. 1017(b)(3); Reg § 1.108-4(b))[11]

Any balance of the discharged debt (excess over the amount the debtor is insolvent) is cancellation of debt (COD) income, as for a wholly solvent debtor (¶1379). (Code Sec. 108(a)(2)(B), Code Sec. 108(a)(3))[12]

A debtor is insolvent for this purpose if, immediately before the debt is discharged, its liabilities exceed the fair market value of its assets. (Code Sec. 108(d)(3))[13]

5. ¶J-7508; ¶1084.04
6. ¶J-7510.1; ¶1084.04
7. ¶J-7513
8. ¶J-7508.1
9. ¶J-7001, ¶J-7200 *et seq.* ¶s 1084, 1084.01

10. ¶J-7401; ¶1084.01
11. ¶J-7404; ¶1084.02
12. ¶J-7401; ¶1084.01
13. ¶J-7403; ¶1084.01

If a reorganization or other transaction described in Code Sec. 381(a) ends a year in which the distributor or transferor corporation excludes COD income under Code Sec. 108(a), any tax attributes to which the acquiring corporation succeeds and the basis of property acquired by the acquiring corporation must reflect the reductions required by Code Sec. 108 and Code Sec. 1017. (Reg § 1.108-7(c), Reg § 1.1017-1(b)(4))

In applying the insolvency exception to grantor trusts and disregarded entities, the "taxpayer" for purposes of defining insolvency, etc., is the owner of the trust or entity, not the grantor trust or disregarded entity itself. [14]

For partners and S corporations, see ¶1384.

¶ 1381 Cancellation of debt (COD) of bankrupt debtor—Form 982.

No amount is included in a debtor's gross income by reason of a discharge of indebtedness in a bankruptcy case (Code Sec. 108(a)(1)(A)), even if the debtor is solvent after the discharge. (Code Sec. 108(a)(2))[15]

The amount of discharged debt that's excluded under this rule must be applied to reduce certain of the debtor's tax attributes (Code Sec. 108(b)(1)) (use Form 982) unless the debtor elects (on Form 982) to apply any or all of the excluded amount *first* to reduce basis in depreciable assets (or real property held as inventory). (Code Sec. 108(b)(5)(A), Code Sec. 1017(b)(3); Reg § 1.1017-1(c))[16] In applying the bankruptcy exception to grantor trusts and disregarded entities, the "taxpayer" for purposes of defining insolvency, etc., is the owner of the trust or entity.[17] For partners and S corporations, see ¶1384.

¶ 1382 Cancellation of "qualified farm indebtedness" of solvent farmers.

A solvent taxpayer whose "qualified farm indebtedness" is discharged (outside bankruptcy) by certain unrelated lenders doesn't have cancellation of debt (COD) income (¶1377), to the extent the discharge doesn't exceed the sum of its adjusted tax attributes plus the aggregate adjusted bases (as of the start of the year after discharge) of its business or income-producing property. (Code Sec. 108(a)(1)(C), Code Sec. 108(g)(1), Code Sec. 108(g)(3)) Any excess is COD income (but the insolvency (¶1380) or bankruptcy (¶1381) rules have precedence). (Code Sec. 108(a)(2))[18]

"Qualified farm indebtedness" is debt incurred directly in connection with taxpayer's farm business if at least 50% of taxpayer's total gross receipts for the three tax years preceding the tax year of the discharge is attributable to farming. (Code Sec. 108(g)(2))[19] For partners and S corporations, see ¶1384.

¶ 1383 Discharge of "qualified real property business indebtedness" (QRPBI)—Form 982.

A solvent taxpayer other than a C corporation whose QRPBI is discharged (outside bankruptcy) can elect to exclude the discharged amount from income, to the extent of the excess (if any) of (1) the outstanding principal amount of the QRPBI immediately before the discharge, over (2) the fair market value immediately before the discharge of the real property securing the QRPBI (i.e., the single item of real property to which the discharged debt is QRPBI), less the outstanding principal amount of any other QRPBI secured by the property at that time. (Code Sec. 108(a)(1)(D), Code Sec. 108(c)(2)(A), Code Sec. 108(c)(3)(C); Reg § 1.108-6(a)) The only property to be taken into consideration for

---

14. ¶J-7403.2
15. ¶J-7402; ¶1084.01
16. ¶J-7404; ¶1084.02

17. ¶J-7403.2
18. ¶J-7405 *et seq.*; ¶1084.01
19. ¶J-7406; ¶1084.01

this purpose is the property that qualified the indebtedness as QRPBI. [20] The excluded amount must be applied (on Form 982) to reduce the basis of taxpayer's depreciable real property. (Code Sec. 108(c)(1)(A))[21]

QRPBI is indebtedness (other than qualified farm indebtedness, ¶1382) incurred or assumed by taxpayer in connection with real property used in a trade or business and secured by the real property (Code Sec. 108(c)(3)(A)) that:

... if incurred or assumed by the taxpayer after '92, is "qualified acquisition indebtedness" (Code Sec. 108(c)(3)(B))—i.e., indebtedness incurred or assumed to acquire, construct, reconstruct, or substantially improve the property (Code Sec. 108(c)(4)); *and*

... taxpayer elects to treat as "qualified real property business indebtedness" (Code Sec. 108(c)(3)(C))[22] on Form 982 attached to the return for the tax year of discharge. (Code Sec. 108(d)(9)(A); Reg § 1.108-5)[23]

QRPBI also includes indebtedness incurred to refinance QRPBI, but only to the extent it doesn't exceed the amount of the indebtedness being refinanced. (Code Sec. 108(c)(3))

Under a safe harbor, IRS will treat certain debt secured by 100% of the ownership interest in a disregarded entity that holds real property as secured by real property. However, a taxpayer that doesn't qualify for the safe harbor requirements can still argue that the debt meets the "secured by" requirement based on the facts and circumstances.

QRPBI doesn't include debt secured by property that's inventory or held by a taxpayer primarily for sale to customers in the ordinary course of its trade or business. [24]

¶ 1384 How cancellation of debt (COD) income exclusions apply to partnership or S corporation debt.

For partnership debt, the insolvency (¶1380), bankruptcy (¶1381), qualified farm indebtedness (¶1382), and qualified real property indebtedness (¶1383) exclusions are applied at the *partner* level, not at the partnership level. (Code Sec. 108(d)(6)) In measuring a partner's insolvency for purposes of the insolvency exclusion, each partner treats as a liability an amount of the partnership's discharged excess nonrecourse debt (i.e., nonrecourse debt in excess of the fair market value of the property securing the debt) based on the allocation of COD income to that partner under Code Sec. 704(b) (¶3720).[25] IRS disagrees with a number of Tax Court cases holding that partners may exclude their share of partnership COD income because the partnership debt was discharged "in a title 11 case" within the meaning of Code Sec. 108(d)(2).[26]

For an S corporation's debt, the exclusions are applied at the corporate level, not at the shareholder level. (Code Sec. 108(d)(7)(A))[27]

¶ 1385 Discounted purchase of debtor's own obligations.

When a debtor buys or otherwise acquires its own obligations for less than face value (i.e., at a discount), it usually realizes taxable income to the extent of the discount. (Reg § 1.61-12(a))[28] This also applies if a party related to the debtor acquires the debtor's indebtedness from an unrelated party. (Code Sec. 108(e)(4)(A); Reg § 1.108-2)[29]

A corporation that repurchases its own bonds (directly or indirectly) has cancellation of debt (COD) income (¶1377) to the extent of the excess of the adjusted issue price over the

---

20. ¶J-7409; ¶1084.01
21. ¶J-7411; ¶1084.01
22. ¶J-7410; ¶1084.01
23. ¶J-7412; ¶1084.01
24. ¶J-7410; ¶1084.01

25. ¶J-7415; ¶1084.03
26. ¶J-7402
27. ¶J-7416; ¶1084.03
28. ¶J-7011; ¶614.114
29. ¶J-7016 *et seq.*; ¶1084.04

repurchase price. (Reg § 1.61-12(c)(2))[30]

For the debtor to be taxed, the obligation must require the unconditional payment of a fixed amount. If the obligation really represents an equity interest, a corporate debtor will be, in effect, acquiring its own stock and thus won't be taxed on the "discount." [31]

Debt instrument reacquired in 2009 and 2010. If the taxpayer elected, debt discharge income from the reacquisition of a discounted applicable debt instrument by the taxpayer or a related party after 2008 and before 2011 is deferred for up to five years, and then included in income ratably over five years. For reacquisitions in 2009, income is includible over the 5-year period beginning with the fifth tax year following the tax year in which it's reacquired; and for reacquisitions in 2010, beginning with the fourth tax year following the tax year in which it's reacquired. (Code Sec. 108(i)(1), Reg § 1.108(i)-0(a))

¶ 1386 Satisfaction of debt with property or services (including "stock for debt").

If a debtor transfers property (other than debt) to, or performs services for, a creditor (or third party) in full satisfaction of the debt, and the property or services are worth the amount owed, there's no *cancellation* of debt (COD) or accompanying COD income since it was actually paid. But a debtor who satisfies debt with services has taxable *compensation* equal to the debt. (Reg § 1.61-12(a))[32]

A debtor who transfers property (other than debt) in satisfaction of the debt has gain (or loss) to the extent the fair market value (FMV) of the property transferred exceeds (or is less than) its basis in the property. The type of gain (or loss), or whether any loss is deductible, is determined under the regular sale or exchange rules (¶2400 *et seq.*). If the property transferred is worth less than the face amount of the debt, the difference is COD income to the debtor.[33]

If a debtor corporation transfers stock, or a debtor partnership transfers a capital or profits interest in that partnership, to a creditor in satisfaction of its recourse or nonrecourse debt, the corporation or partnership is treated as having satisfied the debt with an amount of money equal to the FMV of the stock or the interest. In the case of a partnership, Under a safe harbor, the FMV of the partnership interest in a debt-for-equity exchange will be its liquidation value. Any discharge of debt income recognized under this rule is included in the distributive shares of taxpayers that were partners in the partnership immediately before the discharge. (Code Sec. 108(e)(8), Reg § 1.108-8) So the debtor has taxable income to the extent the principal of the debt exceeds the value of the stock or interest.[34]

¶ 1387 Debt-for-debt exchanges.

A debtor may satisfy an outstanding "old" debt by issuing a "new" debt. The old debt is treated as having been satisfied with an amount of money equal to the issue price of the new debt. (Code Sec. 108(e)(10)(A)) The excess (if any) of the "old" adjusted issue price over the "new" issue price is cancellation of debt (COD) income (¶1377) to the debtor.[35]

For this purpose, "issue price" is determined under the OID rules (¶1314). (Code Sec. 108(e)(10)(B)) However, if the Code Sec. 483 unstated interest rules (¶1304 *et seq.*) (rather than the OID rules) apply, the new debt's issue price is its stated redemption price at maturity (¶1313) less the unstated interest. [36]

---

30. ¶J-7204.1; ¶614.136
31. ¶J-7007
32. ¶J-7040; ¶614.114
33. ¶J-7206; ¶10,014.76

34. ¶J-7015; ¶1084.04
35. ¶J-7205; ¶1084.04
36. ¶J-7205; ¶1084.04

¶ 1388   Home mortgage debt forgiveness before 2018—Form 982.

For indebtedness discharged before Jan. 1, 2018, gross income didn't include any discharge of qualified principal residence indebtedness. (Code Sec. 108(a)(1)(E)) Qualified principal residence indebtedness is acquisition indebtedness under Code Sec. 163(h)(3)(B) with respect to the taxpayers's principal residence (see ¶1730), but with a $2 million limit ($1 million for married individuals filing separately). (Code Sec. 108(h)(2)) It includes indebtedness incurred in the acquisition, construction, or substantial improvement of a principal residence that's secured by the residence, as well as refinancing of debt to the extent the amount doesn't exceed the amount of the refinanced indebtedness. "Principal residence" has the same meaning as under the homesale exclusion rules of Code Sec. 121 (see ¶2442). (Code Sec. 108(h)(5)) The basis of the taxpayer's principal residence was reduced by the excluded amount, but not below zero. (Code Sec. 108(h)(1))[37]

⚠️ *caution:* Check tax.thomsonreuters.com/federaltaxhandbookupdates to see if the above provision has been extended.

---

37. ¶P-3006.2; ¶1084.01

Chapter 3   Deductions—Expenses of a Business

¶ 1500   **Tax Treatment of Start-Up Expenditures.** ▬▬▬▬▬▬▬▬▬

Start-up expenditures (below) must be amortized and can't be deducted unless the taxpayer elects (¶1501) to expense up to $5,000 of these costs with that amount reduced by the excess of total start-up expenditures over $50,000 in the tax year in which the trade or business begins.

The remainder of the start-up expenditures may be amortized (deducted ratably) over a 180-month period. (Code Sec. 195(b)(1))[1]

Start-up expenditures are amounts paid or incurred in connection with:

. . . investigating the creation, acquisition, or establishment of an active trade or business, (Code Sec. 195(c)(1)(A)(i)) but not costs incurred after a taxpayer decides whether to enter a new business, and which new business it will enter or acquire; [2]

. . . creating an active trade or business (Code Sec. 195(c)(1)(A)(ii)); or

. . . any activity engaged in for profit and for the production of income before the day the active trade or business begins, in anticipation of that activity becoming an active trade or business. (Code Sec. 195(c)(1)(A)(iii))

The expenditure must be one that, if paid or incurred in connection with the operation of an existing active trade or business (in the same field as the taxpayer's new business), would be deductible for the year in which paid or incurred. (Code Sec. 195(c)(1)(B))[3]

Start-up expenses don't include any amounts deductible under Code Sec. 163(a) (i.e., as interest expenses); Code Sec. 164 (i.e., as taxes); or Code Sec. 174 (i.e., as research and experimental expenses). (Code Sec. 195(c)(1))[4]

¶ 1501   **Election to expense/amortize start-up expenditures.**

A taxpayer (1) is deemed to have elected to expense/amortize start-up costs under Code Sec. 195(b) (¶1500) for the tax year in which the active trade or business begins, but (2) may forgo the deemed election by clearly electing to capitalize start-up expenditures on a timely filed Federal income tax return (including extensions) for the tax year in which the active trade or business begins. The choice of expensing/amortizing or capitalizing start-up expenditures is irrevocable and applies to all start-up expenditures related to the active trade or business. (Reg § 1.195-1(b))

¶ 1502   **Treatment of deferred start-up expenses on disposition of business.**

If the trade or business is disposed of before the end of the amortization period, any deferred expenses not yet deducted may be deducted to the extent the disposition results in a loss under Code Sec. 165. (Code Sec. 195(b)(2))[5]

¶ 1503   **Fruitless searches for new ventures.**

A corporation (but not a noncorporate taxpayer not engaged in the business of locating or promoting new ventures) that makes expenditures in fruitlessly searching for or investigating a new venture may deduct them as a loss when it abandons the effort. [6] However, once a noncorporate taxpayer has focused on the acquisition of a specific business or

---

1. ¶L-5001; ¶1954
2. ¶L-5013; ¶1954.01
3. ¶L-5011; ¶s 1954, 1954.01

4. ¶L-5011; ¶1954.01
5. ¶L-5023; ¶1954.04
6. ¶L-5019; ¶1954

References beginning with a single letter are to paragraphs in Federal Tax Coordinator 2d and RIA's Analysis of Federal Taxes: Income. Those beginning with numbers are to paragraphs in United States Tax Reporter.

investment, unsuccessful start-up expenses related to an attempt to acquire that business or investment are deductible as business or investment losses under Code Sec. 165 (¶1765).[7]

¶ 1504   Expanding an existing business.

A taxpayer can deduct expenditures made to expand an existing business. The taxpayer must show that the business contemplated and the one already conducted are closely related or "intramural," *and* that the expenditures are ordinary and necessary expenses of the business conducted when the expenses were incurred, and not capital expenditures.

Expansion costs must be capitalized if they provide the taxpayer with long-term benefits, or create separate and distinct assets, or relate to a change in the nature of the taxpayer's activities (e.g., wholesaler opening retail outlet). [8]

¶ 1505   Ordinary and Necessary Business Expenses. ■■■■■■■■■■■

Individuals, corporations, and other taxpayers generally can deduct ordinary and necessary (¶1506) expenses paid or incurred during the tax year in carrying on any trade or business (¶1507). Various limits (e.g., percentage limit on meal and entertainment deductions, see ¶1557) may apply.

¶ 1506   "Ordinary and necessary" requirement.

A deductible business expense must be both ordinary and necessary in relation to the taxpayer's industry. (Code Sec. 162(a))[9]

An expense is *ordinary* if it's customary or usual in the taxpayer's business. [10] But an unusual expense may be ordinary if it's reasonably related to the taxpayer's trade or business. [11] A *necessary* expense is one that's appropriate and helpful in developing and maintaining the taxpayer's business. It need not be essential or indispensable. Usually, the taxpayer's judgment as to what's necessary will be accepted. [12]

Some courts have held that to be deductible under Code Sec. 162, an expense must not only be ordinary and necessary, but also reasonable in amount and reasonable in relation to its purpose. [13]

¶ 1507   Connection to taxpayer's trade or business.

To be deductible as a business expense, an item must be directly connected with or pertain to a trade or business carried on by the taxpayer. (Code Sec. 162(a); Reg § 1.162-1(a))[14]

Serving as an employee is a business (see ¶1616 for deduction limitations). [15] A trade or business need not be the taxpayer's principal occupation. [16]

¶ 1508   Expense must benefit person claiming deduction.

A deductible expense must be an expense of *the taxpayer's* business. Expenses incurred on another's behalf aren't deductible. [17]

A corporation can't deduct payment of the personal expenses of its shareholders [18] or payment of the personal expenses of its officers and employees, except to the extent the

---

7. ¶L-5020; ¶1954
8. ¶L-5101; ¶1624 *et seq.*
9. ¶L-1200 *et seq.*; ¶1624.012
10. ¶L-1201; ¶1624.012
11. ¶s L-1201, L-1209; ¶1624.012
12. ¶L-1201; ¶1624.012

13. ¶L-1202; ¶1624.013
14. ¶L-1002; ¶1624
15. ¶L-3900; ¶1624
16. ¶L-1100 *et seq.*; ¶1624.002
17. ¶L-4400; ¶1624.104
18. ¶L-1214; ¶1624.104

payment represents reasonable compensation (¶1516) or is made for business reasons to provide benefits to employees in general. [19]

A corporate officer can't deduct an expenditure he makes to pay an expense of the corporation.[20]

If a taxpayer pays the debts or other obligations of another, the payment may sometimes qualify as a business expense. [21] Deductions have been allowed where such a payment is made for a good business reason, e.g., to preserve sales-force morale and customer good-will, reestablish or protect credit standing, or avoid loss of business patronage, etc. [22]

¶ 1509   Right to deduction—*Cohan* rule.

Where a taxpayer's records or other proof aren't adequate to substantiate expense deductions, he may be allowed to deduct an estimated amount under the *Cohan* rule. But a court may allow a much smaller deduction than claimed, bearing heavily against a taxpayer whose inexactitude is of his own making. [23] The *Cohan* rule doesn't apply to travel or entertainment expenses, listed property, or business gifts, see ¶1564.

¶ 1510   Expenses of membership organizations.

Organizations that aren't exempt from tax under the rules discussed at ¶ 4100 *et seq.*, which are operated primarily to furnish services or goods to members, can deduct expenses of furnishing services, insurance, goods, or other items to members only to the extent of income derived during the year from members or transactions with members. (Code Sec. 277(a))[24] Any excess of expenses over income isn't deductible, but may be carried over to the following tax year. (Code Sec. 277(a))[25]

¶ 1511   Advertising and business promotion costs.

Advertising and business promotion costs relating to an existing business can be deducted currently, even though the business benefit they generate may extend over a period beyond the year they are incurred or paid. [26]

Production costs of a business catalog that will remain unchanged for several years must be capitalized according to IRS, but some courts disagree. [27] Display equipment (cabinets, signs, etc.) must be capitalized if it has a useful life beyond the tax year. [28] Package design costs (e.g., physical construction of a package containing a consumer product) do not have to be capitalized. (Reg § 1.263(a)-4(b)(3)(v))[29]

¶ 1512   Costs of determining or contesting tax liability.

Costs relating to tax matters that are ordinary and necessary in the course of the conduct of taxpayer's trade or business, including costs of tax advice, are deductible. The deduction applies to expenses incurred in: (1) preparing tax returns, (2) determining tax liability, (3) contesting tax liability, (4) securing tax counsel. (Code Sec. 62(a)(1); Reg § 1.62-1T(d)) This includes expenses incurred by an individual taxpayer in: [30]

- preparing that portion of the individual's tax return that relates to the taxpayer's business as sole proprietor,
- preparing schedules relating to income or loss from rentals or royalties, or farm

19. ¶L-4414; ¶1624.205
20. ¶L-4405; ¶1624.009
21. ¶L-1214; ¶1624.104
22. ¶L-1214 *et seq.*; ¶s 1624.015, 1624.026
23. ¶L-4509 *et seq.*; ¶1624.014
24. ¶L-4301; ¶2774

25. ¶L-4301; ¶2774
26. ¶L-2201; ¶1624.355
27. ¶L-2205; ¶1624.355
28. ¶L-2206; ¶1624.355
29. ¶L-5629, ¶2634.18
30. ¶L-3000 *et seq.*; ¶2124.14

income and expenses, and

- resolving asserted tax deficiencies relating to a business, to rental or royalty income, or to a farm.

From 2018 through 2025, *nonbusiness* tax determination costs are nondeductible because they are subject to the suspension of miscellaneous itemized deductions subject to the 2%-of-AGI floor; see ¶3109. For deductibility of interest on taxes, see ¶¶1708.

¶ 1513   Other deductible costs of carrying on a trade or business.

These include:[31]

... cost of materials and supplies (see ¶1631 for timing of deduction);[32]

... annual license and regulatory fees;[33]

... amounts paid to cancel burdensome contracts;[34]

... cost of moving business equipment and machinery;[35]

... current membership fees (but not admission fees), dues (other than certain social club dues) and assessments paid for business association, etc.;[36]

... training costs; and[37]

... certain education expenses, see ¶2222 *et seq.*

¶ 1514   Compensation Deduction. ▆▆▆▆▆▆▆▆▆▆▆▆▆▆▆▆▆▆▆▆▆▆▆▆

Reasonable amounts (¶1516 *et seq.*) that are paid or incurred in connection with a trade or business as compensation for personal services actually rendered (¶1515) are deductible, subject to a limit for top officers (¶1518). Payments for fringe benefits (¶1523) are deductible as compensation, subject to some limits.

¶ 1515   Compensation paid for personal services.

Compensation (including severance pay)[38] paid or incurred for personal services rendered is deductible as a trade or business expense. (Code Sec. 162(a)(1)) Deductible compensation includes amounts paid to independent contractors, as well as employees. [39]

A parent can deduct reasonable wages he pays his unemancipated minor child for personal services actually rendered as a bona fide employee in the business. [40]

For deductibility of amounts paid for fringe benefits, see ¶1523 *et seq.* For when compensation can be deducted, see ¶1536 *et seq.*

¶ 1516   Reasonableness of compensation.

Compensation is deductible only to the extent it's *reasonable.* Compensation paid to employee-shareholders also must be paid purely for services, or have a purely compensatory purpose, in order to be deductible. (Code Sec. 162(a)(1))[41] The question of reasonableness rarely arises unless the payments are made to a person "related" to the taxpayer — that is, to the members of an employer's family, or to stockholders of the employer, or to members of a stockholder's family. [42]

31. ¶L-4200 *et seq.*; ¶1624.404
32. ¶L-4207 *et seq.*
33. ¶L-4216 *et seq.*
34. ¶L-4213 *et seq.*
35. ¶L-4209 *et seq.*; ¶1624.052
36. ¶L-4231; ¶1624.061

37. ¶L-4232.3
38. ¶H-3600 *et seq.*; ¶1624.205
39. ¶H-3600 *et seq.*; ¶1624.205
40. ¶H-3755; ¶1624.212
41. ¶1624.229
42. ¶s H-3725 *et seq.*, H-3752 *et seq.*; ¶1624.229

The unreasonable portion of compensation is nondeductible. If the recipient is a shareholder, the unreasonable portion may be treated as a dividend. (Reg § 1.162-7(b)(1))[43]

While reasonableness of compensation normally arises in determining whether a business is trying to deduct too high an amount of compensation, IRS finds the concept equally applicable to employment tax cases (e.g., where S corporation shareholder-employees pay themselves a low salary to reduce Medicare and Social Security taxes). [44]

¶ 1517 Factors determining reasonableness.

Reasonable compensation is the amount that would ordinarily be paid for like services by like enterprises under like circumstances. (Reg § 1.162-7(b)(3))[45] Factors determining reasonableness include: (1) duties performed by the employee; (2) character and amount of responsibility; (3) amount of time required; (4) ability and achievements of the employee; (5) volume of business handled by the employee; (6) complexities of the business; (7) relationship of compensation to gross and net income of the business; (8) living conditions in locality; (9) compensation history of the employee; and (10) salary policy as to all employees. [46]

The Seventh Circuit applies a single independent-investor test in evaluating if a stockholder-employee's pay is reasonable (i.e., would an outside investor have paid the compensation amount based on performance). Other courts employ the independent-investor test in conjunction with an analysis of the above factors. [47]

The test of whether compensation is reasonable is normally applied to the compensation paid to the particular individual and not to the total compensation paid to a group of employees.[48] Services rendered in earlier years can be taken into account in determining the reasonableness of compensation paid during the current year. [49] Reasonableness of compensation for part-time services is determined under the usual reasonableness rules. [50]

¶ 1518 Deduction limit for compensation paid to top officers.

A "publicly held corporation" can't deduct applicable employee remuneration (defined below) in excess of $1 million per year paid to a "covered employee." (Code Sec. 162(m)(1))[1] The $1 million limit is reduced (but not below zero) by the amount, if any, paid to the executive but not deductible under the golden parachute rules (¶1534). (Code Sec. 162(m)(4)(F); Reg § 1.162-27(g))[2]

Publicly held corporation. A "publicly held corporation" is any corporation that's an issuer, as defined in section 3 of the Exchange Act, (i) whose securities are required to be registered under section 12 of the Exchange Act, or (ii) that's required to file reports under section 15(d) of the Exchange Act. (Code Sec. 162(m)(2))[3]

Covered employee. A covered employee includes any employee of the taxpayer if: (1) the employee is the PEO or PFO of the taxpayer at any time during the tax year, or was an individual acting in that capacity; (2) the employee's total compensation for the tax year must be reported to shareholders under the Exchange Act because the employee was one of the three highest compensated officers for the tax year other than the PEO or PFO; or (3) the employee was a covered employee of the taxpayer (or any predecessor) for any earlier tax year that began after 2016. (Code Sec. 162(m)(3); Reg § 1.162-27(c)(2))[4]

Applicable employee remuneration. Applicable employee remuneration means a covered

---

43. ¶H-3607; ¶1624.268
44. ¶H-4329
45. ¶H-3701; ¶1624.229
46. ¶H-3706; ¶1624.229
47. ¶H-3721
48. ¶H-3705; ¶1624.229

49. ¶H-3745; ¶1624.229
50. ¶H-3715; ¶1624.229
1. ¶H-3776; ¶1624.009
2. ¶H-3809; ¶1624.009
3. ¶H-3777
4. ¶H-3780; ¶1624.009

employee's aggregate remuneration for services performed (either during the deduction year or during another tax year) which would be deductible entirely for the tax year if the $1 million limit didn't apply. (Code Sec. 162(m)(4)(A)) Applicable employee remuneration includes performance-based compensation and commissions, but doesn't include commissions generated directly by the executive's performance (Code Sec. 162(m)(4)(B); Reg § 1.162-27(d)), certain other performance-based compensation (Code Sec. 162(m)(4)(C); Reg § 1.162-27(e)), certain grandfathered contracts (Code Sec. 162(m)(4)(B)), and qualified plan contributions and certain excludable employee fringe benefits. (Code Sec. 162(m)(4)(C); Reg § 1.162-27(c)(3)(ii))[56] However, under a transition rule, remuneration paid under a written binding contract that was in effect on Nov. 2, 2017 and wasn't modified in any material respect on or after that date doesn't include performance-based compensation and commissions. [7]

Reduced limit for TARP recipients & health insurance providers. The above Code Sec. 162(m) deduction limit is reduced to $500,000 for remuneration paid to covered executives by a recipient of financial assistance under the Troubled Asset Relief Program (TARP), with respect to any period in which any obligation arising from that financial assistance remains outstanding. (Code Sec. 162(m)(5))[8]

For services performed during a tax year in which an employer is a "covered health insurance provider" for any part of the tax year, the employer can't claim a compensation deduction for an "applicable individual" (officer, employee, director, or other worker or service provider such as a consultant) that is in excess of $500,000. A health insurance provider is a covered health insurance provider if at least 25% of its gross premium income from health business derives from health insurance plans that meet certain minimum requirements (Code Sec. 162(m)(6)) and those health insurance premiums received for providing minimum essential coverage are not less than 2% of the employer's gross revenues for that tax year. (Reg § 1.162-31(b)(4)(v)(A); Code Sec. 162(m)(6))[9]

The exceptions in Code Sec. 162(m)(4)(B) for remuneration under existing binding contracts doesn't apply to remuneration paid by TARP recipients or covered health insurance providers. (Code Sec. 162(m)(5)(E), Code Sec. 162(m)(6)(D))

¶ 1519 Services rendered to another.

A taxpayer can't deduct payments for services rendered to someone other than the taxpayer—for example, payments by a shareholder to employees of the corporation for services to the corporation, or by a corporation to its officers for services to subsidiaries and related corporations, or by a corporation to employees of a sub. But salary paid by a parent corporation to its own executives for supervising the operations of a sub is deductible by the parent as an expense of the parent's business. [10]

¶ 1520 Payment of employee debts or expenses.

An employer's payment of an employee's debts or personal expenses is deductible by the employer as compensation paid (if reasonable, see ¶1516), just as if the employee had been paid directly and he had used the money to pay his debts or expenses. [11]

¶ 1521 Contingent compensation.

An employer can deduct contingent compensation, where it's freely bargained for between the employer and the individual before the services are rendered, and not influenced

---

5. ¶H-3781 *et seq.*; ¶1624.009
6. ¶H-3781.1
7. ¶H-3781.2
8. ¶H-3821; ¶1624.009

9. ¶H-3810 *et seq.*; ¶1624.009
10. ¶H-3613; ¶1624.104
11. ¶H-4014; ¶1624.273

by any consideration on the part of the employer other than that of securing the individual's services on fair and advantageous terms. This is so even though the arrangement results in higher compensation than would otherwise be allowed as a deduction. The reasonableness of the amount is determined by the circumstances at the date the contract for services is made, not when the contract is questioned. (Reg § 1.162-7(b)(2), Reg § 1.162-7(b)(3))[12]

¶ 1522 Payment in property other than cash.

The deduction for compensation paid in property, including a bargain sale and including restricted property, is the amount included in the income of the person who performed the services, to the extent the compensation is reasonable. (Code Sec. 83(h))[13] The "amount included" in income is the amount reported by the service provider on an original or amended return, or included in income as a result of an IRS audit. It includes excluded group-term life insurance and foreign income. (Reg § 1.83-6(a)(1))

Under a "deemed inclusion rule," however, a deduction may be taken by an employer (service recipient) if he timely complies with the applicable information reporting requirements. Thus, an employee is *deemed* to have included the property received in income, and a deduction can be claimed by the employer if he timely satisfies the Code Sec. 6041 or Code Sec. 6041A reporting requirements (Reg § 1.83-6(a)(2)), i.e., by timely reporting the transaction to the service provider and federal government on Form W-2 or Form 1099-MISC, whichever applies. If this rule isn't satisfied, an employer must demonstrate that the compensation amount deducted was actually included in the service provider's income.[14]

The deemed inclusion rule can be used where the service provider is a corporation by issuing Form 1099-MISC even though there would otherwise be a general reporting exemption for a service provider that's a corporation. (Reg § 1.83-6(a)(2))

If a transfer is less than $600 in any tax year (in which case the reporting requirements don't apply), or if the transfer is eligible for any other reporting exemption (applicable to a noncorporate service provider), no Form 1099 reporting is required for the service recipient to rely on the deemed inclusion rule.[15]

In addition, to be deductible, a transfer can't be a capital expenditure, a deferred expense, or part of inventory. (Reg § 1.83-6(a)(4))[16]

If payment is in employer stock, no gain or loss results. (Code Sec. 1032)[17] If payment is in property other than the employer's stock, and the value of the property exceeds the employer's basis for the property, the excess is income to the employer (capital gain or ordinary income, depending on the character of the property used). (Reg § 1.83-6(b)) The employer has a loss deduction where the basis of the property exceeds its fair market value[18] (subject to related-taxpayer restrictions on losses).[19]

The deduction is allowed for the tax year of the employer in which, or with which, the employee's tax year ends. (Code Sec. 83(h))[20]

For restricted property, see ¶1216; for noncash fringe benefits, see ¶1523.

---

12. ¶H-3732; ¶1624.229
13. ¶H-3650 *et seq.*; ¶s 834.04, 1624.273
14. ¶H-3650 *et seq.*; ¶s 834.04, 1624.273
15. ¶H-3654; ¶834.04
16. ¶H-3650 *et seq.*; ¶s 834.04, 1624.273

17. ¶H-3659; ¶10,324
18. ¶H-3659
19. ¶H-3659
20. ¶H-3653; ¶834.04

¶ 1523   Compensation paid as noncash fringe benefits.

If an employer furnishes a noncash fringe benefit to an employee as compensation, the employer may deduct only the costs it incurs in providing the property to its employees, not the property's value. The employer may claim a depreciation deduction if it owns the property or a deduction for leasing costs if it rents the property. (Reg § 1.162-25T(a))[21]

Furnishing property to an employee for his personal use is additional compensation to him and gives rise to a deduction by the employer. For example, the employer can deduct depreciation and maintenance expenses it pays on a car, house, etc., furnished for an employee's personal use and treated by the employer as compensation. (Code Sec. 274(e)(2))[22]

Employers may not deduct the expense of a qualified transportation fringe, defined at Code Sec. 132(f) (see ¶1245), provided to an employee. (Code Sec. 274(a)(4)) And, no deduction is allowed for any expense incurred for providing any transportation (or any payment or reimbursement) to an employee for travel between the employee's residence and place of employment, except as necessary to ensure the employee's safety. (Code Sec. 274(l)(1))[23]

¶ 1524   Stock options.

An employer's deduction for a nonstatutory stock option is determined under the Code Sec. 83 payment-in-property rules at ¶1522 (and thus, the employer would deduct the amount the employee must include in income on exercise of the option, where the option has no readily ascertainable value at grant, see ¶1218).[24] The employer isn't allowed a compensation deduction for stock transferred under an incentive stock option or an employee stock purchase plan, unless the employee has income by reason of a disqualified (premature) disposition of the stock (¶1219 *et seq.*). (Code Sec. 421(a), Code Sec. 421(b))[25]

¶ 1525   Premiums on company-owned life insurance, endowment or annuity contracts.

A taxpayer can't deduct premiums on any life insurance policy, or endowment or annuity contract if it is directly or indirectly a beneficiary under the policy or contract. (Code Sec. 264(a)(1)) However, this rule doesn't apply to Code Sec. 72(s)(5) annuity contracts (certain qualified pension plans, retirement annuities, individual retirement annuities and qualified funding assets) or to any annuity contract to which Code Sec. 72(u) (annuity contracts held by other than natural persons) applies. (Code Sec. 264(b)(2)) Premiums are deductible as a noncash fringe benefit where only the insured employee or his beneficiaries will get the proceeds. For contracts issued before June 9, '97, the deduction disallowance only applies to premiums on the life of an officer, employee or any person financially interested in any trade or business carried on by the taxpayer if the taxpayer is directly or indirectly a beneficiary of any part of the policy. [26]

Premiums on group term life insurance are deductible (if the employer isn't directly or indirectly a beneficiary) even though the employee isn't taxed (¶1260) on group term coverage of $50,000 or less. [27]

For interest on business life insurance loans, see ¶1720.

---

21. ¶H-4002; ¶1624.283
22. ¶s H-2150 *et seq.*, H-2160; ¶1624.283
23. ¶L-1612
24. ¶H-2883

25. ¶H-2960; ¶4214.01 *et seq.*
26. ¶H-4031; ¶2644
27. ¶H-4037; ¶s 614.031, 794

¶ **1526**   **Health and accident insurance premiums and direct payment or reimbursement of medical expenses under a plan for employees.**

The employer's payment of health and accident insurance premiums for employees and their families, or the employer's direct payment or reimbursement of actual expenses if under a plan, is deductible. (Reg § 1.162-10(a))[28] Reimbursements are deductible even where the employee is the spouse of a sole proprietor and the medical expenses incurred on behalf of the employee's family include those of the sole proprietor (as the employee's spouse).[29]

¶ **1527**   **Contributions to Archer medical savings account (MSA)—Form 8853.**

Eligible small employers (see ¶1254), their employees, and self-employed individuals may deduct contributions to an Archer medical savings account (MSA). (Code Sec. 106, Code Sec. 220) An eligible self-employed claims deductions (as calculated on Form 8853) for MSAs above the line, to arrive at adjusted gross income. (Code Sec. 62(a)(16)) After 2007, no new contributions can be made to MSAs, except by or for individuals who previously had MSA contributions and employees who are employed by a participating employer. (Code Sec. 220(i))[30]

MSAs are available to employees covered under a high deductible health plan (HDHP) of a small employer (¶1254) and to self-employed individuals covered by a HDHP. An individual isn't eligible for an MSA if he's entitled to benefits under Medicare or covered under any other health plan, unless the other coverage is permitted insurance (e.g., insurance for a specified disease or illness, or fixed payment for hospitalization) or coverage for accidents, disability, dental care, vision care, or long-term care. For employees, contributions can be made by the employee or the employer, but not by both for the same year. An MSA is a tax-exempt entity but is subject to the tax on unrelated business income. (Code Sec. 220(c), Code Sec. 220(d))[31]

For 2018, an HDHP for MSA purposes is a health plan with an annual deductible of at least $2,300 and not more than $3,450 for individual coverage ($4,550 and not more than $6,850 for family coverage); in addition, the maximum out-of-pocket expenses can't exceed $4,550 for individual coverage ($8,400 for family coverage). For 2019, as calculated by Thomson Reuters based on inflation data, an HDHP for MSA purposes is a health plan with an annual deductible of at least $2,350 and not more than $3,500 for individual coverage ($4,650 and not more than $7,000 for family coverage); in addition, the maximum out-of-pocket expenses can't exceed $4,650 for individual coverage ($8,550 for family coverage). (Code Sec. 220(c)(2))[32]

The maximum annual contribution for individual coverage is 65% of the HDHP premium (75% for family coverage). The annual contribution limit is the sum of the limits determined separately for each month the individual is MSA-eligible. (Code Sec. 220(b)(1))[33] A self-employed's deduction for contributions to an MSA can't exceed his earned income from the trade or business that established the HDHP (Code Sec. 220(b)(4)(B)),[34] and an employee's contributions to an MSA can't exceed his compensation from the employer that set up the plan. (Code Sec. 220(b)(4)(A))[35] Contributions can be made until the unextended tax return due date. Excess contributions are subject to a 6% penalty tax (on Form 5329). (Code Sec. 4973(a)(2), Code Sec. 4973(d))[36]

28. ¶s H-4071, H-4073; ¶1624.277
29. ¶L-3510
30. ¶H-1326 *et seq.*; ¶2204 *et seq.*
31. ¶H-1331.1 *et seq.*, ¶H-1335.4; ¶2204.01
32. ¶H-1332; ¶2204.01
33. ¶s H-1335, H-1335.1; ¶2204.01
34. ¶H-1335.3; ¶2204.01
35. ¶H-1335.3; ¶2204.01
36. ¶H-1336.1 *et seq.*; ¶2204.01

For treatment of MSA distributions, see ¶1369.

¶ 1528   Contributions to health savings accounts (HSAs).

Eligible individuals may, subject to statutory limits, make "above-the-line" deductible contributions to a health savings account (HSA). Other persons (e.g., family members) also may contribute on behalf of eligible individuals, as may employers (see ¶1255). (Code Sec. 106, Code Sec. 223) An account holder may deduct contributions to his HSA even if another (e.g., family member) makes the contributions. (Code Sec. 62(a)(19)) An HSA is a tax-exempt entity but is subject to the tax on unrelated business income. (Code Sec. 223(e)(1))

For tax-free HSA distributions for qualifying medical expenses, see ¶1370.

Eligible individuals. These are individuals who are covered under a high deductible health plan (HDHP) (see below) and are not covered under any other health plan which is not a HDHP, unless the other coverage is permitted insurance (insurance for worker's compensation, torts, ownership and use of property such as auto insurance, insurance for a specified disease or illness, or providing a fixed payment for hospitalization) or coverage for accidents, disability, dental care, vision care, or long-term care. An individual won't fail to be treated as an eligible individual solely because he receives hospital care or medical services under any law administered by the Veterans Administration for a service-connected disability. (Code Sec. 223(c))[37]

HSA contributions for an individual aren't deductible if he is claimed as a dependent by another taxpayer for the year. (Code Sec. 223(b)(6)) There's no deduction for an HSA contribution for any month an individual is eligible for and enrolled in Medicare. (Code Sec. 223(b)(7))

HDHP. An HDHP is a health plan with an annual deductible that is not less than $1,350 for 2018 and 2019 for individual coverage and $2,700 for 2018 and 2019 for family coverage. However, an HDHP may have a zero preventive care deductible or a preventive care deductible below the minimum annual deductible. (Code Sec. 223(c)(2)(C)) Preventive care does not generally include any service or benefit intended to treat an existing illness, injury, or condition.

Maximum out-of-pocket expenses for 2018 can't exceed $6,650 for individual coverage and $13,300 for family coverage (for 2019, $6,750 and $13,500, respectively). (Code Sec. 223(c)(2))[38]

Other coverage. Health flexible spending accounts (FSAs, see ¶1267) and health reimbursement arrangements (HRAs, see ¶1371) are "other coverage" that will generally preclude HSA eligibility. However, exceptions apply for: limited purpose FSAs and HRAs (those providing only certain benefits, e.g., dental and vision); suspended HRAs (where the employee elects to forgo reimbursements for the coverage period); FSAs and HRAs imposing annual deductibles, and HRAs providing benefits only after retirement. An otherwise eligible individual may be covered by an HRA which pays and reimburses expenses for (1) vision, dental and preventive care, and (2) premiums for coverage by an accident and health plan.[39] Coverage under a health FSA during the "grace period" (i.e., the period immediately following the end of a plan year during which unused benefits or contributions remaining may be paid or reimbursed to plan participants for qualified expenses) is disregarded coverage for HSA purposes if the balance in the health FSA at the end of the plan year is zero. (Code Sec. 223(c)(1)(B))

Limit on deductible contributions. The maximum annual HSA deductible contribution is

---

37. ¶H-1350.3 *et seq.*; ¶2204.01   39. ¶H-1350.4A
38. ¶H-1350.6; ¶2234.02

the sum of the monthly contribution limits, based on eligibility and health plan coverage on the first day of the month. The monthly limit is 1/12 of the indexed amount for self-only coverage ($3,450 for 2018; $3,500 for 2019) and for family coverage ($6,900 for 2018; $7,000 for 2019). The maximum HSA contribution is increased by an additional catch-up contribution amount (computed on a monthly basis) for individuals age 55 or older as of the last day of the calendar year who are not enrolled in Medicare. The catch-up contribution amount is $1,000. There is no requirement that the individual have earnings. (Code Sec. 223(b))[40] Contributions for a year can be made until the account holder's tax return due date (without extensions) for that year. Excess contributions are subject to a 6% penalty tax (on Form 5329). (Code Sec. 4973(a)(5), Code Sec. 223(f)(3))[41] Maximum annual HSA contributions are reduced by Archer MSA (¶1527) contributions for that year. (Code Sec. 223(b)(4))

For computing the annual HSA contribution, a taxpayer who is an eligible individual in the last month of a tax year is "deemed eligible" during every month of that year. (Code Sec. 223(b)(8)) Thus, he can make contributions for months before he was enrolled in a HDHP. But if he does not remain an eligible individual (except because of disability) during the testing period (from the last month of the tax year to the last day of the 12th month following that month), contributions for months in which he was "deemed eligible" are includible in gross income for the tax year of the first day during the testing period that the taxpayer is not an eligible individual and are subject to a 10% penalty tax. (Code Sec. 223(b)(8)(B))

HSA rollovers and carryover of HSA funds. Amounts in an HSA can be rolled over tax free from an HSA, or from an Archer MSA (¶1527) to an HSA. The rollover must be completed within 60 days after the date on which the account holder receives the amounts from the HSA or Archer MSA and is not taken into account in determining the annual contribution limits for the recipient HSA. Only one tax-free rollover into an HSA is permitted per 1-year period. (Code Sec. 223(f)(5), Code Sec. 220(f)(5))[42]

For one-time rollovers from IRAs, see ¶4353.

Comparability rule for employer contributions. In general, employer contributions to employee HSAs must be the same amount or the same percentage of the HDHP deductible for all employees with the same category of HDHP coverage (self-only, or family coverage, i.e., any coverage other than self-only). But employers may make larger HSA contributions for nonhighly compensated employees than for highly compensated employees (as defined in Code Sec. 414(q), see ¶4315). (Code Sec. 4980G(d)) Employers that provide self + 1, self + 2 and self + 3 family coverage apply the comparability rules separately to each category. The comparability rules apply separately to full time, part-time, and former employees (except for former employees under COBRA continuation coverage). An employer that fails the comparability rule is subject to a 35% penalty tax. The comparability rules do not apply to HSA contributions made through a cafeteria plan. Instead, the Code Sec. 125 discrimination rules apply. (Code Sec. 4980G; Reg § 54.4980G-1 - Reg § 54.4980G-5)

¶ 1529   Medicare Advantage Medical Savings Accounts (MSAs).

Individuals eligible for Medicare can choose either the traditional Medicare program or a Medicare Advantage MSA, which is an MSA as defined in Code Sec. 220(d), (¶1527) but which is designated as a Medicare Advantage MSA by the individual account holder. (Code Sec. 138(b)(1)) A Medicare Advantage MSA is a tax-exempt trust (or a custodial account), similar to an IRA, created exclusively to pay qualified medical expenses of the account

---

40. ¶H-1350, H-1350.7; ¶2234.02
41. ¶H-1350.20; ¶49,734

42. ¶H-1350.9; ¶2234

holder. The Health and Human Services Dept. makes contributions directly to the Medicare Advantage MSA designated by the account holder (the only other type of allowed contribution allowed is a trustee-to-trustee transfer from another Medicare Advantage MSA). Contributions and earnings on amounts held in a Medicare Advantage MSA aren't currently includible in income. (Code Sec. 138(a))

Distributions from a Medicare Advantage MSA for purposes other than qualified medical expenses of the account holder are included in income and are subject to a 50% penalty (except if made because of the account holder's disability or death). (Code Sec. 138(c)(2)) The 15% penalty on the amount includible in gross income for non-qualified distributions from regular Archer MSAs (¶1369) doesn't apply to any payment or distribution from a Medicare Advantage MSA. (Code Sec. 138(c)(2)(A)) Distributions that are excludable from gross income can't be taken as a medical expense deduction. [43]

¶ 1530   Group-health plan continuation coverage (COBRA).

With limited exceptions (including one for small employers), a group health plan of, or contributed to by, an employer must provide that each qualified beneficiary who would lose coverage under the plan because of a qualifying event may elect continuation coverage under the plan within a specified at-least-60-day election period. (Code Sec. 4980B(f)(1))[44]

"Qualified beneficiaries" are the covered employee, his spouse or dependent child, a deceased employee's surviving spouse in certain cases, and a child born to or placed for adoption with the covered employee during the COBRA coverage period. (Code Sec. 4980B(g)(1))[45]

"Qualifying events" include: death of the covered employee; termination or reduction of hours of his employment; divorce or legal separation from the covered employee; cessation of a child's dependency; and the employee's entitlement to certain Medicare benefits. (Code Sec. 4980B(f)(3))[46]

Continuation coverage must be identical to coverage provided under the plan to similarly situated beneficiaries who haven't had a qualifying event. (Code Sec. 4980B(f)(2)(A))[47] Coverage for a qualified beneficiary must begin on the date of the qualifying event and end not earlier than the earliest of: a statutory maximum period, the end of the plan, the failure to pay a premium, or the eligibility for group health plan coverage or Medicare. [48] Coverage of the cost of pediatric vaccines can't be reduced below the coverage provided by the plan as of May 1, '93. (Code Sec. 4980B(f)(1))[49]

Employers (or for a multiemployer plan, the plan) and certain responsible persons are liable for an excise tax (Code Sec. 4980B(e))[50] if, with certain exceptions, a group health plan fails to provide the above coverage. (Code Sec. 4980B(a))[1]

¶ 1531   Self-employed individual's health insurance deduction.

A self-employed individual (or a partner or a more-than-2%-shareholder of an S corporation) can deduct as a business expense 100% of the amount paid during the tax year for medical insurance on himself, spouse, dependents, and to any child of the taxpayer who has not attained age 27 as of the end of the year. (Code Sec. 162(l)(1)) Medicare premiums can be used in figuring the self-employed's deduction for health insurance costs. [2]

No deduction is allowed to the extent the deduction exceeds the individual's earned income as defined in Code Sec. 401(c) (net earnings from self-employment) derived from

---

43. ¶H-1348; ¶1384
44. ¶H-1250 *et seq.*; ¶49,80B4
45. ¶H-1266; ¶49,80B4
46. ¶H-1303; ¶49,80B4
47. ¶H-1272; ¶49,80B4

48. ¶H-1301; ¶49,80B4
49. ¶H-1250 *et seq.*; ¶49,80B4
50. ¶H-1316; ¶49,80B4
1. ¶H-1315; ¶49,80B4
2. ¶1624.403

the trade or business for which the plan providing the coverage is established. (Code Sec. 162(l)(2)(A))[3] For purposes of applying the earned income limit to the deduction of a more-than-2% S corporation shareholder, that shareholder's wages from the S corporation are treated as his earned income. (Code Sec. 162(l)(5)(A))[4]

No deduction is available for any month in which the self-employed individual is eligible to participate in a subsidized health plan maintained by an employer of the taxpayer, the taxpayer's spouse, any dependent, or any child of the taxpayer who hasn't attained age 27 as of the end of the tax year. This test for eligibility is made for each calendar month. This rule is applied separately to (1) plans that provide coverage for qualified long-term care services (¶2144), or are qualified long-term care insurance contracts (¶2145) and (2) plans which don't include such coverage and aren't such contracts. (Code Sec. 162(l)(2)(B)) Thus, an individual eligible for employer-subsidized health insurance may still be able to deduct long-term care insurance premiums, so long as he isn't eligible for employer-subsidized long-term care insurance.[5]

IRS has provided special rules for taxpayers who qualify for both this deduction and the Code Sec. 36B premium tax credit (¶2344).[6]

¶ 1532 Contributions to funded welfare benefit plans.

An employer's contribution to a "welfare benefit fund" is deductible only for the tax year paid, and only to the extent the contribution doesn't exceed the "qualified cost" of the plan for its tax year that relates to (ends with or within) the employer's tax year. (Code Sec. 419(a), Code Sec. 419(b))[7] Contributions for independent contractors are also subject to this rule. (Code Sec. 419(g))[8] The rule, however, doesn't apply to a ten-or-more employer plan if no employer (or related employer) normally contributes more than 10% of total contributions, unless the plan uses experience ratings to determine each employer's contribution. (Code Sec. 419A(f)(6); Reg § 1.419A(f)(6)-1(b)(1))[9]

A welfare benefit fund is a fund that is part of an employer's plan through which the employer provides welfare benefits to employees or their beneficiaries, but doesn't include amounts held under certain kinds of insurance contracts. (Code Sec. 419(e); Reg § 1.419A(f)(6)-1(b)(4))[10]

¶ 1533 Death benefits to employee's beneficiaries.

Payments to the widow or other beneficiaries of a deceased employee, i.e., continuing the decedent's salary for a reasonable period, are deductible by the employer to the extent they qualify as a business expense. A benefit paid as a gift based on the beneficiary's need doesn't qualify as a business expense. (Reg § 1.404(a)-12(b)(2))[11]

¶ 1534 "Golden parachute" payments.

No deduction is allowed for an "excess parachute payment." (Code Sec. 280G)[12] In addition, Code Sec. 4999 imposes a nondeductible 20% excise tax on the recipient of an excess parachute payment. An excess parachute payment is the amount by which a parachute payment (below) exceeds the base amount (below) allocated to it. (Code Sec. 280G(b)(1)) If there's only one parachute payment, the entire base amount is allocated to it.[13]

3. ¶L-3510; ¶1624.403
4. ¶L-3512; ¶1624.403
5. ¶L-3510; ¶1624.403
6. ¶L-3511.1
7. ¶s H-4101, H-4113 *et seq.*; ¶4194 *et seq.*
8. ¶H-4104; ¶4194.01 *et seq.*

9. ¶H-4154; ¶419A4.02
10. ¶H-4105 *et seq.*; ¶4194.02
11. ¶H-4051 *et seq.*; ¶1624.277
12. ¶H-3826; ¶280G4
13. ¶H-3874; ¶280G4

A parachute payment is any payment in the nature of compensation to (or for the benefit of) a disqualified individual (described below) *if*:

(1) the payment is contingent on a change (a) in the ownership or effective control of the corporation, *or* (b) in the ownership of a substantial part of the corporation's assets, *and*

(2) the aggregate present value of all such contingent compensation payments equals, or exceeds, three times the base amount. (Code Sec. 280G(b))[14] This base amount is the average annualized compensation income includible in a disqualified individual's gross income in the 5-tax-year period preceding the tax year in which the change of ownership or control of the corporation occurs. (Code Sec. 280G(b), Code Sec. 280G(d))[15]

A disqualified individual is one who is: (1) an employee, independent contractor, or other person specified in regs who performs personal services for a corporation, *and* (2) is an officer, shareholder or "highly compensated individual." (Code Sec. 280G(c); Reg § 1.280G-1, Q&As 15 to 20)[16] Highly compensated individual means a member of the highest paid 1% of employees or, if less, the highest paid 250 employees. (Code Sec. 280G(c))[17]

A parachute payment doesn't include an amount that the taxpayer can establish, by clear and convincing evidence, is reasonable compensation for services to be rendered on, or after, the date of change in ownership or control. (Code Sec. 280G(b)(4)(A)) The amount of an excess parachute payment can be reduced to the extent that the taxpayer can establish by clear and convincing evidence that the payment is reasonable compensation for personal services actually rendered before the date of change of ownership or control. (Code Sec. 280G(b)(4)(B))[18]

The parachute payment rules don't apply to a corporation (1) that was (immediately before the change in control or assets) a "small business corporation," without regard to whether it has a nonresident alien shareholder (¶3352) or (2) whose stock isn't readily tradeable if shareholder approval has been obtained. (Code Sec. 280G(b)(5)) A corporation that meets the requirements to elect to be treated as an S corporation, but does not elect S status, may nevertheless use the small business exemption. (Reg § 1.280G-1, Q&A 6(a)(1))[19]

Payments to or from a qualified pension or profit-sharing plan, Code Sec. 403(a) annuity, simplified employee pension or SIMPLE plan (¶4369 *et seq.*) aren't parachute payments. (Code Sec. 280G(b)(6); Reg § 1.280G-1, Q&A 8)[20]

¶ 1535   Compensation payments as capital outlays.

Payments otherwise designated as compensation may actually be payments for property. For example, where a partnership sells out to a corporation and the former partners agree to continue to work for the corporation, the salaries of the former partners may be in part payment for the transfer of their business. (Reg § 1.162-7(b)(1))[21]

¶ 1536   Year for deducting compensation.

An employer deducts compensation in the year allowed under its accounting method (¶2816 *et seq.*) with special rules for compensation in property and bargain sales (¶1213 *et seq.*), deferred compensation (¶1537), and contributions to employee benefit plans (¶4323).

If salary is paid or accrued in one year for services to be rendered in a later year, the

---

14. ¶H-3830; ¶280G4
15. ¶H-3864; ¶280G4
16. ¶H-3840; ¶280G4
17. ¶H-3843; ¶280G4

18. ¶H-3876; ¶280G4
19. ¶H-3835; ¶280G4
20. ¶H-3839; ¶280G4
21. ¶H-3604; ¶1624.205

deduction is allowed only over the period during which the services are rendered. This applies to both cash and accrual-basis employers. [22]

For limitations on accrual-basis taxpayers' deductions for compensation paid to related cash-basis taxpayers, see ¶2833.

¶ 1537 When to deduct deferred compensation.

An employer's contributions to a nonqualified deferred compensation plan are deductible in the tax year in which an amount attributable to the contribution is includible in the gross income of employees participating in the plan (Code Sec. 404(a)(5)), even if the employer is an accrual basis taxpayer. [23]

Benefits provided under a welfare benefit fund (Code Sec. 404(b)(2)(B)), and payments of bonuses or other amounts within 2½ months after the close of the tax year in which significant services required for payment have been performed (Reg § 1 404(b) 1T, 2(c)), aren't treated as deferred compensation. [24]

To determine if compensation is deferred compensation, and when deferred compensation is paid, no amount is treated as paid or received until it's actually received by the employee. (Code Sec. 404(a)(11))[25]

If the all events test (¶2830) and recurring item exception (¶2831) are otherwise met, an accrual basis taxpayer may treat its payroll tax liability as incurred in Year 1, regardless of whether the compensation to which the liability relates is deferred compensation deductible under Code Sec. 404 in Year 2. [26]

¶ 1538 When to deduct bonuses paid to employees.

A cash basis employer deducts bonuses only for the year in which the bonuses are actually paid (¶1537).[27]

Bonuses by an accrual basis taxpayer are deductible in the tax year when all the events have occurred that establish the fact of liability to pay the bonus, the amount can be determined with reasonable accuracy, and economic performance has occurred for the liability (¶2831). (Reg § 1.461-1(a)(2)(i))[28]

To deduct a year-end bonus in the accrual year rather than the actual payment year an employer must pay the bonus within a brief period of time after the close of the employer's tax year. If an employer pays bonuses within 2 ½ months after the close of the tax year, then a deduction for the bonuses won't be subject to the deferred compensation rules (¶1537), which would otherwise bar the deduction until the bonus is included in the employee's income. (Reg § 1.404(b)-1T)[29] Payment after 2 ½ months is presumed to be deferred compensation, and that presumption can only be rebutted by showing that: (1) it was either administratively or economically impossible to avoid a later payment, and (2) as of the end of the employer's tax year, the impracticability was unforeseeable. (Reg § 1.404(b)-1T)[30]

For limitations on accrual-basis taxpayers' deductions for compensation paid to related cash-basis taxpayers, see ¶2833.

---

22. ¶H-3934; ¶1624.205
23. ¶H-3677; ¶4044.16
24. ¶s H-3673, H-3674
25. ¶H-3674; ¶4044.16
26. ¶H-3670

27. ¶s H-3901, H-3916; ¶1624.218
28. ¶H-3916
29. ¶H-3919
30. ¶H-3919

¶ 1539   When to deduct vacation pay.

Cash basis employers take a deduction when the vacation pay is paid (¶1537) in accordance with the general rules for cash basis employers. [31]

For an accrual basis employer, vacation pay earned during any tax year but not paid on or before 2 ½ months after the end of the tax year is deductible for the tax year of the employer in which it's paid. (Code Sec. 404(a)(5))[32]

¶ 1540   Deductible Travel Expenses. ▬▬▬▬▬▬▬

Ordinary and necessary expenses incurred by *self-employed taxpayers* while traveling "away from home" (¶1541) in pursuit of a trade or business are deductible. But, unreimbursed expenses of employees and investors for travel away from home are miscellaneous itemized deductions that are disallowed for tax years 2018 - 2025 (see ¶3109).

Those expenses include amounts (other than amounts that are lavish or extravagant) paid for meals (subject to a percentage limit, see ¶1557) and lodging. (Code Sec. 162(a)(2))[33]

A taxpayer isn't away from home unless he or she is away *overnight*, or at least long enough to require rest or sleep. [34]

Deductible business travel expenses include baggage charges, air, rail and bus fares, cost of transporting sample cases or display materials, expenses for sample rooms, cost of maintaining or operating a car, house trailer or airplane, telephone expenses, laundry and dry cleaning costs, taxi fares, etc., from the airport or station to the hotel and back, from one customer to another, transportation from where meals and lodging are obtained to the temporary work assignment, and reasonable tips for any of these expenses. (Reg § 1.162-2(a))[35]

¶ 1541   Home defined for travel expense purposes.

A taxpayer's home for travel expense deduction (¶1540) purposes is his or her "tax home"—the taxpayer's principal place of business, employment station, or post of duty, regardless of where his or her family lives. [36]

Where an individual has no principal place of business or employment but continually changes work locations (e.g., a traveling salesperson), the taxpayer's regular residence is his or her tax "home."[37] If such a taxpayer has no regular place of abode in a real and substantial sense, then the taxpayer has no "home" and can't deduct travel expenses. [38]

The tax home of a taxpayer who regularly works at two or more separate locations is the general area where his or her *principal* employment or business is, determined by taking into account (1) time spent, (2) business activity, and (3) financial return. Income is the most significant factor.[39]

Costs of traveling to and from the minor place of employment, 50% of the cost of meals (but see ¶1557), and the cost of lodging at the minor post are deductible travel expenses. [40]

An indefinite assignment away from home shifts the "tax home" (¶1541) and a taxpayer can't deduct the expenses of travel, meals and lodging while in the location of the "indefinite" assignment.[41] Employment is indefinite if it lasts for more than one year, or there is

---

31. ¶H-3922; ¶4614.01
32. ¶H-3922; ¶4614.15
33. ¶L-1701; ¶1624.114
34. ¶L-1710; ¶1624.147
35. ¶L-1705; ¶1624.114
36. ¶L-1801; ¶1624.125

37. ¶L-1802; ¶1624.125
38. ¶L-2025; ¶1624.125
39. ¶L-1807; ¶1624.141
40. ¶s L-1805, L-2135; ¶1624.141
41. ¶L-1814; ¶1624.130

no realistic expectation that the employment will last for one year or less. [42]

¶ 1542   Local lodging when not away from home.

Local lodging expenses of *self-employed* taxpayers may be deductible as ordinary and necessary business expenses if certain requirements are met. From 2018 to 2025, the unreimbursed local lodging expenses of employees aren't deductible (¶1540).

Under a safe harbor, local lodging expenses are ordinary and necessary business expenses if: (1) the lodging is necessary for the individual to participate fully in or be available for a bona fide business meeting, conference, training activity, or other business function; (2) the lodging is for a period not exceeding five calendar days and does not recur more frequently than once per calendar quarter; (3) if the individual is an employee, his employer requires him to remain at the activity or function overnight; and (4) the lodging is not lavish or extravagant under the circumstances and does not provide any significant element of personal pleasure, recreation, or benefit. (Reg § 1.162-32(b))[43]

¶ 1543   U.S. travel for both business and pleasure.

A travel expense deduction (¶1540) may be claimed for transportation costs to and from the destination, but only if the trip is related primarily to the taxpayer's business. Expenses at the destination allocable to the taxpayer's business are deductible even if the round-trip travel expenses are disallowed because the trip was primarily for pleasure. [44] If the trip is primarily for business, but the taxpayer extends his or her stay for personal reasons, makes side trips, or engages in other nonbusiness activities, the taxpayer may deduct only the expenses, such as lodging and 50% of the cost of meals, that he or she would have incurred if the trip had been totally for business. But no allocation is required for travel costs to and from the business destination. (Reg § 1.162-2(b)(1))[45]

¶ 1544   Foreign travel for both business and pleasure.

If travel is primarily for pleasure, the rules at ¶1543 apply, so that only the amount of nontransportation expenses directly allocable to business is deductible (see ¶1540). But under special rules for foreign travel, even where travel is primarily for business, a portion of the transportation cost is nondeductible if the travel has a pleasure element. The nondeductible part is computed on a time ratio, usually in the proportion of nonbusiness days to all travel days.

This allocation and denial of deduction isn't made if: (1) travel is for one week or less; or (2) less than 25% of the time is spent on nonbusiness activity; or (3) the individual traveling had no substantial control over the arranging of the trip; or (4) a personal vacation wasn't a major consideration in making the trip. (Code Sec. 274(c); Reg § 1.162-2(b), Reg § 1.274-4(f)(5))[46] For foreign conventions, see ¶1545.

¶ 1545   Convention expenses.

Travel expenses incurred in attending a domestic convention are subject to the regular business trip rules (see ¶1540 et seq) if attendance will benefit or advance the taxpayer's business as distinguished from serving some social, political, or other nonbusiness function. (Reg § 1.162-2(d))[47]

No business expense deduction is allowed for expenses allocable to a convention, seminar, or similar meeting held outside the "North American area" (defined below) unless the

---

42. ¶L-1811; ¶1624.130
43. ¶L-1631; ¶1624.114
44. ¶s L-1702, L-2135; ¶1624.119

45. ¶L-1702; ¶1624.119
46. ¶L-1726 *et seq.*; ¶2744.04
47. ¶L-1716; ¶1624.119

taxpayer establishes that the meeting is directly related to the active conduct of his trade or business and that after taking specified factors into account, it's as reasonable for the meeting to be held outside the North American area as within it. (Code Sec. 274(h)(1))

North American area means the U.S., its possessions, the Trust Territory of the Pacific Islands, Canada and Mexico. (Code Sec. 274(h)(3)(A)) U.S. possessions include Puerto Rico and the U.S. Virgin Islands. [48] "North American area" also includes Aruba, Antigua, Bahamas, Barbados, Barbuda, Bermuda, Costa Rica, Curacao, Dominica, the Dominican Republic, Grenada, Guyana, Honduras, Jamaica, Panama, Saint Lucia, Trinidad and Tobago.[49]

For business conventions held aboard a cruise ship, a $2,000 per-individual, per-year deduction limit applies, and the deduction is allowable only if the ship is registered in the U.S. and all ports of call of the cruise ship are located in the U.S. or its possessions. (Code Sec. 274(h)(2))[50] A taxpayer claiming the deduction must attach to his return two specified written substantiation statements (including one signed by the sponsor). (Code Sec. 274(h)(5))[1]

¶ 1546   Travel expense deduction for a companion.

No deduction is allowed (other than moving expenses under very limited circumstances, see ¶1627) for travel expenses paid or incurred for a spouse, dependent, or other individual accompanying the taxpayer (or an officer or employee of the taxpayer) unless: (1) the spouse, etc., is an employee of the taxpayer; (2) the travel of the spouse, etc., is for a bona fide business purpose; and (3) the expenses would otherwise be deductible by the spouse, etc. (Code Sec. 274(m)(3))[2]

The limits on deductions for travel companions don't apply to a companion who (1) is a business associate, (2) comes along for a bona-fide business purpose, and (3) could otherwise deduct the expense if he or she incurred it. (Reg § 1.274-2(g))

If a taxpayer is accompanied by a spouse on a business trip and the spouse's expenses aren't deductible, the deductible expense for transportation and lodging is the single rate cost of similar accommodations for the taxpayer, but the full rental for a car in which both spouses travel is deductible. [3]

¶ 1547   Deduction for luxury water travel is limited.

The travel expense deduction (¶1540) for travel by ocean liner, cruise ship, or other form of "luxury" water transportation is limited to twice the highest domestic per diem allowance of executive branch U.S. government employees (other than high-ranking executive personnel) multiplied by the number of days of luxury water travel. (Code Sec. 274(m)(1)(A)) If the cost includes separately stated amounts for meals and entertainment, these amounts must be reduced by 50% (¶1557). The per diem rule doesn't apply to expenses of a cruise-ship convention or seminar to which the rules at ¶1545 apply (Code Sec. 274(m)(1)(B)(i)), or to:

. . . expenses treated as compensation paid to an employee or otherwise included in the gross income of the recipient;

. . . reimbursed, accounted-for expenses of the taxpayer where the services are performed for someone else, and if performed for an employer, the reimbursement hasn't been treated as compensation;

. . . expenses for recreational or social activities primarily for the benefit of employees;

48. ¶s L-1744, L-1745; ¶2744.04
49. ¶L-1746; ¶2744.04
50. ¶L-1721; ¶2744.04

1. ¶L-1722; ¶2744.04
2. ¶L-1739; ¶2744.035
3. ¶L-1740 *et seq.*; ¶1624.119

. . . services and facilities made available by the taxpayer to the general public; and

. . . services and facilities sold to customers. (Code Sec. 274(m)(1)(B)(ii))[4]

¶ 1548 Above-the-line deduction for overnight travel of reservists.

A member of the Armed Forces reserves who travels over 100 miles from home for an overnight stay connected with the performance of services (e.g., to attend meetings) can deduct travel expenses as an above-the-line adjustment to gross income. The amount deductible is limited to the regular federal per diem rate for lodging, meals, and incidental expenses, and the standard mileage rate for car expenses plus parking fees and tolls. (Code Sec. 62(a)(2)(E)) Expenses for travel that don't take the taxpayer more than 100 miles from home are miscellaneous itemized deductions, not an adjustment to gross income, so they're nondeductible in tax years 2018 through 2025. [5]

¶ 1549 Transportation Expenses. ▬▬▬▬▬

Local transportation expenses (but not commuting expenses; see ¶1550) directly attributable to the conduct of a *self-employed* taxpayer's business are deductible even though he or she isn't away from home overnight. (Reg § 1.162-1(a)) But, unreimbursed local transportation expenses of employees are miscellaneous itemized deductions that are disallowed for tax years 2018 - 2025 (see ¶3109).

These so-called "local travel expenses" include air, train, bus and cab fares and costs of operating automobiles. [6] If a self-employed taxpayer works at two or more places each day, he or she can deduct the cost of getting from one to the other [7]

¶ 1550 Expenses of daily transportation between home and work site.

Expenses of commuting between a taxpayer's residence and regular business location, wherever situated, aren't deductible (Reg § 1.162-2(e), Reg § 1.162-2(f)).[8] But a taxpayer may deduct daily transportation expenses incurred in going between the taxpayer's residence and a temporary (¶1551) work location *outside* the metropolitan area where the taxpayer lives and normally works. [9]

Daily transportation expenses incurred in going between the taxpayer's residence and a temporary (¶1551) work location *within* the same metropolitan area is business transportation if: (1) the taxpayer has one or more regular work locations away from his or her residence; or (2) the taxpayer's residence is his or her principal place of business (¶1620 *et seq.*).[10]

¶ 1551 One-year temporary workplace rule.

A temporary assignment away from home doesn't shift a taxpayer's "tax home." A work location is temporary for purposes of deducting daily transportation costs (¶1550) if employment at the location is realistically expected to last (and in fact does last) for one year or less. If the employment initially is realistically expected to last for one year or less, but at some later date it is realistically expected to exceed one year, that employment is considered temporary (absent facts and circumstances indicating otherwise) only until the date that the taxpayer's realistic expectation changes. [11]

A taxpayer generally isn't treated as being temporarily away from home if his period of employment exceeds one year. (Code Sec. 162(a)) However, where an assignment at a work

---

4. ¶L-1708; ¶2744.05
5. ¶A-2611.4; ¶624.02
6. ¶L-1601; ¶1624.150
7. ¶L-1602; ¶1624.153

8. ¶L-1608 *et seq.*; ¶1624.151
9. ¶L-1605; ¶1624.130
10. ¶L-1605; ¶1624.151
11. ¶L-1606; ¶1624.151

location is expected to last for more than one year, but the taxpayer is realistically expected to be present at that location *for no more than 35 workdays (partial or complete)* during each of the calendar years in that period, the location is temporary for a calendar year in which he actually works there for no more than 35 partial or complete workdays.

A *self-employed* taxpayer may deduct the necessary traveling expenses in getting to his or her temporary assignment and also for the return trip to his tax home after the temporary assignment is completed, and his expenses for lodging and 50% of the cost of meals while he is in the place to which he is temporarily assigned. [12] If he returns home on his nonworking days, he may deduct his travel expenses to his home, but his travel expenses deduction is limited to the amount he would have spent to stay at his temporary location. [13] For an employee, these expenses are miscellaneous itemized deductions that are disallowed for tax years 2018 - 2025 (see ¶3109).

¶ 1552   Automobile expenses.

Unreimbursed employee business expenses (including employee auto expenses) and investment-related expenses (including investment-related auto expenses) are miscellaneous itemized deductions, and therefore not deductible (¶3109). The auto expenses of self-employed taxpayers are deductible as ordinary and necessary business expenses. [14] If a taxpayer makes both personal and business use of his car, he must apportion his expenses between business (deductible) and personal (nondeductible) transportation. [15] Report business auto expenses on Form 2106 or on Form 1040, Schedule C or Form 1040, Schedule C-EZ (self-employeds). [16]

¶ 1553   Transporting tools to work.

A taxpayer may deduct only *additional* expenses incurred because of the need to transport tools, etc., to work *and* only if the additional expenses can be determined accurately. The deduction is only for that portion of the cost of transporting the tools, etc., that exceeds the cost of commuting *by the same mode of transportation* without the tools, etc.[17]

¶ 1554   Business standard mileage rate.

Taxpayers may use the optional business standard mileage rate in computing the deductible costs of operating passenger automobiles owned or leased by them (including vans and pickup or panel trucks) for business purposes. A taxpayer who uses this method multiplies the number of business miles by 54.5¢ per mile for travel during 2018. [18]

A deduction using the standard mileage rate is in lieu of deducting operating and fixed costs, including for depreciation (or leasing costs), maintenance and repairs, tires, gasoline (including taxes), oil, insurance, and registration fees. But deductions for parking fees and tolls are still available. [19]

⊘observation: If operating expenses are high, the standard mileage rate method may produce a smaller deduction than would be obtained by claiming actual expenses plus depreciation or lease payments. However, the standard mileage rate method may yield bigger deductions than the actual expense method if the driver's business mileage is high and his auto is a thrifty, high-mileage model.

In general, the standard mileage rate is used by a taxpayer who owned the vehicle and began applying the standard mileage rate for the first year that the taxpayer placed the

---

12. ¶s L-1810, L-2135; ¶1624.130
13. ¶L-1813
14. ¶L-1901 *et seq.*; ¶1624.150
15. ¶L-1907; ¶1624.157

16. ¶L-1901; ¶1624.157
17. ¶L-1611; ¶1624.152
18. ¶L-1903; ¶1624.157
19. ¶L-1905; ¶1624.157

vehicle in service, or by a taxpayer who leased the vehicle and is using the standard mileage rate for the entire lease period. However, the mileage allowance method can potentially be used after the placed in service year if, in earlier years, the taxpayer deducted actual expenses for the auto. Use of the business standard rate is *not* available for five or more autos that are used simultaneously (e.g., fleet operations) or purchased autos for which the taxpayer has claimed in prior years accelerated depreciation, Code Sec. 179 expensing, or additional first-year depreciation. [20]

A taxpayer may use the optional business standard mileage rate in substantiating reimbursed expenses paid by another. [21] For consequences if the reimbursement is made under an accountable plan, or under a nonaccountable plan, see ¶3104.

¶ 1555 Entertainment Expenses. ▬▬▬▬▬▬▬▬▬▬▬▬▬▬▬▬▬▬▬▬▬▬▬▬▬▬

Except as provided at ¶1556 et seq, no business deduction is allowed for entertainment expenses.

¶ 1556 Exceptions to the non-deductibility of entertainment expenses.

No deduction is allowed for any item for any activity of a type that is generally considered to be entertainment, amusement, or recreation. (Code Sec. 274(a)(1)(A)) Thus, entertainment expenses incurred or paid are nondeductible, regardless of whether they are directly related to or associated with the taxpayer's business, unless one of the following exceptions discussed below applies.

The exceptions to the nondeductibility rule are:

(1) Food and beverages furnished on the taxpayer's business premises primarily for the taxpayer's employees. [22]

(2) The expense (other than club dues) of providing recreational, social, or similar activities primarily for the benefit of the taxpayer's employees, other than highly-compensated employees (defined at ¶4315).[23]

(3) Goods, services, and the use of a facility, if treated as compensation and as wages by the employer for withholding tax purposes. [24]

(4) Expenses connected with meetings of directors, shareholders, employees or trade associations. [25]

(5) Cost of providing entertainment or recreational facilities to the general public as a means of advertising or promoting good will in the community. [26]

(6) Expense of providing entertainment, goods, and services, or use of facilities, that are sold to the public in a bona fide transaction for adequate and full consideration. [27]

(7) Reimbursed and substantiated expenses or allowances of employees where the employer hasn't treated the expenses as wages subject to withholding, and reimbursed, accounted-for entertainment expenses of self-employeds reimbursed or covered with an allowance by the client or customer. (Code Sec. 274(e); Reg § 1.274-2(f)(2)) In these situations, the "directly related" and "associated with" tests apply to the payor. [28]

¶ 1557 Limited deduction for meal expenses—the 50% rule.

Entertainment expenses are generally nondeductible (see ¶1555), regardless of whether they are directly related to or associated with the taxpayer's business.

20. ¶L-1903 *et seq.*; ¶1624.157
21. ¶L-4715; ¶2744.17
22. ¶L-2122; ¶2744.01
23. ¶L-2125; ¶2744.01
24. ¶L-2123; ¶2744.01

25. ¶L-2129; ¶2744.01
26. ¶L-2131; ¶2744.01
27. ¶L-2132; ¶2744.01
28. ¶L-2124; ¶2744.01

No deduction is allowed for any food or beverage expense unless —

(1) the expense isn't lavish or extravagant under the circumstances, and

(2) the taxpayer (or one of taxpayer's employees) is present when the food or beverages are furnished (Code Sec. 274(k)(1)), and

(3) the taxpayer establishes that the expenditure was directly related to the active conduct of taxpayer's business or, for an expenditure directly preceding or following a substantial and bona fide business discussion, was associated with the active conduct of the taxpayer's business. (Code Sec. 274(a), Code Sec. 274(k))[29]

The amount of an otherwise allowable deduction for meal expenses (including meals while on business travel status, ¶1540) is generally reduced by 50%. This reduction applies to any expense for food or beverages. (Code Sec. 274(n)(1)) The 50% limit doesn't apply to:

... Expenses treated as compensation paid to an employee or otherwise included in the gross income of the recipient of the meal. (Code Sec. 274(n)(2)(A); Code Sec. 274(e)(2))

... Meal expenses that were reimbursed. (Code Sec. 274(n)(2)(A); Code Sec. 274(e)(3)) Instead, the percentage limit applied to the person making the reimbursement.

... Traditional recreational expenses for employees (other than those who were highly compensated, see ¶4315). (Code Sec. 274(n)(2)(A); Code Sec. 274(e)(4))

... Expenses for good, services or facilities made available by the taxpayer to the general public. (Code Sec. 274(n)(2)(A); Code Sec. 274(e)(7))

... Expenses for goods, services, or use of facilities, sold to customers by the taxpayer in a bona fide transaction (entertainment sold to customers). (Code Sec. 274(n)(2)(A); Code Sec. 274(e)(8))

... Expenses for goods, services, or facilities provided as entertainment, amusement, or recreation, where the recipient isn't an employee, and the goods and services are includible in the recipient's income as compensation or as a prize or award. Code Sec. 274(n)(2)(A); Code Sec. 274(e)(9))

... Food or beverage expenses of crews of certain drilling rigs and crews of certain commercial vessels (Code Sec. 274(n)(2)(C)), but not fishing vessels.[30]

The deductible percentage of meals for certain transport workers (e.g., air transport employees, truck and bus drivers, railroad employees) while away from home during or incident to the period of duty is 80%. (Code Sec. 274(n)(3))[31]

¶ 1558   Expense Reimbursements.

An employee doesn't pay tax on an advance, reimbursement or other expense allowance received under an "accountable plan" (defined below). The tax treatment of an advance or reimbursement to an independent contractor depends on whether he accounts to his principal for the expense.

An employee doesn't pay tax on an advance, reimbursement or other expense allowance received from his employer (or from a third party) under an "accountable plan." (Reg § 1.62-2(c)(4)) By contrast, an advance, etc., made under a "nonaccountable plan" is fully taxable to the employee and subject to FICA and income tax withholding. (Reg § 1.62-2(c)(5))[32]

An advance, etc., is treated as made under an "accountable plan" if the employee:

(1) receives the advance, etc., for a deductible business expense that he paid or incurred while performing services as an employee of his employer (¶1559),

---

29. ¶s L-2133 *et seq.*, L-2112, L-2118; ¶2744.01   31. ¶L-2145.1; ¶2744.01
30. ¶L-2138 *et seq.*; ¶2744.01   32. ¶J-1050

(2) must adequately account to his employer for the expense within a reasonable period of time (¶1560), and

(3) must return any excess reimbursement or allowance within a reasonable period of time (¶1561).

An advance, etc., that doesn't satisfy all three conditions is treated as paid under a nonaccountable plan—i.e., it is taxed to the employee and is subject to FICA and income tax withholding. (Code Sec. 62(c); Reg § 1.62-2(c)(5))[33] An arrangement that recharacterizes taxable wages as nontaxable reimbursements or allowances (e.g., to provide a tool reimbursement for employees), won't satisfy the deductible business expense requirement (condition (1), above).[34] If an employee does not timely return advances or reimbursements in excess of those that are substantiated, only the excess is treated as made under a nonaccountable plan. (Reg § 1.62-2(c)(3)(ii))[35]

An arrangement that would in part be an accountable plan and in part be a nonaccountable plan if both parts were viewed separately is treated as two expense allowance arrangements.[36] But the entire reimbursement for business-travel meals and incidental expenses (M&IE) is deemed paid under a nonaccountable plan if an employer routinely doesn't track expenses and doesn't require employees either to substantiate actual expenses or pay back amounts exceeding the deemed substantiated amount (¶1560).[37]

Reimbursement of employee expenses for reasonable employment-related cell phone usage is nontaxable in most instances. [38]

¶ 1559 Business connection requirement for employee business expenses.

An arrangement satisfies the "business connection" requirement if it provides advances, allowances (including per diem or mileage allowances, or allowances for meals and incidental expenses only), or reimbursements only for business expenses that are (i) allowable as deductions, and (ii) paid or incurred by the employee in connection with performing services as an employee. (Reg § 1.62-2(d))[39] An advance, reimbursement or allowance that would be treated as made partially under a nonaccountable plan solely because the expense is subject to the 50% deduction limit for business meals and entertainment (¶1557) is treated as made under an accountable plan. (Reg § 1.62-2(h)(1))[40]

¶ 1560 Accounting to employer for expenses.

To the extent an employee business expense such as travel or entertainment isn't deductible unless the substantiation requirements of Code Sec. 274(d) are met (¶1564 *et seq.*), the employee must meet those requirements within a reasonable period of time (¶1561), i.e., submit to the payor information sufficient to substantiate the requisite elements of each expense or use.

For all other business expenses, sufficient information must be submitted to enable the one making the reimbursement to identify the specific nature of each expense and to conclude that the expense is attributable to the employer's business activities. (Reg § 1.62-2(e)(3))

For accounting via per diem allowances and other simplified methods, see ¶1566.

---

33. ¶S-3672
34. ¶L-4703.1A
35. ¶L-4703
36. ¶L-4744

37. ¶L-4704
38. ¶L-4701
39. ¶L-4703.1
40. ¶L-4703.1

¶ 1561   Returning amounts in excess of expenses; when to substantiate.

Under an accountable plan, an employee must be required to return to the payor within a reasonable period of time any reimbursement in excess of substantiated business expenses. (Reg § 1.62-2(f)(1)) The definition of reasonable period of time depends on the facts and circumstances. However, under a safe-harbor rule, (1) an advance within 30 days of the time the employee has the expense, (2) an expense adequately accounted for within 60 days after it was paid or incurred, or (3) an amount returned to the employer within 120 days after the expense was paid or incurred, will be treated as having occurred within a reasonable period of time. (Reg § 1.62-2(g)(2)(i)) If the employee is given a periodic statement (at least quarterly) that asks him to either return or adequately account for outstanding reimbursements and he complies within 120 days of the statement, the amount is adequately accounted for or returned within a reasonable period of time. (Reg § 1.62-2(g)(2))[41]

¶ 1562   Reporting reimbursed employee business expenses.

If an employee's expenses equal advances or reimbursements made under an accountable plan, he reports no income from the expenses and claims no deductions. However, if the employee's actual business expenses exceed nontaxable accountable-plan advances or reimbursements, and he wishes to deduct the excess, he can do so under the rules that follow for deductions under nonaccountable plan reimbursements.

An employee who pays for employment-related business expenses but receives a nonaccountable plan advance or reimbursement (e.g., he isn't required to account to the employer) reports the advance or reimbursement as income and claims otherwise allowable deductions on Form 2106 or Form 2106EZ, and on Form 1040, Schedule A as miscellaneous itemized deductions (suspended for 2018 through 2025; see ¶3109). The employee's meal and entertainment expenses are subject to the 50% limit (¶1557), and total miscellaneous itemized deductions aren't deductible in tax years 2018 through 2025. The employee must be able to substantiate each element of his business expenditures. (Reg § 1.274-5T(f)(3))[42] For listed property, see ¶1569.

¶ 1563   Reimbursed expenses of a self-employed person.

Expenses of a self-employed person incurred on behalf of and reimbursed by a client or customer aren't included in the self-employed's gross income if the self-employed substantiates the expenses to his principal under the rules at ¶1564. But if he doesn't substantiate those reimbursed expenses to his principal, he must include the reimbursements in gross income and may deduct the expenses, subject to the usual limitations (e.g., 50% limit on business meals and entertainment), if he has kept the necessary records and receipts. (Reg § 1.274-5T(h)(1), Reg § 1.274-5T(h)(2))[43]

The client or customer must substantiate business travel or entertainment expenses (and is subject to the 50% limit) if a self-employed person accounts for those expenses to the client or customer and is reimbursed. However, if the self-employed person doesn't account for the expenses, the client or customer doesn't have to substantiate reimbursed expenses (and isn't subject to the 50% limit). (Reg § 1.274-5T(h)(2), Reg § 1.274-5T(h)(4))[44]

A self-employed person (or an employee) may adequately substantiate a meals and incidental expense to an initial payor that initially reimburses the expense, and the initial payor in connection with its performing services for a third party, may be reimbursed

41. ¶L-4746
42. ¶L-4710; ¶2744.16
43. ¶L-4757; ¶2744.16
44. ¶L-4758; ¶2744.16

under a reimbursement or other expense allowance arrangement with the third party. Here, if the initial payor accounts to the third party in the same way that the self-employed (or employee) accounted for the expenses to the initial payor, then the third party bears the expenses and is subject to the percentage limit (¶1557) on the expenses. [45]

¶ 1564 Substantiating T&E and "Listed Property" Expenses. ▬▬▬▬▬▬▬

To deduct travel and entertainment (T&E) expenses, each expense must be substantiated. For listed property, certain elements of each expenditure or business use must be proved.

Taxpayers must substantiate each element of every T&E expense for which a deduction is claimed. (Code Sec. 274(d)(1), Code Sec. 274(d)(2), Code Sec. 274(d)(3)) The elements of away from home travel expenses are explained at ¶1565; entertainment expenses, at ¶1568; and business gifts, at ¶1576.

Taxpayers can't claim deductions or credits for "listed property" (¶1946), such as a passenger auto, unless they substantiate every element of each expenditure and use of the listed property (¶1569) for business or investment purposes. (Code Sec. 274F(d)(4)) For depreciation of "listed property," see ¶1945 *et seq.*

Generally, proper substantiation requires "adequate records" (¶1570 *et seq.*), or a taxpayer statement supported by sufficient corroborating evidence (¶1572), plus documentary evidence where required (¶1571). (Code Sec. 274(d))[46] Approximations or estimates aren't sufficient. (Reg § 1.274-5T(a))[47] However, statistical sampling may be used in some cases to establish the amount of meal and entertainment expenses that isn't subject to the 50% limit (¶1557).[48] All elements of an expenditure or use must be proved. Failure to prove any one will bar the deduction. (Reg § 1.274-5T(c)(1))[49]

In the usual instance, an employee who substantiates expenses to the employer need not account for them to IRS. However, an employee who is "related" to his employer (certain close relatives of an individual employer, or a more than 10% shareholder of a corporate employer) may be asked by IRS to substantiate his expense accounts even though he has accounted to his employer. (Reg § 1.274-5T(f)(5)(ii))[50]

Simplified substantiation procedures apply to expenses of certain federal employees. [1]

¶ 1565 Proving travel and transportation expenses.

The taxpayer must prove all of the following elements by adequate records or by a sufficiently corroborated statement:

(1) The amount of each separate expenditure for traveling away from home, such as the cost of transportation or lodging. The daily cost of breakfast, lunch, and dinner and other incidental travel elements may be aggregated if they are set forth in reasonable categories, such as for meals, oil and gas, taxi fares, etc.

(2) The dates of the departure and return home for each trip, and the number of days spent on business away from home.

(3) The destinations or locality of the travel.

(4) The business reason for the travel or the nature of the business benefit derived or expected to be derived as a result of the travel. (Reg § 1.274-5T(b)(2))[2]

Incidental travel expenses, e.g., tips, aren't subject to these rules. Where records are incomplete and documentary proof is unavailable, the taxpayer may establish the amount

45. ¶L-2138.1
46. ¶L-4600 *et seq.*; ¶2744.10
47. ¶L-4601; ¶2744.10
48. ¶L-4641; ¶2744.10

49. ¶s L-4644, L-4608; ¶2744.10
50. ¶L-4713; ¶2744.16
1. ¶L-4700; ¶624.02
2. ¶L-4630; ¶2744.10

of incidental travel expenses by reasonable approximations. (Reg § 1.162-17(d)(3))[3]

¶ 1566   Substantiation by use of optional meal or incidental expenses allowance.

If a payor (i.e., the employer, its agent, or a third party) pays a per diem allowance in lieu of reimbursing actual expenses for lodging, meal and incidental expenses (M&IE) incurred or to be incurred by an employee for travel away from home, the amount of the expenses that is treated as substantiated for each calendar day (or part of that day) is the lesser of the per diem allowance or the appropriate IRS-approved maximums. An additional requirement is that the employee provides simplified substantiation (time, place and business purpose). Where these tests are met, the reimbursement is treated as made under an accountable plan —it isn't subject to income- or payroll-tax withholding and isn't reported on the employee's Form W-2. Receipts of expenses aren't required. [4]

Incidental expenses include fees and tips given to porters, hotel staff, etc.

An employee who is "related" to his employer (¶1564) *isn't* considered to have accounted to his employer for the full federal per diem allowances for lodging and M&IE, and must substantiate any deductions he claims, but he may use the meals-only per diem (¶1566) and the business standard mileage rate (¶1554).

The following simplified substantiation rules apply to per diems paid under an arrangement that otherwise qualifies as an accountable plan (¶1558):

. . . *Regular federal per diem allowance.* In general, the IRS-approved per-diem maximum is the GSA per-diem rate paid by the federal government to its workers on travel status. This rate varies from locality to locality. [5] For travel outside the continental U.S., a separate lodging expense rate and M&IE rate is available for each locality outside the continental U.S.[6]

. . . *Simplified (high-low) method for substantiating travel allowances.* A simplified method can be used for per diem amounts paid for lodging plus M&IE during travel within the continental U.S. If the regular federal per diem option (above) isn't used, for post-Sept. 30, 2017 travel, the payor may reimburse up to $284 for high-cost localities ($216 for lodging and $68 for M&IE) and $191 for other localities ($134 for lodging and $57 for M&IE). For post-Sept. 30, 2018 travel, the payor may reimburse up to $287 for high-cost localities ($216 for lodging and $71 for M&IE) and $195 for other localities ($135 for lodging and $60 for M&IE)[7]

. . . *Transportation industry per diem.* Employees or self-employeds whose work directly involves moving people or goods (e.g., by plane, bus, truck, ship) and regularly involves travel to different localities with different M&IE rates may, for travel from Oct. 1, 2016 through Sept. 30, 2018, treat $63 as the federal M&IE (meals and incidental expenses) rate for any locality in the continental U.S. and $68 as the M&IE rate for any locality outside the continental U.S. For travel from Oct. 1, 2076 through Sept. 30, 2019, such taxpayers may treat $66 as the federal M&IE (meals and incidental expenses) rate for any locality in the continental U.S. and $71 as the M&IE rate for any locality outside the continental U.S. This method also can be used by payors of a per diem allowance only for M&IE away-from-home expenses to an employee in the transportation industry, if the payment qualifies as a regular meals-only allowance. [8]

. . . *Optional method for incidental expenses only.* Employees and self-employed individuals who don't pay or incur meal expenses for a calendar day (or partial day) of travel away from home may deduct $5 per day as incidental expenses for each away-from-home

3. ¶L-4633
4. ¶L-4717.1; ¶2744.18
5. ¶L-4717; ¶2744.18
6. ¶L-4713
7. ¶L-4718; ¶2744.18
8. ¶L-4721; ¶2744.17

calendar (or partial) day. [9]

A self-employed individual deducts the amount in determining adjusted gross income. His deduction is subject to the percentage limit on meal and entertainment expenses (¶1557).[10]

¶ 1567 Substantiation by use of optional auto allowances.

The following simplified substantiation rules apply to allowances paid under an arrangement that otherwise qualifies as an accountable plan (¶1558):

. . . *Mileage allowance.* An employee who receives a fixed mileage allowance of not more than the optional business standard mileage rate (¶1554) to cover transportation expenses while traveling away from home or for transportation expenses is considered to have made an adequate accounting to his employer if the elements of time, place, and business purpose of the travel are substantiated. (Reg § 1.274-5T(f))[11]

. . . *Fixed and variable rate (FAVR) allowances for autos.* Where an employer provides a mileage allowance under a reimbursement or other expense allowance arrangement for an employee-owned or leased car, the substantiation requirement is satisfied (as to the amount of expense) if the employer reimburses in accordance with a FAVR allowance. A FAVR allowance is periodic fixed payments to cover fixed costs such as depreciation, coupled with periodic variable payments to cover operating costs such as gasoline. Among other things, a FAVR allowance may be paid only to an employee who substantiates at least 5,000 miles driven in connection with the performance of services as an employee, and at least five employees must be covered by the FAVR allowance. [12]

¶ 1568 Proving entertainment expenses.

For entertainment expenses (which are generally nondeductible, subject to a number of exceptions; see ¶1555 et seq), all these elements must be proved:

(1) The amount of each separate expenditure, except that incidental items like cab fares and telephone calls may be aggregated on a separate basis.

(2) The date the entertainment took place.

(3) The name (if any), address or location, and the type of entertainment, such as dinner or theater, if that information isn't clear from the location.

(4) The reason for entertaining, or the nature of the business benefit derived or expected to be derived, and the nature of any business discussion or activity that took place. If deducting entertainment "associated with" the active conduct of business, the date, duration, place and nature of the business discussion, the persons entertained who participated in the business discussion, and the business reason for the entertainment or the nature of business benefit derived or expected to be derived as the result of entertaining.

(5) The occupation or other information about the person or persons entertained, including name, title or other designation, sufficient to establish his business relationship to the taxpayer. (Reg § 1.274-5T(b)(4), Reg § 1.274-5T(b)(3))[13]

---

9. ¶L-4632.1; ¶2744.17
10. ¶L-4632; ¶2744.18
11. ¶L-4715; ¶2744.18

12. ¶L-4725 *et seq.*; ¶2744.18
13. ¶L-4635; ¶2744.10

¶ 1569   Substantiating costs of listed property.

For listed property (¶1564), all the relevant elements from the following list must be proved for each expenditure or business use of the property:

(1) The amount and date of each separate expenditure (for example, the cost and date of acquisition or leasing, the cost and date of maintenance and repairs, etc.).

(2) The amount and date of each use of the item of listed property for business or investment, based on an appropriate measure (mileage for automobiles and other property used for transportation, time for other types of property, unless IRS approves an alternative method), and the total use of the item of listed property for the tax period.

(3) The business purpose for each expenditure or use with respect to the listed property. (Reg § 1.274-5T(b)(6))[14]

For optional business standard mileage rate, see ¶1554.

¶ 1570   Adequate records of T&E expenses and listed-property expenses.

Adequate records of travel and entertainment (T&E) expenses and of listed property (¶1564) expenditures and uses consist of a currently maintained account book, diary, log, statement of expenses, trip sheet, or similar record and, where necessary (¶1571), documentary evidence such as receipts and paid bills, which together are sufficient to establish each element of every expenditure or use that must be substantiated. Information reflected on a receipt need not be duplicated in an account book or other record so long as the account book or other record and the receipt complement each other in an orderly fashion. (Reg § 1.274-5T(c)(2)(i))[15] Both written and computer records are acceptable. (Reg § 1.274-5T(c)(2)(ii)(C)(2))[16]

Where the business purpose of an expenditure is evident from the surrounding facts and circumstances, a written explanation isn't required. (Reg § 1.274-5T(c)(2)(ii)(B))[17]

¶ 1571   Adequate documentary evidence to support lodging expenditures and other expenditures of $75 or more.

Documentary evidence, such as receipts or bills marked paid is required to support all expenditures for (1) lodging while away from home and (2) for any other expenses of $75 or more (except for transportation charges for which documentary evidence is not readily available). (Reg § 1.274-5(c)(2)(iii))[18]

Receipts or other documentary evidence (original documents, faxes, e-mail printouts) [19] must disclose the amount, date, place, and essential character of the expenditure. A canceled check, together with a bill from the payee, ordinarily will establish the cost but may not alone show business purpose. (Reg § 1.274-5(c)(2)(iii))[20]

¶ 1572   Sufficiently corroborated statements used to substantiate expenses.

Taxpayers may substantiate the elements of their expenditures and uses not only by adequate records, but also by their own statements, written or oral, if those statements are supported by sufficient corroborating evidence. (Code Sec. 274(d))[21]

Corroborating evidence may be oral if from a disinterested, unrelated party who has

---

14. ¶L-4644; ¶2744.10
15. ¶L-4616 *et seq.*; ¶2744.13
16. ¶L-4616; ¶2744.13
17. ¶L-4609; ¶2744.13

18. ¶s L-4603, L-4619; ¶2744.13
19. ¶L-4616; ¶2744.13
20. ¶L-4619; ¶2744.13
21. ¶L-4626 *et seq.*; ¶2744.14

knowledge of the expenditure or use in question. Written evidence has greater probative value, especially if its contemporaneous. (Reg § 1.274-5T(c)(1)) A taxpayer's written or oral statement must contain specific, detailed information about the element being substantiated, and the taxpayer must present other corroborating evidence sufficient to establish that element. (Reg § 1.274-5T(c)(3)(i))[22]

¶ 1573   Inadequate substantiation—remedies.

If a taxpayer hasn't fully substantiated a particular element of an expenditure or use, but does establish to IRS's satisfaction that he has substantially complied with the adequate records requirements, IRS may permit the taxpayer to establish the missing element by other evidence that it considers adequate. (Reg § 1.274-5T(c)(2)(v))

Where a taxpayer establishes that, by reason of "the inherent nature of the situation," he was unable to get either fully adequate records, or fully sufficient corroborating evidence in support of his own statement, he will be treated as satisfying the substantiation requirements if he presents other evidence that possesses the highest degree of probative value under the circumstances. (Reg § 1.274-5T(c)(4))[23]

Where a taxpayer establishes that he has maintained adequate records of an expenditure or use, but can't produce them because they have been lost through circumstances beyond his control (e.g., damage by fire, flood, etc.), he may prove his entitlement to a deduction by a reasonable reconstruction of the expenditure or use in question. (Reg § 1.274-5T(c)(5))[24] Destruction of records in marital disputes has been held to fall within this rule.[25]

¶ 1574   Business Gifts and Employee Awards.

The costs of ordinary and necessary business gifts to individuals other than employees are deductible, subject to a $25 per-year per-person limit.

"Gift" means any item excludable from gross income by the recipient under Code Sec. 102 (¶1211), but not excludable under any other income tax provision. (Code Sec. 274(b))[26] However, any item for general distribution having a cost of not more than $4 and on which the giver's name is clearly and permanently imprinted, and signs, display racks, or other promotional material donated to a retailer to be used on his business premises, aren't classified as gifts. (Code Sec. 274(b)(1); Reg § 1.274-3(b)(2))[27]

Since no amount transferred by or for an employer to or for the benefit of an employee is excludable as a gift (under Code Sec. 102) no such amount is deductible as a gift, though it may be deductible under other rules (e.g., as compensation).[28] Certain noncash awards to employees may also be deductible (¶1575).

¶ 1575   Employee achievement awards.

An employer can deduct the cost of employee achievement awards (defined below). (Code Sec. 274(j)) The maximum deduction for awards made to one employee is $400 per year ($1,600 if the award is a qualified plan award, including the cost of awards that aren't qualified plan awards). (Code Sec. 274(j)(2)) The award must be given as part of a meaningful presentation under conditions and circumstances that don't create a likelihood that the payment is disguised compensation. (Code Sec. 274(j)(3))

An employee achievement award is an item of tangible personal property awarded to an employee because of length of service achievement or safety achievement. (Code

22. ¶L-4626; ¶2744.14
23. ¶L-4628; ¶2744.15
24. ¶L-4623; ¶2744.15
25. ¶L-4624

26. ¶L-2306; ¶2744.08
27. ¶L-2306; ¶2744.08
28. ¶H-4009; ¶1624.363

Sec. 274(j)(3))[29] Tangible personal property does not include cash, cash equivalents, gifts cards, gift coupons, gift certificates (other than where from the employer pre-selected or pre-approved a limited selection), vacations, meals, lodging, tickets for theatre or sporting events, stock, bonds or similar items. (Code Sec. 274(j)(3)(A)(ii))[30]

A qualified plan award is an item awarded as part of a permanent, written, nondiscriminatory plan of the employer. (Code Sec. 274(j)(3)(B); Reg § 1.274-3(d))

A length-of-service award won't qualify for deduction under these rules if given during an employee's first five years of employment, or if a length-of-service award was given to the same employee during the same year or any of the earlier four years. (Code Sec. 274(j)(4)(B))

Safety achievement awards don't qualify if given to managerial, administrative, professional or clerical employees, or if such awards previously have been given to more than 10% of other employees during the year. (Code Sec. 274(j)(4)(C))[31]

No deduction is allowed for an employee achievement award (under the normal Code Sec. 162 ordinary and necessary rules or the Code Sec. 212 production of income rules) except under the above rules. (Code Sec. 274(j)(1))[32]

¶ 1576   Substantiating business gift expenses.

To substantiate business gift expenses adequate records or a sufficiently corroborated statement must show: (1) a description of the gift, (2) the taxpayer's cost, (3) when the gift was made, (4) the occupation of or other information about the gift's recipient, including his name, title, or other designation sufficient to establish his business relationship to the taxpayer, and (5) the reason for making the gift or the nature of business benefit derived or expected. (Reg § 1.274-5T(b)(5))[33]

¶ 1577   Rent Expense.

Rent is deductible if paid for the use of property in the taxpayer's trade or business. Rent expense for the production of income is not deductible from 2018 - 2025 due to the suspension of miscellaneous itemized deductions (¶3109).

Rent for the use of real or personal property in the taxpayer's trade, business, or profession, is deductible. (Code Sec. 162(a)(3)) But rent for personal-use property isn't. (Code Sec. 262(a); Reg § 1.262-1(b)(3))[34]

Besides normal cash rent payable periodically, rent includes a lump sum paid as advance rental, bonus, etc.; a percentage of the tenant's receipts or profits; the tenant's payment of the expenses of maintaining the rented property (taxes, insurance, etc.), and payment in property other than money (deductible to the extent of the property's fair market value). [35]

¶ 1578   Rent paid to related lessor.

Rentals paid between parties who are related either as members of a family or by stock ownership may not be deductible to the extent that they exceed the rent that would have been paid in an arm's-length transaction.

A corporation may deduct fair and reasonable rentals paid to corporate shareholders or

29. ¶L-2313; ¶2744.09
30. ¶L-2316
31. ¶L-2315; ¶2744.09
32. ¶L-2313 et seq.; ¶2744.09

33. ¶L-4643; ¶2744.10
34. ¶L-6604; ¶1624.285
35. ¶L-6605 et seq.; ¶1624.285

their relatives. But excessive rentals can be treated as nondeductible dividends. [36] Reasonable rental payments by a shareholder for use of corporate property are deductible. [37]

¶ 1579   Rent under leaseback arrangements.

A transfer by sale or gift coupled with a leaseback may be more advantageous than a mortgage loan and can create tax benefits for the transferor. Tax advantages (including rent deduction) of a sale and leaseback arrangement may be lost if IRS treats it as a mortgage loan, a tax-free exchange, or a sham transaction. [38]

A gift in trust with a leaseback of the property to the grantor will generally be upheld as a valid rental or royalty arrangement by the courts if: (1) the transfer is complete and irrevocable, (2) the trustee is independent, and (3) the rent is reasonable. Reasonableness of rent and the independence of the trustee are questions of fact. [39]

¶ 1580   Rent or purchase; lease with purchase options.

A payment is deductible as rent only if the taxpayer-lessee hasn't taken or isn't taking title to the property and has no equity interest in it. (Code Sec. 162(a)(3)) Thus, payments made under conditional sales contracts aren't deductible as rent. [40]

A lease that contains an option permitting the lessee to buy the property may be construed as a sale so that none of the payments is deductible as rent. Whether the lease is considered to be a sale depends essentially upon the intent of the parties, as shown in the agreement, read in light of the facts and circumstances existing at the time the agreement was made. [41] Important factors indicating sale instead of lease include nominal option price, excessive rent, designating part of the payment as interest, rental plus option price equal to the property's value plus interest, and application of rent payments to the lessee's equity in the property. [42]

¶ 1581   Lease acquisition costs.

Payments made by a lessee to get a business lease aren't currently deductible but must be amortized over the term of the lease. (Reg § 1.162-11(a)) This rule applies whether the tenant is on the cash or accrual basis and even though he has an option to buy the property. [43]

The term of the lease includes all renewal options (and any other period for which the parties reasonably expect the lease to be renewed) if less than 75% of the acquisition cost is attributable to the remaining lease period on the date of acquisition. In determining the term of the lease remaining on the date of acquisition, any period for which the lease may be renewed, extended or continued under an option exercisable by the lessee is not taken into account. (Code Sec. 178)[44]

¶ 1582   Lessor's costs.

Costs incurred by a lessor in leasing his property, or by a lessee in subletting, aren't currently deductible but must be amortized ratably over the term of the lease. [45] For tax treatment of construction allowances, see ¶1341.

The cost of MACRS improvements made by lessors are recoverable over the cost recovery period applicable to the leasehold improvements — regardless of the period of time the

36. ¶L-6702; ¶1624.299
37. ¶L-6710; ¶1624.299
38. ¶L-6300 *et seq.*; ¶1624.299
39. ¶L-6317
40. ¶L-6209; ¶1624.284

41. ¶L-6222 *et seq.*; ¶1624.305
42. ¶L-6200 *et seq.*; ¶1624.305
43. ¶L-6501; ¶1624.323
44. ¶L-6504 *et seq.*; ¶1624.323
45. ¶L-6401; ¶1624.081

property is leased. (Code Sec. 168(i)(8))[46]

A lessor's payments for cancellation of a lease must be amortized and deducted over the remaining term of the *cancelled* lease,[47] except that if the payment is made in order to enter a lease with a new tenant, the payment must be amortized over the term of the *new* lease.[48]

¶ 1583   Year of deduction for rent.

The tax year in which the rent is paid by a cash basis taxpayer or incurred by an accrual basis taxpayer is generally the proper year for deduction.[49] Advance rent paid by accrual basis taxpayers must be apportioned and deducted over the term of the lease or other rental period. For application of the 12-month rule to advance payments by cash basis taxpayers, see ¶1638. For deferred rental agreements, see ¶1584.[50]

¶ 1584   Deferred payments for the use of property or services.

Rent and interest attributable to a deferred rental agreement must be both reported and deducted as if both parties are accrual basis taxpayers. This rule applies to leases of over $250,000 that require either: (1) at least one payment for the use of property to be paid after the close of the calendar year following the calendar year of the use of the property, or (2) increases (or decreases) in the amounts to be paid as rent. (Code Sec. 467)[1]

For lessees, the deductible rental amount for the tax year is the sum of:

(1) rent deemed accrued by allocating rents in accordance with the rental agreement, taking into account the present value of rent to be paid after the close of the period, and

(2) interest for the year on amounts taken into account for earlier tax years (under (1), above), but which are as yet unpaid. (Code Sec. 467(b)(1))[2]

Present value and interest are computed using a rate equal to 110% of the applicable federal rate (¶1118). (Code Sec. 467(e)(4))[3]

If the agreement is silent as to rent allocation or the agreement is a disqualified leaseback or long-term agreement, then constant rental accrual applies. (Code Sec. 467(b)(2), Code Sec. 467(b)(3)) The constant rental amount is an amount paid as of the close of each lease period which would result in a total present value equal to the present value of the total payments required under the lease. (Code Sec. 467(e)(1))[4]

A rental agreement is a disqualified leaseback or long-term agreement if:

(1) it is part of a leaseback transaction to any person who had an interest in the leased property within two years before the leaseback (Code Sec. 467(e)(2)), or the term of the agreement exceeds 75% of a prescribed recovery period (Code Sec. 467(b)(4)), *and*

(2) a principal purpose of the increased rents provided in the agreement is tax avoidance. (Code Sec. 467(b)(4))[5]

An agreement isn't a disqualified leaseback or long-term agreement if it qualifies for any of the various safe harbors, including the uneven rent test, which is met if the rent allocated to each calendar year does not vary from the average rent allocated to all calendar years by more than 10%. (Reg § 1.467-3(c))

46. ¶L-6404; ¶1674.023
47. ¶L-6405; ¶1624.081
48. ¶L-6407; ¶1624.081
49. ¶L-6616; ¶1624.285
50. ¶L-6617; ¶s 1624.081, 1624.285

1. ¶s L-6800, L-6801.13; ¶4674
2. ¶L-6803; ¶4674
3. ¶L-6804
4. ¶L-6805; ¶4674
5. ¶L-6808; ¶4674

Under regs to be issued, similar rules will apply to certain deferred payments for services. (Code Sec. 467(g))[6]

A reasonable rent holiday won't cause an agreement to be treated as a disqualified leaseback or long-term agreement. (Code Sec. 467(b)(5)) A rent holiday of 3 months or less at the beginning of the lease term is disregarded in determining if the rental agreement has increasing or decreasing rent (Reg § 1.467-1(c)(2)(i)(B)), but longer periods have been upheld where reasonable under the circumstances. [7]

¶ 1585 Research and Experimental (R&E) Expenditures.

Taxpayers can choose whether to immediately deduct or to capitalize R&E expenditures. (Code Sec. 174(a)(1))

If the taxpayer adopts current expense treatment, he or she must use it for all qualifying expenses for the year he adopts it and for all later years, unless he gets IRS permission to switch. (Code Sec. 174(a)(3))[8]

For R&E expenditures that aren't chargeable to depreciable or depletable property, instead of current deduction or capitalizing, the taxpayer can elect (use Form 4562) to deduct the expenditures ratably over 60 months or longer, beginning with the month the taxpayer first realizes benefits from the expenditures. (Code Sec. 174(b)(1); Reg § 1.174-4(b)(1))[9]

In general, expenditures that qualify as R&E costs are research and development costs in the experimental or laboratory sense. This includes all costs incident to the development or improvement of a product, including a pilot model, process, formula, invention, technique, patent or similar property. (Reg § 1.174-2(a)) The ultimate success, failure, sale, or other use of the research or property resulting from R&E is not relevant to this definition. (Reg § 1.174-2(a)(1))[10]

All taxpayers, including partners and S corporation shareholders, may elect to deduct all or any portion of these costs ratably over ten years. (Code Sec. 59(e)(1); Reg § 1.59-1)[11]

For limitations on deductions for R&E expenses that also qualify for the research credit or the orphan drug credit, see ¶ 2319 and ¶2328, respectively. For alternative minimum tax treatment of R&E expenditures, see ¶ 3206.

¶ 1586 Legal and Accounting Expenses.

Legal expenses and accounting and related expenses may be deductible.

Attorney's fees, court costs and other legal expenses can qualify as deductible business expenses. Legal expenses aren't deductible if they are either capital expenditures or a personal expense of the taxpayer. (Code Sec. 162, Code Sec. 262(a), Code Sec. 263)[12] Qualified legal expenses can include expenses incurred in litigation, for legal advice, and for the drafting of instruments,[13] but not to acquire, perfect or defend title to property. (Reg § 1.212-1(k))[14] A legal retainer must be capitalized if it is applied to legal expenses associated with the acquisition of a business. [15] No deduction is allowed for attorney fees paid in connection with a sexual harassment suit subject to a nondisclosure agreement. (Code Sec. 162(q))

Fees for bookkeeping and accounting work incurred in the operation of the taxpayer's business are deductible. [16]

---

6. ¶G-3451; ¶4674
7. ¶L-6812; ¶4674
8. ¶L-3117; ¶1744
9. ¶L-3121 *et seq.*; ¶1744
10. ¶L-3117; ¶1744
11. ¶A-8194; ¶594

12. ¶s L-2901, L-2969; ¶1624.040
13. ¶L-2902; ¶1624.040
14. ¶L-2908; ¶2634.01
15. ¶L-2901.1
16. ¶L-2959

For expenses of determining or contesting tax liability, see ¶1512.

¶ 1587   Insurance Premiums. ▬▬▬▬▬▬▬▬

Certain premiums that qualify as trade or business expenses, or as investment expenses, are deductible. See ¶1588 for premiums on nonlife policies, ¶1589 for life insurance premiums, and ¶1590 for when to deduct.

¶ 1588   Insurance premiums on nonlife policies.

Premiums for insurance against various types of risks, such as property damage, are generally deductible as business expenses (Code Sec. 162; Reg § 1.162-1(a)), but premiums on policies on taxpayer's residence, or for other personal use, aren't. (Code Sec. 262(a); Reg § 1.262-1(b))[17] Payments to an insurance company to assume capped costs certain to be incurred in the future isn't insurance for tax purposes. [18]

Self-insurance reserve funds aren't deductible even if taxpayer can't get business insurance coverage for certain business risks. [19] Neither are payments to "captive" insurance subsidiaries or other similar arrangements where there's no true risk shifting. [20] But a limited deduction is allowed for certain payments made to a medical malpractice self-insurance pool. [21]

Premiums are nondeductible capital expenditures where paid for property insurance during construction. So are premiums for title insurance and for public liability and worker's compensation insurance paid in connection with the construction of a building. [22]

¶ 1589   Life insurance premiums.

Life insurance premiums aren't deductible if the taxpayer is directly or indirectly a beneficiary. (Code Sec. 264(a)(1); Reg § 1.264-1) See ¶1525. For example, the cost of a corporation's key person insurance isn't deductible. [23] Premiums paid by an individual for personal life insurance aren't deductible. (Reg § 1.262-1(b)(1))[24] For group-term premiums, see ¶1525.

¶ 1590   Time for deducting insurance premiums.

If a cash basis taxpayer pays an otherwise deductible premium for one year's coverage which applies in part to the following tax year, the entire premium is deductible in the year paid. But if premiums for several years are paid in advance, IRS and most courts require the premium to be amortized and deducted over the life of the policy, though one court has allowed a full deduction to a cash basis taxpayer in the year of payment where the taxpayer had consistently deducted premiums in the year of payment. [25]

For an accrual basis taxpayer, deductibility of an accrued liability for insurance expense is determined under the economic performance rules —that is, when the premium is paid. But where prepaid premiums cover more than one year, an accrual basis taxpayer must prorate the premium paid in advance over the life of the policy. [26]

For the "12-month rule" exception to capitalization of certain intangibles, see ¶1630.

¶ 1591   Bribes, Kickbacks, Fines and Penalties. ▬▬▬▬▬▬▬▬

Certain illegal bribes, kickbacks, rebates and other payments aren't deductible.

17. ¶L-3500 *et seq.*; ¶1624.032
18. ¶L-3517
19. ¶L-3518; ¶1624.032
20. ¶L-3520; ¶1624.032
21. ¶L-3515
22. ¶L-3530
23. ¶L-3407; ¶2644
24. ¶L-3401; ¶2644
25. ¶L-3528; ¶1624.081
26. ¶L-3526 *et seq.*; ¶1624.081

Nor are fines and penalties for violation of a law, including tax penalties.

Public policy isn't a ground for denying a deduction. Unless a payment is nondeductible by law, it's deductible if ordinary and necessary. (Reg § 1.162-1)[27]

¶ 1592   Bribes and other illegal payments.

No deduction is allowed for any illegal bribe, kickback or other illegal payment under any law of the U.S., or of a state (if the state law is generally enforced), that subjects the payor to a criminal penalty or the loss of license or privilege to engage in business, whether or not that penalty or loss of license actually occurs. A kickback includes a payment in consideration of the referral of a client, patient, or customer. (Code Sec. 162(c)(2))[28]

No deduction is allowed for any kickback, rebate, or bribe made by any provider of services, supplier, physician, or other person who furnishes Medicare or Medicaid items or services, if made in connection with the furnishing of such items or services or the making or receiving of such payments. A kickback includes a payment for the referral of a client, patient, or customer. For these payments, deduction is denied regardless of legality. (Code Sec. 162(c)(3))[29]

No business expense deduction is allowed for any illegal bribe or kickback made directly or indirectly to any federal, state, or local public official or employee. If the payment is to an official or an employee of a foreign government, no deduction is allowed if the payment violates the U.S. Foreign Corrupt Practices Act. (Code Sec. 162(c)(1))[30]

Business kickbacks, fee-splitting, etc., that aren't specifically disallowed are deductible if they qualify as ordinary and necessary. [31]

¶ 1593   Illegal businesses and drug trafficking.

The ordinary and necessary expenses incurred in operating an illegal business are deductible, even though payment of the expense and the acts performed by the employees of the business are illegal (e.g., a bookmaker's expenses). [32] But there's no deduction or credit for amounts (including wages) paid or incurred in trafficking in "controlled substances" (Code Sec. 280E), whether or not such trafficking is legal under state law. However, the gross receipts of controlled substance traffickers may be reduced by cost of goods sold.[33]

¶ 1594   Fines and penalties.

No business expense deduction is allowed for fines or similar penalties paid to a government for the violation of any law. (Code Sec. 162(f))[34] For example, state law penalties on public school teachers for striking aren't deductible. Similarly, penalties paid for violating federal environmental protection laws aren't deductible. [35]

Also, penalties paid in connection with federal, state, and local taxes are generally not deductible—for example, penalties for negligence, delinquency, or fraud relating to federal taxes (Reg § 1.162-21(b)), and for failure to withhold federal payroll taxes. [36]

A fine or similar penalty includes an amount paid in settlement of the taxpayer's actual or potential liability for a civil or criminal fine or penalty. (Reg § 1.162-21(b)(1)(iii)) But, compensatory damages paid to a government do not constitute a fine or penalty.

27. ¶L-2609; ¶1624.377
28. ¶L-2606; ¶1624.384
29. ¶L-2608; ¶1624.384
30. ¶L-2601; ¶1624.384
31. ¶L-2601; ¶1624.384

32. ¶L-2631; ¶1624.382
33. ¶L-2632; ¶280E4
34. ¶L-2701 *et seq.*; ¶1624.388
35. ¶L-2701; ¶1624.388
36. ¶L-2709; ¶1624.388

(Reg § 1.162-21(b)(2))

Subject to limited exceptions (e.g., for restitution), no deduction is allowed for any otherwise deductible amount paid or incurred (whether by suit, agreement, or otherwise) to, or at the direction of, a government or specified nongovernmental entity in relation to the violation of any law or the investigation or inquiry by such government or entity into the potential violation of any law. (Code Sec. 162(f))[37]

¶ 1595   Qualified Business Income (Code Sec. 199A "Pass-Through") Deduction. ■

Noncorporate taxpayers may deduct 20% of "qualified business income" (QBI; ¶1596) from a partnership, S corporation, or sole proprietorship, generally defined as the net amount of items of income, gain, deduction, and loss with respect to the trade or business to the extent that such are: (i) effectively connected with the conduct of a trade or business within the U.S. (and from Puerto Rico, if certain requirements are met); and (ii) included or allowed in determining taxable income for the tax year. (Code Sec. 199A) The deduction reduces taxable income, rather than adjusted gross income, but is available whether or not the taxpayer itemizes.

The allowable deduction for any tax year is an amount equal to the lesser of:

(1) the "combined qualified business income amount" (¶1598) of the taxpayer; or

(2) an amount equal to 20% of the excess (if any) of (a) the taxable income of the taxpayer for the tax year, over (b) the net capital gain (as defined in Code Sec. 1(h)) of the taxpayer for such tax year. (Code Sec. 199A(a))[38]

Special rules apply to specified agricultural or horticultural cooperatives (¶1601).

Proposed regs, on which taxpayers may rely, explain the operation and calculation of the deduction. (Prop Reg. § 1.199A-1(a) *et seq.*)

¶ 1596   "Qualified business income" (QBI) defined for the Code Sec. 199A pass-through deduction.

For purposes of the Code Sec. 199A deduction (¶1595), QBI for a tax year is the net amount of qualified items of income, gain, deduction, and loss relating to any "qualified trade or business" (¶1597) of the taxpayer. It doesn't include any qualified real estate investment trust (REIT) dividends, or qualified publicly traded partnership income. (Code Sec. 199A(c)(1)) Qualified items of income, gain, deduction, and loss are items of income, gain, deduction, and loss to the extent these items are effectively connected with the conduct of a trade or business within the U.S. under Code Sec. 864(c) (applied by substituting "qualified trade or business" for "nonresident alien individual or a foreign corporation" or for a "foreign corporation" each place it appears), and are included or allowed in determining taxable income for the tax year. (Code Sec. 199A(c)(3)(A))[39]

If the net amount of qualified income, gain, deduction, and loss relating to qualified trade or businesses of the taxpayer for any tax year is less than zero, the amount is carried over as a loss from a qualified trade or business in the succeeding tax year. (Code Sec. 199A(c)(2))

Exclusions. The following items are not taken into account as qualified items of income, gain, deduction, or loss: any item of short-term capital gain, short-term capital loss, long-term capital gain, or long-term capital loss; any dividend, income equivalent to a dividend, or Code Sec. 954(c)(1)(G) payment in lieu of dividends; any interest income other than interest income that is properly allocable to a trade or business; any Code Sec. 954(c)(1)(C)

---

37. ¶L-2701; ¶1624.388   39. ¶L-4307
38. ¶L-4305

commodity transaction gain or loss or Code Sec. 954(c)(1)(D) foreign currency gain or loss (applied by substituting qualified trade or business for controlled foreign corporation); any item of income, gain, deduction, or loss relating to Code Sec. 954(c)(1)(F) notional principal contracts (determined without regard to the rules coordinating the notional principal contract rules with other categories of foreign personal holding company income and excluding items attributable to notional principal contracts entered into in Code Sec. 1221(a)(7) hedging transactions); any amount received from an annuity that is not received in connection with the trade or business; and any item of deduction or loss properly allocable to an amount described in any of the preceding items in this list. (Code Sec. 199A(c)(3)(B))

In addition, QBI doesn't include: (a) reasonable compensation paid to the taxpayer by any qualified trade or business of the taxpayer for services rendered for the trade or business; (b) any Code Sec. 707(c) guaranteed payment paid to a partner for services rendered for the trade or business; and (c) to the extent provided in regs, any Code Sec. 707(a) payment to a partner outside of his partner capacity for services rendered for the trade or business. (Code Sec. 199A(c)(4))

QBI from Puerto Rico sources. In the case of any taxpayer with QBI from sources within Puerto Rico, if all the income is taxable in the U.S. under Code Sec. 1 for the tax year, then the taxpayer's QBI for the tax is determined by treating Puerto Rico as part of the U.S. (Code Sec. 199A(f)(1)(C)(i)) In the case of any taxpayer subject to this rule, the W-2 wages of the taxpayer relating to any qualified trade or business conducted in Puerto Rico are determined without regard to the Code Sec. 3401(a)(8) exclusion for remuneration paid for services in Puerto Rico. (Code Sec. 199A(f)(1)(C)(ii))

¶ 1597 "Qualified trade or business" definition & limitation for the Code Sec. 199A pass-through deduction.

For purposes of the Code Sec. 199A deduction (¶1595), a qualified trade or business is any trade or business *other than* a "specified service trade or business" or the business of performing services as an employee. (Code Sec. 199A(d)(1))

observation: It appears that a "trade or business" is defined by reference to Code Sec. 162. In such a case, an activity qualifies as a trade or business if the taxpayer's primary purpose for engaging in the activity is for income or profit, and the taxpayer is involved in the activity with continuity and regularity. Thus, a sporadic activity or a hobby doesn't qualify as a trade or business.

Specified service trade or business exclusion. A specified service trade or business is:

(i) any trade or business involving the performance of services described in Code Sec. 1202(e)(3)(A) (e.g., health, law accounting) other than engineering or architecture or which would be so described if the term "employee owners" were substituted for "employees" in that section; or

(ii) any trade or business which involves performance of services that consist of investing and investment management, trading, or dealing in securities described in Code Sec. 475(c)(2), partnership interests, or commodities described in Code Sec. 475(e)(2). (Code Sec. 199A(d)(2))[40]

Proposed regs, on which taxpayers may rely, explain what is a specified service trade or business and a trade or business of an employee. Prop Reg. § 1.199A-5.

Threshold exception to exclusion. If, for any tax year, the taxable income of any taxpayer is less than $157,500 ($315,000 in the case of a joint return), the exclusion for specified service trades or businesses does not apply, and the deduction is available to the taxpayer,

40. ¶L-4311

for that year. If for any tax year, the taxable income of any taxpayer is less than the sum of the $157,500 ($315,000 in the case of a joint return) threshold amount, plus $50,000 ($100,000 in the case of a joint return), a phaseout rule applies to specified service trades or businesses. (Code Sec. 199A(d)(3)(A)(i);) These amounts are inflation-adjusted after 2018.

¶ 1598   "Combined qualified business income amount" defined for the Code Sec. 199A pass-though deduction.

For purposes of the Code Sec. 199A deduction (¶1595), a taxpayer's combined qualified business income amount (defined in Prop Reg. § 1.199A-3(b)) for a tax year is equal to: the sum of the deductible amounts determined for each qualified trade or business (¶1597) carried on by the taxpayer (Code Sec. 199A(b)(1)(A)), plus 20% of the aggregate amount of the qualified REIT dividends and qualified publicly traded partnership income of the taxpayer for the tax year. (Code Sec. 199A(b)(1)(B))[41]

A qualified REIT dividend is any dividend from a real estate investment trust received during the tax year that is not a Code Sec. 857(b)(3) capital gain dividend (Code Sec. 199A(e)(3)(A)) and is not Code Sec. 1(h)(11) qualified dividend income. (Code Sec. 199A(e)(3)(B))

Qualified publicly traded partnership income for any qualified trade or business of the taxpayer is the sum of:

... the net amount of the taxpayer's allocable share of each qualified item of income, gain, deduction and loss (determined after excluding reasonable compensation, guaranteed payments and other payments for services) from a Code Sec. 7704 publicly traded partnership that is not treated as a corporation for tax purposes; (Code Sec. 199A(e)(4)(A)) and

... any gain recognized by the taxpayer upon the disposition of its interest in such a partnership to the extent that the gain is treated as amount realized from a sale or exchange of property other than a capital asset under Code Sec. 751(a). (Code Sec. 199A(e)(4)(B))

¶ 1599   Limitation on Code Sec. 199A pass-through deduction—W-2 wages or basis of qualified property.

For purposes of the Code Sec. 199A deduction (¶1595), unless the taxpayer is below a threshold amount (see below), the deductible amount for a qualified trade or business is limited, i.e., it is the lesser of:

(1) 20% of the taxpayer's qualified business income (QBI) from the qualified trade or business (Code Sec. 199A(b)(2)(A)) or

(2) the greater of (I) 50% of the W-2 wages relating to the qualified trade or business or (II) the sum of (i) 25% of the W-2 wages relating to the qualified trade or business and (ii) 2.5% percent of the unadjusted basis immediately after acquisition of all qualified property. (Code Sec. 199A(b)(2)(B))[42]

W-2 wages. A person's W-2 wages for a tax year is the total of the wages described in Code Sec. 6051(a)(3) and the Code Sec. 6051(a)(8) elective deferrals paid by the person for employment of employees during the calendar year ending during the tax year, but only for amounts properly allocable to QBI. In addition, amounts that are not properly included in a return filed with the Social Security Administration on or before the 60th day after the

---

41. ¶L-4308   42. ¶L-4309

due date (including extensions) for such return are excluded. (Code Sec. 199A(b)(4)) IRS is directed to issue regs regarding how wages and adjusted basis of qualified property are determined in cases of a short tax year or where the taxpayer acquires or disposes of the major portion of a trade or business or the major portion of a separate unit of a trade or business during the tax year. (Code Sec. 199A(b)(5)) Under a proposed Revenue Procedure, IRS would provide three methods of calculating W-2 wages for these purposes which can act as reduction to or limitation on Code Sec. 199A deduction. (Notice 2018-64, 2018-34 IRB)

Qualified property. Qualified property relating to a qualified trade or business for a tax year is tangible property of a character subject to a Code Sec. 167 depreciation allowance that is: (A) held by, and available for use in, the qualified trade or business at the close of the tax year; (B) used at any point during the tax year in the production of QBI; and (C) the depreciable period for which has not ended before the close of the tax year. (Code Sec. 199A(b)(6)(A))

The depreciable period for qualified property of a taxpayer is the period beginning on the date the property was first placed in service by the taxpayer and ending on the later of (i) the date that is 10 years after that date, or (ii) the last day of the last full year in the applicable recovery period that would apply to the property under Code Sec. 168 (i.e., the Modified Accelerated Cost Recovery System (MACRS)), without regard to the Code Sec. 168(g) alternative depreciation system. (Code Sec. 199A(b)(6)(B))

Threshold amount exception. The wage/property limitation doesn't apply for taxpayers below the threshold amount (Code Sec. 199A(b)(3)(A)) of $157,500 ($315,000 in the case of a joint return). (Code Sec. 199A(e)(2)(A)) For tax years beginning after 2018, this amount is adjusted for inflation. (Code Sec. 199A(e)(2)(B)) The limit phases in above the threshold amount. Taxpayers can, but aren't required to, aggregate separate trades or business in applying these limitations. (Prop Reg. § 1.199A-4(a))[43]

If (i) the taxable income of a taxpayer for any tax year exceeds the threshold amount, by less than $50,000 ($100,000 in the case of a joint return) and (ii) the amount in item (2), above (determined without regard to this rule) is less than 20% of the taxpayer's QBI from the qualified trade or business, then that item (2) limitation will not apply. Instead, the 20% of the taxpayer's QBI from the qualified trade or business amount will be reduced by (A) 20% of the taxpayer's QBI from the qualified trade or business (determined without regard to this rule) minus (B) the amount in item (2) (determined without regard to this rule) multiplied by (I) the amount by which the taxpayer's taxable income for the tax year exceeds the threshold amount and divided by (II) $50,000 ($100,000 in the case of a joint return). (Code Sec. 199A(b)(3)(B))[44]

Special rule for income received from cooperatives. In the case of any qualified trade or business of a patron of a specified agricultural or horticultural cooperative, the amount determined under Code Sec. 199A(b)(2) (i.e., the W-2 wages/qualified property limitation) with respect to such trade or business is reduced by the lesser of: (i) 9% of so much of the QBI with respect to such trade or business as is properly allocable to qualified payments received from such cooperative, or (ii) 50% of so much of the W-2 wages with respect to such trade or business as are so allocable. (Code Sec. 199A(b)(7))[45]

¶ 1600 Application of Code Sec. 199A pass-through deduction to partnerships and S corporations.

The qualified business income deduction for noncorporate taxpayers (¶1595) is applied to partnerships and S corporations at the partner or shareholder level. (Code

---

43. ¶L-4309.4 *et seq.*
44. ¶L-4310

45. ¶L-4309 *et seq.*

Sec. 199A(f)(1)(A)(i)) Thus, each partner or shareholder must take into account his allocable share of each qualified item of income, gain, deduction, and loss (Code Sec. 199A(f)(1)(A)(ii)), and is treated as having W-2 wages equal to his allocable share of the W-2 wages of the partnership or S corporation for the tax year (as determined under IRS regs). (Code Sec. 199A(f)(1)(A)(iii)) A partner's or shareholder's allocable share of W-2 wages is determined in the same manner as the partner's or shareholder's allocable share of wage expenses, and a partner's or shareholder's allocable share of the unadjusted basis of qualified property immediately after acquisition of qualified property is determined in the same manner as the partner's or shareholder's allocable share of depreciation. In the case of an S corporation, an allocable share is the shareholder's pro rata share of an item. (Code Sec. 199A(f)(1)(A))[46]

Rules similar to former Code Sec. 199(d)(1)(B)(i) (applicable to the repealed Domestic Production Activities Deduction (DPAD), see ¶1601) apply to apportion W-2 wages and unadjusted basis immediately after the acquisition of qualified property among trusts, estates, and beneficiaries for purposes of the deduction. (Code Sec. 199A(f)(1)(B))[47]

¶ 1601   Application of Code Sec. 199A pass-through deduction to specified agricultural or horticultural cooperative.

For any tax year of a specified agricultural or horticultural cooperative beginning after Dec. 31, 2017, a deduction is allowed under Code Sec. 199A(g) equal to 9% of the lesser of:

(1) the "qualified production activities income" (QPAI; see below) of the taxpayer for the tax year, or

(2) the taxable income of the taxpayer for the tax year, determined without regard to the cooperative's Code Sec. 199A(g) deduction and any deduction allowable under Code Sec. 1382(b) and Code Sec. 1382(c) (relating to patronage dividends, per-unit retain allocations, and nonpatronage distributions) for the tax year. (Code Sec. 199A(g)(1)(A))[48]

For oil-related QPAI, the Code Sec. 199A(g) deduction is reduced by 3% of the least of the cooperative's oil-related QPAI, its QPAI, or its taxable income (as determined above) for the tax year. (Code Sec. 199A(g)(5)(E))[49]

QPAI defined. QPAI generally equals domestic production gross receipts (DPGR), reduced by costs of goods sold allocable to such receipts and other expenses, losses, or deductions allocable to such receipts. (Code Sec. 199A(g)(3)(A)) In turn, DPGR is defined as gross receipts of the cooperative that are derived from any lease, rental, license, sale, exchange, or other disposition of any agricultural or horticultural product that was manufactured, produced, grown, or extracted by the cooperative (or treated as such, in the case of certain activities conducted by the cooperative's patrons) in whole or in significant part within the U.S. (Code Sec. 199A(g)(3)(D))[50]

W-2 wages limitation. The deduction for any tax year can't exceed 50% of the W-2 wages of the taxpayer for the tax year. (Code Sec. 199A(g)(1)(B)) For this purpose, W-2 wages are generally determined in the same manner as under the other provisions of Code Sec. 199A, except that such wages do not include any amount not properly allocable to DPGR (see below). (Code Sec. 199A(g)(2))[1]

"Specified agricultural or horticultural cooperative." A specified agricultural or horticultural cooperative is an organization subject to part I of subchapter T (Code Sec. 1381 through Code Sec. 1383) that is engaged in: (1) manufacturing, producing, growing, or extracting, in whole or significant part any agricultural or horticultural product; or (2)

46. ¶L-4313
47. ¶L-4314
48. ¶L-4315

49. ¶L-4315.5
50. ¶L-4315.2
1. ¶L-4315

marketing agricultural or horticultural products that its patrons have manufactured, produced, grown, or extracted. (Code Sec. 199A(g)(4))[2]

Deduction allowed to patrons. In the case of any qualified trade or business of a patron of a specified agricultural or horticultural cooperative, the deductible amount determined under Code Sec. 199A(b)(2) for such trade or business is reduced by the lesser of (1) 9% of the amount of QBI with respect to such trade or business as is properly allocable to qualified payments received from such specified agricultural or horticultural cooperative, or (2) 50% of the amount of W-2 wages with respect to such qualified trade or business that are properly allocable to such amount. (Code Sec. 199A(b)(7))[3]

Transition rules for certain "qualified payments." For tax years beginning before 2018, taxpayers were allowed a Domestic Production Activities Deduction (DPAD) under former Code Sec. 199 equal to the specified percentage for the tax year of the taxpayer's qualified production activities income for the tax year, subject to certain limits. Under a transition rule, the repeal of the pre-2018 DPAD doesn't apply to a "qualified payment" (generally, any amount of a patronage dividend or per-unit retain allocation) received by a taxpayer from a specified agricultural or horticultural cooperative in a tax year of the taxpayer beginning after Dec. 31, 2017, that's attributable to QPAI for which a deduction is allowable to the cooperative under the pre-2018 DPAD rules for a tax year of the cooperative beginning before Jan. 1, 2018. No deduction is allowed under Code Sec. 199A for such qualified payments. (Consolidated Appropriations Act, 2018; P.L. 115-141). [4]

¶ 1602 Miscellaneous Business Expenses.

Royalty payments (¶1603), circulation costs (¶1604), mine exploration (¶1611) and development (¶1612) costs, and other miscellaneous business costs are deductible subject to certain conditions and limits. A taxpayer may elect to capitalize some deductible expenses, and elect to deduct other expenses that are normally capitalized.

¶ 1603 Royalty payments.

Royalty payments made for the right to use patents, copyrights and similar rights are deductible.[5] Payments to acquire the property itself are capital expenditures. [6] One court has held that a manufacturer may currently deduct sales-based royalties paid under trademark licensing agreements, but IRS disagrees and says such royalties must be capitalized under Code Sec. 263A (¶1640).[7]

¶ 1604 Circulation costs.

Publishers of periodicals can currently deduct (Code Sec. 173)[8] or elect to capitalize (Reg § 1.173-1(c))[9] their expenditures to establish, maintain and increase circulation. A taxpayer may elect (use Form 4562) to amortize circulation costs over three years beginning with the year the expenditure is made. (Code Sec. 59(e)(1); Reg § 1.59-1) For alternative minimum tax treatment of circulation costs, see ¶3211.

¶ 1605 Taxes, interest, and carrying charges—election to capitalize.

Some taxes and carrying charges that would normally be deducted currently or amortized may be capitalized if the taxpayer so elects. [10] For depreciable property, this has the

---

2. ¶L-4315.1
3. ¶L-4316
4. ¶L-4316
5. ¶L-3201; ¶1624.284
6. ¶L-3203; ¶1624.284

7. ¶G-5494
8. ¶L-2213; ¶1734.01
9. ¶L-2215 *et seq.*; ¶1734
10. ¶L-5901; ¶2664

effect of deferring the deduction to later years as depreciation. For nondepreciable property, such as unimproved real estate, the capitalized expenses increase basis and reduce gain (or increase loss) on a later sale of the property. (Code Sec. 266; Reg § 1.212-1(n), Reg § 1.266-1)[11]

The capitalization election may be made:

... for taxes, mortgage interest (subject to the interest capitalization rules at ¶1642) and deductible carrying charges on unimproved and unproductive real property. (Reg § 1.266-1(b))[12]

... by a taxpayer engaged in the development of real estate or the construction of an improvement to real estate, for the following items relating to the project: loan interest; taxes measured by compensation paid to employees and taxes imposed on the purchase of materials, or on the storage, use, or other consumption of materials; and other necessary charges, including fire insurance premiums. (Reg § 1.266-1(b)(1))[13]

... for interest on a loan to finance the purchase, transportation, and installation of machinery and other assets, state and local taxes imposed on the taxpayer, transportation, storage, use or other consumption of the property, and state and local taxes, including sales and use taxes, and state and federal unemployment taxes, and the taxpayer's share of federal social security taxes on the wages of employees engaged in transportation and installation of the assets. (Reg § 1.266-1)[14]

¶ 1606   Architectural and transportation barrier removal expenses.

A taxpayer can elect to treat up to $15,000 of qualified architectural and transportation barrier removal expenses as a deduction rather than as a charge to capital account. (Code Sec. 190(a), Code Sec. 190(c)) To elect, claim the deduction as a separate item identified as such on the timely filed (including extension) return for the tax year for which the election is to apply. (Reg § 1.190-3(a))[15] For the credit for eligible access expenditures, see ¶2323.

¶ 1607   Serial contingent payments for franchises, trademarks, or trade names.

In the case of a transfer of a franchise, trademark or trade name, a deduction is allowed to the transferee for serial payments contingent on the productivity, use, or disposition of the franchise, trademark or trade name transferred. (Code Sec. 1253(d)(1))[16]

¶ 1608   Computer software.

The tax treatment of computer software depends on whether it is bought, licensed, or self-developed.

Purchased software. The cost of software bought by itself, rather than being bundled into hardware costs, is capitalized and amortized over 36 months using the straight-line method. This rule *doesn't* apply to any software that's a Code Sec. 197 intangible (see ¶1967). (Reg § 1.167(a)-14(b)(1))[17] However, the cost of software included or bundled, without being separately stated, in the cost of hardware is capitalized and depreciated as a part of the hardware cost. (Reg § 1.167(a)-14(b)(2))

Licensed software. The cost of software licensed for a specific period of time (unless properly chargeable to capital account) is deducted over that term, in the same way that a business tenant may under Reg § 1.162-11 deduct the cost of acquiring a leasehold over

---

11. ¶L-5901; ¶2664
12. ¶L-5901; ¶2664
13. ¶L-5904; ¶2664
14. ¶s L-5901, L-5905; ¶2664

15. ¶L-3151 *et seq.*; ¶1904 *et seq.*
16. ¶I-8415 *et seq.*; ¶12534.01
17. ¶L-7935; ¶1674.033

the lease term. (Reg § 1.167(a)-14(b)(2))[18] Rental payments for leased software are deducted just like any other rentals. [19]

Self-developed software. Costs of developing computer software (other than software that is a Code Sec. 197 intangible (¶1967)) can be either: (1) consistently expensed currently under Code Sec. 174(a), or (2) consistently treated as capital expenditures recoverable through deductions for ratable amortization over a period of 60 months from the date of completion of the development under Code Sec. 174(b) or over 36 months from the date the software is placed in service under Code Sec. 167(f)(1).[20] Costs of developing software may also qualify as research and experimental expenditures under Code Sec. 174 (see ¶1585).[21]

If costs for developing computer software that the taxpayer elected to treat as deferred expenses under Code Sec. 174(b) (¶1585) result in the development of property subject to depreciation, the 36-month amortization rule applies to the unrecovered costs. (Reg § 1.167(a)-14(b)(1))[22]

¶ 1609   Stock reacquisition expenses.

No deduction is allowed for any amount paid or incurred by a corporation in connection with the reacquisition of its stock (e.g., greenmail) or of the stock of any related person as specially defined in Code Sec. 465(b)(3)(C). Amounts deductible as interest under Code Sec. 163 or as dividends paid under Code Sec. 561 are among expenses not subject to this rule. (Code Sec. 162(k)) The no-deduction rule doesn't apply to deductions for amounts properly allocable to indebtedness (e.g., loan commitment fees) and amortized over the term of the indebtedness. (Code Sec. 162(k)(2)(A)(ii))[23]

¶ 1610   Co-op housing maintenance and lease expenses.

Cooperative housing maintenance and lease expenses are deductible if the cooperative unit is used in a trade or business or for the production of income. However, no deduction is allowed to the co-op stockholder for any payment to the co-op (in excess of the stockholder's share of taxes and interest) to the extent the payment is properly allocable to amounts chargeable to the co-op's capital account. The basis of the stockholder's stock is increased by the amount of any deduction disallowed under this rule. (Code Sec. 216(d))[24]

¶ 1611   Mine exploration costs.

Domestic mine exploration costs incurred before a mine has reached the development stage are nondeductible capital expenditures. However, taxpayers may elect to deduct mining exploration expenditures for minerals (other than oil and gas) that qualify for percentage depletion. (Code Sec. 617)[25]

Deducted exploration costs are subject to recapture when the mine reaches the producing stage, when taxpayer receives a bonus or royalty, or when he disposes of all or part of the property, whichever happens first (except where IRS allows recapture to be postponed on disposition of a *part* interest). (Code Sec. 617(b)(1), Code Sec. 1254(a)(1); Reg § 1.1254-1(b))[26]

All taxpayers, including partners and S corporation shareholders, may elect (use Form 4562) to deduct all or any portion of their deductible mine exploration costs ratably over ten years. (Code Sec. 59(e); Reg § 1.59-1)[27]

---

18. ¶L-5621; ¶1674.033
19. ¶L-5615 *et seq.*; ¶1674.033
20. ¶L-5616; ¶1674.033
21. ¶L-5615; ¶1674.033
22. ¶L-7935; ¶1674.033

23. ¶s L-5305, L-5411; ¶1624.402
24. ¶K-5900 *et seq.*; ¶2164.01
25. ¶N-3103; ¶6174
26. ¶N-3601 *et seq.*; ¶6174.01
27. ¶N-3114; ¶594

Corporations' deductions for exploration costs are cut back 30% if they elect to write off the costs in the year they are incurred. (Code Sec. 291(b)(1)) The amount cut back is amortized over 60 months. (Code Sec. 291(b))[28]

¶ 1612 Mine development costs.

A taxpayer who incurs expenditures to develop minerals other than oil or gas may: (1) deduct those expenditures in the year they were paid or incurred (Code Sec. 616(a));[29] (2) elect to treat them as deferred expenses and deduct them ratably as the units of produced minerals benefited by the expense are sold (Code Sec. 616(b); Reg § 1.616-2(a));[30] or (3) treat them as deferred expenses and elect (use Form 4562) to amortize them ratably over ten years. (Code Sec. 59(e); Reg § 1.59-1)[31]

Corporations' deductions for mine development costs are cut back 30% if the corporation elects to write off the costs in the year incurred. (Code Sec. 291(b)(1)(B)) The amount cut-back is amortized over 60 months. (Code Sec. 291(b))[32]

Deducted mine development costs are recaptured (on Form 4797) as ordinary income on disposition of the property. (Code Sec. 1254(a)(1); Reg § 1.1254-1(b))[33]

¶ 1613 Intangible oil and gas and geothermal well drilling and development costs (IDCs).

Geological and geophysical costs incurred in exploring for oil and gas are capital expenditures.[34] Taxpayers, however, may capitalize, amortize (over 60 months) or expense the so-called intangible drilling and development costs (IDCs) of oil, gas and geothermal wells. (Code Sec. 59(e); Reg § 1.59-1; Code Sec. 263(c); Reg § 1.612-4, Reg § 1.612-5)[35] In general, such intangible costs include only those costs that in themselves don't have a salvage value, such as labor and fuel. [36] For alternative minimum tax treatment of IDCs, see ¶3210.

Deducted IDCs are recaptured (on Form 4797) as ordinary income on disposition of the oil or gas wells. (Code Sec. 1254(a)(1)(A); Reg § 1.1254-1(b))[37]

¶ 1614 Lobbying costs, influencing public on legislation.

Deductible business expenses don't include:

. . . Any amount paid or incurred (1) in influencing legislation; (2) in connection with participation in or intervention in any political campaign or any attempt to influence the general public with respect to elections, legislative matters, or referendums; or (3) in communicating directly with a covered executive branch official on official matters (Code Sec. 162(e)(1)).

. . . The portion of dues paid to a tax-exempt organization allocable to lobbying by the organization for which no deduction is allowed, if the organization informs taxpayer of the nondeductible portion. (Code Sec. 162(e)(3))[38]

Taxpayers must allocate costs to legislative-branch lobbying and executive-branch lobbying in determining the nondeductible amount by consistently using a reasonable method. (Reg § 1.162-28(a)(1), Reg § 1.162-29(c)(2))[39]

---

28. ¶N-3104; ¶2914
29. ¶N-3116; ¶6164
30. ¶N-3123; ¶6164
31. ¶N-3124; ¶6164.04
32. ¶N-3104; ¶2914
33. ¶N-3309 *et seq.*

34. ¶N-3201; ¶6124.001
35. ¶N-3202 *et seq.*; ¶6124.008
36. ¶N-3206; ¶6124.009
37. ¶N-3406; ¶12,544 *et seq.*
38. ¶L-2401 *et seq.*; ¶1624.395
39. ¶L-2400 *et seq.*; ¶1624.395

In-house expenditures of $2,000 or less per year aren't subject to these rules. (Code Sec. 162(e)(4)(B)(i))

¶ 1615　Civil damages.

Civil damages paid under judgments and out-of-court settlements arising out of normal business operations generally are deductible as business expenses [40] if the litigation is directly connected with the taxpayer's business. [41]

No deduction is allowed for two-thirds of treble damage or settlement payments to private parties where the taxpayer (payor) in a criminal proceeding for violation of federal anti-trust law is convicted or pleads guilty or no contest. (Code Sec. 162(g); Reg § 1.162-22)[42] No deduction is allowed for any settlement, payout, or attorneys fees relate to sexual harassment or sexual abuse if such payments are subject to a nondisclosure agreement. (Code Sec. 162(q))[43]

¶ 1616　Business Expenses of Employees and Self-Employeds. ▬▬▬▬▬

From 2018 - 2025, unreimbursed employee business expenses, such as travel expenses, job-search expenses, union dues, work clothes, etc., are generally nondeductible due to the suspension of miscellaneous itemized deductions (¶3109). Expenses of self-employed individuals may, however, be deductible (¶1617).

¶ 1617　Deductions for expenses of self-employed professional individuals.

Self-employed individuals can deduct the expenses of their business or profession, such as supplies, rent, transportation, business, travel, telephone, etc. But a professional who is an employee cannot deduct unreimbursed employee expenses from 2018 - 2025 (see ¶1616).

Self-employed professionals can also deduct expenses peculiar to their professions such as dues to professional organizations, continuing professional education, subscriptions to professional journals, malpractice insurance, and payments to assistants. The cost of professional books, furniture, instruments and equipment are deductible if their useful lives are short.[44] But expenses incurred by business or professional people to build up their reputations are capital expenditures to develop or enhance goodwill, unless the expenses can be tied directly to the production of added income. [45] The following material highlights the rules on deductions for certain types of professionals:

Accountants can't deduct costs of a CPA review course or the CPA exam. [46]

Lawyers have been allowed to deduct bar association dues, but not costs of securing admission to practice (including bar examination fees, expenses to be admitted to second state bar, travel) (Reg § 1.162-5, Reg § 1.212-1(f)), which must be amortized over taxpayer's remaining life expectancy. The cost of bar review courses can't be amortized. [47]

Doctors and dentists can't deduct costs of securing the right to practice, fees on their initial licensing, etc. (Reg § 1.212-1(f))[48] Fees paid to a hospital for staff privileges are amortizable over taxpayer's useful life, or the useful life of the hospital privilege if shorter.[49]

Costs of entering a profession or securing the right to practice are nondeductible. (Reg § 1.212-1(f))[50]

---

40. ¶L-2500 *et seq.*; ¶1624.040
41. ¶L-2502; ¶1624.040
42. ¶L-2714; ¶1624.391
43. ¶L-2511; ¶1624.040
44. ¶L-4101
45. ¶L-4100 *et seq.*; ¶1624.191

46. ¶L-3719; ¶1624.193
47. ¶L-4102; ¶s 1624.193, 1624.195
48. ¶s L-4100, L-4101; ¶1624.193
49. ¶L-4107
50. ¶L-4101; ¶1624.193

¶ 1618   Impairment-related work expenses.

Impairment-related work expenses are deductible (on Form 2106 or Form 2106-EZ). They are ordinary and necessary expenses, including attendant care services (e.g., a blind taxpayer's use of a reader) at the place of employment, to enable an individual who has a handicap to work. (Code Sec. 67(d)) Impairment-related work expenses are not miscellaneous itemized deductions subject to the 2%-of-AGI floor. (Code Sec. 67(b)(6))[1]

¶ 1619   Residence Used in Part for Business—Home Office Deduction. ▬▬▬▬

Self-employed individuals may take home office deductions if tough tests are met. From 2018 - 2025, employees cannot claim home office expense deductions due to the suspension of miscellaneous itemized deductions (¶3109).

The general rule is that no deduction is allowed for the business use of a dwelling unit that's also used by the taxpayer as a residence during the tax year. But exceptions, discussed below, allow deductions under certain circumstances. (Code Sec. 280A(a)) The disallowance rule applies to individuals, trusts, estates, partnerships, and S corporations. However, disallowance doesn't apply to any deduction allowable without regard to its connection with either a business or income-producing activity. (Code Sec. 280A(b)) For example, the deductions allowed under Code Sec. 163 for interest, Code Sec. 164 for certain taxes, and Code Sec. 165 for casualty losses may be claimed without regard to their connection with the taxpayer's trade or business or income-producing activities. In other words, this disallowance applies only to otherwise deductible *business* expenses (Code Sec. 162) and depreciation.[2]

The home office deduction isn't allowed for expenses of an income-producing activity, unless the activity is a trade or business.[3]

Allowable home-office expenses are deducted on Form 1040, Schedule C (most self-employed persons), and Form 1040, Schedule F (farmers).

In situations in ¶1620 et seq, otherwise allowable business expenses are deductible (subject to the limits discussed at ¶1623 and ¶1624) even though they are incurred in connection with the business use of a portion of a taxpayer's residence. In addition, the cost of capital improvements made to the entire residence may be recovered through depreciation to the extent allocable to the portion of the residence used for the taxpayer's business.[4]

Charges (including taxes) for basic local telephone services for the first telephone line for any residence are treated as personal expenses. (Code Sec. 262(b))[5]

¶ 1620   Residence used as principal place of business.

A home office deduction (¶1619) is allowed to the extent allocable to a portion of a residence *used exclusively* and *on a regular basis* (¶1623) as the taxpayer's principal place of business for *any* trade or business of the taxpayer. (Code Sec. 280A(c)(1)(A))[6]

Following are the two ways to meet the principal place of business requirement:

(1) Under the statutory administrative/management activities test,   the principal place of business test is met if a portion of the home is used for the administrative or management activities of any trade or business of the taxpayer, but only if there is no other fixed location where the taxpayer conducts substantial administrative or management activities

---

1. ¶L-3906 *et seq.*; ¶674
2. ¶L-1301 *et seq.*; ¶280A4 *et seq.*
3. ¶L-1305; ¶280A4.013

4. ¶L-1306 *et seq.*; ¶280A4.04
5. ¶L-1307 *et seq.*; ¶2624
6. ¶s L-1317, L-1324; ¶280A4.014

of that trade or business. (Code Sec. 280A(c)(1)) Examples of administrative or management activities are: billing customers, clients or patients; keeping books and records; ordering supplies; setting up appointments; and forwarding orders or writing reports. A taxpayer's administrative or management activities at sites that aren't fixed locations of the business (e.g., car or hotel room), don't count. Moreover, if a taxpayer conducts some administrative or management activities at a fixed location of the business outside the home, he can still claim a home-office deduction as long as those activities aren't substantial (e.g., the taxpayer occasionally does minimal paperwork at another fixed location of the business). A taxpayer's eligibility to claim a home office deduction under the above rules won't be affected by the fact that he conducts substantial non-administrative or non-management business activities at a fixed location outside the home (e.g., meeting with, or providing services to, customers, clients, or patients at a fixed location outside of his home).[7]

🅡*Illustration:* Most of a self-employed plumber's time is spent at customers' homes and offices installing and repairing plumbing. His sole office is in his home and he uses it exclusively and regularly for the administrative or management details of his business (phoning customers, ordering supplies, and keeping his books). The plumber's home office qualifies as a principal place of business.

(2) Under the comparative analysis test, set forth in the Supreme Court's *Soliman* decision, the determination of a taxpayer's principal place of business requires a comparative analysis of: (1) the relative importance of the activities performed at each business location, and (2) the time spent at each place, i.e., time spent at the home compared with time spent in each of the other places where business activities occur. If the nature of the trade or profession requires the taxpayer to meet or confer with clients or patients or to deliver goods or services to a customer, the place where that contact occurs, particularly where that place is a facility with unique or special characteristics, is often important. [8]

¶ 1621 Residence used to meet clients.

A home office deduction (¶1621) is allowed to the extent allocable to a portion of a residence that's *used exclusively* and *on a regular basis* (¶1623) as a place of business (even if not a principal place of business) that is used by patients, clients, or customers in meeting or dealing with the taxpayer in the normal course of his trade or business. (Code Sec. 280A(c)(1)(B)) This permits a doctor, lawyer, sales rep, insurance agent, claims adjuster, etc., to deduct home office expenses even though he operates his business or profession primarily from an office away from his residence. Telephone conversations alone aren't enough; patients, customers, etc., must be physically present for deductions to be claimed under this rule. [9]

¶ 1622 Specialized rules for business use of home.

A home office deduction (¶1619) is allowed:

* For costs allocable to a portion of a separate structure (e.g., artist's studio) not attached to the residence if it's used *exclusively* and *on a regular basis* (¶1623) in connection with the taxpayer's business. (Code Sec. 280A(c)(1)(C))[10]

* To the extent allocable to space in a residence that the taxpayer uses *on a regular basis* to store inventory and/or product samples in his business of selling products at retail or wholesale, if the residence is the sole fixed location of the trade or business. (Code Sec. 280A(c)(2))[11]

---

7. ¶L-1335; ¶280A4.014
8. ¶L-1330 *et seq.*; ¶280A4.014
9. ¶L-1344 *et seq.*; ¶280A4.016

10. ¶L-1347; ¶280A4.017
11. ¶L-1355 *et seq.*; ¶280A4.02

- If a residence is used regularly to provide day care services for compensation to children, handicapped individuals, or persons 65 or over. If there is only part-time use of a portion of the residence, allocation must be made first on the basis of the proportion of total space used to furnish services and then on the basis of the amount of time that space is used for those services compared to the total time the space is available for all uses. The deduction is allowed only if the day care services aren't primarily educational and comply with any applicable state licensing, certification, or approval requirements. (Code Sec. 280A(c)(4))[12]

¶ 1623   "Exclusive" use on a "regular" basis.

For purposes of the home office rules (¶1619 *et seq.*), exclusive use means that the taxpayer must use a specific portion of a residence or detached structure for carrying on his or her business. For example, using a den to write legal briefs and prepare tax returns as well as for personal purposes doesn't meet the exclusive use test. [13] Part of a room used exclusively for business can qualify for the deduction, even though the room isn't divided. [14] Expenses attributable to the exclusive but incidental or occasional trade or business use of a portion of a dwelling unit aren't deductible because the space isn't used on a regular basis. [15]

¶ 1624   Gross income limit on home office deduction.

The home office deduction (¶1619) is limited to the activity's gross income reduced by all other deductible expenses that are allowable regardless of qualified use and by the business deductions that aren't allocable to the use of the home itself. (Code Sec. 280A(c)(5)(A), Code Sec. 280A(c)(5)(B)) Expenses disallowed solely because they exceed business income can be carried forward (Code Sec. 280A(c)(5)), subject to this gross income limitation in the later year. [16]

¶ 1625   Allocation of home office expenses.

Allocation of expenses and depreciation on a house for purposes of the home office deduction (¶1619) is generally based on a comparison of space used for business and personal purposes.

A safe harbor method ($5 per square foot, up to a maximum of 300 square feet) may be used as an alternative to the calculation, allocation, and substantiation of actual home office expenses. [17]

¶ 1626   Rental by employer of space in employee's home.

No home office deduction is allowed for expenses attributable to the rental by an employee of all or part of his home to his employer if the employee uses the rented portion to perform services as an employee of the employer. (Code Sec. 280A(c)(6))[18]

¶ 1627   Moving Expense Deduction for Active Duty Armed Forces Members. ▬▬▬

An active duty member of the armed forces who move under a military order and incident to a permanent change of station (¶1628) can deduct certain moving expenses regardless of the distance moved or the length of time worked at the new station.

---

12. ¶L-1359; ¶280A4.03
13. ¶L-1317 *et seq.*; ¶280A4.011
14. ¶L-1317; ¶280A4
15. ¶L-1324; ¶280A4.012

16. ¶L-1365 *et seq.*; ¶280A4.060
17. ¶L-1310 *et seq.*; ¶280A4.041
18. ¶L-1354; ¶280A4.019

¶ 1628   Moving expenses of active duty members of the armed forces.

A move by an active duty member of the armed forces under a military order and incident to a permanent change of station can qualify for deduction regardless of the distance moved or the length of time worked at the new station. Cash reimbursements or allowances are excludable to the extent of moving and storage expenses actually paid or incurred, as are all in-kind moving and storage services provided by the military. This exclusion also applies to a spouse and dependents when they don't accompany an armed forces member and move to a location different from that *to* which he moves or different from that *from* which he moves. Where the military moves the member and family to or from separate locations and they incur unreimbursed expenses, their moves are treated as a single move to the member's new principal place of work. (Code Sec. 217(g)) No deduction is permitted for any moving or storage expense reimbursed by an excluded allowance. (Reg § 1.217-2(g)(6))[19]

¶ 1629   Deduction vs Capitalization of Tangible Property Costs. ▬▬▬▬▬

In general, repairs and maintenance are deductible currently (¶1630), and materials and supplies are deductible either when used or consumed (if non-incidental), or when paid (if incidental, and other conditions are met) (¶1631). Capitalized expenses generally can't be deducted except through depreciation, expensing, depletion, or amortization deductions.

¶ 1630   Deductible repairs and maintenance costs.

In general, amounts paid for repairs and maintenance to tangible property are currently deductible if they are not otherwise required to be capitalized. (Reg § 1.162-4(a)) Repair costs that don't directly benefit, and are not incurred because of, an improvement do not have to be capitalized, even if made at the same time as a capitalized improvement. (Reg § 1.263(a)-3(g)(1)(i))[20]

illustration: A business may currently deduct as a repair the cost of replacing a truck's broken headlights and mending the driver's seat, even if the work takes place when the truck is taken out of service to overhaul its engine (a capitalized expense).

Taxpayers may elect to capitalize amounts paid for repair and maintenance consistent with their books and records. (Reg § 1.263(a)-3(n)(1))[21]

Regulated taxpayers (e.g., telecommunications companies) may use an optional simplified method to distinguish between repairs and capitalized costs. (Reg § 1.263(a)-3(m))

Routine maintenance safe harbors. Regs provide for a routine maintenance safe harbor for property other than buildings. (Reg § 1.263(a)-3(i)(1)(ii))

Regs also provide for a routine maintenance safe harbor for buildings. (Reg § 1.263(a)-3(i)(1)(i))

For both of these safe harbors, routine maintenance is treated as not improving the unit of property (UOP, see ¶1634) and therefore is currently deductible. (Reg § 1.263(a)-3(i)(1))

Expenses that are not treated as routine maintenance include amounts paid to return a UOP to its former ordinarily efficient operating condition, if the property has deteriorated to a state of disrepair and is no longer functional for its intended use. (Reg § 1.263(a)-3(i)(3))[22]

Effect of uniform capitalization rules. All of the above rules apply only to the extent they

---

19. ¶L-3600 *et seq.*; ¶2174.02
20. ¶L-5601.6; ¶2634.16

21. ¶L-5601.14B; ¶2634.172
22. ¶L-5601.6; ¶2634.16

don't conflict with the uniform capitalization rules (¶1640 *et seq.*). (Reg § 1.263(a)-3(c)(1))

¶ 1631   When to deduct materials and supplies.

The costs of buying or producing *non-incidental* materials and supplies are deductible in the tax year in which they are used or consumed. But *incidental* materials and supplies that are carried on hand, and for which no record of consumption is kept or physical inventories at the beginning and end of the year are not taken, generally are deductible in the tax year in which they are paid for, if taxable income is clearly reflected. (Reg § 1.162-3(a))[23]

"Materials and supplies" means tangible property used or consumed in the taxpayer's business that is not inventory and that falls within *any* of the following categories:

(1) It is a component acquired to maintain, repair, or improve a unit of tangible property owned, leased, or serviced by the taxpayer and that is not acquired as part of any single unit of tangible property; or

(2) It consists of fuel, lubricants, water, and similar items that are reasonably expected to be consumed in 12 months or less, beginning when used in taxpayer's operations; or

(3) It is a unit of property (UOP, see ¶1634) with an economic useful life of 12 months or less, beginning when the property is used or consumed in the taxpayer's operations; or

(4) It is a UOP with an acquisition cost or production cost (as determined under Code Sec. 263A) of $200 or less (or other amount identified in published guidance); or

(5) It is identified in published IRS guidance as materials and supplies. (Reg § 1.162-3(c))[24]

If a taxpayer elects to apply the de minimis safe harbor (¶1634) to amounts paid for the production or acquisition of tangible property, then the taxpayer must, with limited exceptions, apply the de minimis safe harbor to amounts paid for all materials and supplies that meet the de minimis safe harbor requirements. (Reg § 1.162-3(f))[25]

caution: Materials and supplies may have to be capitalized under Code Sec. 263A (¶1640) to property produced or acquired for resale, and Code Sec. 471 (¶2858) may require certain materials and supplies to be included in inventory.

¶ 1632   Rotable, temporary and standby emergency spare parts.

Rotable and temporary spare parts. Rotable spare parts are materials and supplies (see ¶1631) acquired for installation on a unit of property (UOP, ¶1634), removable from that UOP, generally repaired or improved, and either reinstalled on the same or other property or stored for later installation. Temporary spare parts are materials and supplies that are used temporarily until a new or repaired part can be installed and then are removed and stored for later installation. (Reg § 1.162-3(c)(2))[26]

Rotable and temporary spare parts can be handled in one of four ways:

(1) Deduct the costs when the parts are disposed of. (Reg § 1.162-3(a)(1), Reg § 1.162-3(a)(3))[27]

(2) Adopt an optional method for such costs. (Reg § 1.162-3(a)(3), Reg § 1.162-3(e))[28]

(3) Deduct the costs under the elective *de minimis* rule explained at ¶1634. (Reg § 1.162-3(a)(3), Reg § 1.162-3(f))[29]

---

23. ¶L-4207; ¶1624.158
24. ¶G-2453; ¶1624.158
25. ¶G-2453.4; ¶1624.158
26. ¶G-2453.5; ¶1624.158

27. ¶G-2453.5; ¶1624.158
28. ¶G-2453.6; ¶1624.158
29. ¶G-2453.4; ¶1624.158

(4) Elect to capitalize and depreciate the costs. (Reg § 1.162-3(a)(3), Reg § 1.162-3(d))[30]

Standby emergency spare parts. Standby emergency spare parts are materials and supplies (see ¶1631) that meet a list of 11 criteria including that they are: (a) acquired when particular machinery or equipment is acquired (or later acquired and set aside for use in particular machinery or equipment); (b) set aside for use as replacements to avoid substantial operational time loss caused by emergencies due to particular machinery or equipment failure; and (c) located at or near the site of the installed related machinery or equipment so as to be readily available when needed. (Reg § 1.162-3(c)(3)) Options (1), (3) and (4), above, are available for standby emergency spare parts. (Reg § 1.162-3(a)(1), Reg § 1.162-3(a)(3), Reg § 1.162-3(d))

¶ 1633   General rules for capital expenditures.

A taxpayer must capitalize amounts paid: (a) for new buildings or for permanent improvements or betterments made to increase the value of any property or estate; or (b) for restoring property or in making good the exhaustion of the property for which an allowance (e.g., depreciation) is or has been made. (Code Sec. 263(a), Reg § 1.263(a)-1(a))

Examples of expenses that must be capitalized include:

* An amount paid or incurred to facilitate the acquisition of a trade or business, a change in capital structure of a business entity, and certain other transactions. (Reg § 1.263(a)-1(d)) There's a rebuttable presumption that success-based fees (i.e., payments contingent on successfully closing a deal) facilitate the transaction. For success-based fees, taxpayers may elect to (a) allocate 70% to deductible fees paid in business acquisitions or reorganizations to activities that don't facilitate the transaction and deduct such fees currently; and (b) treat the remaining 30% as capitalized activities facilitating the transaction. [31]

* An amount paid to acquire or create interests in land, such as easements, lifo estates, mineral interests, timber rights, or zoning variances.

* An amount assessed and paid under an agreement between bondholders or shareholders of a corporation to be used in a reorganization of the entity or voluntary contributions by shareholders to the capital of the corporation for any corporate purpose. (Reg § 1.263(a)-1(d))[32]

For the Code Sec. 263A rules requiring direct and indirect costs to be capitalized to property produced by the taxpayer and to property acquired for resale, see ¶1640.

¶ 1634   Amounts paid to acquire or produce tangible property.

Unless the materials and supplies rule applies (see ¶1631) or the de minimis rule (discussed below) applies, a taxpayer must capitalize amounts paid to acquire or produce a unit of property (UOP), including leasehold improvement property, land and land improvements, buildings, machinery and equipment, and furniture and fixtures. The taxpayer also must capitalize costs for work (e.g., to make necessary repairs) performed before the date that the UOP is placed in service by the taxpayer. (Reg § 1.263(a)-2(d)(1))[33]

UOP defined. For purposes of the tangible property capitalization rules, the UOP for assets other than buildings generally consists of all the components that are functionally interdependent (i.e., where placing in service of one component is dependent on the placing in service of other component(s)). The UOP for a building generally is the building and its

---

30. ¶G-2453.3; ¶1624.158
31. ¶L-5762.1; ¶2634.80

32. ¶L-5601; ¶2634
33. ¶L-5601.1; ¶2634.01

structural components. (Reg § 1.263(a)-3(e)(2)(i), Reg § 1.263(a)-3(e)(3)(i))[34]

Transaction costs. Amounts paid to facilitate the acquisition (or production) of real or personal property—i.e., paid in the process of investigating or otherwise pursuing the acquisition—must be capitalized and added to the basis of property acquired or produced. (Reg § 1.263(a)-2(f)(3)(i))[35]

⊘observation: Some facilitative expenses may qualify as amortizable start-up expenses under Code Sec. 195; see ¶1500.

Facilitative costs include "inherently facilitative" expenses made up of eleven categories. These include the costs of items such as shipping, moving or appraising property, application fees, sales and transfer taxes, finder's fees, and architectural, engineering, environmental or inspection services related to specific properties, brokers' fees, and services provided by a qualified intermediary in a Code Sec. 1031 exchange. (Reg § 1.263(a)-2(f)(2)(ii))[36]

Costs relating to the process of determining *whether* to acquire realty and *which* realty to acquire generally aren't facilitative expenses (and therefore may be currently deductible), unless they are "inherently facilitative" expenses (e.g., the cost of an engineering study or a broker's fee). (Reg § 1.263(a)-2(f)(2)(iii)) Employee compensation or overhead *doesn't* facilitate the acquisition of real or personal property (but, under Code Sec. 263A, may have to be capitalized to property produced by the taxpayer or acquired for resale). However, the taxpayer may elect to capitalize employee compensation or overhead expenses, or both, related to each acquisition. (Reg § 1.263(a)-2(f)(2)(iv)(B))[37]

For commissions paid on the transfer of property, see ¶1636.

De minimis rules. Under a de minimis safe harbor rule (also known as a book-tax conformity rule), amounts paid to acquire or produce a unit of tangible property, including materials and supplies (but not inventory or land), don't have to be capitalized and may be deducted currently, if the taxpayer so elects and:

- the taxpayer has an applicable financial statement (AFS), such as one required to be filed with the Securities and Exchange Commission, or a certified audited financial statement accompanied by an independent CPA's report and used for credit or reporting purposes;

- the taxpayer has written accounting procedures in place at the beginning of the tax year for expensing amounts paid for such property if it costs less than a specified dollar amount or it has an economic useful life of 12 months or less;

- the taxpayer treats such amounts as expenses on its AFS in accordance with its written accounting procedures; and

- the amount paid for the property does not exceed $5,000 per invoice (or per item as substantiated by the invoice) or other amount identified by IRS in published guidance. (Reg § 1.263(a)-1(f)(1)(i))[38]

A similar rule, but with a $2,500-per-item limit, applies to taxpayers that don't have an AFS. (Reg § 1.263(a)-1(f)(1)(ii))

If the taxpayer elects the de minimis safe harbor, that safe harbor must be applied to all eligible materials and supplies (other than rotable, temporary, and standby emergency spare parts that the taxpayer elects to capitalize, and rotable and temporary spare parts subject to the optional method of accounting for these parts, see ¶1632). (Reg § 1.263(a)-1(f)(1), Reg § 1.263(a)-1(f)(2))

---

34. ¶L-5601.12; ¶L-5601.13;¶2634.01
35. ¶L-5601.4; ¶2634.15
36. ¶L-5601.12; ¶L-5601.13;¶2634.01

37. ¶L-5601.4; ¶2634.15
38. ¶L-5601.5; ¶2634.01

The cost of property to which the de minimis rule applies may be subject to capitalization under Code Sec. 263A (see ¶1640 if the amounts paid for tangible property comprise the direct or allocable indirect costs of other property produced by the taxpayer or property acquired for resale. (Reg § 1.263(a)-1(f)(3)(v))

The existence of the de minimis safe harbor does not mean that a taxpayer cannot establish a de minimis deduction threshold in excess of the safe harbor amount, provided the taxpayer can demonstrate that a higher threshold clearly reflects the taxpayer's income.[39]

¶ 1635   Amounts paid to improve tangible property.

An expense must be capitalized if it betters or improves a unit of property (UOP, ¶1634), restores it, or adapts it to a new and different use.

Capitalized betterment costs . Capitalized betterment costs consist of amounts paid that:

. . . ameliorate a material condition or defect that either existed prior to the taxpayer's acquisition of the UOP or arose during the production of the UOP, whether or not the taxpayer was aware of the condition or defect at the time of acquisition or production; or

. . . is for a material addition, including a physical enlargement, expansion, extension, or addition of a major component) to the UOP or a material increase in the capacity of the UOP; or

. . . is reasonably expected to materially increase the productivity, efficiency, strength, quality, or output of the UOP. (Reg § 1.263(a)-3(j)(1))[40]

Here are two examples of particular costs and whether they must be capitalized as betterments:

* Costs of cleaning up contamination caused by leaking of underground storage tanks installed by prior owner of property are capitalized. (Reg § 1.263(a)-3(j)(3), Ex. 1)

* Removal and replacement of asbestos installed by a taxpayer in a building before its health hazards were known don't result in a betterment. (Reg § 1.263(a)-3(j)(3), Ex. 2)[41]

Capitalized restoration costs. Costs to restore a UOP are capitalized. An amount is treated as a restoration cost only if it:

(1) Replaces a component of a UOP where the taxpayer has (i) properly deducted a loss for that component (other than a casualty loss under Reg § 1.165-7) or (ii) properly taken into account the adjusted basis of the component in realizing gain or loss resulting from the sale or exchange of the component;

(2) Repairs damage to a UOP for which the taxpayer is required to take a basis adjustment as a result of a casualty loss or casualty event under Code Sec. 165;

(3) Returns the UOP to its ordinarily efficient operating condition if the property has deteriorated to a state of disrepair and is no longer functional for its intended use;

(4) Results in the rebuilding of the UOP to a like-new condition after the end of its class life under Code Sec. 168 for alternative depreciation system (ADS) purposes; or

(5) Replaces a part or a combination of parts that comprise a major component or a substantial structural part of a UOP. (Reg § 1.263(a)-3(k)(1)) All the facts and circumstances are to be considered when determining if this condition is met. (Reg § 1.263(a)-3(k)(6)(i))[42]

---

39. ¶L-5601.5; ¶2634.01
40. ¶L-5601.8; ¶2634.16
41. ¶L-5601.8; ¶2634.16
42. ¶L-5601.9; ¶2634.16

Capitalized amounts to adapt property to a new or different use. A taxpayer must capitalize as an improvement an amount paid to adapt a UOP to a new or different use. In general, a "new or different use" means a situation where the adaptation isn't consistent with the taxpayer's intended ordinary use of the property when he placed it in service. (Reg § 1.263(a)-3(l)(1)) For example, the cost of converting a company's manufacturing facility into a showroom facility must be capitalized. (Reg § 1.263(a)-3(l)(3), 1)[43]

Retail/restaurant safe harbor. Under the "remodel-refresh" safe harbor for taxpayers in the retail and restaurant industries, 75% of qualified costs are deductible and 25% are capitalized.[44]

Per-building safe harbor for qualifying small taxpayers. A safe harbor permits qualifying small taxpayers (those with $10 million or less average annual gross receipts in the three preceding tax years (Reg § 1.263(a)-3(h)(3)(i))) to elect to currently deduct improvements made to an eligible building property (one with an unadjusted basis of $1 million or less (Reg § 1.263(a)-3(h)(4))). (Reg § 1.263(a)-3(h)(1)) This safe harbor election applies only if the total amount paid during the tax year for repairs, maintenance, improvements, and similar activities performed on the eligible building does not exceed the lesser of $10,000 or 2% of the building's unadjusted basis. (Reg § 1.263(a)-3(h)(1))[45]

¶ 1636   Commissions paid on transfer of property.

Commissions paid for the *purchase* of real estate or other property aren't deductible as expenses but must be capitalized and added to the cost of the property, whether or not the taxpayer is engaged in the real estate business.[46]

Commissions paid for the *sale* of real estate or other property by a taxpayer who is not engaged in the real estate business must be capitalized but are not added to the property's basis and are not treated as an intangible. Instead, commissions are offset against the selling price to determine the gain or loss realized on a sale. If the seller is in the real estate business, commissions on property sales are deductible business expenses. (Reg § 1.263(a)-1(e))[47]

¶ 1637   Capitalization Rules for Intangible Assets. ▬

Taxpayers generally must capitalize amounts paid to acquire or create intangible assets or facilitate the acquisition or creation of such assets.

This includes amounts paid or incurred to (i) acquire or create an intangible asset, (ii) create or enhance a separate, distinct intangible asset, (iii) create or enhance a "future benefit" identified in published guidance as capitalizable, or (iv) "facilitate" the acquisition or creation of an intangible in (i) through (iii) (e.g., transaction costs). (Reg § 1.263(a)-4(b)(1)) Capitalizable costs cannot be deducted and are generally added to the basis of the intangible. (Reg § 1.263(a)-4) Compensation (including bonuses and commissions) and overhead costs do not facilitate the acquisition, creation or enhancement of an intangible asset. (Reg § 1.263(a)-4(e)(4)(i))[48] These rules do not affect the treatment of amounts specifically provided for in a Code Section other than Code Sec. 162 or Code Sec. 212 (e.g., Code Sec. 174 research expenses). (Reg § 1.263(a)-4(b)(4))

🅁 *observation:* Capitalized costs may be amortizable (e.g., payment to a departing employee for a 3-year noncompete covenant may be deducted ratably over the 3 years).

For the "12-month" and de minimis exceptions to these requirements, see ¶1638. For 15-year amortization of certain intangibles, see ¶1903.

---

43. ¶L-5601.10; ¶2634.16   46. ¶I-2536
44. ¶L-5635   47. ¶I-2537; ¶2634.05
45. ¶L-5601.13A; ¶2634.171   48. ¶L-5751; ¶2634

¶ 1638   De minimis and 12-month rule exceptions to capitalization rules for intangibles.

The following are exceptions to the capitalization rules for intangibles discussed at ¶1637.

De minimis costs—i.e., costs that don't exceed $5,000 —paid to another party to create, originate, enter into, renew, or renegotiate an agreement (Reg § 1.263(a)-4(d)(6)(v)), or paid in the process of investigating a transaction (Reg § 1.263(a)-4(e)(4)(iii)), don't have to be capitalized even if they facilitate a capital transaction and otherwise would be subject to the capitalization rules. Payments made in the form of property are valued at fair market value at the time of payment. The de minimis rule applies on a transaction-by-transaction basis. If transaction costs (other than compensation and overhead) exceed $5,000, none of the costs are treated as de minimis. A pooling method may be used for de minimis transaction costs. Commissions paid to facilitate the acquisition of an intangible aren't treated as de minimis costs (and therefore must be capitalized). [49]

12-month rule. Capitalization is not required for amounts paid to create or facilitate the creation of any right or benefit that does not extend beyond the earlier of (1) 12 months after the first date on which the taxpayer realizes the right or benefit; or (2) the end of the tax year following the tax year in which the payment is made. (Reg § 1.263(a)-4(f)) Amounts paid to terminate an agreement before its expiration date create a benefit for the taxpayer that lasts for the unexpired term of the agreement immediately before the termination date. (Reg § 1.263(a)-4(f)(2)) The 12-month rule doesn't apply to amounts paid to create (or facilitate the creation of) financial interests or amortizable Code Sec. 197 intangibles or to amounts paid to create or enhance a right of indefinite duration. (Reg § 1.263(a)-4(f)(3), Reg § 1.263(a)-4(f)(4)) The 12-month rule does not affect the determination of whether a liability is incurred during the tax year, including the determination of whether economic performance has occurred. (Reg § 1.263(a)-4(f)(6))[50]

¶ 1639   Capitalization of amounts paid or incurred to facilitate certain transactions—expenditures to acquire or create intangible assets or benefits.

A taxpayer must capitalize an amount paid to facilitate the following transactions, whether the transaction is a single step or a series of steps carried out as part of a single plan and without regard to whether gain or loss is recognized:

. . . acquisition of assets that constitute a trade or business (whether the taxpayer is the acquirer or the target).

. . . acquisition by the taxpayer of an ownership interest in a business entity if, immediately after the acquisition, the taxpayer and the business entity are related within the meaning of Code Sec. 267(b).

. . . acquisition by a person other than the taxpayer of an ownership interest in the taxpayer.

. . . restructuring, recapitalization, or reorganization of the capital structure of a business entity, including Code Sec. 368 reorganizations and distributions of stock by the taxpayer under Code Sec. 355.

. . . Code Sec. 351 or Code Sec. 721 transfer (whether the taxpayer is the transferor or transferee).

. . . formation or organization of a disregarded entity.

. . . acquisition of capital.

---

49. ¶L-5757.1, ¶L-5760.2; ¶2634   50. ¶L-5760.5 *et seq.*; ¶2634

... stock issuance.

... borrowing, i.e., any issuance of debt, including in an acquisition of capital or a recapitalization. A borrowing also includes debt issued in a debt-for-debt exchange.

... writing an option. (Reg § 1.263(a)-5(a))

1

¶ 1640 Uniform Capitalization (UNICAP) Rules

Under the Code Sec. 263A UNICAP rules, a taxpayer must include in inventory costs the "allocable costs" of "property" that is inventory (Code Sec. 263A(a)(1)(A)) and capitalize the allocable costs of any other property. (Code Sec. 263A(a)(2)(B))

The *allocable costs* are:

... the direct costs of the property (Code Sec. 263A(a)(2)(A));

... the indirect costs, to the extent of the property's proper share of that part (or all) of the costs allocable to that property. (Code Sec. 263A(a)(2)(B))[2]

Allocable costs include all depreciation deductions for the taxpayer's assets, and interest, but only where the underlying debt was incurred or continued to finance certain produced property, see ¶1642. Taxes are allocable indirect costs. (Code Sec. 263A(a)(2)(B)) Environmental remediation costs incurred by a manufacturer (e.g., to clean land it contaminated with hazardous waste) must be included in inventory costs under these rules. [3]

Allocable costs don't include:

... selling, marketing, advertising and distribution expenses (Reg § 1.263A-1(e)(3)(iii)(A));

... any amounts allowable as a deduction under Code Sec. 174 for research and experimental expenditures (Code Sec. 263A(c)(2));

... any cost to the extent allowable as a deduction under Code Sec. 263(c) (intangible drilling and development costs), Code Sec. 616(a) (mining development expenses) or Code Sec. 617(a) (mining exploration expenses) (Code Sec. 263A(c)(3));

... any qualified creative expense incurred by a "writer," "photographer" or "artist" that would otherwise be deductible. Expenses related to printing photographic plates, motion picture films, or similar items aren't qualified creative expenses (Code Sec. 263A(h));

... "deductible service costs." (Reg § 1.263A-1(e)(3)(iii)(K))[4]

Which property is subject to the UNICAP rules? Under the UNICAP rules, a taxpayer must include in inventory or capitalize the allocable costs for:

... real or tangible personal property (defined below) that the taxpayer *produced* (defined below) (Code Sec. 263A(b)(1));

... real or personal Code Sec. 1221(a)(1) property—inventory and property held primarily for sale to customers in the ordinary course of the taxpayer's trade or business — that the taxpayer acquired for resale. (Code Sec. 263A(b)(2))

Tangible personal property includes a film, sound recording, book, or similar property. (Code Sec. 263A(b))

A taxpayer "produces" tangible property if he constructs, builds, installs, manufactures,

---

1. ¶L-5761; ¶2634.77
2. ¶G-5453; ¶263A4 *et seq.*

3. ¶G-5500.1; ¶263A4 *et seq.*
4. ¶G-5493; ¶263A4.05

develops or improves it. (Code Sec. 263A(g)(1)) Where a taxpayer makes progress or advance payments to a contractor, the taxpayer is treated as producing any property the contractor produces for the taxpayer under the contract, to the extent of those payments (whether paid or incurred by the taxpayer under the contract or otherwise). (Code Sec. 263A(g)(2))

Property acquired for resale includes intangible as well as tangible property. Resellers must capitalize the acquisition cost of property acquired for resale, as well as certain indirect costs properly allocable to property acquired for resale. (Reg § 1.263A-1(e)) However, a reseller isn't required to capitalize handling and storage costs incurred at a retail sales facility. (Reg § 1.263A-3(c))

"Property" doesn't include(and so allocable costs don't have to be capitalized for):

. . . Any property produced by the taxpayer for use by the taxpayer other than in a trade or business or an activity conducted for profit. (Code Sec. 263A(c)(1))

. . . Any property produced by the taxpayer under a long-term contract (Code Sec. 263A(c)(4)) except for certain home construction contracts. (Code Sec. 460(e)(1))

. . . Timber and certain ornamental trees. (Code Sec. 263A(c)(5)(A))

. . . Personal property acquired for resale by certain taxpayers ("small resellers") with average annual gross receipts of $25 million or less. (Code Sec. 263A(i))[5]

Taxpayers who acquire and hold property for resale (such as retailers and wholesalers) may elect a simplified resale method to determine the additional costs properly allocable to the resale property. (Reg § 1.263A-3(d))[6] Qualifying motor vehicle dealerships may (1) treat certain sales facilities as retail sales facilities for purposes of Code Sec. 263A and/or (2) be treated as resellers without production activities for Code Sec. 263A purposes.[7]

For the application of the UNICAP rules to farmers and ranchers, see ¶4519.

¶ 1641 Allocating costs to property under the Uniform Capitalization (UNICAP) rules.

Allocable costs (¶1640) must be allocated to inventory or capitalized as follows:

. . . Direct labor costs are generally allocated by using a specific identification ("tracing") method (Reg § 1.263A-1(g)(2)), but any reasonable method may be used. (Reg § 1.263A-1(f)(4))

. . . Indirect costs should be allocated to particular production, resale, etc., activities using either a specific identification method, the standard cost method, or a method using burden rates, such as ratios based on direct costs, hours, or other items, or similar formulas, so long as the method employed reasonably allocates indirect costs among production, resale, etc., activities. (Reg § 1.263A-1(g)(3)) Taxpayers may be able to use simplified methods such as the simplified production method (Reg § 1.263A-2) and the simplified resale method. (Reg § 1.263A-3)[8]

¶ 1642 Interest capitalization rules.

A taxpayer must capitalize interest he pays or incurs during a production period that is allocable to property he produces if that property (1) has a long useful life (it is real property or property with a class life of 20 years or more); (2) has an estimated production period exceeding two years; or (3) has an estimated production period exceeding one year

---

5. ¶G-5451 *et seq.*; ¶s 263A4 *et seq.*, 263A4.06 *et seq.*
6. ¶G-5452 *et seq.*; ¶263A4.09

7. ¶G-5526.1; ¶263A4.04
8. ¶G-5458; ¶263A4.06

and a cost exceeding $1 million. (Code Sec. 263A(f)(1); Reg § 1.263A-8(b)(1))[9]

The taxpayer must also capitalize any interest on debt allocable to an asset needed to produce the above property. (Code Sec. 263A(f)(3); Reg § 1.263A-8(a)(2)) A taxpayer must capitalize interest whether he produces the property for his own use or for sale.

The "production period" begins on the date production of the property begins and ends on the date it is ready to be placed in service or is ready to be held for sale. (Code Sec. 263A(f)(4)(B))[10]

Interest isn't capitalized for real or personal property acquired solely for resale.

A taxpayer doesn't capitalize interest allocable to property that's not subject to the capitalization rules, such as property produced under a long-term contract (see the discussion of this and other exceptions at ¶1640). (Reg § 1.263A-8(d)(2)(v)(A)) Thus, a taxpayer who produces property under a long term contract capitalizes interest only to the extent he doesn't report income under the percentage of completion method. [11]

Allocating interest to produced property. Interest is allocable to property a taxpayer produces if the taxpayer incurred or continued the underlying debt to finance the construction or production of the property.

A taxpayer is treated as having incurred or continued debt to finance the production of income: (1) where the debt can be specifically traced to production expenditures, and (2) where the debt can't be so traced, but where production or construction expenditures exceed the debt that is directly traceable. (Reg § 1.263A-9(a)(2))

The interest on the debt incurred or continued to finance production is allocated to the property produced as follows: [12]

(1) interest (other than qualified residence interest) on a debt that is directly attributable to production expenditures for the produced property is assigned to that property (Code Sec. 263A(f)(2)(A)(i); Reg § 1.263A-9(a)(2)(i)(A)); and

(2) interest on any other debt is assigned to the produced property to the extent that the taxpayer's interest costs could have been reduced if production expenditures (not attributable to the debt in (1), above) had not been incurred (Code Sec. 263A(f)(2)(A)(ii); Reg § 1.263A-9(a)(2)(i)(B)) (that is, had the expenditures that were incurred for construction been used instead to repay the debt).

Except as provided in regs, a flow-through entity applies the interest allocation rules at the entity level and then, to the extent the entity has insufficient debt to support the production or construction expenditures, at the beneficiary level. (Code Sec. 263A(f)(2)(C))[13]

---

9. ¶L-5920; ¶263A4.11
10. ¶L-5932; ¶263A4.11
11. ¶L-5918; ¶263A4.03

12. ¶L-5926; ¶263A4.11
13. ¶L-5928

Chapter 4　Interest Expense—Taxes—Losses—Bad Debts

¶ 1700　Deduction for Interest. ▬▬▬▬▬▬▬▬▬▬▬▬▬▬▬▬▬▬▬▬▬

Except as provided below, interest paid or accrued during the tax year is generally deductible, whether or not it is incurred in a trade or business. To be deductible, the interest must incurred with respect to a valid debt and the amount of interest must be definitely ascertainable.

However, personal interest is nondeductible (¶1717 *et seq.*). Deductions for business interest (¶1710), investment interest (¶1726 *et seq.*), qualified residence interest (¶1729 *et seq.*), interest incurred in a passive activity (¶1797 *et seq.*) and qualified education loan interest (¶2220 *et seq.*) are subject to limitations.

¶ 1701　Interest is payment for the use or forbearance of money.

Interest is "the compensation allowed by law or fixed by the parties for use, or forbearance, or detention of money."[1]

¶ 1702　Mortgage interest.

Interest on a mortgage on real property (including a condominium or co-op, ¶1716) is deductible, subject to limitations. (Reg § 1.163-1(b))[2] For "points," see ¶1703. For deductibility of prepayment penalties and late payment charges, see ¶1705. For who deducts mortgage interest, see ¶1715.

caution: Interest on a home mortgage must be "qualified residence interest" (¶1729 *et seq.*) to be deductible.

¶ 1703　"Points."

"Points" (loan fees that are a specified percentage of the amount borrowed paid to a lender out of a borrower's own funds to get a loan) are deductible as interest *only* if they are *solely* for the use or forbearance of money and not a charge for services. [3]

For when to deduct points, see ¶1739; for home mortgage points, see ¶1740.

¶ 1704　Finance charges and credit card fees.

Subject to the bar on personal interest deductions (¶1717), amounts designated as finance charges on credit cards, revolving charge accounts, and similar credit arrangements are deductible as interest, since these amounts are based on the amount deferred and the length of the deferral. Credit card fees imposed for cash, check, or overdraft advances are deductible as interest if the payment isn't a service charge. [4]

¶ 1705　Prepayment penalties and late payment charges.

A penalty paid for prepaying a debt (including a mortgage) is deductible as interest, as is a late payment charge that isn't a service charge. [5]

---

1. ¶K-5020 *et seq.* ¶1634
2. ¶K-5043; ¶s 1634.050, 1634.052
3. ¶K-5026; ¶1634.005

4. ¶K-5029; ¶1634.050
5. ¶K-5033, K-5034; ¶1634

References beginning with a single letter are to paragraphs in Federal Tax Coordinator 2d and RIA's Analysis of Federal Taxes: Income. Those beginning with numbers are to paragraphs in United States Tax Reporter.

¶ 1706 Interest and carrying charges on installment purchases and deferred tuition; 6% rule.

Interest on installment purchases that is separately stated or definitely determinable and provable is deductible as interest, subject to the rules for credit cards (¶1704). For deduction of "unstated interest," see ¶1707.

If carrying charges (including finance charges, service charges, etc.) on an installment purchase of personal property or educational services are *separately stated* , but the amount of *interest* included in the charges can't be ascertained, the installment payments are considered to include a 6% interest charge based on the average unpaid balance under the contract during the tax year. (Code Sec. 163(b); Reg § 1.163-2)[6]

¶ 1707 Unstated interest on deferred payment sales.

If property is sold in a deferred payment sale and the parties don't provide for an adequate interest charge on the deferred payments, part of each payment made by the buyer may be treated as "unstated interest" and may be deducted under certain rules, see ¶1304 *et seq.* (Code Sec. 483(a); Reg § 1.483-1)[7]

The unstated interest rules don't apply to (1) purchases of personal use property (Code Sec. 1275(b)(1)) or (2) payments made on account of an installment purchase of personal property where payments include separately-stated carrying charges otherwise treated as interest (¶1706). (Code Sec. 483(d)(3))[8]

¶ 1708 Interest on taxes.

Interest on delinquent tax payments is deductible under Code Sec. 163 to the extent allowable.[9] Thus, interest on sales, excise and similar taxes incurred in connection with a taxpayer's business or investment activities may be deducted. But interest paid by a noncorporate taxpayer on income tax underpayments, or on debt used to pay those taxes, is nondeductible personal interest (¶1717). (Reg § 1.163-9T(b)(2))[10]

No deduction is allowed for any interest paid or accrued on underpayments of tax attributable to the portion of any reportable transaction understatement for which the taxpayer hasn't made adequate disclosure. (Code Sec. 163(m))[11]

¶ 1709 Corporate debt or equity; "thin" capitalization.

The corporate issuer's characterization (at issuance) of a corporate instrument as stock or debt is binding on the issuer and all holders (unless the holder discloses inconsistent treatment on his or her return), but is not binding on IRS. (Code Sec. 385(c))[12] If IRS determines that a corporation's debt obligations should be treated as equity (stock), it will treat "interest" paid on the securities as nondeductible dividends, see ¶1711.

The following factors are relevant in determining whether a corporate obligation is debt or equity for federal tax purposes: the right to enforce payment of principal and interest; presence or absence of a maturity date; source of payments; status equal to or inferior to that of regular corporate creditors; "thin" or inadequate capitalization; intent of parties; and identity of interest between creditor and stockholder. [13]

IRS issued regs under Code Sec. 385 that treat as stock certain related-party interests

6. ¶K-5151; ¶1634.050
7. ¶K-5280 et seq.; ¶K-5283; ¶1634; ¶4834
8. ¶K-5281 et seq.; ¶4834.01
9. ¶K-5048; ¶1634.013
10. ¶K-5513
11. ¶K-5506.1; ¶1634.013
12. ¶K-5791.1 et seq.; ¶3854.01
13. ¶K-5801 et seq.; ¶1634.057

that otherwise would be treated as debt. IRS also issued regs that established threshold documentation requirements that had to be satisfied for certain related-party interests in a corporation to be treated as debt. However, IRS later issued proposed reliance regs that would remove the Code Sec. 385 documentation requirements. (Reg § 1.385-2; Prop Reg. § 1.385-2 [removing Reg § 1.385-2]; Reg § 1.385-3)[14]

¶ 1710   Business interest deduction is limited to 30% of adjusted taxable income, with indefinite carryover.

Generally effective for tax years beginning after 2017, a taxpayer's deduction for business interest for any tax year is limited to the sum of: (i) the taxpayer's business interest income for the year, (ii) 30% of the taxpayer's adjusted taxable income for the year (but not less than zero), plus (iii) the taxpayer's floor plan financing interest (i.e., certain interest paid by vehicle dealers) for the year. (Code Sec. 163(j)(1))[15]

Business interest is any interest paid or accrued on indebtedness properly allocable to a trade or business. Investment interest (¶1727) isn't included in business interest. (Code Sec. 163(j)(5)).[16]

Adjustable taxable income is the taxpayer's taxable income, computed without regard to: (i) items of non-business income, gain, deduction, or loss; (ii) any business interest or business interest income; (iii) any net operating loss deduction (¶1815); (iv) any qualified business income deduction (¶1595); and (v) any deduction for depreciation, amortization, or depletion. (Code Sec. 163(j)(8))[17]

Carryover. Any interest that isn't deductible because of the business interest limitation may be carried forward indefinitely and is treated as business interest in the year to which it is carried. (Code Sec. 163(j)(2)) Special rules apply to partnership carryovers. (Code Sec. 163(j)(4)(B))[18]

Partnerships and S corporations. The business interest limitation applies to partnerships at the partnership level. Any deduction for business interest is taken into account in determining the partnership's nonseparately stated taxable income or loss. Each partner's adjusted taxable income is determined without regard to the partner's distributive share of any of the partnership's items of income, gain, deduction, or loss. (Code Sec. 163(j)(4)(A)) Similar rules apply to S corporations, but without the special carryover rules that apply to partnerships. (Code Sec. 163(j)(4)(D))[19]

Exceptions. The business interest limitation doesn't apply to taxpayers with average annual gross receipts of $25 million or less for the 3-tax-year period ending with the prior tax year. (Code Sec. 163(j)(2))[20]

In addition, the following aren't considered "trades or businesses" for purposes of the business interest limitation: (1) performing services as an employee, (2) an electing real property trade or business (generally, a real property trade or business that elects to not to have the business interest limitation apply), (3) an electing farm business as defined in Code Sec. 263A(e)(4) (see ¶4521), and (4) certain regulated public utilities. (Code Sec. 163(j)(7))[21]

⚠️ *caution:* An electing real property trade or business must use the alternative depreciation system (ADS) to depreciate its non-residential real property, residential rental property, and qualified improvement property. An electing farm business must use ADS to depreciate any property used in the farming business with a recovery period of ten

14. ¶K-5791 *et seq.*; ¶3854.01 *et seq.*
15. ¶K-5430 *et seq.*; ¶1634.061
16. ¶K-5432; ¶1634.061
17. ¶K-5434; ¶1634.061

18. ¶K-5436, K-5437; ¶1634.061
19. ¶K-5443, K-5444; ¶1634.061
20. ¶K-5438; ¶1634.061
21. ¶K-5439 *et seq.*; ¶1634.061

years or more. See ¶1930.

Transition rule. A C corporation with "disqualified interest" that was disallowed for its last tax year beginning before Jan. 1, 2018, under the pre-2018 earnings stripping rules may carry that interest forward as business interest to its first tax year beginning after Dec. 31, 2017.[22]

¶ 1711   No deduction for interest on corporate debt payable in issuer's stock.

No deduction is allowed for interest paid or accrued or original issue discount (OID, ¶1743) on a disqualified debt instrument. (Code Sec. 163(l)(1))

A *disqualified debt instrument* is any corporate debt (or debt issued by a partnership to the extent of its corporate partners) payable in (1) equity (i.e., stock) of the issuer or a related party (under Code Sec. 267(b), ¶2448, or Code Sec. 707(b), ¶3726), or, (2) equity held by the issuer (or any related party) in any other person. (Code Sec. 163(l)(2), Code Sec. 163(l)(6)) But it doesn't include certain debt issued by dealers in securities. (Code Sec. 163(l)(5))[23]

A debt instrument is treated as payable in equity if it is required that, or if at the issuer's or related party's option, (i) a substantial amount of the principal or interest is convertible into equity, (ii) a substantial amount of the principal or interest is determined by reference to the value of the equity, or (iii) the indebtedness is part of an arrangement which is reasonably expected to result in a conversion or determination as described in (i) or (ii). (Code Sec. 163(l)(3))[24]

¶ 1712   Deduction barred for disqualified related party amounts paid or accrued in hybrid transactions or with hybrid entities.

Generally effective for tax years beginning after 2017, taxpayers can't deduct any "disqualified related party amount" paid or accrued under a hybrid transaction or by, or to, a hybrid entity (an entity treated as fiscally transparent for U.S. tax law purposes but not the tax law of the foreign country in which it is resident, or vice versa). (Code Sec. 267A(a)) A disqualified related party amount is, in general, any interest or royalty paid or accrued to a related party to the extent that (a) the amount isn't included in the related party's income under the tax law of the country of which the related party is a resident for tax purposes or is subject to tax, or (b) the related party is allowed a deduction for that amount under the tax law of that country. (Code Sec. 267A(b))[25]

¶ 1713   Who may deduct interest?

Generally, a taxpayer's interest deduction is limited to interest the taxpayer pays or accrues on his or her *own* indebtedness, and is not allowed for interest the taxpayer pays or accrues on debts of others.[26] Joint obligors may each deduct the amount of interest each actually pays on the debt.[27]

A taxpayer who pays interest on a debt as a guarantor, endorser, indemnitor, or other type of secondary obligor is not entitled to an interest deduction. But under limited circumstances, the guarantor may be treated as primarily liable for the debt, and allowed an interest deduction.[28]

---

22. ¶K-5436; ¶1634.061
23. ¶K-5507 *et seq.*; ¶1634.059
24. ¶K-5508; ¶1634.059
25. ¶O-3700; ¶267A4.01

26. ¶K-5120 *et seq.*; ¶1634.015
27. ¶K-5130; ¶1634.015
28. ¶K-5133; ¶1664.450

¶ 1714   Interest paid by a person other than the taxpayer.

A taxpayer can deduct interest on the taxpayer's debt that was paid by another person if the payor is acting (or is treated as acting) as the taxpayer's agent (e.g., where a tenant pays the interest on his or her landlord's mortgage) or if the taxpayer has given some consideration for the payor's payment. [29]

¶ 1715   Who can deduct mortgage interest.

Where a taxpayer isn't directly liable for a mortgage debt, the taxpayer is still entitled to a deduction for the mortgage interest payments that he or she actually makes, subject to the "qualified residence interest" limits (¶1729), if the taxpayer is the legal or equitable owner of the mortgaged property. (Reg § 1.163-1(b)). A taxpayer who is personally liable for a mortgage debt is entitled to a deduction for otherwise deductible mortgage interest payments actually made even if the taxpayer no longer owns the mortgaged property. [30]

Where joint owners of mortgaged property are also jointly liable on the mortgage, each owner may deduct the mortgage interest he actually pays out of his separate funds. If the mortgage interest is paid from a joint bank account in which each has an equal interest, each is presumed to have paid an equal amount, absent evidence to the contrary. [31]

¶ 1716   Cooperative housing corporation's (co-op's) mortgage payments.

Tenant-stockholders of co-ops deduct their share of the co-op's mortgage interest payments (subject to the "qualified residence interest" limits, ¶1729). (Code Sec. 216)[32]

¶ 1717   No deduction for personal interest.

Noncorporate taxpayers can't deduct "personal interest." (Code Sec. 163(h)(1))[33] Personal interest is all interest *other than* (1) interest on trade or business debt; (2) qualified education loan interest (¶2220 *et seq.*); (3) qualified residence interest (¶1729 *et seq.*); (4) passive activity interest (¶1797 *et seq.*); (5) investment interest (¶1727); and (6) interest on certain deferred estate tax payments. (Code Sec. 163(h)(2))[34]

¶ 1718   Net direct interest expense—market discount bonds.

A taxpayer's "net direct interest expense" with respect to any taxable market discount bond (¶1323) is deductible in a tax year only to the extent the expense exceeds the market discount allocable to the days during the year that the taxpayer held the bond. (Code Sec. 1277(a); Code Sec. 1278(a)(1)(C))[35] The disallowed interest expenses are deductible the year the bond is disposed of (Code Sec. 1277(b)(2)(A)) or, earlier if the taxpayer elects, to the extent that the taxpayer has net interest income from the bond. (Code Sec. 1277(b)(1))[36]

"Net direct interest expense" is any excess of (1) interest paid or accrued on debt incurred or continued to buy or carry a market discount bond, over (2) interest (including OID, ¶1311) includible in income for the tax year with respect to the bond. (Code Sec. 1277(c))[37]

---

29. ¶K-5129; ¶1634.018
30. ¶K-5135, K-5136; ¶1634.015
31. ¶K-5130, K-5138
32. ¶K-5140, K-5900 *et seq.*; ¶2164.01
33. ¶K-5510; ¶1634.054

34. ¶K-5511; ¶1634.054
35. ¶K-5341; ¶12,764.02
36. ¶K-5343; ¶12,764.02
37. ¶K-5342; ¶12,764.02

¶ 1719   Net direct interest expense—short-term government obligations.

The "net direct interest expense" (¶1718) for a short-term government obligation is deductible in a tax year only to the extent the expense exceeds the total of (1) the daily portions of the acquisition discount for each day during the year that the taxpayer held the obligation, plus (2) the amount of any other (stated) interest payable on the obligation that accrued during the tax year while the taxpayer held the obligation and that, because of the taxpayer's accounting method, wasn't included in his gross income. (Code Sec. 1282(a))[38]

A deduction for disallowed interest expense generally is deferred until (as with market discount bonds, ¶1718) the taxpayer disposes of the obligation, or earlier if the taxpayer so elects. (Code Sec. 1282(c))[39]

A "short-term obligation" is any bond, debenture, note, certificate, or other evidence of indebtedness that has a fixed maturity date not more than 1 year from the date of issue. (Code Sec. 1283(a)(1))

¶ 1720   Interest on business life insurance, annuity or endowment contract loans.

In general, no deduction is allowed for interest paid or accrued on debt for a life insurance policy owned by the taxpayer covering the life of any individual, or any annuity or endowment contract owned by the taxpayer covering any individual. (Code Sec. 264(a)(4))

A taxpayer *may,* however, deduct a limited amount of interest (if not barred by the rules at ¶1721), subject to certain rate limitations, paid or accrued with respect to policies or contracts covering a "key person" (an officer or 20% owner) to the extent that the aggregate amount of the debt doesn't exceed $50,000. The number of a taxpayer's key persons may not exceed the greater of (1) five individuals or (2) the lesser of 20 individuals or 5% of the taxpayer's officers and employees. (Code Sec. 264(e))[40]

¶ 1721   Single premium life insurance, endowment and annuity contracts; borrowing against life insurance contracts; inside buildup.

Single premium life insurance, endowment and annuity contracts. No deduction is allowed for interest on debt incurred or continued to buy or carry single premium life insurance, endowment or annuity contracts. (Code Sec. 264(a)(2); Reg § 1.264-2) A contract is "single premium" if "substantially all" the premiums are paid within four years from the purchase date, or if an amount is deposited with the insurer for payment of a "substantial" number of future premiums on the contract. (Code Sec. 264(c))[41]

Plan of purchase borrowing against life insurance contracts. No deduction is allowed for interest on debt incurred or continued to buy or carry a life insurance, endowment or annuity contract under a plan of purchase that contemplates the systematic direct or indirect borrowing of part or all of the increases in the contract's cash value from the insurer or another party (e.g., a bank). (Code Sec. 264(a)(3))[42] Borrowing for more than three years is presumed to be a plan. (Reg § 1.264-4(c)(1))[43] However, under exceptions to this rule, interest is deductible, among other circumstances, if the debt is incurred because of an unforeseen loss of income or a substantial increase in financial obligations, or in connection with a taxpayer's trade or business. (Code Sec. 264(d); Reg § 1.264-4(d))

---

38. ¶K-5344; ¶12,814.02
39. ¶K-5343; ¶12,814.02
40. ¶K-5351 *et seq.*; ¶2644

41. ¶K-5570 *et seq.*; ¶2644
42. ¶K-5581 *et seq.*; ¶2644
43. ¶K-5584; ¶2644

Inside buildup —denial of interest deduction for policies held by non-individuals. Generally, the portion of the interest expense allocable to unborrowed policy cash values (i.e., the cash surrender value of all life insurance, annuity, or endowment policies issued after June 8, '97, less loans on the policies) is disallowed. Total interest expense (not just that related to life insurance debt) is allocated to the policy values in a pro rata manner according to the average adjusted basis for all assets. The disallowance rule doesn't apply to policies held by individuals. (Code Sec. 264(f))[44]

¶ 1722   Loans from qualified employer plans.

No deduction is allowed for interest paid on a loan from a qualified employer plan to a participant in the plan, or to a beneficiary of the participant, that isn't treated as a distribution, for the period (1) on or after the first day the individual to whom the loan is made is a key employee (defined in Code Sec. 416(i)), or (2) during which the loan is secured by amounts attributable to elective deferrals under a Code Sec. 401(k) plan (¶4306) or a Code Sec. 403(b) annuity (¶4375 *et seq.*). (Code Sec. 72(p)(3))[45]

¶ 1723   Loans to buy or carry tax-exempt securities.

No deduction is allowed for interest on debt incurred or continued to buy or carry tax-exempt securities (e.g., state or local bonds, ¶1328) (Code Sec. 265(a)(2)), or stock of a mutual fund (¶4201) distributing exempt interest. (Code Sec. 265(a)(4))[46]

¶ 1724   Registration-required obligations.

No deduction is allowed for interest on "registration-required obligations" (defined in Code Sec. 163(f)(2)) that aren't in registered form. (Code Sec. 163(f)(1))[47]

¶ 1725   Interest on corporate acquisition indebtedness.

The amount of a corporation's deductions for interest paid or accrued on indebtedness incurred to acquire the stock or assets of other corporations is limited. The maximum annual deduction is $5 million, less the amount of interest on acquisition indebtedness that is not subject to this limitation. Corporate acquisition indebtedness is debt that meets the tests for acquisition purpose, subordination, convertibility and debt-equity or interest coverage. (Code Sec. 279)[48]

¶ 1726   Investment Interest Deduction Limitation—Form 4952. ▬▬▬▬

The amount of investment interest (¶1727) that a noncorporate taxpayer may deduct in any tax year generally is limited to the taxpayer's "net investment income" (¶1728) for the year. (Code Sec. 163(d)(1)) Form 4952 is used to compute the limitation.[49]

Interest that is disallowed because of this limit can be carried over and deducted in later years, subject to the later year's investment income limit. (Code Sec. 163(d)(2))[50]

¶ 1727   "Investment interest."

"Investment interest" is interest paid or accrued on indebtedness properly allocable to property held for investment. (Code Sec. 163(d)(3)(A)) The deduction limit on investment

---

44. ¶K-5601, ¶K-5604; ¶2644.01
45. ¶K-5506, H-11065 *et seq.*; ¶724.23
46. ¶K-5520 *et seq.*, ¶K-5546; ¶2654
47. ¶K-5550 *et seq.*; ¶1634

48. ¶K-5405 *et seq.*; ¶1634, 2794
49. ¶K-5310 *et seq.*; ¶1634.053
50. ¶K-5321; ¶1634.053

interest (¶1726) doesn't apply to interest expense that must be capitalized (e.g., construction interest) or that is disallowed under Code Sec. 265 (¶1723).[1]

Property held for investment is (1) any property that produces income properly allocable to portfolio income under the passive activity rules (¶1798); and (2) any interest in an activity involving a trade or business in which taxpayer doesn't materially participate, if that activity isn't "passive" (see ¶1798). (Code Sec. 163(d)(5)(A))[2]

¶ 1728   "Net investment income" defined—Form 4952.

A taxpayer's "net investment income" for a tax year is the excess of "investment income" over "investment expenses" for the year. (Code Sec. 163(d)(4)(A))[3] (For the definition of net investment income for alternative minimum tax purposes, see ¶3206.)

"Investment income" is gross income from property held for investment (¶1727) including *net gain* on the disposition of that property. *Net capital gain* is not treated as investment income, unless the taxpayer elects (on Form 4952) to include it in investment income. For the effect of such an election on net capital gain, see ¶2603. Qualified dividend income (defined at ¶1286) is included in investment income only to the extent the taxpayer elects on Form 4952. (Code Sec. 163(d)(4)(B); Reg § 1.163(d)-1)[4]

"Investment expenses" *other than interest* aren't currently deductible due to the suspension of miscellaneous itemized deductions (¶3109). Nonbusiness bad debts (¶1827) directly connected with the production of income are taken into account to the extent they are currently deductible.[5]

Investment income and expenses don't include any amounts taken into account in computing income or loss from a passive activity (¶1797 *et seq.*). (Code Sec. 163(d)(4)(D))[6]

¶ 1729   Qualified Residence Interest.

A taxpayer may claim itemized deductions for qualified residence interest. "Qualified residence interest" is interest (subject to dollar limits) paid or accrued during the tax year on acquisition indebtedness (¶1730) with respect to any qualified residence (¶1732) of the taxpayer. Home equity indebtedness (¶1731) is currently nondeductible from 2018 - 2025, though interest on certain loans *labelled* home equity loans may be deductible based on the use of the proceeds. (Code Sec. 163(h)(3)(A))[7]

¶ 1730   Acquisition indebtedness.

Acquisition indebtedness is debt that is incurred in acquiring, constructing or substantially improving a taxpayer's "qualified residence" (¶1732) (or adjoining land) and is secured by that qualified residence. Debt a taxpayer incurs to refinance his or her acquisition indebtedness also qualifies, but only up to the amount of the refinanced debt. (Code Sec. 163(h)(3)(B)(i))[8]

Generally, the aggregate amount of debt for any period that may be treated as acquisition indebtedness can't exceed $750,000 ($375,000 for a married individual filing a separate return). (Code Sec. 163(h)(3)(F)(i)(II))[9]

However, a $1 million limitation ($500,000 for a married individual filing a separate return) applies (Code Sec. 163(h)(3)(B)(ii)) to:

1. ¶K-5312 *et seq.*; ¶1634.053
2. ¶K-5322; ¶1634.053
3. ¶K-5311; ¶1634.053
4. ¶K-5315 *et seq.*; ¶1634.053
5. ¶K-5320; ¶1634.053

6. ¶s K-5315, K-5320; ¶1634.053
7. ¶K-5471; ¶1634.052
8. ¶K-5484, K-5488; ¶1634.052
9. ¶K-5485; ¶1634.052

(i) debt incurred on or before Dec. 15, 2017; (Code Sec. 163(h)(3)(F)(i)(III))

(ii) binding contracts entered into before Dec. 15, 2017, to close on the purchase of a principal residence before Jan. 1, 2018, where the purchase was completed before Apr. 1, 2018; (Code Sec. 163(h)(3)(F)(i)(IV)) and

(iii) refinancing of qualified residence debt that was incurred on or before Dec. 15, 2017, up to the amount of the refinanced debt. (Code Sec. 163(h)(3)(F)(iii))[10]

Where unmarried taxpayers are co-owners of a qualified residence, the acquisition indebtedness limitation is applied on a per-taxpayer basis and not on a per-residence basis. [11]

For where debt exceeds these limits, see ¶1736.

¶ 1731 Home equity indebtedness.

Home equity indebtedness is any debt (other than acquisition indebtedness, ¶1730) secured by taxpayer's qualified residence (¶1732) to the extent the aggregate amount of the debt doesn't exceed the residence's fair market value (as reduced by the amount of acquisition debt on the residence). (Code Sec. 163(h)(3)(C)(i))

Interest on home equity indebtedness is currently nondeductible from 2018 - 2025. (Code Sec. 163(h)(3)(F)(i)(I)) However, taxpayers can still deduct interest on a loan that is *labelled* a home equity loan, home equity line of credit (HELOC), or second mortgage, if the loan is used to buy, build or substantially improve the taxpayer's home that secures the loan, to the extent the loan doesn't exceed the limitation on acquisition indebtedness (¶1730).[12]

¶ 1732 Qualified residence.

A qualified residence is a taxpayer's principal residence and/or any other residence (second residence) the taxpayer properly elects to treat as qualified, even if the taxpayer didn't use it as a residence that year. But a second residence that a taxpayer rents out to others generally can't qualify unless the taxpayer also uses it as a residence for personal purposes during the year for more than the greater of 14 days or 10% of the number of days it is rented out for a fair rental. (Code Sec. 163(h)(4)(A); Reg § 1.163-10T(p)(3)(iii))

A taxpayer may elect a different residence for each tax year to be the taxpayer's second residence. (Code Sec. 163(h)(4)(A)(i); Reg § 1.163-10T(p)(3)(iv))[13]

A residence for this purpose includes a condominium, cooperative housing corporation (co-op) and a time-share. (Code Sec. 163(h)(4)(B); Reg § 1.163-10T(p)(3); (Reg § 1.163-10T(p)(6))[14] A residence under construction may be treated as a qualified residence for a period of up to 24 months, but only if it otherwise qualifies as of the time it's ready for occupancy. (Reg § 1.163-10T(p)(5))[15] Spouses filing a joint return may treat their common principal residence, as well as property that otherwise qualifies as a second residence and that is owned either jointly or by one spouse only, as a qualified residence. For spouses filing separately, each spouse is entitled to treat only one residence as a qualified residence, unless both spouses consent in writing to permit one spouse to elect both the principal residence and one other residence as qualified residences. (Code Sec. 163(h)(4)(A)(ii))[16]

---

10. ¶K-5485.1; ¶1634.052
11. ¶K-5490.1; ¶1634.052
12. ¶K-5490; ¶1634.052
13. ¶K-5474 *et seq.*; ¶1634.052

14. ¶K-5481; ¶K-5482¶1634.052
15. ¶K-5483
16. ¶K-5480; ¶1634.052

¶ 1733   Mortgage insurance premiums treated as qualified residence interest before 2018—Form 1098.

For amounts paid or accrued before 2018 (and not properly allocable to any period after 2017), premiums paid or accrued by a taxpayer during the tax year for qualified mortgage insurance in connection with acquisition indebtedness (¶1730) for a taxpayer's qualified residence were treated as qualified residence interest, subject to a phase-out based on the taxpayer's adjusted gross income (AGI) (below). (Code Sec. 163(h)(3)(E))[17]

observation: To be deductible, premiums for qualified mortgage insurance have to be paid or accrued in connection with acquisition indebtedness. But, since qualified mortgage insurance isn't a category of acquisition indebtedness, it isn't subject to the limitations on acquisition indebtedness, and doesn't affect the amount of indebtedness that can qualify under those limitations (¶1730).

The amount of mortgage insurance premiums treated as qualified residence interest had to be reduced by 10% of the amount of qualified mortgage insurance for each $1,000 (or fraction thereof) that the taxpayer's AGI for the tax year exceeds $100,000. For married persons filing separately the amount was reduced by 10% for each $500 by which the taxpayer's AGI exceeds $50,000. (Code Sec. 163(h)(3)(E)(ii))[18]

caution: Check tax.thomsonreuters.com/federaltaxhandbookupdates to see if the above provision has been extended.

¶ 1734   Allocation Rules for Interest and Debt. ▆▆▆▆▆▆▆▆

All taxpayers (other than widely-held C corporations) must allocate interest expense for purposes of applying the passive activity loss limitation (¶1798), investment interest limitation (¶1726) and personal interest limitation (¶1717). Interest expense is allocated in the same manner as the debt on which the interest is paid. Debt is allocated by tracing the use of the borrowed money. (Reg § 1.163-8T(a)(3), Reg § 1.163-8T(c)(1), Reg § 1.163-8T(a)(4)(i))[19]

¶ 1735   How debt and interest expense are allocated.

Where the proceeds of a single debt are used for multiple purposes —e.g., to make investments *and* to buy "personal" items —the debt is allocated by tracing disbursements of the debt proceeds to specific expenditures. (Reg § 1.163-8T(a)(3), Reg § 1.163-8T(c)(1))

Debt is allocated to an expenditure for the period (1) beginning on the date the proceeds of the debt are used or treated as used to make the expenditure, and (2) ending on the date the debt is repaid or reallocated, whichever is earlier. (Reg § 1.163-8T(c)(2)(i))[20]

Interest expense that accrues on a debt is generally allocated in the same manner as the debt is allocated, regardless of when the interest is actually paid. (Reg § 1.163-8T(c)(2)(ii)(A))[21]

Where the use of debt proceeds, or of assets bought with debt proceeds, changes, the interest on the debt must be reallocated to the new use. The interest so reallocated will be subject to any appropriate deduction limits (¶1734). (Reg § 1.163-8T(j)(1))[22]

---

17. ¶K-5493 *et seq.*; ¶1634.052
18. ¶K-5493.1; ¶1634.052
19. ¶K-5231, K-5232; ¶1634.055

20. ¶K-5233; ¶1634.055
21. ¶K-5233; ¶1634.055
22. ¶K-5254 *et seq.*; ¶1634.055

¶ 1736 Qualified residence interest not subject to allocation rules.

Qualified residence interest (¶1729 *et seq.*) is deductible without regard to how that interest expense or the underlying debt is allocated under the allocation rules discussed at ¶1734 *et seq.* (Reg § 1.163-8T(m)(3))[23]

But, where the debt exceeds the qualified residence interest limits (¶1730, ¶1731), allocation is required for the excess. (Reg § 1.163-10T(e))[24]

¶ 1737 When Interest May Be Deducted.

The proper time for deducting interest is generally determined by the taxpayer's accounting method. Special rules govern when mortgage "points" (¶1739 *et seq.*), unstated interest (¶1707), and original issue discount (OID; ¶1743 *et seq.*) must be deducted.

¶ 1738 Cash method taxpayer's Interest deduction.

A cash method taxpayer may deduct interest only if it is actually *paid* during the tax year. (Code Sec. 163(a)) (For accrual taxpayers, see ¶1741.) No deduction is allowed if the interest payment is made with funds obtained from the original creditor through a second loan, advance, or any arrangement similar to a loan. [25]

Interest that is contested (i.e., interest the debtor claims he doesn't owe) isn't deductible. But if a cash basis taxpayer transfers money or other property to provide for the satisfaction of the asserted (and otherwise deductible) liability, it's deductible in the year of the transfer. (Code Sec. 461(f))[26] For when prepaid interest (including "points") is deductible, see ¶1739.

¶ 1739 Prepaid interest (including "points").

Generally, interest that is prepaid, including "points," is deductible only in the tax year to which the interest is allocable. (Code Sec. 461(g)(1)) Cash method taxpayers thus generally deduct points ratably over the term of the loan. [27]

A taxpayer who "pays" points by receiving discounted loan proceeds gets no current deduction. Instead, the discount is treated as original issue discount (OID), deductible by the borrower under the OID rules (¶1743). Discounts *not* subject to the OID rules may be deducted ratably as the underlying debt is repaid. [28]

For special rules for certain mortgage points and points on refinancing, see ¶1740.

¶ 1740 "Points" on a home mortgage—cash method taxpayer's deduction in year of payment.

A cash method taxpayer may currently deduct points paid on indebtedness incurred in connection with the purchase or improvement of (and secured by) a principal residence in the tax year of actual payment or may deduct points ratably over the life of the mortgage (¶1739). The charging of points must reflect an established business practice in the geographical area where the loan is made, and the deduction allowed can't exceed the amount generally charged there. (Code Sec. 461(g)(2))[29] Points paid to refinance an existing mortgage are not incurred in connection with the purchase or improvement of a residence, and

---

23. ¶K-5238; ¶1634.055
24. ¶K-5498 *et seq.*
25. ¶K-5170 *et seq.*; ¶s 1634.030, 1634.031
26. ¶G-2442 *et seq.*; ¶4614.56 *et seq.*

27. ¶K-5177, K-5178; ¶s 1634.005, 1634.032, 4614.75
28. ¶K-5176; ¶4614.75
29. ¶K-5178 *et seq.*; ¶s 1634.005, 4614.75

thus are not currently deductible. [30]

Under a safe harbor, cash basis taxpayers may currently deduct amounts paid as points on loans used to acquire a principal residence that meet the above tests *and* are (1) clearly designated on Form HUD-1 as points incurred in connection with the loan; (2) computed as a percentage of the stated principal amount of the debt; *and* (3) paid directly by taxpayer to the lender (or mortgage broker). [31]

Points paid by (or charged to) the seller of a residence in connection with a loan to the buyer (taxpayer) also are deductible by the buyer if he subtracts them from the purchase price in computing the basis of the residence. [32]

If the mortgage ends early (e.g., because of a prepayment, refinancing, foreclosure or similar events), the amount of capitalized and unamortized points remaining in the year in which the loan ends is deductible. [33]

¶ 1741   Accrual basis taxpayer's interest deduction.

An accrual basis taxpayer deducts interest in the year it accrues (see ¶2830 *et seq.*), without regard to when the taxpayer pays the interest. (For cash basis taxpayers, see ¶1738.)

Interest that is contingent on events other than the creditor's demand for payment doesn't accrue until the contingency occurs. [34]

A contested liability isn't accrued or deductible. But if the accrual basis taxpayer transfers money or other property to provide for the satisfaction of the asserted liability, it's deductible in the year of the transfer. (Code Sec. 461(f)) [35]

¶ 1742   Interest under the "Rule of 78's" method.

The Rule of 78's is a method of allocating interest on a loan among time periods during the term of the loan. However, even where a loan agreement provides that interest is earned under the Rule of 78's, no deduction is allowed for interest in excess of the economic accrual of interest. [36]

¶ 1743   Original issue discount (OID).

An issuer of a debt instrument issued with OID (¶1310 *et seq.*) may, regardless of its accounting method, deduct part of the OID (¶1744) in each tax year the instrument is outstanding, even though the OID isn't paid until maturity. (Code Sec. 163(e)(1); Reg § 1.163-3(a)(1), Reg § 1.163-4(a)(1); Reg § 1.163-7(a)) However, a cash method obligor of a *short-term obligation* can only deduct OID (and other interest payable) when it is paid. (Code Sec. 163(e)(2)(C)) [37]

"OID" has the same meaning for this purpose as it does for purposes of requiring the holder to include OID in gross income currently (¶1311), except the de minimis exception (¶1311) and the offset for acquisition premium (¶1320) don't apply (Code Sec. 163(e)(2)(B)) [38] and a special rule applies for certain non-publicly traded debt instruments. (Code Sec. 1275(b)(1)) [39]

---

30. ¶K-5180; ¶s 1634.005, 4614.75
31. ¶K-5179; ¶4614.75
32. ¶P-1720; ¶4614.75
33. ¶K-5183
34. ¶s K-5200, K-5201; ¶s 1634.035, 1634.036

35. ¶G-2643 *et seq.*; ¶4614.56 *et seq.*
36. ¶K-5153; ¶1634.030
37. ¶K-5712, ¶K-5745; ¶1634.051
38. ¶K-5727, K-5746; ¶1634.051
39. ¶K-5724

¶ 1744   Amount of original issue discount (OID) deductible currently.

The amount of OID the issuer of a debt instrument deducts currently (¶1743) is generally determined in the same way as the amount of OID the holder includes in gross income currently using the constant yield method (¶1318). (Code Sec. 163(e)(2)(B); Reg § 1.163-7(a)) An issuer of a debt instrument with a *de minimis* amount of OID may choose to deduct the OID at maturity, on a straight-line basis over the term of the debt instrument, or in proportion to stated interest payments. (Reg § 1.163-7(b)(2)).[40]

¶ 1745   Limits on original issue discount (OID) deduction for applicable high yield debt obligations (AHYDOs).

For certain AHYDOs (with yields at least five percentage points over the applicable federal rate for month of issue) issued after July 10, '89, a C corporation can't deduct a portion of the OID, and the remainder is not deductible until actually paid. However, these rules were suspended for qualified obligations issued after Aug. 31, 2008, and before Jan. 1, 2011. (Code Sec. 163(e)(5))[41]

¶ 1746   Deduction for Taxes.

Certain state, local, U.S. possessions and foreign taxes are deductible whether or not connected with a trade or business; so are some federal taxes, other than federal income taxes.

Only payments that are really taxes (regardless of what they are called) are deductible as taxes. Taxes are charges imposed on persons or property by governmental authority to raise funds for the support of government or for public purposes. The mere fact that a levy is called a "tax" isn't conclusive. Fees imposed primarily as charges for government services, e.g., fees for a driver's license or car inspection, or passport fees, aren't deductible as taxes.[42] Penalties paid to a government for violation of a law aren't taxes. (Code Sec. 162(f))[43]

¶ 1747   Deductible and nondeductible taxes; limit on itemized deductions of taxes.

The following taxes are deductible (subject to the limits on deductions by individuals discussed below):

. . . State, local and foreign real property taxes (but individuals may not deduct foreign real property taxes, see below); (Code Sec. 164(a)(1), Code Sec. 164(b)(6)(A))

. . . State and local personal property taxes (¶1752); (Code Sec. 164(a)(2))

. . . State, local and foreign income, war profits and excess profits taxes; (Code Sec. 164(a)(3))

. . . State and local general sales taxes, if elected in lieu of deducting state and local income taxes (¶1748); (Code Sec. 164(b)(5))

. . . Federal and state generation-skipping transfer (GST) tax imposed on income distributions; (¶5059 *et seq.*) (Code Sec. 164(a)(4), Code Sec. 164(b)(4))

. . . Federal estate tax attributable to income in respect of a decedent; (¶3969)

. . . 50% of the Code Sec. 1401 self-employment tax other than the additional 0.9% Medicare (HI) self-employment tax. (Code Sec. 164(f)(1))[44]

40. ¶K-5745 *et seq.*, ¶K-5748; ¶1634.051
41. ¶K-5754, K-5755.2; ¶1634.051
42. ¶K-4003 *et seq.*; ¶1644

43. ¶K-4009; ¶1644
44. ¶K-4001; ¶K-4403 *et seq.*; ¶1644.03; ¶1644.06; ¶1644.07

observation: Although the Medicare tax rate on self-employment income in excess of the applicable threshold is 3.8%, the deduction for one-half of self-employment taxes is computed based on a 2.9% rate. The additional 0.9% tax won't generate an income tax deduction.

Limits on individuals' deduction. For individual taxpayers, from 2018 - 2025, the aggregate deduction for a tax year for the following taxes is limited to $10,000 ($5,000 for marrieds filing separately): state and local real property taxes; state and local personal property taxes; state, local and foreign income, war profits, excess profits taxes; and state and local general sales taxes (if elected). (Code Sec. 164(b)(6)(B))

However, this limitation does not apply to: state and local real property taxes; state and local personal property taxes; and foreign income, war profits, excess profits taxes, *if* the taxes are paid or accrued in carrying on a trade or business or in an activity described in Code Sec. 212 (expenses incurred for the production of income). (Code Sec. 164(b)(6))

Individuals may not deduct foreign real property taxes at all, unless paid or accrued in carrying on a trade or business or in an activity described in Code Sec. 212. (Code Sec. 164(b)(6))[45]

Before Jan. 1, 2022, real property taxes may be deducted under a safe harbor method by homeowners who receive payments under state programs with funds allocated from the Housing Finance Agency's (HFA's) Hardest Hit Fund. [46]

The above taxes are deductible for individual taxpayers who itemize. For deduction of taxes by individuals who don't itemize, see ¶1749.

For state unemployment and disability taxes, see ¶1750.

caution: For the deductibility of taxes for alternative minimum tax purposes, see ¶3206.

Although taxes not included above (e.g., gasoline, diesel and other motor fuel taxes, Social Security (FICA) and unemployment (FUTA) taxes on employers, motor vehicle registration fees) aren't deductible as *taxes,* they may be deductible as *business expenses* or *expenses for the production of income* (¶1505 *et seq.*). (Code Sec. 164(a); Reg § 1.164-2(f))[47]

Other nondeductible "taxes." The following taxes are not deductible, even if they are incurred with respect to a trade or business or investment-related activity:

(1) Federal income taxes (including amounts withheld from wages, and the alternative minimum tax). (Reg § 1.164-2(a)) (Code Sec. 275(a)(1))

(2) Social Security (FICA) tax on employees, and Railroad Retirement tax on employees and employee representatives. (Code Sec. 275(a)(1); Reg § 1.164-2(a))

(3) Federal war profits and excess profits taxes. (Code Sec. 275(a)(2); Reg § 1.164-2(b))

(4) Federal estate, inheritance, legacy, succession and gift tax (other than GST). (Code Sec. 275(a)(3); Reg § 1.164-2(c))

(5) Income, war profits and excess profits taxes of any foreign country or U.S. possession for which the taxpayer takes the foreign tax credit (¶2362 *et seq.*). (Code Sec. 275(a)(4); Reg § 1.164-2(d))

(6) Excise taxes imposed on: charities, private foundations, qualified pension plans, REITs and RICs, excess golden parachute payments and greenmail gains (Code Sec. 275(a)(6)). (Code Sec. 170(f)(10)(F)(iv))[48]

---

45. ¶K-4001; ¶1644
46. ¶K-4504.1
47. ¶K-4000, L-2350 *et seq.*; ¶1644
48. ¶L-2358; ¶L-2359;¶1644

¶ 1748   State and local sales taxes deductible instead of income tax—Form 1040.

Individual taxpayers can elect (on Schedule A of Form 1040) to deduct state and local *general sales and use* taxes instead of state and local *income* taxes (subject to the dollar limitation described at ¶1747).With limited exceptions, a sales or use tax is *general* if imposed at one rate with respect to the retail sale of a broad range of classes of items. (Code Sec. 164(b)(5); Reg § 1.164-3)[49]

Electing taxpayers can deduct either:

(1) the amount of state and local general sales taxes paid, by accumulating receipts; or

(2) the amount determined under IRS tables, plus the actual amount of sales taxes paid on motor vehicles, boats and other IRS-specified items (e.g., aircraft, homes). (Code Sec. 164(b)(5)(H))[50]

Foreign sales taxes are not deductible under the above rules (Reg § 1.164-3(f)) The elective sales tax deduction doesn't apply to sales taxes paid on items used in a taxpayer's trade or business. [1]

State or local sales or use taxes paid or incurred in connection with the acquisition or disposition of property, and taxes on the transfer of property (e.g., securities, real estate), aren't deductible; the buyer treats them as part of the cost, the seller as a reduction in the amount realized. (Code Sec. 164(a))[2]

¶ 1749   Limitations on deduction for taxes if individual doesn't itemize—Form 1040.

An individual taxpayer generally may deduct taxes only if the taxpayer itemizes (on Schedule A of Form 1040). (Code Sec. 63(d))[3]

For an individual who doesn't itemize, the deduction is limited to the following taxes that are deductible "above the line" (i.e., from gross income in arriving at adjusted gross income, ¶3102): (1) taxes attributable to a trade or business (including taxes on real property) (Code Sec. 62(a)(1)), or to property held for the production of rents or royalties (Code Sec. 62(a)(4)), and (2) 50% of self-employment taxes. (Code Sec. 164(f))[4]

¶ 1750   State unemployment and disability taxes.

Employers' and employees' contributions to state unemployment insurance funds may be deductible under Code Sec. 164(a). Whether contributions to a state unemployment insurance fund or disability plan are deductible as taxes is determined on a state-by-state basis.[5]

¶ 1751   Local benefit assessments.

The deductibility of assessments for public improvements, such as sewers, streets, etc., as taxes depends on the purpose of the assessment. Taxes assessed against local benefits of a kind tending to increase the value of the property assessed are deductible by proper owners as taxes only to the extent the taxes are properly allocable to repairs, maintenance or interest charges. If it can't be determined what part of the tax is for maintenance, repair or interest, the taxes are not deductible, but may be capitalized (¶1629 *et seq.*).

---

49. ¶K-4510 *et seq.*; ¶1644.03
50. ¶K-4511; ¶1644.03
1. ¶K-4510 *et seq.*; ¶1644.03
2. ¶I-2502, K-4500, L-2352.1, P-1174.1; ¶1644.03, 1644.09

3. ¶A-2701; ¶634
4. ¶L-2351; ¶K-4401; ¶624; ¶1644.07
5. ¶K-4003 *et seq.*; ¶L-2353 *et seq.*; ¶1644.03

(Code Sec. 164(c)(1); Reg § 1.164-4(b)(1))[6]

¶ 1752   Personal property taxes.

Personal property taxes imposed by a state or local government are deductible (subject to the dollar limitation described at ¶1747). (Code Sec. 164(a)(2), Code Sec. 164(b)(6)) The tax must be imposed annually on personal property on an ad valorem basis (i.e., based on the value of the personal property). (Code Sec. 164(b)(1))[7]

¶ 1753   Who deducts the tax?

State and local taxes generally are deductible only by the person on whom they are imposed. (Reg § 1.164-1(a))[8]

One who voluntarily pays a tax imposed on another generally isn't entitled to a deduction. But where a corporation pays a tax imposed on a shareholder on his or her interest as a shareholder, and the shareholder does not reimburse the corporation, the deduction is allowed to the corporation and not to the shareholder. (Code Sec. 164(e))[9]

Real property taxes are deductible by the property owner. (For apportionment of real property tax in year of sale, see ¶1762.) A person who owns a beneficial interest in real property may deduct property taxes he pays to protect that interest. [10]

Taxes on property that is leased are deductible by the landlord, even if the tenant makes the payment (which the tenant treats as additional rent expense, ¶1577). (Reg § 1.162-11(a)) But a tenant deducts taxes paid on improvements the tenant makes where the useful life of the improvements will terminate before the end of the lease. [11]

¶ 1754   Married couple's deduction of taxes.

Spouses filing joint federal returns may deduct on that return all deductible taxes paid by either spouse, whether or not they file joint *state* returns.[12]

If the spouses file separate federal and separate state returns, each spouse may deduct only the state income taxes imposed on and actually paid by that spouse. If a joint state return and separate federal returns are filed, then for federal tax purposes, each spouse is entitled to deduct his or her share of the joint state tax prorated according to each spouse's gross income, but not to exceed the amount actually paid by the spouse. [13]

¶ 1755   Property taxes on co-owned property.

An individual's deduction for taxes on property owned with other persons as tenants-in-common may be limited to the individual's pro rata part of the taxes, i.e., the amount attributable to his interest, even if he pays *all* the taxes on the property. This pro rata share limit applies where the tenant is only assessed for his share or has a right to contribution from the other tenants.[14]

Tenants by the entirety (i.e., spouses) and joint tenants with right of survivorship are entitled to deduct in full the taxes they pay on the jointly-owned property. [15]

---

6. ¶K-4600 *et seq.*; ¶1644.03
7. ¶K-4502; ¶1644.03
8. ¶K-4100 *et seq.*; ¶1644.01
9. ¶K-4114; ¶1644.01
10. ¶K-4103; ¶1644.01
11. ¶K-4104
12. ¶s K-4105, K-4107; ¶1644.01
13. ¶s K-4106, K-4108; ¶1644.01
14. ¶K-4112; ¶1644.01
15. ¶K-4112; ¶1644.01

¶ 1756   Cooperative and condominium housing realty taxes.

Tenant-stockholders of cooperative housing corporations (co-ops) deduct their share of the co-op's real property taxes. (Code Sec. 216)[16] Condominium owners deduct the real property taxes on their individual interests, subject to the dollar limitation described at ¶1747.)[17]

¶ 1757   When cash basis taxpayers deduct taxes.

A cash basis taxpayer's taxes are deductible for the tax year the taxes are paid. State and local taxes withheld from the taxpayer's wages are deductible in the year they are withheld.[18]

If the taxpayer pays the tax, the tax is deductible in the year of payment even if the taxpayer contests the liability and seeks to recover the payment (¶1760).[19]

For estimated tax payments and prepaid taxes, see ¶1758. For accrual basis taxpayers, see ¶1759.

¶ 1758   When prepaid taxes and estimated tax payments are deductible.

A cash basis taxpayer may deduct an advance payment of tax in the year of payment as long as it's an actual good faith payment and not a mere deposit. But the advance payment of state taxes that are later refunded won't be deductible unless taxpayer had a reasonable basis, at the time of payment, for believing the taxes were owed. [20]

A deduction in the year of payment is also allowed for advance estimated tax payments made under a pay-as-you-go tax collection system. [21]

¶ 1759   When accrual basis taxpayers deduct taxes.

An accrual basis taxpayer deducts a tax liability in the tax year in which all events have occurred that determine the liability for the tax, the amount of the liability can be determined with reasonable accuracy, and economic performance (¶2831) has occurred. (Code Sec. 461(h); Reg § 1.461-1(a)(2), Reg § 1.461-4(g)(6))[22] For ratable accrual of real property taxes, see ¶1761.

An accrual basis taxpayer who pays an additional state tax for prior years without protest or appeal must deduct that tax for federal tax purposes in the year the tax was originally due, and not when it is later assessed or paid. [23] For when to deduct a contested tax, see ¶1760.

For cash basis taxpayers, see ¶1757.

¶ 1760   When to deduct contested tax.

An accrual basis taxpayer who contests (through an overt act of protest or suit) an assessment can't deduct the contested portion of the tax until the contest is ended and the amount determined. [24]

A cash or accrual basis taxpayer who pays a contested liability without giving up the contest may deduct the tax in the year of payment, if otherwise deductible in that (or an

---

16. ¶K-5900 *et seq.*; ¶2164.01
17. ¶K-4103
18. ¶K-4201 *et seq.*; ¶1644.02
19. ¶K-4201; ¶4614.56
20. ¶K-4203; ¶1644.02

21. ¶K-4204; ¶1644.02
22. ¶G-2673, K-4300 *et seq.*; ¶4614.16, 1644.02
23. ¶K-4320
24. ¶K-4319 *et seq.*; ¶4614.56

earlier) year. (Code Sec. 461(f))[25] But foreign or U.S. possession income, war profits and excess profits tax can't be deducted until the contest is finally determined. (Code Sec. 461(f))[26]

¶ 1761   Election by accrual basis taxpayers to accrue realty taxes ratably—Form 3115.

An accrual basis taxpayer generally deducts real property taxes when paid. An exception to this rule permits an accrual basis taxpayer to elect to accrue any real property tax that is related to a definite time period, ratably over that period (ratable accrual election). (Code Sec. 461(c)(1); Reg § 1.461-4(g)(6)(iii)(A))[27]

A taxpayer can make the ratable accrual election without IRS consent for the first tax year in which the taxpayer incurs real property taxes. The election has to be made by the due date of the return for the election year (including extensions). (Code Sec. 461(c)(2)(A); Reg § 1.461-1(c)(1))

After the first tax year, a taxpayer may make the election to accrue real property taxes ratably at any time, with IRS consent. (Code Sec. 461(c)(2)(B)) Although a written request for IRS consent must be filed within 90 days after the beginning of the first tax year to which the election applies, taxpayers can get an automatic extension that permits an application on Form 3115 at any time during the first tax year. [28] The election is binding unless IRS consents to its revocation. (Reg § 1.461-1(c)(4))[29]

¶ 1762   Apportionment of real property taxes between seller and buyer.

For both cash and accrual taxpayers, the real property tax on property that is sold during the tax year is considered to be imposed

. . . *on the seller* to the extent properly allocable to that part of the real property tax year (period to which the tax relates) ending on the day before the date of sale; and

. . . *on the buyer* to the extent properly allocable to that part of the real property tax year beginning on the date of sale. (Code Sec. 164(d); Reg § 1.164-6)[30]

For when the seller or buyer deducts the sale year realty tax, see ¶1763. For where seller took an excessive deduction, see ¶1764.

¶ 1763   When seller or buyer deducts real property tax.

An *accrual basis* taxpayer (seller or buyer) deducts his share of sale year realty tax (as apportioned, ¶1762) in the income tax year in which the accrual date (date of sale) falls. If an election to accrue realty taxes ratably (¶1761) is in effect for that year, the share of the tax is deductible in the year it accrues under the election. (Code Sec. 164(d)(2)(B); Reg § 1.164-6(d)(6))[31]

A *cash basis* taxpayer (seller or buyer) deducts his portion of the sale year realty tax in the income tax year he pays it. But where the tax isn't payable until after the sale date, or where the other party is liable for the tax under local law, the taxpayer may, at his option, deduct the tax either in the year of sale (whether or not he actually paid it) or in the year of payment, if later. (Reg § 1.164-6(d)(1); Reg § 1.164-6(d)(2))[32]

25. ¶s G-2445, G-2645; ¶s 1644.02, 4614.56
26. ¶K-4322
27. ¶K-4327 *et seq.*
28. ¶s K-4329, K-4330; ¶4614.45

29. ¶K-4334; ¶4614.45
30. ¶K-4117; ¶1644.01
31. ¶s K-4129, K-4130; ¶1644.01
32. ¶K-4127 *et seq.*; ¶1644.01

¶ 1764   Excessive deduction of real property tax before sale.

If the seller (cash or accrual) deducted more than his share of realty taxes on property he sells in a later year, and that "excess" tax payment is allocable to and deductible by the buyer (¶1762), the seller is treated as receiving a recovery in the sale year. The seller must include this "recovery" in gross income for the sale year, to the extent a tax benefit (i.e., the excess deduction) was obtained in that earlier year (¶1205). (Reg § 1.164-6(d)(5))[33]

¶ 1765   Deduction for Losses. ▬

Taxpayers may sustain a loss when their property is transferred, stolen, destroyed, confiscated, abandoned, taken by foreclosure or becomes worthless, and they receive less than adequate compensation for it. This loss may be deductible (¶1766 *et seq.*).

Subject to the limits discussed in the following paragraphs, the at-risk rules (¶1790 *et seq.*) and the passive loss rules (¶1797 *et seq.*), taxpayers may deduct losses they sustain that aren't compensated for by insurance or otherwise. (Code Sec. 165(a))[34]

For losses from a sale or exchange, see ¶ 2400 *et seq.*

¶ 1766   What is a deductible loss?

A deductible loss arises when a taxpayer loses or gives up money, property or rights, or when these items lose value as a result of an identifiable event. [35] It must be shown that the taxpayer sustained a loss of a type that is deductible and that the loss was sustained in the tax year; the amount of the loss also must be shown.

To be deductible, a loss must be evidenced by a closed and completed transaction fixed by identifiable events (Reg § 1.165-1(b)), such as a sale, exchange, foreclosure, stock redemption, abandonment, governmental condemnation, or seizure. Mere fluctuations in an asset's value don't result in deductible losses. [36]

¶ 1767   How much loss is deductible?

The amount of a loss sustained on disposition of property is the adjusted basis of the property, minus the amount of any money and the fair market value of any property received in exchange. (Code Sec. 165(b); Reg § 1.165-1(c))[37] No loss is deductible to the extent the taxpayer was reimbursed or compensated for it (¶1781), or the property has salvage value. (Code Sec. 165(a); Reg § 1.165-1(c))[38] For limit on tax-exempt use losses, see ¶1773. For casualty and theft losses, see ¶1782 *et seq.* and ¶1787 *et seq.*

¶ 1768   Limits on losses of individuals.

Individuals may deduct losses incurred in a trade or business (¶1769) or a transaction entered into for profit (¶1770). (Code Sec. 165(c)(1), Code Sec. 165(c)(2))[39]

From 2018 to 2025, individuals may not deduct personal casualty losses (¶1782) unless incurred in a Federally declared disaster. However, where a taxpayer has personal casualty gains (¶1783), a personal casualty loss is deductible to the extent that it doesn't exceed the gains. (Code Sec. 165(h)(5))[40] Also from 2018 to 2025, due to the suspension of miscellaneous itemized deductions subject to the 2% floor (¶3109), hobby loss deductions

---

33. ¶K-4131
34. ¶M-1000; ¶1654
35. ¶M-1000 *et seq.*; ¶1654.020 *et seq.*
36. ¶M-1101, M-1305 *et seq.*; ¶1654.020 *et seq.*

37. ¶M-1401
38. ¶M-1401; ¶M-1408; ¶1654.304
39. ¶M-1501, M-1510, M-1524; ¶s 1654, 1654.060 *et seq.*
40. ¶M-1900A

are not allowed.

Property that a taxpayer holds partly for personal use and partly for business or income-producing use is treated as two properties, one personal property and one business (or income-producing) property. Loss on the personal part isn't deductible except as discussed above.[41]

¶ 1769   What is a trade or business?

A trade or business is a pursuit or occupation carried on for profit (¶1770), whether or not profit actually results. An isolated transaction isn't a business. [42]

¶ 1770   When a transaction is entered into for profit—Form 5213.

A transaction is entered into for profit if a taxpayer intends to receive income from it overall. If the transaction involves property, the taxpayer's primary motive must be to receive income from it or to profit from disposing of it. A loss deduction is possible where a secondary nonprofit motive exists as long as the profit motive predominates. [43]

An activity is presumed to be engaged in for profit for a tax year if it shows a profit for three or more years during the five-year period ending in the current tax year (or two out of seven years for breeding, showing or racing of horses). (Code Sec. 183(d); Reg § 1.183-1(c))[44] A taxpayer who hasn't engaged in an activity for more than five years (seven, for horse breeding, etc.) can elect (on Form 5213) to postpone the determination as to whether these presumptions apply until the close of the fourth tax year (sixth, for horse breeding, etc.) after the tax year the taxpayer first engages in the activity. (Code Sec. 183(e); Reg § 12.9)[45]

Whether an activity is engaged in for profit is determined on the corporate level for S corporations, and on the partnership level for partners. (Reg § 1.183-1(f))[46]

Deductions that are attributable to an activity that is *not* entered into for profit—i.e., so-called "hobby losses" —are not allowed due to the suspension of itemized miscellaneous deductions subject to the 2%-of-AGI floor (¶3109).[47]

¶ 1771   Vacation home expenses.

Where an individual, trust, estate, partnership or S corporation owns a vacation home or a dwelling unit and uses it for both personal and rental purposes, a deduction of expenses is limited, except for those expenses which are deductible without regard to business use of the property —e.g., mortgage interest and property taxes. (Code Sec. 280A)[48]

The owner's personal use of the home (or portion of it) for even one day in the tax year triggers these "vacation home" limits. (Code Sec. 280A(e)(1))[49]

Subject to a de minimis rule (below), for any tax year in which the owner uses the (rented) vacation home or other dwelling unit for personal purposes, or rents it out for less than a fair rental, the deduction for expenses attributable to the rental of the unit (e.g., maintenance, utilities, depreciation, etc.) can't exceed the percentage of the total expenses for the year "attributable" to the period the unit is rented at a fair rental. (Code Sec. 280A(e)(1))[50] If a taxpayer who rents out a dwelling unit also uses it as a residence,

41. ¶M-1420; ¶s 1654.061, 1654.430
42. ¶L-1100 *et seq.*; ¶1654.060 *et seq.*
43. ¶M-1510 *et seq.*; ¶1654.062
44. ¶M-5818; ¶1834.02
45. ¶M-5821; ¶1834.02
46. ¶M-5802

47. ¶A-2711; ¶674
48. ¶M-6001; ¶280A4
49. ¶M-6005; ¶280A4
50. ¶M-6005, M-6028, ¶ M-6006, *et seq.*; ¶280A4.060, 280A4.072, ¶280A4.065

the deductions for business use (i.e., rental) of the home (other than otherwise deductible expenses, such as mortgage interest and real estate taxes) are limited to net income from the business. (Code Sec. 280A(c)(5))[1]

A home is used as a residence in any tax year the owner's use of the unit (or a portion of it) for personal purposes exceeds the longer of (1) 14 days, or (2) 10% of the period of rental use. (Code Sec. 280A(d)(1))[2] A taxpayer does not use a home for personal use any day during a tax year that occurs before or after a 12-month consecutive period that begins or ends in the tax year, if that 12-month period constitutes a qualified rental period under Code Sec. 280A(d)(4)(B). (Code Sec. 280A(d)(4))[3]

Under a de minimis rule, if a home is rented for less than 15 days a year, the owner can't deduct *any* of the rental expenses, but isn't taxed on any of the rental income. (Code Sec. 280A(g))[4]

¶ 1772 Worthless stock or securities.

A taxpayer may deduct a loss for worthless stock or other securities (i.e., a bond, debenture, note, certificate or other evidence of indebtedness issued by a corporation or a government (or its political subdivision) with interest coupons or in registered form). (Code Sec. 165(g)(1); Reg § 1.165-5)[5]

Total worthlessness of the security is required for the deduction (except in the case of dealers who inventory securities). (Reg § 1.165-4, Reg § 1.165-5)[6]

The taxpayer must show that the security had value at the end of the year preceding the deduction year and that an identifiable event caused a loss in the deduction year. [7] The amount of the loss is, to extent not compensated for (e.g., by insurance), the security's adjusted basis for determining loss on a sale (¶ 2473). (Code Sec. 165(b); Reg § 1.165-1(c))[8]

The deduction is a capital loss if the security is a capital asset to the taxpayer. (Code Sec. 165(g)(1))[9]

An ordinary loss deduction is allowed if the security is (i) not a capital asset (Reg § 1.165-5(b)); (ii) small business corporation stock (¶ 2634 *et seq.*); or (iii) for corporate taxpayers, stock in an "affiliated" corporation (at least 80%-owned by taxpayer), where more than 90% of the affiliate's gross receipts has been from sources other than passive income (e.g., royalties, dividends). (Code Sec. 165(g)(3))[10]

No loss deduction is allowed on a shareholder's surrender of some of his stock to the corporation, whether or not the surrender is pro rata. Instead, the shareholder's basis for stock surrendered is added to the basis of stock retained. [11]

¶ 1773 Limits on "tax-exempt use losses."

Generally, if a taxpayer (i) leases property to a tax-exempt entity or (ii) is a partner in a partnership that owns depreciable property, and the partnership also includes partners that are exempt organizations, subject to some exceptions, the taxpayer cannot claim deductions from the lease transaction in excess of the taxpayer's gross income from the lease or partnership for that tax year. The property subject to the Code Sec. 470 limitations is referred to as "tax-exempt use property." (Code Sec. 168(h), Code Sec. 470)[12] A tax-exempt use loss in excess of gross income may be carried forward to the next tax year,

1. ¶M-6018, M-6022; ¶280A4.060 *et seq.*
2. ¶M-6024; ¶280A4.062, 280A4.064
3. ¶M-6038; ¶280A4.067
4. ¶M-6023; ¶280A4.064
5. ¶M-3301; ¶1654.200 *et seq.*
6. ¶M-3304, G-5021; ¶1654.200 *et seq.*

7. ¶M-3300 et seq., ¶M-3400 et seq.; ¶1654.210
8. ¶M-3305; ¶1654.205
9. ¶M-3301; ¶1654.200
10. ¶M-3308; ¶M-3310 *et seq.*; ¶1654.203
11. ¶M-3501
12. ¶L-6901 *et seq.*; ¶4704

subject to that year s limit. (Code Sec. 470(b))

¶ 1774   Excess business loss disallowance rule.

A noncorporate taxpayer's "excess business loss" is disallowed and carried forward and treated as part of the taxpayer's net operating loss (NOL) carryforward in subsequent tax years.[13] This limitation applies after the application of the passive loss rules (¶1797). (Code Sec. 461(l))

An excess business loss for the tax year is the excess of aggregate deductions of the taxpayer attributable to the taxpayer's trades and businesses, over the sum of aggregate gross income or gain of the taxpayer plus a threshold amount. The threshold amount for a tax year is $500,000 for married individuals filing jointly, and $250,000 for other individuals, with both amounts indexed for inflation. (Code Sec. 461(l)(3))[14] In the case of a partnership or S corporation, the provision applies at the partner or shareholder level. (Code Sec. 461(l)(4))[15]

¶ 1775   Demolition losses.

Generally, no deduction is allowed to the owner or lessee of a building for any loss on demolition of the building, or for any of the demolition expenses. The loss or expenses must be capitalized and added to the basis of the land. (Code Sec. 280B)[16]

¶ 1776   Abandonment loss.

A loss deduction is allowed for loss of usefulness or for obsolescence of nondepreciable property, both tangible and intangible (e.g., land, goodwill), *if* (1) the loss is incurred in a business or transaction entered into for profit; (2) it arises from the sudden termination of usefulness in the business or transaction; *and* (3) the property is permanently discarded from use, or the business or transaction is discontinued. (Reg § 1.165-2)[17]

The loss is an ordinary loss not subject to capital loss limitations. (Reg § 1.165-2(b))[18] The loss can't exceed the adjusted basis (¶ 2473) of the property for determining loss on a disposition. (Reg § 1.165-1(c))[19] For loss on an abandoned security, see ¶1772. For losses on mortgaged property, see ¶1779 and ¶1780.

¶ 1777   Costs of unsuccessful investigation of proposed venture.

A corporation that pays or incurs expenses in *unsuccessfully* searching for or investigating a new venture may deduct those costs as a business loss when it abandons the search or investigation (¶1503). But for a noncorporate taxpayer, these expenses are personal and nondeductible.[20] For expenses of a *successful* investigation, see ¶ 1500 *et seq.*

¶ 1778   Gambling losses–Form 1040.

A taxpayer may deduct gambling losses suffered in the tax year, but only to the extent of that year's gambling gains. (Code Sec. 165(d); Reg § 1.165-10)

Gains include "comps" (i.e., complimentary goods and services taxpayer receives from a casino). Losses from one kind of gambling (e.g., horse bets) are deductible against gains from another kind (e.g., keno).[21]

---

13. ¶M-4451
14. ¶M-4452
15. ¶M-4453
16. ¶M-2200 *et seq.*; ¶s 1654.180, 280B4
17. ¶M-2301; ¶1654.150 *et seq.*

18. ¶M-2353
19. ¶M-2351
20. ¶L-5018 *et seq.*
21. ¶M-6100 *et seq.*; ¶1654.500 *et seq.*

"Gambling losses" are losses from wagering transactions, including any otherwise allowable deduction incurred in carrying on a wagering transaction. (Code Sec. 165(d)) In other words, the gambling loss limitation applies not only to the actual costs of wagers, but to other expenses incurred by the individual in connection with the gambling activity (e.g., transportation to the casino). [22]

Individuals not engaged in the gambling business deduct gambling losses (to extent of gambling gains) only as itemized deductions, and must report gambling gains on Form 1040 even if they are exceeded by gambling losses. [23]

¶ 1779 Mortgagee's loss (or gain) on mortgaged property.

The mortgagee (mortgage lender) treats a loss on mortgaged property as follows:

A loss on *compromise or settlement* of the debt of an insolvent debtor is treated as a bad debt (¶¶1823 *et seq.*). [24]

A mortgagee to whom mortgaged or pledged property is surrendered has a bad debt deduction if the fair market value (FMV) of the property received is less than the debt. The mortgagee has a gain if the FMV of the surrendered property is greater than the debt's basis. [25] For where the surrender is a repossession by the seller, see ¶ 2466.

A loss on a *mortgage foreclosure* is treated as a bad debt equal to the sum of (1) the excess of the debt's basis over the net proceeds from the property foreclosure; (2) accrued interest previously reported as income; plus (3) legal and other expenses. This is true whether the property is sold to the creditor or another purchaser. (Reg § 1.166-6(a)) [26]

¶ 1780 Owner's loss on foreclosure, surrender, or abandonment of mortgaged property; loss on tax sales.

The owner of mortgaged property, whether or not he is the mortgagor and whether or not he is personally liable for the mortgage debt, realizes a loss (occasionally a gain) on foreclosure of the mortgage or surrender of the property. The foreclosure (or surrender) is considered a sale or exchange. [27] The owner-borrower's gain or loss is the difference between adjusted basis of the transferred property and the amount realized. If the owner-borrower isn't personally liable for repaying the debt secured by the transferred property, the amount realized includes the full amount of the debt canceled by the transfer. If the borrower is personally liable, the amount realized doesn't include any cancellation of debt income (¶1377) arising from the debt. But if the FMV of the property is less than the canceled debt, the amount realized includes canceled debt up to the FMV. [28]

Abandonment is generally treated as a sale or exchange. [29]

The tax treatment of an owner whose property is sold for delinquent taxes is similar to the tax treatment for foreclosure, i.e., the tax sale is a sale or exchange. [30]

¶ 1781 When to deduct loss.

A loss is deductible only for the tax year it's sustained. (Code Sec. 165(a)) This is the year the loss occurs, as evidenced by closed and completed transactions and as fixed by identifiable events in that year. (Reg § 1.165-1(d)) [31] For casualty or theft losses, see ¶¶1784 and ¶1789.

---

22. ¶M-6102.1; ¶1654.500
23. ¶J-1651, M-6105
24. ¶M-3709; ¶1664.350 *et seq.*
25. ¶M-3710; ¶1664.353
26. ¶M-3701; ¶1664.353 *et seq.*

27. ¶M-3801; ¶1654.451
28. ¶M-3803
29. ¶M-3808; ¶1654.155
30. ¶M-3806
31. ¶M-1301; ¶1654.111

If taxpayer has a claim for reimbursement on which there is a reasonable prospect of recovery, that "reimbursable" loss can't be deducted until it's reasonably certain whether or not the reimbursement will be made. This may be ascertained by, among other things, settlement, adjudication or abandonment of the claim. (Reg § 1.165-1(d)(2))[32]

¶ 1782   Casualty, Disaster, and Theft Losses–Form 4684. ▬▬▬▬▬▬

The deduction for personal casualty and theft losses is generally suspended from 2018 through 2025, except for personal casualty losses incurred in a Federally declared disaster. (Code Sec. 165(h)(5))[33]

For the amount of casualty loss, see ¶1783. For when to deduct casualty losses, see ¶1784 et seq.

A *casualty* is the complete or partial destruction of property resulting from an identifiable event of a sudden, unexpected or unusual nature such as a fire, storm, shipwreck, car crash, or similar event. Progressive deterioration from a steadily operating cause isn't a casualty. The property must suffer physical damage and not just a decline in value, even if that decline resulted from being in or near an area where casualties have occurred and might occur again. [34]

¶ 1783   Casualty loss deduction—amount of casualty loss–Form 4684.

The amount treated as a loss from a casualty depends on whether the taxpayer held the property for personal or business purposes, as follows:

Personal-use property. The deduction for personal casualty losses is generally suspended for 2018 through 2025, except for personal casualty losses incurred in a Federally declared disaster and, for taxpayers with personal casualty gains, nondisaster personal casualty losses to the extent of the personal casualty gains. (Code Sec. 165(h)(5))[35]

For property held for personal use, the amount of the casualty loss is the *lesser* of (1) the property's adjusted basis (¶2473), or (2) its decline in value (i.e., its fair market value (FMV) immediately before the casualty *minus* its FMV immediately afterward). (Reg § 1.165-7(b)(1))[36]

Business property. For property used in business or held for the production of income, the amount of the casualty loss is determined under the same rules as for personal-use property, except that if the property is *totally* destroyed, the amount of the loss is the property's adjusted basis in all cases. (Reg § 1.165-7(b)(1)(ii))[37]

Measuring decline in value. The decline in a property's value should be ascertained by competent appraisal where possible. [38]

Costs of repairing, replacing, or cleaning up property after a casualty can be used to measure the amount of the loss (decline in value) if: the repair, etc., is necessary to restore the property to its pre-casualty condition; the amount spent isn't excessive; the repairs do no more than take care of the damage suffered; and the post-repair value is no greater than the pre-casualty value. (Reg § 1.165-7(a)(2))[39]

Limits to personal-use property losses. An individual can deduct a casualty loss on personal-use property (where the deduction is available) to the extent that (1) the casualty loss exceeds $100 ("$100 floor"), and (2) all of individual's casualty losses for the tax year exceed 10% of adjusted gross income (AGI) for the year ("10%-of-AGI limit"). (Code

---

32. ¶M-2136; ¶1654.304
33. ¶M-1601;¶1654.300 et seq.
34. ¶M-1701; ¶1654.301
35. ¶M-1900A; ¶1654.300

36. ¶M-1801 et seq.; ¶1654.304
37. ¶M-1802; ¶1654.304
38. ¶M-1809; ¶1654.304
39. ¶M-1815; ¶1654.304

Sec. 165(h))[40]

The casualty loss deduction isn't allowed to the extent the loss is compensated by insurance or otherwise. (Code Sec. 165(a))[41]

¶ 1784 When to deduct casualty losses.

A casualty loss (where deductible, see ¶1783) is considered "sustained" only during the tax year the loss occurs, as fixed by identifiable events occurring in that year. (Code Sec. 165(a); Reg § 1.165-1(d)(1)) A loss may be sustained in the tax year even though repairs or replacements aren't made until a later year. And a loss may be sustained in a year *after* the casualty occurs. [42] For the election to deduct disaster losses early, see ¶1785.

¶ 1785 Early deduction election for disaster losses.

A taxpayer may *elect* to deduct a disaster loss for the tax year *before* the year the loss occurred, instead of for the year the loss occurred (¶1784). (Code Sec. 165(i))[43]

A *disaster loss* is an otherwise deductible loss from a disaster occurring in a Federally declared disaster area. (Code Sec. 165(i)(1), Reg § 1.165-11T(b)(3))[44] A non-casualty loss may be a disaster loss if incurred in the course of a trade or business or profit-seeking transaction. For casualty losses, any other limitations (e.g., the regular $100 floor for personal use property described at ¶1783) continue to apply. (Code Sec. 165(i))[45]

Election. A taxpayer must generally elect to deduct a disaster loss by filing a return, an amended return, or a refund claim within six months after the due date for filing the taxpayer's federal income tax return for the year of the disaster (determined without regard to any extension of time to file). (Reg § 1.165-11T(f)) The election may be revoked on or before the date that is 90 days after the due date for making the election. (Reg § 1.165-11T(g)) A taxpayer can use Form 4684, Schedule D to make an election (or revoke a prior election) to deduct a loss attributable to a Federally declared disaster in the tax year immediately before the disaster year. [46]

¶ 1786 Losses on deposits in insolvent financial institutions—Form 4684.

Losses on deposits in insolvent financial institutions are nonbusiness bad debts, deductible as short-term capital loss when the deposit becomes worthless. In years before 2018, a taxpayer could have benefitted from electing, on Form 4684, to treat these losses as casualty losses (¶1782) or, subject to certain limits, as an ordinary loss (Code Sec. 165(l)), which is a miscellaneous itemized deduction. However, from 2018 to 2025, personal casualty losses (other than those attributable to a Federally declared disaster) and miscellaneous itemized deductions subject to the 2%-of-AGI floor (¶3109) are suspended. [47]

¶ 1787 Theft losses—Form 4684.

Theft losses (reported on Form 4684) are deductible under rules that closely follow those for casualty losses, including the $100/10%-of-AGI floors and the limitation allowing casualty losses to be claimed in 2018 through 2025 only when attributable to a Federally declared disaster (¶1783). (Code Sec. 165(a), Code Sec. 165(h)(1), Code Sec. 165(h)(2))[48] A theft is the unlawful taking and removing of money or property with the intent to deprive

---

40. ¶M-1900 *et seq.*; ¶1654.304
41. ¶M-1408, M-1411, M-1421; ¶1654.304
42. ¶M-1610; ¶1654.111
43. ¶M-2001; ¶1654.520
44. ¶M-2002; ¶1654.520

45. ¶M-2009; ¶1654.304
46. ¶M-2011 *et seq.*; ¶1654.520
47. ¶M-1761, M-1762, M-1765, M-1766; ¶1654.530
48. ¶M-2125

the owner of it, and includes larceny, robbery, embezzlement, burglary, extortion, kidnapping for ransom, blackmail and false representation. (Reg § 1.165-8(d))[49] For determining the amount of a theft loss, see ¶1788.

A theft loss deduction is not allowed for the decline in market value of stock purchased on the open market, where the decline is caused by the disclosure of accounting fraud or other illegal conduct on the part of officers or directors of the corporation that issued the stock.[50]

A taking by a person known to have a claim to the property (e.g., spouse, joint owner) isn't a theft unless there is evidence of criminal intent. [1]

¶ 1788 Amount of theft loss.

For theft of business or investment property, the amount of the *deductible loss* is the adjusted basis of the property minus insurance or other compensation received or recoverable. (Reg § 1.165-8(c))[2]

For theft of personal-use property (the deduction for which is limited from 2018 to 2025 to losses attributable to a Federally declared disaster, see ¶1787), the amount of the *loss* is (1) the lesser of the property's fair market value (FMV) immediately before theft or its adjusted basis, reduced by (2) insurance or other compensation received or recoverable. (Reg § 1.165-8(c)) The $100/10%-of-AGI floors (¶1783) are then applied to determine the amount of the loss that is *deductible*. (Code Sec. 165(c)(3))[3]

If stolen personal-use property is recovered in the deduction year, the amount of the loss is the lesser of (1) the property's adjusted basis, or (2) the decline in its FMV between theft and recovery.[4]

¶ 1789 When to deduct theft loss.

A theft loss (¶1787) is deductible in the year the loss is *discovered,* regardless of when the theft actually occurred. (Code Sec. 165(e)) But the deduction is postponed to the extent the taxpayer, in the year of discovery, had a reimbursement claim on which there was a reasonable prospect of recovery. (Reg § 1.165-8(a))[5]

¶ 1790 At-Risk Limitations. ▪▪▪▪▪▪▪▪▪▪

The "at risk" rules apply to individuals and closely held corporations (¶1791). They limit the deductibility of a loss from an activity (¶1792) to the amount for which the taxpayer is "at risk."(¶1794).

¶ 1791 Taxpayers subject to "at-risk" rules.

The at-risk rules (¶1793) apply to individuals, closely-held C corporations (more than 50% of the value of the corporation's stock is owned by five or fewer individuals at any time during the last half of its tax year) (Code Sec. 465(a)(1)), and estates and trusts. [6] The at-risk rules *don't apply* to C corporations that: (i) are not personal holding companies or personal service corporations (determined by substituting 5% for 10% in Code Sec. 269A(b)(2)); and (ii) are engaged in qualifying active businesses. (Code Sec. 465(c)(7)) The at-risk rules also do not apply to closely-held C corporations engaged in equipment leasing (Code Sec. 465(c)(4)).[7] Although the at-risk rules do not apply to S corporations and

---

49. ¶M-2100 et seq.; ¶1654.351 et seq.
50. ¶M-2111; ¶1654.351
1. ¶M-2104
2. ¶M-2125; ¶1654.370
3. ¶M-2126; ¶1654.370

4. ¶M-2129
5. ¶M-2132; ¶1654.380
6. ¶M-4511, M-4512, M-4515; ¶4654
7. ¶M-4516 *et seq.*; ¶4654

partnerships, they do apply to S corporation shareholders and partners in partnerships.

¶ 1792 "At-risk" activities.

The at-risk rules (¶1793) apply to certain specified activities such as: (i) holding, producing or distributing motion pictures or video tapes; (ii) farming; (iii) equipment leasing; (iv) exploring for, or exploiting, oil and gas resources; or (v) exploring for, or exploiting, geothermal resources; (Code Sec. 465(c)(1)), and a "catch-all" group of activities engaged in by the taxpayer in carrying on a trade or business or in the production of income, other than those specified above (e.g., real estate activities, ¶1796). (Code Sec. 465(c)(3))[8]

Specified activities and those in the catch-all group are subject to different aggregation rules. (Code Sec. 465(c)(3)(B))[9]

¶ 1793 How the at-risk rules work—Form 6198.

For a taxpayer (¶1791) engaged in an at-risk activity (¶1792), any loss from the activity for the tax year is deductible in that year only to the extent that taxpayer is at risk (¶1794) with respect to the activity at the end of the year. (Code Sec. 465(a)) The losses so limited are the excess of the deductions allocable to the activity that otherwise would be allowed for the year, over the income (other than recapture, ¶1795) received or accrued by taxpayer during the year from that same activity. (Code Sec. 465(d))[10]

Any loss thus disallowed is treated as allocable to the same activity in the next tax year, and may be deducted in the later year subject to that year's at-risk limit for the activity. (Code Sec. 465(a)(2)) So, a current year's "loss" may include "suspended" loss accounts from earlier years. (Code Sec. 465(d))[11]

caution: In addition to the at-risk rules, losses and credits from an activity may also be subject to the passive activity rules, discussed at ¶1797 *et seq.*

Form 6198 is used to compute the deductible loss from an at-risk activity. [12]

For the at-risk rules otherwise applicable to real property, see ¶1796.

¶ 1794 Amounts considered "at risk."

A taxpayer is considered at risk for an activity to the extent of:

(1) the amount of money and the adjusted basis of other property the taxpayer contributed to the activity (Code Sec. 465(b)(1)), plus

(2) amounts borrowed with respect to the activity to the extent the taxpayer is personally liable for the repayment of or has pledged property, other than property used in the activity, as security for the borrowed amount. The borrowings can't exceed the fair market value of the taxpayer's interest in the pledged property. No property is treated as security if it is directly or indirectly financed by indebtedness secured by property in (1), above. (Code Sec. 465(b)(1), Code Sec. 465(b)(2))[13]

The taxpayer's amount at risk isn't increased for amounts borrowed from a person who has a non-creditor interest in the activity or from a person considered "related" to such interested parties. (Code Sec. 465(b)(3))[14]

But amounts protected against loss by nonrecourse financing, guarantees, stop loss agreements, or other similar arrangements are not at risk. (Code Sec. 465(b)(4))[15]

---

8. ¶M-4521; ¶4654
9. ¶M-4522 *et seq.*; ¶4654
10. ¶M-4502; ¶4654
11. ¶M-4502; ¶4564
12. ¶M-4501; ¶4654
13. ¶M-4541 *et seq.*; ¶4654
14. ¶M-4557 *et seq.*; ¶4654
15. ¶M-4568 *et seq.*; ¶4654

In determining the amount at risk for any tax year, the amount for that year is reduced by any losses allowed under these limitations in an earlier year. (Code Sec. 465(b)(5))[16]

¶ 1795 Recapture of losses where amount at risk is less than zero.

If a taxpayer's amount at risk (¶1794) is less than zero (e.g., due to distributions to the taxpayer or by debt changing from recourse to nonrecourse), the taxpayer recognizes income to the extent of that negative amount. (Code Sec. 465(e)(1)(A)) But, the amount recaptured is limited to the excess of the losses previously allowed in that activity over any amounts previously recaptured. (Code Sec. 465(e)(2)) The amount added to income under this recapture rule is treated as a deduction allocable to the activity in the first succeeding year, and is allowed if and to the extent the taxpayer's at-risk basis is increased. (Code Sec. 465(e)(1)(B))[17]

¶ 1796 At-risk rules for real property.

A taxpayer engaged in holding real property is subject to the at-risk rules for losses on property placed in service after '86. The at-risk rules also apply to a taxpayer's losses from real estate attributable to an interest in a pass-through entity that is acquired after '86, without regard to when the entity placed the real property in service. [18]

A taxpayer is considered at risk for his share of any "qualified nonrecourse financing" secured by the real property. (Code Sec. 465(b)(6); Reg § 1.465-27(b))[19]

¶ 1797 "Passive Activity" Losses and Credits.

Losses and credits from passive activities (¶1798) may only be used to offset passive activity income (¶1802); thus, they can't be used to offset income from, for example, compensation, interest or dividends. Any losses or credits that are unused in a tax year because of this rule are carried forward until used (¶1798), or until the taxpayer disposes of the interest (¶1814).

Although real estate activities are generally subject to the passive activity loss rules, individuals who actively participate in rental real estate activities may use up to $25,000 of losses from those activities to offset nonpassive income; and rental real estate activities are not treated as a passive activity for real estate professionals who materially participate in the activity (¶1811 *et seq.*).

¶ 1798 Disallowance of passive activity losses and credits—Form 8582; Form 8582-CR; Form 8810

Generally, a taxpayer subject to the passive activity loss rules (¶1799) cannot currently deduct a "passive activity loss" or use a "passive activity credit" (both defined at ¶1800). (Code Sec. 469(a)(1); Reg § 1.469-1T(a)(2))[20]

Carryover loss or credit. The disallowed (or suspended) passive activity losses and passive activity credits are carried over and are allocated among the taxpayer's activities for the following year in a way that reasonably reflects the extent to which each activity continues the loss activity. (Code Sec. 469(b); Reg § 1.469-1(f)(4)(i))[21] Suspended passive activity losses are allowed in full on a taxable disposition of the activity (¶1814).

A *passive activity* is an activity that involves the conduct of a trade or business in which the taxpayer does not materially participate (¶1806). Any rental activity (other than a rental real estate activity of a real estate professional) is passive, regardless of whether the

16. ¶M-4507; ¶4654
17. ¶M-4509; ¶4654
18. ¶M-4533

19. ¶M-4534 *et seq.*; ¶4654
20. ¶M-4600 *et seq.*; ¶4694
21. ¶M-5504, ¶M-5604; ¶4694.45

taxpayer materially participates. (¶1810).

A trade or business includes any activity connected with a trade or business for which expenses are allowable as a deduction under Code Sec. 212, or which involves research or experimental expenditures deductible under Code Sec. 174. (Code Sec. 469(c)(5); Code Sec. 469(c)(6))[22]

Whether a loss is disallowed under these rules is determined *after* the application of the at-risk rules (¶1790 *et seq.*) and the partner (¶3729) and S corporation shareholder (¶3369) basis limitation rules. (Reg § 1.469-2T(d))[23]

The passive activity limits are calculated on Form 8582 (for individuals, estates, and trusts); Form 8582-CR (credits for individuals, estates, and trusts); or Form 8810 (closely held corporations and personal service corporations).

For passive activity losses for alternative minimum tax purposes, see ¶3211.

¶ 1799   Who is subject to the passive activity rules?

The passive activity limits (¶1798) apply to any individual, estate, trust (other than a grantor trust), a personal service corporation (PSC) as specially defined, and a closely held C corporation (subject to special rules). (Code Sec. 469(a)(2), Code Sec. 469(j), Reg § 1.469-1T(b)(2))[24]

Partnerships (unless publicly traded) and S corporations aren't subject to the passive activity rules (¶1798). (Code Sec. 469(a)(2)) But the rules *do* apply to the losses and credits passed through to the partners and shareholders. [25]

Spouses filing a joint return are treated as one taxpayer, with certain exceptions. (Reg § 1.469-1T(j)(1))[26]

¶ 1800   Passive activity loss and credits defined.

A *passive activity loss* for a tax year is the amount by which the aggregate losses from all passive activities (¶1798) for the tax year exceed the aggregate income from all passive activities for that year. (Code Sec. 469(d)(1); Reg § 1.469-2T(b)(1))[27]

For a closely held C corporation, the passive activity loss is determined as above except the loss is further reduced by the corporation's net active income. (Code Sec. 469(e)(2)(A); Reg § 1.469-1T(g)(4))[28]

A *passive activity credit* is the excess of specified credits attributable to passive activities over the regular tax liability allocable to those activities. (Reg § 1.469-3T(a)) The credits subject to the passive activity loss rules include general business credits, alternative motor vehicle credits, and credits for new qualified plug-in electric vehicles. (Code Sec. 469(d)(2)(A))[29]

¶ 1801   Passive activity deductions; loss on disposition.

Any loss recognized on the sale, exchange, or other disposition of an interest in property used in an activity at the time of disposition, or of an interest in an activity held through a pass-through entity, is a passive activity deduction if the activity is a passive activity (¶1798) of the taxpayer for the tax year of the disposition. Any deduction allowed on account of the abandonment or worthlessness of an interest in property or in an activity is treated as a deduction from the activity if the activity is a passive activity of the taxpayer

---

22. ¶M-4802; ¶4694.02
23. ¶M-4603 *et seq.*; ¶4694.30, 4694.31, 4694.47
24. ¶M-4700 *et seq.*; ¶4694
25. ¶s M-4709, M-5302; ¶4694.80

26. ¶M-4702; ¶4694.70
27. ¶M-4601; ¶4694
28. ¶M-5507 *et seq.*; ¶4694.36
29. ¶M-5600 *et seq.*; ¶4694.35

for the tax year of the disposition. (Reg § 1.469-2T(d)(5)(i))[30]

If the interest in property disposed of was used in more than one activity during the 12-month period ending on the date of disposition, the amount realized from the disposition (as well as the adjusted basis of the interest) must be allocated among the activities (with a de minimis exception) on a basis that reasonably reflects those uses. (Reg § 1.469-2T(d)(5)(ii). A partnership interest or S corporation stock is not property used in an activity for purposes of the above rule. (Reg § 1.469-2T(d)(5)(ii))[31]

¶ 1802   Passive activity gross income.

Passive activity gross income is, in general, gross income from a passive activity (¶1798). (Reg § 1.469-2T(c)(1))[32]

The character of a partner's or S corporation shareholder's allocable items of gross income as passive activity gross income is determined, in general, by reference to the partner's or shareholder's participation in the activities that generated the items for the entity's tax year. (Reg § 1.469-2T(e)(1))[33] Passive activity gross income doesn't include portfolio income (e.g., interest, dividends, annuities, or royalties not derived in the ordinary course of a trade or business) (Code Sec. 469(e)(1)(A)(i)(I); Reg § 1.469-2T(c)(3)(i)), compensation for personal services (as specially defined) (Code Sec. 469(e)(3); Reg § 1.469-2T(c)(4)), certain income from intangible property if a taxpayer's personal efforts contributed significantly to the property's creation, a tax refund, or reimbursement of a casualty or theft loss (Reg § 1.469-2T(c)(7)), and certain income from oil and gas properties (Code Sec. 469(c)(3)(B); Reg § 1.469-2(c)(6)).[34]

For when gain on the disposition of a property interest is passive activity gross income, see ¶1803.

¶ 1803   Gain on dispositions in a passive activity—substantially appreciated property exception.

Generally, any gain recognized on the sale, exchange, or other disposition of an interest in property used in a passive activity at the time of disposition, or of an interest in a passive activity held through a pass-through entity, is passive activity gross income (¶1802) for the tax year in which the gain is recognized. Reg § 1.469-2T(c)(2)(i)(A))[35]

Exception for substantially appreciated property. Gain from the disposition of an interest in property that is substantially appreciated (fair market value exceeds 120% of adjusted basis) is not treated as gain from a passive activity unless used in a passive activity for either: (i) 20% of the period the taxpayer held the interest, or (ii) the entire 24-month period ending on the date of disposition. (Reg § 1.469-2(c)(2)(iii))[36] This substantially appreciated property exception, however, does not apply to dispositions of partnership interests or of S corporation stock. Regs provide special rules for disposition of interests in pass-through entities. (Reg § 1.469-2T(e)(3)(ii)(A), Reg § 1.469-2T(e)(3)(iii))[37]

For disposition of an *entire* interest in (or substantially all of) a passive activity, see ¶1814.

¶ 1804   Recharacterization of passive income as nonpassive income.

Regs minimize opportunities for taxpayers to create passive income that can be used to offset passive losses by recharacterizing passive income as nonpassive income in various

---

30. ¶M-5406; ¶4694.32
31. ¶M-5406; ¶4694.32
32. ¶M-5301; ¶4694.21
33. ¶M-5302; ¶4694.80

34. ¶M-5325, ¶M-5332 *et seq.*; ¶4694.22; ¶4694.66
35. ¶M-5304; ¶4694.28
36. ¶M-5306; ¶4694.28
37. ¶M-5708, ¶M-5343; ¶4694.82

situations. Income from the following passive activities isn't treated as income from a passive activity: (i) income from significant participation activities (i.e., activities in which the taxpayer participates for more than 100 hours during the tax year, but doesn't materially participate (defined at ¶1806 *et seq.*); (ii) income from rental of nondepreciable property; (iii) net interest income from an equity-financed lending activity or certain rental property; and (iv) certain royalty income. (Reg § 1.469-2T(f))[38]

¶ 1805   Rules for grouping passive activities.

Taxpayers can group their trade or business activities (¶1798) and rental activities (¶1810) for purposes of the passive activity loss and credit limitation rules as a single activity if the activities are an appropriate economic unit for measuring gain or loss for purposes of the passive activity rules based on all the relevant facts and circumstances. (Reg § 1.469-4(c); Reg § 1.469-4(a))[39]

A rental activity (¶1810) can't be grouped with a trade or business activity unless the activities being grouped together are an appropriate economic unit *and*

... the rental activity is insubstantial in relation to the trade or business activity;

... the trade or business activity is insubstantial in relation to the rental activity; or

... each owner of the trade or business activity has the same proportionate ownership interest in the rental activity. In that case, the part of the rental activity that involves the rental of items of property for use in the trade or business may be grouped with the trade or business activity. (Reg § 1.469-4(b)(2); Reg § 1.469-4(d)(1))[40]

Real property rentals and personal property rentals (other than personal property rentals provided in connection with the real property, or vice versa) can't be grouped together. (Reg § 1.469-4(d)(2))[41]

Once the taxpayer has grouped activities, the taxpayer can't regroup them in later years. However, if a material change occurs that makes the original grouping clearly inappropriate, the taxpayer must regroup the activities. IRS may regroup activities to prevent tax avoidance. (Reg § 1.469-4(e), Reg § 1.469-4(f))[42] Taxpayers must report to IRS their groupings and regroupings of activities and the addition of specific activities within their existing groupings. (Reg § 1.469-4(e)(1))[43]

In a year when there is a disposition of substantially all of an activity, the taxpayer may under specified conditions treat the part disposed of as a separate activity. (Reg § 1.469-4(g))[44]

¶ 1806   What is "material participation" under passive activity loss rules?

A taxpayer materially participates in an activity only if he or she is involved in the activity's operations on a regular, continuous and substantial basis (¶1807 *et seq.*). (Code Sec. 469(h)) A trust materially participates in an activity if a fiduciary, in his or her capacity as such, so participates. A closely held C corporation or personal service corporation materially participates, in general, only if one or more of its shareholders who own more than 50% of its stock (by value) themselves materially participate. (Code Sec. 469(h)(4))[45]

---

38. ¶M-5335; ¶4694.25
39. ¶M-4803, M-4804, M-4807.2; ¶4694.10
40. ¶M-4805; ¶4694.10
41. ¶M-4806; ¶4694.10

42. ¶M-4809; ¶4694.10
43. ¶M-4808.1
44. ¶M-5701.3; ¶4694.50 *et seq.*
45. ¶M-4901 *et seq.*, ¶M-5005, ¶M-5006; ¶4694.06

¶ 1807 Material participation and participation by individuals under passive activity loss rules.

An individual taxpayer materially participates in an activity for a tax year if the taxpayer (or his spouse, whether or not they file jointly) meets one of seven material participation tests:

(1) The individual participates (see below) in the activity for more than 500 hours during the year. (Reg § 1.469-5T(a)(1))

(2) The individual's participation in the activity for the tax year constitutes substantially all of the participation in the activity for the tax year by all individuals (including non-owners). (Reg § 1.469-5T(a)(2))

(3) The individual participates in the activity for more than 100 hours during the tax year and that participation isn't less than the participation in the activity of any other individual (including non-owners) for that year. (Reg § 1.469-5T(a)(3))

(4) The activity is a "significant participation activity" for the tax year, and the individual's aggregate participation in all significant participation activities that year exceeds 500 hours. A "significant participation activity" is a trade or business (¶1798) in which the individual significantly participates (for more than 100 hours), but in which he doesn't otherwise materially participate. (Reg § 1.469-5T(a)(4), Reg § 1.469-5T(c))

(5) The individual materially participated in the activity for any five tax years (consecutive or not) during the 10 immediately preceding tax years. (Reg § 1.469-5T(a)(5))

(6) The activity is a personal service activity, and the individual materially participated in the activity for any three tax years (consecutive or not) before the tax year. (Reg § 1.469-5T(a)(6), Reg § 1.469-5T(d))

(7) The individual meets a facts and circumstances test (¶1808). (Reg § 1.469-5T(a)(7))[46]

Participation means any work done by an individual in connection with an activity in which he owns an interest at the time the work is done, regardless of the capacity in which he does the work. (Reg § 1.469-5(f)(1))[47] However, work done in connection with an activity is disregarded if the work is not of a type that is customarily done by an owner of that type of activity, and one of the principal purposes for the performance of the work is to avoid the passive loss/credit restrictions. (Reg § 1.469-5T(f)(2))[48]

¶ 1808 Facts and circumstances test for material participation under passive activity loss rules.

For purposes of the passive activity loss rules, an individual materially participates (¶1807) in an activity if he participates on a regular, continuous and substantial basis during the year, based on all the facts and circumstances. (Reg § 1.469-5T(a)(7)) An individual who participates in the activity for 100 hours or less during the year doesn't meet this test. (Reg § 1.469-5T(b)(2)(iii))[49]

¶ 1809 Limited partner's material participation under passive activity loss rules.

For purposes of the passive activity loss rules, an individual limited partner is not treated as materially participating (¶1807) in any activity of a limited partnership with respect to his or her interest in that partnership (or to any gain or loss from the activity recognized on a sale or exchange of that interest) *unless* the individual would be treated as

---

46. ¶M-4901 *et seq.*; ¶4694.06
47. ¶M-4902; ¶4694.06
48. ¶M-4903; ¶4694.06
49. ¶M-4912; ¶4694.06

materially participating under the 500-hour, five-tax-years-out-of-ten, or three-year-personal-service-activity tests at ¶1807 (items (1), (5) or (6), respectively), if he or she weren't a limited partner. (Code Sec. 469(h)(2); Reg § 1.469-5T(e)(2))[50] This rule does not apply if the individual owning the limited partner interest is also the general partner. (Reg § 1.469-5T(e)(3)(ii))[1]

¶ 1810   Rental activities as passive activities.

For purposes of the passive activity loss rules, generally, rental activities are treated as passive activities. (Code Sec. 469(c)(2)) This general rule, however, does not apply to individuals who actively participate in rental real estate activities (¶1811) and to certain real estate professionals (¶1813).[2] In addition, under the self-rental rule, taxpayers are prohibited from using net income from the rental of property to offset other passive losses if the property is rented for use in a trade or business in which the taxpayer materially participates. (Reg § 1.469-2(f)(6))[3]

A rental activity is any activity where payments are principally for the use of tangible property (Code Sec. 160(j)(8)), without regard to whether a lease, service contract, or other arrangement is involved. (Reg § 1.469-1T(e)(3)(i)(B)) But, a rental activity doesn't include an activity involving the use of tangible property if:

(1) The average period the customer uses the property is 7 days or less (Reg § 1.469-1T(e)(3)(ii)(A)), or 30 days or less *and* the owner (or someone on the owner's behalf) provides significant personal services (as defined in the regs). (Reg § 1.469-1T(e)(3)(ii)(B))

(2) The owner (or someone on the owner's behalf) provides extraordinary personal services (as defined in the regs), without regard to the average period the customer uses the property. (Reg § 1.469-1T(e)(3)(ii)(C))

(3) The rental of the tangible property is incidental to a nonrental activity of the taxpayer (Reg § 1.469-1T(e)(3)(ii)(D)) (as measured by certain percentage and other tests). (Reg § 1.469-1T(e)(3)(vi))

(4) The taxpayer customarily makes the property available during defined business hours for nonexclusive use by various customers (e.g., a golf course). (Reg § 1.469-1T(e)(3)(ii)(E))

(5) The property is provided for use in an activity conducted by a partnership, S corporation, or joint venture in which the taxpayer owns an interest. (Reg § 1.469-1T(e)(3)(ii)(F))[4]

¶ 1811   Individuals' active participation rental real estate losses up to $25,000 may be used against nonpassive income.

An individual who (1) has at least a 10% interest (by value) in any rental real estate activity (including any interest held by a spouse), and (2) otherwise "actively participates" in that activity (¶1812), may offset up to $25,000 of nonpassive income ($25,000 offset) with that portion of the passive activity loss, or of the deduction equivalent of the passive activity credit, attributable to that activity. (Code Sec. 469(i)(1), Code Sec. 469(i)(2), Code Sec. 469(i)(6)(A), Code Sec. 469(j)(5))[5]

For a married person filing a separate return, the allowance is $12,500 if he or she lives apart from his spouse at all times during the tax year. (Code Sec. 469(i)(5)(A)(i)) The $12,500 allowance doesn't apply to a married person filing a separate return but not living

---

50. ¶M-5003 *et seq.*; ¶4694.06
1. ¶M-5002.1; ¶4694.06
2. ¶M-5100 *et seq.*; ¶4694.60 *et seq.*

3. ¶M-5341; ¶4694.25
4. ¶M-5101 *et seq.*; ¶4694.03
5. ¶M-5131, ¶M-5139; ¶4694.60

apart from his or her spouse at all times during the tax year. (Code Sec. 469(i)(5)(B))[6]

The $25,000 allowance ($12,500 for marrieds filing separately) is reduced (but not below zero) by 50% of the amount by which taxpayer's adjusted gross income (AGI) as specially computed exceeds (1) $100,000 ($50,000 for marrieds filing separately), or (2) $200,000 ($100,000 for marrieds filing separately) in the case of rehabilitation investment credits (¶2307). There's no AGI-based phaseout of the $25,000 ($12,500) offset for low-income housing credits (¶2320). (Code Sec. 469(i)(3), Code Sec. 469(i)(5))[7]

¶ 1812   What is "active participation" for purposes of the $25,000 offset?

To actively participate in a rental real estate activity for purposes of the $25,000 offset (¶1811), a taxpayer must participate (¶1807) in the activity in a significant and bona fide sense. A taxpayer participates if he or she makes management decisions, e.g., approves new tenants, decides on rental terms, approves capital or repair expenditures or arranges for others to provide services (such as repairs). The taxpayer need not have regular, continuous and substantial involvement in operations. But, a merely formal and nominal participation in management, without a genuine exercise of independent discretion and judgment, is insufficient.[8] The active participation test is less stringent than the material participation requirement (¶1806). Active participation isn't required to take low-income housing (¶2320) or rehabilitation investment (¶2307) credits. (Code Sec. 469(i)(6)(B))[9]

The participation of a taxpayer's spouse is taken into account in determining whether the taxpayer actively participates. (Code Sec. 469(i)(6)(D))[10]

A taxpayer isn't treated as actively participating (except as regs may provide) with respect to any interest as a limited partner. (Code Sec. 469(i)(6)(C))[11]

¶ 1813   Rental real estate activities of real estate professionals not treated as automatically passive.

Although rental real estate activities generally are subject to the passive activity loss limitations (¶1798), real estate professionals who materially participate in a rental real estate activity are not subject to the passive activity loss rules (¶1806). (Code Sec. 469(c)(7)(A)(i)) (Reg § 1.469-9(e)(1))[12]

A taxpayer qualifies as a real estate professional for a particular tax year if (1) more than half of the personal services (defined below) the taxpayer performs during that year are performed in real property trades or businesses (defined below) in which the taxpayer materially participates, and (2) the taxpayer performs more than 750 hours of services during that year in real property trades or businesses in which he materially participates. (Reg § 1.469-9(b)(6), Code Sec. 469(c)(7)(B))[13] The activities of spouses can't be combined in determining real estate professional status. (Code Sec. 469(c)(7)(B); Reg § 1.469-9(c)(4))[14]

In determining whether a taxpayer is a real estate professional, each interest in the rental real estate is treated as a separate activity, unless the taxpayer elects (by filing a specified statement with his original income tax return) to treat all interests in rental real estate as one activity. (Code Sec. 469(c)(7)(A); Reg § 1.469-9(g)) The election is binding for the tax year it's made and for all future years in which the taxpayer qualifies.[15]

A closely-held C corporation qualifies as a real estate professional if more than 50% of its

6. ¶M-5131; ¶4694.60
7. ¶M-5142 *et seq.*; ¶4694.60
8. ¶M-5138; ¶4694.60
9. ¶L-12702,¶M-5141; ¶4694.60
10. ¶M-5138; ¶4694.70

11. ¶M-5140; ¶4694.60
12. ¶M-5161; ¶4694.63
13. ¶M-5168; ¶4694.63
14. ¶M-5171; ¶4694.63
15. ¶M-5163 *et seq.*, ¶S-4827.2; ¶4694.63

gross receipts for the tax year are derived from real property trades or businesses in which it materially participates. (Code Sec. 469(c)(7)(D)(i))[16] The Tax Court has held that a trust may qualify as a real estate professional. [17]

Personal services means any work performed by an individual in connection with a trade or business, but not as an investor. (Reg § 1.469-9(b)(4)) Services performed as an employee don't count, unless the individual is a more-than-5%-owner of the employer. (Code Sec. 469(c)(7)(D)(ii))[18]

A real property trade or business is any real property development, redevelopment, construction, reconstruction, acquisition, conversion, rental, operation, management, leasing or brokerage trade or business. (Code Sec. 469(c)(7)(C)) The determination of a taxpayer's real property trades or businesses is based on all relevant facts and circumstances. (Reg § 1.469-9(d)(1))[19]

¶ 1814 Disposition of entire interest or substantially all of the passive activity.

Suspended passive activity losses (¶1798) are deductible in full in the year in which the taxpayer disposes of the taxpayer's entire interest in the passive activity to an unrelated party, in a fully taxable transaction (i.e., a transaction in which all gain or loss on the disposition is recognized). (Code Sec. 469(g)(1))[20]

A taxpayer who disposes of "substantially all" of an activity can deduct the losses associated with the disposed portion. (Reg § 1.469-4(g))[21]

If a taxpayer disposes of an entire interest in a passive activity under the installment method, suspended passive activity losses that exceed the gain are recognized over the term of the installment obligation as the gain on the sale is recognized. (Code Sec. 469(g)(3))[22]

Unlike passive activity losses, unused credits are not allowed on disposition of the activity (Code Sec. 469(g)(1)(A)), but the taxpayer may elect to increase basis of property immediately before the transfer by the amount of unused passive credits that previously reduced the property's basis. (Code Sec. 469(j)(9)).[23]

Special rules apply where the interest in the activity is transferred by reason of death (Code Sec. 469(g)(2)), or where the disposition is by gift. (Code Sec. 469(j)(6))[24]

¶ 1815 Net Operating Losses (NOLs). ████████████████████

An NOL (¶1816) sustained in one year may be used to reduce the taxable income for another year. For losses arising in tax years beginning after 2017, the NOL deduction is limited to 80% of taxable income (¶1817). NOLs arising in tax years ending after 2017 can be carried forward indefinitely, but cannot be carried back (with limited exceptions). NOLs arising in tax years ending before 2018 could generally be carried back two years and forward 20 years, but longer carryback periods applied in some cases. (¶1818) A taxpayer entitled to an NOL carryback can elect not to use it (¶1819).

¶ 1816 Net operating loss (NOL) defined.

An NOL for any tax year is the amount by which the taxpayer's business deductions exceed its gross income, computed without taking into account any NOL carried over from

---

16. ¶M-5172; ¶4694.63
17. ¶M-5168
18. ¶M-5169, M-5170 *et seq.*; ¶4694.63
19. ¶M-5175; ¶4694.63
20. ¶M-5701, ¶M-5704; ¶4694.50

21. ¶s M-5701, M-5701.3; ¶4694.50
22. ¶M-5701.2; ¶4694.50
23. ¶M-5701, ¶M-5703; ¶4694.44, ¶4694.50
24. ¶M-5705 *et seq.*; ¶4694.50

another tax year. (Code Sec. 172(c); Code Sec. 172(d)(1))[25]

¶ 1817   Amount of net operating loss (NOL) deduction; who can use.

The NOL deduction in any tax year is equal to the lesser of:

. . . the aggregate of the NOL carryovers to that year, plus the NOL carrybacks to that year; or

. . . 80% of taxable income, computed without regard to the NOL deduction. (Code Sec. 172(a))

For refunds based on NOL carrybacks, see ¶4853.

An NOL deduction is allowed to individuals, corporations (Code Sec. 172), estates and trusts (Code Sec. 642(d)), and charitable organizations with respect to the unrelated business income tax. (Code Sec. 512(b)(6))

An NOL deduction isn't allowed to partnerships, common trust funds, but the deduction is allowed to the partners and beneficiaries. (Code Sec. 703(a)(2)(D); Code Sec. 584(g)) An NOL deduction isn't allowed to regulated investment companies (Code Sec. 852(b)(2)(B)), or S corporations, but losses are passed through to shareholders. (Code Sec. 1366(a))[26]

For losses arising in tax years beginning before Jan. 1, 2018, the NOL deduction was not limited to 80% of taxable income. Rather, the NOL deduction in any year was equal to the aggregate of the NOL carryovers to the tax year plus the NOL carrybacks to the tax year. [27]

¶ 1818   Net operating loss (NOL) carryover and carryback periods.

For NOLs arising in tax years *ending* after Dec. 31, 2017, NOLs may be carried forward indefinitely, but may not be carried back. However, farming losses may be carried back two years (and carried forward indefinitely). A "farming loss" is the lesser of: (1) the amount that would be the NOL for the tax year taking into account only income and deductions attributable to farming businesses, or (2) the NOL for that tax year. A "farming business" is defined as in Code Sec. 263A(e)(4) for purposes of the uniform capitalization rules (¶4521). In addition, property and casualty insurance companies get a 2-year carryback and 20-year carryforward. (Code Sec. 172(b)(1))[28]

For NOLs arising in tax years ending before 2018, except as noted below (or where a taxpayer elects to forgo a carryback, ¶1819), an NOL could be carried back two years and forward 20 years. [29] A decedent's NOL could be carried back, but not forward. [30]

A 3-year carryback period applied to the following:

. . . NOLs arising from property losses of individuals due to fire, storm, shipwreck, or other casualty, or from theft.

. . . For a small business, or a taxpayer engaged in the trade or business of farming, NOLs attributable to Federally declared disasters (¶1785). A small business is one whose average annual gross receipts under Code Sec. 448(c) are $5 million or less. [31]

In the case of a taxpayer that had a farming loss (as defined in Code Sec. 172(i)) for a tax year, the farming loss could be carried back five years. [32]

An NOL attributable to product liability losses, losses attributable to certain deferred statutory liabilities (e.g., environmental remediation and workers compensation), and/or Gulf Opportunity Zone public utility casualty losses (specified liability losses or SLLs)

25. ¶M-4001 *et seq.*; ¶1724
26. ¶M-4003; ¶1724.02
27. ¶M-4401; ¶1724.01
28. ¶M-4301 *et seq.*; ¶1724.30

29. ¶M-4300; ¶1724.31
30. ¶M-4004; ¶1724.02
31. ¶M-4307, M-4308; ¶1724.434, 1724.436
32. ¶M-4311; ¶1724.437

could be carried back 10 years.

¶ 1819   Election to forgo net operating loss (NOL) carryback.

Where an NOL carryback is available (¶1818), a taxpayer may elect not to use the carryback period and instead only carry over the NOL for the allowed carryforward period. Once the election is made for any tax year (on a statement attached to the return or amended return), it is irrevocable for that year. (Code Sec. 172(b)(3)) The election also applies to alternative minimum tax NOLs (ATNOLs, ¶3208).[33]

¶ 1820   Computing the net operating loss (NOL) for noncorporate taxpayers.

A noncorporate taxpayer has an NOL in a tax year if allowable deductions exceed gross income. In arriving at the NOL for the year, carryback (where available; ¶1818) or carryover deductions from other years, personal exemptions (suspended from 2018 through 2025), and exclusion of gain from qualified small business stock (¶2638) are not allowed. Moreover, deductions for capital losses and nonbusiness deductions are only allowed to a limited extent. (Code Sec. 172(d); Reg § 1.172-3(a))[34]

Where spouses who make a joint return for the deduction year made a joint return for all other tax years involved in computing the NOL deduction, that deduction is computed on the basis of their joint NOLs and combined taxable incomes. (Reg § 1.172-7(c)) Special rules apply if they didn't make joint returns for all applicable years. (Reg § 1.172-7)[35]

¶ 1821   Computing the net operating loss (NOL) for corporate taxpayers.

A corporation's NOL is figured by subtracting its deductions from its gross income, except that, in arriving at the NOL for the year: (1) NOL carrybacks (where available; ¶1818) and carryovers from other years aren't deducted; (2) the deduction for dividends received is taken without limiting it by a percentage of the corporation's taxable income; and (3) the deduction for dividends paid on certain preferred stock of public utilities is computed without limiting it to the year's taxable income. (Code Sec. 172(d); Reg § 1.172-2(a))[36]

¶ 1822   Net operating loss (NOL) intervening year modifications.

If an NOL is not absorbed in the first year to which it is carried (¶1818), then the amount of loss carried to a second year must be reduced not only by the first carryover year's taxable income but also by certain modifications or adjustments attributable to that first year. If the loss is carried to more than two years, then modifications must be made to each of the years to which it's carried ("intervening years") other than the last one. (Code Sec. 172(b)(2); Reg § 1.172-5)[37]

If the adjusted gross income (AGI) or taxable income of an intervening year is otherwise changed because of the modifications, deductions for that year that are based on, or limited to, a percentage of AGI or taxable income must be recomputed on the basis of taxable income or AGI as modified. (Reg § 1.172-5(a)(2)(ii))[38]

For purposes of computing the taxable income of tax years to which an NOL is carried, which is needed to determine the amount of the NOL absorbed in those years, taxable income can't exceed 80% of taxable income computed without regard to the NOL deduction for those intervening years. (Code Sec. 172(b)(2)(C)) But this rule does not apply for losses

---

33. ¶M-4304; ¶1724.33
34. ¶M-4109 *et seq.*; ¶1724.12
35. ¶M-4405 *et seq.*; ¶1724.13

36. ¶M-4105 *et seq.*; ¶1724.11
37. ¶M-4202 *et seq.*; ¶1724, 1724.20 *et seq.*
38. ¶M-4207; ¶1724.20 *et seq.*

arising in tax years beginning before 2018. [39]

¶ 1823   Deduction for Bad Debts.

Bad debts are deductible as ordinary deductions whether or not connected with a taxpayer's business. A deduction is allowed for total worthlessness (¶1825) and, in some cases, for partial worthlessness (¶1826).

An item can't be deductible both as a bad debt and as a loss. If it could be treated as either, it must be treated as a bad debt. [40] For deducting a loss for worthless stock or securities, see ¶1772.

¶ 1824   Time for deducting wholly worthless debt.

A deduction is allowed for the tax year the debt becomes wholly worthless. (Code Sec. 166(a)(1))[41] (For *partial* worthlessness of *business* debts, see ¶1826.) The taxpayer must show the debt had value at the beginning of the year and no value at the end. [42] Worthlessness is a question of fact requiring consideration of all pertinent evidence, including the debtor's financial condition and the value of any security. (Reg § 1.166-2(a))[43]

¶ 1825   Amount of bad debt deduction.

The amount deductible for a wholly worthless debt (¶1824) is its adjusted basis for determining loss on a sale or exchange (¶2400 *et seq.*), regardless of its face value. (Code Sec. 166(b); Reg § 1.166-1(d))[44] Payments received on the debt and prior deductions taken for a debt's partial worthlessness reduce the adjusted basis. [45]

If the creditor (the taxpayer) has no basis in the debt, the taxpayer is not entitled to a bad debt deduction. [46] Worthless debts arising from unpaid wages, salaries, fees, rents, and similar items of taxable income are not deductible as bad debts unless the income that these items represent has been included in the taxpayer's income. (Reg § 1.166-1(e))[47] Where a taxpayer reports receivables at fair market value (FMV) rather than face, the deduction can't exceed FMV. (Reg § 1.166-1(d)(2))[48]

Where a taxpayer fails to prove a debt's exact basis, it may be estimated by a court if the taxpayer proves the right to *some* deduction.[49]

If a debt is compromised because of inability to pay the full amount, the taxpayer deducts the debt's adjusted basis minus any cash and the value of any property received. If the debt is compromised for some other reason, the taxpayer doesn't have a bad debt (but may have a loss). [50]

¶ 1826   Deduction for partially worthless business debts.

A deduction is allowed for partially worthless debts (Code Sec. 166(a)(2)) *only if* (1) the debt is a business debt (¶1827); (2) IRS is satisfied that the debt is recoverable only in part; (3) the amount deducted was *charged off* on the books during the tax year; *and* (4) the debt is not evidenced by a security. (Code Sec. 166(e); Reg § 1.166-5(b))[1]

A taxpayer can charge off and deduct a debt for partial worthlessness as the worthlessness occurs, can defer charge-off and deduction to a later year when partial worthlessness is greater, or can defer deduction until (but not beyond) the year of total worthlessness.

---

39. ¶M-4200.1; ¶1724.23 *et seq.*
40. ¶M-2503; ¶1654.040
41. ¶M-2401; ¶1664
42. ¶M-2701; ¶1664.220
43. ¶M-2702; ¶1664.220
44. ¶M-2402; ¶1664.210
45. ¶s M-2406, M-2407

46. ¶M-2404; ¶1664.210
47. ¶M-2506; ¶1664.210
48. ¶M-2402
49. ¶M-2405
50. ¶M-2408
1. ¶M-2801 *et seq.*; ¶1664.270 *et seq.*

(Reg § 1.166-3(a)(2)(ii); Reg § 1.166-3(b))[2] For deducting "worthless securities" as losses, see ¶1772.

¶ 1827 Effect of classification as business or nonbusiness bad debt.

All debts held by corporations and business debts held by individuals and noncorporate taxpayers are business debts deductible against ordinary income. (Code Sec. 166(a))[3] Nonbusiness bad debts are deductible as short-term capital losses. (Code Sec. 166(d)(1)(B))[4] Both business and nonbusiness debts can be deducted when wholly worthless (¶1824), but only business debts are deductible when partly worthless (¶1826). (Code Sec. 166(a), Code Sec. 166(d)(1)(A))[5]

A *business debt* is either (1) a debt created or acquired in the course of the taxpayer's trade or business, or (2) a debt the loss from the worthlessness of which is incurred in the taxpayer's trade or business. Whether the loss from the worthlessness was incurred in the taxpayer's trade or business depends on the relation the loss bears to the taxpayer's business. If, at the time of the worthlessness, the relation is a "proximate" one to the conduct of the trade or business, the debt qualifies as a business bad debt. The borrower's use of the funds is irrelevant. (Reg § 1.166-5(b))[6]

A *nonbusiness debt* is a debt other than a business debt. (Code Sec. 166(d)(2); Reg § 1.166-5(b))[7]

For the limitation on deduction of capital losses for noncorporate taxpayers, see ¶2608.

¶ 1828 Bad debts of guarantors and shareholders.

Guarantors. A taxpayer who makes a guarantee agreement in the course of his or her trade or business is entitled to a business bad debt deduction for any payment made as guarantor of principal or interest. (Reg § 1.166-9(a))[8]

If a taxpayer (other than a corporation) makes a guarantee agreement in a transaction for profit (but not in the course of his or her business), and makes a payment of principal or interest, the taxpayer is entitled to a nonbusiness bad debt deduction in the year his or her right of subrogation becomes totally worthless. (Reg § 1.166-9(b), Reg § 1.166-9(e)(2))[9] For time for deducting worthless debt, see ¶1824.

Shareholders. An individual shareholder's loan to his or her corporation generally isn't a business debt (¶1827).[10] But a shareholder's loan to his or her corporation can be a business debt if the shareholder is in the business of promoting, financing, and selling corporations.[11]

Shareholder/employee. A loan made by a shareholder/employee to his or her employer may be treated as a business debt if the loan is related to the trade or business of being an employee, required to be made by the employee, or the dominant motive for making the loan was to protect the employee's job. [12]

---

2. ¶M-2416, M-2801; ¶1664.271
3. ¶M-2800; ¶s 1664, 1664.300
4. ¶s M-2401, M-2901; ¶s 1664, 1664.300
5. ¶s M-2401, M-2800; ¶s 1664.210, 1664.270, 1664.300
6. ¶M-2902; ¶1664.301
7. ¶M-2902; ¶1664.301

8. ¶M-3207; ¶1664.450
9. ¶M-3210, M-3214; ¶1664.450
10. ¶M-2904; ¶1664.303
11. ¶M-2911; ¶1664.302
12. ¶M-2911 *et seq.*; ¶1664.309

Chapter 5 Depreciation, Amortization, Property Expensing and Depletion

¶ 1900 The Depreciation Allowance. ▆▆▆▆▆▆▆▆▆▆▆▆▆▆▆▆▆▆▆▆▆▆▆▆▆▆

The Code allows an annual deduction of a portion of the cost of business or income-producing property (not held for sale) with a useful life of more than one year. This deduction (cost recovery) may be for depreciation, amortization or depletion (cost recovery deductions).

For most tangible property, a depreciation deduction is provided under the Modified Accelerated Cost Recovery System (MACRS; ¶1907 *et seq.*) or under useful-life depreciation (see ¶1957). For general depreciation principles. see ¶1901 *et seq.*

For cost recovery for intangibles, see ¶1903, ¶1956, ¶1958 and ¶1966 *et seq.* For depletion deductions for natural resources, see ¶1969 *et seq.* For specialized amortization provisions, see ¶1963 *et seq.*

A bonus first-year depreciation allowance as high as 100% may be claimed for qualified property (¶1932). For certain property, in lieu of all or part of the cost recovery deductions otherwise permitted, all or part of the cost can be deducted in the year in which it is placed in service ("expensed"), see ¶1940 *et seq.*, ¶1960 *et seq.* For a separate election to not capitalize certain tangible property costs (the book-tax conformity election), see ¶1634.

¶ 1901 Claiming the depreciation deduction—Form 4562.

Form 4562 is used to claim depreciation. Taxpayers other than C corporations don't have to complete or attach Form 4562 if (1) the only depreciation (or amortization) claimed is for assets (other than listed property, see ¶1946) placed in service before the tax year, (2) no Code Sec. 179 expense deduction (¶1940) is claimed, and (3) deductions are not claimed for a vehicle reported on a form other than Schedule C or C-EZ.

Failure to claim depreciation doesn't allow a larger deduction in later years (Reg § 1.167(a)-10(a)) unless, where permitted, the failure is treated as an impermissible accounting method, corrected by filing Form 3115 and following the other procedures for changing to a permissible method of accounting in a later year. For changes in computing depreciation or amortization as changes in method of accounting, see ¶2836. An amended return can be used to correct depreciation if the error is (1) a mathematical or posting error, or (2) an improper method used for no more than one tax year. [1]

¶ 1902 What property is depreciable?

Most items of tangible property (Reg § 1.167(a)-2), and certain intangibles (Reg § 1.167(a)-3) (as explained at ¶1903) are depreciable if they:

(1) are used in a trade or business, or held for the production of income, (Code Sec. 167(a))[2]

(2) have an exhaustible useful life that can be determined with reasonable accuracy, (Reg § 1.167(a)-1(a), Reg § 1.167(a)-1(b), Reg § 1.167(a)-2, Reg § 1.167(a)-3);[3] and

(3) aren't inventory or stock in trade. (Reg § 1.167(a)-2)[4]

Land (as distinct from buildings and other land improvements) isn't depreciable. [5]

---

1. ¶G-2103, ¶G-2106.1, ¶G-2109, ¶G-2207.1; ¶4464.21, ¶4464.227, ¶4464.25
2. ¶L-7901; ¶1674.006
3. ¶L-7501, ¶L-7901; ¶1674.006
4. ¶L-7905; ¶1674.006
5. ¶L-7901; ¶1674.006

References beginning with a single letter are to paragraphs in Federal Tax Coordinator 2d and RIA's Analysis of Federal Taxes: Income. Those beginning with numbers are to paragraphs in United States Tax Reporter.

The cost of a life estate or other term interest can be amortized over the term if (1) the interest is acquired by purchase and isn't created by the taxpayer's division of a larger interest, and (2) the remainder interest isn't held by a person related to the taxpayer. [6]

Some courts have held that property can be depreciated under MACRS even if it doesn't have a determinable useful life, but IRS disagrees. [7]

Natural resources such as oil, gas, other minerals in the ground and timber qualify for *depletion* (¶1969 *et seq.*), not depreciation. (Reg § 1.167(a)-2)[8]

Property used solely for personal purposes isn't depreciable (Reg § 1.167(a)-2), but property used only partially for personal purposes is partially depreciable. [9]

¶ 1903   What intangible assets are depreciable.

An intangible asset is depreciable (but not under MACRS, see ¶1908) if it's used in a trade or business or for production of income, has a limited, ascertainable useful life, and the taxpayer can show the cost of that asset. (Reg § 1.167(a)-3(a))

✔caution: Some intangibles (for example, goodwill) can be depreciated or amortized, even though they don't have a limited, ascertainable useful life. For how to depreciate or amortize most depreciable intangibles, see ¶1956, ¶1958 and ¶1966 *et seq.*

If property is acquired subject to a lease, no portion of its adjusted basis can be allocated to the leasehold interest, and the entire adjusted basis is taken into account in determining any depreciation for the property subject to the lease. (Code Sec. 167(c)(2))[10]

¶ 1904   Who is entitled to depreciation deductions?

Ordinarily the property owner is the person entitled to deduct depreciation. [11] This is the person that has the benefits and burdens of ownership, not necessarily legal title. [12] For depreciation of leased property and leasehold improvements, see ¶1922.

If a life tenancy is in depreciable property, the life tenant deducts depreciation as if he were the absolute owner of the property. (Code Sec. 167(d)) After the life tenant's death, the depreciation deduction, if any, is allowed to the remainderman. (Reg § 1.167(h)-1)[13] For rules that limit the depreciation or amortization of life estates and other limited interests in non-depreciable property, see ¶1903.

A tenant-stockholder of a cooperative housing corporation using his proprietary lease in a trade or business or for the production of income can, generally, depreciate the portion of the cost of his stock allocable to depreciable property. (Code Sec. 216(c))[14]

¶ 1905   When depreciation begins and ends.

Depreciation begins when an asset is placed in service (Reg § 1.167(a)-10(b)), i.e., when it's in a condition or state of readiness and availability for a specifically defined function.

A district court held that a retailer's buildings were placed in service when they were ready and available to store and house equipment, racks, shelving and merchandise. It didn't matter that the certificates of occupancy didn't allow customers to enter the buildings until the next year. IRS disagreed and said that it will continue to litigate the issue. [15]

Depreciation ends when the asset is retired from service, or its cost or other basis is fully

6. ¶L-7831 *et seq.*; ¶1674.120 ; ¶2734
7. ¶L-8201, ¶L-10901.1
8. ¶s L-7929, N-2250 *et seq.*; ¶6114 *et seq.*
9. ¶L-7908; ¶1674.006
10. ¶L-7911.1; ¶L-6518.1; ¶1784

11. ¶L-7802; ¶1674.002
12. ¶L-7803 *et seq.*; ¶1674.002
13. ¶L-7830; ¶1674.117
14. ¶K-5921 *et seq.*, ¶L-7828; ¶2164.01
15. ¶L-7601 *et seq.*; ¶1674.085

recovered, or it's sold or otherwise disposed of, whichever occurs first. (Reg §   1.168(i)-8(h); Reg §   1.167(a)-10(b), Reg §   1.167(b)-0(a)) For what transactions are treated as dispositions of MACRS assets, see ¶1906.

For MACRS property (¶1907 *et seq.*), the rules for the beginning and end of depreciation are subject to depreciation conventions (see ¶1926). For useful-life property (¶1957 *et seq.*), a proportionate part of a year's depreciation is allowed for the part of the year in which an asset is placed in service, but only if no depreciation convention is adopted for the asset. (Reg §   1.167(a)-10(b)) No depreciation deduction is allowed for MACRS property placed in service and disposed of in the same year. (Reg §   1.168(d)-1(b)(3)(ii))

¶ 1906   Dispositions of MACRS assets

Regs provide rules for the dispositions of MACRS (see   ¶1907) assets. (Reg §   1.168(i)-8)[16] For separate rules for dispositions from general asset accounts, see   ¶1909.

A disposition of an asset depreciable under MACRS occurs when ownership is transferred or when the asset is permanently withdrawn from use either in a trade or business or in the production of income. A disposition includes sale, exchange, retirement, physical abandonment, destruction, or transfer to a supplies, scrap, or similar account. A disposition doesn't include disposition of a structural component of a building unless the disposition qualifies as a "partial disposition." (Reg §   1.168(i)-8(b)(2))[17]

Partial dispositions include (1) a disposition of a portion of an asset that is also (A) as a result of a casualty loss (see   ¶1779) *et seq.*; (B) a disposition for which gain, determined without regard to depreciation recapture (¶2674), isn't recognized in whole or in part under Code Sec. 1031 (like-kind exchanges) or Code Sec. 1033 (involuntary conversions); (C) a transfer (i) in a corporate or partnership transaction described in Code Sec.   332, Code Sec. 351, Code Sec. 361, Code Sec. 721, or Code Sec. 731, or (ii) between members of an affiliated group filing a consolidated return; or (D) *a sale*, or (2) *any disposition* of a portion of an asset for which the taxpayer *elects* partial disposition treatment. (Reg §   1.168(i)-8(d)(1))[18] Guidance is provided as to when and how to make the election. (Reg §   1.168(i)-8(d)(2))[19]

The regs provide (1) additional guidance as to whether a disposition of an asset has taken place by addressing whether or not, for disposition purposes, an asset is a separate asset or merely part of a larger asset (Reg §   1.168(i)-8(c)(4)), and (2) guidance as to which asset, among similar or identical assets, has been disposed of. (Reg §   1.168(i)-8(g))[20]

¶ 1907   The Modified Accelerated Cost Recovery System (MACRS). ▬▬▬▬

MACRS depreciation is determined under: (1) the general depreciation system (GDS), or (2) the alternative depreciation system (ADS), which is mandatory for some MACRS property and elective for all other MACRS property; see   ¶1929 *et seq.* For "bonus depreciation," see ¶1932 *et seq.*

In both systems, the depreciation deduction is determined by applying the depreciation method (¶1924) to the depreciable basis (¶1921) of the property over the applicable recovery period (¶1923), subject to the applicable placed-in-service conventions (¶1926).[21]

Subject to the exceptions discussed in   ¶1908 (and the expensing and amortization rules discussed at ¶1940 *et seq.* and ¶1960 *et seq.*), most tangible depreciable property (as described at ¶1902) must be depreciated under MACRS. (Code Sec.   168(a))[22]

---

16.   ¶ L-10610 *et seq.*; ¶1684.20 *et seq.*
17.   ¶ L-10612 ; ¶1684.20
18.   ¶ L-10612.1; ¶1684.21
19.   ¶ L-10612.2 *et seq.*; ¶1684.21

20.   ¶ L-10615, L-10616; ¶1684.20, ¶1684.22
21.   ¶L-8100 *et seq.*; ¶1684 *et seq.*
22.   ¶L-8201; ¶1684

¶ 1908 Property excluded from MACRS.

The following property isn't depreciable under MACRS: intangible property, see ¶1903 (Code Sec. 168(a)); property ineligible for MACRS under "anti-churning" rules; property that the taxpayer elects to depreciate under a method not expressed in a term of years, e.g., the income-forecast method (¶1956)); public utility property for which the taxpayer doesn't use the MACRS normalization method of accounting; motion picture films or video tapes, including videocassettes; and master sound recordings. [23] (Code Sec. 168(f))

¶ 1909 General asset accounts for MACRS property.

Taxpayers can elect to maintain one or more general asset accounts (GAAs) for eligible MACRS property. (Code Sec. 168(i)(4))[24] The election is made on a Form 4562 that is included in a timely filed return (including extensions) for the tax year in which the assets are placed in service. (Reg § 1.168(i)-1(l)(2)) For partnerships and S corporations, the election is made at the entity level. (Reg § 1.168(i)-1(l)(1))[25]

Assets grouped in a GAA. Each GAA must include only assets with the same depreciation method, recovery period, and convention that are placed in service in the same tax year (and in the same calendar quarter if the asset is subject to the mid-quarter convention or in the same month for assets subject to the mid-month convention). The following must be grouped into separate GAAs: (1) Passenger autos subject to the luxury auto depreciation dollar limits (¶1950); (2) listed property (¶1946) other than passenger autos; (3) assets not eligible for "bonus depreciation" (including assets for which the taxpayer elected not to claim the bonus depreciation); (4) assets eligible for bonus depreciation can only be grouped into a GAA with assets for which the taxpayer claimed the same percentage of bonus depreciation (e.g., 50%, or 100%); (5) assets for which the depreciation for the placed-in-service year is not determined by using an optional depreciation table (¶1912); (6) certain mass assets subject to a rule allowing the taxpayer to identify which mass asset is disposed of or converted by way of a mortality dispersion table; and (7) certain assets subject to a shorter recovery period or a more accelerated depreciation method because of a change in the assets' use. (Reg § 1.168(i)-1(c)(2))[26]

Mixed use property (i.e., used both for business or income producing use and personal use), and property bought and disposed of during the same tax year can't be in a GAA. [27] Additionally, special rules apply for assets generating foreign source income. (Reg § 1.168(i)-1(c)(1))[28]

Each GAA is depreciated as a single asset, and the depreciation for each GAA is recorded in a separate depreciation reserve account. (Reg § 1.168(i)-1(d))[29]

General rules for dispositions. A disposition from a GAA occurs when ownership of an asset is transferred or the asset is permanently withdrawn from use in the taxpayer's trade or business or in the production of income. A disposition includes the sale, exchange, retirement, physical abandonment, or destruction of an asset or its transfer to a supplies, scrap, or similar account. A disposition doesn't include disposition of a structural component of a building unless the disposition qualifies as a "partial disposition." (Reg § 1.168(i)-1(e)(1)(i))[30] For dispositions of MACRS assets not held in GAAs, see ¶1906.

Partial dispositions are as defined for purposes of the MACRS disposition rules discussed at ¶1906 except that (1) they also include a disposition in an abusive transaction and (2) instead of including dispositions of a portion of an asset made under the election

23. ¶L-8201; ¶1684
24. ¶L-8922 *et seq.*; ¶1684.07 *et seq.*
25. ¶L-8931; ¶1684.07
26. ¶L-8922A *et seq.*; ¶1684.07

27. ¶L-8922; ¶1684.07
28. ¶ L-8922.1; ¶1684.07
29. ¶ L-8922.2; ¶1684.07
30. ¶ L-8930; ¶1684.071

discussed at ¶1906, they include partial disposition treatment for a portion of an asset included in a transaction for which there is made an election described in *Qualifying dispositions* or *Optional termination of entire GAA* below. (Reg § 1.168(i)-1(e)(1)(ii))[31]

The consequences for dispositions, under the above general rules, from a GAA are that:

(1) The asset that's disposed of is treated as having an adjusted basis of zero, so a loss can't be realized on the disposition.

(2) Any amount realized on the disposition is ordinary income to the extent that the sum of the GAA's unadjusted depreciable basis and any expensed cost for assets in the account exceeds any amounts previously recognized as ordinary income upon the disposition of other assets in the account. The recognition and character of any excess amount is determined under other applicable Code provisions (other than the recapture rules).

(3) The disposition does not affect how the GAA is depreciated. Thus, depreciation continues as if the disposed-of asset(s) were still in the GAA. (Reg § 1.168(i)-1(e)(2))[32]

Qualifying dispositions. A taxpayer can elect to terminate GAA treatment for a "qualifying disposition" of an asset. Recognition, amount, and character of gain or loss is determined under the rules generally applicable under the Code (rather than under the rules discussed immediately above), except that Code Sec. 1245/Code Sec. 1250 recapture is limited to the excess of the depreciation (and any expensing) allowed or allowable for the GAA over any amounts previously recognized as ordinary income under the general GAA rules. Adjustments are made to the GAA and its depreciation reserve to reflect the removal of the asset. (Reg § 1.168(i)-1(e)(3)(iii))[33]

A qualifying disposition is: (1) a direct result of a casualty or theft; (2) a deductible charitable contribution; (3) a direct result of a cessation, termination, or disposition of a business, manufacturing, or other income-producing process, operation, facility, plant, or other unit (other than by transfer to a supplies, scrap, or similar account); or (4) a nonrecognition transaction other than (i) a Code Sec. 168(i)(7)(B) "step in the shoes" transaction (¶1911), (ii) a Code Sec. 1031 like-kind exchange or a Code Sec. 1033 involuntary conversion, or (iii) an abusive transaction as defined in Reg § 1.168(i)-1(e)(3)(vii)). (Reg § 1.168(i)-1(e)(3)(iii)(B))[34]

Optional termination of entire GAA. Generally, a taxpayer continues to recover the cost of a GAA over its normal recovery period even though all of its assets have been disposed of. Alternatively, a taxpayer can elect to end GAA treatment, and recover the GAA's adjusted depreciable basis, when it sells the remaining assets in a GAA. Recognition, amount, and character of gain or loss are determined as described above for qualifying dispositions. (Reg § 1.168(i)-1(e)(3)(ii))[35]

Mandatory termination. A GAA must be terminated when all of its remaining assets are transferred in a Code Sec. 168(i)(7)(B), Code Sec. 1031 or Code Sec. 1033 transaction. If less than all of the assets in the GAA are transferred in any of those transactions, GAA treatment terminates only for transferred assets. Additionally, if the taxpayer disposes of an asset from a GAA in certain recapture transactions and abusive transactions, or if the asset is no longer exclusively used for business or income production, GAA treatment for that asset terminates. (Reg § 1.168(i)-1(e)(3), Reg § 1.168(i)-1(g); Reg § 1.168(i)-1(h)(1))[36] A mandatory termination also took place if, for tax years beginning before 2018, see ¶3773, there was a technical termination of a partnership. Reg § 1.168(i)-1(e)(3)(vi))[37]

---

31. ¶ L-8930A; ¶1684.071
32. ¶ L-8924; ¶1684.071
33. ¶ L-8925; ¶1684.072
34. ¶ L-8930; ¶1684.072

35. ¶ L-8926; ¶1684.072
36. ¶L-8922, L-8925.1, L-8925.2, L-8926.1, L-8926.2; ¶1684.07, 1684.072
37. ¶L-8926.1A; ¶1684.072

¶ 1910   Multiple asset accounts for MACRS property.

Taxpayers can account for depreciation of MACRS assets using multiple-asset accounts (MAAs). In general, the only effects of accounting for MACRS assets in MAAs are that (1) annual calculations of depreciation are simplified, and (2) where specific identification of which asset, among similar assets, is being disposed of is impracticable, a taxpayer can alternatively use (A) in most instances, another reasonable method to determine the basis of the disposed of asset, and (B) one of several methods prescribed by IRS to identify the asset and the year that it was placed in service. (Reg §   1.168(i)-7)[38] For other rules for dispositions of MACRS assets, including dispositions of assets from MAAs, see   ¶1906.

¶ 1911   "Step into the shoes" rule for certain carryover-basis property.

If property is acquired in certain nontaxable transfers (such as transactions described in Code Sec. 332 (¶3560), Code Sec. 351 (¶3500) or Code Sec. 361 (¶3548)), the transferee "steps into the shoes" of the transferor for the depreciation period and method of the transferred property. This applies to the extent that the transferee's basis in the property equals the transferor's adjusted basis. (Code Sec.   168(i)(7)(B), Code Sec. 168(i)(7)(C))[39]

¶ 1912   IRS optional MACRS rate tables.

Instead of making the MACRS computations described at   ¶1907 and ¶1924 for either the general or alternate depreciation systems, a taxpayer can, with no notice to IRS, instead rely on tables provided by IRS (reproduced at   ¶1119), subject to the following rules:

(1) All the tables' rates (accelerated or straight-line) are applied to the property's *unadjusted depreciable basis*. For that purpose, unadjusted depreciable basis is the basis for determining gain or loss, not reduced by prior depreciation, and reflecting reductions in basis for: (a) personal-use percentage of the asset for the tax year; (b) any portion of the asset that is expensed under Code Sec.   179 (¶1940); and (c) other initial basis adjustments—e.g., for the Code Sec. 44 disabled-access credit (¶2323), or, unless the taxpayer made an "election-out," for bonus depreciation (¶1932 *et seq.*). (Reg § 1.168(b)-1(a)(3))

(2) The taxpayer must use the tables to compute the annual depreciation allowances for the entire recovery period of the property. However, a taxpayer may not continue to use the tables if there are any adjustments to the basis of the property for reasons other than: (a) depreciation allowed or allowable, or (b) an addition or an improvement to such property that is subject to depreciation as a separate item of property.

(3) Use of the tables is denied for a short tax year and for later tax years for personal property not fully depreciated by the end of the short tax year (¶1925).[40]

⊘illustration: T bought an item of used 7-year property for $10,000, placed it in service on Aug. 11, Year 1, and used the item exclusively in his business. None of the adjustments in (1) above apply, so the unadjusted depreciable basis of the property is $10,000. The percentages for 7-year property using the 200% declining balance method and the half-year convention are found in Table 1, see ¶1119. The depreciation deduction each year of the recovery period is as follows: [41]

---

38. ¶L-8932 *et seq.*, ¶L-10614, L-10616; ¶1684.075, 1684.22, 1684.23

39. ¶L-10401; ¶1684.04

40. ¶L-8602, ¶L-8904 *et seq.*; ¶1684

41. ¶L-8910

Year	Basis	Percentage	Deduction
1	$10,000	14.29%	$1,429
2	10,000	24.49%	2,449
3	10,000	17.49%	1,749
4	10,000	12.49%	1,249
5	10,000	8.93%	893
6	10,000	8.92%	892
7	10,000	8.93%	893
8	10,000	4.46%	446

¶ 1913   Determining the MACRS recovery class for an asset.

The assignment of MACRS property to a recovery class is generally made by reference to that property's class life as of Jan. 1, '86. (Code Sec. 168(i)(1)) The class life of many types of assets is carried in Rev Proc 87-56. The assignment to a MACRS recovery class is determined as follows (Code Sec. 168(e)(1)):

MACRS Recovery Class	Property With a Class Life (in Years) of:
3-Year	4 or less
5-Year	More than 4 but less than 10
7-Year	10 or more but less than 16
10-Year	16 or more but less than 20
15-Year	20 or more but less than 25
20-Year	25 or more

Also, MACRS assigns specified property to the classes described above (see ¶1914 *et seq.*) and as follows: water utility property to the 25-year class; residential rental property to the 27.5-year class; nonresidential real property placed in service before May 13, '93 to the 31.5-year class; nonresidential real property placed in service after May 12, '93 to the 39-year class; any railroad grading and tunnel bore to the 50-year class. (Code Sec. 168(c))[42]

¶ 1914   The 3-year MACRS class.

This class includes:

. . . Depreciable personal property with a class life of four years or less (Code Sec. 168(e)(1)), such as: tractor units for use over-the-road; breeding hogs; special handling devices used in the manufacture of food and beverages; and special tools used in the manufacture of moor vehicles, rubber products, and finished plastic products.

. . . All racehorses placed in service before 2018, racehorses more than two years old when placed in service after 2017, and other horses more than 12 years old when placed in service. (Code Sec. 168(e)(3)(A))

caution: Check tax.thomsonreuters.com/federaltaxhandbookupdates to see if the above dates have been extended.

. . . Qualified rent-to-own (RTO) property (certain consumer durables held for rent). (Code Sec. 168(e)(3)(A)(iii), Code Sec. 168(i)(14))[43]

¶ 1915   The 5-year MACRS class.

This class includes:

. . . Depreciable personal property with a class life of more than four years and less than

---

42. ¶L-8202; ¶1684   43. ¶L-8204; ¶1684.01

ten years (Code Sec. 168(e)(1)), such as: information systems (computers); heavy general purpose trucks; trailers and trailer-mounted containers; breeding or dairy cattle; certain assets used in the drilling of oil and gas wells, construction, the manufacture of textile yarns, apparel, and other finished goods, and the cutting of timber. Also, IRS ruled that support vessels used in offshore oil and gas operations (whether or not used in connection with drilling) are five-year property. [44]

. . . Any automobiles or light-general purpose trucks (Code Sec. 168(e)(3)(B)(i));

. . . Semiconductor manufacturing equipment (Code Sec. 168(e)(3)(B)(ii)) in ADR class 36.0;

. . . Computer-based telephone central office switching equipment (Code Sec. 168(e)(3)(B)(iii));

. . . Qualified technological equipment (Code Sec. 168(e)(3)(B)(iv));

. . . Code Sec. 1245 property used in connection with research and experimentation (Code Sec. 168(e)(3)(B)(v));

. . . Certain energy-related property. (Code Sec. 168(e)(3)(B)(vi), Code Sec. 48(a)(3)(A))

. . . Consumer durable property (such as tangible personal property used in a home) subject to rent-to-own contracts if it isn't qualified rent-to-own property (see ¶1914).

. . . Farm machinery and equipment placed in service after 2017. (Code Sec. 168(e)(3)(B)(vii)).[45]

¶ 1916   The 7-year MACRS class.

This class includes:

. . . Property with a class life of 10 years or more, but less than 16 years (Code Sec. 168(e)(1)), such as: office furniture, fixtures, and equipment; farm machinery and equipment (including vineyard trellising) placed in service before 2018; certain assets (except helicopters) used in air transport; certain assets used in exploration for and production of petroleum and natural gas products, in manufacture of wood products and furniture, and in theme parks, amusement parks and recreation facilities. [46]

. . . Property that doesn't have a class life and isn't specifically assigned to any other MACRS class. (Code Sec. 168(e)(3)(C)(v)).

. . . Any horse not assigned to the three-year class (see ¶1914).

. . . Railroad tracks. (Code Sec. 168(e)(3)(C)(i))[47]

. . . Motorsports entertainment complexes, as defined in Code Sec. 168(i)(15), placed in service before 2018. (Code Sec. 168(e)(3)(C)(ii), Code Sec. 168(i)(15))[48]

caution: Check tax.thomsonreuters.com/federaltaxhandbookupdates to see if the above provision has been extended.

. . . Certain Alaska natural gas pipeline property. (Code Sec. 168(e)(3)(C)(iii), Code Sec. 168(i)(16))[49]

. . . "Natural gas gathering lines" if the taxpayer is the original user. (Code Sec. 168(e)(3)(C)(iv)) No AMT depreciation adjustments apply, see ¶3207. (Code Sec. 56(a)(1)(B))

. . . Assets used to convert corn to fuel grade ethanol. [50]

---

44. ¶L-8205; ¶1684.01
45. ¶L-8205; ¶1684.01
46. ¶L-8206; ¶N-1361; ¶1684.01
47. ¶L-8206; ¶1684.01

48. ¶L-8206.3; ¶1684.01
49. ¶L-8206.2; ¶1684.01
50. ¶L-8206.1; ¶1684.01

¶ 1917   The 10-year MACRS class.

This class includes:

. . . Property with a class life of 16 years or more but less than 20 (Code Sec. 168(e)(1)), such as: water transport equipment not used in marine construction; assets used in petroleum refining, manufacture of grain and grain mill products, sugar and sugar products, and vegetable oils and vegetable oil products. [1]

. . . A single purpose agricultural or horticultural structure (Code Sec. 168(e)(3)(D)(i)).

. . . Any tree or vine bearing fruit or nuts (Code Sec. 168(e)(3)(D)(ii)).

. . . Qualified smart electric meters or qualified smart electric grid systems. (Code Sec. 168(e)(3)(D), Code Sec. 168(i)(18), Code Sec. 168(i)(19))[2]

¶ 1918   The 15-year MACRS class.

This class includes:

(1) Property with a class life of 20 years or more but less than 25 years (Code Sec. 168(e)(1)), such as: land improvements (e.g., sidewalks and roads) that aren't explicitly included in another class and aren't buildings or structural improvements; "modern" golf-course greens; assets such as service-station and car-wash buildings; and concrete footings used to anchor gas station pump canopies.

(2) Municipal wastewater treatment plants (Code Sec. 168(e)(3)(E)(i));

(3) Telephone distribution plants and comparable equipment used for two-way exchange of voice and data communications. (Code Sec. 168(e)(3)(E)(ii))

(4) Any Code Sec. 1250 property (generally, depreciable real property) that is a retail motor fuels outlet (many gas stations qualify, even if they include convenience stores). (Code Sec. 168(e)(3)(E)(iii))[3]

(5) Initial clearing and grading land improvements relating to gas utility property. (Code Sec. 168(e)(3)(E)(iv))[4]

(6) Certain new electrical transmission property (Code Sec. 168(e)(3)(E)(v)), and

(7) Certain new "natural gas distribution lines" placed in service before Jan. 1, 2011. (Code Sec. 168(e)(3)(E)(vi))[5]

(8) For property placed into service before 2018, qualified leasehold improvement property, qualified restaurant property and qualified retail improvement property. Qualified leasehold improvement property is an interior building improvement to nonresidential real property, by a landlord, tenant or subtenant, that is placed in service more than three years after the building is and that meets other requirements. Qualified restaurant property is either (A) a building improvement in a building in which more than 50% of the building's square footage is devoted to the preparation of, and seating for, on-premises consumption of prepared meals (the more-than-50% test), or (B) a building that passes the more-than-50% test. Qualified retail improvement property is an interior improvement to retail space that is placed in service more than three years after the date the building was first placed in service and that meets other requirements. [6]

🖉 *observation:* For property placed in service after 2017, the separate definitions for qualified leasehold improvement property, qualified restaurant property, and qualified

---

1. ¶L-8207; ¶1684.01
2. ¶L-8207; ¶1684.01
3. ¶L-8208, ¶L-8804.1; ¶1684.02

4. ¶L-8208; ¶1684.01
5. ¶L-8208.3, ¶L-8208.4; ¶1684.01
6. ¶L-8208.1, ¶L-8208.2; ¶L-8208.5; ¶1684.02

retail improvement property are eliminated, and replaced with a category called "qualified improvement property" (defined at ¶1943). According to the Joint Explanatory Statement accompanying the conference agreement for the Tax Cuts and Jobs Act, a general 15-year recovery period was intended to have been provided for qualified improvement property. But no such change was reflected in the statutory text, even though the statutory text was amended to provide a definition of qualified improvement property. Thus, until a technical correction is made, the recovery period for qualified improvement property is the same as for nonresidential rental property (see ¶1920).

¶ 1919   The 20-year MACRS class.

This class includes property with a class life of 25 years or more (Code Sec. 168(e)(1)), such as farm buildings (other than single purpose agricultural or horticultural structures (¶1917)) and gas utility distribution facilities. [7]

¶ 1920   Residential and nonresidential buildings under MACRS.

A 27.5-year class is specifically assigned to residential rental property. (Code Sec. 168(c)) Residential real property is defined as a building or structure for which 80% or more of the gross rental income is from dwelling units. A dwelling unit is a house or apartment that provides living accommodations in a building or structure, but doesn't include a unit in a hotel, motel, or other establishment more than half of the units in which are used on a transient basis. (Code Sec. 168(e)(2)(A)).[8] In applying the 80% test, multiple structures that are on the same tract or parcel (or contiguous tracts or parcels) and operated as a single integrated unit are treated as a single building or structure. For example, an apartment building and a hotel were treated as a single building where located on the same tract and operated as a single integrated unit. [9] Otherwise-qualifying residential rental property can include manufactured homes, and, if permanently anchored, mobile homes. Also, housing in a senior citizens' community isn't barred from qualifying merely because services that include assisted living and nursing care are provided.[10]

A 39-year class life is specifically assigned to nonresidential real property (Code Sec. 168(c)), which includes, generally, buildings or structures that aren't residential rental property. (Code Sec. 168(e)(2)(B)[11] Nonresidential real property placed in service before May 13, '93, had a 31.5-year class. [12]

Elevators and escalators are treated as part of a building or structure. Assets that are viewed by IRS as buildings include floating casinos, if intended to remain permanently in place, and open-air parking garages. [13]

Whether an asset is part of a building or structure —and, thus, depreciated over a longer period than if it were treated as a separate asset —may depend on whether the asset would not have qualified as tangible personal property for purposes of prior law's investment tax credit.[14]

☉ observation: Whether an asset is a structural component of a building and, therefore, depreciated over 27.5 years or 39 years (on a straight-line method, see ¶1924) or is, instead, personal property, and, thus, usually depreciated over 5 years (¶1915) or 7 years (¶1916) (usually on an accelerated method, see ¶1917), significantly changes the tax benefit derived from depreciation of the asset. Thus, it is common for taxpayers to

7. ¶L-8209; ¶1684.01
8. ¶L-8211; ¶1684.02
9. ¶L-8211.1; ¶1684.02
10. ¶L-8211; ¶1684.02

11. ¶L-8210; ¶1684.02
12. ¶L-8210.1; ¶1684.02
13. ¶L-8210
14. ¶L-8210

engage tax professionals, usually working with architects, builders or engineers, to produce "cost segregation studies" that, although not binding on IRS, substantiate (1) the taxpayer's treatment of some items of property associated with a building as structural components of a building and some items as belonging to various classes of personal property, and (2) the taxpayer's allocation of costs between the building components and personal property (and among the various classes of personal property).

The depreciation for any additions to, or improvement of, any real property (whether or not recovery property) is determined in the same manner as the depreciation deduction for the real property would be determined if the real property were placed in service at the same time as the addition or improvement. (Code Sec. 168(i)(6)(A))[15]

¶ 1921 Basis of recovery property for computing MACRS depreciation deductions.

If the taxpayer doesn't choose to apply the optional IRS depreciation tables (¶1912), MACRS depreciation deductions are computed on the property's adjusted basis (also referred to by IRS as the "unrecovered basis"), except that salvage value is considered to be zero, i.e., disregarded. (Code Sec. 168(b)(4)) This "unrecovered basis" is adjusted (i.e., ordinarily reduced) by depreciation previously allowed or allowable. [16] For the basis used if the optional IRS depreciation tables are applied, see ¶1912. For mixed-use property, see ¶1902.

¶ 1922 Depreciation of leased property and leasehold improvements by lessees or lessors.

A *lessor* (landlord) deducts depreciation on property that is already on the leased premises when he leases out the property and on any improvements he constructs during the term of the lease. (Reg § 1.167(a)-4) But the lessor can't deduct depreciation where the lease requires the lessee to replace property at the lessee's expense. In that case, the lessor suffers no "depreciable" loss, i.e., wear and tear, etc. [17]

If improvements are made by the lessor for the lessee (e.g., to customize the space) and are irrevocably disposed of or abandoned by the lessor at the termination of the lease, then in determining gain or loss, the improvement is treated as disposed of by the lessor at that time. (Code Sec. 168(i)(8)(B))[18]

A *lessee* (tenant) ordinarily depreciates the cost of improvements he makes, [19] and the depreciation deductions are determined without regard to the lease term. (Code Sec. 168(i)(8)). The costs of acquiring a lease are amortizable, not depreciable, see ¶1581.

Where the lease ends and the lessee doesn't retain the improvement, the lessee has a gain or loss, determined with reference to any remaining un-recovered basis of the property.[20]

observation: A gain would arise where, for example, the tenant is paid an amount to terminate the lease, and the amount exceeds the basis of the leasehold improvements (and lease acquisition costs, if any).

A lessor may advance construction funds to the lessee to help the lessee pay for retail leasehold improvements. If, under the rules explained at ¶1341, a lessee excludes the funds from income, the lessor treats the improvements as its own nonresidential real property, including for purposes of the disposition-of-improvements rule (see above). (Code

---

15. ¶L-9105
16. ¶L-8601; ¶1684
17. ¶L-7808, ¶L-7809; ¶1674.023

18. ¶L-9106; ¶1684.02
19. ¶L-7809; ¶1674.023
20. ¶L-9106; ¶1684.02

Sec. 110(b))[21]

¶ 1923   MACRS depreciation periods—Form 4562

For the 3-year, 5-year, 7-year, 10-year, 15-year and 20-year MACRS classes, the depreciation period is the same as the name of the class (e.g., 5 years for 5-year property). The depreciation period is 25 years for the water utility property class, 27.5 years for the residential rental property class, 39 years for the nonresidential real property class (but 31.5 years if the property is placed in service before May 13, '93) and 50 years for the railroad grading or tunnel bore class. (Code Sec. 168(c))[22]

Shorter depreciation periods apply for "qualified Indian reservation property" placed in service after '93 and before 2018. Taxpayers can elect not to apply the shorter periods. (Code Sec. 168(j))[23]

caution: Check tax.thomsonreuters.com/federaltaxhandbookupdates to see if the above provision has been extended.

Where the 150% declining balance method is elected for MACRS property eligible for the 200% declining balance method, the applicable recovery period is as follows (Code Sec. 168(b)(2)): for property placed in service before '99, the recovery period provided under the "Alternative Depreciation System" (ADS) discussed at ¶¶1929 *et seq.*; for property placed in service after '98, the regular MACRS recovery periods described above. [24]

¶ 1924   MACRS depreciation methods.

There are three depreciation methods used for MACRS property: the 200% and 150% declining balance methods with an appropriate switch to straight-line to maximize deductions, and the straight-line method. (Code Sec. 168(b)) Under the declining balance methods, the depreciation rate (in percentage terms) generally is determined by dividing the declining balance percentage (200% or 150%) by the applicable recovery period. For example, the 200% declining balance method applied to property with a 5-year recovery period results in a depreciation rate of 40% (i.e., 200% ÷ 5). This 40% rate remains constant for each tax year in which the 200% declining balance method is used. [25]

The 200% declining balance method can be used for MACRS property except where the 150% declining balance method or the straight-line method is required or elected as discussed below. (Code Sec. 168(b)(1))

Except where the straight-line method applies, the 150% declining balance method is used for MACRS property that is (1) in the 15-year class (¶1918) or 20-year class (¶1919), (2) a qualified smart electric meter or qualified smart electric grid system, (3) property for which the taxpayer elects (as discussed below). (Code Sec. 168(b)(2)) or (4) property used in a farming business and placed in service before 2018. [26]

The straight-line method must be used for: residential rental property; nonresidential real property; any railroad grading or tunnel bore; any tree or vine bearing fruit or nuts; water utility property Code Sec. 168(b)(3)); if placed in service before 2018, qualified leasehold improvements; qualified restaurant property, or qualified retail improvement property, see ¶1918.[27] For property not required to use the straight-line method, a taxpayer can elect (as discussed below) the straight-line method over the recovery period (¶1923) that applies to the property. (Code Sec. 168(b)(3))[28]

The elections discussed above to use the 150% declining balance method or the straight-

---

21. ¶J-2265; ¶1104
22. ¶L-8802; ¶s 1684.01, 1684.02
23. ¶L-8806; ¶1684.01
24. ¶L-8916, ¶L-8103; ¶1684.01

25. ¶L-8902 *et seq.*; ¶1684.01
26. ¶L-8912; ¶1684.01
27. ¶L-8917; ¶s 1684.01, 1684.02
28. ¶L-8920 *et seq.*; ¶1684.01

line method are made on a class-by-class basis and are irrevocable. (Code Sec. 168(b)(5)) For an alternative depreciation system (ADS) election that changes the depreciation method from accelerated to straight-line, see ¶1929 *et seq.* For computing depreciation under IRS optional MACRS rate tables, see ¶1912. For computing depreciation for alternative minimum tax purposes, see ¶3207 *et seq.*

¶ 1925   Effect of short tax years on MACRS depreciation.

The depreciation allowance for MACRS personal property placed in service or disposed of in a short tax year (short year) can't be determined by using the IRS optional MACRS rate tables. The allowance for the short year is instead determined by: (1) multiplying the property's depreciable basis by the applicable depreciation rate, and (2) multiplying that product by a fraction, the numerator of which is the number of months (including fractions of months) the property is deemed in service during the short year under the applicable convention, and the denominator of which is 12. [29] Depreciation for any year following the short year is determined by consistently using either a prescribed "allocation method" or "simplified method." [30] For a short year other than the first year in the recovery period, the allowance must account for the difference between recovery years and tax years. [31]

¶ 1926   MACRS depreciation conventions.

The mid-month depreciation convention applies in determining MACRS depreciation deductions for the year that the following property is placed in service or disposed of: residential rental property and nonresidential real property discussed at ¶1920, railroad gradings and tunnel bores. Under this rule, property placed in service (or disposed of) during any month is treated as placed in service (or disposed of) at the mid-point of that month in computing MACRS depreciation deductions for the acquisition and disposition years. (Code Sec. 168(d)(2), Code Sec. 168(d)(4)(B))[32]

For all other MACRS property (referred to below as MACRS personal property), the half-year depreciation convention generally applies. It treats all MACRS personal property placed in service or disposed of during a tax year as placed in service or disposed of on the mid-point of that tax year. (Code Sec. 168(d)(1), Code Sec. 168(d)(4)(A))

Except as noted below, the mid-quarter convention applies to all MACRS personal property placed in service during a tax year if more than 40% of the total basis of all of that property placed in service during the year is placed in service during the year's last three months. (Code Sec. 168(d)(3))[33] Under the mid-quarter convention, property is treated as placed in service or disposed of on the mid-point of the applicable quarter. (Code Sec. 168(d)(4)(C))

When determining if the mid-quarter convention applies, the taxpayer excludes:

. . . Amounts expensed under Code Sec. 179; see ¶1940. (Reg § 1.168(d)-1(b)(4)(i))

. . . Nonresidential real property, residential rental property, and any railroad grading or tunnel bore. (Code Sec. 168(d)(3)(B)(i))

. . . Property placed in service and disposed of in the same tax year. (Code Sec. 168(d)(3)(B)(ii))

. . . Property excluded from MACRS under Code Sec. 168(f) (Reg § 1.168(d)-1(b)(1)), such as films, videotapes and sound recordings.

. . . The basis of a business car, if the taxpayer elects for the placed-in-service year to

---

29. ¶L-9002; ¶1684.01
30. ¶L-9003 *et seq.*; ¶1684.01
31. ¶L-9007; ¶1684.01

32. ¶L-8713; ¶1684.01, ¶1684.02
33. ¶L-8707; ¶1684.01

claim deductions using the standard mileage allowance method (¶1554).

. . . That portion of basis attributable to the personal-use of mixed-use assets (e.g., a self-employed's car used for business and personal use). (Reg § 1.168(d)-1(b)(4)(iii))[34]

¶ 1927   MACRS deductions for property after use change.

The following rules apply.[35]

Personal-use property converted to business or income-producing use (e.g., personal residence converted to rental property) is treated as placed in service on the conversion date, and is subject to the Code Sec. 168 depreciation method, recovery period, and placed-in-service convention applicable to the property beginning in the tax year of the conversion. The property's depreciable basis in the change year is the lesser of its fair market value or adjusted depreciable basis when it is converted. This rule doesn't apply when other rules (e.g., rules under Code Sec. 280F(b)(2)(A)) prescribe the depreciation treatment for a change to business use. (Reg § 1.168(i)-4(b))

MACRS property converted from business or income-producing use to personal use generally is treated as a disposition, with depreciation for the conversion year computed by applying the applicable convention (¶1926). However, the conversion doesn't result in gain, loss, or depreciation recapture. (Reg § 1.168(i)-4(c))

For changes in the primary use of an asset after the placed-in-service year, where the asset continues to be MACRS property in the taxpayer's hands (e.g., commercial property converted to residential rental property), MACRS depreciation for the change year is determined as though the change occurred on the first day of that year. (Reg § 1.168(i)-4(d)(2)(iii))

If a use-change results in:

. . . A shorter recovery period and/or a faster depreciation method, adjusted depreciable basis as of the beginning of the change year is depreciated over the shorter recovery period and/or by the faster method beginning with the year of change as though the property were first placed in service in that year. (Reg § 1.168(i)-4(d)(3)) Taxpayers may elect to continue to depreciate the property as though the change in use had not occurred. (Reg § 1.168(i)-4(d)(3)(ii))

. . . A longer recovery period and/or slower depreciation method, adjusted depreciable basis is depreciated over the longer recovery period and/or by the slower method beginning with the year of change as if the property had been originally placed in service with the longer recovery period and/or slower depreciation method. (Reg § 1.168(i)-4(d)(4))

Where use changes during placed-in-service year, the depreciation allowance generally is established by the primary use of the property during that tax year, determined in a consistently applied and reasonable manner. In determining whether property is used within or outside the U.S. during the placed-in-service year, the predominant use of the property governs. (Reg § 1.168(i)-4(e))

General asset accounts. A change in use (other than a change to any personal use) doesn't cause or permit the revocation of a general asset account election (¶1909), but, in some cases the property is removed from its existing general asset account and placed in a separate general asset account. (Reg § 1.168(i)-1(h))[36]

---

34. ¶L-8707; ¶1684.01   36. ¶L-8923; ¶1684.07
35. ¶L-8108, L-9122 *et seq.*, ¶L-9206.1; ¶1684.035

¶ **1928** **Depreciating MACRS property acquired in a like-kind exchange or involuntary conversion.**

MACRS property may be acquired (1) in exchange for MACRS property in a Code Sec. 1031 like-kind property exchange (¶2417 *et seq.*), or (2) to replace involuntarily converted MACRS property in a Code Sec. 1033 involuntary conversion (¶2430 *et seq.*). (Reg § 1.168(i)-6(c)(1))

observation: For exchanges completed after Dec. 31, 2017, a tax-deferred Code Sec. 1031 like-kind exchange works only if the exchanged properties are *real* property (see ¶2418). Thus, the post-2017 exchange of non-realty assets (even if they are of like kind) is treated as a simple sale of the relinquished asset and purchase of the acquired asset. No complex MACRS depreciation calculations are required.

The replacement property is for depreciation purposes divided into the depreciable exchanged basis (i.e., remaining basis of the relinquished property carried over to the replacement property), and the depreciable excess basis (i.e., additional consideration to acquire the replacement property). Where the properties share the same recovery class and depreciation method, the depreciable exchanged basis is written off over what's left of the relinquished property's recovery period; and the depreciable excess basis is in effect treated as a separate property with a recovery period that begins anew. (Reg § 1.168(i)-6(c)(3)(ii))[37]

illustration: In Year 1, ABX Corp. bought a used refrigerator truck (Old Truck), that was 5-year MACRS property (¶1915) for $100,000 and placed it in service that year. In Year 3, ABX acquires a newer-model used truck in exchange for Old Truck by trading in Old Truck and paying $50,000 cash. ABX uses the optional rate tables (¶1912) to compute depreciation and is subject to the half-year convention (¶1926) in Years 1 and 3. ABC claimed $20,000 of depreciation in Year 1 (20%), and $32,000 in Year 2 (32%). For Year 3, ABX may claim a depreciation deduction of $9,600 for Old Truck ($100,000 × .192 [recovery year 3 table percentage for 5-year property] × 6/12 [half-year convention applies]). The remaining depreciable basis of Old Truck (i.e., the depreciable exchanged basis) is $38,400 ($100,000 cost − $20,000 − $32,000 − $9,600), which is depreciated over Year 4−Year 6 (what's left of the original recovery period). ABX's depreciable excess basis in the replacement truck is $50,000, the cash paid by ABX. Per the table percentages, the depreciation allowance for this excess basis is $10,000 for Year 3 (20%), $16,000 for Year 4 (32%), $9,600 for Year 5 (19.2%), $5,760 for Year 6 and Year 7 (11.52%), and $2,880 (5.76%) for Year 8.

If bonus depreciation applies to ABX's replacement truck (see ¶1932 *et seq.*), ABX could claim a bonus depreciation allowance on both the remaining basis of the old truck and the cash paid to acquire the new truck. (Reg § 1.168(k)-1(f)(5)(iii)(A)) But if qualifying property is placed in service and disposed of in an exchange or involuntary conversion in the same tax year, the exchanged or involuntarily converted property isn't eligible for bonus depreciation. (Reg § 1.168(k)-1(f)(5)(iii)(B))[38]

Complex rules apply if the exchanged properties aren't depreciated with the same period and/or method. (Reg § 1.168(i)-6(c)(3)(iii), Reg § 1.168(i)-6(c)(4))[39]

Election out. A taxpayer may elect not to apply the above "split basis" approach to the exchanged properties, and, instead, treat the exchanged basis and excess basis, if any, in the replacement property as placed in service at the time of replacement and the adjusted

---

37. ¶L-10600 *et seq.*
38. ¶L-10602; ¶1684.048

39. ¶L-10601.2A

depreciable basis of the relinquished MACRS property as being disposed of. (Reg § 1.168(i)-6(i))[40]

¶ 1929   The straight-line "alternative depreciation system" (ADS) of MACRS.

The ADS for MACRS property is a straight-line depreciation system, with generally longer depreciation periods than under the general depreciation system (GDS). (Code Sec. 168(g)(2)(C), Code Sec. 168(g)(3)(B)) ADS uses the same depreciation conventions as the GDS (see ¶1907) (Code Sec. 168(g)(2)(B)), see ¶1926, and, like the GDS, disregards salvage value. (Code Sec. 168(g)(2)(A))

Depreciation deductions must be computed under ADS only for certain specified properties, see ¶1930. However, ADS must be used for all properties including properties depreciated under MACRS for purpose of computing earnings and profits of corporations (Code Sec. 312(k)(3)(A)). ADS also applies for purposes of computing the depreciation tax preference under the alternative minimum tax, under the rules explained at ¶3207.[41] ADS may be elected for all other properties — on a class by class basis for personal property and on an individual basis for residential rental and nonresidential real properties. (Code Sec. 168(g)(7)(A))

An ADS election is an irrevocable year-by-year election. (Code Sec. 168(g)(7)(B)) This election is in addition to the straight-line MACRS election (¶1924).

¶ 1930   MACRS property required to be depreciated under ADS.

The following MACRS property must be depreciated under ADS:

... "Luxury" automobiles and other "listed" (i.e., mixed-use) property used 50% or more for personal purposes, see ¶1947. (Code Sec. 280F(b)(1))

... Properties used predominantly outside the U.S. (Code Sec. 168(g)(1)(A)), except certain properties listed in the Code. (Code Sec. 168(g)(4))[42]

... Tax-exempt use property (generally, certain property leased to tax-exempt organizations, governmental units or foreign persons or entities, see Code Sec. 168(h)(3)).[43] (Code Sec. 168(g)(1)(B))

... Tax-exempt bond financed property.[44] ; (Code Sec. 168(g)(1)(C))

... Imported business equipment from countries that discriminate against U.S. goods from the date the equipment is placed on a restricted list by Presidential Executive Order. (Code Sec. 168(g)(1)(D); Code Sec. 168(g)(6))[45]

... For tax years beginning after 2018, (1) nonresidential real property and residential rental property (¶1918), and qualified improvement property (¶1943), held by an electing real property trade or business, as defined in Code Sec. 163(j)(7) (generally, a real property trade or business that elects to not apply new limitations on interest deductions effective for tax years beginning after 2017; see ¶1700) (Code Sec. 168(g)(1)(E); Code Sec. 168(g)(8)) *and* (2) any MACRS property with a recovery period of 10 years or more that is held by a farm business that makes a similar election. (Code Sec. 168(g)(1)(F); Code Sec. 168(g)(8))[46]

... Pre-production costs of farming property excluded from the inventory-capitalization rule of Code Sec. 263A (discussed in ¶1640 *et seq.*).[47]

... Intermodal cargo containers not used predominantly in the direct transportation of

---

40. ¶L-10601.8
41. ¶A-8220; ¶s 564.01, 1684.03
42. ¶L-9406; ¶1684.03
43. ¶L-9600 *et seq.*; ¶s 1684.03, 1684.06

44. ¶L-9500 *et seq.*; ¶1684.03
45. ¶L-9405; ¶1684.03
46. ¶L-9402.1, ¶L-9402.2; ¶1684.03
47. ¶L-9402; ¶s 263A4, 263A4.15, 1684.03

property to or from the U.S.[48]

¶ 1931   ADS depreciation periods.

The prescribed ADS straight-line periods are:

... except as discussed below, the property's "class-life" (¶1913). (Code Sec. 168(g)(3)(B))

... four years—for qualified rent-to-own property (¶1914). (Code Sec. 168(g)(3)(B))

... five years—for automobiles, light-purpose trucks (Code Sec. 168(g)(3)(D)) and qualified technological equipment.[49] (Code Sec. 168(g)(3)(C))

... 10 years—for most new farming equipment and machinery placed in service during 2009 or after 2017. (Code Sec. 168(g)(3)(B))

... 12 years—for personal property with no class life and not governed by any other rule discussed in this list. (Code Sec. 168(g)(2)(C))

... 14 years—new natural gas gathering lines (¶1916) (Code Sec. 168(g)(3)(B))

... 20 years—for any Code Sec. 1250 property (generally depreciable real property) which is a retail motor fuels outlet and initial clearing and grading land improvements relating to gas utility property (¶1918). (Code Sec. 168(g)(3)(B))

... 22 years—certain Alaska natural gas pipeline property (¶1916). (Code Sec. 168(g)(3)(B))

... 30 years—certain new electrical transmission property (¶1918) (Code Sec. 168(g)(3)(B)); and, if placed in service after 2017, residential rental property (¶1920). (Code Sec. 168(g)(2)(C))

... 35 years—certain new natural gas distribution lines placed in service before Jan. 1, 2011 (¶1918). (Code Sec. 168(g)(3)(B))

... 39 years—qualified leasehold improvement property, qualified retail improvement property, and qualified restaurant property that meets the timing requirements for treatment as 15-year MACRS property (¶1918). (Code Sec. 168(g)(3)(B))

... 40 years—for nonresidential real property and (Code Sec. 168(g)(2)(C)), any Code Sec. 1245 real property with no class life. (Code Sec. 168(g)(3)(E)) and, if placed in service before 2018, residential rental property.[50]

Also, the ADS depreciation period is 5 years for semiconductor manufacturing equipment, 9.5 years for computer-based telephone central office switching equipment, 10 years for railroad tracks, 15 years for single-purpose agricultural or horticultural structures, 20 years for trees or vines bearing fruit or nuts, 24 years for a municipal wastewater treatment plant or for telephone distribution plant equipment and 50 years for railroad gradings, tunnel bores, or water utility property. (Code Sec. 168(g)(2)(C), Code Sec. 168(g)(3)(B))[1]

For "tax-exempt use property" (¶1930) subject to a lease, the above depreciation periods can't be less than 125% of the lease term. (Code Sec. 168(g)(1)(B), Code Sec. 168(g)(3)(A))[2]

¶ 1932   Bonus first-year depreciation allowance.

A bonus first-year depreciation allowance applies to "qualified property" (¶1933). The allowance, which is claimed in the first year that the property is placed in service by the taxpayer for use in its trade or business or for the production of income, is equal to the

---

48. ¶s L-9402, L-9407
49. ¶L-9403 *et seq.*; ¶1684.03
50. ¶L-9403; ¶1684

1. ¶L-9403; ¶1684.03
2. ¶L-9602; ¶1684.06

following percentage of the unadjusted depreciable basis (see   ¶1912) of "qualified property" (¶1933):

. . . 100% if *acquired*   (see below) and placed in service after Sept. 27, 2017, and before Jan. 1, 2023 (before Jan. 1, 2024 for certain aircraft and long-production-period property).

. . . 80%, if placed in service after Dec. 31, 2022 and before Jan. 1, 2024 (before Jan. 1, 2025 for certain aircraft and long-production-period property).

. . . 60%, if placed in service after Dec. 31, 2023 and before Jan. 1, 2025 (before Jan. 1, 2026 for certain aircraft and long-production-period property).

. . . 40%, if placed in service after Dec. 31, 2024 and before Jan. 1, 2026 (before Jan. 1, 2027 for certain aircraft and long-production-period property).

. . . 20%, if placed in service after Dec. 31, 2025 and before Jan. 1, 2027 (before Jan. 1, 2028 for certain aircraft and long-production-period property). (Code Sec. 168(k)(1); Code Sec. 168(k)(6)); Code Sec. 168(k)(2)(B); Code Sec. 168(k)(2)(C))[3]

. . . 50% if acquired or placed in service before Sept. 28, 2017 (except that 100% bonus depreciation was available for certain property that (1) was placed in service after Sept. 8, 2010 and before Jan. 1, 2012 (before Jan. 1, 2013 for certain long-production-period property and certain aircraft) and (2) meets certain other requirements) [4]

Property won't be treated as acquired after Sept. 27, 2017 (see above) if it is acquired under a written binding contract entered into before Sept. 28, 2017. And proposed regs, on which taxpayers may rely before they become final, provide guidance as to the written binding contact rule and for more generally determining whether property is acquired after Sept. 27, 2017 for purposes of being eligible for 100% bonus depreciation. [5]

The adjusted basis of the property is reduced by the bonus depreciation allowance before computing the amount otherwise allowable as a depreciation deduction for the tax year and any later tax year. (Code Sec. 168(k)(1)(B)) There is no AMT depreciation adjustment (¶3207) for the entire recovery period of qualified property. (Code Sec. 168(k)(2)(G); Reg § 1.168(k)-1(d)(2)(ii))[6]

For certain plants bearing fruits or nuts (specified plants) for which a taxpayer elects to apply the rules in Code Sec. 168(k)(5), 100% bonus depreciation applies to plants planted or grafted after Sept. 27, 2017 and before Jan. 1, 2027 under slightly modified rules. The deduction begins to phase-down beginning in 2023 in 20% steps (similar to the phase-down described above). Under the election, the placed-in-service date for a specified plant becomes the date of planting or grafting rather than the date on which the plant becomes income-producing. The election accelerates bonus depreciation but not other depreciation (a rule which is relevant after 2022, see above, and to specified plants planted or grafted before Sept. 28, 2017 and after Dec. 31, 2015, when the election was available under the rules for 50% bonus depreciation). IRS guidance provides for (1) how and when to make the election, (2) possible deemed elections for tax years beginning in 2015 and ending in 2016, (3) coordination of the election with expensing permitted under Code Sec. 179 (¶1940), and (4) the extent to which the election is revocable. Additionally the guidance clarifies that the election accelerated the placed-in-service year for bonus depreciation purposes but not as to other depreciation deductions. [7]

For other specialized bonus depreciation provisions, see ¶1939.

Election to defer 100% rate. A taxpayer can elect, for eligible property placed in service in the taxpayer's first tax year ending after Sept. 27, 2017, to apply a 50% bonus depreciation

---

3. ¶L-9311.1; ¶1684.0253
4. ¶L-9311, L-9311.2; ¶1684.025, 1684.0251
5. ¶L-9311; ¶1684.025

6. ¶L-9310 *et seq.*; ¶1684.025 *et seq.*
7. ¶L-9311.1A; ¶1684.0254

rate to the property. (Code Sec. 168(k)(10))[8]

¶ 1933 "Qualified property" eligible for the bonus first-year depreciation allowance.

"Qualified property" eligible for bonus first-year depreciation (¶1932) includes, subject to exclusions (see below), tangible property depreciated under MACRS with a recovery period of 20 years or less, most computer software, water utility property and, if placed in service (and "acquired", see ¶1932) after Sept. 27, 2017, certain television productions, film productions, and live theatrical productions. (Code Sec. 168(k)(2)(A)(i)).[9] In addition to being of a qualifying type, the property must meet an original-use-or-qualifying acquisition requirement, (¶1934), a timely acquisition requirement (but only in the case of certain aircraft or long-production-period property, ¶1935), and a timely placed-in-service requirement (¶1936). Property placed in service (or "acquired", see ¶1932) before Sept. 28, 2017 had to meet an original use requirement instead of an original-use-or-qualifying-acquisition-requirement (see ¶1934).[10]

Exclusions. Property isn't qualified property if it must be depreciated under the alternative depreciation system (see ¶1930, ¶1947). (Code Sec. 168(k)(2)(D)). Also excluded, if placed in service (and "acquired", see ¶1932) after Sept. 27, 2017, is property used by (1) most regulated public utilities and (2) certain businesses that have "floor plan financing indebtedness" (certain vehicle dealers). (Code Sec. 168(k)(9) And for property placed in service before 2018, "qualified restaurant property" (¶1918) isn't qualified property unless the property is also qualified improvement property (¶1943). (Code Sec. 168(e)(7)(B))[11]

¶ 1934 Original-use-or qualifying acquisition requirement for the bonus first-year depreciation allowance for "qualified property."

For property placed in service (and "acquired", see ¶1932) after Sept. 27, 2017, one of the requirements for being qualified property eligible for bonus depreciation, is that property must meet either an original use requirement or a qualifying acquisition requirement. (Code Sec. 168(k)(2)(A)(ii)

Original use requirement. "Original use" is the first use, whether or not that use is *by the taxpayer*. (Reg § 1.168(k)-1(b)(3)(i)) New property first used by a taxpayer for personal use or as inventory and later used by the taxpayer in a trade or business meets the original-use requirement. (Reg § 1.168(k)-1(b)(3)(ii)) There are special rules for reconditioned or rebuilt property, syndication transactions and fractional interests. (Code Sec. 168(k)(2)(E)(iii); Reg § 1.168(k)-1(b)(3))[12]

Qualifying acquisition requirement. Property meets this requirement if (1) it wasn't used by the taxpayer at any time before the acquisition (the no-previous-use-by-the-taxpayer test) and (2) the acquisition of the property meets the requirements of Code Sec. 179(d)(2)(A), Code Sec. 179(d)(2)(B), Code Sec. 179(d)(2)(C) (which for expensing in lieu of depreciation requires that an asset not be acquired in certain types of transactions, e.g., between related persons), and Code Sec. 179(d)(3) (which disallows expensing in lieu of depreciation for properties whose basis is determined by reference to the basis of other property held by the taxpayer). (Code Sec. 168(k)(2)(E)(ii))

✪ observation: The net effect of the "qualifying acquisition requirement" is that most property is eligible for bonus depreciation even if it is bought used.

---

8. ¶L-9311
9. ¶L-9312, L-9312.1, L-9312.2; ¶1684.026, 1684.0271
10. ¶L-9312; ¶1684.026

11. ¶L-9313 *et seq.*; ¶1684.026
12. ¶L-9314; ¶1684.026

Proposed regs. Proposed regs, on which taxpayers may rely before they become final, provide that (A) property fails the no-previous-use-by-the-taxpayer test if the taxpayer had a depreciable interest in the property before acquiring the property and (B) rules for applying the test to consolidated groups. These proposed regs also provide: (1) that certain regs issued under Code Sec. 179 apply in determining whether the requirements of the Code Sec. 179 provisions discussed above apply; (2) rules for applying the qualifying acquisition requirement to related transactions, and (3 that remedial partnership allocations under Code Sec. 704(c) (¶3746) and any basis determined under Code Sec. 732 (concerning partnership distributions, ¶3742 *et seq.*) don't satisfy the original-use-or qualifying-acquisition requirement.[13]

Additionally the proposed regs provide that basis increases under Code Sec. 734(b) (concerning certain partnership distributions, see ¶3769) that are the result of a section 754 election are, as under prior law (see below), ineligible to be qualified property, but, that, in a departure from prior law, *some* basis increases under Code Sec. 743(b) (concerning certain transfers of partnership interests, see ¶3768) that are the result of a section 754 election satisfy the original use or qualifying acquisition requirement.[14]

Property placed in service or acquired before Sept. 28, 2017, qualifies for bonus depreciation only if its original use begins with the taxpayer.[15]

¶ 1935 Time-of-acquisition requirement, for certain long-production-period property and aircraft, for the bonus first-year depreciation allowance for "qualified property."

For certain long-production-period property and certain aircraft, one of the requirements for being qualified property eligible for bonus depreciation (¶1932) is that the property must be acquired by the taxpayer either (1) before Jan. 1, 2027 or (2) under a written contract entered into before Jan. 1, 2027. (Code Sec. 168(k)(2)(B)(i)(III); Code Sec. 168(k)(2)(C)(i))[16]

Special rules apply to property that is treated as acquired by the taxpayer because it is manufactured, constructed or produced by or for the taxpayer. (Code Sec. 168(k)(2)(E); Reg § 1.168(k)-1(b)(4)(iii)) For example, manufacture, construction or production begins when physical work of a significant nature begins. Physical work doesn't include preliminary activities such as planning, designing, securing financing, exploring, or researching. Under a safe-harbor, physical work of a significant nature isn't considered to begin before the taxpayer incurs (in the case of an accrual basis taxpayer) or pays (in the case of a cash basis taxpayer) more than 10% of the total cost of the property, excluding the cost of the preliminary activities. (Reg § 1.168(k)-1(b)(4)(iii)(B))[17]

¶ 1936 Placed-in-service requirement for the bonus first-year depreciation allowance for "qualified property."

To be "qualified property" for purposes of the bonus first-year depreciation allowance (¶1932), otherwise eligible property must be placed in service by the taxpayer before Jan. 1, 2027. (Code Sec. 168(k)(2)(A)(iii)) except that certain aircraft and property with a long production period can be placed in service as late as Dec. 31, 2027. (Code Sec. 168(k)(2)(B)(i)(II); Code Sec. 168(k)(2)(C)(i)) However, in applying the later deadline to long production period property, there is a limitation under which that property qualifies for bonus depreciation only to the extent of adjusted basis attributable to manufacture, construction or production before Jan. 1, 2027. (Code Sec. 168(k)(2)(B)(ii))

13. ¶L-9314; ¶1684.026
14. ¶L-9314; ¶1684.026
15. ¶L-9314; ¶1684.026

16. ¶L-9315
17. ¶L-9315, ¶L-9315B *et seq.*; ¶1684.026

Under Code Sec. 168(k)(2)(H), and in more detail under proposed regs on which taxpayers may rely before they become final, rules specific to certain television productions, film productions, and live theatrical productions apply to determine when the production is placed in service. [18]

Also, there are special rules for syndication transactions and certain non-recognition transactions. (Reg § 1.168(k)-1(b)(5))[19]

For the placed-in-service rule that applies under the Code Sec. 168(k)(5) election for specified plants, see ¶1932.

¶ 1937 Election not to claim the bonus first-year depreciation allowance for "qualified property"—Form 4562.

For "qualified property" eligible for bonus first-year depreciation (¶1932), a taxpayer can elect (1) not to claim bonus first-year depreciation, (2) not to claim. for vehicles that are qualified property, the increase, otherwise applicable to those vehicles, in the usual cap on first-year depreciation for passenger automobiles (including small trucks and vans) (¶1952) (Code Sec. 168(k)(7)) and (3) not to have the ability to make the election, described at ¶1938, to swap bonus and accelerated depreciation for certain credits. This election-out can be made for all property, in one or more classes of property, placed in service in the tax year. For property placed in service before 2016, the election-out also caused the taxpayer to lose the exemption (discussed at ¶1932) from AMT depreciation adjustments. [20]

The election-out must be made on Form 4562, generally by the due date (including extensions) of the return for the tax year in which the taxpayer places the applicable property in service. (Reg § 1.168(k)-1(e)(3)) An election-out can be revoked only with IRS consent, except that if made on a timely filed return, the election-out can be revoked on an amended return filed within six months of the original return's due date (excluding extensions). (Reg § 1.168(k)-1(e)(7))[21]

¶ 1938 Pre-2018 election to swap bonus and accelerated depreciation for certain credits—Form 8827.

For tax years ending after 2015 (as modified by a phase-in rule that applies to tax years beginning before but ending during 2016) and *beginning* before 2018, a corporation could make an election to (1) forego both bonus depreciation (¶1932) (including the bonus-depreciation-related benefit specific to passenger automobiles, see ¶1952) *and* accelerated depreciation (see ¶1924) for qualified property (¶1933) placed in service during the year, in exchange for (2) an increase (i.e., relaxation) of the limitation on otherwise allowable credits against regular tax for AMT paid (AMT credits, ¶2360). The allowable increase was referred to as the "bonus depreciation amount." The increase resulted in the allowance as a refundable credit of otherwise deferred AMT credits. [22]

¶ 1939 Other bonus first-year depreciation rules.

Specialized bonus depreciation allowance provisions include the following:

- 50% bonus first-year depreciation applies for qualified second generation biofuel plant property placed in service after Jan. 2, 2013 and before Jan. 1, 2018. (Code Sec. 168(l))[23]

caution: Check tax.thomsonreuters.com/federaltaxhandbookupdates to see if the

---

18. ¶L-9312.2; ¶1684.026
19. ¶L-9316 *et seq.*; ¶1684.027
20. ¶L-9318 *et seq.*; ¶1684.0291

21. ¶L-9318 *et seq.*; ¶1684.0291
22. ¶L-15213; ¶1684.0293
23. ¶L-9356; ¶1684.081

above provision has been extended.

- 50% bonus first-year depreciation applies for "qualified reuse and recycling property" that is purchased new by the taxpayer and meets other detailed requirements. (Code Sec. 168(m))[24]

¶ 1940   Sec. 179 Expense Election—Form 4562. ▆▆▆▆▆▆▆▆▆▆▆

Many taxpayers are eligible to deduct (in lieu of depreciation) the cost (subject to dollar limits) of most tangible personal property, and certain other property, used in the active conduct of a trade or business.

Taxpayers, except trusts, estates and certain noncorporate lessors (Code Sec. 179(d)(4), Code Sec. 179(d)(5)), can elect on Form 4562 to expense (deduct in lieu of depreciation) the cost (subject to the dollar limits discussed below) of "section 179 property" (see ¶1943). (Code Sec. 179(a), Code Sec. 179(b)(1)) For the election to currently deduct and not capitalize certain tangible property under a *de minimis* election (also known as a book-tax conformity election), see ¶1634.

The maximum amount that can be expensed is $1 million for property placed in service in tax years beginning in 2018 ($1,020,000 in tax years beginning in 2019, as calculated by Thomson Reuters based on inflation data).[25] For the dollar limit for qualified zone property, see ¶1941.

The maximum annual expensing amount generally is reduced dollar-for-dollar by the amount of section 179 property placed in service during the tax year in excess of the "investment ceiling" (Code Sec. 179(b)(2))—for tax years beginning in calendar year 2018, $2,500,000 ($2,550,000 in tax years beginning in 2019, as calculated by Thomson Reuters based on inflation data).[26] For the investment ceiling for qualified zone property, see ¶1941.

The deduction amount is further limited to the amount of taxable income from any of taxpayer's active trades or businesses, computed without regard to the cost of qualified expense property, the deduction for one-half of self-employment tax, NOL carrybacks or carryforwards, and deductions suspended under other Code sections (Code Sec. 179(b)(3); Reg § 1.179-2(c)(1)), e.g., the passive activity rules. (Reg § 1.179-2(c)(6)(iv))

An amount that can't be deducted due to the taxable income limitation is carried over indefinitely until it can be deducted. (Code Sec. 179(b)(3)(B))[27]

For a partner or S corporation shareholder, the deduction limitation, the investment limitation, and the taxable income limitation are applied at both the partnership (or S corporation) level and the taxpayer level. (Code Sec. 179(d)(8); Reg § 1.179-2(c)) However, for purposes of the investment limitation, the cost of qualifying property that a partnership or S corporation placed in service isn't attributed and allocated to the partner or shareholder. (Reg § 1.179-2(b)(3))[28]

A controlled group is treated as a single taxpayer for purposes of the annual dollar limitation. (Code Sec. 179(d)(6); Reg § 1.179-2(b)(1)) However, the single-taxpayer rule doesn't apply to S corporations.[29]

Married taxpayers filing jointly are treated as one taxpayer in applying the expense deduction limit. (Reg § 1.179-2(b)(5)) Married taxpayers filing separately may elect other than a 50-50 allocation of the expense deduction. Absent the election, the 50-50 allocation applies. (Code Sec. 179(b)(4); Reg § 1.179-2(b)(6))[30]

---

24. ¶L-9361; ¶1684.09
25. ¶L-9907, ¶L-9907.1; ¶1794.01
26. ¶L-9907, ¶L-9907.1; ¶1794.01
27. ¶L-9900 *et seq.*; ¶1794 *et seq.*

28. ¶L-9909 *et seq.*; ¶1794.01
29. ¶L-9908; ¶1794.01
30. ¶L-9907; ¶1794.01

An expensing election or specification of property to be expensed can be revoked without IRS consent, but once revoked, can't be re-elected. (Code Sec. 179(c)(2)) Regs as supplemented by later guidance provide that a taxpayer can make or revoke an expensing election on an amended return filed within the time prescribed by law for filing an amended return for the tax year for which the election was made. (Reg § 1.179-5(c)(1))[31] A taxpayer that elected to expense only part of the cost basis of property for a particular tax year (or didn't make any expensing election) can file an amended return and expense any part of the cost basis of property that was not expensed under a prior Code Sec. 179 election. (Reg § 1.179-5(c)(2))[32]

For a limit on the election for SUVs, see ¶1942. For a dollar cap on the election for passenger autos, see ¶1950. For prohibition of the election for "listed property," see ¶1947.

¶ 1941 More generous expensing rules for qualified zone property—before 2018.

The applicable maximum regular Code Sec. 179 expense election amount (described at ¶1940) is increased by $35,000 for "qualified zone property," placed in service, generally, before 2018, of an enterprise zone business. (Code Sec. 1391(d)(1)(A), Code Sec. 1397A(a)(1))[33] Only 50% of expensing-eligible enterprise zone property is taken into account before subtracting the applicable Code Sec. 179 phaseout amount (described at ¶1940). (Code Sec. 1397A(a)(2))[34] Recapture (¶1944) applies if the property ceases to qualify during its normal recovery period. (Code Sec. 1397A(b))[35] Qualified zone property must be used 85% or more in an empowerment zone (certain designated distressed areas) and meet other requirements. (Code Sec. 1397D(a)(1))[36]

✔️*caution:* Check tax.thomsonreuters.com/federaltaxhandbookupdates to see if the above provision has been extended.

¶ 1942 Restricted expensing deduction for heavy SUVs.

In addition to being subject to the overall annual dollar limit on Code Sec. 179 expensing (¶1940), the amount of the cost of a heavy SUV (sport utility vehicle) that can be expensed under Code Sec. 179 is subject to a per-vehicle dollar limit (the SUV limit). (Code Sec. 179(b)(5); Code Sec. 179(b)(6)) The SUV limit is $25,000 for vehicles placed in service in tax years beginning in 2018 ($25,500 in tax years beginning in 2019, as calculated by Thomson Reuters based on inflation data). [37]

The SUV limit applies to any 4-wheeled vehicle that (1) is primarily designed (or can be used) to carry passengers on public streets, roads and highways (except for rail vehicles), and (2) has a GVWR (gross, or loaded, vehicle weight rating) of more than 6,000 pounds but not more than 14,000 pounds. (Code Sec. 179(b)(5)(B)(i))

A vehicle is *not* subject to the SUV limit if it (1) is designed for more than nine individuals in seating rearward of the driver's seat; (2) is equipped with an open cargo area, or a covered box not readily accessible from the passenger compartment, of at least six feet in interior length; or (3) has an integral enclosure, fully enclosing the driver compartment and load carrying device, does not have seating rearward of the drivers seat, and has no body section protruding more than 30 inches ahead of the leading edge of the windshield. (Code Sec. 179(b)(5)(B)(ii))[38]

---

31. ¶L-9932 *et seq.*; ¶1794.04
32. ¶L-9933; ¶1794.04
33. ¶L-9951, ¶J-3396.4; ¶1397A4; ¶14,004.01
34. ¶L-9952; ¶1397A4

35. ¶L-9964; ¶1397A4
36. ¶L-9953, ¶L-9985; ¶1397A4, ¶14,00J4
37. ¶L-9907.2; ¶1794.015
38. ¶L-9907.2; ¶1794.015

For prohibition of the expensing election for passenger autos and other "listed property" not predominantly used in business, see ¶1947.

For dollar caps on the expensing election for passenger autos, see ¶1950.

⨀observation: The portion of the cost of a heavy SUV that isn't expensed under Code Sec. 179 can be depreciated over the 5-year MACRS recovery period (¶1915) *without regard to* the depreciation dollar caps for luxury autos (¶1950). Alternatively, the entire cost of the heavy SUV may be written off in the first year if the vehicle is eligible for the 100% bonus first year depreciation allowance (see ¶1932).

¶ 1943   Property eligible and ineligible for expense election.

Subject to the overall maximum dollar amount and investment ceiling discussed at ¶1940, property eligible for the expense election consists of the following assets, if "purchased" (see below) for use in the active trade or business of the taxpayer:

(1) tangible MACRS property that's Code Sec. 1245 property (generally, most depreciable property other than buildings and other land improvements),

(2) off-the-shelf computer software, and,

(3) by election of the taxpayer, qualified real property (see below). (Code Sec. 179(d)(1)).[39]

Code Sec. 179 property *does not include* property used in the production of income (Code Sec. 212 property), property used outside the U.S., property used by certain tax-exempt organizations, and property used by governmental units or foreign persons or entities (Code Sec. 179(d)(1)). The election also isn't available for the portion of the property's basis that's determined by reference to the basis of other property held at any time by the purchaser (e.g., trade-ins). [40]

Qualified real property. For property placed in service in tax years beginning after 2017, qualified real property (above) is property that is either (1) qualified improvement property or (2) the following improvements to nonresidential real property after the date such property was first placed in service: roofs; heating, ventilation, and air-conditioning property; fire protection and alarm systems; and security systems. (Code Sec. 179(e)) For property placed in service in tax years beginning before 2018, qualified real property consisted of qualified leasehold improvement property, qualified restaurant property, and qualified retail improvement property (all are various types of building improvements, see ¶1918).[41]

Qualified improvement property. Qualified improvement property is any improvement to an interior portion of a building that is nonresidential real property if the improvement is placed in service after the date the building was first placed in service, except for any improvement for which the expenditure is attributable to (1) enlargement of the building, (2) any elevator or escalator, or (3) the internal structural framework of the building. (Code Sec. 168(e)(6)(B))

Purchase. Purchase is any acquisition of property *except* property (1) acquired from certain individuals or entities related to the taxpayer (or from a decedent), or (2) whose basis is determined by reference to the adjusted basis of the person from whom acquired (e.g., gifts).[42] For prohibition of the expensing election for passenger autos and other "listed property" not predominantly used in business, see ¶1947.

---

39. ¶L-9901.1; ¶L-9922 *et seq.*; ¶1794.02
40. ¶L-9922.1, L-9923.1; ¶1794.02

41. ¶L-9901.1; ¶L-9922 *et seq.*; ¶1794.02
42. ¶L-9925; ¶1794.02

¶ 1944 Recapture of amount expensed under Code Sec. 179—Form 4797.

Code Sec. 179 recapture is triggered when the business use of property placed in service in an earlier year is reduced to 50% or less during the recapture period.

The recapture period of the expense election is the entire recovery period of the qualifying Section 179 property. (Code Sec. 179(d)(10))

The recapture amount (reported on Form 4797) is the expense deduction taken minus the MACRS depreciation amount that would have been allowed on the expensed amount up to and through the recapture year. (Reg § 1.179-1(e)(1))[43]

For the application of the general depreciation recapture rules to Code Sec. 179 expensing, see ¶2675 *et seq.*

¶ 1945 "Luxury" Automobiles and "Listed Property." ▬▬▬▬▬▬▬▬▬▬

MACRS depreciation deductions and the Code Sec. 179 expense election are limited for "luxury" business autos and other "listed property." Lessees of listed property are subject to special rules.

The following restrictions on depreciation (and the Code Sec. 179 expense election) apply to listed property (defined at ¶1946):

. . . Depreciation is under the straight-line method, and, generally, over longer recovery periods (and ineligible for bonus depreciation, see ¶1933, and elective expensing, see ¶1940), if it is not used more than 50% for business, see ¶1947 *et seq.*

. . . Depreciation of passenger autos ("luxury autos") is subject to maximum ceiling limitations, see ¶1950.

. . . A taxpayer who leases a "luxury" auto for business must add into income an "inclusion amount," see ¶1954 *et seq.*

. . . A taxpayer who leases listed property, other than a luxury auto, must take into income an "inclusion amount" when the property is no longer used more than 50% for business, see ¶1955.

. . . Specific recapture rules apply to listed property, see ¶2683.

. . . Strict substantiation rules apply to listed property expenses, see ¶1564 and ¶1569.

Lessors of listed property who are regularly engaged in the business of leasing that property aren't subject to the limitations applicable to owners for any listed property they lease or hold for leasing. (Code Sec. 280F(c)(1))[44]

¶ 1946 "Listed property" defined.

"Listed property" consists of:

. . . passenger autos (defined as discussed at ¶1950);

. . . any other property used as a means of transportation (e.g., trucks, buses, trains, boats, airplanes), except for "qualified nonpersonal use vehicles" (defined below);

. . . any property of a type generally used for entertainment, recreation or amusement, including photographic, phonographic, communication and video recording equipment, unless that property is used either exclusively at the taxpayer's regular business establishment, or in connection with the taxpayer's principal trade or business;

. . . for property placed in service before 2018, certain computer and peripheral equipment of employees; and

---

43. ¶L-9935; ¶1794.03   44. ¶L-10201; ¶280F4

... any other property specified by regs. (Code Sec. 280F(d)(4); Reg § 1.280F-6(b))[45]

"Qualified nonpersonal use vehicles" (QNPUVs) are vehicles that by their nature aren't likely to be used more than a *de minimis* amount for personal purposes. (Code Sec. 274(i); Reg § 1.280F-6(f)) QNPUVs include, but aren't limited to, various uniformed services vehicles. (Reg § 1.274-5(k))[46]

¶ 1947 Depreciation and expensing restrictions for listed property used no more than 50% for business—Form 4797.

If, for the year listed property (¶1946) is placed in service, it is used 50% or less in a qualified business use (i.e., it isn't used predominantly on an annual basis in a qualified business use), the listed property: (1) doesn't qualify for the expense election (¶1940) (Reg § 1.280F-3T(c)(1)), (2) is, for all years, depreciable only under straight-line and the "ADS" recovery periods (¶1931), and (3) is ineligible for the bonus first-year depreciation allowance (¶1932). (Code Sec. 168(k)(2)(D)(i), Code Sec. 280F(b)(1))[47]

The actual deduction amount, however, is computed by using the "business/investment use" percentage (defined at ¶1949) and not by the qualified business use percentage. (Reg § 1.280F-6(d)(3)(i))[48]

Any MACRS depreciation and Code Sec. 179 expense election deduction disallowed because of non-business/investment use is lost for all later years. (Code Sec. 280F(d)(2); Reg § 1.280F-4T(a)(1))[49]

If the more-than-50% requirement isn't met in a post-acquisition year (during the property's normal recovery period), the listed property becomes, retroactively to acquisition, straight-line ADS property. (Reg § 1.280F-3T(c)(2))[50] Depreciation previously taken in excess of straight-line (including amounts expensed, ¶1940, and bonus depreciation, ¶1932) is recaptured (on Form 4797). (Code Sec. 280F(b)(2)(A); Reg § 1.280F-3T(b)(2), Reg § 1.280F-3T(d)(2))[1]

¶ 1948 "Qualified business use" for listed property defined.

For purposes of the depreciation and expensing restrictions discussed at ¶1947 and the income inclusion discussed at ¶1955, "qualified business use" generally is any use in a trade or business of the taxpayer. (Code Sec. 280F(d)(6)(B))[2]

The following are excluded from qualified business use:

(1) Code Sec. 212 production-of-income use; (Reg § 1.280F-6(d)(2))

(2) leasing property to any 5% owner of the taxpayer or to any person related to the taxpayer; and

(3) the use of listed property as compensation (A) by a 5% owner or a related person, or (B) if the provider fails to include the value of the compensation in the recipient's gross income, properly report it and, where necessary, treat it as wages subject to withholding. (Code Sec. 280F(d)(6)(C))[3]

The exclusion of items (2) and (3) doesn't apply to an aircraft if at least 25% of the aircraft's total use during the tax year is qualified business use not described at (2) or (3). (Code Sec. 280F(d)(6)(C)(ii))

---

45. ¶L-10002; ¶280F4
46. ¶L-10002, ¶L-4658 *et seq.*; ¶280F4, ¶2744.10
47. ¶L-10018; ¶280F4
48. ¶L-10029; ¶280F4
49. ¶L-10019; ¶280F4

50. ¶L-10021; ¶280F4
1. ¶s L-10021, L-10032; ¶280F4
2. 0¶L-10025 *et seq.*; ¶280F4
3. ¶s L-10025, L-10027; ¶280F4

¶ 1949   "Business/investment use" for listed property defined.

"Business/investment use" (see ¶1947 and ¶1954) is the total of business use and investment use of any listed property for the tax year. For example, if an item of listed property is used 70% in a trade or business and 20% for the production of income, the taxpayer may claim, if the property otherwise qualifies, accelerated depreciation deductions (including the expense election deduction) based on 90% business/investment use. Business or investment use (with an exception concerning automobiles, see below) is determined under the normal rules of Code Sec. 162 and Code Sec. 212. (Reg § 1.280F-6(d)(3)(i), Reg § 1.280F-6(d)(5), Ex 2)[4]

The use of a taxpayer's automobile by another person (even if that other person is a 5% owner or a related person) is treated as business/investment use of the taxpayer if:

(1) its use is directly connected with the taxpayer's business,

(2) the value of that use is properly reported by the taxpayer as income to the other person, and where required, tax is withheld on that income, or

(3) the use of the taxpayer's automobile by that other person results in payment of fair market rent. (Reg § 1.280F-6(d)(3)(iv))

¶ 1950   Depreciation and expensing of business automobiles—"luxury" auto dollar caps.

Autos used in a trade or business normally are depreciated as 5-year MACRS property. (Code Sec. 168(b)(1), Code Sec. 168(e)(3)(B)) However, the deduction normally obtained for an auto by applying the MACRS 5-year property rules, the bonus depreciation allowance (¶1932), and the Code Sec. 179 expensing rules (¶1940), is limited by the so-called "luxury auto" dollar caps. (Code Sec. 280F(a)(1), Code Sec. 280F(d)(1)) The dollar caps (see ¶1951 and ¶1952 for the amounts) are adjusted for inflation, based on the placed-in-service year. (Code Sec. 280F(d)(7))

The dollar caps apply to passenger autos, i.e., four-wheeled vehicles manufactured primarily for use on public streets, roads, and highways, and rated at an unloaded gross vehicle weight of 6,000 pounds or less. For a truck or van, the 6,000-pound test is applied to the truck's or van's gross (loaded) vehicle weight. (Code Sec. 280F(d)(5)(A); Reg § 1.280F-6(c)) Excepted from the dollar caps are ambulances or hearses used directly in a trade or business, taxis and other vehicles used directly in the trade or business of transporting people or property for pay, and trucks or vans specified by IRS regs. (Code Sec. 280F(d)(5)(B)) Thus, qualified non-personal use vehicles (discussed at ¶1946) are excepted. (Reg § 1.280F-6(c)(3)(iii), Reg § 1.280F-6(f))[5]

observation: Sport-utility vehicles (SUVs) are trucks. Thus, SUVs rated at more than 6,000 pounds gross (loaded) vehicle weight are exempt from the dollar caps because they fall outside of the Code Sec. 280F(d)(5) definition of a passenger auto. For the restricted expensing deduction for heavy SUVs, see ¶1942.

¶ 1951   Regular "luxury" auto depreciation and expensing dollar cap amounts.

The "regular" luxury auto dollar caps in depreciation apply to vehicles subject to the caps (see ¶1950) to which bonus first-year depreciation isn't applied (see the observation below). For the increased first-year cap that applies to passenger autos to which bonus first-year depreciation applies, see ¶1952. For additional restrictions on depreciation and

---

4. ¶L-10029; ¶280F4   5. ¶L-10003; ¶280F4

expensing that apply to most vehicles not predominantly used in a qualifying business use, see ¶1947. For the income inclusion amounts instead of deduction limits that apply to leased automobiles and other listed property, see ¶1954 *et seq.*

observation: Few automobiles placed in service in tax years 2018 through 2025 won't qualify for bonus depreciation, mainly because new cars and most all used cars will qualify, see ¶1932 *et seq.*

The regular caps for vehicles first placed in service in 2018, and used 100% for business are as follows: $10,000 for the year in which the vehicle is placed in service, $16,000 for the second year, $9,600 for the third year, and $5,760 for the fourth and later years in the recovery period. (Code Sec. 280F).[6]

Where the "business/investment use percentage" (defined at ¶1949) is less than 100%, the caps are reduced proportionally to correspond to the taxpayer's business/investment use percentage. (Code Sec. 280F(a)(2))[7] Moreover, depreciation after the normal 5-year recovery period (actually six years because of the operation of the applicable convention) is based on unrecovered basis, i.e., adjusted basis determined as if the auto had been used 100% for business, so that the disallowed MACRS depreciation for the earlier years allocable to personal use is lost forever. (Code Sec. 280F(a)(1)(B), Code Sec. 280F(d)(8))

A taxpayer that uses the IRS standard mileage allowance method (discussed at ¶1554) for a tax year isn't subject to the above limitations for that year. [8]

¶ 1952 Depreciation and expensing dollar cap for passenger autos eligible for bonus first-year depreciation.

For passenger autos (including certain trucks and vans) that are eligible for bonus first-year depreciation (¶1932 *et seq.*), the regular first-year dollar cap on depreciation and Code Sec. 179 expensing is increased by $8,000 for an auto or light truck placed in service before 2027. (Code Sec. 168(k)(2)(F)) However, for passenger autos acquired before Sept. 28, 2017, but placed in service during 2018, the regular first-year dollar cap is increased by only $6,400. (Code Sec. 168(k)(2)(F)(iii))[9]

Vehicles eligible for 100% bonus depreciation. These are most vehicles placed in service *and* bought after Sept. 27, 2017 and before Jan. 1, 2023 (see ¶1932) where the taxpayer does not elect out of bonus depreciation (¶1937). Under a safe harbor provided by IRS for when 100% bonus depreciation was last in effect, for years after the placed-in-service year, the depreciation deduction was calculated as if the taxpayer had claimed 50% bonus depreciation.[10]

observation: The safe harbor discussed above was issued because without the safe-harbor, under IRS's view of the interaction between 100% bonus depreciation when last in effect and the passenger auto dollar cap rules, no depreciation was otherwise available for a passenger auto after the placed-service year and before the seventh year in which the passenger auto was in service. IRS guidance is needed as to whether the same analysis and resulting safe harbor applies under the 100% bonus depreciation available for passenger autos bought and placed in service after Sept. 27, 2017.

The depreciation limits for passenger autos (including trucks and vans) placed in service during calendar year 2018, for which bonus depreciation applies, are $18,000 for the placed in service year (but only $16,400 if the vehicle placed in service in 2018 was acquired *before* Sept. 28, 2017), $16,000 for the second tax year, $9,600 for the third tax year, and $5,760 for each succeeding year. (Code Sec. 168(k)(2)(F)(iii))[11]

6. ¶L-10004, ¶L-10004.4; ¶280F4
7. ¶L-10004; ¶280F4
8. ¶L-10013 *et seq.*; ¶280F4

9. ¶L-10004.1A¶L-10004.4; ¶1684.0281,¶280F4
10. ¶L-10004.1B
11. ¶L-10004.1A, ¶L-10004.4, ¶1684.0281,¶280F4

Vehicles eligible for 50% bonus depreciation. These are, generally, new vehicles bought or placed in service before Sept. 27, 2017 (see ¶1932), where the taxpayer does not elect out of bonus depreciation (¶1937). Here, the depreciation deduction for years after the placed-in-service year is the lesser of (1) the depreciation that would be available if the Code Sec. 280F dollar caps didn't apply or (2) the dollar cap for that later year. [12]

¶ 1953 Claiming auto depreciation (Forms 2106, 2106-EZ, 4562, etc.).

Self-employeds and sole proprietors report their vehicle expenses on Form 1040, Schedule C (Form 1040, Schedule C-EZ for certain small businesses) or if they are farmers on Form 1040, Schedule F with Form 4562 attached. For tax years beginning after 2017 and before 2026, unreimbursed employee business expenses (including those for employee owned cars) are nondeductible. (Code Sec. 67(g))[13]

¶ 1954 "Inclusion amount" for leased business autos, trucks, and vans.

Lessees of certain business vehicles (and, under different rules, other listed property, see ¶1955) entering leases of 30 days or more are subject to the MACRS limitations discussed in the preceding paragraphs, although indirectly. Specifically, in every lease year, lessees of vehicles that are subject to the "luxury" auto limits (¶1950) must include in gross income an "inclusion amount," figured from IRS's tables. (Code Sec. 280F(c)(2), Code Sec. 280F(c)(3); Reg § 1.280F-5T(d), Reg § 1.280F-5T(e))[14]

For vehicles first rented in 2018, the inclusion amount for each tax year of the lease is computed as follows (but there's no inclusion amount unless the FMV of the vehicle is more than $50,000): (Reg § 1.280F-7(a)(2))

(1) Find the line from the appropriate table at ¶1120, which includes the fair market value (FMV) of the leased vehicle.

(2) Prorate, with rounding to the nearest dollar, the dollar amount for the number of days in the lease term included in the tax year at issue.

(3) Multiply the prorated dollar amount by the "business/investment use" (see ¶1949) percentage for the vehicle for that tax year. The resulting amount is the inclusion amount.

For the last tax year of a lease that doesn't begin and end in the same tax year, the dollar amount for the preceding year is used. (Reg § 1.280F-7(a)(2)(i))[15]

⊘ *illustration:* On Apr. 1, 2018 a calendar year taxpayer leased and placed in service a vehicle with a FMV of $64,500. The lease is for three years and the business/investment use is 100% in each year. The taxpayer must include the following "inclusion amounts" (from Table at ¶1120) in gross income: for 2018, $31 ($41 inclusion amount × 275/365 rounded); for 2019, $90 (full inclusion amount); for 2020, $134 (full inclusion amount); and for 2021, $33 ($134 inclusion amount × 90/365) rounded. (Reg § 1.280F-7(a)(2)(i))

¶ 1955 Inclusion amount for MACRS leased listed property other than automobiles.

For listed property other than autos, the "inclusion amount" isn't annual (unlike the amount for autos, see ¶1954) but is instead taken into income for the first year the property ceases to be used predominantly (i.e., more than 50%) in a qualified business use

---

12. ¶L-10004.1A, ¶L-10004.4, ¶1684.0281,¶280F4
13. ¶L-10004

14. ¶L-10200 *et seq.*; ¶280F4
15. ¶L-10204, ¶L-10204.2; ¶280F4

(¶1955). (Reg § 1.280F-5T(f))[16]

The amount is the sum of the amounts computed under Steps (1) and (2), below. (Reg § 1.280F-7(b)(2))

STEP (1): Multiply the following three items: (a) the fair market value (FMV) of the property, (b) the business/investment use of the property for the year that use is 50% or less, and (c) the applicable percentage from Table II reproduced at ¶1119. (Reg § 1.280F-7(b)(2)(i))

STEP (2): Multiply the following three items: (a) the FMV of the property, (b) the average of the business/investment use for all tax years (in which the property is leased) that precede the year the business/investment use is 50% or less, and (c) the applicable percentage from Table I reproduced at ¶1119. (Reg § 1.280F-7(b)(2)(ii))

Special rules apply when a lease term begins within nine months of the end of the lessee's tax year or when the lease term is less than one year. (Reg § 1.280F-5T(g))[17]

¶ 1956 Depreciation Deduction Under the Income Forecast Method—Form 8866. ■■■

Depreciation deductions under the income forecast method are figured by multiplying the cost of the property (but only amounts that satisfy the Code Sec. 461(h) economic performance standard, ¶2831) less estimated salvage value, by a fraction, the numerator of which is the year's income generated by the property, and the denominator of which is the total estimated income to be earned before the close of the tenth tax year following the year in which the property was placed in service.[18]

Under the income forecast method, the depreciation deduction for the tenth tax year after the tax year in which the property was placed in service is equal to the taxpayer's entire remaining basis in the property. (Code Sec. 167(g)(1)(C)) Taxpayers using the income forecast method pay (or receive) interest in recomputation years (generally in the third and tenth years after the property was placed in service, unless income earned by the property is within 10% of original estimates; use Form 8866 to compute) based on the recalculation of depreciation under a look-back method (but there's no look-back for property that had a cost basis of $100,000 or less). (Code Sec. 167(g))[19] (For 15-year amortization for films, sound recordings, video tapes, etc., see ¶1967.)

The income forecast (or similar) method (A) can be used only for (1) motion picture films, video tapes, and sound recordings; (2) copyrights; (3) books; (4) patents; and (5) any other property to be specified in regulations, and (B) can't be used to depreciate amortizable section 197 intangibles (see ¶1966). (Code Sec. 167(g)(6))[20]

Rules address the effect on the calculation of depreciation under the income forecast method of "participations and residuals" (costs that, by contract, vary with the amount of income earned from property). (Code Sec. 167(g)(5)(E), Code Sec. 167(g)(7))[21]

¶ 1957 Depreciation Deduction Under the "Useful-Life" Rules. ■■■■■■

Tangible property not depreciable under MACRS (¶1900, ¶1907 through ¶1908) or that was placed in service before '81 is usually depreciable under the useful-life rules. The asset is depreciated (not below salvage value) over the period during which a depreciable asset, or group of similar assets, may reasonably be expected to be useful to the taxpayer in his trade or business or in income production.[22] Under the useful-life rules, a permissible method of depreciation is either one that

---

16. ¶L-10205; ¶280F4
17. ¶L-10206 *et seq.*; ¶280F4
18. ¶L-10704; ¶L-10705.1; ¶1674.100
19. ¶L-10707.4; ¶1674.100

20. ¶L-10704A; ¶1674.100
21. ¶L-10705, ¶L-10707, ¶L-10707.1, ¶L-10707.1A; ¶1674.100
22. ¶L-11800 *et seq.*; ¶1674.040 *et seq.*

is (1) prescribed by Code Sec. 167, or, (2) where a method isn't prescribed by Code Sec. 167, a method that results in a reasonable allowance. (Code Sec. 167(a); Reg § 1.167(b)-0; Reg § 1.167(a)-1(c); Reg § 1.167(b)-2(a))[23] The basis on which depreciation is taken is the adjusted basis under Code Sec. 1011 for the purpose of gain or loss on a sale or other disposition. (Code Sec. 167(c)(1))

¶ 1958 Intangibles excluded from 15-year amortization.

Certain property excluded from Code Sec. 197 (15-year amortization of many intangibles, see ¶1966 *et seq.*) is depreciated as follows:

(1) Computer software, in those situations in which it is excluded from 15-year amortization (see ¶1968), generally is depreciated using the straight-line method with a useful life of 36 months, beginning on the first day of the month that it is placed in service; see ¶1608 for exceptions. (Code Sec. 167(f)(1); Reg § 1.167(a)-14(b)(1))

(2) Rights to service debts secured by residential realty are depreciated using the straight-line method with a useful life of 108 months. (Code Sec. 167(f)(3); Reg § 1.167(a)-14(d)(1))

(3) Amortization of a right (other than one acquired as part of the purchase of a trade or business) to receive a fixed amount of any property under a contract or from a governmental unit is found by dividing its basis by a fraction (amount of tangible property or services received during the year divided by total amount of tangible property or services received or to be received). (Code Sec. 167(f)(2); Reg § 1.167(a)-14(c)(1)(i); Reg § 1.167(a)-14(c)(2)(i)) The cost or other basis of a right to receive an unspecified amount of tangible property or services over a fixed period is amortized ratably over the period of the right. (Code Sec. 167(f)(2); Reg § 1.167(a)-14(c)(1)(ii)) The basis of a right to receive an unspecified amount of an item, other than tangible property or services, over a fixed duration of less than 15 years is amortized over the term of the right. (Code Sec. 167(f)(2); Reg § 1.167(a)-14(c)(2)(ii))

(4) If the purchase price of an interest in a patent or copyright (other than one acquired as part of a purchase of a trade or business) is payable at least annually either as a fixed amount per use or as a fixed percentage of revenue derived, the depreciation deduction is equal to the amount of the purchase price paid or incurred during the year. Otherwise, basis is depreciated either ratably over its remaining useful life or under the income forecast method (¶1956). (Code Sec. 167(f)(2); Reg § 1.167(a)-14(c)(4))

Effective for leases entered into after Mar. 12, 2004, the useful life of property described at items (1), (3) or (4) on the above list that, if it were tangible property, would be "tax-exempt use property" (see ¶1930), can't be less than 125% of the lease term. (Code Sec. 167(f)(1)(C), Code Sec. 167(f)(2))[24]

Also, effective for intangible assets created on or after Dec. 31, 2003 (Reg § 1.167(a)-3(b)(4)), taxpayers may treat an intangible asset as having a useful life of 15 years unless:

... an amortization period or useful life for the intangible asset is specifically prescribed or prohibited by other rules (e.g., 15-year amortization under Code Sec. 197, see ¶1966);

... the intangible asset is described in Reg § 1.263(a)-4(c) (intangibles acquired from another person in a purchase or similar transaction) or Reg § 1.263(a)-4(d)(2) (relating to created financial interests);

... the useful life of the intangible asset can be estimated with reasonable accuracy; or

... the intangible asset is described in Reg § 1.263(a)-4(d)(8) (relating to certain benefits

---

23. ¶L-11711, ¶L-11901; ¶1674.044, ¶1674.100   ¶1674.033
24. ¶L-7935, ¶L-8018, ¶L-8025, ¶L-8030; ¶1674.013, ¶1674.025,

arising from the provision, production, or improvement of realty), in which case the taxpayer may treat the intangible asset as having a useful life equal to 25 years solely for purposes of Reg § 1.167(a)-3(a). (Reg § 1.167(a)-3(b)(1))

The 15-year and 25-year safe harbors don't apply to amounts that must be capitalized by Reg § 1.263(a)-5 (amounts paid to facilitate an acquisition of a trade or business, a change in the capital structure of a business entity, and certain other transactions). (Reg § 1.167(a)-3(b)(2))

Under the safe harbor, the basis of the intangible (determined without regard to salvage value) is amortized ratably over 15 or 25 years beginning on the first day of the month in which the intangible asset is placed in service by the taxpayer. The intangible asset is not eligible for amortization in the month of disposition. (Reg § 1.167(a)-3(b)(3))[25]

¶ 1959 Specialized "useful-life" depreciation methods.

These include:

. . . operating day method used for equipment affected chiefly by wear and tear rather than obsolescence, such as rotary oil drills; [26]

. . . sinking fund method (Reg § 1.167(b)-4(a));[27]

. . . unit-of-production method used for property, the usefulness of which is closely related to its use in production or to a source of supply or similar factor. (Reg § 1.167(b)-0(b), Reg § 1.611-5(a), Reg § 1.611-5(b)(2))[28]

¶ 1960 Special Expensing and Amortization Provisions. ▬▬▬▬▬▬▬▬

Instead of being subject to the ordinary depreciation or expensing rules, certain property is expensed or amortized as described below or at ¶1961 *et seq.*

Research and experimental expenditures connected with a trade or business can be amortized over a 60-month period (among several elective treatments, see ¶1585). Also, start-up expenditures (¶1500), organization costs of a corporation (¶3510) and organization costs of a partnership (¶3706) can be amortized over a 180-month period. Bond premium (¶2165 *et seq.*) and lease acquisition costs are also amortized (¶1581).

Taxpayers can elect to expense 50% of the cost of qualified advanced mine safety equipment property placed in service before 2018. (Code Sec. 179E)

✐caution: Check tax.thomsonreuters.com/federaltaxhandbookupdates to see if the above provision has been extended.

¶ 1961 Expensing election for costs of film, TV, and qualified theatrical production before 2018.

For qualified film and television (TV) productions and qualified theatrical productions that commence before Jan. 1, 2018, taxpayers can elect to deduct production costs in the year the costs are incurred (i.e., to expense them) instead of capitalizing the costs and recovering them through depreciation allowances. (Code Sec. 181(a)(1)) Regs clarify which taxpayers are eligible for the election and the meaning of qualified film and TV production costs. (Reg § 1.181-1, Reg § 1.181-3, Reg § 1.181-5)[29] In general, for each qualifying production, expensing doesn't apply to the portion of the cost that exceeds $15 million. The limit is $20 million if production expenses are "significantly incurred" in areas (1) eligible for designation as a low-income community, or (2) eligible for designation by the Delta

---

25. ¶L-8001; ¶1674.013
26. ¶L-10709; ¶1674.100
27. ¶L-10711

28. ¶L-10702; ¶1674.100
29. ¶L-3140 *et seq.*; ¶1814 *et seq.*

Regional Authority (a federal-state partnership covering parts of certain states) as a low-income community or isolated area of distress. (Code Sec. 181(a)(2)(A))[30]

🌀*caution:* Check tax.thomsonreuters.com/federaltaxhandbookupdates to see if the above provision has been extended.

A qualified film or TV production generally is any production of a motion picture or video tape if at least 75% of the total compensation expended on the production is "qualified compensation." Qualified compensation doesn't include participations and residuals, as defined by Code Sec. 167(g)(7)(B)) and is compensation for services performed in the U.S. by actors, directors, producers, and other relevant production personnel. For property that is one or more episodes in a television series, only the first 44 episodes qualify. Sexually explicit productions, as defined by section 2257 of title 18 of the U.S. Code, don't qualify. (Code Sec. 181(d))[31]

A "qualified live theatrical production" is a live staged production of a play (with or without music) that (1) complies with the 75% qualified compensation rules and sexually explicit production prohibition discussed above, (2) is derived from a written book or script, and (3) is produced or presented by a taxable entity in a venue that meets certain capacity limitations. (Code Sec. 181(e))[32]

Regs explain how and when to make the election. (Reg § 1.181-2) The election can be revoked only with prior consent of IRS. (Code Sec. 181(c)(2))[33] Recapture of the benefits of the expensing can apply if a production no longer qualifies for expensing in tax years after the year for which the expensing election is made. (Reg § 1.181-4(a))[34]

¶ 1962 Expensing for costs of making commercial buildings energy efficient before 2018.

Taxpayers can expense the cost of "energy efficient commercial building property" (Code Sec. 179D(a)) (certain property installed as part of an energy-use reduction plan (Code Sec. 179D(c), Code Sec. 179D(d)) placed in service before 2018. (Code Sec. 179D(h)) The deduction for any building for any tax year can't be more than the excess (if any) of (1) $1.80 × the square footage of the building, over (2) the deductions allowed under Code Sec. 179D(a) for earlier years. (Code Sec. 179D(b))

🌀*caution:* Check tax.thomsonreuters.com/federaltaxhandbookupdates to see if the above provision has been extended.

¶ 1963 Amortization elections for pollution control facilities.

A taxpayer may elect to amortize, over 60 months, part or all of the cost of new identifiable pollution control treatment facilities used in connection with a plant or other property in operation before '76. (Code Sec. 169(a), Code Sec. 169(d)) MACRS depreciation can be taken on any portion that doesn't qualify. (Code Sec. 169(g)) Also, a taxpayer may elect to amortize over an 84-month period *air* pollution control facilities used in connection with an electric generation plant or other property that is primarily coal fired. (Code Sec. 169(d)(5)) For both 60 month amortization and 84 month amortization, certain limits apply. (Code Sec. 169(f), Code Sec. 291(a)(4), Code Sec. 1363(b)(4))[35]

---

30. ¶L-3144 *et seq.*; ¶1814.01
31. ¶L-3142 *et seq.*; ¶1814.07 *et seq.*
32. ¶L-3142.1 *et seq.*; ¶1814.08 *et seq.*

33. ¶L-3146 *et seq.*; ¶1814.05, ¶1814.13
34. ¶L-3147; ¶1814.15
35. ¶L-12600 *et seq.*; ¶1694, ¶2914

¶ 1964   Expensing and amortization of reforestation expenditures—Forms 4562 and Form T.

Taxpayers other than trusts may elect to deduct up to $10,000 ($5,000 if married filing separately) of reforestation costs, and taxpayers (including estates and trusts) may elect to amortize the balance of reforestation costs over 84 months. (Code Sec. 194) Use Form 4562.

Individuals claim deductions under Code Sec. 194 as adjustments to arrive at adjusted gross income. (Code Sec. 62(a)(11))[36] Costs expensed or amortized under Code Sec. 194 are recaptured as ordinary income (to the extent of gain) if there's a disposition of the timber property within ten years. (Code Sec. 1245(a)(2)(C))[37]

Taxpayers must create and maintain separate accounts for each qualified timber property. Elected-for property can't be included in any other timber account (e.g., a depletion block) for which depletion is allowed under Code Sec. 611 (¶1969 *et seq.*). An amortizable timber account can't become part of a depletable account for purposes of deduction under Code Sec. 165(a).[38]

The 84-month amortization is usually reported on Form 4562, but can be reported on Form T (Timber), Forest Activities Schedule, if the taxpayer is required to file Form T. [39]

¶ 1965   24-month amortization for certain oil or gas costs; 7-year amortization for major integrated oil companies.

Geological and geophysical ("G and G") expenses in connection with exploring or developing oil or gas within the U.S. (defined in Code Sec. 638) are amortized over the 24-month period—7-year period for a major integrated oil company —beginning on the date that the expenses are paid or incurred. (Code Sec. 167(h)(1), Code Sec. 167(h)(5)) A half-year convention applies (so 25% of the expenditures are deducted in both Year 1 and Year 3). (Code Sec. 167(h)(2))

Amortization continues over the applicable period even if the underlying property is abandoned or retired. (Code Sec. 167(h)(4), Code Sec. 167(h)(5)) So upon abandonment or retirement, unamortized expenses can't be immediately deducted; neither can they be included in basis for purposes of determining gain or loss. Retirements include sales, exchanges and other withdrawals from service. [40]

Ownership of an oil or gas interest isn't a requirement for being allowed the amortization deduction. So, for example, otherwise-eligible expenses can be amortized by a surveyor that doesn't own oil or gas interests but formulates surveying data for customer use. [41]

The portion of the cost of acquisition of oil and gas assets allocated to seismic data can't be amortized if the data has been used before acquisition to locate the proved or probable wells within the formation to which the data relates. [42]

¶ 1966   Amortization of Intangibles under Code Sec. 197. ▬▬▬▬▬▬

Under Code Sec. 197, the cost of many intangibles, including most intangibles acquired in a business acquisition, is amortized over a 15-year period.

Thus, for property acquired after Aug. 10, '93 (except under certain elections), taxpayers claim deductions on Form 4562 for "amortizable section 197 intangibles" (¶1967) by amortizing the adjusted basis (for purposes of determining gain) of that intangible ratably over

---

36. ¶A-2601, ¶N-6301; ¶624.04
37. ¶N-3704; ¶12,454.03
38. ¶N-6301, ¶N-6310; ¶1944
39. ¶N-6317

40. ¶N-3201 *et seq.*; ¶1674.126
41. ¶N-3201.1
42. ¶N-3201.1

a 15-year period beginning on the *later* of: the first day of the month in which the intangible is acquired, or, for property held in connection with the conduct of a trade or business or a production-of-income activity, the first day of the month in which the conduct of the trade or business or the activity begins. (Code Sec. 197(a); Reg § 1.197-2(f)(1)(i)))[43] For depreciation of intangibles generally and of many intangibles that aren't section 197 intangibles, see ¶1903, ¶1956 and ¶1958.

No loss deduction is permitted on the disposition of an amortizable section 197 intangible if the taxpayer retains one or more other intangibles acquired in the same transaction or series of related transactions along with the intangible disposed of. (Code Sec. 197(f)(1)(A)) On the disposition of the intangible, the bases of the other intangibles acquired in the same transaction or series of related transactions are increased, under a formula, by the amount of the loss barred. (Code Sec. 197(f)(1)(A)(ii))[44]

Anti-churning rules keep taxpayers from converting existing intangibles for which a depreciation or amortization deduction isn't allowable under prior law into amortizable section 197 intangibles. (Code Sec. 197(f)(9))[45]

The amortization period of Code Sec. 197 property that, if it were tangible property, would be "tax-exempt use property" (see ¶1930), can't be less than 125% of the lease term. (Code Sec. 197(f)(10))[46] If more than one amortizable section 197 intangible is disposed of in one transaction, or a series of related transactions, all of the amortizable section 197 intangibles in the transaction (or transactions) —except for any amortizable section 197 intangible with an adjusted basis greater than its fair market value —are treated as a single asset for Code Sec. 1245 recapture purposes (see ¶2677). (Code Sec. 1245(b)(8))[47]

¶ 1967   Amortizable section 197 intangible.

An amortizable section 197 intangible is any section 197 intangible acquired and held in connection with the conduct of a trade or business or a Code Sec. 212 production-of-income activity. (Code Sec. 197(c)(1))[48] Assets can't qualify as amortizable section 197 intangibles before the commencement of a trade or business, e.g., FCC licenses held by entities formed only to hold and lease the licenses, but that have yet to lease the licenses. [49] Amortizable section 197 intangibles include:

. . . goodwill (Code Sec. 197(d)(1)(A); Reg § 1.197-2(b)(1)),[50]

. . . going concern value (Code Sec. 197(d)(1)(B); Reg § 1.197-2(b)(2)),[1]

. . . workforce in place (Code Sec. 197(d)(1)(C)(i); Reg § 1.197-2(b)(3)),[2]

. . . business books and records, operating systems, or any other information base (including lists or other information with respect to current or prospective customers) (Code Sec. 197(d)(1)(C)(ii); Reg § 1.197-2(b)(4)),[3]

. . . any patent or copyright (but see the caution below), process, design, pattern, know-how, format or similar item (Code Sec. 197(d)(1)(C)(iii); Reg § 1.197-2(b)(5)),[4]

. . . customer-based intangibles (Code Sec. 197(d)(1)(C)(iv); Reg § 1.197-2(b)(6)), including the deposit base and any similar asset of a financial institution. (Code Sec. 197(d)(2)(B)) Customer based intangibles are the composition of market, share, and any other value resulting from the future provision of goods or services out of relationships with customers (contractual or otherwise) in the ordinary course of business (Code

43. ¶L-7951; ¶1974
44. ¶L-7977; ¶1974
45. ¶L-7983 *et seq.*; ¶1974
46. ¶L-7951; ¶1974
47. ¶I-10219.1; ¶12,454.05
48. ¶L-7951.1; ¶1974

49. ¶L-7951.1
50. ¶L-7953; ¶1974
1. ¶L-7953; ¶1974
2. ¶L-7954; ¶1974
3. ¶L-7955; ¶1974
4. ¶L-7957; ¶1974

303

Sec. 197(d)(2)(A)),[5]

. . . supplier-based intangibles. (Code Sec. 197(d)(1)(C)(v)) Supplier-based intangibles are the value resulting from the future acquisitions of goods or services out of relationships (contractual or otherwise) in the ordinary course of business with suppliers of goods or services to be used or sold by the taxpayer (Code Sec. 197(d)(3); Reg § 1.197-2(b)(7)),[6]

. . . government granted licenses, permits or other rights (but see the caution below) (Code Sec. 197(d)(1)(D); Reg § 1.197-2(b)(8));[7] and

. . . franchises, trademarks and trade names. (Code Sec. 197(d)(1)(F); Reg § 1.197-2(b)(10))[8]

caution: Certain patents, copyrights, and government granted rights qualify only if acquired with the acquisition of a business.

Costs of acquiring a non-generic domain name (that isn't a trademark, see above) are costs of a customer-based intangible (above) if the name: (1) is associated with a website that is already constructed and will be maintained by the taxpayer; and (2) is acquired for use in a trade or business to provide goods and services through the website. Costs of acquiring a generic domain name are costs of a customer-based intangible if the name meets requirement (1) and is to be used in a trade or business to either generate advertising revenue by selling space on the website or to increase market share by providing goods or services through the website. [9]

Section 197 intangibles also include any other item that is similar to workforce in place, information base, know-how, customer-based intangibles or supplier-based intangibles. (Code Sec. 197(d)(1)(C)(vi))[10]

The following are section 197 intangibles only if acquired in connection with the acquisition of assets constituting a trade or business or a substantial portion of one: [11]

. . . Computer software. (Code Sec. 197(e)(3))[12] (For the exclusion of "off-the-shelf" computer software from 15-year amortization, see ¶1968. For software developed by the taxpayer, see ¶1608.)

. . . Films, sound recordings, video tapes and books. (Code Sec. 197(e)(4)(A); Reg § 1.197-2(c)(4))[13]

. . . Copyrights and patents. (Code Sec. 197(e)(4)(C))[14]

. . . Rights to receive tangible property or services under a contract or granted by the government. (Code Sec. 197(e)(4)(B))[15]

. . . Contract rights and government grants if the right has a fixed duration of less than 15 years, or is fixed in amount and, without regard to Code Sec. 197 would be recoverable under a method similar to the unit of production method. (Code Sec. 197(e)(4)(D); Reg § 1.197-2(c)(13))[16]

Covenants not to compete or similar arrangements are section 197 intangibles if entered into in connection with the acquisition of an interest in a trade or business or a substantial portion of one. The acquisition of the interest can be made in the form of an asset acquisition (including a stock purchase treated as an asset purchase under Code Sec. 338) or a stock or partnership interest acquisition or redemption. (Code Sec. 197(d)(1)(E); Reg § 1.197-2(b)(9))[17] A covenant not to compete agreed to by the seller in connection with

5. ¶L-7961; ¶1974
6. ¶L-7964; ¶1974
7. ¶L-7967; ¶1974
8. ¶L-7968; ¶1974
9. ¶L-7961, ¶L-7968
10. ¶L-7952; ¶1974
11. ¶L-7952; ¶1974

12. ¶L-7958.3; ¶1974
13. ¶L-7959; ¶1974
14. ¶L-7960; ¶1974
15. ¶L-7965; ¶1974
16. ¶L-7970; ¶1974
17. ¶L-7966; ¶1974

an acquisition of an interest (e.g., stock) in a trade or business (as distinct from an acquisition of assets) was held to be not subject to the substantial portion requirement. [18]

¶ 1968 Intangibles excluded from section 197 intangibles.

The following are never treated as section 197 intangibles regardless of how acquired: [19]

. . . interests in corporations, partnerships, trusts and estates. (Code Sec. 197(e)(1)(A))

. . . computer software that's readily available for purchase by the general public, is subject to a non-exclusive license, and hasn't been substantially modified. (Code Sec. 197(e)(3)(A)) For 36-month straight line depreciation, see ¶1958.

. . . futures, foreign currency contracts and notional principal contracts. (Code Sec. 197(e)(1)(B))

. . . land. (Code Sec. 197(e)(2)) But the right to use an American viticultural area (AVA) designation isn't an interest in land, and, thus, *is* a section 197 intangible as a government-granted license, permit or other right (see ¶1967).[20]

. . . leases of tangible property. (Code Sec. 197(e)(5)(A))

. . . debt instruments, except for deposit bases and similar items. (Code Sec. 197(e)(5)(B))

. . . mortgage servicing rights secured by residential real property. (Code Sec. 197(e)(6))

. . . sports franchises, if acquired before Oct. 23, 2004. [21]

. . . any fees for professional services or transaction costs incurred by parties to a transaction with respect to which any part of the gain or loss isn't recognized under the rules for corporate organizations and reorganizations. (Code Sec. 197(e)(7))

. . . accounts receivable. (Reg § 1.197-2(b)(6))

Also, intangibles created by the taxpayer (e.g., customer relationships) (or for the taxpayer by contract) are excluded if they are: (1) not certain rights granted by a governmental unit, covenants not to compete made in connection with acquisition of an interest in a trade or business, or franchises, trademarks and trade names; and (2) not created in connection with a transaction (or a series of related transactions) that involves the acquisition of assets that constitute all, or a substantial portion of, a trade or business. (Code Sec. 197(c)(2); Reg § 1.197-2(d)(2)) The exclusion doesn't apply to self-created intangibles sold and repurchased in an unrelated transaction. [22]

¶ 1969 Depletion Deduction.

All exhaustible natural deposits and timber qualify for deduction of a reasonable allowance for depletion based on the taxpayer's cost or other basis of the resources—cost depletion. (Code Sec. 611; Code Sec. 612) For mines and certain interests in oil or gas wells, the depletion deductions may be computed as a specified percentage of gross income if that is greater than cost depletion. (Code Sec. 613)

A taxpayer may take a depletion deduction only if he owns an "economic interest" in the mineral deposit or the timber. Generally, what is required is that the taxpayer: (1) look to the extraction of the mineral or severance of the timber for a return of capital, and (2) have an interest in the mineral in place or standing timber acquired by investment. (Reg § 1.611-1(b)) A district court held that an employee's contribution of time, skill, and expertise in locating mineral properties for his employer (an oil company) wasn't an investment in mineral property that satisfies (2). [23]

---

18. ¶L-7966
19. ¶L-7952.1, L-7968 *et seq.*; ¶1974
20. ¶L-7972; ¶1974

21. ¶L-7968.1; ¶1974
22. ¶L-7975; ¶1974
23. ¶N-2051 *et seq.*; ¶6114 *et seq.*

A taxpayer can claim (1) percentage depletion on one property and cost depletion on another, or (2) for the same property, cost depletion for one year and percentage for another.[24]

Where the property is entitled to either cost or percentage depletion, the allowable deduction is the greater of the two. (Code Sec. 613)[25] Percentage depletion for oil and gas wells (except for gas from certain domestic geothermal deposits or geopressured brine) is limited to "independent producers and royalty owners," see ¶1972. The allowable deduction is never less than cost depletion. (Code Sec. 611, Code Sec. 612, Code Sec. 613) There's no official form for computing depletion, but Form T must be attached to the income tax return if a deduction for depletion of timber is taken. [26] The basis of the property must be reduced by the depletion deduction allowed or allowable, whichever is larger. [27]

¶ 1970   Cost depletion.

This deduction is based on the property's adjusted basis, the number of recoverable units of mineral at the beginning of the year and units sold or for which payment is received during the year. (Reg § 1.611-2(a)) A safe harbor can be used to determine recoverable oil and gas reserves. [28] The total cost depletion deductions can't exceed the basis for the mineral property [29] (which is *only the mineral property's* cost or other basis plus or minus basis adjustments. (Code Sec. 612; Reg § 1.612-1(b)(1); Code Sec. 1016(a))[30]

¶ 1971   Percentage depletion.

This is a specified percentage of the "gross income from the property" for the tax year. It can never exceed 50% (100% for oil and gas properties) of the property's taxable income (Code Sec. 613(a)) (the excess of gross income from the property over the allowable deductions (exclusive of depletion) attributable to the mining processes (including transportation) on which depletion is claimed. (Reg § 1.613-5(a))[31]

Percentage depletion, reduces basis, but, even if basis is reduced to zero, continues to be deductible as long as there is gross income from the property. Cost depletion is used where higher than percentage depletion. (Code Sec. 613(a))[32] But a corporation's deductible depletion allowance for iron ore or coal (including lignite) is cut back by 20% of the otherwise allowable percentage depletion deduction in excess of the adjusted basis of the property at the close of the tax year (determined without regard to the depletion deduction for the tax year). (Code Sec. 291(a)(2))

The depletion percentages for most minerals are provided in the Code and regs. (Code Sec. 613(b); Reg § 1.613-2(b)).[33] For oil, gas and geothermal deposits, see ¶1972.

Natural resources that don't qualify for percentage depletion include timber (Reg § 1.611-1(a)), minerals from sea water and other inexhaustible sources. (Code Sec. 613(b)(7)) Coal or iron ore disposed of with a retained economic interest that qualifies for capital gain-ordinary loss treatment also doesn't qualify. (Reg § 1.611-1(b)(2))[34] For alternative minimum tax treatment of percentage depletion, see ¶3210.

Cost or percentage depletion must be computed separately for each property. (Code Sec. 612, Code Sec. 613)[35] A "property" is each separate interest owned by the taxpayer in

---

24. ¶N-2004, N-2250 *et seq.*; ¶6114
25. ¶N-2004; ¶6114
26. ¶N-3101 *et seq.*, ¶N-6107; ¶6114.027
27. ¶N-3009; ¶6124.001
28. ¶N-2255.2
29. ¶N-2250 *et seq.*; ¶6114.020 *et seq.*
30. ¶N-3000 *et seq.*; ¶s 6124, 6124.001
31. ¶N-2702; ¶6134.009 *et seq.*
32. ¶N-2300 *et seq.*; ¶6114
33. ¶N-2311; ¶s 2914, 6134 *et seq.*
34. ¶N-2314; ¶s 6114.023, 6314.04
35. ¶N-2901; ¶6114 *et seq.*

each separate tract or parcel of land. (Code Sec. 614(a)) "Interest" means economic interest. It includes working or operating interests, royalties, overriding royalties and net profits interests. It also includes production payments to the extent they aren't treated as loans. (Reg § 1.614-1(a)(2)) Separate properties may be aggregated and treated as a single property. (Code Sec. 614(b), Code Sec. 614(c), Code Sec. 614(e)) An interest in a "mine" may be electively treated as two or more separate properties. (Code Sec. 614(c)(2); Reg § 1.614-3(b))

¶ 1972 Oil, gas and geothermal deposits percentage depletion.

15% depletion is allowed a taxpayer who isn't a retailer or refiner for so much of the "average daily production" of domestic crude oil and domestic natural gas as doesn't exceed the "depletable oil quantity" or "depletable natural gas quantity." "Marginal production" may qualify for a higher percentage depletion rate (not to exceed 25%) if the price of domestic crude oil is below $20 per barrel for the calendar year preceding the calendar year in which the tax year in question begins. (Code Sec. 613A(c)(6)) The maximum depletable amount is 1,000 barrels of oil or 6,000,000 cubic foot of gas per day. A taxpayer who has both types of production must allocate a unified maximum amount between oil and gas at the rate of 6,000 cubic feet of gas per barrel of oil. Over-ceiling production isn't entitled to any depletion. (Code Sec. 613(d), Code Sec. 613A) The deduction can't exceed 65% of the taxpayer's taxable income from all sources. (Code Sec. 613A(d)) The deduction for any costs for which taxpayer claims the 15% enhanced oil recovery credit (¶2322) must be reduced by that credit amount. (Code Sec. 43(d)(1))[36]

Percentage depletion is also available for production of natural heat from geothermal deposits (at a 15% rate) and natural gas production from geo-pressured brine (at a 10% rate) located in the U.S. or its possession. (Code Sec. 613(e), Code Sec. 613A(b)(2))[37]

Percentage depletion isn't available for any lease bonus, advance royalty or other amount payable without regard to production from any oil, gas or geothermal property. (Code Sec. 613(e)(3), Code Sec. 613A(d)(5))[38] This restriction applies only to oil and natural gas, but not other minerals, from oil and gas wells. [39]

The depletable ceiling amounts for independent producers or royalty owners who are related or are under common control are allocated among them. (Code Sec. 613A(c)(8))[40]

36. ¶N-2400 *et seq.*;¶N-2425; ¶613A4
37. ¶N-2316; ¶s 6134.001, 613A4
38. ¶N-2105 *et seq.*; ¶613A4.02

39. ¶N-2400 *et seq.*
40. ¶N-2420; ¶613A4

Chapter 6   Charitable Contributions—Medical Expenses—Alimony—Other Nonbusiness Deductions

¶ 2100   **Charitable Contribution Deduction—Form 1040, Schedule A.** ■■■■■■■

An individual who itemizes can deduct charitable contributions up to 60% for cash contributions made in tax years beginning after Dec. 31, 2017 and before Jan. 1, 2026, 30% or 20% of his adjusted gross income, depending on the type of property contributed and the type of donee (¶2123 *et seq.*). A corporation generally can deduct charitable contributions up to 10% of its taxable income (¶2131). Amounts that exceed the ceilings can be carried forward for five years by both individuals (¶2129) and corporations (¶2131). The deduction allowed for property contributions is usually the property's fair market value, but is reduced for gifts of certain types of property (¶2106 *et seq.*).

For individuals, charitable contributions are deductible only as an itemized deduction on Form 1040, Schedule A. (Reg § 1.170A-1(a))[1] For the charity's requirement to disclose the deductibility of contributions to it, see ¶4120.

¶ 2101   **What is a deductible charitable contribution?**

A deductible charitable contribution generally is one that:

... is to or for the use of a qualified charitable organization (¶2102) (Code Sec. 170(c));

... is paid within taxpayer's tax year, regardless of taxpayer's accounting method (¶2132) (except for certain accrual basis corporations, see ¶2133) (Code Sec. 170(a));

... is within the applicable statutory ceilings for individuals (¶2123 *et seq.*), and corporations (¶2131) (Code Sec. 170(b)); *and*

... meets certain substantiation requirements (¶2134 *et seq.*). (Reg § 1.170A-13)[2]

¶ 2102   **Qualified charitable organizations.**

A qualified charitable organization is one that fits into one of the specified categories *and* which IRS has ruled (or the donor establishes) is eligible to receive deductible contributions.[3] IRS maintains on its website a list of organizations that are eligible to receive tax-deductible charitable contributions, as well information concerning tax-exempt organizations (i.e., in addition to those eligible to receive tax-deductible contributions). [4] Qualified charitable organizations include:

... a corporation, trust, community chest, fund or foundation (including a private foundation) that's organized *and* operated exclusively for charitable, religious, educational, scientific or literary purposes, or for the prevention of cruelty to children or animals, or to foster and conduct national or international amateur sports competition (but only if none of the activities involves providing athletic facilities or equipment); *and* that's organized or created in the U.S. or its possessions, or under their laws; *and* none of whose net earnings inures to the benefit of any private shareholder or individual. Corporate contributions to noncorporate donees must be used in the U.S. or its possessions. (Code Sec. 170(c)(2));[5] Additionally, contributions to disregarded single-member LLCs wholly owned and controlled by a U.S. charity are treated as made to the charity; [6]

---

1. ¶A-2701; ¶1704.01
2. ¶K-2803; ¶1704
3. ¶K-2850 *et seq.*; ¶1704.20

4. ¶K-2945; ¶1704.21
5. ¶K-2862 *et seq.*; ¶1704.20
6. ¶K-2854

References beginning with a single letter are to paragraphs in Federal Tax Coordinator 2d and RIA's Analysis of Federal Taxes: Income. Those beginning with numbers are to paragraphs in United States Tax Reporter.

. . . U.S. states or possessions, their political subdivisions, the U.S., and the District of Columbia, *but only* if the gift is exclusively for public purposes (Code Sec. 170(c)(1));[7]

. . . certain war veterans' organizations (Code Sec. 170(c)(3)),[8] certain domestic fraternal societies, orders or associations (Code Sec. 170(c)(4)),[9] and certain nonprofit cemetery companies. (Code Sec. 170(c)(5)).[10]

¶ 2103   Charitable deductions barred for certain contributions.

No charitable deduction is allowed for the following types of contributions:

. . . To a charity that conducts lobbying activities on matters of direct financial interest to the donor's trade or business, if a principal purpose was to avoid income tax by getting a charitable deduction for expenses for which a business expense deduction would be disallowed (¶1614) had the donor conducted the activities directly. (Code Sec. 170(f)(9))[11]

. . . To an organization disqualified from tax exemption because a substantial part of its activities involves trying to influence legislation, or it participates in any political campaign (Reg § 1.170A-1(j)(5)), see ¶4102 *et seq.*[12]

. . . Made to or for an individual (except for certain students, see ¶2122), unless the individual is an agent for a qualified organization (¶2102).[13]

. . . By church members and earmarked for a specific individual, e.g., to cover the minister's medical expenses. The church must have control over the funds' use for the donation to be deductible.[14]

. . . To a charity to the extent the donor derives an economic benefit (for exception, see ¶2104). Thus, no charitable deduction is allowed for: tuition (or required "donation" of excess "tuition" payment), even for parochial school,[15] or a payment in connection with a person's admission to a senior living or retirement home operated by a charity, to the extent allocable to care to be given (may be partly a *medical* expense, see ¶2146) or the privilege of being admitted.[16] But, contributions to state programs that entitled taxpayer to state tax credits were deductible.[17]

. . . Clothing and household items that aren't in good used condition or better (but deduction may be allowed if amount claimed for the item exceeds $500 and taxpayer includes a qualified appraisal with his return, see ¶2137). IRS may also deny a deduction for any contribution of clothing or a household item with minimal monetary value (e.g., used socks or undergarments). IRS says the price a buyer actually pays for a used item in a store such as a thrift shop is an indication of value, but dismissed as inaccurate "standard value listings" supplied by organizations like the Salvation Army. It also says valuation under a fixed formula or method (e.g., percentage of replacement cost), doesn't work well for used clothing. (Code Sec. 170(f)(16))[18]

¶ 2104   Fundraising events, entertainment, etc., for charity.

Where amounts are paid in connection with admission to fundraising events for charity (e.g., shows, lotteries, and athletic events), the receipt of tickets or other privileges raises a presumption that the payment isn't a gift. Taxpayer must show that a clearly identifiable part of the payment is a gift. Only the part made with the intention of making a gift *and* for which taxpayer receives no consideration qualifies as a contribution.[19] The charity

7. ¶K-2899; ¶1704.25
8. ¶K-2915; ¶1704.27
9. ¶K-2921; ¶1704.26
10. ¶K-2925; ¶1704.28
11. ¶K-2804; ¶1624.395
12. ¶K-2871; ¶1704.30
13. ¶K-2953; ¶1704.20

14. ¶K-2970
15. ¶K-3110, K-3111; ¶1704.38
16. ¶K-3047; ¶1704.38
17. ¶K-3059
18. ¶K-3177.6; ¶1704.41
19. ¶K-3089; ¶1704.38

must show (in its solicitation, tickets, receipts or other related documents) the value (or reasonable estimate) of the event, and how much of the contribution is deductible. [20] For an organization's fundraising disclosure requirements, see ¶4121 *et seq.*

However, the donor may deduct a contribution in full if the benefit is inconsequential or insubstantial. This applies if the charity informs patrons how much is deductible *and* any of these tests is met: (1) the fair market value (FMV) of all benefits received in connection with the payment isn't more than 2% of the payment, or the following dollar figures: $108 for 2018 ($111 for 2019, as calculated by Thomson Reuters based on inflation data), if less; or (2) the payment is at least $54 for 2018 ($55.50 for 2019, as calculated by Thomson Reuters based on inflation data), and in connection with it the donor receives only token benefits (bookmarks, calendars, mugs, posters, tee shirts, etc.) generally costing no more than $10.80 for 2018 ($11.10 for 2019, as calculated by Thomson Reuters based on inflation data), or (3) the charity mails or otherwise distributes free, unordered items to patrons.[21]

A taxpayer may rely on either a contemporaneous written acknowledgment (for contributions of $250 or more, see ¶2136) or a written disclosure statement (for quid pro quo contributions of more than $75, see ¶4121) for the FMV of any goods or services he receives from the charity. A taxpayer can't treat an estimate as the FMV where he knows, or has reason to know, it's unreasonable. (Reg § 1.170A-1(h)(4))[22]

For tax years beginning after 2017, no deduction is allowed for a contribution to a college or university where the donor receives a *right to buy* seating at an athletic event, and the ticket cost itself is nondeductible (Code Sec. 170(l))[23], regardless of whether taxpayer uses it.[24] Amounts paid for raffle tickets, to play bingo, etc., aren't contributions [25] (for deduction as a gambling loss, see ¶1778).

¶ 2105 Charitable contribution vs. business expense.

Transfers to a charity that are directly related to a taxpayer's business and made with a "reasonable expectation of financial return commensurate with" the amount transferred may be deductible as business expenses. But no business expense deduction is allowed for the transfer if *any* part of it is deductible as a charitable contribution. (Reg § 1.162-15(a)(2))[26]

⊘ observation: Business expense treatment may be preferable if the "contribution" would cause the taxpayer's total charitable contributions to exceed the charitable deduction ceiling (¶2123 *et seq.*). Also, some individual taxpayers would benefit more from reducing adjusted gross income (e.g., to avoid or minimize reductions in some otherwise available benefits) than from just reducing taxable income.

¶ 2106 Gift of property.

A gift of property to a qualified charitable donee (¶2102) is a contribution to the extent of the property's fair market value (FMV) at the time of the gift, whether or not it has appreciated (Reg § 1.170A-1(c)), except for gifts of ordinary income-type property (¶2107), and certain gifts of tangible personal property or capital gain property (¶2110).[27] For substantiation requirements, see ¶2134 *et seq.* The property's FMV is reduced for donor-placed restrictions on marketability or use (e.g., 3-year bar on transfer or license of donated patent).[28] No gain is realized on a contribution of appreciated property (for certain

---

20. ¶K-3105; ¶1704.38
21. ¶K-3106; ¶1704.38
22. ¶K-3087.2; ¶1704.38
23. ¶K-3100; ¶1704.38
24. ¶K-3094

25. ¶K-3090; ¶1704.38
26. ¶K-3068 *et seq.*; ¶1624.363
27. ¶K-3150 *et seq.*; ¶1704.40
28. ¶K-3151

bargain sales, see ¶2112).[29]

Taxpayer's charitable deduction for the gift can't exceed the property's FMV (at contribution), even if it's less than his basis. [30] Nor is taxpayer allowed a loss deduction on the difference between the property's basis and FMV. [31] Special rules apply to gifts of patents [32] and taxidermy property. [33]

¶ 2107　Gift of ordinary income-type appreciated property—deduction reduced.

For charitable gifts of ordinary income-type property (below), the amount contributed (property's fair market value (FMV), ¶2106) must be reduced by the amount which would have been recognized as gain other than long-term capital gain if the property had been sold by the donor for its then FMV. (Code Sec. 170(e)(1))[34] However, the reduction does not apply to any gain of a corporation that would not be treated as long-term capital gain under the rules of Code Sec. 291 (¶2680). For exceptions for certain gifts of C corporations, see ¶2108.

Ordinary income-type property is property which, if sold by taxpayer (donor) at its FMV on the date it was contributed, would have resulted in *some* amount of gain other than long-term capital gain. (Code Sec. 170(e)(1)) This includes: inventory or other property held for sale to customers; Code Sec. 306 stock (¶3524 *et seq.*); capital assets held for less than the long-term holding period as of the date contributed; property subject to depreciation, recapture, etc.; property used in taxpayer's trade or business; and art works, letters, memoranda, and similar property created by or for taxpayer. (Reg §　1.170A-4(b))[35]

Taxpayers that aren't C corporations that donated "apparently wholesome food" (i.e., meant for human consumption, and meeting certain quality and labeling standards) inventory to eligible charities, are entitled to the same enhanced deduction available to C corporations (¶2108), except that the deduction can't exceed 15% of aggregate net income for that tax year from all trades or businesses from which those contributions were made, computed without regard to the taxpayer's charitable deductions for the year. (Code Sec. 170(e)(3)(C)(i)(I))[36]

¶ 2108　Enhanced deductions for C corporation gifts for specified purposes.

A C corporation may claim an enhanced ("above-basis") deduction equal to the lesser of (a) basis plus half of the property's appreciation, or (b) twice the property's basis, for:

(1) Contributions of inventory, property held primarily for sale to customers in the ordinary course of its trade or business, or depreciable real property used in its trade or business, if the contribution is to an exempt Code Sec. 501(c)(3) organization (see ¶4102) (other than certain private foundations) that uses the property solely for the care of the ill, the needy or infants, and meets other specified requirements. (Code Sec. 170(e)(3)(A))[37]

(2) Certain contributions of scientific equipment or apparatus constructed by taxpayer to a higher education institution or a tax-exempt organization (but not a private foundation) organized and operated primarily to conduct scientific research. (Code Sec. 170(e)(4))[38]

(3) Contributions of food inventory that are "apparently wholesome food" (i.e., meant for human consumption, and meeting certain quality and labeling standards), limited to

29. ¶K-3208 *et seq.*, ¶K-3179 *et seq.*; ¶1704.43
30. ¶K-3151; ¶1704.41
31. ¶M-1015
32. ¶K-3177.1; ¶1704.42
33. ¶K-3171.1

34. ¶K-3160 *et seq.*; ¶1704.42
35. ¶K-3161; ¶1704.42
36. ¶K-3201.1; ¶1704.42
37. ¶K-3201 *et seq.*; ¶1704.42
38. ¶K-3221 *et seq.*; ¶1704.42

15% of taxable income (as specially computed). (Code Sec. 170(e)(3)(C))[39]

¶ 2109 Property contribution where taxpayer realizes income on gift.

If a taxpayer realizes income (ordinary income or capital gain) on his gift of property, his charitable deduction isn't subject to the reduction described at ¶2107. Thus, he may deduct the full fair market value of donated installment obligations, obligations issued at a discount, or other receivables. (Reg § 1.170A-4(a))[40]

¶ 2110 Limits on contributions of tangible personal property; gifts to certain private foundations.

For certain gifts, the amount treated as contributed and deductible (subject to deduction ceilings, see ¶2123 *et seq.*) is the property's fair market value (FMV) *reduced* by the total amount of the gain that would have been long-term capital gain (determined without regard to Code Sec. 1221(b)(3), see ¶2615) if the property were sold for its then FMV. (Code Sec. 170(e)(1)(B))[41] The donor's deduction is thus limited to his basis for these contributions:

... tangible personal property that's unrelated to the donee's exempt function (e.g., art to a church that then sells it) (Code Sec. 170(e)(1)(B)(i)); and

... any capital gain property except for publicly traded stock (limited to aggregate contributions of not more than 10% of the value of a corporation's outstanding stock by a donor and his family) given to a private foundation that isn't an operating foundation or community foundation and that doesn't make timely qualifying distributions. (Code Sec. 170(e)(1)(B)(ii), Code Sec. 170(e)(5))[42]

For contributions of tangible personal property for which a FMV deduction is claimed, but which isn't used for exempt purposes, if the donee sells or disposes of tangible personal property with a claimed value of at least $5,000: (1) in the year of contribution, the deduction is limited to taxpayer's basis; or (2) after the year of contribution, but within the 3-year period beginning on the contribution date, the donor includes in income the amount of the claimed deduction in excess of his basis in the property. These rules don't apply if the organization makes a proper certification to IRS. A $10,000 penalty applies for fraudulent identifications of property (i.e., stating it's exempt-use property while knowing it was not intended for such use). (Code Sec. 170(e)(1)(B)(i)(II), Code Sec. 170(e)(7), Code Sec. 6720B)[43]

¶ 2111 Liabilities transferred as part of contribution.

The donor's charitable contribution must be reduced by any liability that's assumed (e.g., by the donee) in connection with the gift. (Reg § 1.170A-3(d)) Where the donor transfers property subject to a liability, the amount of that debt is treated as an amount realized for purposes of the bargain sale rules, see ¶2112 (but not for the rule at ¶2109).[44] A reduction also must be made for the prepayment of any interest on the liability attributable to any period after the contribution was made if the donor takes a deduction for interest expense on the same payment. (Code Sec. 170(f)(5))[45]

---

39. ¶K-3201.1; ¶1704.42
40. ¶K-3178
41. ¶K-3160 *et seq.*; ¶1704.42
42. ¶K-3175 *et seq.*; ¶1704.42

43. ¶K-3167 *et seq.*; ¶V-2704.1; ¶1704.42
44. ¶K-3155, K-3198; ¶1704.44
45. ¶K-3157; ¶1704.44

⚫ *observation:* A taxpayer who can't deduct the prepayment as interest, e.g., because it's personal interest, should be able to get a charitable deduction for that payment since the charity has the obligation to make the interest payment after the contribution.

¶ 2112   Bargain sale to charity.

A taxpayer who sells property to (or exchanges it with) a charity and receives less than its fair market value (FMV) may treat the "bargain" element as a charitable contribution. (Code Sec. 1011(b); Reg § 1.170A-4(c)(2)) In computing the deduction, the amount considered contributed (excess of FMV over selling price) must be reduced by the amount of any required adjustment for ordinary income-type appreciated property (¶2107) for the contribution portion. (Reg § 1.170A-4(c), Reg § 1.1011-2(a))[46]

But the donor generally also realizes taxable gain on the sale. His basis for measuring gain is only the portion of his total cost or other basis for the property that the bargain selling price (amount realized) bears to its FMV. (Code Sec. 1011(b); Reg § 1.1011-2) This is basis times the selling price, divided by FMV. (Reg § 1.170A-4(c)(2)(i))[47]

⚫ *illustration:* J owns long-term stock that cost $12,000 and is worth $20,000 when he sells it to charity for $12,000. A contribution deduction of $8,000 ($20,000 − $12,000) is allowable. J's basis for the stock is reduced to $7,200 ($12,000 cost × [$12,000 selling price ÷ $20,000 FMV]) which, applied against his $12,000 selling price, gives J a $4,800 taxable gain.

¶ 2113   Gift of stock to charity followed by redemption ("charitable bail-out").

Owners of closely held corporations may effectively withdraw earnings from their firms tax-free by making a charitable contribution of their corporate stock, which the corporation then redeems. As long as the charity isn't obligated to sell back the stock, the donor can claim a deduction, even if the redemption was preplanned. [48] But, a contribution of stock which is then redeemed from a private foundation may be subject to penalty excise taxes (¶4129).

¶ 2114   Contributions of partial interests in property.

For transfers in trust, a contribution of a partial interest in property (e.g., where the donor transfers only his right to use the property, or his income interest in it) qualifies for a charitable deduction if the interest is:

- a remainder interest transferred to a charitable remainder trust (CRT, ¶2116), or a pooled income fund (¶2117), (Code Sec. 170(f)(2)(A)); or
- an income interest in a charitable lead trust (¶2119). (Code Sec. 170(f)(2)(B))[49]

For transfers not in trust, no charitable deduction is allowed for a contribution of less than the donor's entire interest in the donated property, except to the extent the deduction would have been allowed had the transfer been in trust. (Code Sec. 170(f)(3)(A))[50] Thus, a taxpayer who gives a charity the *right to use* property (e.g., rent-free use of office space), while retaining the property itself, can't take a charitable deduction for the rental or other value of this right.[1] The bar on deductions for transfers not in trust doesn't apply to contributions of:

---

46. ¶K-3190; ¶1704.43
47. ¶K-3194; ¶1704.43
48. ¶K-3186

49. ¶K-3250 *et seq.*; ¶1704.46
50. ¶K-3440.1 *et seq.*; ¶1704.45
1. ¶K-3440.2; ¶1704.45

- A remainder interest in a personal residence or a farm. (Code Sec. 170(f)(3)(B)(i));[2]

- An undivided part of taxpayer's entire interest (even if partial) in property (Code Sec. 170(f)(3)(B)(ii)), such as a remainder or income interest.[3] No deduction is allowed for a contribution of an undivided part of a taxpayer's entire interest in tangible personal property unless, immediately before the contribution, all interests in the property are held by taxpayer or taxpayer and the donee. Additionally, the fair market value (FMV) of any additional contribution of a fractional interest in property is the lesser of: (1) its FMV at the time of the initial fractional contribution, or (2) its FMV at the time of the additional contribution. (Code Sec. 170(o)(1)(A), Code Sec. 170(o)(2)) The deduction is recaptured under certain circumstances. (Code Sec. 170(o)(3)(A), Code Sec. 2522(e)(2)(A));

- A partial interest in property where *all* of taxpayer's interests in the property are given to one or more charities (e.g., income interest to one charity and remainder interest to another charity). (Reg § 1.170A-6(a));[4]

- A partial interest in real property (including remainders and perpetual restrictions) exclusively for "conservation purposes," including a qualifying facade easement. (Code Sec. 170(f)(3)(B)(iii), Code Sec. 170(h)) A facade easement must satisfy a number of requirements, including that it preserve in perpetuity the building's entire exterior and prohibit any change inconsistent with its historical character. No deduction is allowed for a charitable donation of an interest in property which is subject to a mortgage unless the mortgagee subordinates its rights in the property to the right of the charitable donee to enforce the conservation purposes of the gift in perpetuity. (Reg § 1.170A-14(g)(2)) The subordination agreement must be in effect when the easement is granted. And an easement isn't considered to be granted until it's enforceable under state law.[5] The perpetuity requirement is not met if other property can be substituted for the property originally transferred subject to the easement, if the taxpayer retains the right to modify the boundary lines of the donated interest (although the taxpayer may retain the right to modify the boundary lines of tracts *within* the donated interest), if the term of the easement is limited under state law, or if a long-term lessee of a building doesn't have a fee interest in it.[6] Additionally, the easement is held to have no value, and thus no deduction is allowed, if the facade is already subject to restrictions similar to the easement by virtue of being located in a historic district.[7]

¶ 2115 "Personal benefit contract" transactions—Form 8870.

No charitable deduction is allowed for a transfer to or for the use of a charity if the charity directly or indirectly pays or paid any premium on any personal benefit contract (e.g., split-dollar life insurance, see ¶1264) for the transferor. Also, no deduction is allowed if there is an understanding or expectation that any person will directly or indirectly pay any premium on any such contract for the transferor. A charity must pay an excise tax (use Form 8870) if it or any such person pays such premiums. (Code Sec. 170(f)(10))[8]

¶ 2116 Charitable remainder trusts (CRTs)—CRATs and CRUTs.

A CRT is a trust formed to make current distributions to one or more noncharitable income beneficiaries and to pay the entire remainder to charity or use it for a charitable purpose, that's *either* a "charitable remainder annuity trust" (CRAT) or a "charitable remainder unitrust" (CRUT). (Code Sec. 664(d); Reg § 1.664-1)[9]

---

2. ¶K-3440.4 *et seq.*; ¶1704.45
3. ¶K-3451 *et seq.*; ¶1704.45
4. ¶K-3473; ¶1704.45
5. ¶K-3520

6. ¶K-3504 *et seq.*; ¶1704.47
7. ¶K-3527
8. ¶K-3661, K-3667, S-4928.2; ¶1704.305
9. ¶K-3261 *et seq.*, ¶K-3291 *et seq.*; ¶6644 *et seq.*

¶ 2117   Pooled income funds.

A pooled income fund is a trust formed to pay income to one or more noncharitable beneficiaries and the remainder to charity. It must be maintained by the donee charity (no donor or income beneficiary may be a trustee) and meet certain other requirements. (Code Sec. 642(c)(5); Reg § 1.642(c)-5)[10]

¶ 2118   Contributions to donor advised funds (DAFs).

DAFs are charitable accounts set up and sponsored by an organization to which donors contribute and provide advice on the account's distributions and investments, although the sponsoring organization must have final say on the actual distributions and investments. Contributions are deductible if: (1) the sponsoring organization isn't listed in Code Sec. 170(f)(18)(A) (e.g., a war veteran's organization or domestic fraternal lodge); and (2) the donor obtains contemporaneous written acknowledgment from the sponsoring organization certifying it has legal control over the contribution. (Code Sec. 170(f)(18)(B))[11]

¶ 2119   Contribution of income interest in trust—charitable lead trusts.

A charitable deduction is allowed for a contribution of an income interest in trust (remainder to a noncharity) *only* if: (1) the donor is taxable on the trust income, and (2) the donated income interest is either a "guaranteed annuity" or a "unitrust interest." (Code Sec. 170(f)(2)(B); Reg § 1.170A-6) This type of trust is a "charitable lead trust." [12]

¶ 2120   Services for charity and related deductible transportation expenses.

No deduction is allowed for the value of services a taxpayer renders to charity. (Reg § 1.170A-1(g))[13] However, taxpayer is allowed a deduction for his unreimbursed out-of-pocket expenses (for travel expenses, see ¶2121) necessarily incurred in performing services (other than lobbying) free for a charity. (Code Sec. 170(f)(6); Reg § 1.170A-1(g))[14]

A taxpayer who uses his car in performing these services may deduct 14¢ per mile as a contribution (Code Sec. 170(i)) or his actual (unreimbursed) expenses for gas and oil. Parking fees and tolls are deductible in either case, as are deductions otherwise allowable for interest or taxes connected with the car, but not depreciation, insurance, and repairs. [15]

¶ 2121   Charitable travel expenses.

No charitable deduction is allowed for taxpayer's travel expenses (including meals and lodging), whether or not reimbursed, while away from home, unless there is no significant element of personal pleasure, recreation or vacation in the travel. (Code Sec. 170(j)) Even then, deduction is limited to amounts necessarily incurred for meals and lodging while away from home overnight in rendering these services. [16]

¶ 2122   Maintaining student in taxpayer's home.

A charitable deduction is allowed to a taxpayer who, under a written agreement with a charity and without compensation, maintains a student in the 12th grade or lower (not his dependent or relative) in his home. (Code Sec. 170(g); Reg § 1.170A-2)[17] The contribution in any year is the amount so contributed, but not more than $50 times the number of full

---

10. ¶K-3363 *et seq.*; ¶s 1704.46, 6424.03
11. ¶K-3987; ¶1704.285
12. ¶K-3345 *et seq.*; ¶1704.46
13. ¶K-3551; ¶1704.36

14. ¶K-3601 *et seq.*; ¶1704.37
15. ¶K-3614 *et seq.*; ¶1704.37
16. ¶K-3620 *et seq.*; ¶s 1704.37, 2744.01
17. ¶K-3650 *et seq.*; ¶1704.33

calendar months (15 days or more is a "month") during the year for which the individual was a member of taxpayer's household and a full-time student. (Code Sec. 170(g)(2); Reg § 1.170A-2(b))[18]

¶ 2123   Charitable deduction ceilings for individuals.

There's a ceiling on the amount an individual may deduct each year as a charitable contribution, based both on the type of property contributed and the type of charity to which the contribution is made. The ceilings (below) for any tax year are a percentage of taxpayer's "contribution base" (below) for the year, subject to an overall 60% ceiling for all charitable gifts. (Code Sec. 170(b)(1))[19] For carryover of excess contributions, see ¶2129.

If the contributions are all to "50% charities" (see ¶2124), the year's ceiling is 60% of the taxpayer's contribution base for cash contributions made in 2018 through 2025 tax years, except for contributions of appreciated capital gain property (¶2126). (Code Sec. 170(b)(1)(A))

◆✔observation: Charities, contributions to which are subject to a 60% ceiling, are referred to as "50% charities" because the ceiling on the deductibility of contributions to those charities was 50% in tax years beginning before 2018.

[20] If the contributions are all to "30% charities" (see ¶2125), or are "for the use" of *any* charities, the ceiling is 30% of taxpayer's contribution base (except for gifts of appreciated capital gain property, see ¶2128) or, if less, 50% of his contribution base minus his contributions to 50% charities. (Code Sec. 170(b)(1)(B))[21] Cash contributions that are taken into account under the 60% contribution base limit in effect from 2018 through 2025 tax years aren't taken into account for purposes of applying the 50% contribution base limit. (Code Sec. 170(b)(1)(G)(iii)(I))

An individual's "contribution base" for a year is his or her adjusted gross income (¶3102) for the year, but without deducting any net operating loss carryback to that year. (Code Sec. 170(b)(1)(G))[22] For spouses filing joint returns, these ceilings apply to the couple's combined contributions and their combined contribution base. (Reg § 1.170A-8(a)(1))[23]

An individual may elect to deduct certain recent disaster relief efforts up to his or her entire contribution base less other contributions. Qualified contributions exceeding this amount are carried forward for five years as contributions to which the 50%/60% limit applies. A qualified contribution is any cash charitable contribution paid to an organization described in Code Sec. 170(b)(1)(A) (see ¶2124) from Aug. 23, 2017 through Dec. 31, 2017 for relief efforts in the Hurricane Harvey, Irma or Maria disaster areas (Disaster Tax Relief and Airport and Airway Extension Act of 2017, Sec. 504(a)(2)(A), PL 115-63, 9/29/2017) or from Oct. 8, 2017 through Dec. 31, 2018 for relief efforts in the California wildfire disaster area (Bipartisan Budget Act of 2018, Sec. 20104(a)(4)(A), PL 115-123, 2/9/2018). Taxpayers must satisfy substantiation requirements. (Code Sec. 170(b)(1))[24]

For qualified conservation contributions (i.e., contribution of a qualified real property interest to a qualified organization exclusively for conservation), a 50% (rather than 30%) limit on the contribution base, less all other contributions, applies, and the carryforward period (¶2129) is 15 years. [25] For qualified farmers and ranchers (more than 50% of gross income from farming as defined at Code Sec. 2032A(e)(5)), this limit is 100% of the contribution base less all other contributions. For property in agriculture or livestock production to be eligible for the 100% limit, the qualified real property interest has to include a

---

18. ¶K-3651; ¶1704.33
19. ¶K-3670; ¶1704.05
20. ¶K-3671; ¶1704.05
21. ¶s K-3671, K-3674, K-3684 *et seq.*; ¶s 1704.05, 1704.10 *et seq.*

22. ¶K-3672; ¶1704.05
23. ¶K-3673; ¶1704.06
24. ¶K-3670 *et seq.*; ¶1704.05
25. ¶K-3694.1, ¶K-3701.1; ¶1704.11

restriction that the property remains generally available for such production. A 15-year carryover is allowed. (Code Sec. 170(b)(1)(E)).[26]

¶ 2124   50% charities.

✍️observation: Charities, contributions to which are subject to a 60% ceiling (see ¶2123), are referred to as "50% charities" because the ceiling on the deductibility of contributions to them was 50% in tax years beginning before 2018.

For purposes of the deduction ceilings for individuals (¶2123), "50% charities" are (1) churches (or church conventions or associations); (2) tax-exempt educational organizations; (3) tax-exempt hospitals and certain medical research organizations; (4) certain organizations holding property for state and local colleges and universities; (5) a U.S. state or possession, or any political subdivision of any of these, or the U.S. or the District of Columbia, if the contribution is for exclusively public purposes; (6) organizations organized and operated exclusively for charitable, religious, educational, scientific or literary purposes, or for the prevention of cruelty to children or animals, or to foster national or international amateur sports competition if they normally get a substantial part of their support from the government or general public; (7) certain private foundations; (8) certain membership organizations more than one-third of whose support comes from the public; and (9) agricultural research organizations. (Code Sec. 170(b)(1)(A))[27]

¶ 2125   30% charities.

For purposes of the ceilings on an individual's charitable deduction (¶2123), "30% charities" are qualifying charitable organizations (¶2102) that aren't 50% charities (¶2124), e.g., war veterans' organizations, fraternal orders, cemetery companies, and certain private nonoperating foundations. (Code Sec. 170(b)(1)(B);[28]

¶ 2126   Gifts of appreciated capital gain property to 50% charities—30% ceiling.

An individual's deduction ceiling in the tax year for gifts of certain appreciated capital gain property (below) to 50% charities is 30% of his contribution base (¶2123), unless he makes an election to reduce the amount of his contribution (in which case, the 50% ceiling applies, see ¶2127). (Code Sec. 170(b)(1)(C))[29] For ceiling on gifts to 30% charities, see ¶2128.

This rule applies to any capital asset which, if sold for fair market value at contribution, would have given rise to long-term capital gain, *other than* property subject to the reduction at ¶2110. (Code Sec. 170(b)(1)(C))[30]

¶ 2127   Individual's election of 50% ceiling for appreciated property contributions.

An individual donor whose gift of capital gain property to a 50% charity is otherwise subject to the 30% ceiling (¶2126) may elect the 50% ceiling for the gift, *but only* if he or she reduces the amount of his contribution (as described at ¶2107)—i.e., the donor's contribution is limited to his or her basis in the property. (Code Sec. 170(b)(1)(C)(iii))[31]

✍️recommendation: Elect where the appreciation is small (value of increased current deduction is greater than loss of eventual deduction of appreciation) or where the 30% limit will prevent deduction of the appreciation even over the carryover period (¶2129).

---

26. ¶K-3694.2; ¶1704.11
27. ¶K-3720 *et seq.*; ¶1704.08
28. ¶K-3684 *et seq.*; ¶1704.10 *et seq.*

29. ¶K-3686, K-3687; ¶1704.11
30. ¶K-3687; ¶1704.05
31. ¶K-3689; ¶1704.11

Once made, the election applies to all gifts of capital gain property (¶2126) to 50% charities made by the donor in the tax year. In computing carryovers to this year, contributions of this property in an earlier year for which the election was *not* made are reduced as if they were subject to the reduction when made. (Code Sec. 170(b)(1)(C)(iii); Reg § 1.170A-8(d)(2))[32] The election is made by attaching a statement specified in the regs, to the original income tax return for the election year. (Reg § 1.170A-8(d)(2)(iii))[33]

¶ 2128 Gifts of appreciated capital gain property to 30% charities—20% ceiling.

An individual's deduction ceiling for gifts of appreciated long-term capital gain property to 30% charities is 20% of his contribution base (¶2123) (and there's no election like the one for gifts to 50% charities, see ¶2127). (Code Sec. 170(b)(1)(D))[34]

¶ 2129 Carryover of excess charitable contributions by individuals.

If an individual's charitable gifts for a tax year exceed the percentage ceilings for the year (¶2123), the excess may generally be carried forward and deducted for up to five years (subject to the later year's ceiling). (Code Sec. 170(d)(1)) A statement must be filed with the return for the year the carryover is deducted. The carryforward is available even if the individual didn't itemize his deductions in the contribution year. (Reg § 1.170A-10(a)(2))[35]

Contributions are deductible in the following order, up to 50% of the contribution base:

(1) Contributions qualifying for the 50% charity limit (¶2124).

(2) Contributions qualifying for the 30% charity limit (¶2125) up to the lesser of:

. . . 30% of the contribution base, or

. . . (a) 50% of the contribution base minus (b) contributions to 50% limit organizations. For this purpose, (b) includes contributions of capital gain property subject to the 30% limit (¶2126).

(3) Contributions of capital gain property subject to the 30% limit (up to the lesser of 30% of the contribution base or 50% of the contribution base minus other contributions to 50% organizations).

(4) Contributions qualifying for the 20% limit (¶2128) up to the lesser of:

. . . 20% of the contribution base,

. . . 30% of the contribution base minus contributions subject to the 30% limit,

. . . 30% of the contribution base minus contributions of capital gain property subject to the special 30% limit, or

. . . 50% of the contribution base minus the total of contributions to 50% and 30% limit organizations. (Code Sec. 170(b)(1))[36]

Where charitable contributions in more than one limitation category are carried over, the ordering rules determine the deduction limits for each category of contribution. Starting with the first (50% limitation) category, the allowable deduction limit is determined. Current contributions in that category are deducted first. Next, within that category, amounts carried over are deducted, up to the limitation amount for the category. Then, the same process is applied to the next limitation category according to the ordering rules. (Reg § 1.170A-10(b), Reg § 1.170A-10(c)) If there are carryovers from two or more years in any category, the carryover from the earlier year is considered first. [37]

32. ¶K-3706; ¶1704.11
33. ¶K-3690
34. ¶K-3694; ¶1704.11

35. ¶K-3701 *et seq.*, ¶K-3711; ¶1704.13
36. ¶K-3701 *et seq.*; ¶s 1704.05, 1704.13
37. ¶K-3701 *et seq.*; ¶1704.05

¶ 2130   Excess charitable contributions on decedent's final return.

If an individual dies, any charitable contribution that can't be used on the decedent's final return (under the normal ceilings, see ¶2123) is lost. (Reg § 1.170A-10(d)(4)(iii))[38]

¶ 2131   Corporation's charitable deduction ceiling and carryover period.

A corporation's charitable deduction for a tax year can't exceed 10% of its taxable income for the year. Taxable income for this purpose is computed without deductions for charitable contributions or dividends received, net operating loss carrybacks or capital loss carrybacks to the year, (Code Sec. 170(b)(2); Reg § 1.170A-11(a))[39] or adjustments for excess inclusion income stemming from the corporation's residual interest in a REMIC (¶4204) under Code Sec. 860E.[40] To the extent contributions in any year exceed this limit, the excess can be carried forward and deducted for five years. (Code Sec. 170(d)(2))[41]

A corporation that is a qualified farmer or rancher can make a qualified conservation contribution equal to 100% of its taxable income after taking into account other allowable charitable contributions. To be eligible, the corporation's stock can't be readily tradable on an established securities market at any time during the tax year the contribution is made. To be a qualified rancher or farmer, more than 50% of the corporation's gross income for the tax year has to come from the trade or business of farming. A 15-year carryover is allowed. (Code Sec. 170(b)(2)(B))[42] Alaska Native Corporations are allowed to deduct donations of conservation easements up to 100% of taxable income. (Code Sec. 170(b)(2)(C))[43]

A corporation may elect to deduct qualified contributions (defined at ¶2123) made for Hurricane Harvey, Irma or Maria and for California wildfire relief efforts up to its entire taxable income less other contributions. Qualified contributions exceeding this amount are carried forward for five years as contributions to which the 10% limit applies. (Code Sec. 170(b)(2)[44]

¶ 2132   When to deduct charitable contributions.

A charitable contribution is deductible in the tax year it's paid (subject to percentage ceilings, see ¶2123, ¶2131) (Code Sec. 170(a)), regardless of the donor's accounting method (except for accrual method corporations, see ¶2133) or when the gift was pledged. (Reg § 1.170A-1(a))[45] A contribution is "paid" when it's unconditionally delivered to the donee. A contribution by check that's delivered unconditionally is paid when delivered, if it clears in due course. If the check is mailed unconditionally and clears in due course, the contribution is paid when mailed. (Reg § 1.170A-1(b))[46] A contribution charged on a credit card is deductible by a cash basis donor in the year the charge is made, *not* in any later year when the credit card company is paid. [47]

¶ 2133   Corporate election to deduct post-year-end contribution.

An accrual method corporation, other than an S corporation (¶3359), whose board of directors has authorized a charitable contribution during the tax year may elect to deduct all or part of the contribution in that (authorization) year, if the contribution is paid by the 15th day of the fourth month following the close of the year (for tax years beginning before 2026, for C corporations using a tax year ending on June 30, if the contribution is paid by

---

38. ¶K-3710; ¶1704.13
39. ¶K-3830 *et seq.*; ¶1704.14
40. ¶K-3832
41. ¶K-3833; ¶1704.14
42. ¶K-3831.1 *et seq.*; ¶1704.14

43. ¶K-3831.1 *et seq.*; ¶1704.14
44. ¶K-3831.2; ¶14,00S4.01
45. ¶K-3851; ¶1704.02
46. ¶K-3858 *et seq.*; ¶1704.02
47. ¶K-3861; ¶1704.02

the 15th day of the *third* month following the close of the year). (Code Sec. 170(a)(2))[48] The election is made by reporting the contribution in the return and attaching a declaration signed by a principal officer, together with a copy of the directors' resolution authorizing the contribution. (Code Sec. 170(a)(2); Reg § 1.170A-11(b))[49]

¶ 2134 Specialized Rules for Claiming Charitable Contributions. ▬▬▬

Taxpayers (donors) must substantiate their charitable deductions (¶2135), and supply appraisals and other information for certain property contributions. No charitable deduction is allowed for a contribution of $250 or more unless taxpayer substantiates it by a contemporaneous written acknowledgment from the donee (¶2136), and noncash contributions exceeding $500 are also subject to heightened substantiation requirements (¶2137). Special rules apply for contributions of cars, boats, and planes (¶2138), and for gifts of art appraised at $50,000 or more (¶2139).

¶ 2135 Charitable contributions must be substantiated; donor's receipt; Form W-2 for contributions by payroll deduction.

A charitable deduction isn't allowed unless taxpayer can prove his right to it. (Code Sec. 170(a)(1))[50] For *donee's* information return requirement, see ¶4746.

For cash contributions, taxpayer must keep either a cancelled check, receipt or other reliable evidence. (Reg § 1.170A-13(a)(1))[1] A taxpayer can't deduct *any* contribution of a cash, check, or other monetary gift unless he or she maintains as a record of the contribution a bank record (e.g., a statement from a financial institution or cancelled check) or a written communication from the donee organization showing its name, plus the date and amount of the contribution. (Code Sec. 170(f)(17)) For contributions of property (other than cash), taxpayer must have a receipt from the donee and keep records showing the donee's name and describing the gift. (Reg § 1.170A-13(b)(1))[2] For contributions made via payroll deductions, taxpayer must retain a pay stub, Form W-2, or other employer document showing the amount withheld for the purpose of payment to the donee, plus a pledge card or similar donee document showing the donee's name. [3] For contributions made through the Combined Federal Campaign or a similar program (e.g., United Way), the organization receiving the donation may be treated as the donee for substantiation purposes even if it distributes the funds to another organization. The written communication must contain the ultimate recipient's name. [4] Additional substantiation is required for: contributions of $250 or more (¶2136); noncash contributions exceeding $500 (¶2137); and contributions of cars, boats, and planes (¶2138).

¶ 2136 Substantiation requirement for contributions of $250 or more.

No charitable deduction is allowed for any (cash or property) contribution of $250 or more unless taxpayer substantiates it by a contemporaneous written acknowledgment (not just a cancelled check) from the donee (or its agent). (Code Sec. 170(f)(8)(A); Reg § 1.170A-13(f)(1))[5]

In general, the written acknowledgment must state: (1) the amount of cash and a description (but not the value) of any property other than cash contributed; (2) whether the donee provided any goods or services in consideration for the contribution, and if it did, a description and good-faith estimate of their value; and (3) if the goods or services consist

---

48. ¶K-3882 *et seq.*; ¶1704.03
49. ¶K-3883; ¶1704.03
50. ¶K-3901 *et seq.*; ¶1704.50
1. ¶K-3919; ¶1704.50

2. ¶s K-3926, K-3927; ¶1704.50
3. ¶K-3939
4. ¶K-3941
5. ¶K-3933; ¶1704.50

entirely of intangible religious benefits (e.g., admission to a religious ceremony, but not religious school tuition or fees), a statement to that effect. (Code Sec. 170(f)(8)(B); Reg § 1.170A-13(f)(2)) Special requirements apply for gifts to a pooled income fund (¶2117). (Reg § 1.170A-13(f)(13))[6]

The written acknowledgment requirement doesn't apply to transfers to a charitable lead trust (¶2119), charitable remainder annuity trust, or charitable remainder unitrust (¶2116). (Reg § 1.170A-13(f)(13))[7]

Goods or services that have insubstantial value (¶2104), and certain annual membership benefits the charity provides to taxpayer, taxpayer's employees, or the partners of a partnership donor in exchange for the contribution are disregarded in determining the $250 threshold. (Reg § 1.170A-13(f)(8)(i), Reg § 1.170A-13(f)(9)(i))[8] And, separate payments are generally treated as separate contributions. (Reg § 1.170A-13(f)(1))[9]

An employer's payment to a charity of $250 or more withheld from taxpayer's paycheck (the amount withheld from each single paycheck is treated as a separate contribution), may be substantiated by a combination of (1) a pay stub, Form W-2, or other employer-provided document showing the amount withheld for this purpose, and (2) a pledge card or other donee document which states it doesn't provide any consideration for the payroll contributions. (Reg § 1.170A-13(f)(11))[10]

¶ 2137   Proving noncash contributions exceeding $500—Form 8283.

For noncash contributions that are:

(1) more than $500 but not more than $5,000, the donor must substantiate the contribution with a contemporaneous written acknowledgment (CWA) of the gift and attach to its return a description of the contributed property, on Form 8283. This requirement doesn't apply to a C corporation. (Code Sec. 170(f)(11)(B), Reg § 1.170A-16(c))

(2) more than $5,000 but not more than $500,000, the donor must obtain a "qualified appraisal" (one meeting specified IRS requirements) and attach to its return (using Form 8283) information about the property and appraisal (i.e., appraisal summary) as required by IRS. (Code Sec. 170(f)(11)(C))

(3) more than $500,000, the donor must obtain a CWA from the donee, attach a qualified appraisal to its return, and complete a Form 8283. (Code Sec. 170(f)(11)(D), Reg § 1.170A-16(e))

The requirements in (2) and (3), above, don't apply to: patents, copyrights, etc., as described in Code Sec. 170(e)(1)(B)(iii) (¶2106); property described in Code Sec. 1221(a)(1) (e.g., stock in trade, inventory); publicly traded securities; and "qualified vehicle donations" (¶2138). (Code Sec. 170(f)(11)(A)(ii)(I)) IRS will disallow a deduction if the above reporting requirements aren't met, unless the failure was due to reasonable cause. (Code Sec. 170(f)(11)(A))[11]

¶ 2138   Charitable contributions of cars, boats, and planes—Form 1098-C.

Special rules apply for contributions of motor vehicles, boats, and airplanes that aren't in taxpayer's inventory or held for sale in the ordinary course of his business ("qualified vehicle donations"), if the donation's claimed value exceeds $500. (Code Sec. 170(f)(12)) The donor's deduction can't exceed the gross proceeds from the charity's sale proceeds unless:

---

6. ¶K-3933 *et seq.*; ¶1704.50
7. ¶K-3940.3; ¶1704.50
8. ¶K-3934; ¶1704.38

9. ¶K-3934; ¶1704.50
10. ¶K-3940; ¶1704.50
11. ¶K-3942 *et seq.*; ¶1704.50

(1) there's a "significant intervening use" of the vehicle by the charity (actual, significant use to substantially further the charity's regularly conducted activities) before its sale;

(2) the charity materially improves the vehicle (significantly increases its value) before its sale (minor repairs or routine maintenance aren't enough); or

(3) the charity sells it at a price significantly below fair market value (FMV) (or gives it away) to a needy individual, in direct furtherance of its charitable purpose of relieving the poor and distressed or the underprivileged who need vehicles.

If (1), (2), or (3) applies, the donor may claim a deduction for the vehicle's FMV, using the "blue book" value for a similar vehicle (or private party sale amount, until regs are issued).

A deduction for donated vehicles whose claimed value exceeds $500 isn't allowed unless taxpayer substantiates the contribution by a contemporaneous written acknowledgment (CWA) from the donee (on Form 1098-C) and attach it to the Form 8283. (Code Sec. 170(f)(12)(A); Reg § 1 170A-16(o)(1)) It must.

. . . contain the donor's name and taxpayer identification number (TIN), the vehicle identification number (or similar number), and if exception (1), (2), or (3), above, applies, supporting details;

. . . indicate whether the donee provided goods or services in consideration of the vehicle (and, if so, describe them and estimate their value, or, if they consist solely of intangible religious benefits, a statement to that effect);

. . . generally be made within 30 days after the vehicle's sale (within 30 days of the contribution if exception (1), (2) or (3) applies); and

. . . if the charity sells the vehicle and none of the three above exceptions applies, state that the vehicle was sold in an arm's length transaction between unrelated parties, show the gross proceeds, and declare that the deductible amount can't exceed the gross proceeds.[12]

¶ 2139   IRS "Statement of Value" for gifts of art appraised at $50,000 or more.

At taxpayer's request, IRS will issue a Statement of Value that taxpayer may rely on to substantiate the value of an item of art (paintings, sculpture, antique furniture, carpets, rare manuscripts, historical memorabilia, and similar objects) that has been appraised at $50,000 or more and transferred as a charitable gift. Taxpayer must request the statement before filing the return that first reports the gift, and must attach a copy of the statement (or of the request, if the statement hasn't been received yet) to that return. [13]

¶ 2140   Medical Expenses. ▰▰▰▰▰▰▰▰▰▰

For 2018, an individual who itemizes can deduct the amount by which certain unreimbursed medical and dental expenses (¶2144 through ¶2149) paid during the year (see ¶2150) for himself, his spouse, and his dependents (¶2142) exceed 7.5% of his adjusted gross income (10% after 2018, see ¶2141). However, medical expenses aren't deductible if they have been compensated for by insurance or otherwise, see ¶2151.

---

12. ¶K-3948.1 *et seq.*; ¶1704.41   13. ¶T-10080 *et seq.*; ¶1704.50

For whether and when expenses for a decedent's medical care that are paid out of his estate are treated as paid by him (and may be deducted), see ¶2143.

¶ 2141 Medical expense deduction—how much is deductible—Form 1040, Schedule A.

For 2018, the amount of medical expenses (¶2144) an individual can deduct (on Form 1040, Schedule A) is the amount by which unreimbursed payments for those expenses exceed 7.5% of his adjusted gross income (AGI, ¶3102). (There's no ceiling on the deduction.) (Code Sec. 213(a); Code Sec. 213(f))[14]

observation: The deduction is lost if medical expenses don't exceed the "floor."

Any expense allowed as a Code Sec. 21 dependent care credit (¶2348), Code Sec. 35 credit for health insurance costs (¶2343), or Code Sec. 162(l) self-employed medical insurance deduction (¶1531) can't be treated as a medical expense. (Code Sec. 213(e), Code Sec. 35(g)(2), Code Sec. 162(l)(3))[15]

For the percentage floor on deductible medical expenses for purposes of the alternative minimum tax (AMT), see ¶3206.

For tax years ending after 2018, medical expenses will be subject to a 10% floor for both regular tax and AMT purposes.

¶ 2142 Whose medical expenses may taxpayer deduct?

A taxpayer may deduct his own medical expenses, and those of his spouse and dependents if the status as spouse, etc., exists either when the medical care was rendered or when the expenses were paid. (Code Sec. 213(a); Reg § 1.213-1(e)(3)) For this purpose, "dependent" is defined in Code Sec. 152 (see ¶3113) and is determined without the gross income test for qualifying relatives, the rule that a joint return filer can't be a dependent, and the rule that a dependent is ineligible to have dependents. (Code Sec. 213(a); Reg § 1.213-1(a)(3)(i)) A child of divorced parents is considered a dependent of both if Code Sec. 152(e) applies (see ¶3120), so that each parent may deduct the medical expenses he or she pays for the child. (Code Sec. 213(d)(5))[16] An organ donor's medical expenses are deductible by the payor, whether donor or recipient. [17]

¶ 2143 Decedent's medical expenses.

Expenses for a decedent's medical care that are paid out of his estate are treated as paid by him (and may be deducted) in the year incurred if: (1) they're paid within one year after his death, (2) they aren't deducted for federal estate tax purposes, and (3) a statement is filed with the income tax return (or amended return) showing that the expenses weren't allowed for estate tax purposes and that the estate tax deduction is waived. (Code Sec. 213(c))[18]

observation: The choice of an income tax or estate tax deduction depends primarily on the extent to which the expense is deductible for income tax purposes, the decedent's top income tax rate, and the top effective estate tax rate.

---

14. ¶K-2002; ¶2134.14
15. ¶K-2003; ¶s 2134, 2134.04
16. ¶K-2300 *et seq.*; ¶s 2134.01, 2134.02

17. ¶K-2159
18. ¶C-9556; ¶2134.03

¶ 2144 What kinds of medical expenses are deductible?

Deductible medical expenses are amounts paid for the diagnosis, mitigation, treatment, prevention of disease or for the purpose of affecting the body's structure or function (Code Sec. 213(d)(1)),[19] and the costs of nursing services (Reg § 1.213-1(e)(1)(ii))[20] (and related insurance payments, ¶2145, and transportation, ¶2148). Deductible expenses include the costs of:

... Eyeglasses, artificial teeth or limbs (Reg § 1.213-1(e)(1)(ii)), hearing aids, and similar items, as well as breast pumps and supplies that assist lactation. [21]

... Eye surgery to correct defective vision, including laser procedures (e.g., LASIK). [22]

... Discretionary medical procedures affecting the body's structure or function, including legal abortions and procedures to prevent or facilitate pregnancy (e.g., egg donor fees; but in vitro fertilization costs for a taxpayer who wasn't infertile weren't deductible). [23]

... Smoking cessation programs [24] and prescribed drugs designed to alleviate nicotine withdrawal, but not non-prescription nicotine gum and nicotine patches. [25]

... Attending a medical conference on a chronic disease suffered by an individual, his spouse, or dependent (but not meal and lodging costs, ¶2149).[26]

... Legally procured prescription drugs (e.g., not aspirin) and insulin. (Code Sec. 213(b), Code Sec. 213(d)(3)) A controlled substance (such as marijuana) obtained for medical purposes, in violation of the federal Controlled Substances Act, isn't legally procured and is nondeductible, even if state law permits its doctor-prescribed use. [27]

... Weight-loss program for treatment of a specific disease (e.g., obesity, hypertension), but not the cost of diet food.[28]

... Diagnostic tests aiding in the detection of heart attack, diabetes, cancer, and other diseases (but not the collection and storage of DNA, absent a showing of how the DNA will be used for medical diagnosis). These include pregnancy tests, tests on healthy individuals, and tests taken not at the direction of a physician. Such a test will not fail to qualify due to high cost or if a less expensive alternative may be available. [29]

... Service animals used in mental health therapy. [30]

... Sex-change costs (except for breast augmentation undertaken to improve appearance). [31]

... Nonlicensed healthcare providers that provided physician-ordered assistance and supervision to a patient suffering from dementia. [32]

... Nontraditional or alternative medical practices, treatments or services. [33]

Expenses that aren't deductible as medical care include:

... Expenses merely beneficial to the individual's general health. (Reg § 1.213-1(e)(1)(ii))[34]

... Costs of cosmetic surgery or similar procedure (e.g., teeth whitening), unless necessary to ameliorate a deformity arising from, or directly related to, a congenital abnormality, a personal injury resulting from an accident or trauma or a disfiguring disease

19. ¶K-2100 *et seq.*; ¶s 2134.04, 2134.08
20. ¶K-2111; ¶2134.04
21. ¶K-2162; ¶2134.04
22. ¶K-2162
23. ¶K-2110; ¶2134.04
24. ¶K-2117
25. ¶K-2137
26. ¶K-2161
27. ¶K-2137
28. ¶K-2116
29. ¶K-2105.1
30. ¶K-2162
31. ¶K-2101, K-2109
32. ¶K-2122
33. ¶K-2114
34. ¶K-2103; ¶2134.04

(Code Sec. 213(d)(9))—e.g., breast reconstruction surgery after cancer mastectomy. [35]

. . . Payments for illegal operations or treatments. (Reg § 1.213-1(e)(1)(ii))[36]

. . . Insurance premiums paid by an employer-sponsored health insurance plan (cafeteria plan), unless the amounts paid are taxed to the employee (included in taxable compensation box 1 of Form W-2).[37]

Qualified long-term care services are treated as medical care (Code Sec. 213(d)(1)(C)) (unless provided by a relative who isn't a licensed professional, or by a related corporation or partnership. (Code Sec. 213(d)(11))) These services include necessary diagnostic, preventive, therapeutic, curing, treating, mitigating, and rehabilitative services, and maintenance or personal care services, which are required by a chronically ill individual and provided under a plan of care prescribed by a licensed health care practitioner. (Code Sec. 7702B(c)(1))[38]

¶ 2145   Accident and health insurance; Medicare.

The cost of insurance that's deductible as a medical expense is limited to amounts paid for insurance that covers *medical care* as defined at ¶2144. (Code Sec. 213(d)(1)(D))[39]

Amounts paid as *voluntary* premiums under Part B of Medicare (supplementary medical insurance benefits for the aged and disabled) are deductible as medical care, as are voluntary premiums under Medicare Part A (basic Medicare) (Code Sec. 213(d)(1)(D)), and Medicare Part D premiums, but not the *mandatory* employment or self-employment taxes paid for basic coverage under Medicare A. (Reg § 1.213-1(e)(4)(i)(a))[40] IRS has stated that all Medicare parts are insurance that constitutes medical care under Code Sec. 162(l) (see ¶1531).[41] For the business expense deduction for medical care insurance of sole proprietors, partners or 2%-or-more S corporation shareholders who pay Medicare premiums, see ¶1531.

When an insurance contract covers both medical care and other items (e.g., loss of income), no amount is treated as for medical care *unless:* the charge for medical insurance is separately stated, the amount treated as paid for medical insurance doesn't exceed the separately-stated charge, *and* the charge isn't unreasonably large in relation to the total premium for the contract. (Code Sec. 213(d)(6))[42]

Medical expenses include premiums paid for qualified long-term care (LTC) insurance, up to annual limits. For an individual who attained the following age before the close of the tax year the limit is (the 2019 limits as calculated by Thomson Reuters based on inflation data):

. . . 40 or less, the limit is $420 for 2018 (and 2019);

. . . more than 40, but not more than 50, the limit is $780 for 2018 ($790 for 2019);

. . . more than 50, but not more than 60, the limit is $1,560 for 2018 ($1,580 for 2019);

. . . more than 60, but not more than 70, the limit is $4,160 for 2018 (4,220 for 2019); and

. . . more than 70, the limit is $5,200 for 2018 ($5,270 for 2019). (Code Sec. 213(d)(10))[43]

▶ *observation:* The above projections for 2019 were computed under the assumption that a drafting error in the Tax Cuts and Jobs Act, which would clearly produce results at odds with the apparent intent of the statute, will be fixed.

Qualified LTC insurance contracts must provide only coverage of qualified LTC services,

---

35. ¶K-2109; ¶2134.04
36. ¶K-2106; ¶2134.04
37. ¶K-2140
38. ¶K-2122.1; ¶2134.075
39. ¶K-2140 *et seq.*; ¶2134.08

40. ¶K-2140; ¶2134.08
41. ¶L-3510.2
42. ¶K-2141; ¶2134.08
43. ¶K-2141.1; ¶2134.075

must not pay or reimburse expenses to the extent the expenses are reimbursable under Medicare (or would be but for a deductible or coinsurance amount), must be guaranteed renewable, and must meet other detailed requirements. (Code Sec. 7702B(b))[44]

¶ 2146 Deductible costs of care at hospitals and other institutions.

The cost of in-patient care (including meals and lodging, see ¶2149) furnished by a hospital is a deductible medical expense. (Reg § 1.213-1(e)(1)(v))[45] The cost of in-patient care (including meals and lodging) at a medical-care institution that *isn't* a hospital qualifies if the individual is there primarily for the availability of medical care (as defined at ¶2144), and the meals and lodging are a necessity incident to that care. If this test isn't met, only that part of the cost attributable to medical care qualifies. Medical care status depends on the patient's condition and the nature of the services he receives —not on the nature of the institution (e.g., federal, state, local or private). The deduction is allowed for:

. . . costs (including tuition, meals, and lodging) of a mentally or physically handicapped person at a special school (Reg § 1.213-1(e)(1)(v)), e.g., a school for children with learning disabilities like dyslexia. Costs allocable to medical care at a regular school qualify if the school supplies a cost breakdown; [46]

. . . costs of a nursing home or home for the aged. But if the person isn't there principally for medical reasons, only the cost of medical care qualifies. (Reg § 1.213-1(e)(1)(v))[47] A deduction may be available for advance payments for lifetime care if certain requirements are met, and only for the part of the payment allocable to medical care. [48]

¶ 2147 "Medical" capital expenses for equipment or improvements.

Amounts incurred for elevators, swimming pools, and other permanent improvements to taxpayer's property (including capital expenditures to accommodate a residence to a physically handicapped individual) may be deductible medical expenses (¶2144) if the primary purpose is for the medical care of taxpayer, his spouse, or dependents. But the medical deduction is limited to that part of the expenses that exceeds the amount by which the improvement increases the value of taxpayer's property. (Reg § 1.213-1(e)(1)(iii))[49]

Some expenses incurred by or for a physically handicapped individual to remove structural barriers in his residence to accommodate his physical condition (e.g., constructing access ramps, widening doorways, installing support bars) are presumed not to increase the value of the residence and may be deductible in full. (Reg § 1.213-1(e)(1)(iii))[50] Capital expenditures that are related only to the sick person and are detachable from the property aren't permanent improvements, so their full cost can be a medical expense (e.g., detachable inclinators and air conditioners). (Reg § 1.213-1(e)(1)(iii))[1] All the costs of operating or maintaining a medical capital asset are deductible, even if none or only a part of the cost of the asset itself qualifies. (Reg § 1.213-1(e)(1)(iii))[2]

¶ 2148 Transportation expenses for medical care.

The costs of transportation primarily for and essential to medical care (¶2144) qualify as medical expenses. (Code Sec. 213(d)(1)(B)) This includes food and lodging expense (¶2149) while en route to the place of medical treatment (Reg § 1.213-1(e)(1)(iv)), as well as taxi,

---

44. ¶K-2141.2; ¶77,02B4
45. ¶K-2142; ¶2134.04
46. ¶K-2143 *et seq.*; ¶s 2134.10, 2134.11
47. ¶K-2147; ¶2134.11
48. ¶K-2403; ¶2134.03

49. ¶K-2180 *et seq.*; ¶2134.13
50. ¶K-2181; ¶2134.13
1. ¶K-2192; ¶s 2134.04, 2134.12
2. ¶K-2182; ¶2134.13

train, plane, and bus fares and the cost of ambulance services. [3] Deductible medical expenses also include certain out-of-pocket car expenses, e.g., for gas, oil, parking fees, and tolls, but not depreciation, repair, insurance or maintenance. Instead of claiming the actual costs of gas and oil, a taxpayer who uses a car for qualified medical transportation may deduct a flat 18¢ a mile for expenses paid or incurred in 2018. [4] However, no medical expense deduction is permitted for the cost of commuting to and from work, even if taxpayer's illness or disability requires a special method of transportation. [5]

¶ 2149   "Away from home" expenses (meals and lodging)—$50 per night rule.

Expenses for meals and lodging away from home aren't medical expenses unless they're part of the cost of care in a hospital or other institution (¶2146) or medical travel (¶2148).[6] Taxpayer may deduct as a medical expense amounts paid for lodging (not food) while away from home, that's primarily for and essential to medical care in a hospital or equivalent, up to $50 per night for each individual. (Code Sec. 213(d)(2)) No deduction is allowed for lavish or extravagant lodging or where the travel has any significant element of personal pleasure, recreation or vacation. (Code Sec. 213(d)(2)(B))[7]

¶ 2150   When to deduct medical expenses; prepaid insurance.

Only medical expenses actually paid during the tax year are deductible. (Code Sec. 213(a)) Deduction is thus allowed for payments in the year even though the expenses were incurred in an earlier year. (Reg § 1.213-1(a)(1)) If the payment is made by credit card, the amount is deductible in the year the charge is made, regardless of when the credit card bill is paid. [8] Advance payment of anticipated medical expenses doesn't qualify for a current deduction unless there is a contractual obligation to pay in the current year. [9] Certain insurance premiums paid by a taxpayer who is under age 65 during the payment year, for medical care for himself, his spouse, and dependents for the period *after* he reaches age 65, are deductible in the year paid. (Reg § 1.213-1(e)(4)(i)(b))[10]

¶ 2151   Medical expenses compensated for by insurance or otherwise.

Medical expenses aren't deductible if they have been compensated for by insurance or otherwise. (Code Sec. 213(a)) Taxpayer must reduce his medical expenses by amounts so compensated before applying the percentage of adjusted gross income floor (¶2141). But no reduction is required for amounts received as compensation for loss of earnings or as damages for personal injuries. [11] If reimbursements in a tax year exceed medical expenses in that year, no medical deduction is allowed. [12] Any part of the excess that's attributable to an employer's contribution is taxable; the rest is tax-free. [13] If taxpayer is reimbursed for medical expenses in a year after he paid (and deducted) them, he must report the reimbursement as income to the extent attributable to the earlier deduction (Reg § 1.213-1(g))—i.e., to the extent he got a "tax benefit," see ¶1205.[14]

¶ 2152   Tax Treatment of Alimony or Separate Maintenance Payments. ■■■■■■

In general, for divorce or separation instruments executed *before Jan. 1, 2019*, payments of alimony or separate maintenance (¶2153) made under a divorce or separation instrument are taxable to the payee spouse in the year received (Pre-repealed Code Sec. 71(a); Reg § 1.71-1(b)(5)), and are deductible by the payor

3. ¶K-2201; ¶s 2134.04, 2134.09
4. ¶K-2214 *et seq.*; ¶s 2134.04, 2134.09
5. ¶K-2202; ¶2134.09
6. ¶K-2217
7. ¶K-2218; ¶s 2134.04, 2134.09
8. ¶K-2401; ¶2134.03

9. ¶K-2403; ¶2134.03
10. ¶K-2404; ¶2134.03
11. ¶K-2601 *et seq.*; ¶s 2134.14, 2134.15
12. ¶K-2605
13. ¶H-1114; ¶2134.15
14. ¶K-2604; ¶2134.15

spouse in the year paid, as a deduction from gross income. (Code Sec. 62(a)(10), Code Sec. 215(a))[15] Thus, the payor doesn't have to itemize to be allowed the deduction.[16]

These rules don't apply if the spouses file a joint return with each other. (Code Sec. 71(e))[17] For the requirement that the spouses live apart, see ¶2155.

For the requirement that alimony payments be under a divorce or separation instrument, see ¶2154. For child support payments made under a divorce or separation agreement, see ¶2158.

Cash payments by the payor spouse to a third party on behalf of the payee spouse can be alimony, see ¶2156, as can premiums that one spouse pays for insurance on his or her life if the other (payee) spouse owns the policy, see ¶2157. However, a payment isn't alimony if the divorce or separation instrument designates that a payment that would otherwise qualify as alimony is not to be treated as alimony, see ¶2159. And a payor spouse can't deduct payments the payee spouse receives from an alimony trust which aren't includible in the payor's income under the Code Sec. 682 trust rules, see ¶2160.

For the requirement that "excess" (front-loaded) alimony payments be recaptured by the payor spouse, see ¶2161.

For any divorce or separation instrument that's: (1) executed after Dec. 31, 2018, or (2) executed on or before Dec. 31, 2018, and modified after Dec. 31, 2018, if the modification expressly provides for such treatment, the deduction for the payment of alimony won't apply (Code Sec. 215, Code Sec. 62(a)(10)), and the inclusion in gross income for the receipt of alimony payments won't apply. So, the alimony-paying spouse won't be able to deduct the payments, and the alimony-receiving spouse (or the beneficiary of an alimony trust (Code Sec. 682)) won't include them in gross income or pay federal income tax on them. Instead, income used for alimony payments will be taxed at the rates that apply to the payor spouse, rather than those that apply to the recipient spouse. But, IRS intends to issue regs clarifying that Code Sec. 682 will generally continue to apply with regard to trust income payable to a former spouse who was divorced or legally separated under a divorce or separation instrument executed on or before Dec. 31, 2018, unless such instrument is modified after that date and the modification provides that the repeal applies to the modification.[18]

¶ 2153 Alimony requirements.

To qualify as alimony, a payment must be made in cash, under a divorce or separation instrument (¶2154). (Code Sec. 71(b)(1)) A transfer of property other than cash can't be alimony,[19] but cash payments can be designated as "nonalimony" (¶2159). There must be no requirement that payments continue beyond the death of the payee spouse (e.g., to the estate) or that any substitute payment (in cash or property) be made after the death of the payee spouse, i.e., the payments must end at the payee spouse's death. (Code Sec. 71(b)(1)(D)) If this rule isn't satisfied, *none* of the payments (even those made during the payee-spouse's life) are alimony. (Reg § 1.71-1T(b), Q&A 10) If it isn't clear from the divorce or separation agreement whether payments cease at the payee spouse's death, local law controls. A lump sum payment in lieu of future alimony payments makes the payments nondeductible.[20] See ¶2158 for the difference between alimony and child support payments.

---

15. ¶J-1413, K-6001; ¶714 *et seq.*, ¶2158.40
16. ¶A-2621, K-6002; ¶714.10, 2154 *et seq.*
17. ¶K-6001; ¶714.03

18. ¶C-5433
19. ¶K-6005; ¶714.01
20. ¶K-6036 *et seq.*; ¶714.01

¶ 2154   Payments must be under a divorce or separation instrument.

To be alimony, a payment must be made under a divorce or separation instrument (Code Sec. 71(b)(1)(A)), i.e., a (1) decree of divorce or separate maintenance or a written instrument issued incident to the decree (e.g., a pretrial order), (2) written separation agreement, or (3) decree not described in (1) (e.g., a temporary support order). (Code Sec. 71(b)(2))[21] If made under a divorce or separate maintenance decree (or a written instrument incident to the decree), the payment must be made after the decree. (Reg § 1.71-1(b)(1)(i)) If made under a separation agreement, the payment must be made after execution of that agreement. (Reg § 1.71-1(b)(2))[22]

¶ 2155   Separate household requirement for alimony.

Spouses who are legally separated (but not divorced) under a divorce or separate maintenance decree must not live in the same household when the payment is made, or it won't be alimony (¶2153). (Code Sec. 71(b)(1)(C)) But if the spouses aren't legally separated, a payment under a written separation agreement or temporary support order may be alimony even if they are members of the same household. (Reg § 1.71-1T(b), Q&A 9)[23] The spouses aren't treated as members of the same household if one spouse is preparing to leave it, and does leave within one month after the payment. [24]

¶ 2156   "Alimony" payments to a third party.

Payments made in cash by the payor spouse to a third party on behalf of the payee spouse under the terms of the divorce or separation instrument can be alimony (¶2153). (Code Sec. 71(b)(1)(A)) Payments are on behalf of the payee spouse if they satisfy an obligation to that spouse. Thus, cash payments of the payee spouse's rent, mortgage, tax or tuition liabilities that the payor spouse makes as required by the instrument can qualify as alimony, as can payments made to a third party (e.g., a charity) at the payee spouse's written request, if the spouses intend them to be alimony. [25] But payments made to maintain property *owned by the payor spouse* but used by the payee spouse (including mortgage payments, realty taxes, and insurance premiums) *aren't* payments on behalf of the payee spouse (i.e., not alimony), even if made under the terms of the divorce or separation instrument. (Reg § 1.71-1T(b), Q&A 8)[26] A payor spouse who is required by the divorce or separation instrument to pay the mortgage on a home he owns jointly with the payee spouse may deduct one-half of those payments as alimony, if they otherwise qualify (the rest may be deductible as qualified residence interest if paid on a qualified home, see ¶1729 *et seq.*).[27]

¶ 2157   Life insurance contracts as alimony.

Premiums that one spouse pays for insurance on his life as required by the divorce or separation instrument are alimony if the other (payee) spouse owns the policy. [28]

¶ 2158   Support payments for the payor's children aren't alimony.

A payment under a divorce or separation instrument that's "fixed" (or treated as fixed) as support for a child of the payor spouse *isn't* alimony. (Code Sec. 71(c)(1))[29] This applies if the instrument designates a specified amount of money or a part of a payment to be child

---

21. ¶K-6013; ¶714.01
22. ¶K-6018; ¶714.06
23. ¶K-6035; ¶s 714.01, 714.06
24. ¶K-6035; ¶714.01
25. ¶K-6006; ¶714.01

26. ¶K-6007
27. ¶K-6008
28. ¶K-6010; ¶714.01
29. ¶K-6046; ¶714.02

support. The actual amount may fluctuate. (Reg § 1.71-1T(c), Q&A 16)[30] A part of a payment may be *treated* as fixed if the payment is to be reduced on the happening of a specified contingency relating to the child (Code Sec. 71(c)(2)), e.g., on the child's 18th birthday, or when he dies, marries or leaves school. [31] A payment may also be treated as fixed if it ends or is reduced at a time that can clearly be associated with the contingency. (Reg § 1.71-1T(c))[32] If a divorce or separation instrument provides specified amounts for alimony and child support, and the payor spouse pays the payee spouse less than the amount designated for child support, then the *entire* payment is child support; no part is alimony. (Code Sec. 71(c)(3))[33] However, if a fixed amount is paid for family support to a separated spouse, and there is no provision for reduction, e.g., when a child reaches a certain age or graduates from school, the entire amount may be treated as alimony. [34]

> **observation:** The tax rules for child support — i.e., that payers of child support don't get a deduction, and recipients of child support don't have to pay tax on those amounts — weren't changed by the recent law that changed the post-2018 alimony rules (¶2152).

¶ 2159   Designating that payments aren't to be treated as alimony.

If a divorce or separation instrument designates a payment that would otherwise qualify as alimony as *not* to be treated as alimony (e.g., as a property settlement), the payment won't qualify as alimony. (Code Sec. 71(b)(1)(B); Reg § 1.71-1T, Q&A 8)[35]

¶ 2160   Alimony trusts.

A payor spouse can't deduct payments the payee spouse receives from an alimony trust which aren't includible in the payor's income under the Code Sec. 682 trust rules. (Code Sec. 215(d))[36] Under pre-2019 rules, a payee spouse/beneficiary who's divorced or legally separated, or separated under a written separation agreement, includes in gross income the share of trust income that (without this rule) would be includible in the payor spouse's income — effectively shifting liability for tax on the income. But amounts payable for support of the payor spouse's minor children are taxable to the payor spouse. (Code Sec. 682(a))[37]

Generally, for amounts received after 2018 (see ¶2152 for effective dates), the beneficiary of an alimony trust won't include such amounts in gross income or pay federal income tax on them. (Code Sec. 682)) But, IRS has stated that it intends to provide regs that Code Sec. 682 will continue to apply with regard to trust income payable to a former spouse who was divorced or legally separated under a divorce or separation instrument executed on or before 2019, unless such instrument is modified after that date and the modification provides that the revocation applies to the modification.

¶ 2161   Recapture rules—excess front-loading of alimony.

If there are "excess" alimony payments ("front-loading"), the payor spouse must "recapture" the "excess" by including it in gross income for the third post-separation year (below) (Code Sec. 71(f)(1)(A)) (on Form 1040, line 11, cross out "received" and write "recapture").[38] The same amount is deducted by the payee spouse in computing adjusted gross income for *the payee's* third post-separation year (on Form 1040, line 31a; cross out "paid" and write "recapture"). (Code Sec. 71(f)(1)(B))[39] The "recapture" amount is the

---

30. ¶K-6047
31. ¶K-6049; ¶714.02
32. ¶K-6049; ¶714.02
33. ¶K-6048; ¶714.02
34. ¶K-6047

35. ¶K-6033; ¶714.01
36. ¶K-6009; ¶2158.42
37. ¶C-5432 *et seq.*; ¶6824
38. ¶K-6043, K-6044; ¶714.03
39. ¶K-6044; ¶714.03

sum of:

(1) the excess of (a) the alimony or separate maintenance payments in the second post-separation year, over (b) the sum of the payments in the third year, plus $15,000; *plus*

(2) the excess of (a) the payments in the first post-separation year, over (b) the sum of the average of the payments in the second year (minus any excess payment in (1), above) and third year, plus $15,000. (Code Sec. 71(f))[40]

The first post-separation year is the first calendar year in which the payor spouse paid alimony, etc., to the payee spouse. The second and third post-separation years are the succeeding calendar years. (Code Sec. 71(f)(6))[41] There's no recapture if payments cease because either spouse dies or the payee spouse remarries before the close of the third post-separation year. Nor does recapture apply to temporary support payments or payments that fluctuate because of a continuing liability to pay, for at least three years, a fixed portion of income from business, property or services (including self-employment). (Code Sec. 71(f)(5))[42]

¶ 2162   "Nonbusiness" Expenses.

From 2018 to 2025, miscellaneous itemized deductions subject to the 2%-of-AGI floor are not allowed (¶3109), including most "nonbusiness" expense deductions — e.g., ordinary and necessary expenses that, though not connected with a taxpayer's trade or business, are paid or incurred for the collection or production of income; the management, conservation or maintenance of property held for the production of income; or the determination, collection or refund of any tax. (Code Sec. 67(g))

¶ 2163   Tax-exempt income expenses.

A taxpayer may not deduct costs incurred in the production of tax-exempt income (Code Sec. 265(a)(1))[43] (e.g., interest on indebtedness incurred or continued to buy or carry tax-exempt securities, see ¶1723). Expenses attributable to both taxable and tax-exempt income that can't be specifically identified must be prorated. (Reg § 1.265-1(c))[44]

¶ 2164   Premature withdrawal penalties.

An individual may deduct any interest or principal he or she forfeits to a bank or other financial institution as a penalty for premature withdrawal from a time savings account, certificate of deposit or similar deposit. The penalty is deductible from gross income in computing adjusted gross income (Code Sec. 62(a)(9)), see ¶3102.[45]

¶ 2165   Bond Premium Amortization.

Any premium on tax-exempt bonds must be amortized (Code Sec. 171(a)(2); Reg § 1.171-1(c)(1)), but premium on *taxable* bonds is amortized only if the holder so elects (see ¶2166), using the procedure discussed in ¶2168. (Code Sec. 171(a)(1), Code Sec. 171(c); Reg § 1.171-1(c)(2)) The amortized amount reduces basis and, for taxable bonds, is treated as an offset to the interest received. [46]

"Bonds" include a bond, debenture, note, or certificate or other evidence of indebtedness. (Code Sec. 171(d); Reg § 1.171-1(b)) These rules don't apply to certain specified debt obligations. (Reg § 1.171-1(b)(2))[47] Bond premium generally arises when the stated interest rate on the bond is higher than its market yield when purchased. The premium is the

40. ¶K-6044; ¶714.03
41. ¶K-6045; ¶714.03
42. ¶K-6043; ¶714.03
43. ¶K-9000 *et seq.*; ¶2654

44. ¶K-9002; ¶2654
45. ¶A-2618; ¶624
46. ¶K-5611; ¶s 1714.01, 10,164
47. ¶K-5614; ¶1714.01

excess of the holder's basis in the bond immediately after acquisition over the sum of all amounts payable on the bond after the acquisition date (other than payments of qualified stated interest, see ¶1312). (Reg § 1.171-1(d)(1))[48] Basis for this purpose is the holder's basis for determining loss on sale. (Code Sec. 171(b)(1)(A); Reg § 1.171-1(e)(1)(i))[49] If a convertible bond is purchased at a premium, any amount attributable to the conversion feature is excluded from amortizable bond premium. (Code Sec. 171(b)(1))[50] Regs provide special rules for variable rate debt instruments, inflation-indexed debt instruments, and bonds subject to contingencies. (Reg § 1.171-3)[1] For amortization of callable bonds, see ¶2167. For securities dealers, see ¶2169.

¶ 2166 Amortization deduction, basis reduction.

For *tax-exempt* bonds, no deduction is allowed for the amortizable bond premium for a tax year. (Code Sec. 171(a)(2))[2] The bond's basis is reduced by the amortizable bond premium barred as a deduction. (Code Sec. 1016(a)(5)); Reg § 1.1016-5(b)(3))[3] For *taxable* bonds, a taxpayer can elect (¶2168) to deduct amortizable bond premium (Code Sec. 171(a)(1)). The bond premium (computed under a constant-yield method based on yield to maturity (Code Sec. 171(b)(3)(A); Reg § 1.171-1(a)(1))) allocable to an accrual period is deducted as an offset to the qualified stated interest (¶1312) allocable to the period. (Code Sec. 171(e); Reg § 1.171-2(a)(1))[4] Basis is reduced by the offset amount. (Code Sec. 1016(a)(5))[5]

⬥*observation:* If the holder of a taxable bond doesn't elect to amortize bond premium, the basis of the bond remains the original basis in the holder's hands for determining gain or loss on sale or redemption.

¶ 2167 Amortization of callable bonds.

The holder of a taxable bond generally amortizes bond premium by reference to the bond's stated maturity date (see ¶2166), even if the bond is likely to be called. (Code Sec. 171(b)(1)(B)(ii); Reg § 1.171-3(c)(4)(ii)(A), Reg § 1.171-3(e), Ex. 2)[6] The holder can deduct the unamortized bond premium of a called bond (excess of adjusted basis at start of the year over the greater of the amount (a) received on early redemption or (b) due on maturity). (Code Sec. 171(b)(2); Reg § 1.171-3(c)(5)(ii), Reg § 1.171-3(e), Ex. 2)[7]

¶ 2168 Election to amortize bond premium.

The election to amortize bond premium on taxable bonds (¶2165) is made by (a) offsetting interest income with bond premium in the holder's timely filed return for the first tax year to which the election applies, and (b) attaching an election statement to the return. (Code Sec. 171(c)(2); Reg § 1.171-4(a)(1)) IRS consent isn't needed. (Reg § 1.171-5(c)(1)) The election (unless revoked with IRS consent) is binding for the year made and later years, and applies to all taxable bonds (1) held by taxpayer at the beginning of the first tax year to which the election applies, and (2) those acquired after that year by taxpayer. (Code Sec. 171(c)(2); Reg § 1.171-4(b)) A holder who has elected to treat all interest on the bond as original issue discount (¶1311) is treated as having elected to amortize bond premium. (Reg § 1.171-4(a)(2))[8]

48. ¶K-5616; ¶1714
49. ¶K-5611; ¶1714.02
50. ¶K-5622; ¶1714.035
1. ¶K-5624 *et seq.*; ¶1714.036 *et seq.*
2. ¶K-5611; ¶1714
3. ¶P-5043; ¶10,164

4. ¶K-5611; ¶1714.03
5. ¶P-5043; ¶10,164
6. ¶K-5627; ¶1714.03
7. ¶K-5628; ¶1714.03
8. ¶K-5633; ¶1714.04

recommendation: The election provides a current interest income offset, which is preferable to a future capital loss deduction.

¶ 2169   Dealers in securities—bond premium amortization.

Taxable bonds that are stock in trade, held primarily for sale to customers, or includable in inventory if on hand at tax year-end aren't subject to the bond amortization rules (Code Sec. 171(d); Reg § 1.171-1(b)(2)(iv)), but tax-exempt bonds held primarily for sale to customers are. (Code Sec. 75(a))[9]

Chapter 7 Education—Tax Credits, Exclusions, Deductions—ABLE Accounts

¶ 2200 **Education—Tax Credits, Exclusions, Deductions.** ▄▄▄▄

There are several tax breaks designed specifically to help defray the costs of saving and paying for higher education and some pre-college costs.

There are three main categories of tax breaks for education:

(1) Tax credits, see ¶2201 *et seq.*,

(2) Exclusions, see ¶2205 *et seq.*, and

(3) Deductions, see ¶2220 *et seq.*

Other tax breaks. Pre-age-59½ distributions from traditional IRAs and Roth IRAs are excepted from the 10% premature distribution penalty tax to the extent they don't exceed qualified higher education expenses for the distribution year (¶4333, ¶4346). Also, there's an unlimited gift-tax exclusion for gifts made on behalf of another individual directly to a qualifying educational organization (¶5050).

¶ 2201 **Tax Credits for Higher Education.** ▄▄▄▄

Individual taxpayers may claim an income tax credit for the sum of the American opportunity tax credit (AOTC; formerly the Hope scholarship credit, ¶2202), and the Lifetime Learning credit (¶2203) for higher education expenses at accredited post-secondary educational institutions paid for themselves, their spouses, and their dependents. The AOTC is available for qualified expenses of the first four years of undergraduate education; and the Lifetime Learning credit is available for qualified expenses of any post-high school education at "eligible educational institutions." The AOTC can't be claimed in the same tax year as the Lifetime Learning credit for expenses of any one student (see ¶2203). The credits phase out for higher-income taxpayers.

¶ 2202 **American opportunity tax credit (AOTC)—Form 8863.**

Individuals may elect (on Form 8863) a personal, partially refundable AOTC equal to 100% of up to $2,000 of qualified higher education tuition and related (QT&R) expenses (¶2204) plus 25% of the next $2,000 of expenses paid for education furnished to an eligible student in an academic period. So, the maximum AOTC is $2,500 a year for *each* eligible student. (Code Sec. 25A(a)(1); Code Sec. 25A(e); Code Sec. 25A(i))[1]

The AOTC phases out ratably for taxpayers with modified AGI (MAGI, i.e., AGI increased by foreign, possessions, and Puerto Rico income exclusions) of $80,000 to $90,000 ($160,000 to $180,000 for joint filers). (Code Sec. 25A(d)(1))

The AOTC may be claimed for four tax years for each eligible student, and only for students who haven't completed the first four years of post-secondary education as of the beginning of the tax year. (Code Sec. 25A(b)(2)(A); Code Sec. 25A(b)(2)(C); Reg § 1.25A-3(d)(1)(iii)) Also, for at least one academic period during the year, the student must be enrolled for at least half of the normal full-time workload for the student's course of study (Code Sec. 25A(b)(3)(B); Reg § 1.25A-3(d)(1)(ii)), and the student can't have been convicted of a federal or state felony drug offense at the end of the tax year. (Code Sec. 25A(b)(2)(D))

The AOTC (or Lifetime Learning credit, ¶2203) and tax-free Coverdell education savings account (CESA) distributions (¶2205) are allowed for the same student for the same year,

---

1. ¶A-4500 *et seq.*; ¶25A4

References beginning with a single letter are to paragraphs in Federal Tax Coordinator 2d and RIA's Analysis of Federal Taxes: Income. Those beginning with numbers are to paragraphs in United States Tax Reporter.

335

as long as the credit isn't claimed for education expenses used to generate the tax-free CESA distributions. (Code Sec. 530(d)(2)(C)(i))

If a dependency deduction for an individual is allowed to another taxpayer, the dependent can't claim the AOTC, and QT&R expenses paid by the dependent are treated as paid by the person who is allowed the deduction. (Code Sec. 25A(g)(3))

> **observation:** Although the dependency exemption is suspended from 2018 to 2025 (¶3112), Code Sec. 151(d)(5)(B) provides that this suspension isn't taken into account in determining whether a deduction for personal exemptions is "allowed" or "allowable." So, a student who pays his or her own QT&R expenses, for whom a taxpayer could (but for the suspension) claim a dependency exemption, can't claim the AOTC.

If a third party (not the taxpayer, spouse, or dependent) pays a student's QT&R expenses directly to an educational institution, the student is treated as receiving the payment and, in turn, paying the expenses. (Reg § 1.25A-5(b))

If QT&R expenses are prepaid during one tax year for an academic period that begins during the first three months of the next tax year, the academic period is treated as beginning in the earlier year (Code Sec. 25A(g)(4)), and the credit is allowed only in the tax year in which the expenses are paid. (Reg § 1.25A-3(e)) Special rules apply for tuition refunds and excludable tuition assistance received after the tax year in which QT&R expenses are paid. (Reg § 1.25A-5(c), Reg § 1.25A-5(f))

Subject to an exception, 40% of a taxpayer's otherwise allowable AOTC is refundable. None of the credit is refundable if the taxpayer claiming the credit is a child subject to the kiddie tax. (Code Sec. 25A(i)) A resident of a U.S. possession claims the refundable part of the AOTC in that possession.[2]

To claim any education credit (¶2201): the student's name and taxpayer identification number (TIN) must be included on the taxpayer's return (Code Sec. 25A(g)(1)); QT&R expenses must be adjusted for qualified scholarships, etc. (Code Sec. 25A(g)(2)) (¶2204); there can't be a double benefit under the Code (Code Sec. 25A(g)(5)); married taxpayers must file jointly (Code Sec. 25A(g)(6)); nonresident aliens must be treated as a resident alien under a Code Sec. 6013(g) or Code Sec. 6013(h) election (Code Sec. 25A(g)(7)); and the taxpayer must receive a payee statement (Form 1098-T) from the educational institution containing all required information. (Code Sec. 25A(g)(8)) And, the AOTC (but not the Lifetime Learning credit, ¶2202) is barred: (1) unless the taxpayer's and the student's TIN was issued before the return's due date, and the taxpayer includes the employer identification number (EIN) of any institution to which QT&R expenses were paid for the student (Code Sec. 25A(g)(1)); and (2) in certain cases where the AOTC was improperly claimed in a prior year. (Code Sec. 25A(b)(4))

¶ 2203   Lifetime Learning credit (LLC)—Form 8863.

Taxpayers may elect (on Form 8863) an LLC equal to 20% of up to $10,000 of qualified tuition and related expenses (¶2204) paid during the tax year. The maximum credit is $2,000. (Code Sec. 25A(a)(2), Code Sec. 25A(c)(1), Code Sec. 25A(e), Code Sec. 25A(f))[3]

Unlike the American opportunity tax credit (AOTC, ¶2202), which is available on a per-student basis, the LLC is available on a per-family basis, and the maximum amount doesn't vary with the number of students in the family. So, a joint-filing couple with two children could claim no more than a $2,000 LLC, even if each child is a qualifying student with qualifying expenses. For 2018, the credit is phased out ratably for taxpayers with

---

2. ¶A-4525.2; ¶25A4.03   3. ¶A-4500 *et seq.*; ¶25A4

MAGI from $57,000 to $67,000 ($114,000 to $134,000 for joint filers). For 2019, as calculated by Thomson Reuters based on inflation data, the credit is phased out ratably for taxpayers with MAGI from $58,000 to $68,000 ($116,000 to $136,000 for joint filers). (Code Sec. 25A(d), Code Sec. 25A(h))[4]

The same treatment of expenses paid by a dependent and of certain prepayments, and the general requirements for claiming an education credit (e.g., the bar to credit unless marrieds file jointly) described at ¶2202, also apply to the LLC. (Code Sec. 25A(g))

Expenses for a student for whom an AOTC (¶2202) is allowed for the tax year don't qualify for the LLC. (Code Sec. 25A(c)(2))

¶ 2204   Qualified tuition and related (QT&R) expenses for the education credit.

QT&R expenses for the American opportunity tax credit (AOTC, ¶2202) and Lifetime Learning credit (LLC, ¶2203) are tuition and fees (and for the AOTC only, expenses for course materials) required for the enrollment or attendance of the taxpayer, spouse, or a dependent, at a post-secondary educational institution eligible to participate in the federal student loan program. (Code Sec. 25A(f)(1)(A), Code Sec. 25A(f)(2))[5]

QT&R expenses don't include room and board, transportation, insurance, medical expenses, other similar personal, living, or family expenses, or student fees (unless required as a condition of enrollment or attendance). Nor do they include expenses for any course or other education involving sports, games, or hobbies, or noncredit course, unless they're part of the student's degree program (Code Sec. 25A(f)(1)(B); Code Sec. 25A(f)(1)(C); Reg § 1.25A-2(d)(2), Reg § 1.25A-2(d)(3)) (or for the LLC only) help the student acquire or improve job skills. (Code Sec. 25A(c)(2)(B); Reg § 1.25A-2(d)(5))

As to expenses for books, supplies and equipment —for the AOTC, they qualify as QT&R expenses if they're needed for a course of study, whether or not they're purchased from the educational institution as a condition of enrollment[6] —but for the LLC, they qualify as QT&R expenses *only if* required to be paid to the institution as a condition of enrollment or attendance. (Reg § 1.25A-2(d)(2)(ii))

QT&R expenses must be reduced by scholarship amounts excludable from income under Code Sec. 117 (¶2215), educational assistance under chapter 30 through 35 of title 38 U.S. Code or under chapter 1606 of title 10 U.S. Code, and other tax-free payments. But, qualified amounts aren't reduced by amounts paid by gift, bequest, devise, or inheritance. (Code Sec. 25A(g)(2)) No credit is allowed for any expense for which an income tax deduction is allowed. (Code Sec. 25A(g)(5)) Special rules apply for tuition refunds and excludable tuition assistance received after the tax year in which QT&R expenses are paid. (Reg § 1.25A-2(d)(2))

¶ 2205   Coverdell Education Savings Accounts (CESAs). ▬▬▬▬

Taxpayers can contribute up to $2,000 per year to CESAs (formerly "education IRAs") for beneficiaries under age 18 and special needs beneficiaries of any age (¶2207). The account is exempt from income tax (¶2206), and distributions of earnings are tax-free if used for qualified education expenses (¶2208).

¶ 2206   Coverdell Education Savings Accounts (CESAs)—Forms 5305-E and 5305-EA.

A CESA is a trust (Form 5305-E) or custodial account (Form 5305-EA) created exclusively for paying an individual beneficiary's qualified education expenses. (Code

---

4. ¶A-4517.1; ¶25A4.02   6. ¶A-4537; ¶25A4.07
5. ¶A-4537; ¶25A4.07

Sec. 530(b)(1), Code Sec. 530(g)) CESAs are exempt from tax except for the unrelated business income tax. (Code Sec. 530(a)) Allowable annual contributions to CESAs (¶2207) aren't deductible and aren't taxable when withdrawn. Distributions of earnings from CESAs for qualified education expenses are tax-free (¶2208).

CESAs can't invest in life insurance contracts, and, except for common trust or investment funds, trust assets can't be commingled. The account balance must be distributed to the beneficiary within 30 days after the beneficiary turns age 30 (unless the beneficiary has special needs), or, if sooner, to the beneficiary's estate within 30 days after the beneficiary's death (Code Sec. 530(b)(1), Code Sec. 530(d)(8)),[7] unless transferred to a family member's CESA (¶2208).

¶ 2207   Contributions to Coverdell Education Savings Accounts (CESAs).

Annual contributions to CESAs for any beneficiary can't exceed $2,000, must be made in cash, and can't be made after the beneficiary turns age 18 (except for special needs beneficiaries). (Code Sec. 530(b)(1)(A)) CESA contributions for a year may be made as late as the unextended tax return due date for that year. (Code Sec. 530(b)(4))[8]

For individual contributors, the $2,000 limit phases out ratably between $95,000 and $110,000 ($190,000 and $220,000 for joint filers) of modified AGI (MAGI, i.e., AGI plus income excluded under Code Sec. 911, Code Sec. 931, and Code Sec. 933). (Code Sec. 530(c))[9]

observation: A corporation, without regard to any MAGI limits, may contribute to a CESA that has an employee's child as beneficiary. But the contribution would be taxed to the employee.

An individual who has received a military death gratuity or Servicemembers' Group Life Insurance (SGLI) payment can roll it over to one or more CESAs, without regard to the annual contribution limit (Code Sec. 530(d)(9)(A)) or the AGI phase-out limit. The contribution must be made before the end of the one-year period beginning on the date on which the contributor received the payment. (Code Sec. 530(d)(9)(A))[10] The rule allowing only one rollover contribution to a CESA during any 12-month period (¶2208) doesn't apply to this rollover. (Code Sec. 530(d)(9)(B))

Excess contributions are subject to a 6% excise tax in the contribution year and each year that an excess amount is in the account (report on Form 5329, Part V). But, the excise tax doesn't apply to rollover contributions, or contributions (with net earnings attributable to the excess contributions) returned before June 1 of the year following the contribution year. (Code Sec. 4973(e))[11]

For the gift tax treatment of CESAs, see ¶5050.

¶ 2208   Distributions from Coverdell Education Savings Accounts (CESAs).

A distribution from a CESA is included in the distributee's income generally as provided under the annuity rules of Code Sec. 72. (Code Sec. 530(d)(1)) So, distributions consist of a pro-rata share of principal (recovered tax-free) and accumulated earnings (which *may* be excludable under the CESA rules). Distributions from a CESA are entirely excluded if qualified education expenses (QEEs) of the beneficiary equal or exceed total CESA distributions for the year. (Code Sec. 530(d)(2)(A))

---

7. ¶A-4615; ¶A-4628, ¶5304
8. ¶A-4606; ¶5304
9. ¶A-4604; ¶5304

10. ¶A-4619.1; ¶5304.01
11. ¶A-4607; ¶49,734

QEEs include:

. . . higher education tuition, fees, books, and supplies, and, for half-time or greater students, certain room and board charges (Code Sec. 530(b)(2)(A)(i));

. . . elementary and secondary (K through 12) public, private or religious school tuition and expenses, including tutoring, room and board, transportation, uniforms, and extended day programs (Code Sec. 530(b)(2)(A)(ii); Code Sec. 530(b)(3));

. . . special needs services for special needs beneficiaries enrolled in any of the above types of schools (Code Sec. 530(b)(3)(A)); and

. . . contributions to a qualified tuition program (QTP, see ¶2209) on behalf of a designated beneficiary (DB) (Code Sec. 530(b)(2)(B)),[12] but in applying the Code Sec. 72 annuity rules to a CESA distribution that's contributed to a QTP (¶2209) for a DB, any part of the contribution not includible in gross income (because it doesn't exceed the DB's QEEs) won't result in an increase in the investment in the contract (Code Sec. 530(b)(2)(B)).

QEEs are reduced by the same tax-free scholarships and similar payments that reduce qualified tuition and related expenses for education credit purposes (¶2204) (Code Sec. 530(d)(2)(C)(i)(I)), and by the expenses taken into account in determining the education credit (¶2201).[13]

Distributions aren't taxed if rolled over within 60 days (limited to once in a 12-month period) into a CESA for the same beneficiary or a member of the beneficiary's family (as defined at ¶2211) who is under age 30. (Code Sec. 530(d)(5), Code Sec. 530(d)(6))[14] IRS has concluded that only one rollover for a CESA is allowed per individual, per year. [15] A CESA transfer to a beneficiary's family member under a divorce decree or after the beneficiary's death also isn't taxable. (Code Sec. 530(d)(7))

If CESA distributions exceed QEEs in a year, the excludable part of the distributions is the earnings portion of the distributions times a fraction having as its numerator the year's QEEs and as its denominator the year's total distributions. The balance of the earnings portion of the distributions is taxable. (Code Sec. 530(d)(2)(B))[16] Any savings bond redemption proceeds transferred to a CESA in a tax-free transfer under Code Sec. 135 (see ¶2219) *don't* increase the investment in the contract in applying the Code Sec. 72 rules to the CESA distributions. (Code Sec. 135(c)(2)(C))

Any taxable amount also is subject to a 10% additional tax, but not: (1) if made on or after the beneficiary's death or disability, (2) to the extent the taxable amount doesn't exceed (a) the amount of a tax-free scholarship received by the beneficiary, or (b) the "advanced education costs" received by the beneficiary at a U.S. service academy (e.g., U.S. Military Academy), (3) if the distribution is taxable solely because of the rule (see above) reducing the total amount of QEEs by the expenses taken into account in determining the education credit for the year, or (4) if the tax is attributable to income on a contribution withdrawn (with associated income) before June 1 of the year after the contribution year. (Code Sec. 530(d)(4))[17]

If aggregate distributions from CESAs and QTPs (¶2209) in a year exceed an individual's QEEs, the expenses must be allocated among the distributions. (Code Sec. 530(d)(2)(C)) No deduction, credit, or exclusion is allowed under any other Code provision for an education expense used in determining the CESA exclusion. (Code Sec. 530(d)(2)(D))[18]

---

12. ¶A-4610 *et seq.*; ¶5304
13. ¶A-4612; ¶5304
14. ¶A-4619; ¶5304
15. ¶A-4619

16. ¶A-4609; ¶5304
17. ¶A-4618
18. ¶A-4609 *et seq.*; ¶5304

¶ 2209   **Qualified Tuition Programs (QTPs)—529 Plans.** ■■■■■■■■■■

A person can make nondeductible cash contributions to a QTP (or "529 plan") on behalf of a designated beneficiary. The earnings on contributions build up tax-free, and distributions from a QTP are excludable if used to pay for qualified higher education expenses (QHEEs), including some elementary and secondary school tuition.

A QTP is a tax-exempt program established and maintained by a state (including a state agency or instrumentality), or one or more eligible educational institutions (including private ones) under which a taxpayer may:

(1) buy tuition credits or certificates on behalf of a designated beneficiary (DB, ¶2211) which entitle the DB to a waiver or payment of QHEEs (¶2210)—i.e., a prepaid educational services account, or

(2) make contributions to an account set up to meet the DB's QHEEs —i.e., an educational savings account. This option is available only for state (or state agency or instrumentality) programs. (Code Sec. 529(b)(1)(A); Prop Reg. § 1.529-2(c) ["Taxpayers may rely"])[19]

A QTP must require all purchases or contributions to be made in cash (with no dollar limit on contributions), provide separate accounting for each designated beneficiary, prohibit pledging an interest in the program as security, and provide adequate safeguards to prevent contributions exceeding amounts necessary for the DB's qualified higher education expenses.

A QTP must provide that any contributor or DB may, directly or indirectly, direct the investment of any contributions or earnings no more than two times in any calendar year. (Code Sec. 529(b)(4))[20] A QTP maintained by a private educational institution generally must get a ruling that it meets applicable requirements. (Code Sec. 529(b)(1))[21]

For the gift-tax treatment of contributions to a QTP, see ¶5050.

¶ 2210   **Tax treatment of distributions from qualified tuition programs (QTPs).**

Distributions from a QTP are includible in the distributee's income under the Code Sec. 72 annuity rules, if not excluded under any other Code provision. (Code Sec. 529(c)(3)(A))[22]

In-kind distributions (e.g., tuition credits or waivers, payment vouchers) from state-sponsored QTPs aren't includible in gross income if the benefit, if paid for by the distributee, would have been a payment of a qualified higher education expense (QHEE). (Code Sec. 529(c)(3)(B)(i); Prop Reg. § 1.529-1(c), ["Taxpayers may rely"]) [23]

Cash distributions are fully excludable if they don't exceed QHEEs, reduced by expenses for which in-kind distributions were received. If cash distributions exceed QHEEs, the amount otherwise includible under the Code Sec. 72 annuity rules is reduced by the ratio of QHEEs to distributions. (Code Sec. 529(c)(3)(B)(ii))[24]

QHEEs for QTP purposes are: (1) tuition, fees and expenses for books, supplies, equipment required for the enrollment or attendance of a designated beneficiary (DB, ¶2211) at an eligible educational institution (plus up to $10,000 per DB per tax year for expenses for tuition in connection with enrollment or attendance at an elementary or secondary public, private, or religious school); (2) certain expenses for the purchase of computer or peripheral

19. ¶A-4727; ¶5294
20. ¶A-4706; ¶5294
21. ¶A-4729; ¶5294

22. ¶A-4709 *et seq.*; ¶5294.02
23. ¶A-4709; ¶5294.02
24. ¶A-4709; ¶5294.02

equipment, computer software, or internet access and related services; (3) expenses for special needs services; and (4) room and board costs (subject to a limit) for students who are at least half-time. (Code Sec. 529(e)(3); Code Sec. 529(c)(7))[25]

For QTP exclusion purposes, total annual QHEEs are reduced by excludable scholarships or educational assistance received, and by any QHEEs taken into account in determining the American opportunity tax credit and Lifetime Learning credit (¶2201 *et seq.*) allowed to the taxpayer or any other person. (Code Sec. 529(c)(3)(B)(v))[26]

Distributions from a QTP aren't taxed if rolled over within 60 days (limited to once in 12 months) to another QTP (or, for distributions after Dec. 22, 2017 and before Jan. 1, 2026, to an ABLE account up to the ABLE annual contribution limit (see ¶2226)) for the same DB or a family member of the DB (¶2211). (Code Sec. 529(c)(3)(C)(iii))[27] A change in the DB isn't a distribution if the new DB is a member of the old DB's family; see ¶2211. (Code Sec. 529(c)(3)(C)(ii))[28]

A 10% additional tax applies to QTP distributions includible in gross income, in the same way, and with the same exceptions, as for Coverdell education savings account (CESA) distributions (see ¶2208). (Code Sec. 529(c)(6))[29]

If total distributions from a QTP and from a CESA (see ¶2205 *et seq.*) exceed QHEEs otherwise taken into account under the QTP rules (after the above reductions), the taxpayer must allocate the expenses among the distributions for purposes of determining the QTP exclusion. (Code Sec. 529(c)(3)(B)(vi))[30]

¶ 2211   Designated beneficiary (DB) of a qualified tuition program (QTP).

The DB of a QTP (¶2209) is:

(1) the individual so designated at the start of participation in the QTP; (Code Sec. 529(e)(1)(A))

(2) the new DB, if DBs are changed and the new one is a member of the same family (spouses, individuals meeting the relationship tests at ¶3113, spouses of these individuals, and first cousins of the DB); (Code Sec. 529(e)(1)(B), Code Sec. 529(e)(2)) and

(3) the individual receiving the interest in a scholarship, if an interest in a QTP is purchased by a state or eligible educational institution as part of a scholarship program it operates. (Code Sec. 529(e)(1)(C))[31]

¶ 2212   Employer-Provided Educational Benefits; Scholarships and Fellowships. ▬▬

An employee may exclude the value of educational benefits provided by an employer if the benefit qualifies as a working condition fringe (¶2213) or is provided under an educational assistance program (¶2214). Qualified tuition reductions for employees of educational institutions (¶2216) and qualifying scholarships and fellowships (¶2215) also are excludable.

¶ 2213   When education benefits are excluded as working condition fringes.

Employer-provided educational expenses are excludable from an employee's income as a working condition fringe to the extent that, if the employee paid for the benefit, the amount paid would have been deducted as an employee business expense. For the criteria for determining if education is a deductible employee business expense, see ¶2222. (Reg § 1.132-1(f), Reg § 1.132-5(a)(2))[32]

---

25. ¶A-4711; ¶5294
26. ¶A-4709; ¶5294.02
27. ¶A-4721; ¶5294.02
28. ¶A-4721, ¶A-4722; ¶5294.02

29. ¶A-4720; ¶5294.02
30. ¶A-4716; ¶5294.02
31. ¶A-4701; ¶5294
32. ¶H-2052; ¶1324.05

observation: Unreimbursed employee business expenses are currently not deductible because of the suspension of miscellaneous itemized deductions from 2018 through 2025. However, these types of working condition fringe benefits will presumably remain excludible. [33]

¶ 2214 Exclusion for employer-provided educational assistance under a qualified program.

An employee may exclude educational assistance provided under an employer's qualified educational assistance program, up to an annual maximum of $5,250. (Code Sec. 127(a)(2)) The education received need not be job-related. (Reg § 1.127-2(c)(4))

Expenses paid by an employer for education or training provided to the employee that aren't excludable under this provision can only be excluded from income if they qualify as a working condition fringe (¶2213). (Code Sec. 132(j)(8))

"Educational assistance" means the employer's payment for or provision of tuition, fees, books, supplies and equipment under an educational assistance program, including amounts for graduate-level courses. It doesn't include meals, lodging, transportation, or tools or supplies (other than textbooks) that may be retained after the course ends. (Code Sec. 127(c)(1); Reg § 1.127-2(c)(3)) [34]

Eligibility requirements can't discriminate in favor of "highly compensated employees" (see ¶4315). (Code Sec. 127(b)(2); Reg § 1.127-2(e)(1)) [35] No deduction or credit can be taken by the employee for any amount excluded from income. (Code Sec. 127(c)(7)) [36]

¶ 2215 Exclusion for qualifying scholarships and fellowships.

A scholarship or fellowship isn't taxable, to the extent it's a "qualified scholarship" granted to a degree candidate at an educational organization and isn't a stipend (¶2217). (Code Sec. 117(a), Code Sec. 117(c)) [37] A "qualified scholarship" is any amount received as a scholarship and used for tuition and fees required for enrollment at an educational organization, and for required fees, books, supplies and equipment. (Code Sec. 117(b)(2)) [38] An "educational organization" is one that normally maintains a regular faculty, curriculum and regularly enrolled student body in attendance. (Code Sec. 117(b)(2)(A)) [39]

¶ 2216 Exclusion for qualified tuition reductions for school employees.

Qualified tuition reductions for employees of educational institutions are excluded from the recipient's gross income. (Code Sec. 117(d)) A "qualified tuition reduction" is the amount of tuition reduction provided to an employee of an educational organization for below-graduate-level education (not services, see ¶2217) at that or a similar institution, for the employee (whether active, retired, or disabled), or the employee's spouse or dependent children. (Code Sec. 117(d)(2)) But, a tuition reduction for a graduate student engaged in teaching or research can be tax-free. (Code Sec. 117(d)(5)) [40]

A qualified tuition reduction provided with respect to a highly compensated employee (¶4315) is excludable only if it's available to all employees on a nondiscriminatory basis. (Code Sec. 117(d)(3)) [41]

33. ¶H-1701
34. ¶H-2065; ¶1274.01
35. ¶H-2069; ¶1274.01
36. ¶H-2064; ¶1274.01
37. ¶J-1230; ¶1174.01

38. ¶J-1232; ¶1174.01
39. ¶J-1244; ¶1174.01
40. ¶J-1252 *et seq.*; ¶1174.02
41. ¶J-1255; ¶1174.02

¶ 2217   Payments for teaching or research.

The exclusions for qualified scholarships (¶2215) and qualified tuition reductions (¶2216) don't apply to any amount received that represents payment for teaching, research or other services performed by the student as a condition for receiving the qualified benefit. (Code Sec. 117(c)(1))[42] This payment-for-services rule doesn't apply to amounts received under certain health professions scholarship programs (i.e., the National Health Service Corps (NHSC) Scholarship Program and the Armed Forces Health Professions Scholarship and Financial Assistance Program) and, any payments from certain work-learning-service programs that are operated by a work college. (Code Sec. 117(c)(2)).[43]

¶ 2218   Higher Education Exclusion for Savings Bond Income—Form 8815. ■■■■

Subject to a phaseout (below), an individual who pays qualified higher education expenses (QHEEs, ¶2219) during a tax year excludes from that year's gross income any amount of income from the redemption, that year, of any "qualified U.S. savings bond" (Series EE bond issued after '89, or Series I bond). (Code Sec. 135(a), Code Sec. 135(c)(1))[44]

Use Form 8815 to compute the exclusion. Form 8818 (one per bond) may be used to keep a record of the redemptions. [45]

If taxpayer's aggregate redemption proceeds (principal plus interest) for a tax year exceed the QHEEs paid that year, the excluded interest is limited to the otherwise excludable amount times this fraction: the QHEEs paid that year, divided by the year's aggregate redemption proceeds. (Code Sec. 135(b)(1))[46]

Illustration: Taxpayer redeems $8,000 of qualified U.S. savings bonds ($4,000 interest, $4,000 principal) and pays QHEEs of $6,000. The exclusion ratio is 75% ($6,000 ÷ $8,000), so $3,000 of the interest (75% × $4,000) (and the $4,000 principal) is excludable.[47]

The individual must have bought the bond(s) after reaching age 24 (Code Sec. 135(c)(1)(B)) and must be the sole owner (or joint owner with spouse). The exclusion isn't available to the owner of a bond that was bought by another individual (other than a spouse). Nor is it available to a parent who buys the bonds and puts them in the name of a child or other dependent. But the owner may designate an individual (including a child) as the beneficiary for amounts payable at death without losing the exclusion. [48] A married individual must file jointly to get the exclusion. (Code Sec. 135(d)(3))[49]

For 2018, the exclusion phases out for a taxpayer whose modified AGI (MAGI), for the year exceeds $79,550 ($119,300 for joint filers), and is completely phased out when MAGI reaches $94,550 ($149,300 for joint filers). For 2019, as calculated by Thomson Reuters based on inflation data, the exclusion phases out for a taxpayer whose MAGI exceeds $81,100 ($121,600 for joint filers), and is completely phased out when MAGI reaches $96,100 ($151,600).[50]

The exclusion generally applies only if the owner redeems the bonds (Code Sec. 135(a)), i.e., not if the owner transfers them to the educational institution (see ¶2219 for exceptions).[1]

MAGI is AGI determined without the savings bond interest exclusion (see above), the

---

42. ¶J-1258; ¶1174.01
43. ¶J-1258.1; ¶1174.05
44. ¶J-3051 *et seq.*; ¶J-3055; ¶1354
45. ¶J-3051; ¶J-3062; ¶1354.02
46. ¶J-3052; ¶1354.02

47. ¶J-3052; ¶1354.02
48. ¶s J-3055, J-3056; ¶1354.01
49. ¶J-3051; ¶1354
50. ¶J-3053; ¶1354.03
1. ¶J-3051; ¶1354.02

Code Sec. 137 exclusion for employer-provided adoption assistance (¶1252), the Code Sec. 221 deduction for interest on a qualified education loan (¶2220), the Code Sec. 222 deduction for higher education expenses (¶2225), or the Code Sec. 911, Code Sec. 931, and Code Sec. 933 exclusions for income earned abroad (¶4605, ¶4603). (Code Sec. 135(c)(4))[2]

¶ 2219 Qualified higher education expenses (QHEEs) for savings bond exclusion.

For the savings bond exclusion (¶2218), QHEEs are tuition and fees required for the enrollment or attendance of a taxpayer, spouse, or a dependent (¶3113) at an eligible educational institution, (Code Sec. 135(c)(2)(A)) e.g., most colleges, junior colleges, nursing schools and vocational schools. (Code Sec. 135(c)(3)) Expenses for any course or other education involving sports, games or hobbies, unless part of a degree program, don't count. (Code Sec. 135(c)(2)(B))[3] The transfer of redemption proceeds to a qualified tuition program (QTP, ¶2209) or to a Coverdell education savings account (CESA, ¶2207) for the taxpayer, spouse, or dependent also is a QHEE. (Code Sec. 135(c)(2)(C))[4]

Expenses otherwise taken into account must be reduced by amounts received for excludable qualified scholarships (¶2215), certain educational assistance allowances and other tax-exempt payments (other than gifts, bequests, devises or inheritances), and a payment, waiver, or reimbursement of qualified higher education expenses under a QTP. (Code Sec. 135(d)(1))[5] The amount of QHEEs also must be reduced by the amount of such expenses taken into account in figuring the exclusions for distributions from CESA (¶2213) and QTPs (¶2209), and by expenses taken into account in determining the education credits (¶2201) allowed to the taxpayer or any other person for those expenses. This reduction is made before applying the rules reducing the excluded amount where redemption proceeds exceed higher education expenses and where taxpayer's modified AGI exceeds specified dollar amounts) (see ¶2218). (Code Sec. 135(d)(2))[6]

¶ 2220 Deduction for Interest Paid on Qualified Education Loans. ▬▬▬▬

Student loan interest generally is treated as personal interest and so isn't deductible. However, qualifying individuals may, subject to a phaseout, deduct up to $2,500 annually for interest paid on qualified higher education loans. (Code Sec. 221)[7]

The deduction is claimed as an adjustment to gross income to arrive at AGI. (Code Sec. 62(a)(17))[8] There's no deduction for any amount for which a deduction is allowable under any other Code provision (e.g., home equity loan; see ¶1731). (Code Sec. 221(e)(1))[9]

For 2018, the deduction phases out ratably for taxpayers with modified AGI (MAGI) between $65,000 and $80,000 ($135,000 and $165,000 for joint filers). For 2019, as calculated by Thomson Reuters based on inflation data, the deduction phases out ratably for taxpayers with MAGI between $70,000 and $85,000 ($140,000 and $170,000 for joint filers). (Code Sec. 221(b)(2)(B)) MAGI is AGI figured without regard to the deduction for qualified education loan interest, the deduction for qualified higher education expenses, and the exclusions for foreign, possession, and Puerto Rico income. (Code Sec. 221(b)(2)(C)(i))[10]

From 2018 through 2025, while the dependency exemption is suspended (¶3112), a person who would otherwise not be allowed to claim this deduction on account of being claimed as a dependent on another taxpayer's return under Code Sec. 221(c) is presumably

2. ¶J-3054; ¶1354.03
3. ¶s J-3057, J-3061; ¶1354.02
4. ¶J-3059; ¶1354
5. ¶J-3060; ¶1354.02
6. ¶J-3060; ¶1354

7. ¶K-5500 et seq.; ¶2214 et seq.
8. ¶A-2626; ¶K-5501; ¶2214
9. ¶K-5503.2; ¶2214.02
10. ¶K-5502; ¶2214.01

allowed to claim the deduction. The deduction may be claimed only by a person legally obligated to make the interest payments. (Reg § 1.221-1(b))[11] Married couples must file jointly to take the deduction. (Code Sec. 221(e)(2))[12]

For information reporting requirements for interest payments received on qualified education loans, see ¶4746.

¶ 2221   Qualified education loan defined.

A qualified education loan is any debt incurred by the taxpayer solely to pay qualified higher education expenses that are: (1) incurred on behalf of the taxpayer, spouse, or any dependents as of the time the debt was incurred; (2) paid or incurred within a reasonable period of time before or after the debt is incurred; and (3) attributable to education furnished during a period when the recipient was an eligible student (as defined for the American opportunity tax credit purposes, i.e., at least a half-time student, see ¶2202). (Code Sec. 221(d)(1); Code Sec. 221(d)(3))

Revolving lines of credit generally aren't qualified education loans unless the borrower agreed to use the line of credit to pay only qualifying higher education expenses. A qualified education loan includes debt used to refinance debt that qualifies as a qualified education loan, but doesn't include certain debt owed to a related person or a loan under a qualified employer plan. (Code Sec. 221(d)(1))[13]

Qualified higher education expenses include tuition, fees, room and board, and related expenses, but must be reduced by the amount excluded by reason of such expenses under the rules for: employer-provided educational assistance benefits (¶2214), income from U.S. Savings Bonds used to pay higher education expenses (¶2218), Coverdell education savings accounts (¶2205), qualified tuition plans (¶2209), and scholarship or fellowship grants (¶2215). (Code Sec. 221(d)(2)) They also must be reduced by veterans' and armed forces' educational assistance allowances and any other educational assistance excludable from the student's gross income (other than as a gift, bequest, devise or inheritance). (Reg § 1.221-1(e)(2)(ii))[14]

¶ 2222   Education Expenses Related to Business. ▬▬▬▬▬

Self-employeds can deduct educational expenses if the education (1) maintains or improves the skills used in the taxpayer's trade or business, or (2) meets the requirements of applicable law or regs, and, under those requirements, is necessary to keep a job, status, or rate of pay. These expenses may be deducted as ordinary and necessary business expenses. But a taxpayer can't deduct costs incurred to meet minimum requirements for a trade or profession or to qualify for a new trade or profession.[15]

⚫️*caution:* These expenses can't currently be deducted by employees because of the suspension of miscellaneous itemized deductions, which include unreimbursed employee expenses, from 2018 through 2025.

A lawyer who has actually practiced law may generally deduct the expenses of any further legal education on the grounds that it maintains or improves required skills even though the education qualifies the lawyer to practice as a specialist.[16] But a non-lawyer employed in allied fields where a legal education is helpful or customary can't deduct legal education costs. (Reg § 1.162-5(b)(3))[17]

---

11. ¶K-5501.1
12. ¶K-5501
13. ¶K-5504; ¶K-5504.2; ¶2214.02
14. ¶K-5504.3

15. ¶L-3701 *et seq.*, ¶A-2710 *et seq.*; ¶1624.185
16. ¶s L-3724, L-3722; ¶1624.185
17. ¶L-3705; ¶L-3720 *et seq.*

Deductions aren't allowed if the education:

... is needed to meet the minimum requirements for taxpayer's present or intended trade, business or profession (Reg § 1.162-5(b)(2))[18] or

... is undertaken to fulfill general education goals or for other personal reasons, [19] or

... is part of a program of study that will qualify the individual in a new trade or business. (Reg § 1.162-5(b)(3)(i))[20]

Self-employed taxpayers claim education deductions on Schedule C, C-EZ or F of Form 1040.[21]

¶ 2223   Travel and transportation expenses of education.

The expenses of travel as a form of education aren't deductible. (Code Sec. 274(m)(2))[22] But travel expenses necessary to other deductible education expenses are deductible by self-employeds. [23]

caution: These expenses can't currently be deducted by employees because of the suspension of miscellaneous itemized deductions, which include unreimbursed employee expenses, from 2018 through 2025.

Local transportation expenses for deductible education are deductible by self-employeds. These are expenses incurred in going directly from work to school, and, if the taxpayer is regularly employed and goes to school on a strictly temporary basis (e.g., expected to last, and in facts lasts, for one year or less), the costs of returning from school to home, or the round-trip costs of going from home to school and back. [24]

Costs of seminar cruises or tours are disallowed if taken primarily for personal purposes even if part of the time is devoted to qualifying professional education. [25] Even if not for personal purposes, the deduction is limited under the rules at ¶1545.

¶ 2224   Limited above-the-line deduction for educator expenses.

A grade K through 12 teacher, instructor, counselor, principal, or aide in a school for at least 900 hours during a school year ("eligible educator," Code Sec. 62(d)(1)) can claim an "above the line deduction" (i.e., an adjustment to gross income to arrive at AGI) for up to $250 for 2018 (and 2019, as calculated by Thomson Reuters based on inflation data) for business expenses paid: (1) for participation in professional development courses that are either related to the subject taught or the students, and (2) for trade or business expenses paid or incurred for books, supplies (other than nonathletic supplies for courses of instruction in health or physical education), computer equipment (including related software and services) and other equipment, and supplementary materials used in the classroom. (Code Sec. 62(a)(2)(D))

A deduction is allowed only to the extent the amount of expenses exceeds the amount excludable from income under Code Sec. 135 (education savings bonds), Code Sec. 529(c)(1) (qualified tuition programs), or Code Sec. 530(d)(2) (Coverdell education savings accounts). (Code Sec. 62(d)(2))[26]

---

18. ¶L-3713; ¶1624.185
19. ¶L-3704; ¶1624.193
20. ¶L-3715; ¶1624.185
21. ¶L-3741
22. ¶L-3734; ¶1624.185

23. ¶L-3732 *et seq.*, ¶L-3741, ¶A-2710 *et seq.*; ¶1624.185
24. ¶L-3730; ¶1624.185
25. ¶L-3733; ¶2744.04
26. ¶A-2611.2; ¶A-2611.3; ¶624.02

¶ 2225 **Pre-2018 Above-the-Line Deduction for Higher Education Expenses—Form 8917.** ▰▰▰▰▰▰▰▰▰▰▰▰▰▰▰

For tax years beginning before 2018, eligible individuals could deduct (on Form 8917) higher education expenses —generally, "qualified tuition and related (QT&R) expenses" as defined for American opportunity tax credit and Lifetime Learning credit purposes (¶2201), with certain adjustments, of the taxpayer, spouse, or dependents —as an adjustment to gross income to arrive at adjusted gross income (AGI). (Code Sec. 222(a))

The higher education deduction (also called the "tuition and fees deduction") couldn't exceed:

... $4,000 for taxpayers whose modified AGI (MAGI; under Code Sec. 222(b)(2)(C)) for the tax year doesn't exceed $65,000 ($130,000 for joint filers);

... $2,000 for taxpayers whose MAGI exceeds $65,000 ($130,000 for joint filers), but doesn't exceed $80,000 ($160,000 for joint filers); and

... zero for other taxpayers. (Code Sec. 222(b)(2)(B))

💙*caution:* Check tax.thomsonreuters.com/federaltaxhandbookupdates to see if the above provision has been extended.

¶ 2226 **ABLE Accounts for the Disabled or Blind.** ▰▰▰▰▰▰▰▰▰▰▰▰▰▰▰▰▰

The Code allows states to establish tax-exempt "Achieving a Better Life Experience" (ABLE) programs that feature accounts that assist persons with disabilities.

General tax rules. A qualified ABLE account is generally exempt from income tax but is subject to the tax imposed by Code Sec. 511 on the unrelated business income of tax-exempt organizations. (Code Sec. 529A(a))[27] Contributions to an ABLE account aren't deductible for income tax purposes.[28]

Qualified ABLE program defined. A qualified ABLE program is a program established and maintained by a state or state agency or instrumentality that (Code Sec. 529A(b)(1)):

... limits the aggregate contributions from all contributors (including rollover contributions from a 529 plan (see ¶2210) for a tax year to the amount of the annual Code Sec. 2503(b) gift tax exclusion for that tax year ($15,000 for 2018, and also for 2019 as calculated by Thomson Reuters based on inflation data) (Code Sec. 529A(b)(2)); *plus* an additional contribution during tax years 2018 through 2025 (see below);

... provides separate accounting for each designated beneficiary (DB, Code Sec. 529A(b)(3));

... limits the DB's investment direction to no more than two times in a calendar year (Code Sec. 529A(b)(4));

... prohibits the use of any interest or any portion of an interest in the program as security for a loan (Code Sec. 529A(b)(5)); and

... provides adequate safeguards to prevent excess aggregate contributions. (Code Sec. 529A(b)(6))

Additional contribution for tax years 2018 - 2025. For tax years 2018 through 2025, in addition to contributions in an amount up to the annual gift tax exclusion, an ABLE account's DB may contribute, subject to a number of limitations, an additional amount up

---

27. ¶A-4740 *et seq.*, ¶529A4 *et seq.*   28. ¶A-4744

to the lesser of (a) the DB's compensation for the tax year, or (b) the federal poverty line for a one-person household (for 2018 contributions, $12,060). (Code Sec. 529A(b)(2)(B)(ii)) To qualify to make this additional contribution, a DB must be an employee, including a self-employed individual under Code Sec. 401(c), for whom no contribution is made for the tax year to (i) a defined contribution plan under Code Sec. 414(i), (ii) an annuity contract described in Code Sec. 403(b), or (iii) an eligible deferred compensation plan described in Code Sec. 457(b).[29]

Eligible beneficiaries. The DB of an ABLE account is an eligible individual who established the account and is its owner. (Code Sec. 529A(e)(3)) An individual is an eligible individual for a tax year if, during that tax year:

. . . the individual is entitled to benefits based on blindness or disability under the Social Security disability insurance program or the SSI program, and that blindness or disability occurred before the individual's 26th birthday, (Code Sec. 529A(e)(1)(A)) or

. . . a "disability certification" for the individual has been filed with IRS for the tax year. (Code Sec. 529A(e)(1)(B))

Distributions; rollovers. No amount of a distribution from an ABLE account is includible in gross income if distributions from the account don't exceed the DB's "qualified disability expenses" (Code Sec. 529A(c)(1)(B)(i)), which are any expenses related to the eligible individual's blindness or disability that are made for the benefit of an eligible individual who is the DB. (Code Sec. 529A(e)(5))

A taxpayer who receives a distribution from a qualified ABLE program that's includible in gross income is generally subject to an additional 10% tax on the includible part. (Code Sec. 529A(c)(3)(A))[30]

A payment or distribution from an ABLE account isn't taxable to the extent that the amount received is paid, no later than the 60th day after the date of the payment or distribution, into another ABLE account for the benefit of the DB or an eligible individual who's a family member of the DB. (Code Sec. 529A(c)(1)(C)(i))[31]

Upon the death of a DB, amounts remaining in the account (after Medicaid reimbursements) go to the deceased DB's estate or to a beneficiary of the DB, and are subject to income tax on investment earnings, but not the 10% penalty. (Code Sec. 529A(c)(3)(B))[32]

For Saver's Credit for ABLE program contributions for tax years beginning after Dec. 22, 2017, see ¶2358.

---

29. ¶4744.2
30. ¶4747.1

31. ¶4746.1
32. ¶4748

Chapter 8   Tax Credits

¶ 2300   **Tax Credits.** ▆▆▆▆▆▆▆▆▆▆▆▆▆▆▆▆▆▆▆▆▆▆▆▆▆▆▆▆▆▆▆▆▆▆▆▆▆▆

Tax credits are either business credits intended to provide special incentives for the achievement of certain economic objectives, or personal credits, which provide tax benefits to certain taxpayers (e.g., the elderly or disabled, etc.). The foreign tax credit, however, may apply to both business and nonbusiness taxpayers.

The three main categories of tax credits are:

(1) The business incentive credits, see ¶2301 *et seq.*

(2) The personal (refundable and nonrefundable) credits, see ¶2337 *et seq.*

(3) The foreign tax credit, see ¶2362 *et seq.*

For credit for alternative minimum tax (AMT), see ¶2360.

For tax credits attributable to certain "passive" activities, see ¶1797 *et seq.*

¶ 2301   **Business Incentive Credits—General Business Credit (GBC)—Form 3800.** ▆

Certain business incentive credits are combined into one GBC for purposes of determining each credit's allowance limitation for the tax year.

A GBC (claimed on Form 3800) is allowed against income tax for a particular tax year and equals the sum of: (1) the business credit carry *forwards* carried to the tax year, (2) the *current year* GBC, and (3) the business credit carry *backs* carried to the tax year. (Code Sec. 38(a))[1]

The current year GBC is comprised of the:

... investment credit (Code Sec. 38(b)(1)) (¶2306 *et seq.*) (which includes the rehabilitation credit (¶2307), the energy credit (¶2310), the qualifying advanced coal and gasification project credits (¶2311), and the qualifying advanced energy project credit (¶2312);

... pre-2020 work opportunity credit (Code Sec. 38(b)(2)), see ¶2315 *et seq.*;

... pre-2018 second generation biofuel production credit (Code Sec. 38(b)(3)), see ¶2318;

... research credit (Code Sec. 38(b)(4)), see ¶2319;

... low-income housing credit (Code Sec. 38(b)(5)), see ¶2320 *et seq.*;

... enhanced oil recovery (EOR) credit (Code Sec. 38(b)(6)), see ¶2322;

... disabled access credit (DAC) (Code Sec. 38(b)(7)), see ¶2323;

... renewable electricity production credit (Code Sec. 38(b)(8)), see ¶2324;

... empowerment zone employment credit (Code Sec. 38(b)(9)), see ¶2325;

... pre-2018 Indian employment credit (Code Sec. 38(b)(10)), see ¶2326;

... FICA tip credit (Code Sec. 38(b)(11)), see ¶2327;

... orphan drug credit (Code Sec. 38(b)(12)), see ¶2328;

... pre-2020 new markets credit (Code Sec. 38(b)(13)), see ¶2329;

... small employer pension plan startup credit (Code Sec. 38(b)(14)), see ¶2331;

... employer-provided child care credit (Code Sec. 38(b)(15)), see ¶2330;

... pre-2018 railroad track maintenance credit (Code Sec. 38(b)(16), Code Sec. 45G);

... pre-2018 biodiesel fuel credit (Code Sec. 38(b)(17)), see ¶2333;

... the low sulfur diesel fuel production credit (Code Sec. 38(b)(18), Code Sec. 45H)

... marginal oil and gas well production credit (Code Sec. 38(b)(19), Code Sec. 45I);

---

1. ¶L-15200; ¶384.01; ¶384.03

References beginning with a single letter are to paragraphs in Federal Tax Coordinator 2d and RIA's Analysis of Federal Taxes: Income. Those beginning with numbers are to paragraphs in United States Tax Reporter.

... distilled spirits credit (Code Sec. 38(b)(20), Code Sec. 5011(a));

... advanced nuclear power facility production credit (Code Sec. 38(b)(21), Code Sec. 45J(a)) for facilities placed in service before 2021;

... pre-2018 new energy efficient home credit (Code Sec. 38(b)(23)), see ¶2334;

... applicable portion (attributable to depreciable property) of the alternative motor vehicle credit (Code Sec. 38(b)(24)), see ¶2355;

... applicable portion (attributable to depreciable property) of the alternative fuel vehicle refueling property credit (Code Sec. 38(b)(25)), see ¶2356;

... pre-2018 mine rescue training credit (Code Sec. 38(b)(26), Code Sec. 45N);

... differential wage payment credit (Code Sec. 38(b)(28)), see ¶2335;

... carbon sequestration credit (Code Sec. 38(b)(29)), see ¶2314;

... applicable portion (attributable to depreciable property) of the new qualified plug-in electric drive motor vehicles credit (Code Sec. 38(b)(30)), see ¶2356; and

... small employer health insurance credit (Code Sec. 38(b)(31)), see ¶2332.

... 2018 and 2019 employer-paid family and medical leave credit (Code Sec. 38(b)(32)), see ¶2336.

In addition, the "employee retention tax credit" (¶2317) for employers affected by Hurricanes Harvey, Irma, and Maria, as well as those affected by California wildfires, is treated as a credit under Code Sec. 38(b).

The credit for excise tax payments to the Trans-Alaska Pipeline Liability Fund (Code Sec. 4612(e)(1)), the pre-2010 renewal community employment credit (Code Sec. 1400H(a)), and the community development corporation credit for pre-July '99 contributions [2] aren't included in the above Code Sec. 38(b) list, but are also part of the current year business credit.

For when bonus depreciation can be traded for deferred credits, see ¶1932.

¶ 2302 Limitation on general business credits (GBCs) based on tax liability.

The GBC allowed for any tax year (except for separate limitations on the empowerment zone employment credit, the New York Liberty Zone business employee credit, eligible small business credits, and "specified credits," see below) is limited to the excess of taxpayer's "net income tax" over the greater of: (1) the tentative minimum tax for the tax year, or (2) 25% of the amount of the taxpayer's "net regular tax" that exceeds $25,000. (Code Sec. 38(c)(1))[3] Spouses who file separate returns are each limited to $12,500 instead of $25,000, but if the taxpayer's spouse has no carryforward, carryback or current year GBC in the tax year that ends within or with the taxpayer's tax year, the taxpayer gets the full amount of $25,000. (Code Sec. 38(c)(6)(A))[4]

For estates and trusts, the $25,000 amount is reduced to an amount equal to $25,000 multiplied by a fraction (numerator is the estate's or trust's total income not allocated to beneficiaries, denominator is the estate's or trust's total income). (Code Sec. 38(c)(6)(D))[5]

Net income tax is the sum of the regular tax liability and the alternative minimum tax (AMT) (¶3200), reduced by the credits listed below. *For tax years beginning after 2017,* the general business credit limitation for a corporation is applied by treating the corporation as having a tentative minimum tax of zero. (Code Sec. 38(c)(6)(E)) This leaves the tax liability limitation unchanged as applied to individuals but negates the repealed corporate AMT as a limit on allowable business credits for corporations. [6]

2. ¶L-15660 *et seq.*; ¶384.01
3. ¶L-15202; ¶384.02
4. ¶L-15204; ¶384.02

5. ¶L-15207; ¶384.02
6. ¶L-15202; ¶384.02

Net regular tax is the regular tax liability reduced by the sum of the following credits (Code Sec. 38(c)(1)): (1) child and dependent care credit (Code Sec. 21); (2) credit for the elderly and disabled (Code Sec. 22); (3) adoption expense credit (Code Sec. 23); (4) child tax credit (Code Sec. 24); (5) mortgage credit (Code Sec. 25); (6) American Opportunity Tax Credit (except for the portion of the credit treated as a refundable credit) and Lifetime Learning credit (Code Sec. 25A); (7) saver's credit for elective deferrals and IRA contributions (Code Sec. 25B); (8) nonbusiness energy property credit (Code Sec. 25C); (9) foreign tax and possessions tax credit (for American Samoa) (Code Sec. 27, former Code Sec. 936); (10) Puerto Rico economic activity credit (former Code Sec. 30A); (11) alternative motor vehicle credit (Code Sec. 30B); (12) qualified alternative fuel vehicle refueling property credit (Code Sec. 30C); (13) D.C. homebuyer credit for first time homes purchased before 2012 (Code Sec. 1400C); (14) new qualified plug-in electric drive motor vehicles credit (attributable to non-depreciable property); (Code Sec. 30D); and (15) qualified plug-in electric drive motor vehicles acquired before 2012 (attributable to non-depreciable property) (Code Sec. 30(c)(2)(A) before repeal) Tentative minimum tax is the AMT increased by the regular tax that was subtracted in computing the alternative minimum tax. [7]

The empowerment zone employment credit (¶2325) is limited to the excess of the taxpayer's net income tax over the greater of: (1) 75% of its tentative minimum tax, or (2) 25% of so much of its net regular tax liability as exceeds $25,000. This limitation is reduced by the general credits (not including the empowerment zone employment credit, New York Liberty Zone business employee credit, eligible small business (ESB) credits, and other specified credits, see below) allowed for the tax year. (Code Sec. 38(c)(2)) The effect is that the empowerment zone employment credit may be used to offset up to 25% of a taxpayer's AMT.[8]

"Specified credits" may offset 100% of a taxpayer's AMT. (Code Sec. 38(c)(4)) Specified credits include: (Code Sec. 38(c)(4)(B)) (1) the alcohol fuel credit (¶2318); (2) the research credit under Code Sec. 41 for the tax year with respect to an ESB (after application of rules similar to the addition limitation on a partner's and an S corporation shareholder's ESB credits under Code Sec. 38(c)(5)(D)); (3) the low income housing credit for buildings placed in service after 2007 (¶2320); (4) the renewable electricity production credit under Code Sec. 45 (¶2324), to the extent attributable to electricity or refined coal produced; (5) the credit under Code Sec. 45 to the extent attributable to Code Sec. 45(e)(10) (relating to Indian coal production facilities; see ¶2324) for tax years beginning after 2015 (for tax years beginning before 2016, the Indian credit is a specified credit during the 4-year period the property is first placed in service); (6) the FICA tip credit (¶2327); (7) the pre-2018 Code Sec. 45G railroad maintenance credit; (8) the small employer health insurance credit (¶2332); (9) the Code Sec. 45S employer-paid family and medical leave credit (¶2336); (10) the rehabilitation investment credit for qualified rehabilitation expenditures properly taken into account after 2007 (¶2307); (11) the credits determined under Code Sec. 46 to the extent attributable to the energy credit under Code Sec. 48 (¶2310); and (12) the work opportunity tax credit (¶2315).[9]

¶ 2303   Carryback or carryforward of general business credit (GBC).

A 1-year carryback (except for a 5-year carryback applicable for the marginal well production credit under Code Sec. 39(a)(3) and for eligible small business credits determined in the first tax year beginning in 2010 under Code Sec. 39(a)(4)) and a 20-year carryforward applies to the GBC. (Code Sec. 39(a)) No part of any unused current GBC attributable to a component credit may be carried back to tax years before the first tax year that the component credit was allowable. (Code Sec. 39(d))[10]

---

7. ¶L-15202; ¶384.02, 384.03
8. ¶L-15202.1; ¶384.02

9. ¶L-15202.3; ¶384.02
10. ¶L-15209; ¶384.01; ¶384.03

¶ 2304   Deduction for unused qualified business credits after the carryover period.

If any portion of a qualified business credit, i.e. the: investment credit (¶2306 *et seq.*), work opportunity credit (¶2315), alcohol fuels credit (¶2318), research credit (¶2319), enhanced oil recovery credit (¶2322), empowerment zone employment credit (¶2325), Indian employment credit (¶2326), FICA tip credit (¶2327), new markets tax credit (¶2329), small employer pension plan startup credit (¶2331), small employer health insurance credit (¶2332), biodiesel fuels credit (¶2333), low sulfur diesel fuel production credit, and new energy efficient home credit (¶2334), (Code Sec. 196(c)), hasn't been allowed after the carryover period expires, the taxpayer can deduct the unused portion in the first tax year after the last tax year of the carryover period (or in the tax year of the taxpayer's death or cessation if earlier). (Code Sec. 196(a), Code Sec. 196(b)) But, for the investment tax credit (other than the rehabilitation credit), the deduction is 50% of the unused amount. (Code Sec. 196(d))[11]

¶ 2305   Ordering rules for the general business credits (GBCs).

The order in which the component credits of the GBC are used in a tax year or as a carryback or carryforward is determined on the basis of the order they are listed in Code Sec. 38(b) (¶2301) as of the close of the tax year in which the credit is used. (Code Sec. 38(d)(1)) The order in which the component credits of the business investment credit are used is determined on the basis of the order they are listed in Code Sec. 46 as of the close of the tax year in which the credit is used. (Code Sec. 38(d)(2))[12]

¶ 2306   The investment tax credits—Form 3468.

The Code Sec. 46 investment tax credit (claimed on Form 3468) [13] consists of: (1) the rehabilitation investment credit (Code Sec. 47), see ¶2307 *et seq.*;[14] (2) the energy credit (Code Sec. 48(a)), see ¶2310;[15] (3) the qualifying advanced coal project credit (Code Sec. 48A), see ¶2311;[16] (4) the qualifying gasification project credit (Code Sec. 48B), see ¶2311;[17] (5) the qualifying advanced energy project credit (Code Sec. 48C), see ¶2312;[18] and (6) the qualifying therapeutic discovery project credit for qualifying investments made in tax years beginning after 2008 but before 2011(former Code Sec. 48D). [19]

Property qualifying for the investment credit (depreciable or amortizable property) is treated as investment credit property. (Code Sec. 50(a)(5)) But certain otherwise qualified property is denied the applicable credit if it's used:

. . . predominantly outside the U.S., except for property listed in Code Sec. 168(g)(4)—dealing with rolling stock, spacecraft, satellites, etc. (Code Sec. 50(b)(1))

. . . predominantly to furnish, or in connection with the furnishing of, permanent lodging, except for certain nonlodging commercial facilities, lodging facilities used by transients, certified historic structures, and energy property. (Code Sec. 50(b)(2))

. . . by certain tax-exempt organizations. (Code Sec. 50(b)(3)) If property is leased to a partnership or other pass-through entity, a proportionate share of the property is treated as leased to each tax-exempt entity partner (under the rules of Code Sec. 168(h)(5) and (6)) in determining whether any portion of the property is tax-exempt use property. (Code Sec. 50(b)(4))

---

11. ¶L-15212; ¶1964.01
12. ¶L-15208; ¶384.01
13. ¶L-16500 *et seq.*; ¶464
14. ¶L-16100; ¶474
15. ¶L-16400; ¶484

16. ¶L-16450; ¶48A4
17. ¶L-16470; ¶48B4
18. ¶L-16460 *et seq.*; ¶48C4
19. ¶L-15625; ¶48D4

... by the U.S. or other governmental units, except for short-lease property. (Code Sec. 50(b)(4))[20]

A *lessee* of new investment credit property can take the investment credit on the property if the lessor elects to pass it to him. (Code Sec. 50(d)(5); Reg § 1.48-4) The election statement is described in the regs. (Reg § 1.48-4(f), Reg § 1.48-4(g)) The effect is to treat the lessee as having acquired the property for its FMV, but the lessor's basis is used instead when the lessor and lessee are members of a controlled group. The lessee uses the same investment credit life for the property as the lessor. [21] In lieu of a basis adjustment, the lessee must ratably include in gross income an amount equal to the amount of the credit (50% for the energy credit) over the shortest recovery period. (Temp Reg §1.50-1T(b)(2)) But a lessor's election to pass the credit from property with an over 14-year ADR depreciation "class life" to his lessee results in only a partial transfer of the credit if the lease is for a period that is less than 80% of the property's "class life" and isn't a "net lease." (Reg § 1.48-4(a)(2))[22]

If there is a net decrease in the amount of nonqualified nonrecourse financing (under the at-risk rules, ¶1790 *et seq.*) as of the close of a tax year following that in which property was placed in service, the net decrease is treated as an increase in the credit base for the property. Thus, an increase in the taxpayer's at-risk amount for an investment credit property is additional qualified investment. (Code Sec. 49(a)(2))[23]

¶ 2307 Rehabilitation investment credits—Form 3468.

The rehabilitation credit (claimed on Form 3468) for any tax year, during the 5-year period beginning in the tax year in which a qualified rehabilitation building (see ¶2308) building is placed in service, is an amount equal the ratable share for that year. The ratable share for any tax year during the 5-year period is the amount equal to 20% of the qualified rehabilitation expenditures with respect to the qualified rehabilitation building, as allocated ratably to each year during that period. (Code Sec. 47(a))[24]

Transition rule. For qualified rehabilitation expenditures (for either a certified historic structure or a pre-'36 building), for any building owned or leased (as provided under pre-2018 law) by the taxpayer at all times *after* Dec. 31, 2017, the 24-month period selected by the taxpayer (under Code Sec. 47(c)(1)(B)(i), see ¶2308), or the 60-month period selected by the taxpayer under the rule for phased rehabilitation (Code Sec. 47(c)(1)(B)(ii), see ¶2309), is to begin no later than the end of the 180-day period beginning on Dec. 22, 2017, and apply to such expenditures paid or incurred after the end of the tax year in which such 24- or 60-month period ends. (Code Sec. 47(a))[25]

A qualified rehabilitation expenditure is any amount charged to the capital account and incurred in connection with the rehabilitation (including reconstruction, or an addition or improvement) of a qualified rehabilitated building (¶2308) that's depreciable under Code Sec. 168, and is nonresidential real property, residential rental property, or real property with a class life of more than 12.5 years. (Code Sec. 47(c)(2)(A))[26] If bonus first-year depreciation (¶1932) is claimed for the building, the credit may be claimed only if the taxpayer depreciates the remaining adjusted depreciable basis of rehabilitation expenses using the straight line method. (Reg § 1.168(k)-1(f)(10)), Reg § 1.1400L(b)-1(f)(9))[27]

Qualified rehabilitation expenditures don't include: (1) generally, expenditures for which straight-line depreciation isn't used; (2) costs to acquire buildings; (3) expenditures to enlarge existing buildings; (4) expenditures to rehabilitate certain historic buildings; and

20. ¶L-16501; ¶504.01
21. ¶s L-16506, L-17010 *et seq.*; ¶484.10
22. ¶L-17015; ¶484.10
23. ¶L-16505; ¶494

24. ¶L-16101; ¶474
25. ¶L-16103; ¶484.13
26. ¶L-16102; ¶474
27. ¶L-16102.1; ¶1684.025, ¶14,00L4.05

(5) expenditures in connection with the rehabilitation of a building that are allocable to that portion of the building that is (or that is reasonably expected to be) tax-exempt-use property. (Code Sec. 47(c)(2)(B))[28]

In addition to owner-taxpayers of qualified property, the rehabilitation credits are available to lessees for qualified expenditures incurred by them, but only if, on the rehabilitation's completion date, the remaining term of the lease (without regard to renewal) is at least the recovery period under Code Sec. 168(c). (Code Sec. 47(c)(2)(B)(vi))[29]

IRS has provided a safe harbor under which, if certain requirements are met, it will respect allocations of the rehabilitation credits by a partnership to its partners. [30]

¶ 2308   Which buildings qualify for the rehabilitation credit?

A "qualified rehabilitated building" is any building (and its structural components) that:

(1) has been substantially rehabilitated. A substantial rehabilitation is one in which the qualified rehabilitation expenditures during the 24-month period selected by the taxpayer (as prescribed in regs) and ending with or within the year exceed the greater of: (a) $5,000; or (b) the adjusted basis of the building and its structural components as of the first day of the 24-month period, or of the holding period (without regard to reconstruction), whichever is later. (Code Sec. 47(c)(1)(B)(i)) Rehabilitation includes reconstruction; (Code Sec. 47(c)(1)(C))[31]

(2) was placed in service before the beginning of the rehabilitation;

(3) is a certified historic structure; *and*[32]

(4) is depreciable or amortizable. (Code Sec. 47(c)(1)(A))

For any rehabilitation that may reasonably be expected to be completed in phases set forth in architectural plans and specifications completed before the rehabilitation begins, a 60-month (instead of 24-month) period applies. (Code Sec. 47(c)(1)(B)(ii))[33]

¶ 2309   Progress expenditure rehabilitation credit.

If any building being rehabilitated by or for the taxpayer has a normal rehabilitation period of 2 years or more, and it's reasonable to expect the building to be a qualified rehabilitated building (¶2308) in the taxpayer's hands when placed in service (Code Sec. 47(d)(2)), the taxpayer may irrevocably elect (on Form 3468) to account for qualified rehabilitation expenditures made for that property as follows:

(1) where it's reasonable to believe that *more* than half these expenditures will be made directly by the taxpayer, any qualified rehabilitation expenditure is taken into account for the tax year it's properly chargeable to the capital account (i.e., includible in computing the property's basis), and

(2) where it's reasonable to believe that *no* more than half of the qualified expenditures will be made directly by the taxpayer, any qualified rehabilitation expenditure is taken into account in the tax year it's paid. (Code Sec. 47(d)(1); Reg § 1.46-5(g)(1))[34]

28. ¶L-16115; ¶474
29. ¶L-16102; ¶474
30. ¶B-2903B; ¶7044.07
31. ¶L-16106; ¶474

32. ¶ L-16103; ¶474
33. ¶L-16113; ¶474
34. ¶L-16200; ¶474

¶ **2310** **Energy credit—Form 3468.**

A taxpayer can claim (on Form 3468) the following energy credits (in each case, the percentage applies to the basis of eligible energy property placed in service during the year):

(1) 30% (subject to a phaseout) for qualified fuel cell property (Code Sec. 48(a)(2)(A)(i)(I), Code Sec. 48(a)(3)(A)(iv)), the construction of which begin before Jan. 1, 2022. (Code Sec. 48(c)(1)) The credit is not to exceed an amount equal to $1,500 for each 0.5 KW of capacity. The percentage is 26% for qualified fuel cell property the construction of which begins after 2019, and before 2021, reduced to 22% for property the construction of which begins after 2020 and before 2022. The energy property must be placed in service before 2024. (Code Sec. 48(a)(7))[35]

(2) 30% (subject to a phaseout) for solar energy property described in Code Sec. 48(a)(3)(A)(i) (i.e., equipment that uses solar energy to generate electricity, to heat or cool (or provide hot water for) a structure, or to provide solar process heat, but not for heating a swimming pool), the construction of which begins before Jan. 1, 2022. The percentage for property, the construction of which begins after 2019 and before 2021, the energy percentage is reduced to 26%; for property, the construction of which begins after 2020 and before 2022, the energy percentage is further reduced to 22%; and, for property, the construction of which begins before 2022, but is not placed in service before 2024, the energy percentage is 10%. (Code Sec. 48(a)(6))[36]

(3) 30% (subject to a phaseout) for solar energy property described in Code Sec. 48(a)(3)(A)(ii) (fiber-optic solar energy property —i.e., equipment which uses solar energy to illuminate the inside of a structure using fiber-optic distributed sunlight). The percentage is 26% for solar energy property the construction of which begins after 2019, and before 2021, reduced to 22% for property the construction of which begins after 2020 and before 2022. The energy property must be placed in service before 2024. (Code Sec. 48(a)(7))[37]

(4) 30% (subject to a phaseout) for qualified small wind energy property the construction of which begins before 2022, (Code Sec. 48(a)(2)(A)(i)(IV), Code Sec. 48(a)(3)(A)(vi); Code Sec. 48(c)(4)) The percentage is 26% for solar energy property the construction of which begins after 2019, and before 2021, reduced to 22% for property the construction of which begins after 2020 and before 2022. The energy property must be placed in service before 2024. (Code Sec. 48(a)(7))[38]

(5) 10% for equipment used to produce, distribute, or use energy derived from a geothermal deposit. (Code Sec. 48(a)(2)(A)(ii), Code Sec. 48(a)(3)(A)(iii))[39]

(6) 10% for qualified microturbine property for property (Code Sec. 48(a)(2)(A)(ii), Code Sec. 48(a)(3)(A)(iv)) not to exceed $200 for each KW of the property's capacity. [40]

(7) 10% for combined heat and power system property, (Code Sec. 48(a)(2)(A)(ii), Code Sec. 48(a)(3)(A)(v))[41] ; and

(8) 10% for geothermal heat pump systems equipment the construction of which begins before 2022. (Code Sec. 48(a)(2)(A)(ii), Code Sec. 48(a)(3)(A)(vii)).[42]

caution: Check tax.thomsonreuters.com/federaltaxhandbookupdates to see if the above provisions have been extended.

---

35. ¶L-16436; ¶484
36. ¶L-16401; ¶484
37. ¶L-16401A; ¶484
38. ¶L-16436.4

39. ¶L-16425; ¶484
40. ¶L-16437; ¶484
41. ¶L-16436.3; ¶484
42. ¶L-16402; ¶484

No credit is allowed for property unless it's depreciable or amortizable; its construction, reconstruction or erection is completed by the taxpayer or, if acquired by the taxpayer, its original use begins with the taxpayer; and it meets the official quality and performance standards in effect at the time of acquisition. (Code Sec. 48(a)(3))[43] There is no reduction in basis for purposes of determining the energy credit if property is financed in whole or in part by subsidized financing or tax-exempt private activity bonds. (Code Sec. 48(a)(4))[44]

¶ 2311 Credits for qualifying advanced coal projects and gasification projects— Form 3468.

A credit can be claimed for investments in qualifying advanced coal projects. The credit is 30% of the qualified investment for advanced coal-based generation technology projects; 20% of the qualified investment for the tax year in integrated gasification combined cycle projects; and 15% of the qualified investment for the tax year in projects that use other advanced coal-based generation technologies. (Code Sec. 48A(a))[45] A separate investment credit can also be claimed for qualified investment in qualifying gasification projects. The credit is 20% or 30% of the qualified investment for the tax year. (Code Sec. 48B(a)) The Code Sec. 48B credit is not allowed for any qualified investment for which the Code Sec. 48A credit is allowed. (Code Sec. 48B(e))[46]

¶ 2312 Qualified advanced energy project credit—Form 3468.

A taxpayer can claim a 30% credit for investment in qualified property used in a qualifying advanced energy project (Code Sec. 48C), i.e., a project that re-equips, expands, or establishes a manufacturing facility for the production of property designed to: (1) be used to produce energy from the sun, wind, or geothermal deposits or other renewable resources; (2) manufacture fuel cells, microturbines, or an energy storage system for use with electric or hybrid-electric motor vehicles; (3) manufacture electric grids to support the transmission of intermittent sources of renewable energy, including storage of that energy; (4) manufacture equipment for use for carbon capture or sequestration; or (5) refine or blend renewable fuels (but not fossil fuels), to produce energy conservation technologies (including energy-conserving lighting technologies and smart grid technologies). It also includes a facility for the production of new qualified plug-in electric drive motor vehicles (¶2357), components designed specifically for these vehicles; or other advanced energy property designed to reduce greenhouse gas emissions. (Code Sec. 48C(c)(1))[47] Qualified property must be depreciable (tangible) property used in a qualifying advanced energy project and doesn't include property designed to manufacture equipment for use in the refining or blending of any transportation fuel (other than renewable fuels). (Code Sec. 48C(c)(1)) The property's basis is reduced by the amount of credit received.[48] The Code Sec. 48C credit is not allowed for any qualified investment for which the Code Sec. 48, Code Sec. 48A, or Code Sec. 48B credits are allowed. (Code Sec. 48C(e))

¶ 2313 Recapture of investment credits—Form 4255.

If investment credit property is disposed of or ceases to be investment credit property for the taxpayer before the end of the recapture period, the credit taken for all earlier years is recaptured on Form 4255 (i.e., added to the tax liability for the recapture year). (Code Sec. 50(a)(1)) The recapture percentage is 100% during the first full year after the property is placed in service. This percentage decreases by 20 percentage points every succeeding full year. There's no recapture after the fifth full year. (Code Sec. 50(a)(1))[49] Recapture

43. ¶L-16401A; ¶484
44. ¶L-16415; ¶484
45. ¶L-16450; ¶s 48A4
46. ¶L-16470; ¶s 48B4

47. ¶L-16463; ¶48C4
48. ¶L-16461 *et seq.*; ¶48C4
49. ¶L-17312

applies only to credit used to reduce tax liability. If any part of it isn't used, carrybacks and carryovers of the credit must be appropriately adjusted. (Code Sec. 50(a)(3))

No recapture applies to a transfer by reason of death (Code Sec. 50(a)(4)(A)), a mere change in form of doing business (Code Sec. 50(a)(4)(B)), or a transfer between spouses or incident to divorce (under the rules of Code Sec. 1041(a)). (Code Sec. 50(a)(5)(B))[50]

Different recapture computation methods apply to the progress expenditures credit (¶2309) depending on whether the recapture year occurs before or after the progress expenditure property is placed in service. (Code Sec. 50(a)(2))[1]

If the amount of nonqualified nonrecourse financing (¶1796) for at-risk property increases as of the close of the tax year, then the tax for the tax year is increased by the total decrease in credits allowed in earlier tax years that would result if the credit base for the earlier credits had been reduced by the amount of the increase in the nonqualified nonrecourse financing. For purposes of computing recapture, the increase in nonqualified nonrecourse financing is treated as reducing the credit base and correspondingly reducing the qualified investment in the year the property was placed in service. (Code Sec. 49(b)(1)) The transfer of (or an agreement to transfer) any evidence of indebtedness won't be treated as an increase in nonqualified nonrecourse financing, if the transfer occurs (or the agreement is entered into) more than one year after the indebtedness was incurred. (Code Sec. 49(b)(2))[2]

If a taxpayer fails to pay the principal on a level payment nonqualified nonrecourse loan (¶1796) used for qualified energy property, the taxpayer is treated as increasing the amount of nonqualified nonrecourse financing to the extent of the recapture. (Code Sec. 49(b)(3))[3]

¶ 2314   Carbon oxide sequestration credit.

A carbon oxide sequestration credit is allowed for carbon oxide captured. (Code Sec. 45Q) For 2018, the credit is an amount equal to the sum of: (1) $20 per metric ton of qualified carbon oxide which is captured by the taxpayer using carbon capture equipment which is originally placed in service at a qualified facility *before* Feb. 9, 2018 and disposed of by the taxpayer in secure geological storage; (2) $10 per metric ton of qualified carbon oxide which is captured by the taxpayer using carbon capture equipment which is originally placed in service at a qualified facility *before* Feb. 9, 2018 and used by the taxpayer as a tertiary injectant and disposed of by the taxpayer in secure geological storage or utilized in another specified manner (see Code Sec. 45Q(f)(5)); (3) an applicable dollar amount per metric ton of qualified carbon oxide which is captured by the taxpayer using carbon capture equipment which is originally placed in service at a qualified facility *after* Feb. 8, 2018, during the 12-year period beginning on the date the equipment was originally placed in service, and disposed of by the taxpayer in secure geological storage; (4) an applicable dollar amount per metric ton of qualified carbon oxide which is captured by the taxpayer using carbon capture equipment which is originally placed in service at a qualified facility *after* Feb. 8, 2018, during the 12-year period beginning on the date the equipment was originally placed in service, and used by the taxpayer as a tertiary injectant and disposed of by the taxpayer in secure geological storage or utilized in another specified manner (see Code Sec. 45Q(f)(5)). (Code Sec. 45Q(a))[4]

For purposes of the credit, qualified carbon oxide is defined as any carbon dioxide or carbon oxide that meets certain requirements. (Code Sec. 45Q(c))[5]

---

50. ¶L-17301; ¶504.02
1. ¶L-17314; ¶504.02
2. ¶L-17307; ¶494

3. ¶L-16419; ¶494
4. ¶L-18401; ¶45Q4
5. ¶L-18402; ¶45Q4

If any qualified carbon oxide ceases to be used in a required manner, the benefit of the credit can be recaptured. (Code Sec. 45Q(f)(4))

⊘caution: IRS has not yet stated which Form will be used to claim the carbon oxide sequestration credit.

¶ 2315   Work opportunity tax credit (WOTC) before 2020—Forms 5884, 8850.

Generally, the WOTC allows employers who hire members of certain "targeted groups" (see below) before Jan. 1, 2020, and obtain a certification from the relevant State agency as to the individual's status as a member of a targeted group, to get a credit against income tax (using Form 5884) of 40% of first-year wages up to a maximum amount. The maximum amount of first -year wages is generally $6,000 per employee, but is $3,000 for qualified summer youth employees and various amounts for qualified veterans ($6,000 to $24,000, depending on, among other factors, the existence and/or extent of a service-related disability and the overall aggregate periods of unemployment during the one-year period ending on the hiring date.) (Code Sec. 51)[6] The credit percentage is 25% for employees who have completed at least 120, but less than 400, hours of service for the employer. (Code Sec. 51(i)) Where the employee is a long-term family assistance (LTFA) recipient, the WOTC is a percentage of first and second year wages, up to $10,000 per employee. (Code Sec. 51) LTFA recipients include an additional 50% of qualified-second year wages for a maximum credit of $9,000 [(.4 × $10,000) + (.5 × $10,000)]. (Code Sec. 51(e))

The amount of first-year wages taken into account in computing the WOTC for qualified veteran is: $6,000 for a veteran who is a member of a family receiving assistance under a food stamp program for at least three months, all or part of which is during the 12-month period ending on the hiring date; $12,000 for a veteran with a service-connected disability who has a hiring date that isn't more than one year after having been discharged or released from active duty; $24,000 for a veteran with a service-connected disability who has aggregate periods of unemployment during the one-year period ending on the hiring date that equal or exceed six months; $6,000 for a veteran who has aggregate periods of unemployment during the one-year period ending on the hiring date which equal or exceed four weeks, but less than six months; and $14,000 for a veteran who has aggregate periods of unemployment during the one-year period ending on the hiring date which equal or exceed six months. (Code Sec. 51(d)(3))

To be eligible for the WOTC, a new employee has to be certified as a member of a targeted group by a State Employment Security Agency (SESA). The employer can either get the certification by the day the prospective employee begins work or complete a pre-screening notice (using Form 8850) for the employee by the day he is offered employment, and submit it to the SESA (not to IRS) as part of a request for certification within 28 days after the employee begins work. A fast-tracked qualification process applies for certain qualified veterans. (Code Sec. 51(d)(13))

The targeted groups are: (1) qualified IV-A recipients (qualified recipients of aid to families with dependent children or successor program); (2) qualified veterans; (3) qualified ex-felons; (4) designated community residents (i.e., the former "high-risk youths" targeted group but with the maximum age requirement raised and the residency requirement expanded to include rural renewal residents); (5) vocational rehabilitation referrals; (6) qualified summer youth employees; (7) qualified supplemental nutrition assistance benefits recipients; (8) qualified SSI recipients; (9) long-term family assistance recipients, i.e., members of a family that receives or received assistance under a IV-A program for a minimum period of time; and (10) qualified long-term unemployment recipients (i.e., those who have had a period of unemployment that is not less than 27 consecutive weeks, and

---

6. ¶L-17775 *et seq.*; ¶514

includes a period in which the individual was receiving unemployment compensation under State or Federal law). (Code Sec. 51(d))[7]

No WOTC is allowed for employees who are related to the employer or to certain owners of the employer. (Code Sec. 51(i))[8]

Wages paid (a) for federally funded on-the-job training, (Code Sec. 51(c)(2)(A))[9] and (b) to an individual who performed the same or substantially similar services as those of employees participating in or affected by a strike or lockout at the employer's plant do not qualify for the credit. (Code Sec. 51(c)(3))[10] Creditable wages are reduced by any supplementation payments made to the employer for an employee under Social Security Act §482(e). (Code Sec. 51(c)(2)(B))[11]

The WOTC reduces the employer's wage deduction dollar-for-dollar. (Code Sec. 280C(a); Reg § 1.280C-1)[12] But the taxpayer can elect not to take the WOTC. (Code Sec. 51(j))[13]

¶ 2316 Tax-exempt employers' payroll-tax credit for hiring qualified veterans before 2020—Form 5884-C.

Before 2020, a tax-exempt employer (one described in Code Sec. 501(c) and exempt from tax under Code Sec. 501(a)) can claim (on Form 5884-C) a credit for the work opportunity tax credit (WOTC, see ¶2315) that it could have claimed for hiring qualified veterans if it were not tax-exempt (¶2315). The credit is allowed against the OASDI (Social Security) tax (¶3025). (Code Sec. 52(c)(2), Code Sec. 3111(e)) The credit, which can't exceed the OASDI tax otherwise payable for employment of all the tax-exempt's employees during the applicable employment period, is calculated as it would be under Code Sec. 51, but with a number modifications. The general credit percentage of qualifying first-year wages is 26% (instead of 40%); the credit percentage of qualifying wages is 16.25% (instead of 25%) for a qualified veteran who has completed at least 120, but less than 400, hours of service for the employer; and the tax-exempt employer can only take into account wages paid to a qualified veteran for services in furtherance of the activities related to the purposes or function constituting the basis of the organization's exemption under Code Sec. 501. (Code Sec. 3111(e)(2), Code Sec. 3111(e)(3))

Any credit that exceeds the employer Social Security tax for the period the credit is claimed is carried forward.[14]

¶ 2317 Employee retention credits for certain disaster areas—wages paid before 2018.

"Eligible employers" could claim an employee retention credit —an income tax credit of 40% of up to $6,000 of "qualified wages" paid *after* the "specified date" (Aug. 23, 2017, for eligible employees in the Hurricane Harvey disaster zone; Sept. 4, 2017, for eligible employees in the Hurricane Irma disaster zone; Sept. 16, 2017, for eligible employees in the Hurricane Maria disaster zone; Oct. 8, 2017 for eligible employees in the California wildfire disaster zone) but *before* Jan. 1, 2018. The credit was to be treated as a credit listed in Code Sec. 38(b) (i.e., as a component of the general business credit; see ¶2301).[15]

An eligible employer was one: (1) that conducted an active trade or business in a disaster zone as of the specified date (above) for that disaster; and (2) for which the active trade or business was rendered inoperable from damage sustained by the disaster between the

7. ¶L-17776 *et seq.*; ¶514
8. ¶L-17784.2; ¶514
9. ¶L-17784.2; ¶514
10. ¶L-17783.3; ¶514
11. ¶L-17783; ¶514

12. ¶L-17780; ¶514
13. ¶L-17781; ¶514
14. ¶H-4687.8; ¶31,114
15. ¶L-17890 *et seq.*

relevant specified date and Jan. 1, 2018. An eligible employee is one whose principal place of employment with the eligible employer was in the disaster zone as of the relevant specified date.

"Qualified wages" were wages (as defined for the work opportunity credit (WOTC; see ¶2315), but including amounts paid for medical or hospitalization expenses in connection with sickness or accident disability) paid or incurred by an eligible employer for an eligible employee on any day *after* the relevant specified date and *before* Jan. 1, 2018, during the period: (a) beginning on the date on which the employer's trade or business first became inoperable at the principal place of employment of the employee immediately before the disaster, and (b) ending on the date on which the trade or business has resumed significant operations at the principal place of employment.

¶ 2318   Second generation biofuel production credit before 2018—Form 6478.

An *alcohol fuels* credit (computed on Form 6478) was allowed for alcohol (other than that produced from petroleum, natural gas, coal or peat, or with a proof less than 150) (Code Sec. 40(d)(1)) used as a fuel. The second generation biofuel production credit, of $1.01 for each gallon of qualified cellulosic fuel production of the producer for the tax year, applied to a sale or use after Dec. 31, 2008 and before Jan. 1, 2018. (Code Sec. 40(b)(6))[16] (Code Sec. 40(e)(1))

A recapture tax of $1.01 per gallon was imposed on alcohol not used as fuel for one of the specified purposes and reported on Form 720. (Code Sec. 40(d)(3)(C))[17]

caution: Check tax.thomsonreuters.com/federaltaxhandbookupdates to see if the above provision has been extended.

¶ 2319   Research credit—Form 6765.

The research credit (claimed on Form 6765) equals the sum of:

(1) 20% of the excess (if any) of the qualified research expenses (QREs) for the tax year over a base amount, (unless the taxpayer elects the alternative simplified research credit, which then replaced item (1)).

(2) The university basic research credit, i.e., 20% of the basic research payments determined under Code Sec. 41(e)(1)(A).

(3) 20% of the taxpayer's expenditures on qualified energy research undertaken by an energy research consortium. (Code Sec. 41(a))[18]

The base amount is a fixed-base percentage of taxpayer's average annual gross receipts from a U.S. trade or business, net of returns and allowances, for the 4 tax years before the credit year, and can't be less than 50% of the year's QREs. The fixed base percentage for a non-startup company is the percentage (not exceeding 16%) that taxpayer's total QREs are of total gross receipts for tax years beginning after '83 and before '89. (Code Sec. 41(c))[19]

Except when a taxpayer elects the alternative simplified research credit, described below, the Code assigned a fixed-base percentage of 3% in making the base amount computation for each of its first 5 tax years in which a "startup company" has QREs. (Code Sec. 41(c)(3)(B)(ii)(I)) For the second 5 tax years, the fixed-base percentage is a specified amount of the ratio or percentage —increased annually during this second 5-year period — determined by dividing QREs by gross receipts. [20]

16. ¶L-17516.1; ¶404.07
17. ¶L-17507
18. ¶L-15300 *et seq.*; ¶414 *et seq.*

19. ¶L-15309.1
20. ¶L-15309 *et seq.*; ¶414 *et seq.*

To qualify for the research credit, research has to be conducted within the U.S. (including Puerto Rico and U.S. possessions). (Code Sec. 41(d), Code Sec. 41(f)) An expense has to:

(a) qualify as a research and experimental expenditure under Code Sec. 174 (for amounts paid or incurred after 2021, qualify as a "specified" research and experimental expenditure under Code Sec. 174);

(b) relate to research undertaken for the purpose of discovering information that is technological in nature and the application of which is intended to be useful in developing a new or improved business component of the taxpayer; and

(c) be for research in which substantially all of the activities are elements of a process of experimentation that related to a new or improved function, performance, reliability or quality. (Code Sec. 41(d)(1); Reg § 1.41-4(a)(5))

Under Code Sec. 41(d)(4)(E), research with respect to computer software developed by a taxpayer for internal use is generally not considered "qualified research," except as provided in regs. Final regs, effective for tax years beginning after Oct. 3, 2016, govern the internal use software exclusion, providing additional tests that must be satisfied in order for such costs to be eligible for the credit. (Reg § 1.41-4(c)(6)) Certain activities (e.g., marketing, surveys, duplication of existing business components, post-commercial-production activities) aren't qualified expenses. (Code Sec. 41(d)(4)) To pass test (b), above, research has to be intended to eliminate uncertainty about the development or improvement of a business component, and the process of experimentation has to fundamentally rely on principles of the physical or biological sciences, engineering, or computer science. Courts generally apply these tests strictly. [21] The issuance of certain patents is conclusive evidence that a taxpayer has discovered technological-in-nature information that is intended to eliminate uncertainty about the development or improvement of a business component. (Reg § 1.41-4(a)(3)(iii))

IRS has stated that the research credit statute regarding internal use software (i.e., Code Sec. 41(d)(4)(E)) is not self-executing, so notwithstanding any exceptions, internal use software can't be qualified research except as provided in final regs. [22]

QREs are amounts the taxpayer paid or incurred during the tax year "in carrying on any trade or business" (including certain start-up costs) of the taxpayer for: in-house research expenses, which consists of certain wages and supplies, and contract research expenses, i.e., 65% of amounts paid to certain nonemployees, and 100% of the taxpayer's expenditures to eligible small businesses, universities, and federal laboratories for qualified energy research. (Code Sec. 41(b); Reg § 1.41-2)[23]

For purposes of calculating the allowable research credit for persons that acquired the major portion of either a trade or business or a separate unit of a trade or business of another person, the amount of QREs paid or incurred by the acquiring person during the measurement period is increased by certain of the predecessor's expenses, and the acquiring person's gross receipts for the period is increased by certain of the predecessor's gross receipts. The measurement period is, for the tax year of the acquiring person for which the research credit is determined, any period of the acquiring person preceding the tax year which is taken into account for purposes of determining the credit for the year. (Code Sec. 41(f)(3)(A), Code Sec. 41(f)(3)(B))

The credit for each member of a controlled group is determined on a proportionate basis to its share of the aggregate of the QREs, basic research payments, and amounts paid or incurred to energy research consortiums, taken into account by the controlled group for purposes of the research credit. (Code Sec. 41(f)(1)(A)(ii)) A similar rule applies to members

---

21. ¶L-15412
22. ¶L-15437

23. ¶L-15401 *et seq.*; ¶414.01

of a group of commonly controlled trades or businesses. (Code Sec. 41(f)(1)(B)(ii)) Regs provide further guidance on how the research credit is allocated in controlled groups. [24]

Any expense taken into account in computing the orphan drug credit (¶2328) for a tax year can't be taken into account in computing the credit. (Code Sec. 45C(c)(1)) But, any orphan drug expenses for any tax year which are QREs can be taken into account in determining base period research expenses in later tax years. (Code Sec. 45C(c)(2))[25]

No deduction is allowed for that portion of the otherwise deductible QREs or basic research expenses that equals the credit for the tax year. (Code Sec. 280C(c)(1)) If a taxpayer capitalizes rather than deducts expenses, the amount of the expenses capitalized during the year is reduced by the excess of the credit over the amount allowable (without regard to that disallowance) as a deduction for the tax year. (Code Sec. 280C(c)(2))[26] But a taxpayer can avoid the reduction for any tax year by claiming a reduced credit for the year. The election limits the taxpayer to a credit in the amount of the research credit before any reduction less the product of that credit amount times the maximum corporate tax rate. (Code Sec. 280C(c)(3))[27]

A taxpayer can elect an *alternative simplified research credit* equal to 14% of the excess of the QREs for the tax year over 50% of the average QREs for the three tax years preceding the tax year for which the credit was being determined. (Code Sec. 41(c)(4)(A), Reg § 1.41-9(a)) If a taxpayer has no QREs in any one of the three preceding tax years, the alternative simplified research credit is 6% of the QREs for the tax year for which the credit is being determined. (Code Sec. 41(c)(4)(B)) The election applies to the tax year for which it is made and all following tax years unless revoked with IRS's consent. The election can't be made on an amended return if both the Code Sec. 41(a)(1) credit was previously claimed on an original or amended return and the tax year was closed by the period of limitations on assessments. (Code Sec. 41(c)(4)(C); Reg § 1.41-9(b))[28]

The 20% *university basic research credit* component applies to 100% of cash expenditures by corporations (except S corporations, personal holding companies, or service organizations) for basic research over the sum of: (1) the minimum basic research amount, plus (2) the maintenance-of-effort amount. (Code Sec. 41(e); Reg § 1.41-7)[29] The minimum basic research amount (Code Sec. 41(e)(4); Reg § 1.41-7) is the greatest of: (1) 1% of the average amount paid for in-house and contract research expenses during the base period (the three tax years before the first tax year beginning after '83); (Code Sec. 41(e)(7)(B)) (2) the contract research expense for the base period; or (3) 50% of the basic research payments if the taxpayer wasn't in existence for a full year in the base period. [30] The maintenance-of-effort amount is: (a) the average charitable contribution to all educational institutions during the base period (see above) multiplied by the cost-of-living adjustment (Code Sec. 41(e)(5)(C)), *minus* (b) the charitable contributions to educational institutions for the year. (Code Sec. 41(e)(5)(A))[31]

Offset against AMT. For credits determined for tax years that begin after Dec. 31, 2015, eligible small businesses ($50 million or less of gross receipts) may claim the credit against their alternative minimum tax (AMT) liability. (Code Sec. 38(c)(4)(B)(ii))

Offset against payroll tax. For tax years that begin after Dec. 31, 2015, qualified small businesses may elect to claim a portion of their research credit as a payroll tax credit against their employer FICA tax liability, rather than against their income tax liability. Amended returns can be filed before Jan. 1, 2018 for returns filed after Dec. 31, 2015 that didn't indicate an election was made. (Code Sec. 41(h), Code Sec. 3111(f))

---

24. ¶L-15317; ¶414.03
25. ¶L-15621; ¶414.04
26. ¶L-3131; ¶280C4, ¶414.04
27. ¶L-15308; ¶s 280C4, 414.04

28. ¶L-15302.2; ¶414.0107
29. ¶L-15501 *et seq.*; ¶s 414.01, 414.02
30. ¶s L-15508, L-15507; ¶414.02
31. ¶L-15509; ¶414.02

362

A qualified small business is one that, in the case of a corporation or partnership, with respect to any tax year, has gross receipts of less than $5 million, and did not have gross receipts for any tax year preceding the 5-tax-year period ending with the tax year. (Code Sec. 41(h)(3)(A)(i)) An individual can qualify if he meets the two conditions above, taking account the aggregate gross receipts received by the individual in carrying on all his trades or businesses. (Code Sec. 41(h)(3)(A)(ii)) Special aggregation rules apply. And an organization exempt from tax can't be a qualified small business. (Code Sec. 41(h)(3)(B))

The payroll tax credit portion is equal to the least of:

(i) an amount specified by the taxpayer that does not exceed $250,000,

(ii) the research credit determined for the tax year, or

(iii) in the case of a qualified small business other than a partnership or S corporation, the amount of the business credit carryforward under Code Sec. 39 from the tax year (determined before the application of Code Sec. 41(h) to the tax year). (Code Sec. 41(h)(2))

The election can't be made for a tax year if the taxpayer has made such an election for five or more preceding tax years. (Code Sec. 41(h)(4)(B)(ii)) For a partnership or S corporation, an election to apply the credit against OASDI liability is made at the entity level. (Code Sec. 41(h)(4)(C))

The payroll tax portion of the research credit is allowed as a credit against the qualified small business's OASDI tax liability for the first calendar quarter beginning after the date on which it files its income tax or information return for the tax year. The credit can't exceed the OASDI tax liability for a calendar quarter on the wages paid with respect to all employees of the qualified small business. If the payroll tax portion of the credit exceeds the qualified small business's OASDI tax liability for a calendar quarter, the excess is allowed as a credit against the OASDI liability for the following calendar quarter. (Code Sec. 3111(f))

The credit allowed against employer FICA can't be taken account for purposes of determining the amount allowable as a payroll tax deduction. (Code Sec. 3111(f)(4))

¶ 2320 Low-income housing credit for qualified buildings—Forms 8609, 8586.

The low-income housing credit is allowed annually over a 10-year credit period beginning with the tax year the qualified building is placed in service, or, under an irrevocable election (on Form 8609), the next tax year. (Code Sec. 42(f)(1)) The credit period for an existing building can't begin before the first tax year of the tax period for rehabilitation expenses for the building. (Code Sec. 42(f)(5)(A))[32]

The credit equals the qualified building's qualified basis times the applicable percentage (see below) (Code Sec. 42(a)) prescribed by IRS for the month placed in service or elected in agreement with the housing credit agency. (Code Sec. 42(b)(2)(A)) The building owner can't claim a credit amount in excess of the allocation received from the state or housing credit agency for that year. (Reg § 1.42-1T(e)(1))[33]

IRS prescribes percentages that will yield, over a 10-year period, credit amounts that will have a present value equal to 70% of the qualified basis of new buildings (not federally subsidized) and 30% of the qualified basis of existing buildings and federally subsidized new buildings, see following table; however, for any new building that is placed in service by the taxpayer after July 30, 2008 and that is not federally subsidized for the tax year, the applicable percentage can't be less than 9%. (Code Sec. 42(b))[34]

---

32. ¶L-15700 *et seq.*; ¶424.10, 424.55

33. ¶L-15702; ¶424.10

34. ¶L-15718; ¶424.10

Month	Year	70% present value credit	30% present value credit
Nov.	2018	7.72%	3.31%
Oct.	2018	7.67%	3.29%
Sept.	2018	7.68%	3.29%
Aug.	2018	7.66%	3.28%
July	2018	7.68%	3.29%
June	2018	7.68%	3.29%
May	2018	7.65%	3.28%
Apr.	2018	7.66%	3.28%
Mar.	2018	7.63%	3.27%
Feb.	2018	7.57%	3.25%
Jan.	2018	7.55%	3.24%
Dec.	2017	7.55%	3.23%

A credit for rehabilitation expenditures (treated as a separate building (Code Sec. 42(e)(1))) is allowed only if during any 24-month period they are the greater of: 20% of the building's adjusted basis or, for 2018, $6,800 per low-income unit ($7,000 for 2019, as calculated by Thomson Reuters based on inflation data). (Code Sec. 42(e)(3)(A))

To claim the credit, taxpayers must file Form 8586 for each tax year in the 10-year credit period. (Reg § 1.42-1(h))[35] Form 8609 is filed once with the taxpayer's tax return. [36]

A qualified low-income building is a building that at all times during the "compliance period" of 15 tax years beginning with the first tax year of the credit period, is part of a qualified low-income housing project. (Code Sec. 42(c)(2), Code Sec. 42(g), Code Sec. 42(i)(1)) In addition, no credit is allowed unless an extended low income housing commitment (for an additional 15-year period) between the taxpayer and the housing credit agency is in effect at the end of the tax year. (Code Sec. 42(h)(6))[37]

¶ 2321   Recapture of low-income housing credit—Form 8611.

If, at the close of any year in the compliance period (¶2320), the building's qualified basis is less than it was at the close of the earlier tax year, the taxpayer's tax for the year is increased (Code Sec. 42(j)(1), Code Sec. 42(j)(4)(B)) by the sum of:

(1) the total decrease in taxpayer's general business credits for all earlier tax years that would have resulted if the accelerated portion of the credit (below) allowable for the earlier tax years wasn't allowed for all earlier tax years for the decrease in qualified basis, plus

(2) an amount of nondeductible interest on (1), above, computed at the rate charged for overpayment of tax, see ¶4856. (Code Sec. 42(j)(2))

The accelerated portion of the credit for the earlier tax years is the excess of the total credit allowed for the earlier tax years over the total credit that would have been allowable for those years if the total credit that would have been allowable for the entire compliance period were allowable ratably over 15 years. (Code Sec. 42(j)(3))[38]

The disposition of a building (or interest in it) won't result in an increase in tax from credit recapture if it's reasonably expected that the building will continue to be operated as a qualified low-income building for the remaining compliance period for that building. The otherwise applicable statute of limitations is extended until three years after IRS is notified (as specified in guidance) of noncompliance with the low-income housing tax credit rules. (Code Sec. 42(j)(6))[39]

---

35. ¶L-15701 *et seq.*; ¶424.50
36. ¶S-3456; ¶424.50
37. ¶L-15719 *et seq.*; ¶424.60

38. ¶L-16050 *et seq.*; ¶424.85
39. ¶L-16050 *et seq.*; ¶424.85

¶ 2322   Enhanced oil recovery (EOR) credit.

The EOR credit for any tax year is 15% of the taxpayer's qualified EOR costs (under Code Sec. 43(c)(1)) for the tax year. (Code Sec. 43(a)) The credit is phased out by the same ratio as the average per barrel wellhead price of domestic crude oil (reference price) for the last calendar year that ended before the tax year in question exceeds an inflation-adjusted figure (for 2017, $47.62) bears to $6. (Code Sec. 43(b)) Accordingly, because the reference price for the 2017 calendar year ($48.05) exceeds $47.62, only 13.93% of the credit is available for 2018. [40]

observation: The EOR credit had been completely phased out in recent years.

¶ 2323   Disabled access credit (DAC)—Form 8826.

An "eligible small business" (ESB) may elect (on Form 8826) to apply against income tax a DAC of 50% of the amount of "eligible access expenditures" for the tax year that's over $250 and not more than $10,250. (Code Sec. 44(a))

observation: For any tax year, the credit can't exceed $5,000 [50% of ($10,250 – $250)].

For partnerships and S corporations, the limitation applies at the entity and the individual partner or shareholder levels. (Code Sec. 44(d)(3))

An ESB for any tax year is any person who either: (1) has gross receipts of $1 million or less for the past tax year, net of returns and allowances, or (2) employed 30 or less full-time employees (a full-time employee is employed at least 30 hours a week for 20 or more calendar weeks in the tax year) in the past tax year. (Code Sec. 44(b), Code Sec. 44(d)(5))

Eligible access expenditures are amounts paid or incurred so a business can comply with the Americans With Disabilities Act of '90 (ADA, as in effect on Nov. 5, '90). (Code Sec. 44(c)(1)) These expenses include *only* expenses that are necessary to comply with ADA, that are paid or incurred: (1) for the purpose of removing architectural, communication, physical or transportation barriers in connection with any facility first placed in service before Nov. 6, '90, which prevent a business from being accessible to, or usable by, disabled individuals; (2) to provide qualified interpreters or other effective methods of making aurally delivered materials available to hearing impaired individuals; (3) to provide qualified readers, taped texts and other effective methods of making visually delivered materials available to visually impaired individuals; (4) to acquire or modify equipment or devices for disabled individuals; or (5) to provide other similar services, modifications, materials or equipment. (Code Sec. 44(c))[41]

¶ 2324   Credit for producing electricity from renewable resources—Form 8835.

A renewable electricity production credit (claimed on Form 8835) is allowed for electricity produced by taxpayers from: (1) wind, (2) closed-loop biomass, (3) open-loop biomass, (4) geothermal energy, (5) municipal solid waste, (6) marine and hydrokinetic renewables (e.g., waves and tides), (7) qualified hydropower production, (8) small irrigation power and (9) solar energy. (Code Sec. 45(c)) The electricity production credit is generally available for a 10-year period beginning on the placed-in-service date of the qualifying facility for electricity produced during that period. (Code Sec. 45(a)(2)(A)) The 10-year credit period for a qualified hydropower facility begins on the date that the qualifying efficiency improvements or additions to capacity are placed in service. (Code Sec. 45(d)(9)(C))

---

40. ¶L-17615; ¶434.01 *et seq.*   41. ¶L-17900 *et seq.*; ¶444

Facilities producing electricity from wind qualify for the credit (subject to a phaseout) if the facility's construction begins before 2020; for a facility, the construction of which begins after 2016 and before 2018, the credit is reduced by 20%; for a facility, the construction of which begins after 2017 and before 2019, the credit is reduced by 40%; and for a facility, the construction of which begins after 2018 and before 2020, the credit is reduced by 60%. (Code Sec. 45(b)(5)) For facilities producing electricity from the resources in (2) through (7) (including landfill gas and trash facilities using municipal solid waste) to be qualified facilities, the facility's construction must begin before 2018. (Code Sec. 45(d))[42] Qualified small irrigation power facilities had to be placed in service before Oct. 3, 2008. Qualified facilities for solar energy had to be placed in service before 2006. (Code Sec. 45(d))[43]

Facilities placed in service by the later of (1) a calendar year no more than four years after the calendar year during which construction of the facility began or (2) Dec. 31, 2018 will be considered to satisfy the continuity safe harbor for establishing when construction has begun. This applies to any project, for which an electricity production credit is claimed, placed in service after Jan. 2, 2013. [44]

For 2018, the credit is 2.4¢ per kilowatt hour (KWH). (Code Sec. 45(a)) But, for electricity produced and sold at any qualifying facility using open-loop biomass, small irrigation power, landfill gas, trash, or hydropower, marine or hydrokinetic the amount of the credit is reduced to 1.2¢ per KWH. (Code Sec. 45(b)(4)) The credit is allowed for qualified electricity sold to an unrelated person (Code Sec. 45(a)(2)(B))[45] and produced from U.S. (or U.S. possession) facilities (see above). The credit is allocated to a taxpayer in proportion to his ownership interest in the gross sales from the qualifying facility. (Code Sec. 45(e))[46] The safe harbor under which partnership allocations of wind energy production credits are respected does *not* apply to partnership allocations of Code Sec. 48 energy credits, see ¶2310.[47]

The credit is proportionately phased out when the national average price of electricity produced from the applicable renewable resource exceeds a specified, inflation-adjusted threshold price per KWH. (Code Sec. 45(b)(1)) Accordingly, there is no phaseout for 2017. [48]

A credit applies for the domestic production of refined coal from a qualified facility placed in service after Oct. 22, 2004 and before 2012. (Code Sec. 45(c)(7), Code Sec. 45(d)(8)) The refined coal credit is equal to $6.909 for 2017 ($7.03 for 2018) per ton of qualified refined coal and phases out as the market price of refined coal exceeds certain threshold levels. (Code Sec. 45(d)(8)) No phaseout applies for 2017 or 2018. [49]

A credit based on the production of Indian coal is available to producers of Indian coal at Indian coal facilities during the 12-year period beginning on Jan. 1, 2006 (i.e., before 2018). (Code Sec. 45(e)(10)(A)) .[50]

caution: Check tax.thomsonreuters.com/federaltaxhandbookupdates to see if the above provision has been extended.

Taxpayers can elect to have qualified property of certain qualified facilities treated as energy property eligible for a 30% investment credit under Code Sec. 48 (¶2310). Qualified property is tangible property or other tangible property (not including a building or its structural components), but only if the property is used as an integral part of the qualified facility: for which depreciation (or amortization) is allowable; which is constructed, reconstructed, erected, or acquired by the taxpayer; and the original use of which begins with

42. ¶L-17771.10 *et seq.*; ¶454 *et seq.*
43. ¶L-17751 *et seq.*; ¶454
44. ¶L-17771.10 *et seq.*; ¶454 *et seq.*
45. ¶L-17754; ¶454
46. ¶L-17755; ¶454

47. ¶B-2903A
48. ¶L-17760 *et seq.*; ¶454
49. ¶L-17771.7B; ¶454.16
50. ¶L-17771.8; ¶454.17

the taxpayer. (Code Sec. 48(a)(5)) The qualified facilities are those Code Sec. 45(d) facilities (other than refined or Indian coal facilities or solar facilities) placed in service after 2008 and construction of which begins before 2018 that are otherwise eligible for the Code Sec. 45 credit (see above), and for which no such credit has been allowed. Subject to a phaseout, an election is also available for a qualified wind facility for which the construction begins before 2020; for a wind facility, the construction of which begins after 2016 and before 2018, the credit is reduced by 20%; for a facility, the construction of which begins after 2017 and before 2019, the credit is reduced by 40%; and for a facility, the construction of which begins after 2018 and before 2020, the credit is reduced by 60%. (Code Sec. 48(a)(5)(E)) The irrevocable election (on Form 3468) is made on a timely filed return (including extensions) for the tax year in which the facility is placed in service. [1]

No Code Sec. 45 credit is allowed for energy property for which a nontaxable grant (for income and alternative minimum tax purposes) is made by the Treasury Secretary in lieu of the credit for property placed in service (a) during 2009, 2010, or 2011; or (b) after 2011 and before the credit termination date but only if construction of the property began during 2009, 2010, or 2011. If the credit is allowed, recapture applies. The basis of the property is reduced by 50% of the amount of the grant. (Code Sec. 48(d))[2]

¶ 2325   Empowerment zone employment credit before 2018—Form 8844.

Before 2018, employers could claim (on Form 8844) an empowerment zone employment credit for any tax year equal to 20% of up to $15,000 of "qualified zone wages" paid or incurred during the calendar year that ended with or within that tax year, for a maximum per-employee credit of $3,000. (Code Sec. 1396(a), Code Sec. 1400(d))[3] Qualified zone wages didn't include wages taken into account for the work opportunity tax credit (WOTC, ¶2313), and the $15,000 maximum was reduced by the amount of wages taken into account for the WOTC. (Code Sec. 1396(c)(3))[4] The credit also reduced an employer's wage deduction for the year. (Code Sec. 280C(a))[5]

caution: Check tax.thomsonreuters.com/federaltaxhandbookupdates to see if the above provision has been extended.

¶ 2326   Indian employment credit before 2018—Form 8845.

For tax years beginning before Jan. 1, 2018 (Code Sec. 45A(f)),[6] the Indian employment credit (claimed on Form 8845) was 20% of the excess, if any, of the sum of qualified wages and qualified employee health insurance costs (not in excess of $20,000 per employee) paid or incurred (other than paid under salary reduction arrangements) to qualified employees (enrolled Indian tribe members and their spouses who meet certain requirements) during the tax year (Code Sec. 45A(a)(1), Code Sec. 45A(b)(2)) over the sum of these same costs paid or incurred in calendar year '93 —determined as if the Indian employment credit had been in effect in '93. (Code Sec. 45A(a)(2); Code Sec. 45A(c))

caution: Check tax.thomsonreuters.com/federaltaxhandbookupdates to see if the above provision has been extended.

1. ¶L-16401.1; ¶484.01
2. ¶L-17773; ¶454.19
3. ¶L-15630 *et seq.*; ¶13,964
4. ¶L-15632; ¶13,964
5. ¶L-15639.2; ¶13,964
6. ¶L-15670 *et seq.*; ¶45A4

¶ 2327   FICA tip credit—Form 8846.

A food and beverage establishment is allowed a credit (on Form 8846) for the amount of the employer's FICA tax obligation (7.65%) attributable to employee tips received for providing, delivering, or serving food or beverages (whether or not the tips are reported as required by Code Sec. 6053). However, no credit is given for tips used to meet the federal minimum wage rate. (Code Sec. 45B) Employers determine their Code Sec. 45B credit using the minimum wage in effect on Jan. 1, 2007 (Code Sec. 45B(b)(1)) (i.e., $5.15).[7] No deduction is allowed for any amount taken into account in determining the FICA tip credit. (Code Sec. 45B(c)) A taxpayer can elect out of the credit for any tax year. (Code Sec. 45B(d))[8]

¶ 2328   Qualified clinical testing expense ("orphan drug") credit—Form 8820.

A taxpayer that incurs qualified clinical testing expenses (QCTEs) for drugs for rare diseases may claim (on Form 8820) a credit equal to 25% of those expenses for the tax year. (Code Sec. 45C)[9] QCTEs are amounts which, with certain modifications, would qualify as qualified research expenses for the research credit (¶2319). (Code Sec. 45C(b)(1))

Deductions (or amounts chargeable to capital account) for QCTEs are reduced by the amount of the allowable orphan drug credit. (Code Sec. 280C(b)(1), Code Sec. 280C(b)(2))

Taxpayers can elect to take a reduced orphan drug credit in lieu of reducing allowable deductions. (Code Sec. 280C(b)(3))

¶ 2329   New markets tax credit before 2020—Form 8874.

Before 2020, a "new markets tax credit" applies for qualified equity investments to acquire stock in a community development entity (CDE). Nationally, the maximum annual amount of qualifying equity investments is capped at $3.5 billion each calendar year from 2010 through 2019; but no amount can be carried over to any calendar year after 2024. (Code Sec. 45D) A CDE is any domestic corporation or partnership (1) whose primary mission is serving or providing investment capital for low-income communities or low-income persons, (2) that maintains accountability to residents of low-income communities through representation on governing or advisory boards of the CDE, and (3) is certified by Treasury as an eligible CDE. A qualified equity investment is stock or a similar equity interest acquired directly from a CDE for cash. Substantially all (at least 85%, reduced to 75% for the final year of the 7-year credit period) of the cash has to be used by the CDE to make investments in, or loans to, qualified active businesses located in low-income communities or certain financial services to businesses and residents in low-income communities. A qualified equity investment made by an LLC (classified as a partnership) can include cash from a nonrecourse loan or a recourse loan to the LLC that the LLC invests as equity in a qualified CDE, where the loan is indebtedness for federal income tax purposes. (Code Sec. 45D; Reg § 1.45D-1(c)(5))[10]

The new markets tax credit (claimed on Form 8874) is: (a) 5% for the year in which the equity interest is purchased from the CDE and for the first two anniversary dates after the purchase (for a total credit of 15%), *plus* (b) 6% on each anniversary date thereafter for the following four years (for a total of 24%).[11] The credit is recaptured if the entity fails to continue to be a CDE or the interest is redeemed within seven years, unless it is allowed to, and did, correct its failure. (Code Sec. 45D(g); Reg § 1.45D-1(e))[12]

---

7. ¶L-17860 *et seq.*; ¶45B4
8. ¶L-17860 *et seq.*; ¶45B4
9. ¶L-15615 *et seq.*; ¶45C4

10. ¶L-17920 *et seq.*; ¶L-17924 ; ¶45D4 *et seq.*
11. ¶L-17922; ¶45D4
12. ¶L-17928; ¶45D4.10

¶ 2330   Credit for employer-provided child care—Form 8882.

A tax credit for "employer-provided child care" (Code Sec. 45F(a)) is allowed for the sum of the following expenses (up to $150,000) for the tax year Code Sec. 45F(b)):[13]

(1) *25% of qualified child care expenses,* which are expenses to buy, build, rehabilitate, or expand property to be used as part of an employer's qualified child care facility, for which a deduction for depreciation (or amortization) is allowable, and which isn't part of the taxpayer's (or an employee's) principal residence. Qualifying child care expenses also include operating costs of a taxpayer's qualified child care facility (including costs related to employee training, scholarship programs, and to providing increased compensation to employees with higher levels of child care training), and amounts paid under a contract with a qualified child care facility to provide child care services to the taxpayer's employees. (Code Sec. 45F(c)(1)(A)) Qualified child care expenses don't include expenses in excess of the FMV of the care; *and* (Code Sec. 45F(c)(1)(B))

(2) *10% of qualified child care resource and referral expenses* (i.e., amounts paid or incurred under a contract to provide child care resource and referral services to an employee).[14]

Generally, a qualified child care facility is one principally used to provide child care assistance, and which meets the requirements of the state or local government in which it is located, including its licensing as a child care facility. (Code Sec. 45F(c)(2)(A)) The facility must be open to the taxpayer's employees during the tax year, and, if it is the taxpayer's principal trade or business, at least 30% of its enrollees must be the dependents of the taxpayer's employees. [15]

The provision of child care resource and referral services or facilities can't discriminate in favor of highly compensated employees (within the meaning of Code Sec. 414(q)) (see ¶4315). (Code Sec. 45F(c)(2)(B), Code Sec. 45F(c)(3))[16]

A taxpayer claiming a Code Sec. 45F credit for acquiring, constructing, rehabilitating, or expanding a qualified child care facility must reduce its basis in the facility by the amount of the credit. (Code Sec. 45F(f)(1)(A))[17] No deduction or credit is allowed for any amount taken into account in determining Code Sec. 45F credit. (Code Sec. 45F(f)(2))[18]

Recapture rules apply for the first 10 years after the facility is placed in service. (Code Sec. 45F(d))[19]

For purposes of the credit, all persons treated as one employer under Code Sec. 52(a) or Code Sec. 52(b) are treated as one taxpayer. [20] Regs are to address credit allocations between an estate or trust and its beneficiaries, and among partners of a partnership. (Code Sec. 45F(e))[21]

¶ 2331   Small employer pension plan startup credit—Form 8881.

Eligible small employers that adopt a new qualified defined benefit or defined contribution plan (including a Code Sec. 401(k) plan, SIMPLE plan, or SEP) may claim a credit. The credit equals 50% of administrative and retirement-related education expenses for the plan for each of the first three plan years, with a maximum credit of $500 for each year. The first credit year is the tax year that includes the date the plan becomes effective, or, electively, the preceding tax year. (Code Sec. 45E(a), Code Sec. 45E(b), Code

13. ¶L-17872; ¶45F4
14. ¶L-17870 *et seq.*; ¶45F4
15. ¶L-17874; ¶45F4
16. ¶L-17875; ¶45F4
17. ¶L-17876; ¶45F4

18. ¶L-17877; ¶45F4
19. ¶L-17878; ¶45F4.01
20. ¶L-17879
21. ¶L-17870; ¶45F4

Sec. 45E(d)(3))[22]

The pension plan startup credit is available only to businesses that did not employ, in the preceding year, more than 100 employees with compensation of at least $5,000. But, an employer isn't an eligible employer if, during the 3-tax year period immediately preceding the first tax year for which the credit is otherwise allowable, it or any member of any controlled group including the employer (or any predecessor of either) established or maintained a qualified employer plan to which contributions were made, or benefits were accrued, for substantially the same employees that are in the qualified employer plan. (Code Sec. 45E(c))[23] For purposes of Code Sec. 45E, all persons treated as a single employer under Code Sec. 52(a) or Code Sec. 52(b) or Code Sec. 414(m) or Code Sec. 414(o) are treated as one taxpayer. (Code Sec. 45E(e)(1))[24] To be eligible for the credit, the plan must cover at least one nonhighly compensated employee. (Code Sec. 45E(d)(1)) If the credit is for the cost of a payroll-deduction IRA plan, it must be made available to all employees who have worked with the employer for at least three months. [25]

No deduction is allowed for that portion of the qualified startup costs paid or incurred for the tax year which is equal to the credit. (Code Sec. 45E(e)(2))[26] An eligible employer may elect not to have the credit apply for any tax year. (Code Sec. 45E(e)(3))[27]

¶ 2332   Small employer health insurance credit–Forms 8941; 990-T.

An eligible small employer (ESE) may claim, subject to a phaseout, a credit equal to 50% of nonelective contributions for health insurance for its employees. (Code Sec. 45R) The credit is allowed for the credit period —the 2-consecutive-tax year period beginning with the first tax year beginning after for which the ESE files an income tax return with an attached Form 8941. (Code Sec. 45R(e)(2), Reg § 1.45R-1(a)(3)) The credit reduces the ESE's Code Sec. 162 deduction. (Code Sec. 45R(e)(5))[28]

Eligible employers. An ESE is generally an employer that: (1) has no more than 25 full-time equivalent employees (FTEs) employed during its tax year; (2) has employees who have average annual wages of no more than an indexed dollar amount ($53,200 for 2018, $54,200 for 2019, as calculated by Thomson Reuters based on inflation data); and (3) has in effect a qualifying arrangement in which the employer has to contribute at least 50% of the premiums. (Code Sec. 45R(d)(1), Reg § 1.45R-2(a))

The FTEs of an ESE are determined by dividing (a) the total hours of service (up to 2,080 hours, determined using either an employee's actual hours of service, a days-worked equivalency method, or a weeks-worked equivalency method) by (b) 2,080. (Code Sec. 45R(d), Reg § 1.45R-2(a))[29] The average annual wages of an ESE for any tax year is the amount determined by dividing the aggregate amount of wages that were paid by the ESE to employees during the tax year by the number of the ESE's FTEs and rounding that amount to the next lowest multiple of $1,000. (Code Sec. 45R(d)(3))[30]

Regarding self-employed individuals, including partners and sole proprietors, 2% S corporation shareholders, and 5% owners of the employer (within the meaning of Code Sec. 416(i)(1)(B)(i)): (1) they aren't treated as employees; (2) their wages or hours are not counted in determining either the number of FTEs or the amount of average annual wages; and (3) premiums paid on their behalf are not counted in determining the credit. (Code Sec. 45R(e)) Similarly, an employee-spouse of any of the following isn't taken into account: (1) a more-than-2% S shareholder; (2) a more-than-5% owner of a business; (3) a partner owning more than a 5% interest in a partnership; and (4) a sole proprietor.

---

22. ¶L-15690 *et seq.*; ¶45E4   27. ¶L-15699; ¶45E4
23. ¶L-15692; ¶45E4   28. ¶L-15681; ¶45R4
24. ¶L-15699.1   29. ¶L-15682 *et seq.*; ¶45R4.02
25. ¶L-15694   30. ¶L-15689; ¶45R4.06
26. ¶L-15698; ¶45E4

Credit amount. The credit equals 50% (35% for a tax-exempt ESE, see below) of the lesser of:

(1) the aggregate amount of nonelective contributions (i.e., an employer contribution other than one under a Code Sec. 125 salary reduction arrangement) the ESE made on behalf of its employees during the tax year under a contribution arrangement for premiums for qualified health plans offered by the employer to its employees through a Small Business Health Options Program (SHOP) exchange; (Code Sec. 45R(b)(1)) or

(2) the aggregate amount of nonelective contributions which the ESE would have paid if each employee were enrolled in a plan with a premium equal to the average premium for the small group market in the state (or in an area in the state) in which the employer is offering health insurance coverage. (Code Sec. 45R(b)(2))[31]

The above credit amount is reduced for an ESE if: (i) it has more than 10 FTEs; or (ii) the average annual full-time equivalent wages per employee are more than $26,600 for 2018 ($27,100 for 2019, as calculated by Thomson Reuters based on inflation data). The otherwise applicable credit is reduced (but not below zero) by the sum of: (1) that credit amount multiplied by a fraction, the numerator of which is the total number of the employer's FTEs in excess of 10, and the denominator of which is 15; and (2) the credit amount multiplied by a fraction, the numerator of which is the average annual wages in excess of $26,600 for 2018 ($27,100 for 2019) and the denominator of which is $26,600 for 2018 ($27,100 for 2019). (Code Sec. 45R(c)(1), Code Sec. 45R(c)(2))

observation: The phaseout of the credit amount under Code Sec. 45R(c) operates in such a way that an employer with exactly 25 FTEs, or with average annual wages exactly equal to $53,200 for 2018 ($54,200 for 2019) is not in fact eligible for the credit.

Qualifying arrangement. A ESE must generally make premium payments on behalf of its employees for qualified health plans offered by the employer to its employees through a SHOP Exchange. (Code Sec. 45R(d)(4), Reg § 1.45R-2(a), Reg § 1.45R-1(a)(15)) Employer contributions to, or amounts made available under, a health reimbursement arrangement (HRA), health flexible spending arrangement (health FSA), or a health savings account (HSA) are not taken into account in determining the premium payments by the employer for a tax year. (Reg § 1.45R-3(g)(2)(ii))[32]

Tax-exempt ESEs. The applicable percentage for an eligible small tax-exempt employer (tax-exempt ESE) is 35%. For tax-exempt ESEs, the credit is a refundable tax credit (claimed on Form 990-T) limited to the amount of the employer's payroll taxes (income tax and Medicare tax withheld from employees' wages and the employer share of Medicare tax on employees' wages) during the calendar year in which the tax year begins. (Code Sec. 45R(b); Code Sec. 45R(f), Reg § 1.45R-3(e))

observation: Employers can deduct employee health insurance expenses not qualifying for the small employer health insurance credit as ordinary and necessary business expenses for employee compensation. Thus, an ESE's deductible expenses presumably can include amounts paid: a) in excess of the percentage of the expenses qualifying for the credit, or b) related to certain individuals such as certain business owners and their dependents that aren't treated as employees.

In certain cases, IRS offers relief to employers that can't offer a qualified health plan through a SHOP exchange because their principal business address is in a county without an available plan. [33]

---

31. ¶L-15689.7; ¶45R4.06
32. ¶L-15689.4A; ¶L-15689.5M; ¶45R4.03

33. ¶L-15689.7A *et seq.*

¶ 2333   Biodiesel fuel credit before 2018—Form 8864.

For fuels produced and sold or used before 2018 (Code Sec. 40A(g)), a taxpayer could claim a credit (on Form 8864) equal to the sum of: (1) a biodiesel mixture credit of $1 per gallon of biodiesel used in the production of a qualified biodiesel mixture; (2) a biodiesel credit of $1 per gallon of biodiesel, not in a mixture, used as a fuel in the taxpayer's trade or business, or sold at retail and placed in a vehicle fuel tank; and (3) for an eligible small agri-biodiesel producer, a small agri-biodiesel producer credit of 10¢ per gallon of agri-biodiesel, up to a 15 million gallon maximum: (a) used by the producer or sold by the producer for use in the production of a qualified biodiesel mixture in a trade or business or as fuel in a trade or business, or (b) sold at retail and placed in a vehicle fuel tank by the producer or a person buying from the producer. (Code Sec. 40A(a), Code Sec. 40A(b))[34] The credit is inapplicable to fuel produced outside the U.S. for use outside the U.S. (Code Sec. 40A(d)(5))[35] Renewable diesel is treated like biodiesel. (Code Sec. 40A(f))[36]

✓caution: Check tax.thomsonreuters.com/federaltaxhandbookupdates to see if the above provision has been extended.

¶ 2334   New energy efficient home credit before 2018—Form 8908.

For homes acquired before 2018, eligible contractors that constructed new energy-efficient homes meeting certain requirements could qualify for a $2,000 credit (claimed on Form 8908) per qualifying home. (Code Sec. 45L(a), Code Sec. 45L(g))[37] Certain manufactured homes qualified for a $1,000 credit. (Code Sec. 45L(a)(2), Code Sec. 45L(c)(3))[38]

A property's basis was reduced by the amount of credit. (Code Sec. 45L(e))[39]

✓caution: Check tax.thomsonreuters.com/federaltaxhandbookupdates to see if the above provision has been extended.

¶ 2335   Differential wage payment credit—Form 8932.

Eligible small business employers (ESBEs) that pay differential wages (i.e., payments for periods that employees are called to active duty with the U.S. uniformed services, see ¶3005) to a qualified employee can claim a credit (on Form 8932) equal to 20% of up to $20,000 of differential pay made to a qualified employee during the tax year. (Code Sec. 45P) A qualified employee is one who was an employee for the 91-day period immediately before the period for which any differential wage payment was made. (Code Sec. 45P(b)(2)) An ESBE is one that under a written plan, provided eligible differential wage payments to each of its qualified employees. For tax years beginning before 2016, to qualify as an ESBE, the employer had to employ on average less than 50 employees on business days during the tax year; for tax years beginning after 2015, no such limit applies. (Code Sec. 45P(b)(3))[40]

The credit can't be claimed by a taxpayer that has failed to comply with the employment and reemployment rights of members of the uniformed services (as provided under Chapter 43 of Title 38 of the United States Code). (Code Sec. 45P(d)) No deduction can be taken for that part of compensation which is equal to the credit, and the amount of any otherwise allowable income tax credit for compensation paid to an employee has to be reduced by the differential wage payment credit allowed for the employee. (Code Sec. 280C(a))[41]

34. ¶L-17570 *et seq.*; ¶40A4
35. ¶L-17585; ¶40A4.05
36. ¶L-17585.1; ¶40A4.05
37. ¶L-17941; ¶45L4

38. ¶L-17949; ¶45L4
39. ¶L-17949.14; ¶45L4
40. ¶L-15675 *et seq.*; ¶45P4
41. ¶L-15678.2; ¶45P4

¶ 2336   Employer-paid family and medical leave credit for 2018 and 2019.

For wages paid in tax years beginning after 2017 and before 2020, a general business credit may be claimed equal to 12.5% of the amount of wages paid to qualifying employees during any period in which the employees are on family and medical leave (FMLA) if the rate of payment is at least 50% of the wages normally paid to an employee, up to a maximum of 12 weeks of leave with respect to any employee for the tax year. (Code Sec. 45S(b)(3)) The credit is increased by 0.25 percentage points (but not above 25%) for each percentage point by which the rate of payment exceeds 50%. [42]

To qualify for the credit, an employer must have a written policy containing certain requirements, and all "qualifying" full-time employees must be given at least two weeks of annual paid family and medical leave (all less-than-full-time qualifying employees must be given a commensurate amount of leave on a pro rata basis). (Code Sec. 45S) A qualifying employee must have been employed by the employer for one year or more, and, for the preceding year, had compensation not in excess of an amount equal to 60% of the "highly compensated employee" threshold under Code Sec. 414(q)(1)(B)(i) (for 2018, 60% of $120,000, or $72,000). A taxpayer can't take both a credit and a deduction for amounts for which the paid family and medical leave credit is claimed. (Code Sec. 280C(a)) [43]

¶ 2337   Personal (Refundable and Nonrefundable) Credits. ▬▬▬▬▬▬▬

Taxpayers, whether or not in business, may qualify for one or more personal credits. Some credits are refundable —i.e., the excess of the credit over tax liability is refunded to the taxpayer —while some are partly refundable, and some are nonrefundable.

The *refundable* credits are the:

. . . Earned income tax credit (EITC), see ¶2338 *et seq.*;

. . . Health coverage tax credit for displaced workers and PBGC pensioners (before 2020), see ¶2343;

. . . Premium assistance credit, see ¶2344;

. . . Credit for income tax withheld, see ¶2345;

. . . Credit for excess social security tax withheld, see ¶2346;

. . . Child tax credit (CTC; partly refundable), see ¶2351;

. . . Alternative minimum tax (AMT) refundable credit for individuals, see ¶2360;

. . . American opportunity tax credit (AOTC; partly refundable), see ¶2202;

. . . Credit for capital gain tax paid by a regulated investment company (RIC), see ¶4201; and

. . . Credit for excise tax on certain nontaxable uses of fuels. (Code Sec. 6420, Code Sec. 6421, Code Sec. 6427)

The *nonrefundable* credits are the:

* Credit for the elderly and the permanently and totally disabled, see ¶2347;
* Credit for child and dependent care expenses, see ¶2348 *et seq.*;
* Credit for adoption expenses, see ¶2349;
* Child tax credit (but see above), see ¶2351;
* Credit for certain home mortgage interest, see ¶2352;
* AOTC credit (see above) and Lifetime Learning credit, see ¶2201 *et seq.*;

---

42. ¶L-17881.1;¶45S4.01   43. ¶L-17880 *et seq.*;¶45S4.01

- Pre-2018 nonbusiness energy property credit, see ¶2353;
- Residential energy efficient property credit (before 2022), see ¶2354;
- Pre-2018 new qualified fuel cell motor vehicle credit, see ¶2355;
- Pre-2018 credit for alternative fuel vehicle refueling property, see ¶2356;
- New qualified plug-in electric drive motor vehicles (NQPEDMV) credit, see ¶2357;
- Pre-2018 two-wheeled plug-in electric vehicle (QPEV) credit, see ¶2357;
- "Saver's" credit for elective deferrals and IRA contributions, see ¶2358;
- AMT credit, see ¶2360; and
- Credit for qualified tax credit bonds (QTCBs), see ¶2361.

For the limit on the combined amount of certain personal nonrefundable credits, see ¶2359.

For the treatment of a refund or advance payment of a refundable credit, see ¶4860.

¶ 2338 Earned income tax credit (EITC)—overview—Schedule EIC.

An eligible individual (¶2340) is allowed an EITC equal to the credit percentage of earned income (up to an "earned income amount") for the tax year. (Code Sec. 32(a)(1)) The EITC for a tax year (determined under IRS tables) can't be more than the excess (if any) of (1) the credit percentage of the earned income amount, over (2) the phaseout percentage of AGI (or earned income, if greater) over a phaseout amount. (Code Sec. 32(a)(2)) For 2018 and 2019 (as calculated by Thomson Reuters based on inflation data), these amounts are (phaseout amounts in table are for other than joint returns): [44]

FOR 2018

Qualifying Children:	The Credit % is:	The Earned Income Amount is:	The Phaseout % is:	The Phaseout Amount is:
No qualifying children	7.65%	$6,780	7.65%	$8,490
1 qualifying child	34%	$10,180	15.98%	$18,660
2 qualifying children	40%	$14,290	21.06%	$18,660
3 or more qualifying children	45%	$14,290	21.06%	$18,660

The 2018 phaseout amounts for joint filers are $14,170 for no qualifying children, and $24,350 for one or more qualifying children. [45]

The maximum EITC for 2018 is $519 (no qualifying children), $3,461 (one qualifying child), $5,716 (two qualifying children), and $6,431 (three or more qualifying children). [46] It's completely phased out at the following amounts of earned income (or AGI, if greater):

. . . no qualifying children, $15,270 ($20,950 for joint filers),

. . . one qualifying child, $40,320 ($46,010 for joint filers), and

. . . two qualifying children, $45,802 ($51,492 for joint filers).

. . . three or more qualifying children, $49,194 ($54,884 for joint filers). [47]

---

44. ¶A-4201 *et seq.*; ¶324 *et seq.*
45. ¶A-4202; ¶324.01

46. ¶A-4201; ¶324.01
47. ¶A-4202

FOR 2019

Qualifying Children:	The Credit % is:	The Earned Income Amount is:	The Phaseout % is:	The Phaseout Amount is:
No qualifying children	7.65%	$6,920	7.65%	$8,650
1 qualifying child	34%	$10,370	15.98%	$19,030
2 qualifying children	40%	$14,570	21.06%	$19,030
3 or more qualifying children	45%	$14,570	21.06%	$19,030

The 2019 phaseout amounts for joint filers are $14,450 for no qualifying children, and $24,820 for one or more qualifying children. [48]

The maximum EITC for 2019 is $529 (no qualifying children), $3,526 (one qualifying child), $5,828 (two qualifying children), and $6,557 (three or more qualifying children). [49] It's completely phased out at the following amounts of earned income (or AGI, if greater):

... no qualifying children, $15,565 ($21,365 for joint filers),

... one qualifying child, $41,095 ($46,885 for joint filers), and

... two qualifying children, $46,703 ($52,493 for joint filers).

... three or more qualifying children, $50,164 ($55,954 for joint filers). [50]

Taxpayers claiming the credit must file Form 1040 and attach Schedule EIC. [1] No EITC is allowed if the taxpayer has excess disqualified income, see ¶2341.

The EITC is refundable. [2]

No EITC is allowed for 10 years after a year in which the credit was claimed fraudulently (2 years for erroneously claimed credit due to reckless or intentional disregard of the rules). If the EITC is denied under deficiency procedures, including administrative procedures (but not mathematical or clerical errors), no credit is allowed for any later tax year unless the taxpayer provides information IRS requires to demonstrate eligibility (Code Sec. 32(k); Reg § 1.32-3(b)) (use Form 8862). (Reg § 1.32-3(c))[3] For due diligence requirements for return preparers, see ¶4890.

¶ 2339　Earned income defined for earned income tax credit (EITC) purposes.

Earned income for EITC purposes includes wages, salaries, tips, and other employee compensation, but only if those amounts are includible in gross income for the tax year; plus net earnings from self-employment less the Code Sec. 164(f) deduction for half of self-employment tax (¶1747), for the year. (Code Sec. 32(c)(2)(A)) Taxpayers may elect to treat nontaxable combat pay (¶1222) as earned income. (Code Sec. 32(c)(2)(B)(vi))[4]

If the earned income of a "qualified individual" (one whose principal place of abode on the "applicable date" —Aug. 23, 2017 for Hurricane Harvey, Sept. 4, 2017 for Hurricane Irma, and Sept. 16, 2017 Hurricane Maria —was either (a) located in that hurricane's Disaster Zone; or (b) located in its Disaster Area and the individual was displaced from the principal place of abode due to the hurricane) in the tax year that includes the "applicable date" is lower than the taxpayer's earned income for the preceding tax year, the individual

48. ¶A-4202; ¶324.01
49. ¶A-4201; ¶324.01
50. ¶A-4202
1. ¶A-4201; ¶324.01

2. ¶A-4201; ¶324.01
3. ¶A-4205 *et seq.*; ¶324.02
4. ¶A-4222 *et seq.*; ¶324.05

can elect to substitute the preceding year's earned income amount. (Sec. 504(c), PL 115-63, 9/29/2017) Similar relief applies for "qualified individuals" (any individual whose principal place of abode during any portion of the period from Oct. 8, 2017, to Dec. 31, 2017, was located (a) in the California wildfire disaster zone, or (b) in the California wildfire disaster area—but outside the California wildfire disaster zone —and such individual was displaced from the principal place of abode due to the applicable wildfires) affected by California wildfires. (Sec. 20104(c), PL 115-123, 2/09/2018)

Earned income is reduced by any net loss in earnings from self-employment (Reg § 1.32-2(c)(2)) and *doesn't* include any amount received as a pension or an annuity (including social security or VA benefits), any amount subject to the 30% withholding tax on U.S. income (not connected with U.S. business) of nonresident alien individuals (Code Sec. 32(c)(2)(B)), unemployment or worker's compensation (Reg § 1.32-2(c)(2)), amounts earned while an inmate in a penal institution, or amounts received for "workfare" services to the extent subsidized by a state program. (Code Sec. 32(c)(2)(B)(iv)) Earned income is determined without regard to community property laws. (Code Sec. 32(c)(2))[5]

¶ 2340   Eligible individual defined for earned income tax credit (EITC) purposes.

An individual who has a "qualifying child" (¶2342) for the tax year is an eligible individual. (Code Sec. 32(c)(1)(A)(i)) An individual who doesn't have a qualifying child for the tax year is an eligible individual *if*:

. . . the individual's principal place of abode is in the U.S. for more than half the tax year (U.S. Armed Forces personnel are considered to have a U.S. abode while stationed outside the U.S. on extended active duty (Code Sec. 32(c)(4))),

. . . the individual or spouse (if any) is older than 24 but younger than 65 before the end of the tax year, *and*

. . . the individual can't be claimed as another's dependent for a tax year beginning in the same calendar year as the individual's tax year. (Code Sec. 32(c)(1)(A)(ii))[6]

An individual can't be an eligible individual for a tax year if the individual: is another's qualifying child (¶2342) (Code Sec. 32(c)(1)(B)); elects to exclude foreign earned income (¶4605) (Code Sec. 32(c)(1)(C)); or is a nonresident alien (unless the individual elects under Code Sec. 6013(g) or Code Sec. 6013(h) to be treated as a U.S. resident). (Code Sec. 32(c)(1)(D))[7]

Married individuals are eligible for only one EITC on their combined earned income and must file a joint return to claim the credit. (Code Sec. 32(d)) IRS will not follow a Tax Court decision which, contrary to the Code, allowed the credit to a married taxpayer filing separately. [8]

Except for short-period returns due to an individual's death, only individuals filing a return for a full 12-month year can claim the credit. (Code Sec. 32(e))[9]

To qualify as an eligible individual, a taxpayer must include the taxpayer identification number (TIN: social security number, not an individual taxpayer identification number (ITIN) or adoption taxpayer identification number (ATIN)) of the taxpayer and spouse, and the name, age, and TIN (not ITIN or ATIN) of any qualifying child on the return for the tax year. (Code Sec. 32(m), Code Sec. 32(c)(1)(E), Code Sec. 32(c)(1)(F), Code Sec. 32(c)(3)(D))[10]

---

5. ¶A-4222 *et seq.*; ¶324.05
6. ¶A-4209, A-4217; ¶324.02
7. ¶A-4209; ¶324.02

8. ¶A-4221; ¶324.02
9. ¶A-4209; ¶324.02
10. ¶A-4219; ¶324.02

¶ 2341   No earned income tax credit (EITC) for individuals with excessive investment income.

A taxpayer with "disqualified income" over $3,500 for 2018 ($3,600 for 2019, as calculated by Thomson Reuters based on inflation data) can't claim the EITC. (Code Sec. 32(i)(1))[11]

Disqualified income means:

(1) interest or dividends to the extent includible in gross income for the year (Code Sec. 32(i)(2)(A));

(2) tax-exempt interest (as defined for return disclosure rules) received or accrued in the year (Code Sec. 32(i)(2)(B));

(3) the excess (if any) of (a) gross income from nonbusiness rents or royalties, over (b) the sum of noninterest deductions clearly and directly allocable to that gross income plus properly allocable interest deductions (Code Sec. 32(i)(2)(C));

(4) capital gain net income for the year (but not gain treated as long-term capital gain under Code Sec. 1231(a)(1), ¶2669) (Code Sec. 32(i)(2)(D)); and

(5) the excess, if any, of total income from all passive activities for the year (without regard to amounts otherwise included in earned income, or other disqualified income) over total losses from all passive activities for the year (as so determined). (Code Sec. 32(i)(2)(E))[12]

¶ 2342   Qualifying child defined for earned income tax credit (EITC) purposes.

A "qualifying child" for EITC purposes means a qualifying child of the taxpayer, as defined for the dependency exemption in Code Sec. 152(c) (¶3114) but without the requirement that the child not have provided more than half of the child's own support, and without regard to a custodial parent's release of the dependency exemption (¶3120). (Code Sec. 32(c)(3)(A))[13]

¶ 2343   Health coverage tax credit (HCTC) for health insurance costs of eligible individuals—Form 8885.

Before Jan. 1, 2020 (Code Sec. 35(b)(1)(B)), an "eligible individual" can elect (file Form 8885 with Form 1040) a refundable HCTC equal to 72.5% of the amount paid by the taxpayer for "qualified health insurance" coverage of the taxpayer and qualifying family members (spouse and dependents (Code Sec. 35(d)) for eligible coverage months beginning in the tax year. (Code Sec. 35(a))[14] Qualified health insurance includes individual health insurance, COBRA continuation coverage, VEBA coverage, and certain state-based coverage options. Individual health insurance *excludes* coverage enrolled in through an Exchange established under the Affordable Care Act. (Code Sec. 35(e)) Qualifying family members can claim the HCTC for up to 24 months after the eligible individual enrolled in Medicare, divorces, or dies. (Code Sec. 35(g)(10))[15]

A taxpayer can't receive the HCTC for any eligible coverage month unless the taxpayer elects application of the HCTC rules for that month no later than the due date (including extensions) for the tax return for the tax year. (Code Sec. 35(g)(11))[16]

Eligibility is determined on a monthly basis. An "eligible individual" is an (1) "eligible

---

11. ¶A-4204; ¶324.02
12. ¶A-4205; ¶324.02
13. ¶A-4210 *et seq.*; ¶324.02

14. ¶A-4231 *et seq.*; ¶354
15. ¶A-4235.3; ¶354
16. ¶A-4239.2

Trade Adjustment Allowance (TAA) recipient" as defined in Code Sec. 35(c)(2),[17] (2) "eligible alternative TAA recipient" as defined in Code Sec. 35(c)(3),[18] or (3) "eligible PBGC pension recipient" (i.e., an individual who has reached age 55 as of the first day of the month (but isn't entitled to Medicare), and is receiving a benefit for the month that is, in any part, paid by the Pension Benefit Guaranty Corporation (PBGC) under title IV of the Employee Retirement Income Security Act of '74, dealing with plan terminations (Code Sec. 35(c)(4))). (Code Sec. 32(c)(1))[19]

A month is an eligible coverage month if on the first day of the month the taxpayer is an "eligible individual," is covered by qualified health insurance for which the individual paid the premium, doesn't have other specified subsidized coverage (defined in Code Sec. 35(f)), and isn't imprisoned under federal, state, or local authority. (Code Sec. 35(b))[20]

Married taxpayers filing separate returns can claim the credit. For joint returns, the eligibility requirements are considered met for any month if one spouse meets them. [21]

An individual who can be claimed as a dependent on another's tax return can't claim the HCTC. (Code Sec. 35(g)(4))[22]

¶ 2344   Premium tax credit (PTC) for health insurance purchased on Exchange— Form 8962.

Individuals whose household income is within certain limits and who aren't eligible for other qualifying coverage or "affordable" employer-sponsored health insurance plans that provide "minimum value," are allowed a refundable PTC (known as a health care affordability tax credit or premium assistance credit) to subsidize the purchase of certain health insurance plans through a State-established American Health Benefit Exchange (Code Sec. 36B(a), Code Sec. 36B(c)(1)) or, as provided in regs (and upheld by the Supreme Court), through federally-facilitated Exchanges. (Reg § 1.36B-1(k)) (Code Sec. 36B(c)(1)(C))[23]

The amount of the PTC is the lesser of: (a) the premiums for the plan or plans in which the taxpayer or one or more members of the taxpayer's family enroll; or (b) the excess of the premiums for the applicable second lowest cost "silver plan" covering the taxpayer's family offered by the Exchange, over the taxpayer's contribution amount. The taxpayer's contribution amount (i.e., "required share") is determined by multiplying the taxpayer's household income by an applicable percentage for the tax year. That percentage is based on the taxpayer's income level relative to the federal poverty line (FPL), subject to a "fail safe" adjustment after 2018, under which the post-2018 inflation adjustment applies for a calendar year only if the aggregate amount of PTCs and cost-sharing reductions for the preceding calendar year exceeds 0.504% of the gross domestic product for the preceding calendar year. IRS has determined that the fail safe exception applies for 2019, so no additional adjustment is required for 2019. (Code Sec. 36B(b)(2),Code Sec. 36B(b)(3))[24]

An individual is eligible for the PTC if the individual:

. . . purchases coverage through an Exchange;

. . . has household income (see below) that falls between 100% and 400% of the FPL for a family of the size involved. Eligibility for the credit is based on the FPL for the preceding year, so eligibility for a credit in 2018 is determined based on household income and FPL guidelines for 2017 —e.g., for the 48 contiguous states and Washington, D.C. (separate figures apply for Alaska and Hawaii), household income between $12,060 and $48,240 for one individual; between $16,240 and $64,960 for a family of two; and between

17. ¶A-4232; ¶354
18. ¶A-4233; ¶354
19. ¶A-4234; ¶354
20. ¶A-4231; ¶354

21. ¶A-4231; ¶354
22. ¶A-4231; ¶354
23. ¶A-4241.0 *et seq.*; ¶36B4.01 *et seq.*
24. ¶A-4243.5 *et seq.*; ¶36B4.02 *et seq.*

$24,600 and $98,400 for a family of four.

recommendation: Because the 400% limitation is a "cliff" (e.g., a taxpayer whose income is 401% of FPL doesn't qualify for any credit), taxpayers who qualify for the credit should determine whether they are close to the 400% limit and, if so, consider trying to reduce their household income.

. . . isn't able to get "affordable coverage" through an eligible employer plan that provides "minimum value";

. . . isn't actually enrolled in an employer-sponsored plan (regardless of minimum value or affordability);

. . . isn't eligible for coverage through a government program, such as Medicaid, Medicare, TRICARE or CHIP (but mere eligibility, without actual enrollment, for Medicaid or CHIP based on the pregnancy of a woman enrolled in a qualified health plan, or eligibility for CHIP "buy-in" programs, won't disqualify the individual from taking the credit);

. . . files a joint return, if married (however, taxpayers who are victims of domestic violence or spousal abandonment that file married filing separately will meet this requirement, limited to a 3-consecutive-year period) (Reg § 1.36B-2(b)(2)); and

. . . isn't claimed as a dependent by another person. (Code Sec. 36B)[25]

observation: Although the dependency exemption is suspended from 2018 to 2025 (¶3112), Code Sec. 151(d)(5)(B) provides that this suspension isn't taken into account in determining whether a deduction for personal exemptions is "allowed" or "allowable."

Household income is an individual's modified adjusted gross income (MAGI) plus the aggregate MAGIs of all other individuals who; (a) are counted in determining the taxpayer's family size (i.e., taxpayer, spouse, and dependents); and (b) are required to file an income tax return for the tax year. For this purpose, MAGI doesn't include Supplemental Security Income (SSI). (Code Sec. 36B(d)(2); Reg § 1.36B-1(e)(1))

An employee who is provided a "qualified small employer health reimbursement arrangement" (QSEHRA, or small employer HRA, as defined in Code Sec. 9831(d)(2)) that qualifies as "affordable coverage" for any given coverage month isn't eligible for a PTC for that month. (Code Sec. 36B(c)(4)(A)) But if the QSEHRA doesn't constitute affordable coverage, the employee is eligible for a PTC for a coverage month, but the amount of the PTC is reduced under Code Sec. 36B(c)(4)(C).[26]

An eligible employer-sponsored plan is "affordable" if the portion of the annual premium the employee must pay for self-only coverage doesn't exceed 9.56% for the 2018 plan year (9.86% for the 2019 plan year) of the taxpayer's household income. (Code Sec. 36B(c)(2)(C); Reg § 1.36B-2(c)(3)(v))[27]

An employer-sponsored plan provides minimum value if the plan covers at least 60% of the expected total allowed costs for covered services. (Code Sec. 36B(c)(2)(C)(ii), Reg § 1.36B-2(c)(3)(vi)) Employers must provide employees with a summary of benefits and coverage that indicates whether the plan provides minimum value. [28]

The PTC is generally payable in advance by the Exchange directly to the insurer on the individual's behalf, with the taxpayer reconciling, on a timely filed return, the actual credit due to the taxpayer. Or, individuals can elect to purchase health insurance out-of-pocket and apply to IRS for the credit at the end of the tax year. Either way, an individual must file an income tax return with Form 8962 attached to claim the credit for the year. If a taxpayer's credit amount exceeds the advance payments paid, the taxpayer may receive

---

25. ¶A-4243 *et seq.*; ¶36B4.01 *et seq.*
26. ¶A-4246; ¶36B4.01

27. ¶A-4246.2B *et seq.*; ¶36B4.03
28. ¶A-4246.2B *et seq.*; ¶36B4.03

the excess as an income tax refund. If the advance payment exceeds the credit amount, the taxpayer owes the excess as an additional tax liability (with certain inflation-adjusted repayment limitations on repayment for taxpayers with household income under 400% of the FPL).[29]

By Jan. 31 of the year after the year of coverage, the Exchange must send individuals an information statement (on Form 1095A) showing the amount of their premiums and advance PTC payments. Individuals should notify the Exchange about changes in circumstances that can affect the amount of the PTC (e.g., increases or decreases in household income; marriage; divorce; birth or adoption of a child; other changes to a household composition; and gaining or losing eligibility for employer-sponsored or government-sponsored health care coverage). (Code Sec. 36B(f)(2), Reg § 1.36B-4(a)(3))[30]

IRS has provided special rules on the interplay between a self-employed individual's deduction of health insurance costs under Code Sec. 162(l) and the PTC. (Reg § 1.36B-4(a)(3)(iii), Reg § 1.162(l)-1(a)) In that situation, two optional methods can be used to compute the credit.[31]

¶ 2345   Credit for income tax withheld.

The recipient of wages, pensions, annuities, gambling winnings, etc., is allowed a credit for the amount of income tax withheld from those amounts in a calendar year, for the last tax year beginning in that calendar year. (Code Sec. 31(a); Reg § 1.31-1(a))[32] For amounts withheld under the backup withholding rules (¶3044 *et seq.*), the credit is allowed for the tax year in which the income is received. (Code Sec. 31(c))[33]

If spouses file separate returns, each must claim credit for the actual amount of tax withheld from salary or wages. In a community property state, each spouse may claim a credit for half the tax withheld on community wages. (Code Sec. 31(a); Reg § 1.31-1(a))[34]

¶ 2346   Credit for excess social security tax withheld.

If more than the maximum social security tax (¶1108) is withheld from an employee's wages for a calendar year because the employee worked for two or more employers, the excess is a credit against income tax on the employee's return for the year. (Code Sec. 31(b)(1), Code Sec. 6413(c)(1); Reg § 1.31-2(a)(2), Reg § 31.6413(c)-1) If two spouses both work, the ceiling is applied separately to each. If more than the maximum was withheld by one employer, the employee can't claim the credit; the employer must refund the over-collection.[35]

¶ 2347   Credit for the elderly and permanently and totally disabled—Schedule R.

The credit is available to a "qualified individual" —i.e., one who: (1) is 65 or older at the end of the tax year, or (2) is under 65 at the end of the tax year, retired on permanent and total disability, received taxable disability income during the tax year, and hasn't reached mandatory retirement age on the first day of the tax year. (Code Sec. 22(b))[36]

Permanently and totally disabled means the individual is unable to engage in any substantial gainful activity because of a medically determinable physical or mental impairment that can be expected to result in death, or that has lasted or can be expected to last for a continuous period of at least 12 months. (Code Sec. 22(e)(3))[37] IRS requires a physician's statement (part of Schedule R of Form 1040 or Form 1040A) certifying the disability

29. ¶A-4241 *et seq.*; ¶36B4.01
30. ¶A-4248 *et seq.*; ¶36B4.06
31. ¶A-4248.1A, ¶L-3511.1
32. ¶A-4005 *et seq.*; ¶314.01
33. ¶J-9009; ¶s 314.01, 34,064

34. ¶A-4006; ¶314.01
35. ¶A-4002; ¶314.02
36. ¶A-4101; ¶224
37. ¶A-4102; ¶224.02

to be kept as part of taxpayer's records (but not filed). For joint returns, the statement is required for each spouse under 65 who is retired on permanent and total disability. [38]

Disability income is gross income from amounts received as (or in lieu of) wages while out of work due to a permanent and total disability. (Code Sec. 22(c)(2))[39]

Married individuals must file jointly to claim the credit unless they qualify as married living apart, ¶3126. (Code Sec. 22(e)(1)) A nonresident alien (NRA) isn't eligible for the credit (Code Sec. 22(f)), unless the NRA has a U.S. spouse and elects under Code Sec. 6013(g) or Code Sec. 6013(h) to be treated as a U.S. resident. (Reg § 1.37-1(d))[40]

The credit is 15% of an "initial amount" (Step 1 below), reduced by amounts based on the taxpayer's AGI (Step 2) and on the taxpayer's income from tax-free pensions and annuities (Step 3) (for Form 1040, use Schedule R):

Step (1): The "initial amount" is:

. . . $5,000 for a single person, 65 or over;

. . . $5,000 for spouses filing jointly, one spouse is a qualified individual, 65 or over;

. . . $7,500 for spouses filing jointly, both spouses are qualified individuals, 65 or over;

. . . $3,750 for a married person, 65 or over, filing separately. (Code Sec. 22(c)(2)(A))

For *individuals under 65*, the "initial amount" is the *lesser* of the above initial amount, or:

- single persons/married filing separately: taxpayer's disability income for the year;

- joint returns, both spouses under 65 and disabled: spouses' combined disability incomes;

- joint returns, one spouse under 65 and disabled, other spouse 65 or older: sum of $5,000 plus disabled spouse's disability income;

- joint returns, both spouses under 65, one spouse disabled: disabled spouse's disability income. (Code Sec. 22(c)(2)(B))

Step (2): If AGI exceeds a threshold amount ($7,500 for single persons; $10,000 for joint returns; $5,000 for married filing separately), the "initial amount" must be reduced by one-half of the excess. (Code Sec. 22(d)) The reduction applies regardless of the taxpayer's age.

⊘observation: Step (2) eliminates the credit for joint filers at AGI of $25,000 (both spouses 65 or over) or $20,000 (if one is), and for a single person at AGI of $17,500.

Step (3): The initial amount as adjusted under Step (2) must be further reduced by the sum of the amounts received by the individual (for a joint return, by either spouse) as a pension or annuity or as a disability benefit that's: (a) excluded from gross income and payable under title II of the Social Security Act, the Railroad Retirement Act, or a law administered by the VA; or (b) excluded from gross income under any non-Code provision of law. (Code Sec. 22(c)(3)(A))[41] Social security benefits (¶1277) (Code Sec. 86(f)(1)) and worker's compensation that reduces such benefits (Code Sec. 22(c)(3)(B)) are received as a pension or annuity. [42]

---

38. ¶A-4102
39. ¶A-4103; ¶224.02
40. ¶A-4101

41. ¶A-4105, A-4106; ¶224.02
42. ¶A-4107; ¶224.02

¶ 2348   Credit for household and dependent care expenses—Form 2441.

The credit may be claimed by an individual taxpayer (on Form 2441) who: (1) has one or more qualifying individuals and (2) incurs employment-related expenses enabling the taxpayer to be gainfully employed. (Code Sec. 21(a)(1); Reg § 1.21-1(a))[43]

The credit is equal to 35% of employment-related expenses, for taxpayers with AGI of $15,000 or less. The percentage decreases by 1% for each $2,000 (or fraction) of AGI over $15,000, but not below 20%. (Code Sec. 21(a)(1), Code Sec. 21(a)(2); Reg 1.21-1(a))[44] The maximum amount of employment-related expenses that may be used to compute the credit is $3,000 for one qualifying individual, or $6,000 for two or more qualifying individuals. (Code Sec. 21(c); Reg § 1.21-2(a)(1)) These maximums must be reduced, dollar-for-dollar, by the total amount excludable from gross income under Code Sec. 129 (dependent care assistance exclusion, ¶1268). (Code Sec. 21(c); Reg § 1.21-2(a))[45]

An otherwise eligible taxpayer may claim the credit for a qualifying individual who lives with the taxpayer for more than half the year, even if the taxpayer doesn't provide more than half the household maintenance costs. (Code Sec. 21(a); Reg § 1.21-1(b))[46]

Qualifying individuals for a taxpayer's dependent care credit are:

. . . a taxpayer's under-age-13 dependent (as defined in Code Sec. 152(a)(1) for the dependency exemption, ¶3114) (Code Sec. 21(b)(1)(A), Reg § 1.21-1(b)(1));

. . . a taxpayer's dependent who is physically or mentally incapable of self care and who has the same principal place of abode as the taxpayer for more than half the tax year. For this purpose, "dependent" is defined in Code Sec. 152 (¶3113), but without the gross income test for qualifying relatives, the rule that a joint filer can't be a dependent, and the rule that a dependent can't have dependents (Code Sec. 21(b)(1)(B); Reg § 1.21-1(b)(1)); or

. . . the taxpayer's spouse, if the spouse is physically or mentally incapable of self care and has the same principal place of abode as the taxpayer for more than half the tax year. (Code Sec. 21(b)(1)(C); Reg § 1.21-1(b)(1))[47]

Employment-related expenses qualifying for the credit are expenses for household services or for the care of qualifying individuals that are incurred to enable the taxpayer to be gainfully employed (for earned income limit, see below). Costs of a housekeeper, maid, babysitter, or cook ordinarily qualify. (Code Sec. 21(b)(2)(B); Reg § 1.21-1(d))[48]

Payments for services provided outside the taxpayer's household count only if incurred for a qualifying individual who either is a dependent under age 13, or regularly spends at least 8 hours each day in taxpayer's household. (Code Sec. 21(b)(2)(B); Reg § 1.21-1(e)(1))[49] Also, for services performed by a *dependent care center*, the center must comply with all applicable state or local laws and regs. (Code Sec. 21(b)(2)(C); Reg § 1.21-1(e)(2))[50]

➢ *observation:* The credit isn't available for expenses of full institutional care unless incurred for a dependent under age 13.

Payments to taxpayer's relatives or household members don't qualify if the person paid is: a dependent (under Code Sec. 151(c)) of the taxpayer or spouse, a child of the taxpayer (under Code Sec. 152(f)(1)) under 19 at the end of the tax year, taxpayer's spouse, or the parent of taxpayer's child who's a qualifying individual. (Code Sec. 21(e)(6); Reg § 1.21-4(a))[1]

43. ¶A-4301 *et seq.*; ¶214
44. ¶A-4301; ¶214
45. ¶A-4302, A-4303; ¶214.04
46. ¶A-4301; ¶214.03
47. ¶A-4312; ¶214.02

48. ¶A-4319 *et seq.*; ¶214.03
49. ¶A-4325; ¶214.03
50. ¶A-4327; ¶214.03
1. ¶A-4331; ¶214.01

The amount of employment-related expenses that may be taken into account can't exceed: (1) for an individual who isn't married at the end of the tax year, the individual's earned income, or (2) for an individual who is married at the end of the tax year, the lesser of individual's, or spouse's, earned income for the year (even if married for only part of the year). (Code Sec. 21(d)(1); Reg § 1.21-2(b))[2]

A spouse who is a full-time student or who is a qualifying individual because incapable of self-care is deemed to have earned income of $250 per month if there's one qualifying individual in the household, and $500 a month if there are two or more qualifying individuals. But this deemed earned income rule applies to only one spouse for any given month. (Code Sec. 21(d)(2); Reg § 1.21-2(b)(4))[3]

The credit is available to married couples only on a joint return. (Code Sec. 21(e)(2); Reg § 1.21-3(a))[4] A married individual living apart from a spouse may claim the credit on a separate return if the individual maintains a household for which the individual furnishes over half the maintenance costs for the tax year, the household is a qualifying individual's principal place of abode for more than half the tax year, and the other spouse is absent for the last six months of the tax year. (Code Sec. 21(e)(4), Reg § 1.21-3(b))[5]

Divorced or legally separated parents claim the credit for a child under under age 13 or physically or mentally incapable of self-care as follows: if the child receives more than half the child's support during the year from the child's parents, and is in the custody of one or both of the parents for more than half the calendar year, the child is a qualifying individual for the parent with longer custody. That parent may claim the credit even if that parent can't claim the child as a dependent and even if that parent released the dependency exemption (¶3120) to the other parent. (Code Sec. 21(e)(5); Reg § 1.21-1(b)(5))[6]

The care provider's name, address, and taxpayer identification number (TIN) must be included on taxpayer's return. The TIN isn't required for tax-exempt care providers (write "tax-exempt" instead). (Code Sec. 21(e)(9)) The care provider should give this information and certify the TIN on Form W-10. If the care provider doesn't comply with a request, the taxpayer should furnish whatever information is available, and include a statement that the other required information was requested but wasn't given. (Code Sec. 21(e)(9))[7]

No credit is permitted for a qualifying individual unless the individual's TIN is included on the return claiming the credit. (Code Sec. 21(e)(10))[8]

¶ 2349 Adoption expense credit rules—Form 8839.

An individual may claim a credit (use Form 8839 with Form 1040) for qualified adoption expenses (Code Sec. 23(a)(1)), which are reasonable and necessary adoption fees, court costs, attorney fees, and other expenses that are directly related to and the principal purpose of which is for the taxpayer's legal adoption of an eligible child (an individual under age 18, or physically or mentally incapable of self-care.) (Code Sec. 23(d)) The credit is a nonrefundable personal credit allowed against the income tax and alternative minimum tax. The total amount that may be taken as a credit for all tax years for the adoption of a child is $13,810 for 2018 ($14,080 for 2019, as calculated by Thomson Reuters based on inflation data). (Code Sec. 23(b)(1))[9]

For 2018, phaseout begins with amounts over $207,140 and the credit is fully eliminated at $247,140 (for 2019, credit phases out over $211,170 to $251,170, as calculated by Thomson Reuters based on inflation data). (Code Sec. 23(b)(2))[10]

---

2. ¶A-4304, A-4305; ¶214.05
3. ¶A-4306; ¶214.06
4. ¶ A-4310; ¶214.07
5. ¶A-4311; ¶214.07
6. ¶A-4314; ¶214.07

7. ¶A-4334; ¶214.09
8. ¶A-4333; ¶214
9. ¶A-4401, A-4407, A-4410; ¶234
10. ¶A-4404; ¶234

If the expenses are paid or incurred before the tax year the adoption becomes final, the credit is allowed for the year after the year when they're paid or incurred. For expenses paid or incurred during or after the tax year the adoption becomes final, the credit is allowed for the year they're paid or incurred. (Code Sec. 23(a)(2))[11]

For an adoption of a child with special needs (defined in Code Sec. 23(d)(3)), the taxpayer is treated as having paid (in the tax year the adoption becomes final) the maximum credit amount regardless of actual expenses. (Code Sec. 23(a)(3))[12]

The credit's not allowed for a foreign adoption unless it becomes final. Expenses paid or incurred in the tax year the adoption is finalized or in earlier years are allowed in the year finalized. Expenses paid or incurred after that year are taken into account when paid or incurred. (Code Sec. 23(e)) Taxpayers may treat certain adoptions as final if the competent authority enters a decree of adoption or a home state enters a decree of re-adoption. Under a safe harbor, IRS won't challenge another country's treatment of an adoption as final if it enters a final decree of adoption, or the Secretary of State issues a specified certificate. [13]

No adoption expense credit is allowed if a deduction or credit (or exclusion, ¶1252) is otherwise allowed, or government funds are received, for the expense. (Code Sec. 23(b)(3)).[14]

To get the credit, married individuals must file jointly (unless legally separated or living apart). (Code Sec. 23(f)(1))[15] The taxpayer's return must include (if known) the name, age and taxpayer identification number (TIN) of the child. (Code Sec. 23(f)(2))[16]

If the adoption expense credit exceeds the "applicable limitation" (i.e., the limit imposed by Code Sec. 26(a), ¶2359, for the tax year, reduced by nonrefundable personal credits other than the adoption expense credit, the residential energy efficient property credit, and the prior-law D.C. first-time homebuyer's credit) for the year, the excess is carried over to each of the next five years. (Code Sec. 23(c)(1))[17]

¶ 2350   Child tax credit (CTC).

From 2018 to 2025, a taxpayer may claim a CTC (on Form 1040) for each "qualifying child" of $2,000 per qualifying child, as well as a partial credit for each dependent of the taxpayer other than a qualifying child, see below. (Code Sec. 24(a); Code Sec. 24(c))[18]

A "qualifying child" is a qualifying child of the taxpayer as defined in Code Sec. 152(c), who is under 17 and a U.S. citizen or resident alien. (Code Sec. 24(c))[19]

From 2018 to 2025, the CTC is phased out for taxpayers with modified adjusted gross income (MAGI) above $400,000 for joint filers and $200,000 for all others, (Code Sec. 24(b))[20] and no CTC is allowed for a child for a tax year unless the taxpayer's return includes the child's name and taxpayer identification number (TIN). (Code Sec. 24(e))[21]

From 2018 to 2025, a $500 nonrefundable credit is available for each dependent (as defined in Code Sec. 152) of the taxpayer other than a qualifying child, who is a U.S. citizen, national or resident. (Code Sec. 24(h)(4)(A)) This "partial" credit can also be claimed for a qualifying child for whom the full credit under Code Sec. 24(a) is not allowed because taxpayer didn't include a TIN. (Code Sec. 24(h)(4))

---

11. ¶A-4402; ¶234
12. ¶A-4401; ¶234
13. ¶A-4402, A-4403; ¶234
14. ¶A-4409; ¶234
15. ¶A-4412, A-4413; ¶234
16. ¶A-4414; ¶234

17. ¶A-4406; ¶234
18. ¶A-4051; ¶244
19. ¶A-4053; ¶244
20. ¶A-4052; ¶244
21. ¶A-4059; ¶244

For refundability, see ¶2351.

No credit is allowed for a short tax year unless due to taxpayer's death. (Code Sec. 24(f))[22]

For limits on combined amount of nonrefundable personal credits, see ¶2359.

¶ 2351 Child tax credit (CTC) is partially refundable—Form 8812.

The CTC is refundable, but only to the extent of the *greater of*: (1) 15% of taxable earned income above $2,500 (above $3,000 for tax years after 2025), or (2) for a taxpayer with three or more qualifying children, the excess of the taxpayer's social security taxes for the tax year over the taxpayer's earned income tax credit (¶2338) for the year. For 2018 (and 2019, as calculated by Thomson Reuters based on inflation data), the refundable portion of the CTC for any qualifying child is limited to $1,400. For tax years after 2025, the $1,400 threshold doesn't apply.Credits for dependents who aren't qualifying children are nonrefundable. (Code Sec. 24(d); Code Sec. 24(h)) IRS calls the amount of the CTC that's refundable (on Schedule 8812, to Form 1040) the "additional child tax credit." A taxpayer who elects to exclude any amount from gross income under the Code Sec. 911 foreign earned income/foreign housing exclusions (¶4605, ¶4606) can't claim the refundable credit for that tax year. (Code Sec. 24(d)(3))[23]

Earned income is defined in Code Sec. 32 (¶2339), and includes amounts excluded from gross income under Code Sec. 112 (combat zone pay, see ¶1222). (Code Sec. 24(d)(1)) Certain victims of 2017 Hurricanes Harvey, Irma, and Maria who are "qualified individuals" may elect to use the previous year's earned income, if higher, for purposes of the child tax credit (¶2339) (Sec. 504(o), PL 115-63, 9/29/2017) Similar rules apply to qualified individuals who were victims of the 2017 California wildfires. (Sec. 20104, PL 115-123, 2/09/2018) [24]

¶ 2352 Credit for mortgage interest under the qualified mortgage credit (MCC) program—Form 8396, Form 8828.

Under a state or local government qualified MCC program, certificate holders claim a credit (on Form 8396) (Code Sec. 25) equal to the MCC rate multiplied by the interest paid or accrued by the taxpayer during the tax year on a mortgage. (Code Sec. 25(a)(1)) If the MCC rate exceeds 20%, the credit is limited to $2,000. (Code Sec. 25(a)(2)) A 3-year carryover is allowed for certain excess amounts. (Code Sec. 25(e))[25] The credit is subject to recapture on Form 8828 if the taxpayer sells or otherwise disposes of any interest in the residence within nine years after the mortgage was provided. (Code Sec. 143(m))[26] If the credit exceeds the applicable limitation for the year, the excess is carried over to each of the next three years. The applicable limitation is the limitation imposed by Code Sec. 26(a) (¶2359) for the tax year, reduced by the nonrefundable personal credits (other than the MCC credit, the adoption expense credit, the residential energy efficient property credit, and the D.C. first-time homebuyer credit) for the year. (Code Sec. 25(e)(1))[27]

¶ 2353 Nonbusiness energy property credit before 2018—Form 5695.

For property placed in service before 2018, a taxpayer may claim (on Form 5695) a nonbusiness energy property tax credit equal to the sum of: (1) 10% of the cost of "qualified energy efficiency improvements" under Code Sec. 25C(c) and (2) the amount of "residential energy property expenditures" under Code Sec. 25C(d). (Code Sec. 25C(a)) There is a lifetime credit limit of $500 (with no more than $200 due to windows and skylights) less

22. ¶A-4051; ¶244
23. ¶A-4055; ¶244.02
24. ¶A-4055; ¶244.02

25. ¶A-4008 *et seq.*; ¶254 *et seq.*
26. ¶I-4901 *et seq.*; ¶1434.02
27. ¶A-4010; ¶254.01

the total credits allowed to the taxpayer for all earlier tax years ending after 2005. (Code Sec. 25C(b)) The expenses had to be for property originally placed in service by the taxpayer and made on or in connection with a dwelling unit located in the U.S. owned and used by taxpayer as a principal residence (under the Code Sec. 121 homesale exclusion) at the time of installation. (Code Sec. 25C(c), Code Sec. 25C(d))[28]

caution: Check tax.thomsonreuters.com/federaltaxhandbookupdates to see if the above provision has been extended.

¶ 2354   **Residential energy efficient property (REEP) credit—Form 5695.**

For property placed in service before Jan. 1, 2020, an individual is allowed a nonrefundable 30% personal tax credit (on Form 5695) for the purchase of REEP —i.e., qualified solar electric property (that uses solar power to generate electricity in a home), qualified solar water heating property (i.e., property to heat water for use in a home if at least half of the energy it uses is derived from the sun), qualified fuel cell property (as defined in Code Sec. 48(c)(1), up to a maximum $500 credit for each 0.5 kilowatt (kw) of capacity), qualified small wind energy property (wind turbine to generate electricity for a home), and qualified geothermal heat pump expenses (to heat water for use in a residence if at least half of the energy used is derived from the sun). (Code Sec. 25D(a), Code Sec. 25D(d), Code Sec. 25D(g)) For property placed in service in 2020, the credit rate is 26%; and for property placed in service in 2021, the credit rate is 22%. (Code Sec. 25D(g))[29]

The REEP must be installed for use in a dwelling that's located in the U.S. and used as the taxpayer's residence (Code Sec. 25D(d)), and can't be used to heat a swimming pool or hot tub. (Code Sec. 25D(e)(3)) The credit can be claimed for either an existing home or a newly constructed home. A taxpayer can claim the credit for property described above that is installed on or in a second or vacation home. IRS has allowed the credit for the cost of solar panels (and a partial ownership interest in related equipment) installed in an off-site community-shared solar project. [30]

Taxpayers can rely on an appropriate manufacturer's certification that a component meets energy requirements, unless IRS withdraws it before taxpayer's purchase. [31]

The credit covers installation and labor costs (Code Sec. 25D(e)(1)) and includes sales tax. An expense is treated as made when the original installation is completed, except an expense for the construction or reconstruction of a structure is treated as made when the taxpayer's original use of the constructed or reconstructed structure begins. (Code Sec. 25D(e)(8))[32] If the equipment is used less than 80% for nonbusiness purposes, only the expenses properly allocable to nonbusiness use are taken into account. (Code Sec. 25D(e)(7))[33]

For the limit on the combined amount of certain personal nonrefundable credits, see ¶2359.

If the credit is allowed for an expense for a property, the basis increase is reduced by the credit allowed (¶2477). (Code Sec. 25D(f), Code Sec. 1016(a)(34))[34]

caution: Check tax.thomsonreuters.com/federaltaxhandbookupdates to see if the above provision has been extended.

---

28. ¶A-4751 *et seq.*; ¶25C4
29. ¶A-4781, A-4782; ¶25D4
30. ¶A-4782, A-4785; ¶25D4
31. ¶A-4782.1

32. ¶A-4783; ¶25D4
33. ¶A-4784; ¶25D4
34. ¶A-4788; ¶25D4

¶ 2355 New qualified fuel cell motor vehicle credit before 2018—Form 8910.

For the purchase of a fuel cell vehicle before 2018, taxpayers may claim (on Form 8910) a new qualified fuel cell motor vehicle credit (i.e., the alternative motor vehicle credit (AMVC)) for qualifying vehicles placed in service during the tax year. (Code Sec. 30B(a))

caution: Check tax.thomsonreuters.com/federaltaxhandbookupdates to see if the above provision has been extended.

The credit equals a base credit amount that depends upon the vehicle's weight class plus, for passenger cars or light trucks (vehicles weighing 8,500 pounds or less), an amount that depends upon the vehicle's rated fuel economy compared to a base fuel economy. A qualifying fuel cell vehicle has to be propelled by power derived from one or more cells that convert chemical energy directly into electricity by combining oxygen with hydrogen fuel stored on board the vehicle. (Code Sec. 30B(b))[35]

The credit is allowed to the vehicle's owner (or lessor) (Code Sec. 30B(b)) or, for vehicles sold to and used by certain tax-exempt entities, the seller. (Code Sec. 30B(h)(6))[36]

¶ 2356 Credit for alternative fuel vehicle property before 2018—Form 8911.

A taxpayer is allowed a tax credit against income tax for the tax year equal to 30% of the cost of any qualified alternative fuel vehicle refueling (QAFVR) property placed in service by the taxpayer before Jan. 1, 2018. (Code Sec. 30C(a), Code Sec. 30C(g)) The credit per tax year can't exceed $30,000 for depreciable property, and $1,000 for nondepreciable property. (Code Sec. 30C(b))[37]

caution: Check tax.thomsonreuters.com/federaltaxhandbookupdates to see if the above provision has been extended. F

QAFVR property—i.e., certain property for the storage or dispensing of a clean-burning fuel or electricity into the fuel tank or battery of a motor vehicle—is defined in repealed Code Sec. 179A (dealing with clean-fuel vehicles and certain refueling property) but with certain modifications, e.g., property installed on property used as the taxpayer's principal residence (under Code Sec. 121) didn't need to be depreciable. Property used outside the U.S. doesn't qualify. (Code Sec. 30C(c), Code Sec. 30C(e)(3))[38]

¶ 2357 Electric vehicle credit—Form 8936.

A taxpayer can claim (on Form 8936) a credit for each new qualified plug-in electric drive motor vehicle (NQPEDMV) placed in service during the tax year. (Code Sec. 30D(a))[39] For a conversion credit, see ¶2355.

To qualify for the credit, a vehicle must have a gross vehicle weight rating (GVWR) of less than 14,000 pounds; and be propelled to a significant extent by an electric motor that draws electricity from a battery that has a capacity of at least 4 kilowatt (kw) hours, and be capable of being recharged from an external source of electricity. (Code Sec. 30D(d)(1)) The taxpayer must be the original user of the vehicle (which must be used predominantly in the U.S. (Code Sec. 30D(f)(4)), and must have acquired it for use or lease and not for resale. (Code Sec. 30D(d)(1))[40] The vehicle must meet certain provisions of the Clean Air Act. (Code Sec. 30D(f)(7))

The amount of the NQPEDMV credit is the sum of: (1) $2,500; plus (2) for a vehicle that

---

35. ¶L-18024; ¶30B4.01
36. ¶L-18021; ¶30B4
37. ¶L-18046; ¶30C4

38. ¶L-18049; ¶30C4.02
39. ¶L-18031; ¶30D4
40. ¶L-18032.3; ¶30D4.04

draws propulsion energy from a battery with not less than five kw hours of capacity, $417 for each kw hour of capacity in excess of 5 kw hours, but not in excess of $5,000. Thus, the maximum credit is $7,500, regardless of weight. (Code Sec. 30D(b))[41]

The credit (as computed above) phases out beginning in the second calendar quarter following that in which a manufacturer sells its 200,000th plug-in electric drive motor vehicle for use in the U.S. after 2009 (50% credit reduction in second and third quarter; 75% in fourth and fifth quarter; 0 credit allowed thereafter). (Code Sec. 30D(e))[42]

Any portion of the credit attributable to depreciable property is treated as part of the general business credit (¶2301). The remaining portion is a nonrefundable personal credit. (Code Sec. 30D(c)(1))[43] For limits on combined amount of nonrefundable personal credits, see ¶2359.

The vehicle's basis, and any other allowable deduction or credit, must be reduced by the amount of the NQPEDMV credit allowed. (Code Sec. 30D(f)(1), Code Sec. 30D(f)(2))[44]

Qualified 2-wheeled plug-in electric vehicle credit before 2018. For property placed in service before 2018, a taxpayer may claim (on Form 8834) a credit equal to 10% of the cost of each qualified plug-in electric two-wheeled vehicle (QPEV) placed in service during the tax year and acquired in the tax year. The maximum credit for a vehicle is $2,500. (Code Sec. 30D(g))[45]

caution: Check tax.thomsonreuters.com/federaltaxhandbookupdates to see if the above provision has been extended.

¶ 2358   "Saver's" credit for elective deferrals and IRA contributions—Form 8880.

An eligible lower-income taxpayer can claim a nonrefundable credit (use Form 8880 with Form 1040) for a percentage of up to $2,000 of qualified retirement savings contributions—"the saver's credit." (Code Sec. 25B(a)) The applicable percentage (50%, 20%, or 10%) depends on filing status and AGI. (Code Sec. 25B(b))

For tax years beginning in 2018, the amounts are:

... Joint filers: $0 to $38,000, 50%; $38,000 to $41,000, 20%; and $41,000 to $63,000, 10% (no credit if AGI is above $63,000).

... Heads of households: $0 to $28,500, 50%; $28,500 to $30,750, 20%; and $30,750 to $47,250, 10% (no credit if AGI is above $47,250).

... All other filers: $0 to $19,000, 50%; $19,000 to $20,500, 20%; and $20,500 to $31,500, 10% (no credit if AGI is above $31,500).

For tax years beginning in 2019, the amounts are:

... Joint filers: $0 to $38,500, 50%; $38,500 to $41,500, 20%; and $41,500 to $64,000, 10% (no credit if AGI is above $64,000).

... Heads of household: $0 to $28,875, 50%; $28,875 to $31,125, 20%; and $31,125 to $48,000, 10% (no credit if AGI is above $48,000).

... All other filers: $0 to $19,250, 50%; $19,250 to $20,750, 20%; and $20,750 to $32,000, 10% (no credit if AGI is above $32,000).

The taxpayer's AGI is determined without regard to the foreign, possessions, and Puerto Rico income exclusions. (Code Sec. 25B(e))

41. ¶L-18031.2; ¶30D4.015   44. ¶L-18033.2, L-18033.3; ¶30D4.06
42. ¶L-18031.2; ¶30D4.02   45. ¶L-18041; ¶30D4.08
43. ¶L-18034, L-18034.1; ¶30D4.07

To be eligible, an individual must have reached age 18 by the end of the tax year, and can't be either a full-time student or claimed by another as a dependent for the tax year beginning in the calendar year the individual's tax year begins. (Code Sec. 25B(c))[46]

The credit applies to: elective contributions to Code Sec. 401(k) plan (including SIMPLE 401(k)), Code Sec. 403(b) annuity, Code Sec. 457 plan, SIMPLE IRA plan, or salary reduction SEP; contributions to traditional or Roth IRA; voluntary after-tax employee contributions to qualified retirement plan or Code Sec. 403(b) annuity; and, for amounts contributed in tax years beginning 2018 – 2025, contributions to ABLE account (¶2226) by designated beneficiary. (Code Sec. 25B(d)(1))[47] The credit is in addition to any otherwise applicable deduction or exclusion. [48][49]

The amount of any credit-eligible contribution is reduced (not below zero) by distributions received by the individual (and spouse, for joint returns) from any of the above savings arrangements during a testing period (i.e.: the tax year for which the credit is claimed, the two preceding tax years, and the period after the end of the tax year and before the due date (including extensions) for filing the taxpayer's return for that year) to the extent they're either taxable or are Roth IRA distributions that aren't rolled over. (Code Sec. 25B(d)(2)) Distributions listed in Code Sec. 25B(d)(2)(C), such as qualified plan loans not treated as distributions, don't reduce a credit-eligible contribution. [50]

For limits on the combined amount of nonrefundable personal credits, see ¶2359.

¶ 2359   Limit on combined amount of nonrefundable personal credits.

The total amount of nonrefundable personal credits (below) allowed for the tax year can't exceed the sum of: (1) the taxpayer's regular tax liability (below) for the tax year reduced by the foreign tax credit (¶2362), (Code Sec. 26(a)(1)) plus (2) the tax imposed by Code Sec. 55(a) (i.e., the alternative minimum tax (AMT)) for the year. (Code Sec. 26(a)(2)).[1]

observation: Thus, all otherwise allowable nonrefundable personal credits can be used to reduce AMT (as well as regular tax). Under this rule, the taxpayer can claim up to the amount of the sum of the regular tax and the AMT as nonrefundable personal credits.

observation: Allowing the nonrefundable personal credits to reduce AMT (as well as regular tax) benefits middle income individuals who: (a) have low taxable income (and thus a low regular tax); (b) are subject to the AMT because the standard deduction and certain itemized deductions generally aren't allowed in computing the AMT; and (c) have substantial nonrefundable personal credits such as the child tax credit.

The Code Sec. 26(a) limitation applies to the dependent care credit (¶2348); credit for the elderly and permanently and totally disabled (¶2347); adoption expense credit (¶2349); the child tax credit (¶2350); mortgage credit certificate (MCC) credit (¶2352); American Opportunity Tax Credit (AOTC) (¶2202) and Lifetime Learning credit (¶2203); saver's credit (¶2358); pre-2018 nonbusiness energy property credit (¶2353); residential energy efficient property (REEP) credit (¶2354); and the nonbusiness portions of: (a) the pre-2018 credit for 2-wheeled (pre-2014 for 3-wheeled) qualified plug-in electric vehicle (QPEV) credit, (b) the pre-2018 alternative motor vehicle credit (AMVC), ¶2355), (c) the new qualified plug-in electric drive motor vehicles property (NQPEDMV) credit (¶2357), and (d) the pre-2012 first-time D.C. homebuyer credit. [2]

---

46. ¶A-4452; ¶25B4
47. ¶A-4453; ¶25B4
48. ¶A-4451
49. ¶A-4451; ¶25B4

50. ¶A-4454; ¶25B4
1. ¶A-4901; ¶264
2. ¶A-4902; ¶264

observation: The limitation under Code Sec. 26(a) is the starting point for determining the credit carryover for the adoption expense, MCC, AOTC, REEP, and prior-law D.C. first-time homebuyer credits.

Regular tax liability means the tax imposed by Chapter 1 *except* (Code Sec. 26(b)): (1) AMT (Code Sec. 55); (2) penalty taxes on certain premature distributions (Code Sec. 72(m)(5)(B), Code Sec. 72(q), Code Sec. 72(t), Code Sec. 72(v)); (3) tax on nonqualified withdrawals from capital construction funds (Code Sec. 7518(g)(6)); (4) accumulated earnings tax (Code Sec. 531); (5) personal holding company tax (Code Sec. 541); (6) certain recoveries of foreign expropriation losses (Code Sec. 1351(d)(1)); (7) tax on certain built-in gains of S corp. (Code Sec. 1374); (8) tax on passive investment income of S corp. with Subchapter C E&P over 25% of gross receipts (Code Sec. 1375); (9) tax on transfers of high-yield interest to disqualified holders of financial asset securitization trusts (FASITs) (Former Code Sec. 860K); (10) 30% tax on U.S.-source income earned by nonresident aliens and foreign corporations (Code Sec. 871(a), Code Sec. 881); (11) interest, paid as additional income tax, imposed on tax deferred by: (a) installment sales of timeshares and residential lots, and (b) certain installment sales of nondealer property in excess of $150,000 (Code Sec. 453(l)(3), Code Sec. 453A(c)); (12) recapture of federal subsidy from use of mortgage bonds and mortgage credit certificates (Code Sec. 143(m)); (13) tax on transfers of residual interests in a real estate mortgage investment conduit (REMIC) to disqualified organization (Code Sec. 860E(e)); (14) branch profits tax (Code Sec. 884); (15) additional tax on distributions not used for medical purposes from Archer MSA, health savings account (HSA), and Medicare Advantage MSA (Code Sec. 220(f)(4), Code Sec. 223(f)(4), Code Sec. 138(c)(2)); (16) additional tax on distributions from Coverdell education savings accounts not used for higher education expenses (Code Sec. 530(d)(4)); (17) recapture of prior-law first-time homebuyer credit (Code Sec. 36(f)); (18) 10% penalty taxes for failure to maintain high deductible health plan (HDHP) coverage, including: (i) tax for rollovers from flexible spending accounts and health reimbursement accounts into HSAs, (Code Sec. 106(e)(3)(A)(ii)) (ii) the tax for contributions to HSAs, (Code Sec. 223(b)(8)(B)(i)(II)), and (iii) the tax for rollovers from IRAs to HSAs (Code Sec. 408(d)(9)(D)(i)(II)); (19) 10% recapture tax on taxpayer required to recapture charitable deduction claimed for gift of fractional interest in tangible personal property (Code Sec. 170(o)(3)(B)); (20) interest and tax for violations of Code Sec. 409A nonqualified deferred compensation (NQDC) rules, off-shore trust and financial health trigger funding rules, and tax on NQDC from certain tax-indifferent entities (Code Sec. 409A(a)(1)(B), Code Sec. 409A(b), Code Sec. 457A(c)(1)(B)); (21) additional tax on ABLE account distributions not used for qualified disability expenses (Code Sec. 529A(c)(3)(A)); and (22) base erosion and anti-abuse tax (¶3316) (Code Sec. 59A).[3]

¶ 2360   Credit for alternative minimum tax (AMT)—Forms 8801, 8827.

The minimum tax credit (MTC or AMT credit) is equal to (compute on Form 8801, Form 8827 for corporations pre-2018 as the corporate AMT has been repealed for tax years beginning after 2017) the adjusted net minimum tax (ANMT) the taxpayer paid in all earlier tax years for "deferral preferences" (for a corporation, also "exclusion preferences"), less the allowable MTCs for those years. (Code Sec. 53(a), Code Sec. 53(b)) The allowable credit for a tax year is limited (subject to the rule below for individuals and at ¶1932) to the excess of: (1) taxpayer's regular tax liability (¶2359) reduced by the sum of allowable nonrefundable credits, *over* (2) the tentative minimum tax (¶3201), for the year. (Code Sec. 53(c))[4]

For a small corporation exempt from AMT for a tax year before 2018, the regular tax liability otherwise used in computing the year's credit limitation is reduced by 25% of the amount over $25,000. (repealed Code Sec. 55(e)(5))[5]

A *noncorporate taxpayer's* ANMT for a tax year equals: (a) the AMT for the year, *less* (b) the amount of AMT that would have arisen if the only applicable AMT preferences and adjustments were "exclusion preferences." (Code Sec. 53(d)(1)(B))[6]

A *corporation's* ANMT for a tax year before 2018 equals item (a), above. (Code Sec. 53(d)(1)(B))[7] *For tax years beginning after 2017,* a corporation's MTC (1) may offset regular tax liability for any tax year, and (2) is refundable for any tax year beginning after 2017 and before 2022 in an amount equal to 50% (100% for tax years beginning in 2021) of the excess MTC for the tax year, over the amount of the credit allowable for the year against regular tax liability. Thus, the full amount of the corporation's MTC is allowed in tax years beginning before 2022. (Code Sec. 53(d)(2), Code Sec. 53(e)(1))

"Deferral preferences" are all the AMT preferences and adjustments except those for: (i) depletion, (ii) tax-exempt interest, (iii) itemized deductions of noncorporate taxpayers, (iv) the standard deduction, (v) personal exemptions, and (vi) the exclusion of gain from qualified small business stock. (Code Sec. 53(d)(1)(B)(ii)) "Exclusion preferences" are the AMT preferences/adjustments that aren't deferral preferences. [8]

¶ 2361   Qualified tax credit bonds (QTCBs) issued before 2018.

For bonds issued after Dec. 31, 2017, the authority to issue tax-credit bonds and direct pay bonds under Code Sec. 54A, Code Sec. 54B, Code Sec. 54C, Code Sec. 54D, Code Sec. 54E, Code Sec. 54F, and Code Sec. 6431 is prospectively repealed. [9]

The following rules apply to bonds issued before 2018. Taxpayers holding QTCBs on specified "credit allowance dates" during the tax year are entitled to a nonrefundable credit (rather than interest payments) against regular income tax and alternative minimum tax (AMT) liability. The credit accrues quarterly and is includible in gross income as interest is paid on the bond. The amount of the credit is determined by multiplying the bond's credit rate by its face amount. The credit rate is determined by IRS and is a rate that allows the bonds to be issued without discount and interest cost to the issuer. A QTCB is a specified type of bond that is part of an issue that meets requirements relating to expenditures, reporting, arbitrage, maturity, and financial conflicts of interest. (Code Sec. 54A)[10] These bonds can be QTCBs:

... *Qualified forestry conservation bonds (QFCBs)* issued by qualified issuers (states and Code Sec. 501(c)(3) organizations) to finance qualified forestry conservation projects. (Code Sec. 54A(d)(1)(A), Code Sec. 54B)[11]

... *New clean renewable energy bonds (New CREBs)* issued for capital expenditures incurred by government bodies, public power providers, or cooperative electric companies to finance qualified renewable energy facilities. (Code Sec. 54A(d)(1)(B), Code Sec. 54C)[12]

... *Qualified energy conservation bonds (QECBs)* issued by a state or local government for qualified conservation purposes. (Code Sec. 54A(d)(1)(C), Code Sec. 54D)[13]

... *Qualified zone academy bonds (QZABs)* issued by a state or local government for repairing and renovating schools as well as for school equipment and teacher training. (Code Sec. 54A(d)(1)(D), Code Sec. 54E)[14]

---

5. ¶A-8807; ¶534
6. ¶A-8802; ¶534
7. ¶A-8802; ¶534
8. ¶A-8804; ¶534
9. ¶L-15530 *et seq.*; ¶54A8.4

10. ¶L-15530 *et seq.*; ¶54A8.4
11. ¶L-15550 *et seq.*; ¶54B8.4
12. ¶L-15560 *et seq.*; ¶54C8.4
13. ¶L-15570 *et seq.*; ¶54D8.4
14. ¶L-15580 *et seq. et seq.*; ¶1397E8.4

. . . *Qualified school construction bonds (QSCBs)* issued by a state or local government for constructing, rehabilitating, or repairing a public school facility, or for acquiring land where a facility is to be constructed. (Code Sec. 54A(d)(1)(E); Code Sec. 54F)[15]

☁caution: Although there's no specific termination date for issuance of New CREBs, QECBs, QZABs, or QSCBs, a zero national bond volume limitation for QSCBs for years after 2010 and for QZABs for years after 2016 means that the bonds can be issued after this date only if unused national bond volume limitations from previous years can be carried forward.

Direct Pay Tax Credit Bonds. For New CREBs, QECBs, QZABs (but not QZABs issued under a post-2010 national bond volume limitation or carryforward of such), or QSCBs, the issuer may make an irrevocable election (on Form 8038-CP) for the bond to be treated as a "Direct Pay Tax Credit Bond" under Code Sec. 6431, entitling the issuer to receive a direct payment from IRS of an amount based on a market-determined interest rate, on the bond's interest payment dates. Special limits apply to new CREBs or QECBs. If the issuer elects the direct payment option, the holder can't claim any otherwise available QTCB credit for the bond, and is taxed on any bond interest paid. Any income tax deduction otherwise allowed to the issuer is reduced by the amount of the payment made under Code Sec. 6431 for the interest. (Code Sec. 6431(f))[16]

¶ 2362   Foreign Tax Credit. ▬▬▬▬▬▬▬▬▬▬▬▬

U.S. taxpayers who pay income taxes to foreign governments may generally credit them dollar-for-dollar against their U.S. tax liability on their worldwide income.

Taxpayers may elect to take a foreign tax credit against U.S. income tax for income tax paid to a foreign country or U.S. possession, or deduct them. (Code Sec. 901, Code Sec. 27, Code Sec. 164(a)(3); Reg § 1.901-1(a))[17] Foreign income taxes may not, however, be deducted in the same year that a credit is claimed for any foreign income tax and excess eligible foreign taxes eligible for carryover cannot be claimed in a year in which a deduction for current foreign taxes is taken. The deduction of other foreign taxes doesn't effect the creditability of foreign income taxes. (Code Sec. 164(a), Code Sec. 275(a)(4), Code Sec. 904(c); Reg § 1.901-1(c), Reg § 1.901-1(h)(2))[18]

The credit is allowed to U.S. citizens, domestic corporations, U.S. residents and bona fide residents of Puerto Rico for the entire tax year as to foreign or possessions taxes paid or accrued during the tax year. (Code Sec. 901(b)(1), Code Sec. 901(b)(2), Code Sec. 901(b)(3)) Nonresident aliens and foreign corporations can claim the credit for foreign or possessions tax only on certain income effectively connected with a U.S. business (¶4631). (Code Sec. 901(b)(4), Code Sec. 906)[19]

A person described above who is a member of a partnership, a beneficiary of an estate or trust, or a shareholder of an electing regulated investment company (RIC) may credit his or her share of foreign tax paid or accrued by the partnership, estate, trust or RIC. (Code Sec. 901(b)(5), Code Sec. 853(a)) Trusts and estates are allowed the foreign tax credit for taxes not allocable to beneficiaries. (Code Sec. 642(a), Code Sec. 901(n)(3))[20]

The Code Sec. 936 possessions tax credit has generally been phased out, but remained effective for American Samoa for the first twelve tax years of a corporation beginning after Dec. 31, 2005 and before Jan. 1, 2018. [21]

☁observation: Check tax.thomsonreuters.com/federaltaxhandbookupdates to see if the above provision has been extended.

---

15. ¶L-15590 *et seq.*; ¶54F8.40
16. ¶L-15547 *et seq.*; ¶64,318.40
17. ¶O-4001; ¶9014.04
18. ¶O-4002; ¶K-4701; ¶2754

19. ¶O-4101 *et seq.*; ¶9014.01
20. ¶O-4103; ¶9014.01
21. ¶O-1500.1; ¶9314.06

A foreign tax is only creditable by the taxpayer upon whom foreign law imposes legal liability for the tax, even if another person pays the tax. (Reg § 1.901-2(f)) In addition, foreign tax credits may be suspended under a matching rule to prevent the separation of creditable foreign taxes from the associated foreign income when certain related persons account for the associated income in another tax period (a tax credit splitting event). IRS provides an exclusive list of arrangements that qualify as splitting events. (Code Sec. 909, Reg § 1.909-2)[22]

¶ 2363   When and how to claim foreign tax credit—Forms 1116, 1118.

The credit is claimed on Form 1116 by an individual, trust or estate, and on Form 1118 by a corporation. (Reg § 1.905-2(a)(1))[23] A cash basis taxpayer may elect to credit *all* qualified foreign taxes on an accrual basis, but the election is binding with respect to all taxes for that year, whenever paid. (Code Sec. 905(a); Reg § 1.905-1(a))[24]

¶ 2364   What taxes qualify for a foreign tax credit?

Income taxes, war profits taxes and excess profits taxes paid or accrued during the tax year to a foreign country or a U.S. possession qualify for the foreign tax credit. (Code Sec. 901) However, a tax conditioned on its eligibility for the credit (a soak up tax) or used by the foreign country to provide a subsidy doesn't qualify. (Reg § 1.901-2(c)) A payment also qualifies if it is *in lieu* of taxes on income. (Code Sec. 903) Taxes on wages, dividends, interest and royalties generally qualify. (Reg § 1.901-2)[25] In the case of certain elections and transactions that create additional asset basis for cost recovery in the U.S. (e.g., qualified stock purchases, acquisitions of partnership interests with a Code Sec. 754 election in place), a portion of the foreign income tax paid on the income or gain attributable to the underlying foreign assets is disqualified. (Code Sec. 901(m))[26]

Taxes that may not be credited include those imposed by and paid to certain countries that the U.S. doesn't recognize or have diplomatic relations with or that have been designated as a country supporting acts of international terrorism; but these taxes may be taken as itemized deductions. (Code Sec. 901(j)) The credit is also reduced or denied to international boycott participants (see ¶4624). (Code Sec. 908)[27]

The credit is generally denied for a foreign withholding tax if the underlying property wasn't held for a minimum holding period, or to the extent that the recipient is obligated to make related payments with respect to positions in substantially similar or related property. (Code Sec. 901(l))[28]

¶ 2365   Limitations on the foreign tax credit.

The total credit for foreign taxes for a year is limited to the amount of U.S. tax that would be imposed on the taxpayer's foreign source income. (Code Sec. 904(a))[29] Separate calculations are required for different categories of income (see ¶2366).

An individual may elect an exemption from the limitation (by not filing the Form 1116) on *de minimis* amounts if the individual has $300 or less ($600 in the case of joint filers) of creditable foreign taxes and no foreign source income other than qualified passive income, so long as the amounts are shown on Form 1099 or other statement. However, there is no carryover of excess foreign taxes to or from a tax year for which the election is made. (Code

---

22. ¶O-4104; ¶O-4113 *et seq.*; ¶9014.02; ¶9094

23. ¶O-5501; ¶9054.02

24. ¶O-5504; ¶9054.01

25. ¶O-4200 *et seq.*; ¶9014.02

26. ¶O-4013 *et seq.*

27. ¶O-4004; ¶O-4005; ¶K-4701; ¶9014.07; ¶9084

28. ¶O-4009 *et seq.*; ¶9014.08

29. ¶O-4401 *et seq.*; ¶9044 *et seq.*

Sec. 904(j))[30]

A loss netting rule requires a taxpayer to reduce foreign source capital gain by U.S. capital losses and the limitation is reduced to take into account any preferential rates for capital gain and qualifying dividends (¶1286). (Code Sec. 904(b)(2), Code Sec. 904(b)(3); Reg § 1.904(b)-1) In certain cases, noncorporate taxpayers may elect not to apply the adjustment for rate differentials. (Reg § 1.904(b)-1(b)(3))[31]

If foreign income taxes paid or accrued exceed the amount that may be credited for the tax year, the excess may be carried back one year and forward 10 years. (Code Sec. 904(c)) Taxes are treated as carried over to the extent of any unused limitation in a year in which the taxpayer does not elect the credit and the taxpayer may file an amended return to claim the foreign tax credit for that year. (Reg § 1.904-2(d)) The carryback and carryover rule does not apply to foreign taxes on global intangible low-taxed income (GILTI, see ¶4614). (Code Sec. 904(c))[32]

Additional limitations apply to foreign taxes on foreign mineral income (Code Sec. 901(e); Reg § 1.901-3)[33] and foreign oil and gas extraction income. (Code Sec. 907)[34]

On a joint return, the credit is based on total taxes paid or accrued by both spouses. (Reg § 1.901-1(e))[35]

¶ 2366   Separate limitations for specified income categories ("separate limitation categories").

The foreign tax credit limitation (see ¶2365) is computed separately for (1) global intangible low-taxed income (GILTI, see ¶4614), (2) foreign branch income (i.e., the business profits of a U.S. person which are attributable to one or more qualified business units in one or more foreign countries), (3) passive category income (i.e., generally any income which would be foreign personal holding company (FPHC) income (¶4613) but not export financing interest or high-taxed income), and (4) general category income (i.e., income other than amounts included in the previous three categories). Additional categories may be mandated by other Code provisions. (Code Sec. 904(d); Reg § 1.904-4(m))

Dividends, interest, rents, and royalties received by a U.S. shareholder from a controlled foreign corporation (CFC) receive look-through treatment and so are characterized according to the source of the income to the CFC. Similarly, subpart F inclusions are only treated as passive category income to the extent the amount included is attributable to passive category income of the CFC. Look-through treatment also applies to dividends from non-controlled 10% owned foreign corporations (¶2369). (Code Sec. 904(d)(3); Reg § 1.904-5)[36]

¶ 2367   Resourcing of foreign source income as U.S. source and recapture of overall foreign and domestic losses.

Certain income derived from U.S. owned foreign corporations (in which U.S. persons hold at least 50% by vote or value) is recharacterized as U.S.-source for purposes of the foreign tax credit limitation rules (see ¶2365). Recharacterization applies to certain includible Subpart F income (¶4613) and income from a qualifying electing fund (QEF) (¶4620). It also applies to interest and dividends, unless less than 10% of the corporation's earnings and profits for the tax year are attributable to sources within the U.S. However, where a treaty treats income derived from a U.S. owned foreign corporation as foreign-source that the above rule treats as U.S. source, the taxpayer may elect to treat the income as foreign

---

30. ¶O-4412, ¶O-4413; ¶9044.04
31. ¶O-4404 et seq.; ¶9044.01
32. ¶O-4601 et seq.; ¶9044.02
33. ¶O-5100 et seq.; ¶9014.02

34. ¶O-5200 et seq.
35. ¶O-4410; ¶9014.01
36. ¶O-4326 et seq.; ¶O-4369;¶9044.01

source, subject to a separate foreign tax credit limitation (see ¶2366). (Code Sec. 904(h))[37]

An overall foreign loss (OFL) is created whenever a taxpayer's foreign losses exceed foreign gross income (disregarding any NOLs, foreign expropriation losses, and losses which arise from fire, storm, shipwreck, or other casualty, or from theft). OFLs are recaptured by recharacterizing a portion of the taxpayer's foreign source taxable income for each succeeding tax year as U.S. source income. This portion is generally the lesser of the unrecaptured OFL and 50% of the taxpayer's taxable foreign source income for that succeeding tax year. This recharacterization reduces the credit limitation until the OFL is completely offset. Ordering rules apply to match OFLs to the various separate limitation income categories. A taxpayer who disposes of property used in a trade or business predominantly outside the U.S. or of stock of certain CFCs recognizes the gain as foreign-source income to the extent of any unrecaptured OFLs. (Code Sec. 904(f)) Corporations track these amounts on Form 1118, Schedule J. [38]

An equivalent rule recharacterizes the U.S.-source income of a taxpayer as foreign-source income for purposes of the foreign tax credit limitation to the extent of the taxpayer's prior overall domestic loss (ODL). (Code Sec. 904(g))[39]

¶ 2368   Exchange rate for translating foreign tax payments.

A cash-basis taxpayer uses the currency exchange rate in effect on a payment date. An accrual taxpayer translates foreign taxes at the average exchange rate for the year to which the taxes relate unless the taxes are paid more than two years after, or any time before, the tax year to which they relate, or if the taxes are denominated in an inflationary currency. A taxpayer may elect to use the spot rate for foreign taxes not paid in the taxpayer's functional currency. (Code Sec. 986(a)(1); Reg § 1.905-3T(b))[40]

¶ 2369   Deemed-paid credit for foreign tax paid or accrued by a foreign affiliate.

A U.S. corporate shareholder (or an individual U.S. shareholder who makes the corporate tax election) of a controlled foreign corporation (CFC) may claim a deemed-paid credit with respect to foreign taxes paid or accrued by the CFC when amounts are included in the gross income of the shareholder under Subpart F. (Code Sec. 960(a), Code Sec. 962(a)) However, with respect to global intangible low-taxed income (GILTI, see ¶4614), this credit is limited to 80% of the attributable foreign taxes. (Code Sec. 960(d)) Qualified electing fund (QEF) inclusions (see ¶4620) of a U.S. corporate shareholder of a QEF are treated similarly to Subpart F amounts for these purposes. (Code Sec. 1293(f)) If any portion of a distribution from a CFC to a U.S. corporate shareholder is excluded from gross income as previously taxed income (PTI), the shareholder is deemed to have paid so much of the foreign CFC's foreign income taxes as are properly attributable to that portion, and have not previously been deemed paid by the shareholder under these rules. (Code Sec. 960(b)) The foreign tax credit limitation (see ¶2365) is increased for additional taxes paid or deemed paid on distributions of PTI. (Code Sec. 960(c)) A holding period requirement applies for purposes of qualifying for the deemed-paid credit except in the case of securities dealers or brokers in the active conduct of a foreign securities dealer business. (Code Sec. 901(k))

If a domestic corporation chooses to claim a foreign tax credit for any tax year, an amount equal to the taxes deemed paid by that corporation under the above rules (determined without regard to the 80% limitation for GILTI-related taxes) for the tax year is treated for income tax purposes (other than for purposes of the deduction of U.S. source

37. ¶O-4501 *et seq.*; ¶9044.01
38. ¶O-4700 *et seq.*; ¶9044.01
39. ¶O-4720 *et seq.*; ¶9044.01
40. ¶O-5300 *et seq.*; ¶9864.01

dividends from foreign corporations and the deduction for foreign source dividends from foreign corporations (see ¶3315)) as a dividend received by that domestic corporation from the foreign corporation. (Code Sec. 78)[41]

---

41. ¶O-4900 *et seq.*; ¶784; ¶9604 *et seq.*

Chapter 9   Sales and Exchanges—Tax-Free Exchanges—Basis

¶ 2400   **Gain or Loss on Sales or Exchanges.** ▃▃▃▃▃▃▃▃▃▃▃▃▃▃▃

Taxpayers realize gain to the extent the amount realized from a sale or exchange exceeds their adjusted basis (usually cost, increased for improvements and decreased for depreciation or amortization). If the adjusted basis of the property disposed of exceeds the amount realized (¶2401), the difference is a loss. (Code Sec. 1001(a))[1] With limited exceptions (e.g., when property is subject to the mark-to-market rules discussed at ¶2646), a taxpayer doesn't realize gain or loss when property merely goes up or down in value.

🅡🅐 *observation:* Whether realized gain or loss is recognized in the tax year of sale or exchange depends on whether it was realized in a taxable or tax-deferred transaction.

¶ 2401   **Amount realized.**

The amount realized on a sale or other disposition of property is the amount of money plus the fair market value (FMV) of any property received by the seller. (Code Sec. 1001(b))[2] Where the buyer of property assumes a debt of the seller, or pays one (e.g., pays seller's taxes or legal fees), the amount of the debt is added to the amount realized by the seller. (Reg § 1.1001-2(a))[3] FMV is the price at which the property would change hands between a willing buyer and a willing seller, neither being under any compulsion to buy or sell and both having reasonable knowledge of relevant facts. (Reg § 1.170A-1(c)(2), Reg § 1.412(c)(2)-1(c)(1), Reg § 1.1445-1(g)(7))[4]

If a taxpayer sells an asset, selling expenses (e.g., brokers' commissions) ordinarily reduce the amount realized, thus reducing any realized gain or increasing any loss realized on the sale.[5]

For the effect of unstated interest on a deferred payment sale or installment sale of property, see ¶1304.

¶ 2402   **Amount realized on sale of property subject to a debt.**

If property is sold subject to a mortgage or other debt, the amount of the liability is included in the sales price whether or not the seller is personally liable on the debt. This is so whether or not the buyer assumes the debt.[6]

In determining the gain or loss on property, its fair market value is treated as being not less than the amount of the nonrecourse debt to which it's subject. (Code Sec. 7701(g))[7]

¶ 2403   **Open transactions.**

When a seller receives payment in the form of a property right or obligation whose value depends on future events, if the seller can prove that the right or obligation has no ascertainable value, he reports gain only when the proceeds from the obligation exceed his basis, and loss is fixed only when further payments can't reasonably be expected.[8] For contingent payment sales and open sales under the installment sale rules, see ¶2455.

---

1. ¶I-2501; ¶10,014
2. ¶I-2502; ¶10,014
3. ¶I-2517; ¶10,014.03
4. ¶P-6002; ¶10,114.25

5. ¶I-2537; ¶10,014.02
6. ¶I-2517; ¶10,014.03
7. ¶I-2522
8. ¶G-6567 *et seq.*; ¶4534.49

References beginning with a single letter are to paragraphs in Federal Tax Coordinator 2d and RIA's Analysis of Federal Taxes: Income. Those beginning with numbers are to paragraphs in United States Tax Reporter.

¶ 2404   Repossession of real estate by a secured seller.

When real property is sold and the sale gives rise to a debt to the seller secured by the real property (a purchase-money mortgage or similar lien), and the seller later repossesses the property (through voluntary transfer or foreclosure) because of actual or imminent default by the buyer, then (1) no loss results to the seller from the repossession or reacquisition, nor does the mortgage debt become worthless; and (2) the seller's gain on repossession is limited to the money and the value of property (other than the repossessed property) received by the seller with respect to the original sale to the extent these amounts haven't already been reported as income. The resulting gain can't exceed the gain on the original sale. (Code Sec. 1038)[9]

If gain isn't recognized under the homesale exclusion rules (¶ 2442) and the seller repossesses the home and then resells it within 1 year after the date of the repossession, the above rules don't apply and the resale of the home is treated as part of the transaction constituting the original sale of the residence. (Code Sec. 1038(e))[10] If the resale isn't made within 1 year, the regular repossession rules above apply, and the seller recognizes gain, including gain previously excluded under the homesale exclusion rules (¶2442 *et seq.*).[11]

¶ 2405   Personal property repossessed.

Gain or loss to the seller on repossession of personal property sold in a deferred payment transaction, not reported on the installment method, is the difference between the fair market value of the property when repossessed and the basis of the defaulted obligation, with that basis decreased by amounts paid on the note and increased for costs incurred in connection with the repossession. Gain or loss is reported in the year of repossession.[12]

¶ 2406   When cash basis taxpayers report gain or loss.

A cash basis seller reports gain on a sale or exchange in the tax year the sales proceeds are received, actually or constructively. A loss is reported in the tax year the transaction is completed by a fixed, identifiable event. (Code Sec. 451(a); Reg § 1.451-1(a))[13]

¶ 2407   When accrual basis taxpayers report gain or loss.

An accrual basis seller reports gain or loss in the tax year a sale is completed and an unqualified right to the purchase price arises —usually when title passes to the buyer but, generally not later than the tax year in which the income is taken into account for financial accounting purposes (Code Sec. 451(b)), see ¶2823 *et seq.*[14] For securities sales, see ¶2409.

¶ 2408   Delivery of deed or title in escrow.

Where both the deed (or other evidence of title) and the purchase price are placed in escrow pending examination and approval of the title by the buyer, a sale isn't completed (and gain or loss isn't realized) until the buyer signifies approval. Until then, the seller doesn't have an unqualified right to payment. Once the buyer approves title, the seller can't postpone reporting gain by directing the escrow agent to hold the payment. But if the deed is delivered in escrow as security for the performance of an unconditional obligation of the buyer (usually payment of the purchase price), the sale is completed when the deed

---

9. ¶G-6851 *et seq.*; ¶10,384
10. ¶G-6877 *et seq.*; ¶10,384
11. ¶G-6877

12. ¶G-6801
13. ¶I-2601; ¶4514.001
14. ¶I-2602; ¶4464.07

is delivered and the buyer enters into possession of the property. [15]

¶ 2409   Sales and exchanges of securities.

Gain or loss on the sale of securities arises when the seller has sold or committed himself to sell specific shares. [16] Gain or loss on the exchange of securities arises when the taxpayer acquires a right to specific securities. [17]

In stock exchange transactions, cash and accrual basis taxpayers realize gain or loss on the trade date, and not on the later settlement date. [18] For short sales, see ¶ 2629.

No gain or loss is recognized by owners of securities when they loan the securities in return for the agreement of the borrower to return identical securities, but the agreement must not reduce the transferor's risk of loss or opportunity for gain in the transferred securities. (Code Sec. 1058(a))[19]

Transactions structured to appear to be loans are sometimes found to be sales where they have the practical effect of sales, e.g., certain forward share and/or lending agreements where the taxpayer no longer has any substantial risk of loss. [20]

¶ 2410   Sales of load mutual funds with reinvestment right.

A load charge incurred in buying mutual fund shares is disregarded (in whole or in part) in computing gain or loss on the disposition of those shares within 90 days, if the buyer was given a reinvestment right under which shares in the same (or another) mutual fund could be bought at less than the usual load charge. The load charge is disregarded to the extent of the reduction in the load charge on the later purchase. (Code Sec. 852(f))[21]

¶ 2411   Significant modification of debt instrument treated as an exchange.

A significant modification of a debt instrument results in an exchange of the original debt instrument for a modified instrument that differs materially either in kind or in extent. (Reg § 1.1001-3(b))[22]

  ☉ observation: The like-kind exchange rules (¶2417 *et seq.*) don't apply to exchanges of any personal property (including bonds, notes, or other evidences of indebtedness). Exchanges of corporate bonds, but not of government bonds, can be tax-free under the reorganization provisions (¶3534), but only to the extent the principal amount isn't increased. Thus, in most cases, an exchange (or modification, which is considered an exchange for tax purposes) results in the holder's recognizing gain or loss. For example, if a modification of a debt instrument results in a reduction of the debt, the debtor has cancellation of debt income. (¶1377)

Examples of significant modifications in the terms of a debt instrument are:

. . . a change in the yield of a debt instrument, if the yield varies from the annual yield on the unmodified instrument (determined as of the date of the modification) by more than the greater of: 1/4 of 1% (25 basis points), or 5% of the annual yield of the unmodified instrument (.05 × annual yield). (Reg § 1.1001-3(e)(2)(ii))

  ☉ observation: 5% of the annual yield will be more than 1/4 of 1% if the annual yield of the unmodified instrument was more than 5%.

. . . a change to the timing of payments (including any resulting change in the amount of

15. ¶I-1112; ¶4514.087; ¶4514.101
16. ¶I-2615
17. ¶I-2616
18. ¶I-2615.1; ¶4514.112

19. ¶I-1311, I-3802; ¶10,584
20. ¶I-1311 *et seq.*
21. ¶P-5038 *et seq.*; ¶8524.02
22. ¶I-1050 *et seq.*; ¶10,014.83

payments), if it results in the material deferral of scheduled payments. (Reg § 1.1001-3(e)(3)(i))[23]

A modification of a debt instrument can sometimes cause it to be recharacterized as an instrument or property right that isn't debt, but a deterioration in the debtor's financial condition isn't taken into account in making that determination unless there is a substitution of a new obligor or the addition or deletion of a co-obligor. (Reg § 1.1001-3(f)(7)(ii))[24]

Qualifying taxpayers can elect to treat a substitution of certain publicly traded debt instruments for new ones as a realization event even if the substitution doesn't result in a significant modification of the terms of the old debt instrument, and therefore isn't an exchange for tax purposes. Electing taxpayers don't recognize any realized gain or loss on the date of the substitution. Instead, gain or loss generally is taken into account as income or deductions over the term of the new debt instruments. [25]

¶ 2412   Tax-Free Exchanges of Stock.

A taxpayer doesn't recognize gain or loss on exchanges of common or preferred stock for other common or preferred stock of the same corporation (¶2413). A corporation doesn't recognize gain or loss when it sells or exchanges its own stock for property or services (¶2414). Certain U.S. obligations can be exchanged tax-free (¶2415), as well as certain insurance policies and annuities (¶2416).

¶ 2413   Stock exchanged for stock of same corporation.

No gain or loss is recognized on the exchange of common stock for other common, or preferred stock for other preferred, of the same corporation. (Code Sec. 1036(a)) It's tax-free whether between a shareholder and the corporation or between 2 shareholders, and even if voting stock is exchanged for nonvoting stock. (Reg § 1.1036-1(a))[26] But, nonqualified preferred stock (¶3542) is treated as property other than stock for this purpose. (Code Sec. 1036(b))[27]

An exchange of common stock for preferred stock in the same corporation isn't tax-free. (Reg § 1.1036-1(a))[28] However, reorganization exchanges of stock for stock or stock and securities of the same or different corporations can be tax-free, see ¶3527 *et seq.*

¶ 2414   Corporation's sale or exchange of its own stock for property or services.

A corporation doesn't recognize gain or loss on the sale or exchange of its stock (including treasury stock) for money, other property, or services. (Code Sec. 1032(a); Reg § 1.1032-1)[29] It also doesn't recognize gain or loss on the lapse of an option (warrant) to buy or sell its stock (including treasury stock). (Code Sec. 1032(a); Reg § 1.1032-3(d))[30]

¶ 2415   Tax-free exchanges of U.S. obligations.

IRS regs can provide for the tax-free exchange of one U.S. obligation (bond, note, etc.) for another. (Code Sec. 1037(a); Reg § 1.1037-1) The Treasury designates the specific obligations it will exchange for the previously issued obligations without recognition of gain or loss. [31]

23. ¶I-1058 *et seq.*; ¶10,014.83
24. ¶I-1075.1; ¶10,014.83
25. ¶I-1081.8; ¶10,014.83
26. ¶I-3301; ¶10,364
27. ¶I-3301.1; ¶10,364

28. ¶I-3301; ¶10,364
29. ¶I-3201, I-3208; ¶10,324
30. ¶I-6517; ¶10,324
31. ¶I-3400 *et seq.*; ¶10,374

¶ 2416   Tax-free exchanges of insurance policies and annuities.

No gain or loss is recognized upon the exchange by the owner (or by a beneficiary on the death of the owner) of a life insurance contract for another or for an endowment or annuity contract, an endowment contract for an annuity or endowment contract providing for regular payments beginning at a date not later than the beginning date under the old contract, or an annuity contract for another. To qualify for tax-free exchange treatment, the insured or annuitant must remain the same. (Code Sec. 1035; Reg § 1.1035-1(c)) The direct transfer of a part of funds from one annuity contract to another annuity contract qualifies as a nontaxable exchange under Code Sec. 1035 if certain conditions are met. Thus, the direct exchange of part of the cash surrender value of an annuity contract for a new annuity contract issued by a 2nd insurance company is tax-free even though the original annuity contract continued to exist. [32]

To the extent provided in regs, the rules allowing a tax-free exchange of insurance policies and annuities don't apply to any exchange having the effect of transferring property to a non-U.S. person. (Code Sec. 1035(c)) [33]

No gain or loss is recognized on the exchange of a life insurance contract or an annuity contract for a qualified long-term care contract. (Code Sec. 1035(a)) [34]

¶ 2417   Like-Kind (Code Sec. 1031) Real Property Exchanges—Forms 8824, 8849. ■

No gain or loss is recognized on the exchange of real property held for productive use in a trade or business or for investment if the real property is exchanged solely for like-kind (¶2418) real property that is to be held either for productive use in a trade or business or for investment. Whether real property is trade or business or investment property is determined by the taxpayer's intent at the time of the exchange (¶2419). Multi-party exchanges and deferred exchanges can qualify. However, gain, but not loss, is recognized if boot (¶2421) is also received.

This nonrecognition provision doesn't apply to any exchange of real property held primarily for sale. (Code Sec. 1031(a)(2)) [35]

Nonrecognition under Code Sec. 1031 is mandatory if the conditions are met. [36]

Report a like-kind exchange on Form 8824. If gain is recognized on the exchange because boot (money and/or non-like-kind property) is received, also report the transaction on Form 8849 and Schedule D of the applicable tax form (e.g., Form 1040, Form 1041, Form 1065, or Form 1120), Form 4797, or Form 6252 (whichever applies). [37]

For exchanges completed before Jan. 1, 2018, in addition to exchanges of like-kind real property, exchanges of like-kind personal or intangible property were also tax-free. Under a transition rule, the real-property-only limitation didn't apply to an exchange if the property disposed of or the property received by the taxpayer in the exchange was disposed of or received before Jan. 1, 2018. [38]

¶ 2418   Like-kind defined.

"Like-kind" refers to the nature, character, or class of the property, not to its grade or quality. Thus, an exchange of real estate for real estate is an exchange of "like-kind" property. (Reg § 1.1031(a)-1(b)) [39] It doesn't matter where the real estate is located or whether it's improved or not, but foreign and U.S. real property can't be like-kind. (Code

---

32. ¶J-5302 *et seq.*; ¶10,354
33. ¶J-5306.1; ¶10,354
34. ¶J-5301; ¶10,354
35. ¶I-3050 *et seq.*; ¶10,314 *et seq.*

36. ¶I-3052
37. ¶I-3051
38. ¶I-3050 *et seq.*¶10,314
39. ¶I-3059; ¶10,314.02

Sec. 1031(h)[40] State law classification of property as real or personal isn't determinative for like-kind exchange purposes. [41] While the exchange of a leasehold in real property for real property is generally not a like-kind exchange, under safe harbor rules, an exchange of real property for a 30-year leasehold on real property is a like-kind exchange. (Reg § 1.1031(a)-1(c))[42] Also, an undivided fractional interest in real property can qualify as like-kind replacement property for other real property. [43] Development rights that a corporation intended to acquire as replacement property were like-kind to a fee interest in relinquished property. [44]

¶ 2419   Property held for productive use in a trade or business or for investment.

Both the real property exchanged ("relinquished property") and the property received in the exchange ("replacement property") must be primarily held either for productive use in a trade or business or for investment. (Code Sec. 1031(a)(1))[45] Whether real property is trade or business or investment property is determined by the taxpayer's intent at the time of the exchange. [46]

Property held for productive use in a trade or business can be exchanged for property held for investment. Similarly, property held for investment can be exchanged for property held for productive use in a trade or business. [47]

IRS won't challenge whether a dwelling unit (e.g., a vacation home) qualified as property held for productive use in a trade or business or for investment purposes if the unit (whether relinquished property or replacement property) met certain ownership, rental, and personal use tests. [48] Also, property used for business and personal purposes couldn't be treated as 2 separate assets for purposes of determining whether the trade or business or investment requirement was satisfied. [49]

¶ 2420   Multi-party (including deferred) nontaxable exchanges.

If a taxpayer wants to (or will only) exchange his or her real property for like-kind replacement property, but the party who wants taxpayer's property (the relinquished property) doesn't own the like-kind property, the taxpayer can still set up a tax-free exchange if the other party acquires the like-kind replacement property and taxpayer then exchanges the relinquished property for that like-kind property.

✐illustration: A holds Whiteacre for investment. A doesn't want to sell it if that would result in tax, but would exchange it for Blackacre. B wants Whiteacre. C owns Blackacre and is willing to sell, but doesn't want Whiteacre. B buys Blackacre from C for cash. A transfers Whiteacre to B for Blackacre. The exchange is nontaxable to A.

An exchange can be nontaxable (if the time limits at ¶2423 are met) even where a taxpayer transfers the relinquished property in exchange for a written promise by the transferee to deliver like-kind replacement property to the taxpayer in the future, i.e., a deferred or non-simultaneous exchange.

A multiparty tax-free exchange can be set up by using a qualified intermediary (QI) (someone other than the taxpayer or a "disqualified person," e.g., taxpayer's agent) to facilitate the transaction. (Reg § 1.1031(k)-1(g)(4))[50] Reverse exchanges (replacement property is acquired before the relinquished property is transferred) can be implemented using qualified exchange accommodation arrangements (QEAAs) under IRS-approved safe-

---

40. ¶I-3068; ¶I-3069;¶10,314.04
41. ¶I-3059.1
42. ¶I-3076; ¶10,314.03
43. ¶I-3092.1
44. ¶I-3073
45. ¶I-3083; ¶10,314.01

46. ¶I-3084; ¶10,314.01
47. ¶I-3083; ¶10,314.01
48. ¶I-3083.2 *et seq.*; ¶10,314.01
49. ¶I-3088.1
50. ¶I-3119, I-3120; ¶10,314.10

harbor rules. However, the safe-harbor rules don't apply to replacement property owned by the taxpayer within the 180-day period ending on the date of transfer of ownership of the property to an exchange accommodation titleholder (EAT). IRS recognizes, however, that under case law, some reverse exchanges can still qualify even if they don't meet the safe-harbor requirements.[1]

Where property or cash is set aside in a qualified escrow account, qualified trust, or similar account ("exchange funds") pending completion of a deferred like-kind exchange, the exchange funds are generally treated as an exchange facilitator loan, i.e., a demand loan from the taxpayer to the exchange facilitator (i.e., the QI, transferee, escrow holder, trustee, or other party holding exchange funds for the taxpayer in the deferred exchange), and all items of income, deduction, and credit (including capital gains and losses) attributable to the exchange funds are taken into account by the exchange facilitator. (Reg § 1.468B-6(c)(1))[2] If all earnings attributable to the exchange funds are paid to the taxpayer under the terms of the agreement, then the taxpayer takes all items of income, deduction, and credit into account. (Reg § 1.468B-6(c)(2))[3]

¶ 2421 Taxing "boot" in otherwise tax-free exchange.

If a taxpayer receives boot —money or any other property that doesn't qualify for nonrecognition of gain—in an otherwise nontaxable exchange of stock (¶2413), insurance policies (¶2416), like-kind real property (¶2417), or U.S. obligations (¶2415), then gain to the taxpayer is recognized (is taxable) in an amount not exceeding the value of the boot received (Code Sec. 1031(b)), but loss to the taxpayer isn't recognized (isn't deductible) to any extent. (Code Sec. 1031(c))[4]

Illustration: In a like-kind exchange, T exchanges business real estate worth $500,000 and having an adjusted basis of $200,000 for business real estate worth $400,000 plus $100,000 cash. T's realized gain is $300,000 ($400,000 + $100,000 − $200,000 basis), but the gain recognized is limited to the boot ($100,000). The tax on the remaining $200,000 of realized gain is deferred.

Where a taxpayer gives money in a nontaxable exchange, no gain is recognized. But, if the boot given is property other than money, gain or loss can be recognized. Thus, where stock that has depreciated in value is given in connection with a nontaxable exchange of real estate, loss on the stock is recognized to the extent the stock's adjusted basis exceeds its fair market value. (Reg § 1.1031(d)-1(e))[5]

¶ 2422 Assumption of liabilities in a tax-free exchange.

Liabilities assumed are treated as boot (¶2421) in a nontaxable exchange. Whether a liability is "assumed" in the exchange is determined under Code Sec. 357(d) (¶3506). (Code Sec. 1031(d)) A taxpayer who assumes the liability is the one giving the boot, while a taxpayer whose liability is assumed *receives* the boot.[6] If each party assumes a liability of the other, only the net liability is boot given or received. (Reg § 1.1031(b)-1(c))

Illustration: In a like-kind exchange, A exchanges real property worth $700,000 (basis of $200,000) that is subject to a $200,000 mortgage, with B for replacement real property that is worth $600,000 (basis of $300,000) that is subject to a $100,000 mortgage. A recognizes gain of $100,000 since the mortgage on A's replacement property is $100,000 less than the mortgage on the relinquished property. B recognizes no gain on the transaction.

1. ¶I-3095 *et seq.*; ¶10,314.10
2. ¶J-1379.1 *et seq.*; ¶468B4.2
3. ¶J-1379.1J *et seq.*; ¶468B4.2

4. ¶I-3160; ¶10,314.11
5. ¶I-3163; ¶10,314.11
6. ¶I-3165; ¶10,314.12

¶ 2423   Time limits for deferred like-kind exchanges.

Like-kind exchange treatment (¶2417) is barred if the replacement property isn't identified (e.g., unambiguously described in a written document) on or before 45 days after the transfer, or isn't received within 180 days after the transfer or by the due date (with extensions) of the return for the year of transfer, if earlier. (Code Sec. 1031(a)(3); Reg § 1.1031(k)-1(b))[7] There's no good faith exception to these deadlines,[8] but IRS can extend the deadlines for exchanges affected by disasters.[9] There is also a safe harbor method of reporting gain or loss for certain taxpayers who initiate deferred exchanges but fail to complete the exchange because a qualified intermediary (QI) defaults on its obligation to acquire and transfer replacement property to the taxpayer.[10]

¶ 2424   Related-party like-kind exchanges—Form 8824.

Where a taxpayer exchanges like-kind property with a related taxpayer under Code Sec. 267(b) (¶2448) or Code Sec. 707(b)(1) (¶3726) and, within 2 years of the date of the last transfer that was part of the exchange, either party disposes of the property received in the exchange, then gain or loss not recognized in the exchange is recognized on the date the later disposition occurs. A disposition includes indirect transfers. Exceptions are made for death, certain involuntary conversions, and non-tax-avoidance transactions. (Code Sec. 1031(f))[11] Form 8824 must be filed for the year of the exchange and also for the 2 years following the exchange.[12]

A qualified intermediary (QI; ¶2420) can't be used to circumvent the limitations that would have applied to a direct exchange between related parties. For example, an exchange was part of a transaction structured to avoid the related party rules (and didn't qualify for nonrecognition treatment) where: (1) a taxpayer (T) transferred appreciated property to a QI, which (2) sold it to an unrelated party and used the proceeds to purchase like-kind property from a party related to T, then (3) transferred that property to T.[13]

¶ 2425   Like-kind exchanges of multiple properties.

These are like-kind exchanges in which more than one "exchange group" (see below) is created, or exchanges in which only one exchange group is created but there is more than one property being transferred or received within that exchange group. To compute gain, (1) separate the properties transferred into exchange groups, (2) offset all liabilities assumed by the taxpayer as part of the exchange by all liabilities of which the taxpayer is relieved as part of the exchange, with the excess liabilities assumed or relieved allocated among the exchange groups, and (3) apply the like-kind exchange rules separately to each exchange group to determine the amount of gain recognized in the exchange and the basis of the properties received in the exchange. (Reg § 1.1031(j)-1(a)(2)(i))[14]

Each "exchange group" consists of the properties transferred and received in the exchange, all of which are of a like kind or like class. (Reg § 1.1031(j)-1(b)(2)(i))[15]

☑ observation: In exchange of real properties and personal properties (i.e., property ineligible to be exchanged tax-free), all real properties would presumably be included in one exchange group as like-kind property. Any personal property would be treated in the same manner as boot (money or other property).

---

7. ¶I-3099; ¶10,314.08
8. ¶I-3101
9. ¶S-8012
10. ¶I-3120.2 *et seq.*
11. ¶I-3132 *et seq.*; ¶10,314.07

12. ¶I-3132
13. ¶I-3137; ¶10,314.07
14. ¶I-3187 *et seq.*; ¶10,314.10
15. ¶I-3138 *et seq.*; ¶10,314.10

¶ 2426 Rollover of Gain from Certain Sales. ▬▬▬▬

Eligible taxpayers can elect to roll over gain from (1) the sale of qualified empowerment zone assets (¶2427), (2) the sale of qualified small business stock (QSBS; ¶2428), and (3) certain gain from the sale of property that is invested in a Qualified Opportunity (QO) Fund (¶2429).

¶ 2427 Election to rollover gain from qualified empowerment zone (QEZ) assets.

A taxpayer can elect to defer recognition of capital gain on the sale of a QEZ asset held for more than 1 year where replacement QEZ assets are purchased within 60 days. (Code Sec. 1397B(a), Code Sec. 1391(d)(1)(A)(i))[16]

The rollover rules don't apply to any gain treated as ordinary income or any gain attributable to real property, or an intangible asset, which isn't an integral part of an enterprise zone business. (Code Sec. 1397B(b)(2))[17]

If the rollover is elected, capital gain from the sale of a QEZ asset is recognized only to the extent that the amount realized from the sale exceeds the cost of any QEZ asset (with respect to the same zone as the asset sold) purchased during the 60-day period beginning on the sale date, reduced by any part of the cost previously taken into account under this rollover rule. (Code Sec. 1397B(a))[18]

The basis of the replacement zone asset is reduced by gain not recognized on the rollover, but this rule doesn't apply for purposes of Code Sec. 1202 (exclusion for gain on the sale of small business stock; see ¶2638). (Code Sec. 1397B(b)(4))[19]

The holding period of the replacement zone asset includes the holding period of the original zone asset, except for determining whether the 1-year holding period under Code Sec. 1397B(a) is satisfied. (Code Sec. 1223(13); Code Sec. 1397B(b)(5))[20]

¶ 2428 Rollover election for gain from sale of qualified small business stock (QSBS).

Taxpayers other than corporations can elect to roll over capital gain from the sale of QSBS (¶2639) held for more than 6 months, so that gain is recognized only to the extent that the amount realized exceeds (1) the cost of QSBS bought during the 60-day period beginning on the sale date, reduced by (2) any part of the cost previously taken into account under the rule. (Code Sec. 1045(a))

Rules similar to those under Code Sec. 1202(g) (for determining which holders of interests in pass-through entities are eligible for the 50% exclusion of gain from the sale of QSBS, see ¶2638) apply to the rollover of gain from the sale of QSBS by a pass-through entity. (Code Sec. 1045(b)(5))[21]

The holding period of the replacement stock includes the holding period of the stock sold, but not for purposes of determining whether the 6-month holding period required for rollovers is met. To qualify as small business stock, the issuing corporation must meet an active business test during substantially all of the taxpayer's holding period for the stock. For purposes of the rollover provision, the replacement stock must meet this active business requirement for the 6-month period following the purchase. (Code Sec. 1045(b)(4))[22]

For adjustments to basis of the replacement QSBS, see ¶2506.

---

16. ¶I-3431; ¶13,97B4
17. ¶I-3435 *et seq.*; ¶13,97B4
18. ¶I-3431 *et seq.*; ¶13,97B4
19. ¶I-3433; ¶13,97B4
20. ¶I-3437; ¶13,97B4
21. ¶I-9201; ¶10,454
22. ¶I-9204; ¶10,454

¶ 2429   Deferral and exclusion of gains invested in Qualified Opportunity (QO) Fund before 2027.

At the taxpayer's election on the sale or exchange of any property to an unrelated person:

(1) gross income for the tax year doesn't include gain up to the aggregate amount invested by the taxpayer in a QO Fund during the 180-day period beginning on the date of the sale or exchange (the temporary deferral election);

(2) gain excluded under (1) is included in gross income as provided by Code Sec. 1400Z-2(b) (see below); and

(3) the permanent exclusion of certain gain from the investment in the QO Fund is determined under Code Sec. 1400Z-2(c) (the permanent exclusion election). (Code Sec. 1400Z-2(a)(1))[23]

No elections can be made for a sale or exchange if a Code Sec. 1400Z-2 election previously made with respect to the sale or exchange is in effect. (Code Sec. 1400Z-2(a)(2))[24]

A QO Fund is, in general, any investment vehicle organized as a corporation or partnership for the purpose of investing in QO Zone property that holds at least 90% of its assets in QO Zone property (as defined in Code Sec. 1400Z-2(d)).[25] A QO Zone is a low-income community population census tract that has been nominated by the CEO of a state and certified by IRS as such under procedures described at Code Sec. 1400Z-1(b). Each population census tract in Puerto Rico that is a low-income community is considered to be certified and designated as a QO Zone. A designation ends at the close of the 10th calendar year beginning on or after the date of designation. (Code Sec. 1400Z-1(b))[26] IRS issued a complete list of all population census tracts it has designated as QO Zones. [27]

Gain temporarily deferred under item (1) above is included in income in the tax year that includes the earlier of: the date on which the investment is sold or exchanged, or Dec. 31, 2026. The amount of gain included is the lesser of (a) the deferred gain or the FMV of the investment, over (b) the basis in the investment (¶2507). (Code Sec. 1400Z-2(b)(1))[28]

Gain excluded under the temporary deferral election is included in income in the tax year that includes the earlier of: the date on which the investment is sold or exchanged, or Dec. 31, 2026. (Code Sec. 1400Z-2(b)(1))[29]

Permanent exclusion. At the taxpayer's election for an investment held for at least 10 years, the basis of the property equals the FMV of the investment on the date it is sold or exchanged, Code Sec. 1400Z-2(c)) thereby excluding from income any post-acquisition capital gains on investments in QO Funds that are held for at least 10 years. [30]

For basis of an investment in QO Funds, see ¶2507.

¶ 2430   Involuntary Conversions—Forms 4797 and 8949. ■■■■■■■

No gain is recognized when property is compulsorily or involuntarily converted (¶2432) into property similar or related in service or use. (Code Sec. 1033(a)(1)) Where property is involuntarily converted into money (e.g., insurance proceeds for the property) or into property that isn't similar or related in service or use, the taxpayer can defer tax on any gain if he so elects and buys replacement property (¶2438) or acquires control of a corporation that owns the replacement property (or

23. ¶I-8821; ¶14,00Z-24
24. ¶I-8823; ¶14,00Z-24
25. ¶I-8828; ¶14,00Z-24
26. ¶I-8824; ¶14,00Z-14

27. ¶I-8838
28. ¶I-8838; ¶14,00Z-14
29. ¶I-8838; ¶14,00Z-14
30. ¶I-8827; ¶14,00Z-24

acquires the property within a specified time).

The cost of the replacement property must be equal to or more than the net proceeds from the converted property, and the replacement must generally be made within 2 years after the close of the first tax year in which any part of the gain is realized. (Code Sec. 1033) A loss on an involuntary conversion is recognized or not recognized without regard to the involuntary conversion rules. (Reg § 1.1033(a)-1(a))[31] Use Form 8949 to report gain or loss from an involuntary conversion. Form 4797 is used to report an involuntary conversion of assets used in a trade or business. [32]

¶ 2431 Nonrecognition of gain on involuntary conversions.

Where property is involuntarily converted into other property similar or related in service or use to the converted property, no gain is recognized. (Code Sec. 1033(a)(1)) But, if the taxpayer receives dissimilar property or cash when his or her property is involuntarily converted, the taxpayer must buy "replacement" property (¶2438)[33] or 80% control of a corporation owning or acquiring replacement property within a specified time. [34] Gain is recognized only to the extent the amount realized on the conversion exceeds the cost of the replacement property. (Code Sec. 1033(a)(2)(A))[35]

If a principal residence is involuntarily converted and gain is excluded under Code Sec. 121 (¶2442), then the amount realized under the involuntary conversion provisions is the amount realized less the excluded gain. (Code Sec. 121(d)(5)(B))[36]

A business that realized gain from a state disaster relief grant to reimburse it for disaster-related damage to real and personal property can elect to defer the gain to the extent that an amount equal to the grant proceeds is used to timely purchase property similar or related in service or use to the destroyed or damaged property. [37]

¶ 2432 Involuntary conversion defined.

An involuntary conversion is the compulsory or involuntary conversion of property into similar property, dissimilar property or money as a result of the property's destruction, theft, seizure, requisition or condemnation (actual or threatened). (Code Sec. 1033(a))[38]

Involuntary conversions include the following: sales in actual or threatened condemnation (¶2435); certain sales (or the destruction) of livestock due to disease (Code Sec. 1033(d)); the sale or exchange of livestock (in excess of the number taxpayer would sell if he followed his usual business practices) solely on account of drought, flood, or other weather-related conditions (Code Sec. 1033(e)(1));[39] the sale or transfer of property to the federal government, a state or local government, or an Indian tribal government to implement hazard mitigation (Code Sec. 1033(j));[40] and the sale of publicly traded stock under a state escheat law. [41] However, payments for the temporary use of a taxpayer's property by the government where the taxpayer continues to own the property are treated as rental income and not payments in exchange for the property. [42]

¶ 2433 Principal residence or contents converted due to federally declared disaster.

If the taxpayer's principal residence, or any of its contents, is located in a disaster area and is compulsorily or involuntarily converted because of a "federally declared disaster,"

31. ¶I-3701; ¶10,334
32. ¶I-3733
33. ¶I-3700 *et seq.*; ¶10,334
34. ¶I-3743; ¶10,334.23
35. ¶I-3701; ¶10,334.31
36. ¶I-4565; ¶1214.14

37. ¶I-3702
38. ¶I-3702; ¶10,334.01
39. ¶N-1216 *et seq.*; ¶10,334.08
40. ¶I-3716.1; ¶10,334.01
41. ¶I-3712
42. ¶I-9021

any gain resulting from the receipt of insurance proceeds for personal property that was part of the contents of the residence and wasn't "scheduled property" for insurance purposes isn't recognized, regardless of the use to which the taxpayer puts those proceeds. (Code Sec. 1033(h)(1))[43] "Federally declared disaster" and "disaster area" are defined in Code Sec. 165(i)(5). (Code Sec. 1033(h)(3)) Insurance proceeds received for the home or its "separately scheduled" contents are treated as received for a single item of property, and any property which is similar or related in service or use to the residence so converted (or its contents) is treated for purposes of the involuntary conversion rules as property similar or related in service or use to that single item of property. [44]

For when an extended replacement period applies, see ¶2441.

¶ 2434 Insurance compensation for loss of use of involuntarily converted property.

Insurance proceeds that compensate for the loss of the right to use property due to loss or destruction may qualify for nonrecognition as involuntary conversion proceeds, but the proceeds of a use and occupancy insurance contract that expressly insures against actual lost profits don't qualify and are treated as taxable income. (Reg § 1.1033(a)-2(c)(8))[45]

¶ 2435 Condemnations—actual or threatened.

A disposition under the threat or imminence of condemnation is treated as an involuntary conversion. (Code Sec. 1033(a)(2)(E)(ii))

Threat or imminence of condemnation exists (1) when taxpayer is informed, orally or in writing, by a representative of a governmental body or an authorized public official, that the body or official has decided to acquire the property, and taxpayer has reasonable grounds to believe that condemnation proceedings will be initiated if he doesn't voluntarily sell, or (2) where the taxpayer gets information as to a decision to acquire the property for public use through a report in the news media, if a representative of the governmental body or public official involved confirms the published report and taxpayer has reasonable grounds to believe that the necessary steps to condemn will be taken if he doesn't sell. [46] Sales to third parties (as distinguished from the condemning agency) also qualify as involuntary conversions if made under the threat or imminence of condemnation. [47]

¶ 2436 Amount of condemnation awards.

Condemnation proceeds can't be greater than the amount specifically awarded for the requisitioned property. It may, however, be less if there are any legal or other expenses or special assessments which must be deducted. Sums withheld from the award to pay liens on the property don't reduce the amount realized. [48]

¶ 2437 Severance damages for partial condemnations.

Where only part of a property is condemned, the owner may be paid severance damages as compensation for a loss of value in the part of the property retained. Severance damages may be paid, for example, because of impairment of access to the property retained. Payments are considered severance damages only if specifically agreed to in the condemnation proceeding; otherwise, the entire award is considered made for the condemned property. Where severance damage proceeds are used to acquire replacement property, the

---

43. ¶I-3772.1 *et seq.*; ¶10,334.40
44. ¶I-3772.2; ¶10,334.40
45. ¶I-3724; ¶10,334.12

46. ¶I-3703; ¶10,334.02
47. ¶I-3706
48. ¶I-3764; ¶10,334.31

taxpayer can elect not to recognize any gain from the receipt of the severance damages. [49]

¶ 2438   Replacement property that is similar or related in service or use.

The replacement property must be similar or related in service or use to the property replaced. (Code Sec. 1033(a)(1)) "Similar or related in service or use" means the use of the replacement property must be substantially similar to the use of the replaced property. But, it's not necessary that the replacement property duplicate the converted property. [50]

As an alternative to direct replacement of the converted property, the taxpayer can acquire control of a corporation owning replacement property. (Code Sec. 1033(a)(2)(A)) If this method is used, however, the "like-kind" replacement rule for real property (¶2440) isn't available. The replacement property must qualify under the "similar use" rule. (Code Sec. 1033(g)(2))[1]

If leased property is replaced with other leased property, the similarity of the replacement property is determined on the basis of the nature of the owner's (lessor's) relation to the properties rather than the actual end use made of the properties by the lessees. If the replacement property involves similar business risks, management and landlord services, etc., it is similar even if the lessee's use of the replacement property differs from the lessee's use of the old. [2]

Tangible property acquired and held for productive use in a trade or business is treated as similar or related in service or use to property that (a) was held for investment or for productive use on a trade or business (including inventory), and (b) was involuntarily converted as a result of a federally declared disaster. (Code Sec. 1033(h)(2))[3]

illustration: If a business loses its delivery truck in a federally declared disaster, it can defer tax on any gain realized by timely (¶2441) reinvesting the insurance proceeds in a production machine.

If, because of drought, flood, or other weather-related conditions or soil contamination or other environmental contamination, it isn't feasible for a taxpayer to reinvest the proceeds from compulsorily or involuntarily converted livestock (¶2432) in property similar or related in use to the old livestock, he can reinvest the proceeds in other property used for farming purposes. In the case of soil contamination or other environmental contamination, "other property used for farming purposes" includes real property. (Code Sec. 1033(f))[4]

¶ 2439   Related-person exception to nonrecognition rule.

Nonrecognition treatment for gain in an involuntary conversion isn't permitted if a taxpayer described below acquires replacement property or stock from a related party (under Code Sec. 267(b) (¶2448), or Code Sec. 707(b)(1) (¶3726)):

. . . C corporations.

. . . A partnership if 1 or more C corporations own, directly or indirectly under Code Sec. 707(b)(3) (¶3728), more than 50% of the capital interest or the profits interest of the partnership at the time of the involuntary conversion.

. . . Any other taxpayer (including an individual) if, with respect to property which is involuntarily converted during the tax year, the aggregate realized gain on property on which there is realized gain exceeds $100,000. (Code Sec. 1033(i))[5]

But, nonrecognition does apply to the extent the related party acquired the replacement

49. ¶I-3768 *et seq.*; ¶10,334.14
50. ¶I-3725; ¶10,334.22
1. ¶I-3743; ¶10,334.22
2. ¶I-3730

3. ¶I-3772.6; ¶10,334.2205
4. ¶N-1220; ¶10,334.08
5. ¶I-3733.1, I-3733.2; ¶10,334.221

property or stock from an unrelated party, within the period (¶2441) allowed for the acquisition of replacement property or stock. (Code Sec. 1033(i)(1))[6]

For a partnership (or S corporation), this denial of nonrecognition rule applies to a partnership (or S corporation) and to each partner (or S shareholder). Thus, the annual $100,000 limit applies to both the entity and each partner (or S shareholder). [7]

¶ 2440   Replacement of condemned real estate.

A replacement of condemned real estate held for productive business use or for rental or investment qualifies for nonrecognition treatment if the replacement property is property of a like-kind. (Code Sec. 1033(g)(1)) Determination of whether replacement property is of like-kind is made under the rules at ¶2417, rather than the "similar use" rule. For example, improved realty isn't similar in use to unimproved realty (Reg § 1.1033(a)-2(c)(9)(i)), but the 2 properties are of like-kind, see ¶2418.[8]

The like-kind rule doesn't apply to real estate held primarily for sale (Code Sec. 1033(g)(1)) or where control of a corporation owning replacement property is acquired. (Code Sec. 1033(g)(2))[9]

¶ 2441   Replacement period for involuntarily converted property.

Converted property must be replaced within a period:

(1) beginning with (a) the date the property was destroyed, stolen, condemned, etc., or (b) the date condemnation or requisition was first threatened or became imminent, whichever is earlier (Code Sec. 1033(a)(2)(B)), and

(2) ending (a) 2 years after the close of the first tax year in which any part of the gain is realized (3 years in the case of condemnation or threat of condemnation of real property described at ¶2440; 4 years for principal residences converted due to federally declared disasters, see ¶2433), or (b) at a later date allowed by IRS upon application by the taxpayer. (Code Sec. 1033(a)(2)(B), Code Sec. 1033(g)(4), Code Sec. 1033(h)(1)(B))[10]

If a taxpayer sells livestock on account of drought, flood, or other weather-related conditions (see ¶2438) which result in the area being designated as eligible for assistance by the federal government, the replacement period is extended to 4 years. IRS can extend this 4-year period on a regional basis if the weather-related conditions continue for more than 3 years. (Code Sec. 1033(e)(2)) For persistent droughts, IRS has extended the replacement period until the end of taxpayers' first tax year ending after the first drought-free year (as specially defined) for applicable regions. [11]

¶ 2442   Exclusion of Gain on Principal Residence. ▮▮▮▮▮▮▮▮

A taxpayer can exclude up to $250,000 of gain ($500,000 for certain joint filers) from the sale of his or her principal residence owned and used by the taxpayer as a principal residence for at least 2 of the 5 years before the sale. (Code Sec. 121(a))[12]

The exclusion doesn't apply if, during the 2-year period ending on the sale date, the exclusion applied to another homesale by the taxpayer. (Code Sec. 121(b)(3); Reg § 1.121-2(b)(1))[13]

Married taxpayers filing jointly (¶4705) for the year of sale can exclude up to $500,000 of gain if (1) either spouse owned the home for at least 2 of the 5 years before the sale, (2) both spouses used the home as a principal residence for at least 2 of the 5 years before the

6. ¶I-3733.1; ¶10,334.221
7. ¶I-3733.2; ¶10,334.221
8. ¶I-3727; ¶10,334.22 et seq.
9. ¶I-3727; ¶10,334.22

10. ¶I-3734; ¶10,334.26
11. ¶N-1216.2 et seq.; ¶10,334.08
12. ¶I-4520et seq.; ¶1214 et seq.
13. ¶I-4539; ¶1214 et seq.

sale, and (3) neither spouse is ineligible for a full exclusion because of the once-every-2-year limit. (Code Sec. 121(b)(2)(A); Reg § 1.121-2(a)(3))[14] A surviving spouse can qualify for the up-to-$500,000 exclusion if the sale occurs not later than 2 years after the other spouse's death, if the requirements for the $500,000 exclusion were met immediately before the spouse's death, and the survivor hasn't remarried before the sale. (Code Sec. 121(b)(4))[15]

For the excludable amount where married taxpayers aren't eligible for the full $500,000 exclusion, see ¶2444.

Gain from the sale or exchange of property that is attributable to periods of "nonqualified use' isn't eligible for the exclusion. (Code Sec. 121(b)(5)(A))[16] Nonqualified use refers to any period after 2008 during which the property isn't used as the principal residence of the taxpayer, or his spouse, or former spouse. (Code Sec. 121(b)(5)(C)(i))[17] Exceptions to the definition of 'period of nonqualified use' include (1) use occurring in the 5-year testing period after the date the residence was last used as a principal residence, (2) temporary absence (not to exceed an aggregate period of 2 years), and (3) any period during which the taxpayer or his spouse is serving on qualified official extended duty (not to exceed an aggregate period of 10 years), see ¶2445. (Code Sec. 121(b)(5)(C)(ii))[18]

The gain allocated to periods of nonqualified use is the total amount of gain, multiplied by a fraction, the numerator of which is the aggregate periods of nonqualified use during the period the taxpayer owned the property, and the denominator of which is the period the taxpayer owned the property. (Code Sec. 121(b)(5)(B))[19]

The exclusion also doesn't apply to gain attributable to post-May 6, '97 depreciation (Code Sec. 121(d)(6)),[20] and that gain isn't taken into account in determining the amount of gain allocated to qualified use. (Code Sec. 121(b)(5)(D))[21]

The exchange or involuntary conversion (destruction (but only if the residence is totally destroyed), as well as condemnation) of a principal residence is treated as a sale for purposes of the homesale exclusion. (Code Sec. 121(d)(5)(A))[22]

If property is used for both residential and business (or investment) purposes, no allocation of gain is required if both the residential and non-residential portions of the property are within the same dwelling unit, but gain isn't excludable to the extent of any post-May 6, '97, depreciation. However, gain is allocated if the part of the home for which the use requirement isn't met is separate from the dwelling unit. (Reg § 1.121-1(e)(1))[23]

Individuals subject to the expatriate tax rules (¶4640) can't claim the exclusion. (Code Sec. 121(e))[24]

For a taxpayer who acquired a home in a like-kind exchange (¶2417 *et seq.*) in which any gain wasn't recognized, or a donee of that taxpayer, the exclusion doesn't apply for the 5-year period beginning with the date of the acquisition. (Code Sec. 121(d)(10))[25]

A taxpayer can elect out of the exclusion. (Code Sec. 121(f))[26]

If all of the homesale gain is excluded, the transaction isn't reported on the return. But, entries on Form 8949 are necessary if there is taxable gain on the homesale (e.g., realized gain exceeds the excludable amount). [27]

---

14. ¶I-4536; ¶1214.02
15. ¶I-4538.1; ¶1214.02
16. ¶I-4568.1; ¶1214.07
17. ¶I-4568.3; ¶1214.07
18. ¶I-4568.4; ¶1214.07
19. ¶I-4568.2; ¶1214.07
20. ¶I-4568; ¶1214.06

21. ¶I-4568.7; ¶1214.07
22. ¶I-4565; ¶1214.14
23. ¶I-4532 *et seq.*; ¶1214.06
24. ¶I-4569; ¶1214.18
25. ¶I-4561.1; ¶1214.14
26. ¶I-4570; ¶1214.20
27. ¶I-4521; ¶1214

¶ 2443   Reduced exclusion for partially qualifying principal residence sales.

A reduced maximum exclusion can apply to taxpayers who sell their principal residence but (1) fail to qualify for the 2-out-of-5-year ownership and use test, or (2) previously sold another home within the 2-year period ending on the sale date of the current home in a transaction to which the exclusion applied (¶2442). If a taxpayer's failure to meet either rule occurs because he must sell the home due to a change of place of employment, health or, to the extent provided by regs, other unforeseen circumstances, then he can claim a reduced exclusion. Under these circumstances, the maximum gain that can be excluded is equal to the full $250,000 or $500,000 exclusion times a fraction having as its numerator the shorter of (a) aggregate periods of ownership and use of the home by the taxpayer as a principal residence during the 5 years ending on the sale date, or (b) the period of time after the last sale to which the exclusion applied, and before the date of the current sale, and having 2 years (or its equivalent in months) as its denominator. (Code Sec. 121(c))[28]

illustration: S, a single taxpayer, owned and used a home as a principal residence for the last 18 months. S sells the home because S has a new job in another city. S realizes $50,000 on the sale. Since S doesn't meet the 2-year ownership and use tests and the sale is due to a change in place of employment, S qualifies for the reduced exclusion. The amount of gain excluded by S can't exceed $187,500 ($250,000 × 1.5 ÷ 2). S can exclude all of the gain ($50,000) from the sale.

The up-to-10-year suspension for qualifying military services or Foreign Service members or intelligence community employees (¶2445) can be elected to determine the amount of the reduced exclusion. (Code Sec. 121(d)(9)(A))[29]

To claim a reduced exclusion, the sale or exchange must be made because of a change of place of employment, health, or unforeseen circumstances. If a safe harbor in the regs applies, a sale is deemed to be made by reason of a change in place of employment, health, or unforeseen circumstances. If a safe harbor doesn't apply, a sale or exchange is by reason of a change in place of employment, health, or unforeseen circumstances only if the primary reason for the sale or exchange is one of those reasons. (Reg § 1.121-3(b))[30]

A sale or exchange is because of a change in place of employment, if, in the case of a qualified individual (taxpayer, spouse, co-owner of the residence, or a person whose principal place of abode is in the same household as the taxpayer), the primary reason for the sale or exchange is a change in the location of the individual's employment (including self-employment). Under the distance safe harbor, this condition is treated as met if (1) the new place of employment is at least 50 miles farther from the residence sold or exchanged than was the former place of employment (for the formerly unemployed, 50 miles between the new place of employment and the residence sold or exchanged), and (2) the change in place of employment occurs during the taxpayer's ownership and use of the home as his principal residence. (Reg § 1.121-3(c))[31]

The health condition is met if the primary reason for the sale is to (1) obtain, provide, or facilitate the diagnosis, cure, mitigation, or treatment of disease, illness, or injury of a qualified individual, or (2) obtain or provide medical or personal care for a qualified individual suffering from a disease, illness, or injury. A qualified individual includes those listed above under change of employment, plus (a) a parent, grandparent, stepmother, stepfather, child, grandchild, stepchild, adopted child, brother, sister, stepbrother, stepsister, half brother, half sister, mother-in-law, father-in-law, brother-in-law, sister-in-law, son-in-law, daughter-in-law, uncle, aunt, nephew, or niece even if they aren't his dependents; and (b) descendants of the taxpayer's grandparent (e.g., first cousins). A sale or

---

28. ¶I-4557; ¶1214.08
29. ¶I-4557.1; ¶1214.08

30. ¶I-4541; ¶1214.08
31. ¶I-4542 *et seq.*; ¶1214.08

exchange doesn't qualify for the health condition if it is merely beneficial to the general health or well-being of the individual. Under a safe harbor, the health condition is treated as met if a doctor recommends a change of residence for the health reasons listed above in (1) or (2). (Reg § 1.121-3(d); Reg § 1.121-3(f))[32]

⚫*observation:* Qualified individuals in (a) and (b) above are defined in Reg § 1.121-3(f) by reference to paragraphs (1) through (8) of former Code Sec. 152(a). Presumably that reference still applies even though Code Sec. 152(a) now contains only two paragraphs.

A sale or exchange is caused by unforeseen circumstances if the primary reason for the sale or exchange is an event that the taxpayer couldn't reasonably have anticipated before buying and occupying the residence. A sale or exchange by reason of unforeseen circumstances (other than a circumstance covered by a safe harbors listed in regs, such as an involuntary conversion, or death of a qualified individual, or designated by IRS as an unforeseen circumstance in published guidance or in a ruling issued to a specific taxpayer) doesn't qualify for the reduced exclusion if the primary reason for the sale or exchange is a preference for a different residence or an improvement in financial circumstances. (Reg § 1.121-3(e))[33]

¶ 2444   Amount excludable if married taxpayers ineligible for full exclusion.

If married taxpayers filing a joint return aren't eligible for the $500,000 maximum exclusion (¶2442), the amount of the exclusion that they can claim is the sum of each spouse's maximum exclusion determined on a separate basis as if they had not been married. But, for this purpose, each spouse is treated as owning the house during the period that either spouse owned the house. (Code Sec. 121(b)(2)(B))[34]

¶ 2445   Ownership and use tests to qualify for homesale exclusion.

The full homesale exclusion applies only if a taxpayer owned the home and used it as a principal residence for at least 2 of the 5 years ending on the date of the sale. (Code Sec. 121(a))

A taxpayer is treated as the owner and seller of a residence held by a trust during the period that he or she is treated as the owner of the trust or the part of the trust that includes the residence under the rules of Code Sec. 671 through Code Sec. 679 (grantors and others treated as substantial owners, see ¶3955 *et seq.*). Similar treatment applies to certain single-owner entities (e.g., LLC) where the entity is disregarded for federal tax purposes. (Reg § 1.121-1(c)(3))[35]

Each unmarried taxpayer who jointly owns a principal residence can be eligible to exclude from gross income up to $250,000 of gain that is attributable to that taxpayer's interest in the property. (Reg § 1.121-2(a)(2))[36]

Gain from the sale or exchange of partial interests (other than interests remaining after the sale or exchange of a remainder interest) in the taxpayer's principal residence is excludable if the interest sold or exchanged includes an interest in the dwelling unit. Only 1 maximum limitation amount of $250,000 ($500,000 for certain joint returns) applies to the combined sales or exchanges of partial interests. (Reg § 1.121-4(e))[37]

An individual's bankruptcy estate (¶3972) in a chapter 7 or 11 bankruptcy case under title 11 of the U.S. Code succeeds to and takes into account his homesale exclusion if the individual otherwise satisfies the requirements. (Reg § 1.1398-3)[38]

---

32. ¶I-4543 *et seq.*; ¶1214.08
33. ¶I-4547 *et seq.*; ¶1214.08
34. ¶I-4537; ¶1214.02
35. ¶I-4529 *et seq.*; ¶1214.12

36. ¶I-4535; ¶1214.02
37. ¶I-4567; ¶1214.16
38. ¶C-9718.01; ¶13,984.01

Under the following circumstances, a taxpayer can 'tack on' someone else's ownership and/or use period to his or her own period.

. . . An unmarried individual whose spouse (¶4705) was deceased on the sale date can tack on the decedent's ownership and use period to his or her own period. (Code Sec. 121(d)(2))[39]

. . . An individual who receives a home in a Code Sec. 1041(a) transaction (¶2447), such as a tax-free transfer from a spouse (or former spouse), can tack on the transferor's ownership period to his or her own ownership period. (Code Sec. 121(d)(3)(A))[40]

. . . An individual is treated as using a home as his or her principal residence during any period of ownership that the individual's spouse (see ¶4705) or former spouse is granted use of the property under a divorce or separation instrument. (Code Sec. 121(d)(3)(B))[41]

However, if a taxpayer voluntarily demolishes his or her principal residence and builds a new principal residence on the same land, the period that the taxpayer owned and used the demolished principal residence isn't taken into account in determining qualification for the exclusion on the sale of the new principal residence. [42]

If a taxpayer becomes physically or mentally incapable of self-care and, during the 5-year period ending on the home's sale date, owns and uses the home as a principal residence for periods aggregating at least 1 year, the taxpayer is treated as using the home as a principal residence during any time in the 5-year period in which he or she owns the home and lives in a facility (including a nursing home) licensed by a state or political subdivision to care for someone in the taxpayer's condition. (Code Sec. 121(d)(7))[43]

A member of the uniformed services or the Foreign Service, and an employee of the intelligence community can elect to suspend the 5-year period for measuring ownership and use during any period that service member and his or her spouse (¶4705) is serving on extended duty at least 50 miles from the residence or while residing under orders in government quarters. (Code Sec. 121(d)(9)(A)) The suspension can't last more than 10 years. (Code Sec. 121(d)(9)(B))[44] A Peace Corps volunteer or his or her spouse serving outside the U.S. can also make that election. (Code Sec. 121(d)(12))[45]

¶ 2446   Sales and Exchanges Between Related Taxpayers.

No gain or loss is recognized on a transfer of property between spouses (or former spouses incident to divorce; ¶2447). No deduction is allowed for any loss from the sale or exchange of property between specified related taxpayers (¶2448). A loss from a transfer between members of the same controlled group is generally deferred until the property is transferred outside the group (¶2450).

¶ 2447   Gain or loss not recognized on transfer to spouse.

No gain or loss is recognized on a transfer of property to (or in trust for the benefit of) the transferor's spouse, or to a former spouse incident to a divorce. (Code Sec. 1041(a))[46] Certain transfers to third parties on behalf of (i.e., in satisfaction of an obligation or liability of) the spouse or former spouse qualify for nonrecognition. (Reg § 1.1041-1T(c), Q&A-9)[47] However, nonrecognition doesn't apply to transfers in trust where liability exceeds basis (Code Sec. 1041(e)),[48] to transfers in trust of installment obligations (Code Sec. 453B(g)),[49] or where the transferee spouse is a nonresident alien. (Code Sec. 1041(d))[50]

---

39. ¶I-4559; ¶1214.10
40. ¶I-4558; ¶1214.10
41. ¶I-4558; ¶1214.10
42. ¶I-4527
43. ¶I-4563; ¶1214.14
44. ¶I-4528.1; ¶1214.14

45. ¶I-4528.7; ¶1214.14
46. ¶I-3601; ¶10,414
47. ¶I-3604; ¶10,414
48. ¶I-3608; ¶10,414
49. ¶I-3609; ¶10,414
50. ¶I-3611; ¶10,414

A transfer of property is incident to divorce if it occurs within 1 year after the date the marriage ceases (Code Sec. 1041(c)(1)) or the transfer is related to the cessation of the marriage. (Code Sec. 1041(c)(2)) A transfer is related to the cessation if the transfer is under a divorce or separation instrument and the transfer occurs not more than 6 years after the date the marriage ceases. For later transfers, there's a presumption that the transfer isn't related to the cessation. (Reg § 1.1041-1T(b), Q&A-7)[1]

¶ 2448   Losses from sales and exchanges between related taxpayers.

No deduction is allowed for losses from sales or exchanges between certain related taxpayers. (Code Sec. 267(a)) The following are related taxpayers:

Members of the seller's family, but only brothers and sisters (whole or half blood), spouse, ancestors, and lineal descendants. (Code Sec. 267(a), Code Sec. 267(b)(1), Code Sec. 267(c)(4))[2] In-laws aren't considered members of the seller's family. [3]

Controlled corporations. A taxpayer and a controlled corporation, and a fiduciary and a corporation controlled by the trust or grantor. "Control" is direct or indirect ownership of more than 50% in value of the outstanding stock. (Code Sec. 267(b)(2), Code Sec. 267(b)(8))[4]

Controlled group member. Corporations that are members of the same controlled group of corporations. (Code Sec. 267(b)(3))[5] Loss from a sale or exchange between members of a controlled group is deferred, as explained at ¶2450.

A corporation and a partnership, if the same persons own more than 50% in value of the outstanding stock of the corporation, and more than 50% of the capital interest, or the profits interest, in the partnership. (Code Sec. 267(b)(10))[6]

An S corporation and another S corporation, if the same persons own more than 50% in value of the outstanding stock of each corporation. (Code Sec. 267(b)(11))[7]

An S corporation and a C corporation, if the same persons own more than 50% in value of the outstanding stock of each corporation. (Code Sec. 267(b)(12))[8]

An estate and a beneficiary of that estate, except in the case of a sale or exchange in satisfaction of a pecuniary bequest. (Code Sec. 267(b)(13))[9]

Trustees, grantors, and beneficiaries, that is, the grantor and the fiduciary of a trust; the fiduciary and the beneficiary of a trust; the fiduciaries of 2 different trusts with the same grantor; a fiduciary of one trust and the beneficiary of another trust with the same grantor; and a trust fiduciary and a corporation more than 50% in value of the outstanding stock of which is owned directly or indirectly by or for the trust or its grantor. (Code Sec. 267(b)(4), Code Sec. 267(b)(5), Code Sec. 267(b)(6), Code Sec. 267(b)(7), Code Sec. 267(b)(8))[10]

Exempt organizations. A person and an exempt organization controlled, directly or indirectly, by that person or the members of his family. (Code Sec. 267(b)(9))[11]

In applying the related taxpayer rules, ownership of stock is attributed to the taxpayer as follows:

(1) A stockholder is considered to own a proportionate share of the stock owned by the corporation.

(2) A partner is considered to own a proportionate share of the stock owned by the partnership.

---

1. ¶I-3613; ¶10,414
2. ¶I-3512; ¶2674.03
3. ¶I-3515; ¶2674.03
4. ¶I-3519; ¶2674.03
5. ¶I-3522; ¶2674.05
6. ¶I-3532; ¶2674.03
7. ¶I-3531; ¶2674.03
8. ¶I-3531; ¶2674.05
9. ¶I-3533; ¶2674.03
10. ¶I-3527; ¶2674.03
11. ¶I-3530; ¶2674.03

(3) An individual owning some stock in a corporation is considered the owner of stock owned by his partner.

(4) A beneficiary is considered to own a proportionate share of the stock owned by the trust or estate.

(5) An individual is considered to own stock owned by members of his family, as defined above, whether or not he's the actual owner of stock in the same corporation. (Code Sec. 267(c); Reg § 1.267(c)-1)[12]

¶ 2449 Disallowed loss can reduce gain on a later sale by related buyer.

A related buyer can reduce his gain on property he resells at a gain by the loss disallowed to his seller if these conditions are met: (1) a loss deduction was barred under the rules on related taxpayers (¶2448); (2) the resale or exchange is at a gain, and the property is either the property on which the loss was disallowed or property the basis of which is determined by reference to the basis of that property; (3) the loss deduction on the original sale to the taxpayer wasn't barred under the wash sale rules (¶2461); and, for sales and exchanges of property acquired after Dec. 31, 2015, loss with respect to the property that has been sold or exchanged is subject to federal income tax in the hands of the transferor immediately before the transfer. (Code Sec. 267(d); Reg § 1.267(d)-1)[13]

Illustration: H sells to his wife, W, for $55,000, farmland with an adjusted basis for determining loss to H of $80,000. The loss of $25,000 isn't allowable to H. W exchanges the farmland, held for investment purposes, with an unrelated individual for 2 city lots, also held for investment purposes. The basis of the city lots in W's hands ($55,000) is a substituted basis determined by reference to the basis of the farmland. Later, W sells the city lots for $100,000. Although W's realized gain is $45,000 ($100,000 minus $55,000), W's recognized gain is only $20,000, the excess of the realized gain of $45,000 over the loss of $25,000 not allowable to H. (Reg § 1.267(d)-1(a)(4), Ex (4))

¶ 2450 Loss between members of controlled group are deferred.

With some exceptions, a loss from a transfer between members of the same controlled group is deferred (rather than denied). The loss is recognized when the property is transferred outside the group if the loss would be recognized under consolidated return principles. (Code Sec. 267(f)(2))[14]

For purposes of any Code section other than Code Sec. 267 which refers to a relationship which would result in a disallowance of losses under Code Sec. 267, deferral under Code Sec. 267(f)(2) is treated as a disallowance. (Code Sec. 267(f)(4); Reg § 1.267(f)-1)[15]

¶ 2451 Gain on sale of employer stock to ESOP or EWOC.

A taxpayer (but not a C corporation) or taxpayer's executor who sells qualified securities (certain common stock) to an employee stock ownership plan (ESOP) or eligible worker-owned cooperative (EWOC) that holds specified percentages of the securities, can elect nonrecognition of gain if the seller buys "qualified replacement property" (QRP) or securities of another corporation that doesn't exceed certain passive income limits) within a specified period of time. The seller's gain is recognized only to the extent the sale proceeds exceed the cost of the QRP. Nonrecognition treatment applies only if the gain on the sale of the stock would otherwise have been long-term capital gain. (Code Sec. 1042)[16] However, with some exceptions (e.g., for gifts), gain not recognized on the sale to the ESOP is

---

12. ¶I-3516; ¶2674.04
13. ¶I-3541; ¶2674.01
14. ¶s E-8250, I-3524 *et seq.*; ¶2674.05

15. ¶I-3504.1; ¶2674
16. ¶H-12103 *et seq.*; ¶10,424

recognized on the disposition of the QRP. (Code Sec. 1042(e))[17]

The deferral of gain under Code Sec. 1042 also applies to the sale of stock of a qualified refiner or processor to an eligible farmers' cooperative. (Code Sec. 1042(g)(1))

¶ 2452   Installment Sales and Other Deferred Payment Sales. ■■■■■■

Under the installment method, a nondealer (unless he elects out; see ¶2456) reports gain on a sale as payments are received, instead of reporting all the gain in the year of sale (¶2453).

For sales that don't qualify for installment reporting, see ¶2454. For contingent payment sales, see ¶2455. For character of gain when depreciable property is sold, see ¶2457. For sales and other dispositions of installment notes, see ¶2458. For an installment sale to a related person who resells the property, see ¶2459. For pledge and interest rule, see ¶2460. For unstated interest on installment sales, see ¶1304 *et seq.*

¶ 2453   Reporting gain under the installment sale rules—Form 6252.

The installment sale rules are used to report gain on the disposition of non-dealer property by both cash-method and accrual-method taxpayers where at least 1 payment is to be received after the close of the tax year in which the disposition occurs unless the taxpayer elects not to use the installment method (see ¶2456) or the transaction is one for which the installment method can't be used (see ¶2454). (Code Sec. 453)[18] The amount of a payment included in the seller's income is that part of the installment payments received in the year that the gross profit realized or to be realized bears to the total contract price (the "gross profit ratio"). (Code Sec. 453(c); Reg § 15A.453-1(b)(2)(i))[19]

illustration: Taxpayer sells personal-use property for a gross profit of $20,000 at a contract price of $80,000. The gross profit ratio is 25% ($20,000 ÷ $80,000). Therefore, 25% of each payment collected on the sale (including the down payment) is gain and is included in gross income for the tax year it's collected. The ratio remains constant for all installment payments received on the sale.

Payments include:

(a) amounts actually received by the seller, e.g., cash, other property, foreign currency, marketable securities, or evidences of indebtedness of persons other than the buyer. (Reg § 15A.453-1(b)(3)(i))[20] Evidences of indebtedness of the buyer are treated as payment if they are payable on demand or readily tradable; (Code Sec. 453(f)(4))[21]

(b) the buyer's payments of the seller's selling expenses; [22] and

(c) the amount by which qualifying debt assumed or taken subject to by the buyer exceeds the seller's basis. (Reg § 15A.453-1(b)(3)(i))[23]

Gross profit is the selling price less the property's adjusted basis (as increased by selling expenses). (Reg § 15A.453-1(b)(2)(v)) The selling price is the gross selling price without reduction to reflect any existing mortgage or other encumbrance on the property (whether assumed or taken subject to by the buyer) and without reduction to reflect any selling expenses. Neither interest (whether stated or unstated) nor OID is part of the selling price. (Reg § 15A.453-1(b)(2)(ii))[24]

Gain recaptured under Code Sec. 1245 (¶2677) or Code Sec. 1250 (¶2679), including gain attributable to the Code Sec. 179 expense election (¶1940 *et seq.*), or so much of the unrealized receivables under Code Sec. 751 (¶3750) as relates to Code Sec. 1245 or Code

---

17. ¶H-12111; ¶10,424
18. ¶G-6000 *et seq.*; ¶4534 *et seq.*
19. ¶G-6052 *et seq.*; ¶4534.21
20. ¶G-6151 *et seq.*; ¶4534.22 *et seq.*

21. ¶G-6163; ¶4534.23
22. ¶G-6151
23. ¶G-6155; ¶4534.27
24. ¶G-6053 *et seq.*; ¶4534.21

Sec. 1250, is ordinary income in the year of sale. Only gain that isn't recapture income is taken into account under the installment method. (Code Sec. 453(i))[25] The recaptured amount is added to the adjusted basis of the property for purposes of determining basis recovered and gain recognized from each installment. [26]

While gain on the sale of a partnership interest qualifies for installment reporting, gain attributable to inventories and unrealized receivables held by the partnership does not. [27]

The *total contract price* is the selling price, reduced by debt on the property that the buyer assumes (or takes subject to), but only to the extent of the seller's basis in the property. (Reg § 15A.453-1(b)(2)(iii))[28]

¶ 2454   When the installment method can't be used.

The installment method can't be used by dealers in property, real or personal. (Code Sec. 453(b)(2))[29] However, the installment method can be used for:

• dispositions by farmers (not merchants) of any property used or produced in the trade or business of farming (Code Sec. 453(l)(2)(A)); and

• dispositions to an individual in the ordinary course of a taxpayer's trade or business of the following, but only if interest is paid on the tax deferred when the installment method is used: (Code Sec. 453(l)(2)(B))

. . . a timeshare right to use, or a timeshare right to an ownership interest in, residential real property for not more than 6 weeks per year, or a right to use specified campgrounds for recreational purposes (timeshare rights or ownership interests held by the spouse, children, grandchildren or parents of an individual are treated as held by the individual), or

. . . any residential lots, but only if the taxpayer (or any related person) isn't to make any improvements with respect to the lots. [30]

The installment method can't be used for:

. . . sales of stock or securities traded on an established securities market (Code Sec. 453(k)(2)(A)), but it can be used for unregistered restricted stock sold in a private placement;[31]

. . . sales at a loss; [32]

. . . sales of depreciable property between persons related within the Code Sec. 1239(b) rules (¶2674), and between controlled partnerships (as defined in Code Sec. 707(b)(1)(B), ¶3726 *et seq.*), unless it's established to IRS's satisfaction that the sale didn't have as 1 of its principal purposes the avoidance of federal tax. (Code Sec. 453(g))[33]

¶ 2455   Contingent payment installment sales.

The installment method is used to report contingent payment sales (sales or other dispositions of property in a tax year in which the total selling price can't be determined at the close of that tax year), unless the taxpayer elects not to use the installment method (¶2456). (Reg § 15A.453-1(c)(1)) In general, basis is allocated to payments received and to be received by treating the stated maximum selling price as the selling price. (Reg § 15A.453-1(c)(2)(i)) However, if:

---

25. ¶G-6097 *et seq.*; ¶4534.05
26. ¶G-6097; ¶4534.05
27. ¶G-6010; ¶4534.05
28. ¶G-6060; ¶4534.21
29. ¶G-6601; ¶4534.01

30. ¶G-6603 *et seq.*; ¶4534.01
31. ¶G-6016 *et seq.*; ¶4534.01
32. ¶G-6015; ¶4534.01
33. ¶G-6201 *et seq.*; ¶4534.17

. . . the maximum selling price can't be determined, but the maximum period over which payments may be received is fixed, the seller's basis is allocated to the tax years in which payments may be received in equal annual increments. (Reg § 15A.453-1(c)(3)(i))

. . . the agreement neither specifies a maximum selling price nor limits payments to a fixed period, the transaction can be a sale or payments under the agreement may be rent or royalty income. If the transaction is a sale, basis (including selling expenses) generally is recovered in equal annual increments over a period of 15 years starting with the date of sale. (Reg § 15A.453-1(c)(4))[34]

A seller may (if IRS grants permission) use an alternative basis recovery method if it's able to demonstrate that applying the normal basis recovery rule would substantially and inappropriately defer recovery of basis and the alternative method would likely result in basis recovery at a rate at least twice as fast. (Reg § 15A.453-1(c)(7))[35]

¶ 2456   Electing out of the installment method.

An election not to have the installment method apply to a sale is made by reporting an amount realized equal to the selling price (including the full face amount of any installment obligation) on the tax return filed for the year the sale occurs. The election out must be made on or before the due date (including extensions) for filing the return for the year of sale. A late election is allowed only if IRS concludes taxpayer had good cause for the failure to timely elect. An election out may be revoked only with IRS's consent. (Code Sec. 453(d); Reg § 15A.453-1(d)(3))[36]

recommendation: Consider electing out of the installment method if the seller will be in a much higher tax bracket in post-sale years than in the sale year, or if he is selling a property with large suspended passive activity losses so these losses can be used immediately to offset nonpassive income (¶1814).

A taxpayer who elects out of the installment method recognizes gain on the sale under his accounting method. The amount realized attributable to a debt instrument received is the debt instrument's issue price as determined under the OID rules discussed at ¶1314. (Reg § 1.1001-1(g))[37]

¶ 2457   Character of installment gain on sale of depreciable realty.

When depreciable real property is sold by a noncorporate taxpayer, the gain may be partially 25%-rate gain (unrecaptured section 1250 gain subject to a maximum tax of 25%, see ¶2604), and partially adjusted net capital gain (taxed at a lower rate, see ¶2603). If there are both types of gain, the 25%-rate gain is taken into account as payments are received before any adjusted net capital gain is included. (Reg § 1.453-12(a)) See ¶2600 *et seq.* for the taxation of capital gains. [38]

illustration: T sells depreciable real property for a total price of $150,000. T has a total gain of $30,000, $20,000 of which is 25%-rate gain, and $10,000 of which is adjusted net capital gain. The sales price is payable in 5 equal annual installments of $30,000, with the 1st installment due in the year of sale. T takes $6,000 of gain into account as each installment is paid. The entire gain of $6,000 on the receipt of the 1st 3 installments, and $2,000 of the gain on the receipt of the 4th installment, is taxed as 25%-rate gain. The remaining $4,000 of gain on the 4th installment and the entire $6,000 of gain on the 5th installment is taxed at the applicable rate for adjusted net capital gain.

---

34. ¶G-6250 *et seq.*; ¶4534.30
35. ¶G-6279 *et seq.*; ¶4534.30
36. ¶G-6350 *et seq.*; ¶4534.08

37. ¶G-6550 *et seq.*; ¶4534.45 *et seq.*
38. ¶G-6102; ¶4534.57

Net Code Sec. 1231 gain that would otherwise be taxed as long-term capital gain, is taxed as ordinary income to the extent of non-recaptured net Code Sec. 1231 losses for the preceding 5 years (¶2669). If net Code Sec. 1231 gain for a tax year consists of both 25%-rate gain and adjusted net capital gain, the 25%-rate gain is recharacterized as ordinary income first. This rule also applies to installment payments. (Reg § 1.453-12(d), Ex. 3)[39]

¶ 2458   Sale, exchange, or satisfaction of installment obligations.

For installment obligations satisfied at face value, gain or loss is computed under the general rules (¶2453) for computing income on the installment method. [40]

If an installment obligation is satisfied at other than face or is sold or exchanged, gain or loss is the difference between the basis of the obligation and the amount realized. If it's distributed, transmitted, or disposed of other than by sale or exchange, gain or loss is the difference between its basis and its fair market value (FMV) (Code Sec. 453B(a)),[41] except that if it's distributed in a complete liquidation of a subsidiary to which Code Sec. 337(a) applies (¶3560), no gain or loss is recognized. (Code Sec. 453B(d))[42] If there's a repossession by the seller of the personal property sold following the buyer's default (i.e., a disposition of the installment obligation by the seller), [43] the seller's gain or loss is: (1) the FMV of the property, plus anything received from the buyer in addition to the repossessed property; *minus* (2) the seller's basis in the installment obligation, plus any expense in connection with the repossession. [44] Transmission of an installment obligation at death doesn't result in gain or loss to the decedent. (Code Sec. 453B(c); Reg § 1.451-1(b)(2))[45]

A reduction of the purchase price, or a modification of an installment obligation by changing the payment terms (e.g., reducing the purchase price and interest rate, and deferring or increasing the payment dates) isn't a disposition of the obligation. [46]

The basis of an obligation is the excess of its face value over the amount equal to the income that would be returnable if the obligation were fully satisfied. (Code Sec. 453B(b))[47]

observation: Thus, the basis of the installment obligations is the adjusted basis of the property sold less any part of that basis allocated to a payment made at the time of sale.

¶ 2459   Installment sale to related person who then resells.

If a person disposes of property in an installment sale (1st disposition) to a related person (see below) who then disposes of the property (2nd disposition) within 2 years of the 1st disposition, and before all payments are made on the 1st disposition, the amount the related person (i.e., the buyer in the 1st disposition) realizes as a result of the 2nd disposition is treated as being received by the original seller at the time of the 2nd disposition. (Code Sec. 453(e)(1), Code Sec. 453(e)(2))

The amount treated as received by the person making the 1st disposition because of the 2nd disposition can't be more than:

. . . the lesser of the total amount realized on any 2nd disposition of the property occurring in the tax year, or the total contract price for the 1st disposition; minus

. . . the sum of the aggregate amount of payments received with respect to the 1st disposition before the close of the tax year in which the 2nd disposition occurs, and the aggregate amount treated as received with respect to the 1st disposition because of

39. ¶G-6105; ¶4534.58
40. ¶G-6052; ¶4534.22
41. ¶G-6454 *et seq.*; ¶453B4.05
42. ¶G-6489; ¶453B4.11
43. ¶G-6476; ¶453B4.07

44. ¶G-6481; ¶453B4.07
45. ¶G-6507; ¶453B4.13
46. ¶G-6486
47. ¶G-6456; ¶453B4.07

earlier dispositions of installment obligations by related persons. (Code Sec. 453(e)(3))[48]

For purposes of these rules, if the 2nd disposition isn't a sale or exchange, the property's fair market value is treated as the amount realized. (Code Sec. 453(e)(4))[49]

A "related person" is someone whose stock would be attributed to the initial seller under Code Sec. 318(a) (¶3523), other than under the option attribution rules, or a person who bears a relationship to the initial seller under Code Sec. 267(b) (¶2448) for purposes of the rules disallowing the deduction of losses on sales between related persons. (Code Sec. 453(f)(1))[50]

Exceptions include involuntary conversions, deaths, corporations' reacquisition of their own stock, and where IRS rules out tax avoidance. (Code Sec. 453(e)(6), Code Sec. 453(e)(7))[1]

Except for marketable securities, the 2-year period stops running when puts, options, or short sales, etc., are involved. (Code Sec. 453(e)(2))[2]

¶ 2460 Installment sales of certain property for more than $150,000—"pledge and interest" rule.

The following rules apply to an installment sale of "any" property (except personal use or farm property, and dealer sales of timeshares or residential lots) where the selling price is over $150,000: (Code Sec. 453A)[3]

(1) If an installment obligation from the sale plus all other installment obligations that arose from dispositions during the tax year and are still outstanding at the close of the tax year total over $5 million, the seller must pay, as additional tax, interest at the underpayment rate (¶4868) on the deferred tax attributable to those installment obligations. Once interest is required on an obligation that arises during any year, interest must be paid for any later tax year if any of the obligation is still outstanding at the close of that later year.

(2) If an installment obligation from the sale becomes security for any indebtedness, the net proceeds of the indebtedness are treated as a payment of the obligation as of the later of the time the indebtedness becomes secured or the proceeds of the indebtedness are received by the seller. (Code Sec. 453A(d)(1)) Payment of indebtedness is treated as secured by an interest in an installment obligation to the extent that an arrangement allows the taxpayer to satisfy all or part of the debt with the installment obligation (i.e., gives him the *right* to repay the loan by transferring the installment note to his creditor). (Code Sec. 453A(d)(4))

¶ 2461 Wash Sales; Loss Disallowance Rule. ▬▬▬▬▬

No loss deduction is allowed for any loss from any sale or other disposition of stock or securities (including contracts or options to acquire or sell stock or securities) if, within a period beginning 30 days before and ending 30 days after the sale, the taxpayer acquires, or has entered into a contract or option to acquire, substantially identical stock or securities. (Code Sec. 1091(a); Reg § 1.1091-1(a))[4]

illustration: June 1: T buys 100 shares of Corp A stock for $15 per share. Dec. 1: T buys 100 shares of Corp A stock for $10 per share. Dec. 31: T sells the 100 shares of Corp A stock bought on June 1 for $10 per share realizing a $500 loss. T can't deduct the loss because he bought substantially identical stock within 30 days before the sale. The same

---

48. ¶G-6401 *et seq.*; ¶4534.18
49. ¶G-6403; ¶4534.18
50. ¶G-6416; ¶4534.18
1. ¶G-6411 *et seq.*; ¶4534.18

2. ¶G-6408, G-6409; ¶4534.18
3. ¶G-6300 *et seq.*; ¶453A4
4. ¶I-3901; ¶10,914

result would occur if the 2nd purchase had been made on the following Jan. 30.

caution: This rule can ensnare investors (e.g., investors in mutual funds) who participate in automatic dividend reinvestment plans since the automatic reinvestment of dividends within the prohibited period is a purchase of substantially identical securities.

Loss is also disallowed where the repurchase is made either by an IRA (¶4340) or by a Roth IRA (¶4356), established for the exclusive benefit of the original purchasing taxpayer or his beneficiaries. [5]

"Substantially identical securities" requires something less than precise correspondence. Stock or securities of different issuers or obligors aren't substantially identical. Stock or securities of the same issuer are substantially identical if they are substantially the same in all important particulars. [6]

observation: It is often possible to recognize losses by selling a security and investing the proceeds in a similar but not substantially identical security (e.g., sell common stock in one drug company and buy stock in another drug company, or sell stock in one exchange-traded fund (ETF) and buy stock in another ETF that invests in the same types of securities).

The wash sale rule also disallows a loss on the closing of a short sale of stock or securities, or the sale, exchange, or termination of a securities futures contract to sell, if, within the period beginning 30 days before the date the short sale is closed and ending 30 days after that date: (1) substantially identical stock or securities are sold, or (2) another short sale of (or securities futures contracts to sell) substantially identical stock or securities is entered. (Code Sec. 1091(e))[7]

Special rules apply to residual interests in REMICs (Code Sec. 860F(d)),[8] and to tax straddles. (Reg § 1.1092(b)-1T, Reg § 1.1092(b)-5T)[9]

The wash sale rules don't apply to: (a) any losses on shares in a floating net asset value money market fund.[10], or (b) a dealer in stocks or securities if the loss is sustained in a transaction made in the ordinary course of that business. (Code Sec. 1091(a))[11]

For the basis and holding period of the acquired stock, see ¶2500 and ¶2658.

¶ 2462   Basis of Property. ▬▬▬▬▬▬▬▬▬▬▬▬

Basis is generally the cost (¶2463) of property, subject to certain adjustments (¶2473), for tax purposes. It is the point of departure for determining gain or loss on the disposition of the property, for computing annual deductions for depreciation, amortization, depletion, casualty losses, bad debts, and losses from "at-risk" activities, and for many other tax computations.

In general, basis for computing loss and gain is the same, whatever the transaction may be. But, the basis for computing loss differs from the basis for computing gain for (1) property converted from personal use to business or income-producing use (¶2472), and (2) property acquired by gift (¶2509).

For basis in corporate transactions and in nontaxable exchanges, see ¶2481 *et seq.*

For basis of property acquired by gift, or from a decedent or a spouse, see ¶2508 *et seq.*

---

5. ¶I-3906
6. ¶I-3914 *et seq.*; ¶10,914
7. ¶I-3904, I-3905; ¶10,914
8. ¶I-3902, I-3903; ¶860A4

9. ¶I-7540 *et seq.*; ¶10,924
10. ¶I-3916
11. ¶I-3917; ¶10,914

¶ 2463   Cost as basis.

A property's original basis is the taxpayer's cost, except where otherwise specifically provided (Code Sec. 1012) (¶2496 *et seq.*) or where a transaction isn't made at arm's length (see below). Cost is the amount paid in cash or other property, and liabilities incurred (¶2464). (Reg § 1.1012-1(a))[12] Payments made in connection with the acquisition of property, e.g., commissions and legal fees, are included in basis as part of the property's cost. [13]

IRS and most courts say that the cost basis of property received in an arm's-length taxable exchange is the fair market value (FMV) of the property *received* in the exchange, at the time of the exchange, unless the FMV of the property received can't be determined with a fair degree of certainty. Then, the FMV of the property given up will be used as a way of valuing the property received. However, some courts say the cost basis of property received in an arm's-length taxable exchange is the FMV of the property given up, not the property received. [14]

If property isn't bought in an arm's-length deal, its basis is its FMV. This can occur in sham transactions, or where the buyer, for personal reasons, overpays for the property (e.g., to help out a friend). [15]

¶ 2464   Mortgages and other liabilities as part of basis.

Taxpayer's cost (¶2463) of property (basis) includes the amount of a mortgage or other liability assumed in connection with the purchase, plus the amount of any liabilities that the purchased property is subject to (whether or not the taxpayer assumes the liabilities). [16] Redeemable ground rents are treated as mortgages. (Code Sec. 1055)[17]

illustration: J buys a building for $20,000 cash and an $80,000 mortgage. J's basis is $100,000. It would also be $100,000 if instead J assumed an existing $80,000 mortgage. And it would be $100,000 if, J paid $20,000 cash and J acquired the building subject to a mortgage without assuming it, or if J agreed to pay a seller's debt of $80,000.

Mortgages or other liabilities aren't part of the cost if they are contingent *and* there's a clear indication they would never have to be paid or that taxpayer doesn't intend to pay. [18]

¶ 2465   Effect of original issue discount (OID) and unstated interest on basis.

If the OID rules (¶1743 *et seq.*) or the unstated interest rules (¶1707) apply so that a part of a debt included in the buyer's cost for the property is treated as OID or unstated interest, the basis doesn't include any OID or unstated interest. (Reg § 1.483-1(a)(2))[19]

¶ 2466   Basis of repossessed mortgaged real estate.

A seller's basis in repossessed property is equal to the adjusted basis of the mortgage debt (determined under Code Sec. 453 and Code Sec. 1011) to the seller (as of the date of repossession), *plus* the sum of: (1) the repossession gain, and (2) the amount of money and the fair market value of other property (other than the buyer's obligations) which the seller transfers in connection with the repossession. If the mortgage debt isn't discharged on repossession, the seller's basis in the mortgage debt is zero. (Code Sec. 1038(c))[20]

---

12. ¶P-1119; ¶10,124 *et seq.*
13. ¶P-1102; ¶10,124.03
14. ¶P-1114; ¶10,124.46
15. ¶P-1108; ¶10,124.22
16. ¶P-1104 *et seq.*; ¶10,124.04

17. ¶P-1175; ¶10,554
18. ¶P-1134; ¶10,124.04
19. ¶s P-1138, P-1139; ¶4834
20. ¶G-6872 *et seq.*; ¶10,384

¶ 2467　Basis of property received in satisfaction of debt or claim.

The cost basis of property received in whole or partial satisfaction of a debt or claim is the amount of the debt, etc. satisfied, but not more than the property's fair market value. [21]

¶ 2468　Property acquired through exercise of options—basis.

The basis of property acquired by exercising an option or warrant other than an option granted for services is (a) the basis of the option, plus (b) the option price. [22]

¶ 2469　Holder's basis in certain debt instruments acquired at a discount.

A holder's basis in a debt instrument issued with original issue discount (OID) is increased by the OID currently included in gross income (¶1310 *et seq.*). (Code Sec. 1272(c)(2))[23] This rule also applies for inflation-indexed debt instruments (¶1330); however, the basis of the instruments is reduced for deflation adjustments. [24]

Short-term debt instruments. If the holder includes the daily portions of acquisition discount (or OID) in gross income, that holder increases his basis in the debt instrument by the amount so included. (Code Sec. 1283(d)(1))[25]

Tax-exempt obligations issued with OID. A holder's basis is increased by the amount of OID that the holder would have had to include in gross income currently if the obligation had not been tax-exempt. (Code Sec. 1288(a)(2), Code Sec. 1288(b)(3))[26]

Market-discount bonds. Where an election is made to include accrued market discount in income currently (see ¶1324), the bond's basis is increased by the amount of income included. (Code Sec. 1278(b)(4))[27]

For determining cost of, and original basis in, property received in exchange for an OID debt instrument, see ¶2465.

¶ 2470　Intangible assets—cost basis.

The basis of goodwill, a patent, a copyright, or a covenant not to compete is the amount taxpayer paid for it. [28]

Where a patent is obtained from the government, the basis is the cost of development, such as research and experimental expenditures (but not if deducted currently), drawings, attorneys' and governmental fees, etc. The value of any time spent on an invention isn't part of an inventor's basis. The basis of a copyright acquired from the government is the cost of securing the copyright, including the cost of producing the work covered by the copyright, but not including the value of the author's time. [29]

Accounts receivable in the hands of a cash basis taxpayer have a zero basis. [30]

¶ 2471　Basis allocation, including "applicable asset acquisitions"—Form 8594.

If a single transaction involves a number of separate properties, the total cost is allocated to establish the cost of the individual properties. The total basis is allocated to each item in proportion to the fair market value (FMV) of each item at the time of acquisition. [31]

21. ¶P-1116
22. ¶P-1165 *et seq.*; ¶10,124.13
23. ¶P-5044; ¶12,714.01
24. ¶P-5044.1
25. ¶P-5047; ¶12,814.01
26. ¶P-5048; ¶12,884

27. ¶J-4573 *et seq.*; ¶12,764.02
28. ¶P-1178, P-1179, P-1180; ¶10,124.38
29. ¶P-1178; ¶1674.025
30. ¶P-1121
31. ¶P-1300 *et seq.*; ¶10,124.55

However, for an applicable asset acquisition (defined below), the residual method is used to allocate the purchase price among 7 classes of assets. Under the residual method, the purchase price is reduced first by the amount of cash and cash equivalents (Class I). The amount remaining is allocated among the following assets in proportion to (but not in excess of) their FMV on the purchase date, in the following order: actively traded personal property (Class II); certain mark-to-market assets and debt instruments (Class III); stock in trade, inventory (Class IV); all assets not in any other class (Class V); all Code Sec. 197 intangibles (¶1967) except those in the nature of goodwill and going concern value (Class VI); and Code Sec. 197 intangibles in the nature of goodwill and going concern value (Class VII). (Reg § 1.1060-1(c)(2))[32]

The parties to an applicable asset acquisition can agree in writing to an allocation of consideration for, or a determination of the FMV of, any asset in the acquisition. The agreement is generally binding on the parties. But, the existence of a written agreement doesn't restrict IRS from challenging those allocations or values. (Code Sec. 1060(a); Reg § 1.1060-1(c)(4), Reg § 1.1060-1(e))[33] A party to the agreement can challenge the terms of the agreement only by showing fraud, mistake, undue influence, etc. [34]

An *applicable asset acquisition* is any direct or indirect transfer of a group of assets that is a trade or business in the hands of either the seller or buyer if (except for certain like-kind exchanges) the buyer's basis in the transferred assets is determined wholly by reference to the buyer's consideration. (Code Sec. 1060(c); Reg § 1.1060-1(b)(1))[35]

The buyer and seller have to provide IRS with specified information about the assets on Form 8594. (Code Sec. 1060(b); Reg § 1.1060-1(e)(1))[36]

¶ 2472 Personal use property converted to business use.

When a residence or other nonbusiness property is converted from personal use to business or income-producing use, for purposes of calculating losses or depreciation (but not gain), the basis for the property on the date of its conversion is the *lower* of its adjusted basis or fair market value on that date. This basis is thereafter adjusted for depreciation, etc., after conversion. (Reg § 1.167(g)-1)[37]

¶ 2473 Adjusted basis.

Basis is increased or decreased to reflect certain events, such as capital improvements or depreciation, whether the original basis was cost or something else. [38]

The basis of property is adjusted (increased) to include the amount of the capital expenditures with respect to the property. (Code Sec. 1016(a)(1))[39] A lessee's basis for his leasehold is increased by his capital expenditures. [40] However, a lessee's capital improvements don't increase or diminish the lessor's basis of the leased property. (Code Sec. 1019)[41]

Basis can be increased for items that are ordinarily deductible as expenses if the taxpayer has capitalized those items, e.g., taxes and carrying charges, see ¶1630.

For the requirement that brokers report on Form 1099-B information about a customer's basis (including information about organizational actions such as stock splits that would affect the basis) in stock and securities, see ¶4746.

For adjusted basis for AMT purposes, see ¶3209.

For basis adjustments for investments in Qualified Opportunity Funds, see ¶2507.

---

32. ¶P-1406.1
33. ¶P-1400 *et seq.*; ¶10,604
34. ¶I-8612
35. ¶P-1402 *et seq.*; ¶10,604
36. ¶S-4301; ¶10,604

37. ¶P-1908; ¶1674.037
38. ¶P-1700 *et seq.*; ¶s 10,114, 10,164.01
39. ¶P-1801; ¶10,164.01
40. ¶L-6510; ¶10,164
41. ¶P-1809; ¶10,194

In determining the basis of a life insurance or annuity contract (entered into after Aug. 25, 2009), no basis adjustment is made for mortality, expense, or other reasonable charges incurred under the contracts (known as "cost of insurance"). (Code Sec. 1016(a)(1)) This reverses the position of IRS in Rev. Rul. 2009-13 that, on the sale of a cash value life insurance contract, the insured's (seller's) basis is reduced by the cost of insurance. [42]

¶ 2474   Contributions and returns of capital—effect on basis.

A shareholder's contribution to the capital of a corporation increases the basis in his corporate stock.[43] A partner's contribution of cash or other property to the partnership increases the basis in his partnership interest (¶3732 *et seq.*).

Basis is also reduced for receipts representing a return of capital (Code Sec. 1016(a)(1); Reg § 1.1016-2(a)), such as damages taxpayer received for injury to property. [44]

¶ 2475   Depreciation, amortization, etc. adjustments to basis.

Basis is reduced for depreciation, cost recovery, Code Sec. 179 expensing, pre-2010 commercial revitalization deductions under former Code Sec. 1400I, or amortization deductions with respect to the property. The amount of the reduction is the larger of (1) the amount of the depreciation, cost recovery, amortization, or depletion deductions *allowable* under the law, or (2) the amount that was actually *allowed* and resulted in a reduction of tax. (Code Sec. 1016(a)(2))[45]

Basis is reduced for the Code Sec. 179D energy efficient commercial building property deduction for property placed in service after 2005 and before 2018. (Code Sec. 1016(a)(31))[46]

caution: Check tax.thomsonreuters.com/federaltaxhandbookupdates to see if the Code Sec. 179D deduction has been extended.

Allowable depreciation (or cost recovery) is the amount the taxpayer was legally entitled to deduct, whether or not he actually took more or less and whether or not a tax benefit results. Where a taxpayer didn't adopt a depreciation method under Code Sec. 167, the amount allowable is figured under the straight-line method. (Code Sec. 1016(a))[47]

The depreciation (or cost recovery) *allowed* is the amount claimed on a tax return and allowed by IRS. [48]

In the case of business autos for which the optional business standard mileage rate (see ¶1554) is used, depreciation is considered to have been allowed at a rate of 23¢ per mile for 2012 and 2013, 22¢ for 2014, 24¢ for 2015 and 2016, and 25¢ for 2017 and 2018. [49]

¶ 2476   Partial losses due to casualty or theft.

If property is partly lost or destroyed through casualty or theft, basis is reduced by (1) the amount of insurance or other reimbursement received, and (2) the amount of deductible loss. But if a loss is *not* deductible (see ¶1782 *et seq.*), basis isn't reduced.

Expenses with respect to that property, e.g., to remove debris and to restore the property to pre-casualty condition, increase basis, unless they are deducted as repairs. [50]

---

42. ¶J-5058; ¶10,164
43. ¶F-1916; ¶10,164.02
44. ¶P-1821; ¶10,164.03
45. ¶P-1901; ¶10,164.25
46. ¶L-3176; ¶10,164

47. ¶P-1902; ¶10,164.25
48. ¶P-1903; ¶10,164.25
49. ¶P-1909; ¶1624.157
50. ¶P-1811; ¶1654.304

¶ 2477 Basis of credit property reduced by certain credits allowed.

The basis of investment credit property (¶2306), for purposes of computing depreciation or cost recovery deductions and gain or loss, is reduced by 100% of the amount of the credit for which the property qualifies. (Code Sec. 50(c)(1))[1] The basis of energy credit property (¶2310) is reduced by 50% of the allowed credit. (Code Sec. 50(c)(3)(A))[2]

The basis of property is also reduced for certain other credits, such as: the Code Sec. 25C nonbusiness energy property credit for property placed in service before 2008 or after 2008 and before 2018 (¶2353) (Code Sec. 1016(a)(33))[3]; the Code Sec. 25D residential energy efficient property credit for property placed in service before 2022 (¶2354) (Code Sec. 1016(a)(34))[4]; the Code Sec. 30B alternative motor vehicle credit (¶2355) (Code Sec. 1016(a)(35))[5]; the Code Sec. 30D credit for certain electric vehicles (¶2357) (Code Sec. 1016(a)(37))[6]; the Code Sec. 45F credit for employer-provided child care assistance (¶2330) (Code Sec. 1016(a)(28))[7]; and the Code Sec. 45L energy efficient homes credit for homes acquired before 2018 (¶2334). (Code Sec. 1016(a)(32))[8]

⚓**caution:** Check tax.thomsonreuters.com/federaltaxhandbookupdates to see if any of the expired credits discussed above have been extended.

¶ 2478 Recaptured tax credits—effect on basis.

Where certain tax credits are recaptured, a percentage of the recapture amount is added back to basis immediately before the event causing the recapture. A "recapture amount" is any increase in tax (or adjustment in carrybacks or carryovers) due to the credit recapture provision. (Code Sec. 50(c)(2), Code Sec. 50(c)(3)(B))[9]

¶ 2479 Special lessor-lessee rule doesn't require basis-reduction adjustment.

A lessor of certain credit property who elects to pass the credit for the leased property to the lessee isn't required to make the basis-reduction adjustment (¶2477). (Code Sec. 50(d)(5), Reg § 1.50-1T(h)(1))[10]

¶ 2480 How credits affect basis in partnership interest or S corporation stock.

The basis of a partner's interest in a partnership or of an S corporation shareholder's stock is adjusted to reflect a partner's or shareholder's share of the required adjustments to the basis of partnership or S corporation property when credits are either allowed or recaptured. (Code Sec. 50(c)(5))[11]

¶ 2481 Property Acquired in Nontaxable Exchanges. ▬▬▬▬

The basis of property received (replacement property) in a nontaxable exchange, depending on the type of transaction, generally is the same as its basis in the hands of the transferor or is the same as the basis of the property transferred (relinquished property) by the recipient in the exchange. If gain is recognized in part on the transaction, the basis of the property received may have to be adjusted.

For corporate transactions that affect basis, see ¶2482 *et seq.* For other nontaxable transactions, see ¶2501 *et seq.* For basis of replacement property after an involuntary

1. ¶P-2000 *et seq.*; ¶504.03
2. ¶P-2005; ¶504.03
3. ¶P-1710.4; ¶10,164
4. ¶P-1710.5; ¶10,164
5. ¶L-18023; ¶10,164
6. ¶P-1710.6; ¶10,164
7. ¶P-1710.1; ¶10,164
8. ¶P-1710.01; ¶10,164
9. ¶P-2007; ¶504.03
10. ¶P-2008
11. ¶P-2009

conversion, see ¶2503.

¶ 2482   Corporation's basis in property received in a tax-free transfer.

The basis of property received by a controlled corporation in a tax-free transfer, whether upon the incorporation of the corporation or otherwise (see ¶3500 *et seq.*), is equal to the basis of the property in the transferor's hands increased by any gain recognized by the transferor on the transfer. (Code Sec. 362(a))[12]

The corporation's basis in property acquired from a shareholder as a contribution to capital equals the basis of that property in the shareholder's hands increased by any gain recognized by the shareholder on the transfer. (Code Sec. 362(a))[13]

For limitations on an increase in basis due to the assumption of a liability and/or a built-in loss, see ¶2484.

¶ 2483   Acquirer's basis in property received in a tax-free reorganization.

The basis of property received by the acquiring corporation in a tax-free reorganization (¶3527), is the transferor's (target's) basis increased by any gain recognized to the target. However, if the property consists of stock or securities of the target, this rule applies only if the property was acquired in exchange for stock or securities of the acquirer or the acquirer's parent corporation. (Code Sec. 362(b))[14]

For when an acquirer must reduce basis in assets received in a tax-free reorganization if the transferor has cancellation of debt income in connection with the transfer, see ¶1380.

For limitations on basis increase due to the assumption of a liability, see ¶2484.

¶ 2484   Limit on basis increase due to assumption of liability or built-in loss.

For purposes of the basis increase for a tax-free transfer to a controlled corporation (¶2482) or a reorganization exchange (¶2483), the property's basis can't be increased above its fair market value (FMV) due to gain recognized by the transferor as a result of a liability assumed by the transferee. For this purpose, FMV is determined without regard to Code Sec. 7701(g) (which generally provides that a property's FMV isn't less than the amount of nonrecourse debt to which it is subject). (Code Sec. 362(d)(1))[15]

Also, to prevent the importation of built-in losses, if property transferred was not taxable in the transferor's hands but is taxable in the transferee corporation's hands, and the total basis for the property in the transferee's hands would otherwise (if not for the basis limitation rule) exceed its FMV, then the basis for each property in the transferee's hands is its FMV. (Code Sec. 362(e)(1); Reg § 1.362-3) If this rule doesn't apply, a second carryover basis limitation rule (not limited to property as to which the transferor would not have recognized gain or loss) limits the total basis for property transferred by any transferor to its FMV, with the basis of each property transferred reduced by its allocable part of the transferor's net built-in loss. (Code Sec. 362(e)(2); Reg § 1.362-4(b)) However, the transferor and transferee can jointly elect to reduce the basis of the stock received by the transferor instead of the basis of the assets transferred. (Code Sec. 362(e)(2)(C); Reg § 1.362-4(d)) IRS has prescribed how to make the election. (Reg § 1.362-4(d))[16]

---

12. ¶F-1851; ¶3624.01
13. ¶F-1851; ¶3624.05
14. ¶F-4305; ¶3624.04

15. ¶F-1852; ¶3624.01
16. ¶F-1871 *et seq.*; ¶3624.02, 3624.03

¶ 2485   Target's basis in property received in a tax-free reorganization.

The basis of property (other than stock and securities of another corporation that is a party to the reorganization, see ¶3541 *et seq.*) received under a plan of reorganization by the target equals the fair market value of the property on the exchange date. (Code Sec. 358(a)(2), Code Sec. 358(f))[17]

¶ 2486   Corporation's basis in property acquired in a taxable acquisition of property for its stocks or bonds.

In cases other than tax-free contributions or reorganizations, the basis of property a corporation acquires in exchange for its stock is the stock's fair market value at the time of the exchange.[18] The cost to a corporation of property it acquires in exchange for its bonds is the face amount of the bonds.[19] For bonds with OID or unstated interest, see ¶2465.

¶ 2487   Basis of property to distributee shareholders or security holders.

For purposes of determining basis, property received by a distributee in connection with a transfer to a controlled corporation, a reorganization, or a corporate division (¶3500 *et seq.*) is either nonrecognition property or other property. Nonrecognition property is property received without recognition of gain or loss to the recipient (stock in the transferee corporation in the case of a transfer to a controlled corporation, and stock or securities in the distributing corporation in tax-free reorganizations and corporate divisions). (Code Sec. 358(a)(1)) Other property is anything except nonrecognition property and money.

The basis of nonrecognition property is the same as the basis of the property given up in the exchange, except that basis is (1) decreased by any money received, by the fair market value of any other property received, and by any loss recognized by the distributee on the exchange; and (2) increased by any part of the distribution that is treated as a dividend, and by any other gain recognized by the distributee on the exchange. (Code Sec. 358(a)(1))[20] The basis is allocated among the nonrecognition property received in the transaction without recognition of gain or loss. If no stock or securities of the issuing corporation are issued and distributed in the transaction, shareholders that own actual shares in the issuing corporation can designate the shares of stock of the issuing corporation to which the basis, if any, of the stock or securities surrendered will attach. (Reg § 1.358-2(a)(2))[21]

Where, as part of the consideration for the transfer of the distributee corporation's property to the acquirer, another party to the deal assumes a liability of the distributee, the assumption of that liability is treated as though it were money received by the distributee on the reorganization exchange (for basis purposes only). (Code Sec. 358(d)(1))[22]

✔*observation:* Thus, the basis of the nonrecognition property received by the distributee on the exchange is reduced by an amount equal to the liabilities assumed.

IRS can provide adjustments for divisive reorganization transactions (¶3545) among affiliated group members. (Code Sec. 358(g))[23]

---

17. ¶F-4304; ¶3584.02
18. ¶P-1158; ¶10,124.47
19. ¶P-1160
20. ¶F-4034; ¶3584.02

21. ¶F-4036; ¶3584.03
22. ¶F-4035; ¶3584.04
23. ¶F-4632; ¶3554.07

¶ 2488   Basis of other property received in tax-free transfer or reorganization.

The basis of property, other than stock or securities, received by a shareholder upon a tax-free transfer to a controlled corporation, a reorganization, or a corporate division (¶3500 *et seq.*) is its fair market value as of the date of the transaction. (Code Sec. 358(a)(2))[24]

¶ 2489   Basis of property received in complete liquidation of corporation.

If property is received in a complete liquidation and any gain or loss is recognized on the receipt of the property, its basis in the hands of the shareholder-distributee is its fair market value at the time of the distribution. (Code Sec. 334(a))[25]

¶ 2490   Basis in stock after partnership incorporates.

If a partnership incorporates, the basis of the corporation in the partnership's assets and the basis of the former partners in their stock in the corporation depends on the method used to incorporate.

If the partnership transfers all of its assets subject to its liabilities to a newly formed corporation in return for all its stock, then distributes the stock to the partners, the corporation's basis in the partnership's assets is equal to the partnership's basis in the assets before the transaction, and each partner's basis in the stock of the corporation (¶3743) is equal to the adjusted basis of that partner's interest in the partnership.

If the partnership distributes all of its assets subject to liabilities to the partners, who in turn transfer them to the new corporation for its stock, the corporation's basis in its assets is the same as the partners' basis in the assets before their contribution to the corporation, and the partners' basis in the stock of the corporation is the same as their basis in the assets distributed in liquidation reduced by liabilities assumed by the corporation.

If the partners transfer their partnership interests to the new corporation in exchange for its stock and the corporation then liquidates the partnership, the corporation's basis in its assets is equal to the partners' basis in their partnership interests before the transaction, and the partners' basis in their stock is equal to their basis in their partnership interests reduced by the liabilities assumed by the corporation. [26]

¶ 2491   Property received as a dividend—basis.

The basis for property received as a dividend, including stock or stock rights received as a taxable stock dividend, is its fair market value on the date of distribution. (Code Sec. 301(d))[27] For basis allocation for a nontaxable stock dividend, see ¶2492.

¶ 2492   Basis allocation for nontaxable stock dividend.

If a shareholder gets a nontaxable dividend of stock or stock rights, the (adjusted) basis of the old stock (that is, of the stock on which the dividend was distributed) is allocated between the old and new stock (or rights) in proportion to the fair market value (FMV) of each on the date of distribution. (Code Sec. 307(a)) Where only part of the stock dividend is nontaxable, the basis of the old stock is allocated between the old stock and that part of the new stock (or rights) which isn't taxable, in proportion to the FMV of each on the date of distribution. The date of distribution is, in both cases, the date on which the new stock (or

---

24. ¶F-1804, F-4034, F-5014; ¶3584.02
25. ¶F-13119; ¶3344.01

26. ¶s F-1011, F-1805
27. ¶P-5400 *et seq.*; ¶3014.03

the stock rights) was distributed, not the record date. (Reg § 1.307-1(a))[28]

🅡**illustration:** S bought 1 share of voting common for $45. The corporation distributed 2 new shares of voting common for each share held. This gave S 3 shares of voting common with a basis of $15 each. If S had owned 2 shares before the distribution, one purchased for $30 and the other for $45, S would have 6 shares: 3 with a basis of $10 each, and 3 with a basis of $15 each.

If the FMV of stock rights at the time of distribution is less than 15% of the FMV of the stock on which they were distributed, the basis for the rights received is zero unless the taxpayer elects to allocate basis to the rights. (Code Sec. 307(b)(1); Reg § 1.307-2)[29]

¶ 2493 Basis of stock acquired through dividend reinvestment plans (DRPs).

If a corporation allows shareholders to receive dividends in either cash or stock, then, depending on the situation, the receipt of stock is treated either as the receipt of a taxable stock dividend, because the shareholder has the choice of receiving either cash or stock, or as the receipt of a cash dividend which the shareholder used to buy stock (in some cases, at a discount). If the transaction is treated as a stock dividend, the shareholder's basis is equal to the value of the shares received at the time of the receipt. But, if the transaction is treated as a cash dividend, the shareholder's basis in the shares is equal to the amount of cash he could have received.[30] The basis of stock acquired after 2011 in connection with a DRP, while held as part of the DRP, is determined using 1 of the methods available for determining the basis of mutual fund stock. (Code Sec. 1012(d)(1)) Thus, the average basis method for mutual fund shareholders (¶2498) is available for shares of stock acquired after 2011 in connection with a DRP, but only if the shares are identical (i.e., have the same CUSIP number, or other acceptable security identifier number). (Reg § 1.1012-1(e)(1))[31]

¶ 2494 Effect of extraordinary dividends on corporate shareholder's basis.

If a corporation receives an extraordinary dividend with respect to a share of stock that it hasn't held for more than 2 years before the dividend announcement date, the basis of the stock is reduced (but not below zero) by the non-taxed part (i.e., the excess (if any) of: (a) the distribution amount over (b) the part of the dividend that is included in gross income, reduced by the amount of any dividend received deduction allowable under Code Sec. 243, or Code Sec. 245). (Code Sec. 1059) Where a redemption is treated as an extraordinary dividend, the basis in the nonredeemed shares is also reduced if the redemption is part of a partial liquidation of the redeeming corporation, or isn't pro rata as to all shareholders, but not if the redemption wouldn't have been treated (in whole or in part) as a dividend if an option hadn't been taken into account under the Code Sec. 318(a)(4) option attribution rules or the Code Sec. 304(a) related-party stock purchase rules.[32]

¶ 2495 Effect of Sec. 245A dividends received deduction on corporate shareholder's basis.

If a corporation that is a "U.S. shareholder" of a 10% owned specified foreign corporation receives a dividend from that foreign corporation, a deduction is allowed for the foreign-source portion of the dividend under Code Sec. 245A (see ¶3315). A domestic corporation that receives that dividend in any tax year, solely for purposes of determining loss on any disposition of stock of that foreign corporation in that tax year or any later tax year, must reduce its basis in that stock (but not below zero) by the amount of the Code

---

28. ¶P-5301; ¶3074.01 *et seq.*
29. ¶P-5303; ¶3074.03
30. ¶P-5402

31. ¶P-5201.4; ¶10,124.7701
32. ¶P-5100 *et seq.*; ¶10,594

Sec. 245A deduction allowable to the domestic corporation on that stock. (Code Sec. 961(d)) However, no reduction in basis is required to the extent the basis in the specified 10% owned foreign corporation's stock was already reduced under Code Sec. 1059 (¶2494).[33]

¶ 2496   Identifying shares or bonds transferred.

Where a taxpayer can adequately identify which shares of stock or which bonds are transferred, the basis used is the basis of that stock or those bonds (specific identification). Shares of stock or bonds are adequately identified where it can be shown that the shares or bonds that were delivered to the transferee are from a lot acquired on a certain date or for a certain price. (Reg § 1.1012-1(c)(1); Reg § 1.1012-1(c)(2); Reg § 1.1012-1(c)(6))[34]

If a number of lots were acquired and the ones sold can't be adequately identified, a first-in, first-out (FIFO) rule applies. If the earliest lot purchased or acquired is held in a stock certificate that represents multiple lots of stock, and the taxpayer doesn't adequately identify the lot from which the stock is sold or transferred, the stock sold or transferred is charged against the earliest lot included in the certificate. (Reg § 1.1012-1(c)(1)(i)) Where shares are held in more than 1 account, the FIFO rule applies only to the particular account from which the shares were transferred. [35]

¶ 2497   Adequate identification of shares vs. wrong delivery.

In certain situations, if a taxpayer specifically identifies certain shares of stock or bonds as the ones to be transferred (¶2496), and certain other conditions are met, these will be treated as the ones transferred even though some other lot is actually delivered. This rule applies (1) for sales of stock or bonds held by a broker or agent (Reg § 1.1012-1(c)(3)(i)), (2) where a single certificate represents different lots of stock (Reg § 1.1012-1(c)(3)(ii)), and (3) for certain transfers by a trustee, executor or administrator. (Reg § 1.1012-1(c)(4))[36]

¶ 2498   Methods for determining basis of mutual fund shares.

A taxpayer who sells mutual fund shares held by a custodian or agent in an account can elect to determine the basis of the shares sold by determining the average basis using the "single-category method." (Reg § 1.1012-1(e)(7)(i)) Generally, the single-category method groups in one category all shares regardless of holding period (but treats shares sold as sold on a first-in-first-out (FIFO) basis so that shares that qualify for long-term capital gain or loss treatment are treated as sold before shares that would get short-term treatment). A shareholder who doesn't elect the average-basis method must use the normal FIFO method for determining which shares were sold, see ¶2496.

Unless a single-account election is in effect, a taxpayer can not average together the basis of identical stock held in separate accounts that the taxpayer sells, exchanges, or otherwise disposes of. (Reg § 1.1012-1(e)(7)(i))[37]

¶ 2499   Determining basis for certain securities held in brokerage accounts.

In the case of a sale, exchange or other disposition, the broker reported basis in a "specified security" (defined below) is determined under the conventions prescribed in existing regs and applied to each separate account, on an account-by-account basis. (Code Sec. 1012(c)(1)) Reported basis is computed using a first-in-first-out (FIFO) method, the specific-identification method, or the average-basis convention (Reg § 1.1012-1) (¶2496, ¶2498).[38]

---

33. ¶O-2423.1 ¶9614.04
34. ¶P-5202 *et seq.*; ¶10,124.78
35. ¶P-5212 *et seq.*; ¶10,124.7701

36. ¶P-5200 *et seq.*; ¶10,124.77 *et seq.*
37. ¶P-5214 *et seq.*; ¶10,124.7801
38. ¶P-5201.1; ¶10,124.7701

A "specified security" is stocks, notes and other debt, certain commodity contracts and derivatives, and other securities deemed appropriate by IRS. (Code Sec. 6045(g)(3)(B))[39]

¶ 2500 Basis of stock acquired in wash sale.

Where a loss is disallowed under the wash sale rule (¶2461), the basis of the acquired stock takes account of the unrecognized loss in the following manner: (Code Sec. 1091(d))

(1) If the sales price is less than the repurchase price, the basis of the new stock is the basis of the stock sold plus the difference between the repurchase and the sales prices.

Illustration (1): T owns 100 shares of X Corp stock which cost $100 per share. On May 1, T sells the 100 shares at $80 per share. On May 20, T buys 100 shares of X at $90 per share. No loss is allowed on the May 1 sale. The basis of each share acquired May 20 is $110, i.e., the basis of the shares sold ($100) plus the $10 difference between the repurchase and sale prices ($90 − $80). (Reg § 1.1091-2(a))

(2) If the sales price is more than the repurchase price, the basis of the new stock is the basis of the stock sold minus the difference between the sale and the repurchase prices. [40]

Illustration (2): If, in Illustration (1), the May 1 sale price had been $90 per share and the May 20 repurchase price was $80 per share, the basis of each share acquired May 20 would be $90, i.e., the basis of shares sold ($100) minus the difference between the sale and repurchase prices ($90 − $80). (Reg § 1.1091-2(a))

¶ 2501 Basis of properties received in a nontaxable exchange.

The basis of replacement property received in a like-kind exchange and nontaxable exchanges of stock in the same corporation (¶2413), U.S. obligations (¶2415), and life insurance and annuity contracts (¶2416) where no part of the gain is recognized is the adjusted basis of the relinquished property. (Code Sec. 1031(d))

If money is received as part of the exchange and some gain is recognized, the replacement property's basis is decreased by the money received and increased by any gain recognized. Reg § 1.1031(d)-1(b)) Basis is increased by the amount of any money paid. (Reg § 1.1031(d)-1(a))

In determining the basis, liabilities assumed by the other party are treated as money (boot) received by the taxpayer. (Reg § 1.1031(d)-2)

If other property (boot) is received and some gain is recognized, basis is allocated (based on fair market value) to all the properties received. (Reg § 1.1031(d)-1(c))

If boot is given as part of the exchange, and gain or loss is recognized on transfer of the boot, the basis of the nonrecognition property received is the total basis of all the properties given, increased by any recognized gain on the boot, or decreased by any recognized loss on the boot. (Reg § 1.1031(d)-1(e))[41]

¶ 2502 Basis after tax-free exchange of multiple properties.

In a nontaxable exchange of multiple properties (¶2425), the aggregate basis of properties received in each of the "exchange groups" is allocated proportionately to each property in the group based on its fair market value. (Reg § 1.1031(j)-1(c))[42]

---

39. ¶P-5201.3; ¶60,454.08
40. ¶P-5019; ¶10,914

41. ¶I-3176 *et seq.*; ¶10,314.13
42. ¶I-3193; ¶10,314.14

¶ 2503   Basis of replacement property after involuntary conversion.

If property is involuntarily converted directly into similar property and gain on the conversion isn't recognized under Code Sec. 1033(a)(1) (¶2431), the basis of the replacement property is the basis of the converted property (1) decreased by the amount of any money received that wasn't reinvested in similar property (¶2438), and (2) increased by the amount of gain recognized, or decreased by the amount of loss recognized. (Code Sec. 1033(b)(1)) Where a taxpayer's property is involuntarily converted into money or other property that isn't similar or related in use and, within the prescribed period (¶2441), the taxpayer buys replacement property that is similar or related in service or use to the converted property and elects not to recognize any part of the gain, the basis of the replacement property is its cost, reduced by the amount of unrecognized gain. If more than 1 piece of replacement property is bought, the basis (cost less nonrecognized gain) is allocated to each piece in proportion to its cost. (Code Sec. 1033(b)(2))[43] If a taxpayer satisfies the replacement property requirement by buying a controlling stock interest in a corporation (¶2431), the corporation reduces its basis in its assets by the amount by which the taxpayer reduces its basis in the stock. (Code Sec. 1033(b)(3))[44]

¶ 2504   Basis of replacement for stock sold to ESOP or EWOC.

If the seller of qualified securities to an employee stock ownership plan (ESOP) or eligible worker-owned cooperative (EWOC) reinvests in qualified replacement property and elects gain nonrecognition (¶2451), basis is reduced by the gain not recognized. If more than 1 item of replacement property is bought, basis reduction is allocated among each item (as the cost of that item bears to the cost of all items). (Code Sec. 1042(d))[45]

¶ 2505   Basis for Specialized Small Business Investment Company (SSBIC) rollovers.

Any gain not recognized under the now-repealed SSBIC rollover rules (that applied to gain from certain pre-2018 sales of publicly traded securities rolled over into SSBICs) reduced the taxpayer's basis in any SSBIC investment made during the 60-day rollover period. If taxpayer made more than one SSBIC investment during this period, the bases of those other investments were reduced in the order they were acquired. [46]

¶ 2506   Basis for Qualified Small Business Stock (QSBS) rollovers.

Gain from the sale of QSBS that isn't recognized because of the Code Sec. 1045(a) rollover election (see ¶2428) reduces (in the order acquired) the basis for determining gain or loss of any QSBS that's purchased by the taxpayer within the 60-day rollover period beginning on the sale date. (Code Sec. 1045(b)(3))[47]

¶ 2507   Basis of investments in Qualified Opportunity (QO) Funds.

Except for the increases to basis described below, a taxpayer's basis in the investment in a QO Fund (¶2429) is zero. For an investment held for at least 5 years, the basis of the investment is increased by 10% of the amount of gain temporarily deferred. For an investment held for at least 7 years, basis is increased by an additional 5% of the amount of gain deferred. The basis is also increased by the amount of gain recognized at the end of the temporary deferral period. (Code Sec. 1400Z-2(b)(2)(B))[48]

---

43. ¶P-1154; ¶10,334.33
44. ¶P-1154.1; ¶10,334.231
45. ¶H-12110; ¶10,424

46. ¶I-3791; ¶10,448.4
47. ¶I-9206; ¶10,454
48. ¶I-8826; ¶14,00Z-24

434

¶ 2508   **Property Acquired by Gift, from a Decedent, or from a Spouse.** ▬▬▬▬

Special rules apply to determine the basis of property acquired by gift, from a decedent, or from a spouse. Property acquired by gift or certain transfers in trust generally has a carryover basis, see ¶2509 *et seq*. Property acquired from a decedent generally has a fair market value basis, see ¶2513 *et seq*. Property acquired from a spouse (or former spouse) generally has a carryover basis, see ¶2524.

¶ 2509   **Basis of property acquired by gift or transfer in trust.**

A donee's original or unadjusted basis (that is, the basis before adjustments made while the donee owned it) for property the donee acquires by gift is the same as the property's adjusted basis in the donor's hands, or in the hands of the last preceding owner who didn't acquire the property by gift. But if the property's fair market value (FMV) at the date of the gift is lower than that adjusted basis, then the property's basis for determining *loss* is its FMV on that date. (Code Sec. 1015(a))[49]

Since 2 different methods determine basis of property acquired as a gift, it's possible that neither gain nor loss determined in reference to basis will be realized when the donee sells or exchanges the property. (Reg § 1.1015-1(a)(2))[50]

⬤*Illustration:* T acquires by gift income-producing property with an adjusted basis of $100,000 at the date of gift. The FMV on the date of gift is $90,000. T later sells the property for $95,000. T has neither gain nor loss since the basis for determining gain is $100,000 and the basis for determining loss is $90,000.

If a transfer in trust is made for consideration (whether full and adequate, or less), the basis is the same as it would be in the grantor's hands, increased by the amount of gain or decreased by the amount of loss recognized to the grantor upon the transfer under the law applicable to the year in which the transfer was made. (Code Sec. 1015(b))[1]

For part sales and part gifts, see ¶2510.

¶ 2510   **Basis after transfer that is part purchase, part gift.**

Where a transfer of property is part purchase and part gift, the transferee's basis is the greater of cost or the transferor's adjusted basis for the property at the time of the transfer. In either event, basis is increased to the extent of any gift tax paid (¶2512). However, for determining loss, the basis can't exceed the property's fair market value at the time of transfer. (Reg § 1.1015-4)[2]

¶ 2511   **Basis rules for donees of partial interests.**

If 2 or more donees receive gifts of partial interests in the same property, the basis of each interest is its proportionate part of the donor's basis. To determine the part of total basis allowable to life tenants and remaindermen, see ¶2523. (Reg § 1.1015-1(b))[3]

¶ 2512   **Increase in basis for gift tax paid by donor.**

If the property's fair market value at the date of the gift is greater than the donor's adjusted basis, the donee's basis (i.e., the donor's basis) is increased by any gift tax paid that is attributable to the net appreciation in the gift's value. This part is determined by multiplying the gift tax paid by a fraction whose numerator is the net appreciation in

---

49. ¶P-3103; ¶P-3104; ¶10,154.01
50. ¶P-3105
1. ¶P-3112; ¶10,154.16

2. ¶P-1113; ¶10,154
3. ¶P-3131; ¶10,154.06

value of the gift and whose denominator is the amount of the gift. (Code Sec. 1015(d)(6))

If a gift consists of more than 1 item of property, the gift tax paid with respect to each item is computed by allocating to each item a proportionate part of the gift tax paid. If more than 1 gift was made during the calendar year, the total tax paid is apportioned to each gift to determine the amount paid on each gift. (Code Sec. 1015(d)(2))

The gift tax paid on a split gift (¶5056) is the sum of the taxes, computed separately, paid with respect to each spouse's half of the gift. (Code Sec. 1015(d)(3); Reg § 1.1015-5(b)(3))[4]

¶ 2513   Basis of property acquired from a decedent.

The basis of property acquired from a decedent by inheritance, bequest, devise, etc. (¶2516), that hasn't been sold, exchanged, or otherwise disposed of before the decedent's death, is generally equal to its fair market value (FMV) at the date of the decedent's death (i.e., a stepped-up basis). (Code Sec. 1014(a)(1)) However, if:

(1) the fiduciary elects to value the decedent's gross estate at the alternate valuation date (¶5016), the basis of the property is its FMV at that date (Code Sec. 1014(a)(2)).

(2) the fiduciary elects for estate tax purposes the special use valuation method of valuing farm or other closely held business real property included in the decedent's gross estate (¶5017), the basis of the real property is its value determined for purposes of the special use valuation election (rather than its FMV). (Code Sec. 1014(a)(3))[5]

(3) land acquired at death is subject to a qualified conservation easement, it is excluded from the decedent's gross estate (see ¶5016), and its basis (to the extent that it's subject to the easement) is the basis in the decedent's hands. (Code Sec. 1014(a)(4))[6]

FMV on the date of the decedent's death (or the alternate valuation date, if applicable) doesn't apply to determine the basis of property that's:

. . . appreciated property acquired by the decedent by gift in the 1-year period ending on his death, and that is reacquired by the donor (or the donor's spouse) from the decedent, see ¶2515;

. . . included in the decedent's estate but disposed of by the taxpayer before the decedent's death, see ¶2517;

. . . stock in a domestic international sales corporation (DISC) or former DISC (Code Sec. 1014(d)), or of certain foreign entities; or

. . . a right to receive income in respect of a decedent (Code Sec. 1014(c)), see ¶3965.[7]

. . . acquired from a decedent who died in 2010 if the executor elected the modified carryover basis rules (and exemption from the estate tax). [8]

FMV of property at the decedent's death or at the alternate valuation date is the FMV as determined by an appraisal for federal estate tax purposes. If no federal estate tax return is required to be filed, the FMV of the property appraised as of the date of death for purposes of state inheritance or other transmission taxes (e.g., legacy taxes) is used to determine FMV. However, if no federal estate tax return is filed, the alternate valuation date can't be used to determine FMV. (Reg § 1.1014-3(a))[9]

---

4. ¶P-3107 *et seq.*; ¶10,154.01
5. ¶P-4001 *et seq.*; ¶s 10,144, 10,144.05
6. ¶P-4021.1; ¶10,144.055

7. ¶P-4001 *et seq.*; ¶10,144.02
8. ¶P-4060; ¶10,224
9. ¶P-4022; ¶10,144.03

¶ 2514   When estate tax value is also income tax basis.

For property with respect to which an estate tax return is filed after July 31, 2015 and whose inclusion in the decedent's estate increases the estate's estate tax liability (reduced by allowable credits), the basis of that property for income tax purposes can't exceed: (A) in the case of property, the final value of which has been determined for purposes of the estate tax, that value; and (B) in the case of property not described in (A) and with respect to which a statement (Form 8971) has been furnished under Code Sec. 6035(a) (see ¶4746), the value on Form 8971. (Code Sec. 1014(f); Prop Reg. § 1.1014-10 ["Taxpayers may rely"])[10] If the final estate tax value is later determined and that value is different from the value reported on Form 8971, the taxpayer can't rely on the Form 8971 initially furnished for the value of the property. Before the determination of final estate value, the recipient of property can't claim an initial basis in excess of the value on Form 8971. Final estate value is considered to occur when IRS doesn't contest the value shown on the return, the executor doesn't contest a value specified by IRS, or a court order or settlement agreement with IRS specifies value. (Prop Reg. § 1.1014-10(c) ["Taxpayers may rely"])[11]

For property with respect to which an estate tax return was filed before Aug. 1, 2015, or whose inclusion in the decedent's estate doesn't increase the estate's estate tax liability (reduced by credits allowable against the tax), the value for estate tax purposes is only presumptively correct for basis purposes. Except where facts have been misrepresented, neither taxpayer nor IRS is barred from using a value for basis purposes that differs from the value accepted for estate tax purposes. However, where a discount is allowed in valuing property (e.g., artwork) for estate tax purposes, full value generally won't be allowed in valuing the same property for income tax purposes. [12]

¶ 2515   Appreciated property reacquired by donor from donee-decedent.

If: (1) appreciated property was acquired by the decedent by gift during the 1-year period ending at death, and (2) that property is acquired from the decedent by (or passes from the decedent to) the donor of the property (or the donor's spouse), the basis of the property in the hands of the donor (or spouse) is the adjusted basis of the property in the decedent's hands immediately before his death. (Code Sec. 1014(e)(1))[13]

¶ 2516   When is property considered acquired from a decedent?

Property is acquired from a decedent if it is acquired by bequest, devise, or inheritance, or by the decedent's estate from the decedent. (Code Sec. 1014(b)(1); Reg § 1.1014-2(a)(1))[14] Property acquired from a decedent includes certain pre-death transfers and other classes of property (¶2520 *et seq.*). Qualified terminable interest property (QTIP) includible in a surviving spouse's estate (¶5008) is treated as passing from that surviving spouse for purposes of determining the remaindermen's basis. (Code Sec. 1014(b)(10))[15] But, property acquired from a decedent *excludes*:

. . . property the fiduciary acquires after the decedent's death. The basis of that property to the fiduciary (or a distributee if it's distributed) is its cost or other basis with appropriate adjustments. (Reg § 1.1014-3(c))[16]

. . . property bought from a decedent's estate. Its basis to the buyer is its cost or other basis with appropriate adjustments. [17]

. . . income in respect of a decedent (IRD, see ¶3965). (Code Sec. 1014(c)) Its basis is equal

---

10. ¶P-4022; ¶10,144.03
11. ¶P-4022.1; ¶10,144.03
12. ¶P-4022, P-4023, P-4024; ¶10,144.03
13. ¶P-4002; ¶10,144.02

14. ¶P-4102; ¶10,144.01
15. ¶P-4104; ¶10,144.01
16. ¶P-4054; ¶10,144.02
17. ¶P-4118

to the decedent's basis (if any). [18]

. . . property transferred by the executor, administrator or trustee to a beneficiary in discharge of a specific pecuniary bequest. The beneficiary's basis is the fair market value of the property on the date of the transfer. (Reg § 1.1014-4(a)(3))[19]

¶ 2517   Property acquired from decedent and included in decedent's gross estate.

Property is considered acquired from a decedent if it was acquired from a decedent by reason of: death, form of ownership, or other conditions and the property is required to be included in determining the value of the decedent's gross estate whether or not an estate tax return is required or an estate tax is payable. These acquisitions include acquisitions as surviving joint tenant or tenant by the entirety (¶2518), acquisitions through exercise of a general power of appointment (¶2521), and gifts within 3 years of death (if includible in the gross estate for estate tax purposes, see ¶5002). (Reg § 1.1014-2(b))[20] If property is acquired before the decedent's death, the basis is reduced by the amount actually allowed to the taxpayer as deductions for depreciation, obsolescence, amortization, and depletion for the period before the decedent's death. (Code Sec. 1014(b)(9))[21] If property received as a gift (including a gift in trust) is disposed of by the donee before the donor's death, the property isn't treated as acquired from a decedent and the donee's basis is determined under the rules for gifts, see ¶2509. But property received in exchange for the gift property, or property acquired through reinvesting proceeds of sale of the gift property (or property acquired in further exchange or reinvestments), is treated as acquired from a decedent if it is properly includible in the gross estate. (Reg § 1.1014-3(d))[22]

¶ 2518   Tenants by the entirety and joint tenants as property acquired from a decedent.

Property that a person acquires as the surviving tenant by the entirety or as a surviving joint tenant is property acquired from a decedent (¶2517) to the extent the property is includible in the decedent's gross estate (¶5010 *et seq.*). The part of the property that's treated as acquired from the decedent gets a stepped-up basis (¶2513 *et seq.*).[23] The reduction in basis for depreciation and similar deductions is required only for depreciation, etc., allowed to the surviving joint owner, whose new basis is at issue. (Code Sec. 1014(b)(9)) Local law applies to determine how depreciation is allocated to spouses who file joint returns. (Reg § 1.1014-6(a)(2))[24]

¶ 2519   Community property as property acquired from a decedent.

Where a spouse dies owning community property and at least one-half of the entire community interest is includible in the deceased spouse's gross estate (whether or not an estate tax return is required or an estate tax is payable), the surviving spouse's interest is treated as property acquired from a decedent (¶2517). (Code Sec. 1014(b)(6))[25]

observation: Under the above rule, the surviving spouse's share of the community property plus the decedent's share (included in the decedent's estate) is treated as property acquired from the decedent. Thus, both shares get a stepped-up basis.

---

18. ¶P-4003; ¶10,144.02
19. ¶P-4055; ¶10,124.07
20. ¶P-4103; ¶10,144.01
21. ¶P-4027; ¶10,144.01

22. ¶P-3124; ¶10,144.02
23. ¶P-4115; ¶10,144.01
24. ¶P-4028 *et seq.*; ¶10,144.01
25. ¶P-4112; ¶10,144.01

¶ 2520 Inter vivos trust with power to revoke, alter, etc. as property acquired from a decedent

Property acquired from a decedent (¶2517) includes property that the decedent during his lifetime transferred in trust to pay the trust income to, or on the order of, the decedent, where the decedent also reserved to himself at all times before his death the right to make any change in the enjoyment of the trust through the exercise of a power to alter, amend, or terminate the trust (whether alone or with the consent of another not having an interest adverse to his). (Code Sec. 1014(b)(3))[26]

¶ 2521 Basis of property passing under a general power of appointment.

Property acquired from a decedent (¶2517) includes property passing without full and adequate consideration under a general power of appointment exercised by the decedent in his or her will. (Code Sec. 1014(b)(4))[27]

¶ 2522 Basis of postponed or contingent remainder Interests.

Taxpayer's basis for property acquired from a decedent (¶2517) is determined on the date of the decedent's death under the rules at ¶2513 *et seq.*, whether or not, at the decedent's death, the taxpayer's interest was conditional or contingent, and whether or not the taxpayer can immediately possess and enjoy the property. (Reg § 1.1014-4(a)(2))[28]

✪ observation: If an estate tax return is filed, and the alternate valuation date (¶2513) is elected, the value would be determined as of the alternate valuation date.

¶ 2523 Multiple interests In one property acquired from a decedent—basis of property.

Where more than 1 person has an interest in property acquired from a decedent (¶2517), the basis in the property is determined and adjusted without regard to the multiple interests. Therefore, a life tenant adjusts basis for depreciation as if he were the absolute owner. His basis adjustments are an adjustment in the hands of every person who receives an interest by reason of the decedent's death. (Reg § 1.1014-4(b))[29]

¶ 2524 Basis of property transferred between spouses or incident to a divorce.

A transferee-spouse is treated as acquiring the property by gift; the transferee's basis in the property received is the transferor-spouse's adjusted basis in the property. (Code Sec. 1041(b)) This rule applies even where the transaction is a sale between the spouses or where the transferee-spouse pays the transferor-spouse (as required under the divorce settlement) for the transfer of title to the property to the transferee-spouse. (Reg § 1.1041-1T(a), Q&A-2) This carryover basis rule applies whether the adjusted basis of the transferred property is less than, equal to, or greater than its fair market value at the time of transfer and applies for purposes of determining loss as well as gain, upon later sale by the transferee. (Reg § 1.1041-1T(d), Q&A-11)[30] Exceptions apply to certain transfers in trust (where liabilities assumed by the trust exceed the transferor's adjusted basis) (Code Sec. 1041(e)), and to transfers of installment obligations into a trust (Code Sec. 453B(g)).[31] The transferor must, at the time of the transfer, give the transferee records sufficient to determine the adjusted basis and holding period of the property at the date of transfer. (Reg § 1.1041-1T(e), Q&A-14)[32]

---

26. ¶P-4109; ¶10,154.17
27. ¶P-4110; ¶10,144.01
28. ¶P-4018
29. ¶P-4014 *et seq.*; ¶10,144.06

30. ¶P-1146; ¶10,414
31. ¶P-1147; ¶10,414
32. ¶P-1153; ¶10,414

Chapter 10   Capital Gains and Losses—Section 1231— Depreciation Recapture

¶ 2600   Capital Gains and Losses. ▃▃▃▃▃▃

The tax treatment of capital gains and losses depends on whether the gains and losses are long-term or short-term and on whether the taxpayer is a corporation or not. For noncorporate taxpayers, the maximum tax rate on net long-term capital gains is lower than the top rate on ordinary income. That maximum tax depends on the type of capital asset sold, and the taxpayer's marginal tax rate (the top rate on the taxpayer's ordinary income). Corporate long-term capital gains, and short-term gains of both corporations and noncorporate taxpayers, are taxed at the same rates as their ordinary income. The deduction for capital losses is limited. Unused noncorporate capital losses may be carried over indefinitely (¶2609) and unused corporate capital losses can generally be carried back for 3 years and forward for 5 years, see ¶2611.

The main features of the income tax treatment of capital gains and losses are:

. . . Short-term capital gains and losses are netted, long-term capital gains and losses are netted, and then long- and short-term are netted with each other (¶2601 *et seq.*). Further netting may be required if a noncorporate taxpayer has capital losses and long-term capital gain subject to differing maximum tax rates. (¶2606)

. . . A net capital gain (excess of net long-term capital gain over net short-term capital loss) of a noncorporate taxpayer is generally taxed more favorably than ordinary income. The maximum tax rate depends on whether the net capital gain is adjusted net capital gain (¶2602), unrecaptured section 1250 gain (¶2604), collectibles gain (¶2605) or section 1202 gain (¶2605).

. . . Section 1231 nets gains and losses to arrive at a net of long-term capital gain or ordinary loss (¶2607 and ¶2669 *et seq.*).

. . . Recapture provisions restrict the possibility of converting ordinary income into capital gains via cost recovery or depreciation (¶2675 *et seq.*).

Capital gains and losses are gains and losses from sales or exchanges (¶2664) of capital assets (¶2612). Capital gain treatment also applies to gains in certain transactions involving assets that aren't capital assets, e.g., depreciable property used in business (¶2670).[1]

> ⊘ *observation:* Not all losses (capital or ordinary) are deductible. Individuals can only deduct losses incurred in business or transactions for profit, or resulting from a federally declared disaster in tax years beginning after 2017 and before 2026 (¶1782). So, a loss on a sale of a personal residence is a nondeductible capital loss.

With limited exceptions, report capital gains and losses on Form 8949, and then carry the totals over to Schedule D of the applicable form (e.g., Form 1040 for individuals, Form 1041 for trusts and estates, Form 1065 for partnerships, Form 1120 for corporations and Form 1120-S for S corporations) where the net short-term and long-term capital gain or loss is computed. Taxpayers may report the total of their capital gains and losses transactions on the applicable schedule and provide details on attachments such as brokers' statements. Individuals whose only capital gains are capital gains distributions (other than unrecaptured section 1250 gain (¶2604), collectibles gain (¶2605), or section 1202 gain (¶2605)) reported on Form 1099-DIV don't have to file a Form 8949 or Schedule D. They enter capital gains on Form 1040 and complete a capital gain tax worksheet in the

---

1. ¶I-5100 *et seq.*; ¶12,214 *et seq.*

References beginning with a single letter are to paragraphs in Federal Tax Coordinator 2d and RIA's Analysis of Federal Taxes: Income. Those beginning with numbers are to paragraphs in United States Tax Reporter.

instructions.

For the deduction when stock or securities become worthless, see ¶1772.

¶ 2601 Tax effect of capital asset sales and exchanges.

If a capital asset is held for not more than the short-term holding period (¶2655), the gain or loss from its sale or exchange is short-term. If held for more than the short-term holding period, gain or loss is long-term. (Code Sec. 1222)[2]

Short-term capital gains and losses are netted to get net short-term capital gain or net short-term capital loss. (Code Sec. 1222(5), Code Sec. 1222(6))

Long-term capital gains and losses are netted to get net long-term capital gain or net long-term capital loss. (Code Sec. 1222(7), Code Sec. 1222(8))

There's a further netting if 1 group shows a loss and the other a gain:

If capital losses exceed capital gains , see ¶2608 *et seq.* (noncorporate) or ¶2611 (corporate).

If net long-term capital gains exceed net short-term capital losses , the excess is net capital gain (Code Sec. 1222(11)), taxed under the rules at ¶2602 to ¶2608 (individuals and other noncorporate taxpayers) or at ¶2610 *et seq.* (corporate taxpayers). *If net short-term capital gains exceed net long-term capital losses,* the excess is taxed (both for noncorporate and corporate taxpayers) at the same rate as ordinary income. [3]

A taxpayer who has an excess of capital gains over capital losses (whether long-term or short-term) for the tax year, has "capital gain net income" (Code Sec. 1222(9)), which is included in gross income. [4]

¶ 2602 Noncorporate taxpayer's tax on net capital gain.

For 2018, the 0% tax rate applies to adjusted net capital gain *up to* $77,200 for joint filers and surviving spouses, $51,700 for heads of household, $38,600 for single filers, $38,600 for married taxpayers filing separately, and $2,600 for estates and trusts. The corresponding 2019 amounts, as calculated by Thomson Reuters based on inflation data, are $78,750, $52,750, $39,350, $39,350, and $2,650.

For 2018, the 15% tax rate applies to adjusted net capital gain over the amount subject to the 0% rate, and up to $479,000 for joint filers and surviving spouses, $452,400 for heads of household, $425,800 for single filers, $239,500 for married taxpayers filing separately, and $12,700 for estates and trusts. The corresponding 2019 amounts, as calculated by Thomson Reuters based on inflation data, are $488,850, $461,700, $434,550, $244,400, and $12,950.

For 2018, the 20% tax rate applies to adjusted net capital gain over $479,000 for joint filers and surviving spouses, $452,400 for heads of household, $425,800 for single filers, $239,500 for married taxpayers filing separately, and $12,700 for estates and trusts. The corresponding 2019 amounts, as calculated by Thomson Reuters based on inflation data, are $488,850, $461,700, $434,550, $244,400, and $12,950. (Code Sec. 1(j)(5))

Unrecaptured section 1250 gain continues to be taxed at a maximum rate of 25%, and 28% rate gain at a maximum rate of 28%. (Code Sec. 1(h)(1))

Sellers of interests in S corporations, partnerships, and trusts held for more than 1 year recognize collectibles gain if the entity owns the appreciated assets at the time of sale. (Code Sec. 1(h)(5)(B)) Regs explain how to figure the seller's deemed collectibles gain and

---

2. ¶I-5103, I-5104; ¶s 12,224.01, 12,224.02
3. ¶I-5100

4. ¶I-5106; ¶12,224.03

his or her residual long-term gain or loss and use the same approach for sales of interests in various entities. (Reg § 1.1(h)-1) See ¶3758 for the regs' approach in the context of sales of partnership interests, which also may cause a partner to recognize unrecaptured section 1250 gain. However, sales of interests in S corporations and trusts don't trigger unrecaptured section 1250 gain —only collectibles gain and residual long-term capital gain or loss. [5]

The 3.8% surtax on net investment income of noncorporate taxpayers whose modified adjusted gross income is over specified thresholds includes capital gains, see ¶3143.

For netting rules where a noncorporate taxpayer has capital losses, see ¶2606.

¶ 2603 Adjusted net capital gain defined.

Adjusted net capital gain is net capital gain (¶2601) determined without taking qualified dividend income (see ¶1286) into account less the amount that the taxpayer takes into account as investment income under Code Sec. 163(d)(4)(B)(iii) (see ¶1728), reduced (but not below zero) by the sum of:

... unrecaptured section 1250 gain (¶2604), and

... 28% rate gain (as defined at ¶2605), and increased by

the amount of qualified dividend income. (Code Sec. 1(h)(3))[6]

🔹*observation:* Effectively, adjusted net capital gain is the sum of that part of a taxpayer's net capital gain, if any, that is eligible to be taxed at a maximum rate of 20% or less (see ¶2602), plus the amount of qualified dividend income.

¶ 2604 Noncorporate taxpayer's unrecaptured section 1250 gain.

Unrecaptured section 1250 gain is taxed at a maximum rate of 25%. It is the excess (if any) of:

(1) the amount of long-term capital gain (¶2601) not otherwise treated as ordinary income, and which would be treated as ordinary income if Code Sec. 1250(b)(1) recapture applied to all depreciation (rather than only to depreciation in excess of straight line), and the applicable percentage under Code Sec. 1250(a) (¶2679) were 100%, over

(2) the excess (if any) of the amount of losses taken into account in computing 28% rate gain (¶2605) over the amount of gains taken into account in computing 28% rate gain. (Code Sec. 1(h)(6))[7]

The amount in (1), above, from sales exchanges and conversions described in Code Sec. 1231(a)(3)(A) (i.e., section 1231 gain) for any tax year can't exceed the net section 1231 gain (¶2669) for that tax year. (Code Sec. 1(h)(6)(B))

🔹*observation:* Under MACRS, real property must be depreciated using the straight-line method (¶1924), so any gain on the sale or exchange of such property attributable to depreciation will be unrecaptured section 1250 gain if held for more than 1 year.

🔹*illustration:* Y, an individual, sells nonresidential real property on Aug. 15 for $200,000, realizing a gain of $50,000. This is Y's only transaction involving a capital asset for the year. Y held the property for more than 1 year. Y depreciated the property using MACRS, and claimed $25,000 of depreciation during Y's ownership. There is no depreciation recapture under Code Sec. 1250(b)(1) because Y didn't claim accelerated depreciation. However, $25,000 of Y's gain, representing depreciation deductions claimed by Y, is unrecaptured section 1250 gain.

5. ¶I-5110.14; ¶14.08
6. ¶I-5110.10; ¶14.08

7. ¶I-5110.8; ¶14.08

For how to handle unrecaptured section 1250 gain where a sale of real property is reported on the installment method, see ¶2457. For how unrecaptured section 1250 gain can arise on sale of a partnership interest, see ¶3758.

¶ 2605   Noncorporate taxpayer's 28% rate gain.

The term 28% rate gain means the sum of collectibles gain and losses and section 1202 gain less the sum of collectibles loss, the net short-term capital loss for the tax year, and the long-term capital loss carryover to the tax year. (Code Sec. 1(h)(4))[8]

observation: The way 28% rate gain is defined causes a long-term capital loss carryover from an earlier tax year to always be used first to offset 28% rate gain, see ¶2606.

Collectibles gain or loss is gain or loss from the sale or exchange of a collectible which is a capital asset held for more than 1 year, but only to the extent such gain or loss is taken into account in computing gross income. (Code Sec. 1(h)(5)) Any work of art, rug or antique, metal or gem, stamp or coin, alcoholic beverage, or any other tangible personal property specified by IRS for this purpose is a collectible. [9]

For how collectibles gain can arise on the sale of interests in a partnership, S corporation, or trust, see ¶2602.

Section 1202 gain is the excess of (1) the gain that would be excluded from gross income on the sale of certain qualified small business stock (QSBS) under Code Sec. 1202, if the percentage limitations of Code Sec. 1202(a) (see ¶2638) didn't apply, over (2) the gain actually excluded under Code Sec. 1202. (Code Sec. 1(h)(7))[10]

observation: If any portion of the gain on the sale of QSBS is excluded from gross income, the part includible in gross income is taxed at a maximum rate of 28%.

See ¶3206 for AMT treatment of section 1202 gain.

¶ 2606   Netting rules where taxpayer has capital losses.

The following netting and ordering rules apply where the taxpayer has capital losses:

(1) Short-term capital losses are applied first to reduce short-term capital gains, if any. If there's a net short-term capital loss, it first reduces any net long-term gain from the 28% group, then gain from the 25% group, and finally reduces adjusted net capital gain.

(2) Long-term capital losses are handled as follows:

. . . A net loss from the 28% group (including long-term capital loss carryovers from prior years) first reduces gain from the 25% group, then reduces adjusted net capital gain.

. . . A net loss from a group in which net gain would be treated as adjusted net capital gain first reduces net gain from the 28% group, then from the 25% group. [11]

illustration: T has a loss of $40,000 from the sale of stock, collectibles gain of $25,000, and unrecaptured section 1250 gain of $25,000. T's net capital gain is $10,000 (total gain of $50,000 less $40,000 loss). T's $40,000 loss from the sale of stock completely offsets the collectibles gain of $25,000, and offsets $15,000 of the $25,000 of unrecaptured section 1250 gain. T has unrecaptured section 1250 gain of $10,000.

8. ¶I-5110.11; ¶14.08
9. ¶I-5110.12; ¶14.08

10. ¶I-5110.13; ¶14.08
11. ¶I-5107; ¶14.08

¶ 2607   Noncorporate taxpayer's nonrecaptured net section 1231 losses.

If any Section 1231 gain is treated as ordinary income under Code Sec. 1231(c) (i.e., Section 1231 gain treated as ordinary income to the extent of nonrecaptured Section 1231 losses, see ¶2669), the amount to be treated as ordinary income is allocated first to any net section 1231 gain in the 28% group, then to any section 1231 gain in the 25% group, and then to any net section 1231 gain in the 0%/15%/20% group. [12]

¶ 2608   Capital losses of noncorporate taxpayers.

A noncorporate taxpayer may deduct capital losses only to the extent of capital gains plus (if the losses exceed the gains) the lower of:

    (1) $3,000 ($1,500 for married individuals filing separate returns), or

    (2) the excess of the losses over the gains. (Code Sec. 1211(b))[13]

Illustration: B has a short-term capital loss of $100 and a long-term capital loss of $3,600 for the tax year. B's total capital loss for the tax year is $3,700. This capital loss is deductible from ordinary income up to a maximum of $3,000. See ¶2609 for carrying over the excess capital loss.

A noncorporate taxpayer's capital losses for a tax year consist of the capital losses sustained during the year plus the total of all capital losses sustained in other years that are carried to that tax year (¶2609). (Code Sec. 1212(b); Reg § 1.1211-1(b)(1))[14]

¶ 2609   Noncorporate capital loss carryovers.

If an individual, trust or estate has a net capital loss that exceeds the maximum deductible in the current year (¶2608), the excess is carried forward to later years indefinitely until used. (Code Sec. 1212(b)) Carrybacks aren't allowed. [15] A decedent's capital loss that can't be used on his or her final income tax return is lost; it can't be carried over. [16]

The capital loss keeps its original character as long- or short-term when carried over. For purposes of determining the amount of excess long- or short-term capital loss that is carried over, short-term capital loss is applied first to offset ordinary income, and long-term capital loss is applied only to the extent that the amount that can be offset exceeds the total short-term capital loss for the year (including any short-term capital loss carried over from an earlier year). (Code Sec. 1212(b))[17]

¶ 2610   Capital gains of corporate taxpayers.

Corporate taxpayers must include capital gains in full in gross income but only to the extent that they exceed capital losses. [18]

¶ 2611   Corporation's capital losses.

Corporations may deduct capital losses only to the extent of their capital gains. Excess capital losses can't be deducted from a corporation's ordinary income. (Code Sec. 1211(a))[19]

A corporation's capital losses in excess of its capital gains for the current year are carried back 3 years, but only to the extent the loss isn't attributable to a foreign expropriation capital loss and to the extent that the carryback doesn't increase or produce an NOL

12. ¶I-9003.1
13. ¶I-5112; ¶12,114
14. ¶I-5113; ¶12,124 *et seq.*
15. ¶I-5122; ¶12,124.01

16. ¶I-5133
17. ¶I-5123; ¶12,124.01
18. ¶I-5116; ¶12,114
19. ¶I-5121; ¶12,114

for the tax year to which it's carried back. (Code Sec. 1212(a)(1)(A)) A net capital loss can't be carried back to a tax year in which the corporation was either a regulated investment company (RIC) or a real estate investment trust (REIT). (Code Sec. 1212(a)(4))

The carryforward period is 5 years (10 years for foreign expropriation capital losses, and there is no limit on how long a RIC may carry forward capital losses). (Code Sec. 1212(a)(1)(B);Code Sec. 1212(a)(1)(C); Code Sec. 1212(a)(3))[20]

A capital loss carryback or carryover is treated as a short-term capital loss whether or not it was short-term when sustained (Code Sec. 1212(a)(1)) except that the capital losses of a RIC retain their character as short-term or long-term when carried over. (Code Sec. 1212(a)(3)(A)) A carryover from 1 year can't be included in computing a new net capital loss for another year. (Code Sec. 1222(10))[21]

¶ 2612   Assets to Which Capital Gain and Loss Rules Apply. ▰▰▰▰▰▰

The capital gain or loss rules apply to assets that are capital in nature. An asset's character depends upon what it is and what use it has in the taxpayer's hands.

Capital assets include all assets held by the taxpayer   *except*:

(1) Stock in trade of the taxpayer or other property of a kind that would properly be included in the inventory of the taxpayer if on hand at the close of the tax year, or property held by the taxpayer primarily for sale to customers in the ordinary course of his or her trade or business. (Code Sec. 1221(a)(1))[22]

(2) Depreciable property, amortizable Code Sec. 197 intangibles, and real property used in the taxpayer's trade or business, see ¶2669 *et seq.* (Code Sec. 1221(a)(2))[23]

(3) Copyrights, literary, artistic, or musical works (unless, for musical works or copyrights in them, the election discussed at ¶2615 is made); certain letters, memoranda, or similar property; and, patents, inventions, models or designs (whether or not patented), secret formulas or processes. (Code Sec. 1221(a)(3))[24]

(4) Accounts or notes receivable acquired in the ordinary course of a trade or business for services rendered or from the sale of any properties described in (1) or (2), above. (Code Sec. 1221(a)(4))[25]

(5) U.S. government publications (e.g., Congressional Record) received from the government without charge or below the price sold to the public, in the hands of the recipient and carryover-basis transferees. (Code Sec. 1221(a)(5))[26]

(6) Commodities derivative financial instruments held by a commodities derivatives dealer (except for certain instruments not connected to the dealing activity). (Code Sec. 1221(a)(6))[27]

(7) Any hedging transaction, see ¶2616. (Code Sec. 1221(a)(7))[28]

(8) Supplies of a type regularly used or consumed by the taxpayer in the ordinary course of the taxpayer's trade or business. (Code Sec. 1221(a)(8))[29]

Property held for personal use is a capital asset, as is property used for the production of income. (Reg § 1.1221-1(b)) Examples of capital assets include stock and securities held for investment,[30] including tax-exempt bonds [31] (¶2621). A payment received in exchange for the right to ordinary income isn't a capital asset. [32] Depending on the circumstances, a contractual right to purchase land can be a capital asset. [33]

---

20. ¶I-5125 *et seq.*; ¶12,124.04
21. ¶I-5125 ; ¶12,124.04
22. ¶I-6100 *et seq.*; ¶12,214.01 *et seq.*
23. ¶I-6006 ; ¶12,314 *et seq.*
24. ¶I-6601 *et seq.*; ¶12,214.45
25. ¶I-6127 *et seq.*; ¶12,214.48
26. ¶I-6002

27. ¶I-6291 ; ¶12,214.76
28. ¶I-6231*et seq.* ; ¶12,214.80
29. ¶I-6140; ¶12,214.18
30. ¶I-6201; ¶12,214.21
31. ¶I-7801
32. ¶I-6824.1
33. ¶I-6317

For the sale of: real property, see ¶2613 *et seq.*; SBIC and RIC stock, see ¶2619 *et seq.*; debt instruments, see ¶2621; investments by a dealer in securities, see ¶2622; a business, see ¶2625; and life estates, terms for years, etc., see ¶2626.

For options and straddles, see ¶2617 *et seq.* For transfers of patents, trademarks, etc., see ¶2623 *et seq.*

¶ 2613   Sale of real property.

Real property held primarily for sale in the ordinary course of the taxpayer's trade or business doesn't qualify as a capital asset. Whether particular real estate sold is a capital asset is decided on a case by case basis taking into consideration many factors including the number and taxpayer's frequency of sales, subdividing and promotional activities. [34]

¶ 2614   5-year land subdivision rule for taxpayers other than C corporations.

A taxpayer other than a C corporation won't be treated as holding land primarily for sale to customers merely because the taxpayer subdivided a tract of land into lots or parcels and engaged in advertising, promotion, selling activities, or the use of sales agents in selling lots in the subdivision, if the taxpayer:

. . . hasn't previously held any part of the same land primarily for sale to customers in the ordinary course of business, and, in the year of sale doesn't hold any other real estate for sale to customers;

. . . doesn't (while he holds the land or as part of a contract of sale with the buyer) make "substantial improvements" on the land that substantially increase the value of the lot sold (except, if elected, improvements needed to make marketable land that has been held for 10 years or more); and

. . . either has owned the land for 5 years or more, or acquired it by inheritance or devise. (Code Sec. 1237(a); Reg § 1.1237-1(a)(2), Reg § 1.1237-1(a)(5), Reg § 1.1237-1(b)(1))[35]

However, if more than 5 lots or parcels in the same tract are sold or exchanged, gain from any sale or exchange (which occurs in or after the tax year in which the 6th lot or parcel is sold or exchanged) of any lot or parcel covered by the above 5-year rule will be treated as ordinary income to the extent that 5% of the selling price exceeds the expenses of the sale. (Code Sec. 1237(b)(1); Reg § 1.1237-1(e)(2))[36]

⚡*illustration:* A divides a tract covered by the 5-year rule into 6 parcels. If A sells all 6 parcels in Year 1, gain from the sale of each parcel is treated as ordinary income to the extent that 5% of the selling price exceeds the expenses of the sale. However, if A doesn't sell the 6th parcel until Year 2, the 5% rule applies only to the gain from the sale of that parcel.

The rules discussed above don't apply to the sale or exchange of otherwise qualifying subdivided land that is business property, and the capital gain-ordinary loss rules of Code Sec. 1231 (see ¶2669) apply. (Reg § 1.1237-1(f))[37]

¶ 2615   Patents, copyrights, literary, musical, artistic compositions, etc.

A patent, invention, model or design (whether or not patented), secret formula or process, copyright, literary, artistic, and (except as noted below) musical composition, etc., aren't capital assets or Section 1231 assets if the taxpayer is either (1) the author or creator of property through his or her own personal efforts, or (2) the donee of the author

---

34. ¶I-6300 *et seq.*; ¶12,214.31
35. ¶I-6400 *et seq.*; ¶12,374.01

36. ¶I-6420; ¶12,374.05
37. ¶I-6424; ¶12,374.07

or creator, or one who otherwise has a basis for the property determined in whole or in part by reference to the basis in the donor's hands.

A letter, memorandum or similar property prepared or produced for a taxpayer isn't a capital asset to the taxpayer (or the taxpayer's donee or other carryover-basis transferee). (Code Sec. 1221(a)(3))[38]

A taxpayer may elect to treat a sale or exchange of musical compositions or copyrights in musical works created by the taxpayer's personal efforts (or having a basis determined by reference to the basis in the hands of a taxpayer whose personal efforts created them) as the sale or exchange of a capital asset. (Code Sec. 1221(b)(3)) A taxpayer must make the election on Form 8949 and Schedule D (Form 1040) by treating the sale or exchange as the sale or exchange of a capital asset on or before the due date (including extensions) of his or her return for the tax year of the sale or exchange. (Reg § 1.1221-3(b)) The election is revocable with IRS consent. IRS automatically grants taxpayers a 6-month extension from the due date of the taxpayer's income tax return (excluding extensions) to revoke an election, if the taxpayer timely filed the income tax return and, within the 6-month extension period, files an amended return that treats the sale or exchange as the sale or exchange of property that isn't a capital asset. (Reg § 1.1221-3(c))[39]

¶ 2616　Hedging transactions.

The term "capital asset" doesn't include property that's part of a hedging transaction. (Code Sec. 1221(a)(7); Reg § 1.1221-2(a)) A hedging transaction is a transaction that a taxpayer enters into in the normal course of the taxpayer's trade or business, primarily to reduce the risk of price changes or currency fluctuations with respect to ordinary property, or to reduce the risk of interest rate or price changes or currency fluctuations with respect to borrowings or ordinary obligations. (Reg § 1.1221-2(b)) Property is ordinary property only if its sale or exchange by the taxpayer couldn't produce capital gain or loss regardless of the holding period. An obligation is an ordinary obligation if performance or termination of the obligation by the taxpayer could not produce capital gain or loss. (Reg § 1.1221-2(c)(2))[40] Thus, hedging in corn futures (to stabilize the cost of corn inventory) as an integral part of a taxpayer's inventory-purchase system produces ordinary income and loss.[41]

A taxpayer must identify a transaction (including recycling an existing hedge) as a hedging transaction before the close of the day he enters it. (Reg § 1.1221-2(f)(1))[42]

The accounting method used for a hedging transaction must clearly reflect income and reasonably match the transaction's timing with the timing of the item(s) being hedged. Special rules give the accounting methods for various transactions. (Reg § 1.446-4)[43]

¶ 2617　Options to buy or sell.

Gain or loss from the sale or exchange of a noncompensatory option to buy or sell property is considered a gain or loss from the sale or exchange of a capital asset if the optioned property is (or would be if acquired) a capital asset in the taxpayer's hands. (Code Sec. 1234(a)(1); Reg § 1.1234-1(a))[44] If the holder of an option incurs a loss because he fails to exercise the option, the option is considered to have been sold or exchanged on the date it expires. (Code Sec. 1234(a)(2); Reg § 1.1234-1(b))[45]

---

38. ¶I-6601 *et seq.*; ¶12,214.08
39. ¶I-6601; ¶12,214.45
40. ¶I-6231 *et seq.*; ¶12,214.80
41. ¶I-6268

42. ¶I-6250; ¶12,214.80
43. ¶G-2519 *et seq.*; ¶4464.01
44. ¶I-6504; ¶12,344
45. ¶I-6510; ¶12,344

A dealer in options is considered a dealer in the property subject to the option, and any gain or loss received from sale or exchange of the option is ordinary. (Reg § 1.1234-1(d))[46]

¶ 2618 "Put" and "call" options; straddles.

There are no tax consequences to the buyer or writer of an option until the option is exercised, otherwise closed out, or lapses. The holder treats the premium paid as a nondeductible capital expenditure at the time of payment. The premium isn't included in income of the writer at the time of receipt.[47] The premium received by the writer for granting a "put" or "call" option that's not exercised ("lapses"), so that the writer simply keeps the money, is generally treated as ordinary income, and gain or loss to the writer on repurchase of an option ("closing transaction") is also generally ordinary. (Reg § 1.1234-1(b)) However, gain or loss to a nondealer from a lapse or closing transaction involving options in stocks, securities, commodities or commodity futures is treated as short-term capital gain or loss. (Code Sec. 1234(b); Reg § 1.1234-3)[48]

Where a put is exercised, the premium received by the writer for granting the option is deducted from the option price for the property in determining the net basis to the writer of the property purchased. The holder deducts the premium from the amount received from the writer, in computing the gain or loss realized on the sale. Where a call is exercised, the premium received by the writer (i.e., seller) for granting the option is added to the sale proceeds received. This is included in the holder's (buyer's) basis for the property.[49]

illustration: A bought a 180-day put from B for $5,000 that gave A the right to sell 1,000 shares of stock to B for $50,000. The stock originally cost A $25,000. The put was timely exercised. A has a gain of $20,000 on the sale ($50,000, less $30,000 ($5,000 paid for put and $25,000 original cost of stock). B's basis in the stock is $45,000 ($50,000 paid to A on the exercise of the put, less $5,000 received by B from A for the put).

When the put or call is bought from the original holder (or the original holder's assignee), the buyer is treated as a holder, and the amount paid by him to the original holder is likewise treated as a premium. However, the original holder isn't treated as a writer, and must include that premium in his or her amount realized upon disposition of the option, see ¶2617.[50]

observation: Thus, if a holder (other than a dealer) of a put or call option on publicly traded stock closes out a position by selling the option on an exchange, the gain or loss is a capital gain or loss.

A "straddle" option combines a put and a call. (Reg § 1.1234-3(b)(4))[1] The allocation of a premium received for a straddle or multiple option between or among the component options is made on the basis of the relative market value of the component options at the time of their issuance or on any other reasonable and consistently applied basis which is acceptable to IRS. (Reg § 1.1234-3(e))[2]

¶ 2619 Sale of small business investment company (SBIC) stock.

Losses from the sale, exchange or worthlessness of SBIC (¶4205) stock are deductible by a shareholder as an ordinary loss attributable to the shareholder's business. (Code Sec. 1242; Reg § 1.1242-1) Gains on the sale or exchange of SBIC stock are capital gains.[3]

46. ¶I-6509; ¶12,344.03
47. ¶s I-6521, I-6522; ¶12,344 *et seq.*
48. ¶I-6515; ¶12,344 *et seq.*
49. ¶s I-6530, I-6531; ¶s 12,344.03, 12,344.04

50. ¶I-6523; ¶s 12,344.03, 12,344.04
1. ¶I-6526; ¶12,344.06
2. ¶I-6528; ¶12,344.06
3. ¶I-9543; ¶12,424 *et seq.*

¶ 2620   Sale of regulated investment company (RIC) stock.

A loss realized on the sale or exchange of stock in a RIC is a long-term capital loss to the extent of any long-term capital gain realized via a distribution made with respect to the stock, if the taxpayer held the stock for 6 months or less. Also, the loss of a shareholder who receives an exempt-interest dividend on stock which is held for 6 months or less is disallowed to the extent of the exempt interest dividend received by the shareholder. Rules for periodic liquidations differ. (Code Sec. 852(b)(4))[4]

¶ 2621   Type of gain on a sale or exchange of debt instruments.

Debt instruments issued with original issue discount (OID). If a debt instrument is issued with OID (¶1311) and, if at the time of original issue there was an intention to call the debt instrument before maturity, any gain realized on the sale or exchange of the instrument is treated as ordinary income to the extent the gain doesn't exceed the OID reduced by the part of the OID previously included in the income of any holder. For purposes of this rule, any part of the OID that would have been included in the income of the holder had there been no acquisition premium is treated as if it had been included. (Code Sec. 1271(a)(2)(A)) This rule doesn't apply to tax-exempt obligations or to the sale or exchange by a holder who purchased the debt instrument at a premium. (Code Sec. 1271(a)(2)(B))[5]

Sale or exchange of short-term government obligations. On the sale or exchange of any short-term government obligation, any gain realized that doesn't exceed an amount equal to the ratable share of the acquisition discount is treated as ordinary income (Code Sec. 1271(a)(3)(A)) unless the seller was required to include the discount in gross income currently under the rules at ¶1325. (Code Sec. 1283(d)(3))[6]

Sale or exchange of short-term nongovernment obligations. On the sale or exchange of any short-term nongovernment obligation, any gain realized that doesn't exceed an amount equal to the ratable share of OID is treated as ordinary income (Code Sec. 1271(a)(4)(A)), unless the seller was required to include the discount in gross income currently under the rules at ¶1325. (Code Sec. 1283(d)(3))[7]

Sale or exchange of tax-exempt bonds. The sale or exchange of tax-exempt obligations is a taxable event, even if the interest on the bonds is exempt. The seller has gain to the extent that the amount realized exceeds adjusted basis (¶2473) in the bonds. The seller's basis for this purpose means the price he or she paid, even if the bonds were purchased at a discount. However, the holder of a tax-exempt bond issued with OID can increase his adjusted basis in the bond by the amount of OID accrued during the period the bond is held. If the bond is bought at a premium over face value, the holder must reduce his or her adjusted basis in the bond by the amount by which the premium is amortized under the rules discussed at ¶2165.[8]

¶ 2622   Investments by dealer in securities.

A securities dealer who buys securities for resale to customers may also hold securities purchased as investments for the dealer's own account. But gain from the sale or exchange of those securities won't be capital gain unless (1) the security is clearly identified in the dealer's records as a security held for investment on the day it is acquired, and (2) the security isn't held by the dealer primarily for sale to customers in the ordinary course of a trade or business at any time after the acquisition date. (Code Sec. 1236(a))[9]

---

4. ¶E-6162; ¶8524.02
5. ¶I-8001; ¶12,714
6. ¶I-8004; ¶12,714.05

7. ¶I-8005; ¶12,714.05; ¶12,814
8. ¶I-4001 *et seq.*
9. ¶I-6209; ¶12,364.01

A loss is a capital loss if the security has ever been clearly identified in the dealer's records as held for investment, even though held primarily for sale at the time of its disposition. (Code Sec. 1236(b); Reg § 1.1236-1(b))[10]

¶ 2623 Transfer of patents.

If an individual inventor or his financial backer transfers (other than by gift, inheritance or devise) all substantial rights to a patent, or an undivided interest (e.g., a half, a third) in those rights, the transfer is considered a sale or exchange of a long-term capital asset, even though the transferor hasn't held the patent rights for the period required for long-term treatment (see ¶2655), and even though the payments to the seller are: (1) made periodically during the buyer's use of the property; or (2) contingent on the productivity, use or disposition of the buyer's rights in the property (i.e., are like royalties). (Code Sec. 1235(a); Reg § 1.1235-1(a))[11] However, effective control of the transferee would prevent treatment as a transfer of all substantial rights. [12]

It's not necessary that the patent or patent application be in existence at the time of that transfer for long-term capital gain treatment to apply. (Reg § 1.1235-2(a))[13]

This treatment doesn't apply to a transfer by the inventor's employer (Code Sec. 1235(b)(2)(A)),[14] or to transfers made (directly or indirectly) to or by certain persons related to the inventor. (Code Sec. 1235(b)(2)(B); Reg § 1.1235-2(f))[15]

¶ 2624 Franchise, trademark, or trade name transfers.

The transfer of a franchise, trademark, or trade name isn't a sale or exchange of a capital asset if the transferor retains any significant power, right or continuing interest (such as the right to terminate at will, prescribe standards of quality, or require the transferee to sell only the transferor's products). (Code Sec. 1253(a), Code Sec. 1253(b)(2))[16] Thus, ordinary income treatment applies to payments received by a transferor that are contingent on production, use, or disposition of a franchise, etc. (Code Sec. 1253(c))[17]

For deduction and amortization of these payments, see ¶1607 and ¶1967.

¶ 2625 Sale of businesses.

Sole proprietorship. If a sole proprietorship is sold, there isn't a sale of just 1 asset (i.e., the business), but rather, there's a sale of the individual assets that *comprise* the business. Thus, gain or loss on some assets is ordinary while on others it is capital. [18]

Allocation of selling price on sale of business. If assets of a going business are sold, the selling price is allocated among the assets (including goodwill) for purposes of determining gain or loss (and the type of gain or loss, e.g., capital gain or ordinary income) separately for each. Allocation is made under the rules for determining the buyer's basis in each of them, see ¶2471.[19]

Goodwill and covenants not to compete. Goodwill is a capital asset, unless it is treated as an amortizable section 197 intangible (see ¶1966 *et seq.*). If the Code Sec. 197 rules don't apply, proceeds from the sale of a business that are allocable to goodwill are taxed under the capital gain and loss rules, [20] and payments for a covenant not to compete that is severable from the sale of goodwill results in ordinary income. [21]

---

10. ¶I-6215; ¶12,364.01
11. ¶I-8301; ¶12,354
12. ¶I-8325; ¶12,354.06
13. ¶I-8307; ¶12,354.08
14. ¶I-8322; ¶12,354.04
15. ¶s I-8301, I-8325; ¶12,354.06

16. ¶I-8401; ¶12,534 *et seq.*
17. ¶I-8412; ¶12,534.01
18. ¶I-8501; ¶12,214.53
19. ¶I-8506 *et seq.*; ¶12,214.51
20. ¶I-8601; ¶12,214.55
21. ¶I-8603; ¶12,214.56

¶ 2626   Life estates, term of years, etc.

A life tenant, a tenant for a term of years, or an income beneficiary of a trust is generally entitled to capital gain on the sale of that interest. [22] However, where the interest was acquired by gift, from a decedent, by a transfer in trust, or by a transfer from a spouse (or a former spouse incident to divorce), that part of the basis that's determined under the Code rules for those types of acquisitions (e.g., fair market value basis where acquired from a decedent) isn't taken into account in computing gain or loss on the sale or exchange of the interest, unless the entire interest in the underlying property is transferred in the same transaction. (Code Sec. 1001(e); Reg § 1.1001-1(f))[23]

¶ 2627   Constructive Sales of Appreciated Financial Positions. ▰▰▰▰

The constructive sale rules restrict a taxpayer's ability to defer recognition of gain on appreciated property he owns even though he locks in his gain and limits risk of loss through the use of "short sales against the box" and similar transactions. In general, the taxpayer is treated as constructively selling property he owns if he borrows and sells the same or substantially identical property.

A taxpayer must recognize gain upon entering into a constructive sale of any appreciated financial position in stock, a partnership interest, or certain debt instruments. (Code Sec. 1259) In general, an appreciated financial position is any position with respect to any stock, debt instrument, or partnership interest if there would be gain if the position were sold, assigned, or otherwise terminated at its fair market value (FMV). (Code Sec. 1259(b)(1)) Except as provided at ¶2628, a constructive sale of an appreciated position occurs when the taxpayer (or a related person):

(1) enters into a short sale of the same or substantially identical property,

(2) enters into an offsetting notional principal contract with respect to the same or substantially identical property,

(3) enters into a futures or forward contract to deliver the same or substantially identical property,

(4) in the case of an appreciated financial position that's a short sale or a contract described in (2) or (3) above with respect to any property, acquires the same or substantially identical property, or

(5) to the extent provided in regs, enters into 1 or more other transactions (or acquires 1 or more positions) that have substantially the same effect as a transaction described in (1), (2), (3), or (4) above. (Code Sec. 1259(c)(1))[24]

Persons are "related" with respect to a transaction if their relationship is described in Code Sec. 267(b) (¶2448) or Code Sec. 707(b) (¶3726), and the transaction is entered into with a view toward avoiding the purposes of the constructive sale rules. (Code Sec. 1259(c)(4))[25]

The constructive sale rules don't apply to a short sale of stock that the seller borrows if he doesn't hold substantially identical property at the time of the sale. However, if he acquires the same stock that he borrowed and sold, and has a gain, the constructive sale rules apply on the acquisition date even if the acquired stock isn't delivered to the lender. [26]

As a result of a constructive sale,

. . . the taxpayer recognizes gain as if the position were sold, assigned, or otherwise

---

22. ¶I-7014; ¶12,214.66
23. ¶P-3129; ¶10,144.07
24. ¶I-7732; ¶12,594

25. ¶I-7733; ¶12,594
26. ¶I-7732; ¶12,594

terminated at its FMV value on the constructive sale date (Code Sec. 1259(a)(1)), and . . . for purposes of applying the Code for periods after the constructive sale, (1) an appropriate adjustment is made in the amount of gain or loss later realized on the position for the gain taken into account because of the constructive sale rule, and (2) a new holding period for the position begins as if the taxpayer had acquired the position on the date of the constructive sale. (Code Sec. 1259(a)(2))[27]

☑️illustration: On May 1, 2017, S bought 100 shares of ABC stock for $10,000. On Sept. 3, 2017, S sold short 100 shares of ABC stock for $16,000. S made no other transactions involving ABC stock for the rest of 2017 and the first 30 days of 2018. S's short sale is treated as a constructive sale of an appreciated financial position because a sale of the ABC stock on the date of the short sale would have resulted in a gain. S recognizes a $6,000 short-term capital gain from the constructive sale and has a new holding period in the ABC stock that begins on Sept. 3, 2017.

The term "appreciated financial position" does *not* include (1) certain positions with respect to nonconvertible debt if the holder is unconditionally entitled to receive a specified principal amount and certain specified conditions with respect to interest are met (Code Sec. 1259(b)(2)(A)); (2) any hedge with respect to a position described in (1), above (Code Sec. 1259(b)(2)(B)); and (3) any position which is marked to market under any Code section or the regs thereunder. (Code Sec. 1259(b)(2)(C))[28]

¶ 2628   Exceptions to constructive sale rules.

A taxpayer isn't treated as having made a constructive sale solely because the taxpayer enters a contract for the sale of any stock, debt instrument, or partnership interest which isn't a marketable security if the contract settles within 1 year after the date the contract is entered. (Code Sec. 1259(c)(2))[29] In addition, any transaction which would otherwise cause a constructive sale during the tax year is disregarded if:

(1) it's closed on or before the 30th day after the close of the tax year it was entered,

(2) the taxpayer holds the appreciated financial position to which the transaction relates (e.g., the stock where the transaction is a short sale) throughout the 60-day period beginning on the date the transaction is closed, and

(3) at no time during that 60-day period is the taxpayer's risk of loss reduced with respect to the position (applying the principles of Code Sec. 246(c)(4), relating to suspension of the holding period where the risk of loss is diminished for purposes of the dividends received deduction, see ¶3310). (Code Sec. 1259(c)(3)(A))[30]

☑️observation: If a taxpayer meets the above requirements, a "short sale against the box" isn't a constructive sale as long as he remains at risk with respect to the appreciated financial position for 60 days after the closing.

¶ 2629   Short Sales. ▄▄▄▄▄▄▄▄

In a short sale, an investor sells a security for delivery in the future. The short seller may meet his or her obligation to deliver by buying the security on the delivery ("closing") date. If the security has declined in value by the time the short seller closes or covers the sale, he or she has a gain equal to the sale price minus cost; if the value has increased, the purchase price is higher than the sale price, and the short seller has a loss. The nature of the gain or loss on a short sale depends upon the nature of the property used to close the short transaction.

---

27. ¶I-7731; ¶12,594
28. ¶I-7741 *et seq.*; ¶12,594

29. ¶I-7736; ¶12,594
30. ¶I-7737; ¶12,594

If the property used to close the short sale is a capital asset in the hands of the short seller, the gain or loss on the transaction is capital gain or loss. (Code Sec. 1233(a); Reg § 1.1233-1(a)(1))[31] Where the property used to close the short sale is a capital asset, the period the taxpayer held the property determines whether the gain or loss is long or short term, unless the limits at ¶2630 *et seq.* apply. (Reg § 1.1233-1(a)(3))[32]

caution: Entering into certain short sales may result in a taxpayer recognizing gain under the constructive sale rules (¶2627 *et seq.*).

Entering into a securities futures contract (¶2651) to sell is treated as a short sale and the settlement of the contract is treated as the closing of the short sale for determining whether gain or loss is long- or short-term and for the holding period rules at ¶2658. (Code Sec. 1233(e)(2)(E))[33]

For the effect of the wash sale rules on short sales, see ¶2461.

¶ 2630   Limits on long-term capital gains on short sales.

Capital gain realized in a short sale is short-term, regardless of the actual holding period, where the seller either: (1) as of the date of the short sale, has owned for not more than 1 year (determined without regard to the effect of the short sale on the holding period, see ¶2658) property that's "substantially identical" (¶2461) to that which he used to close the sale, or (2) after the short sale and on or before its closing, he acquires substantially identical property. (Code Sec. 1233(b); Reg § 1.1233-1(c)(2)) This doesn't apply to any capital gain on property in excess of the amount of substantially identical property. This keeps the taxpayer from turning what would normally be a short-term capital gain into a long-term capital gain. [34]

The above rule applies only to stocks, securities, and commodity futures, but doesn't include any position subject to the straddle rules of Code Sec. 1092(b). (Code Sec. 1233(e)(2)(A))[35]

¶ 2631   Capital loss limits on short sales.

If property "substantially identical" (¶2461) to that sold short was held by the taxpayer for more than 1 year as of the sale date, any loss on closing of the short sale is long-term capital loss, regardless of how long he held the property used to close the sale. (Code Sec. 1233(d)) This doesn't apply to any capital loss on property used to close the short sale in excess of the amount of substantially identical property. (Code Sec. 1233(e)(1))[36] This rule applies only to stocks, securities and commodity futures, but doesn't include any position to which the straddle rules of Code Sec. 1092(b) apply. (Code Sec. 1233(e)(2)(A))[37]

¶ 2632   Commodity futures and hedging transactions.

Commodity transactions are generally subject to the same rules for short sales as stocks and securities. A commodity future is a contract to buy some fixed amount of a commodity at a future date at a fixed price. Gain or loss from the short sale of a commodity future is capital gain or loss if the future used to close the short sale is a capital asset to the taxpayer. However, the short sale rules don't apply where the sale of the commodity future is a bona fide hedging transaction (¶2616). (Code Sec. 1233(g); Reg § 1.1233-1(b))[38]

---

31. ¶I-7704; ¶12,334.01
32. ¶I-7708; ¶12,334.01
33. ¶I-7712.2; ¶12,334.09
34. ¶I-7710; ¶12,334.03

35. ¶I-7709; ¶12,334.03
36. ¶I-7714; ¶12,334.03
37. ¶I-7709; ¶12,334.03
38. ¶I-7724; ¶12,334.12, ¶12,334.14

¶ 2633   Gain recognition required when property sold short becomes worthless.

If a taxpayer enters into a short sale of property, and that property becomes substantially worthless, the taxpayer recognizes gain in the same manner as if the short sale were closed when the property becomes substantially worthless. (Code Sec. 1233(h)(1))[39]

If property becomes substantially worthless during a tax year and a short sale of the property remains open at that time, the period for assessing any deficiency attributable to any part of the gain on the transaction doesn't expire before the earlier of: (1) the date 3 years after the date IRS is notified by the taxpayer (in a manner that IRS prescribes in regs) of the property's substantial worthlessness, or (2) the date 6 years after the date the return for the tax year during which the position became substantially worthless is filed. Also, the deficiency may be assessed before the expiration of the assessment period in spite of any other law that would otherwise prevent the assessment. (Code Sec. 1233(h)(2))[40]

¶ 2634   Section 1244 ("Small Business Corporation") Stock. ■■■■■■■■

Loss on the sale, exchange or worthlessness of Section 1244 stock is deductible, within limits, as an ordinary loss, even though gain on the stock is capital gain (¶2635). This ordinary deduction is available only to an individual to whom the stock was issued by a small business corporation (¶2637), or an individual who was a partner in a partnership at the time the stock was issued to a partnership by a small business corporation. Transferees of these original purchasers don't qualify. (Code Sec. 1244(a); Reg § 1.1244(a)-1(b)(2))[41]

The aggregate amount of the ordinary loss is limited to $50,000 on separate returns and $100,000 on joint returns each year. Spouses may deduct the $100,000 maximum in a joint return even if only 1 spouse owned the stock. (Code Sec. 1244(b))[42]

A loss on qualifying Section 1244 stock is deductible as an ordinary loss attributable to the shareholder's business. As such, the loss is deductible in full from gross income and may give rise to a net operating loss. Losses exceeding the limits must be treated as regular capital losses. (Code Sec. 1244(d)(3))[43]

See ¶2636 for how to claim the Section 1244 ordinary loss.

¶ 2635   Qualifying for Section 1244 ordinary loss treatment.

To qualify as Section 1244 stock, all of the following tests must be met: (Code Sec. 1244(c))[44]

... The stock must be stock (common or preferred, voting or nonvoting) issued by a domestic "small business" corporation (¶2637).[45]

... The stock must have been issued for money or property (other than stock and securities). Stock issued for the cancellation of corporate debt (not evidenced by a security or issued for services) qualifies, but not stock issued for services rendered or to be rendered to, or for the benefit of, the issuing corporation. (Reg § 1.1244(c)-1(d)(1))[46]

... The issuing corporation must have shown that over 50% of its aggregate gross receipts within the 5 most recent tax years ending before the date of the loss (or within the period before the date of the loss if the corporation was in existence for less than 5 tax years at that time) came from sources other than rents, royalties, dividends, interest,

---

39. ¶I-7707.1; ¶12,334.02
40. ¶T-4221.2; ¶12,334.02
41. ¶I-9503; ¶12,444.02
42. ¶I-9505; ¶12,444.01

43. ¶I-9502; ¶12,444
44. ¶I-9508 *et seq.*; ¶12,444.03
45. ¶I-9508 *et seq.*; ¶12,444.03
46. ¶I-9511, I-9512; ¶12,444.03

annuities, and sales or exchanges of stock or securities. (Code Sec. 1244(c)(1)(C))[47]

¶ 2636   How to claim the Section 1244 ordinary loss—Form 4797.

Claim the ordinary loss on Form 4797 (attached to Form 1040). No information statement is required to be filed with the return but records must be maintained to establish a loss and whether the stock qualifies as Section 1244 stock. (Reg § 1.1244(e)-1(b))[48]

¶ 2637   Small business corporation (SBC) defined.

A corporation is an SBC if at the time the stock is issued its "capital receipts" don't exceed $1 million. Capital receipts means the aggregate amount of money and other property received by the corporation for stock, as a contribution to capital, and as paid-in surplus. This includes amounts received for the Section 1244 stock and for all stock issued previously. The corporation can designate which shares issued in a year capital receipts exceed $1 million are to be treated as Section 1244 stock. The designation must be made by the 15th day after the end of the tax year. If no designation is made, part of the loss on stock issued that year may qualify as ordinary loss under allocation rules contained in the regs. (Code Sec. 1244(c)(3)(A); Reg § 1.1244(c)-2(b))[49]

¶ 2638   Exclusion of Gain from Qualified Small Business Stock (QSBS). ▬▬▬

Under the rules described below, a non-corporate taxpayer may exclude all (or, in some cases, part) of the gain realized on the disposition of QSBS (¶2639) held for more than 5 years. (Code Sec. 1202(a))

For QSBS acquired after Sept. 27, 2010, noncorporate taxpayers may exclude all of the gain on the disposition of QSBS stock. For QSBS acquired after Feb. 17, 2009 and before Sept. 28, 2010, noncorporate taxpayers can exclude 75% of any gain realized on the disposition of QSBS. For QSBS acquired before Feb. 18, 2009, noncorporate taxpayers may exclude 50% of the gain on the disposition of QSBS. (Code Sec. 1202(a))[50]

The acquisition date is the first day on which the stock was held by the taxpayer determined after the application of the holding period rules provided in Code Sec. 1223 permitting the tacking of holding periods for substituted basis property, see ¶2662. (Code Sec. 1202(a)(3); Code Sec. 1202(a)(4))

The exclusion is 60%, rather than 50%, for periods that the 75% or 100% exclusion doesn't apply, for gain on the sale of empowerment zone stock (but not District of Columbia Enterprise Zone stock) acquired after Dec. 21, 2000, held for more than 5 years, and not attributable to periods after 2018. The empowerment zone stock must be in a corporation that qualifies as an enterprise zone business under Code Sec. 1397C(b) during substantially all of the taxpayer's holding period. (Code Sec. 1202(a)(2))[1]

However, a taxpayer (or a related party) who takes an offsetting short position before the required 5-year holding period is completed cannot exclude gain from the disposition of QSBS. (Code Sec. 1202(j))[2]

For each corporation in which the taxpayer invests, the total amount of gain eligible for the applicable exclusion for a tax year may not exceed the greater of:

. . . $10 million ($5 million for marrieds filing separately) (Code Sec. 1202(b)(1)(A), Code Sec. 1202(b)(3)(A)) reduced by taxpayer's total gain on dispositions of the corporation's stock that he took into account in earlier years. (Code Sec. 1202(b)(1)(A)) To apply this

47. ¶I-9524 *et seq.*; ¶12,444.03
48. ¶I-9537, I-9538; ¶12,444.05
49. ¶I-9518 *et seq.*; ¶12,444.04

50. ¶I-9100 *et seq.*; ¶12,024
1. ¶I-9100.1C; ¶12,024
2. ¶I-9115; ¶12,024.03

limit to later years, the amount of eligible gain is allocated equally between spouses who file jointly (Code Sec. 1202(b)(3)(B)); or

... 10 times the aggregate adjusted bases of any of the corporation's QSBS that taxpayer disposed of during the year, but not including any additions to basis after the date it was originally issued. (Code Sec. 1202(b)(1))[3]

The exclusion is denied where the corporation redeems stock from the taxpayer or a related person during certain periods, or buys its own stock in excess of certain amounts during specified periods. (Code Sec. 1202(c)(3))[4]

Additional rules apply where passthrough entities hold the stock. (Code Sec. 1202(g))[5]

For the rollover of gain from QSBS to other QSBS, see ¶2428.

For alternative minimum tax treatment of the exclusion, see ¶3206.

¶ 2639 Qualified small business stock (QSBS) defined.

QSBS is any stock (but not an option to acquire stock) in a C corporation which is originally issued after Aug. 10, '93 if:

... as of the date of issuance, the corporation is a qualified small business. (Code Sec. 1202(c)(1)(A)) This means a domestic C corporation whose total gross assets (treating all members of the same parent-subsidiary controlled group as 1 corporation) at all times after Aug. 10, '93 and before the issuance, and immediately after the issuance (taking into account amounts received in the issuance), don't exceed $50,000,000, and that meets certain reporting requirements (Code Sec. 1202(d));

... the taxpayer claiming the exclusion acquired the stock at its original issuance for money or other property (not stock) or as compensation for services provided to the corporation (other than services performed as an underwriter) (Code Sec. 1202(c)(1)(B)); *and*

... during substantially all of taxpayer's holding period for the stock, the corporation is a C corporation (other than certain excluded corporations) *and* meets an active business test. (Code Sec. 1202(c)(2)(A), Code Sec. 1202(e))[6]

¶ 2640 Tax-Free Capital Gains for Investment in Renewal Communities and DC Zone Assets.

Taxpayers could exclude capital gains realized from the sale of certain qualifying community renewal (¶2641) or DC Zone (¶2642) assets held for more than 5 years.

¶ 2641 Tax-free capital gains from sale of qualified community assets held for more than 5 years.

Taxpayers could exclude 100% of their "qualified capital gain" recognized on the sale or exchange of a "qualified community asset" if the asset was (1) acquired after 2001 and before 2010 and (2) held for more than 5 years. (Former Code Sec. 1400F)

"Qualified capital gain" was gain recognized on the sale or exchange of a capital asset, or property used in a trade or business (under Code Sec. 1231(b), see ¶2670. It didn't include gain: (1) in periods before 2002 or after 2014; (2) recaptured under Code Sec. 1245 (¶2677) or Code Sec. 1250 (¶2679); (3) on real property, or intangible assets, that wasn't integral to a "renewal community business" (defined in Former Code Sec. 1400G); and (4) attributable in whole or part to certain related-party transactions. (Former Code

---

3. ¶I-9112 *et seq.*; ¶12,024.01
4. ¶I-9102; ¶12,024

5. ¶I-9116; ¶12,024.03
6. ¶I-9101 *et seq.*; ¶12,024.02

Sec. 1400F(c))

A qualified community asset was qualifying stock in a U.S. corporation, a qualifying capital or a profits interest in a U.S. partnership, or qualifying community business property (defined in Former Code Sec. 1400F(b)).[7]

¶ 2642   Tax-free gain from the sale or exchange of DC Zone assets.

Gross income didn't include qualified capital gain from the sale or exchange of any "DC Zone asset" held for more than 5 years. Qualified capital gain was any gain recognized on the sale or exchange of a capital asset, or property used in the trade or business. (Former Code Sec. 1400B(a), Code Sec. 1400B(b)(1), Code Sec. 1400B(e)(1))

Qualified capital gain didn't include gain: (1) in periods before '98 or after 2016; (2) treated as ordinary income under the recapture rules of Code Sec. 1245 (¶2677) or Code Sec. 1250 (¶2679) if Code Sec. 1250 applied to all depreciation rather than the additional depreciation; (3) attributable to real property, or an intangible asset, that wasn't an integral part of a DC Zone business; or (4) attributable, directly or indirectly, in whole or in part, to a related-party transaction (under Code Sec. 267(b) (¶2448) or Code Sec. 707(b)(1)) (¶3727)). (Former Code Sec. 1400B(e))

¶ 2643   Tax Straddles and Section 1256 Contracts. ■■■■■■■■

Losses on certain unregulated straddles (¶2644) are deferred to the extent taxpayer has offsetting unrecognized gain (¶2645). Related interest and carrying charges must be capitalized. Regulated futures contracts and other Section 1256 contracts (¶2647) are subject to the "mark-to-market" rule (¶2646) which treats unrealized capital gain or loss from the contract for the year as 60% long-term and 40% short-term. Hedging transactions are excepted from these rules (¶2650).

There are a number of rules provided to restrict tax avoidance opportunities in commodity futures straddles and to curb certain tax shelters involving tax straddles. [8]

Under the constructive sale rules (¶2627), a taxpayer must recognize gain (but not loss) upon entering into a constructive sale of any appreciated financial position in stock, a partnership interest, or certain debt instruments. (Code Sec. 1259). The constructive sale rules generally are intended to apply to transactions that are identified as hedging or straddle transactions under other Code provisions such as Code Sec. 1092(a)(2) (dealing with a special rule for straddles that are identified as straddles at the close of a tax year), Code Sec. 1092(b)(2) (dealing with regs with respect to identified mixed straddles, ¶2648), Code Sec. 1092(e) (dealing with an exception for hedging transactions), and Code Sec. 1256(e) (dealing with the nonapplication of the mark-to-market rules to hedging transactions, ¶2650).[9]

The interest and carrying charges properly allocable to personal property that is part of a straddle aren't deductible, but must be charged to the capital account of the property for which they were paid or incurred. (Code Sec. 263(g)(1)) However this requirement doesn't apply to any identified hedging transactions (¶2650). (Code Sec. 263(g)(3))[10]

¶ 2644   Straddle defined.

A straddle is "offsetting positions" with respect to personal property. (Code Sec. 1092(c)(1)) A "position" is an interest, including a futures or forward contract or option, in personal property. (Code Sec. 1092(d)(2)) Personal property includes stock only if the stock is of a type which is actively traded and at least 1 of the positions offsetting the

---

7. ¶I-8801 *et seq.*; ¶14,00F4   9. ¶I-7746
8. ¶I-7500 *et seq.*; ¶10,924   10. ¶L-5985; ¶2634

stock is a position with respect to that stock or substantially similar or related property, or the stock is in a corporation formed or used to take positions in personal property which offset positions taken by any shareholder. (Code Sec. 1092(d)(3)(A))

A taxpayer holds "offsetting positions" if he or she has reduced the risk of loss from holding the property by holding 1 (or more) other positions, whether or not the items of personal property involved in the different positions are the same kind. (Code Sec. 1092(c)(2)(A))[11]

If a taxpayer is the obligor under a debt instrument on which 1 or more payments are linked to the value of personal property or a position with respect to personal property, then the taxpayer's obligation under the debt instrument is a position with respect to personal property and may be part of a straddle. (Reg § 1.1092(d)-1(d))[12]

¶ 2645 Recognition of losses postponed on certain nonregulated futures straddles (loss deferral rule).

Loss deductions on nonregulated straddles, that is, those straddle positions not on the "mark-to-market" system (see ¶2646), are limited to the amount by which the losses exceed "unrecognized gains" on any offsetting straddle positions. Losses in excess of the limitation (deferred losses) are carried forward to the next year and are subject to the deferral rules in that year. (Code Sec. 1092(a)(1))[13]

¶ 2646 Regulated futures contracts, etc. (Section 1256 contracts), under "mark-to-market" system.

Taxpayers must report (on Form 6781) gains and losses from regulated futures contracts and other "Section 1256 contracts" (¶2647) on an annual basis under the "mark-to-market" rule. All Section 1256 contracts must be marked-to-market at year end. Each Section 1256 contract held by a taxpayer is treated as if it were sold for fair market value on the last business day of the tax year. (Code Sec. 1256(a)(1)) If a taxpayer holds Section 1256 contracts at the beginning of a tax year, any gain or loss later realized on the contracts must be adjusted to reflect any gain or loss taken into account with respect to the contracts in an earlier year. (Code Sec. 1256(a)(2))

Any capital gain or loss on a Section 1256 futures contract that is marked-to-market is treated as if 40% of the gain or loss is short-term capital gain or loss, and as if 60% of the gain or loss is long-term capital gain or loss. (Code Sec. 1256(a)(3))[14]

The wash sale rules (¶2461) don't apply to losses taken into account when a Section 1256 contract is marked to market. (Code Sec. 1256(f)(5))[15]

¶ 2647 Section 1256 contracts defined.

Section 1256 contracts include: regulated futures contracts, foreign currency contracts, nonequity options, dealer equity options, and dealer securities futures contracts (¶2651). (Code Sec. 1256(b))[16] For a partnership that's a qualified fund, Section 1256 contracts include bank forward contracts, foreign currency futures contracts, and similar instruments prescribed by IRS regs. (Code Sec. 988(c)(1)(E)(iv)(I))[17] A Court of Appeals, disagreeing with IRS and the Tax Court, said a foreign currency option is a foreign currency transaction that is treated as a Section 1256 contract. [18]

11. ¶I-7503 *et seq.*; ¶10,924
12. ¶I-7532
13. ¶I-7501; ¶10,924
14. ¶I-7602, ¶I-7603.3; ¶12,564 *et seq.*

15. ¶I-7602; ¶12,564.02
16. ¶I-7604; ¶12,564.01
17. ¶I-7607; ¶9884.01
18. ¶I-7611

Section 1256 contracts don't include (1) any securities futures contract, or option on a securities futures contract, unless the contract or option is a dealer securities futures contract, or (2) any interest rate swap, currency swap, basis swap, interest rate cap, interest rate floor, commodity swap, equity swap, equity index swap, credit default swap, or similar agreement. (Code Sec. 1256(b)(2))[19]

¶ 2648   Election for mixed straddles—Form 6781.

If straddles are composed of at least 1 position in a Section 1256 contract (¶2647) and 1 or more positions in interests in property that aren't Section 1256 contracts, a taxpayer may elect on Form 6781 to exclude all positions in the mixed straddle (including Section 1256 contracts) from the mark-to-market rules, in which case they will be subject to the loss deferral, wash sale, and short sale rules, and the straddle won't be a mixed straddle. (Code Sec. 1256(d))[20] If that election isn't made, so that the straddle is a mixed straddle, a taxpayer may elect to offset gains and losses in the mixed straddle by either separately identifying the positions of the mixed straddle or establishing a mixed straddle account. (Reg § 1.1092(b)-4T)[21]

Unrealized gain or loss on a position held before establishing an identified mixed straddle is taken into account at the time, and has the character, provided by the Code provisions that would apply if the identified mixed straddle had not been established. (Reg § 1.1092(b)-6(a))[22]

¶ 2649   Carryback election for losses from Section 1256 contracts—Form 6781.

Taxpayers other than corporations, estates, and trusts can elect to carry net Section 1256 losses back 3 years and apply them against net Section 1256 gains for the period. The carryback is available only if, after netting Section 1256 contracts and other positions subject to the mark-to-market rule with capital gains and losses from other sources, there is a net capital loss for the tax year which, but for the election, would be a capital loss in the succeeding year. The lesser of that net capital loss or the net loss resulting from the application of the mark-to-market rules is the net Section 1256 loss which may be carried back. Capital losses carried back must be treated as 40% short-term capital losses and 60% long-term capital losses. The losses must be absorbed in the earliest year to which they may be carried back. Any remainder is then carried forward to the next year. The losses may be applied in the carryback year against the lesser of net Section 1256 contracts gain or capital gain net income for that year. (Code Sec. 1212(c))

Capital losses that are carried forward, to the extent they were determined under the mark-to-market rule, continue to be treated as losses from Section 1256 contracts in the year to which they are carried. (Code Sec. 1212(c)(6)(B))[23]

¶ 2650   Hedging transactions not covered by the mark-to-market rules.

The "mark-to-market" rules don't apply to "hedging transactions" as defined in Code Sec. 1256(e)(2). (Code Sec. 1256(e)(1))[24]

¶ 2651   Securities Futures Contracts. ▬▬▬▬▬▬▬

Gain or loss on the sale, exchange, or termination of a securities futures contract (as defined in Code Sec. 1234B(c)) generally has the same character as gain or loss from transactions in the underlying security. (Code Sec. 1234B(a)(1))

---

19. ¶I-7604; ¶12,564.01
20. ¶I-7616; ¶12,564.03
21. ¶I-7571 *et seq.*; ¶10,924

22. ¶I-7570; ¶10,924
23. ¶I-7606; ¶12,124.02
24. ¶I-7620; ¶12,564.05

For example, if the underlying asset would be a capital asset in the taxpayer's hands, gain or loss from the sale of the contract is capital gain or loss. This rule doesn't apply to (1) securities futures contracts that aren't capital assets because they are Code Sec. 1221(a)(1) inventory assets, or are identified as Code Sec. 1221(a)(7) hedging transactions, or (2) any income derived in connection with a contract which would otherwise not be capital gain. (Code Sec. 1234B(a)(2))[25]

Except as provided in regs under Code Sec. 1092(b), or Code Sec. 1234B, or in Code Sec. 1233, capital gain or loss from the sale, exchange, or termination of a securities futures contract to sell property is treated as short-term capital gain or loss. (Code Sec. 1234B(b))

If the security to which a securities futures contract that isn't a Code Sec. 1256 contract (see ¶2647) relates is acquired in satisfaction of that contract, the taxpayer's holding period for the security includes the period for which the taxpayer held the contract if the contract was a capital asset in the taxpayer's hands. (Code Sec. 1223(14))[26]

A dealer securities futures contract is treated as a Code Sec. 1256 contract. (Code Sec. 1256(b)(1)(E)) A dealer securities futures contract is any securities futures contract and any option to enter into such a contract that (1) is entered into by the dealer (or, in the case of an option, is purchased or granted by the dealer) in the normal course of his or her activity of dealing in such contracts or options, as the case may be, and (2) is traded on a qualified board or exchange. (Code Sec. 1256(g)(9)(A))[27]

¶ 2652   Conversion and Constructive Ownership Transactions.

Capital gain on the disposition of property that was part of a conversion transaction (i.e., functionally equivalent to a loan) is treated as ordinary income (¶2653). Certain gains from derivative contracts (constructive ownership transactions) with respect to financial assets are recharacterized as ordinary income (¶2654).

¶ 2653   Gain recharacterized on conversion transactions similar to loans.

Gain recognized on the disposition or other termination of any position held as part of a conversion transaction (defined below), that would otherwise be treated as capital gain, is treated as ordinary income, to the extent it doesn't exceed the applicable imputed income amount. (Code Sec. 1258(a))[28] The applicable imputed income amount equals the excess of (1) taxpayer's net investment in the transaction multiplied by 120% of (a) the applicable federal rate (¶1118), compounded semiannually, for the period covered by the transaction, if the transaction has a definite term, or of (b) the federal short-term rates (compounded daily) in effect under Code Sec. 6621(b) for the period of the conversion transaction, if the term of the transaction is indefinite, over (2) the amount already so treated with respect to the same transaction. (Code Sec. 1258(b), Code Sec. 1258(d)(2))[29]

When a taxpayer disposes or terminates all positions of an identified (as part of the same transaction on taxpayer's books and records) netting transaction within a 14-day period in 1 tax year, all gains and losses on those positions realized within that period are netted to determine the amount of gain treated as ordinary income. (Reg § 1.1258-1(b))[30]

A conversion transaction is any transaction where substantially all of taxpayer's expected net return is attributable to the time value of his or her net investment, and which is:

---

25. ¶I-6280 *et seq.*; ¶12,34B4

26. ¶I-8924.1; ¶12,234.27

27. ¶I-7615.1; ¶12,564.01

28. ¶I-8200 *et seq.*; ¶12,584

29. ¶I-8208; ¶12,584

30. ¶I-8209.1 *et seq.*; ¶12,584

. . . the holding of any property (whether or not actively traded) and substantially con-temporaneous making of a contract to sell that or substantially identical property at a price determined in accordance with the contract (Code Sec. 1258(c)(2)(A));

. . . a straddle (¶2644) of actively traded personal property (Code Sec. 1258(c)(2)(B));

. . . any other transaction that is marketed or sold as producing capital gains, and sub-stantially all of the expected return from that transaction is attributable to the time value of the taxpayer's net investment in the transaction (Code Sec. 1258(c)(2)(C)); or

. . . any other transaction specified in regs to be issued. (Code Sec. 1258(c)(2)(D))[31]

Conversion transactions don't include transactions of options dealers and commodities traders in the normal course of their trade or business. (Code Sec. 1258(d)(5)(A))[32]

¶ 2654 Certain long-term capital gains from constructive ownership transactions are recharacterized as ordinary income.

The amount of long-term capital gain a taxpayer can recognize from certain derivative contracts (constructive ownership transactions (defined in Code Sec. 1260(d))) for certain financial assets is limited, and an interest charge is imposed on the tax underpayment for each year that the constructive ownership transaction was open. (Code Sec. 1260) If a taxpayer has gain from a constructive ownership transaction with respect to any financial asset and that gain would otherwise be treated as a long-term capital gain, then (1) the gain is treated as ordinary income to the extent it exceeds the net underlying long-term capital gain, and (2) to the extent gain is treated as long-term capital gain, the determination of the capital gain rate (or rates) applicable to the gain under Code Sec. 1(h) (i.e., the individual capital gains rates) is determined on the basis of the respective rate (or rates) that would have applied to the net underlying long-term capital gain. (Code Sec. 1260(a))[33]

¶ 2655 Holding Period.

The length of time that a capital asset is held before its sale or exchange deter-mines whether the proceeds from the sale or exchange are taxable as long-term capital gain or loss or as short-term capital gain or loss.

The length of time an asset is held is also crucial in qualifying for Section 1231 (capital gain/ordinary loss) treatment, see ¶2670.

Holding a capital asset for the short-term holding period (1 year or less) results in short-term capital gain or loss on the sale or exchange of that asset. (Code Sec. 1222(1), Code Sec. 1222(2)) Holding a capital asset for the long-term holding period (more than 1 year) results in long-term capital gain or loss on the sale or exchange of that asset. (Code Sec. 1222(3), Code Sec. 1222(4))[34]

The holding period is computed in terms of calendar months, not days. [35] It begins on the day after the day of acquisition and ends on the day of sale, exchange or other disposition. Thus, the taxpayer excludes the day of acquisition but includes the date of disposition. [36]

illustration: To meet the more-than-one-year long-term holding period, a capital asset acquired on Feb. 15 must be held until Feb. 16 of the next year.

For the holding period for:

. . . a partnership interest, see ¶2656.

. . . a profits interest (carried interest) in a partnership, see ¶2657

---

31. ¶I-8205; ¶12,584
32. ¶I-8210 *et seq.*; ¶12,584
33. ¶I-8251; ¶12,604

34. ¶I-8901; ¶12,234
35. ¶I-8904; ¶12,234.01
36. ¶s I-8904, I-8906; ¶12,234.01

... stocks and securities, see ¶2658.

... property acquired through options, see ¶2659.

... property inherited from a decedent, see ¶2660.

... property acquired by a gift, see ¶2661.

... property received in a tax-free exchange, see ¶2662.

... property received to replace property lost in an involuntary conversion, see ¶2663.

¶ 2656   Holding period of partnership interest.

A partner doesn't have a divided holding period in his partnership interest unless he acquired parts of it at different times or in exchange for property transferred at the same time but resulting in different holding periods. (Reg § 1.1223-3(a)) The holding period of a part of a partnership interest is determined based on a fraction equal to the fair market value (FMV) of the part of the partnership interest received in the transaction to which the holding period relates over the FMV of the entire partnership interest (determined immediately after the transaction). (Reg § 1.1223-3(b))[37]

⊘ *Illustration:* A contributes $50,000 and a nondepreciable capital asset that he's held for 2 years to a partnership for a 50% interest in it. A's basis in the capital asset is $50,000, and its FMV is $100,000. After the exchange, A's basis in his or her interest in the partnership is $100,000, and the FMV of the interest is $150,000. A's holding period in the one-third of the interest received for cash begins on the day after the contribution. Under Code Sec. 1223(1), A has a 2-year holding period in the two-thirds of the interest received in the partnership for the capital asset.

¶ 2657   Holding period for partnership profits interest (carried interest).

Partnership interests received in connection with the performance of substantial services in a regular trade or business raising capital, or investing in or developing certain assets (known as "carry" or "carried interest"), must be held for more than 3 years to qualify for long-term capital gain rates. If an "applicable partnership interest" (API; see below) is held by the taxpayer for 3 years or less, gain will be treated as short-term gain taxed at ordinary income rates. (Code Sec. 1061)[38] This treatment applies notwithstanding Code Sec. 83 or any election in effect under Code Sec. 83(b), see ¶1216 *et seq.*

An API is any interest in a partnership that, directly or indirectly, is transferred to (or is held by) the taxpayer in connection with the performance of substantial services by the taxpayer, or any other related person, in any "applicable trade or business." An applicable trade or business is any activity conducted on a regular, continuous, and substantial basis that consists in whole or part of (i) raising or returning capital, and (ii) either (a) investing in (or disposing of) specified assets (or identifying specified assets for such investing or disposition), or (b) developing specified assets. (Code Sec. 1061(c)(2)(B)) An interest held by an individual who is employed by another entity that is conducting a trade or business (that isn't an applicable trade or business) isn't an API if the individual provides services only to that other entity. (Code Sec. 1061(c)(1)) An API also doesn't include a partnership interest held (directly or indirectly) by a corporation (other than an S corporation (Notice 2018-18)), or a capital interest based on the amount of capital contributed or the value of the interest subject to tax under Code Sec. 83 upon receipt or vesting of that interest. (Code Sec. 1061(c)(4))[39]

---

37. ¶I-8934.1; ¶12,234.29
38. ¶B-1480 *et seq.* ¶10,614

39. ¶B-1482 *et seq.* ¶10,614

Transfer of API to related person. A taxpayer who transfers an API, directly or indirectly, to a related person must include in gross income as short-term capital gain as much of the taxpayer's net long-term capital gain attributable to the sale or exchange of an asset held for not more than 3 years as is allocable to the interest. The amount included as short-term capital gain on the transfer is reduced by the amount treated as short-term capital gain on the transfer for the tax year under Code Sec. 1061(a) (that is, amounts aren't double-counted). (Code Sec. 1061(d)(1)) A person is related to the taxpayer for these purposes if the person (1) is a member of the taxpayer's family within the meaning of Code Sec. 318(a)(1) (generally spouse, children, grandchildren, and parents), or (2) performed a service within the current or preceding 3 calendar years in any applicable trade or business in or for which the taxpayer performed a service. (Code Sec. 1061(d)(2))[40]

¶ 2658   Holding period for stocks and securities.

The holding period for stocks and securities acquired by purchase, whether on a registered securities exchange or in the "over-the-counter" market, is determined by reference to the "trade date" on which the stock or security is acquired and the "trade date" on which it is sold. The "settlement dates" aren't considered.[41]

The holding period for stock or securities acquired from a corporation by the exercise of rights begins on, and includes, the day the rights are exercised. (Code Sec. 1223(5); Reg § 1.1223-1(f))[42]

The holding period for property "substantially identical" to that sold short in a transaction to which the rule at ¶2630 applies is considered to begin on the day the short sale is closed or, if earlier, on the date the property is sold, given away or otherwise disposed of. (Code Sec. 1233(b)(2))[43]

The holding period for stock, stock rights or other property received as a taxable dividend begins on the date the distribution is actually or constructively received.[44] If the distribution is tax-free, the holding period for the stock, etc., includes the period that the underlying stock was held. (Code Sec. 1223(4); Reg § 1.1223-1(e))[45]

The holding period for restricted stock (or property) begins after it is substantially vested, unless an election (¶1217) is made to include the property in income in the year of transfer, in which case it begins just after the transfer. (Code Sec. 83(f); Reg § 1.83-4(a))[46]

Where the loss on a sale of stock or securities is disallowed under the "wash sale" rules (¶2461), the holding period for the new similar stock includes the holding period for the old stock that was sold. (Code Sec. 1223(3))[47]

The holding period for U.S. Treasury bonds and notes is measured from the acquisition date; for those sold at auction, this is the date the Treasury gives notice of acceptance to bidders; for those sold in a subscription offering at a specified interest rate, it's the date the buyer submits an offer.[48]

If an individual rolls over gain from qualified small business stock (QSBS) by way of the timely acquisition of other QSBS stock (¶2428), the holding period for the acquired QSBS stock includes the holding period for the sold QSBS stock. (Code Sec. 1223(13))[49]

---

40. ¶B-1484¶10,614
41. ¶I-8914 *et seq.*; ¶12,234.07
42. ¶I-8924; ¶12,234.25
43. ¶I-7720; ¶12,334.03
44. ¶I-8918; ¶12,234.25

45. ¶I-8921; ¶3054.02
46. ¶I-8916; ¶834 *et seq.*
47. ¶I-8929; ¶12,234.25
48. ¶I-8915
49. ¶I-9207; ¶12,234.24

¶ 2659   Holding period for property acquired through options.

The holding period for property acquired through the exercise of an option begins the day after the option is exercised. [50]

¶ 2660   Holding period for property inherited from a decedent.

The holding period of property acquired from a decedent starts with the date of death. [1] However, property acquired from a decedent which is sold within the short-term capital gain holding period after the decedent's death is considered to be held for the *long*-term capital gain holding period if the person selling the property has a basis that is determined under Code Sec. 1014 (by reference to the property's fair market value on the date of death or the alternate valuation date). (Code Sec. 1223(9))[2]

The long-term holding period is also met where special use valuation property (¶5017) is acquired by a "qualified heir" from the decedent's estate, and is sold within the short-term holding period to another "qualified heir." (Code Sec. 1223(10))[3]

The holding period of the surviving spouse's share of community property that vested at the time of the acquisition by the community (as opposed to the share inherited from the deceased spouse) starts from the date of acquisition. [4]

¶ 2661   Holding period for gifts.

The holding period for property acquired by gift includes the donor's holding period if the property has the same basis for gain or loss (see ¶2462 *et seq.*) in whole or in part in the donee's hands as it would have in the donor's hands. (Code Sec. 1223(2), Reg § 1.1223-1(b)) But if the donee sells the property at a loss based on its market value on the date of the gift (and not the donor's basis), the holding period starts on the day after the date of the gift, i.e., the day after the property is acquired under the rule at ¶2655.[5]

¶ 2662   Holding period for tax-free exchange property.

The holding period for property received in a partially or wholly tax-free exchange (¶2412) includes the holding period for the property surrendered. This "tacking on" applies where the new property has the same basis, in whole or in part, as the old property (Code Sec. 1223(1)), e.g., like-kind exchanges (¶2417), tax-free stock distributions (¶2658), involuntary conversions (¶2663), or incorporations and tax-free corporate reorganizations (¶3500 *et seq.*).[6]

¶ 2663   Holding period for replacements for property lost or damaged in an involuntary conversion.

The holding period of the original property is tacked on to that of property acquired to replace property lost or damaged in an involuntary conversion (¶2430 *et seq.*), where gain isn't recognized.[7]

---

50. ¶I-8949; ¶12,234.10
1. ¶I-8944; ¶12,234.21
2. ¶I-8942; ¶12,234.21
3. ¶I-8943; ¶12,234.21

4. ¶I-8945
5. ¶I-8966; ¶12,234.22
6. ¶I-8960 *et seq.*; ¶12,234.18
7. ¶I-8963; ¶12,234.18

¶ 2664   Sales and Exchanges. ▬▬▬▬▬▬▬▬▬▬▬▬▬▬▬▬▬▬▬▬▬▬

Unless a transaction involving a capital asset is treated as a sale or exchange, any resulting gain or loss doesn't qualify as capital gain or loss.

A sale is a transfer of property for an amount of money or a money equivalent that is fixed or determinable. An exchange is a transfer of property for property other than money or a cash equivalent. (Reg § 1.1002-1(d))[8]

To qualify as a sale or exchange, the transaction must be complete, and bona fide in all respects. If it's real in substance as well as form, it qualifies as a sale or exchange even though it was designed to reduce taxes. [9] However, it may be treated as a sham for tax purposes if (a) there is no business motive for the transaction other than getting tax benefits, and (b) the transaction has no economic substance. (Code Sec. 7701(o))[10]

Where shareholders deal with their corporation, or family members sell or exchange property among themselves, IRS scrutinizes the deal closely. If a sale or exchange is a sham, IRS can disallow ac ny of the sought-after tax benefits. [11]

Retirement of debt instruments. In general, amounts received by a holder on retirement of a debt instrument are treated as received in exchange for the debt instrument. (Code Sec. 1271(a)(1))[12]

⊕*observation:* Since the retirement is treated as an exchange, see ¶2621 for the effect on gain recognized on retirement when there is an intent to call a debt instrument issued with OID before maturity.

Payment of debt with property. A debtor realizes gain or loss when he transfers property to his creditor in complete or partial satisfaction of his debt. The transfer is treated as a sale or exchange of the property by the debtor. Gain or loss is the difference between the amount of debt satisfied and the basis of the transferred property. [13]

Conversion of bonds. No gain or loss is realized upon the conversion of bonds into stock of the *same* corporation under a conversion privilege set forth in the terms of the bond. [14] However, if a bond is convertible into the stock of another corporation, the exercise of the conversion privilege results in an exchange on which gain or loss is recognized. [15]

For whether certain terminations are treated as the sale of a capital asset, see ¶2665.

For the cancellation of a lease or distribution agreement as a sale or exchange, see ¶2666.

For whether a sale with a leaseback, reservations, or restrictions is a sale or exchange, see ¶2667.

For transactions that are in part a gift and part a sale, or a conditional gift, see ¶2668.

¶ 2665   Gain or loss from certain terminations treated as capital gain or loss.

Gain or loss attributable to the cancellation, lapse, expiration, or other termination of the following is treated as gain or loss from the sale of a capital asset:

    (1) A right or obligation (other than a securities futures contract (¶2651)) with respect to property which is (or on acquisition would be) a capital asset in the taxpayer's hands (Code Sec. 1234A(1)), or

    (2) A section 1256 contract (¶2647) not described in (1) above which is a capital asset in

---

8. ¶I-1002, I-1104; ¶12,224.07
9. ¶I-1212 *et seq.*; ¶12,224.07
10. ¶M-5901; ¶77,014.35
11. ¶I-1201 *et seq.*

12. ¶I-1901; ¶12,714
13. ¶I-1501 *et seq.*; ¶10,014.76
14. ¶I-1909; ¶10,014.42
15. ¶I-1909

the taxpayer's hands. (Code Sec. 1234A(2))

These rules don't apply to the retirement of any debt instrument (whether or not through a trust or other participation arrangement). (Code Sec. 1234A)[16] Also, they don't apply to a forfeited deposit received on a canceled sale of Section 1231 property (¶2670).[17]

¶ 2666 Cancellation of lease or distribution agreement as sale or exchange.

Amounts received by a lessee or tenant for the cancellation of a lease, or by a distributor of goods for the cancellation of a distributorship agreement, are considered amounts received *in exchange* for the lease or agreement. (Code Sec. 1241)[18]

observation: Thus, capital gain-ordinary loss treatment (¶2669) is available for gain or loss from the cancellation of a business lease or distributorship held long-term. However, if the lease was for the tenant's home, a gain would be taxed as a capital gain, but any loss wouldn't be deductible.

¶ 2667 Sale with leaseback, reservations or restrictions.

The fact that a sale of property is accompanied by a leaseback doesn't bar recognizing the sale as closed for tax purposes. [19] However, a leaseback of realty (including renewal options) extending for 30 years or more may be considered an exchange of like-kind property (¶2418) on which gain or loss isn't recognized. [20] A sale restricting the buyer's use of the property may be recognized as a completed sale, as where stock is sold subject to security-device restrictions, [21] but if the rights retained are significant enough, the seller may be considered as selling only a partial interest or as granting a license to use. [22]

¶ 2668 Part gift, part sale; conditional gifts.

If an owner combines a gift with a sale (e.g., to a family member), gain is realized to the extent the price received exceeds the owner's adjusted basis. However, no loss is recognized if the amount received is less than the owner's basis. (Reg § 1.1001-1(e))[23]

If a donor gives appreciated property to a donee on condition the donee pay the donor's gift tax, there's a sale by the donor for the amount of the gift tax. To the extent the gift tax paid by the donee exceeds the donor's basis, the donor has income. [24]

¶ 2669 Capital Gain—Ordinary Loss Rule—Form 4797. ▬▬▬▬

Under Code Sec. 1231, if there's a net gain for the tax year from (1) sales and exchanges of property used in a trade or business (Section 1231 assets as defined at ¶2584), and (2) involuntary or compulsory conversions of certain assets used in the trade or business or held in connection with a trade or business or a transaction entered for profit, it's treated as long-term capital gain, except as discussed below. A net loss is treated as an ordinary loss. (Code Sec. 1231(a); Reg § 1.1231-1(b))[25] Section 1231 gains and losses are reported and netted on Form 4797.

A net Section 1231 gain is treated as ordinary income to the extent of nonrecaptured net Section 1231 losses. (Code Sec. 1231(c)(1))

A nonrecaptured net Section 1231 loss is the net Section 1231 loss for the 5 most recent preceding tax years that hasn't been offset by a net Section 1231 gain in an intervening

16. ¶I-6275 *et seq.*; ¶12,34A4
17. ¶I-6276
18. ¶I-1400 *et seq.*; ¶12,414
19. ¶I-1122
20. ¶I-3077

21. ¶I-1125
22. ¶I-1602 *et seq.*
23. ¶I-1006; ¶10,014.06
24. ¶I-1007
25. ¶I-9001; ¶12,314

tax year. (Code Sec. 1231(c)(2)) Net Section 1231 gain is the excess of the Section 1231 gains over the Section 1231 losses. Net Section 1231 loss is the excess of the Section 1231 losses over the Section 1231 gains. (Code Sec. 1231(c)(3), Code Sec. 1231(c)(4))[26]

illustration: X Corp., a calendar year taxpayer, had a net Section 1231 loss of $1 million in 2014 that was offset against ordinary income. X Corp. had no net Section 1231 gain in 2015, 2016, or 2017, but has a net Section 1231 gain in 2018 of $1.4 million (consisting of a $2 million gain on condemnation of land, and a $600,000 loss on the sale of machinery). $1 million of the net Section 1231 gain for 2018 is treated as ordinary income, and the remaining $400,000 is treated as long-term capital gain.

If the recognized losses from involuntary conversions arising from fire, storm, shipwreck or other casualty, or from theft, exceed the recognized gain, they aren't included in the Section 1231 computations. (Code Sec. 1231(a)(4)(C), Code Sec. 1231(c)(5))[27]

observation: This means that losses from such involuntary conversions will be treated as ordinary losses, but won't reduce the amount of net Section 1231 gains realized from other transactions eligible for capital gain treatment. However, if there is a net gain from such involuntary conversions, that net gain will be eligible for Section 1231 treatment. Capital gain treatment under Section 1231 is also barred to the extent that the depreciation recapture rules apply, see ¶2675 *et seq.*

For the applicability of Section 1231 treatment to timber cutting, see ¶2671; to timber, coal or U.S. iron ore sold with a retained economic interest, see ¶2672; and to advance payments for timber, coal or domestic iron ore, see ¶2673.

¶ 2670   Section 1231 assets defined.

Section 1231 assets are certain assets used in taxpayer's trade or business that were held for more than 1 year at the time of disposition. Except as explained below, these assets include depreciable tangible and intangible personal property, and real property, whether or not depreciable. They include timber, certain livestock (other than poultry), and unharvested crops that are transferred with land. (Code Sec. 1231(b))

They don't include: (1) inventory, (2) property held primarily for sale to customers in the ordinary course of the taxpayer's business, (3) patents, inventions, models or designs (whether or not patented), secret formulas or processes, copyrights, artistic, literary, or musical compositions (unless, for musical compositions or copyrights in them, the election discussed at ¶2615 is made), letters or memoranda, or similar property, in the hands of the creator or other taxpayer described in Code Sec. 1221(a)(3), and (4) U.S. government publications obtained without charge or below the price sold to the general public. (Code Sec. 1231(b)(1); Reg § 1.1231-1(c))[28]

Property held for rent usually is treated as property used in business, but IRS (with the support of some, but not all, courts) denies this status where rental activity is slight. [29]

¶ 2671   Timber cutting treated as sale or exchange—Form T.

A taxpayer who owned timber, or had a contract right to cut it, for more than 1 year before it was cut, may elect to treat the cutting as a sale or exchange qualifying for Section 1231 capital gain-ordinary loss treatment. Taxpayers who elect must file Form T with their returns unless they only have an occasional sale of timber. Once made, the election can be revoked only with IRS's consent unless it was made for a tax year ending before Oct. 23, 2004, in which case it can be revoked for any later tax year without IRS's consent.

---

26. ¶I-9003; ¶12,314.15
27. ¶I-9004; ¶s 12,314.09, 12,314.15

28. ¶I-9007 *et seq.*; ¶12,314 *et seq.*
29. ¶I-9013; ¶12,314.02 *et seq.*

(Code Sec. 631(a); Code Sec. 1231(b)(2); ; Reg § 1.631-1)[30]

¶ 2672   Timber, coal or U.S. iron ore sold with a retained economic interest.

A disposition of timber, coal or U.S. iron ore held more than 1 year qualifies for Section 1231 treatment if disposed of under a contract in which the taxpayer retains an economic interest. (Code Sec. 631(b), Code Sec. 631(c), Code Sec. 1231(b)(2); Reg § 1.631-2(a)(1), Reg § 1.631-3(a)(1))[31] For timber sales, Section 1231 treatment can apply if the owner makes an outright sale of the timber even if no economic interest is retained. (Code Sec. 631(b))[32]

When the disposition qualifies for Section 1231 treatment, no cost depletion deduction (¶1970) is allowed. (Reg § 1.611-1(b)(2)) And, for dispositions of coal and iron ore, no percentage depletion deduction is allowed if the maximum tax rate for the year on net capital gain is less than the maximum rate for ordinary income. (Code Sec. 631(c))[33]

¶ 2673   Advance payments for timber, coal or domestic iron ore.

Advance or minimum royalty payments or other amounts received or accrued before cutting of timber or before the mining of coal or iron ore (disposed of with a retained economic interest) are treated as realized from a sale subject to Section 1231 if the contract of disposal provides that they are to be applied as payment for timber cut later or coal or iron ore mined later. (Reg § 1.631-2(d)(1), Reg § 1.631-3(c)(1)) But if the right to cut or to mine ends or is abandoned before the timber, coal or iron ore is cut or mined, those advance payments are ordinary income. (Reg § 1.631-2(d)(2), Reg § 1.631-3(c)(2))

If the taxpayer elects to treat the date of payment as the date of disposal of timber (Code Sec. 631(b); Reg § 1.631-2(b)(1)), Section 1001 applies only if the timber is held for the required period at the time of the advance payment. (Reg § 1.631-2(c)(2)) If the election isn't made, the required holding period is measured as of the time it's cut. (Reg § 1.631-2(d)(1))[34] This election is made by attaching a specified statement to the return (filed not later than the due date, including extensions) for the year payment is received. (Reg § 1.631-2(c))[35]

¶ 2674   Sale of Depreciable Property to Related Parties—Capital Gain Bar. ████

In a direct or indirect sale or exchange of property between related persons, any gain recognized is treated as ordinary income if that property is, in the transferee's hands, subject to the Code Sec. 167 allowance for depreciation, or is an amortizable Code Sec. 197 intangible asset. (Code Sec. 197(f)(7), Code Sec. 1239(a))

This rule also applies to property that would be subject to depreciation except that the buyer has elected amortization instead of depreciation (Reg § 1.1239-1(a)), and to patent applications. (Code Sec. 1239(e))[36]

Related persons are:

(1) a person and all entities that are controlled entities with respect to that person (see below) (Code Sec. 1239(b)(1));

(2) a taxpayer and any trust in which the taxpayer or the taxpayer's spouse is a beneficiary (unless the interest is a remote contingent interest) (Code Sec. 1239(b)(2));

(3) an executor of an estate and a beneficiary of the estate (except in the case of a sale or exchange in satisfaction of a pecuniary bequest) (Code Sec. 1239(b)(3));

---

30. ¶N-6201 *et seq.*; ¶6314 *et seq.*
31. ¶N-7001 *et seq.*; ¶6314
32. ¶N-7001; ¶6314
33. ¶N-7021

34. ¶N-7025 *et seq.*; ¶6314 *et seq.*
35. ¶N-7026
36. ¶I-8702; ¶12,394

(4) an employer and any person related to the employer (within the meaning of (1) through (3) above) (Code Sec. 1239(d)(1)); and

(5) a welfare benefit fund controlled directly or indirectly by anyone in (4), above (Code Sec. 1239(d)(2)).[37]

A controlled entity ((l), above) means, with respect to any person:

. . . a corporation more than 50% of the value of the stock of which is owned (directly or indirectly) by or for the person (Code Sec. 1239(c)(1)(A)),

. . . a partnership more than 50% of the capital interest or profits interest in which is owned (directly or indirectly) by or for the person (Code Sec. 1239(c)(1)(B)), or

. . . any entity that is a related person to the person under Code Sec. 267(b)(3) (controlled group of corporations), Code Sec. 267(b)(10) (certain related corporations and partnerships), Code Sec. 267(b)(11) (S corporations controlled by the same person), or Code Sec. 267(b)(12) (S corporations and C corporations controlled by the same person). (Code Sec. 1239(c)(1)(C))

And, under Code Sec. 267(c), there is attribution for stock owned by children, grandchildren, ancestors and siblings, as well as by the spouse. (Code Sec. 1239(c)(2))[38]

¶ 2675   Depreciation Recapture.

Two provisions restrict the possibility of converting ordinary income into capital gains by use of depreciation or amortization deductions.

One applies to personal property that is Section 1245 property (¶2676); the other to real property that is Section 1250 property (¶2678). (Code Sec. 1245(a)(3), Code Sec. 1250(c)) Recapture applies only to the extent of gain on a sale or other "disposition" (¶2682) of property. (Code Sec. 1245(a)(1), Code Sec. 1250(a)) Compute recapture on Form 4797.

For the treatment of basis reduction for the investment credit, see ¶2681.

For transactions and event that trigger or escape depreciation recapture, see ¶2682.

For recapture rules for listed property, see ¶2683.

¶ 2676   What is Section 1245 property?

Section 1245 property includes:

(1) all MACRS property other than residential real property (27.5-year class) and nonresidential real property (39-year class; 31.5-year class if placed in service before May 13, '93);

(2) all ACRS property other than 19-year, 18-year or 15-year real property: (a) that is residential rental property, (b) that is foreign-held realty, (c) with respect to which an optional (straight-line) cost recovery period was elected, or (d) that includes any 1 of certain categories of subsidized low-income rental housing;

(3) other property subject to the depreciation rules of Code Sec. 167 or the amortization rules of Code Sec. 197 (¶1967) that's personal property, certain real property (not including buildings) to the extent of certain amortization (or Code Sec. 179) deductions taken.[39]

Section 1245 property includes property, other than a building or its structural components, used as an integral part of manufacturing, production or extraction, or for furnishing transportation, communication or other public utility services, and research or storage facilities used in connection with any of these activities. It also includes single purpose

37. ¶I-8703 *et seq.*; ¶12,394
38. ¶I-8708; ¶12,394

39. ¶I-10101 *et seq.*; ¶12,454.01

agricultural or horticultural structures, and storage facilities (except buildings and their structural components) used in distributing petroleum or any primary product of petroleum. (Code Sec. 1245(a)(3); Reg § 1.1245-3))[40]

For recapture rules for Section 1245 property, see ¶2677.

¶ 2677   Recapture rules for Section 1245 property.

A gain on the disposition (¶2682) of Section 1245 property (¶2676) is treated as ordinary income to the extent of depreciation or amortization allowed or allowable on the property. (Code Sec. 1245(a))[41] The following deductions are treated as amortization for purposes of the Section 1245 recapture rules: the expense deduction under Code Sec. 179 (¶1940 *et seq.*); the deductions for certain refining costs under Code Sec. 179B and Code Sec. 179C (for property placed in service before 2010 (or before 2014 if constructed under a written binding contract entered into before 2010); the deduction for the cost of energy efficient commercial buildings under Code Sec. 179D (¶1962); the deduction for 50% of the cost of qualified advanced mine safety equipment property under Code Sec. 179E (¶1960); the deduction for the costs incurred of qualified film and TV productions under Code Sec. 181 (¶1961); qualified architectural and transportation barrier removal expenses under Code Sec. 190 (¶1606); and reforestation expenses under Code Sec. 194 (¶1964). (Code Sec. 1245(a)(2)(C))[42]

The environmental remediation expensing deduction (Code Sec. 198(e)),[43] and the amortization of a Section 197 intangible (¶1967) (Code Sec. 197(f)(7)) also are subject to recapture under Code Sec. 1245.[44]

The amount of gain treated as ordinary income on the disposition is limited to the lower of:

(1) the recomputed basis of the property minus the adjusted basis of the property. (Code Sec. 1245(a)(1)(A)) Recomputed basis is the adjusted basis of the property increased by the recapturable depreciation and amortization deductions reflected in the adjusted basis (Code Sec. 1245(a)(2)); or

(2) in the case of a sale, exchange or involuntary conversion, the amount realized minus the adjusted basis of the property; or in the case of any other disposition, the fair market value of the property minus the adjusted basis of the property. (Code Sec. 1245(a)(1)(B))[45]

If a taxpayer disposes of more than 1 amortizable Code Sec. 197 intangible (¶1967) in a transaction or a series of related transactions, all of the amortizable intangibles are treated as 1 Code Sec. 1245 property for purposes of the recapture rules. However, this rule doesn't apply to an intangible if its adjusted basis exceeds its fair market value. (Code Sec. 1245(b)(8))[46]

A taxpayer who disposes of qualified real property (¶1943) for which a Code Sec. 179 election has been made (¶1940 *et seq.*) may use any reasonable allocation method to determine the part of the gain that is attributable to Code Sec. 1245 property, i.e., to the part of the unadjusted basis of the property that was reduced by the Code Sec. 179 expense deduction. The remaining unadjusted basis of the property is allocated to Code Sec. 1250 property, see ¶2679.[47]

---

40. ¶I-10101; ¶12,454.01
41. ¶I-10200 *et seq.*; ¶12,454
42. ¶I-10204; ¶12,454.05
43. ¶L-6160.4; ¶1984

44. ¶L-7981.2; ¶1974
45. ¶I-10200 *et seq.*; ¶12,454.05
46. ¶I-10219.1; ¶12,454.05
47. ¶I-10220.1 *et seq.*; ¶12,454.05

¶ 2678   What is Section 1250 property?

All real property subject to depreciation that isn't Section 1245 property is Section 1250 property. (Code Sec. 1250(c)) Thus, Section 1250 property includes:

(1) MACRS residential real property (in the 27.5-year class) and nonresidential real property (in the 39-year class; 31.5-year class if placed in service before May 13, '93).

(2) The types of ACRS real property that aren't Section 1245 property, see ¶2676.

(3) The following real property placed in service before '81: (a) depreciable intangible real property; (b) all depreciable buildings and their structural components; and (c) other depreciable real property excluded from the definition of Section 1245 property (¶2676). (Reg § 1.1250-1(e)(3))[48]

For recapture rules for Section 1250 property, see ¶2679.

For 20% additional depreciation on dispositions of realty by corporations, see ¶2680.

¶ 2679   Recapture rules for Section 1250 property.

Gain on the disposition of Section 1250 property is treated as ordinary income to the extent of the lower of (1) the "applicable percentage" of the additional depreciation allowed or allowable on the property, or (2) in the case of a sale, exchange or involuntary conversion, the excess of the amount realized over the adjusted basis, or in the case of any other disposition, the fair market value of the property over its adjusted basis. For Section 1250 property held longer than 1 year, the additional depreciation is the excess of the actual depreciation taken over the depreciation figured using the straight line method. If held less than a year, it's all the depreciation taken. (Code Sec. 1250(a); Code Sec. 1250(b))[49] Thus, Section 1250 recapture doesn't apply to residential rental or nonresidential real property depreciated under MACRS since such property is depreciated using the straight line method, see ¶1920. Section 1250 recapture does apply to the pre-2010 commercial revitalization deduction. (Former Code Sec. 1400I(f)(2)) [50]

The applicable percentage is generally 100% for depreciation attributable to periods after '75, but is lower on the disposition of low income housing and other special rental housing property.[1]

For the allocation between Code Sec. 1245 and Code Sec. 1250 of recapture income on the sale of qualified real property (¶1943) for which the Code Sec. 179 election (¶1940 *et seq.*) was made, see ¶2677.

For treatment of a noncorporate taxpayer's unrecaptured section 1250 gain, see ¶2604.

¶ 2680   Additional 20% recapture on disposition of realty by corporations.

For sales or other dispositions (of both residential and nonresidential property), 20% of the amount by which the gain recapturable if Section 1245 rules applied exceeds the gain recaptured under Section 1250 is treated as ordinary income (to the extent of gain) to a corporation. (Code Sec. 291(a))[2] This rule applies to an S corporation only if it was formerly a C corporation for any of the 3 immediately preceding tax years. (Code Sec. 1363(b)(4))[3]

---

48. ¶I-10112 *et seq.*; ¶12,504.01
49. ¶I-10400 *et seq.*; ¶12,504 *et seq.*
50. ¶L-12709; ¶14,00I4

1. ¶I-10417 *et seq.*; ¶12,504.06
2. ¶I-10422 *et seq.*; ¶2914
3. ¶I-10422; ¶13634.01

¶ 2681 Treatment of basis reduction for investment credit.

In determining the recapturable amount, the reduction of basis for the investment credit is treated as a deduction allowed for depreciation. (Code Sec. 50(c)(4)(A))[4] However, this basis reduction is disregarded in computing straight-line depreciation for purposes of determining "additional depreciation" subject to recapture for Section 1250 property. (Code Sec. 50(c)(4)(B))[5]

¶ 2682 Transactions and events that trigger or escape depreciation recapture.

The following is a list of transactions and events that either trigger or escape depreciation recapture:[6]

* A sale in a sale and leaseback transaction, a sale under a conditional sales contract, and a transfer of title back to the seller, creditor, or new purchaser upon foreclosure of a security interest trigger recapture. But, a transfer of legal title to a creditor upon creation of a security interest, or to a debtor upon termination of a security interest, escapes recapture. (Reg § 1.1245-1(a)(3), Reg § 1.1250-1(a)(2)(i))

* For like-kind exchanges and involuntary conversions, Section 1245 depreciation isn't recaptured unless gain is recognized or non-Section 1245 property is acquired (Code Sec. 1245(b)(4); Reg § 1.1245-4(d)); and Section 1250 depreciation isn't recaptured except where gain is recognized, stock is bought to acquire control of a corporation owning replacement property, or non-Section 1250 property is acquired. (Code Sec. 1250(d)(4); Reg § 1.1250-3(d))

* Conversion to personal use (except for Code Sec. 179 property, see ¶1944) doesn't trigger recapture, but a later sale will. (¶1927)

* Termination or disposition of a lease where depreciation was taken by the lessee (or sublessee) generally triggers recapture. (Reg § 1.1245-2(a)(3)(i))

* Incorporation of a business triggers recapture only if gain is otherwise recognized. (Code Sec. 1245(b)(3), Code Sec. 1250(d)(3); Reg § 1.1245-4(c), Reg § 1.1250-3(c))

* Corporate distributions in kind (including liquidating distributions) generally trigger recapture, except in a tax-free complete liquidation of a subsidiary with carryover basis, where recapture is triggered upon disposition by the parent-transferee. (Code Sec. 1245(b)(3), Code Sec. 1250(d)(3); Reg § 1.1245-4(c), Reg § 1.1250-3(c))

* Corporate split-ups and reorganizations generally don't trigger recapture, except to the extent that gain is otherwise recognized on transfer of the property. (Code Sec. 1245(b)(3), Code Sec. 1250(d)(3); Reg § 1.1245-4(c), Reg § 1.1250-3(c))

* S corporation elections or termination of S status don't trigger recapture.

* Sale of a partnership interest triggers recapture. Contributions to a partnership generally don't trigger recapture, but may if property is subject to a liability. (Code Sec. 1245(a), Code Sec. 1245(b)(3), Code Sec. 1250(a), Code Sec. 1250(d)(3); Reg § 1.1245-4(c), Reg § 1.1250-3(c))

* Gifts generally don't trigger recapture, but recapturable depreciation carries over to donee. (Code Sec. 1245(b)(1), Code Sec. 1250(d)(1); Reg § 1.1245-4(a), Reg § 1.1250-3(a))

* For transfers by reason of death, recapturable depreciation is neither triggered nor carried over. (Code Sec. 1245(b)(2), Code Sec. 1250(d)(2); Reg § 1.1245-4(b), Reg § 1.1250-3(b))[7]

* When a trust or estate realizes gain from the distribution of depreciable property in

---

4. ¶I-10204
5. ¶I-10507

6. ¶10501 *et seq.*
7. ¶I-10002, I-10301 *et seq.*; ¶12,454 *et seq.*, ¶12,504.01

satisfaction of a fixed-dollar bequest, or from a distribution property in satisfaction of a bequest of other property, recapture is triggered. (Reg § 1.1245-4(b), Reg § 1.1250-3(b))[8]

For the effect of depreciation recapture on installment sales, see ¶2453.

¶ 2683   Special recapture rules for listed property.

A reduction of business use of listed property (¶1945 *et seq.*) from more-than-50% to 50% or less triggers recapture of excess depreciation previously taken. (Code Sec. 280F(b)(2)(A)) "Excess depreciation" means depreciation allowable for years before the first year in which the property wasn't predominantly used in a qualified business use, over the amount of depreciation which would have been allowable for those years if the property hadn't been predominantly used in a qualified business (¶1947 *et seq.*) for the year it was acquired and if there had been no Section 179 expense election for the property. (Code Sec. 280F(b)(2)(B))[9]

---

8. ¶C-7154; ¶s 12,454.03, 12,504.01   9. ¶L-10032; ¶280F4

Chapter 11   Tax Accounting—Inventories

¶ 2800   **Accounting Periods.** ▰▰▰▰▰▰▰▰▰▰▰▰▰

Each taxpayer must compute taxable income and file a return on the basis of an accounting period called a tax year (¶2801). An S corporation generally must use a calendar year as its tax year unless it elects (¶2813) to use a fiscal year (¶2810), as does a personal service corporation (¶2811). A partnership generally must use a "majority interest tax year" (¶2812) unless it makes the fiscal year election.

¶ 2801   **Tax year.**

Taxpayers must compute their taxable income on the basis of their tax year. (Code Sec. 441(a); Reg § 1.441-1(a)) "Tax year" is the taxpayer's annual accounting period (on the basis of which the taxpayer regularly computes his income in keeping his books) (Code Sec. 441(c)), but only if that's the calendar year or a fiscal year. (Code Sec. 441(b)(1))[1]

The calendar year is the 12-month period ending on Dec. 31. (Code Sec. 441(d)) In general, a taxpayer must use the calendar year if it keeps no books, has no annual accounting period, has an accounting period that doesn't qualify as a fiscal year (Code Sec. 441(b)(2), Code Sec. 441(g)), or hasn't established a fiscal year. (Reg § 1.441-1(b)(1)(iv))[2]

A fiscal year is any 12-month period ending on the last day of a month other than December, or the 52-53 week tax year described at ¶2802. (Code Sec. 441(e))[3] If a return is properly made for a period of less than 12 months (see ¶2804), the tax year is the short tax year for which the return is made. (Code Sec. 441(b)(3))[4]

Certain taxpayers must use a required tax year. (Code Sec. 441(f)(3), Code Sec. 441(f)(4); Reg § 1.441-1(b)(2))

¶ 2802   **Tax year of 52-53 weeks.**

This tax year varies from 52 to 53 weeks and always ends on the same day of the week. That day must be either the day of the week that last occurs in a calendar month or the day that falls nearest to the end of the calendar month (in which case the last day of the tax year may fall in the next month). (Code Sec. 441(f)(1); Reg § 1.441-2(a)(1)) A taxpayer may elect a 52-53 week tax year if it otherwise satisfies Code Sec. 441 and its regs. (Reg § 1.441-2(a)(3))[5]

Wherever the applicability of any provision of the Code, or filing date, is expressed in terms of tax years beginning, including, or ending with reference to a specified date that's the first or last day of the month, the actual opening and closing dates of 52-53 week years are disregarded. The year is considered to begin on the first day of the calendar month beginning nearest to the first day of that tax year, and to end on the last day of the calendar month ending nearest to the last day of that tax year. (Code Sec. 441(f)(2)(A))[6]

If a pass-through entity or its owner, or both, use a 52-53-week tax year and the tax years of both end with reference to the same calendar month, then, for purposes of determining the tax year in which pass-through items are taken into account by its owner, the owner's tax year is deemed to end on the last day of the pass-through's tax year. (Reg § 1.441-2(e)(1)) Similarly, if the tax year of a personal service corporation (PSC) and an employee-owner end with reference to the same calendar month, then for purposes of

---

1. ¶G-1000 *et seq.*; ¶4414
2. ¶s G-1001, G-1003; ¶4414
3. ¶G-1004; ¶4414

4. ¶s G-1001; ¶4414
5. ¶G-1101; ¶4414
6. ¶G-1103; ¶4414

References beginning with a single letter are to paragraphs in Federal Tax Coordinator 2d and RIA's Analysis of Federal Taxes: Income. Those beginning with numbers are to paragraphs in United States Tax Reporter.

determining the tax year in which an employee-owner takes into account items that are deductible by the PSC and includible in the owner's income, the employee-owner's tax year is deemed to end on the last day of the PSC's tax year. (Reg § 1.441-2(e)(2))

¶ 2803 Establishing a tax year.

A new taxpayer generally may adopt any tax year that satisfies Code Sec. 441 and its regs by simply filing its first federal income tax return using that tax year. (Reg § 1.441-1(c)(1)) However, a newly formed partnership, S corporation, or personal service corporation that wants to adopt a tax year other than its required tax year, a tax year elected under Code Sec. 444 (¶2813), or a 52-53 week tax year (¶2802) that ends with reference to its required tax year or one elected under Code Sec. 444 must establish a business purpose and get IRS approval. (Reg § 1.441-1(c)(2)) Use Form 1128 following IRS procedures. [7]

If taxpayer's "annual accounting period" (¶2801), as established by the basis on which taxpayer keeps his books, is the calendar year or a fiscal year, his tax year is that annual accounting period. (Code Sec. 441(b)(1), Code Sec. 441(c)) Otherwise, the taxpayer must use the calendar year as his tax year. (Code Sec. 441(b)(2), Code Sec. 441(g)) [8]

A new taxpayer using a 52-53 week tax year (¶2802) must file a statement (specified in the regs) with the return for its first 52-53 week tax year. (Reg § 1.441-2(b)(1)(ii)) [9]

¶ 2804 Short tax years.

A taxpayer must use a tax "year" of less than 12 months if the taxpayer: (1) isn't in existence for what would otherwise be his full tax year (Code Sec. 443(a)(2)); [10] or (2) properly changes his annual accounting period (¶2814). (Code Sec. 443(a)(1)) [11] But if the short year arises because of the taxpayer's death, his last return may be filed and the tax paid as if he had lived to the end of his last tax year. (Reg § 1.443-1(a)(2)) [12] For filing requirements for short years, see ¶ 4716 and ¶ 4724.

¶ 2805 Computing tax for a short year.

If the short year results from a change of the taxpayer's annual accounting period, the short period's taxable income must be annualized. (Code Sec. 443(b)) Under the general method of annualization, gross income for the short period (less allowable deductions for it) is multiplied by 12 (months) and divided by the number of months in the short period. The result is the annualized taxable income on which tentative tax is computed. The tax due is arrived at by multiplying the tentative tax by the number of months in the short period and dividing by 12. (Code Sec. 443(b)(1); Reg § 1.443-1(b)(1)(i)) [13] Special annualization rules apply to the alternative minimum tax (AMT). (Code Sec. 443(d)) [14]

There are exceptions to the annualization requirements for self-employment tax, accumulated earnings tax, personal holding company tax, undistributed foreign personal holding company income, and income of regulated investment companies. [15]

The net operating loss (NOL) deduction can reduce actual income for the short period before computing short period income on an annual basis. Therefore, if the NOL deduction wipes out short period actual income, there would be nothing to annualize and therefore no short period taxable income. [16]

The income is *not* annualized if the short year is caused by the taxpayer not being in

7. ¶4414
8. ¶G-1051; ¶4414
9. ¶s G-1054, G-1753; ¶4414
10. ¶G-1153; ¶4434
11. ¶G-1155; ¶4434

12. ¶G-1154; ¶4434
13. ¶G-1166; ¶4434
14. ¶A-8119; ¶4434
15. ¶G-1163; ¶4434
16. ¶G-1166; ¶4434

existence for a full tax year. (Code Sec. 443(b)) In this case, tax is computed as if the short period were a full year. (Reg § 1.443-1(a)(2))[17]

If a taxpayer changes to or from a 52-53 week year, income for the short period must be annualized, with this exception: If the short period is 359 days or more, it is treated as a full tax year; while if it is six days or less, it is added to the following tax year. (Reg § 1.443-1(b)(1)(ii))[18]

¶ 2806   Optional look-back method of computing tax for the short period.

The annualizing method at ¶2805 may create a tax hardship for taxpayers who have a disproportionately large amount of taxable income in the short period. To avoid this, taxpayers may use an optional method that computes the tax for the full 12 months starting at the beginning of the short year and prorates the tax according to the amount of income earned in the short period. (Code Sec. 443(b)(2)) This method is available only on a claim for credit or refund, filed no later than the due date (including extensions) of taxpayer's return for the first tax year that ends on or after the day that is 12 months after the first day of the short period. (Reg § 1.443-1(b)(2)(v)(a))[19]

¶ 2807   Tax year of sole proprietorship.

A sole proprietorship must use the same tax year as the proprietor. Thus, a calendar year employee who later operates as a sole proprietorship must use the calendar year for the proprietorship unless he gets IRS consent to use a fiscal year. [20]

¶ 2808   Tax years of trusts and estates.

Trusts must use the calendar year, except for trusts exempt from tax under Code Sec. 501(a), wholly charitable trusts described in Code Sec. 4947(a)(1) (Code Sec. 644),[21] and grantor trusts.[22] Estates may adopt either a calendar year or a fiscal year. [23]

¶ 2809   Tax years of Domestic International Sales Corporations (DISCs).

DISCs must use the tax year of the shareholder (or group of shareholders with the same 12-month tax year) with the highest percentage of voting power. (Code Sec. 441(h)(1))[24]

¶ 2810   Tax year of S corporation.

An S corporation (¶3350 *et seq.*), unless it makes the election at ¶2813, or elects a 52-53 week tax year (¶2802) ending with reference to its required year, must have a "required year," i.e., a calendar year or any other accounting year for which it shows a business purpose satisfactory to IRS; use Form 2553. (Code Sec. 1378; Reg § 1.441-1(b)(2)(i)(L), Reg § 1.441-1(b)(2)(ii)(B), Reg § 1.1378-1(a))[25]

¶ 2811   Tax year of personal service corporation (PSC).

The tax year of a PSC (¶3330) must be a calendar year unless it makes the election at ¶2813, elects a 52-53 week tax year ending with reference to the calendar year or the year elected under the rules at ¶2813, or can satisfy IRS that there's a business purpose for a different tax year. (Code Sec. 441(i)(1); Reg § 1.441-1(b)(2)(i)(B), Reg § 1.441-3(a))[26]

---

17. ¶G-1162; ¶4434
18. ¶G-1108; ¶4434
19. ¶G-1170 *et seq.*; ¶4434
20. ¶G-1062; ¶4414
21. ¶G-1400; ¶6454

22. ¶G-1401; ¶6454
23. ¶C-7008; ¶4414
24. ¶O-2041; ¶4414
25. ¶G-1250; ¶13,784
26. ¶G-1300; ¶4414

A PSC is, as defined under the rules permitting IRS to reallocate PSC income and deductions (¶2854), any corporation whose principal activity is the performance of personal services that are substantially performed by employee-owners. But for this purpose, PSC doesn't include S corporations, and the term "owner-employee" includes all employees with *any* stock ownership in the corporation. In determining ownership, attribution from a corporation (under Code Sec. 318(a)(2)(C)) is applied if *any* stock is owned by the shareholder in that corporation. (Code Sec. 441(i)(2))[27] Certain independent contractors who own stock in the corporation and perform personal services for or on behalf of it are treated as employees. (Reg § 1.441-3(g)(2))[28]

The performance of personal services is considered the corporation's principal activity if the corporation's compensation cost for a testing period for activities that are considered the performance of personal services exceeds 50% of its total compensation cost for the period. (Reg § 1.441-3(e)(1)) The testing period is the preceding tax year (or, for a corporation's first tax year, the period beginning the first day of the first tax year and ending the last day of that tax year or, if earlier, the last day of the calendar year in which that tax year began). (Reg § 1.441-3(c)(2)) Personal services are substantially performed by employee-owners if, during the testing period, more than 20% of the corporation's compensation cost (excluding qualified plan or SEP contributions) attributable to the performance of personal services is attributable to personal services performed by employee-owners. (Reg § 1.441-3(f), Reg § 1.441-3(e)(2)(ii))[29]

¶ 2812   Tax year of partnership—"majority interest tax year."

Unless a partnership makes the election at ¶2813, or can satisfy IRS that there's a business purpose for a different tax year (Code Sec. 706(b)(1)(C)),[30] it must adopt:

(1) the "majority interest tax year" (Code Sec. 706(b)(1)(B)(i))—the tax year of one or more of the partners having an aggregate interest in partnership profits and capital of more than 50% on each testing day (the first day of the partnership's tax year as otherwise determined, or days prescribed by IRS) (Code Sec. 706(b)(4)(A));

(2) the tax year of all its principal (5%-or-more) partners, if there's no majority interest tax year (Code Sec. 706(b)(1)(B)(ii)); or

(3) the "least-aggregate-deferral" year, if there's no majority interest tax year and the principal partners don't have the same tax year. (Code Sec. 706(b)(1)(B)(iii); Reg § 1.706-1(b)(2)(i)(C))[31]

A partnership may have a tax year other than its required year if it makes an election under Code Sec. 444 (¶2813), elects to use a 52-53-week tax year (¶2802) that ends with reference to its required year or a tax year elected under Code Sec. 444, or establishes a business purpose for it and gets IRS approval. (Reg § 1.706-1(b)(2)(ii))

A partnership that's required to change to a majority-interest tax year isn't required to change to another tax year for either of the two tax years following the year of change. (Code Sec. 706(b)(4)(B))[32]

A partnership tax year ends as dictated by its accounting period, except that it closes earlier: (1) for a partner who sells his entire interest or whose interest is completely liquidated (Code Sec. 706(c); (Reg § 1.706-1(c)(2)(i)), and (2) for all its partners on the date the partnership terminates for tax purposes. (Reg § 1.706-1(c)(1))[33]

27. ¶G-1302; ¶4414
28. ¶G-1306; ¶4414
29. ¶G-1303; ¶4414
30. ¶G-1200 *et seq.*; ¶7064.01

31. ¶G-1200 *et seq.*; ¶7064.01
32. ¶G-1201; ¶7064.01
33. ¶G-1224, G-1225; ¶7064.02

¶ 2813   Section 444 election of tax year other than required tax year—Form 8716; Form 8752; Form 1120, Schedule H.

An S corporation, personal service corporation (PSC), or partnership may elect (on Form 8716) to have a tax year other than the required tax year (Code Sec. 444(a)), but only if the deferral period (i.e., the number of months between the beginning of elected fiscal tax year and the following Dec. 31) for the tax year elected isn't longer than three months. (Code Sec. 444(b)(1); Reg § 1.444-1T(b))[34]

A partnership or S corporation that elects has to make a "required payment" (report on Form 8752) that approximates the tax that the partners or S corporation shareholders would have paid on short-period income if the election hadn't been made. (Code Sec. 7519; Reg § 1.444-3T)[35]

A PSC that elects a fiscal tax year but doesn't make required minimum distributions to its employee-owners before the end of the calendar year must postpone part or all of its corresponding deduction to its next fiscal tax year. (Code Sec. 280H) To figure the required minimum distribution and maximum deductible amount, use Form 1120, Schedule H. [36]

¶ 2814   How to change accounting periods—Form 1128.

A taxpayer must get prior IRS approval to change accounting periods unless authorized by the Code or is a change listed at ¶2815. (Reg § 1.441-1(e), Reg § 1.442-1(a))[37]

IRS will approve a request for a change in tax years only if the taxpayer establishes a substantial business purpose for it, [38] and agrees to any terms, conditions or adjustments required to effect it, including any that IRS feels are necessary to avoid a substantial distortion of the taxpayer's income. (Reg § 1.442-1(b)(1))[39]

To request IRS approval, file Form 1128 within the time and in the manner provided in IRS administrative procedures. (Reg § 1.442-1(b)(1), Reg § 1.442-1(h)(3))[40] Fiscal year individuals must follow an exclusive procedure to change to a calendar year. [41]

If a taxpayer changed its annual accounting period within 48 months before the last month of the requested tax year, a copy of the previous change application, the ruling letter, and any related correspondence from IRS, must be attached to the application. [42]

Special rules apply to the carryback and carryforward of certain capital losses and farming NOLs generated in the short period necessary to effect a change of tax year. [43]

¶ 2815   "No prior approval needed" changes of accounting period.

A taxpayer that has adopted a tax year generally must continue to use it unless it obtains IRS approval to change or is otherwise authorized to change without IRS approval under the Code (e.g., Code Sec. 444, ¶2813) or regs. (Reg § 1.442-1(a))[44] A taxpayer may change his annual accounting period without IRS approval, or with "automatic" IRS approval, where the taxpayer:

. . . changes to a 52-53 week tax year that ends with reference to the same calendar month as the month ending his previous tax year (Reg § 1.441-2(b)(2));[45]

. . . marries a person with a different tax year (Reg § 1.442-1(d)(1));[46]

34. ¶G-1500 *et seq.*; ¶4444
35. ¶s G-1500, G-1550; ¶75,194
36. ¶G-1600; ¶280H4
37. ¶G-1800; ¶4424
38. ¶G-1803 *et seq.*; ¶4424
39. ¶G-1812 *et seq.*; ¶4424
40. ¶G-1701.1; ¶4424
41. ¶G-1726; ¶4424
42. ¶G-1882
43. ¶G-1827 *et seq.*; ¶4424
44. ¶G-1701; ¶s 4424, 7064.01
45. ¶G-1101; ¶4414
46. ¶G-1708; ¶4424

. . . is an individual with a fiscal year tax year who changes to a calendar year tax year; [47]

. . . is a partnership changing its tax year to meet the tests described at ¶2812;[48]

. . . is a C corporation that meets certain tests; [49]

. . . is an S corporation changing its tax year to meet the tests described at ¶2810;[50]

. . . is a personal service corporation changing to a calendar year or a 52-53 week tax year ending with reference to a calendar year; (Reg § 1.441-3(b)(2))[1] or

. . . is a subsidiary corporation required to change its tax year to that of members of its affiliated group that file a consolidated return. (Reg § 1.442-1(c))

¶ 2816   Accounting Methods.

Methods of tax accounting are the methods and systems by which taxpayers determine the amount of their income, gains, losses, deductions and credits, as well as the time when those items must be realized and recognized. Various methods of tax accounting are permissible, but each must be used consistently and clearly reflect income. See ¶2817 for establishing a method of accounting, and ¶2818 for limits on choice of accounting method.

¶ 2817   Establishing a method of accounting.

Because a taxpayer's book accounting method determines his accounting method, a taxpayer establishes a tax accounting method by setting up books, keeping accounts, and preparing income tax returns under any of the permissible methods. The method first used in accounting for business income and deductions in connection with each trade or business, as evidenced in the taxpayer's income tax return in which the income or deductions are first reported, must be followed consistently after that. (Reg § 1.446-1(d)(1))[2] Books and records can be maintained on certain electronic storage systems. [3]

A taxpayer may use one method of accounting to keep personal books and another to keep the books for his trade or business. But the two must be strictly separated. (Reg § 1.446-1(c)(1)(iv)(b))

A taxpayer whose only income is wages doesn't have to keep formal books in order to establish an accounting method, but may establish a method of accounting by means of tax returns (or copies) or other records. (Reg § 1.446-1(b)(2))[4]

A new taxpayer may adopt a method of accounting in connection with filing the first income tax return. An existing taxpayer entering into a business that's separate and distinct from any trade or business that the taxpayer previously carried on (including through a disregarded entity) may adopt a method of accounting for the separate and distinct business in connection with filing the first tax return reporting income from that business. (Reg § 1.446-1(e)(1))[5]

Use of different accounting methods that create or shift profits or losses between the taxpayer's various trades or businesses (e.g., by using inventory adjustments, sales, purchases or expenses) resulting in a distortion of the taxpayer's income isn't allowed. (Reg § 1.446-1(d)(3))[6]

Taxpayers may use any combination of the cash, accrual, and specifically permitted special methods of accounting if the combination clearly reflects income and is consistently used. (Reg § 1.446-1(c)(1)(iv))[7]

47. ¶G-1725; ¶4424
48. ¶G-1222; ¶4424
49. ¶G-1800 *et seq.*; ¶4424
50. ¶G-1250.1; ¶13,784
1. ¶G-1301; ¶4424
2. ¶G-2051; ¶4464.01

3. ¶G-2019; ¶60,014
4. ¶G-2051
5. ¶G-2051; ¶4464.01
6. ¶G-2052; ¶4464.01
7. ¶G-2003; ¶4464.09

¶ 2818   Limits on choice of accounting methods and small business exceptions.

Inventory limitation. The accrual method (¶2823 *et seq.*) is mandatory for purchases and sales (unless IRS consents to a change) where inventories must be used, (Code Sec. 471(a), Reg § 1.446-1(c)(2)(i)) that is, where the production, purchase or sale of merchandise is an income-producing factor. (Reg § 1.446-1(a)(4)(i))[8] However, a major exception to inventory accounting applies for businesses (other than tax shelters prohibited from using the cash receipts and disbursements method) that satisfy a "gross receipts test" —i.e., whose average annual gross receipts for the three-tax-year period preceding the testing year don't exceed $25 million for 2018 ($26 million for 2019, as calculated by Thomson Reuters using inflation data). (Code Sec. 471(c)(1)(A))[9]

If a taxpayer meets the gross receipts test, its method of accounting for inventory won't be treated as failing to clearly reflect income if it: (Code Sec. 471(c)(1)(B))[10]

. . . treats inventory as non-incidental materials and supplies, or

. . . conforms to the taxpayer's method of accounting reflected in an "applicable financial statement" (AFS) for that tax year, or the taxpayer's books and records prepared in accordance with its accounting procedures if it doesn't have an AFS for the tax year.

An AFS is a financial statement: (Code Sec. 471(c)(2), Code Sec. 451(b)(3))[11]

(A) that is certified as prepared in accordance with generally accepted accounting principles (GAAP) and meets certain other requirements;

(B) is made on the basis of international financial reporting standards and filed with a foreign government agency equivalent to the U.S. Securities and Exchange Commission, but only if the taxpayer has no financial statement described in item (A), above; or

(C) is filed with any other regulatory or governmental body specified by IRS, but only if the taxpayer has no statement described in items (A) or (B), above.

For any taxpayer that isn't a corporation or a partnership, the $25 million gross receipts test (as inflation indexed) is applied as if each trade or business of that taxpayer were a corporation or a partnership. (Code Sec. 471(c)(3)) Any change in method of accounting made under Code Sec. 471(c) is treated for purposes of Code Sec. 481 as initiated by the taxpayer and made with IRS consent. (Code Sec. 471(c)(4))[12]

Limitations on use of cash method. C corporations and partnerships with a C corporation partner (but not farming businesses (see ¶4505) or qualified personal service corporations), and tax shelters generally may not use the cash method of accounting (see ¶2819 *et seq.*). (Code Sec. 448(a), Code Sec. 448(b)) However, a corporation or partnership with a C corporation partner that meets the gross receipts test described above (or for the period of its existence if less than 3 years) is exempt from that limitation. (Code Sec. 448(b), Code Sec. 448(c)) Gross receipts for short tax years must be annualized. Persons treated as a single employer under the controlled group or affiliated service group rules are treated as one person for purposes of the gross receipts test. (Code Sec. 448(c)(2)) Accounting method changes made under these liberalizations are treated for purposes of Code Sec. 481 as initiated by the taxpayer and made with IRS consent. (Code Sec. 448(d)(7))

Other limitations. Tax shelters can't use the cash method in any event. (Code Sec. 448(a))[13] The limitation on the cash method doesn't apply to farming businesses (except tax shelters) (Code Sec. 448(b)(1)), but for special farm accounting rules, see ¶4505

---

8. ¶G-5000 *et seq.*; ¶4714
9. ¶G-5004; ¶4714.05
10. ¶G-5004; ¶4714.05

11. ¶G-5004; ¶4714.05
12. ¶G-5004; ¶4714.05
13. ¶G-2054; ¶4484

et seq.[14] For purposes of these restrictions, an accounting method that records some but not all items on the cash method (i.e., a hybrid method) is treated as the cash method of accounting. (Reg § 1.448-1T(a)(4))[15] Tax-exempt trusts are treated as C corporations with respect to unrelated trade or business income. (Code Sec. 448(d)(6))[16]

¶ 2819   The Cash Method of Accounting.

Under the cash basis method of accounting, income is reported when cash or property is actually or constructively received (¶2821), and deductions are taken in the year cash or property is paid or transferred.[17] It doesn't matter when the income was earned or when the expense was incurred.

For income a taxpayer receives under a claim of right, see ¶1204. For restrictions on use of the cash method by certain taxpayers (and exceptions for small businesses), see ¶2818.

¶ 2820   When is a check income?

A check issued by a solvent payor is income when received by a cash basis payee, unless there's a restriction on the payee's right to cash the check.[18] Receipt of a check by an agent is considered receipt by the principal.[19]

¶ 2821   Constructive receipt of income.

Income not actually received is constructively received and reportable if it's within the taxpayer's control. Cash basis taxpayers must report money unconditionally subject to their demand as income, even if they haven't received it.[20] There's no constructive receipt if the amount is available only on surrender of a valuable right,[21] or if there are substantial limits on the right to receive it. (Reg § 1.451-2(a))[22]

¶ 2822   Timing of deductions under the cash method.

Cash method taxpayers generally take deductions (if otherwise allowable) in the year the items are paid. (Reg § 1.461-1(a)(1))[23] There's no constructive payment doctrine.[24]

Where an expense (e.g., rent or an insurance premium) relates to a period covering more than 12 months, IRS and most courts agree that the deduction must be spread over the period to which the expense applies.[25] For an exception for points paid on a home mortgage, see ¶1740. For deduction of prepaid taxes, see ¶1758.

A check is payment when delivered, not when cashed, if it's honored when it's first presented for payment.[26]

¶ 2823   The Accrual Method of Accounting.

Under the accrual method, income accrues and is reported in the year all events have occurred that determine the taxpayer's right to receive it (¶2830), and the amount can be determined with reasonable accuracy (Reg § 1.451-1(a)), even if it's received in a later year. The right to receive the income must not be contingent on a future event; it must be reasonably susceptible of accurate estimate, and reasonably expected to be received in due course.[27]

Starting with tax years beginning in 2018, the all-events test for any item of gross

---

14. ¶G-2057; ¶s 614.053, 4474
15. ¶G-2054; ¶4484
16. ¶G-2055; ¶4484
17. ¶G-2410 *et seq.*; ¶s 4464.05, 4514.003
18. ¶G-2415; ¶s 4514.003, 4514.004
19. ¶G-2419
20. ¶G-2424; ¶4514.036
21. ¶G-2426; ¶4514.036
22. ¶G-2425; ¶4514.036
23. ¶G-2436 *et seq.*; ¶4614.01
24. ¶G-2443
25. ¶L-3526 *et seq.*, ¶L-6616 *et seq.*; ¶1624.081
26. ¶G-2438; ¶4614.02
27. ¶G-2471; ¶4514.012

income generally isn't treated as met any later than when it is taken into account as revenue in an applicable financial statement (AFS), if the taxpayer has one for a tax year, or other financial statement specified by IRS for this purpose. (Code Sec. 451(b)(1)(A)) This requirement does not apply to taxpayers that don't have an AFR or IRS-specified financial system. An AFS is a financial statement certified as being GAAP compliant and of a type filed with the SEC (10-K, etc.) or an audited financial statement used for certain substantial nontax purposes if there is no SEC-filed statement, or one filed with other federal agencies for nontax purposes or certain foreign government agencies, if no better statements exist. (Code Sec. 451(b)(3)) IRS intends to issue proposed regs providing that market discount is not includible in income under Code Sec. 451(b).[28]

However, accrual basis taxpayers do not need to accrue income from the performance of services that, based on their experience, will not be collected if, among other things, interest isn't charged on the debt and there is no penalty for late payment. This "nonaccrual experience method" is available only for: (1) amounts owing for services in the fields of health, law, engineering, architecture, accounting, actuarial science, performing arts, or consulting, or (2) other services, if for the 3-tax-year period preceding the testing year the taxpayer's average annual gross receipts didn't exceed $25 million for 2018 ($26 million for 2019, as calculated by Thomson Reuters using inflation data). Uncollectible amounts may be determined using specified safe-harbor methods. (Code Sec. 448(d)(5)) A taxpayer's nonaccrual experience method must be tested against actual experience unless he has adopted one of the six safe harbor methods in the regs (Reg § 1.448-2(d)) or a book safe harbor provided in IRS guidance. [29]

For deductions under the accrual method, see ¶2830.

¶ 2824 Contingent rights to income.

Where the right to income is contingent on a future event, an accrual basis taxpayer doesn't have to recognize the income until that event occurs. [30]

Advance payments to a retailer under which it agreed to purchase specified amounts from its supplier were held by a court to be income on receipt. But another court found similar cash advances by a wholesaler to a retailer in exchange for a volume purchase commitment not includible on receipt; they were contingent on the purchases being made. Generally adopting the latter approach, IRS allows taxpayers to adopt an advance trade discount method of accounting in which advance trade discounts aren't recognized as income on receipt by accrual method taxpayers with inventories, but instead are taken into account in the amount and manner that the taxpayer accounts for the discount in its financial statements. [31]

Where litigation is involved and liability to the taxpayer is admitted, the income must be recognized if the taxpayer can accurately estimate the amount of recovery. [32] But if liability isn't admitted, the income accrues when the litigation is concluded or settlement reached, whichever is earlier. [33] An offer in compromise is income when the dispute is settled or the offer is unconditionally accepted. [34]

¶ 2825 Income accrual for disputed liability for goods.

If an accrual method taxpayer overbills a customer due to clerical error and the customer discovers the error and disputes its liability in the following year, gross income accrues in the year of sale for the correct amount. An accrual method taxpayer does not

---

28. ¶G-2472.2; ¶4514.011
29. ¶G-2501 *et seq.*; ¶4514.023 *et seq.*
30. ¶s G-2484, G-2485; ¶s 4514.011, 4514.012
31. ¶G-2483

32. ¶G-2506; ¶s 4514.021, 4514.055
33. ¶G-2506; ¶4514.055
34. ¶s G-2506, G-2507; ¶4514.058

accrue income in the year of sale if, during that year, the customer disputes its liability because incorrect goods were shipped. However, income does accrue in the year of sale if excess quantities of goods are shipped and the customer agrees to pay for them. [35]

¶ 2826   Dealers' reserves.

Dealers commonly discount customers' notes with a finance company that keeps a portion of the amount due the dealer as security against possible default by the customer. A dealer that uses the accrual method must include the full amount of the discount price, undiminished by the portion retained by the finance company —the "dealer reserve" —in income as soon as the notes are sold to the finance company. This is so even if the dealer assigned the notes to the finance company "without recourse." [36]

¶ 2827   Deferral method for certain advance payments.

An accrual basis taxpayer that receives an advance payment generally must include it in gross income for the tax year of receipt. However, it may elect for a category of advance payments (including, after 2017 tax years, payments for goods) to defer inclusion in gross income of specified advances to the next succeeding tax year, to the extent they are not otherwise required to be recognized in revenue (or, in certain cases, are not earned) in the year of receipt (see ¶2823). (Code Sec. 451(c)(1)) The election must be made in the form and manner provided by IRS, and is effective for the tax year for which it is first made and all later year years unless IRS consents to its revocation. (Code Sec. 451(c)(2))[37] Unless IRS provides otherwise, the following payments don't qualify for this deferral: rent, certain insurance premiums, payments on financial instruments, payments under warranty or guaranty contracts, payments of property in exchange for services, and certain payments subject to tax or withholding on income related to nonresident alien individuals or foreign persons or corporations. (Code Sec. 451(c)(4)(B))[38] For the taxpayer's first tax year beginning after 2017, a change to this accounting method for advance payments is treated as initiated by the taxpayer and made with IRS consent. The election to defer inclusion of advance payments doesn't apply to advance payments received during a tax year if the taxpayer ceases to exist during (or with the close of) that tax year. (Code Sec. 451(c)(3))[39] Alternately, a taxpayer, under the full inclusion method of accounting for advance payments, can include the full amount of advance payments in gross income in the tax year of receipt, whether or not the taxpayer earns the full amount of advance payments in that tax year.[40]

> *illustration:* Accrual method, calendar year C Corp sells and repairs TVs. On July 1, 2018, C Corp receives an advance payment for a 2-year contract under which it will repair or replace broken parts in a customer's TV. In its applicable financial statement, C Corp recognizes ¼ of the payment in revenues for 2018, ½ in revenues for 2019, and ¼ in revenues for 2020. Under the deferral method, C Corp includes ¼ of the payment in gross income for 2018 and the remaining ¾ of the payment in gross income for 2019.

> *observation:* Given the deferral possibilities outlined above, cash-basis service providers who bill in advance should consider switching to the accrual method, taking into account both the benefits of ongoing deferral and the costs and effort of making the accounting method change.

Reliance on prior guidance. Notice 2018-35 provides that until expected guidance on the treatment of advance payments in Code Sec. 451 is issued and becomes effective, taxpayers

---

35. ¶G-2511.1
36. ¶G-2513; ¶4514.017
37. ¶G-2548; ¶4514.191*et seq.*

38. ¶G-2548.4 *et seq.*; ¶4514.191
39. ¶2548.3
40. ¶G-2548 *et seq.*; ¶4514.191

may continue to rely on Rev Proc 2004-34 for the treatment of advance payments. During this time, IRS will not challenge a taxpayer's use of Rev Proc 2004-34 to satisfy the requirements of Code Sec. 451, although it will continue to verify on examination that taxpayers are properly applying that procedure.

¶ 2828 Advance payments received under construction contracts.

Advance payments under long-term construction contracts are reported by accrual method taxpayers when the income is properly accruable under their method of accounting.[41] But that method must be used for all tax reporting and for credit purposes. (Reg § 1.451-5(b))[42]

An accrual basis taxpayer or a taxpayer using one of the long-term contract methods (¶2844 *et seq.*) can defer reporting an advance payment received under an agreement for the sale or other disposition in a future tax year of goods held primarily for sale to customers, or for the building, installing, constructing or manufacturing of items, where the work isn't completed in the year the advance payment is received. (Reg § 1.451-5(a)(1)) Deferral also applies to advance payments for services to be performed under the agreement as an integral part of the above activities, and for gift certificates. (Reg § 1.451-5(a)(2))[43] Amounts due and payable under the contract are treated as advance payments received. (Reg § 1.451-5(a))[44]

There's a limited deferral for certain inventoriable goods. Where a payment for goods is received several years before they are delivered, taxpayer can postpone reporting the advance payments for one year past the year total advance payments first equal or exceed the anticipated cost of the goods. Thereafter, all prepayments received are reported and actual or expected costs deducted. (Reg § 1.451-5(c))[45] A taxpayer who defers reporting advance payments for merchandise must attach an annual information schedule to its tax return for each year. (Reg § 1.451-5(d))[46]

Use Form 3115 (¶2837) to get IRS consent to switch to deferral. (Reg § 1.451-5(e))[47]

¶ 2829 Advance payments or security deposits.

Amounts received as security aren't taxable until used. A deposit that guarantees the customer's payment of amounts owed to the creditor isn't a deposit but an advance payment includible in income (unless deferred, see ¶2827 and ¶2828), while a deposit securing someone's property is a true security deposit and not an advance payment. [48]

¶ 2830 Timing of expense deductions—all-events test.

Expenses are deductible under the accrual method in the period in which: (1) all events have occurred that determine the fact of the liability; (2) the amount of the liability can be determined with reasonable accuracy; and (3) economic performance (see ¶2831) has occurred. (Code Sec. 461(h)(4); Reg § 1.461-1(a)(2)) Requirements (1) and (2) are referred to as the "all events" test.

Under requirement (1), no accrual can be made where the liability has not actually been incurred, is contingent upon an uncertain future event, or is contested and not paid. Once the fact of the liability is established, accrual under this requirement is generally not postponed because of events in later years, the accrual isn't thereafter paid, or the amount of the liability is later adjusted. The fact of a liability —generally, the earlier of the event

---

41. ¶G-2592 *et seq.*; ¶s 4514.121, 4514.191
42. ¶G-2595
43. ¶s G-2592, G-2594
44. ¶G-2599; ¶4514.121
45. ¶G-2596; ¶4514.166
46. ¶G-2597
47. ¶G-2598
48. ¶J-1435 *et seq.*; ¶s 4514.193, 4514.194

fixing the liability (e.g., the required performance) or when payment is due —isn't established by executing a contract for services to be provided in the future. The "all events" test isn't satisfied, and a liability isn't established, by a statistical probability, however high, that the taxpayer will ultimately pay the expense; rather, the test requires that nothing further be needed to create a fixed liability. For bonuses that are payable to a group of employees that can't revert to the employer, IRS has ruled that the fact of the liability can be shown, even though the employer doesn't know the identity of any particular bonus recipient or the amount payable to that individual recipient until after the end of the tax year. A reasonable estimate of the liability must be accrued for the tax year in which it was incurred; if there is a difference between the estimate and the amount finally determined, the difference must be added to or deducted from income when the final determination is made. [49]

IRS held that a manufacturer's contractual liability to pay certain trade promotion rebates to customers became fixed and determinable under the all events test in the year that the underlying goods were purchased; the later filing of a rebate claim was a mere formality that didn't delay accrual of the liabilities. [50] But, IRS disagreed with (nonacquiesced in) a Third Circuit case holding that discounts against future purchases that were redeemable after the year were currently deductible as unconditionally fixed "near-certain" obligations; IRS reasoned that the future purchase by the customer was a condition precedent to liability for the discount. [1]

Where the accrual doesn't involve a current expense, but results in the creation of an asset having a useful life extending substantially beyond the end of the tax year, the deduction must be taken as depreciation, amortization, etc. (Reg § 1.461-1(a)(2))[2]

An accrual basis taxpayer may deduct a properly accrued expense, regardless of whether it has been paid. [3]

¶ 2831   Economic performance.

Accrual basis taxpayers won't be considered to have met the all-events test (¶2830), until economic performance has occurred. (Code Sec. 461(h))[4] Economic performance occurs when the property or service to which the accrual relates is actually provided or used. (Code Sec. 461(h)(2))[5] If a liability arises out of the providing of services or property to the taxpayer by another person, economic performance occurs as the services or property are provided. (Code Sec. 461(h)(2)(A)(i), Reg § 1.461-4(d)(2)(i)) Thus, economic performance for a liability to pay compensation generally occurs as the employee renders his services. If a taxpayer's liability arises out of the use of property, economic performance occurs ratably over the period of time that the taxpayer is entitled to the use of the property. (Code Sec. 461(h)(2)(A)(iii), Reg § 1.461-4(d)(3)(i)) Payment constitutes economic performance for: (i) liabilities arising under a workers compensation act or out of any tort, breach of contract, or violation of law; (ii) rebates and refunds; (iii) awards, prizes and jackpots; (iv) insurance, warranty and service contracts; and (v) taxes (other than real property taxes for which a Code Sec. 461(c) election (¶1761) has been made and creditable foreign taxes); and (vi) any other liabilities where specific economic performance rules aren't provided in a reg, revenue ruling or revenue procedure. (Reg § 1.461-4(g)(1) - Reg § 1.461-4(g)(7))

Exceptions. A taxpayer is allowed to treat property or services as provided when he pays for them, but only if he can reasonably expect the property or services to be provided by the other person within 3 1/2 months after the payment is made. (Reg § 1.461-4(d)(6)(ii))[6]

49. ¶G-2620 *et seq.*; ¶4614.15
50. ¶G-2620 *et seq.*; ¶4614.15
1. ¶G-2630
2. ¶G-2620; ¶4614.15

3. ¶G-2620; ¶4614.15
4. ¶G-2653; ¶4614.15
5. ¶G-2656; ¶4614.15
6. ¶G-2656; ¶4614.15

In addition, certain "recurring" expenditures may be treated as incurred in the year the all-events test is otherwise met, even though economic performance doesn't occur until the following year. This applies if:

(1) economic performance occurs on or before the date taxpayer files a timely (including extensions) return for the tax year the expense is accrued or, if shorter, 8 $\frac{1}{2}$ months after the close of that year; and

(2) the item is recurring and taxpayer consistently treats items of that kind as incurred in the tax year the all-events test (excluding the economic performance test) is met; and

(3) the item is either not a material item or its accrual in the year before economic performance results in a more proper match against income than if it were accrued in the year of economic performance. (Code Sec. 461(h)(3)(A); Reg § 1.461-5(b))[7]

The recurring item exception is allowed for payroll taxes on compensation and, under a safe harbor, for bonuses and vacation pay. [8] The recurring item exception doesn't apply to liabilities for interest; workers compensation, tort, breach of contract, and violation of law; or other liabilities described in (vi), above, for which payment is economic performance, or incurred by a tax shelter. (Code Sec. 461(i)(1); Reg § 1.461-5(c))[9]

The 3 $\frac{1}{2}$ month rule, as well as the 8 $\frac{1}{2}$ month recurring item exception, apply only to property or services completely provided within that period; a prorated deduction isn't allowed where all services to be performed aren't provided within that period. [10]

Taxpayers who are recipients of services under "Ratable Service Contracts" can treat economic performance as occurring ratably under a safe harbor and deduct the cost of regular and routine services as the services are provided under the contract. A Ratable Service Contract is one where: (a) the contract provides for similar services to be provided on a regular basis (such as daily, weekly, or monthly); (b) each occurrence of the service provides independent value, such that the benefits of receiving each occurrence of the service isn't dependent on the receipt of any previous or subsequent occurrence of the service, and; (c) the term of the contract doesn't exceed 12 months (without regard to contract renewal provisions). If a single contract includes services that satisfy these requirements and services (or other items) that do not, the services (or other items) that do not satisfy the requirements must be separately priced in the contract for the contract to qualify as a Ratable Service Contract. [11]

¶ 2832 Accruing contested liability.

An otherwise deductible expense isn't allowable, as long as the taxpayer denies and contests the liability, until the contest is resolved by agreement or final court decision. [12] However, a deduction is allowed in the year of transfer (payment) where:

(1) the taxpayer contests an asserted liability;

(2) the taxpayer transfers money or other property to satisfy the liability;

(3) the contest with respect to the asserted liability exists after the transfer; and

(4) but for the contest, a deduction would be allowed for the tax year of the transfer (or an earlier year). (Code Sec. 461(f)) The contest need not involve court proceedings. [13]

Except as provided under Code Sec. 468B, economic performance does not occur when a taxpayer transfers money or property to a trust, escrow account, or court to provide for the satisfaction of a contested workers compensation, tort, or a liability that arises out of a

---

7. ¶G-2686; ¶4614.15
8. ¶K-4302.1; ¶4614.17
9. ¶G-2458; ¶4614.15
10. ¶G-2656

11. ¶G-2659.1
12. ¶G-2643; ¶s 4614.56, 4614.59
13. ¶G-2645; ¶s 4614.56, 4614.59

breach of contract or violation of law and requires a payment or a series of payments to another person unless the trust, escrow account, or court is the claimant, or the taxpayer's payment discharges the taxpayer's liability to the claimant. (Reg § 1.461-2(e)(2)(ii))[14]

¶ 2833   Accrual basis taxpayer's payables to related cash basis taxpayer.

An accrual basis taxpayer can deduct expenses and interest owed to a related cash basis person only when payment is made and the amount involved is includible in the gross income of the cash basis payee. (Code Sec. 267(a)(2)) In other words, an accrual basis taxpayer is treated as on the cash method for purposes of deducting amounts owed to a related cash basis person. [15]

The rule applies in general to all deductible expenses if the timing of the deduction depends on the taxpayer's method of accounting or on electing to expense the item. But it doesn't apply to defer the deduction of otherwise deductible original issue discount or below-market loan interest. (Reg § 1.267(a)-2T(b), Q&A-2) Nor does it apply to defer the deduction of otherwise deductible depreciation or amortization, except as to amounts owed to a related person for interest, rent, or for the performance or nonperformance of services (which amount the payor capitalized or treated as a deferred expense). (Reg § 1.267(a)-2T(b), Q&A-4)[16]

¶ 2834   Changes of Accounting Methods.

Taxpayers generally may change their accounting methods (¶2836) only with IRS consent and on IRS-imposed terms (¶2835). However, automatic consent is available in certain circumstances where IRS-set procedures are followed (¶2842).

¶ 2835   IRS permission to change method of accounting.

Generally, once a taxpayer has adopted an accounting method, he must continue to use it until: IRS requires him to change the method; or he requests, and gets, IRS permission to change. (Code Sec. 446(e); Reg § 1.446-1(e)(2)) This is so even if the taxpayer has been using an incorrect method, or a method that doesn't clearly reflect income. [17] Taxpayers can't, without IRS consent, retroactively change from an erroneous to a permissible accounting method by filing amended returns, even if the time for amending the return for the first year in which the erroneous method was used hasn't expired. [18]

Taxpayers under examination [19] or before an appeals office [20] or federal court [21] may request prospective accounting method changes in certain circumstances.

For automatic consent procedures for certain accounting method changes, see ¶2842. For changes to inventory methods, see ¶2875.

¶ 2836   What is a change in accounting method?

A change in accounting method is a change of the taxpayer's overall method of accounting or a change in the treatment of a material item of income or expense. Changes in overall methods of accounting include changes:

... from the cash to accrual basis, or vice-versa;

... from the long-term contract method to the cash or accrual method, or vice-versa;

... from one basis of inventory valuation to another; and

---

14. ¶G-2645; ¶4614.56
15. ¶G-2700 *et seq.*; ¶2674
16. ¶G-2701 *et seq.*; ¶2674
17. ¶G-2201; ¶4464

18. ¶G-2201; ¶s 4464.21, 4464.22
19. ¶G-2237; ¶4464.22
20. ¶G-2256.1; ¶4464.22
21. ¶G-2257.1; ¶4464.22

. . . to or from a specialized basis, e.g., the crop basis. (Reg § 1.446-1(e)(2)(ii))[22]

A material item is any item that involves the proper time for the inclusion of the item in income or the taking of a deduction. It doesn't include corrections of mathematical or posting errors, or errors in computing tax liability. (Reg § 1.446-1(e)(2)(ii))[23]

Depreciation changes that aren't accounting method changes include: adjustments in the useful life of a depreciable or amortizable asset for which depreciation is determined under Code Sec. 167 (other than under current (or former) Code Sec. 168, Code Sec. 1400I, and Code Sec. 1400L); changes in computing depreciation or amortization allowances in the tax year in which the use of an asset changes in the hands of the same taxpayer; changes in depreciation caused by certain revocations of elections and late elections; and changes in the placed-in service date. (Reg § 1.446-1(e)(2)(ii), Reg § 1.167(e)-1(a)(2))

However, most changes in computing depreciation (or amortization) are treated as accounting method changes. Changes that are accounting method changes include changes: in depreciation or amortization methods, recovery periods or conventions, e.g., half-year to midquarter (but a switch from 200% or 150% declining balance to straight line is allowable without IRS's consent in the first tax year in which it produces a higher allowance); from regular MACRS to the alternative depreciation system; in claiming bonus first-year depreciation without electing; from treating property as nondepreciable or nonamortizable to depreciable or amortizable (or vice versa); and from depreciating or amortizing an item to deducting it as an expense (or vice versa). (Reg § 1.167(e)-1(a)(1), Reg § 1.446-1(e)(2)(ii))[24]

¶ 2837 Applying for a change in accounting method—Form 3115.

An application for change generally must be filed with IRS on the latest version of Form 3115 by the end of the tax year of the change. (Reg § 1.446-1(e)(3)(i))[25] However, automatic consent accounting method change requests (¶2842) may be made on Form 3115:

(1) with a timely filed (including extensions) original income tax return for the change year (file a copy with the IRS National Office), or

(2) within six months of the original tax return due date (excluding extensions) for the change year, if the taxpayer (a) timely filed (including extensions) its return for the change year; (b) files an amended return within the 6-month extension period; (c) attaches the original Form 3115 to the amended return; (d) files a copy with the national office at the same time or sooner; and (e) writes "FILED PURSUANT TO Reg § 301.9100-2" at the top of the application. [26]

Extensions won't be granted except in unusual and compelling circumstances. The taxpayer must include all information required by the form, and state that he agrees to the conditions set by IRS and will take into account any required adjustments (¶2838).[27]

For an exception to filing Form 3115 for accounting method changes for the tangible property regs, see ¶2837.

¶ 2838 Adjustments required on change—Code Sec. 481(a) adjustments.

In any year in which taxpayer uses a different tax accounting method from the method used in the preceding year, Code Sec. 481(a) adjustments must be made to prevent items of income or expense from being duplicated or entirely omitted. (Reg § 1.446-1(e)(3)(i))[28] The adjustments must take into account inventories, accounts receivable, accounts payable, and any other necessary items. (Reg § 1.481-1(b))[29] The adjustments can be positive

---

22. ¶G-2103; ¶4464.21; ¶4464.24
23. ¶G-2104; ¶4464.24
24. ¶G-2106.1; ¶4464.25
25. ¶G-2225; ¶4464.22

26. ¶G-2203.9; ¶4464.225
27. ¶G-2220 *et seq.*; ¶4464.22
28. ¶G-2215; ¶4464.21
29. ¶G-2290 *et seq.*; ¶4814

(increasing taxable income), or negative (decreasing taxable income). (Reg § 1.481-1(c))[30]

IRS may determine that certain changes in accounting methods must be made without a Code Sec. 481(a) adjustment (for example, on a cut-off basis) where, in general, only the items arising on or after the beginning of the year of change (or other operative date) are accounted for under the accounting method for which consent is granted. Any items arising before the year of change (or other operative date) continue to be accounted for under the taxpayer's former accounting method.

¶ 2839   When Code Sec. 481(a) adjustments are taken into account.

Except as noted below or where the Code or another federal statute provides otherwise, the Code Sec. 481(a) adjustment required as a result of an accounting method change (¶2838) must be taken into account in the year of change —i.e., the first tax year in which the taxpayer's method of accounting is different from that used in the previous tax year. (Code Sec. 481(a); Reg § 1.481-1(a)(1)) This applies to both positive and negative adjustments. (Reg § 1.481-1(c))[31]

Instead of taking the Code Sec. 481(a) adjustment into account in the year of change, a taxpayer may take it into account over an appropriate period agreed to (in writing) by IRS. (Code Sec. 481(c); Reg § 1.481-4(a), Reg § 1.481-4(b)) The adjustment must be taken into account ratably over the years included in the adjustment inclusion period (¶2840).[32]

¶ 2840   Adjustment inclusion periods prescribed by IRS—four-year/one-year rules.

The Code Sec. 481(a) adjustment period for voluntary accounting method changes, including automatic consent changes (¶2842), is one tax year for negative adjustments and four tax years for positive adjustments beginning with the year of change. [33] However, taxpayers may elect to account for a positive adjustment in the year of change if it's less than $50,000. Cooperatives generally must take the adjustment into account for the year of change. Taxpayers that terminate their existence or cease to engage in a trade or business must take any remaining balance into account in the year of the cessation or termination. Except for last-in-first-out (LIFO) discontinuance, acceleration of a Code Sec. 481(a) adjustment isn't required on conversion from C to S corporation status, or vice versa. [34]

If an accounting method issue (i.e., an issue regarding whether the taxpayer's accounting treatment of an item is proper, but only if changing the taxpayer's treatment of that item could constitute a change in accounting method) results from an examination, any resulting positive Code Sec. 481(a) adjustment is made in the earliest tax year under examination, with a one-year Code Sec. 481(a) adjustment period. [35]

Special rules govern Code Sec. 481 adjustments attributable to S elections revoked during the 2-year period beginning Dec. 22, 2017, if the corporation's stock is owned by the same shareholders and in the same proportion on the revocation date as it was on Dec. 22, 2017 (¶3376). The adjustments are taken into account ratably over a 6-tax-year period beginning with the year of change. (Code Sec. 481(d))[36] See ¶3376 for treatment of post-revocation distributions.

---

30. ¶G-2304; ¶4814
31. ¶G-2360; ¶4814
32. ¶G-2309; ¶4814
33. ¶G-2311; ¶4814

34. ¶G-2308; ¶4814
35. ¶G-2308; ¶4464.21
36. ¶G-2373; ¶4814

¶ 2841 Relief for high-impact adjustments.

Where Code Sec. 481(a) adjustments increase taxable income of the change-over year by more than $3,000, the taxpayer can compute his tax for that year using whichever of these two methods produces the lower tax:

(1) *3-year allocation* —The tax that would have resulted if $1/3$ of the increase had been included in taxable income in each of the two preceding years and in the change-over year. (Code Sec. 481(b)(1); Reg § 1.481-2(a))

(2) *Allocation of specific years under new method of accounting* —Where the taxpayer establishes his taxable income under the new method of accounting for one or more tax years consecutively preceding the year of change (in which the old method was actually used), the tax is reduced to the amount that would have been paid if:

(a) the tax for the preceding years was figured under the new method, and

(b) the then-remaining adjustments were allocated to the change-over year. (Code Sec. 481(b)(2); Reg § 1.481-2(b))[37]

In making the above computations, the entire Code Sec. 481(a) adjustment required as a result of the accounting method change is taken into account. (Reg § 1.481-1(d))[38]

¶ 2842 Automatic consent procedures for certain accounting method changes.

IRS provides automatic procedures for obtaining IRS consent to make certain accounting method changes. Guidance on these is contained in *Rev Proc 2015-13*, as modified by later guidance such as *Rev Proc 2018-40*, which provides procedures for small business taxpayers changing to the cash method, excepted from inventory accounting, UNICAP, and long-term construction contract percentage-of-completion method, etc., by the 2017 Tax Cuts and Jobs Act (TCJA). For changes within their scope, these procedures generally provide the exclusive means of obtaining an accounting method change. Taxpayers who before Aug. 3, 2018 filed under non-automatic procedures for TCJA-related changes governed by *Rev Proc 2018-40's*, automatic procedure may request to switch to the automatic procedure.[39] Some of the more commonly applicable "automatic consent" items are those involving: permissible to permissible accounting method for depreciation; uniform capitalization methods of small resellers; cash or hybrid method to accrual method; series E or EE U.S. savings bonds; timing of incurring liabilities for employee compensation, workers' compensation, and payroll taxes; change from last-in-first-out (LIFO); retail safe harbor method (and certain other methods) for estimating inventory shrinkage; and capitalizing costs incurred in acquiring or creating intangible assets. IRS has also provided automatic consent procedures for changes under the Code Sec. 162 and Code Sec. 263 capitalization regs (e.g., changes under Reg § 1.168(i)-1, Reg § 1.168(i)-7, and Reg § 1.168(i)-8), for sales-based royalties and vendor charge backs changes, and to conform with FASB and IASB financial accounting standards concerning revenue recognition from customer contracts.[40] There are generally no user fees for automatic-consent accounting method change requests.[41] For applying for an automatic consent accounting method change, see ¶2837.

¶ 2843 Reserves for Estimated Expenses and Contingent Liabilities. ▬▬▬

Taxpayers often maintain accounting reserves for various future liabilities. Except as provided below, no deduction is allowed for additions to these reserves, even if they are required by state law or contract.

---

37. ¶G-2401; ¶4814
38. ¶G-2401; ¶4814
39. ¶G-2203 *et seq.*; ¶4464

40. ¶G-2040 *et seq.*
41. ¶G-2203.13

Deduction or exclusion from income for additions to reserves for estimated expenses or contingent liabilities is allowed when expressly authorized by the Code (e.g., depreciation)[42] or as a reserve for trading stamps or premium coupons (Reg § 1.451-4(a)) (but hybrid coupons that can either be redeemed for products or used for discounts on product purchases don't qualify as premium coupons), [43] or for container deposits. However, the use of this method for container deposits applies only where the containers are leased or loaned (*not* sold). Thus, no reserve is permitted for refundable deposits on empty beverage containers under states' environmental and conservation laws. The deposits are includible in income when received and refunds are deductible when paid. [44]

¶ 2844   Long-Term Contracts.

Taxpayers must account for long-term contracts (except for certain home and other real property construction contracts, see ¶2845) under the percentage-of-completion method (¶2847), subject to an election to use a modified percentage-of-completion method ("10% method," see ¶2848). (Code Sec. 460)[45]

A long-term contract is any contract for the manufacture, building, installation, or construction of property, if not completed in the tax year in which entered into. (Code Sec. 460(f)(1); Reg § 1.460-1(b)(1)) Whether the taxpayer reasonably expected that the contract would be completed within the tax year is not relevant. [46] But a manufacturing contract isn't long-term unless it involves manufacture of a unique item (of a type not normally included in inventory), or an item that normally requires more than 12 months to complete.[47] (Code Sec. 460(f)(2))

For how to account for long-term contracts for alternative minimum tax purposes, see ¶3210.

¶ 2845   Completed contract method for home and real property construction contracts.

The completed contract method may be used instead of the percentage-of-completion method for: (1) home construction contracts (specially defined in (Reg § 1.460-6(b)(2)); and (2) other real property construction contracts if (a) the taxpayer (other than a tax shelter) estimates at contract inception that it will be completed within two years, and (b) the taxpayer satisfies a $25 million average three-year gross receipts test ($26 million for 2019, as calculated by Thomson Reuters using inflation data, see ¶2818) for contracts entered into after Dec. 31, 2017 in tax years ending after that date. (Code Sec. 460(e); Reg § 1.460-1(a)(2), Reg § 1.460-3(b))[48] Under the completed contract method, a taxpayer doesn't report income until a contract is complete, even though payments are received in years before completion. (Reg § 1.460-1(b)(10))[49]

¶ 2846   Allocation of costs to long-term contracts.

All costs that directly benefit, or are incurred by reason of, a long-term contract (including research and experimental costs) must be allocated to the contract in the same manner as costs were allocated to extended-period long-term contracts entered into before Mar. 1, '86, under Code Sec. 451 and former Reg. § 1.451-3(d), except that past service pension costs must be allocated to the contract. Also, in the case of a cost-plus contract or a federal long-term contract or subcontract, any other costs (e.g., general and administrative expenses) must be allocated to the contract if identified by the taxpayer (or a related person)

---

42. ¶s G-2733, G-2737; ¶4514.017
43. ¶G-2742; ¶s 4514.161, 4514.163
44. ¶G-2740
45. ¶s G-3100, G-3229; ¶4514.125

46. ¶G-3103; ¶4604
47. ¶s G-3102, G-3106; ¶4604
48. ¶G-3209; ¶4604
49. ¶G-3245; ¶4514.127

as being attributable to it under the contract, or under federal, state, or local law or regulation. (Code Sec. 460(c)(1), Code Sec. 460(c)(2))[50] Interest costs are allocated to long-term contracts in a way that's similar to the way interest costs are allocated under the uniform capitalization rules (Code Sec. 263A(f)) (¶1640) that apply to property produced by a taxpayer. (Code Sec. 460(c)(3); Reg § 1.460-5(b)(2)(v))[1]

The allocation rules don't apply to any expenses for unsuccessful bids and proposals; marketing, selling, and advertising expenses; or independent research and development (IR&D) expenses. IR&D expenses don't include expenses directly attributable to a long-term contract in existence when the expenses are incurred, or expenses under an agreement to perform research and development. (Code Sec. 460(c)(4), Code Sec. 460(c)(5))[2] Costs of a guaranty, warranty, or maintenance agreement aren't treated as part of a long-term contract. (Reg § 1.460-1(d)(2))

Alternatively, a taxpayer may elect to use the simplified cost-to-cost allocation method, under which a contract's completion factor is determined based upon only direct material costs; direct labor costs; and depreciation, amortization, and cost recovery allowances on equipment and facilities directly used to manufacture or construct the subject matter of the contract. Material or labor costs associated with a subcontractor's activities must be allocated to the contract. A taxpayer electing this method must use it to apply the lookback method (¶2849) and to determine alternative minimum taxable income. Elect the simplified cost-to-cost method for all long-term contracts entered into during the tax year by using it on the original federal income tax return for the election year. The election isn't available if the percentage-of-completion method (¶2847) is not used for all long-term contracts or if the 10% method (¶2848) is used. (Code Sec. 460(b)(3)(A); Reg § 1.460-5(c))[3]

Home construction and real property construction contracts (¶2845) are not required to use the above cost allocation rules other than the interest allocation rules. They can use any permissible method. (Code Sec. 460(e))[4]

¶ 2847 Percentage-of-completion method.

Under this method, a long-term contract's percentage of completion must be determined by comparing costs allocated to the contract and incurred before the close of the tax year, with estimated total contract costs. (Code Sec. 460(b)(1)(A)) For qualified property with a recovery period of 7 years or less that is (i) acquired before Sept. 28, 2017, and placed in service before 2020 (before 2021 for certain property with a long production period), or (ii) acquired after Sept. 27, 2017 (but not if acquired under a written binding contract entered into before Sept. 28, 2017), and placed in service before 2027 (2028 for long production period property), bonus depreciation (¶1932) isn't taken into account in applying the percentage of completion method. (Code Sec. 460(c)(6)) Events that occur after the end of the tax year that are reasonably subject to estimate as of the last day of the tax year are taken into account.[5]

Gross income recognized in a particular year under the percentage-of-completion method equals total revenue expected from the contract times the cumulative percentage of the contract completed as of the end of the tax year, less the total cumulative amount of contract revenue required to be included in gross income in all preceding tax years. (This can result in a deductible loss for a year if total estimated contract costs increase.) (Reg § 1.460-4(b)(2))[6]

If the total contract price has not been included in gross income by the completion year,

50. ¶G-3143 *et seq.*; ¶s 4514.132, 4604
1. ¶G-3150; ¶s 4514.132, 4604
2. ¶G-3154 *et seq.*; ¶4604
3. ¶G-3138; ¶4604

4. ¶G-3209 *et seq.*; ¶4604
5. ¶G-3143; ¶4604
6. ¶G-3126 *et seq.*; ¶4604

the taxpayer must include the remaining portion of the total contract price in gross income for the following tax year. (Reg § 1.460-4(b)(3))

When the contract is completed (or, for amounts received or accrued after completion, when those amounts are received or accrued), the taxpayer must either pay (or be entitled to receive) interest computed under the look-back method discussed at ¶2849. (Code Sec. 460(b)(1)(B))[7]

Small construction contract exception. The percentage-of-completion method is generally not required to be used for real estate construction or improvement contracts if (1) the estimated time of contract's completion when the contract is entered into is within two years of its start, and (2) the taxpayer's average annual gross receipts for the previous three tax years was not more than $25 million for 2018 ($26 million for 2019, as calculated by Thomson Reuters using inflation data; see ¶2818); $10 million for contracts entered into before 2018). This exception is not available to tax shelters prohibited from using the cash method of accounting. (Code Sec. 460(e)(1)(B))[8]

¶ 2848　　Modified percentage-of-completion method—"the 10% method."

For purposes of the percentage-of-completion method (¶2847), a taxpayer may elect not to recognize income under the contract and not to take into account any costs allocable to the long-term contract for any tax year if, as of the end of the tax year, less than 10% of the estimated total contract costs have been incurred. (Code Sec. 460(b)(5)) Elect by using the 10% method for all long-term contracts entered into during the tax year on the original federal income tax return for the election year. If elected, the method is used to apply the look-back method (¶2849) and to determine alternative minimum taxable income. It can't be used if the simplified cost-to-cost method (¶2846) is used. (Reg § 1.460-4(b)(6)(ii))[9]

¶ 2849　　Look-back method for interest on tax—Form 8697.

In the tax year a long-term contract (with exceptions, below) is completed, the taxpayer must compare the amount of taxes paid in previous years under the percentage method with the tax that would have been owed if actual, rather than anticipated, costs and contract price had been used to compute gross income. Interest at the "adjusted overpayment rate" (overpayment rate (¶4856) for the calendar quarter in which the "interest accrual period" begins) for any "interest accrual period" (period beginning the day after the return due date, without extensions, and ending on the return due date of the following tax year) is owed by or payable to the taxpayer (use Form 8697) if there is, respectively, an underpayment or overpayment for any tax year. (Code Sec. 460(b)(2), Code Sec. 460(b)(7))[10] For pass-through entities, see ¶2850.

Taxpayers may elect (for all contracts completed in the election year and all future years, revocable only with IRS consent) not to apply the look-back method if, at the close of each contract year before the tax year in which the look-back method would otherwise have to be applied, the cumulative taxable income (or loss) under the contract (using estimated contract price and costs) is within 10% of the cumulative look-back income or loss under the contract. (Code Sec. 460(b)(6)) Elect by attaching a statement to a timely filed (including extensions) original return for the election year. (Reg § 1.460-6(j))[11]

The look-back method doesn't apply to any contract whose gross price (at completion) doesn't exceed the lesser of $1 million or 1% of taxpayer's average annual gross receipts for the three tax years preceding the tax year the contract was completed if the contract is completed within two years of its start date. (Code Sec. 460(b)(3)(B))[12] Nor does it apply to

---

7. ¶G-3156; ¶4604
8. ¶G-3210; ¶4604.12
9. ¶G-3229 *et seq.*; ¶4604

10. ¶G-3161 *et seq.*; ¶4604
11. ¶G-3203.1; ¶4604
12. ¶G-3158; ¶4604

home construction contracts or others described at ¶2845. (Reg § 1.460-6(b)(2))[13]

¶ 2850   Simplified look-back marginal-impact method for pass-through entities.

For partnerships, S corporations and trusts (that aren't 50% or more held directly or indirectly by five or fewer persons), a simplified look-back marginal-impact method is applied at the entity level if substantially all the income from the contract is U.S.-source. The amount of taxes treated as overpaid or underpaid under a contract in any year is found by multiplying the amount of contract income over- or under-reported for the year by the top marginal tax rate applicable for the year. (Code Sec. 460(b)(4); Reg § 1.460-6(d)(1))[14] Individuals, C corporations and owners of closely-held pass-through entities may elect to use this method. Also, widely-held pass-through entities may use it for foreign contracts. (Reg § 1.460-6(d)(4))[15]

¶ 2851   Long-term contract following mid-contract change in taxpayer.

The tax treatment following a mid-contract change in taxpayer of a long-term contract depends on whether the change is a "constructive completion transaction" or a "step-in-the-shoes transaction." In a constructive completion transaction, the old taxpayer is treated as completing the contract and the new taxpayer as entering into a new contract on the transaction date. This approach applies to any transaction not subject to the step-in-the-shoes approach. (Reg § 1.460-4(k)(2)) In general, with a step-in-the-shoes transaction, the old taxpayer's obligation to account for the contract terminates on the transaction date and is assumed by the new taxpayer. The new taxpayer assumes the old taxpayer's methods of accounting for the contract, with both the contract price and allocable contract costs based on amounts taken into account by both parties. Special rules apply to the treatment of certain partnership transactions. (Reg § 1.460-4(k), Reg § 1.460-6(g))[16]

¶ 2852   Reconstruction of Income by IRS. ▪▪▪▪▪▪▪▪▪▪▪▪▪▪▪▪

Where taxpayer's records are inadequate, IRS can reconstruct taxpayer's income by whatever method will in its opinion most clearly reflect income.

The methods most often used are:

The net worth method. Here, IRS attempts to establish an opening net worth or total value of the taxpayer's assets at the beginning of a given year. It then proves increases in the taxpayer's net worth for each later year during the period under examination and calculates the difference between the adjusted net values of the taxpayer's assets at the beginning and end of each of the years involved. The taxpayer's nondeductible expenditures, including living expenses, are added to these increases. If the resulting figure for any year is substantially greater than the taxable income reported by the taxpayer for that year, IRS treats the excess as unreported taxable income. [17]

Bank deposit method. The bank deposit method assumes that all deposits represent income unless the taxpayer can show otherwise. [18]

Percentage markup method. IRS determines taxpayer's net income by applying certain percentages, e.g., gross profit to sales, or net income to gross income, or net income to sales, derived from other taxpayers in the same kind of business. [19]

---

13. ¶G-3159
14. ¶G-3195 *et seq.*; ¶4604
15. ¶G-3201; ¶4604
16. ¶G-3246; ¶4604.04

17. ¶G-2912; ¶s 4464.41, 4464.42
18. ¶G-2941; ¶s 4464.41, 4464.67
19. ¶G-2948; ¶s 4464.41, 4464.76

¶ 2853   Reallocations of Income by IRS. ■■■■■■■■■■■■

IRS is authorized (under Code Sec. 482) to distribute, apportion, or allocate gross income, deductions, credits or allowances among two or more organizations, trades, or businesses owned or controlled by the same interests in order to prevent tax evasion or to reflect the true taxable income of any of those entities. A similar rule also allows IRS to reallocate tax items (under Code Sec. 269A) for a personal service corporation.

IRS can reallocate income under Code Sec. 482 regardless of the entities' *motives* for shifting it, and can reallocate even if the shift was unintentional. (Reg § 1.482-1(c))[20]

If an allocation is made for a transaction between controlled taxpayers, IRS will also take into account the effect of any other non-arm's length transaction between the same controlled taxpayers in the same tax year which will result in a setoff against the original allocation. (Reg § 1.482-1(g)(4)(i)) Procedures have been issued for notifying IRS of a proposed setoff.[21]

The tax treatment of services transactions ensures that valuable intangibles cannot be transferred outside the U.S. for less than arm's length consideration, and update guidance on the transfer pricing methods to determine the arm's-length price in services transactions. (Reg § 1.482-9)[22]

Under advance pricing agreements (APAs) with IRS, taxpayers can prospectively determine and apply transfer pricing methodologies to international transactions by related foreign or domestic taxpayers (and resolve other related issues). [23]

¶ 2854   Reallocation of personal service corporation (PSC) income.

To prevent tax avoidance or evasion or to clearly reflect income, IRS may allocate all income, deductions, credits, exclusions and other allowances between a PSC and its employee-owner who owns more than 10% of the PSC stock (on any day in the tax year) if: substantially all of its services are performed by or for one other corporation, partnership, or entity (including related parties) and are availed of principally to avoid federal income tax by securing for any employee-owner significant tax benefits that he wouldn't otherwise have. (Code Sec. 269A(a))[24] A PSC is a corporation whose principal activity is the performance of personal services, substantially all of which are performed by employee-owners for one other corporation, partnership, or entity (including related parties). The Code Sec. 318 attribution rules apply for purposes of the 10% test, except that for purposes of applying the Code Sec. 318(a)(2)(C) rules, attribution is triggered by 5% rather than 50% stock ownership. (Code Sec. 269A(b)(2))[25]

¶ 2855   Deduction for Previously Reported Income Repayments. ■■■■■■■■

Taxpayers who must repay amounts previously reported as income may deduct the repayments in the year they are made. [26] If the amount repaid exceeds $3,000, the taxpayer may recover the tax paid on that amount in the year the income was reported if that provides a greater tax benefit (¶2856).

For a cash basis taxpayer, the year of the deduction, and accordingly the year the special computation might be available, is the year the previously reported income was repaid. If the taxpayer reported the income as constructively received, the year of deduction is the year the taxpayer's claim to the income had to be relinquished. (Reg § 1.1341-1(e))[27]

20. ¶G-4018; ¶4824
21. ¶G-4108; ¶4824.08
22. ¶G-4200; ¶G-4500; ¶4824.04, ¶4824.06
23. ¶G-4700 *et seq.*; ¶4824.07
24. ¶G-4751; ¶269A4
25. ¶G-4766; ¶269A4
26. ¶G-3001; ¶13,414
27. ¶G-3027; ¶13,414.01

For an accrual basis taxpayer, the deduction year is the year liability for repayment becomes fixed. If the taxpayer received the income reported, the deduction year is the year it's finally established the taxpayer had no unrestricted right to it. (Reg § 1.1341-1(e))[28]

¶ 2856 Repayments that exceed $3,000.

If the amount of the deduction allowed for a tax year (¶2855) with respect to an item reported as income in an earlier tax year is more than $3,000, and:

. . . that item was included in gross income in the earlier year because it appeared that the taxpayer then had an unrestricted right to it, and

. . . the deduction is allowed because it was shown after the close of the earlier year that taxpayer did *not* have an unrestricted right to all or part of that item,

then the tax for the year in which the deduction is allowed is the lesser of:

(1) the tax for that year computed with the deduction, or

(2) the tax for that year computed *without the deduction,* minus the decrease in tax for the earlier year resulting solely from excluding the deductible repayment. (Code Sec. 1341(a))

This relief for repayments exceeding $3,000 doesn't apply:

. . . where repayment is required because of a liability that arose later, as distinguished from absence of an unrestricted right to the income previously reported; [29]

. . . where an item was originally included in gross income by reason of the sale or other disposition of stock-in-trade, or other property includible in inventory if on hand at close of the earlier tax year, or property held primarily for sale to customers in the ordinary course of business—i.e., it doesn't apply to sales returns and allowances and similar items (Code Sec. 1341(b)(2); Reg § 1.1341-1(f));

. . . to deductions attributable to bad debts or to legal fees and other expenses incurred in contesting the repayment of income previously included. (Reg § 1.1341-1(g), Reg § 1.1341-1(h))[30]

¶ 2857 Inventories. ▄▄▄▄▄▄▄▄▄▄

Where producing, buying or selling merchandise is an income-producing factor, inventories are needed to determine the correct cost of goods sold, subject to a major exception for small businesses.

Inventories serve to allocate the expense of buying merchandise to the year in which that merchandise is sold. [31] They must be used whenever IRS finds their use is needed to clearly determine a taxpayer's income. (Code Sec. 471) Generally, this is the case where the "production, purchase or sale of merchandise" is an income-producing factor. (Reg § 1.471-1)[32] A taxpayer that must use inventories also must use the accrual method of accounting for its purchases and sales. (Reg § 1.446-1)[33] Taxpayers (other than tax shelters prohibited from using the cash method) that meet a 3-year-average $25 million gross receipts test for their 2018 tax year ($26 million for 2019, as calculated by Thomson Reuters using inflation data) are exempted from the inventory-use requirement (Code Sec. 471(c)) provided their method of accounting either (1) treats inventory as non-incidental materials and supplies, or (2) conforms to the taxpayer's financial accounting treatment of inventories (Code Sec. 471(c)(1)(B)) (see ¶2818 for details and conditions, and the less

28. ¶G-3028; ¶13,414.01
29. ¶G-2308; ¶13,414
30. ¶s G-3032, G-3034, G-3035; ¶13,414.01

31. ¶G-5000 *et seq.*; ¶4714
32. ¶G-5001; ¶4714
33. ¶G-2089; ¶4464.07

generous prior-law exceptions).[34] Until it releases further guidance, IRS will not assert that construction contractors engaged in paving, painting, roofing, drywall and landscaping must maintain inventory accounts for their supplies.[35]

⚫*caution:* Under the uniform inventory inclusion and capitalization rules (¶1640 *et seq.*), certain direct and indirect costs are either included in inventory or capitalized.

¶ 2858   What goods are included in inventory?

Inventories include all merchandise that is held for sale in the ordinary course of business or that is to become a physical part of merchandise intended for sale. Inventories generally cover finished or partly finished goods as well as raw materials and supplies acquired for sale or that will physically become a part of merchandise intended for sale. For items to be included in inventory, taxpayer must have title. (Reg § 1.471-1)[36] Prescription drugs and similar items administered by healthcare providers are not merchandise. [37]

Merchandise shipped on approval or sold on sample is kept in the seller's inventory until its acceptance. Consigned goods or goods in the hands of others for processing (e.g., dyeing) and returnable in kind are kept in the consignor's inventory. A seller's inventory includes goods he has contracted to sell but not yet segregated and applied to the contract, while a buyer's inventory includes merchandise in transit to him or that for other reasons hasn't been reduced to possession but to which he has title. But a buyer does *not* include in inventory goods ordered for future delivery.[38]

Containers that are to be *sold* with the merchandise they contain should be included in the seller's inventory, regardless of whether they are returnable. If the containers are merely leased or loaned with a deposit received to guarantee their return, they aren't included in inventory since they aren't part of the merchandise held for sale. In that case they can be inventoried at cost the same as supplies, considered as fixed assets and depreciated, or, if they have a useful life of less than a year, currently deducted. [39]

¶ 2859   Valuing inventory.

The two most commonly recognized bases of valuing inventories are: (1) cost, and (2) the lower of cost or market. (Reg § 1.471-2(c))[40] Farmers may use other valuation methods, see ¶4513 *et seq.* For inventories of dealers in securities, see ¶2873. Consistency from year to year in whatever inventory procedure is adopted is of first importance. (Reg § 1.471-2(b))[41]

¶ 2860   Valuation of unsalable, slow-moving and traded-in goods.

Any goods in inventory that are unsalable at normal prices or in the normal way because of damage, imperfections, style changes, etc., can at the taxpayer's option be written down—that is, valued at selling prices less direct costs of disposition —whether the cost or the lower of cost or market method is used. If the goods consist of raw materials or partly finished goods held for use or consumption, they must be valued upon a reasonable basis, considering the usability and condition of the goods, but in no case at less than scrap value. (Reg § 1.471-2(c))[42] Selling price means the actual price at which goods are offered for sale during a period ending not later than 30 days after the date of inventory. (Reg § 1.472-2(c))[43] Normal but slow-moving inventory (i.e., goods in excess of current demand) can't be written down based on arbitrary cut-off time periods. [44]

---

34. ¶G-5004; ¶4714.05
35. ¶G-5001A
36. ¶G-5006 *et seq.*; ¶4714
37. ¶G-5001
38. ¶G-5009; ¶4714
39. ¶G-5010; ¶4714

40. ¶G-5101; ¶s 4714.21, 4714.41, 4714.51
41. ¶G-5002; ¶4714.21
42. ¶G-5159; ¶4714.35
43. ¶G-5161; ¶4714.35
44. ¶G-5164

¶ 2861 Prohibited valuation methods and practices.

The following aren't permitted in valuing inventory:

(1) Deducting from inventory a reserve for price changes or an estimated depreciation in the value of inventory (but for permissible estimates of inventory shrinkage, see ¶2862).

(2) Valuing work in process, or other parts of the inventory, at a nominal price or at less than its proper value.

(3) Omitting portions of the stock on hand.

(4) Using a constant price or nominal value for so-called normal quantity of material or goods in stock.

(5) Segregating indirect production costs into fixed and variable classifications and allocating only the variable costs to the cost of goods produced while treating fixed costs as currently deductible (the "direct cost" method).

(6) Treating all or substantially all indirect production costs (whether classified as fixed or variable) as currently deductible (the "prime cost" method). (Reg § 1.471-2(f))[45]

¶ 2862 Estimates of inventory shrinkage.

A method of determining inventories doesn't fail to clearly reflect income solely because it uses estimates of inventory shrinkage that are confirmed by a physical count only after the last day of the tax year if the taxpayer: (1) normally does a physical count at each location on a regular and consistent basis, and (2) makes proper adjustments to inventories and to its estimating methods if estimates are greater or less than actual shrinkage. (Code Sec. 471(b)) Use the automatic consent procedure (¶2842), with some modifications, to change to the retail safe harbor method of estimating inventory shrinkage (using a historical ratio of shrinkage-to-sales to estimate shrinkage occurring between the last physical inventory and the end of the tax year), or to a method that clearly reflects income other than the retail safe harbor method if the method being changed from didn't estimate inventory shrinkage. [46]

¶ 2863 What is inventory cost?

The cost of goods on hand at the start of an accounting period is the amount at which they were valued in the closing inventory of the period before. (Reg § 1.471-3(a))[47]

The cost of the goods purchased ordinarily is the invoice price reduced by trade or other discounts. Strictly cash discounts approximating a fair interest rate may be deducted at the option of the taxpayer if the method is consistently followed. (Reg § 1.471-3(b))[48] To this net invoice price should be added transportation or other necessary charges incurred in acquiring possession of the goods. (Reg § 1.471-3(b))[49]

The costs of goods produced by the taxpayer include, in addition to the opening inventory, costs of raw materials and supplies entering into or consumed in manufacture, regular and overtime direct labor costs, and the indirect costs required to be included under the "full absorption" method. (Reg § 1.471-3(c))[50]

For the uniform capitalization rules for including costs in inventory, see ¶1640 *et seq.*

---

45. ¶G-5124; ¶4714.21
46. ¶G-5120.1; ¶4714.38
47. ¶G-5102; ¶4714.41

48. ¶G-5107, G-5108; ¶4714.41
49. ¶G-5103, G-5110; ¶4714.41
50. ¶s G-5102 *et seq.*, G-5402; ¶4714.41

¶ 2864   Valuing inventory using the lower of cost or market method.

Under this method, market value on the inventory date is compared with the cost of each item. The lower of the two is the inventory value of the item. Total inventory is the aggregate of the inventory values so computed for each item in the inventory. It is *not* the lower of the total cost or total market value of all items. (Reg § 1.471-4(c))[1]

¶ 2865   Market value defined.

Market value normally means the current bid price prevailing at the inventory date for the particular merchandise in the volume usually purchased by the taxpayer. Market price is applied to: (1) goods purchased and on hand, and (2) the basic elements of cost (materials, labor and overhead) of goods in process of manufacture and of finished goods on hand. (Reg § 1.471-4(a))[2]

Market price may not be applied to goods on hand or in process if the merchandise is covered by a firm sales contract at fixed prices (i.e., not legally subject to cancellation by either buyer or seller). If, under the contract, the taxpayer is protected against actual loss, the goods must be inventoried at cost with no deduction for inventory decline. (Reg § 1.471-4(a)) Moreover, goods covered by firm sales contracts at the end of the year must be valued at cost even though the contracts are cancelled after the close of the year at the customer's request.[3] If the contract gives the seller an almost certain loss, IRS says the seller isn't allowed to write the inventory down but must value it at cost, thus taking the loss when actually realized (Reg § 1.471-4(a)), but some courts disagree.[4]

A taxpayer may write down inventory below market if, in the regular course of business, he has offered the merchandise for sale at below-market prices. (Reg § 1.471-4(b))

If no market exists, or if quotations are nominal because of an inactive market, the taxpayer must use whatever evidence of a fair market price at the date or dates nearest his inventory date as may be available, e.g., specific purchases and sales made by the taxpayer or others in reasonable volume and in good faith, or compensation paid for cancellation of contracts for purchase commitments. (Reg § 1.471-4(b))[5]

¶ 2866   Inventory cost identification methods.

Under the specific identification method, goods are matched with their invoices (less appropriate discounts) to find the cost of each item.[6]

Where it isn't possible or practicable to identify each item of inventory with its cost, an assumption must be made to determine which items were sold and which remain in inventory. Although only two methods of costing intermingled merchandise are specifically approved (the "first-in, first-out" (FIFO) and the "last-in, first-out" (LIFO) methods, ¶2867), any method that comes within the best accounting practice of the particular business and clearly reflects income is acceptable. Two permissible cost identification methods are averaging the cost of each type or grade of goods in the inventory (¶2869), and mainly relying on the taxpayer's accounting records to arrive at the correct inventory value (¶2871). The base stock method (the assumption that a certain portion of inventory will be maintained from year to year and therefore need not be revalued) isn't permitted.[7]

The inventory price index computation (IPIC) method, under which inventory price indexes are computed with reference to consumer or producer price indexes published by

---

1. ¶G-5150; ¶4714.51
2. ¶G-5151; ¶4714.51
3. ¶G-5154 *et seq.*; ¶4714.51
4. ¶G-5154 *et seq.*; ¶4714.51

5. ¶G-5157; ¶4714.51
6. ¶s G-5121, G-5265; ¶4714.41
7. ¶G-5125 *et seq.*; ¶4714.41

the U.S. Bureau of Labor Statistics (BLS) (Code Sec. 472(f); Reg § 1.472-8(e)(3)), is intended to simplify the use of the dollar-value LIFO method (¶2869).[8]

¶ 2867 FIFO (first-in, first-out) and LIFO (last-in, first-out) methods.

Under the FIFO method, the cost of goods that are so intermingled they cannot be identified with specific invoices is considered to be the cost of goods most recently purchased or produced. (Reg § 1.471-2(d))[9]

Under the LIFO method of inventory valuation, the most recently purchased merchandise is treated as the first sold. (Code Sec. 472(b)(1))[10] LIFO may generally be used only where inventory is valued at cost. (Reg § 1.472-2(b))[11] If a taxpayer had written down inventory to a lower market value, the difference between that value and cost must be restored to income ratably over a 3-year period (beginning with the year of the election to LIFO). (Code Sec. 472(d))[12]

In order to use LIFO for tax purposes, the enterprise must also use LIFO in its reports to partners, stockholders, etc., and for credit purposes. (Code Sec. 472(c))[13]

Qualifying heavy equipment dealers using LIFO or FIFO may, like auto dealers, use replacement cost to determine the cost of their heavy parts inventory under safe harbor rules.[14]

¶ 2868 Electing last-in, first-out (LIFO)—Form 970.

File Form 970 (or other acceptable statement) with the return for the tax year as of the close of which LIFO is first to be used (Reg § 1.472-3)[15] or re-elected in the fifth or later tax year after changing from LIFO (otherwise IRS permission is needed for the change, see ¶2835 *et seq.*) Once made, the election applies to all later years unless IRS grants permission to change. (Reg § 1.472-5)[16] Automatic consent procedures (¶2842) apply to adoption of certain specialized LIFO methods and to changes from LIFO.

¶ 2869 Dollar-value last-in, first-out (LIFO) and simplified dollar-value LIFO.

Under this method, a taxpayer who deals in a large variety of products may value inventory by the use of the dollar value rather than natural units. The assumption is that items in the inventory are homogeneous. The taxpayer is therefore required to break up the inventory into a series of "pools" —the natural business unit pool or multiple pools. (Reg § 1.472-8)[17] Any taxpayer electing to use the dollar-value LIFO method can elect to compute an inventory price index in accordance with the Inventory Price Index Computation method (Reg § 1.472-8(e)(3)(ii), see ¶2866.

An eligible small business may elect to use a simplified dollar-value method of pricing inventories for purposes of the LIFO method. Under this method, the cost of each grade of goods is averaged. (Code Sec. 474(a)) An eligible small business is one whose average annual gross receipts don't exceed $5 million for the 3-tax-year period ending immediately before the tax year. (Code Sec. 474(c))[18]

8. ¶G-5253; ¶4724
9. ¶G-5121; ¶4714.41
10. ¶G-5200; ¶4724
11. ¶G-5212; ¶4724
12. ¶G-5208; ¶4724
13. ¶G-5307; ¶4724

14. ¶G-5248.4
15. ¶G-5202; ¶4724
16. ¶G-5201; ¶4724
17. ¶G-5245 *et seq.*; ¶4724
18. ¶G-5302 *et seq.*; ¶4744

¶ 2870   Retailers' inventory.

Retailers can convert the retail selling price of ending inventory to an approximation of cost (retail cost method) or an approximation of lower of cost or market (retail LCM method). (Reg § 1.471-8(a))[19] Price change adjustments are determined by reference generally to U.S. Bureau of Labor Statistics price indexes. (Reg § 1.472-1(k))[20]

¶ 2871   Book (perpetual) inventory method.

Under this method, inventory accounts are charged with the actual cost of goods purchased or produced, and credited with the cost of goods used, transferred or sold. The net amount is considered to be the cost of the goods on hand, if the balances shown on the books are adjusted at reasonable intervals to conform to physical inventories. (Reg § 1.471-2(d))[21]

¶ 2872   Miners' and manufacturers' inventory.

Miners and manufacturers who use a single process or uniform series of processes, and derive a product of two or more kinds, sizes or grades with a unit cost substantially alike, may allocate a share of total cost to each kind, size or grade as a basis for pricing inventories. (Reg § 1.471-7)[22]

¶ 2873   Securities and commodities dealers' inventories—mark-to-market rules.

Any security that's inventory in the hands of a securities dealer must be included in inventory at its fair market value (FMV). (Code Sec. 475(a)(1)) In the case of a non-inventory security that's held at the close of a tax year, the dealer must recognize gain or loss as if the security were sold for its FMV on the last business day of that year, and any gain or loss must be taken into account for that tax year, generally as ordinary income or loss. (Code Sec. 475(a)(2), Code Sec. 475(d)(3)) For this purpose, FMV cannot be less than the amount of nonrecourse debt to which the property is subject. [23] A "security" doesn't include any security held for investment, certain other securities, and hedges of those securities (but only if the hedge is clearly identified as a hedge in the dealer's records before the close of the business day on which it was acquired, originated or entered into). (Code Sec. 475(b))[24] A security also doesn't include nonfinancial customer paper arising from the sale of nonfinancial goods or services by sellers or providers of those goods or services that are held by them (or related parties) at all times since issue. (Code Sec. 475(c)(4))[25] Commodities dealers may elect (under interim procedures [26]) to apply the mark-to-market rules to commodities held by them in the same way that the rules apply to securities held by securities dealers. (Code Sec. 475(e)(1)) Once made, the election may be revoked only with IRS consent. (Code Sec. 475(e)(3))[27] Where the Code Sec. 475 rules don't apply, a securities dealer inventories securities at: (1) cost, (2) lower of cost or market, or (3) market value. (Reg § 1.471-5)[28]

A dealer is one who regularly buys and sells securities to customers (or enters into or terminates positions in securities with customers) in the ordinary course of business. (Code Sec. 475(c)(1))[29] If one's sole business is trading in securities he's not a dealer [30] (but for the mark-to-market election by traders, see ¶2874).

19. ¶G-5351; ¶4724.06
20. ¶G-5362; ¶4724.06
21. ¶G-5119; ¶4714.21
22. ¶G-5020; ¶4714.85
23. ¶I-7652; ¶4754
24. ¶I-7657 *et seq.*; ¶4754

25. ¶I-7657.1; ¶4754
26. ¶I-7669; ¶4754.02
27. ¶I-7667 *et seq.*; ¶4754.01
28. ¶G-5021; ¶s 4754, 4714.67
29. ¶G-5023; ¶4754
30. ¶I-7656.1; ¶4754

¶ 2874   Mark-to-market election for securities and commodities traders.

A securities or commodities trader may elect [31] to have these mark-to-market rules apply to the trade or business: (1) gain or loss is recognized on any security (or commodity) held in connection with the business at the close of any tax year as if it were sold for its fair market value on the last business day of the tax year, and (2) gain or loss is taken into account (Code Sec. 475(f)(1)(A), Code Sec. 475(f)(2)) as ordinary income or loss. Once made, the election may be revoked only with IRS consent. (Code Sec. 475(f)(3)) These rules don't apply to securities or commodities that have no connection to the electing person's trading activities if they are clearly identified as such before the close of the day acquired. (Code Sec. 475(f)(1)(B)) Securities and commodities subject to this election aren't subject to the constructive sale rules of Code Sec. 1259 (¶2627). (Code Sec. 475(f)(1)(C))[32]

¶ 2875   Changing inventory method—Form 3115.

A change in the method of valuing inventory, except a change to LIFO (¶2868) and certain specialized LIFO methods (¶2842), requires IRS approval. This includes adoption of either: (1) cost, or (2) cost or market, whichever is lower, where the taxpayer has been on a different basis, and changes to and from the various methods of determining inventory costs. Use Form 3115, under the rules at ¶2837. (Reg § 1.446-1(e))[33] An automatic consent procedure also applies for certain taxpayers changing *from* LIFO (¶2842).[34]

---

31. ¶I-7675; ¶4754.02
32. ¶I-7670 *et seq.*; ¶4754.01

33. ¶G-2101 *et seq.*, ¶G-5201 *et seq.*; ¶4464.21
34. ¶G-5217 *et seq.*; ¶s 263A4.10, 4464.21, 4724

Chapter 12   Withholding Tax on Wages and Other Income Payments

¶ 3000   Withholding on Wages.

Employers must withhold income tax from wages paid to employees (¶3003), but not from amounts paid to independent contractors (¶3004). "Wages" include most forms of taxable compensation (¶3005 *et seq.*). Employees are entitled to minimum, and sometimes additional (¶3017), withholding exemptions or allowances. Withheld tax must be paid through electronic funds transfers.

Businesses can shift their withholding responsibilities to IRS-certified professional employer organizations (PEOs), see ¶3002.

For withholding on certain federal payments (e.g., social security payments), see ¶3010. For other nonpayroll withholding, see ¶3032. For withholding from U.S. source amounts paid to nonresident aliens and foreign corporations, see ¶4648.

¶ 3001   Withholding by employers.

Employers must withhold. (Code Sec. 3402(a)(1); Reg § 31.3402(a)-1(b))[1] An employer is any person or organization for whom an individual performs any service as an employee. (Code Sec. 3401(d)) An employer includes any person paying wages to a former employee, (Reg § 31.3401(d)-1(b)) and includes tax-exempt organizations. (Reg § 31.3401(d)-1(d))[2] Employers who outsource some or all of their payroll responsibilities remain liable for all taxes, penalties and interest due. [3]

If the actual employer doesn't have control over the payment of wages, the person who does have control must withhold. (Code Sec. 3401(d)(1)) A lender, surety or other person is personally liable for the employee income tax required to be withheld if he or she: (1) directly pays wages to another's employees (Code Sec. 3505(a)), or (2) supplies funds specifically for the payment of the wages of another's employees knowing the employer can't or doesn't intend to pay payroll taxes. In the case of (2), liability is limited to 25% of the amount supplied (inclusive of interest). (Code Sec. 3505(b); Reg § 31.3505-1(b))

For professional employer organizations taking on the responsibilities of an employer, with respect to wages paid for services performed by an employee, see ¶3002.

A disregarded single-owner entity is treated as a separate entity (i.e., as a corporation) for purposes of employment taxes and related reporting requirements. (Reg § 1.1361-4(a)(7), Reg § 301.7701-2(c)(2)) An owner of a disregarded entity treated as a sole proprietorship is subject to self-employment taxes. (Reg § 301.7701-2(c)(2)) Similarly, partners in a partnership that owns a disregarded entity aren't employees of the disregarded entity for employment tax purposes and are, instead, subject to self-employment taxes. (Reg § 301.7701-2T)[4]

If a person pays wages on behalf of a nonresident employer not engaged in trade or business in the U.S., that person must withhold. (Code Sec. 3401(d)(2))[5]

¶ 3002   Professional employer organizations (PEOs).

Small businesses often contract with a PEO, also known as an employee leasing company, to ensure compliance with workplace laws and regulations. A PEO may compute

---

1. ¶H-4222; ¶34,024
2. ¶H-4226; ¶34,014.60
3. ¶V-1664
4. ¶D-1531; ¶D-1165
5. ¶H-4229.2; ¶34,014.60

References beginning with a single letter are to paragraphs in Federal Tax Coordinator 2d and RIA's Analysis of Federal Taxes: Income. Those beginning with numbers are to paragraphs in United States Tax Reporter.

each employee's social security tax, withholding tax, worker's compensation, and 401(k) contributions, pay the employees, make the customer's tax deposits and/or file the customer's employment tax returns.

When an employer contracts with a PEO to make withholding tax payments, the employer might still be liable for making the payments if the PEO fails to. [6]

An IRS-certified professional PEO (CPEO) is treated as the employer of any "work site employee" performing services for any customer of the CPEO, but only for remuneration paid by the CPEO to that work site employee. (Code Sec. 3511(a)(1)) For purposes of employment taxes, a CPEO is treated as the employer of any "covered employee" (generally, any individual other than a self-employed individual who performs services for the customer and who's covered by a CPEO contract between the CPEO and the customer), whether or not a work site employee, but only for remuneration paid by the CPEO to that covered employee. (Prop Reg. § 31.3511-1(a)(1) "Taxpayers may rely") [7]

To be a CPEO, a PEO has to satisfy various requirements intended to ensure that the PEO properly remits wages and employment taxes. (Code Sec. 7705)[8] The PEO is also subject to an annual fee of $1,000. (Code Sec. 7528(b)(4))[9]

¶ 3003   Employees defined.

Every individual who performs services subject to the will and control of an employer, both as to what is to be done and how it's to be done, is an employee for withholding purposes. It doesn't matter that the employee has considerable discretion and freedom of action, so long as the employer has the *legal right* to control both the method and the result of the services. (Reg § 31.3401(c)-1(b)) For how IRS determines whether a worker is an employee or independent contractor, see ¶3004.

It doesn't matter that the employee is designated a partner, agent or independent contractor, or how payments are measured or paid or what they're called. (Reg § 31.3401(c)-1(e))[10]

No distinction is made between classes of employees. Managers and other supervisory personnel are employees. An officer of a corporation is an employee (Code Sec. 3401(c)), but a director in his capacity as director isn't an employee. (Reg § 31.3401(c)-1(f))[11]

Persons in business for themselves aren't employees. For example, self-employed physicians, lawyers, dentists, veterinarians, construction contractors and others who offer their services to the public aren't employees. (Reg § 31.3401(c)-1(c))[12]

Qualified real estate agents and direct sellers are treated as independent contractors. (Code Sec. 3508(a))[13]

Statutory employees, such as certain drivers, life insurance salespersons, home workers, and other salespersons, who are treated as employees for FICA purposes (Code Sec. 3121(d)(3)) but aren't common law employees, aren't employees for income tax purposes.[14]

observation: A person not treated as an employee for income tax purposes can't be covered under employee plans, e.g., medical reimbursement and group-term life insurance plans.

If payment is made for services rendered and the payor isn't sure whether the payee is an employee or independent contractor, the payor may get an IRS ruling by filing Form

---

6. ¶H-4229.3
7. ¶H-4861; ¶35,114
8. ¶H-4864; ¶H-4869; ¶77,054
9. ¶T-10002
10. ¶H-4251; ¶34,014.37

11. ¶H-4252; ¶s 34,014.39, 34,014.40
12. ¶H-4258; ¶34,014.47, 34,014.48, 34,014.50, 34,014.61
13. ¶H-4283; ¶34,014.37
14. ¶H-4559; ¶624.03

SS-8.[15] Adverse rulings can be reviewed by the Tax Court (Code Sec. 7436) after IRS sends an adverse notice of determination.[16]

Employees who have been misclassified as independent contractors by an employer use Form 8919 to figure and report the employee's share of uncollected Social Security and Medicare taxes due on their compensation. The worker performing the services must meet one of several criteria supporting his belief that he's an employee, e.g., receipt of an SS-8 determination letter.[17]

¶ 3004 How IRS determines employee or independent contractor status.

To determine whether a worker is an independent contractor or an employee, IRS examines the relationship between the worker and the business, and considers all evidence of control and independence. The facts that provide this evidence fall into the following three categories:

(1) *Behavioral control* covers facts that show whether the business has a right to direct and control how the work is done through instructions, training, or other means. Employees are generally given instructions on when and where to work, what tools to use, where to purchase supplies, what order to follow, etc.

(2) *Financial control* covers facts that show whether the business has a right to control the financial and business aspects of the worker's job. This includes the extent to which the worker has unreimbursed business expenses; the extent of his investment in the facilities being used; the extent to which he makes his services available to the relevant market; how he's paid; and the extent to which he can realize a profit or incur a loss.

(3) *Type of relationship* includes written contracts describing the relationship the parties intended to create; the extent to which the worker is available to perform services for other, similar businesses; whether the business provides the worker with employee-type benefits, such as insurance, a pension plan, vacation pay, or sick pay; the permanency of the relationship; and the extent to which services performed by the worker are a key aspect of the company's regular business.

IRS's 3-category approach essentially distills the 20-factor test IRS had used to determine whether a worker was an employee or an independent contractor.[18]

A consultant can simultaneously be an employee and an independent contractor when working on two projects for the same company. IRS will separately examine the relationship between the worker and the business for each performance of services.[19]

In certain cases in which a taxpayer has a reasonable basis for treating an individual as a non-employee (e.g., judicial precedent, IRS ruling, past audit allowance), a special statutory rule (section 530 of the '78 Revenue Act) may allow non-employee treatment regardless of the above factors.[20]

A voluntary compliance program allows employers to prospectively reclassify — as employees — those workers they have erroneously treated as independent contractors. The program features settlement terms and provides audit relief for previous years. Eligible taxpayers apply by filing Form 8952, at least 60 days before they want to begin treating the workers as employees.[21]

---

15. ¶H-4282; ¶34,014.37
16. ¶U-2143; ¶74,364
17. ¶S-1709.1
18. ¶H-4259

19. ¶H-4258.1
20. ¶H-4303 *et seq.*; ¶34,014.375
21. ¶H-4282.1

¶ 3005   Wages subject to withholding.

"Wages" cover all types of employee compensation, including salaries, fees, bonuses, commissions and fringe benefits. It's immaterial whether payments are based on the hour, day, week, month, year or on a piecework or percentage plan, or whether they're called wages, salaries, fees, etc. (Code Sec. 3401(a); Reg § 31.3401(a)-1(a)(2), Reg § 31.3401(a)-1(a)(3))[22] Bonuses received for signing employment contracts are wages, as are payments received for canceling employment contracts. [23] Wages also include amounts includible in an employee's gross income for failure to comply with the Code Sec. 409A deferred compensation rules (¶1273). (Code Sec. 3401(a)) For withholding purposes they are treated as paid in the year they are includable in gross income. [24]

Noncash wages are the fair market value of the goods, lodging, meals or other consideration given for services. (Reg § 31.3401(a)-1(a)(4))[25]

Vacation allowances[26] and back pay, including retroactive wage increases, are wages. (Reg § 31.3401(a)-1(b)(3))[27] The Supreme Court has held that severance pay is subject to FICA tax.[28] An appellate court has ruled that an age discrimination settlement payment received by a taxpayer was wages. [29] Amounts received as "front pay" are wages subject to withholding, according to IRS, but some courts have disagreed. Front pay is an amount paid to an individual for pay he would have received after a settlement date or court award but for the employer's wrongful conduct and the circumstances — e.g., extreme animosity between the parties — that make it impractical to place the employee in the position. [30] IRS isn't bound by the settlement allocation of payments under a class action lawsuit and can instead convert portions of a settlement allocated to penalty and interest payments into wages subject to employment taxes. [31]

Supplemental unemployment compensation benefits are treated as wages for income tax purposes (Code Sec. 3402(o)(1)(A), Code Sec. 3402(o)(2)),[32] but they aren't subject to FICA if certain conditions are met. [33] Differential wage payments are also wages for income tax purposes and are treated as supplemental wage payments (¶3012). These are payments to employees for periods that they are called to active duty with the U.S. uniformed services (for more than 30 days) that represent all or part of the wages that they would otherwise received from the employer. (Code Sec. 3401(h)) They aren't subject to FICA and FUTA withholding.[34] "Short-week" benefits paid to workers who worked fewer than 36 hours in a week or who couldn't work due to weather are also treated as wages when certain conditions are met.[35]

Under Code Sec. 3401(i), withholding is required at the highest individual rate when stock subject to a Code Sec. 83(i) election (¶1216) is included in income. [36]

Withholding is computed on gross wages before any deductions by the employer for social security tax, pensions, union dues, insurance, etc. (Reg § 31.3401(a)-1(b)(5))[37]

Employers are required to withhold an additional 0.9% Medicare tax on wages (see ¶1108), and are liable for the tax that it fails to withhold from wages or collect from the employee. The obligation applies only to wages in excess of $200,000 that the employee receives from the employer. An employer isn't required to notify an employee when it begins withholding the additional tax, and should begin withholding in the pay period in

---

22. ¶H-4326; ¶34,014.01, 34,014.02, 34,014.09
23. ¶H-4360.2, ¶H-4361.1
24. ¶H-4326, ¶H-4333.1; ¶34,014.025
25. ¶H-4327; ¶34,014.09
26. ¶H-4364; ¶34,014.04
27. ¶H-4355; ¶34,014.09
28. ¶H-4664
29. ¶H-4355

30. ¶H-4360.1
31. ¶J-5810
32. ¶H-4351
33. ¶H-4664
34. ¶H-4372; ¶34,014.11
35. ¶H-4664
36. ¶H-4334
37. ¶H-4331

which it pays wages to the employee exceeding the $200,000 threshold and not earlier. If the $200,000 threshold is exceeded, the additional tax must be withheld even if the employee ultimately won't owe the tax because the taxpayer and spouse file a joint return and won't meet the $250,000 threshold for joint filers. The employer disregards any wages paid to the employee by another employer. Wages paid by two or more employers aren't combined to reach the threshold unless the payor is a common paymaster. IRS provides FAQs explaining employers' withholding obligations. [38]

¶ 3006 Tips.

Wages include tips. (Code Sec. 3401(f)) But, withholding isn't required on cash tips of less than $20 a month received by an employee, or for tips paid in any medium other than cash (such as passes, tickets or other goods or commodities). (Code Sec. 3401(a)(16); Reg § 31.3401(a)(16)-1) But, if cash tips amount to $20 or more in a month, none of the cash tips are exempt. The $20 test is applied separately with respect to cash tips received by the employee for his or her services to each employer. (Reg § 31.3401(a)(16)-1)[39] (For the business tax credit for employer FICA tax paid on tips for food and beverage service, see ¶2327.)

¶ 3007 Exempt "wages"—fringes, reimbursed expenses, domestic service, etc.

The following aren't wages subject to income tax withholding:

... Fringe benefits, if it's reasonable to believe that the employee will be able to exclude them from income as a qualified scholarship, a no-additional-cost service, a qualified employee discount, a working condition fringe, a de minimis fringe, a qualified transportation fringe, a qualified moving expense reimbursement, an on-premises athletic facility, or an employee achievement award. (Code Sec. 3401(a)(19))[40] (For the employer's election not to withhold on a vehicle fringe benefit, see ¶3008.)

... Amounts specifically advanced or reimbursed to employees for traveling or other ordinary and necessary expenses incurred or reasonably expected to be incurred in the employer's business. But they must be either paid separately, or specifically identified if combined with wages in a single payment. (Reg § 31.3401(a)-4(a)) If a reimbursement or other expense allowance arrangement meets the requirements of Code Sec. 62(c) (¶3104, i.e., an "accountable plan"), payments that don't exceed the substantiated expenses aren't wages and aren't subject to withholding. Payments that aren't substantiated within a reasonable period of time or are in excess of substantiated expenses are wages and subject to withholding. Per diem or mileage allowances at a rate in excess of the deemed substantiated amount are subject to withholding. If the arrangement doesn't meet the Code Sec. 62(c) requirements (i.e., a "nonaccountable plan"), all amounts paid are wages and subject to withholding. (Reg § 31.3401(a)-4(a), Reg § 31.3401(a)-4(b), Reg § 1.62-2(h)(1), Reg § 1.62-2(h)(2))[41]

... Moving expense reimbursements, if a corresponding deduction is allowable under the normal Code Sec. 217 rules (limited to members of the U.S. Armed Forces for 2018 – 2025), see ¶1627, (determined without regard to the Code Sec. 274(n) percentage limit on meal expenses). (Code Sec. 3401(a)(15))[42]

... Tips, under the circumstances at ¶3006.

... Benefits paid by a labor union to workers unemployed because of a strike or lockout. [43]

... Payments for agricultural labor except if during the year: (1) cash payments to an employee are $150 or more, or (2) the employer pays all such employees $2,500 or more

---

38. ¶H-4701.1; ¶31,114
39. ¶H-4341; ¶34,014.31
40. ¶H-4400 *et seq.*; ¶s 34,014.09, 34,024

41. ¶H-4340; ¶34,014.03
42. ¶H-4418; ¶34,014.30
43. ¶H-4354; ¶34,014.10

(unless the employee is a hand harvest laborer who is paid on a customary basis, commutes daily to the farm from his permanent residence and was employed in agriculture less than 13 weeks during the prior year). (Code Sec. 3401(a)(2), Code Sec. 3121(a)(8))[44]

. . . Payments for domestic service in a private home, local college club, or fraternity or sorority chapter. (Code Sec. 3401(a)(3))[45]

. . . Certain payments for services by a U.S. citizen for an employer outside the U.S. (Code Sec. 3401(a)(8)(A)(i))[46]

. . . Premiums paid by an employer for group term insurance on an employee's life. (Code Sec. 3401(a)(14))[47]

. . . Payments to or on behalf of an employee or his beneficiary to or from a qualified plan (except payments for services rendered by an employee of the plan) (Code Sec. 3401(a)(12)(A)); to or under a qualified annuity plan (Code Sec. 3401(a)(12)(B)); under a SIMPLE retirement account (Code Sec. 3401(a)(12)(D)); to or under a governmental section 457 plan (Code Sec. 3401(a)(12)(E)); or, if it's reasonable to believe the employee will be entitled to exclude the payment, for contributions to a simplified employee pension for an employee. (Code Sec. 3401(a)(12)(C))[48]

. . . Payments made under educational assistance or dependent care programs if it's reasonable to believe that the employee can exclude them. (Code Sec. 3401(a)(18))[49]

. . . Payment of deceased employee's accrued wages to his estate or beneficiaries. [50]

. . . Combat zone compensation excludible under Code Sec. 112. (Code Sec. 3401(a)(1))[1]

. . . Employer contributions to medical savings accounts. (Code Sec. 3401(a)(21), Code Sec. 3401(a)(22))[2]

. . . Qualified adoption expenses paid under an employer's adoption assistance program. [3]

. . . Disqualifying dispositions of stock acquired through the exercise of an incentive stock option or an option under an employee stock purchase plan (ESPP) (Code Sec. 421(b)) or with respect to any amount treated as compensation as a result of the ESPP discount option rule which treats a part of the gain on a disposition of stock acquired through the exercise of an option under an ESPP as compensation income if the option price at which the stock was acquired was between 85% and 100% of its fair market value at the time the option was granted. (Code Sec. 423(c))[4]

¶ 3008   Employer's election not to withhold on vehicle fringe benefit.

Employers may elect not to withhold on an employee's use of an employer-provided vehicle where that use is wages to the employee. The employer must notify the employee of the election and include the amount of the benefit on a timely furnished Form W-2. (Code Sec. 3402(s))[5]

¶ 3009   Withholding on sick pay—Form W-4S.

If the recipient of sick pay that isn't wages requests the payor (on Form W-4S) to withhold a specified amount of at least $20 from each payment, the payor must withhold that amount. (Code Sec. 3402(o)(1)(C); Reg § 31.3402(o)-3(b)) An employee doesn't have to request withholding if his employer makes the sick payments since employers are required

44. ¶H-4426; ¶34,014.18
45. ¶H-4450 *et seq.*; ¶34,014.19
46. ¶s H-4442, H-4443; ¶34,014.23
47. ¶H-1518 *et seq.*, ¶J-8548; ¶34,014.29
48. ¶H-10500 *et seq.*; ¶34,014.27
49. ¶H-4401; ¶34,014.05

50. ¶H-4350; ¶34,014.07
1. ¶H-4447; ¶34,014.17
2. ¶H-4326; ¶34,014.67
3. ¶H-1451
4. ¶H-4448.2
5. ¶s H-4411, H-4412; ¶34,024.27

to withhold income tax from sick pay. [6]

¶ 3010 Voluntary withholding agreements—Forms W-4 and W-4V.

Household workers, and other employees who aren't subject to income tax withholding, may elect to have tax withheld, if their employers agree. (Code Sec. 3402(p)) Other employees can also have their withholding increased voluntarily. (Code Sec. 3402(i))

The rules generally applicable to mandatory withholding, including withholding rates and tables, apply to the voluntary withholding. An employee requests voluntary withholding by filing a Form W-4 with his employer —unless he wants the voluntary withholding to apply for a *limited period of time*. In that case, he must also give the employer a statement that includes the date the voluntary withholding is to terminate.

A voluntary withholding agreement may be terminated by the employer or employee by giving advance notice to the other in accordance with the regs. (Reg § 31.3402(p)-1)[7]

A taxpayer can request voluntary withholding at a rate of 7%, 10%, 15%, or 25% on certain federal payments, including Social Security benefits, crop disaster payments, and Commodity Credit Corporation loans (Code Sec. 3402(p)(1)), and at a 10% rate on unemployment compensation payments (¶1279). (Code Sec. 3402(p)(2)) Use Form W-4V.[8]

¶ 3011 Fringe benefits.

Fringe benefits must be treated as paid at least annually. Except for transfers of either personal property of a kind normally held for investment or real property (which must be reported when they are actually paid), an employer may elect to treat fringe benefits as paid quarterly, semiannually, annually, or on another basis. An employer may also treat a fringe benefit as paid in installments, even if the entire benefit is paid at one time. Benefits provided in a calendar year must be treated as paid by Dec. 31 of that year. [9]

Employers may treat fringe benefits as part of regular wages for the payroll period and compute withholding on the total, or instead withhold 20% of the value of the benefit from regular wages. (Reg § 31.3501(a)-1T, Q&A-10) Any noncash fringe benefit provided in a calendar quarter may be treated as provided on the last day of that quarter. (Reg § 31.3501(a)-1T, Q&A-1)[10]

For when withholding isn't required on a presumptively tax-free fringe benefit, see ¶3007. For the election to not withhold on the value of a vehicle fringe benefit provided to the employee, see ¶3008.

¶ 3012 Supplemental wage payments.

Withholding on bonuses, commissions, overtime pay or other supplemental wages paid:

. . . *with regular wages*, should be determined as if the total supplemental and regular wages were a single payment for the regular payroll period; (Reg § 31.3402(g)-1(a))

. . . *at a different time*, can be determined by adding the supplemental wages either to the regular wages for the current payroll period or to the last preceding payroll period within the same calendar year; (Reg § 31.3402(g)-1(a))

. . . *where tax has been withheld on regular wages* , generally can be determined by using a flat rate of not less than 25% without allowance for exemptions and without reference to any regular wage payment. (Reg § 31.3402(g)-1(a)) Where tax has been withheld on

6. ¶H-4337; ¶H-4481 *et seq.*; ¶34,024.25
7. ¶H-4477 *et seq.*; ¶34,024.19
8. ¶H-4483 *et seq.*; ¶34,024.25
9. ¶H-4403; ¶34,024
10. ¶H-4404 *et seq.*; ¶s 34,024, 34,024.27

regular wages (during the calendar year of the payment or the preceding one), withholding generally can be determined (at the employer's option) by using a flat rate of 25% without allowance for exemptions and without reference to any regular wage payment, if the supplemental wages are either paid at a different time than the regular wages or are separately stated on the employer's payroll records. (Reg § 31.3402(g)-1(a))[11]

But, for supplemental wage payments totalling more than $1 million for a calendar year, the withholding rate is increased to the maximum tax rate under Code Sec. 1 (i.e., 37%). (Reg § 31.3402(g)-1(a)(2))[12]

The employer has the option of treating either the entire supplemental payment or just that which brings the total payment over $1 million as subject to this mandatory withholding. (Reg § 31.3402(g)-1(a)(4)(iv))[13]

Where tax isn't withheld from regular wages for employees who receive both regular wages and supplemental wages (e.g., tips), the flat supplemental withholding rate can't be used; the tips are added to the current or preceding regular wage payment and withholding is computed at the regular graduated rates. (Reg § 31.3402(g)-1(a)(5))[14] A payment qualifies as supplemental wages even if no regular wages have been paid to the employee.

Extra pay for working during a vacation period is treated as a supplemental wage payment. (Reg § 31.3402(g)-1(c))[15] Employers have the option to treat tips and overtime pay as either regular or supplemental wages. (Reg § 31.3402(g)-1(a)(1)(v))[16]

IRS provides guidance on withholding on supplemental wages in a variety of situations.[17] An employee can't ask an employer to withhold additional amounts, other than those required to be withheld, from supplemental wages, with respect to the mandatory and optional flat rate methods of withholding. But, an employee has some control over withholding if the aggregate procedure is used. [18]

¶ 3013   Computing the amount withheld—percentage and wage bracket methods.

There are two principal systems of withholding: (1) the percentage or exact method, and (2) the wage bracket method. IRS provides tables to use for each. [19] Whichever method is used, the employer applies the withholding allowances and marital status indicated by the employee, see ¶3015 *et seq.* For variations of these two methods, see ¶3014.

If an employer fails to withhold income tax and the employee's portion of FICA taxes because the employer failed to treat the payee as an employee, for prior years the withholding rate is generally reduced to 1.5% of wages for income tax withholding, and only 20% of the regular amount to be withheld for FICA will generally have to be withheld. Certain exceptions apply. (Code Sec. 3509)[20]

¶ 3014   Alternative withholding methods.

IRS also authorizes withholding on the basis of: (1) annualized wages, (2) cumulative wages, (3) part-year employment, (4) average estimated wages, and (5) any other method that results in substantially the same amount of withholding as the percentage method. (Methods (2) and (3) are at the employee's request.) (Code Sec. 3402(h))[21]

---

11. ¶s H-4531, H-4539, H-4544.1; ¶34,024.13
12. ¶H-4542; ¶34,024.13
13. ¶H-4538.3 *et seq.*; ¶34,024.13
14. ¶H-4538.4
15. ¶H-4538.5; ¶34,024.13
16. ¶H-4538.3 *et seq.*; ¶34,024.13

17. ¶H-4540
18. ¶H-4539
19. ¶H-4493 *et seq.*; ¶34,024.02 *et seq.*
20. ¶H-4225; ¶35,094
21. ¶H-4492; ¶34,024.18

¶ 3015   Employee's withholding allowance certificate—Form W-4.

⚫️*caution:* The regs cited below were issued before the enactment of the Tax Cuts and Jobs Act (TCJA, P.L. 115-97, 12/22/2017), and refer to the pre-2018 withholding rules which were based on pre-2018/post-2025 personal exemptions (¶3112). However, the same rules appear on IRS's website at "Topic Number 753 - Form W-4 - Employee's Withholding Allowance Certificate" (as of Oct. 16, 2018), so presumably taxpayers may continue to apply them.

An employer should ask each new employee to fill out a Form W-4 withholding allowance certificate before employment begins. (Code Sec. 3402(f)(2)(A)) Employers must take into account the marital status and exemptions and allowances of each employee on the basis of that Form W-4. A certificate filed by a new employee is effective on the first payment of wages. (Code Sec. 3402(f)(3)) If an employee fails to furnish a certificate, the employer must withhold tax as if the employee were a single person with no withholding allowances. (Reg § 31.3402(f)(2)-1(a))[22]

An employer can establish a system for its employees to file Form W-4 electronically. (Reg § 31.3402(f)(5)-1(c))[23]

¶ 3016   Withholding allowances.

For tax years beginning after Dec. 31, 2017 and before Jan. 1, 2026, the personal exemption amount under Code Sec. 151 is zero (¶3112); and instead of being entitled to an "exemption" for each item under Code Sec. 3402(f)(1), an employee is entitled to a "withholding allowance" based on:

(A) whether the employee is an individual for whom a deduction is allowable with respect to another taxpayer under Code Sec. 151;

(B) if the employee is married, whether the employee's spouse is entitled to an allowance, or would be so entitled if the spouse were an employee receiving wages, under (A) (above) or (D) (below), but only if the spouse doesn't have in effect a withholding allowance certificate claiming the allowance;

(C) the number of individuals for whom a child tax credit (¶2350 *et seq.*) may be claimed;

(D) any additional amounts the employee elects to take into account under Code Sec. 3402(m) (additional withholding allowances), but only if the employee's spouse doesn't have in effect a withholding allowance certificate making the election;

(E) the standard deduction allowable to the employee (one-half of the standard deduction for an employee who is married (as determined under Code Sec. 7703), and whose spouse is an employee receiving wages subject to withholding; and

(F) Whether the employee has withholding allowance certificates in effect for more than one employer.

(Code Sec. 3402(f)(1) before amend by Sec. 11041(c)(2), PL 115-97, 12/22/2017; Code Sec. 3402(f)(2))[24]

The 2018 Form W-4 (see ¶3015) contains worksheets for figuring personal allowances (including for the child tax credit and certain other credits) and a worksheet for those who plan to itemize deductions, claim certain adjustments to income, or have a large amount of nonwage income.[25]

---

22. ¶H-4516; ¶34,024.09 *et seq.*
23. ¶H-4523.1; ¶34,024.11

24. ¶H-4505; ¶34,024.10
25. ¶H-4505; ¶34,024.10

A taxpayer working for more than one employer must allocate his allowances on separate Forms W-4 filed with each employer. (Code Sec. 3402(f)(7); Reg § 31.3402(m)-1(f)(2))[26]

¶ 3017   Standard deduction for withholding allowance.

In addition to the factors listed at ¶3016, the withholding allowance is based on the standard deduction allowable to the employee. The allowance is based on one-half of the standard deduction for an employee who is married under Code Sec. 7703, and whose spouse is an employee receiving wages that are subject to withholding. (Code Sec. 3402(f)(1)(E); Reg § 31.3402(f)(1)-1(e))[27]

Personal allowances, allowances for certain credits, such as the child tax credit, earned income tax credit, education tax credits, or dependent care credits, and allowances for itemized deductions and adjustments to income (such as deductions for IRA contributions) can be figured on worksheets for Form W-4, or using IRS's withholding calculator. (Code Sec. 3402(m)[28]

¶ 3018   Employees with no tax liability.

An employee with no tax liability can be exempt from income tax withholding. To qualify, the employee certifies on Form W-4 to the employer that he or she expects to have no federal income tax liability for the current year, *and* had no federal income tax liability in the preceding year. (Code Sec. 3402(n))[29]

An employee who can be claimed as a dependent on someone else's tax return (whether or not actually claimed) can't claim exemption from withholding if his or her income exceeds $1,050 for 2018 ($1,100 for 2019, as calculated by Thomson Reuters using inflation data) and includes more than $350 for 2018 (and for 2019, as calculated by Thomson Reuters using inflation data) of unearned income, such as interest and dividends. Special calculations must be made by an employee who is 65 or older and/or blind. [30]

¶ 3019   Amending withholding certificate—Form W-4.

caution: The regs cited below were issued before the enactment of the Tax Cuts and Jobs Act (TCJA; P.L. 115-97, 12/22/2017), and refer to the pre-2018 withholding rules, which were based on pre-2018/post-2025 personal exemptions (¶3112).

If, on any day during the calendar year, an employee's withholding allowance (¶3016) is in excess of the withholding allowance to which the employee would be entitled had the employee submitted a true and accurate withholding allowance certificate to the employer on that day, the employee must furnish the employer with a new Form W-4 within 10 days. If, on any day during the calendar year, an employee's withholding allowance is greater than the withholding allowance claimed, the employee may —but is not required to—furnish the employer with a new Form W-4. (Code Sec. 3402(f)(2)(B))[31] A taxpayer's withholding may need to be adjusted if the taxpayer has a change in life that affects his or her withholding allowances, such as a change in marital status.

An amended Form W-4 must be filed by Dec. 1 if the number of allowances is expected to *decrease* for next year. If the change resulting in the decrease occurs in Dec., the amended Form must be furnished within ten days of the date of the change. The number of allowances drops if a spouse or dependent died during the year or an individual will no longer qualify as a dependent. [32]

---

26. ¶H-4516; ¶34,024.10
27. ¶H-4506; ¶34,024.10
28. ¶H-4511; ¶34,024.09
29. ¶H-4519; ¶34,024.24

30. ¶H-4519; ¶34,024.24
31. ¶H-4524
32. ¶H-4525; ¶34,024.11

If the number of allowances is expected to increase next year, an employee can amend his W-4 by Dec. 1. If the change arises in Dec., the amended W-4 may be filed on or after the date of the change. (Code Sec. 3402(f)(2)(C); Reg § 31.3402(f)(2)-1(c)) This W-4 doesn't take effect and isn't to be made effective with respect to any payment of wages in the calendar year it's furnished. (Code Sec. 3402(f)(3)(B)(iii))[33]

¶ 3020   Employer withholding tax return—Forms 941 and 944.

Every employer (except household employers, see ¶3031) must file with IRS a quarterly return reporting withheld income taxes on Form 941. (Reg § 31.6011(a)-1, Reg § 31.6011(a)-4) Employers must submit copies of W-4s to IRS only when directed to do so by written notice or as directed in published guidance. (Reg § 31.3402(f)(2)-1(g)(1)) Where a serious underwithholding problem is found to exist for a particular employee, IRS will notify the employer to withhold income tax from that employee at a more appropriate rate (i.e., issue a "lock-in letter"). (Reg § 31.3402(f)(2)-1(g)(2))[34]

In certain cases (e.g., for taxpayers who must separately account, see ¶3026) IRS can require monthly wage withholding returns. (Reg § 31.6011(a)-5(a)(1))[35]

Form 941 must be filed by Apr. 30, July 31, Oct. 31 and Jan. 31 for the calendar quarters ending Mar. 31, June 30, Sept. 30 and Dec. 31, respectively, unless monthly filing is required. But the returns may be filed ten days later if timely deposits in full payment of the tax are made. (Reg § 31.6071(a)-1(a))[36] Form 941 reflects the 0.9% Medicare surtax (¶1108).[37]

Form 941, Schedule D, can be used to explain reporting discrepancies after (1) statutory mergers and consolidations, and (2) acquisitions satisfying the requirements for predecessor-successor status. [38]

Employers with annual employment tax liabilities of $1,000 or less who have received written notification from IRS that they qualify for the "Form 944 program" can file Form 944 annually, if they choose, instead of Form 941. (Reg § 31.6011(a)-4(a)(4)(i))[39] Employers that request to participate in the program must receive notice to file Form 944 before they may file. Once notice is received, they must file Form 944 for each year and can't file Form 941 until they are notified that their filing requirement has been changed to Forms 941 either because they contacted IRS to request that their filing requirement be changed to Form 941 or they no longer qualify for the Form 944 program. (Reg § 31.6011(a)-1(a)(5))[40]

For nonpayroll withholding (backup withholding, withholding for pension, annuities, and gambling winnings, etc.), see ¶3032.

¶ 3021   Errors in withholding and payment of tax.

Where underwithholding of FICA and income tax is ascertained before the return is filed, the employer must report and pay the correct amount of tax by the due date of the return. (Reg § 31.6151-1, Reg § 31.6205-1(b)(1), Reg § 31.6205-1(c)(1))[41]

Rules are provided for making corrections (in some cases on an interest-free basis) after the return is filed. [42] Form 941-X is used to correct errors in a previously filed Form 941. [43]

---

33. ¶H-4526; ¶34,024.11
34. ¶S-2603; ¶s 34,034, 35,014.002
35. ¶S-2604; ¶60,114.011
36. ¶S-4918; ¶60,114.011
37. ¶H-4687
38. ¶S-3195.1

39. ¶S-4918; ¶60,114.011
40. ¶S-4918.3; ¶60,114.011
41. ¶S-5525; ¶35,014.005
42. ¶S-5526; ¶35,014.005
43. ¶S-5533; ¶35,014.007

¶ 3022   Wage and tax statement—Form W-2.

Along with other information, Form W-2 includes the amount of wages paid by the employer to the employee and the taxes withheld from the wages during the calendar year. (Code Sec. 6051(a)) An employer must show the value of the employee's health insurance coverage sponsored by the employer (Code Sec. 6051(a)(14)). The aggregate cost of employer-sponsored coverage must be reported on Form W-2, with an exception for small employers (defined as those that were required to file less than 250 Forms W-2 for the preceding calendar year).[44] The W-2 must also include information and deferrals and inclusions under Code Sec. 83(i) (¶1216).[45]

An employer in business must give each employee copies of Form W-2, on or before Jan. 31 of the year after the calendar year for which the wages were paid. If an employee leaves the job before the end of the calendar year and isn't expected to return within the calendar year, Form W-2 must be given to him not later than 30 days after the employer receives a written request for it from the employee, if that 30-day period ends before Jan. 31. (Code Sec. 6051; Reg § 31.6051-1(d))[46]

¶ 3023   Nonreceipt of Form W-2 by employee—Form 4852.

If an employee doesn't receive a Form W-2, he should ask his employer for it. If the employer doesn't provide the form, the taxpayer should contact IRS, which will ask the employer to send a copy or duplicate form. If the employee hasn't received a Form W-2 in time to file his tax return, he should file a return estimating wages and the income tax withheld on Form 4852.[47]

¶ 3024   Earned income credit notice to employees with no tax withheld—Notice 797.

An employer must notify any employee who hasn't had any tax withheld from his wages (other than an employee who certifies, see ¶3018, that he has no tax liability) that the employee may be eligible for a refund because of the earned income credit (¶2338 *et seq.*). IRS Notice 797 or a written statement containing an exact reproduction of the wording in Notice 797 must be used and furnished within one week of the date the employee should receive a timely Form W-2 or, if none is required, before Feb. 8th of the following calendar year. (Reg § 31.6051-1(h))[48]

¶ 3025   Payroll taxes.

The Federal Insurance Contributions Act (FICA) imposes two taxes, the Old Age, Survivors and Disability Insurance (OASDI) tax and the Medicare Hospital Insurance (HI) tax. These taxes are imposed on employers for wages paid with respect to employment and on employees for wages received with respect to employment. The OASDI tax rate is 6.2% on wages up to an annually-adjusted "wage base" (see ¶1108).[49]

The HI tax rate generally is 1.45% on all wages, regardless of amount. An additional 0.9% HI tax applies to certain high wage earners; see ¶1108.

44. ¶S-3152; ¶S-3312; ¶60,514
45. ¶S-3152
46. ¶S-4930; ¶60,514

47. ¶S-3193
48. ¶H-4851 *et seq.*; ¶s 324.04, 60,514
49. ¶H-4687; ¶35,014.07

¶ 3026   Separate accounting for employment tax.

IRS can require an employer who fails to collect, account for, deposit, etc., income or related employment taxes or make timely deposits or file returns to make deposits in a special trust account. (Code Sec. 7512; Reg § 301.7512-1(b))[50]

¶ 3027   Deposit of employment taxes.

An employer is either a monthly or semi-weekly depositor. (Reg § 31.6302-1(a))

An employer is a monthly depositor for the entire calendar year if the aggregate amount of employment taxes reported for the lookback period (i.e., the 12-month period ended the preceding June 30) is $50,000 or less. (Reg § 31.6302-1(b)(2)(i), Reg § 31.6302-1(b)(4)) These employers must deposit taxes on or before the 15th day of the following month. (Reg § 31.6302-1(c)(1))[1]

An employer is a semi-weekly depositor for the entire calendar year if the aggregate amount of employment taxes reported for the lookback period (i.e., the 12-month period ended the preceding June 30) exceeds $50,000. (Reg § 31.6302-1(b)(3), Reg § 31.6302-1(b)(4)) The employer must deposit taxes on or before the following dates. (Reg § 31.6302-1(c)(2))[2]

If the wage payment date is:

. . . Wednesday, Thursday, and/or Friday, the deposit date is on or before the following Wednesday.

. . . Saturday, Sunday, Monday, and/or Tuesday, the deposit date is on or before the following Friday.

If a return period (quarterly or annual) ends during a semi-weekly period, the employer must designate on his deposit coupon the proper return period for which the deposits relates (the period in which the payment is made). If the return period ends during a semi-weekly period during which the employer has two or more payment dates, two deposit obligations may exist. (Reg § 31.6302-1(c)(2)(ii))[3]

Notwithstanding the above rules, under the "one-day rule," if on any day an employer has $100,000 or more of employment taxes accumulated, these taxes must be deposited by the close of the next banking day. (Reg § 31.6302-1(c)(3)) The day after a monthly depositor becomes subject to the one-day rule it becomes a semi-weekly depositor for the remainder of that calendar year and for the following calendar year. (Reg § 31.6302-1(b)(2)(ii))[4]

If a tax deposit day isn't a banking day, deposits are timely if made on the next day that is a banking day. (Reg § 31.6302-1(c)(4)) In addition, if one of the three weekdays following the close of a semi-weekly period is a bank holiday, the employer has an extra banking day to deposit taxes. (Reg § 31.6302-1(c)(2)(iii))[5]

Deposits are considered timely if mailed (postmarked, or date marked by a designated delivery service, see ¶4754) at least two days before the due date if the deposit is actually received by the bank. (Code Sec. 7502(e)) But a deposit of $20,000 or more by a person who is required to make a deposit more than once a month must be actually received by the due date. (Code Sec. 7502(e)(3))[6]

In general, taxpayers must deposit taxes by electronic funds transfer (¶3029).

---

50. ¶S-5541 *et seq.*; ¶75,124
1. ¶S-5503; ¶63,014
2. ¶S-5506; ¶63,014
3. ¶S-5507; ¶63,014

4. ¶S-5510; ¶63,014
5. ¶S-5512; ¶63,014
6. ¶T-10777 *et seq.*; ¶63,014, 75,024

¶ 3028   Deposit safe harbor and de minimis rules.

Under the single deposit safe harbor, an employer will be considered to have satisfied his deposit obligations if:

(1) the amount of any shortfall (the excess of the amount required to be deposited over the amount deposited for the applicable period —monthly, semi-weekly or daily) doesn't exceed the greater of $100 or 2% of the amount of employment taxes required to be deposited (Reg § 31.6302-1(f)(1)(i), Reg § 31.6302-1(f)(2)), and

(2) the employer deposits the shortfall on or before the shortfall make-up date. (Reg § 31.6302-1(f)(1)(ii) For a monthly depositor, this is no later than the due date for the quarterly return. For a semi-weekly or a one-day depositor, this is on or before the first Wednesday or Friday (whichever is earlier) falling on or after the 15th day of the month following the month the deposit was required to be made. (Reg § 31.6302-1(f)(3))[7]

An employer with accumulated employment taxes of less than $2,500 for a return period (quarterly or annual) doesn't have to make deposits and can instead remit his full liability with a timely filed return for the period. (Reg § 31.6302-1(f)(4))[8]

¶ 3029   Tax deposits by electronic funds transfer (EFT).

Unless exempted, all of the following are required to be deposited via EFT: FICA and FUTA taxes and withheld income taxes; corporate income and estimated taxes; unrelated business income taxes of tax-exempt organizations; private foundation excise taxes; taxes withheld on nonresident aliens and foreign corporations; estimated taxes on certain trusts; railroad retirement taxes; nonpayroll taxes, including backup withholding; and certain excise taxes. (Code Sec. 6302(h); Reg § 31.6302-1(h)(2)(iii))[9]

A taxpayer required to deposit by EFT must use the Electronic Federal Tax Payment System (EFTPS) to make federal tax deposits.[10] Taxpayers must enroll in EFTPS before they can make EFT deposits. Enroll on-line at www.eftps.gov.[11]

Federal income taxes (including estimated taxes) (Reg § 1.6302-4), estate (Reg § 20.6302-1) and gift taxes (Reg § 25.6302-1), and various excise taxes (Reg § 40.6302(a)-1) may be made voluntarily by EFT.[12]

A taxpayer required to deposit taxes by EFT that (without reasonable cause) deposits by other means is subject to the Code Sec. 6656 failure to deposit penalty.[13]

¶ 3030   Motion picture industry employment taxes.

Motion picture payroll service companies that qualify as "motion picture project employers" are treated as the employer of their film and television production workers for FICA and FUTA purposes. As a result, all remuneration paid by a motion picture project employer to a worker during a calendar year is subject to a single FICA wage base and a single FUTA wage base. (Code Sec. 3512)[14]

¶ 3031   Payment of Domestic Service Employment Tax ("Nanny Tax")—Form 1040, Schedule H.

Employers of domestic service employees must file annual returns of "domestic service employment taxes" on a calendar-year basis (Code Sec. 3510(a)(1)) on or

7. ¶S-5513 *et seq.*; ¶63,014
8. ¶S-5516; ¶63,014
9. ¶S-5620 *et seq.*; ¶63,014
10. ¶S-5621
11. ¶S-5630
12. ¶S-5629
13. ¶V-1658
14. ¶H-4687.1; ¶35,124

before the 15th day of the fourth month following the close of the employer's tax year. (Code Sec. 3510(a)(2))

Household employers report withheld income and FICA tax for their household employees on their individual income tax return (Form 1040, Schedule H) and need employer identification numbers (EINs, apply on Form SS-4). [15]

Annual Form 940 (FUTA) doesn't have to be filed for domestic employees. There is no requirement to make deposits of domestic service employment taxes, or to pay installments of these taxes under Code Sec. 6157 (Code Sec. 3510(a)(3)), dealing with quarterly payment of FUTA tax. Rather, they can be paid in a lump sum when the employer's income tax return is filed.

"Domestic service employment taxes" are: (1) any FICA and FUTA taxes on remuneration paid for domestic service in a private home of the employer (for dollar threshold see below), and (2) and any income tax on these payments that's withheld under the Code Sec. 3402(p) voluntary withholding agreement rules (¶3010) (for the otherwise applicable exemption from income tax withholding on domestic service employment, see ¶3007). (Code Sec. 3510(c))[16]

Domestic service is service of a household nature performed in and about the private home of the person for whom the services are performed. (Reg § 31.3121(a)(7)-1(a), Reg § 31.3401(a)(3)-1(a))[17]

Noncash payments for domestic services in an employer's private home are excluded from FICA wages. Cash remuneration paid by an employer for domestic service in the employer's private home isn't FICA wages if the cash remuneration paid during the year is less than the "applicable dollar threshold" —$2,100 in 2018 and 2019. (Code Sec. 3121(a)(7), Code Sec. 3121(x))[18]

⊘observation: The dollar threshold applies separately to each domestic employee. So, for example, if an employer pays just under $2,100 each to a babysitter and a housekeeper in 2018, no FICA tax is due for either.

Domestic service performed in the private home of the employer in any year by an individual under the age of 18 during any portion of the year is excepted from employment for FICA if the service isn't the principal occupation of the employee. (Code Sec. 3121(b)(21))[19]

Form W-2. An employer must furnish Form W-2 to household employees whose wages are subject to Social Security taxes even if they aren't subject to income tax withholding. (Reg § 31.6051-1(b)(1)) Use a Form W-3 transmittal to file even one Form W-2. [20]

¶ 3032   Nonpayroll Withheld Taxes. ▆▆▆▆▆▆▆▆▆

Income tax on gambling winnings, payments subject to backup withholding, retirement plan payments, IRAs, annuities and certain other deferred compensation is withheld under "nonpayroll withheld taxes" rules.

The employment tax deposit rules of ¶3027 *et seq.* apply to determine the time and manner of making deposits of nonpayroll withheld taxes. (Reg § 31.6302-4(a))[21] Whether a taxpayer is a monthly or a semi-weekly depositor for a calendar year is based on an annual determination and generally depends on the aggregate amount of nonpayroll withheld taxes reported by the taxpayer for the "lookback period" —i.e., the second calendar year preceding the current calendar year. So, the lookback period for calendar year 2018 is

15. ¶S-2608; ¶35,104
16. ¶S-2608.3; ¶35,104
17. ¶H-4654
18. ¶H-4653 *et seq.*; ¶35,104

19. ¶H-4611.1
20. ¶S-3159
21. ¶S-5582 *et seq.*; ¶63,014

calendar year 2016. A new taxpayer is treated as having nonpayroll withheld taxes of zero for any calendar year in which the taxpayer didn't exist. (Reg § 31.6302-4(c)(2)(iv))[22]

A taxpayer is a monthly depositor of nonpayroll withheld taxes for a calendar year if the amount of nonpayroll withheld taxes accumulated in the lookback period is $50,000 or less. A taxpayer ceases to be a monthly depositor of nonpayroll withheld taxes on the first day after the taxpayer is subject to the "one-day rule" (¶3027) with respect to nonpayroll withheld taxes. At that time, the taxpayer immediately becomes a semi-weekly depositor of nonpayroll withheld taxes for the remainder of the calendar year and the succeeding calendar year. (Reg § 31.6302-4(c)(2)(ii))

A taxpayer is a semi-weekly depositor of nonpayroll withheld taxes for a calendar year if the amount of nonpayroll withheld taxes accumulated in the lookback period exceeds $50,000. (Reg § 31.6302-4(c)(2)(iii))

Nonpayroll withheld taxes are income taxes withheld from: gambling winnings (¶3034) (Reg § 31.6302-4(b)(1)); retirement pay for services in the Armed Forces under Code Sec. 3402 (Reg § 31.6302-4(b)(2); retirement plan payments, IRAs, annuities and certain other deferred compensation (¶3035) (Reg § 31.6302-4(b)(3)); and under the backup withholding rules (¶3044). (Reg § 31.6302-4(b)(5))[23]

For the requirement that some taxpayers deposit nonpayroll withheld taxes by electronic funds transfer (EFT), see ¶3029.

¶ 3033   Annual nonpayroll tax return—Form 945.

Taxpayers who withhold income tax from nonpayroll payments must report the withholding annually on Form 945. The return must be filed on or before Jan. 31 following the calendar year. But, if timely deposits of tax have been made, the return may be filed by Feb. 10. (Reg § 31.6071(a)-1(a)(1))[24]

¶ 3034   Withholding on gambling winnings—Form W-2G and Form 5754.

Payors must withhold 24% on proceeds of more than $5,000 (Code Sec. 3402(q)(1)) from:

(1) a wagering transaction in a parimutuel pool with respect to horse races, dog races or jai alai if the amount of the proceeds is at least 300 times as large as the amount wagered; (Code Sec. 3402(q)(3)(C)(ii))

(2) a wager placed in a state-conducted lottery; (Code Sec. 3402(q)(3)(B))

(3) a sweepstakes, wagering pool or lottery (other than a state-conducted lottery); (Code Sec. 3402(q)(3)(C)(i)) or

(4) all other wagering transactions if the amount of the proceeds is at least 300 times as large as the amount wagered. (Code Sec. 3402(q)(3)(A))[25]

"Proceeds" means amount received from the wager reduced by the amount of the wager. (Code Sec. 3402(q)(4)(A))[26] Amounts paid with respect to identical wagers are treated as paid with respect to a single wager. (Reg § 31.3402(q)-1(c)(1)(ii))[27]

A person who receives gambling winnings subject to withholding must provide certain information on Form W-2G or Form 5754 and give it to the payor. (Code Sec. 3402(q)(6); Reg § 31.3402(q)-1(e))[28]

The above withholding rules don't apply to slot machines, keno and bingo winnings. (Code Sec. 3402(q)(5)) But, backup withholding (¶3044) may apply. [29] A payor must file a

---

22. ¶S-5585; ¶63,014
23. ¶S-5581; ¶63,014
24. ¶S-2609.1 *et seq.*, S-4918
25. ¶J-8603; ¶34,024.26

26. ¶J-8606 *et seq.*; ¶34,024.26
27. ¶J-8610; ¶34,024.26
28. ¶J-8614; ¶34,024.26
29. ¶J-8604; ¶34,024.26

Form W-2G for every person the payor pays $1,200 or more in winnings from slot machines or bingo, or $1,500 or more from Keno (after deducting the cost of the winning Keno game). (Reg § 1.6041-10(b)(1)(i))[30]

Casinos and other sponsors of poker tournaments must report tournament winnings of more than $5,000. Sponsors who comply with the reporting requirement won't need to withhold. But, if the reporting requirement isn't met, IRS will enforce it and also require the sponsor to pay any tax that should have been withheld. [31]

Withholding on Indian casino profits. Withholding equal to a payment's proportionate share of annualized tax is required under tables provided by IRS (Reg § 31.3402(r)-1(a)(2)) on payments to Indian tribal members from the net revenue of most gambling activities of the tribe. (Code Sec. 3402(r))[32]

¶ 3035 Pension, Annuity and Other Withholding.

Withholding of 20% is required on any designated distribution (¶3037) that's an eligible rollover distribution (¶3036), unless there's a direct trustee-to-trustee transfer. Withholding is required on periodic and lump-sum payments from certain employee plans and certain annuities. But, certain recipients may elect not to have tax withheld (¶3039 *et seq.*).

¶ 3036 Mandatory 20% withholding on eligible rollover distributions.

Unless a distributee elects to have the distribution paid directly to an eligible retirement plan under the Code Sec. 401(a)(31)(A) trustee-to-trustee rules (¶4308), a payor must withhold 20% of any designated distribution that's an "eligible rollover distribution" as defined by Code Sec. 402(f)(2)(A). The Code Sec. 3405(a) and Code Sec. 3405(b) elective withholding rules (¶3037 *et seq.*) don't apply to an eligible rollover distribution. (Code Sec. 3405(c); Reg § 31.3405(c)-1, Q&A-1)[33]

An eligible rollover distribution (reported by the payor on Form 1099-R) (Reg § 31.3405(c)-1, Q&A-16) is any distribution to an employee from a qualified trust (not from an IRA, SEP, or SIMPLE plan) *other than:*

... a required distribution under Code Sec. 401(a)(9);

... any distribution that's one of a series of substantially equal periodic payments made (a) not less frequently than annually for the life (or life expectancy) of the employee (or joint lives or expectancies of the employee and his designated beneficiary), or (b) for a specified period of ten years or more; or

... a hardship distribution from a 401(k) or 403(b) plan. (Code Sec. 3405(c)(3), Code Sec. 402(c)(4), Code Sec. 402(f)(2)(A), Code Sec. 403(b)(8)(B); Reg § 1.402(c)-2, Q&A-3[34]

No withholding is required if the total distribution paid to the distributee under the plan within one tax year is expected to be less than $200. (Reg § 31.3405(c)-1, Q&A-14)[35]

¶ 3037 Required withholding for designated distributions.

Withholding is required for designated distributions (Code Sec. 3405(d)(1)),[36] but the recipient generally may elect out (¶3039) unless the distribution is an eligible rollover distribution (¶3036). Designated distributions are periodic as well as nonperiodic (including lump-sum) payments from pension, profit sharing, stock bonus or other employer deferred compensation plans, as well as from IRAs (other than Roth IRAs) and commercial

---

30. ¶S-3697.1; ¶60,414
31. ¶J-8603; ¶34,024.26
32. ¶J-8617; ¶34,024.261
33. ¶J-8577 *et seq.*; ¶34,054

34. ¶J-8586; ¶4024.04
35. ¶s J-8584; ¶35,054
36. ¶J-8501 *et seq.*; ¶34,054

annuities, whether or not the contract was purchased under an employer's plan for employees. (Code Sec. 3405(e)) Annuity payments and other distributions under a state or local government deferred compensation plan, other than a Code Sec. 457 plan, including the Civil Service Retirement System are subject to income tax withholding as well. (Reg § 35.3405-1T, Q&A-22 and 23)[37]

The payor of a designated distribution must withhold and is liable for the payment of the tax (unless the payee elects out). But, in the case of a qualified pension, profit sharing, stock bonus, annuity, or 457 governmental plan, the plan administrator has the responsibility, unless he directs the payor to withhold and provides the payor with the information set out in the regs. In that case, the responsibility reverts to the payor. (Code Sec. 3405(d); Reg § 35.3405-1T, Q&A E-3)[38]

¶ 3038   Withholding from periodic payments.

Tax is withheld in accordance with a recipient's withholding certificate. If none is in effect, the amount withheld will be determined under rules prescribed by IRS. (Code Sec. 3405(a)(4); Reg § 35.3405-1T, Q&A B-2)[39]

¶ 3039   Election out of withholding on periodic payments—Form W-4P.

A recipient of periodic payments (except for certain U.S. citizens and expatriates living abroad, see ¶3043) may elect not to have any tax withheld. The election remains in effect until revoked. (Code Sec. 3405(a)(2))[40] Elect (or revoke) on Form W-4P.[41]

If the recipient doesn't furnish his taxpayer identification number (TIN) to the payor or if IRS has notified the payor that the TIN furnished is incorrect, an election out of withholding isn't effective. (Code Sec. 3405(e)(12))[42]

For periodic payments that are "eligible rollover distributions," see ¶3036.

¶ 3040   Withholding from nonperiodic distributions.

The payor of any nonperiodic distribution that isn't an eligible rollover distribution subject to 20% mandatory withholding (¶3036) must withhold an amount equal to 10% of that distribution (Code Sec. 3405(b)(1)),[43] unless the recipient elects out of withholding (¶3041).

¶ 3041   Electing out of withholding on nonperiodic distributions—Form W-4P.

A payee (except for recipients of eligible rollover distributions (¶3036), and certain U.S. citizens and expatriates living abroad (¶3043)) may elect exemption from withholding for any nonperiodic distribution. The election is made on Form W-4P on a distribution-by-distribution basis. (Code Sec. 3405(b)(2))[44]

If the recipient doesn't furnish his taxpayer identification number (TIN) to the payor or if IRS has notified the payor that the TIN furnished is incorrect, an election out of withholding isn't effective. (Code Sec. 3405(e)(12))[45]

37. ¶J-8504 *et seq.*; ¶34,054
38. ¶J-8518 *et seq.*; ¶34,054
39. ¶J-8525; ¶34,054
40. ¶J-8526; ¶34,054
41. ¶J-8528; ¶34,054

42. ¶J-8513
43. ¶J-8533; ¶34,054
44. ¶J-8539; ¶34,054
45. ¶J-8513; ¶34,054

¶ 3042 Payor must notify payee of right to elect to have no tax withheld.

For periodic payments, the notice to make, renew, or revoke the election out of withholding is required no earlier than six months before and no later than the date of the first payment. For nonperiodic payments, the notice should be given not earlier than six months before the distribution and not later than the time that will give the payee reasonable time to elect out. (Code Sec. 3405(e)(10)(B); Reg § 35.3405-1T, Q&A D-4 and D-9)[46] The notice must state that withholding will apply unless the payee elects otherwise, and if he elects no withholding, estimated tax may apply. A sample statement is in the regs. (Reg § 35.3405-1T, Q&A D-21 and D-25)[47]

¶ 3043 Electing out of withholding where payment is delivered outside the U.S.

An election out of withholding can't be made for any periodic or nonperiodic payment that is to be delivered outside the U.S. and its possessions (Code Sec. 3405(e)(13)(A)) *unless* the recipient certifies to the payor that the recipient is neither a U.S. citizen, a resident alien, nor a nonresident alien who in the last 10 years has lost his U.S. citizenship in order to avoid U.S. taxes and is therefore subject to Code Sec. 877. (Code Sec. 3405(e)(13)(B))[48]

¶ 3044 When Backup Withholding Is Required. ▮▮▮▮▮▮▮▮

A payor of any reportable payment (¶3045) must withhold 24% of the payment if:

(1) The payee has failed to furnish his taxpayer identification number (TIN) to the payor (Code Sec. 3406(a)(1)(A)) or furnishes an "obviously incorrect number," (Code Sec. 3406(h)(1)) i.e., one without nine digits or which includes letters of the alphabet. (Reg § 31.3406(h)-1(b))

(2) IRS or a broker has notified (the "B-notice") the payor that the TIN furnished by the payee is incorrect. (Code Sec. 3406(a)(1), Code Sec. 3406(d)(2))

(3) There has been a notified payee underreporting with respect to interest and dividends. (Code Sec. 3406(a)(1)(C))

(4) The payee has failed to make the exemption certification (on Form W-9) with respect to interest and dividends. (Code Sec. 3406(a)(1)(D))[49]

Backup withholding doesn't apply to any payment made to an organization exempt from tax under Code Sec. 501(a) (with certain exceptions); the U.S., a state, the District of Columbia, a U.S. possession, or their political subdivisions; a foreign government or its political subdivisions; an international organization; any wholly-owned agency or instrumentality of any of the above political entities; or any other person specified in regs. (Code Sec. 3406(g)(1)) Payments to a fiduciary or nominee account, or to an exempt recipient (Reg § 31.3406(d)-5(b)), aren't subject to backup withholding.[50]

¶ 3045 Reportable payments.

Reportable payments include most payments for which information returns are required, such as an interest or dividend payment. (Code Sec. 3406(b)(1))[1] Original issue discount (OID) is treated as a payment of interest for backup withholding purposes, but the amount withheld is limited to the cash paid. (Reg § 31.3406(b)(2)-2(a))[2] Code Sec. 6050W reportable payment transactions (¶4746) are subject to backup withholding.[3]

---

46. ¶J-8528 *et seq.*, ¶J-8539 *et seq.*; ¶34,054
47. ¶J-8541, J-8543; ¶34,054
48. ¶J-8554; ¶34,054
49. ¶J-9001; ¶34,064

50. ¶J-9109; ¶34,064
1. ¶J-9101; ¶34,064
2. ¶J-9111.1; ¶34,064
3. ¶J-9126.2; ¶34,064.01

Reportable payments are treated as if they were wages. Amounts deducted and withheld are treated as if they were deducted and withheld from wages. (Code Sec. 3406(h)(10))[4]

¶ 3046   How to stop backup withholding.

A payee can stop backup withholding once it has started by showing that there was no underreporting, correcting any underreporting, showing that backup withholding will cause undue hardship and that it's unlikely he will underreport again, or showing that a bona fide dispute exists as to whether there has been any underreporting. (Reg § 35a.3406-2(g)(1), Reg § 31.3406(c)-1(g)) If IRS determines that backup withholding should stop, it will give the payee a written certification to that effect and notify payors and brokers to stop withholding. (Reg § 35a.3406-2(h)(1), Reg § 35a.3406-2(d)(1), Reg § 31.3406(c)-1(g)(1))

Withholding must stop as of the close of the day before the "stop date" (generally 30 days after receipt of the stop notice from IRS or a copy of the certification IRS gave the payee, whichever is earlier). (Code Sec. 3406(e)(5)) The payor may elect to shorten or eliminate the 30-day period. (Code Sec. 3406(e)(5)(C); Reg § 35a.3406-2(e)(2)(iii), Reg § 31.3406(c)-1(e)(2)(i)(B))[5]

---

4. ¶J-9009   5. ¶J-9607; ¶34,064

Chapter 13 Individual's Tax Computation—Kiddie Tax— Self-Employment Tax—Net Investment Income Tax—Estimated Tax

¶ 3100 How Income Tax on Individuals Is Computed. ■■■■■■■■

An individual's annual income tax liability on taxable income (¶3101) is computed using either the tax rate schedules or (if taxable income is less than $100,000) the tax tables, see ¶1101 *et seq.* This tax liability may be increased by other taxes, e.g., self-employment tax or alternative minimum tax, and is reduced by certain credits.

For taxation of unearned income of children subject to the kiddie tax, see ¶3128 *et seq.*

For the threshold amounts of gross income that must be reached before a tax return must be filed, see ¶4701.

¶ 3101 Steps in computing taxable income.

An individual taxpayer first computes gross income —generally all income from all sources (Code Sec. 61), see ¶1200 *et seq.*

From gross income, taxpayer subtracts the deductions specified at ¶3102 to reach adjusted gross income (AGI). (Code Sec. 62)

Finally, taxpayers who itemize reduce AGI by allowable deductions. (¶3112) (Code Sec. 63(a)), see ¶3109 *et seq.* Nonitemizers reduce AGI by the standard deduction (¶3110) and the 20% deduction for qualified business income (¶1595*et seq.*).(Code Sec. 63(b))[1]

¶ 3102 Deductions taken "above the line" to reach adjusted gross income (AGI).

Subtract the following deductions from gross income to reach AGI: (Code Sec. 62(a), Reg § 1.62-1T)[2]

... Trade or business expenses (¶1507), other than unreimbursed employee business expenses (¶3104). For business-related deductions of "statutory employees," see ¶3103.

... Employee expenses that are reimbursed by the employer or a third party (¶3104).

... One-half of self-employment tax (¶1747), other than the additional 0.9% self-employment tax (¶1108).

... Employee business expenses of certain performing artists (¶3105) and of state and local government officials compensated on a fee basis (¶3106).

... For 2018 (and 2019, as calculated by Thomson Reuters using inflation data), deduction of up to $250 of qualifying expenses of educators (¶2224).

... Certain unreimbursed travel expenses of National Guard and Reserve members (¶1548).

... Losses from the sale or exchange of property (¶2400).

... Deductions for property held for production of rents or royalties. (Code Sec. 62(a)(4))

... Contributions to tax-favored retirement plans for the self-employed (¶4316).

... Contributions to individual retirement accounts (IRAs) or annuities (¶4340).

... The "total taxable amount" of a retirement plan lump-sum distribution with respect to a participant born before '36, to the extent included in recipient's gross income

---

1. ¶A-2500 *et seq.*; ¶634   2. ¶A-2601; ¶624

References beginning with a single letter are to paragraphs in Federal Tax Coordinator 2d and RIA's Analysis of Federal Taxes: Income. Those beginning with numbers are to paragraphs in United States Tax Reporter.

(¶4328).

. . . Amounts forfeited on premature withdrawal of savings accounts or deposits (¶2164).

. . . Alimony and separate maintenance payments, generally for divorce or separation instruments executed before 2019 (¶2152 *et seq.*).

. . . Repayments of supplemental unemployment compensation. (Code Sec. 62(a)(12))

. . . Jury duty pay remitted to an employer (¶3107).

. . . Depreciation and depletion deductions of a life tenant or an income beneficiary of a trust, or of an heir, legatee or devisee of an estate (¶3925).

. . . Amortization or expensing of reforestation expenditures (¶1964).

. . . Certain foreign housing costs of individuals having income earned abroad (¶4607).

. . . Self-employed medical insurance premiums (¶1531).

. . . Pre-2018 moving expenses (¶1627 *et seq.*).

. . . Contributions to an Archer medical savings account (Archer MSA, ¶1527).

. . . Deduction for interest on qualified education loans (¶2220 *et seq.*).

. . . Pre-2018 deduction for higher education expenses (¶2225).

. . . Contributions to a health savings account (HSA, ¶1528).

. . . Attorney fees and court costs of civil rights suits, whistleblower awards, and, for post-2017 tax years, awards under section 21F of the Securities Exchange Act of 1934 (¶3108).

¶ 3103 Business-related expenses of "statutory employees."

For purposes of computing adjusted gross income (AGI), the allowable deductions attributable to the services rendered by a statutory employee (drivers, life insurance salespersons, home workers and other salespersons meeting certain conditions) are treated as trade or business expenses (deductible on Schedule C, rather than as itemized deductions).[3]

¶ 3104 Reimbursed and unreimbursed employee expenses.

In computing adjusted gross income (AGI), an employee can deduct from gross income employee expenses for which the employee's reimbursed by the employer, its agent, or third party (for whom the employee performs services as an employee of the employer) under an express agreement for reimbursement or other expense allowance under an accountable plan. (But there's no normal "deduction," since the reimbursement is excluded from the employee's gross income —i.e., no deduction for the expense to the extent there's no inclusion of the reimbursement.) (Code Sec. 62(a)(2)(A); Reg § 1.62-2(c)(4))[4] The expense must be otherwise allowable as a deduction (i.e., not a personal expense). [5]

If the reimbursement is for less than the total expenses paid or incurred by the employee, employees may not deduct these unreimbursed expenses for 2018 – 2025, due to the suspension of miscellaneous itemized deductions for those years. [6]

A reimbursement or other expense allowance arrangement under an accountable plan is one that meets tests for (1) business connection, (2) substantiation, and (3) return of amounts in excess of expenses. (Reg § 1.62-2(c)(2)) See ¶1558 *et seq.* for details.

A payor can have more than one arrangement as to one employee. (Reg § 1.62-2(c)(1))[7]

For an above-the-line deduction for expenses of educators, see ¶2224.

---

3. ¶A-2603; ¶624.03
4. ¶A-2604; ¶624.02
5. ¶A-2602; ¶624.02

6. ¶A-2605; ¶624.02
7. ¶L-4703.2

¶ 3105 Expenses of certain performing artists—Form 2106.

Expenses of certain performing artists are deductible (use Form 2106 or Form 2106-EZ) in arriving at adjusted gross income (AGI), notwithstanding the disallowance of un-reimbursed employee business expenses as above-the-line deductions. (Code Sec. 62(a)(2)(B)) To qualify, the taxpayer must have earned at least $200 as a performing artist from each of at least two employers during the tax year. (Code Sec. 62(b)(1)(A), Code Sec. 62(b)(2)) Also, the allowable expenses must exceed 10% of gross income from the services, and AGI for the year (before deducting these expenses) can't exceed $16,000. (Code Sec. 62(b)(1)(B), Code Sec. 62(b)(1)(C)) A married performing artist who lives with a spouse at any time during the year must file a joint return to deduct these expenses to reach AGI. (Code Sec. 62(b)(3)(A)) The two-employer requirement and 10%-of-gross-income test are applied separately to each spouse, but the $16,000 test is applied to their combined income. (Code Sec. 62(b)(3)(B))[8]

¶ 3106 Business expenses of state and local officials paid on a fee basis.

Employee business expenses relating to service as an official of a state or local government (or a political subdivision thereof) are deductible in computing AGI, if the official is compensated on a fee basis. (Code Sec. 62(a)(2)(C))[9]

¶ 3107 Jury duty pay remitted to an employer.

An individual may deduct jury pay from gross income if the individual is required to remit any of the jury pay to the employer in exchange for compensation for the period the individual was performing jury duty. (Code Sec. 62(a)(13))[10]

¶ 3108 Attorney fees & court costs of civil rights suits, whistleblower awards, and false claims under securities laws.

Any deduction allowable under Chapter 1 for attorney fees and court costs paid by, or on behalf of, the taxpayer in connection with the following is deductible from gross income:

. . . an action involving a claim (1) of unlawful discrimination (defined in Code Sec. 62(e)), (2) of a violation of subchapter III of chapter 37 of title 31, United States Code (Claims Against the U.S. Government), or (3) made under Sec. 1862(b)(3)(A) of the Social Security Act (42 U.S.C. 1395y(b)(3)(A)) (private cause of action under the Medicare Secondary Payer statute), but only up to the amount includible in taxpayer's gross income for the tax year on account of the judgment or settlement. (Code Sec. 62(a)(20))[11]

. . . any Code Sec. 7623(b) whistleblower award or, for post-2017 tax years, award under section 21F of the Securities Exchange Act of 1934, a state law false or fraudulent claim meeting requirements of section 1909(b) of the Social Security Act, or section 23 of the Commodity Exchange Act, but only up to the amount includible in taxpayer's gross income for the tax year on account of the award. (Code Sec. 62(a)(21))[12]

¶ 3109 Itemized deductions.

Itemized deductions are all the allowable Chapter 1 deductions *other than* the deductions taken from gross income to reach adjusted gross income (AGI) (¶3102), and the 20% deduction for qualified business income (¶1595*et seq.*). (Code Sec. 63(d))[13]

---

8. ¶A-2611; ¶624.02
9. ¶A-2611.1; ¶624.02
10. ¶A-2623; ¶624.04

11. ¶A-2628; ¶624.04
12. ¶A-2629; ¶624.04
13. ¶A-2700 *et seq.*; ¶634

caution: For itemized deductions under the alternative minimum tax, see ¶3206.

Miscellaneous itemized deductions (i.e., itemized deductions other than those listed in Code Sec. 67(b)) are disallowed for tax years beginning after 2017 and before 2026. (Code Sec. 67(g))

¶ 3110   Standard deduction.

The standard deduction is the sum of the basic standard deduction, and the additional standard deduction, as adjusted each year for inflation. (Code Sec. 63(c)(1))[14] Here are the basic standard deduction amounts (2019 amounts calculated by Thomson Reuters using inflation data):[15]

Basic Standard Deduction

Filing Status	2018	2019
Joint filers and surviving spouses	$24,000	$24,400
Heads of household	18,000	18,350
Singles	12,000	12,200
Marrieds filing separately	12,000	12,200

The basic standard deduction of individuals who can be claimed as dependents by another taxpayer can't exceed the greater of (a) $1,050 for 2018 ($1,100 for 2019, as calculated by Thomson Reuters using inflation data), or (b) $350 for 2018 (and 2019, as calculated by Thomson Reuters using inflation data), plus the individual's earned income. But the basic standard deduction can't be more than the regular basic standard deduction amount shown above ($12,000 for 2018; $12,200 for 2019, as calculated by Thomson Reuters using inflation data). (Code Sec. 63(c)(5))[16]

The standard deduction is zero for: a married individual filing separately whose spouse itemizes deductions; a nonresident alien individual; an individual filing a short-year return due to an accounting period change; and, an estate or trust, common trust fund, or partnership. (Code Sec. 63(c)(6))[17]

Elderly and blind taxpayers get additional standard deductions. (Code Sec. 63(c)(3)) A taxpayer who is 65 before the end of the tax year, or blind at the end of the tax year, is entitled to an additional standard deduction. An individual is considered to have reached age 65 on the day before the individual's actual 65th birthday. [18] Here are the additional standard deduction amounts (2019 amounts calculated by Thomson Reuters using inflation data): (Code Sec. 63(f)(1), Code Sec. 63(f)(2), Code Sec. 63(f)(3), Code Sec. 63(c)(4))[19]

Additional Standard Deduction

Filing Status	2018	2019
Marrieds and surviving spouses	$ 1300	$ 1300
Heads of household	1,600	1,650
Singles	1,600	1,650

One who's elderly *and* blind gets an additional standard deduction for each status. (Code Sec. 63(c)(3))[20]

A married individual who files a separate return can claim a spouse's additional standard deduction if the spouse has no gross income and isn't the dependent of another taxpayer. (Code Sec. 63(f)(1)(B), Code Sec. 63(f)(2)(B), Code Sec. 151(b))[21]

An individual claiming an additional standard deduction for blindness who isn't totally

---

14. ¶A-2801; ¶634
15. ¶A-2803; ¶634
16. ¶A-2804; ¶634
17. ¶A-2802; ¶634

18. ¶A-2806
19. ¶A-2806, A-2807; ¶634
20. ¶A-2806; ¶634
21. ¶A-2806

blind must get (and keep, but not file) a certification from an eye doctor or registered optometrist. If the eye condition will never improve, the statement should state this. [22]

On a decedent's final return, the fiduciary may claim the full amount of the appropriate standard deduction regardless of the date of death. [23]

caution: For the standard deduction under the alternative minimum tax, see ¶3206.

¶ 3111   Election to itemize deductions in computing taxable income.

No itemized deductions are allowed unless an election to itemize is made on the return. (Code Sec. 63(e)) A taxpayer who elected to itemize and wants to switch to the standard deduction, or vice versa, can. But the change isn't allowed unless a separately filing spouse makes a consistent change, and both spouses consent in writing to assessment of any deficiency resulting from the change. (Code Sec. 63(e)(3); Reg § 1.63-1)[24]

¶ 3112   Deduction for personal exemptions—suspended for 2018 – 2025.

For 2018 through 2025, the deduction for personal exemptions —including deductions for dependents under Code Sec. 152—is suspended; i.e., it's reduced to zero for those years. (Code Sec. 151(d)(5)) The personal exemption phaseout ("PEP") is also accordingly suspended for those years.

But, for purposes of any Code provision other than Code Sec. 151, the reduction to zero isn't taken into account. This means that for tax years 2018 through 2025, even though the personal exemption is zero, if a Code provision refers to a taxpayer being allowed a deduction (or an individual with respect to whom a taxpayer is allowed a deduction) under Code Sec. 151, then Code Sec. 151 will still apply for that purpose. This is the case for, among other provisions: the Code Sec. 24 child tax credit (¶2351), the earned income credit (¶2338), and qualification for head-of-household filing status (¶3127). IRS says that the amount treated as the exemption amount for these purposes is $4,150 for 2018 ($4,200 for 2019, as calculated by Thomson Reuters using inflation data).

¶ 3113   "Dependent" defined.

A person qualifies as a taxpayer's dependent (i.e., for tax rules that incorporate the definition of "dependent," notwithstanding the 2018 – 2025 suspension of the dependency exemption; see ¶3112) if the person is the taxpayer's qualifying child (¶3114) or qualifying relative (¶3116). (Code Sec. 152(a))[25] An individual who is a taxpayer's dependent for a tax year is treated as having no dependents for the individual's tax year beginning in the calendar year when the taxpayer's tax year begins. (Code Sec. 152(b)(1)) But, for purposes of this rule, the individual isn't considered a dependent of a person if that person isn't required to file an income tax return and either doesn't file a return, or files a return solely to claim a refund of estimated or withheld taxes. (Prop Reg § 1.152-1(a)(2)(i) ["Taxpayers may apply"])[26]

Also, an individual isn't treated as a taxpayer's dependent if the individual makes a joint return with the individual's spouse for the tax year beginning in the calendar year when the taxpayer's tax year begins. (Code Sec. 152(b)(2))[27]

A dependent must be a U.S. citizen, national, or resident, or a resident of Canada or Mexico at some time in the calendar year in which the taxpayer's tax year begins. (Code Sec. 152(b)(3)(A), Reg § 1.152-2(a)(1))[28] But an adopted child who isn't a U.S. citizen or

---

22. ¶A-2808
23. ¶C-9603; ¶60,124.04
24. ¶A-2702; ¶634
25. ¶A-3601; ¶1524

26. ¶A-3626; ¶1524)
27. ¶A-3622; ¶1524
28. ¶A-3623; ¶1524

resident (or a resident of Canada or Mexico) isn't excluded from the definition of dependent if: (i) for the taxpayer's tax year, the child has the same principal place of abode as the taxpayer; (ii) for the taxpayer's tax year, the child is a member of the taxpayer's household; and, (iii) the taxpayer is a U.S. citizen or national. This rule is limited to adopted children, and doesn't apply to stepchildren of a U.S. citizen who have not been adopted or lawfully placed for adoption. (Code Sec. 152(b)(3)(B))[29]

¶ 3114   "Qualifying child" defined.

A taxpayer's "qualifying child" (i.e., for tax rules that incorporate the definition of "dependent," notwithstanding the 2018 – 2025 suspension of the dependency exemption; see ¶3112) for a tax year is an individual who: (1) bears a relationship to the taxpayer specified below; (2) has the same principal place of abode as the taxpayer for more than half the tax year (except that a child of divorced or separated parents can be treated as the noncustodial parent's qualifying child if the custodial parent has released the claim to the child's dependency exemption to the noncustodial parent under Code Sec. 152(e)); (3) hasn't reached a specified age (see below); (4) hasn't provided over half the child's own support for the calendar year in which the taxpayer's tax year begins; and (5) hasn't filed a joint return (other than for a refund claim) with the individual's spouse for the tax year beginning in the calendar year in which the taxpayer's tax year begins. (Code Sec. 152(c)(1), Code Sec. 152(e)(1))[30] For tie-breaking rules, see ¶3115.

The following relationships of an individual to the taxpayer meet requirement (1), above:

. . . a child (defined below) of the taxpayer, or a child's descendant (Code Sec. 152(c)(2)(A)), or

. . . a brother, sister, stepbrother, stepsister, half-brother, or half-sister of the taxpayer or a descendant of those relatives. (Code Sec. 152(c)(2)(B), Code Sec. 152(f)(4))[31]

For this purpose, the term "child" means an individual who is:

• a son, daughter, stepson, or stepdaughter of the taxpayer (Code Sec. 152(f)(1)(A)(i)), or

• an eligible foster child of the taxpayer (Code Sec. 152(f)(1)(A)(i)), i.e., an individual placed with the taxpayer by an authorized placement agency or by judgment, decree, or other order of any court of competent jurisdiction. (Code Sec. 152(f)(1)(C))

For this purpose, a registered domestic partner (or partner in other formal relationship that isn't a marriage under state law) is the stepparent of the partner's child if so treated under the law of the state in which the partners reside. [32]

In determining if an individual is taxpayer's son, daughter, stepson, stepdaughter, brother, or sister, one who's legally adopted by an individual, or lawfully placed with one for legal adoption by him, is treated as a child of that individual by blood. (Code Sec. 152(f)(1)(B))[33]

An individual meets the age requirement in (3), above, if the individual:

. . . is younger than the taxpayer and hasn't reached age 19 as of the end of the calendar year in which the taxpayer's tax year begins;

. . . is younger than the taxpayer and is a student who hasn't reached age 24 as of the end of that calendar year (Code Sec. 152(c)(3)(A)); or

. . . is permanently and totally disabled, as defined in Code Sec. 22(e)(3) (¶2347), at any time during that calendar year. (Code Sec. 152(c)(3)(B))[34]

---

29. ¶A-3624; ¶1524
30. ¶A-3605.2; ¶1524
31. ¶A-3605.3; ¶1524

32. ¶A-3605.3; ¶1524
33. ¶A-3612; ¶1524
34. ¶A-3605.4; ¶1524

👁️*observation:* If a child of the taxpayer doesn't meet the definition of a "qualifying child," for example, because the child doesn't meet the age test, the child may still qualify as a dependent under the "qualifying relative" test, ¶3116.

¶ 3115 "Qualifying child"—tie-breaking rules where two or more taxpayers claim a qualifying child.

If an individual can be claimed as a qualifying child (¶3114) by two or more taxpayers for a tax year beginning in the same calendar year, the following tie-breaking rules apply (i.e., for tax rules that incorporate the definition of "dependent," notwithstanding the 2018 – 2025 suspension of the dependency exemption; see ¶3112):

(1) If two or more taxpayers may claim an individual as a qualifying child for a tax year beginning in the same calendar year, the individual will be treated as the qualifying child of the taxpayer who is: (a) a parent of the individual, or (b) if item (a) doesn't apply, the taxpayer with the highest adjusted gross income (AGI) for that tax year. (Code Sec. 152(c)(4)(A)) If more than one taxpayer who can claim an individual as a qualifying child is a parent of the individual, then any one of those parents may claim the individual as a qualifying child. (Prop Reg. § 1.152-2(g)(1)(i) ["Taxpayers may apply"])

(2) If the parents don't file a joint return together, the child will be treated as the qualifying child of: (a) the parent with whom the child resided for the longest period of time during the tax year, or (b) if the child resided with both parents for the same amount of time during the tax year, the parent with the higher AGI. (Code Sec. 152(c)(4)(B)) The same rule will apply where a child is a qualifying child of both parents who are registered domestic partners or partners in a similar formal relationship that isn't a marriage under state law.

(3) If an individual's parents can claim the individual as a qualifying child but no parent does, another taxpayer may claim the individual as a qualifying child, but only if that taxpayer's AGI is higher than the highest AGI of any parent of the individual. (Code Sec. 152(c)(4)(C))[35]

¶ 3116 "Qualifying relative" defined.

A "qualifying relative" for a tax year (i.e., for tax rules that incorporate the definition of "dependent," notwithstanding the 2018 – 2025 suspension of the dependency exemption; see ¶3112) is an individual:

(1) who bears a specified relationship to the taxpayer (see below);

(2) whose gross income for the calendar year in which that tax year begins is less than the exemption amount ($4,150 for this purpose for 2018; $4,200 for 2019, as calculated by Thomson Reuters using inflation data, see ¶3112);

(3) with respect to whom the taxpayer provides over half of the individual's support (¶3118) for the calendar year in which that tax year begins (for multiple support agreements, see ¶3117); and

(4) who isn't a qualifying child (¶3114) of that taxpayer or of any other taxpayer for any tax year that begins in the calendar year in which that tax year begins. (Code Sec. 152(d)(1))[36]

A registered domestic partner is a dependent of the partner if the requirements of Code Sec. 151 and Code Sec. 152 are met. Registered domestic partners who live in community property states are unlikely to meet the requirements of (2) and (3) above. [37]

---

35. ¶A-3605.5 *et seq.*; ¶1524
36. ¶A-3605.6; ¶1524

37. ¶A-3608.1; ¶1524

The following relationships of an individual to the taxpayer meet the relationship test (item (1), above): a child or a descendant of a child, including foster and adopted children who will qualify under the rules in ¶3114; a brother, sister, half-brother, half-sister, stepbrother, or stepsister; the father or mother, or an ancestor of either; a stepfather or stepmother; a nephew or niece; an uncle or aunt; a son-in-law, daughter-in-law, father-in-law, mother-in-law, brother-in-law, or sister-in-law; and an individual (other than one who, at any time in the tax year, was the taxpayer's spouse, determined without regard to Code Sec. 7703) whose principal place of abode is the taxpayer's home and who is a member of the taxpayer's household for the taxpayer's tax year. (Code Sec. 152(d)(2), Code Sec. 152(f)(4))[38]

¶ 3117 Multiple support agreement—Form 2120.

For purposes of the support test for qualifying relatives (¶3116), i.e., for tax rules that incorporate the definition of "dependent," notwithstanding the 2018 – 2025 suspension of the dependency exemption (see ¶3112), over one-half of an individual's support (¶3118) for a calendar year is treated as received from the taxpayer if:

(1) no one person contributed over half of that support;

(2) over half of that support was received from two or more persons each of whom, but for the fact that that person alone didn't contribute over half of that support, would have been entitled to claim the individual as a dependent for a tax year beginning in that calendar year;

(3) the taxpayer contributed over 10% of that support; *and*

(4) each person described in (2), other than the taxpayer, who contributed over 10% of that support files a written declaration that the person won't claim the individual as a dependent for any tax year that begins in that calendar year. (Code Sec. 152(d)(3))[39]

¶ 3118 "Support" defined.

Support (i.e., for tax rules that incorporate the definition of "dependent," notwithstanding the 2018 – 2025 suspension of the dependency exemption; see ¶3112) includes:[40]

. . . food and clothing;

. . . recreation, including toys, summer camp, horseback riding, entertainment, vacations;

. . . medical and dental care, including premiums on accident and health insurance;

. . . child care expenses, even though a credit is also allowed for these expenses;

. . . allowances, gifts;

. . . lodging—when furnished in kind, measured by its fair market value rather than actual cost (Reg § 1.152-1(a)(2));[41]

. . . education—these costs include board, uniforms at military schools, and tuition, even where free schooling is available. Scholarship payments received by a dependent are treated as support furnished by someone other than the taxpayer, but aren't counted in determining if the taxpayer furnished more than half the dependent's support if the dependent is the taxpayer's child (including stepchild, foster child, or child adopted or placed for adoption) who's a full-time student at an educational institution. (Code Sec. 152(f)(5), Reg § 1.152-1(c))[42]

Under proposed regs that taxpayers can apply prior to finalization, a surviving child's

38. ¶A-3606; ¶1524
39. ¶A-3731; ¶1524
40. ¶A-3701 *et seq.*; ¶1524.06
41. ¶A-3701 *et seq.*, A-3714 *et seq.*; ¶1524.09
42. ¶A-3721; ¶1524.07

Social Security benefit payment used to support the child is considered as paid by the child for the child's own support (Prop Reg. § 1.152-4(a)(3)(ii)(B) ["Taxpayers may apply"]), [43] and governmental payments and need-based subsidies for an item of support are support provided by a third party, the government. (Prop Reg. § 1.152-4(a)(3)(i), ["Taxpayers may apply"]) But governmental payments that are based on a taxpayer's earnings and contributions into the Social Security system are support provided by the individual for whose benefit the payments are made, to the extent those payments are used for that individual's support. (Prop Reg. § 1.152-4(a)(3)(ii)(A) ["Taxpayers may apply"]) [44]

Armed Forces dependency allotments — the amount contributed by the government *and* the amount withheld from the pay of the member of the Armed Forces — are treated as contributed by the member. [45]

¶ 3119   Allocating support of several contributors to several dependents.

Where more than one member of a household contributes toward expenses that are equally applicable to all members of the household (i.e., for tax rules that incorporate the definition of "dependent," notwithstanding the 2018 – 2025 suspension of the dependency exemption; see ¶3112), the contributors are presumed (absent contrary evidence) to have pooled their contributions toward the support of all members. The total contributed is divided equally among the members as amounts paid for their support, unless there is proof of how much was actually spent for particular members. [46]

¶ 3120   Treatment of child as "qualifying child" or "qualifying relative" by noncustodial parent—Form 8332.

A child is treated as being the "qualifying child" (¶3114) or "qualifying relative" (¶3116) of the noncustodial parent for a calendar year (i.e., for tax rules that incorporate the definition of "dependent," notwithstanding the 2018 – 2025 suspension of the dependency exemption; see ¶3112) if:

(1) the child receives over half of the child's support during the calendar year from the parents;

(2) the child's parents: (a) are divorced or legally separated under a decree of divorce or separate maintenance; (b) are separated under a written separation agreement; or (c) live apart at all times during the last six months of the calendar year, whether or not they are or were married;

(3) the child is in the custody of one or both parents for over half the calendar year; and

(4) the custodial parent signs a written declaration (on Form 8332) stating that he or she won't claim that child as a dependent for the tax year beginning in that calendar year, which the noncustodial parent attaches to his or her return *or* a pre-'85 decree of divorce or separate maintenance or written separation agreement between the parents provides that the noncustodial parent can claim the child as a dependent, and the noncustodial parent provides at least $600 for support of the child during the year. (Draft Form 1040 Instructions; Sept. 26, 2018) Code Sec. 152(e)(1), Code Sec. 152(c)(2),Reg § 1.152-4(b))[47]

⊘ observation: While the dependency exemption deduction is currently suspended (¶3112), a note on Form 8332 states that it still "applies to some tax benefits, including the child tax credit, additional child tax credit, and credit for other dependents." (Draft Form 8332; July 19, 2018)

---

43. ¶A-3712
44. ¶A-3712
45. ¶A-3711; ¶1524.09

46. ¶A-3708
47. ¶A-3851; ¶1524.10

A child is in the custody of one or both parents for more than one-half of the calendar year (item (3), above) if one or both parents have the right under state law to physical custody of the child for more than one-half of the calendar year. (Reg § 1.152-4(c)) But a child isn't in the custody of either parent for this purpose after the child reaches the age of majority and is emancipated under state law. [48]

The custodial parent is the parent with whom the child resides for the greater number of nights during the calendar year. (Code Sec. 152(e)(4)(A),Reg § 1.152-4(d))[49]

The above rules apply despite: the Code Sec. 152(c)(1)(B) requirement that a qualifying child have the same principal place of abode as the taxpayer for more than half the year, ¶3114; the Code Sec. 152(c)(4) tie-breaking rules, ¶3115; or the Code Sec. 152(d)(1)(C) support test for qualifying relatives, ¶3116. (Code Sec. 152(e)(1),Reg § 1.152-4(b)(1))[50]

In certain cases, IRS treats a child of parents who are divorced, separated, or living apart as the dependent of both parents for purposes of Code Sec. 105(b) (employer-provided medical expense reimbursements, ¶1254), Code Sec. 132(h)(2)(B) (excludable fringe benefits, ¶1241), Code Sec. 213(d)(5) (deductible medical expenses, ¶2142), Code Sec. 220(d)(2) (Archer Medical Savings Accounts (MSAs), ¶1527), and Code Sec. 223(d)(2) (Health Saving Accounts (HSAs), ¶1528) when the custodial parent hasn't released the claim to the exemption for the child under Code Sec. 152(e)(2).[1]

The above rules relating to release don't apply where, under the Code Sec. 152(d)(3) rules for multiple support agreements (¶3117), more than half the child's support is treated as having been received from a taxpayer. (Code Sec. 152(e)(5))[2]

For purposes of these rules, if a parent remarries, support of a child received from this remarried parent's spouse is treated as received from the parent. (Code Sec. 152(e)(6))[3]

¶ 3121   Relationship test—effect of death or divorce.

For purposes of tax rules that incorporate the definition of "dependent" (notwithstanding the 2018 − 2025 suspension of the dependency exemption; see ¶3112), death or divorce doesn't end relationships established by marriage. So, for example, the relationship of son-in-law and father-in-law survives the spouse's death. (Reg § 1.152-2(d))[4]

¶ 3122   Tax status of kidnapped children.

Solely for the purposes listed below, a taxpayer's child who is presumed by law enforcement authorities to have been kidnapped by a non-family member, and who had, for the tax year in which the kidnapping occurred, the same principal place of abode as the taxpayer for more than half of the portion of that year before the kidnapping date, is treated as meeting the requirement in Code Sec. 152(c) that a "qualifying child" have the same principal place of abode as the taxpayer for more than half the tax year for all tax years ending during the period that the individual is kidnapped. (Code Sec. 152(f)(6)(A)) This rule applies for purposes of the child tax credit; surviving spouse or a head of a household status; and the earned income credit. (Code Sec. 152(f)(6)(B)) Comparable treatment applies to certain qualifying relatives (¶3116). (Code Sec. 152(f)(6)(C))[5]

¶ 3123   Tax rate schedules for individuals.

There's a tax rate schedule for:

(1) Single persons (not married at year's end), including certain marrieds living apart

---

48. ¶A-3852
49. ¶A-3853; ¶1524.10
50. ¶A-3851; ¶1524.10
1. ¶A-3861; ¶1524.10

2. ¶A-3851; ¶1524.10
3. ¶A-3851; ¶1524.10
4. ¶A-3606; ¶1524.03
5. ¶A-3601.1; ¶1514.02

(¶3126), see ¶1102. These rates are more favorable than those for marrieds filing separate returns, but less favorable than head-of-household and (generally) joint return rates.

(2) Married couples filing joint returns, and certain widows and widowers who qualify as "surviving spouses" (¶3125), see ¶1103. These are often the most favorable rates.

(3) Heads of household, see ¶1105—more favorable rates than those for single persons.

(4) Married persons filing separately, see ¶1104—least favorable rates. (Code Sec. 1)[6]

For 2018 through 2025, the individual tax rates are 10%, 12%, 22%, 24%, 32%, 35%, and 37%. (Code Sec. 1)[7]

¶ 3124   Tax tables.

IRS has prepared tax tables, based on the tax rates. (Code Sec. 3(a)(1))[8] The draft 2018 table for Form 1040 filers with taxable income less than $100,000 is reproduced at ¶1111. The tables aren't used by those who file a short-period return because they changed their accounting period. (Code Sec. 3(b)(1))[9]

¶ 3125   When surviving spouse (qualifying widow/er) gets lower joint return rates.

A surviving spouse (qualifying widow/er) whose spouse died during either of the surviving spouse's two tax years immediately preceding the tax year (Code Sec. 2(a)(1)) is taxed at joint return rates (Code Sec. 1(a)(2)) if the surviving spouse:

. . . hasn't remarried at any time before the end of the tax year (Code Sec. 2(a)(2)(A)),

. . . "maintains" (pays over 50% of the costs of) a household as the surviving spouse's home that's the "principal place of abode" of a dependent (a) who is taxpayer's son or daughter (including adopted children, but not foster children), stepson, or stepdaughter, and (b) for whom taxpayer would have been entitled to a dependency deduction (¶3112 et seq) for the tax year (Code Sec. 2(a)(1)(B)), and

. . . could file a joint return with the deceased for the year of death. (Code Sec. 2(a)(2)(B))[10]

observation: The surviving spouse rules *don't* apply for the year the spouse died. For when a joint return can be filed (and joint return rates used) in such year, see ¶4705 and ¶4708.

A special rule applies for spouses of individuals in "missing status" as a result of "combat zone" or "qualified hazardous duty area" service. If an MIA or POW is officially determined to be dead, and so is removed from the missing status rolls, surviving spouse status doesn't depend on the actual date of death. The relevant date is the date of the official determination, or, if earlier, two years after the date of official termination of combat activities in that zone. If a later actual death is established, that date will control. (Code Sec. 2(a)(3))[11]

¶ 3126   Certain married individuals living apart treated as unmarried.

A married taxpayer is considered single for tax purposes if the taxpayer meets all of the following tests (Code Sec. 7703(b); Reg § 1.7703-1(b)):

(1) Files a separate return.

---

6. ¶A-1101 *et seq.*; ¶14.08
7. ¶A-1102; ¶14.08
8. ¶A-1100; ¶34 *et seq.*

9. ¶A-1181; ¶34.02
10. ¶A-1700 *et seq.*; ¶24.02
11. ¶A-1703; ¶24.02

(2) Maintains as the taxpayer's home a household that for more than half the tax year is the principal place of abode of a child (defined in Code Sec. 152(f)(1), ¶3114) for whom he's entitled to a dependency deduction for the year, or would be so entitled if the taxpayer hadn't released the exemption to the noncustodial parent (¶3120). (Code Sec. 7703(b)(1))

(3) Furnishes over half the cost of maintaining the household. (Code Sec. 7703(b)(2))

(4) During the last six months of the tax year, the taxpayer's spouse isn't a member of the household. (Code Sec. 7703(b)(3))[12]

🅡 *observation:* Individuals treated as unmarried under this "abandoned spouse" rule can use the single or head-of-household rates.

Either or both spouses can qualify as "unmarried" by meeting the tests. If only one spouse qualifies, the other spouse must use married-filing-separately rates. [13]

A taxpayer who doesn't meet the above rules is considered married even though living apart from a spouse, unless legally separated under a decree of divorce or separate maintenance. (Reg § 1.7703-1(a))[14]

¶ 3127   Head-of-household status.

To qualify as a head of household for a tax year, a taxpayer must:

(1) be unmarried (or treated as unmarried, ¶3126) at the end of the year;

(2) not be a surviving spouse (Code Sec. 2(b)(1), Reg § 1.2-2(b)(1));

(3) not be a nonresident alien at any time that year (Code Sec. 2(b)(3)(A); *and*

(4) maintain a household: (a) that's the taxpayer's home, and for more than half of the tax year, the principal place of abode of a child or other dependent who is a "member of that household" (Code Sec. 2(b)(1)(A)), or (b) (not necessarily the taxpayer's own) that for the tax year is the principal place of abode for either the taxpayer's father or mother. (Code Sec. 2(b)(1)(B))[15]

The same individual can't be used to qualify more than one taxpayer as head of household during the same tax year. (Reg § 1.2-2(b)(2))[16]

A qualifying child for this purpose is defined in Code Sec. 152(c) (¶3114), but without regard to Code Sec. 152(e) (custodial parent's release of exemption, ¶3120). But a taxpayer isn't eligible for head of household status if the child is married at the end of taxpayer's tax year and isn't taxpayer's dependent because the child filed a joint return and/or isn't a U.S. citizen or resident. (Code Sec. 2(b)(1)(A)(i))[17] If registered domestic partners who reside in a community property state pay all the costs of maintaining a household from community funds, each partner has incurred half the cost, and neither can qualify. Even if one partner pays more than half by contributing separate funds, that partner cannot file as head of household if that partner's only dependent is the other registered domestic partner. [18]

¶ 3128   Tax on Unearned Income of Children—Kiddie Tax. ▬▬▬▬▬▬

For tax years beginning after 2017 and before 2026, the taxable income of a child attributable to earned income is taxed under the rates for single individuals (¶1102), and taxable income of a child attributable to net unearned income (¶3131) is taxed according to the brackets applicable to trusts and estates (¶1106). This

---

12. ¶A-1610 *et seq.*; ¶77,034.01
13. ¶A-1502; ¶14.01
14. ¶A-1611; ¶77,034.01
15. ¶A-1401.1 *et seq.*; ¶24.03

16. ¶A-1401.1 ;¶24.03
17. ¶A-1406 *et seq.*; ¶24.03
18. ¶A-1416 *et seq.*

rule applies to the child's ordinary income and the child's income taxed at preferential rates. (Code Sec. 1(j)(4))

observation: The amount of tax paid by the child under the post-2017 kiddie tax rules is no longer determined by the parents' tax situation (see below).

¶ 3129 Child subject to kiddie tax.

The kiddie tax applies to a child if: (1) the child is under age 19 by the close of the tax year, or is a full-time student age 19 to 23; (2) the child's unearned income exceeds an inflation-adjusted prescribed amount ($2,100 for 2018; $2,200 for 2019, as calculated by Thomson Reuters using inflation data); and (3) the child doesn't file a joint return. For a child age 18, or a child age 19 to 23 who is a full-time student, the kiddie tax rules apply only if the child's earned income doesn't exceed one-half of the amount of the child's support. (Code Sec. 1(g)(2))[19]

¶ 3130 Computing the kiddie tax—Form 8615.

For tax years beginning in 2018 through 2025, children to whom the kiddie tax rules apply (¶3129), who have over the prescribed amount of unearned income for the year (¶3129), are taxed on that excess at the ordinary and capital gain rates applicable to estates and trusts. (Code Sec. 1(j)(4))[20]

Specifically, for a child to whom the kiddie tax rules apply (see ¶3129) for a tax year, in determining the amount of tax imposed on the child, the otherwise applicable income tax table (i.e., generally, the tax rate schedule for single individuals, see ¶1111) is applied with the following changes: (1) the maximum taxable income taxed at a rate below 24% can't be more than the sum of: (a) the child's "earned taxable income" (see below), plus (b) the minimum taxable income for the 24% bracket in the estates and trusts income tax table for the tax year (i.e., for 2018, $2,550; for 2019, $2,600, as calculated by Thomson Reuters using inflation data, see ¶1106); (2) the maximum taxable income taxed at a rate below 35% can't be more than the sum of: (a) the child's "earned taxable income," plus (b) the minimum taxable income for the 35% bracket in the estates and trusts income tax table for the tax year (i.e., for 2018, $9,150; for 2019, $9,300, as calculated by Thomson Reuters using inflation data, see ¶1106); and (3) the maximum taxable income taxed at a rate below 37% can't be more than the sum of: (a) the child's "earned taxable income," plus (b) the minimum taxable income for the 37% bracket in the estates and trusts income tax table for the tax year (i.e., for 2018, $12,500; for 2019, $12,750, as calculated by Thomson Reuters using inflation data, see ¶1106). (Code Sec. 1(j)(4))[21]

observation: Applying the estate and trust tax income tax rates under the kiddie tax rules in many cases will produce a higher tax bill because the income ranges (brackets) under the estate and trust income tax table are much smaller than those for individuals.

Further, for purposes of applying the capital gains rates (¶2602): (a) the maximum zero rate amount (¶2602) can't be more than the sum of: (i) the child's earned taxable income, plus (ii) the maximum zero rate amount for estates and trusts in effect for the tax year (i.e., for 2018, $2,550; for 2019, $2,600, see ¶1106); and (b) the maximum 15% rate amount (see ¶2602) can't be more than the sum of: (i) the child's earned taxable income plus (ii) the maximum 15% rate amount for estates and trusts in effect for the tax year (i.e., for 2018, $12,500; for 2019, $12,750, see ¶1106). (Code Sec. 1(j)(4)(C))[22]

The child's "earned taxable income" means, for any child for any year, the child's

---

19. ¶A-1301; ¶14.09
20. ¶A-1301 *et seq.*; ¶14.09
21. ¶A-1301 *et seq.*; ¶14.09
22. ¶A-1301; ¶14.09

taxable income reduced (but not below zero) by the child's "net unearned income" (see ¶3131). (Code Sec. 1(j)(4)(D))[23]

Parents of a child subject to the kiddie tax will have to give the child their taxpayer identification number (TIN) so it can be included on the child's return. (Code Sec. 1(g)(6))[24] If a child can't get the required information from a parent, the child (or legal representative) will be able to request the necessary information from IRS. (Code Sec. 6103(e)(1)(A)(iii); Reg § 1.1(i)-1T, Q&A22)[25]

✔*caution:* For the child's alternative minimum tax, see ¶3204.

¶ 3131   "Net unearned income" for kiddie tax purposes.

For the kiddie tax rules (¶3130), "net unearned income" is the portion of the child's "AGI not attributable to earned income" (i.e., investment income), reduced by the sum of the following amounts (collectively, the "reduction amount") (Code Sec. 1(g)(4)(A); Reg § 1.1(i)-1T):

(1) the amount in effect for the tax year under Code Sec. 63(c)(5)(A) (Code Sec. 1(g)(4)(A)(ii)(I); Reg § 1.1(i)-1T, Q&A6), relating to one component of the standard deduction for a child who can be claimed as a dependent —i.e., $1,050 for 2018 ($1,100 for 2019, as calculated by Thomson Reuters using inflation data) (¶3110);

(2) the greater of (a) the amount in (1) or (b) the amount of the itemized deductions directly connected with the production of the unearned income if the child itemizes deductions (Code Sec. 1(g)(4)(A)(ii)(II); Reg § 1.1(i)-1T, Q&A6);

(3) adjustments to income attributable to the unearned income, such as the penalty on early withdrawal of savings. [26]

✔*observation:* For children who don't itemize deductions, the "reduction amount" for net unearned income is generally $2,100 for 2018 ($2,200 for 2019).

But a child's net unearned income can't exceed the child's taxable income. (Code Sec. 1(g)(4)(B))[27]

Earned income means earned income as defined in Code Sec. 911(d)(2)—i.e., income attributable to wages, salaries, or other amounts received as compensation for personal services. (Code Sec. 1(g)(4)(A)(i); Reg § 1.1(i)-1T, Q&A6) Distributions from certain qualified disability trusts are treated as earned income. (Code Sec. 1(g)(4)(C))) But the taxable part of social security or pension benefits paid to the child are unearned income. (Reg § 1.1(i)-1T, Q&A9) Unearned income also includes taxable interest, dividends, capital gains (including capital gain distributions), rents, royalties, etc. [28]

¶ 3132   Parents' election to be taxed on child's unearned income—Form 8814.

✔*caution:* It's not clear, after changes made by the Tax Cuts and Jobs Act (PL 115-97, 12/22/2017) to the kiddie tax rules for tax years 2018 – 2025 (see ¶3130), whether Congress intended for the election to report the income of a child subject to the kiddie tax on the parents' return, to be available in 2018 – 2025. As of the date of publication, IRS has made available a draft 2018 version of the form (Form 8814) that's used to make the election, providing some indication that it will apply; and the discussion below, using 2018 figures, presumes that it will apply.

A parent can irrevocably elect (on Form 8814) to include in the parent's gross income for

23. ¶A-1301; ¶14.09
24. ¶S-1544; ¶14.09
25. ¶S-6403; ¶61,034.04

26. ¶A-1305; ¶14.09
27. ¶A-1305; ¶14.09
28. ¶A-1301.1, A-1307; ¶14.09

the tax year the child's gross income in excess of $2,100 for 2018 ($2,200 for 2019, as calculated by Thomson Reuters using inflation data). (Code Sec. 1(g)(7)(B)(i); Reg § 301.9100-8(a)(4)(i)) The child is then treated as having no gross income for the year and isn't required to file a return. (Code Sec. 1(g)(7)(A))[29]

For 2018, the election applies only if the child's gross income is only from interest, dividends, and capital gain distributions; it's more than $1,050 and less than $10,500 (for 2019, $1,100 and $11,000, as calculated by Thomson Reuters using inflation data); the child made no estimated tax payments for, and didn't apply any overpayments to, the year; and backup withholding didn't apply. (Code Sec. 1(g)(7)(A))[30]

For 2018, the electing parent's tax equals the sum of: (1) the tax on the parent's taxable income after taking into account the child's gross income over $2,100, plus (2) 10% of the lesser of (a) $1,050, or (b) the excess of the child's gross income over $1,050. The corresponding 2019 figures are $2,200, $11,000 and $1,100, as calculated by Thomson Reuters using inflation data. (Code Sec. 1(g)(7)(B)(ii))[31] Any interest income that is a tax preference item of the child is treated as that of the electing parent. (Code Sec. 1(g)(7)(B)(iii))[32]

⊘illustration: S, age 6, receives $5,000 in interest income in 2018. The requirements for making the election to report his income on his parents' return are satisfied, and his parents make the election. So they include $2,900 of S's gross income on their tax return ($5,000 gross income, minus $2,100 (2 × $1,050)). They also must pay an additional tax of $105 (i.e., 10% of the lesser of (a) $1,050, or (b) $3,950 ($5,000 − $1,050)). Assuming a 25% tax bracket applies to the parents, the added tax under the election would be $830, i.e., $725 (25% × $2,900) + $105.

¶ 3133   Self-Employment (SE) Tax—Schedule SE ▬▬▬▬▬▬

Self-employeds pay social security (OASDI) and Medicare (hospital insurance) taxes as part of their income tax.

These taxes are imposed (compute on Form 1040, Schedule SE) on self-employment income (¶3134). (Code Sec. 1401(a), Code Sec. 1401(b)).[33] For contribution bases and rates for the SE tax, including the 0.9% additional Medicare self-employment tax, see ¶1109. For who is subject to the SE tax, see ¶3138.

¶ 3134   Self-employment (SE) income subject to SE tax.

SE income consists of net earnings from self-employment (¶3135). But in computing an individual's SE tax (¶3133), the maximum amount of SE income subject to OASDI tax for a tax year (whether 12 months or less) is the contribution base (¶1109) for the calendar year in which the tax year begins, minus wages received in the same tax year. If net earnings from self-employment are less than $400 ($100 for a church employee (Code Sec. 1402(j)(2)(B))), SE income for that year is zero. (Code Sec. 1402(b); Reg § 1.1402(b)-1)[34]

⊘observation: Since a 7.65% deduction (¶3135) is allowed from net profits (i.e., net earnings from self-employment before that deduction), an individual can have actual net profits of up to $433.13 (92.35% of $433.13 = $400) without triggering SE tax.

A mitigation provision can come into play where wages were erroneously reported as self-employment income or vice versa. (Code Sec. 6521)[35]

---

29. ¶A-1326; ¶14.11
30. ¶A-1327; ¶14.11
31. ¶A-1330; ¶14.11
32. ¶A-1330; ¶14.11

33. ¶A-6001; ¶14,024
34. ¶A-6031 *et seq.*; ¶14,024.02
35. ¶T-3634; ¶14,024.18, 65,214.01

¶ 3135   Net earnings from self-employment.

This is gross income, under the individual's income tax accounting method, from a trade or business carried on by the individual, less allowable deductions for that business, plus the distributive share of partnership taxable income (whether or not distributed) or loss from a partnership of which the individual's a member. (Code Sec. 1402(a); Reg § 1.1402(a)-1)[36]

A deduction is allowed for 7.65% of net earnings from self-employment for the tax year (determined without this deduction), computed without regard to the 0.9% additional Medicare self-employment tax (see ¶1109). (Code Sec. 1402(a)(12))[37]

An individual with more than one business must combine the net earnings from each to determine self-employment income. The gains and loss from the businesses are netted, so a loss in one reduces a gain in another. (Reg § 1.1402(a)-2(c))[38] If an individual has a part-time business and a regular job as an employee, only the income from the part-time business is included in determining net earnings. [39]

In computing net earnings from self-employment, the following deductions *aren't* allowed:

. . . deduction for a self-employed's health insurance costs (Code Sec. 162(l)(4));

. . . deduction for net operating losses (Code Sec. 1402(a)(4));

. . . nonbusiness deductions. [40]

Net earnings from self-employment *don't include*:

• certain income received by a retired partner under a written plan of the partnership (Code Sec. 1402(a)(10));[41]

• dividends or interest on investments (Code Sec. 1402(a)(2));[42]

• gains (or losses) from disposition of a capital asset or other property that's not inventory or held for sale to customers (Code Sec. 1402(a)(3));[43] but options and commodities dealers must include gains and losses derived from dealing or trading in options and regulated futures subject to mark-to-market rules in SE net earnings (Code Sec. 1402(i));[44]

• gain or loss of a securities or commodities trader that is treated as ordinary solely by reason of the election of mark-to-market treatment (Code Sec. 475(f)(1)(D));[45]

• qualified disaster relief (or mitigation) payments (Code Sec. 139(d));[46]

• rents from real estate (and personal property leased with it) held for investment. (Code Sec. 1402(a)(1)) But rents are included in net earnings if received by real estate dealers in the normal course of business (Reg § 1.1402(a)-4(a)),[47] or if the rent is for living quarters where *services* (e.g., maid service) are also rendered primarily for the occupant's convenience (Reg § 1.1402(a)-4(c)(2)), such as in hotels, boarding houses, tourist camps or homes, parking lots, warehouses and storage garages; [48]

• rents paid in crop shares unless paid under an arrangement where the landowner (or tenant) materially participates in crop production or controls and directs the farming operation and pays the farmer at a fixed rate as an employee (Reg § 1.1402(a)-4(b));[49]

• certain termination payments received by former insurance salesmen (Code

36. ¶A-6100 *et seq.*; ¶14,024.07
37. ¶A-6114; ¶14,024
38. ¶A-6103; ¶14,024
39. ¶A-6103; ¶14,024
40. ¶A-6113; ¶14,024
41. ¶A-6166; ¶14,024.16
42. ¶A-6108; ¶14,024.05

43. ¶A-6109; ¶14,024.06
44. ¶A-6112; ¶14,024.06
45. ¶A-6112.1; ¶4754.01
46. ¶A-6105; ¶1394
47. ¶A-6105, A-6106; ¶14,024.04
48. ¶A-6107; ¶14,024.04
49. ¶A-6202 *et seq.*; ¶14,024.04

Sec. 1402(k));[50]

* a shareholder's share of an S corporation's income (whether distributed or not) or loss.[1]

A passive activity loss that's disallowed for income tax purposes isn't taken into account in computing net earnings from self-employment. (Reg § 1.469-1T(d)(3))[2]

Holding public office isn't an SE trade or business, except for certain state or local officials paid solely on a fee basis (¶3138). (Code Sec. 1402(c)(1))[3]

¶ 3136 Partner's self-employment tax.

A partner's net earnings from self-employment are, generally, the partner's distributive share of the partnership's taxable income arising out of the trade or business of the partnership plus the partner's guaranteed payments. (Code Sec. 1402(a); Reg § 1.1402(a)-1(a)(2), Reg § 1.1402(a)-1(b))[4]

The distributive share of any item of income or loss of a limited partner is excluded. But this exclusion doesn't apply to guaranteed payments to that partner for services actually rendered to or on behalf of the partnership, to the extent the payments are shown to be remuneration for those services. (Code Sec. 1402(a)(13))[5]

¶ 3137 Married couple's self-employment (SE) tax.

SE tax is computed on the separate self-employment income of each spouse, whether or not they file joint returns. But the spouses are jointly and severally liable for SE tax due on a joint return. (Code Sec. 6017; Reg § 1.6017-1(b))[6]

¶ 3138 Who is subject to self-employment (SE) tax?

The SE tax is a tax on self-employed individuals (U.S. citizens and resident aliens). (Code Sec. 1401, Code Sec. 1402(b)) Income earned as an employee isn't subject to SE tax (Code Sec. 1402(c)(2)),[7] with these exceptions:

. . . Members of the clergy, see ¶3139.

. . . Persons 18 or older employed to sell magazines and newspapers to the public at a fixed price, whose pay is the excess of the fixed price over their cost. (Code Sec. 1402(c)(2)(A))[8]

. . . U.S. citizens employed by a foreign government, its wholly owned instrumentality, or an international organization (e.g., the U.N.). (Code Sec. 1402(c)(2)(C))[9]

. . . Fishing boat crew who work on a boat that normally has fewer than 10 crew members and who get no fixed remuneration other than a share of the catch and certain small cash payments. (Code Sec. 1402(c)(2)(F))[10]

. . . Sharecroppers whose earnings depend on production. [11]

. . . State or local government officials whose pay is *solely* fees, unless the services are covered by social security under a federal-state agreement. (Code Sec. 1402(c)(2)(E))[12]

Statutory employees (¶3103) don't pay SE tax (they pay FICA instead) even if treated as self-employed for income tax purposes. (Code Sec. 1402(d), Code Sec. 3121(d)(3))[13]

50. ¶A-6032.1; ¶14,024.155
1. ¶A-6084
2. ¶M-4603; ¶4694.47
3. ¶A-6095; ¶14,024.13
4. ¶A-6150 *et seq.*; ¶14,024.16
5. ¶A-6157; ¶14,024.16
6. ¶S-1812; ¶60,174

7. ¶A-6092; ¶14,024.09
8. ¶A-6087.1; ¶14,024.09
9. ¶A-6097; ¶14,024.09
10. ¶A-6090; ¶14,024.14
11. ¶A-6209; ¶14,024.04
12. ¶A-6092; ¶14,024.13
13. ¶A-6081; ¶14,024.09

Members of certain religious sects who conscientiously oppose social security and file an exemption (Form 4029) are exempt. (Code Sec. 1402(g); Reg § 1.1402(h)-1)[14]

¶ 3139 Members of the clergy.

Members of the clergy, members of religious orders, and Christian Science practitioners are subject to self-employment tax on services performed in the exercise of their ministry (Code Sec. 1402(c)(4), Code Sec. 1402(c)(5)) *unless* they have taken a vow of poverty (Code Sec. 1402(c))[15] or irrevocably elect (on Form 4361) *not* to be covered. (Code Sec. 1402(e))[16]

¶ 3140 Farmers' self-employment (SE) tax.

Self-employed persons must pay SE tax on the income from their farming operations. (Code Sec. 1402(a)) Unless received by an individual who is getting social security retirement or disability payments, IRS holds that conservation reserve program (CRP) payments are includible in SE income. (Code Sec. 1402(a)(1)) Where the payment is to a landlord who doesn't materially participate in production or management of the property, IRS holds the payment is rental and not SE income. But the Eight Circuit holds that CRP payments made to non-farmers are rental income, excludable from the SE self-employment tax; IRS disagrees and will not follow in any circuit for CRP payments after 2007. [17]

Since a farmer has an optional method of computing SE tax on farm income (¶3141), the farmer may have to distinguish farm income from other self-employment income. Farm income comes from an operation on a farm in which more than half the time is devoted to farming activities. (Reg § 1.1402(a)-13)[18]

¶ 3141 Optional methods for computing self-employment (SE) earnings.

The optional method—referred to as the "nonfarm optional method" for nonfarming businesses and the "farm optional method" for farming businesses —is as follows: for 2018, if an individual's gross income from the business is not more than $7,920 ($8,160 for 2019), the individual may elect to treat 66 2/3% of that gross income as SE net earnings from the business. For 2018, if it's more than $7,920 and net profits from the business are less than $5,717.38, the individual may elect to treat $5,280 as SE net earnings from the business. The corresponding figures for 2019 are $8,160, $5,890.63, and $5,440. But if net profits are $5,717.38 or more for 2018 ($5,890.63 for 2019), the individual must use the net profits. (Code Sec. 1402(a), Code Sec. 1402(l); Reg § 1.1402(a)-15(a)(1))[19]

The optional nonfarm method may be used only if: net profits from the nonfarming business are less than $5,717.38 for 2018 ($5,890.63 for 2019) *and* less than 72.189% of gross nonfarm income, SE net earnings were at least $400 in 2 of the prior 3 years, *and* taxpayer has used this method for fewer than 5 years (consecutive or not). (Code Sec. 1402(a), Code Sec. 1402(h))[20]

An individual may use the optional farm method for 2018 if gross farm income is not more than $7,920 ($8,160 for 2019) , or net farm profits are less than $5,717.38 ($5,890.63 for 2019). (Code Sec. 1402(a), Code Sec. 1402(h))[21]

An individual with both farm and nonfarm incomes may use both methods (if otherwise allowed): the farm optional method for the farm income and the nonfarm optional method for the nonfarm income. For 2018, if both methods are used, the combined total SE net earnings can't be more than $5,280 ($5,440 for 2019). (Code Sec. 1402(a); Reg § 1.1402(a)-

---

14. ¶A-6327 *et seq.*; ¶14,024.15
15. ¶A-6301; ¶14,024.10
16. ¶A-6321; ¶14,024.10
17. ¶A-6208

18. ¶A-6201 *et seq.*; ¶614.051
19. ¶A-6117; ¶14,024.20
20. ¶A-6121; ¶14,024.20
21. ¶A-6122; ¶14,024.20

15)[22]

Elect the optional method by computing (on Schedule SE, Form 1040) SE net earnings under that method. The election may be made or revoked after the return is filed, on an amended return. (Code Sec. 1402(a); Reg § 1.1402(a)-16)[23]

¶ 3142   3.8% Net Investment Income Tax (NIIT)—Form 8960. ▬▬▬▬▬▬▬

Certain unearned, passive, and trading income, plus certain net gain, of individuals, trusts, and estates is subject to a 3.8% net investment income tax (NIIT).

For individuals, the NIIT, also called the unearned income Medicare contribution tax, is 3.8% of the lesser of:

(1) net investment income (NII, ¶3143); or

(2) the excess of modified adjusted gross income (MAGI) over an unindexed threshold amount ($250,000 for joint filers or surviving spouses, $125,000 for a married individual filing a separate return, and $200,000 in any other case). (Code Sec. 1411(a)(1), Code Sec. 1411(b), Reg § 1.1411-2(b)(1), Reg § 1.1411-2(d)(1))[24]

Illustration (1): For 2018, A, an unmarried U.S. citizen, has MAGI of $190,000, which includes $50,000 of NII. A isn't liable for the NIIT because the threshold amount for a single individual is $200,000. (Reg § 1.1411-2(b)(2))

Illustration (2): For 2018, B, an unmarried U.S. citizen, has MAGI of $220,000, which includes $50,000 of NII. B pays a NIIT of $760 (3.8% x $20,000). The $20,000 figure is the lesser of the $50,000 NII or the $20,000 excess of MAGI over the $200,000 threshold amount. (Reg § 1.1411-2(b)(2))

MAGI is adjusted gross income (AGI) plus any amount excluded as foreign earned income under Code Sec. 911(a)(1) (net of the deductions and exclusions disallowed with respect to the foreign earned income). (Code Sec. 1411(d), Reg § 1.1411-2(c)(1)(ii))

Any federal income tax credit that may be used to offset a tax imposed by subtitle A of the Code may be used to offset the NIIT, but if a credit is allowed only against income tax, it may not be credited against the NIIT unless specifically provided. [25]

For an estate or trust, the NIIT is 3.8% of the lesser of (1) undistributed NII or (2) the excess of adjusted gross income (AGI, as defined in Code Sec. 67(e)) over the dollar amount at which the highest income tax bracket applicable to an estate or trust begins (see ¶1106). (Code Sec. 1411(a)(2), Reg § 1.1411-3(a)(1))[26]

¶ 3143   What is net investment income (NII)?

For net investment income tax (NIIT) purposes, NII is investment income less deductions properly allocable to NII. Investment income is:

. . . gross income from interest, dividends, annuities, royalties, and rents, unless derived in the ordinary course of a trade or business to which the NIIT *doesn't* apply,

. . . other gross income derived from a trade or business to which the NIIT *does* apply, and

. . . net gain (to the extent taken into account in computing taxable income) attributable to the disposition of property other than property held in a trade or business to which the NIIT *doesn't* apply. (Code Sec. 1411(c), Reg § 1.1411-4(a))[27]

---

22. ¶A-6119; ¶14,024.20
23. ¶A-6125; ¶14,024.20
24. ¶A-6361 *et seq.*; ¶14,114.01 *et seq.*

25. ¶A-6361.1 *et seq.*; ¶14,114.01
26. ¶C-5801; ¶C-9581; ¶14,114.02
27. ¶A-6363; ¶14,114.01

The NIIT applies to a trade or business only if it's a Code Sec. 469 passive activity of the taxpayer, or a trade or business of trading in (a) financial instruments or (b) commodities, as defined in Code Sec. 475(e)(2). (Code Sec. 1411(c)(2))

Gain or loss from a disposition of an interest in a partnership (¶3758) or S corporation (¶3367) is taken into account by the partner or shareholder as NII only to the extent of the net gain or loss that the transferor would take into account if the entity had sold all its property for fair market value immediately before the disposition. (Code Sec. 1411(c)(4))[28]

Deductions taken into account in determining NII include adjustments to income, itemized deductions, and losses. Unless provided elsewhere in the NIIT regs, only the properly allocable deductions listed in Reg § 1.1411-4(f) may be taken into account in determining NII. (Reg § 1.1411-4(f)) If a properly allocable deduction is allocable to both NII and excluded income, taxpayers may use any reasonable method to determine the portion that's properly allocable to NII. (Reg § 1.1411-4(g)(1))[29]

🅡 *observation:* To minimize NIIT at year-end, some taxpayers should minimize (e.g., through deferral) additional NII for the rest of the year, others should try to reduce MAGI other than unearned income, and others should minimize both NII and other types of MAGI.

Items excluded from NII. Investment income for NIIT purposes doesn't include any amount subject to the self-employment tax (¶1109) or amounts distributed from retirement plans (¶4346). (Code Sec. 1411(c)(5), Reg § 1.1411-9(a), Code Sec. 1411(c)(6), Reg § 1.1411-8(a)) NII doesn't include items excluded from gross income for income tax purposes. "Excluded income" means items that are: (i) excluded from gross income for income tax purposes, such as interest on state and local bonds (¶1328) and gain from the sale of a principal residence (¶2442); (ii) not included in NII under Reg § 1.1411-4 and Reg § 1.1411-10, such as wages, unemployment compensation, Alaska Permanent Fund Dividends, alimony, and Social Security benefits; (iii) specifically excluded by Code Sec. 1411, its regs, or other IRS guidance, e.g., gains from the disposition of property used in a trade or business that isn't passive activity or trading activity, and distributions from certain qualified plans. So operating income from a nonpassive business, unemployment compensation, Social Security benefits, alimony, tax-exempt interest, Alaska Permanent Fund Dividends, distributions from certain qualified plans, self-employment income, and wages aren't NII. (Reg § 1.1411-1(d)(4))[30]

Although NII doesn't include income or net gain derived in the ordinary course of a trade or business (other than a passive activity or trading business), any item of gross income from the investment of working capital is treated as not derived in the ordinary course of a trade or business for the NIIT any net gain attributable to the investment of working capital is treated as not derived in the ordinary course of a trade or business. So that gross income and net gain is subject to the NIIT Code Sec. 1411(c)(3), Reg § 1.1411-6(a))[31]

¶ 3144 Who is subject to the net investment income tax (NIIT)?

The 3.8% NIIT applies to individuals, trusts, and estates. (Code Sec. 1411(a)) A bankruptcy estate in which the debtor is an individual is treated as a married taxpayer filing a separate return. (Reg § 1.1411-3(b)(2))

The NIIT doesn't apply to: nonresident aliens (special rules apply to nonresident aliens married to U.S. citizens or residents); bona fide residents of a U.S. territory (but the NIIT does apply if the individual is required to file U.S. income tax return after application of

---

28. ¶A-6373; ¶14,114.05
29. ¶A-6367 *et seq.*; ¶14,114.03

30. ¶A-6368 *et seq.*; ¶14,114.04
31. ¶A-6372 ; ¶14,114.01

Code Sec. 931, Code Sec. 932, or Code Sec. 933); trusts, all the unexpired interests in which are devoted to charitable purposes described in Code Sec. 170(c)(2)(B); trusts exempt from tax under Code Sec. 501; charitable remainder trusts (CRTs) exempt from tax under Code Sec. 664 (¶2116); or "grantor trusts" (but the income and deductions of the trusts are taken into account in determining the owners' NII). (Code Sec. 1411(e)) (Reg § 1.1411-2(a), Reg § 1.1411-3(b)) Electing small business trusts (ESBTs, ¶3354) and CRTs are subject to special rules. (Reg § 1.1411-3(c))[32]

¶ 3145 Individual Estimated Tax.

An individual must make four quarterly installment payments of estimated tax based on the amount of the "required annual payment" to avoid an underpayment penalty. The required annual payment is the lower of 90% of the tax shown on the current year return or 100% (110%, for high income individuals) of the tax shown on the prior year return. There's no penalty if the tax shown on the return (after withholding) is less than $1,000, or if other specified exceptions or waivers apply.

To avoid the penalty, an individual must: (1) pay each "required installment" (¶3148) by its due date (¶3151), (2) meet an exception (¶3155), *or* (3) get a waiver (¶3156).[33]

✔caution: The 3.8% net investment income tax (¶3142) isn't subject to withholding, so individuals who are subject to that tax should increase either their withholding or their estimated tax payments to avoid the underpayment penalty.

¶ 3146 How to pay estimated tax—Form 1040-ES.

Estimated tax payments can be made by check or money order using payment voucher Form 1040-ES (Form 1040-ES (NR) for nonresident aliens) and phone or online using a credit (MasterCard, VISA, American Express, or Discover) or debit card. Taxpayers also have the option to pay estimated taxes online under the electronic federal tax payment system (EFTPS). Individuals must first register to use the system online at www.eftps.gov or by calling 1-800-555-4477 and ordering an enrollment kit. (Reg § 301.6311-2)[34]

Estimated tax liability is computed as the expected taxes on expected taxable income for the year, minus the tax withheld (or to be withheld) from the year's wages and the expected tax credits (Code Sec. 6654(f), Code Sec. 6654(g); Reg § 1.6654-5(a)), taking into account the taxes, credits, and other amounts listed in Reg § 1.6654-1(a)(4). (Reg § 1.6654-5(b))[35]

¶ 3147 Married individuals' estimated tax.

A married person determines estimated tax liability based on the married person's separate income. Spouses making joint estimated tax payments apply the rules on a joint basis. Joint estimated tax payments don't affect the choice of joint or separate income tax returns.[36] Joint payments can be apportioned between the spouses' separate returns. (Reg § 1.6654-2(e)(5))[37]

¶ 3148 Amount of required installment.

Unless the annualized income method (¶3149) is used, the amount of each required installment is 25% of the "required annual payment." For most individuals, the required annual payment is the lower of: (1) 90% of the tax shown on the current year's return (or, if no return is filed, 90% of the current-year tax), or (2) 100% of the tax shown on the

---

32. ¶C-5802 ; ¶14,114.01
33. ¶S-5200 *et seq.*; ¶66,544 *et seq.*
34. ¶S-5253; ¶63,114

35. ¶S-5201; ¶66,544.01
36. ¶S-5254; ¶66,544.01
37. ¶S-5255; ¶66,544.01

previous year's return, if that tax year was a 12-month year and the taxpayer filed a return (even a late one) for that year. (Code Sec. 6654(d)(1))[38]

Different rules apply to high-income individuals. If an individual's previous year's return showed adjusted gross income exceeding $150,000 ($75,000 for marrieds filing separately), the required annual payment is the lower of (1), above, or 110% of the tax shown on the previous year's return. (Code Sec. 6654(d)(1)(C))[39]

¶ 3149 Annualized income method.

For any installment for which the taxpayer establishes that the "annualized income installment" (below) is less than the required installment determined under the rules at ¶3148, the annualized income installment becomes the required installment. (Code Sec. 6654(d)(2)(A)(i)) The annualized income installment is the excess (if any) of:

(1) an amount equal to the "applicable percentage" (below) of the annualized tax (computed by placing taxable income, alternative minimum taxable income (AMTI), and adjusted self-employment income (below) on an annualized basis) for the months in the tax year ending before the due date for the installment, over

(2) the sum of any earlier required installments for the tax year. (Code Sec. 6654(d)(2)(B))[40]

The applicable percentages are 22.5%, 45%, 67.5% and 90%, respectively, for the first, second, third and fourth required installments. (Code Sec. 6654(d)(2)(C)(ii))[41]

Adjusted self-employment income means self-employment income (¶3134) except that wages for calendar months ending before the installment due date must be annualized as in (1), above. (Code Sec. 6654(d)(2)(C)(iii))[42]

If, for an installment, the annualized income installment is the required installment because it's less than the installment determined under the rules at ¶3148, the excess must be recaptured—i.e, added to the next required installment that isn't an annualized income installment. (Code Sec. 6654(d)(2)(A)(ii))[43]

¶ 3150 Withholding as payment of estimated tax.

Any withholding is treated as a payment of estimated tax. An equal part of the withheld tax is considered paid on each installment date unless the individual establishes the dates the amounts were actually withheld. (Code Sec. 6654(g)(1))[44]

recommendation: An individual who underpays an early required installment can avoid or reduce the underpayment penalty by increasing withholding for the rest of the year.

¶ 3151 Time for paying installments.

Calendar year individuals (not farmers and fishermen (¶3152) or nonresident aliens (¶3153)) must pay estimated taxes in four installments, due Apr. 15, June 15, Sept. 15 of the current year, and Jan. 15 of the next year. (Code Sec. 6654(c)) But an individual who first has income subject to the tax after Mar. 31 makes the first payment by the due date for the period in which the individual has the income. [45] The last installment, ordinarily due on Jan. 15, needn't be paid if the individual files a return and pays the tax shown on it

38. ¶S-5204; ¶66,544.03
39. ¶S-5204.1; ¶66,544.03
40. ¶S-5219 *et seq.*; ¶66,544.04
41. ¶S-5235; ¶66,544.04
42. ¶S-5225; ¶66,544.04
43. ¶S-5229; ¶66,544.04
44. ¶S-5248; ¶66,544.02
45. ¶S-5241, S-5242; ¶66,544.02

by Jan. 31. (Code Sec. 6654(h))[46]

For fiscal year taxpayers, the due dates are the 15th day of the 4th, 6th, and 9th month of the fiscal year and the 15th day of the first month of the next tax year. (Code Sec. 6654(k))[47]

¶ 3152 Farmers and fishermen.

A farmer or fisherman doesn't have to pay estimated tax for a year if the taxpayer files the return and pays the tax shown on it by Mar. 1 of the next year. Otherwise, the taxpayer must make one estimated tax payment for the year, due Jan. 15 of the next year.[48] The required installment calculation (¶3148) uses $66^2/3\%$ (not 90%) of the current year tax. (Code Sec. 6654(i)(1))[49]

An individual is a farmer or fisherman if at least 66 $^2/3\%$ of the farmer/fisherman's gross income for the current or preceding tax year is from farming or fishing. (Code Sec. 6654(i)(2))[50]

¶ 3153 Nonresident aliens—Form 1040-ES (NR).

Nonresident aliens required to file U.S. income tax returns (¶4643) must pay three required installments for the year, due on June 15, Sept. 15, and Jan. 15 of the next year. (Code Sec. 6654(j)(2))[1] The required installments (compute on Form 1040-ES(NR)) are 50%, 25%, and 25%, respectively, of the required annual payment (¶3148). (Code Sec. 6654(j)(3)(A)) The applicable percentages under the annualized income method (¶3149) are 45%, 67.5%, and 90%, respectively. (Code Sec. 6654(j)(3)(B))[2]

¶ 3154 Penalty for underpayment of estimated tax—Form 2210, Form 2210F.

The penalty for underpayment equals the product of the interest rate (using simple interest) (Code Sec. 6622(b)) on deficiencies (¶4868), times the amount of the underpayment (below), for the period of the underpayment (below). (Code Sec. 6654(a))[3]

The *amount of the underpayment* is the excess of the "required installment" (¶3148) over any amount paid on or before the due date of the installment. (Code Sec. 6654(b)(1))[4] It's adjusted to reflect the number of days the underpayment is outstanding. [5]

The *period of underpayment* runs from that due date to the earlier of: (1) Apr. 15 following the end of the tax year, or (2) the date the underpayment is paid. (Code Sec. 6654(b)(2)) For these purposes, a payment is credited against unpaid installments in the order the installments are required to be paid. (Code Sec. 6654(b)(3))[6]

Form 2210 (Form 2210F for farmers and fishermen) may be used to compute the penalty,[7] or IRS will compute it and send a bill. [8] For exceptions, see ¶3155. For waivers, see ¶3156.

¶ 3155 Exceptions to underpayment penalty.

The underpayment penalty (¶3154) doesn't apply:

(1) if the tax shown on the return (or the tax due if no return is filed) is less than $1,000 after reduction for withholding tax paid (Code Sec. 6654(e)(1)),[9] or

---

46. ¶S-5260; ¶66,544.02
47. ¶S-5243; ¶66,544.02
48. ¶S-5247; ¶66,544.06
49. ¶S-5237; ¶66,544.06
50. ¶S-5238; ¶66,544.06
1. ¶S-5246; ¶66,544.07
2. ¶S-5236; ¶66,544.07

3. ¶S-5260; ¶66,544.02
4. ¶S-5261, S-5262; ¶66,544.02
5. ¶S-5260; ¶66,544.02
6. ¶S-5263; ¶66,544.02
7. ¶S-5265
8. ¶S-5260
9. ¶S-5265

(2) if the individual was a U.S. citizen or resident for the entire preceding tax year, had no tax liability for that year, and that year was a 12-month year (Code Sec. 6654(e)(2)),[10] or

(3) for the 4th installment, if the individual (not a farmer or fisherman, ¶3152) files the return by the end of the 1st month after the tax year (Jan. 31 for calendar year taxpayers), and pays in full the tax computed on the return (Code Sec. 6654(h)),[11] or

(4) in certain cases while a Title 11 bankruptcy case is pending. (Code Sec. 6658(a))[12]

¶ 3156   Waiver of penalty.

The underpayment penalty (¶3154) may be waived by IRS if:

(1) failure to pay was due to casualty, disaster, or other unusual circumstances where penalty would be inequitable or against good conscience (Code Sec. 6654(e)(3)(A)),[13] or

(2) underpayment was due to reasonable cause (not willful neglect), and the taxpayer retired (after reaching age 62) or became disabled during the year for which the payments in question were required or in the preceding tax year. (Code Sec. 6654(e)(3)(B))[14]

---

10. ¶S-5265; ¶66,544.05
11. ¶S-5260; ¶66,544.02
12. ¶V-7378; ¶66,584

13. ¶S-5265; ¶66,544.05
14. ¶S-5265; ¶66,544.05

Chapter 14   Alternative Minimum Tax

¶ 3200   **Alternative Minimum Tax.** ▬▬▬▬▬▬▬▬▬▬▬▬▬▬▬▬▬▬▬▬▬▬▬▬▬▬

The alternative minimum tax (AMT) equals the excess (if any) of the tentative minimum tax over the regular tax (¶3201).

The AMT was designed to prevent a taxpayer from avoiding all tax liability by using exclusions, deductions, and credits. Under it, AMT rates are applied to AMT income determined after the taxpayer "gives back" an assortment of tax benefits. AMT is paid only if, and to the extent, it exceeds the taxpayer's regular tax. A taxpayer's total tax liability for the year will equal the taxpayer's regular tax liability, plus AMT liability. (Code Sec. 55(a))[1]

Any noncorporate taxpayer subject to the regular tax is also subject to the AMT. (Code Sec. 55(a), Code Sec. 55(b)) Partnerships (Code Sec. 701) and S corporations (Code Sec. 1363(a)) aren't subject to AMT, but their partners and shareholders are. [2]

For a minimum tax credit (the "AMT credit") applied against regular tax, see   ¶2360.[3]

For tax years beginning before 2018, the AMT also applied to corporations, with a small corporation exception.[4] For a refundable AMT credit for corporations for 2018 –2021, see ¶2360.[5]

¶ 3201   **Computing the AMT—Form 6251; Form 1041, Schedule I.**

The alternative minimum tax (AMT) on noncorporate taxpayers equals the excess (if any) of the tentative minimum tax (see below) for the tax year, over the regular tax (see below) for the tax year. (Code Sec. 55(a)) AMT is computed on Form 6251 for individuals, and Schedule I of Form 1041 for fiduciaries (estates and trusts). [6]

For taxpayers other than a married person filing separately, the tentative minimum tax for 2018 equals 26% of the "taxable excess" (defined below) that doesn't exceed $191,100, plus 28% of the taxable excess above $191,100, reduced by the AMT foreign tax credit (AMTFTC), ¶3212, for the year. For 2019, as calculated by Thomson Reuters using inflation data, the tentative minimum tax equals 26% of the taxable excess that doesn't exceed $194,800, plus 28% of the taxable excess above $194,800, reduced by the AMTFTC. (Code Sec. 55(b)(1)(A)(i); Code Sec. 55(d)(4)(B)(i)) For marrieds filing separately, the amount used to compute tentative minimum tax is 50% of the amount used for marrieds filing jointly. (Code Sec. 55(b)(1)(A)(iii)) Tentative minimum tax on net capital gain and qualified dividend income is computed using the long-term capital gain rates that apply for regular tax purposes (Code Sec. 55(b)(3)) (¶2602). "Taxable excess" is the excess of alternative minimum taxable income (AMTI, ¶3202) for the tax year over the applicable AMT "exemption amount" (¶3203). (Code Sec. 55(b)(1)(A)(ii))[7]

The regular tax for this purpose is the regular tax liability used for determining the limitation on various nonrefundable credits for the tax year (¶2359), reduced by the regular (i.e., not the AMT) foreign tax credit (¶2362) and without including any investment credit or low-income housing credit recapture (¶2313, ¶2321), or Code Sec. 45(e)(11)(C) income tax increase for a farmer's cooperative from electricity production credits passed through to patrons. (Code Sec. 55(c)(1))[8]

In computing regular tax liability for AMT purposes, income averaging for farmers and

1. ¶A-8100 *et seq.*; ¶554
2. ¶A-8130 *et seq.*; ¶554
3. ¶A-8801 *et seq.*; ¶534
4. ¶A-8103 ; ¶A-8140 *et seq.*; ¶554

5. ¶A-8807.1; ¶534
6. ¶A-8101; ¶554.01
7. ¶A-8101, ¶A-8102; ¶554.01
8. ¶A-8105; ¶554.01

References beginning with a single letter are to paragraphs in Federal Tax Coordinator 2d and RIA's Analysis of Federal Taxes: Income. Those beginning with numbers are to paragraphs in United States Tax Reporter.

fishermen isn't taken into account. (Code Sec. 55(c)(2))[9]

⚫ observation: That is, the "regular tax" used to determine if the farmer or fisherman is subject to AMT is computed as if income averaging had not been used. So, the use of 3-year income averaging doesn't trigger or increase AMT liability.

¶ 3202   Alternative minimum taxable income (AMTI).

AMTI is computed by taking the taxpayer's regular taxable income for the tax year and (i) adding or subtracting AMT "adjustments" (¶3205 *et seq.*) and (ii) adding AMT "preferences" (¶3210). (Code Sec. 55(b)(2))[10] The alternative minimum tax (AMT) can apply if a taxpayer only has adjustment items; a taxpayer without preference items must still compute AMTI with the adjustments. [11]

All Code provisions that apply in determining regular taxable income also apply in determining a taxpayer's AMTI (Reg § 1.55-1(a)), e.g., the limitations on the use of capital losses by noncorporate taxpayers (¶2608, ¶2609) also apply for AMT purposes. [12]

A noncorporate taxpayer's net capital gain and qualified dividend income are included in AMTI, but are taxed at the same capital gains rates as apply for regular tax purposes (¶3201).[13]

The at-risk rules (¶1790), and the partnership (¶3729) and S corporation (¶3369) loss limitation rules, are applied in computing AMTI taking into account all AMT adjustments and preferences. (Code Sec. 59(h))[14]

The pass-through Code Sec. 199A(a) deduction for qualified business income (QBI) (¶1595 *et seq.*) allowed in determining AMTI is computed without regard to any AMT adjustments. (Prop Reg. § 1.199A-1(e)(4) [" . . . taxpayers may rely," Prop Reg. § 1.199A-1(f)(1)])[15]

If a taxpayer's regular tax is determined by reference to an amount other than taxable income (e.g., unrelated business taxable income of an exempt organization, ¶4124), that amount is treated as taxable income in determining AMTI. (Code Sec. 55(b)(2))[16]

There are rules for the apportionment of items that are treated differently for AMT purposes among holders of interests in regulated investment companies (RICs), real estate investment trusts (REITs), and common trust funds. (Code Sec. 59(d))[17]

¶ 3203   Alternative minimum tax (AMT) exemption amounts.

The AMT exemption amounts used in computing AMT (¶3201) are:

. . . *Married individuals filing jointly and surviving spouses: for 2018,* $109,400, less 25% of AMTI exceeding $1,000,000 (zero exemption when AMTI is $1,437,600 or more); *for 2019, as calculated by Thomson Reuters using inflation data,* $111,700, less 25% of AMTI exceeding $1,020,600 (zero exemption when AMTI is $1,467,400 or more).

. . . *Unmarried individuals: for 2018,* $70,300, less 25% of AMTI exceeding $500,000 (zero exemption when AMTI is $781,200 or more); *for 2019, as calculated by Thomson Reuters using inflation data,* $71,700, less 25% of AMTI exceeding $510,300 (zero exemption when AMTI is $797,100 or more). But see ¶3204 for a child subject to kiddie tax.

. . . *Married individuals filing separately: for 2018,* $54,700, less 25% of AMTI exceeding

---

9. ¶A-8105; ¶554.01
10. ¶A-8101; ¶554.01
11. ¶A-8109
12. ¶A-8108; ¶554.01
13. ¶A-8102

14. ¶A-8115 *et seq.*; ¶594
15. ¶A-8103.1
16. ¶A-8107; ¶554.01
17. ¶A-8112; ¶594

$500,000 (zero exemption when AMTI is $718,800 or more. But, AMTI for marrieds filing separately must be increased (for 2018) by the lesser of: $54,700 or 25% of the excess of AMTI (determined without this exemption reduction) over $718,800. *For 2019, as calculated by Thomson Reuters using inflation data,* $55,850, less 25% of AMTI exceeding $510,300 (zero exemption when AMTI is $733,700 or more. But, AMTI for marrieds filing separately must be increased (for 2019) by the lesser of: $55,850 or 25% of the excess of AMTI (determined without this exemption reduction) over $733,700. (Code Sec. 55(d), Code Sec. 55(d)(1), Code Sec. 55(d)(3))[18]

... *Estates and trusts: for 2018,* $24,600, less 25% of AMTI exceeding $81,900 (zero exemption when AMTI is $180,300); *for 2019, as calculated by Thomson Reuters using inflation data,* $25,000, less 25% of AMTI exceeding $83,500 (zero exemption when AMTI is $183,500). (Code Sec. 55(d)(4)(B)(ii))[19]

In no case can the AMT exemption amount be less than zero. (Code Sec. 55(d))[20]

¶ 3204   AMT exemption amount of a child subject to the kiddie tax.

For 2018, the AMT exemption amount for a child subject to the kiddie tax (¶3129) can't exceed the child's earned income (under Code Sec. 911(d)(2)) for the tax year plus $7,600 ($7,750 for 2019, as calculated by Thomson Reuters using inflation data). (Code Sec. 59(j)) But this exemption amount can't be more than the child's regular AMT exemption, i.e., the unmarried individual's $70,300 (before a phaseout) exemption amount for 2018 ($71,700 [before phaseout] for 2019, as calculated by Thomson Reuters using inflation data) (¶3203).[21]

¶ 3205   AMT adjustments and preferences defined.

Adjustments differ from preferences, in computing alternative minimum taxable income (AMTI, ¶3202). Adjustments involve *substituting* AMT treatment of an item for the regular tax treatment. Preferences involve *adding* the difference between the AMT treatment and the regular tax treatment. Some (but not all) adjustments can be negative amounts —i.e., they may result in AMTI that's less than taxable income. Preferences can't be negative amounts.[22]

For AMT adjustments, see ¶3206 *et seq.*, for AMT preferences, see ¶3210, and for certain losses denied for the AMT, see ¶3211.

A taxpayer can avoid preference/adjustment treatment for certain costs by electing amortization (use Form 4562), rather than a current deduction. (Code Sec. 59(e); Reg § 1.59-1)[23]

¶ 3206   AMT adjustments.

The following adjustments (¶3205) apply in computing alternative minimum taxable income (AMTI) (¶3202) of *individual taxpayers:*

(1) *Itemized deductions adjustment.* Itemized deductions for AMT purposes are computed the same as for regular tax purposes, *except:*

(a) Property, income, and state and local general sales taxes that are deductible for regular tax purposes only as itemized deductions (on Form 1040, Schedule A) aren't deductible in computing AMTI. (Code Sec. 56(b)(1)(A)(ii)) But, these taxes if deductible in computing adjusted gross income for regular tax purposes (i.e., in computing income

---

18. ¶A-8162; ¶554.01
19. ¶A-8164; ¶554.01
20. ¶A-8162; ¶A-8164; ¶554.01

21. ¶A-8163; ¶594
22. ¶A-8191; ¶564, ¶574
23. ¶A-8194 *et seq.*; ¶594

from a trade or business or farming activity (on Schedule C or F), or taxes that are an expense of producing income (on Schedule E), ¶1749), are deductible in computing AMTI. (Code Sec. 56(b)(1)(A))[24]

(b) Qualified housing interest (instead of qualified *residence* interest (QRI), ¶1729) is deductible in computing AMTI. (Code Sec. 56(b)(1)(C), Code Sec. 56(e)) So, home equity indebtedness isn't allowed for AMT purposes unless it's used to buy, build, or substantially improve the taxpayer's principal residence or one other qualified dwelling.[25] (For 2018–2025, AMT and regular tax treatment of home equity debt are essentially the same.[26])

(c) Net investment income (NII) (for limit on deduction of investment interest) is generally computed the same as for regular tax (¶1728), but qualified housing interest (instead of QRI) is excluded, and AMT adjustments and preferences are taken into account. And, tax-exempt bond interest that's an AMT preference item (¶3210) is included in NII. (Code Sec. 56(b)(1)(C))[27]

(d) Miscellaneous itemized deductions (currently suspended from 2018 through 2025; ¶3109), aren't allowed. (Code Sec. 56(b)(1)(A)(i))[28]

(e) The Code Sec. 68 3%/80% reduction in itemized deductions (in effect after 2025), doesn't apply in computing AMT. (Code Sec. 56(b)(1)(F))[29]

(2) *Standard deduction and personal exemptions adjustments.* The standard deduction (¶3110) and the deduction for personal exemptions (currently suspended from 2018 through 2025, in effect thereafter), *including those of trusts and estates* (¶3112), *aren't* allowed for the AMT. (Code Sec. 56(b)(1)(E))[30]

(3) *State, etc., tax recoveries adjustment.* If an itemized deduction for state, etc., taxes paid is permitted for regular tax purposes but denied for AMT purposes ((1)(a), above), and any portion of that tax is refunded, the refund isn't included in AMTI. (Code Sec. 56(b)(1)(D))[31]

(4) *Research and experimental (R&E) expenditures adjustment.* The deduction allowed is the amount that results from capitalizing Code Sec. 174(a) R&E expenditures (¶1585) and amortizing them on a straight-line basis over 10 years. (Code Sec. 56(b)(2)(A)(ii), Code Sec. 59(e)(6)) This doesn't apply to expenses incurred in an activity in which the taxpayer materially participates under Code Sec. 469(h) (¶1806). (Code Sec. 56(b)(2)(D))[32]

(5) *Circulation expenditures.* The AMT circulation expenditures deduction is the amount that results from capitalizing the costs and amortizing them over three years (¶1604). (Code Sec. 56(b)(2))[33]

(6) *Incentive stock option (ISO) adjustment.* The Code Sec. 83 restricted property rules (¶1216)—and not the favorable Code Sec. 421 rules that apply for regular tax (¶1220)—apply in determining AMTI, unless the stock is acquired and disposed of in the same tax year. (Code Sec. 56(b)(3))[34] The amount included in AMTI (but not regular income) equals the excess of the stock's fair market value on the exercise date over the exercise (strike) price. This applies to vested stock, and to nonvested stock for which the taxpayer makes a Code Sec. 83(b) election (¶1217).[35]

Adjustments for these items apply in computing the AMTI of *all taxpayers:*

24. ¶A-8308; ¶564.02
25. ¶A-8310 *et seq.*; ¶564.02
26. ¶K-5471; ¶1634.052
27. ¶A-8313; ¶564.02
28. ¶A-8314; ¶564.02
29. ¶A-8306; ¶564.02

30. ¶A-8305, ¶A-8315; ¶564.02
31. ¶A-8309; ¶564.02
32. ¶A-8316; ¶564.02
33. ¶A-8245; ¶564.02
34. ¶A-8302, ¶A-8303; ¶564.02
35. ¶A-8302, ¶H-2508.2

...*Depreciation* adjustment, see ¶3207.

...*Alternative tax net operating loss deduction (ATNOLD)* adjustment, see ¶3208.

...*Mine exploration and development costs.* The AMT deduction is the amount that results from capitalizing the costs allowed under Code Sec. 616(a) or Code Sec. 617(a) for the tax year without the Code Sec. 291(b)(1) 30% cutback (¶1611, ¶1612), and amortizing them ratably over 10 years. (Code Sec. 56(a)(2)(A), Code Sec. 59(e)(6))[36]

...*Certain long-term contracts.* For long-term contracts (except home construction contracts) adjustment), AMTI is computed using the percentage-of-completion method of accounting (¶2847). For small construction contracts (under Code Sec. 460(e)(1), ¶2845), use the Code Sec. 460(b)(3) simplified cost allocation method (¶2850) to find the percentage of contract completed. (Code Sec. 56(a)(3); Reg § 1.460-4(f))[37]

...*Pollution control facilities.* In computing AMTI, the Code Sec. 169 deduction for amortization of pollution control facilities (¶1963) placed in service after '98 is determined under Code Sec. 168 using the straight-line method of depreciation. For facilities placed in service after '86 and before '99, the AMT deduction is the amount allowable under the Alternative Depreciation System (ADS, ¶1929). (Code Sec. 56(a)(5))[38]

...*Adjusted basis* adjustment, see ¶3209.

...*Alcohol fuel credit* amount that's included in gross income (¶1206) isn't included in AMTI. (Code Sec. 56(a)(7))[39]

¶ 3207 Depreciation adjustment for AMT.

Except as provided below, the following AMT adjustment (¶3205) rules apply to all taxpayers subject to the AMT, for depreciable property placed in service after '86 (and after July 31, '86 and before '87, for which the taxpayer elected to have the MACRS rules, ¶1907 *et seq.*, apply):

(1) For property placed in service before '99, AMT depreciation for Code Sec. 1250 property (¶2678) and property depreciated under the straight-line method for regular tax purposes is computed using the Alternative Depreciation System (ADS, ¶1929). For property subject to accelerated depreciation for regular tax purposes, AMT depreciation is computed using ADS recovery periods and the 150% declining balance method (switching to straight-line in the year that method yields a higher allowance).

(2) For property placed in service after '98, AMT depreciation is computed using the 150% declining balance method (switching to straight-line in the year that method yields a higher allowance), except straight-line is used for Code Sec. 1250 property and other property for which straight-line is used for regular tax purposes. (Code Sec. 56(a)(1)(A), Code Sec. 56(a)(1)(C)(ii)) The recovery period is the same as for regular tax purposes. [40]

The AMT adjustment (i.e., the amount to be added or subtracted in computing alternative minimum taxable income (AMTI) (¶3202)) generated by the above calculations is determined by subtracting the amount of AMT depreciation for all property covered by the above rule from the MACRS depreciation for that property. [41]

The above rules don't apply to: (a) certain property to which the MACRS rules don't apply; (b) natural gas gathering lines placed in service after Apr. 11, 2005 (Code Sec. 56(a)(1)(B), Code Sec. 56(a)(1)(C));[42] (c) qualified property that is eligible for a special depreciation allowance under Code Sec. 168(m) (qualified reuse and recycling property, ¶1939) or Code Sec. 168(n) (qualified disaster assistance property, ¶1939) (Code

---

36. ¶A-8235; ¶564.01
37. ¶A-8202 *et seq.*; ¶564.01
38. ¶A-8237; ¶564.01
39. ¶A-8247; ¶564.01

40. ¶A-8220; ¶564.01
41. ¶A-8220; ¶564.01
42. ¶A-8221 *et seq.*; ¶564.01

Sec. 168(m)(2)(D), Code Sec. 168(n)(2)(D));[43] (d) qualified property that is or was eligible for bonus first-year depreciation under Code Sec. 168(k) (¶1933), Code Sec. 1400L(b) (qualified New York Liberty Zone property), Code Sec. 1400N(d) (GO Zone property), or Code Sec. 168(l) (qualified second generation biofuel plant property placed in service before 2018, ¶1939); (Code Sec. 168(k)(2)(G), Code Sec. 1400L(b)(2)(E), Code Sec. 1400N(d)(4), Code Sec. 168(l)(6));[44] and (e) qualified Indian reservation property placed in service after '93 and before 2018. (Code Sec. 168(j)(3))[45]

¶ 3208   Alternative tax net operating loss deduction (ATNOLD) for AMT.

For AMT purposes, an ATNOLD is allowed instead of the regular tax net operating loss (NOL) deduction (RNOLD, ¶1815 *et seq.*). A taxpayer's ATNOLD generally can't reduce the taxpayer' alternative minimum taxable income (AMTI, ¶3202) by more than 90% of the AMTI. (Code Sec. 56(a)(4))[46]

In general, the ATNOLD is the same as the RNOLD *except that:*

(1) the amount of the ATNOLD is limited to 90% of AMTI, determined without regard to the ATNOLD and the pre-2018 Code Sec. 199 production activities deduction. But the 90%-of-AMTI limitation doesn't apply to carrybacks and carryovers of amounts attributable to: 2008 or 2009 NOLs for which an extended carryback period was elected under former Code Sec. 172(b)(1)(H) (¶1818), pre-2010 qualified disaster losses, or certain other disaster losses such as qualified GO Zone losses (¶1818) (Code Sec. 56(d)(1)(A), Code Sec. 56(d)(3), former Code Sec. 1400N(k)(1)(B)), which can offset up to 100% of AMTI;[47] and

(2) the ATNOL is determined with AMT adjustments (¶3206 *et seq.*) and reduced by AMT preferences (¶3210) (but only to the extent the preference increased the NOL for the year). (Code Sec. 56(d)(2))[48]

An election to forego the regular NOL carryback period (generally, for NOLs arising in tax years before 2018, ¶1819) also applies for ATNOLD purposes. (The election must be made for regular tax purposes to get it for AMT purposes.) [49]

The difference between the regular tax basis and AMT basis (¶3209) of stock acquired under an incentive stock option (ISO) isn't an adjustment and doesn't result in an ATNOL.[50]

Since the alternative minimum tax (AMT) doesn't apply to corporations for tax years beginning after Dec. 31, 2017, the ATNOLD for AMT purposes doesn't apply to corporations for tax years beginning after that date.

¶ 3209   Different AMT adjusted basis for some property.

For AMT purposes, the adjusted bases of the following types of property are computed by taking into consideration the AMT adjustment (¶3205) listed below with the property:

(1) Depreciable property subject to the Code Sec. 56(a)(1) depreciation adjustment (¶3207).

(2) Property subject to the Code Sec. 56(b)(2) adjustment for circulation or research and experimental expenditures (¶3206) paid or incurred after '86.

(3) Property subject to the Code Sec. 56(a)(2) adjustment for mine exploration or development expenditures (¶3206) paid or incurred after '86.

---

43. ¶A-8221 *et seq.*; ¶1684.029, ¶1400L4.07, ¶1684.08
44. ¶A-8221 *et seq.*; ¶1400L4.07, ¶1684.08
45. ¶L-8806; ¶1684.01
46. ¶A-8210 *et seq.*; ¶564.01

47. ¶A-8212, ¶A-8213; ¶564.01
48. ¶A-8211; ¶564.01
49. ¶A-8216; ¶564.01
50. ¶A-8211

(4) Pollution control facilities subject to the Code Sec. 56(a)(5) adjustment (¶3206), if placed in service after '86. (Code Sec. 56(a)(6))

(5) Stock acquired under an incentive stock option (ISO) (¶3206). Generally, the basis of the stock is determined under the Code Sec. 83 rules rather than the Code Sec. 421 rules. (Code Sec. 56(b)(3)) So, the taxpayer gets a cost basis in the ISO stock for regular tax purposes, and a fair market value basis in the stock for AMT purposes (¶1220).[1]

¶ 3210   AMT preference items.

(1) *Tax-exempt interest* on certain private activity bonds (not certain housing bonds or bonds issued in 2009 or 2010), less related expenses that aren't deductible for regular tax purposes, is an AMT preference item (¶3205). (Code Sec. 57(a)(5))[2]

(2) *Depletion.* Except for independent oil and gas producers and royalty owners, the excess of percentage depletion (¶1971) over the property's adjusted basis (disregarding the current year's depletion) at the end of the year is a preference item. (Code Sec. 57(a)(1))[3]

(3) *Excess intangible drilling costs* (IDCs) are a preference item. This is the excess of the allowable Code Sec. 263(c) IDC deduction for the tax year for oil, gas, and geothermal wells (¶1613), over the amount that would have been allowable had the costs been capitalized and amortized ratably over 120 months. For integrated oil companies, the preference equals this excess, reduced by 65% of the net income received from all oil, gas, and geothermal properties. For other taxpayers, the preference applies only to the extent that, had it applied fully, it would have increased alternative minimum taxable income (AMTI, ¶3202) by more than 40% of the AMTI for the tax year (without the IDC preference or the alternative tax NOL deduction, ¶3208). The preference is computed separately for oil and gas properties, and for geothermal properties. (Code Sec. 57(a)(2), Code Sec. 57(b), Code Sec. 59(e)(6))[4]

(4) *Qualified small business stock (QSBS) exclusion.* For gain on the disposition of QSBS that's partly excluded from gross income (¶2638 *et seq.*), 7% is treated as a preference item. (Code Sec. 57(a)(7)) But, for QSBS to which the 100% exclusion applies, the excluded portion of the gain isn't treated as a preference item. (Code Sec. 1202(a)(4)(C))[5]

¶ 3211   Denial of certain losses for AMT.

(1) *Farm losses.* For the AMT, no loss is permitted from any "tax shelter farm activity" of a noncorporate taxpayer, except to the extent the taxpayer is insolvent at the end of the tax year. A tax shelter farm activity is (a) a farming syndicate (¶4511), or (b) any other "passive activity" (¶1798) consisting of farming unless the taxpayer materially participates in it. (Code Sec. 58(a), Code Sec. 58(c)(1))[6]

(2) *Passive losses.* The rules limiting the regular tax deduction of losses from passive activities (¶1797 *et seq.*) apply for AMT purposes *except that:*

. . . AMT preferences and adjustments (¶3205 *et seq.*) are taken into account;

. . . qualified housing interest (¶3206) (rather than qualified residence interest) is omitted from the passive loss calculation (Code Sec. 58(b)); and

. . . the amount of losses disallowed under the regular tax limitation is reduced by the amount, if any, by which the taxpayer is insolvent at year end. (Code Sec. 58(c)(1))[7]

---

1. ¶A-8193; ¶564.01 *et seq.*
2. ¶A-8201, ¶574
3. ¶A-8233; ¶574
4. ¶A-8238 *et seq.*; ¶574

5. ¶A-8304 *et seq.*; ¶574
6. ¶A-8242; ¶584
7. ¶A-8244; ¶584

¶ 3212   AMT foreign tax credit (AMTFTC).

The AMTFTC is subtracted in the computation of a noncorporate taxpayer's AMT (¶3201). (Code Sec. 55(b)(1)(A)(i), Code Sec. 55(b)(1)(B)(ii))[8]

The AMTFTC is computed the same as the regular foreign tax credit (¶2362), *except* that in applying the Code Sec. 904 limitation on the amount of the credit: (1) alternative minimum taxable income (AMTI, ¶3202) is substituted for taxable income (but see below); (2) the "pre-credit tentative minimum tax" is substituted for "the tax against which the foreign tax credit is taken"; and (3) the AMT rate (¶3201) is used in determining "high-taxed" income instead of the regular tax highest tax rate. (Code Sec. 59(a)(1), Code Sec. 59(a)(2); Reg § 1.904-4(k))[9]

If a taxpayer so elects for the first tax year for which the taxpayer claims an AMTFTC (Code Sec. 59(a)(3)(B)(i)), the AMTFTC limitation is figured in a simplified way, based on the proportion that regular taxable income from sources outside the U.S. (but not in excess of the taxpayer's entire AMTI) bears to the entire AMTI for the tax year. (Code Sec. 59(a)(3)(A)) Letting taxpayers use foreign source regular taxable income to compute the limitation eliminates the need to reallocate and reapportion every deduction. Once made, the election applies to all tax years and can be revoked only with IRS consent. (Code Sec. 59(a)(3)(B)(ii))[10]

---

8. ¶A-8181;¶594
9. ¶A-8181; ¶594

10. ¶A-8182; ¶594

Chapter 15   Corporations—Accumulated Earnings Tax— Personal Holding Companies—Consolidated Returns—Estimated Tax—S Corporations

¶ 3300   Taxation of Corporations.

A corporation is an entity distinct from its shareholders. How a corporation is taxed depends on whether it is a C corporation (¶3301 *et seq.*) or an S corporation (¶3350 *et seq.*).

¶ 3301   What is a corporation for tax purposes—Form 8832?

Under regs that set forth a "check-the-box" system of classifying entities for federal tax purposes, the following business entities are mandatorily classified as corporations:

. . . A business entity organized under a federal or state statute, or under a statute of a federally recognized Indian tribe, if the statute describes or refers to the entity as incorporated or as a corporation, body corporate, or body politic.

. . . An association as determined under Reg § 301.7701-3 (see below).

. . . A business entity organized under a state statute, if the statute describes or refers to the entity as a joint-stock company or joint-stock association.

. . . An insurance company.

. . . A state-chartered business entity conducting banking activities, if any of its deposits are insured under the Federal Deposit Insurance Act.

. . . A business entity wholly owned by a state or any of its political subdivisions.

. . . A business entity that's taxable as a corporation under a provision of the Code other than Code Sec. 7701(a)(3), such as a publicly traded partnership (see ¶3302).

. . . Certain foreign business entities ("per se" corporations) (Reg § 301.7701-2(b)(8)) and business entities formed under the laws of U.S. territories and possessions. (Reg § 301.7701-2(b))[1]

Under the "check-the-box" regs, if a joint undertaking is an entity separate from its owners for federal tax purposes, the entity is a business entity and not a trust, and the business entity is an "eligible entity" (i.e., not mandatorily classified as a corporation), it may elect its classification for federal tax purposes. An eligible entity with at least two members may elect to be classified as a partnership or as an association (i.e., a corporation). An eligible entity with a single owner may elect to be classified as an association or to be disregarded as an entity separate from its owner. [2] An eligible entity that wishes to elect a classification other than its default classification, or any eligible entity that wishes to change its classification, does so by filing Form 8832 with the IRS Center designated on the form.[3]

An entity organized in more than one jurisdiction is treated as a corporation for federal tax purposes if it is so treated in any of those jurisdictions. (Reg § 301.7701-2(b)(9))[4]

¶ 3302   Publicly traded partnerships (PTPs) as corporations.

A PTP is taxable as a corporation (¶3303). (Code Sec. 7704(a))[5] A partnership is a PTP if interests in the partnership either: (1) are traded on an established securities market

1. ¶D-1101 *et seq.*; ¶77,014.14
2. ¶D-1151; ¶77,014.15
3. ¶D-1158; ¶77,014.15
4. ¶D-1101.1; ¶77,014.13
5. ¶D-1321; ¶77,044

References beginning with a single letter are to paragraphs in Federal Tax Coordinator 2d and RIA's Analysis of Federal Taxes: Income. Those beginning with numbers are to paragraphs in United States Tax Reporter.

(including a national exchange, a regional or local exchange, certain foreign exchanges, and an interdealer quotation system), or (2) are readily tradable on a secondary market or its substantial equivalent. (Code Sec. 7704(b); Reg § 1.7704-1)[6]

However, a PTP won't be treated as a corporation if at least 90% of its gross income for the tax year is specified passive-type "qualifying" income, and certain other requirements are met. (Code Sec. 7704(c))[7]

¶ 3303 How C Corporations Are Taxed. ■■■■■■■■■■■■■■■■■■■■■■

For tax years after 2017, a flat 21% rate applies.

For the rates at which a C corporation's income is taxed for 2017, and for the amount at which the graduated rates are phased out, see ¶1113. For limits on the use of graduated rates and other tax benefits for members of a controlled group of corporations, see ¶3338 *et seq.*.

For tax years beginning before 2018, some C corporations were also subject to an alternative minimum tax (¶3200 *et seq.*).

For tax years beginning after 2017, the corporate AMT has been repealed.

For penalty taxes imposed on corporations with earnings accumulations in excess of the reasonable needs of the business, see ¶3317 *et seq.*

For the personal holding company tax, see ¶3321 *et seq.*

For taxation of corporations making certain outbound transfers, see ¶3568.

¶ 3304 C corporation's taxable income.

A C corporation's taxable income equals its gross income less the deductions allowed by the Code. (Code Sec. 63)[8] Generally, a C corporation's gross income doesn't include contributions to its capital. (Code Sec. 118) IRS has provided a number of safe harbors for treating certain types of grants as capital contributions. For a C corporation's gain or loss from distributing property to its shareholders, see ¶3526.

For contributions made after Dec. 22, 2017, subject to an exception for certain contributions made by a government entity under a master development plan approved before that date, the term "contributions to capital" generally does not include: (i) any contribution in aid of construction or any other contribution as a customer or potential customer, or (ii) any contribution by any governmental entity or civic group (other than a contribution made by a shareholder as such). (Code Sec. 118(b))

¶ 3305 Computing a C corporation's tax.

A C corporation's tax is computed by applying the Code Sec. 11 rate(s) in effect for its tax year (¶1113) to its taxable income (¶3304) for that year, and then subtracting any available tax credits (¶2300 *et seq.*).[9]

Special rules apply for computing the tax for years that straddle a rate change (Code Sec. 15(a))[10] and for short tax years, see ¶2805.

¶ 3306 Deduction for Dividends from Domestic and Certain Foreign Corporations. ■

For tax years after 2017, subject to specific disallowances, reductions, and limitations (¶3309 *et seq.*), a C corporation may deduct 50% of the dividends received or accrued from *domestic* corporations (65% for dividends received or accrued from a

---

6. ¶D-1343; ¶77,044.03   9. ¶D-1001 *et seq.*; ¶114.01
7. ¶D-1363 *et seq.*; ¶77,044   10. ¶D-1009 *et seq.*; ¶154.01
8. ¶D-1001; ¶634

corporation at least 20% of the stock of which, not counting preferred stock described in Code Sec. 1504(a)(4), is owned, by vote and value, by the corporate shareholder). (Code Sec. 243(a)(1); Code Sec. 243(c))[11]

Members of an affiliated group (as specially defined) that file separate returns may deduct 100% of the dividends received from other group members if certain requirements are met. (Code Sec. 243(a)(3), Code Sec. 243(b))[12]

For a small business investment company's dividends-received deduction, see ¶4205.

The deduction applies to taxable dividends (¶1283 *et seq.*) (Code Sec. 243(a)), "boot" dividends (¶3542), consent dividends (¶3335)[13] and the "dividend equivalent" portion of applicable high yield debt obligations (¶1745). (Code Sec. 163(e)(5)(B))[14] For dividends that aren't deductible, see ¶3314.

For the post-2017 deduction allowed for dividends received from a specified 10%-owned foreign corporation, see ¶3315.

¶ 3307 Dividends from regulated investment companies (RICs).

A corporate shareholder that receives a properly designated dividend (other than capital gain or exempt-interest dividends) from a RIC is eligible for the dividends-received deduction (DRD) to the extent the RIC would have been allowed to deduct the amount as a DRD if it were taxed as a regular corporation. (Code Sec. 243(d)(2), Code Sec. 854(b)(3))[15]

¶ 3308 Dividends from foreign corporations and possession corporations.

A U.S. corporation that owns at least 10% (by vote and value) of the stock of a foreign corporation (other than a passive foreign investment company) may deduct the applicable percentage (50% or 65% for tax years after 2017) see ¶3306) of the *U.S.-source* portion of the dividends it receives from that foreign corporation. (Code Sec. 245(a)(1), Code Sec. 245(a)(2))[16]

The U.S.-source portion of any dividend is the amount that bears the same ratio to the dividend that the payor's post-'86 undistributed U.S. earnings bears to its total post-'86 undistributed earnings. (Code Sec. 245(a)(3), Code Sec. 245(a)(4), Code Sec. 245(a)(5))[17] Special rules apply for dividends paid out of pre-'87 earnings. [18]

A 100% dividends-received deduction is allowed (instead of the above percentages) if all the foreign corporation's gross income is effectively connected with its U.S. business in the year the dividends are earned, and all its outstanding stock is owned by the U.S. payee both in that year and in the payee's tax year in which the dividends are received. (Code Sec. 245(b))[19]

For the post-2017 deduction allowed for dividends received from a specified 10%-owned foreign corporation, see ¶3315.

For domestic international sales corporation (DISC) dividends, see ¶3314.

¶ 3309 Taxable income limit on dividends-received deduction (DRD).

For tax years after 2017, in the case of dividends that are subject to the 50% or 65% (but not the 100%) rule (¶3306), the DRD may not exceed 50% or 65% of the corporation's "taxable income." For this purpose, taxable income is computed without regard to the

---

11. ¶D-2201; ¶D-2205 *et seq.*; ¶2434.01
12. ¶D-2223 *et seq.*; ¶2434.01
13. ¶D-2209 *et seq.*; ¶2434.01
14. ¶D-2221; ¶1634.051
15. ¶D-2216, ¶E-6163; ¶8524.02

16. ¶D-2244; ¶2434.03
17. ¶s D-2244, D-2246; ¶2434.03
18. ¶D-2246; ¶2434.03
19. ¶D-2247; ¶2434.03

deductions for capital loss carrybacks, NOLs, dividends received, and income attributable to domestic production activities, and without any basis reduction for extraordinary dividends (¶2494). (Code Sec. 246(b)(1))[20]

In 2017, if a taxpayer receives both 80% and 70% dividends, this limitation is applied in two stages. First, the 65% deduction for dividends from 20% –owned corporations is restricted to 80% of taxable income. Second, for dividends qualifying for the 50% deduction, the limitation is 50% of the taxable income reduced by dividends from 20% or greater owned corporations.[21]

A corporation with a net operating loss (NOL) for the tax year is not subject to this limitation. (Code Sec. 246(b)(2))[22]

For the post-2017 deduction allowed for dividends received from a specified 10%-owned foreign corporation, see ¶3315.

¶ 3310   Holding period requirements.

No dividends-received deduction (DRD) is allowed for any dividend on any share of stock held by the taxpayer for 45 days or less during the 91-day period beginning on the date that is 45 days before the date on which the stock becomes ex-dividend (i.e., the latest purchase date for collecting a dividend) with respect to the dividend (90 days or less out of the relevant 181-day period for any preferred stock with respect to which the taxpayer gets dividends that are attributable to a period or periods aggregating in excess of 366 days). (Code Sec. 246(c)) In other words, a DRD is allowed only if the taxpayer's holding period for the dividend paying stock is satisfied over a period immediately before or immediately after the taxpayer becomes entitled to receive the dividend. [23]

In determining how long the shareholder has held the stock, the day of disposition but not the day of acquisition is taken into account. (Code Sec. 246(c)(3)(A))[24]

The shareholder's holding period for the stock is reduced for any period during which he:

(1) has an option to sell, is under a contractual obligation to sell, has made (and not closed) a short sale of, or is the grantor of an option to buy, substantially identical stock or securities (as defined under the "wash sale" rules, see ¶2461). (Code Sec. 246(c)(4)(A), Code Sec. 246(c)(4)(B); Reg § 1.246-3(c)(2))[25]

(2) has diminished the risk of loss by holding one or more other positions with respect to substantially similar or related property (i.e., the fair market values (FMVs) of the stock and the property primarily reflect a single firm or enterprise, and changes in the stock's FMV are reasonably expected to approximate (directly or indirectly) changes in the property's FMV), where changes in the FMVs of the stock and the positions are reasonably expected to vary inversely. (Code Sec. 246(c)(4)(C); Reg § 1.246-5)[26]

The Code Sec. 245A post-2017 dividends received deduction (¶3315) is generally available only to taxpayers who have held shares of the specified 10%-owned foreign corporation for more than 365 days during a 731-day period. (Code Sec. 246(c)(5))[27]

¶ 3311   No dividends-received deduction (DRD) where shareholder is obligated to make certain payments.

A corporate shareholder gets no DRD for any dividends received on any stock acquired after July 18, 1984 to the extent the shareholder is under an obligation (by a short sale or

---

20. ¶D-2251 *et seq.*; ¶2434.04
21. ¶D-2253; ¶2434.04
22. ¶s D-2251, D-2252; ¶2434.04
23. ¶D-2263; ¶2434.04

24. ¶D-2263; ¶2434.04
25. ¶s D-2264, D-2266; ¶2434.04
26. ¶D-2268 *et seq.*; ¶2434.04
27. ¶O-2953

otherwise) to make related payments with respect to positions in substantially similar or related property (see ¶3310). (Code Sec. 246(c)(1)(B))[28]

¶ 3312 Deduction for foreign-derived intangible income (FDII) and global intangible low-taxed income (GILTI).

For tax years that begin after Dec. 31, 2017 and before Jan. 1, 2026, subject to a limitation based on taxable income (Code Sec. 250(a)(2)), a domestic corporation may deduct an amount equal to the sum of:

(1) 37.5% of the FDII (Code Sec. 250(b)) of the domestic corporation for the tax year, plus

(2) 50% of (i) the GILTI (¶4614) amount (if any) which is included in the gross income of the domestic corporation under Code Sec. 951A for the tax year, and (ii) the amount treated as a dividend received by the corporation under Code Sec. 78 which is attributable to the amount described in item (i). (Code Sec. 250)[29]

For tax years that begin after Dec. 31, 2025, the above percentages decrease to (1) 21.875%; and (2) 37.5%, respectively. (Code Sec. 250(a)(3))[30]

¶ 3313 Deduction reduced for dividends on debt-financed portfolio stock.

For tax years after 2017, the 50% and 65% dividends-received deduction (but not the 100% deduction) (¶3306) is reduced for dividends on debt-financed portfolio stock with a holding period that began after July 18, 1984. As reduced, the applicable percentage for deducting these dividends equals: (1) 50% (65% for dividends from 20%-owned corporations), multiplied by (2) 100% minus the "average indebtedness percentage." (Code Sec. 246A(a), Code Sec. 246A(b)) The reduction for any dividend may not exceed the interest deduction (including short sale expense) allocable to that dividend. (Code Sec. 246A(e))[31]

¶ 3314 Dividends from certain corporations aren't deductible.

No dividends-received deduction is allowed for dividends from:

. . . a corporation that's exempt from tax as a charitable organization under Code Sec. 501 or as a farmer's cooperative under Code Sec. 521. (Code Sec. 246(a)(1))[32]

. . . a domestic international sales corporation (DISC; ¶4604) or former DISC to the extent paid out of accumulated DISC income or previously taxed income, or amounts considered distributed in the year of qualification as a DISC. (Code Sec. 246(d))[33]

. . . a real estate investment trust (REIT). (Code Sec. 243(d)(3))[34]

. . . a mutual savings bank, savings and loan associations and other banks allowed a deduction under Code Sec. 591. (Code Sec. 243(d)(1))[35] However, certain dividends from federal home loan banks qualify to the extent set out in a specified formula. (Code Sec. 246(a)(2))[36]

28. ¶D-2261; ¶2434.04
29. ¶O-3000 *et seq.*
30. ¶O-3005
31. ¶D-2255; ¶2434.05
32. ¶D-2213; ¶2434.04

33. ¶D-2212; ¶2434.04
34. ¶D-2215; ¶2434.01
35. ¶D-2211; ¶2434.01
36. ¶s D-2214, D-2219; ¶2434.04

¶ 3315 "Participation exemption" system—deduction for dividends received from a specified 10%-owned foreign corporation.

Generally effective for distributions made after 2017, a domestic corporation (not a REIT or RIC) that is a U.S. shareholder of a specified 10%-owned foreign corporation can, if certain requirements are met, take a deduction in an amount equal to the foreign-source portion of any dividend received from the specified 10% owned foreign corporation. (Code Sec. 245A(a)) For this purpose, a U.S. shareholder is a U.S. person that owns 10% or more of the total vote or value of shares of all classes of stock of the foreign corporation. (Code Sec. 951(b)) Amounts treated as dividends under Code Sec. 1248 (¶4616) and Code Sec. 964(e) are treated as dividends for purposes of the Code Sec. 245A dividends received deduction.[37]

The foreign-source portion of a dividend from a specified 10%-owned foreign corporation is that amount which bears the ratio to the dividend as the undistributed foreign earnings of the specified 10%-owned foreign corporation bears to the total undistributed earnings of such foreign corporation. (Code Sec. 245A(c)) Undistributed earnings are the E&P of the specified 10%-owned foreign corporation as of the close of the tax year without any reduction for dividends distributed during the tax year. (Code Sec. 245A(c)(2)) Undistributed foreign earnings are undistributed earnings reduced by post-'86 undistributed earnings described in Code Sec. 245(a)(5)(A) that are attributable to income effectively connected with the conduct of a trade or business in the U.S., and any dividends received from an 80%-owned domestic corporation described in Code Sec. 245(a)(5)(B) (but by treating RICs and REITs as domestic corporations). (Code Sec. 245A(c)(3))[38]

No foreign tax credit (¶2362) or deduction is allowed for any taxes paid or accrued with respect to a dividend that qualifies for the deduction,[39] and the domestic corporation's basis in the 10% owned foreign corporation's stock is reduced (but not below zero) by the amount of the deduction allowable on that stock. (Code Sec. 961(d))[40]

The deduction is not available with respect to a hybrid dividend received by a U.S. shareholder from a controlled foreign corporation (CFC). (Code Sec. 245A(e)(1)) A "hybrid dividend" is an amount received from a CFC for which a deduction would otherwise be allowed under Code Sec. 245A(a) and for which the CFC received a deduction (or other tax benefit) with respect to any income, war profits, or excess profits taxes imposed by any foreign country or possession of the U.S. (Code Sec. 245A(e)(4)) The deduction is also not available for any amount that a shareholder of a PFIC that has made a qualifying electing fund (QEF) election treats as a deemed dividend under Code Sec. 1291(d)(2)(B). (Code Sec. 245A(f))[41]

¶ 3316 Base erosion minimum tax—payments to foreign related parties.

Under Code Sec. 59A, a tax is imposed on "base erosion payments" paid or accrued in tax years beginning after 2017 of corporate taxpayers (other than RICs, REITs, and S corporations) with (i) substantial gross receipts, which for this purpose means average gross receipts of at least $500 million for the three-tax-year period ending with the preceding year; and (ii) a "base erosion percentage" under Code Sec. 59A(e)(1)(C) of at least 3% (2% for certain banks and securities dealers). The tax is structured as an alternative minimum tax that applies when a multinational company reduces its regular U.S. tax liability to less than a specified percentage of its taxable income, after adding back deductible base eroding payments and a percentage of tax losses claimed that were carried from

---

37. ¶O-2950 *et seq.*
38. ¶O-2951
39. ¶O-2951

40. ¶O-2423.1
41. ¶O-2952

another year. The tax applies to deductible payments to foreign affiliates from domestic corporations, as well as on foreign corporations engaged in a U.S. trade or business in computing the tax on their effectively connected income.

An applicable taxpayer who is subject to the tax under Code Sec. 59A is required to pay a tax equal to the "base erosion minimum tax amount" for the tax year. (Code Sec. 59A(a)) This amount is the excess of 10% of the taxpayer's "modified taxable income" (5% in tax years beginning in calendar year 2018) over its regular tax liability, reduced (not below zero) by specified credits. (Code Sec. 59A(b))[42]

¶ 3317   Accumulated Earnings Tax. ▂▂▂▂▂▂▂▂▂▂▂▂

With limited exceptions (see below), every corporation that accumulates earnings and profits, rather than distributing them, in order to avoid the imposition of income tax on its shareholders (¶3318), is subject to an annual accumulated earnings (penalty) tax equal to 20% of its "accumulated taxable income" for the year (¶3319). The tax is in addition to the regular corporate tax, but is not self assessed and arises only on a deficiency assessment.

The tax generally applies to all corporations, regardless of the number of shareholders and regardless of whether the corporation is widely held. [43] It also applies to foreign corporations on their U.S.-source income if *any* of their shareholders is subject to U.S. income tax on distributions. (Reg § 1.532-1(c))[44]

Personal holding companies (¶3321), tax-exempt corporations, passive foreign investment companies, and S corporations are specifically exempt from the accumulated earnings tax. (Code Sec. 532(b), Code Sec. 1363(a))

¶ 3318   "Reasonable needs" of the business.

For purposes of the accumulated earnings tax (¶3317), a corporation that accumulates earnings and profits (E&P) beyond the reasonable needs of its business is considered to have done so to avoid tax on its shareholders *unless* it proves otherwise by the preponderance of the evidence. (Code Sec. 533(a))[45]

An accumulation is in excess of the reasonable needs of a business if it exceeds the amount that a prudent business person would consider appropriate for the present purposes of the business and for its reasonably anticipated future needs. (Code Sec. 537; Reg § 1.537-1(a), Reg § 1.537-1(b)(1))[46] The reasonable needs of a corporation's business include the Code Sec. 303 death tax redemption needs of the business (Code Sec. 537(a)(2)[47] and the excess business holdings redemption needs of the business. (Code Sec. 537(a)(3))[48]

Corporations facing an accumulated earnings tax may use a formula to compute the amount reasonably needed for working capital to test their liability for the penalty. The Tax Court in *Bardahl Manufacturing Corp* held that necessary working capital should be determined by: (1) calculating a corporation's operating cycle percentage (the period of time, expressed as a percentage of a year, needed to convert cash to inventory, inventory to sales and accounts receivable, and accounts receivable to cash), and then (2) multiplying that percentage by the corporation's total operating expenses for the year . [49]

---

42. ¶D-1250 *et seq.*
43. ¶D-2602; ¶5324
44. ¶D-2607; ¶5324
45. ¶D-2704; ¶s 5324.01, 5374

46. ¶D-2779, D-2783, D-2792; ¶s 5314, 5374
47. ¶D-2828;¶5374
48. ¶D-2830; ¶5374
49. ¶D-2848; ¶5374

¶ 3319   Accumulated taxable income.

For purposes of computing the accumulated earnings tax (¶3317), a corporation's accumulated taxable income is its taxable income, adjusted as described below,   *minus:* (1) the dividends-paid deduction (¶3332), and (2) the accumulated earnings credit (¶3320). (Code Sec. 535(a))[50]

The corporation's taxable income is *reduced* by:

. . . federal income and excess profits taxes accrued during the tax year (not the accumulated earnings tax or the personal holding company tax) (Code Sec. 535(b)(1));

. . . taxes of foreign countries and U.S. possessions accrued or deemed paid by a domestic corporation and included in the foreign tax credit (¶2362 *et seq.*) (Code Sec. 535(b)(1));[1]

. . . charitable contributions in excess of the deduction ceiling (¶2131) (Code Sec. 535(b)(2));[2]

. . . net capital gains (less attributable taxes) (Code Sec. 535(b)(6)(A));[3] and

. . . net capital losses. (Code Sec. 535(b)(5)(A))[4]

Taxable income is *increased* by:

. . . special corporate deductions (e.g., for dividends received (¶3306 *et seq.*), but not for organizational expenditures) (Code Sec. 535(b)(3));

. . . net operating loss deduction (¶1815 *et seq.*) (Code Sec. 535(b)(4)); and

. . . capital loss carryback or carryover (¶2611). (Code Sec. 535(b)(7)(B))[5]

¶ 3320   Accumulated earnings credit.

For purposes of computing accumulated taxable income (¶3319) for a corporation other than a mere holding or investment company, the accumulated earnings credit equals the *greater* of:

(1) $250,000 ($150,000 for a corporation whose principal function is the performance of health, legal, engineering, accounting, or certain other services) *plus* dividends paid during the first 2 1/2 months of the tax year *minus* accumulated earnings and profits (E&P) at the end of the preceding tax year (Code Sec. 535(c)(2), Code Sec. 535(c)(4)); or

(2) an amount equal to that part of the E&P for the tax year that is retained for the reasonable needs of the business (i.e., the amount in excess of the dividends-paid deduction (¶3332, Code Sec. 535(c)(4)), *minus* the net capital gain deduction, if any, allowed in adjusting the corporation's taxable income (¶3319). (Code Sec. 535(c)(1))[6]

¶ 3321   Personal Holding Company (PHC) Penalty Tax. ▮▮▮▮▮▮▮▮▮▮▮

For any year in which a corporation is a PHC, it is liable for an additional 20% penalty tax on its undistributed PHC income (¶3322), reported on Form 1120, Schedule PH. (Reg § 1.6012-2(b))[7] With exceptions (¶3323), a corporation is a PHC for the tax year if the following "PHC tests" are met: (i) it is closely held (i.e., at any time during the last half of the year, more than 50% of the value of its outstanding stock is owned, directly or indirectly, by not more than five individuals, see ¶3324); and (ii) at least 60% of the adjusted gross income of which is "PHC income" (¶3326).[8]

50. ¶D-2901; ¶5354.01
1. ¶D-2913; ¶5354.01
2. ¶D-2906; ¶5354.01
3. ¶D-2908; ¶5354.01
4. ¶D-2911; ¶5354.01

5. ¶D-2907; ¶5354.01
6. ¶D-2915; ¶5354.01
7. ¶D-3601; ¶5454.02
8. ¶D-3203; ¶5424

The foreign tax credit isn't allowed against the PHC tax. (Reg § 1.545-2(a)(3))[9]

¶ 3322 Undistributed personal holding company (PHC) income subject to the PHC penalty tax.

A corporation's undistributed PHC income that is subject to the PHC penalty tax (¶3321) is its taxable income (Code Sec. 545(a)),[10] adjusted as described below.

. . . The following amounts are *subtracted* from taxable income:

. . . Federal income tax accrued during the year, and U.S. possession and foreign income taxes not deductible in computing taxable income. (Code Sec. 545(b)(1))[11]

. . . Excess charitable contributions, i.e., amounts over the *corporate* ceiling up to the amount allowed under the *individual* ceiling (¶2123 *et seq.*). (Code Sec. 545(b)(2))[12]

. . . Net capital gain (i.e., excess of net long-term capital gain over net short-term capital loss), minus income taxes attributable to that excess. (Code Sec. 545(b)(5))[13]

. . . The preceding tax year's net operating loss (NOL) carryforward. (Code Sec. 545(b)(4))[14]

. . . The dividends-paid deduction (¶3331 *et seq.*). (Code Sec. 545(a))[15]

. . . The following amounts are *added* to taxable income:

. . . Special corporate deductions. (¶3306 *et seq.*). (Code Sec. 545(b)(3))[16]

. . . NOL deduction. (Code Sec. 545(b)(4))[17]

. . . Expenses and depreciation exceeding income from property (unless income was highest obtainable). (Code Sec. 545(b)(6))[18]

¶ 3323 Corporations exempt from personal holding company (PHC) classification.

The following entities are not subject to the PHC penalty tax (¶3321):

. . . S corporations (¶3350 *et seq.*); (Code Sec. 1363(a))

. . . tax-exempt corporations; (Code Sec. 542(c)(1))

. . . banks or domestic building and loan associations; (Code Sec. 542(c)(2))

. . . life insurance companies; (Code Sec. 542(c)(3))

. . . surety companies; (Code Sec. 542(c)(4))

. . . certain active lending or finance companies; (Code Sec. 542(c)(6), Code Sec. 542(d))

. . . small business investment companies (¶2619), provided no shareholders own, directly or indirectly, a 5%-or-more interest in a small business concern to which the investment company provides funds; (Code Sec. 542(c)(7))

. . . corporations subject to the jurisdiction of a court in a bankruptcy case or in a receivership, foreclosure or similar proceeding in a federal or state court, if the proceedings aren't primarily to avoid the PHC tax; (Code Sec. 542(c)(8)) and

. . . foreign corporations. (Code Sec. 542(c)(5))[19]

9. ¶D-3619; ¶9014
10. ¶D-3603; ¶5454
11. ¶D-3606; ¶5454
12. ¶D-3609; ¶5454
13. ¶D-3610; ¶5454
14. ¶D-3614; ¶5454

15. ¶D-3800; ¶5454
16. ¶D-3613; ¶5454
17. ¶D-3614; ¶5454
18. ¶D-3615; ¶5454
19. ¶D-3301; ¶5424.02

¶ 3324   Determining stock ownership.

For purposes of determining liability for the personal holding company (PHC) penalty tax (¶3321), an individual is the owner of any stock he owns directly or indirectly (Code Sec. 542(a)(2)), or constructively under the following rules:

(1) Stock owned by or for a corporation, partnership, estate or trust is considered owned proportionately by its shareholders, partners or beneficiaries. (Code Sec. 544(a)(1))[20]

(2) Stock owned by or for an individual's family or partner is considered owned by the individual. An individual's family includes only his brothers and sisters (whether by the whole or half blood), spouse, ancestors and lineal descendants. (Code Sec. 544(a)(2))[21]

(3) If any person has an option to acquire stock, the stock subject to the option is considered owned by that person. An option to acquire the option, and each one of a series of these options, is considered an option to acquire the stock. (Code Sec. 544(a)(3))[22]

Stock that may be considered owned by an individual under either rule (2) or rule (3) is considered owned by him under rule (3). (Code Sec. 544(a)(6))[23]

Rules (2) and (3) apply only if the result is to make the corporation a PHC or to make income PHC income (¶3326). (Code Sec. 544(a)(4))[24]

Stock *constructively* owned by a person under rule (1) or rule (3) is considered *actually* owned by that person for purposes of again applying rule (1), or applying rule (2), to make *another* person the *constructive* owner of the same stock. (Code Sec. 544(a)(5))[25]

Only outstanding stock (i.e., not Treasury stock) is counted. (Reg § 1.542-3(b))[26] Outstanding securities convertible into stock are considered outstanding stock *but only if* converting them would make the corporation a PHC or the income PHC income (except where there are differing conversion dates none of the convertibles may be counted as stock unless all outstanding securities having the same or an earlier conversion date are also included). (Code Sec. 544(b))[27]

¶ 3325   Adjusted ordinary gross income used in personal holding company (PHC) tests.

For purposes of determining liability for the PHC penalty tax (¶3321), *adjusted ordinary gross income* is ordinary gross income (below) minus certain interest income, with these adjustments: for each of the separate categories of rents, mineral, oil and gas royalties, working interests in an oil or gas well and property produced by the taxpayer, gross income from the category is reduced (but not below zero) by certain expenses allocated to each category. (Code Sec. 543(b)(2))[28]

Ordinary gross income is gross income minus all gains from the sale or other disposition of capital assets and Code Sec. 1231(b) assets. (Code Sec. 543(b)(1))[29]

¶ 3326   Personal holding company (PHC) income used in PHC tests.

For purposes of determining liability for the PHC penalty tax (¶3321), PHC income is the portion of adjusted ordinary gross income (¶3325) that consists of: dividends; interest; annuities; rents (¶3327); mineral, oil and gas royalties; copyright, patent, etc., royalties

---

20. ¶D-3406; ¶5444.01
21. ¶D-3408; ¶5444.01
22. ¶D-3410; ¶5444.01
23. ¶D-3411; ¶5444.01 *et seq.*
24. ¶s D-3408, D-3410; ¶5444.01

25. ¶D-3411; ¶5444.01
26. ¶D-3402; ¶5424.04
27. ¶D-3412; ¶5444.01 *et seq.*
28. ¶D-3506; ¶5424.03
29. ¶D-3505; ¶5424.03

(but not certain "active business computer software royalties"); produced film rents; compensation for more-than-25% shareholder's use of corporate property (¶3328); amounts received under personal service contracts (¶3329); and amounts received from estates and trusts.[30]

¶ 3327 Rents.

The adjusted income from rents is personal holding company (PHC) income (¶3326) for purposes of determining liability for the PHC penalty tax (¶3321), unless: (1) it is 50% or more of adjusted ordinary gross income (¶3325); *and* (2) certain other *undistributed* PHC income, as specially defined, is 10% or less of ordinary gross income (¶3325). This "specially defined" PHC income *includes* copyright royalties and adjusted income from mineral, oil and gas royalties but *excludes* rents and compensation for a 25%-or-more shareholder's use of corporate property. The 10% test is met if the total of (a) dividends paid during the tax year, plus (b) late-paid dividends (¶3333), plus (c) consent dividends (¶3335), equals or exceeds the amount, if any, by which "PHC income" exceeds 10% of ordinary gross income. (Code Sec. 543(a)(2))[31]

Rents are compensation (however designated) for the use of, or the right to use, property (Code Sec. 543(a)(1)(A), Code Sec. 543(b)(3)), *except* for: compensation for a shareholder's use of corporate property that is PHC income (¶3328), copyright royalties, produced film rents, or compensation for the right to use any tangible personal property manufactured or produced by the corporation, if during the tax year it's engaged in substantial manufacturing or production of property of the same type. (Code Sec. 543(b)(3)) For this purpose, rents also include payments for a negative easement (i.e., to leave property undeveloped). [32]

¶ 3328 Compensation for use of corporate property by a 25%-or-more shareholder.

Amounts received by the corporation from a shareholder as compensation for the use of, or right to use, tangible property of the corporation are included in the corporation's personal holding company (PHC) income (¶3326) for purposes of determining liability for the PHC penalty tax (¶3321), if, during the tax year, 25% or more in value of the corporation's outstanding stock is owned by or for an individual entitled to use that property (directly or through a sublease). (Code Sec. 543(a)(6)(A)) But this doesn't apply if the corporation's PHC income (as specially defined, see ¶3327) doesn't exceed 10% of its ordinary gross income (¶3325).[33]

¶ 3329 Receipts under personal service contract.

For purposes of determining liability for the personal holding company (PHC) penalty tax (¶3321), PHC income (¶3326) includes amounts received under a contract pursuant to which the corporation furnishes personal services, and amounts received from the sale or other disposition of the contract, if:

(1) some person other than the corporation has the right to designate (by name or description) the individual who performs the services, or if the individual who is to perform the services is so designated in the contract, *and*

(2) at some time during the tax year, 25% or more in value of the corporation's outstanding stock is owned, directly or indirectly, by or for that individual. (Code Sec. 543(a)(7); Reg § 1.543-1(b)(8)(i))[34]

---

30. ¶D-3507; ¶5434
31. ¶D-3522; ¶5434.07
32. ¶D-3524; ¶s 5434.06, 5434.07, 5434.09

33. ¶D-3527 *et seq.*; ¶5434.06
34. ¶D-3531; ¶5434.05

¶ 3330   Qualified Personal Service Corporations (PSCs). ▬▬▬▬▬▬

For tax years beginning before 2018, qualified PSCs were subject to special rules, e.g., they were subject to a flat 35% tax rate (¶3303) and were required to use the cash accounting method. For tax years beginning after 2017, a 21% rate applies (¶1113). A corporation is a qualified PSC if it meets two tests:

(1) Substantially all of its activities involve the performance of services in the fields of health, law, engineering, architecture, accounting, actuarial science, performing arts, or consulting. "Substantially all" means that 95% or more of the time spent by the corporation's employees, serving in their capacity as employees, is devoted to performing such services. Brokerage services, including commission-based financial services, are excepted from consulting services.

(2) Substantially all (95% or more) of the stock by value (not including treasury shares) is held directly or indirectly by: employees performing the services or retired employees who had performed such services; or the estates of such employees, or any other person who, during the two-year period starting with the date that such an employee died, acquired that individual's stock because his death. (Code Sec. 448(d)(2); Reg § 1.448-1T(e)(4))[35]

For the rules on allowable accounting methods, see ¶2818. For the tax year of PSCs, see ¶2811.

¶ 3331   Dividend Distributions to Reduce Special Taxes on Corporations. ▬▬▬▬▬

A deduction for dividends paid is allowed in computing the accumulated earnings penalty tax (¶3317) and personal holding company (PHC) penalty tax (¶3321), and in determining a corporation's qualification as a regulated investment company (¶4201) or real estate investment trust (¶4202). A deduction is also allowed in some cases for undistributed amounts shareholders consent to report as dividends.

Depending on the entity involved, the dividends-paid deduction may consist of:

(1) dividends paid during the tax year (¶3332),

(2) "late paid" dividends (¶3333),

(3) liquidating dividends (¶3334),

(4) consent dividends (¶3335),

(5) dividend carryover —only for PHCs (¶3336), and

(6) deficiency dividends (¶3337)—only for PHCs. (Code Sec. 561 *et seq.*; Reg § 1.561-1)[36]

¶ 3332   Dividends paid during the tax year.

The dividends-paid deduction includes dividends (¶1285) paid and actually received by the shareholder during the tax year. (Code Sec. 561(a)(1); Reg § 1.561-2(a)(1))[37]

No deduction is allowed if the dividend is preferential, i.e., it must be pro rata. (Code Sec. 562(c); Reg § 1.562-2(a))[38]

The amount of "dividends" paid is the amount by which the distribution reduces the corporation's earnings and profits (E&P). (Code Sec. 316(a), Code Sec. 562(a))[39]

A personal holding company's (PHC's, ¶3321 *et seq.*) dividends-paid deduction may equal its undistributed PHC income, even if this exceeds its E&P. (Code Sec. 316(b)(2), Code

---

35. ¶G-2058 *et seq.*; ¶4484
36. ¶D-3800; ¶5614
37. ¶D-3810; ¶5614.01

38. ¶D-3819 *et seq.*; ¶5624.06
39. ¶D-3807; ¶3164, 5614, 5624

Sec. 562(a))[40]

¶ 3333   Deduction for "late paid" dividends.

A corporation (except for corporations with a June 30 tax year, see below) may treat dividends paid after the close of the tax year but within the first 4 ½ months of the next year as paid on the last day of the earlier year for the accumulated earnings tax (¶3317 *et seq.*) and, if elected (on the earlier year return), personal holding company (PHC) tax (¶3321 *et seq.*). For a C corporation with a tax year ending on June 30, for tax years beginning before 2026, a dividend paid after the close of the tax year but within the first 3½ months of the next year, is considered paid during the tax year. (Code Sec. 563(a), Code Sec. 563(b))[41]

¶ 3334   Liquidating distributions.

Corporations (including mutual funds and real estate investment trusts) other than personal holding companies (PHCs) may include liquidating distributions in their dividends-paid deduction, to the extent the distribution is properly chargeable to earnings and profits (E&P). (Code Sec. 562(b)(1)(A))[42] Where there's a deficit in E&P at the start of the tax year of distribution, no dividends-paid deduction is allowed if current E&P for that year doesn't exceed the deficit. (Reg § 1.562-1(b)(1))[43] A liquidation for this purpose includes a redemption of stock to which Code Sec. 302 applies (¶3515 *et seq.*), other than a redemption by a mere investment or holding company. (Code Sec. 562(b)(1))[44]

If a *complete* liquidation of a corporation other than a PHC occurs within 24 months after the plan of liquidation is adopted, any distribution under the plan within the 24-month period is treated as a dividend for this purpose, to the extent of the corporation's E&P for the tax year of the distribution, computed without regard to capital losses. (Code Sec. 562(b)(1)(B)) Thus, the dividends-paid deduction is allowed for the amount of the distribution up to current E&P, even if there's an E&P deficit at the start of the year. (Reg § 1.562-1(b)(1))[45]

For PHCs only, distributions made within 24 months after the plan of liquidation is adopted qualify for the dividends-paid deduction. [46] Distributions (in this period) to *corporate* shareholders qualify to the extent the undistributed PHC income for the tax year of the distribution is allocable to corporate shareholders. (Code Sec. 562(b)(2))[47] Distributions to *noncorporate* shareholders qualify if the corporation designates the amount distributed as a dividend and notifies the shareholders that it must be reported as a dividend. (Code Sec. 316(b)(2)(B), Code Sec. 562(b)(2))[48]

¶ 3335   Consent dividends—Form 972 and Form 973.

A corporation may claim a dividends-paid deduction for amounts with respect to "consent" stock (below) that are not actually paid out as dividends if those who are shareholders on the last day of its tax year consent (on Form 972) to report these hypothetical amounts as dividend income on their tax returns. (Code Sec. 565(a); Reg § 1.565-1(a), Reg § 1.565-1(b))[49]

This amount is treated for all tax purposes as if it had been distributed in money to the consenting shareholder on the last day of the corporation's tax year, and contributed to the

---

40. ¶D-3807; ¶s 3164.03, 5614
41. ¶D-3825 *et seq.*; ¶5634
42. ¶D-3828; ¶5624.02
43. ¶D-3835; ¶5624.02
44. ¶D-3829; ¶s 5624.02, 5624.05

45. ¶D-3836; ¶5624.02
46. ¶D-3837; ¶s 3164.03, 5624.02
47. ¶D-3844 *et seq.*; ¶5624.02
48. ¶D-3838 *et seq.*; ¶s 3164.03, 5624.02
49. ¶s D-3851, D-3854, D-3861; ¶5654

corporation's capital by the shareholder on the same day. (Code Sec. 565(c))[50]

Consent stock includes common stock, and preferred stock with unlimited participation rights. (Code Sec. 565(f); Reg § 1.565-6(a)(1))[1]

The corporation must file the Form 972 duly executed by each consenting shareholder, and a return on Form 973, with its income tax return not later than the due date (with extensions) of the return. (Reg § 1.565-1(b)(3))[2]

¶ 3336   Dividend carryover for personal holding companies (PHCs).

A PHC may increase its dividends-paid deduction for the tax year by the excess of: (1) dividends paid in the two preceding tax years, over (2) its undistributed PHC income for those years. (Code Sec. 564; Reg § 1.564-1)[3]

¶ 3337   Personal holding company (PHC) deficiency dividend deduction—Form 976.

If a corporation is "determined" (i.e., by a final court decision, closing agreement, or signed agreement with IRS relating to PHC tax liability, Code Sec. 547(c))[4] to be liable for a deficiency in PHC tax (¶3321 *et seq.*) for any tax year, it may reduce or eliminate the deficiency (or get a refund of part or all of any deficiency paid) by making a "deficiency dividend" distribution and then claiming a deduction (on Form 976) for it. This deduction is allowed only for purposes of determining the *PHC tax* for that year (but not any interest, additional amounts or assessable penalties computed with respect to the PHC tax). (Code Sec. 547(a))[5]

The deduction isn't allowed if the determination finds that any part of the deficiency is due to fraud or willful failure to file a timely income tax return. (Code Sec. 547(g))[6]

¶ 3338   Limitation on Tax Benefits for Members of "Controlled Groups." ■■■■■

If two or more corporations constitute a controlled group of corporations (below), the corporate tax rate schedule (¶1113) is applied to the group as one, and the group is allowed only one credit in computing the accumulated earnings (¶3317) and, for tax years before 2018, one exemption in computing alternative minimum taxes (the corporate AMT having been repealed for tax years after 2017) (¶3200 *et seq.*).[7] However, a group member that incurs a loss for a tax year may not apply that loss to reduce the amount of the combined taxable income (or, for tax years before 2018, combined alternative minimum taxable income) of the controlled group for purposes of determining the amount of the additional tax or the reduction in the exemption amount. (Reg § 1.1561-2(a)(1))[8]

A controlled group of corporations is a group of two or more corporations connected through stock ownership and may consist of a parent-subsidiary group, a brother-sister group, or a combined group (a combined parent-subsidiary/brother-sister group).

A *parent-subsidiary controlled group* consists of one or more chains of corporations connected through stock ownership with a common parent where:

...the common parent owns stock having at least 80% of the total combined voting power of all classes of stock entitled to vote, or at least 80% of the total value of shares of all classes of stock, of at least one other corporation in the chain; *and*

...at least 80% of the stock (combined voting power or value) of each corporation in the

50. ¶D-3853; ¶5654
1. ¶s D-3859, D-3861; ¶5654
2. ¶D-3867; ¶5654
3. ¶D-3869; ¶5644
4. ¶D-3705; ¶5474

5. ¶s D-3703, D-3716; ¶5474
6. ¶D-3719; ¶5474
7. ¶E-10301; ¶15,614
8. ¶E-10303; ¶15,614

chain (other than the parent) is owned by one or more of the other corporations in the chain. (Code Sec. 1563(a)(1); Reg § 1.1563-1(a)(2))[9]

A *brother-sister controlled group* consists of two or more corporations if (a) more than 50% of the total combined voting power of all classes of stock, or (b) more than 50% of the value of all shares of stock, of each corporation is owned by five or fewer persons who are individuals, estates, or trusts, taking into account the stock ownership of each person only to the extent the stock ownership is identical for each corporation. (Code Sec. 1563(a)(2), Code Sec. 1563(f)(5); Reg § 1.1563-1(a)(3))[10]

Specific constructive ownership rules apply in determining whether these stock ownership tests are met. (Code Sec. 1563(d))

¶ 3339 Consolidated Returns by Affiliated Groups.

An affiliated group (defined at ¶3340) can elect to file a single consolidated return instead of each group member filing a separate return.

Any affiliated group of one or more chains of "includible" corporations (¶3340) connected through the requisite stock ownership with a common parent may file a consolidated return in place of separate returns by each member. (Code Sec. 1501—Code Sec. 1505)[11] Generally, once this election to file a consolidated return is made, the group must continue to file a consolidated return. (Reg § 1.1502-75(a)(2))[12]

Tax saving considerations usually determine whether to file a consolidated return. Advantages of consolidated returns include:

. . . operating losses of one group member offset operating profits of other members. [13]

. . . capital losses of one group member offset capital gains of other members. [14]

. . . deferral of income on intercompany distributions. [15]

. . . group's ability to use of foreign taxes paid by a member in excess of its limitation on foreign tax credits. [16]

. . . the 70% or 80% dividends-received deduction for dividends received from unrelated corporations, that may not be fully usable on a separate return basis because of the income limitation rule, may be fully used in a consolidated return. (¶3306)[17]

Regs prescribe detailed rules for treating items of income, gain, deduction and loss of members from intercompany transactions. The rules are designed to clearly reflect the group's taxable income (and tax liability) as a whole by preventing intercompany transactions from creating, accelerating, avoiding, or deferring consolidated taxable income or consolidated tax liability. (Reg § 1.1502-13)[18] There is also significant case law preventing the deduction of duplicate losses. [19]

¶ 3340 "Affiliated group" defined.

In order to qualify as an affiliated group:

(1) the common parent must directly own at least 80% of the total voting power and 80% of the total value of the stock in at least one other "includible" corporation; *and*

(2) one or more of the other includible corporations must directly own at least 80% of the stock (by vote or value) in each of the remaining includible corporations (i.e., not the

9. ¶E-10601; ¶15,634
10. ¶E-10613, ¶15,634
11. ¶E-7500 *et seq.*; ¶15,014
12. ¶E-10000; ¶15,024.16
13. ¶E-7503; ¶15,024
14. ¶E-7503; ¶15,024

15. ¶E-8300 *et seq.*; ¶15,024.03
16. ¶E-9750 *et seq.*; ¶15,024.12
17. ¶E-8905; ¶2434.01
18. ¶E-8250 *et seq.*; ¶15,024.03
19. ¶E-8501 *et seq.*

parent). (Code Sec. 1504(a))[20]

All corporations connected through these stock ownership requirements are "includible" corporations *except*:

. . . tax-exempt organizations;

. . . life insurance companies, except (under certain conditions) where two or more insurance companies are themselves an affiliated group;

. . . regulated investment companies (i.e., mutual funds) and real estate investment trusts (REITs, ¶4201 *et seq.*);

. . . foreign corporations, except for certain Mexican or Canadian subs of a U.S. parent;

. . . corporations that have a Code Sec. 936 election (possessions tax credit) in effect for the tax year;

. . . domestic international sales corporations (DISCs, ¶4604);

. . . S corporations. (Code Sec. 1504(b), Code Sec. 1504(c))[21]

¶ 3341   Forms for consolidated reporting—Form 851, Form 1120, and Form 1122.

A consolidated return is made by the common parent on Form 1120 with an attached Form 851 (affiliation schedule), and a Form 1122 (consent) signed by each subsidiary unless a consolidated return was filed (or required) for the preceding tax year. (Reg § 1.1502-75(b), Reg § 1.1502-75(h))[22] If a group member fails to file Form 1122, IRS can nonetheless treat that member as having joined in the making of a consolidated return if the facts and circumstances warrant such treatment. (Reg § 1.1502-75(b)(2)) In addition, in Rev Proc 2014-14, IRS provided requirements for obtaining an automatic determination that a subsidiary is to be treated as if it had filed Form 1122. [23]

¶ 3342   Consolidated groups—unified loss rules.

When a member of a consolidated group claims a loss on the disposition or worthlessness of a share of another member's stock, the unified loss rules determine what portion of that loss is allowable. The unified loss rules apply when a consolidated group member transfers stock of a subsidiary (S), and after taking into account all applicable rules, the share is a loss share (i.e., its basis exceeds its value). In such a case: (1) the members' basis in the transferred S stock is redetermined to reduce any disparity between the members' bases in the S stock; (2) if the transferred share is still a loss share, the transferor members' basis in the transferred loss share is reduced; and (3) if the transferred share is still a loss share, attributes of S and of its lower-tier subsidiaries are reduced. Thus, the selling group is now entitled to claim its stock loss, but the departing member must reduce its tax attributes immediately after it leaves the group, thereby precluding that member (or the consolidated group it joins) from enjoying a second tax benefit. (Reg § 1.1502-36)[24]

Special anti-avoidance rules under Reg § 1.1502-35 bar the circumvention of the basis redetermination and loss suspension rules, [25] including rules that prevent groups from avoiding the loss suspension rule by "reimporting" losses to the group. (Reg § 1.1502-35(g)(3))[26]

Special rules apply when assets are distributed to multiple group members from a liquidating member in a Code Sec. 332 liquidation. (Reg § 1.1502-80(g))[27]

---

20. ¶E-7601; ¶s 15,024.16, 15,024.17
21. ¶E-7646; ¶s 15,024, 15,024.17
22. ¶E-7754 *et seq.*; ¶15,024.16
23. ¶E-7757; ¶15,024.16

24. ¶E-8574 *et seq.*; ¶3374.025
25. ¶E-8566; ¶3374.025
26. ¶E-8569; ¶3374.025
27. ¶E-7552.2 ; ¶15,024.03

¶ 3343   Dual Consolidated Losses. ▮

A corporation that is subject to tax on its worldwide income in the U.S. and a foreign jurisdiction (e.g. a company incorporated in the U.S. but managed and controlled in another country) is referred to as a "dual resident corporation" (DRC). If a DRC is a resident of a foreign country that permits its losses to offset the income of other commonly controlled foreign corporate residents, then the DRC could use a single loss to offset both foreign and U.S. taxable income. [28] The use of a dual consolidated loss to offset the income of a domestic affiliate is permitted only if the loss does not offset the income of a foreign corporation under foreign law. (Code Sec. 1503(d))[29]

¶ 3344   Corporate Estimated Tax—"Required Annual Payment." ▮

A corporation owing $500 or more in income tax for the tax year must make estimated tax payments —i.e., installment payments (¶3346) of its "required annual payment"—or be subject to a penalty. (Code Sec. 6655(f))

A corporation's required annual payment equals the *lesser* of:

(1) 100% of the tax shown on its return for the year (or if no return is filed, 100% of its tax for that year); or

(2) 100% of the tax shown on its return for the preceding tax year (except as noted below). (Code Sec. 6655(d)(1)(B))[30]

A corporation's required annual payment can't be based on the preceding year's tax if:

... it didn't file a return for the preceding tax year showing a liability for tax (Code Sec. 6655(d)(1)) (a return showing zero tax, e.g., because of a net operating loss (NOL), isn't a return showing a liability for tax);

... the preceding tax year was less than 12 months (Code Sec. 6655(d)(1)); or

... it's a "large corporation (see below)." (Code Sec. 6655(d)(2)(A)) However, a large corporation may use its prior year's tax to determine the amount of its first required installment for any tax year, but it must recapture any resulting reduction in that first installment, by increasing its next required installment by the amount of the reduction. (Code Sec. 6655(d)(2)(B))[31]

A corporation is "large" in any tax year if it (or any predecessor corporation) had taxable income of $1,000,000 or more for any of the three immediately preceding tax years. For this purpose, taxable income doesn't include carryback or carryover of NOLs or capital losses. Special rules apply to controlled groups. (Code Sec. 6655(g)(2))[32]

For quick refunds where a corporation pays *too much* in estimated tax, see ¶4854.

¶ 3345   What is "tax" for estimated tax purposes?

A corporation's "tax" for estimated tax purposes is the excess of: (1) the sum of its regular corporate income tax (or, if applicable insurance company tax), base erosion anti-abuse tax (¶3316), and, for foreign corporations, the tax on gross transportation income (¶4638), over (2) the sum of its tax credits. (Code Sec. 6655(g)(1))[33] For tax years before 2018, the corporate alternative minimum tax (repealed for tax years after 2017; see ¶3303) was included in (1), and the base erosion anti-abuse tax was not.

For S corporations, regular corporate taxes also include: built-in gains tax (¶3362) or tax on net capital gains for certain S corporations (¶3361), tax on excess passive income

---

28. ¶E-9200 *et seq.*; ¶15,024.005
29. ¶E-9201 *et seq.*; ¶15,024.005
30. ¶S-5329 *et seq.*; ¶66,554

31. ¶S-5329 *et seq.*; ¶66,554
32. ¶S-5335 *et seq.*; ¶66,554
33. ¶S-5325; ¶66,554

(¶3365), and tax on recapture of pre-S election investment credit (Code Sec. 6655(g)(4)(A)), but not the last-in, first-out (LIFO) recapture tax (¶3364).[34]

Special rules apply for foreign corporations, insurance companies and tax-exempt organizations (for unrelated business income tax). (Code Sec. 6655(g)(1), Code Sec. 6655(g)(3))[35]

¶ 3346   **"Required installments" of corporate estimated tax—Form 8109.**

Generally, a corporation pays its estimated tax electronically, if required (see ¶3029), otherwise with Form 8109 in four equal "required installments" of its "required annual payment" (¶3344).[36] (Code Sec. 6655(c)(1), Code Sec. 6655(d)(1)(A)) For a calendar year corporation, the installments are due as follows: first, Apr. 15; second, June 15; third, Sept. 15; fourth, Dec. 15, assuming that those days do not fall on a Saturday, Sunday, or legal holiday. (Code Sec. 6655(c)(2)) For a fiscal year corporation, they are due on the 15th day of the corresponding months of the tax year (Code Sec. 6655(i)(1)) (i.e., the fourth, sixth, ninth and twelfth months).[37]

For lower installments in certain situations, see ¶3347 and ¶3348.

¶ 3347   **Use of lower "annualized income installment" as required installment— Form 8842.**

A corporation may use an "annualized income installment" as its estimated tax installment, if that's less than the "required installment" (¶3346). (Code Sec. 6655(e)(1)(A))[38]

For tax years beginning after 2017, the annualized income installment is the excess (if any) of: (1) the applicable percentage of the tax for the year and modified taxable income computed by placing on an annualized basis (as provided by regs) the taxable income for months in the tax year ending before the due date for the installment; *over* (2) the sum of any earlier required installments for the tax year. (Code Sec. 6655(e)(2)(A), Code Sec. 6655(e)(2)(B); Reg § 1.6655-2)[39] For tax years beginning before 2018, alternative minimum taxable income (AMTI) was included in the computation of the required annual installment under the annualized income method. (The corporate AMT has been repealed for tax years beginning after 2017; see ¶3303.)

Alternatively, a corporation may elect on Form 8842, by the due date of the first installment (Reg § 1.6655(e)-1(b)), to determine its annualized income based on its income for *either:* (1) the first two months (first installment), first four months (second), first seven months (third) and first ten months (fourth); *or* (2) the first three months (first), first five months (second), first eight months (third), and first eleven months (fourth). (Code Sec. 6655(e)(2)(C))[40]

Any reduction in an installment resulting from using the annualization method must be made up (recaptured) by increasing the amount of the next required installment that *isn't* determined under the annualization method by the amount of the reduction. (Code Sec. 6655(e)(1)(B))[41]

¶ 3348   **Use of lower "adjusted seasonal installment" as required installment.**

A corporation may use an "adjusted seasonal installment" as its estimated tax installment if it's less than the required installment (¶3346) or the annualized income installment (Code Sec. 6655(e)(1)(A)), but only if the corporation's "base period percentage" (below) for any six consecutive months of the tax year is at least 70%. (Code

34. ¶S-5401; ¶66,554
35. ¶S-5321 *et seq.*, S-5421 *et seq.*; ¶66,554
36. ¶T-10796; ¶75,034
37. ¶S-5324.1; ¶66,554
38. ¶S-5304; ¶66,554
39. ¶S-5342 *et seq.*; ¶66,554
40. ¶S-5342 *et seq.*; ¶66,554
41. ¶S-5347; ¶66,554

Sec. 6655(e)(3)(B); Reg § 1.6655-3)[42]

A corporation computes its adjusted seasonal installment by: (1) computing the taxable income for all months during the tax year before the filing month (i.e., the month the installment is required to be paid), (2) dividing this amount by the base period percentage for those preceding months, (3) determining the tax on the result, (4) multiplying that tax by the base period percentage for the filing month and all preceding months in the tax year (Code Sec. 6655(e)(3)(C), Code Sec. 6655(e)(3)(D)(ii)), and subtracting the aggregate of all earlier required installments. (Code Sec. 6655(e)(3)(A); Reg § 1.6655-3(c))[43]

The "base period percentage" for any specific period of months is the average percentage that the corporation's taxable income for the corresponding months in each of the three preceding tax years bears to its taxable income for those three years. (Code Sec. 6655(e)(3)(D)(i); Reg § 1.6655-3(d))[44]

Any reduction in an installment resulting from the adjusted seasonal method must be made up (recaptured), by increasing the amount of the next required installment that *isn't* determined under the adjusted seasonal method by the amount of the reduction. (Code Sec. 6655(e)(1)(B))[45]

¶ 3349 Penalty for failure to pay estimated tax—Form 2220.

A corporation that underpays its estimated tax must add to its income tax an amount equal to the underpayment interest rate (¶4868) times the amount of the underpayment, for the period of the underpayment. (Code Sec. 6655(a)) Compute on Form 2220.[46]

The amount of the underpayment is the excess of the required installment (¶3346) over the amount (if any) of the installment paid on or before its due date. (Code Sec. 6655(b)(1))[47]

The period of the underpayment runs from the due date for the installment to the earlier of: (1) the 15th day of the third month (fourth month for C corporation tax years that begin after Dec. 31, 2015 (after Dec. 31, 2025 for C corporation tax years that end on June 30)) after the close of the tax year, or (2) with respect to any portion of the underpayment, the date the portion is paid. (Code Sec. 6655(b)(2), Code Sec. 6655(g)(4)(E)) For this purpose, a payment of estimated tax is credited against unpaid required installments in the order those installments were due. (Code Sec. 6655(b)(3))[48]

No estimated tax penalty is imposed for any tax year if the tax shown on the return for that year (or if no return is filed, the tax liability) is less than $500. (Code Sec. 6655(f))[49] Nor is the penalty imposed for a period in which the failure to pay the required installment(s) results from a pending Title 11 bankruptcy case. (Code Sec. 6658(a))[50]

¶ 3350 S Corporations.

An eligible corporation may elect to be taxed as an S corporation which, with limited exceptions, isn't taxed at the corporate level. Instead, its items of income, loss, deduction and credit are passed through to, and taken into account by, its shareholders in computing their individual tax liabilities (¶3367).

For S election eligibility, see ¶3351 *et seq.*

---

42. ¶S-5344; ¶66,554
43. ¶S-5345 *et seq.*; ¶66,554
44. ¶S-5346; ¶66,554
45. ¶S-5348; ¶66,554
46. ¶S-5358; ¶66,554

47. ¶S-5359; ¶66,554
48. ¶S-5324; ¶66,554
49. ¶S-5359; ¶66,554
50. ¶V-7378

¶ 3351   S election eligibility.

An S corporation is a corporation for which an election to be taxed under Subchapter S of the Code is in effect. (Code Sec. 1361(a)(1))[1] Only a small business corporation may elect to be an S corporation. (Code Sec. 1362(a)(1)) A corporation (or an unincorporated entity that's taxable as a corporation) qualifies as a small business corporation if: [2]

(1) It is a domestic corporation (created under the law of the U.S. or of any state). (Code Sec. 1361(b)(1))[3]

(2) It is not *ineligible.* (Code Sec. 1361(b)(1); Reg § 1.1361-1(d))

A corporation is ineligible if it is:

. . . a financial institution that uses a reserve method of accounting for bad debts,

. . . taxable as an insurance company (with certain exceptions),

. . . a domestic international sales corporation (DISC) or former DISC (¶4604) (Code Sec. 1361(b)(2)), or

. . . a taxable mortgage pool. (Reg § 301.7701(i)-4(c)(1))[4]

(3) It doesn't have more than 100 shareholders, see ¶3353. (Code Sec. 1361(b)(1)(A); Reg § 1.1361-1(e))[5]

(4) All shareholders are individuals, decedents' estates, bankruptcy estates, trusts described at ¶3354, or tax-exempt Code Sec. 501(c)(3) charitable organizations (Code Sec. 1361(b)(1)(B); Reg § 1.1361-1(f)), except that an otherwise eligible S corporation can be wholly owned by another S corporation, see ¶3352. A partnership can hold S corporation stock as a nominee for an eligible shareholder. (Reg § 1.1361-1(e)(1))[6] With a very limited exception for certain banks that are S corporations, Individual Retirement Accounts (including one designated as a Roth IRA) may not be shareholders in an S corporation. (Reg § 1.1361-1(h)(1)(vii), Reg § 1.1361-1(h)(3)(i)(G))

(5) No shareholder is a nonresident alien (Code Sec. 1361(b)(1)(C)), or married to a nonresident alien who has a current ownership interest in his stock under local law (unless the spouses elect under Code Sec. 6013(g) to be taxed as U.S. residents (¶3112)). (Reg § 1.1361-1(g)(1))[7] *For tax years beginning after 2017,* a nonresident alien may, however, be a potential current beneficiary of an Electing Small Business Trust (ESBT; see ¶3354).[8]

(6) It has only one class of stock, see ¶3355. (Code Sec. 1361(b)(1)(D); Reg § 1.1361-1(b)(1))[9]

¶ 3352   S corporation subsidiaries—Form 8869.

S corporations may have 80%-or-more owned C ("regular") corporation subsidiaries and wholly-owned S corporation subsidiaries. (Code Sec. 1361(b))

A C corporation subsidiary is treated as a separate taxpayer. If it operates profitably, it pays tax on its income. If it operates at a loss, it cannot pass the loss through to the S corporation. A C corporation subsidiary may file a consolidated return with other C corporations with which it is affiliated. The S corporation cannot be included in this return (¶3340).

---

1. ¶D-1421; ¶13,614 *et seq.*
2. ¶D-1431; ¶13,614
3. ¶D-1432; ¶13,614.01
4. ¶D-1434 *et seq.*; ¶ 77,014.32
5. ¶D-1441; ¶13,614.02
6. ¶D-1445; ¶13,614.03
7. ¶D-1457; ¶13,614.03
8. ¶D-1482
9. ¶D-1496; ¶13,614.04

An S corporation cannot have a corporate shareholder. (Code Sec. 1361(b)(1)(B); Reg § 1.1361-1(f)) This rule ordinarily prevents a subsidiary from being an S corporation. However, an S corporation can have an S corporation subsidiary if it owns 100% of the subsidiary's stock, the sub is not an ineligible corporation, and the S corporation parent elects (on Form 8869)[10] to treat the subsidiary as a qualified subchapter S subsidiary (QSub). (Code Sec. 1361(b)(3)(B); Reg § 1.1361-2, Reg § 1.1361-3)[11]

A QSub isn't treated as a separate corporation for federal tax purposes; rather, its assets, liabilities, and items of income, deduction, and credit are treated as those of the parent S corporation. (Code Sec. 1361(b)(3)(A); Reg § 1.1361-4)[12] However, except to the extent otherwise provided by IRS, QSubs are treated as separate entities for purposes of making information returns. (Code Sec. 1361(b)(3)(E))[13]

If a QSub loses its qualification, it is treated as if it sold an undivided interest in its assets (based on a percentage of the stock sold) and transferred the remaining assets to itself in a tax-free incorporation. Thus, if an S corporation sells 21% of the stock of its QSub to an unrelated party, it will recognize 21% of the gain on the QSub's assets. (Code Sec. 1361(b)(3)(C); Reg § 1.1361-5)[14] If QSub status terminates, the corporation or its successor may not elect QSub status or S corporation status before its fifth year beginning after the first tax year for which the termination was effective, without IRS consent. (Code Sec. 1361(b)(3)(D); Reg § 1.1361-5(c))[15] IRS may waive inadvertent or invalid QSub elections and terminations of elections. (Code Sec. 1362(f))[16] For late election relief, see ¶3358.

A QSub generally uses the parent S corporation's employee identification number (EIN). If the election terminates, the sub must get an EIN; but if the entity either had an EIN before becoming a QSub or got an EIN while it was a QSub, it must use that EIN. (Reg § 301.6109-1(i))[17]

¶ 3353   Number of shareholders.

In applying the 100-shareholder limit (¶3351), everyone who owns stock is counted separately, even if the stock is owned jointly with someone else (e.g., joint tenant, tenant in common), except as follows:

(1) Spouses (and their estates) are treated as one shareholder, no matter how the stock is held (separately, jointly, etc.). (Code Sec. 1361(c)(1)(A)(i); Reg § 1.1361-1(e)(2))[18]

(2) Where stock is owned by a grantor trust and also by the grantor directly, they are treated as one shareholder. [19]

(3) All members of a family and their estates are treated as one shareholder. Family members include the common ancestor, lineal descendants of the common ancestor, and the spouses (or former spouses) of the lineal descendants or common ancestor. But, an individual isn't considered a common ancestor if, on the applicable date (see below), the individual was more than six generations removed from the youngest generation of shareholders who would (but for this limitation) be family members. For this purpose, a spouse (or former spouse) is treated as being of the same generation as the individual to which such spouse is (or was) married. Adopted children are treated as children if they are (i) legally adopted, (ii) lawfully placed with an individual for legal adoption, or (iii) eligible foster children (defined under Code Sec. 152(f)(1)(C), ¶3114). (Code Sec. 1361(c)(1)) The applicable date is the latest of: the date the S election was made; the earliest date that a family member holds stock in the S corporation; or Oct. 22, 2004.

10. ¶D-1539; ¶13,614.05
11. ¶D-1540; ¶13,614.05
12. ¶D-1531; ¶13,614.05
13. ¶D-1532; ¶13,614.05
14. ¶D-1536; ¶13,614.05
15. ¶D-1538; ¶13,614.05
16. ¶D-1564.1; ¶13,624.03
17. ¶D-1532; ¶13,614.05
18. ¶D-1447; ¶s 13,614.02, 13,614.03
19. ¶D-1461; ¶s 13,614.02, 13,614.03

(Code Sec. 1361(c)(1)(B)(ii))[20]

Each potential current beneficiary (i.e., one who may receive a discretionary distribution of income or principal during the relevant period) of an electing small business trust (¶3354) is treated as a shareholder in applying the limit. The trust is treated as the shareholder for periods when there's no potential current beneficiary. (Code Sec. 1361(c)(2)(B)(v); Reg § 1.1361-1(m)(4)) However, unexercised powers of appointment are not taken into account in determining potential current beneficiaries. In addition, a person who first becomes a potential current beneficiary during the 1-year period ending with the date of the trust's disposition of all of its stock in an S corporation isn't a potential current beneficiary of that corporation. (Code Sec. 1361(e)(2))[21]

¶ 3354   Trusts as shareholders.

Only the following trusts may be S corporation shareholders:

(1) Grantor trusts—domestic trusts that are treated as being owned by an individual ("grantor") who is a U.S. citizen or resident, during the period the trust holds the S corporation stock. The grantor, not the trust, is treated as the shareholder. (Code Sec. 1361(c)(2); Reg § 1.1361-1(h)) But after the grantor dies, the trust may continue as the shareholder for two years. (Code Sec. 1361(c)(2)(A)(ii))[22]

(2) Code Sec. 678 trusts—where a person other than the grantor is treated as the substantial owner of the trust, during the period the trust holds the S corporation stock. The deemed owner, who must be a U.S. citizen or resident, is treated as the shareholder. (Code Sec. 1361(c)(2); Reg § 1.1361-1(h))[23]

(3) Voting trusts, but each beneficiary is counted as a separate shareholder. (Code Sec. 1361(c)(2); Reg § 1.1361-1(h))[24]

(4) Testamentary trusts, for two years beginning with the day when stock was transferred to the trust under the testator's will. (Code Sec. 1361(c)(2)(A)(iii); Reg § 1.1361-1(h)(1)(iv))[25]

(5) "Qualified Subchapter S trusts" (QSSTs), if the beneficiary elects (on Form 2553, in certain circumstances) to be treated as the owner of the trust so that it is eligible to hold the S stock (as in (1), above), and is treated as the shareholder. (Code Sec. 1361(d); Reg § 1.1361-1(j)) For late election relief, see ¶3358.

A QSST can be converted to an electing small business trust (ESBT) if certain conditions are met.[26]

(6) "Electing Small Business Trusts" (ESBTs) —these trusts are subject to fewer restrictions than QSSTs but carry a heavy tax cost, see ¶3908. (Code Sec. 1361(c)(2)(A)(v), Code Sec. 1361(e); Reg § 1.1361-1(m)) To elect, the trustee must sign and file a specified statement with the service center with which the corporation files its income tax return. In the case of a newly electing S corporation, the trustee can attach the ESBT's consent to the Form 2553.[27] An ESBT can be converted to a QSST if certain conditions are met .[28] For late election relief, see ¶3358. *For tax years beginning after 2017,* nonresident aliens can potentially be current beneficiaries of an ESBT. (Code Sec. 1361(c)(2)(B)(v))[29]

(7) Tax-exempt Code Sec. 401(a) qualified plan trusts. (Code Sec. 1361(c)(6))[30]

20. ¶D-1447.1; ¶13,614.02
21. ¶D-1484 *et seq.*; ¶13,614.03
22. ¶s D-1460, D-1461; ¶13,614.03
23. ¶D-1461; ¶13,614.03
24. ¶D-1492; ¶13,614.03
25. ¶D-1491; ¶13,614.03

26. ¶D-1489; ¶13,614.03
27. ¶D-1482; ¶13,614.03
28. ¶D-1490; ¶13,614.03
29. ¶D-1482
30. ¶D-1493; ¶13,614.03

¶ 3355   One class of stock.

A corporation is treated as having only one class of stock (¶3351) if:

... all outstanding shares of its stock confer identical rights to distribution and liquidation proceeds, based on certain governing provisions (e.g., corporate charter, by-laws, state law, etc.) (Reg § 1.1361-1(l)(1), Reg § 1.1361-1(l)(2)(i)); and

... it hasn't issued any instrument or obligation or entered into any arrangement that's treated as a second class of stock. (Reg § 1.1361-1(l)(4))[31]

The one-class-of-stock rule isn't violated *solely* because of differences in voting rights. Thus, voting and nonvoting common can be issued. (Code Sec. 1361(c)(4))[32]

Buy-sell agreements among shareholders, redemption agreements and agreements restricting the transferability of stock generally won't violate the one-class-of-stock rule *unless:* (1) a principal purpose of the agreement is to circumvent the rule, and (2) it establishes a purchase price for the stock that's significantly above or below its fair market value (FMV). (Reg § 1.1361-1(l)(2)(iii))[33]

A call option, warrant or similar instrument is, with certain exceptions, treated as a second class of stock if it's substantially certain to be exercised and has a strike price substantially below the stock's FMV on the date it's issued, transferred to an ineligible shareholder, or materially modified. (Reg § 1.1361-1(l)(4)(iii)(A))[34]

Straight debt isn't treated as a second class of stock if specified safe harbor rules are met. (Code Sec. 1361(c)(5)(A), Code Sec. 1361(c)(5)(B))[35] However, any instrument, obligation or arrangement is, with certain exceptions, treated as a second class of stock if: (1) it constitutes equity or otherwise results in the holder being treated as the owner of stock under general tax law, and (2) its principal purpose is to circumvent these rules. (Reg § 1.1361-1(l)(4))[36] Restricted bank director stock is not taken into account for the one class of stock requirement. (Code Sec. 1361(f)(1))[37]

¶ 3356   How to elect S corporation status—Form 2553.

The S election is made by the corporation (Code Sec. 1362(a)(1)) by filing a Form 2553 signed by its authorized officer, with the required shareholder consents (¶3357) (and IRS user fee), at the IRS Service Center designated on the form. (Reg § 1.1362-6(a)(2))[38]

An S election for a tax year may be made during the preceding tax year, or by the 15th day of the third month of the tax year for which it's to be effective. (Code Sec. 1362(b)(1)) If this first tax year is less than two months and 15 days, the election must be made no later than two months and 15 days after the first day of that year. (Code Sec. 1362(b)(4))[39]

An S election will be effective retroactively to the first day of a tax year *only if:*

... on all days in the tax year before the day the election is made, the corporation would have been eligible to elect (Code Sec. 1362(b)(2)(B)(i)), *and*

... all persons who were shareholders at any time during the tax year before the day of the election, but who aren't shareholders on that date, consent (along with persons who *are* shareholders, see ¶3357). (Code Sec. 1362(b)(2)(B)(ii))[40]

If either of the above conditions isn't met, the election is treated as made for the next tax

---

31. ¶D-1496 *et seq.*; ¶13,614.04
32. ¶D-1499; ¶13,614.04
33. ¶D-1507 *et seq.*; ¶13,614.04
34. ¶D-1523; ¶13,614.04
35. ¶D-1517; ¶13,614.04

36. ¶D-1512 *et seq.*; ¶13,614.04
37. ¶D-1444.1; ¶13,614.02
38. ¶D-1552, ¶T-10004; ¶s 13,624, 13,624.01
39. ¶s D-1565, D-1568; ¶13,624.01
40. ¶D-1566; ¶13,624.01

year. (Code Sec. 1362(b)(2))[41]

A partnership that converts to a corporation under check-the-box rules (¶3301) or a state law conversion statute may make an S election effective for the corporation's first tax year.[42]

IRS may waive invalid elections (e.g., because of an inadvertent failure to get all the necessary consents (¶3357) or to qualify to elect S status). (Code Sec. 1362(f))[43] For late election relief, see ¶3358.

¶ 3357   Shareholder consents.

All shareholders owning stock in the corporation on the day it elects S status must consent to the election. (Code Sec. 1362(a)(2); Reg § 1.1362-6(b)(2)(i))[44] The consents may be given on Form 2553 (¶3356), or on separate statements attached to it. (Reg § 1.1362-6(b))[45]

A shareholder's failure to file a timely consent won't invalidate an otherwise valid timely filed election if consents are filed within an extended period of time as granted by IRS, and IRS is satisfied that: (1) there was reasonable cause for the failure; (2) the extension was requested within a reasonable time; and (3) its interests won't be jeopardized by treating the election as valid. (Reg § 1.1362-6(b)(3)(iii)(A))[46] Special rules apply for requests for automatic relief when a community property spouse fails to timely consent to an S corporation election.[47]

¶ 3358   Relief for late S corporation and related elections.

IRS has provided exclusive simplified methods for taxpayers to request relief for late S corporation elections, electing small business trust (ESBT) elections, qualified Subchapter S trust (QSST) elections, qualified Subchapter S subsidiary (QSub) elections, and late corporate classification elections under Reg § 301.7701-3(c)(1)(v)(C) which the taxpayer intended to take effect on the same date that an S corporation election for the entity was to take effect. (Rev Proc 2013-30) If certain requirements are met, a taxpayer can obtain relief without having to obtain a private letter ruling (PLR). However, if the taxpayer doesn't qualify for the simplified method in Rev Proc 2013-30, the taxpayer may still seek relief through a PLR. In considering the taxpayer's PLR request, IRS has the authority to treat an election as timely made if it determines, among other things, that there was reasonable cause for the failure to timely elect. [48]

¶ 3359   "Taxable income" of an S corporation.

An S corporation's taxable income is computed in the same manner as an individual's taxable income *except that*: (Code Sec. 1363(b))[49]

(1) Items of income (including tax-exempt interest), loss, deduction or credit must be separately stated if their separate treatment by a shareholder could affect his tax liability. (Code Sec. 1363(b)(1))

(2) The corporation can't take the following deductions allowed to individuals: personal exemptions; foreign taxes; charitable contributions; net operating loss (NOL) deduction; additional itemized deductions; and oil and gas depletion. (Code Sec. 1363(b)(2))

---

41. ¶D-1566; ¶13,624.01
42. ¶D-1456
43. ¶D-1564.1; ¶13,614.03
44. ¶D-1554; ¶13,624.01
45. ¶D-1556; ¶13,624.01

46. ¶D-1564.2; ¶13,624.03
47. ¶D-1572.3; ¶13,624.03
48. ¶D-1572.1 *et seq.*; ¶13,624.03
49. ¶D-1591; ¶13,634.01

(3) A deduction is allowed for the amortization of the corporation's organizational expenditures under Code Sec. 248 (¶3510). (Code Sec. 1363(b)(3))[50]

(4) The Code Sec. 291 rules that reduce certain corporate tax benefits apply to an S corporation (or any predecessor) that was a C corporation for any of the three immediately preceding tax years. (Code Sec. 1363(b)(4))[1]

Except as otherwise provided in the Code, or to the extent inconsistent with the Subchapter S rules, the Subchapter C rules (transfers to related corporations, redemptions, reorganizations, liquidations, etc., see ¶3500 *et seq.*) apply to an S corporation and its shareholders. (Code Sec. 1371(a))[2] But there are these modifications:

. . . With respect to liquidating distributions, no gain or loss is recognized on distributions of installment obligations where the shareholders' receipt of them (as part of a 12-month complete liquidation) isn't treated as payment for their stock by reason of Code Sec. 453(h)(1). (Code Sec. 453B(h)(1))[3]

. . . Except for the organizational expenditures deduction (above), Code provisions governing the computation of taxable income which apply only to corporations (e.g., dividends-received deduction, ¶3306) don't apply to S corporations. (Code Sec. 1363(b))[4]

. . . Limitations on the amount allowed for: (1) expensing certain depreciable assets (Code Sec. 179(d)(8)), and (2) writing off reforestation expenses (Code Sec. 194(b)(2)(B)) are determined at both the corporate and shareholder level. [5]

. . . Generally, an item (e.g., an NOL) cannot be carried over from a year the corporation was a C corporation to a year the corporation was an S corporation (except in computing the built-in gains tax, see ¶3362). (Code Sec. 1371(b)(1))[6]

¶ 3360 Deductions for fringe benefits—Form W2.

In applying the Code's fringe benefit rules, an S corporation is treated as a partnership and its more-than-2% shareholders are treated as partners. (Code Sec. 1372) Fringe benefits furnished by an S corporation to its more-than-2% shareholder-employees are treated like partnership guaranteed payments [7] and reported on Form W-2. [8]

¶ 3361 Taxation of S corporations.

An S corporation is generally exempt from federal income taxes. (Code Sec. 1363(a))[9] Instead, the corporation's income is passed through, and taxed, to its shareholders (¶3367). But some S corporations may be subject to corporate-level taxes on recognized built-in gains (¶3362); excess net passive income (¶3365); last-in, first-out (LIFO) recapture (¶3364); and recapture of investment credit. [10] For an S corporation's liability to make estimated tax payments, see ¶3344 *et seq.*

¶ 3362 Built-in gains tax—Form 1120S, Schedule D.

An S corporation is subject to a corporate-level built-in gains tax in any tax year beginning in the recognition period in which it has a "net recognized built-in gain" (¶3363). (Code Sec. 1374(a)) The recognition period is the 5-year period beginning with the first day of the first tax year for which the corporation was an S corporation. (Code Sec. 1374(d)(7))[11] But the tax is imposed only on S corporations that were formerly C corporations. (Code

50. ¶D-1594; ¶13,634.01
1. ¶D-1595; ¶13,634.01
2. ¶D-1600; ¶13,714
3. ¶s D-1600, D-1601; ¶453B4.11
4. ¶D-1595; ¶13,634.01
5. ¶D-1596; ¶1794.01

6. ¶D-1603; ¶13,714.01
7. ¶D-1621; ¶13,724
8. ¶S-3178
9. ¶D-1641; ¶13,634
10. ¶D-1640; ¶13,714.03
11. ¶D-1655; ¶13,744.01

Sec. 1374(c)(1))[12]

In addition, the built-in gains tax may be imposed where an S corporation acquires property in a transaction and its basis in the property is determined by reference to the basis that the property had in the hands of a C corporation (a §1374(d)(8) transaction). (Code Sec. 1374(d)(8)(A); Reg § 1.1374-1(e), Reg § 1.1374-8(a))[13]

The built-in gains tax (computed on Form 1120S, Schedule D) equals the highest corporate rate (¶1113) times the net recognized built-in gain. (Code Sec. 1374(b)(1))[14]

In this computation, net recognized built-in gains are taken into account only to the extent of the excess of the net *unrealized* built-in gain over net recognized built-in gains for earlier tax years in the recognition period. (Code Sec. 1374(c)(2); Reg § 1.1374-2(a))[15] Net unrealized built-in gain means the excess (if any) of: (1) the fair market value of the S corporation's assets (including inventory) over (2) the aggregate adjusted basis of the assets, at the start of its first tax year as an S corporation ("S tax year"). (Code Sec. 1374(d)(1))[16]

Regs prevent gain or loss from being counted twice for the built-in gains tax when a C corporation converting to S status owns stock in a subsidiary that's later liquidated. (Reg § 1.1374-3)[17]

¶ 3363   Net recognized built-in gain defined.

The *net recognized built-in gain* for any tax year in the recognition period (¶3362) is the *lesser of:* (1) the amount that would be the S corporation's taxable income for that year if only recognized built-in gains (below) and recognized built-in losses are taken into account, and (2) the taxable income for that year determined without taking into account net operating loss (NOL) carryovers or special corporate deductions, e.g., for dividends received. (Code Sec. 1374(d)(2)(A))[18] However, if (1) is more than (2), the excess is treated as recognized built-in gain in the next tax year, but only if the S election was made after Mar. 31, 1988. (Code Sec. 1374(d)(2)(B); Reg § 1.1374-2(c))[19]

Recognized built-in gain means any gain recognized (and certain related amounts taken into account) during the recognition period on the disposition of any asset held on the first day of the corporation's first S tax year (¶3362), but only to the extent the gain doesn't exceed the excess (if any) of the asset's fair market value over its adjusted basis, on that first day. (Code Sec. 1374(d)(3); Reg § 1.1374-4)[20]

Special rules apply to determine an S corporation's recognized built-in gain on the disposition of transferred-basis and exchanged-basis property acquired after it became an S corporation. (Code Sec. 1374(d)(8); Reg § 1.1374-8)[21]

¶ 3364   Last-in, first-out (LIFO) recapture amount.

A C corporation that maintained its inventory using the LIFO method for its last tax year before the S corporation election is effective must include a "LIFO recapture amount" in its income for that last C corporation year. (Code Sec. 1363(d)(1))[22] LIFO recapture also applies to QSub elections (¶3352). (Reg § 1.1363-2(a))[23] In addition, a C corporation that transfers LIFO inventory to an S corporation in a nonrecognition transaction must include a LIFO recapture amount in income the year of the transfer. (Reg § 1.1363-2(a))[24]

12. ¶D-1643; ¶13,744.01
13. ¶D-1650; ¶13,744.01
14. ¶D-1657; ¶13,744.01
15. ¶D-1657; ¶13,744.01
16. ¶D-1658; ¶13,744.01
17. ¶D-1651; ¶13,744.01
18. ¶D-1644; ¶13,744.01

19. ¶D-1645; ¶13,744.01
20. ¶D-1646 *et seq.*; ¶13,744.01
21. ¶D-1650 *et seq.*; ¶13,744.01
22. ¶D-1581; ¶13,634.02
23. ¶D-1581
24. ¶D-1583; ¶13,634.02

The "LIFO recapture amount" is the excess (if any) of the inventory amount under FIFO (first-in, first-out) over the inventory amount under LIFO, at the close of the last C corporation tax year. (Code Sec. 1363(d)(3))[25]

Any resulting increase in tax is payable in four equal installments over four tax years. The first installment must be paid on or before the due date (without regard to extensions) for the tax return for the last year for which the corporation was a C corporation. The other three installments must be paid on or before the due date for the corporation's return for the three succeeding tax years. (Code Sec. 1363(d)(2))[26]

A C corporation holding LIFO inventory indirectly through a partnership must recognize a lookthrough LIFO recapture amount if it either elects to be an S corporation or transfers its partnership interest to an S corporation in a nonrecognition transaction. (Reg § 1.1363-2(b))[27]

¶ 3365 Tax on excess net passive income.

A corporate-level tax is imposed on an S corporation's "excess net passive income" (below) for any tax year in which it has: (1) accumulated earnings and profits (i.e., E&P from a year it was taxed as a C corporation) at the close of the tax year, and (2) passive investment income (¶3366) that exceeds 25% of gross receipts (¶3366). This tax is imposed at the highest regular corporate rate (¶1113) (Code Sec. 1375(a)),[28] but IRS can waive the tax if the S corporation shows that its determination of no year-end C corporation E&P was made in good faith, and that within a reasonable time after it was determined otherwise, those E&P were distributed. Code Sec. 1375(d))[29]

Net passive income is passive investment income reduced by deductions directly connected with the production of that income. (Code Sec. 1375(b)(2)) A deduction item that is attributable partly to passive investment income and partly to other income is allocated on a reasonable basis. (Reg § 1.1375-1(b)(3)(ii))[30] But passive investment income may not be reduced by the net operating loss (NOL) deduction or any of the special corporate deductions (e.g., for dividends received). (Code Sec. 1375(b)(2))[31]

Excess net passive income means the amount that bears the same ratio to total net passive income for the year as: (1) the amount by which passive investment income for the tax year exceeds 25% of gross receipts for the year ("excess passive investment income"), bears to (2) total passive investment income for the tax year. However, an S corporation's excess net passive income for the year can't exceed its taxable income for the year computed as though it were a C corporation but without any NOL deduction or any of the special corporate deductions described above. (Code Sec. 1375(b)(1))[32]

¶ 3366 "Passive investment income" and "gross receipts" defined.

For purposes of the tax on excess net passive income (¶3365) and involuntary terminations (¶3375), passive investment income means gross receipts derived from royalties, rents, dividends, interest, and annuities. (Code Sec. 1362(d)(3)(C); Code Sec. 1375(b)(3))[33]

However, in the case of a bank, a bank holding company, a financial holding company, or a depository institution holding company, passive investment income does not include (1) interest income earned by the bank or holding company or (2) dividends on assets that must be held by the bank or holding company. (Code Sec. 1362(d)(3)(C)(v)(I))[34]

25. ¶D-1582; ¶13,634.02
26. ¶D-1585; ¶13,634.02
27. ¶D-1582.1; ¶13,634.02
28. ¶D-1690 *et seq.*; ¶13,754
29. ¶D-1696; ¶13,754.01

30. ¶D-1693 *et seq.*
31. ¶D-1693; ¶13,754
32. ¶D-1692; ¶13,754
33. ¶D-1713 *et seq.*; ¶s 13,624.02, 13,754
34. ¶D-1737; ¶13,624.02

Gross receipts are the total amount received or accrued under the S corporation's accounting method before reduction for returns, allowances, cost, or deductions. But gross receipts don't include amounts received in nontaxable sales or exchanges except to the extent gain is recognized by the corporation. (Code Sec. 1362(d)(3), Code Sec. 1375(b)(3))[35]

Special rules apply to determine gross receipts from the sale of capital assets. [36]

¶ 3367   Taxation of S corporation's shareholders.

An S corporation's income is taxed directly to its shareholders by allocating the corporation's items of income, loss, deduction and credit for each day in its tax year pro rata among the persons who were shareholders on that day. (Code Sec. 1366(a)(1); Reg § 1.1366-1(a); Code Sec. 1377(a)(1))[37]

Items of income, loss, deduction and credit are separately allocated to each shareholder whenever separate treatment could affect the tax liability of a shareholder. (Code Sec. 1366(a)(1)(A); Reg § 1.1366-1(a)) Under regs, the following S corporation items must be taken into account separately:

. . . The combined net amount of gains and losses from sales or exchanges of capital assets grouped by applicable holding periods, Code Sec. 1(h) tax rates, and by any other classification that may be relevant in determining the shareholder's tax liability.

. . . The combined net amount of gains and losses from sales or exchanges of Code Sec. 1231 property grouped by applicable holding periods, Code Sec. 1(h) tax rates, and by any other classification that may be relevant in determining the shareholder's tax liability.

. . . The charitable contributions, grouped by the Code Sec. 170(b) percentage limitations (see ¶2123 *et seq.*), made by the corporation within its tax year.

. . . The foreign taxes paid (or accrued) by the corporation.

. . . Each of the separate items involved in determining credits, except credits for certain uses of gasoline and special fuels.

. . . Each of these separate items: Code Sec. 165(d) gains and losses from wagering transactions; Code Sec. 175 soil and water conservation expenditures; Code Sec. 179 expense election deductions; Code Sec. 213 medical, dental, etc. expenses; additional itemized deductions for individuals under Code Sec. 212 *et seq.*; and any other deductions subject to the Code Sec. 67 or Code Sec. 68 limitations on itemized deductions.

🅡*observation:* Miscellaneous itemized deductions under Code Sec. 67(b) are suspended from 2018 through 2025. (¶3109)

. . . Any of the corporation's items of portfolio income or loss, and related expenses, as defined in the regs under Code Sec. 469.

. . . The corporation's tax-exempt income.

. . . For tax years before 2018 (the corporate AMT having been repealed for tax years after 2017, see ¶3303), the corporation's alternative minimum tax adjustments described in Code Sec. 56, and Code Sec. 58 and tax preference items described in Code Sec. 57.

. . . Any item identified in IRS guidance (including forms and instructions) as an item required to be separately stated. (Reg § 1.1366-1(a)(2))[38]

The character of any item in the shareholder's hands is determined as if the item had been realized directly from the source from which the corporation realized it, or incurred in the same manner as incurred by the corporation. (Code Sec. 1366(b); Reg § 1.1366-1(b))[39]

---

35. ¶s D-1702, D-1703; ¶13,624.02
36. ¶D-1701 *et seq.*; ¶13,624
37. ¶D-1761 *et seq.*; ¶13,664

38. ¶D-1765; ¶13,664
39. ¶D-1762; ¶13,664

A shareholder's share of an S corporation's items is taken into account in his tax year that includes the last day of the corporation's tax year (¶2810). (Code Sec. 1366(a)(1); Reg § 1.1366-1(a)(1))[40]

When shareholders perform services for an S corporation, dividends paid to the shareholders in lieu of reasonable compensation for these services can be treated as wages subject to employment taxes, regardless of whether the shareholder also receives a salary.[41]

If a shareholder sells all of his S corporation stock during the corporation's tax year and all affected shareholders (all terminating shareholders and their transferees) consent (by attaching a specified statement to Form 1120S for the tax year during which the shareholder's interest is terminated), the corporation's tax year can be split into two tax years, the first of which ends on the date the seller's interest is terminated. Items will be allocated between those tax years according to the corporation's normal method of accounting. (Code Sec. 1377(a)(2); Reg § 1.1377-1(b))[42] This also applies where the S corporation elects to terminate its tax year because of a "qualifying disposition." (Reg § 1.1368-1(g))[43]

Any gain or loss from a shareholder's disposition of an interest in an S corporation is taken into account by the shareholder as net investment income for purposes of the 3.8% surtax on unearned income (¶3142 *et seq.*) *only* to the extent of the net gain or loss that the transferor would take into account if the entity had sold all its property for fair market value immediately before the disposition. (Code Sec. 1411(c)(4))

If a shareholder dies (or a trust terminates) before the end of an S corporation tax year, his (or its) pro rata part of the corporation's items is reported on his (its) final return. (Code Sec. 1366(a)(1))[44]

¶ 3368 Amount passed through to shareholders reduced for corporate-level taxes.

The amount of any corporate-level built-in gains tax (¶3362) that's imposed on an S corporation is treated as a loss sustained by the corporation during the tax year. The character of the loss is determined by allocating it proportionately among the recognized built-in gains giving rise to the tax. (Code Sec. 1366(f)(2); Reg § 1.1366-4(b)) If a corporate-level tax is imposed on an S corporation's excess net passive income (¶3365), each item of passive investment income that's passed through to a shareholder is reduced by a pro rata part of that tax. (Code Sec. 1366(f)(3); Reg § 1.1366-4(c))[45]

¶ 3369 Shareholders' deductions and losses limited to basis.

All deductions and losses of an S corporation (e.g., capital losses and net operating losses) are passed through to and (except as otherwise limited by the Code) deductible by shareholders. However, a shareholder may deduct his pro rata share of these passed-through items only to the extent of his adjusted basis (¶3371) in his S corporation stock, determined by taking into account the increases in basis for his share of the S corporation income during the year, and the decreases in basis for nondividend distributions for the year, plus any debt owed to him by the corporation.

Any deduction or loss that can't be deducted (for lack of basis) is suspended and may be carried over to be used whenever the shareholder has basis to apply against all or part of the amount the shareholder carried over. (Code Sec. 1366(d)(2); Reg § 1.1366-2(a)(2))[46]

40. ¶D-1764; ¶13,774
41. ¶H-4329
42. ¶D-1769; ¶13,774
43. ¶D-1771; ¶13,684.09

44. ¶D-1768; ¶13,664
45. ¶D-1767; ¶13,664.02
46. ¶D-1785; ¶13,664

Special rules apply where the S corporation is in bankruptcy or is insolvent. (Code Sec. 108(d)(7)(B))[47]

If an S corporation's stock, or the debt it owes to a shareholder, becomes worthless in any tax year of the corporation or shareholder, the corporate items for that year will be taken into account by the shareholders and the adjustments to basis of stock or debt will be made, before the worthlessness is taken into account. (Code Sec. 1367(b)(3))[48]

¶ 3370   Consistent treatment on shareholder's return and S corporation's re-turn— Form 8082.

A shareholder must on his own return treat a Subchapter S item in a manner that is consistent with the treatment of that item on the corporation's return (Form 1120S). A shareholder that treats a Subchapter S item differently must notify IRS of the inconsistency (Code Sec. 6037) on Form 8082.[49]

¶ 3371   Shareholder's basis in S corporation's stock or debt.

A shareholder's basis in the stock of an S corporation is *increased* by his share of the corporation's income items that are passed through to him —i.e., its separately and non-separately computed income items (including tax-exempt income) and the excess of the deduction for depletion over the basis of depletable property. (Code Sec. 1367(a)(1); Reg § 1.1367-1(b)) An S corporation shareholder may increase basis of indebtedness of the S corporation to the shareholder for bona fide loans to the S corporation (determined under general tax principles), but gets no basis increase for debts of the corporation that he guarantees. (Code Sec. 1366(d)(1); Reg § 1.1366-2)[50] Debt discharge income of an S corpo-ration that is excluded from its income is not income to a shareholder and does not increase shareholder basis in the S corporation's stock. [1] Basis in stock is *decreased* (but not below zero) by: the shareholder's share of the corporation's items of deduction, loss and nondeductible expenses (except those chargeable to the capital account); the shareholder's depletion deduction for oil and gas property; and distributions to the shareholder that aren't taxable as dividends. (Code Sec. 1367(a)(2); Reg § 1.1367-1(c))[2]

For charitable contributions made by an S corporation, shareholders reduce their basis in the S corporation stock by their pro rata shares of the adjusted basis (as opposed to the fair market value) of the contributed property. (Code Sec. 1367(a)(2))

In any tax year of an S corporation when the total of the amount of items (other than distributions) that reduce a shareholder's basis in stock exceeds the amount that would reduce that basis to zero, the balance is applied to reduce the basis (but not below zero) of any shareholder debt in the S corporation. (Code Sec. 1367(b)(2)(A); Reg § 1.1367-2(b))[3]

If the shareholder's basis in S corporation debt in any tax year is reduced below his original basis in it, that basis must be increased to (but not above) its original amount, before the shareholder's basis in *stock* is increased. (Code Sec. 1367(b)(2)(B); Reg § 1.1367-2(b))[4] For purposes of the basis adjustment rules, shareholder advances aggregating less than $25,000 and not evidenced by separate written instruments and repayments on the advances are treated as a single indebtedness. (Reg § 1.1367-2(a)(2))[5]

47. ¶D-1785, J-7416; ¶1084.03
48. ¶D-1789; ¶13,674
49. ¶D-1801; ¶60,374
50. ¶D-1775; ¶13,664
1. ¶D-1863; ¶13,674

2. ¶D-1865; ¶13,674
3. ¶D-1868; ¶13,674
4. ¶D-1869; ¶13,674
5. ¶D-1868;¶13,674.10

¶ **3372** **Tax treatment of S corporation distributions.**

The amount of a distribution from an S corporation to a shareholder equals the amount of cash distributed plus the fair market value (at distribution) of any other property distributed. (Code Sec. 301(c), Code Sec. 1368(a))[6]

If an S corporation has no accumulated earnings and profits (E&P), the amount distributed reduces the shareholder's basis in his stock (¶3371). If the amount exceeds basis, the excess is treated as payment in exchange for stock, i.e., as capital gain. (Code Sec. 1368(b)(2))[7]

If IRS finds that the salary paid to an S corporation shareholder-employee is unreasonably low, it may reclassify dividend payments made to the shareholder as salary. [8]

If an S corporation has accumulated E&P, its distributions are treated as follows: [9]

(1) The portion of the distribution that doesn't exceed the accumulated adjustments account (AAA, see ¶3374) is taxed the same as a distribution from an S corporation with no accumulated E&P (above). If more than one distribution is made in a tax year, and the total amount distributed exceeds the amount in the AAA at the end of that year, the balance in that account is allocated among the distributions in proportion to the size of each distribution. (Code Sec. 1368(c)(1))[10]

(2) The portion of the distribution that remains after applying (1) is treated as a dividend to the extent it doesn't exceed the S corporation's accumulated E&P. (Code Sec. 1368(c)(2))

(3) Any portion of the distribution remaining after applying (2) is treated the same as a distribution by an S corporation with no accumulated E&P. (Code Sec. 1368(c)(3))[11]

The tax effects of an S corporation's distributions to shareholders with respect to stock are determined only after taking into account:

(i) adjustments that increase the basis of the shareholder's stock and

(ii) adjustments to the AAA, other than for distributions to shareholders and without regard to any net negative adjustments, for the S corporation's tax year. (Code Sec. 1368(d); Reg § 1.1368-1(e)(2))[12]

observation: The effect of taking the basis increases, but not the decreases, into account is that the shareholder may receive more nontaxable distributions, at the cost of a decrease in the amount of loss that he may deduct.

An S corporation may elect, with the consent of all affected shareholders (i.e., those to whom distributions are made), to treat distributions as made out of accumulated E&P *before* being made out of the AAA. (Code Sec. 1368(e)(3); Reg § 1.1368-1(f)(2))[13]

¶ **3373** **S corporation's earnings and profits (E&P).**

An S corporation, unlike a C corporation, generally does not generate E&P. [14] Any E&P carried over from prior C corporation years, or acquired from a C corporation in a reorganization, remain unadjusted while the corporation retains S status, except: (Code Sec. 1371(c)(1))

---

6. ¶D-1813; ¶13,684
7. ¶D-1815; ¶s 13,684, 13,684.07
8. ¶H-4329
9. ¶s D-1817, D-1816; ¶13,684.01
10. ¶D-1816, D-1819; ¶13,684.01

11. ¶s D-1817, D-1816; ¶13,684.01
12. ¶D-1818
13. ¶D-1835; ¶13,684.03
14. ¶D-1631; ¶13,684.01 *et seq.*

. . . E&P is reduced to reflect distributions that are taxable to the shareholders as dividends. (Code Sec. 1371(c)(3))

. . . E&P is adjusted (up or down) to reflect the effect of redemptions, liquidations, tax-free reorganizations and corporate divisions. (Code Sec. 1371(c)(2))

. . . E&P is reduced to reflect any tax paid by an S corporation because of the recapture of a pre-S election investment credit. (Code Sec. 1371(d)(3))[15]

. . . E&P is adjusted for LIFO recapture tax. (¶3364) (Code Sec. 1363(d)(5))[16]

For purposes of determining the S corporation's accumulated E&P, all pre −'86 S corporation generated E&P has been eliminated for tax years beginning after May 25, 2007. [17]

¶ 3374   Accumulated adjustments account (AAA).

The AAA is a corporate account consisting of the corporation's income that was previously taxed to its shareholders and not distributed. An S corporation's AAA [18] is increased each tax year by:

(1) Separately computed items of income (other than income that is exempt from tax).

(2) Nonseparately computed income.

(3) The excess of deductions for depletion over the basis of property subject to depletion. (Code Sec. 1368(e)(1); Reg § 1.1368-2(a)(2))[19]

The AAA is decreased each tax year by:

(a) Items of separately computed loss and deduction.

(b) Nonseparately computed loss.

(c) Nondeductible expenses (other than expenses chargeable to capital account) unless related to tax-exempt income.

(d) The amount of the shareholder's deduction for depletion under Code Sec. 611 with respect to oil and gas wells.

(e) Distributions from an S corporation that has no E&P and distributions that are made out of the AAA.

(f) The amount that was treated as paid out of the AAA on redemptions that were treated as payments in exchange for stock under Code Sec. 302(a) or Code Sec. 303(a). This equals the amount in the account before the redemption multiplied by a fraction, the numerator of which is the number of redeemed shares and the denominator of which is the total number of outstanding shares before the redemption. (Code Sec. 1368(e)(1); Reg § 1.1368-2(a)(3))[20]

Special ordering rules apply with regard to the above mentioned increases and decreases. (Reg § 1.1368-2(a)(5))[21]

Where there is a net negative adjustment for the tax year, any net loss for the year is disregarded in adjusting the AAA for purposes of distributions made during the tax year. (Code Sec. 1368(e)(1)(C))[22]

The balance in an S corporation's AAA at the end of a tax year may be reduced below zero if the items that reduce the AAA exceed the sum of the AAA plus the items that increase the AAA (items (1) − (3), above). (Code Sec. 1368(e)(1)(A)) Income in a later year will cause the AAA to become positive only after the negative balance has been restored.

15. ¶D-1633; ¶13,714.03
16. ¶D-1581
17. ¶D-1632; ¶13,684.07
18. ¶D-1823; ¶13,684.02

19. ¶D-1824; ¶13,684.02
20. ¶D-1825, D-1827; ¶13,684.02
21. ¶D-1829; ¶13,684.02
22. ¶D-1826.1

(Reg § 1.1368-3)[23]

The AAA isn't to be adjusted (i.e., reduced) for federal taxes attributable to any tax year when the S corporation was a C corporation. (Code Sec. 1368(e)(1))[24]

If distributions made during the year exceed the AAA at the close of the tax year, then the AAA is allocated pro rata among the distributions (Code Sec. 1368(c); Reg § 1.1368-2(b)(1))[25]

Special rules apply to distributions after the S election is terminated. (Code Sec. 1371(e))[26] Although the AAA continues during a "post-termination transition period" (PTTP), IRS has ruled that where an S election is terminated, and then re-elected, the undistributed AAA doesn't survive the break in S status. [27]

¶ 3375 Involuntary termination of S election.

A corporation's S election is terminated if either:

(1) The corporation ceases to meet all of the S corporation eligibility requirements discussed at ¶3351. (Code Sec. 1362(d)(2)(A)) The termination is effective as of the day the eligibility requirement is no longer met (Code Sec. 1362(d)(2)(B));[28] or

(2) The S corporation's passive investment income (¶3366) exceeds 25% of its gross receipts for three consecutive tax years and at the end of each of those years, the corporation had accumulated earnings and profits (E&P, ¶3365). The termination is effective as of the first day of the first tax year beginning after the third of these years. (Code Sec. 1362(d)(3)(A))[29]

IRS can waive inadvertent terminations or invalid elections if certain conditions are met. (Code Sec. 1362(f)) Regs explain how to request relief. (Reg § 1.1362-4(c))[30] QSubs are eligible for the same relief (as discussed above) for an inadvertently invalid QSub election or inadvertent termination. (Reg § 1.1362-4)

¶ 3376 Voluntary revocation of the S election; rescission.

A corporation's S election may be revoked with the consent of holders of a majority of the corporation's issued and outstanding stock (including non-voting stock). (Code Sec. 1362(d)(1); Reg § 1.1362-2(a)(1))[31]

If no effective date is specified, a revocation is effective for the tax year in which made, if made by the 15th day of the third month of that year. Otherwise, it will be effective as of the first day of the next tax year. (Code Sec. 1362(d)(1)(C))[32] However, if the revocation specifies that it is to be effective on a date that is on or after the date it's made, it will be effective on that date even if it causes the corporation's tax year to be split. (Code Sec. 1362(d)(1)(D))[33]

For S elections that are revoked by an "eligible terminated S corporation" (as defined under Code Sec. 481(d)(2)) during the 2-year period beginning Dec. 22, 2017, special rules govern both: (i) adjustments made under Code Sec. 481 that are attributable to the revocation; and (ii) the treatment of post-revocation distributions under Code Sec. 1371(f). Specifically, if an eligible terminated S corporation makes a cash distribution after the post-termination transition period, the accumulated adjustments account is allocated to the distribution, and the distribution is chargeable to accumulated earnings and profits, in the

23. ¶D-1830; ¶13,684.02
24. ¶D-1823; ¶13,684.02
25. ¶D-1819; ¶13,684.02
26. ¶D-1846 *et seq.*; ¶13,714.04
27. ¶D-1846; ¶13,774
28. ¶D-1911; ¶13,624.02

29. ¶D-1914; ¶13,624.02
30. ¶D-1928; ¶13,624.03
31. ¶D-1901; ¶13,624.02
32. ¶D-1903; ¶13,624.02
33. ¶D-1905; ¶13,624.02

same ratio as the amount that the accumulated adjustments account bears to the amount of such accumulated earnings and profits. An eligible terminated S corporation is a C corporation that: (1) was an S corporation on Dec. 21, 2017 that revoked its S corporation election during the two-year period beginning on Dec. 22, 2017; and (2) the owners of the stock of the corporation on the date the revocation is made, are the same owners (and in identical proportions) as on Dec. 22, 2017. [34]

A corporation may *rescind* the revocation at any time before it becomes effective. A rescission may be made only with the consent of each person who consented to the revocation and of each person who became a shareholder during the period from the day after the date the revocation was made through the date the rescission is made. (Reg §   1.1362-2(a)(4))[35]

¶ 3377   When new S election can be made after termination or revocation.

After a revocation or termination of its S election, a corporation must wait five years before making a new S election unless IRS consents to an earlier election. (Code Sec. 1362(g))[36]

---

34. ¶D-1846.1
35. ¶D-1907 *et seq.*; ¶13,624.02

36. ¶s D-1951, D-1953; ¶13,624.02

Chapter 16　Corporate Transactions— Organization—Distributions—Reorganization— Acquisitions—Liquidations

¶ 3500　Incorporations and Transfers to Controlled Corporations—Code Sec. 351. ■

Incorporating a business or transferring property to a controlled corporation can be partly or wholly tax-free if technical requirements are satisfied. [1] No gain or loss is recognized if property (¶3501) is transferred to a corporation solely in exchange for stock (¶3502) of that corporation, if, immediately after the transfer, the transferor or transferors are in control (¶3503) of the corporation. (Code Sec. 351(a))[2] A transfer of property may be respected as a Code Sec. 351 exchange even if followed by later transfers of the property as part of a prearranged, integrated plan. However, IRS can deny Code Sec. 351 treatment if warranted to reflect the substance of the transaction as a whole. [3]

For exceptions to nonrecognition on transfers to controlled corporations, see ¶3504 (receipt of boot), ¶3505 (assumption of liabilities by transferee corporation), ¶3507 (transfers to investment companies), and ¶3508 (transfers in bankruptcy).

See ¶3509 for gain or loss to a corporation on the issuance of its stock, and ¶3510 for the deductibility of a corporation's organization costs.

For transfers to foreign corporations, see ¶3568.

For the basis of property received in the exchange, see ¶2481 *et seq.*

¶ 3501　Property.

Property that may be transferred tax-free under Code Sec. 351 includes cash, tangible property and intangible personal property, e.g., stock, partnership interests, patent rights, and working interests in oil and gas properties. [4]

Property doesn't include: (i) services to the transferee corporation (Code Sec. 351(d)(1)); (ii) transferee corporation debt not evidenced by a security (Code Sec. 351(d)(2)); or (iii) unpaid interest on transferee corporation debt accrued during the transferor's holding period for the debt. (Code Sec. 351(d)(3))[5]

¶ 3502　Stock.

For purposes of transfers to controlled corporations, property must be transferred *solely in exchange for stock*, which does not include (1) stock rights, options or warrants (Reg § 1.351-1(a)), or (2) nonqualified preferred stock. (Code Sec. 351(g)) (¶3542) Shares in an association, joint stock company or insurance company are treated as stock. (Code Sec. 7701(a)(7))

¶ 3503　Control.

For purposes of transfers to controlled corporations, *control* means at least 80% of the transferee's combined voting power and at least 80% of all other classes of the transferee's stock (¶3539). (Code Sec. 368(c))[6] The transferor group must hold at least 80% of the voting

---

1. ¶F-1000 *et seq.*; ¶3514 *et seq.*
2. ¶F-1001; ¶3514.01
3. ¶F-1014

4. ¶F-1101 *et seq.*; ¶3514.03
5. ¶F-1102 *et seq.*; ¶3514.03
6. ¶s F-1200 *et seq.*, F-5501 *et seq.*; ¶3514.05

References beginning with a single letter are to paragraphs in Federal Tax Coordinator 2d and RIA's Analysis of Federal Taxes: Income. Those beginning with numbers are to paragraphs in United States Tax Reporter.

power immediately after the transfer; but not every transferor must hold voting stock. [7]

¶ 3504   Gain on receipt of cash or property ("boot").

If transferors receive *boot* (¶3542) as well as stock in a Code Sec. 351 transfer, nonrecognition is limited and the transferor (i) recognizes gain up to the amount or fair market value of the boot, and (ii) does not recognize any loss. (Code Sec. 351(b))[8]

¶ 3505   Assumption of liabilities.

If a corporation assumes liabilities (¶3506 *et seq.*) in connection with an otherwise tax-free exchange, it is still tax-free (Code Sec. 357(a))[9] subject to the following exceptions.

- *Tax avoidance rule.* If the principal purpose for the assumption of liabilities is tax avoidance or isn't a bona fide business purpose, the full amount of *all* assumed liabilities are treated as cash received by the transferor (even those assumed for nontax avoidance or valid business purposes) and taxed as boot (¶3504). (Code Sec. 357(b)(1))[10]

- *Excess liabilities rule.* If the total liabilities assumed exceed the transferor's adjusted basis in the transferred property, gain is recognized to the extent of the excess. (Code Sec. 357(c)(1))[11]

Where both anti-abuse rules apply, tax avoidance takes precedence and all liabilities are treated as boot. (Code Sec. 357(c)(2)(A))[12]

The excess liabilities rule does not apply to any liability that (i) would give rise to a deduction when paid by the transferor, or (ii) would be a liquidating payment to a partner described in Code Sec. 736(a), see ¶3761. (Code Sec. 357(c)(3)(A))[13]

The excess liabilities rule applies to transfers in a divisive Type D reorganization under Code Sec. 361. It does not apply, however, to acquisitive reorganizations in which the transferor corporation goes out of existence (and cannot benefit from the transferee's assumption of liabilities), i.e., Code Sec. 351 transfers that also qualify as either (1) a Type A or Type C reorganization, or (2) a nondivisive Type D or Type G reorganization that meets the requirements of Code Sec. 354(b)(1) (discussed at ¶3530 *et seq.*).[14]

The amount of a liability assumed in a Code Sec. 351 exchange reduces the transferor's basis in the stock received, regardless of whether the transferor recognizes any gain or loss on the exchange. (Code Sec. 358(a), Code Sec. 358(d)(1)) However, the transferor's basis in the stock will not be reduced by the assumption of any liability described in Code Sec. 357(c)(3) that would have been deductible by the transferor had it not been assumed or which would have been a liquidating payment to a partner. (Code Sec. 358(d)(2))[15]

If a transferor's basis in stock received in a Code Sec. 351 exchange exceeds the fair market value (FMV) of the stock, the basis is reduced (but not below FMV) by the amount of any liability that (i) is assumed in exchange for the stock, and (ii) did not otherwise reduce that basis by reason of the assumption. However, basis is not reduced if the trade or business with which the liability is associated is transferred as part of the exchange to the person assuming the liability. (Code Sec. 358(h); Reg § 1.358-5)[16]

7. ¶F-1202
8. ¶F-1501; ¶3514.10
9. ¶F-1509; ¶3574.01
10. ¶F-1511 *et seq.*; ¶3574.02
11. ¶F-1515 *et seq.*; ¶3574.03

12. ¶F-1519; ¶3574.03
13. ¶F-1521; ¶3574.03
14. ¶F-4203 *et seq.*; ¶3574.03
15. ¶F-1803; ¶F-1521; ¶3584.04
16. ¶F-1803.1

¶ 3506   When a liability is treated as assumed.

Except as provided in regs,

(1) A recourse liability is treated as having been assumed by the transferee if, based on all facts and circumstances, the transferee has agreed to and is expected to satisfy it, regardless of whether the transferor has been relieved of the liability. (Code Sec. 357(d)(1)(A))

(2) A nonrecourse liability is treated as having been assumed by the transferee of any asset subject to the liability (Code Sec. 357(d)(1)(B)), except that the amount so treated is reduced by the lesser of:

(i) the amount of the liability that the owner of other untransferred assets subject to the same liability has agreed with the transferee to, and is expected to, satisfy, or

(ii) the FMV of those other untransferred assets determined without regard to Code Sec. 7701(g) (providing generally that the FMV of property subject to nonrecourse debt is not less than the debt (¶2402)). (Code Sec. 357(d)(2))[17]

⊘observation: If the owner of untransferred assets securing nonrecourse debt doesn't agree to pay any of it, the amount of the liability treated as assumed by the transferee isn't reduced at all. Thus, liabilities may exceed basis and cause gain recognition.

For the limit on basis increase for assumption of liabilities, see ¶2484.

¶ 3507   Transfers to investment companies (swap funds).

Gain or loss is recognized on the transfer of property to an investment company in exchange for its stock (Code Sec. 351(e); Reg § 1.351-1(c)(1)).[18] A transfer is to an investment company if the transfer diversifies a transferor's interests, and the transferee is (1) a regulated investment company (RIC), (2) a real estate investment trust (REIT), or (3) a corporation more than 80% of the value of whose total investment assets are marketable securities, interests in RICs or REITs, or stocks and securities (including specified types of property, such as money, that are treated as stocks or securities) (Code Sec. 351(e)(1); Reg § 1.351-1(c)(1)).[19] This rule does not apply if each transferor transfers a portfolio of already diversified assets. (Reg § 1.351-1(c)(6))[20]

¶ 3508   Transfer of debtor's property in a bankruptcy or similar proceeding.

The Code Sec. 351 nonrecognition rule does not apply to transfers in a bankruptcy, receivership, foreclosure or similar proceeding (including agency receivership proceedings involving banks), but only to the extent the stock received by the debtor in exchange for assets is used to satisfy the debtor's indebtedness. (Code Sec. 351(e)(2))[21]

¶ 3509   Gain or loss to corporation on issuance of stock.

A corporation does not recognize gain or loss on the exchange of its stock (including treasury stock) for property or money. (Code Sec. 1032(a))[22] Similarly, no gain or loss is recognized in otherwise taxable transactions where a corporation acquires stock directly or indirectly from the issuing corporation in what otherwise would be a transferred basis

---

17. ¶F-1509.2; ¶3574.01
18. ¶F-1301; ¶3514.06
19. ¶F-1302*et seq.*; ¶3514.06

20. ¶F-1307.1; ¶3514.06
21. ¶F-1308; ¶3514.07
22. ¶I-3201; ¶10,324

transaction and immediately transfers the stock to acquire money or other property (including services), and no party receiving the issuing corporation stock receives a substituted basis in the stock of the issuing corporation. (Reg § 1.1032-3(b), Reg § 1.1032-3(c))[23] For stock issued to a creditor in satisfaction of a corporation's debt, see ¶1386.

¶ 3510   Deductibility of costs of organizing a corporation.

A corporation is deemed to have made an election to deduct up to $5,000 of its organizational expenditures in the tax year it begins business. The $5,000 amount is reduced (but not below zero) by the amount, if any, by which its organizational expenditures exceed $50,000. Remaining organizational expenditures are deductible ratably over the 180-month period beginning with the month it begins business. (Code Sec. 248(a); Reg § 1.248-1(a)) A corporation may irrevocably forgo the deemed election by clearly electing to capitalize *all* organizational expenditures on a timely filed Federal income tax return (including extensions) for the tax year in which it begins business. (Reg § 1.248-1(c))

Such expenses include fees for legal services, incorporation fees, temporary directors' fees and organizational meeting costs. Costs relating to capital structure, e.g., of issuing stock, can't be deducted or otherwise recovered. (Code Sec. 248(b); Reg § 1.248-1(b))[24]

¶ 3511   Corporate Distributions; Earnings and Profits (E&P). ▬▬▬▬▬

A distribution of property (i.e., money, securities, and any other property except stock of the distributing corporation) by a corporation to its shareholders is treated as a dividend and is taxable as ordinary income to the extent it is made out of current and accumulated E&P (¶1283 *et seq.*). The part of the distribution in excess of E&P is treated as a return of capital to the extent of the shareholder's basis in the stock of the distributing corporation. The remainder of the distribution, if any, is generally taxed as capital gain. (Code Sec. 301(c); Code Sec. 316(a))[25]

The amount of a distribution is reduced by an associated liability only if it is assumed by the shareholder within the meaning of Code Sec. 357(d). (¶3506) (Reg § 1.301-1(g))[26]

For adjustments in E&P for corporate distributions, see ¶3512, for depreciation, see ¶3513, and for other E&P adjustments, see ¶3514.

For the tax treatment of the distributing corporation, see ¶3526 *et seq.*

¶ 3512   How distributions affect earnings and profits (E&P).

With certain exceptions discussed below, distributions of property by a corporation with respect to its stock reduce E&P by the following amounts:

(1) The amount of money distributed. (Code Sec. 312(a)(1))[27]

(2) The principal (face) amount of the corporation's obligations (i.e., its own notes, bonds, etc.) distributed without original issue discount (OID) (¶1310 *et seq.*) (or the aggregate issue price of the obligations for distributions of obligations having OID). (Code Sec. 312(a)(2))[28]

(3) The adjusted basis of other distributed property (Code Sec. 312(a)(3)) as determined for purposes of computing E&P. However, since a corporation's distribution of appreciated property (other than its own obligations) increases its E&P by the excess of the property's fair market value (FMV) over its adjusted basis, E&P is decreased by the FMV of the appreciated property. ((Code Sec. 312(b))[29]

---

23. ¶I-3213; ¶10,324
24. ¶L-5201 *et seq.*; ¶2484
25. ¶J-2351 *et seq.*; ¶3014
26. ¶J-2354; ¶3014.02

27. ¶F-10502; ¶3124.02
28. ¶F-10503; ¶3124.02
29. ¶F-10505 *et seq.*; ¶3124.02

However, special rules apply to certain types of distributions, including the following:

(1) Redemption distributions that are treated as payment in exchange for stock (¶3515) reduce E&P by an amount not in excess of the ratable share of the distributing corporation's E&P attributable to the redeemed stock. (Code Sec. 312(n)(7))[30]

(2) Reorganizations and other tax-free distributions don't reduce E&P if the distributee does not recognize any gain. (Code Sec. 312(d)(1)(A); Reg § 1.312-11(b), Reg § 1.312-11(c))[31]

(3) The distribution to a distributee by or on behalf of a corporation of its stock or securities, of stock or securities in another corporation, or of property, is not a distribution of E&P if no gain to the distributee is recognized, or if the distribution is not subject to tax in the hands of the distributee by reason of Code Sec. 305(a). (Code Sec. 312(d)(1)(B)) But if a distribution of stock is *taxable* to the shareholders (¶1294), E&P is reduced by the FMV of the taxable part of the stock or rights. (Reg § 1.312-1(d))[32]

(4) Distributions to 20% corporate shareholders may require adjustments to E&P solely for purposes of determining the distributee's income and stock basis. (Code Sec. 301(e))[33]

Basis can be different for E&P and taxable income (TI) purposes if the corporation uses different depreciation or cost recovery methods for computing E&P and TI. (¶3513).[34]

¶ 3513 Effect of depreciation on earnings and profits (E&P).

Depreciation deductions for E&P purposes are often lower than the corresponding deductions for computing taxable income. (¶1900 *et seq.*) For modified accelerated cost recovery system (MACRS) property (other than property expensed under Code Sec. 179 and certain other expensing provisions), the E&P deduction is computed under the alternative depreciation system (ADS), even if a different system is used in computing taxable income. (Code Sec. 312(k)(3)(A))[35] For Accelerated Cost Recovery System (ACRS) property placed in service before '87, the E&P deduction is computed by using the straight-line method over the regular or alternative ACRS recovery periods, which may be longer than those used in computing taxable income. [36] The E&P deduction for depreciable property placed in service before '81 is computed by using the straight-line or similar method (e.g., units of production), even if an accelerated method is used in computing taxable income. [37] For property expensed under Code Sec. 179 and certain other expensing provisions, the cost is deducted from E&P ratably over five tax years. (Code Sec. 312(k)(3)(B))[38]

¶ 3514 Other adjustments to earnings and profits (E&P).

Other common adjustments are made to E&P to reflect economic gain or loss.

. . . Circulation expenses must be capitalized and treated as part of the basis of the asset to which they relate, even if they are deducted currently in computing taxable income (TI). (Code Sec. 312(n)(3))[39]

. . . Completed contract method of accounting can't be used for E&P purposes. The percentage of completion method must be used instead. (Code Sec. 312(n)(6))[40]

. . . Construction period carrying charges (interest, property taxes, etc.) must be capitalized as part of the assets to which they are allocable. (Code Sec. 312(n)(1)(A)) The capitalized amounts must be written off for E&P purposes, as is the asset itself. [41]

---

30. ¶F-10701; ¶3124.07
31. ¶F-10801; ¶3124.02
32. ¶F-10509 *et seq.*; ¶3124.02
33. ¶F-10601 *et seq.*; ¶3014
34. ¶F-10300 *et seq.*; ¶3124.01 *et seq.*
35. ¶F-10303; ¶3124.04

36. ¶F-10307
37. ¶F-10309
38. ¶F-10304; ¶3124.04
39. ¶F-10206; ¶3124.07
40. ¶F-10008; ¶3124.07
41. ¶F-10208; ¶3124.07

. . . Depletion is determined on a *cost,* not percentage, basis. (Reg § 1.312-6(c)(1))[42]

. . . Exempt income (e.g., state or local bond interest) increases E&P. (Reg § 1.312-6(b))[43]

. . . Income tax liabilities reduce E&P as of the close of the tax year for an accrual basis corporation, and, according to some courts, a cash basis corporation. (IRS and other courts say a cash basis corporation reduces E&P only when the tax (including estimated tax) is *paid*.)[44]

. . . Installment sales are accounted for without regard to the installment method, i.e., principal amounts must be treated as received in the year of sale. (Code Sec. 312(n)(5))[45]

. . . Intangible drilling and development costs that are deductible when paid or incurred for TI purposes (other than costs incurred in connection with a nonproductive well) must be capitalized and deducted ratably over a 60-month period. (Code Sec. 312(n)(2)(A))[46]

. . . Life insurance proceeds increase E&P if the corporation is the beneficiary, even if not includible in TI.[47]

. . . E&P is increased or decreased by the amount of any increase or decrease in the LIFO (last-in, first-out) recapture amount as of the close of each tax year. (Code Sec. 312(n)(4))[48]

. . . Loss carryovers and carrybacks don't reduce E&P of the year to which they are carried and reductions of loss carryovers do not increase E&P in a later carryover year. [49]

. . . Losses recognized, but not allowed as a deduction (e.g., losses under the related party rules (¶2447), and capital losses (¶2611)) decrease E&P by the disallowed amount. A wash sale loss does not reduce E&P since it is not recognized. (Reg § 1.312-7(b)(1)[50]

. . . Mineral exploration and development costs that are deductible for taxable income purposes must be capitalized and deducted ratably over a 120-month period. (Code Sec. 312(n)(2)(B))[1]

. . . Organizational expenses must be capitalized and treated as part of the basis of the asset to which they relate, even if they are amortized in computing TI (as described at ¶3510). (Code Sec. 312(n)(3))[2]

. . . Premiums paid for life insurance on corporate officers reduce E&P, even if they are not deductible in computing TI.[3]

¶ 3515   Stock Redemptions.

The redemption by a corporation of its own stock from a shareholder in exchange for cash or property is treated as a taxable dividend distribution to the shareholder (¶1283 *et seq.*) unless it qualifies as a sale or exchange for sale or exchange treatment, in which case it is treated as a sale or exchange for which capital gain treatment is allowed (if the stock is a capital asset in the hands of the taxpayer) whether or not the stock acquired is cancelled, retired, or held as treasury stock. (Code Sec. 317(b))[4] The following redemptions will be treated as a sale or exchange of stock:

(1) *Substantially disproportionate redemptions* . (¶3516)

(2) *Complete redemptions* of a shareholder's interest. (¶3517)

(3) *Redemptions not essentially equivalent to a dividend* . (¶3519)

(4) *Redemptions in partial liquidation* of a noncorporate shareholder. (¶3520)

---

42. ¶F-10314; ¶3124.04
43. ¶F-10101; ¶s 3124.01, 3124.07
44. ¶F-10223 *et seq.*; ¶3124.03
45. ¶F-10405; ¶3124.07
46. ¶F-10221; ¶3124.07
47. ¶F-10102
48. ¶F-10212; ¶3124.07

49. ¶F-10012; ¶3124.03
50. ¶F-10403; ¶3124.05
1. ¶F-10220; ¶3124.07
2. ¶F-10204; ¶3124.07
3. ¶F-10234
4. ¶F-11001; ¶3174.01

(5) *Redemptions of a decedent's stock* to pay death taxes. (¶3521) (Code Sec. 302(a))[5]

For the treatment of stock sales between related corporations as redemptions, see ¶3522.

For constructive ownership rules applicable to redemptions, see ¶3523.

¶ 3516   Substantially disproportionate redemptions.

A redemption is *substantially disproportionate* if it satisfies both of the following tests:

(1) *80% test.* Immediately after the redemption, the ratio of the shareholder's voting stock to the corporation's total outstanding voting stock is less than 80% of that ratio immediately before the redemption. The same 80% test must also be met with regard to the corporation's *common stock,* voting and nonvoting, based on the fair market value of the aggregate shares of each class of common stock. (Code Sec. 302(b)(2)(C))

(2) *50% test.* Immediately after the redemption, the shareholder owns less than 50%, by vote, of the corporation's total voting stock. (Code Sec. 302(b)(2)(B))[6]

A redemption solely of nonvoting stock doesn't qualify as substantially disproportionate. However, if voting stock is redeemed at the same time in a redemption that qualifies as substantially disproportionate, the redemption of the nonvoting stock (other than Section 306 stock, see ¶3524 *et seq.*) will also be substantially disproportionate. (Reg § 1.302-3(a))[7]

¶ 3517   Complete redemptions—termination of a shareholder's interest in the corporation.

To qualify as a complete redemption, all stock in the corporation that is owned, or treated as owned under the constructive ownership rules (¶3523) (unless waived (¶3518)), by the shareholder must be redeemed. (Code Sec. 302(b)(3))[8]

A redemption on the installment basis can qualify as a complete redemption if the corporation and the shareholder are bound by a purchase agreement to complete the redemption by a certain date and for a maximum price. [9]

¶ 3518   Family attribution rules waived on complete terminations.

An individual who receives a distribution that is otherwise in complete redemption of all the stock he actually owns will not be treated as constructively owning the stock owned by a spouse, child, grandchild or parent if:

(1) He has no personal financial interest in the corporation (prohibited interest), other than as a creditor, immediately after the redemption;

(2) He no longer serves as director, officer or employee;

(3) He doesn't acquire any prohibited interest (except by inheritance) or position within ten years after the redemption;

(4) He didn't acquire any of the redeemed stock from close family members, and didn't transfer any stock to them, within ten years before the redemption, except acquisitions or transfers not principally motivated by tax avoidance; *and*

(5) He attaches a separate statement (in duplicate) to his income tax return for the redemption year stating that he hasn't acquired any new prohibited interest (except by inheritance) and that he will notify the district director within 30 days after acquiring any new interest. (Code Sec. 302(c)(2); Reg § 1.302-4)[10]

---

5. ¶F-11101 *et seq.*; ¶3024.02
6. ¶F-11203 *et seq.*; ¶3024.04
7. ¶F-11212; ¶3024.04

8. ¶F-11301 *et seq.*; ¶3024.05
9. ¶F-11307
10. ¶F-11313 *et seq.*; ¶3024.05

Waiver of family attribution allows an individual to completely redeem his interest without all related persons redeeming their stock and applies only for purposes of determining that a distribution is a complete redemption. There is no need for the waiver if the redemption would otherwise qualify as payment in exchange for stock. (Code Sec. 302(b)(6))[11]

A partnership, estate, trust or corporation (entity) can waive family attribution if the partner, beneficiary or shareholder (related person) owns stock solely as a function of the family constructive ownership rules. Such ownership is not reattributed to the entity if both the entity and the related person satisfy the conditions for a waiver and agree to be jointly and severally liable for any tax deficiency resulting from any acquisition of an interest within the 10-year period. (Code Sec. 302(c)(2)(C))[12]

¶ 3519 Redemptions not essentially equivalent to a dividend.

A redemption is not essentially equivalent to a dividend if it results in a meaningful reduction in the redeemed shareholder's proportionate interest in the distributing corporation, without regard to how it affects the distributing corporation. (Reg § 1.302-2(b))[13] A redemption of a sole shareholder and a pro rata redemption cannot qualify as not essentially equivalent to a dividend since they do not reduce a shareholders' proportionate interest in the distributing corporation. [14]

A redemption from a shareholder with over 50% of the voting power usually results in a meaningful reduction if that shareholder's voting power is reduced to 50% or less. [15] Additionally, a redemption of voting stock from a substantial minority shareholder results in a meaningful reduction if, after the redemption, the number of shareholders the redeemed shareholder must act in concert with to control the corporation is increased [16]; and a redemption of voting stock from a low percentage minority shareholder is usually treated as a meaningful reduction so long as there is some reduction in proportionate interest. [17]

Redemptions of nonvoting preferred stock from shareholders who own no common stock and no voting stock always result in a meaningful reduction in interest. [18]

The constructive ownership rules (¶3523) apply in determining the redeemed shareholder's stock ownership before and after the redemption (Code Sec. 302(c)(1)), even if no stock is actually owned after the redemption. [19]

¶ 3520 Redemptions in partial liquidation of a noncorporate shareholder.

A partial liquidating distribution in redemption of stock of a noncorporate shareholder is treated as a sale or exchange even if it is made pro rata. A redemption distribution is treated as made in partial liquidation if it is (1) made with respect to a noncorporate shareholder, (2) not essentially equivalent to a dividend determined at the corporate level (i.e., it results from a contraction of the corporate business), and (3) made under a plan within the tax year in which the plan is adopted or the next tax year. (Code Sec. 302(b)(4), Code Sec. 302(e)(1))[20]

¶ 3521 Redemption of decedent's stock to pay death taxes.

Distributions in redemption of stock included in a decedent's gross estate for federal estate tax purposes are treated as payment for stock up to the sum of: (1) all death taxes

11. ¶F-11311; ¶3024.05
12. ¶F-11314; ¶3024.05
13. ¶F-11402; ¶3024.03
14. ¶F-11407; ¶3024.03
15. ¶F-11418; ¶3024.03

16. ¶F-11424; ¶3024.03
17. ¶F-11425
18. ¶F-11429 *et seq.*
19. ¶F-11410 *et seq.*; ¶3024.03
20. ¶F-11500 *et seq.*; Reg § 1.346-1(a); ¶3024.06

(federal and state), including interest, and (2) funeral and administration expenses allowable as federal estate tax deductions (Code Sec. 303(a)),[21] *but only if*:

(1) the value of the redeeming corporation's stock included in the estate exceeds 35% of the decedent's adjusted gross estate, with the stock of two or more corporations treated as stock of a single corporation if 20% or more of the value of the outstanding stock of each corporation is included in the decedent's gross estate (Code Sec. 303(b)(2));[22]

(2) the redemption distribution takes place after the decedent's death and within three years and 90 days after the estate tax return is filed (or due, if filed early), or, in some cases, later specified dates (Code Sec. 303(b)(1));[23] and

(3) the redeemed shareholder bears the burden of the taxes or expenses. (Code Sec. 303(b)(3))[24]

¶ 3522   Stock sales between related corporations.

If shareholders control two corporations and sell stock of one controlled corporation (Issuer) to the other (Acquirer) in return for cash or other property, the sale is treated as a stock redemption, rather than as a sale. The redemption will be treated as a dividend, unless it qualifies for nondividend treatment under one of the exceptions listed at ¶3515. (Code Sec. 304(a))[25]. If the Acquirer is a brother corporation (see below) of the Issuer, the sale is treated as a redemption by the Acquirer. (Code Sec. 304(a)(1)) If the Issuer is a parent (see below) of the Acquirer, the sale is treated as a redemption by the Issuer. (Code Sec. 304(a)(2))[26]

If the sale is treated as a dividend, the amount taxable to the shareholder is determined as if it were distributed *first* by the Acquirer to the extent of its earnings and profits (E&P), and *then* by the Issuer to the extent of its E&P. (Code Sec. 304(b)(2))[27] The parties to transactions subject to Code Sec. 304 entered into with a principal purpose of avoiding its application to certain corporations, however, may be recast for purposes of determining the dividend amount. (Reg § 1.304-4)[28] In the case of a *foreign* Acquirer, (a) the amount of E&P that can support a deemed dividend is limited to E&P attributable to stock of a U.S. shareholder accumulated while Acquirer was a controlled foreign corporation (CFC) (¶4611 *et seq.*) and (b) its E&P is not taken into account if more that 50% of the consequent dividend would be *neither* subject to U.S. tax for the year of the dividend, *nor* includible in the E&P of a CFC. (Code Sec. 304(b)(5))[29]

If a deemed distribution from a stock sale between brother-sister corporations is treated as a dividend, (1) the stock that was sold is deemed to have been transferred by Issuer to Acquirer for stock of Issuer in a tax-free transfer to a controlled corporation, and (2) Acquirer is deemed to have redeemed the stock that is treated as having been issued to it in the constructive transfer, preventing Issuer from using the dividends-received deduction to shelter any part of the deemed distribution. (Code Sec. 304(a)(1))[30]

A corporation is a parent if it controls another corporation. (Code Sec. 304(a)(2)) A brother-sister relationship exists where the same person(s) control(s) each of two corporations. (Code Sec. 304(a)(1)) Control means ownership of stock possessing at least 50% of the total combined voting power of all classes of the voting stock, or at least 50% of the total value of all classes of stock. (Code Sec. 304(c)(1))[31] Constructive ownership rules similar to those at ¶3523 apply with modifications. (Code Sec. 304(c)(3))[32]

21. ¶F-11600 *et seq.*; ¶3034.01
22. ¶F-11603 *et seq.* ¶3034.01
23. ¶F-11613; ¶3034.01
24. ¶F-11617; ¶3034.01
25. ¶F-11704; ¶s 3044.02, 3044.03
26. ¶F-11701 *et seq.*; ¶3044 *et seq.*

27. ¶F-11706; ¶3044.03
28. ¶F-11707; ¶3044.05
29. ¶F-11719.2; ¶F-11719.3; ¶3044.04
30. ¶F-11716; ¶3044.03
31. ¶F-11711; ¶3044.01
32. ¶F-11720 *et seq.*; ¶3044.01

The parent-subsidiary redemption rules apply even if, as a result of the constructive ownership rules, a brother-sister relationship also exists, and the brother-sister redemption rules apply where the parent's control over the subsidiary results from constructive and not actual ownership. (Reg § 1.304-2(c))[33]

¶ 3523   Constructive ownership.

For purposes of the stock redemption rules, a person is treated as owning not only his own direct holdings, but also those of certain closely related taxpayers: (Code Sec. 302(c))

... An individual is considered as owning stock owned, directly or indirectly, by his spouse (unless divorced or legally separated), children (including adopted children), grandchildren and parents. (Code Sec. 318(a)(1))[34]

... Stock owned by or for an S corporation, partnership or estate is considered as owned proportionately by its shareholders, partners, or beneficiaries. (Code Sec. 318(a)(2)(A), Code Sec. 318(a)(5)(E)) Stock owned by or for an S corporation shareholder, partner or estate beneficiary is attributed in full to the S corporation, partnership or estate. (Code Sec. 318(a)(3)(A), Code Sec. 318(a)(5)(E))[35]

... Stock owned by or for a trust is considered owned by its beneficiaries in proportion to their actuarial interest in the trust. (Code Sec. 318(a)(2)(B)(i)) Stock owned by or for a trust beneficiary is attributed in full to the trust unless the beneficiary's interest in the trust is a remote contingent interest. (Code Sec. 318(a)(3)(B)(i))[36]

... A 50%-or-more shareholder in a C corporation is considered as owning his proportionate share of stock in other corporations owned by the C corporation. (Code Sec. 318(a)(2)(C)) A C corporation is considered as owning all the stock (except its own) owned by its 50%-or-more shareholder. (Code Sec. 318(a)(3)(C); Reg § 1.318-1(b)(1))[37]

... The holder of an option to buy stock is treated as the owner of the stock covered by the option. (Code Sec. 318(a)(4))[38] This includes an option that isn't exercisable until after the lapse of a fixed time. [39]

Stock constructively owned is considered to be actually owned for purposes of further attribution (Code Sec. 318(a)(5)(A)),[40] *except* as follows (where so-called double or sidewise attribution is prohibited):

... Stock constructively owned by a person under the family attribution rules won't be attributed further to make another family member the constructive owner of that stock. (Code Sec. 318(a)(5)(B))[41]

illustration: If a father and son each own 50 shares in a corporation, each is treated as owning all 100 shares. But the father's constructive ownership of the son's shares can't be further attributed from the father to his daughter.

... Stock constructively owned by a partnership, estate, trust or corporation can't be further attributed from the partnership, etc., to make another (partner, heir, beneficiary or shareholder) the constructive owner of that stock. (Code Sec. 318(a)(5)(C))[42]

¶ 3524   Section 306 Stock. ▬▬▬▬▬▬▬▬▬▬▬▬

Code Sec. 306 prohibits capital gain treatment on the disposition of certain preferred stock received either as a nontaxable stock dividend or in certain substituted basis transactions when ordinary income treatment would have applied if

33. ¶F-11723
34. ¶F-11803 *et seq.*; ¶3184.02
35. ¶F-11812 *et seq.*; ¶3184.03
36. ¶F-11827 *et seq.*; ¶3184.04
37. ¶F-11808 *et seq.*; ¶3184.05

38. ¶F-11834; ¶3184.06
39. ¶F-11835
40. ¶F-11805; ¶3184.07
41. ¶F-11804; ¶3184.07
42. ¶s F-11811, F-11814, F-11824, F-11832; ¶3184.07

cash had been distributed instead. Exemptions apply to dispositions that do not ordinarily bail out a corporation's earnings and profits. [43]

Proceeds from a redemption of Section 306 stock (defined at ¶3525) are treated as a current distribution of property subject to the regular Code Sec. 301 dividend rules (see ¶1283 *et seq.*). (Code Sec. 306(a)(2))[44]

If Section 306 stock is sold or otherwise disposed of in a transaction other than a redemption, the entire amount realized is treated as ordinary income to the extent the fair market value on the distribution date would have been a dividend had the corporation distributed cash instead of stock. Ordinary income treatment is thus limited to the corporation's E&P at the time of the distribution rather than the sale. (Code Sec. 306(a)(1)(A))[45]

Gain is recognized to the extent the amount received exceeds the sum of the amount treated as ordinary income plus the adjusted basis of the stock, but loss is not recognized. (Code Sec. 306(a)(1)(B); Code Sec. 306(a)(1)(C))[46] The ordinary income is treated as qualified dividend income for individuals and other noncorporate taxpayers (¶1286).[47]

An amount realized on the disposition of Section 306 stock will not be treated as a dividend in the case of:

. . . A complete disposition of the shareholder's interest in the corporation, including stock attributed under the Code Sec. 318(a) constructive ownership rules. (Code Sec. 306(b)(1)(A))

. . . A redemption (i) of all of a shareholder's Section 306 stock terminating the shareholder's corporate ownership, or (ii) from a noncorporate shareholder in partial liquidation of the corporation. (Code Sec. 306(b)(1)(B)).

. . . A redemption in a complete liquidation of the corporation. (Code Sec. 306(b)(2))

. . . A transaction in which gain or loss is not recognized on the disposition of the Section 306 stock (in which case the stock retains the Section 306 taint in the transferee's hands). (Code Sec. 306(b)(3))

. . . A transaction, if the issuance and/or subsequent disposition of the stock was not pursuant to a plan having one of its principal purposes the avoidance of federal income tax. (Code Sec. 306(b)(4))[48]

For stock treated as Section 306 stock, see ¶3525.

¶ 3525   Stock treated as Section 306 stock.

Section 306 stock includes:

(1) Stock received as a stock dividend, other than common stock issued with respect to common stock, if any part was not taxable on its receipt; usually preferred stock distributed on common stock. (Code Sec. 306(c)(1)(A))[49]

(2) Stock other than common stock received in a reorganization, spin-off, split-up or split-off, to the extent that (a) the transaction was substantially the same as the receipt of a stock dividend, or (b) the stock was received in exchange for Section 306 stock. (Code Sec. 306(c)(1)(B))[50]

(3) Stock (unless described in (2) above) whose basis is determined by reference to the basis of Section 306 stock. (Code Sec. 306(c)(1)(C))[1]

(4) Preferred stock (but not nonqualified preferred stock (see ¶3542)) received in a Code

---

43. ¶F-12100 *et seq.*; ¶3064 *et seq.*
44. ¶F-12106; ¶3064.02
45. ¶ F-12101 *et seq.*; ¶3064.02
46. ¶F-12103; ¶3064.02
47. ¶F-12101; ¶3064.02

48. ¶F-12108 *et seq.*; ¶3064.02
49. ¶F-12122; ¶3064.01
50. ¶F-12124 *et seq.*; ¶3064.01
1. ¶F-12128; ¶3064.01

Sec. 351 transfer (except for certain bank transfers) if receipt of cash (in lieu of the stock) would have been treated as a dividend to any extent after applying the related corporation redemption rules (¶3522). (Code Sec. 306(c)(3))[2]

Section 306 stock does not include any stock of any class which, at the time of distribution, would not in any part have been a dividend if cash had been distributed instead because there were no earnings and profits. (Code Sec. 306(c)(2))[3]

¶ 3526   Nonliquidating Corporate Distributions.

In determining the tax effects to a corporation of nonliquidating distributions (dividends or distributions in redemption of the corporation's stock) to its shareholders, the following rules apply:

... A corporation doesn't recognize gain or loss on distributions of its stock or rights to acquire its stock. (Code Sec. 311(a)(1)).[4]

... A corporation does not recognize loss on any distribution of property to its shareholder. (Code Sec. 311(a)(2))[5]

... A corporation recognizes gain when it makes a nonliquidating distribution of appreciated property (other than its own obligations) to its shareholders as if the property had been sold, at the time of the distribution, to the distributee for its then fair market value (FMV). (Code Sec. 311(b)(1))[6]

... If distributed property is subject to any debt, or the shareholder assumes any debt in connection with the distribution, the FMV of the property is treated as not less than the amount of that debt. (Code Sec. 311(b)(2))[7] If the liability is unsecured, it is allocated among all the distributed assets (including any asset that secures another liability) according to the assets' relative FMVs. [8]

recommendation: Instead of distributing property with a basis in excess of its value to its shareholders, a corporation should consider selling that property to a third party so the loss can be recognized in computing its taxable income.

For how nonliquidating distributions affect earnings and profits (E&P), see ¶3512.

¶ 3527   Corporate Reorganizations.

If one corporation transfers property to another corporation solely in exchange for stock or securities of the other corporation and the exchange is made under a plan of reorganization, neither will recognize gain or loss on the exchange if the transaction complies with strict statutory and regulatory requirements. The following are the different types of reorganizations: Type A: Merger or consolidation (¶3530); Type B: stock for stock (¶3531); Type C: Assets for stock (¶3532); Type D: Transfer of assets to subsidiary (¶3533); Type E: Recapitalization (¶3534); Type F: Change of identity (¶3535); Type G: Bankruptcy (¶3536); and triangular reorganization where the acquirer's parent is a party (¶3537).

For conditions common to all reorganizations, see ¶3528.

For reorganizations involving investment companies, see ¶3529.

For the tax effects of the transfer of property acquired in a reorganization, see ¶3538.

For how shareholders and corporate parties are taxed in a reorganization, see ¶3540 *et seq.*

---

2. ¶F-12123; ¶3064.01
3. ¶F-12132; ¶3064.01
4. ¶F-14002 *et seq.*; ¶3114.02
5. ¶F-14002; ¶3114.02

6. ¶F-14004 *et seq.*; ¶3114.01
7. ¶s F-14005, F-14402; ¶3114.01
8. ¶F-14006

For the deductibility of reorganization costs, see ¶3544.

¶ 3528 Conditions common to all reorganizations.

The following definitions and requirements apply to all reorganization types, with exceptions noted. Failure to meet any requirement may disqualify a reorganization and result in gain recognition and/or dividend treatment. [9]

Plan of reorganization. An exchange must be under a plan of reorganization. (Code Sec. 354(a)(1); Reg § 1.368-2(g))[10] The plan must be adopted by each party to the reorganization (see below) and each party must include a statement on its return pursuant to regs. (Reg § 1.368-3(a))[11]

Party to a reorganization. A corporation whose stock or securities are exchanged must be a party to the reorganization for nonrecognition treatment to apply. (Code Sec. 354(a)(1))[12] This includes any corporation resulting from a reorganization and, in the case of an acquisition by one corporation of the stock or properties of another, both corporations. The parent of the acquiring corporation in a Type B, C, or G reorganization is a party to the reorganization if its stock is the consideration for the acquisition of assets or stock. A parent of the surviving corporation in a statutory merger is a party to the reorganization if its stock is used as consideration and the transaction qualifies as a Type A reorganization under Code Sec. 368(a)(2)(D) or Code Sec. 368(a)(2)(E). If assets or stock received in a Type A, B, C, or G reorganization are dropped down under Code Sec. 368(a)(2)(C), the corporation controlling the transferee is a party to the reorganization. (Code Sec. 368(b)) (Reg § 1.368-2(f))[13]

Continuity of interest. The regulatory continuity of proprietary interest doctrine incorporates the judicial requirement that the former target shareholders retain a significant equity participation in the target corporation after the reorganization. A proprietary interest in the target is sufficiently preserved if (1) it is exchanged for a proprietary interest in the issuing corporation, (2) it is exchanged by the acquiring corporation for a direct interest in the target corporation enterprise, or (3) it otherwise continues as a proprietary interest in the target corporation. (Reg § 1.368-1(e))[14]

Continuity of business enterprise. An acquiring corporation must either (1) continue the target's historic business (generally, its most recent business unless the most recent business was entered under the plan of reorganization), or (2) use a significant part of the target's historic business assets in a business. The business may be conducted by, or the assets held through, one or more members of the acquiring corporation's qualified group, i.e., one or more chains of corporations connected through stock ownership, if the acquiring corporation has 80% control of at least one of them and each of the other corporations is controlled by one of the other corporations). (Reg § 1.368-1(d))[15]

Business purpose. A transaction that is structured as a reorganization but has no business purpose is not in the nature of a reorganization and is not treated as such. [16]

The continuity of interest and continuity of business enterprise requirements do not apply to recapitalizations involving a single corporation (Type E reorganizations, ¶3534)[17] or change-in-identity (Type F) reorganizations (¶3535). (Reg § 1.368-1(b))[18]

---

9. ¶F-3500 *et seq.*; ¶3684
10. ¶s F-4009; ¶3684.09
11. ¶F-4118; ¶3684.09
12. ¶F-4001; ¶3684.08
13. ¶F-4013; ¶3684.08

14. ¶s F-3501, F-3600 *et seq.*; ¶3684.10
15. ¶F-3701 *et seq.*; ¶3684.11
16. ¶F-3800 *et seq.*; ¶3684.12, ¶79,006.07
17. ¶F-3626; ¶3684.05
18. ¶F-3709; ¶3684.06

¶ 3529   Reorganizations involving investment companies.

If two or more investment companies are parties to a transaction, the transaction cannot qualify as a nonrecognition reorganization with respect to either company or the holders of its stock and securities unless it was a regulated investment company (¶4201), a real estate investment trust (¶4202), or a corporation that meets specific diversified investment company requirements. (Code Sec. 368(a)(2)(F))[19]

¶ 3530   Type A: Merger or consolidation.

A Type A reorganization is a merger or consolidation effected under statutory law (including foreign laws). (Code Sec. 368(a)(1)(A); Reg § 1.368-2(b)(1)(ii))[20] The merger of a disregarded entity into a corporation doesn't qualify as a tax-free statutory merger or consolidation, although the merger of a corporation into a disregarded entity may qualify. (Reg § 1.368-2(b)(1)(iii))[21]

¶ 3531   Type B: Acquisition of stock in exchange for stock.

A Type B reorganization is the acquisition by one corporation of stock in a second (target) corporation in exchange *solely for voting stock* of the acquiring corporation (or voting stock of its parent in the case of a triangular Type B reorganization (¶3537)), if the acquiring corporation is in *control* (¶3539) of the target immediately after the exchange. (Code Sec. 368(a)(1)(B)) An acquiring corporation that transfers property other than voting stock in connection with a Type B reorganization plan doesn't violate the *solely for voting stock* requirement as long as the target's *stock* is acquired solely for voting stock. [22]

¶ 3532   Type C: Acquisition of a target's assets for stock.

A Type C reorganization is the acquisition by one corporation of *substantially all* of the properties of a target corporation in exchange for voting stock of the acquiring corporation (or the stock of its parent in the case of a triangular C reorganization (¶3537)). Except as noted below, liabilities assumed by the acquiring corporation are disregarded. (Code Sec. 368(a)(1)(C))[23]

There is no definition of *substantially all* of a target's properties or rules on what part of the assets the target can safely retain. However, for purposes of a favorable IRS ruling, the target must transfer at least 90% of the fair market value (FMV) of the net assets and at least 70% of the FMV of the gross assets that it held immediately before the transfer. [24]

A transaction won't qualify as a C reorganization unless the target, under the plan of reorganization, liquidates and distributes to its shareholders all stock, securities and other property received under the plan, as well as its other properties. IRS may waive this distribution requirement under certain conditions. (Code Sec. 368(a)(2)(G))[25]

To satisfy the *solely for voting stock* requirement, at least 80% of the FMV of property received must be acquired solely for voting stock. The remainder of the property may be acquired for cash or other property. If any cash or other property is transferred, liabilities assumed with respect to acquired properties are treated as cash. (Code Sec. 368(a)(2)(B))[26] Preexisting ownership by an acquiring corporation of a part of the target's stock does not, in and of itself, prevent the solely for voting stock requirement from being satisfied.

19. ¶F-2101 *et seq.*; ¶3684.14
20. ¶F-2201 *et seq.*; ¶3684.01
21. ¶F-2201.2 *et seq.*; ¶3684.01
22. ¶F-2500 *et seq.*; ¶3684.02

23. ¶F-2600 *et seq.*; ¶3684.03
24. ¶F-2618, F-2620
25. ¶F-2629 *et seq.*; ¶3684.03
26. ¶F-2613; ¶3684.03

(Reg § 1.368-2(d)(4))[27]

¶ 3533 Type D: Transfer of assets to subsidiary.

A Type D reorganization is the transfer by one corporation of all or part of its assets to a second corporation, if, immediately after the transfer, the transferor and/or its shareholders are in control (¶3539) of the transferee corporation *and* the transferor satisfies a distribution requirement by:

. . . distributing all of the assets (including stock and securities) of the transferee to its shareholders under a plan of reorganization as a part of the transferor's liquidation (*acquisitive* or *nondivisive* D); or

. . . distributing the stock and securities of the transferee in a tax-free spin-off, split-off or split-up (corporate separation, or *divisive* D (¶3545 *et seq.*). (Code Sec. 368(a)(1)(D))[28]

The distribution requirements of Code Sec. 368(a)(1)(D) and Code Sec. 354(b)(1)(B) are deemed satisfied even if no stock is actually distributed in cases where the same person or persons own(s) directly or indirectly all of the stock of the transferor and transferee corporations in the same proportions. Except in certain related party triangular reorganizations, if fair market value (FMV) is paid for the assets, the transferee is deemed to issue a nominal share of stock to the transferor, which is deemed further distributed as necessary to reflect actual ownership. (Reg § 1.368-2(l)(2))[29]

An acquiring corporation's transfer of target corporation assets to a controlled subsidiary as part of a plan of reorganization may not disqualify an otherwise qualifying D reorganization. (Reg § 1.368-2(k))[30]

A Type D reorganization may also qualify as a Type C, in which case it will be treated only as a Type D. (Code Sec. 368(a)(2)(A))[31]

¶ 3534 Type E: Recapitalization.

A Type E reorganization is a recapitalization (Code Sec. 368(a)(1)(E)) or change in the capital structure of a single corporation. It may be achieved through an exchange of stock for stock, bonds for bonds, stock for bonds, or bonds for stock. Recapitalizations include:

. . . An issuance of preferred stock in discharge of outstanding bonds;

. . . An exchange of one class of common for another class of common, or preferred for common (provided that new preferred is not Section 306 stock (¶3523), and provided that the fair market value of the post-reorganization stock equals that of the pre-organization stock), or vice-versa;

. . . An exchange of old bonds for new bonds with a different face value, interest rate, etc.;

. . . Changes in stock or securities effected by a change in the corporate charter. (Reg § 1.368-2(e))[32]

¶ 3535 Type F: Change in Identity.

A Type F reorganization is limited to a change in identity, form or place of organization *of one corporation* and may be accomplished using various methods. (Code Sec. 368(a)(1)(F))[33]

---

27. ¶F-2617; ¶3684.03
28. ¶s F-2004, F-2700 *et seq.*; ¶3684.04
29. ¶F-2708 *et seq.*; ¶3684.041
30. ¶F-2702.1

31. ¶F-2710; ¶3684.04
32. ¶F-3000 *et seq.*; ¶3684.05
33. ¶F-3100 *et seq.*; ¶3684.06

¶ 3536   Type G: Bankruptcy.

A Type G reorganization is the transfer by a corporation of all or part of its assets to another corporation (including a bridge bank) under a court-approved reorganization plan in a Title 11 or similar case (e.g., bankruptcy, receivership, or foreclosure), but only if stock or securities of the corporation to which the assets are transferred are distributed in a transaction that qualifies under Code Sec. 354, Code Sec. 355, or Code Sec. 356. (Code Sec. 368(a)(1)(G), Code Sec. 368(a)(3)(A))[34] The acquirer can use parent stock to acquire the debtor corporation in a triangular Type G reorganization. (Code Sec. 368(a)(2)(D))[35]

¶ 3537   Triangular reorganizations.

Tax-free treatment applies to the following triangular reorganizations in which the acquirer's parent is a party to the transaction:

(1) *Forward triangular merger.* Where the acquirer uses parent stock to acquire *substantially all* of the target's assets (¶3532), the transaction is a forward triangular merger. If certain requirements are met, a forward triangular merger qualifies as a Type A reorganization. (Code Sec. 368(a)(2)(D))[36]

(2) *Triangular C reorganization.* Where the acquiring corporation acquires substantially all the assets of the target corporation solely in exchange for all or a part of the voting stock of the acquirer's parent, the transaction qualifies as a triangular Type C reorganization. (Code Sec. 368(a)(1)(C))[37]

(3) *Triangular B reorganization.* A triangular reorganization qualifies for Type B treatment if the acquirer acquires target stock solely in exchange for parent stock. [38]

(4) *Reverse triangular merger.* Where target shareholders exchange stock of the target constituting control for voting stock of the parent of the merged corporation and the target holds substantially all of its own properties and of those of the merged subsidiary after the merger, the merger is a reverse triangular merger. (Code Sec. 368(a)(2)(E))[39] A reverse triangular merger is tax-free despite a later sale of half of the target's operating assets.[40] If certain requirements are met, a reverse triangular merger that doesn't qualify as a Type A reorganization may qualify as a Type B reorganization. (Reg § 1.368-2(j)(6), Ex 4)[41]

¶ 3538   Transfer of property acquired in a reorganization.

An otherwise tax-free reorganization is not disqualified by one or more later (or successive) transfers of assets or stock, provided that (i) there is continuity of business enterprise (¶3528), (ii) target's corporate existence is not terminated in connection with the drop-down, and (iii) the drop-down does not cause the target to cease to be a member of the qualified group. (Reg § 1.368-2(k))[42]

¶ 3539   Control defined.

For purposes of the rules for reorganizations (other than nondivisive Type Ds), *control* is the ownership of: (i) stock possessing at least 80% of the total combined voting power of all voting stock, and (ii) at least 80% of the total number of shares of each class of nonvoting stock. (Code Sec. 368(c))[43] For nondivisive Type Ds, *control* is defined under the related

---

34. ¶F-3200 *et seq.*; ¶3684.07
35. ¶F-3207; ¶3684.07
36. ¶F-2301 *et seq.*; ¶3684.01
37. ¶F-2651 *et seq.*; ¶3684.135
38. ¶F-2551; ¶3684.08

39. ¶F-2401 *et seq.*; ¶3684.01
40. ¶F-2413
41. ¶F-2410
42. ¶F-2308, ¶F-3251; ¶3684.135
43. ¶F-4502, ¶F-5500 *et seq.*; ¶3684.13

corporation redemption rules (i.e., 50%, rather than 80%, ownership, see ¶3522). If the corporate division requirements of Code Sec. 355 (¶3546) are satisfied, control isn't affected by later transfers by shareholders of the distributed controlled corporation stock or by the issuance by the corporation whose stock was distributed of additional stock. (Code Sec. 368(a)(2)(H))[44]

¶ 3540 How shareholders are taxed in a reorganization.

If, under a plan of reorganization, the holder of stock or securities receives only stock in a corporation that's a party to the reorganization, the recipient recognizes no gain or loss. Nonrecognition also applies when securities of a corporate party to the reorganization are received in exchange for other securities, if the principal (face) amount of the securities received isn't more than the face amount given up. (Code Sec. 354(a)(1); Code Sec. 354(a)(2)(A))[45] Nonqualified preferred stock (¶3542) received for stock that isn't nonqualified preferred stock is not treated as stock or securities unless it's received in a recapitalization (¶3534) of a family-owned corporation. (Code Sec. 354(a)(2)(C))[46] Stock rights (except rights to acquire nonqualified preferred stock not received as part of a family corporation recapitalization) are treated as securities with no principal amount. (Reg § 1.354-1(e), Reg § 1.355-1(c), Reg § 1.356-6(a)(2), Reg § 1.356-6(b)(1))[47] For the treatment of nonqualified preferred stock and excess securities as boot, see ¶3542.

Type D and Type G reorganizations are not tax-free unless (i) the transferee corporation receives substantially all of the transferor's assets, and (ii) the stock, securities and other property received by the transferor, as well as its remaining assets, are distributed by the transferor under the reorganization plan. (Code Sec. 354(b))[48]

If nonrecognition would apply but for the fact that property other than stock or securities (i.e., boot (¶3542)) is also received in the exchange, gain is recognized up to the sum of the boot received. (Code Sec. 356(a)(1))[49] A loss on one block of stock exchanged in a reorganization may not reduce gain on another block. [50] Gain recognized in a reorganization with boot is treated as a dividend if the exchange has the effect of a distribution (see ¶3515). The gain is treated as ordinary income to the extent of the taxpayer's ratable share of the accumulated earnings and profits of the distributing corporation, and the balance is treated as gain from the sale or exchange of property. (Code Sec. 356(a)(2))[1]

For basis of property received in the exchange, see ¶2487.

¶ 3541 How the corporate parties are taxed in a reorganization.

No gain or loss is recognized by a corporation that is a party to a reorganization (¶3528) and that exchanges property solely for stock or securities of another corporation that is also a party to that reorganization. (Code Sec. 361(a))[2] If the corporation receives other property or money (boot, see ¶3542) in addition to stock or securities, then if the corporation distributes all of the boot, it doesn't recognize gain on the exchange (but may recognize gain on the distribution of appreciated property, see below). However, if the corporation does not distribute any part of the boot, gain is recognized on the exchange, but only to the extent of the undistributed boot. (Code Sec. 361(b))[3]

Gain or loss isn't recognized on the distribution of *qualified property* received under the plan of reorganization. Qualified property is stock (or the right to acquire stock) in the distributing corporation, and stock or obligations of another party to the reorganization

---

44. ¶F-4502; ¶3684.13
45. ¶F-4001, F-4022; ¶s 3544.01, 3544.03
46. ¶F-4001.1, F-4001.2; ¶s 3544.01, 3544.03
47. ¶F-4012; ¶F-4012.1; ¶3544.06
48. ¶s F-2701, F-3205; ¶3544.02

49. ¶F-4017; ¶3564.02
50. ¶F-4018
1. ¶F-4017; ¶3564.02
2. ¶F-4100 *et seq.*; ¶3614.01
3. ¶F-4106 *et seq.*; ¶3614.01

that are received in the reorganization exchange. Gain (but not loss) is recognized on the distribution of property that isn't qualified property. (Code Sec. 361(c))[4]

For acquirer's basis in property received in the exchange, see ¶2483. For target's basis, see ¶2485.

¶ 3542   Boot.

Boot is money or the fair market value (FMV) of property other than stock or securities of a party to the reorganization (¶3528) that's received by the target in exchange for its property, or by target shareholders in exchange for their stock, under the plan of reorganization.[5] Nonqualified preferred stock received for stock other than nonqualified preferred stock is boot unless received in a recapitalization of a family-owned corporation. (Code Sec. 356(e))[6] Nonqualified preferred stock is generally preferred stock that the issuer is required to redeem, or is more likely than not to redeem, or preferred stock with a dividend rate that varies with changes in interest rates or similar indices. (Code Sec. 351(g)(2))[7] For the effect of liabilities on characterization of property as boot, see ¶3543.

Securities in corporations not parties to the reorganization are always boot and gain is taxable to the extent of the securities' FMV. In the case of securities in corporations that are parties to the reorganization, only the excess face amount of securities received over the face amount of securities surrendered is boot. If no securities are surrendered, the FMV of any securities received is boot. (Code Sec. 354(a)(2), Code Sec. 356(d)) A stock right treated as a security having no principal amount (¶3540) isn't boot whether or not securities are surrendered in the exchange. (Reg § 1.356-3(b))[8]

¶ 3543   Assumption and transfer of liabilities.

Where a party to a reorganization (¶3528) exchanges property for stock or securities in a corporation and the corporation assumes the transferor's liabilities, the assumed liabilities are not treated as boot (¶3542) for the purpose of *recognizing* gain. (Code Sec. 357(a))[9] However, if the principal purpose for the assumption of the liabilities is tax avoidance, or is something other than a bona fide business purpose, *all the liabilities assumed* are treated as cash (i.e., boot) in both computing *and* recognizing gain. (Code Sec. 357(b))[10]

If, in the case of a Type D reorganization (¶3533) in which stock or securities of the transferee corporation are distributed in a qualifying tax-free separation under Code Sec. 355 (¶3545), the sum of the liabilities assumed exceeds the total adjusted basis of the property transferred, the excess is taxed as a gain from the sale or exchange of property (capital gain or ordinary income, depending on the character of the property in the hands of the transferor). (Code Sec. 357(c))[11]

For what constitutes assumption of a liability, see ¶3506.

¶ 3544   Deductibility of reorganization costs.

Generally, expenses incurred in connection with a corporate reorganization, including borrowing costs, are capital expenditures (¶1637) and not deductible business expenses. If a proposed reorganization is abandoned, the costs are deductible in the year of abandonment.[12]

IRS has provided a safe harbor allowing taxpayers to allocate 70% of the success-based

---

4. ¶F-4108 *et seq.*; ¶3614.03
5. ¶F-4017; ¶3564.01
6. ¶F-4001.1; ¶F-4001.2; ¶3564.01
7. ¶F-1531; ¶3514.13
8. ¶F-4021 *et seq.*; ¶3564.01

9. ¶F-4201; ¶3574.01
10. ¶F-4202; ¶3574.02
11. ¶F-4203; ¶3574.03
12. ¶L-5401, ¶L-5416; ¶2484

fees (¶1633) paid in business acquisitions or reorganizations to activities that don't facilitate the transaction and deduct such fees currently. The remaining 30% is treated as going to activities that facilitate the transaction and must be capitalized. However, an acquired taxpayer that elects to treat a stock sale as an asset sale under Code Sec. 338(h)(10) (¶3567) can't elect the safe harbor. [13]

¶ 3545 Spin-Offs, Split-Offs and Split-Ups.

If certain requirements are met (¶3546), a corporate division may be accomplished on a tax-free basis in the form of a (1) *spin-off*, i.e., a pro rata distribution of a controlled corporation's stock to the distributing corporation's shareholders without requiring the shareholders to surrender any of their distributing corporation stock; (2) *split-off*, i.e., a pro rata or non pro rata distribution of a controlled corporation's stock to one or more of the distributing corporation's shareholders in exchange for stock held in the distributing corporation; or (3) *split-up*, i.e., a transfer of all the businesses of a distributing corporation to controlled corporations followed by a distribution of the stock of the controlled corporations to the distributing corporation's shareholders and the liquidation of the distributing corporation. The distribution of controlled corporation stock to the distributing corporation's shareholders can be pro rata or non pro rata. [14]

For how boot is taxed to shareholders in a spin-off, split-off, or split-up, see ¶3547.

For how the distributing corporation is taxed, see ¶3548.

¶ 3546 Requirements for a tax-free spin-off, split-off or split-up.

The following requirements for nonrecognition apply to spin-offs, split-offs, or split-ups.

(1) The distributing corporation (P) must distribute to its shareholders "with respect to" their stock, or to its security holders in exchange for their securities, solely stock or securities in a corporation (S) that it "controls" (¶3539) immediately before the distribution. (Code Sec. 355(a)(1)) Nonqualified preferred stock (¶3542) received in exchange for stock other than nonqualified preferred stock is not treated as stock or securities for this purpose. (Code Sec. 355(a)(3)(D))[15]

(2) The transaction must not be used principally as a device for distributing earnings and profits (E&P) of either P or S. (Code Sec. 355(a)(1)(B)) The regs identify "device factors" (the presence of which are evidence of a device) and nondevice factors, and certain distributions that aren't ordinarily considered to have been used principally as a device even though device factors are present. (Reg § 1.355-2(d))[16]

(3) One or more of P's pre-distribution shareholders must end up with an amount of stock that establishes a continuity of interest (¶3528) in both P and S, though not necessarily proportionately (see (6), below). (Reg § 1.355-2(c)(1))[17]

(4) Both P and S (or each controlled subsidiary) must be engaged in the active conduct of a trade or business immediately after the distribution. (Code Sec. 355(b)(1)(A), Code Sec. 355(b)(2)(A)) For this purpose, all members of the corporation's separate affiliated group are treated as one corporation. (Code Sec. 355(b)(3)(A))[18] The trades or businesses must have been actively conducted throughout the 5-year period ending on the date S's stock is distributed. (Code Sec. 355(b)(2)(B))[19]

(5) The active trade or business (see 4 above) must not have been acquired during the 5-year period ending on the date S's stock is distributed in a transaction in which gain or

---

13. ¶L-5762.1A; ¶2634.80
14. ¶F-4600 *et seq.*; ¶3554.01
15. ¶F-4607 *et seq.*; ¶3554.01
16. ¶F-4701 *et seq.*; ¶3554.011

17. ¶F-4613; ¶3554.03
18. ¶F-4800 *et seq.*; ¶3554.02
19. ¶F-4818; ¶3554.02

loss was recognized in whole or in part. (Code Sec. 355(b)(2)(C))[20]

(6) A distribution doesn't qualify as a tax-free Code Sec. 355 division if immediately after the transaction (including any series of related transactions) (1) either the distributing or controlled corporation is a disqualified investment corporation, and (2) any person that did not hold 50% or more by vote or value in the disqualified investment corporation immediately before the transaction holds a 50% or greater interest (voting or value). (Code Sec. 355(g))[21]

(7) A distribution generally won't qualify as a tax-free Code Sec. 355 division if either the distributing or controlled corporation (but not both) is a real estate investment trust (REIT; ¶4202). (Code Sec. 355(h))[22]

(8) P must distribute either all its stock or securities in S, or at least an amount of S stock that's treated as "control" (¶3539). The distributions don't have to be pro rata or under a plan of reorganization. However, if P retains *any* stock or securities in S, tax avoidance must not be a principal purpose for the retention. (Code Sec. 355(a)(1)(D), Code Sec. 355(a)(2))[23]

In addition, one or more corporate business purposes must support the transaction for nonrecognition treatment to apply. (Reg § 1.355-2(b)) IRS established guidelines for whether a corporate business purpose exists. [24]

If a parent corporation (P) transfers property (including property that is an active trade or business) to its subsidiary (D), and if, under the same plan, D distributes the stock of its controlled subsidiary (C) to P (a "north-south" transaction) whether the transaction is treated for federal income tax purposes as a Code Sec. 351 tax-free exchange followed by a Code Sec. 355 tax-free distribution depends on whether the transactions are treated as separate (tax-free) or integrated (taxable). [25]

Gain may be recognized when a distribution of stock (or stock and securities) of a controlled corporation is part of the same plan that includes a planned 50% acquisition of a predecessor or successor of the distributing or controlled corporation. (Reg § 1.355-8T)[26]

¶ 3547 Boot taxed to shareholders in Sec. 355 transactions.

The receipt of boot in an otherwise tax-free spin-off, split-off or split-up (¶3546) may trigger shareholder tax. Boot includes cash and the fair market value of:

... Any property (including stock warrants, short-term notes, etc.) *except* (and subject to the limitations below) stock or securities (other than nonqualified preferred stock (¶3542) (Code Sec. 356(e)) in the spun-off corporation (S) (Code Sec. 356(a));

... Any excess in the face amount of securities of S received over the face amount of securities in distributing corporation (P) which are surrendered. (Code Sec. 355(a)(3)(A), Code Sec. 356(d)(2)(C)) Stock rights are treated as securities having no principal amounts. (Reg § 1.355-1(c))

... Stock in S that P acquired in a partially or wholly taxable transaction during the five-year period preceding the distribution. (Code Sec. 355(a)(3)(B))[27]

Boot received in a spin-off (where no stock or securities of P are surrendered) is treated like a Code Sec. 301 dividend (¶1284). (Code Sec. 356(b))[28]

Boot received in a split-off or split-up (where stock or securities of P are surrendered) is taxable to the recipient to the extent gain is recognized, but not in excess of the value of

20. ¶F-4822 *et seq.*; ¶3554.02
21. ¶F-5401 *et seq.*; ¶3554.035
22. ¶F-5451; ¶3554.075
23. ¶F-4602 *et seq.*; ¶3554.01
24. ¶F-4900 *et seq.*; ¶3554.03

25. ¶F-4608.1
26. ¶F-5333 *et seq.*; ¶3554.069 *et seq.*
27. ¶F-5003 *et seq.*; ¶3554.04, 3564.02
28. ¶F-5002; ¶3564.02

the boot received. (Code Sec. 356(a)(1)) If, however, the exchange "has the effect of the distribution of a dividend," it is treated as a dividend to the extent of the taxpayer's ratable share of accumulated earnings and profits. The remainder, if any, of the recognized gain is generally treated as capital gain. (Code Sec. 356(a)(2))[29] In determining whether boot has the effect of a dividend, the transaction is treated as though the shareholder had retained the P stock which he actually surrendered in exchange for S stock, and had received the boot in exchange for an amount of P stock with a value equal to the amount of the boot; the redemption rules (¶3515 *et seq.*) are then applied to determine whether the boot is treated as a dividend. [30] No loss is recognized, whether or not boot is received. (Code Sec. 355(a), Code Sec. 356(c))[31]

For shareholders' basis in property received, see ¶2487.

¶ 3548   How distributing corporation is taxed.

Except as stated below, no gain or loss is recognized by a distributing corporation (P) on distributions to which the tax-free corporate separation rules of Code Sec. 355 apply (Code Sec. 355(c)(1), Code Sec. 361).

(1) Gain is recognized by P on the distribution of appreciated property other than qualified property (i.e., stock and securities of S) in the same manner as if the property were sold for its fair market value (FMV). The FMV of distributed property is considered to be not less than the amount of any liability to which the property is subject or which is assumed by a shareholder in connection with the distribution. (Code Sec. 355(c)(2))[32]

(2) If the distribution is *disqualified* (as defined below), stock and securities of S are not treated as qualified property, and P recognizes gain on their distribution in the same manner as gain is recognized in (1), above. (Code Sec. 355(d)(1) *et seq.*)[33]

(3) If, following the distribution, there is an acquisition of an interest greater than or equal to 50% in either S or P under a plan or in a series of transactions, P generally must recognize gain as if it had sold the stock or securities of S to the distributee for FMV immediately before the distribution. (Code Sec. 355(e)) Regs discuss factors for and against a finding of a plan or a series of related transactions. (Reg § 1.355-7)[34]

Except as provided in regs, tax-free division treatment isn't available for distributions from one affiliated group member to another in a plan under which any person acquires (directly or indirectly) an interest greater than or equal to 50% in either P or S, determined after application of Code Sec. 355(e). (Code Sec. 355(f))[35]

A distribution is disqualified (unless it doesn't violate the purpose of Code Sec. 355(d) (Reg § 1.355-6(b)(3)(i))) if (1) immediately after the distribution, any shareholder (or any two or more shareholders acting under a plan) holds (actually or constructively) at least 50% of the stock of P or S, and (2) that stock was purchased (or acquired) within the immediately preceding 5-year period, or was received as a distribution on P stock purchased (or acquired) during that period. (Code Sec. 355(d))[36]

¶ 3549   Carryovers of Tax Items. ▬▬▬▬▬▬

A corporation that acquires the assets of another corporation in certain tax-free reorganizations or liquidations also succeeds to and takes into account numerous tax items (¶3550) of the transferor (predecessor) corporation.

A predecessor's tax items are carried over to the successor corporation in a:

---

29. ¶F-5002; ¶3564.02
30. ¶F-4026; ¶3564.02
31. ¶F-4018; ¶3564.02
32. ¶F-5101 *et seq.*

33. ¶F-5201 *et seq.*; ¶s 3554.01, 3554.04
34. ¶F-5301; ¶3554.05
35. ¶F-4630 *et seq.*; ¶3554.07
36. ¶F-5202 *et seq.*; ¶3554.04

. . . Type A (¶3530), C (¶3532) or F (¶3535) reorganization;

. . . Type D (¶3533) or G (¶3536) reorganization, but only if the transferor transfers substantially all its assets to the acquiring corporation and then (in effect) completely liquidates; or

. . . Complete liquidation of an 80% subsidiary (¶3560). (Code Sec. 381(a))[37]

The carryover rules do not generally apply to divisive reorganizations, but items may be carried over under general principles of corporate succession. (Reg §   1.381(a)-1(b)(3))[38]

¶ 3550   Tax items that are carried over.

When the Code's carryover provisions apply, the acquiring corporation succeeds to and takes into account the following tax items of the transferor (Code Sec. 381(c)): accounting method; amortization of bond discount or premium; capital loss carryovers; charitable contributions carryover; depreciation allowance and method; earnings and profits (E&P); employee benefit plan contributions; general business credit; installment method; inventory method; involuntary conversions; minimum tax credit; mining development and exploration expenses; net operating loss carryovers; percentage depletion on extraction of ores or minerals from waste or residue of earlier mining; personal holding company (PHC) deficiency dividend; PHC dividend carryover; real estate investment trust (REIT) or regulated investment company (RIC) deficiency dividend; tax benefit items; and items under Subchapter U (Code Sec. 1391 *et seq.*) dealing with enterprise zones, as regs provide. [39]

Tax items to which an acquiring corporation succeeds, including the basis of property acquired, must reflect reductions for cancellation of debt. (Reg §   1.108-7(c))[40]

¶ 3551   Tax Avoidance Acquisition Bar to Tax Benefits. ■■■■■■■■■■■

Under Code Sec. 269, any deduction, credit or other allowance may be disallowed where, for the principal purpose of tax avoidance:

. . . Any person or persons acquire, directly or indirectly, stock having at least 50% of the total combined voting power of all classes of a corporation's voting stock, or at least 50% of the total value of all classes of its stock; or

. . . Any corporation acquires, directly or indirectly, property of another corporation not controlled, directly or indirectly, by the acquirer (or its shareholders) immediately before the acquisition, if the acquirer takes a carryover basis in the property. (Code Sec. 269(a))[41]

IRS may also disallow a deduction, credit, or other allowance where a target that a corporation acquired in a qualified stock purchase (¶3565) *without* making a Code Sec. 338 election (¶3564) is liquidated primarily for tax avoidance or evasion, under a plan of liquidation adopted within two years after the acquisition date. (Code Sec.   269(b))[42]

¶ 3552   Limits on Use of Built-in Gains of One Corporation to Offset Losses of Another. ■■■■■■■■■■■

If a corporation acquires directly (or through one or more other corporations) control (as defined at ¶3340) of another corporation, or acquires the assets of another corporation in a Type A, C, or D reorganization, and either corporation is a gain corporation, then any income of either corporation attributable to recognized built-in gain within a 5-year period beginning on the date of the ownership change (¶3556) can't be offset by any pre-acquisition loss of the other corporation.

---

37. ¶F-7000 *et seq.*; ¶3814 *et seq.*
38. ¶F-7005; ¶F-7013; ¶3814.01
39. ¶F-7012, F-7098, F-7099; ¶3814.02

40. ¶J-7404.2; ¶1084.02
41. ¶F-7900 *et seq.*; ¶2694
42. ¶F-7912; ¶2694

(Code Sec. 384(a); Code Sec. 384(c)(5))[43] Similar rules limit the use of any excess credit or net capital loss. (Code Sec. 384(d))[44]

The above offset prohibition doesn't apply to any pre-acquisition loss of any corporation if that corporation and the gain corporation were members of the same controlled group at all times during the 5-year period ending on the acquisition date (or shorter period of either corporation's existence). (Code Sec. 384(b))[45]

¶ 3553 The Code Sec. 382 Limitation on Loss Carryovers After Ownership Change. ∎

If an ownership change (¶3556) occurs with respect to a "loss corporation," that corporation's taxable income for any post-change year can be offset by pre-change losses and credits (¶3555) only to the extent of a certain percentage of the value of the corporation at the time of the change.

Thus, a loss corporation that is entitled to use a net operating loss (NOL) carryover in, or that has an NOL for, the tax year in which an ownership change (¶3556) occurs, may offset taxable income for any tax year ending after the ownership change by pre-change loss carryforwards only to the extent of the "Section 382 limitation" for that year (Code Sec. 382(a); Code Sec. 382(k)(1)).[46] The "Section 382 limitation" is equal to the value of the loss corporation immediately before the ownership change multiplied by the long-term tax-exempt rate (¶3554). (Code Sec. 382(b)(1))[47] Except in the case of redemptions or other corporate contractions, and some capital contributions, that value is the value of its stock immediately before the ownership change. (Code Sec. 382(e)(1), Code Sec. 382(e)(2), Code Sec. 382(l)(1)(A), Code Sec. 382(l)(4))[48]

If a loss corporation has net unrealized built-in gain on assets held immediately before the change date in excess of a defined amount, the Section 382 limitation may be increased by recognized built-in gains on an asset within the 5-tax year recognition period (beginning on the date of the ownership change), but only to the extent of the excess of the asset's fair market value over its adjusted basis on that date. Pre-paid income is not treated as built-in gain. The limitation may also be increased by certain recognized Code Sec. 338 gains. (Code Sec. 382(h)(1), Code Sec. 382(h)(6)) The disallowed part of a recognized built-in loss can be carried forward like an NOL subject to the Section 382 limitation in later years as if it were a pre-change NOL. IRS guidance describes two alternative safe harbors to determine built-in income and deduction items after an ownership change. [49]

The Section 382 limitation doesn't apply to the loss corporation's taxable income for the part of the change year before the ownership change occurs. (Code Sec. 382(b)(3))[50] Nor does it apply if the loss corporation is under the jurisdiction of a court in a bankruptcy, receivership, foreclosure, or similar proceeding (unless it elects not to have this exception apply). (Code Sec. 382(l)(5); Reg § 1.382-9(i))[1] Special rules apply for consolidated (Reg § 1.1502-90 to Reg § 1.1502-96,Reg § 1.1502-98 to Reg § 1.1502-99),[2] and controlled (Reg § 1.382-8) groups,[3] and for successive ownership changes. (Reg § 1.382-5(d))[4]

¶ 3554 Long-term tax-exempt rate.

The long-term tax-exempt rate is the highest of the adjusted federal long-term rates for any month in the three-calendar month period ending with the month in which the ownership change occurs. (Code Sec. 382(f))[5] The long-term tax-exempt rate for ownership

---

43. ¶s F-7851, F-7852; ¶3844
44. ¶F-7851 *et seq.*; ¶3844.04
45. ¶F-7860 *et seq.*; ¶3844.01
46. ¶F-7201; ¶F-7203¶3824.01
47. ¶F-7251; ¶3824.12
48. ¶F-7301 *et seq.*; ¶3824.12
49. ¶F-7340 *et seq.*; ¶3824.25

50. ¶F-7255 *et seq.*; ¶3824.12
1. ¶F-7700 *et seq.*; ¶3824.26
2. ¶E-9061 *et seq.*; ¶15,024.04
3. ¶F-7035 *et seq.*; ¶3824.24
4. ¶F-7257; ¶3824.12
5. ¶F-7336; ¶3824.12

changes in:

   . . . Nov. 2018 is 2.43%.

   . . . Oct. 2018 is 2.29%.

   . . . Sept. 2018 is 2.32%.

   . . . Aug. 2018 is 2.32%.

   . . . July 2018 is 2.32%.

   . . . June 2018 is 2.31%.

   . . . May 2018 is 2.30%.

   . . . Apr. 2018 is 2.30%.

   . . . Mar. 2018 is 2.18%.

   . . . Feb. 2018 is 1.97%.

   . . . Jan. 2018 is 1.96%.

   . . . Dec. 2017 is 1.96%. [6]

¶ 3555   Pre-change losses and credits subject to Section 382 limitation.

The Section 382 limitation applies to (1) any net operating losses (NOLs) of the old loss corporation that are carried forward to the tax year ending with the ownership change or in which the change date occurs; (2) any NOL of the old loss corporation for the tax year in which the ownership change occurs to the extent the loss is allocable to the period in that year on or before the change date; (3) any recognized built-in loss in a recognition period tax year (¶3553); (4) any pre-change capital loss described in (1) −(3); and (5) any pre-change credits (below). (Reg § 1.383-1(c)(2); Code Sec. 382(d)(1); Reg § 1.382-2(a)(2))[7] Pre-change credits are excess foreign taxes under Code Sec. 904(c), unused Code Sec. 38 business credits, and the available Code Sec. 53 minimum tax credit, to the extent attributable to periods ending on or before the change date. (Reg § 1.383-1(c)(3))[8]

For the order in which pre-change losses and credits are absorbed, see ¶3557.

¶ 3556   Ownership change defined.

There is an ownership change if, immediately after any owner shift involving a 5% shareholder or an equity structure shift, the stock of the loss corporation owned by one or more 5% shareholders has increased by more the 50 percentage points over these shareholders' lowest percent ownership at any time during a three-year testing period. (Code Sec. 382(g)(1))[9] A 5% shareholder is any person holding 5% or more by value of the stock of the corporation at any time during the testing period. (Code Sec. 382(k)(7)) The percent of stock owned is determined on the basis of value, and nonvoting preferred stock is generally not taken into account. (Code Sec. 382(k)(6))[10] Certain nonstock interests may be treated as stock. (Reg § 1.382-2T(f)(18)(iii))[11] Special aggregation rules apply to treat groups of shareholders as single shareholders. (Reg § 1.382-2T(j))[12]

¶ 3557   Order of loss absorption for Section 382 limitation.

A loss corporation must absorb its Section 382 limitation in the following order for each post-change year: (1) pre-change losses that are built-in capital losses recognized during that year, (2) pre-change losses that are capital loss carryovers, (3) pre-change losses that are built-in ordinary losses recognized during that year, (4) pre-change losses that are net

---

6. ¶F-7336; ¶3824.12

7. ¶F-7363; ¶F-7386; ¶s 3824, 3824.01, 3824.25; ¶3834.01

8. ¶F-7408; ¶3834.01

9. ¶F-7441; ¶3824.02

10. ¶F-7505 *et seq.*; ¶s 3824.01, 3824.10

11. ¶F-7603; ¶3824.10

12. ¶F-7510 *et seq.*; ¶3824.15

operating loss carryovers, (5) pre-change credits for excess foreign taxes carried forward under Code Sec. 904(c), (6) pre-change credits that are unused general business credits carried over under Code Sec. 39, and (7) pre-change credits that are unused minimum tax credits under Code Sec. 53. (Reg § 1.383-1(d)(2))[13]

The losses absorb the Section 382 limitation on a dollar-for-dollar basis, but the credits must be converted to a "deduction equivalent" for this purpose. (Reg § 1.383-1(e)(2))[14]

¶ 3558　Corporate Liquidations. ▖▖▖▖▖▖▖▖▖▖▖▖▖▖▖▖▖▖▖▖▖▖▖▖▖▖▖▖▖▖▖▖▖▖▖▖

A liquidating corporation recognizes taxable gain or loss on distributions of property as if the property had been sold to the distributee for its fair market value (FMV). (Code Sec. 336(a)) If the distributed property is subject to a liability, or if any shareholder assumes a liability of the liquidating corporation in connection with the distribution, the property's FMV is treated as not less than the amount of the liability. (Code Sec. 336(b))[15] The liquidating corporation's shareholders generally recognize capital gain or loss on the receipt of the distributions (¶3559).

Exceptions apply for gain or loss on liquidating distributions made (i) by an 80%-owned subsidiary to its parent (¶3560), and (ii) in connection with tax-free reorganizations (¶3541). (Code Sec. 336(c))[16]

For the taxation of asset transfers to an exempt entity or a change to exempt entity status, see ¶3562. For the deductibility of costs of corporate dissolution and liquidation, see ¶3563.

¶ 3559　Shareholder's tax on liquidating distributions.

Amounts received by a shareholder in a distribution in complete liquidation of a corporation are treated as payment in exchange for the stock (i.e., capital gain or loss). (Code Sec. 331(a))[17] Gain or loss is the total amount distributed minus the shareholder's basis in his stock. (Reg § 1.331-1(b)) The amount of the distribution is the sum of the cash plus the fair market value of any other property (reduced by any liability assumed) received by the shareholder in exchange for his stock. (Code Sec. 1001(b))[18]

A shareholder who receives a series of distributions in complete liquidation of a corporation reports gain only after the cost or other basis of all of his stock has been recovered. [19]

For basis of property received in the distribution, see ¶2489.

¶ 3560　Liquidation of 80% subsidiaries.

When a parent corporation completely liquidates its 80%-owned subsidiary, the *parent* (as shareholder) doesn't recognize gain or loss on the liquidating distributions (Code Sec. 332(a)), whether *cash* or other property is distributed, if: (i) the parent owns at least 80% of the subsidiary stock by vote and value on the date the plan of liquidation is adopted and until the final liquidating distribution is received (Code Sec. 332(b)(1)); (ii) the distributions are made under a plan of *complete* liquidation, and in complete redemption of all of the subsidiary's stock (Code Sec. 332(b)(2), Code Sec. 332(b)(3)); and (iii) the distributions are made within one tax year of the subsidiary, or within three years from the close of the tax year during which the first of the series of distributions under the plan of liquidation is made. (Code Sec. 332(b); Reg § 1.332-4(a))[20] However, any gain or loss realized by the parent on the satisfaction of the subsidiary's debt to the parent is recognized to the parent

13. ¶F-7360, F-7405; ¶3834.01
14. ¶F-7361 *et seq.*, ¶F-7404; ¶3834.01
15. ¶F-14401 *et seq.*; ¶3364.01
16. ¶F-4112, ¶F-14401 *et seq.*; ¶3364.01, ¶3614

17. ¶F-13101; ¶3314.01
18. ¶F-13108; ¶3314.01
19. ¶F-13112; ¶3314.01
20. ¶F-13200 *et seq.*; ¶3324 *et seq.*

at the time of the liquidation.(Reg § 1.332-7)[21]

If the 80% subsidiary liquidation qualifies for nonrecognition treatment, the parent takes a carryover basis in the distributed assets. (Code Sec. 334(b)(1))[22]

Where a distribution from a regulated investment company (RIC) or a real estate investment trust (REIT) qualifies as a distribution in complete liquidation of the RIC or REIT under Code Sec. 332(b), the corporation receiving the distribution is required to include in income as a dividend from the RIC or REIT an amount equal to the dividends-paid deduction allowable to the RIC or REIT by reason of the distribution. (Code Sec. 332(c))[23]

Minority shareholders of a subsidiary must generally recognize gain or loss under the regular liquidation rules (¶3559). (Reg § 1.332-5)[24]

¶ 3561   How 80% subsidiary is taxed on liquidating distributions.

A sub doesn't recognize any gain or loss on liquidating distributions to its 80% distributee-parent, but it does recognize gain (not loss) on distributions to minority shareholders. (Code Sec. 336(d)(3), Code Sec. 337(a))[25]

However, if property of a C corporation becomes the property of a regulated investment company (RIC) or real estate investment trust (REIT) by the qualification of that C corporation as a RIC or REIT or by the transfer of assets of that C corporation to a RIC or REIT, then the RIC or REIT will be subject to tax on the net built-in gain on the sale of that property within the five-year recognition period provided for S corporations under Code Sec. 1374 (¶3362). (Reg § 1.337(d)-7(b)) This rule does not apply if the C corporation makes a "deemed sale election" to recognize gain and loss as if it sold the converted property to an unrelated party at its fair market value. (Reg § 1.337(d)-7(c)(1)) Temp regs provide the deemed sale election is treated as made on certain transactions that occur within 10 years of a Code Sec. 355 distribution (¶3546). (Reg § 1.337(d)-7T(c)(6))

✔️*observation:* Treasury is considering revising Reg § 1.337(d)-7T to limit gain recognition to the assets of the smaller corporation on deemed sales resulting from reorganizations that occur within 10 years of a Code Sec. 355 spinoff. However, as of the date the print version of the 2019 Federal Tax Handbook went to press, no action had been taken, and whether and when any such action may occur is uncertain.

The regs contain exceptions to the above rules for the following:

... Gain otherwise recognized. (Reg § 1.337(d)-7(d)(1))

... Reelection of RIC or REIT status. (Reg § 1.337(d)-7(d)(2))

... Like-kind exchanges and involuntary conversions. (Reg § 1.337(d)-7(d)(3))[26]

¶ 3562   Taxation of asset transfers to exempt entity or change to exempt entity status.

With some exceptions, a corporation recognizes gain or loss on the transfer of its assets to a tax-exempt entity and on a change of its status to tax-exempt. (Reg § 1.337(d)-4)[27]

¶ 3563   Deductibility of costs of corporate dissolution and liquidation.

Filing fees, attorney's and accountant's fees and other expenditures, including payments for tax advice, incurred in connection with the complete liquidation and dissolution

---

21. ¶F-13216 *et seq.*
22. ¶F-13227 *et seq.*; ¶3344.01
23. ¶F-13209.1; ¶3324.02
24. ¶F-13223; ¶3324.01

25. ¶F-14504; ¶3374.01
26. ¶E-6851 *et seq.*; ¶3374.03
27. ¶F-14609 *et seq.*; ¶3374.03

of a corporation are generally deductible in full by the dissolved corporation. [28]

¶ 3564   Code Sec. 338 Election to Treat a Stock Purchase as an Asset Purchase. ■■■

A corporate acquirer that makes a qualified stock purchase (¶3565) of the stock of another corporation (target) may be able to get a stepped-up basis for the target's assets by making a Code Sec. 338 election to treat the stock purchase as an asset purchase.

If a Code Sec. 338 election is made, the target is treated (for tax purposes only) as two corporations: an old target and a new target. The old target is treated as if it sold its assets as of the close of the acquisition date for their fair market value (FMV) in a single transaction (Code Sec. 338(a)),[29] and the new target is treated as though it had purchased all of the assets of the old target as of the beginning of the day after the acquisition date (Code Sec. 338(a)(2)) for an amount equal to the sum of: the grossed-up basis of the acquiring corporation's recently purchased stock, the basis of the acquiring corporation's nonrecently purchased stock, the target's liabilities, and other relevant items. This sum (as adjusted) is the target's "adjusted grossed-up basis" for the assets. (Code Sec. 338(b)(1), Code Sec. 338(b)(2); Reg § 1.338-4(a), Reg § 1.338-5(b)(1))[30]

The acquirer may step up its basis in the target's assets by making a "gain recognition election" with respect to its nonrecently purchased stock. (Code Sec. 338(b)(3); Reg § 1.338-5(d)(3))[31] Regs specify how basis is allocated among the target's assets. (Code Sec. 338(b)(5); Reg § 1.338-6)[32]

observation: Because a Code Sec. 338 election requires the target to recognize gain from the "sale" of its assets and the seller to recognize gain on the sale of the stock, it can best be used where the target has losses to offset gains, owns predominantly depreciated property, or will benefit from stepped-up basis through deductions for depreciation or amortization.

The acquirer must make the Code Sec. 338 election on Form 8023 on or before the 15th day of the 9th month beginning after the month of the acquisition. (Code Sec. 338(g)(1))[33] Once made, the election is irrevocable. (Code Sec. 338(g)(3))[34]

For the consistency requirement, see ¶3566. For an election where target is a member of a consolidated group, see ¶3567. For the Code Sec. 338(h)(10) and Code Sec. 336(e) elections to treat stock sales as asset transfers, see ¶3567.

¶ 3565   "Qualified stock purchase" (QSP) requirement.

The Code Sec. 338 election may be made only if the acquiring corporation makes a QSP of the target (Code Sec. 338(a)), i.e., the acquiring corporation purchases, in one or more transactions during a 12-month acquisition period, the target's stock, and the shares so purchased have at least 80% of the target's total combined voting power and at least 80% of the value of all the target's stock. (Code Sec. 338(d)(3))[35]

¶ 3566   Consistency as to purchases from target or target affiliate.

Consistency rules prevent acquiring corporations from receiving a basis step-up in only selected assets where (1) a corporation acquires both target stock and target assets, (2) a Code Sec. 338 election is not made, and (3) the asset acquisition resulted in a stepped-up basis of target stock (or receipt of a dividend eligible for the 100% dividends received

---

28. ¶L-5500 *et seq.*; ¶2484
29. ¶F-8201, F-8202; ¶3384.05
30. ¶F-8501 *et seq.*; ¶3384.09
31. ¶F-8511; ¶3384.09

32. ¶F-8601 *et seq.*; ¶3384.10
33. ¶F-8701 *et seq.*; ¶3384.01
34. ¶F-8706; ¶3384.01
35. ¶F-8101; ¶3384

deduction) to the seller. The stock consistency rule applies to all qualified stock purchases of members of an affiliated group during the consistency period (generally, the period beginning one year before the 12-month acquisition period and ending one year after the acquisition date). The asset consistency rule applies where the purchasing corporation acquires assets of the target or a target affiliate at any time during the consistency period, unless the acquisition is pursuant to a sale in the ordinary course of the seller's business or if certain other conditions apply. (Code Sec. 338(e), Code Sec. 338(f); Code Sec. 338(h)(4)(A)), (Reg § 1.338-8)[36]

¶ 3567 Code Sec. 338(h)(10) and Code. Sec. 336(e) elections to treat stock acquisitions as asset transfers.

observation: Although Code Sec. 338(h)(10) elections and Code Sec. 336(e) elections both treat stock acquisitions as asset acquisitions resulting in a single level of tax, the requirements of the elections differ. A transaction can be structured to qualify for either election, but not both.

In the case of a qualified stock purchase (¶3565) of the stock of a member of a selling consolidated group, or stock sold by a selling affiliate or S corporation shareholders, the acquiring corporation and the sellers can jointly elect to have the sellers recognize (and report) gain or loss as though the target sold all of its assets in a single taxable transaction. (Code Sec. 338(h)(10); Reg § 1.338(h)(10)-1(c))[37]

A Code Sec. 338(h)(10) election results in the following tax consequences:

. . . No gain or loss will be recognized by the sellers on the actual sale of target stock in a qualified stock purchase.

. . . The target is treated as if, at the close of the acquisition date but after the deemed sale, it had distributed all of its assets in complete liquidation under Code Sec. 331 (¶3559), or under the 80% subsidiary liquidation rules (¶3560).

. . . If the acquirer owns nonrecently purchased target stock, it is deemed to have made a "gain recognition election" with respect to that stock.

. . . The acquirer's adjusted gross-up basis in the target is determined under the rules described at ¶3564, with adjustments. (Reg § 1.338(h)(10)-1(d))[38]

A Code Sec. 336(e) election provides for essentially similar asset sale treatment in the case of qualified stock dispositions by selling corporations or S corporation shareholders. (Reg § 1.336-1, Reg § 1.336-2)[39]

¶ 3568 Transfers to Foreign Corporations—Code Sec. 367 Transfers. ▮▮▮▮▮

Transfers of property to foreign corporations (outbound transfers) that would otherwise be tax-free under the transfer to controlled corporation (¶3500), reorganization (¶3528), or liquidation (¶3558) rules are treated as transfers to non-corporate transferees in determining the extent that gain is recognized on the transfer, unless one of the following exceptions applies: (Code Sec. 367(a)(1), Code Sec. 367(c)).[40]

observation: The following rules apply to transfers of foreign corporations after Dec. 31, 2017. Different rules applied for pre-Jan. 1, 2018 transfers.

. . . *Certain transfers of foreign corporation stock or securities.* The transfer of foreign corporation stock or securities by a U.S. person to another foreign corporation is not

---

36. ¶F-8901 *et seq.*; ¶3384.11
37. ¶F-8800 *et seq.*; ¶3384.075
38. ¶F-8800 *et seq.*; ¶s 3384.075, 3384.09

39. ¶F-14450 *et seq.*; ¶3364.02
40. ¶F-6000 *et seq.*; ¶3674 *et seq.*

taxable under Code Sec. 367(a) if (i) the U.S. person owns less than 5% of the vote and value of the transferee stock immediately after the transfer, or (ii) the U.S. person enters into a gain recognition agreement ("GRA," see below) with respect to the transferred stock or securities. (Code Sec. 367(a)(2); Reg § 1.367(a)-3(b)(1))[41] The transfer of foreign corporation stock as part of a Type E recapitalization qualifies for nonrecognition. (Reg § 1.367(a)-3(a)(2)(i))[42]

. . . *Certain transfers of U.S. corporation stock or securities.* The transfer of U.S. stock or securities to a foreign corporation is not taxable under Code Sec. 367(a) if (i) U.S. transferors receive 50% or less of the vote and value of the transferee stock in the transaction; (ii) U.S. persons who are officers or directors of the U.S. target or 5% transferee shareholders do not own more than 50% of the transferee stock; (iii) either the U.S. transferor is not a 5% transferee shareholder, or, if the U.S. transferor is a 5% transferee shareholder, it enters into a GRA; and (iv) the transferee has been actively engaged in business for at least three years. (Reg § 1.367(a)-3(c))[43]

The above exceptions for transfers of foreign stock do not generally apply to Code Sec. 361(a) and Code Sec. 361(b) outbound transfers incident to a reorganization. (Code Sec. 367(a)(5))[44] However, regs contain an elective exception under which, if five or fewer domestic corporations are in Code Sec. 368(c) control (¶3539) of the transferor corporation and subject to basis adjustment regs, the exceptions may apply to *asset* reorganizations under Code Sec. 361(a) or Code Sec. 361(b). (Reg § 1.367(a)-7)[45]

Transfers of foreign loss branches. If a domestic corporation transfers substantially all of the assets of a foreign branch (within the meaning of Code Sec. 367(a)(3)(C) in effect before Dec. 22, 2017) to a specified 10% owned foreign corporation with respect to which it is a U.S. shareholder (¶3315) after the transfer, the domestic corporation includes in gross income for the tax year which includes the transfer an amount equal to the transferred loss amount (as defined in Code Sec. 91(b)) for the transfer. (Code Sec. 91(a)) The transferred loss amount is reduced (but not below zero) by the amount of gain recognized by the taxpayer on account of the transfer (other than amounts recognized due to the recapture of overall foreign loss (¶2367)). (Code Sec. 91(c)) Under a transition rule, the amount of gain taken into account under Code Sec. 91(c) must be reduced by the amount of gain which would be recognized under Code Sec. 367(a)(3)(C) (as in effect before Dec. 22, 2017) with respect to losses incurred before Jan. 1, 2018. [46]

Qualification under some exceptions may require a GRA under which the U.S. transferor generally agrees to include in income any gain not recognized on the original transfer of stock or securities to the foreign corporation if the foreign transferee disposes of the stock or securities within five years. Some nonrecognition transactions, however, are not triggering events when certain requirements are satisfied. (Reg § 1.367(a)-8) The amount of gain recognized under a GRA when a disposition or other event requires recognition under more than one GRA is determined under an ordering rule. (Reg § 1.367(a)-8(c)(1)(ii))[47]

Outbound distributions of subsidiary stock under Code Sec. 355 are generally treated as exchanges and result in recognition of gain (but not loss) unless the distribution is made to a qualified U.S. person, i.e., a domestic corporation or a U.S. citizen or resident. (Code Sec. 367(e)(1); Reg § 1.367(e)-1)[48] Outbound parent-subsidiary liquidation distributions generally result in recognition of both gain and loss to the liquidating subsidiary. (Code Sec. 367(e)(2); Reg § 1.367(e)-2)[49]

The taxable transfer treatment under Code Sec. 367(a) doesn't apply for Code Sec. 351 or

---

41. ¶F-6202 *et seq.*; ¶3674.02
42. ¶F-6201; ¶3674.02
43. ¶F-6209 *et seq.*; ¶3674.02
44. ¶F-6207; ¶3674.02
45. ¶F-6239 *et seq.*; ¶3674.02

46. ¶F-6128.1
47. ¶F-6300 *et seq.*; ¶3674.02
48. ¶F-6801; ¶3674.05
49. ¶F-6901 *et seq.*; ¶3374.01

Code Sec. 361 transfers of intangibles to foreign corporations. Instead, the transferor is treated as receiving deemed payments over the life of the intangible and a lump sum payment if there is a disposition of the property. For this purpose, intangible property includes goodwill (foreign and domestic), going concern value, and workforce in place (including its composition and terms and conditions (contractual or otherwise) of its employment). (Code Sec. 367(d))[50])

---

50. ¶F-6005; ¶F-6504; ¶3674.03

Chapter 17   Partnerships

¶ 3700   **Partnership defined—Form 8832.** ▪▪▪▪▪▪▪▪▪▪▪▪

A "partnership" includes a syndicate, group, pool, joint venture or other unincorporated organization through, or by means of which, any business, financial operation or venture is carried on if it isn't, within the meaning of the Code, a corporation, trust or estate. (Code Sec. 761(a))[1] For tax purposes, a partnership is a business entity with two or more members that has elected, or defaulted to (below), partnership classification under the "check-the-box" entity classification regs. (Reg § 301.7701-2(c))[2]

Under default provisions, unless a domestic eligible entity elects otherwise, it's a partnership if it has two or more members. (Reg § 301.7701-3(b)(1)(i))[3] In general, an eligible entity that wishes to elect a classification other than its default classification, or that wishes to change its classification, does so by filing Form 8832. (Reg § 301.7701-3(c)(1)(i))[4] A partnership that changes to an association is deemed to contribute all of its assets and liabilities to the association in exchange for stock in it. Then, the partnership is deemed to liquidate by distributing the stock to its partners. (Reg § 301.7701-3(g)(1)(i))[5] An eligible entity classified as a partnership becomes disregarded as an entity separate from its owner when the entity's membership is reduced to one member. (Reg § 301.7701-3(f)(2))[6]

For tax years of a partnership, see ¶2812.

For partnership tax returns (including Schedule K-1 (Form 1065)), see ¶4731.

¶ 3701   **Electing large partnerships, Before 2018—Form 1065-B.**

For tax years beginning before 2018, simplified flow-through reporting (Form 1065-B) applied for an electing large partnership, i.e., a partnership with at least 100 partners in the prior tax year that elected simplified reporting under former Code Sec. 771 through former Code Sec. 777. (former Code Sec. 775(a)(1))[7] These rules differed from the regular rules for partnerships (¶3713 *et seq*) in that, for example, fewer partnership items passed through to partners (former Code Sec. 772)[8] and limitations on deductions and credits generally were applied at the partnership level. (Code Sec. 773)[9]

¶ 3702   **Limited liability companies (LLCs)—Form 8832.**

LLCs are a creation of state law. LLCs are owned (and in some cases managed) by members who aren't personally liable for the LLC's debts or obligations. [10]

Under the "check-the-box" entity classification rules (¶3700), if an LLC isn't mandatorily classified as a corporation, it's an "eligible entity" that may elect (on Form 8832) to be classified for tax purposes either as a partnership or as a corporation (Reg § 301.7701-2(c)), except that a single-member LLC that doesn't elect to be a corporation is treated as a disregarded entity and its activities are treated in the same manner as a sole proprietorship, branch or division. (Reg § 301.7701-2(a), Reg § 301.7701-2(c)(2)(i))[11]

📌*observation:* Pass-through of tax attributes and limited liability are also available to S corporations, but S corporations are subject to many restrictions (see ¶3350 *et seq.*)

---

1. ¶B-1000 *et seq.*; ¶7614.01, 7614.03
2. ¶D-1151; ¶77,014.15
3. ¶D-1152; ¶77,014.15
4. ¶D-1158; ¶77,014.15
5. ¶D-1170; ¶77,014.155
6. ¶D-1171; ¶77,014.165

7. ¶B-4401 *et seq.*; ¶7754
8. ¶B-4402 *et seq.*; ¶7724
9. ¶B-4410 *et seq.*; ¶7734
10. ¶D-1150 *et seq.*
11. ¶D-1167; ¶77,014.15

References beginning with a single letter are to paragraphs in Federal Tax Coordinator 2d and RIA's Analysis of Federal Taxes: Income. Those beginning with numbers are to paragraphs in United States Tax Reporter.

that don't apply to LLCs.

¶ 3703   Family partnerships.

If capital isn't a material income-producing factor, a family member is recognized as a partner only if he contributes substantial services. [12]

If capital is a material income-producing factor in the enterprise, a valid family partnership may be created by gift of a capital interest. (Code Sec. 761(b))[13]

The donee-partner's distributive share of partnership income is included in his gross income, provided that: (1) it must be determined after allowance of reasonable compensation for services rendered to the partnership by the donor, and (2) the donee's share attributable to donated capital must not be proportionately greater than the donor's share attributable to his capital. (Code Sec. 704(e)(1))[14]

A capital interest purchased from a partner by the partner's spouse, ancestor, lineal descendant, or any trust for the primary benefit of such persons is considered to be a gift of the partnership interest by the seller to the buyer. (Code Sec. 704(e)(2))[15]

A donee or purchaser of a capital interest in a family partnership isn't recognized as a partner unless the transfer to him is bona fide. (Reg § 1.704-1(e)(1)(iii))[16]

A minor child generally won't be recognized as a partner unless either: (1) the child is shown to be competent (despite legal disability under state law) to manage his or her own property, or (2) control of the child's interest is exercised by a fiduciary for the child's sole benefit, subject to any required judicial supervision. (Reg § 1.704-1(e)(2)(viii))[17]

¶ 3704   Election to be excluded from partnership rules.

Certain unincorporated organizations can elect to be excluded from the partnership rules, i.e., exempt from Subchapter K of the Code (or only some of those provisions under a partial exclusion election). The election is available only if the income of each separate member of the partnership can be adequately determined without computation of partnership taxable income. (Code Sec. 761(a); Reg § 1.761-2(a)(1))[18] The election is available for:

... "Investing partnerships" whose members own property as co-owners, reserve the right separately to dispose of their share of property, and aren't engaged in the active conduct of a business; (Reg § 1.761-2(a)(2))[19]

... "Operating agreement groups" under which a number of co-owners engage in the joint production, extraction or use of property, but not for the purpose of selling services or property produced or extracted; and (Reg § 1.761-2(a)(3))[20]

... Syndications formed for a short period by dealers in securities to underwrite, sell or distribute an issue of securities. (Code Sec. 761(a)(3))[21]

¶ 3705   Partnerships vs. other forms of doing business.

Partnerships are "pass-through entities" — that is, their income is subject to tax only once, at the partner level. They share this characteristic with S corporations, but not C corporations (whose income is taxed twice, once at the corporate and again at the shareholder levels). Partnerships offer several advantages over S corporations, including: no limitations on the identity or number of partners; greater flexibility in allocating the

12. ¶B-3422; ¶7044.12
13. ¶B-3402; ¶7044.12
14. ¶B-3423; ¶7044.13
15. ¶B-3403; ¶7044.15
16. ¶B-3408; ¶7044.15
17. ¶B-3416; ¶7044.14
18. ¶B-1200 *et seq.*; ¶7614.02
19. ¶B-1204; ¶7614.02
20. ¶B-1205; ¶7614.02
21. ¶B-1210; ¶7614.02

enterprise's profits, losses and credits (by means of special allocations, see ¶3720 *et seq.*); and a partner's basis in his partnership interest includes the partner's share of partnership liabilities (see ¶3753 *et seq.*).

¶ 3706 Organization and syndication fees.

No deduction is allowed to a partnership or to any partner for any amounts paid or incurred to organize a partnership or to promote the sale of, or to sell, an interest in that partnership, except as described below. (Code Sec. 709(a))[22]

If it so elects, a partnership may deduct, for the tax year in which it begins business, an amount equal to the lesser of: (1) the amount of organizational expenses with respect to the partnership, or (2) $5,000, reduced (but not below zero) by the amount by which such organizational expenses exceed $50,000. The remainder of such organizational expenses may be deducted ratably over the 180-month period beginning with the month the partnership begins business. If the partnership liquidates before the end of the 180-month period, any unamortized organization expenses may be deducted then. (Code Sec. 709(b)(2))

Syndication expenses aren't amortizable and must be capitalized. They are expenses connected with the marketing of interests in the partnership. (Reg § 1.709-2(b)) Syndication expenses can't be deducted as a loss when the partnership is liquidated (Reg § 1.709-1(b)(3)) or the syndication effort is abandoned. [23]

For an election to deduct start-up costs, see ¶1500.

¶ 3707 Partnership anti-abuse rules.

If a partnership is formed or used in connection with a transaction with a principal purpose of substantially reducing the present value of the partners' total tax liability in a manner that is inconsistent with the intent of subchapter K, IRS may recast the transaction as appropriate to achieve a tax result that is consistent with the intent of subchapter K.[24] These anti-abuse rules apply only with respect to federal income taxes. (Reg § 1.701-2(h))[25]

IRS also may treat a partnership as an aggregate of its partners, in whole or in part (except as described below), as appropriate in order to carry out the purpose of any provision of the Code or regs. (Reg § 1.701-2(e)(1)) But IRS may not treat a partnership as an aggregate to the extent that:

(1) a Code or reg provision prescribes the treatment of a partnership (in whole or in part) as an entity; and

(2) that treatment and the ultimate tax results, taking into account all the relevant facts and circumstances, are clearly contemplated by that provision. (Reg § 1.701-2(e)(2))[26]

¶ 3708 Treatment of Contributions to a Partnership. ▬▬▬

In general, no gain or loss is recognized when a partner makes contributions to a partnership's capital, whether made on formation of the partnership or later. (Code Sec. 721; Reg § 1.721-1)

However, this rule doesn't apply where: a partner acts in his individual capacity (vs. as a partner) in a transaction with the partnership (¶3724); a partner contributes property to a partnership and the partnership assumes a liability of the partner, with the resulting

---

22. ¶B-1301; ¶7094
23. ¶B-1306; ¶7094.04
24. ¶B-1251; ¶7014
25. ¶B-1250 *et seq.*; ¶7014
26. ¶B-1255; ¶7014

decrease in the partner's liabilities being treated as a distribution of money to the contributing partner (¶3738); disguised sales;[27] or in the situations listed at ¶3709 *et seq.*[28] Also, IRS has regulatory authority (1) to provide for gain recognition in cases where the gain would otherwise be transferred to foreign partners (Code Sec. 721(c)) and (2) to treat intangibles transferred to a foreign partnership as sold. (Code Sec. 721(d)) Tax-free contributions to a partnership will not trigger depreciation recapture. (Code Sec. 1245(b)(3), Code Sec. 1245(b)(6), Code Sec. 1250(d)(3)),[29] Similarly, an investment credit isn't recaptured as long as the transfer is a mere change in the form of conducting the business of the contributing partner. (Reg § 1.47-3(f)(6), Ex (5))[30]

For gain or loss on the distribution of contributed built-in gain or loss property, see ¶3746.

¶ 3709   Partnership Investment Companies.

Gain, but not loss, is recognized where a transfer of appreciated stocks, securities or other property is made to a partnership that would be treated as an investment company under Code Sec. 351 were the partnership a corporation. (Code Sec. 721(b)) The partnership is treated as an investment company if, after the exchange, over 80% of the value of its assets (excluding cash and nonconvertible debt) is held for investment and consists of readily marketable stocks or securities (or interests in real estate investment trusts or regulated investment companies). This exception doesn't apply where the transaction doesn't result in a diversification of the transferor's investment. [31]

¶ 3710   Contribution of services.

Where a taxpayer receives a capital interest in a partnership in exchange for services, that interest is taxable compensation income to him. When the income must be recognized depends on the facts and circumstances, including whether there are any restrictions on the taxpayer's right to withdraw from the partnership or otherwise dispose of the partnership interest. (Reg § 1.721-1(b)(1))[32]

Where a taxpayer receives a profits interest in a partnership (even if substantially unvested) in exchange for services, IRS won't treat the transaction as giving rise to compensation income, unless: (1) the profits interest relates to a substantially certain and predictable stream of income from partnership assets; (2) the partner disposes of the profits interest within two years; or (3) the profits interest is a limited partnership interest in a publicly traded partnership. Cases hold that no income is includible where the profit interest has only speculative value. [33]

¶ 3711   Partnership's basis in property contributed to it.

Property received by a partnership from a contributing partner takes the same basis in the partnership's hands as it had in the contributing partner's hands at the time of the contribution (increased by any gain recognized if the partnership is an "investment company partnership," see ¶3709). (Code Sec. 723; Reg § 1.723-1)[34]

¶ 3712   Partnership's holding period for contributed property.

A partnership's holding period for property contributed to it includes the contributing partner's holding period. (Code Sec. 1223(2); Reg § 1.723-1)[35]

27. ¶B-2100 *et seq.*; ¶7074.02
28. ¶B-1401; ¶7214
29. ¶s I-10311, I-10503; ¶7214.01
30. ¶L-17418; ¶474.03
31. ¶B-1410

32. ¶B-1407 *et seq.*; ¶7214.01
33. ¶B-1408; ¶7214.01
34. ¶B-1418; ¶7234.01
35. ¶B-1419; ¶7234.01

¶ **3713**   **Partnership Income and Deductions.** ▬▬▬▬▬

A partnership is essentially a conduit that passes through to each partner his or her share of income and deductions generated by the partnership.

Thus, the partners, not the partnership, are taxed on the partnership's income. (Code Sec. 701) The partnership only files an information return (Form 1065, see ¶4731) showing each partner's distributive share of the partnership income, deductions, gains, losses, etc. Each partner includes his share of these items on his own return. (Code Sec. 702)[36]

Partnership taxable income is computed the same as an individual's, except that certain items are separately stated (see ¶3714) and the following deductions aren't allowed: standard deduction (Code Sec. 63(c)(6)(D)); personal exemptions; charitable contributions; nonbusiness expenses, medical expenses, alimony, retirement savings under Code Sec. 219, and taxes and interest paid to cooperative housing corporations; capital loss carryovers; net operating loss deduction; taxes paid to a foreign country or U.S. possession that can be taken as a credit or as a deduction (income and similar taxes); and oil and gas well depletion. (Code Sec. 703(a)(2); Reg § 1.703-1(a)(2))[37]

¶ **3714**   **"Separately stated" items of income and deductions.**

Partnerships are required to "state separately" —that is, to compute as separate items—certain classes of income and deductions. These are then directly "passed through" to the partnership's partners, who take them into account for tax purposes by including their distributive share of each of the classes as separate items on their tax returns (Code Sec. 702(a))

Key items that must be separately stated include: charitable contributions; certain dividends; foreign and U.S. possession taxes eligible for the foreign tax credit; income, gains and losses from the sale or exchange of unrealized receivables and substantially appreciated inventory; items that are specially allocated under the partnership agreement (¶3720 *et seq.*); long- and short-term capital gains and losses; nonbusiness production of income expenses; recoveries of tax benefit items; and Code Sec. 1231 gains and losses.

Partnerships must also separately state —and partners must separately take into account their distributive share of—any partnership item, if separately stating that item would result in a tax liability for any partner different from that partner's tax liability if the item weren't separately stated. (Reg § 1.702-1(a)(8))[38]

For a discussion of the separately stated items relating to the qualified business income deduction for tax years beginning after 2017 and before 2026, see ¶1595 *et seq.*

¶ **3715**   **Items not required to be separately stated.**

After determining which of its items of income, gains, losses, deductions and credits must be separately stated, a partnership computes its taxable income or loss based on items that don't have to be separately stated. The partnership's partners, in computing their income tax liabilities, take into account their distributive shares of the partnership's nonseparately stated income or loss, as well as their distributive shares of each separately stated item. (Code Sec. 702(a)(8); Reg § 1.702-1(a)(9))[39]

---

36. ¶B-1900 *et seq.*; ¶7014
37. ¶B-1901; ¶7034.01

38. ¶B-1903; ¶7024.01
39. ¶B-1904; ¶7024.01

¶ 3716   Character of partnership income.

Each item passed through to the partners and separately stated on their returns has the same character as if realized or incurred directly by the partnership. (Code Sec. 702(b); Reg § 1.702-1(b))[40]

¶ 3717   Consistent treatment on partner's and partnership's return—Form 8082.

A partner must, on his own return, treat a partnership item in a manner that's consistent with the treatment of that item on the partnership's return. (Code Sec. 6222(a)) A partner that treats a partnership item differently must notify IRS of the inconsistency on Form 8082. (Code Sec. 6222(b))[41]

For tax years beginning before Jan. 1, 2018, the above consistency rule didn't apply to certain small partnerships that weren't covered by the unified audit and review procedures for partnerships (¶4840). (Former Code Sec. 6231(a)(1)(B))[42]

¶ 3718   When partnership income is reported by the partners.

Each partner reports his distributive share of the partnership income, deductions and other items (including guaranteed salary and interest payments) for a partnership tax year on his individual return for his tax year with or within which ends the partnership tax year (discussed at ¶2812). (Code Sec. 706(a); Reg § 1.706-1(a))[43]

If two partnership years end within the partner's year, the income for both years is included in that year even though partnership income for a period of more than twelve months is then included in the partner's income. [44]

¶ 3719   Elections.

Elections affecting partnership taxable income must be made by the partnership except for certain elections involving discharge of indebtedness, foreign tax credits, mining exploration costs, and the election by nonresident alien individuals and foreign corporations regarding income from U.S. real property, which are made at the partner level. [45]

¶ 3720   Partnership Allocations. ▆▆▆▆▆▆▆▆▆▆

A partnership's allocations (the partners' distributive shares) of partnership income, gains, losses, deductions and credits are normally determined by the partnership agreement. (Code Sec. 704(a))

If the partnership agreement does make allocations of partnership items, these will be respected for tax purposes if:

. . . they have substantial economic effect, see ¶3721; or

. . . they are in accord with the partners' interests in the partnership; or

. . . they are treated as being in accord with the partners' interests in the partnership. (Code Sec. 704(b); Reg § 1.704-1(b)(1))[46]

If, however, the partnership agreement fails to make such allocations, they must be determined in accord with the partners' interests in the partnership. (Code Sec. 704(b)(1))

---

40. ¶B-1905; ¶7024.02
41. ¶B-1801; ¶62,214
42. ¶T-2104; ¶62,214.10
43. ¶B-1701; ¶7064

44. ¶B-1701
45. ¶B-1907; ¶7034.02
46. ¶B-2401; ¶7044

Retroactive allocations —that is, allocations that give particular partners shares of partnership items of income, expense, etc., that were paid or accrued before these partners joined the partnership —aren't permitted. (Code Sec. 706(d)(1))[47]

Special allocation rules apply for certain items that cannot have economic effect, such as: certain tax preferences relating to pre-MACRS depreciation; [48] income, gains, losses, etc., with respect to property whose book value differs from its adjusted basis; [49] tax credits and credit recapture amounts; [50] creditable foreign taxes and amounts relating to foreign tax credits;[1] "excess percentage depletion;" [2] the basis of partnership oil and gas properties; [3] recapture income under Code Sec. 1245 and Code Sec. 1250;[4] and allocations attributable to the partnership's nonrecourse debt.[5] Special safe harbors apply to allocations of the Code Sec. 45 wind energy production credit and the Code Sec. 47 rehabilitation credit. [6]

Subject to exceptions (Reg § 1.706-4(b)), partnership allocations must take into account the varying interests of the partners during the year. (Code Sec. 706(d)(1)) In general, if there is a change in any partner's interest in the partnership during the year, the partnership determines each partner's distributive share of partnership income, gain, loss, deduction or credit for such tax year by using the "interim closing method" or the "proration method," under which a partnership allocates its items among the partners in accordance with either their partnership interests during each segment of the tax year or their pro rata shares of the items for the entire tax year, respectively. (Reg § 1.706-4(d)) A partnership may use different methods for different ownership changes in the same year provided that the overall combination of methods is reasonable. [7] Certain "extraordinary items" are allocated using special rules, as are "allocable cash basis items" under Code Sec. 706(d)(2)(B).[8]

¶ 3721 Determining whether an allocation has substantial economic effect.

An allocation of partnership income, gain, loss, deduction or credit among partners has substantial economic effect if it passes a two-part test applied as of the end of the partnership year to which the allocation relates.

First, the allocation must have economic effect. (Reg § 1.704-1(h)(2)(i)) This means that it must be consistent with the underlying economic arrangement of the partners. An allocation will be treated as having economic effect only if, throughout the full term of the partnership, the partnership agreement states:

(1) the partners' capital accounts are to be determined and maintained according to the capital account maintenance rules set forth in the regs (see ¶3722);

(2) when the partnership liquidates, or a partner's interest is liquidated, liquidating distributions are to be made according to the partners' positive capital account balances; and

(3) a partner with a deficit balance in his capital account after the liquidation of his partnership interest is unconditionally obligated to restore the amount of the deficit to the partnership. (Reg § 1.704-1(b)(2)(ii))[9]

Second, the economic effect of the allocation must be substantial. (Reg § 1.704-1(b)(2)(i)) The economic effect of an allocation is substantial if there's a reasonable possibility that it

---

47. ¶B-3201; ¶7064.02
48. ¶B-2901
49. ¶B-2902; ¶7044.07
50. ¶B-2903; ¶7044.07
1. ¶B-2903.1 *et seq.*; ¶7044.07
2. ¶B-2904; ¶7044.07
3. ¶B-2905; ¶7044.07

4. ¶B-2906 *et seq.*; ¶7044.07
5. ¶B-3001; ¶7044.08
6. ¶B-2903A; ¶B-2903B; ¶7044.07
7. ¶B-3201; ¶7064.02
8. ¶B-3204 *et seq.*; ¶7064.02
9. ¶B-2503 *et seq.*; ¶7044.03

will affect substantially the dollar amounts to be received by the partners from the partnership, independent of the tax consequences. (Reg § 1.704-1(b)(2)(iii))[10]

> **observation:** Generally speaking, the economic effect test is designed to ensure that partnership allocations of income and gain ultimately correspond to real distributions of money and property, and that allocations of deductions, losses and credits ultimately correspond to the partners' actual liabilities for partnership expenses and losses. The substantiality test is designed to ensure that the economic effects of an allocation don't arise principally from the tax character of the allocated item —for example, from the fact that an income item is tax-exempt or foreign-sourced, or that a loss is from the sale of partnership property used in its trade or business.

Determining whether the economic effect of an allocation is substantial where partners are look-through entities (e.g., partnerships, S corps, trusts or estates) or members of a consolidated group is done by taking into account the tax consequences that result from the interaction of an allocation with the tax attributes of any person that is an owner (or for a trust or estate, the beneficiary) of an interest in the partner. (Reg § 1.704-1(b)(2)(iii)(d)(1))[11]

¶ 3722   Partner capital account maintenance rules.

For partner capital accounts to be determined and maintained properly for purposes of the economic effect rules (see ¶3721), each partner's account must be increased by cash contributed by the partner (including cash treated as contributed when the partner assumes partnership liabilities), and by the fair market value of property contributed by the partner (net of liabilities secured by the property). The account must also be increased by the partner's allocable share of partnership income and gain, including tax-exempt income, book income (not tax income) for property whose book value differs from basis, and unrealized income with respect to accounts receivable and certain other accrued but unpaid items.

Each account must be decreased by cash distributed to the partner (including cash treated as distributed when the partnership assumes partner liabilities), and by the fair market value of property distributed to the partner (net of liabilities secured by the property). The account must also be decreased by the partner's allocable share of partnership expenditures that are neither deductible nor capitalizable, and partnership loss and deduction, including book (not tax) loss for property whose book value differs from basis, and unrealized deductions for accounts payable and certain other accrued but unpaid items.

Capital account adjustments may also be required when partnership property is revalued or distributed, and on the transfer of a partnership interest. For example, partnership property may be revalued (and capital accounts adjusted) if property is contributed by, or distributed to, a partner in exchange for a partnership interest. Revaluation is also allowed where a partnership interest is granted as payment for services or when a noncompensatory option to acquire a partnership interest is issued.

An adjustment may also be required if an optional basis adjustment election is in effect (see ¶3767) and property is distributed or an interest is transferred. (Reg § 1.704-1(b)(2)(iv))[12]

---

10. ¶B-2700 *et seq.*; ¶7044.02
11. ¶B-2702; ¶7044.05

12. ¶B-2600 *et seq.*; ¶7044.04

¶ 3723   Partner's Dealings with Partnership. ▮▮▮▮▮▮▮

Partners may deal with their partnerships in other than their capacity as partners (¶3724). "Guaranteed payments" to partners are generally treated as made to nonpartners (¶3725). Certain sales between partners and their partnerships establish the character of any gain, and require the deferral of loss (¶3726 *et seq.*).

¶ 3724   "Separate entity" transactions between partner and partnership.

If a partner provides services for or transfers property to his partnership, he may be treated as dealing with the partnership either as a member or as an outsider. If there's a related allocation and distribution of partnership income (direct or indirect), and the transaction on the whole is properly characterized as a sale or exchange between a partnership and an outsider, it will be treated that way for tax purposes. (Code Sec. 707(a)(2)(A), Code Sec. 707(a)(2)(B))[13] Contribution and distribution transactions that occur within two years of one another are generally presumed to be a sale of property unless the facts and circumstances clearly establish otherwise. (Reg § 1.707-3(c)(1))

¶ 3725   Guaranteed payments.

Guaranteed payments are payments to a partner for services or capital *without regard to partnership income.*[14] Guaranteed payments for a partner's services or capital are treated like salary payments to employees or interest payments to creditors, not like partnership distributions. (Code Sec. 707(c); Reg § 1.707-1(c))[15]

For a guaranteed payment to be deductible as a business expense by the partnership, it must qualify as a business expense as if the payment had been made to a person who wasn't a partner. In determining whether a partnership may deduct or must capitalize a guaranteed payment, the regular capital expenditure rules apply. (Code Sec. 707(c))[16]

When a partnership makes a guaranteed payment using property other than cash, it is treated as a sale or exchange of that property by the partnership on which gain is recognized, and not a partnership distribution treated as discussed at ¶3737.[17]

¶ 3726   Losses on sales and exchanges with controlled partnership.

No deduction is allowed for losses from sales or exchanges between:

. . . a partnership and a person owning, directly or indirectly, over 50% of the capital interest, or profits interest, in the partnership; or

. . . two partnerships in which the same persons own over 50% of the capital or profits interests.

For constructive ownership rules, see ¶3728.

If property on which a loss was disallowed under the above rule is later sold by the transferee at a gain, the gain is taxable only to the extent it exceeds the loss previously disallowed. (Code Sec. 707(b)(1); Reg § 1.707-1(b)(1))[18]

¶ 3727   Gain on sale or exchange with controlled partnership.

The character of the property in the hands of the transferee, immediately after the transfer, determines the character of a *gain to the transferor* on a direct or indirect sale or

---

13. ¶B-2000 *et seq.*; ¶7074.01
14. ¶B-2005; ¶7074.04
15. ¶B-2006 *et seq.*; ¶7074.04

16. ¶B-2009; ¶7074.04
17. ¶B-2006
18. ¶B-2016; ¶7074.03

exchange of property between:

. . . a partnership and a person owning, directly or indirectly, over 50% of the capital interest, or profits interest, in the partnership; or

. . . two partnerships in which the same persons own, directly or indirectly, more than 50% of the capital interest or profits interest in each. (Code Sec. 707(b)(2); Reg § 1.707-1(b)(2))[19]

For constructive ownership rules, see ¶3728.

Thus, if the property is a noncapital asset in the hands of the transferee, the transferor will have ordinary income on the sale. (Code Sec. 707(b)(2); Reg § 1.707-1(b)(2))[20]

¶ 3728   Constructive ownership of partnership interests.

In determining the percentage of ownership of partnership interests for purposes of ¶3726 and ¶3727, the constructive ownership rules for stock under Code Sec. 267(c) (¶2448) apply (substituting "capital or profits interest" for "stock"), except that a partner isn't considered as owning the interest of his partners (unless they are relatives, etc.). (Code Sec. 707(b)(3))[21]

¶ 3729   Limitations on a Partner's Deductible Loss. ▬▬▬▬▬▬▬▬

A partner's deduction for partnership losses may not exceed the adjusted basis of his interest in the partnership (¶3732 *et seq.*) at the end of the partnership's loss year. (Code Sec. 704(d)) However, partners (although not partnerships) are allowed loss carrybacks and carryovers.

Where a partnership has more than one class of losses (e.g., capital losses, Code Sec. 1231 losses, and operating losses) in the same year and a partner's total share of those losses exceeds the adjusted basis of his partnership interest, the limitation is allocated proportionately to each type of loss. (Reg § 1.704-1(d))

Excess losses disallowed to a partner in any year are carried over, and are deductible by him at the end of the partnership year in which the adjusted basis of the partner's interest at the end of the year exceeds zero (before reduction by that year's loss). (Reg § 1.704-1(d)(4))[22]

For limits on a partner's loss under the at-risk rules, see ¶1791 *et seq.*, and under the passive activity rules, see ¶1799 *et seq.*

¶ 3730   Basis adjustments made before applying loss limitations.

In determining whether a partner's deductible share of partnership loss exceeds (and is thus limited by) his basis in his partnership interest (¶3729), the basis adjustments described at ¶3734 are made first. (Reg § 1.704-1(d)(2))[23]

¶ 3731   Loss carrybacks and carryovers.

A carryover or carryback of net operating losses isn't allowed to a partnership, but a partner may carry back or carry over his share of the partnership's net business loss for any year to the extent it can't be used by that partner in the year it's passed through to him. (Code Sec. 702)[24]

---

19. ¶B-2017; ¶7074.03
20. ¶B-2017; ¶7074.03
21. ¶B-2018; ¶7074.03

22. ¶B-3500 *et seq.*; ¶7044.10
23. ¶B-3501 *et seq.*; ¶7044.10
24. ¶B-3508; ¶7024.01

¶ 3732   Basis of Partnership Interest. ▬▬▬▬▬▬▬▬

A partner's basis for his interest in a partnership ("outside basis") depends on how he or she acquired it. It may be the amount of cash contributed to the partnership, the adjusted basis of the property contributed, or the amount paid to purchase it.

For the initial basis of partnership interest, see ¶3733. For adjustments to basis, see ¶3734. For alternative adjusted basis computation, see ¶3735.

¶ 3733   Initial basis of partnership interest.

A partner's interest acquired by a tax-free contribution of money or property to the partnership has a basis equal to the amount of money plus the partner's adjusted basis in the property when contributed. (Code Sec. 722)[25] If the contributed property is subject to indebtedness or if liabilities of the partner are assumed by the partnership, the basis of the contributing partner's interest is reduced by the portion of the indebtedness assumed by the other partners. (Reg § 1.722-1)[26]

A partner's capital interest acquired for services has a basis equal to the value of the capital interest acquired. (Reg § 1.722-1; Reg § 1.721-1(b))[27]

A partner's interest acquired by purchase or inheritance has a basis determined under the general basis rules (¶2462 *et seq.*). (Code Sec. 742; Reg § 1.742-1)[28]

A partner may have a divided holding period in his partnership interest, see ¶2656. (Reg § 1.1223-3)[29]

¶ 3734   Adjustments to basis of partner's interest.

The basis of a partner's interest is increased by: further contributions (but not by his own personal note given to the partnership);[30] the cost of additional interests purchased or inherited (¶3733) (Code Sec. 742); any increase in his share of partnership liabilities (since the increase is treated as a contribution of money to the partnership, see ¶3753);[31] his distributive share of partnership income, including tax-exempt income and any excess of net long-term capital gains over losses (Code Sec. 705(a)(1)); and his distributive share of the excess of percentage depletion deductions over the basis of the depletable property. (Code Sec. 705(a)(1))[32]

The basis of a partner's interest is reduced (but not below zero) by: the adjusted basis allocable to any part of his interest sold or otherwise transferred;[33] the amount of money and the adjusted basis of partnership property distributed to him in nonliquidating distributions (Code Sec. 705(a)(2), Code Sec. 733);[34] any decrease in his share of partnership liabilities (since the decrease is treated as a distribution of money by the partnership, see ¶3753); his distributive share of partnership losses (including capital losses) *and* nondeductible expenditures not chargeable to capital account (Code Sec. 705(a); Reg § 1.705-1(a)) (for the partner's distributive share of losses in excess of his adjusted basis, see ¶3729); and his percentage depletion deduction for partnership oil and gas property to the extent the deduction doesn't exceed his allocated proportionate share of the property's basis. (Code Sec. 705(a)(3));[35] In determining the amount of the partner's loss, the partner's distributive shares under Code Sec. 702(a) of partnership charitable contributions

25. ¶B-1502; ¶7224.01
26. ¶B-1506; ¶7224.01
27. ¶B-1502; ¶7224.02
28. ¶B-1501; ¶7424.01
29. ¶I-8934.1; ¶12,234.29
30. ¶B-1504; ¶7054.01

31. ¶B-1506; ¶7524
32. ¶B-1507; ¶7054.01
33. ¶B-3805
34. ¶B-1505; ¶7334.01
35. ¶B-1507; ¶7054.02

and taxes paid or accrued to foreign countries or U.S. possessions are taken into account. (Code Sec. 704(d)(3)(A)) However, in the case of a charitable contribution of property with a fair market value that exceeds its adjusted basis, the partner's distributive share of the excess is not taken into account. (Code Sec. 704(d)(3)(B)) For tax years beginning before Jan. 1, 2018, charitable deductions were not subject to the basis limitation. [36]

Regs prevent the acceleration or duplication of losses through a partnership's assumption of obligations that are not treated as resulting in a deemed cash contribution or distribution by or to the partner under the rules discussed at ¶3753 *et seq.* These obligations are called "Reg § 1.752-7 liabilities." Where such a liability is assumed by a partnership from a partner in a property contribution by a partner to a partnership in exchange for a partnership interest (a Code Sec. 721(a) contribution), the liability is treated as having a built-in loss (see ¶3746) equal to the amount of the liability as of the date of the partnership's assumption of the liability. (Reg § 1.752-7; Reg § 1.704-3)[37]

Regs prevent inappropriate increases or decreases in the basis of a corporate partner's interest in a partnership resulting from the partnership's disposition of the corporate partner's stock. (Reg § 1.705-2)[38]

¶ 3735   Alternative adjusted basis computation.

The adjusted basis of a partner's interest may be determined under a "short-cut" method by reference to what would be his proportionate share of the adjusted basis of the partnership property upon a termination of the partnership (Code Sec. 705(b)) where: (1) it isn't practicable to use the regular rule, or (2) IRS is satisfied the result under the alternative method won't vary substantially from that under the regular rule. (Reg § 1.705-1(b))[39]

¶ 3736   Distributions to a Partner. ▰▰▰▰▰▰▰▰▰▰▰▰▰▰▰

A partnership generally doesn't recognize gain or loss on a distribution to a partner (¶3737), but the partner often will recognize gain or loss (¶3738).

¶ 3737   Partnership's gain or loss on distribution.

No gain or loss is recognized to a partnership on a current or liquidating distribution to a partner of money or other property, except where a disproportionate distribution is treated as a sale by the partnership, see ¶3749. (Code Sec. 731(b))[40]

¶ 3738   Partner's gain or loss on receipt of distribution.

Gain or loss isn't recognized to a partner on receipt of a current or liquidating distribution from a partnership, except as follows:

. . . Gain is recognized to the extent that *money* (defined to include marketable securities, see ¶3739) distributed exceeds the adjusted basis of the partner's interest in the partnership immediately before the distribution. (Code Sec. 731(a))[41] This is treated as a gain from sale or exchange of the partner's interest. (Reg § 1.731-1(a)(3))[42] A reduction in a partner's liabilities (due either to the partnership's assumption of them or a reduction in the partner's share of partnership liabilities) is treated as a money distribution. (Code Sec. 752(b))[43]

. . . Loss is recognized to the extent the adjusted basis of the partner's interest exceeds the sum of any money, and the basis to the distributee of any unrealized receivables and

---

36. ¶B-3506
37. ¶B-1506.1; ¶7524.04
38. ¶B-1504.1; ¶7054.03
39. ¶B-1514; ¶7054.04

40. ¶B-3601; ¶7314.01
41. ¶B-3602; ¶7314.01
42. ¶B-3602; ¶7314.01
43. ¶B-3608; ¶7524.01

inventories received if the distribution is in liquidation of the partner's interest in the partnership *and* no other property is distributed. This is treated as a loss from sale or exchange of the partner's interest in the partnership. (Code Sec. 731(a))[44]

If gain or loss is recognized under one of the above rules, the partnership may elect to, or may have to, adjust the basis of its assets, as explained at ¶3767 *et seq.*

The above rules on recognition of a partner's gains and losses don't apply to (Code Sec. 731(c); Reg § 1.731-1(c)):[45]

. . . disproportionate distributions treated as sales or exchanges of property, see ¶3749;

. . . liquidation payments made to a retiring partner or to a deceased partner's successor in interest treated as a share of income or as guaranteed payments, see ¶3761;

. . . recognition of precontribution gain under Code Sec. 737, see ¶3746.

¶ 3739 Distribution of marketable securities treated as cash.

Subject to exceptions, a distribution of marketable securities (stock and other equity instruments, evidences of indebtedness, precious metals commodities, options, forward or futures contracts, notional principal contracts and derivatives) is treated as a distribution of money. The securities are taken into account at their fair market value (FMV) as of the date of the distribution. (Code Sec. 731(c); Reg § 1.731-2)

Gain is recognized by a distributee partner to the extent that the cash and the FMV of the marketable securities exceed the basis of the partner's interest in the partnership. But where a partner realizes a loss on a distribution of marketable securities, the loss isn't recognized. These rules are applied after the application of the rules that treat a shift in the partners' interests in accounts receivables and substantially appreciated inventory as a sale. (Code Sec. 731(a))[46]

The amount of marketable securities taken into account under the above rule is reduced (but not below zero) by the excess (if any) of:

(1) the partner's distributive share of the net gain that would be recognized if all marketable securities of the same class and issuer as the distributed securities held by the partnership were sold (immediately before the transaction to which the distribution relates) by the partnership for FMV, over

(2) the partner's distributive share of the net gain attributable to the marketable securities of the same class and issuer as the distributed securities held by the partnership immediately after the transaction, determined using the FMV described in (1) above. (Code Sec. 731(c)(3)(B))

All marketable securities held by the partnership are treated as marketable securities of the same class and issuer as the distributed securities. (Reg § 1.731-2(b))[47]

¶ 3740 Partner's holding period.

A partner's holding period for property distributed to him in kind includes the period the partnership held the property. (Code Sec. 735(b)) If contributed to the partnership by a partner, the recipient partner's holding period also includes the period that the property was held by the contributing partner before contribution. (Reg § 1.735-1(b))[48]

---

44. ¶B-3603; ¶7314.01
45. ¶B-3605; ¶7314.01
46. ¶B-3602.1 *et seq.*; ¶7314.01

47. ¶B-3602.2; ¶7314.01
48. ¶B-3706; ¶7354.02

¶ 3741   Character of certain contributed property.

When a partner contributes what was an unrealized receivable in his hands to a partnership, the partnership's gain or loss on disposition of the item will still be ordinary income or loss. (Code Sec. 724(a)) The same rule applies to contributed inventory, but in this case, ordinary income or loss will result only if the assets are disposed of by the partnership within five years of the contribution. (Code Sec. 724(b))[49]

If a partner contributes a capital asset with a basis higher than its fair market value, and the partnership disposes of it within five years of the contribution, the partnership's loss will be capital to the extent of the basis/value variance at contribution. (Code Sec. 724(c))[50]

If any of the above property is disposed of by the partnership in a nontaxable disposition, the above rules apply to the substituted basis property that results. (Code Sec. 724(d)(3))[1]

¶ 3742   Partner's basis for property received in nonliquidating distributions.

The basis to a partner of property distributed to him, in kind, other than in liquidation of his partnership interest, is the same as the property's adjusted basis to the partnership immediately before the distribution. But the basis of the property to the partner may not exceed the adjusted basis of his interest in the partnership reduced by any money distributed to him in the same transaction. (Code Sec. 732(a); Reg § 1.732-1(a))[2]

¶ 3743   Partner's basis for property distributed in liquidation.

A partner's basis for property distributed in liquidation of his partnership interest is the same as the adjusted basis for his partnership interest reduced by any money distributed to him in the same transaction. However, the partner's basis in inventory and unrealized receivables cannot exceed the basis the partnership had in such items. (Code Sec. 732(b), Code Sec. 732(c); Reg § 1.732-1(b))[3]

¶ 3744   Basis adjustments to assets of corporation whose stock is distributed to corporate partner.

A corporate partner that receives a distribution of stock in another corporation ("distributed corporation") must, subject to limitations and exceptions, reduce the basis of the distributed corporation's assets if:

. . . the corporate partner "controls" (by 80% vote and value) the distributed corporation immediately after the distribution or at any time thereafter, and

. . . the partnership's adjusted basis in the stock of the distributed corporation immediately before the distribution exceeded the corporate partner's adjusted basis in such stock immediately after the distribution. (Code Sec. 732(f)(1))[4]

The basis reduction equals the excess described above and is applied to the property held by the distributed corporation following the distribution, if the corporate partner then has control of the distributed corporation. (Code Sec. 732(f)(1))[5]

Regs provide that if (i) two or more corporate partners receive a distribution of stock in

---

49. ¶B-1420; ¶7244
50. ¶B-1421; ¶7244
1. ¶B-1422; ¶7244.01
2. ¶B-3701; ¶7324.01

3. ¶B-3702; ¶7324.01
4. ¶B-3704; ¶7324.03
5. ¶B-3704; ¶7324.03

another corporation and (ii) the corporation whose stock was distributed by the partnership is or becomes a member of the distributee partners' consolidated group following the distribution, the basis reduction rules apply only to the extent that the partnership's adjusted basis in the distributed stock immediately before the distribution exceeds the aggregate basis of the distributed stock of the corporation in the hands of corporate partners that are members of the same consolidated group (as defined in Reg § 1.1502-1(h)) immediately after the distribution. (Reg § 1.732-3(b))[6]

The basis reduction cannot exceed the lesser of:

(A) the amount by which (i) the sum of the aggregate adjusted bases of the property and the amount of money of the distributed corporation exceeds (ii) the corporate partner's adjusted basis in the stock of the distributed corporation, or

(B) the adjusted basis of any property of the distributed corporation (determined before the reduction). (Code Sec. 732(f)(3))[7]

If, in applying the basis-reduction rule, the amount by which basis is to be reduced exceeds the aggregate adjusted bases of the property of the distributed corporation, then the excess is recognized by the corporate partner as long-term capital gain and increases its basis in the stock of the distributed corporation. (Code Sec. 732(f)(4))[8]

¶ 3745 ## Allocation of basis to distributed property when limited by basis of partner's interest.

In (i) a current distribution in which the partner's basis in his partnership interest is less than the partnership's basis in the property distributed and (ii) a liquidating distribution, the partner's basis in his partnership interest (reduced by any money received) must be allocated among the distributed property in the following manner:

(1) First, to any unrealized receivables and inventory items in an amount equal to the adjusted basis of each such property to the partnership. (Code Sec. 732(c)(1)(A)(i)) If the basis to be allocated is less than the sum of the adjusted bases of these properties in the hands of the partnership, a basis decrease is applied as described below. (Code Sec. 732(c)(1)(A)(ii); Reg § 1.732-1(c)(2)(i))

(2) To the extent any basis isn't allocated under (1), basis is allocated to other distributed properties. This allocation is made by assigning to each property its adjusted basis in the hands of the partnership (Code Sec. 732(c)(1)(B)(i); Reg § 1.732-1(c)(2)(ii) and then increasing or decreasing the basis to the extent any increase or decrease in basis is required in order for the adjusted bases of the other distributed properties to equal the remaining basis to be allocated under the rules described below. (Code Sec. 732(c)(1)(B)(ii); Reg § 1.732-1(c)(2)(ii))

Any basis *increase* is allocated (i) first to properties with unrealized appreciation in proportion to their respective amounts of unrealized appreciation before such increase to the extent of each property's unrealized appreciation (Code Sec. 732(c)(2)(A); Reg § 1.732-1(c)(2)(ii)) and (ii) to the extent the required increase isn't allocated under (i), in proportion to the respective fair market values of the properties. (Code Sec. 732(c)(2)(B); Reg § 1.732-1(c)(2)(ii))

Any basis *decrease* is allocated (a) first to properties with unrealized depreciation in proportion to their respective amounts of unrealized appreciation before such decrease to the extent of each property's unrealized depreciation (Code Sec. 732(c)(3)(A); Reg § 1.732-1(c)(2)(i)) and (b) to the extent the required decrease isn't allocated under (a), in proportion

---

to the respective bases of the properties (as adjusted under (a)). (Code Sec. 732(c)(3)(B); Reg § 1.732-1(c)(2)(i))[9]

¶ 3746   Built-in gain or loss property—seven-year rule.

If the basis of property contributed to a partnership by a partner is different from the property's fair market value (FMV) at the time of contribution (i.e., there is built-in gain or loss), then the following rules apply:

If the partnership distributes the contributed property to a partner or partners *other than the contributing partner* within seven years of the contribution, then the distributed property is treated as sold by the partnership for its FMV at the time of the distribution, and the contributing partner must recognize any gain or loss from this constructive sale in an amount equal to the amount of gain or loss that would have been allocated to him if the property had actually been sold. (Code Sec. 704(c)(1)(B); Reg § 1.704-4(a)(5), Ex (1))[10]

Where property is distributed to the partner *who contributed the property,* the partner will recognize as gain the lesser of (a) the excess of the FMV of the property over the adjusted basis of the partner's interest in the partnership immediately before the distribution (reduced, but not below zero, by any money or marketable securities received), or (b) the partner's net precontribution gain, *i.e.,* the gain that would have been recognized by the distributee partner under the rules discussed, above, if all property held by the partnership immediately before the distribution that had been contributed to it by the distributee partner within seven years of the distribution, was distributed to another partner. (Code Sec. 737(a), Code Sec. 737(b))[11] Distributions of property previously contributed by the distributee partner aren't taken into account for purposes of determining (a) and (b), above. (Code Sec. 737(d)(1))[12]

Special rules apply if the partnership distributes to the contributing partner property that's of "like kind" to the contributed property (within the meaning of Code Sec. 1031, see ¶2417) to limit recognition of gain by the contributing partner. (Code Sec. 704(c)(2))[13]

The rules requiring gain recognition on distributions described above do not apply when a partnership transfers all of its assets and liabilities to a partnership in exchange for an interest in the transferee partnership, and distributes the interest to its partners in liquidation as part of the same plan (a merger). With respect to a later distribution of "built-in gain" property that was transferred, the seven-year period is measured from the date that the property was originally contributed to the transferor partnership, and not from the date of the transfer to the transferee partnership. However, the merger is considered a contribution of assets, so a new seven-year period begins but only with respect to the appreciation in value that occurred while the property was held by the transferor partnership.[14]

Income, gain, loss and deductions with respect to property contributed to the partnership after Mar. 31, 1984 are shared among the partners so as to take into account the difference between the property's FMV and its basis at the time of the contribution. (Code Sec. 704(c)(1)(A)) Built-in gain or loss must be allocated using a reasonable method, i.e., the traditional method following the ceiling rule or with curative allocations, the remedial allocation method or another method appropriate to the circumstances. (Reg § 1.704-3(a)(1)) Under anti-abuse rules, an allocation isn't reasonable if made with a view to shifting the tax consequences of built-in gain or loss among partners (including indirect partners), in a way that substantially reduces the present value of the partners' aggregate tax liability. (Reg § 1.704-3(a)(10))

9. ¶B-3703; ¶7324.01
10. ¶B-3125; ¶7044.09
11. ¶B-3171 *et seq.*; ¶7374

12. ¶B-3178; ¶7374.03
13. ¶B-3151 *et seq.*; ¶7044.09
14. ¶B-3157; ¶7044.097

If any property contributed to a partnership after Oct. 22, 2004 has a built-in loss, then:

... the built-in loss is taken into account only in determining the amount of items allocated to the contributing partner, and

... except as provided in regs, in determining the amount of items allocated to other partners, the basis of the contributed property in the hands of the partnership is treated as being equal to its FMV at the time of the contribution. (Code Sec. 704(c)(1)(C))

If a partnership makes an installment sale of built-in gain or loss property, the installment obligation it receives is treated as built-in gain or loss property. (Reg § 1.704-3(a)(8)(ii))[15]

¶ 3747 Character of unrealized receivables and inventory to a distributee-partner.

Gain or loss on disposition of unrealized receivables and inventory by a distributee-partner is:

... in the case of *unrealized receivables*, ordinary gain or loss; (Code Sec. 735(a)(1))

... in the case of *inventory items* (whether or not substantially appreciated) sold or exchanged within five years from the date of the distribution, ordinary gain or loss. (Code Sec. 735(a)(2)) If disposed of after five years from the date of distribution, the character of the gain or loss depends upon the character of the item in the partner's hands on the date of disposition. (Reg § 1.735-1(a)(2))[16]

¶ 3748 Disproportionate Distributions.

Disproportionate distributions (¶3749) of partnership property that include "unrealized receivables" (including recapturable deductions, certain transfers of franchises, trademarks or trade names, see ¶3750) and "substantially appreciated inventory" (see ¶3751) (collectively, "hot assets") may trigger ordinary income, gain or loss to both the partnership and its partners.

¶ 3749 Disproportionate distributions defined.

A disproportionate distribution of partnership assets to a partner is treated as a sale or exchange that may result in recognition of gain or loss to the partner and the partnership. The rule applies to all distributions, both liquidating and nonliquidating, except for: (1) a distribution of contributed property to the same partner who contributed it; and (2) liquidation payments to a retiring or deceased partner that are treated as ordinary income under the rules at ¶3761. (Code Sec. 751(b))[17]

A distribution is "disproportionate" if a partner receives more than his proportionate share of "hot assets" (see ¶3748) and less of his proportionate share of other property (including money), or vice versa. In such a case, a partner, in effect, sells or exchanges part or all of his share in property of one category for property of the other category, see ¶3752. The general rules on partnership distributions apply to the balance of the distribution not treated as a sale or exchange. (Reg § 1.751-1(b))[18]

The partners may agree as to which particular assets in one category are considered to have been sold or exchanged for particular assets in the other category, but absent such an agreement, a proportionate part of each asset relinquished in one category will be considered to have been sold or exchanged for excess assets received in the other. (Reg § 1.751-

---

15. ¶B-3100; ¶7044.09
16. ¶B-3705; ¶7354.01

17. ¶B-3905 *et seq.*; ¶7514.01
18. ¶B-3906 *et seq.*; ¶7514.01

$1(g))$[19]

Under proposed regs on which taxpayers may rely, a distribution of partnership property (including money) is a "Code Sec. 751(b) distribution," and may give rise to an income recognition requirement (see ¶3752) if it gives rise to a "Code Sec. 751(b) amount" for any partner. A partner's Code Sec. 751(b) amount is the greatest of: (i) the amount by which the partner's net Code Sec. 751 unrealized gain immediately before the distribution exceeds the partner's net Code Sec. 751 unrealized gain immediately after the distribution; (ii) the amount by which the partner's Code Sec. 751 unrealized loss immediately after the distribution exceeds the partner's net Code Sec. 751 unrealized loss immediately before the distribution; and (iii) the amount of the partner's net Code Sec. 751 unrealized gain immediately before the distribution, increased by the total amount of the partner's net Code Sec. 751 unrealized loss immediately after the distribution (where neither of those numbers equals zero).[20] (Prop Reg. § 1.751-1(b)(2), [Taxpayers may rely])

For this purpose, a partner's interest in the partnership's Code Sec. 751 property would include allocations of tax items under Code Sec. 704(c) principles. (Prop Reg. § 1.751-1(b)(1)(i), [Taxpayers may rely])

¶ 3750   "Unrealized receivables."

Unrealized receivables include any contractual or other rights to payment for:

. . . goods delivered, or to be delivered, to the extent the proceeds would be treated as amounts received from the sale or exchange of noncapital assets;

. . . services rendered, or to be rendered.

Such receivables are included only to the extent not previously includible in income under the method of accounting used by the partnership. (Code Sec. 751(c))[21]

¶ 3751   "Inventory items" and "substantially appreciated" inventory items.

Inventory items include property properly includible in inventory and property held primarily for sale to customers in the ordinary course of business (Code Sec. 751(d)(1)), as well as:

. . . any other property that would produce ordinary income on sale or exchange by the partnership (Code Sec. 751(d)(2)), including accounts receivable for goods or services and unrealized receivables as described at ¶3750 (Reg § 1.751-1(d)(2)(ii)); and

. . . any other property held by the partnership that would be inventory items, as defined above, if held by the selling or distributee-partner. (Code Sec. 751(d)(3)) However, this rule doesn't apply to property actually distributed to a partner. (Reg § 1.751-1(d)(2)(iii))[22]

Inventory items are "substantially appreciated" in value if the fair market value of *all* such items (including unrealized receivables) exceeds 120% of their adjusted basis to the partnership. (Code Sec. 751(b)(3)(A)) The 120% limit is computed by excluding any item acquired principally to avoid meeting it. (Code Sec. 751(b)(3)(B))

If the test is met on the basis of all inventory items, a distribution of any inventory item is a distribution of a substantially appreciated one, even though the particular item may not have appreciated at all. If the test isn't met on the basis of all items, no distribution of an inventory item is a distribution of a substantially appreciated item. (Reg § 1.751-1(d)(1))[23]

---

19. ¶B-3902 *et seq.*; ¶7514.01
20. ¶B-3907.1
21. ¶B-3914; ¶7514.02

22. ¶B-3921; ¶7514.02
23. ¶B-3922; ¶7514.02

¶ 3752   Gain or loss on disproportionate distribution.

If a distributee-partner receives *more* than his share of unrealized receivables and substantially appreciated inventory items and *less* than his share of other property (including money), he is considered to have sold or exchanged the portion of his share of the other property that he relinquished for the excess unrealized receivables and substantially appreciated inventory items he received. (Reg § 1.751-1(b)(2)(i), Reg § 1.751-1(b)(2)(iii))

The partnership (as constituted after the distribution) is considered to have sold or exchanged the excess unrealized receivables and substantially appreciated inventory items distributed to the partner in exchange for the other property he relinquished. (Reg § 1.751-1(b)(2)(i), Reg § 1.751-1(b)(2)(ii))[24]

Rules analogous to those described above apply where the distributee partner receives a disproportionate distribution of *less* than his share of unrealized receivables and substantially appreciated inventory items and *more* than his share of other property (including money). (Reg § 1.751-1(b)(3))[25]

Under proposed regs on which taxpayers may rely, in the case of a Code Sec. 751(b) distribution described at ¶3749, the partnership may choose a reasonable approach that is consistent with the purpose of Code Sec. 751 (i.e., to prevent a partner from converting its rights to ordinary income into capital gain) under which each partner with a Code Sec. 751(b) amount would recognize ordinary income (or would take it into account by eliminating a basis adjustment) equal to the Code Sec. 751(b) amount immediately before the Code Sec. 751(b) distribution. However, in certain circumstances, a distributee partner would also be allowed or required to recognize capital gain. (Prop Reg. § 1.751-1(b)(3), [Taxpayers may rely])[26]

¶ 3753   Liabilities of Partnerships and Partners. ▬▬▬▬▬

Changes in partners' shares of partnership liabilities are treated as cash contributions to, or distributions by, the partnership. Partners' shares of partnership liabilities depend on whether the liability is recourse (¶3754) or nonrecourse (¶3755).

Specifically, if a partner's share of partnership liabilities increases, or if he or she assumes any partnership liabilities, it's treated as a contribution of money from the partner to the partnership. (Code Sec. 752(a); Reg § 1.752-1(b))[27]

If a partner's share of the partnership liabilities decreases, or if the partnership assumes any of his liabilities, it's treated as a distribution of money to the partner. (Code Sec. 752(b); Reg § 1.752-1(c))[28]

An unassumed liability to which property is subject is considered a liability of the owner of the property (e.g., the partnership) to the extent of its fair market value. (Code Sec. 752(c))[29]

For these purposes and for determining "Reg § 1.752-7 liabilities" (see ¶3734), a liability is any fixed or contingent obligation to make payment without regard to whether the obligation is otherwise taken into account for tax purposes. Obligations include, but are not limited to, debt obligations, environmental obligations, tort obligations, contract obligations, pension obligations, obligations under a short sale, and obligations under derivative financial instruments such as options, forward contracts, and futures contracts. (Reg § 1.752-1(a)(4)(ii))[30]

---

24. ¶B-3909 *et seq.*; ¶7514.01
25. ¶B-3911; ¶7514.01
26. ¶B-3907.2
27. ¶B-1601; ¶7524.01

28. ¶B-1602; ¶7524.01
29. ¶B-1608; ¶7524.01
30. ¶B-1607; ¶7524.01

¶ 3754   Share of recourse liabilities.

A partnership debt is a recourse liability to the extent that any partner bears the economic risk of loss for the liability.[31] A partner's share of a recourse liability is the part of the economic risk of loss for the liability the partner bears. (Reg § 1.752-1(a)(1))[32]

Generally, a partner bears the economic risk of loss for a partnership liability to the extent that he (or a related person) would be obligated to pay the creditor or contribute to the partnership (and wouldn't be entitled to reimbursement) in the case of a constructive liquidation. (Reg § 1.752-2(b)(1))[33] However, IRS may disregard a partner's purported obligation to make a payment under anti-abuse rules. (Reg § 1.752-2(j); Reg § 1.752-2T(j))

¶ 3755   Share of nonrecourse liabilities.

If no partner bears the economic risk of loss for a partnership liability (e.g., unassumed mortgages), the liability is nonrecourse. (Reg § 1.752-1(a)(2)) Nonrecourse liabilities of a partnership are first allocated among all the partners to reflect their shares of:

(a) "partnership minimum gain," the excess of partnership nonrecourse liabilities over the basis (or, if the assets are recorded on the books at a value different from basis, the book value of the assets) of the partnership assets those liabilities encumber; and

(b) the gain that would be allocated to the partners under Code Sec. 704(c), or under similar principles in connection with a revaluation of partnership property, if, in a taxable transaction, the partnership disposed of all property subject to a nonrecourse liability in satisfaction of those liabilities and for no other consideration.

Any excess is allocated among the partners in proportion to their interests in partnership profits. The partnership agreement may specify the partners' profit interests as long as those interests are reasonably consistent with allocations (which have substantial economic effect) of some significant item of partnership income or gain among the partners. Alternatively, the excess may be allocated in accordance with the manner in which it's expected that the deductions attributable to the nonrecourse debt will be allocated. In addition, the excess may be allocated first to the contributing partner to the extent any built-in-gain with respect to that property exceeds the amount allocated to that partner under (b), and thereafter under one of the other methods described above. (Reg § 1.752-3(a))[34]

¶ 3756   Transfer and Liquidation of Partnership Interest. ████████████████

The transfer or liquidation (¶3743 *et seq.*) of a partnership interest, while generally resulting in capital gain or loss, is subject to special rules that may turn part of the gain or loss from capital to ordinary (¶3759).

¶ 3757   Liquidation vs. sale of partner's interest.

Withdrawal of a partner from a partnership ordinarily may be accomplished either by a partner's sale or liquidation of his interest in the partnership.

Where a partner's interest is liquidated, payments are taxable to that partner as guaranteed payments or income distributions to the extent they exceed the value of his interest in the partnership property (¶3761 *et seq.*).[35]

Where a partner *sells* his interest, payments to him that exceed his basis for his interest

---

31. ¶B-1651; ¶7524.03
32. ¶B-1653 *et seq.*; ¶7524.03
33. ¶B-1654 *et seq.*; ¶7524.03

34. ¶B-1670; ¶7524.03
35. ¶B-3811, B-4102; ¶7364.01

are capital gain except to the extent of payments for unrealized receivables and inventory items (¶3758 *et seq.*). (Code Sec. 741; Reg § 1.741-1)[36]

¶ 3758 Sale or exchange of partnership interest.

If a partner sells or exchanges all or a part of his interest in the partnership after holding it for more than one year, he may recognize ordinary income, collectibles gain (¶2605), section 1250 gain, or residual long-term capital gain or loss. (Reg § 1.1(h)-1(a)) He recognizes ordinary income (¶3759) to the extent his gain is attributable to unrealized receivables (¶3750) and inventory (¶3751). (Code Sec. 741, Code Sec. 751(a), Code Sec. 751(c))[37]

The capital gain or loss is the difference between:

. . . the amount realized *reduced* by the portion attributable to unrealized receivables and inventory; and

. . . the transferor-partner's adjusted basis for the partnership interest transferred *reduced* by the portion attributable to unrealized receivables and inventory. (Reg § 1.741-1(a))[38]

Any gain or loss from a partner's disposition of an interest in a partnership is taken into account by the partner as net investment income for purposes of the 3.8% surtax on unearned income (¶3142 *et seq.*) *only* to the extent of the net gain or loss that the transferor would take into account if the entity had sold all its property for fair market value immediately before the disposition. (Code Sec. 1411(c)(4))

The seller's collectibles gain is the amount that would be allocated to him if the partnership had sold all of its collectibles for fair market value in a fully taxable transaction immediately before the sale of the interest in the entity. (Reg § 1.1(h)-1(b)(2)(ii)) The seller must take into account under Code Sec. 1(h)(6)(A)(i) in determining his unrecaptured section 1250 gain (¶2604) the amount of "section 1250 capital gain" that would be allocated to him if the partnership had sold all of its section 1250 property in a fully taxable transaction immediately before the transfer of the partnership interest. (Reg § 1.1(h)-1(b)(3)(ii)) The amount of residual long-term capital gain or loss recognized by a selling partner is the amount of long-term capital gain or loss that the partner would recognize under Code Sec. 741 (as explained above) minus (1) the collectibles gain allocable to the sold interest, and (2) the section 1250 gain allocable to the sold interest. (Reg § 1.1(h)-1(c))

¶ 3759 Ordinary gain or loss.

To the extent that money or property received by a partner in exchange for all or part of his partnership interest is attributable to his share of partnership unrealized receivables or inventory items—collectively Code Sec. 751 property—the gain or loss is ordinary income or loss. (Code Sec. 751(a))

The income or loss realized by a partner on the sale or exchange of his interest in Code Sec. 751 property is the amount of income or loss from Code Sec. 751 property (including any remedial allocations) that would have been allocated to the partner (to the extent attributable to the partnership interest sold or exchanged) if the partnership had sold all of its property in a fully taxable transaction for cash in an amount equal to the fair market value (FMV) of such property (taking into account the Code Sec. 7701(g) rule that the FMV must be not less than the amount of the nonrecourse debt to which the property is subject) immediately before the partner's transfer of the interest in the partnership. Gain or loss

---

36. ¶B-3801 *et seq.*; ¶7414.01
37. ¶B-3850 *et seq.*; ¶7414.01

38. ¶s B-3802, B-3901; ¶7414.01

attributable to Code Sec. 751 property is ordinary. The difference between the amount of capital gain or loss that the partner would realize absent Code Sec. 751 and the amount of ordinary income or loss is capital gain or loss on the sale of his partnership interest. (Reg § 1.751-1(a)(2))[39]

The basis for unrealized receivables includes all attributable costs or expenses paid or accrued but not previously taken into account under the partnership's method of accounting. (Reg § 1.751-1(c)(2)) The basis of any potential gain from the following property (treated as unrealized receivables) is zero: (1) mining exploration expenditures recapture under Code Sec. 617; (2) gain from stock of a domestic international sales corporation (DISC) or a former DISC under Code Sec. 995(c); (3) depreciation recapture under Code Sec. 1245 and Code Sec. 1250; (4) gain from stock of a controlled foreign corporation under Code Sec. 1248(a); (5) gain from disposition of farm land under Code Sec. 1252(a)(1); (6) gain from transfers of franchises, trademarks, or trade names under Code Sec. 1253(a); or (7) oil, gas, or geothermal wells intangible drilling and development cost recapture under Code Sec. 1254. (Reg § 1.751-1(c)(5))[40]

¶ 3760   Sale of partnership business vs. sale of partnership assets.

A transaction can be structured either as a sale of assets or as a sale of the partnership interests. However, where all the assets of the partnership are sold (except for cash or insignificant assets) and the partnership does not engage in business after the transfer, the transaction will be treated as a sale of the partnership interests. [41]

¶ 3761   Payments After Partner's Death or Retirement. ▬▬▬▬▬▬▬▬

When a partner either retires or dies and payments are made in liquidation of his partnership interest, the payments are broken down into several categories, which are treated as ordinary income or capital gains.

These payments may be for the partner's interest in the fair market value of the partnership assets, his interest in unrealized receivables, or payments under an agreement akin to mutual insurance. These amounts have to be separately considered. [42]

Liquidation payments received by a retiring partner, a partner expelled from a partnership, or by a deceased partner's successor in interest are treated as distributions taxable under the rules for regular distributions discussed at ¶3738 if they are for the partner's interest in partnership property, see ¶3762. (Code Sec. 736(b)(1))[43] Payments for *substantially appreciated* inventory (¶3751) may result in ordinary income under the rules governing disproportionate distributions (see ¶3752). (Reg § 1.736-1(b)(1))

Liquidation payments that aren't in exchange for partnership property are treated either as distributive shares of partnership income (if the amount is determined with regard to partnership income) or as guaranteed payments (if the amount is determined without regard to partnership income). (Code Sec. 736(a); Reg § 1.736-1(a)(3))[44]

¶ 3762   Payment for interest in partnership property.

Payments for partnership property don't include payments to a retiring or deceased general partner in a partnership in which capital isn't a material income-producing factor for (i) unrealized receivables (which for this purpose includes only accounts receivable and unbilled amounts) or (ii) goodwill (unless the partnership agreement provides for payments for goodwill). (Code Sec. 736(b)(2), Code Sec. 736(b)(3))[45]

---

39. ¶B-3901; ¶7514.01
40. ¶B-3903; ¶7514.02
41. ¶B-3809
42. ¶B-4102 *et seq.*; ¶7364.01

43. ¶B-4103; ¶7364.02
44. ¶B-4106; ¶7364.03
45. ¶B-4104; ¶7364.02

¶ 3763   Allocation of payments between income and property.

The allocation of payments between income and property is an issue that arises when payments are made over two or more years. Retirement or death payments must be allocated between the portion received in exchange for partnership property and the balance, received in the form of guaranteed payments or as a distributive share of partnership income. This allocation may be made in any manner in which the remaining partners and the withdrawing partner (or a deceased partner's successor in interest) agree. However, the *total* allocated to property must not exceed the fair market value of the property at the date of death or retirement. (Reg § 1.736-1(b)(5)(iii))

In the absence of an allocation agreement, payments will be allocated between income and property as follows:

. . . Payments that aren't fixed in amount are first treated as made in exchange for the partner's interest in partnership property to the extent of the value of that interest. Additional amounts are ordinary income. (Reg § 1.736-1(b)(5)(ii))

. . . Payments fixed in amount and to be received over a fixed number of years are apportioned year by year in accordance with the overall ratio of property payments to total payments. (Reg § 1.736-1(b)(5)(i))[46]

A payment for goodwill is treated as a payment made in exchange for partnership property where payment for goodwill is provided by the partnership agreement. (Reg § 1.736-1(b)(3))[47]

¶ 3764   Withdrawing partner's share of final year's income.

A retiring partner must recognize his distributive share of the partnership income for the partnership year in which he retires. His share of the partnership income for the year is allocable to him only for the portion of the year he was a member of the partnership. (Reg § 1.736-1(a)(4))[48]

¶ 3765   Income of deceased partner.

The tax year of a partnership closes with respect to a deceased partner on the date of his death. Thus, partnership items for the short partnership tax year that closes on the partner's death are included in his final return. (Code Sec. 706(c)(2))[49]

¶ 3766   Continuation of retiring or deceased partner's partner status.

A retiring partner or a deceased partner's successor in interest who receives retirement or death payments is regarded as a partner until his entire interest in the partnership is liquidated. Thus, even a two-person partnership isn't terminated until the retiring or deceased partner's interest is liquidated. (Reg § 1.708-1(b)(1)(i), Reg § 1.736-1(a)(6))[50]

¶ 3767   Special Basis Adjustments to Partnership Property. ▬▬▬

A partnership's basis in its assets ("inside basis") is unaffected by partnership distributions and transfers of partnership interests unless there is a substantial basis reduction or the partnership makes a special basis election (¶3772). Under certain circumstances, the transferee of a partnership interest may elect to adjust

46. ¶B-4110; ¶7364.01
47. ¶B-4104; ¶7364.02
48. ¶B-4107; ¶7064.02

49. ¶B-4201; ¶7064.02
50. ¶B-4112; ¶7084.03

the basis of property distributed to him as if the partnership had made the special basis election (¶3770).

¶ 3768   Post-transfer adjustments to basis.

A transfer of a partnership interest by reason of a sale or exchange or the death of a partner causes a basis adjustment of the partnership's property if (i) a basis adjustment election under Code Sec. 754 is in effect, or (ii) the partnership has a substantial built-in loss immediately after the transfer. (Code Sec. 743(a)) A partnership is treated as having a substantial built-in loss if:

(1) the partnership's adjusted basis in the partnership property exceeds by more than $250,000 the fair market value (FMV) of that property, or

(2) for transfers of partnership interests after 2017, the transferee partner would be allocated a loss of more than $250,000 if the partnership assets were sold for cash equal to their FMV immediately after the transfer. (Code Sec. 743(d)(1))[1]

A contribution of cash or property to the partnership does not cause a basis adjustment to the partnership's property, regardless of whether a basis adjustment election is in effect. (Reg § 1.743-1(a))[2] If the election is in effect, the partnership's basis in its property with respect to the transferee partner is increased by any excess of the partner's basis in his interest over his share of the basis of partnership property (or decreased if his basis in his interest is lower). (Reg § 1.743-1(b))[3] Regs provide rules for allocating the basis adjustment among the partnership's assets. (Reg § 1.755-1)[4]

¶ 3769   Post-distribution adjustments to basis of undistributed property.

The basis of partnership property is not adjusted when the partnership makes a distribution to a partner unless a basis adjustment election under Code Sec. 754 is in effect, or the partnership has a substantial basis reduction with respect to the distribution. (Code Sec. 734(a)) A substantial basis reduction exists where the sum of (i) the amount of the partner's loss on the distribution, and (ii) the basis increase to the distributed properties, is over $250,000. (Code Sec. 734(d))[5] If an adjustment is made on a partnership distribution, the partnership's basis in its retained property (1) is increased by the amount of gain recognized by the distributee partner on the distribution, and the amount by which the basis of the distributed property in the hands of the partnership before the distribution exceeds the basis of the property in the hands of the distributee partner (Code Sec. 734(b)(1)), and (2) is decreased by the amount of loss recognized by the distributee partner on the distribution and the amount by which the basis of the distributed property in the hands of the distributee partner exceeds the basis the partnership had in the property before the distribution. (Code Sec. 734(b)(2)(B))[6] Regs provide rules for allocating the basis adjustment among the partnership's assets. (Reg § 1.755-1)[7]

In allocating any basis reduction in partnership property under Code Sec. 734(b) as a result of a distribution, no allocation may be made to stock in a corporation that is a partner in the partnership, or to the stock of any person related to the corporation, and any amount not allocable to stock is allocated to other partnership property. Where the reduction that must be allocated to other partnership property exceeds the aggregate adjusted basis of the other partnership property immediately before the required allocation, gain is recognized by the partnership to the extent of the excess. (Code Sec. 755(c))[8]

---

1. ¶B-4009.1
2. ¶B-4010; ¶7434
3. ¶B-4009; ¶7434
4. ¶B-4051 *et seq.*; ¶7554

5. ¶B-4002.1; ¶7344
6. ¶B-4002; ¶7344.01
7. ¶B-4055 *et seq.*; ¶7554
8. ¶B-4054.1; ¶7554

Where the basis of a partnership's recovery property is increased as a result of a distribution of property by the partnership, the increased portion of the basis is taken into account for depreciation purposes as if it were newly purchased recovery property placed in service when the distribution or transfer occurs. Any applicable recovery period and method may be used to determine the recovery (depreciation) deduction for the increased portion of the basis. However, no change is allowed in determining the recovery (depreciation) deduction for the portion of the basis of recovery property for which there is no increase. (Reg § 1.734-1(e)(1))[9]

Where the basis adjustment requires a decrease in the basis of partnership recovery property, the basis decrease must be accounted for over the remaining recovery period of the property beginning with the recovery period in which the basis is decreased. (Reg § 1.734-1(e)(2))[10]

¶ 3770 Partner's basis adjustments.

Where a partnership interest is transferred and the partnership later distributes property, but hasn't made the election described at ¶3768, the transferee-partner may elect to have the basis of the property distributed to him adjusted as if the partnership had made the election. The election to make the adjustment applies only for purposes of determining the basis of distributed property (other than money) in the partner's hands. It doesn't enable the partner to amend prior income tax returns to recompute income based on an adjusted basis. (Code Sec. 732(d)) Accordingly, in computing the adjustment, there is no reduction for any depletion or depreciation of that portion of the basis of partnership property arising from the basis adjustment, because no depletion or depreciation on the basis adjustment for the period before the distribution is allowed or allowable unless the partnership had an election described at ¶3768 in effect. (Reg § 1.732-1(d)(1)(iv))[11]

The transferee-partner may make this election only with respect to property (other than money) distributed to him within two years after he acquired his interest by transfer. (Code Sec. 732(d))[12]

The adjustment is *required* (without regard to the 2-year limit) if, at the time the transferee-partner acquired the transferred partnership interest, all three of the following conditions existed:

(1) The fair market value of all partnership property (other than money) exceeded 110% of its adjusted basis to the partnership;

(2) Allocation of basis under Code Sec. 732(c) (general rule for allocation of basis of distributed properties) upon a liquidation of his interest immediately after the transfer of the interest would have resulted in a shift of basis from property not subject to depreciation, depletion or amortization to property that is so subject; and

(3) The post-transfer adjustment as if the election at ¶3768 had been made would change the basis to the transferee-partner of the property actually distributed. (Code Sec. 732(d); Reg § 1.732-1(d)(4))[13]

¶ 3771 Basis of unrealized receivables and inventory items distributed to a partner.

If unrealized receivables or inventory items are distributed to a *transferee partner* who has a special basis adjustment for those assets under either the post-transfer adjustment

---

9. ¶B-4007; ¶7344.01
10. ¶B-4007; ¶7344.01
11. ¶B-4029; ¶7324.01

12. ¶B-4029; ¶7324.01
13. ¶B-4033; ¶7324.01

rule (¶3768) or the distributed property adjustment rule (¶3769), the partnership's adjusted basis, immediately before distribution, of any unrealized receivables or inventory items distributed to such a partner takes into account the following portions of the post-transfer or distributed property basis adjustments that the distributee partner has for those assets:

. . . The entire amount of the post-transfer or distributed property basis adjustments *if* the distributee-partner receives his entire share of the fair market value of the unrealized receivables or inventory items of the partnership.

. . . The same proportion of the post-transfer or distributed property basis adjustments as the value of the unrealized receivables or inventory items distributed to him bears to his entire share of the total value of all those items of the partnership, *if* the distributee-partner gets less than his entire share of those items. (Reg §   1.732-2(c))[14]

¶ 3772   Electing basis adjustments.

The election to adjust the basis of the partnership assets on a distribution, sale, or transfer of a partnership interest (¶3768, ¶3769) is made by the partnership filing a statement of election with the partnership return for the tax year during which the transfer of interest or the distribution of property occurs. (Code Sec. 754; Reg § 1.754-1(b)) Once made, the election applies to all current and future distributions and transfers until revoked. (Code Sec. 754; Reg § 1.754-1(a))[15]

A transferee-partner who wishes to make the distributed property adjustment (¶3770) must elect as follows:

. . . If the distribution includes any depreciable, depletable, or amortizable property, elect with the return for the distribution year.

. . . If it doesn't include any such property, elect not later than the first tax year in which the basis of any of the distributed property is pertinent in determining the transferee-partner's tax. (Reg § 1.732-1(d)(2), Reg § 1.732-1(d)(3))[16]

¶ 3773   Termination of a Partnership.

A partnership terminates for tax purposes (whether or not it has terminated under applicable local law) when:

(1) it stops doing business as a partnership, or

(2) for partnership tax years beginning before 2018, 50% or more of the total interest in partnership capital and profits changes hands by sale or exchange (or by distribution, unless excepted by regs) within 12 consecutive months (a "technical termination"). (Code Sec. 708, Code Sec. 761(e); Reg § 1.708-1(b)(1))[17]

Under the regs, a pre-2018 technical termination resulted in a liquidation and reformation of the partnership. [18]

The cessation of doing business as a partnership may result from a cessation of the business or from the fact that there is only one continuing partner in the partnership. [19]

¶ 3774   Split-up of partnership.

If a partnership splits up into two or more partnerships, each resulting partnership is considered a continuation of the old partnership as long as the members of the resulting partnership had more than a 50% interest in the capital and profits of the old partnership.

---

14. ¶B-4018
15. ¶B-4023 *et seq.*; ¶7544 *et seq.*
16. ¶B-4031; ¶7324.01

17. ¶B-4301; ¶B-4303; ¶7084; ¶7084.02
18. ¶B-4305; ¶7084.02
19. ¶B-4302; ¶7084.01

A resulting partnership whose members had an interest of 50% or less in the old partnership is treated as a new partnership.

If the members of none of the resulting partnerships had more than a 50% interest in the old partnership, the old partnership is considered terminated as of the date of the division, and all the resulting partnerships are treated as new partnerships. (Code Sec. 708(b)(2)(B); Reg § 1.708-1(d)(2))[20]

Any members of the original partnership who do not become members of a resulting partnership that is treated as a continuation of the original partnership are considered to have had their partnership interests liquidated as of the date of the division. (Reg § 1.708-1(d)(1))

For divisions, the resulting partnership (referred to as the divided partnership) that is treated as a continuation of the prior partnership must file a return for the entire tax year of the partnership that has been divided and must retain the employer identification number (EIN) of the prior partnership. All other resulting partnerships that are regarded as continuing and new partnerships must file separate returns for the tax year beginning on the day after the date of the division with new EINs for each partnership. (Reg § 1.708-1(d)(2))

---

20. ¶B-4308; ¶7084.06

Chapter 18   Trusts—Estates—Decedents

¶ 3900   **Taxation of Trusts and Estates—Form 1041.** ▬▬▬▬▬▬▬

Trusts and estates are generally treated as separate taxpayers and, with some important qualifications, are taxed in the same way as individuals.

Trust and estate income is normally taxed to the fiduciary (that is, to the trust or estate itself) if retained by the trust, or to the beneficiary if distributed. Thus, if the fiduciary passes on income to the beneficiary, the trust or estate deducts the distributed income which then becomes taxable to the beneficiary. A special yardstick called "distributable net income" (DNI) (see ¶3933 and ¶3935) is used to limit both the amount deducted by the trust or estate as a distribution, and the amount taxed to the beneficiary. (Code Sec. 643, Code Sec. 651, Code Sec. 652, Code Sec. 661, Code Sec. 662)[1]

The income that's passed on to the beneficiary has the same tax attributes in the beneficiary's hands as when received by the fiduciary (¶3944).

Trusts and estates compute their tax under a tightly-compressed, 5-bracket tax rate schedule (¶1106) that quickly reaches the top marginal rate. (Code Sec. 1(e))[2]

Trusts and estates can't use the tax tables for individuals to figure their tax. (Code Sec. 3(b)(2)) For 2018, the 20% maximum rate for capital gains and qualified dividends applies to estates and trusts with income above $12,700, the 0% rate applies to amounts up to $2,600, while the 15% rate applies to amounts over $2,600 and up to $12,700. For 2019, as calculated by Thomson Reuters using inflation data, the 20% maximum rate for capital gains and qualified dividends applies to estates and trusts with income above $12,950, the 0% rate applies to amounts up to $2,650, while the 15% rate applies to amounts over $2,650 and up to $12,950.

caution: For treatment of trusts and estates for AMT purposes, see ¶3200 *et seq.*

A foreign trust or estate is taxed as if it were a nonresident alien individual who isn't present in the U.S. at any time (see ¶4625 *et seq.*), subject to special rules for trusts. (Code Sec. 641(b))[3]

For income tax returns of trusts and estates (Form 1041), see ¶4732 *et seq.* Form 1041 must be e-Filed using Form 8453-FE, U.S. Estate or Trust Declaration for an IRS e-File Return. Beneficiaries must report items consistently with the entity's return or notify IRS (on Form 8082) of the inconsistency. (Code Sec. 6034A(c)).[4]

For the 3.8% surtax on a trust's or estate's unearned income, see ¶3954.

For the tax years of trusts and estates, see ¶2808.

Optional Form 1041-V, Payment Voucher is used to include information about the taxpayer's remittance of the balance due on Form 1041. IRS encourages its use if payment is made by check or money order. Payment may also be made electronically. [5]

¶ 3901   **Election to treat revocable trust as part of estate—Form 8855.**

An election can be made to have an individual's revocable trust treated as part of his or her estate for income tax purposes. (Code Sec. 645) If there is an executor, the trustee and the executor make the election by filing Form 8855. If there is no executor, the trustee makes the election by filing Form 8855. (Reg § 1.645-1(c))[6]

---

1. ¶C-2600 *et seq.*, ¶C-7000 *et seq.*; ¶6414
2. ¶s C-1003 *et seq.*, C-7002 *et seq.*; ¶6414
3. ¶C-1014 *et seq.*, ¶O-10118; ¶6414
4. ¶s C-3081, C-9081; ¶60,34A4
5. ¶S-1654
6. ¶C-1021 *et seq.*; ¶6454

References beginning with a single letter are to paragraphs in Federal Tax Coordinator 2d and RIA's Analysis of Federal Taxes: Income. Those beginning with numbers are to paragraphs in United States Tax Reporter.

¶ 3902   **Estimated tax payments by trusts and estates—Form 1041-ES.**

Trusts and certain estates must make estimated income tax payments (using Form 1041-ES and vouchers unless the Electronic Federal Tax Payment System (EFTPS) is used) under rules similar to those that apply to individuals, with certain adjustments. (Code Sec. 6654(l)(1))[7] Trusts and estates generally have 45 days to compute their estimated tax payments under the annualization rules. (Code Sec. 6654(l)(4))[8]

Estates and grantor trusts that receive the residue of a probate estate are exempt from making estimated tax payments for their first two tax years after the date of decedent's death. (Code Sec. 6654(l)(2))[9] Charitable trusts subject to tax under Code Sec. 511 are subject to corporate, not individual estimated taxes. (Code Sec. 6654(l)(3), Code Sec. 6655(g)(3))[10]

Where an electing small business trust (ESBT) election (see ¶3908) is effective on a date other than the first day of the trust's tax year, the trust is considered one trust for estimated tax purposes. (Reg § 1.1361-1(m)(3)(v))[11]

A trust or estate with a short tax year must pay estimated tax installments on or before the 15th day of the 4th, 6th and 9th month of such tax year, and the 15th day of the first month of the following year. For a short tax year in which the trust or estate terminates, installments due before the last day of the short year must be paid, and a final installment must be paid by the 15th day of the first month following the month the short year ends. [12]

¶ 3903   **Election to treat estimated tax payments as paid by beneficiary—Form 1041-T.**

A trustee may elect (on Form 1041-T) to treat any part of the trust's estimated tax payments as paid by a beneficiary. Any amount so treated is considered paid or credited to the beneficiary on the last day of the trust's tax year and is considered an estimated tax payment made by the beneficiary on Jan. 15, following the trust's tax year. (Code Sec. 643(g)(1))[13]

This election is available to an estate for a tax year reasonably expected to be its last tax year. (Code Sec. 643(g)(3))

Elect on or before the *65th day* after the tax year. (Code Sec. 643(g)(2)) Attach Form 1041-T to Form 1041 only if the election is made with Form 1041. Otherwise, file Form 1041-T separately. The election is irrevocable. (Reg § 301.9100-8(a)(4))[14]

⊘ observation: The income tax return of a trust or estate is due 3 ½ months after the close of its tax year, see ¶4732. Thus, the election must be made before the return due date.

¶ 3904   **Trust's termination.**

When a trust terminates, it ends as a separate tax entity and no longer reports gross income or claims the deductions, credits, etc. (Reg § 1.641(b)-3(d))

Though the duration of a trust may depend on the occurrence of a particular event under the trust instrument, e.g., the life beneficiary reaching a specified age, for tax purposes the trust will nevertheless continue for a reasonable period beyond this time to allow for the

---

7. ¶S-5300 *et seq.*; ¶66,544.08
8. ¶S-5304; ¶6434.08
9. ¶s S-5302, S-5203; ¶66,544.08
10. ¶s S-5301, S-5420; ¶66,554

11. ¶S-5301
12. ¶S-5311; ¶6434.08
13. ¶S-5309; ¶66,544.08
14. ¶S-5310; ¶6434.08

orderly completion of administration. (Reg § 1.641(b)-3(b))[15]

For unused deductions allowed to a beneficiary on a trust's termination, see ¶3949.

¶ 3905   Estate's termination.

An estate's status as a separate taxpayer exists only during the period of administration or settlement of the estate. (Code Sec. 641(a)(3)) This is the period actually required to perform the ordinary duties of administration, such as collecting assets and paying legacies and debts.[16] If estate administration is unduly prolonged, IRS considers the estate terminated for tax purposes after expiration of a reasonable period for performance by the executor of all the duties of administration. (Reg § 1.641(b)-3(a))[17]

For unused deductions allowed to a beneficiary on an estate's termination, see ¶3949.

¶ 3906   Trust taxed as business entity.

The fact that any organization is technically cast in the trust form won't change the real character of the organization if it is more properly classified as a business entity under Reg § 301.7701-2. (Reg § 301.7701-4(b))[18]

¶ 3907   Liquidating trusts.

Liquidating trusts are ordinary trusts if their primary purpose is to liquidate the assets transferred to them. They are corporations if liquidation is only an incidental or ultimate intention and the primary objective is to continue normal business operations for an indefinite time. (Reg § 301.7701-4(d))[19]

¶ 3908   Electing small business trusts (ESBTs) for holding S stock.

ESBTs may hold stock of an S corporation. For the portion of an ESBT consisting of S stock, the normal pass-through rules don't apply; instead, the trust is taxed at a flat rate of 39.6% on its taxable ordinary income as specially computed, and its capital gains are taxed at the preferential rates that apply for individuals. Interest paid or accrued on debt incurred to acquire S stock is taken into account in determining the income of the S portion of an ESBT. (Code Sec. 641(c)) A grantor trust may elect to be an ESBT and if it does, the trust consists of a grantor portion, an S portion, and a non-S portion. The items of income, deduction, and credit attributable to the grantor portion are taxed to the deemed owner of that portion. The S portion is taxed under the special rules of Code Sec. 641(c), while the non-S portion is subject to the normal trust rules. (Reg § 1.641(c)-1)[20]

¶ 3909   Environmental remediation trusts.

An environmental remediation trust is treated as a grantor trust. Each contributor is taxed on the portion of the trust relating to his or her contributions. (Reg § 301.7701-4(e))[21]

¶ 3910   Funeral trusts—Form 1041-QFT.

A trustee of a qualified funeral trust may elect simplified tax treatment for the trust on Form 1041-QFT, if it would otherwise be treated as a grantor trust. (Code Sec. 685)[22]

---

15. ¶C-1012; ¶6414.07
16. ¶C-7010; ¶6414.03
17. ¶C-7011 *et seq.*; ¶6414.03
18. ¶C-5003; ¶77,014.13

19. ¶C-5015; ¶77,014.17
20. ¶C-5700 *et seq.*; ¶6414.08
21. ¶C-5035.1; ¶77,014.12
22. ¶C-1013.1; ¶6854

¶ 3911   Multiple trusts.

If a grantor creates multiple trusts, each trust is treated as a separate taxpayer. Separate trusts may be created even though there is only one trust instrument and only one trustee.[23]

Two or more trusts are treated as one if: (1) the trusts have substantially the same grantor or grantors and substantially the same primary beneficiary or beneficiaries, and (2) a "principal purpose" (see below) of the trusts is avoidance of federal income tax. (Code Sec. 643(f)) However, if a trust was irrevocable on Mar. 1, '84, this consolidation rule applies only to that portion of the trust attributable to contributions to corpus after Mar. 1, '84.[24]

IRS has issued proposed regs, the substance of which is basically the same as the rule provided in Code Sec. 643(f), which clarify that a "principal purpose" for establishing the trusts, or for contributing additional cash or property to the trusts, would be to avoid income tax. For these purposes, a "principal purpose" would be presumed if the creation or funding of the trust results in a significant income tax benefit, unless there is a significant non-tax purpose that could not have been achieved without the creation of separate trusts. (Prop Reg. § 1.643(f)-1)[25]

observation: The threshold amount under Code Sec. 199A (¶1595) is determined at the trust level, so absent additional legislation, taxpayers could maximize the threshold amount by dividing assets among multiple trusts, each of which would claim its own threshold amount. Code Sec. 643(f) and the proposed regs prevent this abuse.

¶ 3912   Charitable remainder annuity trusts (CRATs) and charitable remainder unitrusts (CRUTs).

These types of charitable trusts (¶2116) are not subject to income tax. However, if these trusts have unrelated business taxable income (UBTI), they must pay an excise tax equal to 100% of the UBTI. (Code Sec. 664(c); Reg § 1.664-1(a)(1))[26]

¶ 3913   Pooled income fund (PIF).

A PIF formed to pay income to noncharitable beneficiaries and the remainder to charity (¶2117) generally is taxed under the trust rules [27] even if it isn't a trust under local law. (Reg § 1.642(c)-5(a)(2))[28] However, a PIF is allowed a charitable deduction for long-term capital gain that is, under the terms of its governing instrument, permanently set aside for charitable purposes during the tax year. (Code Sec. 642(c)(3); Reg § 1.642(c)-2(c)) No amount of net long-term capital gain will be considered "permanently set aside for charitable purposes" if, under the terms of the PIF's governing instrument and applicable local law, the trustee has the power, whether or not exercised, to satisfy the income beneficiaries' right to income by the payment of either (1) an amount equal to a fixed percentage of the fair market value of the PIF's assets, whether determined annually or averaged on a multiple year basis; or (2) any amount that takes into account unrealized appreciation in the value of the PIF's assets. (Reg § 1.642(c)-2(c))[29]

---

23. ¶C-5150 *et seq.*; ¶6434.07
24. ¶C-5154; ¶6434.07
25. ¶C-5153; ¶6434.07
26. ¶C-5039; ¶6644

27. ¶s C-2312, C-2316
28. ¶C-5040
29. ¶C-2316; ¶6424.03

¶ 3914 Gross income of trusts and estates.

What would be gross income in the hands of an individual is gross income when received by a trust or estate. (Reg § 1.641(a)-2)[30]

Gross income includes income accumulated or held for future distribution under the terms of a will or trust, income that's currently distributable, income received by a decedent's estate during administration or settlement, and income that, in the fiduciary's discretion, may be either accumulated or distributed. (Code Sec. 641(a))[31]

¶ 3915 Income from real estate passing directly to heirs.

Where under local law, real property is subject to an estate's administration, the income from it is that of the estate for the period that the estate is under administration. [32]

Where state law vests legal title to decedent's real estate upon death directly in the decedent's heirs, devisees, or other beneficiaries, income from the real estate is taxed to the beneficiaries and not the estate. (Reg § 1.661(a)-2(e))[33]

¶ 3916 Gain or loss on distribution of property in kind.

Gain or loss is realized by a trust or estate (or the other beneficiaries) by reason of a distribution of property in kind if the distribution is in satisfaction of a right to receive a specific dollar amount, specific property other than that distributed, or income, if income is required to be distributed currently. In addition, gain or loss is realized if the trustee or executor makes the Code Sec. 643(e) election to recognize gain or loss. (Reg § 1.661(a)-2(f))[34]

Trusts and estates may not deduct a loss on property to which a Code Sec. 643(e)(3) election applies because of the rule barring losses on sales between related parties. See ¶2448.

¶ 3917 Estate income from community property.

If a decedent dies leaving community property, the income from one-half of the property is taxable to the estate, and the income from the other half is taxable to the surviving spouse. [35]

¶ 3918 Deductions and credits of trusts and estates.

Deductions and credits of trusts and estates are basically those allowed to individuals except for the special deduction rules discussed in the following paragraphs. (Code Sec. 641(b); Reg § 1.641(b)-1)[36]

¶ 3919 2% floor on miscellaneous itemized deductions.

For tax years before 2018, for purposes of this floor (see ¶3109), the adjusted gross income (AGI) of a trust or estate was computed the same as for an individual, except that the following were allowed as deductions in arriving at AGI: (1) costs paid or incurred in connection with the administration of the trust or estate (¶3920) that wouldn't have been incurred if the property weren't held in the trust or estate; (2) the trust's or estate's

---

30. ¶s C-2100 *et seq.*, C-7100 *et seq.*; ¶6414
31. ¶s C-2101, C-7101; ¶6414 *et seq.*
32. ¶C-7105
33. ¶C-7109

34. ¶s C-2151, C-7151; ¶6614.01
35. ¶C-7108; ¶6414.06
36. ¶s C-2200 *et seq.*, C-7200 *et seq.*; ¶6414

personal exemptions (¶3926); and (3) distribution deductions (¶3932 and ¶3934). (Code Sec. 67(e)) Thus, those expenses were not subject to the 2% floor on miscellaneous itemized deductions.

From 2018 - 2025, miscellaneous itemized deductions subject to the 2% floor have been suspended (¶3109). However, IRS intends to issue regulations to clarify that non-grantor trusts may continue to deduct expenses under Code Sec. 67(e)(1) and allowable amounts under Code Sec. 67(e)(2) during these years. Also, the appropriate portion of a "bundled fee" (see below) will continue to be deductible for purposes of determining a non-grantor trust's adjusted gross income. (Notice 2018-61, Sec. 3, 2018-31 IRB 278) [37]

Ownership costs, and similar other costs, *are* subject to the 2% floor, whereas certain tax preparation costs (those not commonly and customarily incurred by individuals) are not subject to the floor. (Reg § 1.67-4(b)) Investment advisory fees incurred by a non-grantor trust, that exceed the amount of fees that would be charged to an individual investor, are not subject to the 2% floor (and are fully deductible). (Reg § 1.67-4(b)(4))

A "bundled fee" (a single fee, such as a fiduciary's commission, which includes costs subject to the 2% floor and costs (in more than de minimis amounts) not subject to the 2% floor) paid by a non-grantor trust or an estate has to be allocated between the costs subject to the 2% floor and the costs that are not subject to the 2% floor. (Reg § 1.67-4(c)(1))[38]

Amounts that wouldn't be allowable as miscellaneous itemized deductions if paid directly by an individual can't be indirectly deducted through grantor trusts. (Code Sec. 67(c); Reg § 1.67-2T(g)(1), Reg § 1.67-2T(g)(2))

¶ 3920   Administration expenses.

Reasonable amounts paid or incurred by the fiduciary of an estate or trust on account of administration expenses, including fiduciaries' fees and litigation expenses, that are ordinary and necessary in the performance of duties of administration are deductible. (Reg § 1.212-1(i)) Deductible items include commissions and legal fees, whether allocable to corpus or income.[39] For the election to deduct these expenses against income or estate tax, see ¶3923.

¶ 3921   Interest deduction.

An estate or trust may deduct interest to the same extent as an individual, see ¶1700 *et seq*. Thus, an estate or trust is subject to the bar on the deduction of "personal" interest. (Code Sec. 163(h)) The bar applies to interest on deferred estate tax on a closely held business interest (Code Sec. 163(k)), but not to interest on deferred estate tax on a reversionary interest (see ¶5038). (Code Sec. 163(h)(2)(E))[40]

¶ 3922   Expenses allocable to exempt income.

No deduction may be taken for *any* expenses allocable to tax-exempt income. (Code Sec. 265; Reg § 1.212-1(i))[41]

¶ 3923   Election to take either income tax or estate tax deduction.

Administration expenses, including commissions and other selling expenses, and casualty and theft losses during administration may be taken either: (1) as a deduction (or as an offset against the sales price of property in determining gain or loss) in computing the

37. ¶C-2202 *et seq.*, C-7202 *et seq.*; ¶674
38. ¶C-2202 *et seq.*, C-7202 *et seq.*; ¶674
39. ¶s C-2217, C-7215; ¶s 2124.09, 6424
40. ¶K-5513; ¶s 1634.013, 1634.054
41. ¶s C-2217, C-2219, C-7217; ¶2654

estate's taxable income for *income tax* purposes, or (2) as a deduction in computing the decedent's taxable estate for *estate tax* purposes, but not both. (Code Sec. 642(g)) To take the income tax deduction, the executor should file in duplicate (a) a statement that the amount involved hasn't already been taken as a deduction for federal estate tax purposes, and (b) a waiver of the right to take it as an estate tax deduction. (Reg § 1.642(g)-1)[42]

Some items or portion of an item can be deducted for income tax purposes if the statement and waiver are filed, while a similar item or different portion of the same item can be taken for estate tax purposes. (Reg § 1.642(g)-2)[43]

Similar rules apply for purposes of the GST tax. (Code Sec. 642(g))[44]

¶ 3924 Deductions that can be claimed for both income and estate tax purposes.

The rule barring deductions for *both* income tax and estate tax purposes (¶3923) doesn't apply to obligations of the decedent for interest, taxes and expenses that are allowable as deductions in respect of a decedent as explained at ¶3968 (Reg § 1.642(g)-2), or items that qualify for deduction on the estate tax return as claims against the estate. [45]

¶ 3925 Depreciation and depletion.

Depreciation and depletion deductions of trust or estate property must be apportioned.

For a *trust*, these deductions are generally apportioned between the beneficiaries and the trustee on the basis of the trust income allocable to each. (Code Sec. 167(d), Code Sec. 611(b)(3), Code Sec. 642(e))[46] But if the trustee is required or permitted by the trust instrument or local law to maintain a reserve for the deduction, the deduction belongs to the trust to the extent that income is actually set aside for the reserve. Apart from this, the regs bar any deduction by the trust or a beneficiary that exceeds the trust's or beneficiary's allocable share of trust income. (Reg § 1.167(h)-1(b), Reg § 1.611-1(c)(4))[47]

For an *estate*, the deductions are apportioned between the estate and the beneficiaries on the basis of the estate income allocable to each, regardless of the terms of the will. (Code Sec. 167(d), Code Sec. 611(b)(4))[48]

¶ 3926 Estate exemption.

An estate is entitled to an exemption of $600. (Code Sec. 642(b))[49]

A trust that's required to distribute all of its income currently has a $300 exemption (even for a year in which it makes a corpus distribution or a charitable contribution). All other trusts generally deduct a $100 exemption. (Code Sec. 642(b); Reg § 1.642(b)-1)[50]

For tax years beginning after Dec. 31, 2017 and before Jan. 1, 2026, when the Code Sec. 151(d) individual exemption amount is zero, the exemption amount for a qualified disability trust is $4,150, adjusted for inflation after 2018 ($4,200 for 2019, as calculated by Thomson Reuters using inflation data), subject to the applicable phaseout (starting at modified adjusted gross income above $266,700 for 2018, $271,250 for 2019, as calculated by Thomson Reuters using inflation data).

42. ¶C-7226 *et seq.*; ¶6424.07
43. ¶C-7232; ¶6424.07
44. ¶C-7227; ¶6424.07
45. ¶s C-7234, C-7235; ¶6914.04
46. ¶C-2222 *et seq.*; ¶6424.06

47. ¶C-2214, C-2224; ¶6424.06
48. ¶C-7220; ¶s 1674.119, 6424.06
49. ¶C-7207; ¶6424.01
50. ¶C-2206; ¶6424.01

¶ 3927   Standard deduction.

The standard deduction of a trust or estate is zero. (Code Sec. 63(c)(6)(D))[1]

¶ 3928   Net operating loss (NOL).

Trusts and estates are entitled to the NOL deduction under Code Sec. 172 (¶1815 *et seq.*). (Code Sec. 642(d)) In computing the NOL, the charitable deduction and the deduction for distributions are disregarded. (Reg § 1.642(d)-1)[2]

¶ 3929   Charitable contributions—Form 1041-A.

An estate or trust may deduct any amount of gross income, without limitation, that, under the terms of the governing instrument is *paid* during the tax year for a charitable purpose. (Code Sec. 642(c)(1); Reg § 1.642(c)-1(a)) A provision in a governing instrument or local law that specifically provides the source from which amounts are to be paid, permanently set aside, or used for a purpose specified in Code Sec. 642(c), must have economic effect independent of income tax consequences in order to be respected for Federal tax purposes. (Reg § 1.642(c)-3(b)(2), Reg § 1.643(a)-5(b)) A contribution made out of income accumulated in earlier years is deductible, but only if no deduction was allowed for any previous year for the amount currently contributed. However, for a donation of property purchased from income in a prior year, the entity may claim a charitable deduction only for the property's adjusted basis and not its higher fair market value. [3] Courts have agreed that the amount of the deduction must be limited to the adjusted basis of the property because a deduction for unrealized gains would be inconsistent with the Code's general treatment of gross income. [4]

These deductions aren't subject to the 2% floor on miscellaneous itemized deductions, see ¶3109. (Code Sec. 67(b)(4)) File Form 1041-A for a trust that claims a charitable deduction under Code Sec. 642(c). Use Form 8868 for an extension, see ¶4126.

IRS ruled that a trust wasn't entitled to a charitable deduction under Code Sec. 642(c)(1) where the contributions that were made to charitable organizations were possible only because of modifications made to the trust under a state court order. [5]

Estates are allowed to deduct any amount of gross income, without limit, which under the terms of the governing instrument is, during the tax year, permanently *set aside* for a charitable purpose. (Code Sec. 642(c)(2); Reg § 1.642(c)-2(a), Reg § 1.642(c)-2(b))[6]

Trusts are denied the set-aside deduction, except for pooled income funds. (Code Sec. 642(c)(2), Code Sec. 642(c)(3); Reg § 1.642(c)-2(b), Reg § 1.642(c)-2(c))[7]

Contributions made out of tax-exempt income, such as state or municipal bond interest, aren't deductible. (Reg § 1.642(c)-3(b), Reg § 1.643(a)-5(b))[8]

¶ 3930   Election to accelerate charitable deduction.

A trust or estate can elect to treat a contribution actually paid in one tax year as paid in the preceding tax year. The election must be made not later than the due date (including extensions) of the income tax return for the tax year *following the tax year* to which the deductions are pushed back. (Code Sec. 642(c)(1))[9] The election is made by attaching a

---

1. ¶s C-2204, C-7205; ¶634
2. ¶s C-2226, C-7222; ¶6424.05
3. ¶s C-2301 *et seq.*, C-7301 *et seq.*; ¶6424.02
4. ¶C-2307
5. ¶C-2302

6. ¶C-7311; ¶6424.02
7. ¶C-2312 *et seq.*; ¶6424.03
8. ¶s C-2308, C-7308; ¶6424.02
9. ¶s C-2303, C-7304; ¶6424.02

statement to the return or amended return for the year to which the deductions are pushed back. (Reg § 1.642(c)-1(b))[10]

¶ 3931 Deduction for distributions to beneficiaries of trusts and estates.

Distributions to beneficiaries are deductible up to the "distributable net income" (DNI) of the trust or estate for the tax year. (Code Sec. 651(b), Code Sec. 661(a))[11] The distribution deduction of a trust depends on whether the trust is a simple trust or a complex trust.

A "simple" trust (¶3932) is one that makes no distribution other than of current income and the terms of which require all of its income to be distributed currently and do not provide for charitable or similar contributions. A "complex" trust (¶3934) permits accumulation of income or charitable contributions or distributes principal. [12]

A trust may shift its character from simple to complex and vice versa. (Reg § 1.651(a)-1, Reg § 1.661(a)-1)[13]

¶ 3932 Distributions deduction of a simple trust.

This deduction for a simple trust is the amount of its income for the tax year that's required to be distributed currently, up to the ceiling of its distributable net income (DNI) for the year (¶3933). (Code Sec. 651(b)) Tax-exempt income is excluded both from accounting income and DNI in figuring the deduction. (Reg § 1.651(b)-1)[14]

¶ 3933 Distributable net income (DNI) of a simple trust.

The starting point is *taxable* income, i.e., gross income minus deductions. These adjustments are then made to taxable income:

(1) Add back the deduction for personal exemption and any deduction for distributions. (Code Sec. 643(a)(1), Code Sec. 643(a)(2); Reg § 1.643(a)-1, Reg § 1.643(a)-2)

(2) Subtract any extraordinary dividends (in cash or property) and taxable stock dividends that the trustee doesn't pay or credit because he determines they are allocable to principal. (Code Sec. 643(a)(4); Reg § 1.643(a)-4)

(3) Subtract any capital gains that are allocated to principal and aren't paid, credited or required to be distributed during the tax year. Add back any capital losses, except to the extent they are taken into account in computing capital gains that are paid, credited or required to be distributed during the tax year. Add back any gain excluded under Code Sec. 1202 on the sale of qualified small business stock. (Code Sec. 643(a)(3); Reg § 1.643(a)-3(b))[15]

Gains from the sale or exchange of capital assets are included in DNI to the extent they are allocated to: (i) income; (ii) corpus, but treated consistently by the fiduciary on the trust's books, records, and tax returns as part of a distribution to a beneficiary; or (iii) corpus, but actually distributed to the beneficiary or used by the fiduciary in determining the amount that is distributed or required to be distributed to a beneficiary. (Reg § 1.643(a)-3(b))[16]

¶ 3934 Distributions deduction of a complex trust or estate.

A complex trust or estate deducts, up to its distributable net income (DNI) ceiling for the year (¶3935), the sum of:

---

10. ¶s C-2305, C-7305; ¶6424.02
11. ¶s C-2501, C-8001; ¶6514
12. ¶C-2601; ¶6434.02
13. ¶C-2501; ¶6514.01

14. ¶C-2603 *et seq.*; ¶6514.01
15. ¶C-2606 *et seq.*; ¶6434.01
16. ¶C-2608; ¶6434.01

(1) any income for the tax year required to be distributed currently (¶3936); and

(2) any other amounts, whether income or principal, properly paid or credited or required to be distributed for that tax year (¶3937). (Code Sec. 661(a); Reg § 1.661(a)-2(a))[17]

No distributions deduction may be taken for any portion of DNI that represents an item, such as tax-exempt interest, that isn't included in the gross income of the trust or estate. (Code Sec. 661(c); Reg § 1.661(c)-1) Unless the instrument or local law requires another allocation, the distribution is considered to contain the same proportion of tax-exempt items entering into DNI as the total tax-exempt income bears to total DNI. (Code Sec. 661(b); Reg § 1.661(b)-1)[18]

¶ 3935   Distributable net income (DNI) for a complex trust or estate.

The DNI of a complex trust or an estate is its taxable income with these adjustments:

(1) No deduction for distributions or personal exemption is allowed. (Code Sec. 643(a)(1))

(2) Capital gains are excluded unless: allocated to income; allocated to corpus, but treated consistently by the fiduciary as part of a distribution to a beneficiary; allocated to corpus but actually distributed to the beneficiary or used by the fiduciary in determining the amount that is distributed or required to be distributed to a beneficiary; or allowed as a charitable deduction. Capital losses are excluded except to the extent they enter into a determination of any capital gains paid, credited or required to be distributed to a beneficiary during the tax year. Add back any gain excluded under Code Sec. 1202 on the sale of qualified small business stock. (Code Sec. 643(a)(3); Reg § 1.643(a)-3(b))

(3) Tax-exempt interest, reduced by allocable, nondeductible expenses, is included except to the extent allocable to the charitable deduction. (Code Sec. 643(a)(5); Reg § 1.643(a)-5)[19]

¶ 3936   "Income required to be distributed currently."

Income required to be distributed currently means accounting income of the trust or estate determined under the trust instrument or will and applicable local law. It doesn't include items of gross income that the fiduciary allocates to corpus. (Code Sec. 643(b))

An allocation of amounts between income and principal under applicable local law will be respected if local law provides for a reasonable apportionment between the income and remainder beneficiaries of the total return of the trust for the year, including ordinary and tax-exempt income, capital gains, and appreciation. (Reg § 1.643(b)-1)

A distribution required to be made out of income or corpus, such as an annuity, is considered to be out of currently distributable income to the extent it's paid out of income for the tax year. (Code Sec. 661(a)(1); Reg § 1.661(a)-2(b))

Currently distributable income is deductible for the tax year of the trust or estate in which it is received even though, as a matter of practical necessity, it isn't distributed until after the end of that year. (Reg § 1.651(a)-2(a), Reg § 1.651(a)-2(b))[20]

---

17. ¶s C-2701, C-8101; ¶6614.01
18. ¶s C-2707, C-8107

19. ¶s C-2702 *et seq.*, C-8102 *et seq.*; ¶6434.01
20. ¶s C-2504 *et seq.*, C-8003 *et seq.*; ¶s 6434.03, 6514.01, 6624.01

¶ 3937   "Other amounts properly paid or credited or required to be distributed."

Other amounts properly paid or credited or required to be distributed must be actually distributed or at least made available on demand by the beneficiary. Even though designated by the fiduciary as a payment of *principal* of the trust or estate, a distribution actually paid or made available is deductible by the fiduciary as a distribution of "other amounts." It isn't necessary that the distribution actually be made out of income. (Code Sec. 661(a); Reg § 1.661(a)-2(c))[21] An amount that a trust has elected to treat as an estimated tax payment by a beneficiary (¶3903) is a deductible distribution. (Code Sec. 643(g))[22]

¶ 3938   Deduction for distribution of property in kind.

Distributions of property in kind qualify for deduction as other amounts paid. (Reg § 1.661(a)-2(c)) If the trust or estate elects to recognize gain or loss (¶3916), the property distributed is taken into account at its fair market value for purposes of the distribution deduction. If the election isn't made, the property is taken into account only to the extent of the lesser of the basis of the property in the hands of the beneficiary (¶3947) or the fair market value of the property. (Code Sec. 643(e)(2), Code Sec. 643(e)(3))[23]

¶ 3939   Family support allowances.

Family support allowances (for a decedent's widow(er) or dependent) paid by an estate under a court order or decree, or under local law, are treated as distributions deductible by the estate, subject to the regular distributable net income (DNI) deduction ceiling. (Reg § 1.661(a)-2(e), Reg § 1.662(a)-2(c))[24]

¶ 3940   Nondeductible distributions.

No distributions deduction is allowed for:

. . . distributions to charity (Reg § 1.663(a)-2);[25]

. . . the value of any interest in real estate, title to which passes directly from decedent to the decedent's heirs and devisees (Reg § 1.661(a)-2(e));[26]

. . . a gift or bequest of specific property or of a specific sum of money that is paid or credited all at once or in not more than three installments —an amount that can be paid only from income isn't considered a gift or bequest of a specific sum of money and is therefore includible in the distributions deduction (Code Sec. 663(a)(1));[27]

. . . any amount reported as a distribution in an earlier year's return because it was credited or required to be distributed in the earlier year (Code Sec. 663(a)(3); Reg § 1.663(a)-3);[28] or

. . . any amount paid or credited within the first 65 days of the current year which the fiduciary elected to treat as paid or credited in the preceding year, see ¶3941.

¶ 3941   Election to deduct "late paid" distributions—the "65-day rule."

The fiduciary of a complex trust and the executor of an estate can elect, by checking a box on Form 1041, to treat an amount properly paid or credited within the first 65 days of any tax year of the entity as paid or credited on the last day of the preceding tax year.

21. ¶s C-2524 *et seq.*, C-8014 *et seq.*; ¶s 6614.01, 6624.01
22. ¶C-2530; ¶6434.08
23. ¶s C-2525, C-8015; ¶6434.05
24. ¶C-8011; ¶6614.01

25. ¶s C-2533, C-8026; ¶6614.01
26. ¶C-8027
27. ¶s C-2531 *et seq.*, C-8022 *et seq.*; ¶6614.01
28. ¶s C-2534, C-8028; ¶6614.01

(Code Sec. 663(b))[29] This gives the trustee or executor time to determine income earned by the trust for the year, and the opportunity to deduct distributions of that income on the return for the year earned.

The amount to which the election applies can't exceed the greater of: (1) the entity's accounting income for the year for which the election is made, or (2) its distributable net income (DNI) for that year, in each case reduced by any amounts paid, credited, or required to be distributed in that year other than amounts considered paid or credited in a preceding tax year by reason of the "65-day" rule. (Reg § 1.663(b)-1(a))[30]

¶ 3942   Amount taxed to beneficiary of a simple trust.

The beneficiary of a simple trust is generally taxed on the *lower* of these two items:

(1) the amount of trust income for the tax year of the trust required to be distributed to the beneficiary currently whether distributed or not; or

(2) the beneficiary's proportionate share of the trust's distributable net income (DNI). (Code Sec. 652(a); Reg § 1.652(a)-1)

DNI is computed as explained at ¶3933, except that for this purpose it includes tax-exempt interest minus allocable deductions. (Code Sec. 643(a)(5)) Tax-exempt income items, however, aren't taxable to the beneficiary because of the character rule explained at ¶3944. Income from sources outside the U.S. is included for foreign trusts. (Code Sec. 643(a)(6))[31]

¶ 3943   Amount taxed to beneficiary of a complex trust or estate.

The beneficiary of a complex trust or of an estate includes in gross income the sum of the following amounts, subject to the distributable net income (DNI) ceiling (see below) and the elimination of tax-exempt items under the character rule (¶3944):

(1) income required to be distributed to the beneficiary currently (though not actually distributed), which includes an annuity or other amount required to be paid out of income or corpus, to the extent it is paid out of income for the tax year; and

(2) all other amounts (whether from income or principal) properly paid, credited or required to be distributed to the beneficiary for the tax year (Code Sec. 662(a))[32] including income from property distributed in kind, see ¶3947. (Reg § 1.662(a)-3(b))

A beneficiary of a complex trust or an estate need not report as income more than the beneficiary's share of DNI, so that the total amount of income reported by all beneficiaries cannot exceed the total DNI of the trust or estate for the tax year. For this purpose, the beneficiaries are divided into two groups or "tiers:"

(1) The first tier is composed of beneficiaries entitled to income distributions currently, that is "income required to be distributed currently."

(2) The second tier is composed of beneficiaries receiving or entitled to receive other "noncurrent" distributions. (Code Sec. 662(a); Reg § 1.662(a)-3(c))[33]

First-tier beneficiaries report, in the aggregate, the amount of their current distributions, up to the amount of DNI for the tax year of the trust or estate, computed as explained at ¶3935 without any charitable deduction. Thus, if the total of first-tier distributions is equal to or less than DNI (without charitable deduction), each first-tier beneficiary reports his or her full share of the distributions. (Code Sec. 662(a)(1))[34]

29. ¶C-2713, ¶C-8113; ¶6634.03
30. ¶C-2713, ¶C-8113; ¶6634.03
31. ¶C-3001; ¶s 6524, 6524.02, 6434.01

32. ¶s C-3006 *et seq.*, C-9001 *et seq.*; ¶6624
33. ¶s C-3010, C-9006; ¶6624
34. ¶s C-3011 *et seq.*, C-9007 *et seq.*; ¶6624

But if the total of first-tier distributions exceeds DNI (without charitable deduction) each beneficiary reports an amount equal to his or her pro rata share of DNI (without charitable deduction). (Code Sec. 662(a)(1); Reg § 1.662(a)-2(b))[35]

Second-tier beneficiaries report, in the aggregate, the amount of their second-tier distributions up to the DNI of the trust or estate as reduced for first-tier distributions of current income. For this purpose, DNI is computed *with* allowance of any charitable deduction.

If the total of second-tier distributions equals or is less than the ceiling (DNI as reduced for first-tier distributions), each second-tier beneficiary reports his or her full share of the second-tier distributions. But, if the total of second-tier distributions exceeds the ceiling, each second-tier beneficiary reports only his or her pro rata share of the ceiling amount. (Code Sec. 662(a)(2); Reg § 1.662(a)-3(c))[36]

¶ 3944 Character of trust's and estate's income in beneficiary's hands.

For simple trusts, complex trusts and estates, the amounts taxable to the beneficiaries have the same character (e.g., as tax-exempt income) in the hands of the beneficiaries as the amounts had when received by the trust or estate. (Code Sec. 652(b), Code Sec. 662(b); Reg § 1.652(b)-1, Reg § 1.662(b)-1)[37]

Unless the instrument specifically allocates different classes of income to different beneficiaries, amounts distributed are treated as consisting of the same proportion of each class of items entering into the computation of distributable net income (DNI) as the total of each class bears to the total DNI of the trust or estate. (Code Sec. 652(b), Code Sec. 662(b); Reg § 1.652(b)-1, Reg § 1.662(b)-1)[38]

Deductions that enter into the computation of DNI are allocated among the classes as follows:

. . . Deductions *directly* attributable to a particular class of income (interest, rents, dividends, capital gains, etc.) are allocated to that class.

. . . If deductions *directly* attributable to a class of income exceed that class, the excess may be allocated to any other class (including capital gains) included in DNI in the manner shown below for deductions not directly attributable, except that excess deductions directly attributable to tax-exempt income cannot be used to reduce any other class of income.

. . . Deductions not directly attributable to a specific class of income can be allocated to any item of income (including capital gains) included in DNI, but a part must be allocated proportionately to tax-exempt income. Examples of these "neutral" deductions are trustees' commissions (both income and corpus), and state income and personal property taxes. (Reg § 1.652(b)-3)[39]

A *charitable deduction* by an estate or complex trust is allocated just before the other deductions. Allocation follows the terms of the instrument or local law, or if these are silent, the charitable deduction is allocated to each class of income items in the proportion that the total of each class bears to the total of all classes. (Reg § 1.643(a)-5(b), Reg § 1.662(b)-2)[40]

¶ 3945 Beneficiaries' separate shares treated separately.

If a complex trust or an estate accumulates income for one beneficiary and distributes principal to another beneficiary, the normal tax rules would impose a tax burden on the

---

35. ¶s C-3011, C-9008; ¶6624
36. ¶s C-3013, C-9009; ¶6624
37. ¶s C-3002, C-3016, C-9012; ¶s 6524.03, 6624.03

38. ¶s C-3003, C-3016, C-9012; ¶s 6524.02, 6624.02
39. ¶s C-3004, C-3017, C-9013; ¶s 6524, 6524.02, 6624.02
40. ¶s C-3018, C-9015; ¶6624

recipient of principal since that recipient in effect must pay tax on income accumulated for the other beneficiary. To prevent this, the "separate share rule" treats substantially separate and independent shares of different beneficiaries of a single trust or estate as though each share represented a separate trust or estate. This applies *only* in computing distributable net income (DNI) as a ceiling on the amount deductible by the trust or estate and taxable to the beneficiaries (Code Sec. 663(c); Reg § 1.663(c)-1(b)), and is mandatory. (Reg § 1.663(c)-1(d))[41] Code Sec. 663(c), Reg § 1.663(c)-1(a))[42] A surviving spouse's elective share is a separate share, [43] as is a pecuniary formula bequest unless it's not entitled to income or to share in appreciation or depreciation and can paid or credited in more than three installments. (Reg § 1.663(c)-4(b))[44]

¶ 3946　　When a beneficiary is taxed.

Amounts required to be distributed currently are taxed to the beneficiary when they are required to be distributed even though not actually distributed. Other distributions are taxed to a beneficiary when they are made or credited, or required to be made. (Code Sec. 652(a), Code Sec. 662(a); Reg § 1.662(a)-3(a))[45]

If a beneficiary's tax year is different from that of the estate or trust, the beneficiary includes his or her share of the trust or estate income in the return for the tax year in which the tax year of the trust or estate ends. (Code Sec. 652(c), Code Sec. 662(c))[46]

Upon termination of an estate, a beneficiary must include in his or her calendar year return income received from the estate during both the estate's fiscal year and final short year where both years end within his or her calendar year. [47]

Where the 65-day rule is elected (¶3941), the beneficiary is considered as receiving the distribution in his or her tax year that includes the close of the trust's or estate's tax year in which the distribution is considered made. (Reg § 1.663(b)-1(a)(2)(ii))[48]

¶ 3947　　Distributions in kind includible in a beneficiary's income.

For property distributed in kind, the amount taken into account under Code Sec. 662(a)(2) (¶3943) for purposes of determining the amount includible in the beneficiary's income, and for purposes of determining basis in the property, depends on whether the estate or trust elected to recognize gain or loss on the distribution (see ¶3916).

If the estate or trust elects, the property is taken into account at its fair market value (FMV). (Code Sec. 643(e)(3))

If the estate or trust doesn't elect, the property is taken into account only to the extent of the lesser of: (1) the FMV of the property, or (2) its basis in the hands of the beneficiary. (Code Sec. 643(e)(2))[49]

The beneficiary's basis for property distributed in kind is the adjusted basis of the property in the hands of the estate or trust immediately before the distribution, adjusted for any gain or loss recognized by the estate or trust on the distribution. (Code Sec. 643(e)(1))[50]

¶ 3948　　Nontaxable gifts and bequests.

A beneficiary isn't taxable on any amount paid or credited as a gift or bequest of specific property or of a specific sum of money, and that is paid or credited all at once or in not

---

41. ¶C-2711 *et seq.*; ¶6634.01
42. ¶C-8111; ¶6634.01
43. ¶C-8112.1; ¶6634.01
44. ¶C-8112.2; ¶6634.01
45. ¶s C-3025, C-9017; ¶s 6524.01, 6624.01

46. ¶s C-3026, C-9018; ¶s 6524.04, 6624.04
47. ¶C-9018
48. ¶C-3028, ¶C-9019; ¶6634.03
49. ¶s C-3009, C-9004; ¶6434.05
50. ¶s C-3009, C-9004; ¶6614.01

more than three installments. (Code Sec. 663(a)(1))[1]

¶ 3949 Beneficiaries' deductions on estate or trust termination.

Beneficiaries who succeed to property of a trust or estate on its termination can deduct as a miscellaneous itemized deduction the unused deductions in excess of gross income for the last tax year of the trust or estate, other than the personal exemption and charitable contributions. The deduction is allowed only for the beneficiary's tax year in which the trust or estate terminates. The deduction is taken into account in computing the beneficiary's items of tax preference. (Code Sec. 642(h); Reg § 1.642(h)-2(a))[2]

¶ 3950 Taxation of beneficiaries of charitable remainder trusts (CRTs).

Amounts paid to an income beneficiary of a CRT retain the character they had in the hands of the trust, with this qualification: each payment is treated as consisting of (1) ordinary income, to the extent of the trust's ordinary income for that year and undistributed ordinary income for earlier years, (2) capital gain, to the extent of capital gain for that year and undistributed capital gain (determined on a cumulative net basis) for earlier years, (3) other income (e.g., tax-exempt interest), to the extent of that income for that year and undistributed amounts for earlier years, and (4) trust corpus. (Code Sec. 664(a), Code Sec. 664(b); Reg § 1.664-1(d)(1)) Within categories (1) and (2), items are assigned to different classes to reflect rate differences (e.g., qualified dividends and different capital gain classes). (Reg § 1.664-1(d)(1)(i)(b))[3]

¶ 3951 Determining basis in a term interest in a charitable remainder trust (CRT) for sale or other disposition.

The basis of a term interest (an interest, present or future, in the income from property or the right to use property which will terminate or fail on the lapse of time, on the occurrence of an event or contingency, or on the failure of an event or contingency to occur) in a CRT of a taxable beneficiary is the portion of the adjusted uniform basis assignable to that interest, reduced (but not below zero) by an amount determined by applying the same share of that portion to the sum of (1) the amount of the trust's undistributed net ordinary income; and (2) the amount of the trust's undistributed net capital gain. (Reg § 1.1014-5(c))[4]

¶ 3952 Distribution of accumulated trust income—"throwback" rules.

The throwback rules tax beneficiaries on distributions of income accumulated by the trust before the year of distribution, as though the income had been distributed currently to the beneficiaries in the years received by the trust. (Reg § 1.665(a)-0A(a)(1))[5]

The throwback rules apply to foreign trusts, domestic trusts previously treated as foreign trusts (except as provided in regs), and domestic trusts created before Mar. 1, '84, that would be treated as multiple trusts under Code Sec. 643(f). (Code Sec. 665(c))

The throwback rules generally apply only to complex trusts. Estates aren't subject to the throwback rules. (Code Sec. 666; Reg § 1.665(a)-0A(d))[6]

The fiduciary of a trust subject to the throwback rules must complete Schedule J (Form 1041) and attach it to the trust's return. [7]

---

1. ¶s C-2531, C-8022; ¶6634.02
2. ¶s C-3033 *et seq.*, C-9053 *et seq.*; ¶6434.04
3. ¶C-3051; ¶6644.01
4. ¶P-3130.1; ¶10,014.90

5. ¶C-4001; ¶6664
6. ¶C-4002; ¶6664
7. ¶C-4001; ¶6664

Distributions of income accumulated before the birth of the beneficiary or before the beneficiary reaches age 21 are exempt from the throwback rules. But this exclusion doesn't apply to distributions from a foreign trust or to certain distributions from multiple trusts. (Code Sec. 665(b))[8] Distributions not exceeding accounting income are also exempt. (Code Sec. 665(b))[9]

¶ 3953   Beneficiary's tax under throwback rules—Form 4970.

The beneficiary includes in his or her income for the current year:

. . . the amount of the accumulation distribution considered distributed; and

. . . the trust's income tax considered distributed. (Code Sec. 667(a), Code Sec. 666(b))[10]

The beneficiary's total tax liability for the current year is:

(1) a partial tax on the beneficiary's taxable income *reduced* by the total amounts considered distributed to the beneficiary under the throwback rules; *plus*

(2) a partial tax on the amounts considered distributed under the throwback rules (Code Sec. 667(a)); *plus*

(3) in the case of a foreign trust, a special nondeductible interest charge. (Code Sec. 667(b))[11]

The beneficiary's partial tax under (2) is computed (on Form 4970) under a special "shortcut" method and is then reduced by any estate tax or generation-skipping transfer tax attributable to the partial tax. (Code Sec. 667(b)(6))[12]

¶ 3954   3.8% surtax on "unearned income" of estate or trust—Form 8960.

Certain unearned income of individuals (¶3144), estates, and trusts is subject to a surtax on "unearned income" (i.e., it's payable on top of any other tax payable on that income). For an estate or trust, the surtax is 3.8% of the lesser of (1) undistributed net investment income (¶3143) or the excess of adjusted gross income (as defined in Code Sec. 67(e), see ¶3919) over the dollar amount at which the highest income tax bracket applicable to an estate or trust begins. (Code Sec. 1411(a)(2)) The tax does not apply to trusts all the unexpired interests in which are devoted to charitable purposes; trusts exempt from tax under Code Sec. 501; or charitable remainder trusts exempt from tax under Code Sec. 664. (Code Sec. 1411(e)) Proposed reliance regs clarify many aspects of the 3.8% surtax including issues unique to estates and trusts. The 3.8% tax is computed on Form 8960 and reflected on and paid with Form 1041. [13]

¶ 3955   Grantor or others taxed as owner of trust—grantor trust rules.

A trust grantor or another person with power over a trust or its property may be taxed on its income as the "owner" of the trust. Under IRS guidance, a grantor trust is ignored as a separate entity apart from the owner for all federal income tax purposes. These grantor trust rules are discussed at ¶3956 *et seq.*[14] These rules don't apply to charitable remainder trusts or pooled income funds. (Reg § 1.671-1(d))[15] These rules generally apply only to the extent they result in amounts being currently taken into account in computing the income of a U.S. citizen, resident or domestic corporation. (Code Sec. 672(f); Reg § 1.672(f)-1, Reg § 1.672(f)-2, Reg § 1.672(f)-3)

✪observation: Thus, the grantor trust rules generally don't apply where they would

---

8. ¶C-4007; ¶6664
9. ¶C-4008; ¶6664
10. ¶C-4101; ¶6664
11. ¶C-4101; ¶6664

12. ¶C-4100 *et seq.*; ¶6664
13. ¶C-5800; ¶C-9850; ¶14,114.02
14. ¶C-5200 *et seq.*; ¶6714
15. ¶C-5216; ¶6714

treat a foreign person as owner of the trust. This ensures that either the U.S. or the foreign jurisdiction taxes the trust income.

For this purpose, a grantor includes any person who creates a trust, or directly or indirectly makes a gratuitous transfer of property, including cash, to a trust. (Reg § 1.671-2(e))[16]

These rules may be applicable to the entire trust or, where appropriate, to only a specific portion of a trust. (Reg § 1.671-3(a))[17] If a grantor or other person is considered to be the owner of the *entire* trust, he or she computes his or her own personal income tax by taking into account all trust income, deductions and credits, as though the trust didn't exist. (Reg § 1.671-3(a)(1)) But, where a grantor is treated as owner solely because of his or her interest in trust *income*, the grantor takes into account only the share of trust items that would be reported by a current income beneficiary. (Reg § 1.671-3(c))[18]

For purposes of taxing the grantor as the owner of a trust, the grantor is treated as holding any power or interest held by any individual who was the spouse of the grantor at the time of the creation of the power or the interest, or who became the spouse of the grantor after the creation, but only for periods after the individual became the spouse. (Code Sec. 672(e)(1)) This rule applies only to transfers in trust made after Mar. 1, '86. [19]

A "defective grantor trust" is a trust intentionally structured so that the grantor, rather than the trust or its beneficiaries, will be taxed on the trust's income without the trust being included in the grantor's estate. A defective grantor trust can lower income taxes where the grantor is in a lower bracket than the beneficiary or some income would be accumulated in the trust and taxed at the highly compressed trust tax brackets. The grantor's payment of income tax on trust income taxed to him is not a gift to the beneficiaries. If a defective grantor trust or applicable state law requires the trustee to reimburse the grantor for the income tax on trust income, the full value of the trust property will be included in the grantor's gross estate for trusts created after Oct. 3, 2004. [20]

Where a grantor established an irrevocable trust and gave a distribution committee the power to make distributions, the committee's discretionary distributions would not cause the grantor or any of the other beneficiaries to be treated as the trust's owner for income tax purposes, if distributions to the grantor required the consent of adverse parties, and distributions at the grantor's sole discretion were limited by an ascertainable standard. [21]

observation: The trust discussed above was likely established as a non-grantor trust for state income tax avoidance purposes. These trusts are commonly referred to as "ING" trusts, or Incomplete Non-Grantor Trusts, and are often established in a state (such as Delaware or Nevada) that does not tax a trust's accumulated income and capital gains. These trusts should not include a reversion to the grantor, so that the grantor is not considered to be the owner of the trust.

¶ 3956   Grantor's power to revoke.

If the grantor of a trust reserves the power to take back title to the trust funds, the grantor is considered the owner of the trust, whether or not the grantor actually exercises that power. (Code Sec. 671, Code Sec. 676) The power to get back the trust funds may be a power to revoke, terminate, alter or amend, or to appoint. (Reg § 1.676(a)-1)

The grantor is taxed if the grantor can exercise the power alone, if it can be exercised only by another who is regarded as a "nonadverse party" (see below), or if it can be

---

16. ¶C-5201; ¶6714
17. ¶C-5207 *et seq.*; ¶6714
18. ¶C-5209 *et seq.*; ¶6714

19. ¶C-5204 *et seq.*; ¶6724.02
20. ¶C-5200; ¶6714
21. ¶C-5311

exercised by both the grantor and a "nonadverse party" together. (Code Sec. 676(a))[22] The grantor is not taxed if the power can be exercised only by or with consent of an adverse party. (Code Sec. 672(a), Code Sec. 676(a); Reg § 1.676(a)-1)[23]

An "adverse party" is any person with a substantial beneficial interest in the trust (including a general power of appointment over trust property) which would be adversely affected by the exercise or non-exercise of his or her power with regards to the trust. (Code Sec. 672(a)) A beneficiary is ordinarily an adverse party. (Reg § 1.672(a)-1(b)) A "nonadverse party" has either no beneficial interest, or one that is not substantial, or one which would not be adversely affected by the exercise of his or her power with regard to the trust. (Code Sec. 672(b); Reg § 1.672(b)-1)[24]

¶ 3957   Income for grantor, spouse or dependent.

The grantor of a trust is treated as its owner and taxed on its income, if the trust income is:

. . . distributed actually or constructively to the grantor or the grantor's spouse;

. . . held or accumulated for future distribution to the grantor or the grantor's spouse; or

. . . applied to pay premiums on life insurance policies taken out on the life of the grantor or the grantor's spouse (and not irrevocably payable to charities). (Code Sec. 677(a))

The income isn't taxable to the grantor if the application of the income to any of these purposes requires the approval of an adverse party (¶3956). (Reg § 1.677(a)-1(b))[25]

If trust income is *actually* used to support a beneficiary (other than the grantor's spouse) whom the grantor is legally obligated to support, such as the grantor's minor children, the grantor is taxable on that income. But the mere fact that trust income *may* be so used doesn't make the grantor taxable, unless the use is discretionary with the grantor as an *individual* (not trustee). (Reg § 1.677(b)-1(d), Reg § 1.677(b)-1(e), Reg § 1.677(b)-1(f))[26]

¶ 3958   Reversionary interests.

For transfers in trust made after Mar. 1, '86, the grantor of a trust is generally taxable as the owner on its income if the grantor has a reversionary interest in the corpus or income and, as of the inception of the trust, the value of that interest is more than 5% of the value of the trust. (Code Sec. 673(a)) The value of the reversionary interest must be determined by assuming the maximum exercise of discretion in favor of the grantor. (Code Sec. 673(c))

Any postponement of the date specified for the reacquisition of possession or enjoyment of the reversionary interest is treated as a new transfer in trust starting with the date the postponement is effective and terminating with the date prescribed by the postponement. However, income for any period isn't included in income of the grantor by reason of this rule if it wouldn't be includible in the absence of the postponement. (Code Sec. 673(d))

The grantor isn't treated as the owner where the reversionary interest takes effect on the death before age 21 of a beneficiary who (1) is a lineal descendant of the grantor, and (2) holds all present interests in the trust. (Code Sec. 673(b))[27]

---

22. ¶C-5301; ¶6764
23. ¶C-5303; ¶6764
24. ¶C-5312 *et seq.*; ¶6724.01

25. ¶C-5401; ¶6774.01
26. ¶C-5423; ¶6774.04
27. ¶C-5450 *et seq.*; ¶6734.01

¶ 3959   Power to control beneficial enjoyment (including "sprinkling" and "spray" powers).

Trust income is generally taxable to the grantor as the owner of the trust property if the beneficial enjoyment of trust corpus or income is subject to a power of disposition that may be exercised by him personally, or by a nonadverse party (¶3956), or both, and requires no consent or approval of an adverse party (¶3956). (Code Sec. 674)[28]

Similarly, the grantor will be taxed if he retains certain administrative powers, such as borrowing powers and dealing with the trust for less than full consideration. (Code Sec. 675)[29]

But certain relatively broad powers to shift benefits may be given to "independent" trustees without causing the grantor to be treated as owner. These so called "sprinkling" and "spray" powers permit the trustee to distribute, apportion or accumulate income, or to pay out corpus to or among beneficiaries (Code Sec. 674(c)), but not to add beneficiaries except to include after-born or after-adopted children. These powers vested solely in trustees won't cause the grantor to be taxed as the owner of the trust if the grantor isn't eligible as a trustee or co-trustee and no more than half the trustees vested with the power are related or subordinate parties subservient to the grantor's wishes. (Code Sec. 674(c), Code Sec. 674(d); Reg § 1.674(d)-2(b))

Also, a power to distribute, apportion or accumulate income won't subject the grantor to tax if the grantor and the grantor's spouse (living with the grantor) are ineligible to exercise the power as trustee or co-trustee and the power is limited by a reasonably definite external standard set forth in the trust instrument. (Code Sec. 674(d); Reg § 1.674(d)-1)[30]

¶ 3960   Person other than the grantor as owner (including "Crummey" powers).

A trustee, beneficiary, or some other person may be taxable on the income as the owner, if that person:

. . . has a power exercisable solely by him or her to vest the corpus, or income from it, in him or herself; or

. . . has previously modified or released such a power and afterward retains control which would make the grantor taxable under the rules discussed at ¶3955 *et seq.* (Code Sec. 678)[31]

A holder of a "Crummey" power (see ¶5049) is treated as owner under the above rule. [32]

¶ 3961   Foreign trust grantors or other transferors—Form 3520, Form 3520-A.

If a U.S. person (e.g., a grantor) makes a transfer to a foreign trust with a U.S. beneficiary, the income of the trust (including foreign source income) will be taxed currently to the transferor as the owner of the trust. (Code Sec. 679(a)(1); Reg § 1.679-1) This rule doesn't apply where the transfer is: (a) by reason of death, (b) for fair market value, or (c) to a foreign employee benefit or charitable trust. (Code Sec. 679(a); Reg § 1.679-4)

A trust is treated as having a U.S. beneficiary for a tax year unless (1) under the terms of the trust, no part of the trust's income or corpus may be paid or accumulated during the tax year to or for the benefit of a U.S. person, and (2) if the trust is terminated at any time during the tax year, no part of the income or corpus could be paid to or for the benefit of a

---

28. ¶C-5531; ¶6744
29. ¶C-5551 *et seq.*; ¶6754
30. ¶C-5542 *et seq.*; ¶6744

31. ¶C-5571; ¶6784
32. ¶C-5574; ¶6784

U.S. person. An amount is treated as accumulated for the benefit of a U.S. person even if the U.S. person's interest in the trust is contingent on a future event. (Code Sec. 679(c)(1))

If a U.S. person directly or indirectly transfers property to a foreign trust, there is a rebuttable presumption that the trust has a U.S. beneficiary unless the U.S. person submits information as required by IRS and demonstrates to its satisfaction that requirements (1) and (2) in the above paragraph are met. (Code Sec. 679(d)) If any person has the discretion to make a distribution from a trust to, or for the benefit of, any person, the trust is treated as having a U.S. beneficiary unless: (i) the trust terms specifically identify the class of persons to whom the distributions may be made; and (ii) none of those persons is a U.S. person during the tax year. (Code Sec. 679(c)(4)) If any U.S. person who directly or indirectly transfers property to the trust is directly or indirectly involved in any agreement or understanding that may result in the income or corpus of the trust being paid or accumulated to or for the benefit of a U.S. person, that agreement or understanding is treated as a term of the trust. (Code Sec. 679(c)(5)) For purposes of determining whether a foreign trust has a U.S. beneficiary, a loan of cash or marketable securities (or the use of any other trust property) directly or indirectly to or by any U.S. person (whether or not the U.S. person is a beneficiary under the terms of the trust) is treated as paid or accumulated for the benefit of a U.S. person, unless the U.S. person repays the loan at a market rate of interest (or pays the fair market value of the use of the property) within a reasonable period of time. (Code Sec. 679(c)(6))[33]

The above rules also apply to (1) certain foreign persons who transfer property to a foreign trust and later become a U.S. person (Code Sec. 679(a)(4); Reg § 1.679-5(a)) and (2) a U.S. person who transferred property to a domestic trust that becomes a foreign trust during the transferor's life. (Code Sec. 679(a)(5); Reg § 1.679-6(b))[34]

A U.S. person who is treated as an owner of any portion of a foreign trust must provide information as IRS may require with respect to the trust. (Code Sec. 6048(b)(1))

Specifically, a U.S. person (and an executor of the estate of a U.S. decedent) that is treated as the owner of a foreign trust must file Form 3520 to report certain transactions with foreign trusts, ownership of foreign trusts under the grantor trust rules, and receipt of certain large gifts or bequests from certain foreign persons. [35]

Further, a foreign trust with a U.S. owner must file Form 3520-A to satisfy the annual information reporting requirements. [36]

¶ 3962   Beneficiary treated as grantor to the extent of gifts to foreign grantor.

Where a foreign person would ordinarily be treated as the owner of any portion of a trust, *and* the trust has a beneficiary who is a U.S. person, the beneficiary generally is treated as the grantor of that portion to the extent the beneficiary has after Nov. 5, '90, made transfers by gift (directly or indirectly) to the foreign grantor. Gifts which are excluded from the calculation of gift tax under Code Sec. 2503(b) (generally, annual gifts of present interests of up to $15,000 for 2018, and for 2019 as calculated by Thomson Reuters using inflation data); see ¶5049) aren't included. (Code Sec. 672(f)(5); Reg § 1.672(f)-5) This rule applies even if the beneficiary wasn't a U.S. person at the time of the transfer. [37]

¶ 3963   Decedent's Income and Deductions. ▆▆▆▆▆▆▆

The last tax year of a decedent ends with the date of death. (Reg § 1.451-1(b))[38]

For a *cash basis* decedent, include only the income received, actually or constructively, up to the end of the day of death (Code Sec. 691(a); Reg § 1.451-1(b)(1), Reg § 1.691(a)-

---

33. ¶C-5600 *et seq.*; ¶6794
34. ¶s C-5603.1, C-5603.2; ¶6794
35. ¶S-3644; ¶60,484

36. ¶S-3645.2; ¶60,484
37. ¶C-5218.31; ¶6724.03
38. ¶C-9601; ¶6914

1(b)), and deduct expenses only to the extent paid before death (except for the special deduction for the unrecovered investment in an annuity contract, see ¶3964, and certain medical expenses paid within one year after death, see ¶2143).[39]

For an *accrual basis* decedent, include income and deductions computed on the accrual method. But an amount of income or deduction accrued *solely* by reason of death isn't includible on the final return. (Code Sec. 451(b), Code Sec. 461(b))[40]

Post-death income and deductions "in respect of a decedent" must be reported by decedent's estate or others who acquire the decedent's rights or obligations (¶3965 *et seq.*).

¶ 3964 Deduction for unrecovered investment in annuity contract.

A decedent's unrecovered investment in an annuity contract is an itemized deduction (*not* subject to the 2%-of-AGI floor) (Code Sec. 67(b)(10)) for the decedent's last tax year, if the annuity payments cease by reason of death. (Code Sec. 72(b)(3)(A))[41]

¶ 3965 Income in respect of a decedent (IRD, after-death income).

IRD covers income (including capital gain) which a decedent had a right to receive but that: (1) wasn't actually or constructively received by a cash basis decedent, or (2) wasn't accrued by an accrual basis decedent. IRD includes insurance renewal commissions, a monthly pension paid to deceased employee's spouse, taxable distributions from a qualified employee plan or IRA, a death benefit under a deferred annuity contract, partnership income of a deceased partner (Reg § 1.742-1) and S corporation income of a deceased shareholder. (Code Sec. 1367(b)(4))[42]

¶ 3966 Installment obligations, including self-cancelling installment notes (SCINs).

Uncollected installment obligations held by the decedent and disposed of at death are income in respect of a decedent (IRD, Code Sec. 453B(c); Reg § 1.691(a)-5(a)) and not reported on the decedent's final return. (Code Sec. 691(a)(4)) The amount of the IRD is the excess of the face amount of the obligation over its basis in the hands of the decedent. (Code Sec. 453B(b), Code Sec. 691(a)(4)) On collecting the face amount, the executor, beneficiary or other recipient includes in gross income the same proportion of the payment that would have been reported by the decedent if he or she had lived and received the payment. (Reg § 1.691(a)-5(a))

If the executor or beneficiary transfers the installment obligation, the amount included in gross income for the tax year of the transfer is the fair market value of the obligation at the time of the transfer plus any excess of sales proceeds over fair market value (if it's sold) minus an amount equal to the basis of the obligation in the hands of the decedent (adjusted to reflect the receipt of any installment payments since the decedent's death). (Code Sec. 691(a)(4); Reg § 1.691(a)-5(b))

If the installment obligation is transferred to the obligor or is cancelled by the executor, any previously unreported gain from the installment sale will be recognized by the seller's estate. (Code Sec. 691(a)(5)) The result is the same where payments due on an installment note are extinguished at the holder's death under a provision contained in the sales agreement and installment note, i.e., a "death-terminating" installment note or a SCIN. [43]

39. ¶s C-9556, C-9605; ¶6914
40. ¶s C-9606, C-9608; ¶6914.03
41. ¶C-9608; ¶674

42. ¶C-9505 *et seq.*; ¶s 6914, 6914.03
43. ¶C-9528; ¶6914

¶ 3967   Who is taxed on income in respect of a decedent (IRD)?

A decedent's IRD not includible on the decedent's last return must be reported, for the tax year when received, by:

... the decedent's estate, if it acquired the right to receive the item of income from the decedent;

... the person who, by reason of the decedent's death, acquires the right to the income whenever this right isn't acquired by the decedent's estate from the decedent; or

... the person who acquires the right from the decedent by bequest, devise or inheritance, if the amount is received after distribution by the decedent's estate of the right to the income. (Code Sec. 691(a)(1))[44]

The character of IRD is the same as it would have been in the hands of the decedent, if the decedent had lived and received the income. (Code Sec. 691(a)(3); Reg § 1.691(a)-3(a))[45]

¶ 3968   Decedent's deductions and credits available to estate or beneficiaries.

Deductions for a decedent's business expenses, expenses for the production of income, interest, taxes, depletion and the credit for foreign taxes are available to the decedent's estate if the estate is liable for the obligation giving rise to the deduction or credit, and it isn't allowable in the decedent's final (or any previous) return. If not available to the estate, the deduction or credit may be taken by the person who acquires an interest in the decedent's property from the decedent by reason of the decedent's death, or by bequest, devise or inheritance, subject to the obligation. (Code Sec. 691(b))[46]

¶ 3969   Deduction for estate tax attributable to income in respect of a decedent (IRD).

The decedent's right to IRD is frequently included in his or her gross estate for federal estate and GST tax purposes although it's taxed as income to the recipient. As a relief, the recipient of the IRD can deduct the estate and GST tax attributable to inclusion of the right to income in the gross estate. (Code Sec. 691(c)(1); Reg § 1.691(c)-1(a)) This relief is available to an individual only if he or she itemizes deductions, but the deduction isn't subject to the 2%-of-AGI floor. (Code Sec. 67(b)(8))[47]

If IRD includes capital gains or qualified dividends, the Code in effect treats the deduction as an offset against the capital gains or qualified dividends. For purposes of computing (1) the Code Sec. 1211 limitation on capital losses, (2) the maximum tax on a noncorporate taxpayer's capital gains or qualified dividends under Code Sec. 1(h), (3) the alternative tax on a corporation's capital gains, and (4) the full or partial exclusion of gain realized on the disposition of qualified small business stock, the amount of any gain taken into account that is treated as IRD must be reduced (but not below zero) by the amount of the allowable deduction for estate tax attributable to that gain. (Code Sec. 691(c)(4))[48]

Annuity payments received by the surviving annuitant of a joint and survivor annuity are IRD of the deceased annuitant to the extent that the payments are includible in gross income of the survivor. The portion of the estate tax attributable to the survivor's annuity is allowable as a deduction to the survivor over the survivor's life expectancy (determined under IRS tables). (Code Sec. 691(d); Reg § 1.691(d)-1(c))[49]

---

44. ¶C-9501; ¶6914
45. ¶C-9506; ¶6914.05
46. ¶C-9551; ¶6914.04

47. ¶C-9557 *et seq.*; ¶674
48. ¶C-9563; ¶6914.07
49. ¶C-9569; ¶6914.07

¶ **3970**   **Bankruptcy Estate for Bankrupt Individual.** ▆▆▆▆▆▆

The bankruptcy estate of an individual is treated as a separate taxable entity for income tax purposes, subject to special rules.

Specifically, the separate entity rules apply if a bankruptcy case involving an *individual* debtor (not a corporation or partnership) is brought under Chapter 7 (relating to liquidations) or Chapter 11 (reorganizations) of Title 11 of the U.S. Code. (Code Sec. 1398(a))[50]

For income tax returns of bankruptcy estates (Form 1040 and Form 1041), see ¶4736.

¶ **3971**   **Debtor's election to close tax year.**

An individual debtor can elect to close his or her tax year as of the day before the date the bankruptcy case commences. (Code Sec. 1398(d)(2)(A), Code Sec. 1398(d)(3)) If the election is made, the debtor's tax year that otherwise would include the commencement date is divided into two "short" tax years. The first year ends on the day before the commencement date; the second begins on the commencement date. (Code Sec. 1398(d)(2)(A))[1]

¶ **3972**   **Taxation of bankruptcy estate.**

The gross income of the bankruptcy estate of an individual consists of: (1) any gross income of the individual debtor (other than any amount received or accrued as income by the debtor before the commencement of the case), that under the substantive law of bankruptcy (Title 11 of the U.S. Code), is property of the bankruptcy estate, and (2) the gross income of the estate beginning on and after the date the case commenced. (Code Sec. 1398(e)(1))[2]

Except as otherwise provided, the taxable income of the bankruptcy estate is computed the same as in the case of an individual. (Code Sec. 1398(c)(1))[3] The estate is allowed a personal exemption deduction equal to that of an individual (two exemptions for married debtors jointly filing for bankruptcy)[4] and the same standard deduction as married individuals filing separately. (Code Sec. 1398(c)(3)) The tax rate schedule applicable to the estate is the same as for married individuals filing separate returns. (Code Sec. 1398(c)(2))[5]

The estate succeeds to various income tax attributes of the debtor (including certain carryovers and unused passive activity and at-risk losses). (Code Sec. 1398(g); Reg § 1.1398-1, Reg § 1.1398-2)[6]

¶ **3973**   **Deduction of business and administrative expenses.**

An amount paid or incurred by the bankruptcy estate is deductible or creditable by the estate to the same extent that the item would be by the debtor had the debtor remained in the same trades, businesses or activities after the case commenced as before and had the debtor paid or incurred the amount. (Code Sec. 1398(e)(3))[7]

The estate can deduct: (1) any administrative expense allowed under 11 U.S. Sec. 503 (11 USCS 503), and (2) any court fees and costs assessed against the estate under Chapter 123 of Title 28 of the U.S. Code. (Code Sec. 1398(h)(1))[8]

---

50. ¶C-9701; ¶13,984
1. ¶C-9802 *et seq.*; ¶13,984.05
2. ¶C-9711; ¶13,984.01
3. ¶C-9708; ¶13,984.01
4. ¶C-9709; ¶13,984.01

5. ¶C-9707; ¶13,984.01
6. ¶C-9718; ¶13,984.02
7. ¶C-9714; ¶13,984.01
8. ¶C-9715; ¶13,984.01

¶ 3974   Carrybacks and carryovers.

Any deduction for administrative and related expenses not used in the current year can be carried back by the estate three years and carried forward seven years (Code Sec. 1398(h)(2)), but only to a tax year of the *estate*, not of the debtor. (Code Sec. 1398(h)(2)(D))

The administrative expense carrybacks and carryovers that may be carried to a particular tax year are "stacked" after the net operating loss deductions (allowed by Code Sec. 172) are computed for the particular year. (Code Sec. 1398(h)(2)(C))[9]

If the bankruptcy estate itself incurs a net operating loss (apart from losses passing to the estate from the individual debtor), the bankruptcy estate can carry back its net operating losses not only to earlier tax years of the estate, but also to tax years of the debtor before the year in which the case commenced. (Code Sec. 1398(j)(2)(A))[10]

¶ 3975   Tax attributes on termination of estate.

On termination of the bankruptcy estate, the debtor generally succeeds to various tax attributes of the estate (including certain carryovers). (Code Sec. 1398(i))[11]

---

9. ¶C-9720; ¶s 1724.05, 13,984.01   11. ¶C-9812; ¶13,984.02
10. ¶C-9721; ¶s 1724.05, 13,984.01

Chapter 19 Exempt Organizations

¶ 4100   Tax-Exempt Organizations. ▬▬▬▬▬▬

Certain nonprofit organizations are exempt from federal income taxation, but they may be taxable on income from unrelated businesses they conduct.

Exempt organizations include, among other entities:

. . . religious, charitable, scientific, literary and educational organizations, organizations testing for public safety, organizations that foster national or international amateur sports competition, those organized and operated for preventing cruelty to children or animals (¶4102) (Code Sec. 501(c)(3)), qualified charitable risk pools, (Code Sec. 501(n)) cooperative hospital (Code Sec. 501(e)) and educational organization, service organizations; (Code Sec. 501(f))[1]

. . . religious and apostolic organizations (¶4105);

. . . nonprofit civic organizations operated exclusively for social welfare, and local employees' associations whose net earnings are used solely for charitable, educational or recreational purposes (Code Sec. 501(c)(4));[2]

. . . labor, agricultural or horticultural organizations (Code Sec. 501(c)(5), Code Sec. 501(g));[3]

. . . chambers of commerce, business leagues, real estate boards, boards of trade or professional football leagues not organized for profit or private benefit (Code Sec. 501(c)(6));[4]

. . . social clubs organized for pleasure, recreation and other nonprofitable purposes (¶4107) (Code Sec. 501(c)(7)) and fraternal beneficiary societies, orders or associations operating under the lodge system and providing life, sick, accident or other benefits to members and their dependents (Code Sec. 501(c)(8));[5]

. . . voluntary employees' beneficiary associations (VEBAs) providing benefit payments to members and their dependents (Code Sec. 501(c)(9));[6]

. . . supplemental unemployment benefit plans (SUBs) (Code Sec. 501(c)(17));[7]

. . . qualified employee benefit trusts (¶4308);

. . . organizations (including mutual insurance companies) providing worker's compensation (Code Sec. 501(c)(27)(B))[8]; and

. . . state sponsored high-risk health coverage organizations (Code Sec. 501(c)(26)).[9]

¶ 4101   Feeder organizations.

An organization operated for the primary purpose of carrying on a business for profit (not just holding title to property) is taxable on all its income, even if all its profits are payable to exempt organizations. (Code Sec. 502(a); Reg § 1.502-1(a))[10] But this type of "feeder" organization is exempt if it's controlled by and furnishes its services *solely* to: a single exempt organization, an exempt parent organization and its exempt subs, or exempt subs having a common parent. (Reg § 1.502-1(b))[11]

---

1. ¶D-4100 *et seq.*; ¶5014.04
2. ¶D-5100 *et seq.*; ¶5014.13
3. ¶D-4600 *et seq.*; ¶5014.14
4. ¶D-4800 *et seq.*; ¶5014.15
5. ¶D-4300 *et seq.*; ¶5014.17
6. ¶D-4400 *et seq.*; ¶5014.18

7. ¶D-4500; ¶5014.26
8. ¶D-6346
9. ¶D-6320; ¶5014.39
10. ¶D-7101; ¶5024
11. ¶D-7103; ¶5024.01

References beginning with a single letter are to paragraphs in Federal Tax Coordinator 2d and RIA's Analysis of Federal Taxes: Income. Those beginning with numbers are to paragraphs in United States Tax Reporter.

¶ 4102   Religious, charitable, educational and similar organizations.

A corporation, community chest, fund, foundation, or other organization is exempt if:

. . . it's both organized *and* operated exclusively for: religious, charitable, scientific, literary or educational (including certain child care) purposes; public safety testing; prevention of cruelty to children or animals; or fostering national or international amateur sports competition; (Code Sec. 501(c)(3); Reg § 1.501(c)(3)-1(a))

. . . no part of its net earnings inures to benefit any private shareholder or individual; *and*

. . . no substantial part of its activities consists of carrying on propaganda or otherwise attempting to influence legislation, i.e., lobbying (subject to an election, see ¶4103), or intervening in any political campaign for or against any candidate. (Code Sec. 501(c)(3))[12]

Special qualification requirements apply to any Code Sec. 501(c)(3) organization that operates at least one hospital facility. (Code Sec. 501(r),[13] Code Sec. 6033(b))

¶ 4103   Lobbying expenditures election for Code Sec. 501(c)(3) organizations—Form 5768.

Certain Code Sec. 501(c)(3) organizations (other than church-related ones or private foundations) may elect (on Form 5768) to make limited lobbying expenditures without losing their exempt status. (Code Sec. 501(h))[14] The election is effective for all tax years that end after it's made, and that begin before it's revoked. (Code Sec. 501(h)(6))[15]

An electing charity's permissible lobbying expenditures for any tax year can't exceed ("general limit") the *lesser of:* (1) $1 million, or (2) the sum of 20% of the first $500,000 it paid or incurred for exempt purposes (including related administrative costs) for the year, plus 15% of the second $500,000, plus 10% of the third $500,000, plus 5% of any additional such expenditures. (Code Sec. 4911(c)(2); Reg § 56.4911-1(c)(1)) Also, only 25% of this lobbying amount may go to influencing legislation ("grass roots expenditures"). (Code Sec. 4911(c)(4); Reg § 56.4911-1(c)(2))[16] Charities must keep records of these expenditures (and show them on their annual returns, see ¶4126). (Reg § 56.4911-6)[17]

In any tax year an electing charity's lobbying expenditures exceed either the general or the grass roots limit, a 25% excise tax is imposed on that excess. If both limits are exceeded, the tax is imposed on the greater excess. (Code Sec. 4911(a), Code Sec. 4911(b))[18] Pay the tax on Form 4720. Use Form 8868 for an extension (¶4126).[19] Also, an electing charity can lose its tax exemption if its lobbying expenditures over a 4-year period exceed 150% of either limit. (Code Sec. 501(h)(1), Code Sec. 501(h)(2))[20]

¶ 4104   Excise tax on Code Sec. 501(c)(3) organizations' political and lobbying expenditures—Form 4720.

A Code Sec. 501(c)(3) organization is subject to a 2-tier excise tax on its *political expenditures*. An initial tax of 10% of the expenditure is imposed on the organization, and an initial 2.5% tax (up to $5,000 per expenditure) is imposed on any organization manager who willfully and without reasonable cause agreed to the expenditure. (Code Sec. 4955(a), Code Sec. 4955(c)(2); Reg § 53.4955-1(b))[21] Use Form 4720 to report these taxes, and Form 8868 for an extension. (¶4126)[22] Additional taxes are imposed on both the organization

---

12. ¶D-4101; ¶5014.05
13. ¶D-4141.1
14. ¶D-6500 *et seq.*, ¶D-6571; ¶5014.12, ¶60,334
15. ¶D-6501; ¶5014.12;
16. ¶D-6507 *et seq.*; ¶49,114
17. ¶D-6571

18. ¶D-6532 *et seq.*; ¶5014.12, 49,114
19. ¶S-2512
20. ¶D-6572 *et seq.*; ¶5014.12
21. ¶D-6421 *et seq.*; ¶49,554
22. ¶S-2512

(100%) and management (50%, up to $10,000 per expenditure) if the expenditure isn't corrected within a reasonable time. (Code Sec. 4955(b), Code Sec. 4955(c)(2))[23]

A Code Sec. 501(c)(3) organization (other than charities making the lobbying expense election (¶4103), private foundations and church-related organizations) whose *lobbying expenditures* for a tax year cause it to lose its tax exemption is subject to a 5% tax on those disqualifying amounts. The 5% tax also is imposed on any organization manager who agreed to the expenditure knowing that disqualification could result. (Code Sec. 4912)[24][25]

IRS may also seek to enjoin a Code Sec. 501(c)(3) organization from engaging in flagrant political activities. (Code Sec. 7409(a); Reg § 301.7409-1(a))[26]

¶ 4105   Religious or apostolic associations.

Even if an organization carries on business activities so that it can't be exempt under Code Sec. 501(c)(3) (as *exclusively* for exempt purposes), it still can be exempt as a *religious or apostolic association.* The organization may thus be exempt if it has a common or community treasury, and if its income (whether or not distributed) is taxed pro rata to its members, as a dividend received, for the organization's tax year ending with or within the member's tax year. (Code Sec. 501(d); Reg § 1.501(d)-1)[27]

¶ 4106   Civic leagues for social welfare.

A civic league is exempt if it isn't organized or operated for profit; it is operated exclusively for the promotion of social welfare; no part of its net earnings inures to the benefit of any private shareholder or individual; (Code Sec. 501(c)(4)) and no substantial part of its activities consists of providing commercial-type insurance. (Code Sec. 501(m)(1))[28]

¶ 4107   Social clubs.

For a social club to be exempt, it must be organized and operated substantially for pleasure, recreation or other nonprofit purposes, its governing instruments or written policies can't provide for discrimination based on color, race or religion, and no part of its earnings may benefit any private shareholder. (Code Sec. 501(c)(7))[29]

Up to 35% of a social club's gross receipts (including investment income) may be from sources outside of its membership. Within this 35%, not more than 15% of gross receipts may be from the general public's (i.e., not members or their guests) use of the club's facilities or services. [30]

If the club fails the 35% or 15% tests (and a facts and circumstances test) in any tax year, all of its income, even amounts (reduced by allocable costs) received from members, is subject to tax in that year. (Code Sec. 277)[31]

¶ 4108   Nondiscrimination requirements for voluntary employees' beneficiary associations (VEBAs) and supplemental unemployment benefit trusts (SUBs).

A VEBA or SUB won't be exempt unless it satisfies nondiscrimination rules similar to those applicable to qualified employee benefit plans (¶4314). (Code Sec. 501(c)(17)(A), Code Sec. 505(a)(1), Code Sec. 505(b)(1))[32]

23. ¶D-6421 *et seq.*; ¶49,554
24. ¶D-6417 *et seq.*; ¶49,124
25. ¶S-2512
26. ¶V-2713; ¶74,094
27. ¶D-5601; ¶5014.33

28. ¶D-5100 *et seq.*; ¶5014.13
29. ¶D-4201; ¶5014.16
30. ¶D-4206; ¶5014.16
31. ¶D-4206; ¶5014.16
32. ¶s D-4418, D-4501, D-6351; ¶5054

¶ 4109   Political organizations—Forms 1120-POL, 990, 8871, 8872, 8453-X.

A political organization is a party, committee, association, fund (including certain news-letter funds) or other organization (whether or not incorporated) that's organized and operated primarily to accept contributions and/or make expenditures for an "exempt function," e.g., influencing or attempting to influence the selection, nomination, election or appointment of any individual to public office. (Code Sec. 527(e)(1), Code Sec. 527(e)(2), Code Sec. 527(g))[33] Subject to exceptions, political organizations must (1) give notice of status electronically (use Form 8871 and Form 8453-X), (2) provide periodic reports of contributions and expenditures, electronically in some cases (use Form 8872), and (3) file annual returns. Although generally tax-exempt (Code Sec. 527(a)), a political organization is taxed, at the *highest* corporate rate, on income (minus connected expenses) that isn't from its exempt function. (Code Sec. 527(b)(1), Code Sec. 527(c))[34] A political organization, whether or not tax-exempt, that has more than $100 of taxable income must file an annual income tax return on Form 1120-POL. (Code Sec. 6012(a)(6)) Subject to exceptions, a tax-exempt political organization (other than a qualified state or local political organization) with $25,000 or more of annual gross receipts must file Form 990. Qualified state or local political organizations must file Form 990 (see ¶4126) if they have annual gross receipts of $100,000 or more. (Code Sec. 6033(g)(1)) .[35]

¶ 4110   Homeowners' associations—Form 1120-H.

Associations for the management of residential real estate and condominiums and timeshare associations (but not cooperative housing corporations) that meet an organization and operation test and an income test may elect (by filing Form 1120-H) to be treated as exempt organizations. (Code Sec. 528(a), Code Sec. 528(c))[36] Electing associations are taxed at a 30% (32% for timeshare associations) rate on income other than amounts received as dues, fees or assessments from members. (Code Sec. 528(b))[37] This taxable income must be reported on Form 1120-H.[38]

¶ 4111   Loss of exemption for exempt employee trusts engaging in prohibited transactions.

Some employee trusts (including church and governmental plans) will lose or be denied their exemption from income tax (and are subject to an excise tax, see ¶4336) if they engage in "prohibited transactions." (Code Sec. 503(a)(1))[39]

A prohibited transaction occurs if a trust engages in an activity with its creator, a substantial contributor, or person related to either, in which it (1) lends any part of its income or corpus without receiving adequate security and a reasonable rate of interest; (2) pays any compensation in excess of a reasonable allowance for personal services actually rendered; (3) makes any part of its services available on a preferential basis; (4) makes any substantial purchase of securities or any other property for more than adequate consideration; (5) sells any substantial part of its securities or any other property for less than adequate consideration; or (6) engages in any other transaction that results in a substantial diversion of its income or corpus. (Code Sec. 503(b))[40] :

33. ¶s D-5002, D-5021; ¶5274
34. ¶D-5008; ¶5274
35. ¶S-1921; ¶5274
36. ¶D-5701 *et seq.*; ¶5284

37. ¶D-5712; ¶5284
38. ¶S-1922; ¶5284
39. ¶D-6700 *et seq.*; ¶5034.01
40. ¶D-6702 *et seq.*; ¶5034.02

¶ 4112   Excise tax on excess benefit transactions by disqualified persons and organization managers—Form 4720.

Penalty excise taxes are imposed on disqualified persons and organization managers who benefit from an excess benefit transaction with a Code Sec. 501(c)(3) or Code Sec. 501(c)(4) organization (other than a private foundation), or that was such an organization at any time within five years before the transaction. (Code Sec. 4958(a); Reg § 53.4958-1) An excess benefit transaction is one in which the exempt organization provides a benefit directly or indirectly to or for the use of a disqualified person (any person in a position to exercise substantial influence over the organization at any time during the five years before the transaction (Code Sec. 4958(f); Reg § 53.4958-4)), or certain related parties, that exceeds the value of the consideration, including services, received in exchange. (Code Sec. 4958(c))[41]

The disqualified person is liable for a tax of 25% of the excess benefit (200% if the transaction is not corrected by the time a deficiency notice is mailed or the tax is assessed). (Code Sec. 4958(a)(1), Code Sec. 4958(b); Reg § 53.4958-1)[42] An organization manager (officer, director, trustee, etc.) who knowingly participates in an excess benefit transaction is liable for a tax of the lesser of 10% or $20,000. (Code Sec. 4958(a)(2), Code Sec. 4958(d)(2))[43] Distributions from a donor advised fund to a donor, donor advisor, or related person are automatically treated as excess benefit transactions. (Code Sec. 4958(c)(2)) Excess benefit transactions of Code Sec. 509(a)(3) supporting organizations are determined under special rules. (Code Sec. 4958(c)(3))[44] IRS may abate the first-tier taxes for reasonable cause. (Code Sec. 4962(b))[45] Persons liable for excess benefit transaction excise taxes report them on Form 4720. (Reg § 53.6071-1(f)) Use Form 8868 for an extension (¶4126).

¶ 4113   Excise tax on tax-exempt organizations that pay "excess compensation."

For tax years beginning after 2017, an "applicable tax-exempt organization" is liable for a 21% excise tax on remuneration exceeding $1 million paid to a "covered employee," and on "excess parachute payments" made to a covered employee. (Code Sec. 4960) An applicable tax-exempt organization is generally one exempt from tax under Code Sec. 501(a), a farmer's cooperative organization under Code Sec. 521(b)(1), a state or political subdivision that has income excluded from tax under Code Sec. 115(1), or a political organization under Code Sec. 527(e)(1). (Code Sec. 4960(c)(1)) A covered employee is any current or former employee of an applicable tax-exempt organization if the employee is (a) one of the five highest compensated employees of the organization for the tax year, or (b) was a covered employee of the organization, or any predecessor of the organization, for any tax year beginning after Dec. 31, 2016. (Code Sec. 4960(c)(2))[46] An excess parachute payment is the amount by which a parachute payment (defined in Code Sec. 4960(c)(5)(B)) exceeds the base amount (determined under rules similar to Code Sec. 280G(b)(3); ¶1534) allocated to it. (Code Sec. 4960(c)(5)(A))[47]

¶ 4114   Excise tax on investment income of private colleges and universities.

For tax years beginning after 2017, a 1.4% excise tax is imposed on net investment income of certain private colleges and universities with at least 500 tuition-paying students during the preceding tax year, more than 50% of whom are located in the U.S., and

---

41. ¶D-6650 *et seq.*; ¶49,584
42. ¶D-6652; ¶49,584
43. ¶D-6653; ¶49,584
44. ¶D-6654; ¶49,584

45. ¶D-6652; ¶49,624
46. ¶D-4115.1
47. ¶D- 4115.2

with assets at the end of the preceding tax year (other than those used directly in carrying out the institution's exempt purpose) of at least $500,000 per student. (Code Sec. 4968)[48]

¶ 4115 Excise tax on entities that are parties to, and managers who knowingly approve, prohibited tax shelter transactions.

Excise taxes are imposed on (1) certain tax-exempt entities that are parties to "prohibited tax shelter transactions" (Code Sec. 4965(a)(1)) and (2) "entity managers" of tax-exempt entities who approve the entity as a party (or otherwise cause the entity to be a party) to a prohibited tax shelter transaction and know or have reason to know that the transaction is a prohibited tax shelter transaction. (Code Sec. 4965(a)(2); Reg § 53.4965-1 through Reg § 53.4965-9)[49]

¶ 4116 Mandatory disclosure of participation in prohibited tax shelter transactions—Form 8886-T.

Every tax-exempt entity described in Code Sec. 4965(c) that is a party to a prohibited tax shelter transaction (¶4115) must disclose to IRS (on Form 8886-T): (a) that the entity is a party to the prohibited tax shelter transaction; and (b) the identity of any other party to the transaction which is known to such tax-exempt entity. (Code Sec. 6033(a)(2))[50] For 2018, the penalty for failing to comply is $100 for each day during which such failure continues, not to exceed $52,000 (for 2019, $105 and $53,000, respectively, as calculated by Thomson Reuters using inflation data) for any one disclosure. IRS may make a written demand on any entity or manager subject to the penalty for nondisclosure, specifying a reasonable future date by which the required disclosure must be filed. For 2018, failure to comply with the demand is subject to an additional penalty of $100 for each day after the expiration of the time specified in the demand during which such failure continues, not to exceed $10,000 (for 2019, $105 and $10,500, respectively, as calculated by Thomson Reuters using inflation data) for any one disclosure. (Code Sec. 6652(c)(3)(B)(ii))[1]

Any taxable party to a prohibited tax shelter transaction must disclose by statement to any tax-exempt entity that is a party to the transaction that it's a prohibited tax shelter transaction. (Code Sec. 6011(g))[2]

¶ 4117 Donee acknowledgment of qualified vehicle donations—Form 1098-C.

An organization that receives a charitable contribution of a "qualified vehicle" (¶2138) must provide the donor with a contemporaneous written acknowledgment of the contribution if the claimed value is more than $500, and report the information to IRS (use Form 1098-C) or face a penalty, which also applies for furnishing a false or fraudulent acknowledgment. It also must indicate whether the donee provided any goods or services in consideration for the vehicle, and, if so, a description and good faith estimate of their value, or, if they consist solely of intangible religious benefits, a statement to that effect. (Code Sec. 170(f)(12)(B))[3]

¶ 4118 Application for exemption—advance rulings—Forms 1023, 1023-EZ, 1024.

An organization must apply in writing (on Form 1023 for Code Sec. 501(c)(3) organizations, Form 1024 for most others, and with the appropriate user fee, but see below for Code Sec. 501(c)(4) organizations) for an IRS ruling or determination that it's exempt from federal income tax. (Reg § 1.501(a)-1(a)(2)) A parent organization's exemption doesn't

48. ¶D-8171 *et seq.*
49. ¶D-8301; ¶49,654
50. ¶S-2895; ¶60,334

1. ¶V-2538; ¶66,524.01
2. ¶S-4433; ¶60,114.023
3. ¶K-3948.2; ¶67,204

cover its subsidiary. [4] But organizations under the general control of a central organization may apply on a group basis. [5] When applying for tax-exempt status, sponsoring organizations must notify IRS of any donor advised fund they maintain or intend to maintain. (Code Sec. 508(f))[6] Small charities (U.S. charities with assets of $250,000 or less, and annual gross receipts of $50,000 or less) may use Form 1023-EZ to apply for Code Sec. 501(c)(3) tax-exempt status. [7]

Newly-formed organizations seeking to operate under Code Sec. 501(c)(4) are to provide IRS with the required notice of their intent to operate as such by filing Form 8976 (online) within 60 days of their formation. IRS, in turn, must acknowledge receipt of the Form 8976 within 60 days after it is submitted. (Code Sec. 506; Reg § 1.506-1T; Prop Reg. § 1.506-1)[8]

¶ 4119   Modification or revocation of exemption.

IRS may modify or revoke rulings and determination letters that granted exempt status to an organization. (Reg § 601.201(n)(6)) The revocation may be retroactive, in which case deficiencies and penalties may be imposed for open years. [9]

¶ 4120   Disclosure of nondeductibility of contributions.

Certain exempt organizations that aren't eligible to receive deductible contributions must expressly state that fact (in a conspicuous and easily recognizable format) in every fund-raising solicitation. (Code Sec. 6113)[10]

¶ 4121   Disclosure requirement for quid pro quo contributions.

Certain charities that are eligible to receive deductible contributions must, in connection with soliciting or receiving a quid pro quo contribution in excess of $75, inform the donor in writing that his charitable deduction is limited to the excess of his contribution over the value of the goods or services provided by the charity (with a good faith estimate of the value of those goods and services). (Code Sec. 6115; Reg § 1.6115-1)[11]

¶ 4122   Disclosure of annual return and exemption application—Form 990s, 990-PF, 990-T, 4720.

A Code Sec. 501(c) or Code Sec. 501(d) organization must make a copy of its annual returns (Form 990) for the last three years and its exempt status application and supporting documents available for inspection during business hours, but religious or apostolic organizations don't have to make K-1s available. (Code Sec. 6104(a), Code Sec. 6104(b), Code Sec. 6104(d); Reg § 301.6104(a)-1)[12] The organization must provide a copy of the application without charge, except reasonable reproduction and mailing costs, to any individual who requests it. Copies must be provided within 30 days, for written requests, or immediately for in-person requests. (Code Sec. 6104(d)(1)) Requests don't have to be honored if the information has been made widely available or if the request is determined by IRS to be part of a harassment campaign. (Code Sec. 6104(d)(4); Reg § 301.6104(d)-3, Reg § 301.6104(d)-3)[13] These requirements apply to annual information returns (Form 990-PF and Form 4720) of private foundations, which also must disclose names and addresses of contributors. (Reg § 301.6104(d)-1(b)(4)(ii))[14] Returns of certain political organizations (¶4109) also are subject to disclosure requirements. (Code Sec. 6104(a), Code Sec. 6104(b), Code Sec. 6104(d))[15] Code Sec. 501(c)(3) organizations (¶4102) must make

4. ¶T-10450 *et seq.*; ¶5014.01
5. ¶T-10481; ¶5014.01
6. ¶T-10462.1; ¶5014.01
7. ¶T-10461.1; ¶5074
8. ¶D-5101.1; ¶5064
9. ¶s T-10485, T-10486

10. ¶D-4004 *et seq.*; ¶61,134
11. ¶K-3126 *et seq.*; ¶61,154
12. ¶S-6601 *et seq.*; ¶61,044
13. ¶61,044
14. ¶S-6603; ¶61,044
15. ¶S-6642 *et seq.*; ¶61,044

available for public inspection copies of their annual unrelated business income tax (UBIT) returns (Form 990-T) for the 3-year period following the filing of the return. (Code Sec. 6104(d)(1)(A)(ii))

¶ 4123 Unrelated business income tax (UBIT)—Form 990-T.

Exempt organizations (other than U.S. corporate instrumentalities and certain other exempt organizations) are subject to a tax on income (¶4124) from any unrelated business (defined below). (Code Sec. 511(a), Code Sec. 512(a), Code Sec. 512(b)(12); Reg § 1.511-2(a)(1))[16] Form 990-T is used to report and pay UBIT. (Reg § 1.6012-2(e), Reg § 1.6012-3(a)(5))[17] Imposition of UBIT doesn't affect the organization's exempt status. (Code Sec. 501(b), Code Sec. 511)[18]

An unrelated business is a trade or business (i.e., carried on for the production of income, whether or not profit results) regularly carried on (including seasonally) by the organization, that isn't substantially related (aside from providing funds) to the exercise or performance of its exempt purpose or function. (Code Sec. 513(a), Code Sec. 513(c); Reg § 1.513-1)[19] An unrelated trade or business doesn't include the activity of soliciting and receiving qualified sponsorship payments (payments from a person engaged in a trade or business for which the person won't get any substantial return benefit other than the use or acknowledgment of the donor's name or logo as part of a sponsored event or certain goods or services that have an insubstantial value). (Code Sec. 513(i); Reg § 1.513-4)[20]

For exempt Supplemental Unemployment Benefit trusts (SUBs), qualified employee pension, etc., trusts, and nonexempt trusts, *any* business it regularly carries on is "unrelated." (Code Sec. 513(b))[21] But an unrelated business doesn't include an activity where substantially all the work is performed for the organization without compensation, e.g., by volunteers. (Code Sec. 513(a)(1))[22]

The rules on assessment, collection, and penalties applicable to income tax, including estimated tax and foreign tax credit, apply. (Code Sec. 515, Code Sec. 6655(g)(3)(A); Reg § 1.511-3(a)) The corporate tax rates and filing dates apply if the organization is a corporation, and those for trusts if it's a charitable trust. (Code Sec. 511(a), Code Sec. 511(b))[23]

Tax-exempt organizations must make estimated tax payments on their unrelated business taxable income. (Code Sec. 6655(g)(3))[24]

¶ 4124 Unrelated business taxable income (UBTI) defined.

UBTI is the gross income derived from any unrelated trade or business (¶4123), less directly connected allowable deductions, but with certain exceptions (below), additions and limitations (Code Sec. 512(a), Code Sec. 512(b)), including a specific deduction of $1,000. (Code Sec. 512(b)(12))[25] *For tax years beginning after 2017,* tax-exempt organizations with more than one unrelated trade or business generally must calculate their UBTI separately for each trade or business, such that losses from one may not be used to offset income of another. (Code Sec. 512(a)(6))[26]

IRS has issued guidance for calculating UBTI for separate businesses. [27]

---

16. ¶D-6800 *et seq.*; ¶5114 *et seq.*
17. ¶S-2101; ¶5114
18. ¶D-6801; ¶5114
19. ¶D-6804 *et seq.*; ¶5134.01
20. ¶D-6819 *et seq.*; ¶5134.02
21. ¶D-6807; ¶5134

22. ¶D-6836; ¶5134
23. ¶D-6928 *et seq.*
24. ¶S-5421; ¶66,554
25. ¶D-6900 *et seq.*; ¶5124
26. ¶D-6922.1
27. ¶D-6922.1

Social clubs, voluntary employees' beneficiary associations (VEBAs), supplemental unemployment benefit plans (SUBs), and veterans organizations are allowed special exclusions. (Code Sec. 512(a)(3))[28] A charitable organization's income or gain from ownership of S corporation stock is UBTI. (Code Sec. 512(e))[29]

Dividends (except certain insurance income received from a controlled foreign corporation (Code Sec. 512(b)(17))), interest, rents, royalties, annuities, payments for securities loans, loan commitment fees, and gains or losses from property dispositions are excluded from UBTI, as are gains or losses from the lapse or termination of options to buy or sell securities or real property, or from the forfeiture of good-faith deposits to buy, sell, or lease real property in connection with the organization's investment activities, (Code Sec. 512(b))[30] and annual dues of up to $165 for 2018 ($169 for 2019, as calculated by Thomson Reuters using inflation data) per member received by agricultural or horticultural organizations. (Code Sec. 512(d))[31]

But to the extent the dividends, etc., are attributable to property acquired through debt financing ("debt-financed property," see ¶4125), they *are* included in UBTI. The includible portion (computed separately for each property) equals a percentage (not over 100%) of the dividends, etc., derived from the property during the tax year, based on the ratio of: (1) the average acquisition indebtedness, to (2) the average adjusted basis of debt-financed property, for the year. (Code Sec. 514(a)(1))[32] This same percentage also is used to compute the allowable deductions for that property (other than capital loss carryovers or depreciation). (Code Sec. 514(a)(2), Code Sec. 514(a)(3))[33]

For tax years beginning after 2017, UBTI of a tax-exempt organization also includes any expenses paid or incurred for qualified transportation fringe benefits under Code Sec. 132(f), for a parking facility used in connection with qualified parking under Code Sec. 132(f)(5)(C), or for any on-premises athletic facility under Code Sec. 132(j)(4)(B), if such amounts aren't deductible under Code Sec. 274 and aren't directly connected with an unrelated trade or business which is regularly carried on by the organization. (Code Sec. 512(a)(7))[34]

¶ 4125   Property acquired through debt financing—"debt-financed property."

Debt-financed property, with certain exceptions, is any property held to produce income (including gains from its disposition, as well as rents, dividends and other recurring income) (Code Sec. 514(b); Reg § 1.514(b)-1(a)), for which there's an acquisition indebtedness at any time during the tax year.

"Acquisition indebtedness" for any property generally means: (1) the unpaid amount of indebtedness incurred by the organization in acquiring or improving the property; and (2) indebtedness incurred at other times which *but for* the acquisition or improvement wouldn't have been incurred (if incurred after the acquisition, etc., the debt must have been reasonably foreseeable at that time). (Code Sec. 514(c))[35]

Any mortgage or other lien on the acquired property is considered incurred in that acquisition, whether or not it's assumed by the organization. (Code Sec. 514(c)(2)(A))[36]

¶ 4126   Exempt organization returns—Forms 990, 8868.

In general, every organization that's exempt from tax (with limited exceptions for churches and organizations whose gross receipts fall under a prescribed threshold), or whose exemption application is pending, must file an annual information return (Form 990

---

28. ¶D-6929 *et seq.*; ¶5124
29. ¶D-6916.1
30. ¶D-6901 *et seq.*; ¶5124
31. ¶D-6847; ¶5124
32. ¶D-6901 *et seq.*; ¶5144

33. ¶s D-7007, D-7010; ¶5144
34. ¶D-6917.1
35. ¶D-7040 *et seq.*; ¶5144
36. ¶D-7043; ¶5144

series) and keep the records and make sworn statements as required by IRS. (Code Sec. 6033; Reg § 1.6033-2)[37] Code Sec. 509(a)(3) supporting organizations must file annual information returns (Code Sec. 509(a)(3)) containing specific information (Code Sec. 6033(l))[38] Certain exempt organizations that acquire interests in life insurance contracts must file an information return or face a penalty. (Code Sec. 6050V, Code Sec. 6724(d)(1)(B)(xiv), Code Sec. 6721(e)(2)(D))[39] For private foundations, see ¶4133.

The return must show the organization's total lobbying and political expenditures for the year (Code Sec. 6033(b)(8)), (except political expenditures of nonpolitical organizations taxed under Code Sec. 527(f) (Code Sec. 6033(e)(1)(B)(iii)))[40] and the total amount of dues and similar receipts to which the expenditures are allocable. There are exceptions for Code Sec. 501(c)(3) organizations' in-house expenditures not exceeding $2,000 (Code Sec. 6033(e)(1))[41] and certain nondeductible dues. [42]

Form 990 includes a core form to be completed by all organizations, and schedules to be completed depending on an organization's type and activities. IRS has released Publication 4839, and has posted numerous materials on its web site to help tax-exempt organizations in filing Form 990.

IRS allows an exempt organization (other than a private foundation or Code Sec. 509(a)(3) supporting organization) whose annual gross receipts aren't normally in excess of $50,000 to electronically file the simpler Form 990-N (the "e-Postcard") instead of Form 990.[43]

Information returns of parent tax-exempt organizations must include information about transactions with controlled entities. (Code Sec. 6033(h))[44]

Sponsoring organizations must disclose information about donor advised funds on information returns. (Code Sec. 6033(k))

Form 990 must be for the organization's annual accounting period or, if it has none, the calendar year. (Reg § 1.6033-2(b)) It must be filed on or before the 15th day of the fifth full calendar month after the close of the annual accounting period. (Reg § 1.6033-2(e))[45]

An exempt organization required to file a return on Form 990 (except for Form 990-C), Form 1041-A, Form 4720, Form 5227, Form 6069, or Form 8870 may obtain an automatic 6-month filing extension by filing on or before the return due date a Form 8868 showing the full amount properly estimated as tax, and remitting the full amount of properly estimated unpaid tax. (Reg § 1.6081-9T(a))

An exempt organization that fails to file the required information return or notice for three consecutive years will automatically lose its exempt status and must reapply to be recognized as an exempt organization. [46] Organizations that lost their exempt status for this reason may have their tax-exempt status retroactively reinstated. [47]

Most exempt organizations must file an information return (with Form 990) on liquidation, dissolution, termination or contraction if they were exempt for any of their last five years. (Code Sec. 6043(b))[48]

Tax-exempt organizations must electronically file their Forms 990 if they have $10 million or more in total assets and file 250 or more returns a year. Private foundations and charitable trusts must e-file Forms 990-PF, regardless of their asset size, if they file at least 250 returns. (Reg § 301.6033-4)[49]

IRS Publication 4779 provides information on the steps to be taken when an exempt

---

37. ¶S-2801 *et seq.*; ¶60,334
38. ¶S-2823.1
39. ¶S-2896; ¶60,50V4
40. ¶S-2853; ¶60,334
41. ¶s S-2858.1, S-2858.2; ¶60,334
42. ¶S-2858.3; ¶60,334
43. ¶S-2802; ¶66,524

44. ¶S-2862.2
45. ¶S-4928; ¶60,334
46. ¶S-2802; ¶60,334
47. ¶S-2802.1B
48. ¶S-2883; ¶60,334
49. ¶S-2822.2; ¶60,334

organization is merged or terminated.

¶ 4127 Private Foundations and Donor Advised Funds. ▪▪▪▪▪▪▪▪

Private foundations are generally exempt from income tax, but are subject to excise taxes, notification requirements and other restrictions.

A private foundation is any domestic or foreign religious, scientific, charitable, etc., organization described in Code Sec. 501(c)(3) (¶4102) *other than* organizations that:

(1) are "50% charities" (¶2124), except operating foundations and membership organizations (Code Sec. 509(a)(1));[50]

(2) meet detailed public support tests (Code Sec. 509(a)(2), Code Sec. 509(d));[1]

(3) operate exclusively for the benefit of one or more of the above organizations (as Type I, Type II, or Type III supporting organizations) and aren't controlled by disqualified persons (¶4129, other than foundation managers) (Code Sec. 509(a)(3));[2]

(4) are organized and operated exclusively for testing for public safety. (Code Sec. 509(a)(4))[3]

Strict accountability requirements apply to qualify as a Type III supporting organization (Code Sec. 509(f)(1), Reg § 1.509(a)-4(f)(5), Reg § 1.509(a)-4(i));[4] and Type I and Type II supporting organizations lose their status as non-private foundations if they accept gifts from prohibited persons. (Code Sec. 509(f)(2)(A))[5]

A Code Sec. 501(c)(3) organization (other than a church or an organization whose annual gross receipts don't exceed $5,000) is presumed to be a private foundation unless it notifies IRS to the contrary (Code Sec. 508(b), Code Sec. 508(c))[6] on Form 1023 within 15 months from the end of the month it was organized. (Reg § 1.508-1(b)(2))[7]

IRS has established a specific procedure for organizations classified as supporting organizations under Code Sec. 509(a)(3) that seek reclassification under Code Sec. 509(a)(1) or Code Sec. 509(a)(2).[8]

¶ 4128 Taxable trusts and foreign organizations subject to private foundation rules—Forms 1041-A, 5227.

Certain charitable trusts and split interest trusts, and foreign organizations meeting the private foundation definition (¶4127), may be subject to the private foundation excise taxes (¶4129) and rules on prohibited acts, but not the notification requirements. (Code Sec. 4947, Code Sec. 4948) File Form 1041-A for a split interest trust. Use Form 8868 for an extension, see ¶4126. Use Form 5227 to report the financial activities of a split-interest trust and to determine if it is treated as a private foundation and is subject to excise tax. Use Form 8868 for an extension, see ¶4126.[9]

¶ 4129 Excise taxes on private foundations—Forms 990-PF, 4720.

Private foundations may be subject to the following excise taxes:

Net investment income. An *exempt* private foundation is liable for an excise tax of 2% on its net investment income for the tax year. (Code Sec. 4940(a); Reg § 53.4940-1)[10] The tax is reduced to 1% if the foundation makes certain charitable distributions (Code Sec. 4940(e))[11] and is eliminated altogether for certain operating foundations. (Code

50. ¶D-7203; ¶5074
1. ¶s D-7204, D-7207, D-7209; ¶5074
2. ¶D-7212 *et seq.*; ¶5074
3. ¶D-7202; ¶5074
4. ¶D-7211; ¶D-7213.0 *et seq.*;¶5074; ¶5074.01
5. ¶D-7211; ¶5074

6. ¶s D-7216, D-7217; ¶5074
7. ¶T-10464; ¶5074
8. ¶T-10492
9. ¶s D-7300 *et seq.*, D-7400 *et seq.*; ¶s 49,474, 49,484
10. ¶D-7501; ¶49,404
11. ¶D-7503; ¶49,404

Sec. 4940(d))[12] For a *taxable* foundation, the excise tax equals the amount (if any) by which: (1) the sum of 2% of its net investment income (computed as if it were exempt) plus the unrelated business income tax (¶4124) that would have been imposed on it had it been exempt, *exceeds* (2) the income tax actually imposed on it for the tax year. (Code Sec. 4940(b))[13] Report the tax on Form 990-PF. (Reg § 53.6011-1(d))[14]

Self-dealing. An excise tax is imposed when a disqualified person (substantial contributors, foundation managers, and specified owners, family members and related entities of these, as well as government officials) (Code Sec. 4946(a)(1)) engages in any of certain acts of self-dealing with a private foundation. [15]

For *each* act of self-dealing (Code Sec. 4941(a), Code Sec. 4941(b)),[16] the disqualified person (except a foundation manager) is subject to an initial tax of 10% on the amount (not exceeding the amount he actually benefits) involved (Code Sec. 4941(a)(1); Reg § 53.4941(a)-1(a))[17] and a 200% additional tax if the self-dealing isn't timely corrected. (Code Sec. 4941(b)(1))[18] Any foundation manager who knowingly participates in the act is subject to an initial 5% tax. (Code Sec. 4941(a)(2))[19] and, if he refuses to agree with all or part of the correction, an additional 50% tax. (Code Sec. 4941(b)(2))[20] Managers may be jointly and severally liable, but their maximum liability for any one act is $20,000 in initial tax and $20,000 in additional tax. (Code Sec. 4941(c))[21] Report the initial taxes on Form 4720. (Reg § 53.6011-1(b))

Failure to distribute income. A foundation (other than an operating foundation) that fails to distribute its income for a tax year by the end of the *next* year is subject to an initial tax equal to 30% of the income (based on a minimum investment return) (Code Sec. 4942(a); Reg § 53.4942(a)-1(a)), which IRS may abate for reasonable cause (Code Sec. 4962(a))[22] and a 100% additional tax if the foundation fails to distribute the income by the date the initial tax is assessed or IRS issues a 90-day letter for it. (Code Sec. 4942(b))[23] Distributions by nonoperating private foundations to certain supporting organizations are not qualifying distributions. (Code Sec. 4942(g)(4))[24] Report the initial taxes on Form 4720. (Reg § 53.6011-1(b))

Excess business holdings. A foundation that has any excess business holdings is subject to an initial tax (which IRS may abate for reasonable cause) equal to 10% of those excess holdings, based on their value on the day during the tax year when those holdings were the greatest. (Code Sec. 4943(a), Code Sec. 4962)[25] For tax years after 2017, an exception applies if the foundation owns all of the business enterprise's voting stock at all times during the tax year and acquired its interests other than by purchase, the business distributes all net operating income for a tax year to the foundation within 120 days after the close of that year, and other requirements are met. (Code Sec. 4943(g)) If the foundation fails to timely correct its holdings, an additional 200% tax is imposed. (Code Sec. 4943(b))[26] The excess business holding tax applies to donor advised funds (Code Sec. 4943(e))[27] and the excess business holdings rules apply to certain supporting organizations. (Code Sec. 4943(f))[28] Report the initial taxes on Form 4720. (Reg § 53.6011-1(b))

Investments that jeopardize a foundation's charitable purpose. An excise tax is imposed if a foundation makes investments that jeopardize its charitable purpose. An initial tax of 10% of the amount invested is imposed on the foundation *and* on any foundation manager who knowingly participated in the investment. (Code Sec. 4944(a))[29] Additional taxes are

12. ¶D-7504; ¶49,404
13. ¶D-7506; ¶49,404
14. ¶S-2511; ¶60,334
15. ¶D-7600 *et seq.*; ¶s 49,414; 49,464
16. ¶s D-7606, D-7608; ¶49,414.02
17. ¶D-7601; ¶49,414.02
18. ¶D-7602; ¶49,414.02
19. ¶D-7602; ¶49,414.02
20. ¶D-7602; ¶49,414.02

21. ¶s D-7603, D-7604; ¶49,414.02
22. ¶s D-7701, D-8201; ¶s 49,424, 49,614
23. ¶s D-7701, D-7706; ¶49,424.01
24. ¶D-7711; ¶49,424.03
25. ¶s D-7800 *et seq.*, D-8201; ¶s 49,434, 49,614
26. ¶D-7801; ¶49,434
27. ¶D-7801; ¶49,434
28. ¶D-7800 *et seq.*; ¶49,434
29. ¶s D-7901, D-7903; ¶s 49,444, 49,614

imposed on the foundation (25%) if the investment is not timely removed from jeopardy (Code Sec. 4944(b)(1))[30] and on any manager (5%) who refuses to agree to removing the investment from jeopardy. (Code Sec. 4944(b)(2))[31] Foundation managers may be jointly and severally liable for these taxes, but the initial tax on management for any one investment is limited to $10,000, and the additional tax to $20,000. (Code Sec. 4944(d))[32] The initial taxes are reported on Form 4720. (Reg § 53.6011-1(b))

Propaganda, legislative activities and other taxable expenditures. An excise tax is imposed for engaging in propaganda or legislative activities or for making other taxable expenditures. An initial tax equal to 20% of the amount of the taxable expenditure is imposed on the foundation, and a 5% initial tax is imposed on any foundation manager who willfully agreed to the expenditure. (Code Sec. 4945(a))[33] An additional tax is imposed on the foundation (100%) if the expenditure isn't timely corrected, and on any foundation manager (50%) who refuses to agree to part or all of the correction. (Code Sec. 4945(b))[34] Foundation managers may be jointly and severally liable, but the maximum tax that may be imposed on them for any one taxable expenditure is $10,000 of initial tax and $20,000 of additional tax. (Code Sec. 4945(c)) These taxes don't apply if the political expenditures tax (¶4104) applies. (Code Sec. 4955(e))[35] Report the initial taxes on Form 4720. (Reg § 53.6011-1(b))

Use Form 8868 for an extension to file the above forms, see ¶4126.

¶ 4130   Termination of private foundation status; termination tax—Form 990-PF.

Except as otherwise provided below, an organization's status as a private foundation may terminate only if either: (1) the organization notifies IRS of its intent to terminate, or (2) the organization is guilty of willful repeated acts or omissions or of a willful and flagrant act or omission resulting in liability for any of the excise taxes on private foundations (see ¶4129), and IRS notifies the organization that it's liable for tax on termination of its status as a private foundation. (Code Sec. 507(a))[36]

The organization must pay a tax (use Form 990-PF, see ¶4133) on termination of its private foundation status. Unless abated by IRS, the tax equals the lesser of: (1) the aggregate tax benefit (as adequately substantiated by the foundation) resulting from its Code Sec. 501(c)(3) status, or (2) the value of its net assets. (Code Sec. 507(c), Code Sec. 507(g))[37]

Absent willful repeated acts or omissions or willful and flagrant acts or omissions resulting in private foundation excise tax liability, a private foundation's status may be terminated without imposition of the tax on termination if: (a) it distributes all its net assets to one or more public charities that have been in existence as such for at least 60 calendar months before the distribution; or (b) it notifies IRS of its intent to terminate, and the organization becomes a public charity for a continuous 60-month period. (Code Sec. 507(b))[38]

¶ 4131   Excise tax on taxable distributions from donor advised funds—Form 4720.

If a taxable distribution is made from a donor advised fund (see below):

(1) a tax equal to 20% of the amount distributed is imposed and must be paid by the donor advised fund's sponsoring organization (Code Sec. 4966(a)(1)); and

---

30. ¶D-7905; ¶49,444
31. ¶D-7906; ¶49,444
32. ¶D-7907; ¶49,444
33. ¶D-8001; ¶s 49,454, 49,614
34. ¶D-8001; ¶49,454.02

35. ¶D-8003; ¶49,554
36. ¶s D-7220, D-7222; ¶5074
37. ¶D-7228; ¶5074
38. ¶D-7223; ¶5074

(2) a tax equal to 5% of the amount distributed is imposed if any fund manager agreed to the making of a distribution knowing that it was a taxable distribution. The tax must be paid by any fund manager who agreed to the making of the distribution. (Code Sec. 4966(a)(2))[39]

The maximum amount of tax imposed by item (2) as to any one taxable distribution is $10,000. (Code Sec. 4966(b)(2))[40]

Subject to exceptions, a *donor advised fund* is a fund or account which is:

(1) separately identified by reference to contributions of a donor or donors,

(2) owned and controlled by a sponsoring organization, and

(3) as to which a donor (or any person appointed or designated by the donor) has, or reasonably expects to have, advisory privileges as to the distribution or investment of amounts held in the fund or account by reason of the donor's status as a donor. (Code Sec. 4966(d)(2))[41]

¶ 4132   Excise taxes imposed on prohibited benefits received by a donor, donor advisor, or related person from a donor advised fund—Form 4720.

If a distribution from a donor advised fund (¶4131) results in a donor, donor advisor, or a related person ("Subsection (d) person," as set forth in Code Sec. 4967(d)) receiving directly or indirectly a more than incidental benefit as a result of the distribution:

(1) A tax equal to 125% of the amount of the prohibited benefit is imposed on the advice of any Subsection (d) person who recommended the distribution, payable by that Subsection (d) person or the person who benefited from it. (Code Sec. 4967(a)(1))

(2) A tax equal to 10% of the amount of the prohibited benefit (not to exceed $10,000) is imposed on the agreement of any fund manager to knowingly make such a distribution, payable by that fund manager. (Code Sec. 4967(a)(2), Code Sec. 4967(c)(2))[42]

However, the above taxes are not imposed for any distribution that is subject to tax under Code Sec. 4958 (i.e., the excess benefit transaction rules, ¶4112). (Code Sec. 4967(b))

¶ 4133   Annual return of private foundations—Form 990-PF.

A private foundation must file an annual information return on Form 990-PF (Reg § 1.6033-2(a)(2)(i)) on or before the fifteenth day of the fifth month following the close of the tax year. (Reg § 1.6033-2(e))[43] For return disclosure requirements, see ¶4122. Certain private foundations must file returns electronically. (Reg § 301.6033-4)

39. ¶D-8152 *et seq.*; ¶49,664
40. ¶D-8152; ¶49,664
41. ¶D-8155; ¶49,664.02

42. ¶D-8160 *et seq.*; ¶49,674
43. ¶s S-2801, S-4928; ¶60,334

Chapter 20   RICs (Mutual Funds), REITs, REMICs, Banks and Other Special Corporations

¶ 4200   Special Corporations and Other Entities.

Regulated investment companies (¶4201), real estate investment trusts (¶4202), and real estate mortgage investment conduits (¶4204) are generally not subject to tax, but serve as pass-through entities.

Other corporations that are subject to special tax treatment include Small Business Investment companies (¶4205), cooperatives (¶4206), banks and other financial institutions (¶4209), common trust funds maintained by banks or trust companies (¶4210), and insurance companies (¶4211).

¶ 4201   Regulated investment companies (RICs)—mutual funds—Form 1120-RIC.

A RIC is a domestic corporation that at all times in the tax year is registered with the SEC as a management company or unit investment trust, has an election in effect to be treated as a business development company under the '40 Investment Company Act, or is a mutual or common trust fund other than an "investment company" under that Act. (Code Sec. 851(a))[1] It must also meet gross income, (Code Sec. 851(b)(2))[2] diversification, (Code Sec. 851(b)(3))[3] and E&P tests, (Code Sec. 852(a)(2))[4] satisfy the distribution requirement (Code Sec. 852(a)(1))[5] *and* elect on its return (Form 1120-RIC) to be taxed as a RIC. (Code Sec. 851(b)(1))[6]

If it makes the required distributions, a RIC is taxed only on: (1) the undistributed portion of its ordinary net income, at the regular corporate rates; and (2) the undistributed portion of its net long-term capital gains, at the corporate capital gains rate. (Code Sec. 852(b))[7] The RIC isn't taxed on the amounts it distributes to shareholders, thus allowing it to pass through ordinary income, net capital gains, qualified dividend income eligible for capital gain treatment (see ¶1286), dividend income eligible for the corporate dividends-received deduction, and certain other items to them (see ¶1296) without any tax at the RIC level (if requirements are met). (Code Sec. 852(b))[8] For "late-paid" and year-end dividends, see ¶4203.

The RIC's *undistributed* capital gains may also be designated (on Form 2439) and passed through to the shareholders (but the RIC pays tax (on Form 2438) on the retained gains). The effects of designation are that the shareholders: (1) include their shares of the undistributed capital gains in income, (2) get a credit or refund for their shares of the tax the RIC paid on these amounts (so that only one tax is paid), and (3) get a basis step-up in their shares equal to the difference between the amount of the includible capital gains from the dividend and the tax the shareholder is deemed to have paid with respect to those shares. (Code Sec. 852(b)(3)(D))[9]

The RIC must report capital gains distributions or undistributed capital gains by specifying the rate group of the capital gains passed through to the shareholder, i.e., as 20% rate gain, 25% rate gain for unrecaptured Code Sec. 1250 gains, 28% rate gain for collectibles gains, and Code Sec. 1202 gain for gains on the sale of qualified small business stock held for more than five years. [10]

---

1. ¶E-6001 *et seq.*; ¶8514
2. ¶E-6003; ¶8514.02
3. ¶E-6007, E-6010; ¶8514.04
4. ¶E-6021; ¶8524.01
5. ¶E-6101; ¶8524.01

6. ¶E-6002; ¶8514.01
7. ¶E-6100 *et seq.*; ¶8524.10
8. ¶E-6150; ¶8524.02
9. ¶E-6157; ¶8524.02
10. ¶E-6153

References beginning with a single letter are to paragraphs in Federal Tax Coordinator 2d and RIA's Analysis of Federal Taxes: Income. Those beginning with numbers are to paragraphs in United States Tax Reporter.

¶ 4202　Real estate investment trusts (REITs)—Form 1120-REIT.

A REIT must be a calendar-year (Code Sec. 859) corporation, trust or association that meets certain requirements as to the source of income, earnings and profits, type of its investments, nature of its activities, and its relationships with financially interested parties (Code Sec. 856(a)), and certain recordkeeping and distribution requirements. (Code Sec. 857(a)) And it must elect on its return (Form 1120-REIT) to be a REIT. (Code Sec. 856(c)(1); Reg § 1.856-2(b))[11]

⊘*observation:* REITs are designed to do for real estate investors what mutual funds (RICs, see ¶4201) do for investors in securities — i.e., pool resources and get a return on capital without paying a corporate tax on the gain.

REITs are generally taxed only on amounts not distributed to their shareholders or beneficiaries, as follows: (1) at *regular* corporate rates on undistributed earnings and profits and net capital gains, and (2) at the *highest* corporate rate on net income from foreclosure property. (Code Sec. 857(b))[12] A REIT may pass through the character of its capital gains and qualified dividend income eligible for capital gain treatment (see ¶1286) to its shareholders, see ¶1297. In addition, a REIT's *undistributed* capital gains may be passed through to the shareholders (on Form 2439). The REIT pays tax on the retained gains (on Form 2438) and the shareholders: (1) include their shares of the undistributed capital gains in income, (2) get a credit or refund for their shares of the tax the REIT paid on these amounts (so that only one tax is paid), and (3) get a basis step-up in their shares equal to the difference between the amount of the includible capital gains from the dividend and the tax the shareholder is deemed to have paid with respect to those shares. (Code Sec. 857(b)(3)(C))[13] For "late-paid" and year-end dividends, see ¶4203.

¶ 4203　RIC (mutual fund) and REIT dividends paid after close of tax year; year-end dividends.

A RIC (¶4201) or REIT (¶4202) may elect to treat all or part of any dividend paid after the end of a tax year ("late-paid dividends") as paid during the year, if the dividend is declared and paid within the required statutory periods. (Code Sec. 855(a), Code Sec. 858(a))[14]

A dividend declared by a RIC or REIT in October, November or December of any calendar year, that's payable to shareholders of record on a specified date in one of those months, is considered to have been paid on Dec. 31 if the dividend is actually paid during January of the following calendar year. (Code Sec. 852(b)(7), Code Sec. 857(b)(9))[15]

For shareholders' tax on these dividends, see ¶1296 (RICs) and ¶1297 (REITs).

¶ 4204　Real estate mortgage investment conduits (REMICs)—Form 1066.

REMICs are fixed mortgage pools with multiple classes ("regular" and "residual" (Code Sec. 860G(a)(1), Code Sec. 860G(a)(2); Reg § 1.860G-1)) of investment interests that have elected REMIC status (on Form 1066). (Code Sec. 860D; Reg § 1.860D-1)[16] REMICs, which are treated as partnerships for procedural purposes (Code Sec. 860F(e)),[17] generally aren't taxable. (Code Sec. 860A(a))[18] The REMIC's income is allocated to, and taken into account by, the holders of its interests. (Code Sec. 860A(b)) REMICs report on Form 1066.[19]

---

11. ¶E-6501, E-6523; ¶8564.02
12. ¶E-6600 *et seq.*; ¶8574.01
13. ¶E-6617.7; ¶8574.02
14. ¶s E-6201, E-6701; ¶s 8554, 8584
15. ¶s E-6202, E-6704; ¶s 8554.01, 8574.02

16. ¶s E-6901, E-6903; ¶860A4
17. ¶E-6927; ¶860A4
18. ¶E-6917; ¶860A4
19. ¶E-7000 *et seq.*; ¶s 860A4.01, 860A4.02

Although not subject to federal *income* tax, a REMIC is subject to penalty taxes on: income from foreclosure property (Code Sec. 860G(c)), contributions after the start-up date (Code Sec. 860G(d)), and prohibited transactions (Code Sec. 860F(a)), and an excise tax (reported on Form 8831) on certain transfers of residual interests. (Code Sec. 860E(e))[20]

¶ 4205 Small business investment companies (SBICs).

SBICs are licensed and operated under the Small Business Investment Act of '58. [21] They are subject to these special tax rules:

... Loss on stock received through the conversion of convertible debentures originally acquired for long-term equity capital supplied to small business concerns is a fully deductible ordinary loss. (Code Sec. 1243)[22]

... An SBIC's gain or loss on sale of bonds, debentures, etc., (regardless of issuer) is ordinary gain or loss. (Code Sec. 582(c); Reg § 1.582-1(d))[23]

... Dividends the SBIC receives from taxable domestic corporations are 100% deductible. (Code Sec. 243(a)(2))[24]

... An SBIC is exempt from personal holding company tax (¶3321 *et seq.*), unless at any time in the tax year any shareholder of the SBIC owns, directly or indirectly, a 5%-or-more interest in the companies financed by the SBIC. (Code Sec. 542(c)(7))[25]

¶ 4206 Cooperatives (co-ops).

A co-op is an entity in which the same persons are both owners and customers. Although some co-ops are *classified* as "exempt," most co-ops are taxed like any ordinary business corporation, and at the regular corporate rates, but with a specific deduction for patronage dividends (¶4207). (Code Sec. 1382(b)) "Exempt" farmers' co-ops also may deduct certain nonpatronage distributions (¶4208). (Code Sec. 1382(c))[26]

¶ 4207 Patronage dividends and per-unit retain allocations.

Both "exempt" farmers' co-ops and nonexempt co-ops exclude (deduct) from their income amounts paid as patronage dividends or per-unit retain allocations. (Code Sec. 1381(a), Code Sec. 1382(b))[27] For deduction of nonpatronage dividends, see ¶4208. For how the patrons or shareholders treat these amounts, see ¶1298.

A patronage dividend represents distributions of net earnings among the cooperators and other patrons on the basis of each person's patronage. (Code Sec. 1388(a))[28] It may be paid in money, a certificate of indebtedness, or other property, including a qualified written notice of allocation.[29]

A per-unit retain allocation is an allocation by a co-op to a patron with respect to products marketed for him. (Code Sec. 1388(f))[30]

A written notice of allocation must disclose the dollar amount allocated to the patron and the portion that is a patronage dividend. (Code Sec. 1388(b); Reg § 1.1388-1(b))[31]

---

20. ¶E-6920 *et seq.*; ¶E-7106; ¶s 860A4.05, 860A4.06, 860A4.07
21. ¶I-9541; ¶12,424
22. ¶I-9542; ¶12,424
23. ¶I-9544
24. ¶D-2243; ¶12,424
25. ¶D-3311; ¶5424.02

26. ¶E-1100 *et seq.*; ¶13,814.01
27. ¶E-1100 *et seq.*; ¶13,814.01
28. ¶E-1104; ¶13,814.05
29. ¶E-1120; ¶13,814.01
30. ¶E-1126; ¶13,814.14
31. ¶E-1123; ¶13,814.02

¶ 4208　Nonpatronage distributions deductible by exempt co-ops.

In addition to patronage distributions (¶4207), an "exempt" farmers' co-op may also deduct: dividends paid during the tax year on its capital stock and on any other evidence of proprietary interest in the co-op, (Code Sec. 1382(c)(1); Reg § 1.1382-3(b)) distributions to patrons on a patronage basis out of earnings from nonpatronage sources, (Code Sec. 1382(c)(2)(A); Reg § 1.1382-3(c), Reg § 1.1382-3(c)(3)) and payments in redemption of nonqualified written notices of allocation issued to patrons on a patronage basis with respect to earnings from nonpatronage sources. (Code Sec. 1382(c)(2)(B); Reg § 1.1382-3(d))[32]

¶ 4209　Taxation of banks and other financial institutions.

Banks are generally taxed like regular corporations (Reg § 1.581-1), except that:[33]

Gains and losses from sales or exchanges of bonds, debentures, notes or certificates or other evidences of indebtedness (including any regular or residual interest in a REMIC, see ¶4204) are treated as ordinary gains and losses. (Code Sec. 582(c)(1)) Sales of stock and securities are subject to the regular wash sale provisions (¶2461).[34]

Interest paid or credited on deposits or CDs is deductible (special rules apply to frozen deposits).[35] But no deduction is allowed for any portion of interest expense that's allocable (comparing the bank's adjusted bases in taxable and exempt investments) to investment in tax-exempts. (Code Sec. 265(b)(1), Code Sec. 265(b)(2))[36] However, interest allocable to tax-exempts acquired (or treated as acquired) before Aug. 8, '86, is 80% deductible (100% deductible if acquired before '83). (Code Sec. 291(a)(3), Code Sec. 291(e)(1)(B))[37]

Bad debts. Banks generally must treat bad debts (e.g., losses on loans) by taking a specific deduction ("charge-off") for the debt, but non-large banks can choose to deduct additions to bad debt reserves. (Code Sec. 585(a))[38] Banks using reserves must use the experience method to compute the additions. Under this method, the additions can't bring the reserve above the bank's loans outstanding at year-end, times a six-year moving average percentage (ratio of total bad debts to total outstanding loans). (Code Sec. 585(b))[39]

Losses a bank incurs on account of its deposits in other banks must be specifically deducted, whether or not it uses the reserve method for other bad debts. [40]

Worthless securities. A bad debt deduction is allowed to banks for total or partial worthlessness (¶1772) of debts evidenced by securities. (Code Sec. 582(a)) Under the charge-off method, a bank's debt is conclusively presumed to be worthless where the charge-off is made under specific orders or in conformance with established policies, of federal or state supervisory authorities, or is in accordance with a properly made "conformity" election. (Reg § 1.166-2(d))[41]

Mutual savings banks or stock associations, savings and loan associations, building and loan associations, and cooperative banks are subject to special tax rules. [42] Gain or loss from the sale or exchange of any qualifying Fannie Mae and Freddie Mac preferred stock by any applicable financial institution (those referred to in Code Sec. 582(c) or financial institution holding companies) is treated as ordinary income or loss. (§ 301 of Division A, P.L. 110-343, 10/3/2008)[43]

---

32. ¶s E-1140, E-1141, E-1142; ¶13,814.01
33. ¶E-3000 *et seq.*, ¶E-3300 *et seq.*; ¶5814
34. ¶E-3022 *et seq.*; ¶5824
35. ¶E-3105; ¶5914
36. ¶E-3108; ¶2654
37. ¶s E-3111, E-3124; ¶2914

38. ¶E-3201, ¶E-3224
39. ¶E-3227; ¶5854
40. ¶E-3139
41. ¶E-3201 *et seq.*; ¶5824
42. ¶E-3300 *et seq.*; ¶5814
43. ¶E-3022.1 *et seq.*; ¶5854

¶ 4210   Common trust funds.

A common trust fund isn't subject to tax (Code Sec. 584(b)) but must file a return (on Form 1065) and pass through its income or loss and other items attributable to each participant. (Reg § 1.6032-1)[44] A common trust fund is a fund maintained by a bank or trust company exclusively to collectively invest and reinvest moneys that it, in its capacity as a trustee, executor, administrator, guardian or custodian, contributes to the fund. (Code Sec. 584(a))[45]

¶ 4211   Taxation of insurance companies.

Life insurance companies are taxed, at the regular corporate rates, on their "life insurance company taxable income" (LICTI). (Code Sec. 801(a))[46] LICTI is life insurance company gross income minus general deductions and, if applicable, the pre-2018 small life insurance company deduction under former Code Sec. 806. (Code Sec. 803(a), Code Sec. 804)[47] Gain from the redemption at maturity of certain market discount bonds is taxed under a special rule. [48]

A corporation (whether stock, mutual, or mutual benefit) is taxed as a life insurance company if: (1) it's an insurance company, (2) it's engaged in the business of issuing life insurance and annuity contracts, and (3) it meets a reserve test. (Code Sec. 816(a))[49]

Nonlife insurance companies (stock and mutual) are taxed like corporations generally (¶3303 *et seq.*), with certain deductions particular to insurance. Gross income is investment and underwriting income, and gain or loss from property dispositions. (Code Sec. 831, Code Sec. 832)[50] Certain small nonlife insurance companies may elect to be taxed only on investment income, (Code Sec. 831(b))[1] and others may be exempt. (Code Sec. 501(c)(15))[2]

---

44. ¶s E-3600 *et seq.*, S-4105; ¶s 5844, 60,324
45. ¶E-3600 *et seq.*; ¶5844
46. ¶E-4801; ¶8014
47. ¶E-4801 *et seq.*; ¶s 8034, 8044
48. ¶E-4819

49. ¶E-5401; ¶8164
50. ¶E-5500 *et seq.*; ¶8324.01
1. ¶E-5503; ¶8314
2. ¶D-5901

Chapter 21   Pension and Profit-Sharing Plans—401(k) Plans—Roth 401(k) Plans—IRAs—Roth IRAs— SEPs—SIMPLE Plans

¶ 4300   Employee Benefit Plans.

Qualified pension, profit-sharing and stock bonus plans offer substantial tax benefits to sponsor-employers and their employees.

The principal tax advantages are:

. . . the employer gets an immediate deduction for contributions under the plan (Code Sec. 404);[1]

. . . the income earned by funds while held under the plan is tax-exempt (Code Sec. 501(a));[2]

. . . the employee isn't taxed on his share of the fund until amounts are distributed to him (usually after retirement), ¶4327 *et seq.*, (Code Sec. 402; Reg § 1.402(a)-1);[3]

. . . amounts transferred in a direct trustee-to-trustee transfer are excluded from income (¶4348) (Code Sec. 402(c)(6)) and eligible rollover distributions can be rolled over tax-free to eligible retirement plans (¶4348) (Code Sec. 402(c)(1));[4]

. . . tax is deferred on qualifying distributions of appreciated employer stock until the stock is sold, see ¶4329. (Code Sec. 402(e)(4))[5]

For the small-employer retirement plan start-up tax credit, see   ¶2331.

¶ 4301   Pension plans.

A qualified pension plan provides systematically for the payment of definitely determinable benefits to employees (and their beneficiaries) after retirement over a period of years, usually for life. [6] Retirement benefits are generally measured by such factors as years of the employee's service and compensation received. (Reg §   1.401-1(b)(1)(i))[7] Benefits under a defined benefit plan are "definitely determinable" if they are determined actuarially, on a basis that precludes employer discretion. (Code Sec. 401(a)(25))[8] A money-purchase plan —contributions geared to a fixed formula (e.g., 10% of compensation), rather than to profits—is a pension plan if the plan "designates" its intent to be a money purchase pension plan. (Code Sec. 401(a)(27)(B); Reg § 1.401-1(b)(1)(i))[9]

Defined benefit plans also include so-called "hybrid plans," such as cash balance plans and pension equity plans (PEPs). Special rules apply to these plans. (Code Sec.   411(b)(5)[10] ; Reg § 1.411(b)(5)-1(b) through Reg § 1.411(b)(5)-1(e))[11]

¶ 4302   Profit-sharing and stock bonus plans.

A qualified profit-sharing plan must have a definite, predetermined formula for allocating contributions made under the plan among the participants, and for distributing the funds accumulated under the plan only after a fixed number of years, the attainment of a stated age or upon the occurrence of some event (such as disability, retirement, death or severance of employment). (Reg § 1.401-1(b)(1)(ii))[12]

1. ¶H-10000 *et seq.*; ¶4014
2. ¶H-10500 *et seq.*; ¶4014
3. ¶H-11006 *et seq.*; ¶4014
4. ¶H-8250 *et seq.*; ¶s 4014.27, 4024.04
5. ¶H-11500 *et seq.*; ¶s 4014, 4024.02
6. ¶H-5328; ¶4014.02

7. ¶H-5328; ¶4014.02
8. ¶H-5328; ¶4014.10
9. ¶s H-5205, H-5337; ¶4014.02
10. ¶H-7239.2 *et seq.*; ¶4114.33
11. ¶H-7239.4 *et seq.*; ¶4114.3303 *et seq.*
12. ¶H-5337 *et seq.*; ¶4014.03

References beginning with a single letter are to paragraphs in Federal Tax Coordinator 2d and RIA's Analysis of Federal Taxes: Income. Those beginning with numbers are to paragraphs in United States Tax Reporter.

Contributions can be made to a qualified profit-sharing plan whether or not the employer has current or accumulated profits, and whether or not the employer is a tax-exempt organization. (Code Sec. 401(a)(27)(A))[13]

A qualified stock bonus plan provides benefits in the form of the employer-corporation's own stock. Stock bonus plans must generally satisfy the qualification requirements that apply to profit sharing plans, plus some additional requirements. [14]

¶ 4303   Employee stock ownership plans (ESOPs).

An ESOP is a qualified defined contribution plan that is either a stock bonus plan, or a combination stock bonus and money purchase plan, that invests primarily in employer securities (Code Sec. 4975(e)(7)), and is formally designated as an ESOP. [15]

To ensure that S corporation ESOPs benefit a broad range of employees, restrictions apply under Code Sec. 409(p) that generally prohibit the accrual or allocation of S corp. stock to certain disqualified persons in an ESOP where 10% owners hold 50% or more of the interests in the S corp. (Code Sec. 409(p); Reg § 1.409(p)-1)[16]

Dividends on employer securities that are distributed from an ESOP under Code Sec. 404(k) must be reported on a Form 1099-R that does not report any other distributions, rather than on Form 1099-DIV. [17]

¶ 4304   Annuity plans.

The tax advantages of a qualified plan can be obtained without a trust by using contributions to buy retirement annuities directly from an insurance company. (Code Sec. 403(a)(1), Code Sec. 404(a)(2))[18]

Taxpayers may buy deferred "longevity" annuities ("Qualified Longevity Annuity Contracts," or QLACs) under qualified defined contribution plans, Code Sec. 403 plans, Code Sec. 408 individual retirement annuities and accounts (IRAs), and eligible governmental Code Sec. 457 plans. (Reg § 1.401(a)(9)-5; Reg § 1.401(a)(9)-6; Reg § 1.408-8, Q&A-12; Reg § 1.403(b)-6(e))[19]

¶ 4305   "Thrift" and "savings" plans.

A thrift plan is in the nature of a profit-sharing plan and provides for participant contributions of a specified percentage (the same for all participants) of their salaries. This employee contribution is then matched by the employer, either dollar for dollar or in some other specified manner, out of profits. [20]

A savings plan permits employees to make voluntary employee contributions which aren't limited to any specific percentage of compensation. [21]

These plans may allow withdrawal of the voluntary employee contributions (plus earnings) before retirement or termination. However, these contributions are subject to nondiscrimination testing, see ¶4306.[22]

¶ 4306   401(k) plans—elective deferral.

Cash or deferred arrangements (CODAs), popularly known as "401(k) plans," allow an employee to choose whether the employer should pay a certain amount directly to the

---

13. ¶H-5337; ¶4014.03
14. ¶H-5209; ¶4014.04
15. ¶H-9300 *et seq.*; ¶49,754
16. ¶H-5337; ¶4014.03
17. ¶S-3419.1

18. ¶H-5212 *et seq.*; ¶4034
19. ¶H-8280.30 *et seq.*; ¶H-12264.12; ¶H-12290.42A; ¶4014.153
20. ¶H-5214
21. ¶H-5215
22. ¶H-5313

employee in cash, or should instead pay that amount on the employee's behalf to a qualified trust under a profit-sharing plan, a stock bonus plan, a pre-ERISA money purchase plan, or a rural cooperative defined contribution pension plan. (Code Sec. 401(k))[23]

For 2018, an employee may elect to defer a maximum of $18,500 ($19,000 for 2019)on a pre-tax basis under a 401(k) plan, SEP, or Code Sec. 403(b) tax-sheltered annuity (¶4375). (Code Sec. 402(g)(1), Code Sec. 402(g)(5))[24] Individuals who attain age 50 by the end of the plan year may make (if their plan permits (Reg § 1.414(v)-1(a))) additional pre-tax "catch-up" contributions of up to $6,000 for 2018 and 2019. (Code Sec. 414(v)(2)(B)(i), Code Sec. 414(v)(2)(C)) The maximum catch-up amounts apply to all qualified plans, tax sheltered annuity plans, SEPs and SIMPLE plans of an employer on an aggregated basis, as if all plans were a single plan. (Code Sec. 414(v)(2)(D))[25]

If all the requirements are met, any amount set aside under the CODA is not taxed to the employee currently but instead is taxed at the time of distribution. However, elective deferrals and designated Roth contributions (¶4363) are included in wages for purposes of social security and Medicare taxes. (Code Sec. 3121(v)(1)(A))[26]

Excess deferrals are included in the employee's gross income. (Code Sec. 402(g)(1)(A); Reg § 1.402(g)-1(d)(1)) They will be taxed again on distribution unless distributed to the employee in a corrective (nontaxable) distribution during the tax year or by the Apr. 15th following the close of the employee's tax year. (Code Sec. 402(g)(2)(C); Reg § 1.402(g)-1(e)(8))[27]

A 401(k) plan must meet all the normal tax qualification rules (¶4308), including the nondiscrimination rules (¶4314), and, in addition, all of the following requirements:

(1) amounts must not be distributable except by reason of (a) retirement, death, disability or other separation from employment, including certain transfers in connection with the sale of a business, (b) hardship (see below) or attainment of age 59 1/2 (for profit-sharing or stock bonus plans), (c) in a lump sum on termination of the plan, or (d) in a lump sum, on the employer's disposition of (i) substantially all of its trade or business assets, or (ii) a subsidiary (Code Sec. 401(k)(2)(B))[28] (for loans from 401(k) plans, see ¶4332);

(2) employer contributions made under the employee's election must be nonforfeitable at all times (Code Sec. 401(k)(2)(C));[29]

(3) a covered employee must be able to elect to have the employer make plan contributions on the employee's behalf or make the payment directly to the employee in cash (Code Sec. 401(k)(2)(A))[30] (automatic contributions are permitted for employees who don't affirmatively elect to receive cash, see below); [31]

(4) elective deferrals under the plan (as aggregated with all other plans, etc., of the employer) must be prohibited from exceeding the above indexed dollar limits; [32] and

(5) special nondiscrimination rules that require the plan to satisfy one of two "actual deferral percentage (ADP) tests," so highly compensated employees can't elect to defer a disproportionately higher amount of their salary, must be met. (Code Sec. 401(k)(3)(A))[33] Similar requirements —actual contribution percentage (ACP) tests —apply to limit employer matching or employee contributions made on behalf of highly compensated employees. (Code Sec. 401(m))[34]

A 401(k) plan is treated as meeting these requirements if it's a "SIMPLE" plan

23. ¶H-8975 *et seq.*; ¶4014.17
24. ¶H-9151; ¶4024
25. ¶H-9246; ¶4144.26
26. ¶H-4624
27. ¶H-9155 *et seq.*; ¶s 4014.176, 4154.015
28. ¶H-9201 *et seq.*; ¶4014.17

29. ¶H-8975.12; ¶4014.17
30. ¶H-8975.12; ¶4014.17
31. ¶H-9053.1I
32. ¶s H-9150, H-9159; ¶4014.17
33. ¶H-6579 *et seq.*; ¶4014.17
34. ¶H-6555 *et seq.*; ¶4014.212

(¶4369) that meets specified matching or nonelective contribution tests and other requirements. (Code Sec. 401(k)(11))[35]

An alternative nondiscrimination safe harbor based on employer matching or nonelective contributions also is available. (Code Sec. 401(k)(12))[36]

Similar rules apply to employer and matching contributions under Code Sec. 401(m). (Code Sec. 401(m)(3))[37]

A nondiscrimination safe harbor applies for automatic enrollment 401(k) programs (called qualified automatic contribution arrangements, or "QACAs") that meet certain contribution, vesting, and withdrawal requirements. (Code Sec. 401(k)(13)(A))

Similar rules apply for 403(b) plans, see ¶4375.

A 401(k) plan can include a qualified Roth contribution program; see ¶4363.

An in-service distribution on account of hardship may be made only if the employee has "an immediate heavy financial need" and the distribution is "necessary to meet such need." But a distribution may be considered for hardship only to the extent that, as shown by the employee, the need can't be relieved by certain alternate sources, e.g., loans, insurance. (Reg § 1.401(k)-1(d)(2))[38] *For plan years beginning after 2018,* hardship distributions may be made from contributions to a profit-sharing or stock bonus plan cash or deferred arrangement; certain employer nonelective contributions; employer matching contributions; and earnings on all of them. Also, failure to take an available plan loan won't disqualify an employee from receiving a hardship distribution. (Code Sec. 401(k)(14))[39]

401(k) plans may permit hardship distributions of elective contributions for certain medical, tuition, funeral etc. expenses of a named plan beneficiary, or of a person who has an unconditional right to all or a part of the participant's account balance on the participant's death.[40]

Hardship distributions are not rollover-eligible, see ¶4348.

For the special rules that apply to "qualified hurricane distributions" from, and rollovers to, 401(k) (and other qualified) plans, see ¶4333.

¶ 4307   Defined contribution and defined benefit plans.

Certain rules governing employee benefit plans specifically apply either to "defined contribution plans" or to "defined benefit plans."

A "defined contribution plan" provides for individual accounts for participants and for benefits based on those accounts. (Code Sec. 414(i)) Included are money purchase pension plans, profit-sharing plans and stock bonus plans.

A "defined benefit plan" is a pension plan other than a defined contribution plan. (Code Sec. 414(j)) It provides for the payments of definitely determinable benefits to the employee over a period of years, usually for life, after retirement. (Reg § 1.401-1(b)(1)(i))[41]

Employers with 500 or fewer employees may establish a combined defined benefit-401(k) plan (a "DB(k) plan"). (Code Sec. 414(x)(2))[42]

¶ 4308   Qualification requirements for a qualified employee plan.

The chief requirements for tax qualification of an employee benefit plan and tax-exempt trust are:

35. ¶H-9087; ¶4014.1735
36. ¶H-9053.1; ¶4014.21
37. ¶H-9050 *et seq.*; ¶4014.176
38. ¶H-9211 *et seq.*; ¶4014.17

39. ¶H-8975.12, ¶H-8978.3
40. ¶H-9211 *et seq.*; ¶4014.17
41. ¶H-5200 *et seq.*; ¶s 4014.02, 4014.03
42. ¶H-9252; ¶4144.27

(1) The plan must be a definite written program [43] that's communicated to the employees. (Reg § 1.401-1(a)(2))[44]

(2) The plan must be established by the employer for the *exclusive* benefit of the employees or their beneficiaries. (Code Sec. 401(a)(1))[45]

(3) The plan must generally provide that benefits can't be assigned, except for transfers under a qualified domestic relations order (QDRO) and judgments or settlements for certain ERISA crimes and violations. (Code Sec. 401(a)(13); Reg § 1.401(a)-13(g)(2))[46]

(4) The plan must meet special tests based on coverage and eligibility of employees to participate (¶4312).

(5) The plan must not discriminate in favor of highly compensated employees with respect to contributions or benefits (¶4314).

(6) The plan must be properly funded (¶4319), and must meet certain vesting requirements (¶4311).

(7) Under a defined benefit plan, forfeitures must not be applied to increase the benefits of the employees. (Code Sec. 401(a)(8))[47]

(8) A pension plan (and certain other plans) must in general pay a married participant's benefits in the form of a qualified joint and survivor annuity (QJSA), unless the participant elects otherwise (with written spousal consent). The monthly survivor benefit must be at least 50% of the joint benefit. (Code Sec. 417(b))[48] Plans that offer a QJSA must offer, as an option, a joint and survivor benefit that provides at least a 75% survivor benefit. (Code Sec. 417(a)(1)(A), Code Sec. 417(g)) Plans subject to the QJSA requirements must provide, to a participant who waives the QJSA, the chance to elect a qualified optional survivor annuity (QOSA). (Code Sec. 417(a)(1)(A)(ii))[49]

(9) In the event of a merger or consolidation with, or transfer of assets or liabilities to, any other plan, each participant must be entitled to a termination benefit at least equal to his pre-merger termination benefit. (Code Sec. 401(a)(12))[50]

(10) The plan may not provide for contributions or benefits that exceed specified overall limits (Code Sec. 401(a)(16))[1] (¶4317).

(11) The plan must provide that benefit payments begin (unless otherwise elected) no later than the 60th day after the plan year in which occurs the latest of: (a) the date the participant reaches age 65 (or earlier retirement age), (b) the 10th anniversary of the employee's participation in the plan, or (c) the date the participant terminates service. (Code Sec. 401(a)(14); Reg § 1.401(a)-14(a))[2]

Qualified pension plans may allow employees age 62 or older to receive in-service distributions. (Code Sec. 401(a)(36); Reg § 1.401(a)-1(b)(1)(i))[3]

(12) The plan must provide certain required minimum distribution rules (Code Sec. 401(a)(9) (¶4334).

(13) A pension plan can't allow withdrawal of employer contributions before termination of employment, or of the plan.[4] But employer contributions accumulated in a profit-sharing plan may be distributed after a fixed number of years (not less than two years). (Reg § 1.401-1(b)(1)(ii))[5] A profit-sharing plan may also permit withdrawal of employer contributions for hardship[6] or by participants with at least 60 months of participation. [7]

(14) Every plan must provide that a distributee of an eligible rollover distribution may

43. ¶H-5301; ¶4014.05
44. ¶H-5303; ¶4014.05
45. ¶H-5304; ¶4014.09
46. ¶H-8200 *et seq.*; ¶4014.14
47. ¶H-7502; ¶4014.11
48. ¶H-8611; ¶4174.02
49. ¶H-8623.1 *et seq.*; ¶4174.02; ¶4174.035
50. ¶H-8800 *et seq.*; ¶4014.07

1. ¶H-5901 *et seq.*; ¶4154
2. ¶H-8271; ¶4014.15
3. ¶H-8273.2; ¶4014.141
4. ¶H-5310
5. ¶H-5346
6. ¶H-5348
7. ¶H-5346

elect to have the distribution transferred directly to an eligible retirement plan (¶4348). (Code Sec. 401(a)(31)(A); Reg § 1.401(a)(31)-1)[8] Plans also must adhere to certain involuntary cash-out rollover rules (see ¶4348). (Code Sec. 401(a)(31)(B))

(15) The plan can't reduce plan benefits (including death or disability) to account for post-separation social security benefit increases. (Code Sec. 401(a)(15))[9]

(16) A plan may take into account only the first $275,000 for 2018 ($280,000 for 2019) of each employee's annual compensation. (Code Sec. 401(a)(17))[10]

(17) Defined benefit plans other than government plans must meet minimum participation requirements (¶4312) (Code Sec. 401(a)(26)) in addition to the coverage and eligibility requirements (¶4313).[11]

(18) If a plan member elects to have an eligible rollover distribution paid directly to a specified eligible retirement plan, the plan must make the distribution in the form of direct trustee-to-trustee transfer. (Code Sec. 401(a)(31))[12]

(19) A qualified trust that's a retirement plan must provide that the survivors of a participant who dies while performing qualified military service are entitled to any additional benefits (other than benefit accruals relating to the period of qualified military service) under the plan as if the participant had resumed and then terminated employment on account of his death. (Code Sec. 401(a)(37))[13]

For the cash-out requirements under the minimum survivor annuity rules, which allow participant accounts of $5,000 or less to be distributed, the present value of plan benefits is calculated using the "applicable mortality table" and the "applicable interest rate." (Code Sec. 417(e)(3)) The "applicable interest rate" is the adjusted first, second, and third segment rates for the month before the distribution date (or as IRS regs prescribe). [14] The "applicable mortality table" is a mortality table, modified as appropriate by IRS, based on the mortality table specified for the plan year. [15]

¶ 4309 Distributions pursuant to domestic relations orders.

The rules prohibiting the assignment or alienation of qualified plan benefits do not apply to the creation, assignment, or recognition of a right to any benefit payable with respect to a participant under a domestic relations order that is determined to be a "qualified domestic relations order" (i.e., a "QDRO"). (Code Sec. 401(a)(13)(B)) A domestic relations order is any judgment, decree, or order (including approval of a property settlement agreement) that: (i) relates to the provision of child support, alimony payments, or marital property rights to a spouse, former spouse, child, or other dependent of the participant, and (ii) is made under a state domestic relations law (including a community property law). (Code Sec. 414(p)(1))[16]

The term "QDRO," which (i) provides an exception to the anti-alienation rules, and (ii) may place the responsibility for the taxation of plan distributions on an alternate payee who is a spouse or former spouse of a plan participant, means a "domestic relations order" (see above) that: (1) creates or recognizes the existence of an alternate payee's right, or assigns to an alternate payee (see below) the right, to receive all or a portion of a plan participant's benefits payable under a plan, (2) clearly specifies certain facts, such as the amount or percentage of, and manner that, the participant's benefits are to be paid to the alternate payee, and (3) does not alter the amount or form of benefit. (Code Sec. 414(p)(1)(A), Code Sec. 414(p)(2), Code Sec. 414(p)(3))[17]

8. ¶H-8250 *et seq.*
9. ¶H-5311; ¶4014.22
10. ¶H-5919; ¶4014.18
11. ¶H-5700 *et seq.*; ¶4014.25
12. ¶H-8251; ¶4014.27

13. ¶H-9963 *et seq.*; ¶4014.28
14. ¶H-8705.1; ¶4174.06
15. ¶H-8704; ¶4174.06
16. ¶H-8207; ¶H-8208; ¶4144.20
17. ¶H-8209; ¶4144.20

An "alternate payee" includes any spouse, former spouse, child, or other dependent of a participant who is recognized by a QDRO as having a right to receive all, or a portion of, the benefits payable under a plan with respect to the participant. (Code Sec. 414(p)(8))[18]

A spouse (or former spouse) who has a right to receive all or a part of a distribution under a QDRO as an alternate payee, is treated as the distributee of any distribution received under the QDRO. However, a distribution to a participant's non-spouse dependent (who also may be an alternate payee) is taxed to the participant. (Code Sec. 402(e)(1)(A)) Similar rules apply to distributions from Code Sec. 457 plans. (Code Sec. 414(p)(12))[19]

Lump-sum distributions made to alternate payees who are spouses (or ex-spouses) of participants are eligible for preferential tax treatment (see ¶4328) so long as the distributions would qualify for the preferential tax treatment if made to the participant. Further, any amounts paid or distributed under a qualified plan to an alternate payee who is the spouse (or former spouse) of the participant under a QDRO may be rolled over (see ¶4348 *et seq.*) as if the alternate payee were the participant. Thus, a QDRO distribution made to an employee's spouse (or former spouse) as an alternate payee is an eligible rollover distribution. (Code Sec. 402(e)(1)(B))[20]

In the case of a distribution made to the spouse (or former spouse) of the plan participant as alternate payee under a QDRO, net employee contributions (together with other amounts treated as the participant's investment in the contract) are apportioned between the participant and the alternate payee. The apportionment is made pro rata, on the basis of the present value of all benefits of the participant under the plan and the present value of all benefits of the alternate payee under the plan (as alternate payee with respect to the participant under a QDRO). (Code Sec. 72(m)(10))[21]

¶ 4310   Incidental benefits.

Life or accident and health insurance features that are incidental to the primary benefit of a qualified plan, may be included to a limited extent. (Reg § 1.401-1(b)(1)(i), Reg § 1.401-1(b)(1)(ii))[22] IRS regs address the tax treatment of payments for accident or health insurance made by qualified retirement plans. (Reg § 1.402(a)-1(e))[23]

¶ 4311   Vesting of benefits.

Plans must provide that a participant's right to his accrued benefit (defined below) vests at certain rates during the years of his employment. Benefits derived from employee contributions must be 100% vested at all times. (Code Sec. 411(a); Reg § 1.411(a)-1(a)(2)) Benefits derived from employer contributions must become nonforfeitable when the employee reaches normal retirement age (defined below). (Code Sec. 411(a)) A defined benefit plan also must meet one of two alternative minimum vesting standards for vesting in benefits derived from employer contributions before normal retirement age: (1) a 5-year cliff schedule requiring full vesting after five years of service, or (2) a 3-to-7 year graded schedule requiring 20% vesting after three years of service and 20% additional vesting in each of the following years. (Code Sec. 411(a)(2); Reg § 1.411(a)-3T) For a defined contribution plan, slightly faster vesting (3-year cliff or 2-to-6 year graded) applies to all employer contributions (non-elective employer contributions as well as matching contributions). (Code Sec. 411(a)(2)(B))[24]

For hybrid defined benefit plans (¶4301), IRS regs provide guidance on the accelerated 3-

---

18. ¶H-8209.1; ¶4364.08
19. ¶H-11008; ¶4364.08
20. ¶H-11439
21. ¶H-11049

22. ¶H-8104 *et seq.*; ¶4014.13
23. ¶H-11076.1; ¶4024.05
24. ¶H-7400 *et seq.*; ¶s 4114, 4114.01

year vesting for employer contributions. (Reg § 1.411(a)(13)-1(c))[25]

Accrued benefit means the participant's annual benefit (or its actuarial equivalent) starting at normal retirement age (defined benefit plans) or the balance in the participant's account (defined contribution plans). (Code Sec. 411(a)(7)(A))[26]

Normal retirement age is the earlier of the time a participant attains normal retirement age under the plan or the later of: (1) the time the participant reaches age 65, or (2) the 5th anniversary of the individual's participation in the plan. (Code Sec. 411(a)(8))[27]

IRS regs allow plans to set normal retirement age lower than age 65, so long as this age isn't earlier than the earliest age that is reasonably representative of the typical age for the industry in which the covered workforce is employed. Age 62 is a safe harbor for this requirement. (Reg § 1.401(a)-1(b)(2))[28]

¶ 4312   Coverage and eligibility requirements.

A qualified plan other than a government plan must meet special tests designed to ensure adequate coverage of rank and file employees and avoid discrimination.

The plan must, on at least one day in each quarter of its tax year, either: (1) benefit 70% of the employees who aren't "highly compensated" (¶4315), (2) benefit a percentage of nonhighly compensated employees that is at least 70% of the highly compensated benefiting, or (3) meet a test under which the average benefit for the nonhighly compensated is at least 70% of the average benefit for the highly compensated. (Code Sec. 410(b)(1)) This "average benefits test" also requires that the plan benefit employees under a nondiscriminatory classification. (Code Sec. 410(b)(2))[29] However, a plan maintained by an employer that has no employees other than highly compensated employees for a year is treated as meeting the coverage requirement for the year. (Code Sec. 410(b)(6)(F))[30]

A qualified plan can't require as a condition of participation that any employee complete a period of service extending beyond the later of the date he: (1) reaches age 21, or (2) completes one year of service (or two years, if the plan provides full and immediate vesting for all participants). (Code Sec. 410(a)(1)(A), Code Sec. 410(a)(1)(B)(i))[31]

¶ 4313   Minimum participation requirement—the 50-employee/40% test.

A defined benefit plan other than a governmental plan isn't qualified unless, on each day of the plan year, the plan benefits at least the lesser of (a) 50 employees of the employer, or (b) the greater of 40% of employees, or 2 employees (or 1 employee if there is only 1 employee). (Code Sec. 401(a)(26)(A))[32] Instead of meeting the test on each day of the plan year, compliance on a single representative "snapshot" day during the year is sufficient. (Reg § 1.401(a)(26)-7(b))[33]

¶ 4314   Contributions or benefits must be nondiscriminatory.

Contributions or benefits under a plan other than a governmental plan must not discriminate in favor of "highly compensated employees," see ¶4315. (Code Sec. 401(a)(4))[34] To comply, a plan must satisfy three requirements: (1) either the contributions or benefits under the plan must be nondiscriminatory in amount, (2) the plan's optional forms of benefit, ancillary benefits (e.g., disability benefits), and other rights and features (e.g., plan

---

25. ¶H-7239.22; ¶4114.3320
26. ¶H-7200 *et seq.*; ¶4114.06
27. ¶H-7404; ¶4114.08
28. ¶H-7404; ¶4114.08
29. ¶H-5410 *et seq.*; ¶s 4104.11, 4104.12

30. ¶H-5410; ¶4104.12
31. ¶s H-5804, H-5807 *et seq.*; ¶4104.02
32. ¶H-5701 *et seq.*; ¶4014.25
33. ¶H-5704; ¶4014.25
34. ¶H-6100 *et seq.*; ¶4014.19

loans and investment alternatives) must be made available to employees in a nondiscriminatory manner, and (3) the effect of the plan under certain plan amendments, grants of past service credit, and plan terminations must be nondiscriminatory. (Reg § 1.401(a)(4)-1(b))[35] Defined benefit plans can be cross-tested for discrimination on the basis of equivalent employer contributions to profit-sharing plans, and vice versa. (Reg § 1.401(a)(4)-8) "Catch-up" elective deferrals by older employees (¶4306) are not subject to nondiscrimination requirements, above, but all eligible employees must have the opportunity to make these "catch-up" contributions (the "universal availability" requirement). (Code Sec. 414(v)(3)(B))[36]

¶ 4315 Who is a highly compensated employee (HCE)?

An HCE is an employee who (1) was a 5% owner at any time during the determination year or the preceding year, or (2) for the preceding year, received more than $120,000 in compensation from the employer in 2018 ($125,000 in 2019), and, if the employer elects, also was in the "top-paid group" (top 20%) of employees for that year. (Code Sec. 414(q))[37]

¶ 4316 Plans covering self-employed persons (Keogh plans).

A person who is a "self-employed individual," i.e., derives "earned income" from a business or profession that he owns or conducts, or who has earned income from a partnership in which he is a partner, or has other self-employment income (such as director's fees), can establish and be covered by a qualified retirement plan (sometimes called a Keogh plan). (Code Sec. 401(c)(1))[38] Earned income for this purpose consists essentially of earnings attributable to personal services, whether from a sole proprietorship, partnership or other unincorporated venture, derived from the trade or business with respect to which the plan is established. (Code Sec. 401(c)(2), Code Sec. 401(d))[39]

¶ 4317 Overall limits on plan contributions and benefits.

A plan can't be qualified if it provides for contributions or benefits that exceed the overall limits described below.

Benefits under a defined benefit plan will disqualify the plan if the "annual benefit" for each participant beginning at age 65 exceeds the lesser of: (1) $220,000 for 2018 ($225,000 for 2019), but actuarially reduced if benefit begins before age 62, and increased if the benefit begins after age 65, or (2) 100% of the participant's average compensation for his three high consecutive years of active plan participation. (Code Sec. 415(b); Reg § 1.415(b)-1(a)(1))[40] The maximum dollar benefit is reduced if the employee has less than ten years of plan participation when retirement benefits begin. (Code Sec. 415(b)(5)) This reduction doesn't apply to pro rata benefit increases under a terminating plan if there is no discrimination in favor of highly compensated employees. (Code Sec. 4980(d)(4)(C))[41] Neither the dollar nor the percentage limitation applies if the annual benefit payable under a defined benefit plan doesn't exceed $10,000 and the employer has never had a defined contribution plan in which the employee participated. (Code Sec. 415(b)(4))[42]

Annual additions under a defined contribution plan may not exceed the lesser of: (1) $55,000 for 2018 ($56,000 for 2019), or (2) 100% of the participant's compensation. (Code Sec. 415(c)(1)) Annual additions include employer contributions, employee contributions other than qualified cost-of-living contributions to a defined benefit plan (Code

---

35. ¶H-6350 *et seq.*; ¶4014.19
36. ¶H-9247.1; ¶4144.26
37. ¶H-6702; ¶s 4144.21, 4154.015
38. ¶s H-5218, H-9500 *et seq.*; ¶4014.24

39. ¶H-9512 *et seq.*; ¶4014.24
40. ¶H-5950; ¶4154.02
41. ¶H-5962; ¶4154.02
42. ¶H-5965; ¶4154.02

Sec. 415(k)(2)(A)), and employee forfeitures. (Code Sec. 415(c); Reg § 1.415(c)-1(a)(1))[43]

Mandatory employee contributions that are made to a defined benefit plan are treated as contributions made to a defined contribution plan, and are therefore subject to the Code Sec. 415(c) contribution limit. An individual medical account that is part of a pension or annuity plan under Code Sec. 401(h), and an account established to provide post-retirement medical benefits or life insurance for a key employee under Code Sec. 419A(d)(1), are treated as defined contribution plans, so that contributions to these accounts are also subject to the Code Sec. 415(c) limit.[44]

Special rules apply the limits to certain ESOPs. (Code Sec. 415(c)(6); Reg § 1.415(c)-1(f))[45]

Benefits provided to alternate payees under any qualified domestic relations order (QDRO) relating to a participant's benefits must be aggregated with benefits provided to the participant from all defined benefit and defined contribution plans in applying the Code Sec. 415 limitations.[46]

¶ 4318   Additional qualification requirements for "top-heavy" plans.

A "top-heavy" plan is one that primarily favors officers, shareholders, partners and other key employees. If more than 60% of the accrued benefits in a defined benefit plan, or more than 60% of the aggregate of the account balances in a defined contribution plan, are for "key employees," the plan is top-heavy and must meet additional requirements for minimum vesting, and minimum benefits or contributions for non-key employees, in determining contributions or benefits. (Code Sec. 416(a))[47] SIMPLE retirement plans (¶4369) and Code Sec. 401(k) plans that meet safe-harbor nondiscrimination requirements, aren't subject to the top-heavy rules. (Code Sec. 416(g)(4)(G), Code Sec. 416(g)(4)(H))[48]

Top-heavy plans are subject to special vesting rules. (Code Sec. 416(b))[49] Further, top-heavy defined benefit plans must provide non-key employes with a minimum annual benefit that's not integrated with social security. (Code Sec. 416(c)(1))[50] And, for top-heavy defined contribution plans, the employer must make contributions of at least 3% of compensation for each non-key employee (including employer matching contributions). (Code Sec. 416(c)(2))[1]

¶ 4319   Minimum funding requirements.

To qualify for tax advantages, defined benefit plans and money purchase plans (including target benefit plans) must meet minimum funding standards. To the extent the minimum funding standard is not met, the employer must pay nondeductible taxes on the amount of the deficiency until the deficiency is eliminated.

A plan is treated as satisfying the minimum funding standard for a plan year if:

(1)   for a single-employer defined benefit plan, the employer makes contributions to, or under, the plan for the plan year which, in total, are not less than the Code Sec. 430 minimum required contribution for the plan year;

(2)   for a single-employer money purchase plan, the employer makes contributions to, or under, the plan for the plan year, which are required under the plan's terms;

(3)   for a multiemployer plan, the employers make contributions to, or under, the plan, for any plan year which, in the aggregate, are sufficient to ensure that the plan does not

---

43. ¶H-6000 *et seq.*; ¶4154.06
44. ¶H-6000 *et seq.*; ¶4154.06
45. ¶H-6016; ¶4154.09
46. ¶s H-5950, H-6000, H-8217 *et seq.*; ¶4154.02
47. ¶H-8000 *et seq.*; ¶4164

48. ¶H-8001 *et seq.*; ¶4164.02
49. ¶H-7423; ¶4164.04
50. ¶H-8025; ¶4164.05
1. ¶H-8032; ¶4164.06

have an accumulated funding deficiency under Code Sec. 431 as of the end of the plan year. (Code Sec. 412(a)(2))[2]

For single-employer defined benefit plans, the minimum required contribution generally depends on whether the value of plan assets covers the plan's "funding target," which is the present value of all benefits accrued, earned, or otherwise allocated to years of service before the first day of the plan year. (Code Sec. 430(d)(1); Reg § 1.430(d)-1(b)(2))[3]

If the value of plan assets (less any prefunding balance or funding standard carryover balance) is less than the funding target, the minimum required contribution is the sum of the plan's target normal cost and the shortfall and waiver amortization charges for the plan year. (Code Sec. 430(a)(1); Reg § 1.430(d)-1(b)(2)) If the value of plan assets (less any prefunding balance or funding standard carryover balance) equals or exceeds the funding target, the minimum required contribution is the plan's target normal cost for the plan year reduced (but not below zero) by the amount of the excess. (Code Sec. 430(a)(2); Reg § 1.430(d)-1(b)(2))

A plan's target normal cost is the present value of the benefits that are expected to accrue or to be earned during the plan year, plus any plan-related expenses expected to be paid from plan assets, and less any mandatory employee contributions expected to be made during the plan year. (Code Sec. 430(b)(1)(A); Reg § 1.430(d)-1(b)(1))[4]

To determine a plan's target normal cost and funding target, plan liabilities are calculated by discounting future payments to present value using required interest rates based on corporate bonds. Plans must discount future liabilities using three different interest rates (segment rates), depending on the length of time until the liabilities must be paid. A short-term interest (segment) rate is used to calculate the present value of liabilities that will come due within 5 years. A midterm interest (segment) rate is used for liabilities that will come due in 5 to 15 years, and a long-term interest (segment) rate is applied to liabilities that will come due in more than 15 years. These rates are derived from a "yield curve" of investment-grade corporate bonds averaged over the most recent 24 months (i.e., the interest rates are "smoothed" over a 24-month period).

If the rates determined under the regular rules (see above) are outside of a specified percentage corridor (90% to 110% of the 25-year average for calendar years 2012 through 2017, then increasing annually until 2020 and thereafter, when the specified percentage corridor will be 70% to 130% of the 25-year average), the segment rate is adjusted. The average segment rate is the average of the segment rates determined under the regular rules for the 25-year period ending September 30 of the calendar year preceding the calendar year in which the plan year begins. (Code Sec. 430(h)(2)(C)(iv); Highway and Transportation Funding Act of 2014 ("HATFA") §2003(a))[5]

Typically, a plan will have a funding shortfall for a plan year if its funding target for the year exceeds the value of the plan's assets. The shortfall amortization base for a plan year is (1) the plan's funding shortfall, less (2) the present value, determined using one of several permissible rates, of the total of the shortfall amortization installments that have been determined for the current plan year and any succeeding plan years. The total of these installments is referred to as the shortfall amortization charge. [6]

Plans in "at risk status" (generally, plans that are less than 80% funded) must use additional actuarial assumptions to determine their funding target and target normal cost. (Code Sec. 430(i); Reg § 1.430(i)-1)[7]

Underfunded defined benefit plans must also satisfy funding-based limits on the accrual

---

2. ¶H-7601; ¶4124.02
3. ¶H-7752.1; ¶4304
4. ¶H-7751.1; ¶4304.01

5. ¶H-7751.2A; ¶4304.011
6. ¶H-7751.3; ¶H-7751.2; ¶4304.01
7. ¶H-7759.1 *et seq.*; ¶4304.01 *et seq.*

and payment of benefits, such as plant shutdown benefits, plan amendments that increase liabilities for benefits, the payment of accelerated benefit distributions, etc. (Code Sec. 436; Reg § 1.436-1)[8]

The due date for payment of minimum required contributions to defined benefit plans, other than multiemployer plans, is 8 1/2 months after the close of the plan year. Thus, for calendar year plan years, the due date for payment of the minimum required contribution for plan Year 1 is Sept. 15 of Year 2. A payment that's made before the first day of the plan year cannot be applied toward the minimum required contribution for that plan year. An accelerated schedule of quarterly installments of a plan's contributions applies where the plan had a funding shortfall for the preceding plan year. Any payment of the minimum required contribution that is made on a date other than the valuation date must be adjusted for interest accruing for the period between (i) the valuation date, and (ii) the payment date, at the plan's effective rate of interest for the plan year, with a special adjustment required for a small plan. (Code Sec. 430(j); Reg § 1.430(j)-1)[9]

¶ 4320   Returning veteran's pension rights.

An employee who returns to a civilian employer following qualified military service is entitled to restoration of certain qualified plan benefits that would have accrued but for the absence due to military service. Qualified military service of a reemployed person must not be treated as a break in service, and must be considered service with the employer for purposes of determining the nonforfeitability and the accrual of the individual's benefits. (Code Sec. 414(u)(8)(B))[10] "Make-up" contributions in excess of the usual contribution and deduction limits for the year made, and suspension of plan loan repayment during uniformed service do not cause loss of a plan's qualified status. (Code Sec. 414(u)(1); Code Sec. 414(u)(4))[11] Plans must permit returning employees to make additional elective deferrals and employee contributions, and must make matching contributions that would have been required had the deferral been made during the period of military service. (Code Sec. 414(u)(2)(A)) Report make-up contributions on Form W-2 or a separate statement identifying the type of plan, years involved, and amounts. [12]

For retirement plans that are subject to Code Sec. 414(u): (1) an individual receiving a differential wage payment (¶3005) has to be treated as an employee of the employer making the payment; (2) the differential wage payment has to be treated as compensation; and (3) the plan won't be treated as failing to meet certain nondiscrimination requirements by reason of any contribution or benefit that is based on the differential wage payment (but other nondiscrimination requirements apply). (Code Sec. 414(u)(12)(A))

Death benefits. Qualified retirement plans, including Code Sec. 403(b) tax-deferred annuities and Code Sec. 457(b) plans, must provide that, where a plan participant dies while performing qualified military service, the participant's survivors are entitled to any additional benefits (other than benefit accruals relating to the period of qualified military service) that would have been provided under the plan had the participant resumed employment and then terminated employment on account of death. However, benefit accruals for the period of qualified military service are excepted from these additional benefits. [13]

¶ 4321   How to get IRS approval of plan—Form 5300; Form 5307.

Although advance IRS approval isn't required, it's desirable and customary to seek it by requesting an opinion letter (or determination letter) on special forms issued by IRS (e.g.,

---

8. ¶H-7730.5 *et seq.*; ¶4364.04 *et seq.*
9. ¶H-7770.1 *et seq.*; ¶4304.02
10. ¶H-9951

11. ¶H-9952 *et seq.*
12. ¶H-9956
13. ¶H-9963 *et seq.*

Form 5300).[14]

IRS limits the issuance of determination letters for individually-designed plans to initial plan qualification, qualification upon plan termination, and certain other limited circumstances. (Rev Proc 2016-37, 2016-29 IRB) [15]

Master and prototype plans. Instead of establishing a plan on its own, an employer may adopt (use Form 5307) a qualified plan using an IRS-approved master or prototype plan prepared and sponsored by trade or professional associations, banks, insurance companies or regulated investment companies (mutual funds). [16] IRS has replaced its determination and opinion letter program with a streamlined opinion letter process for plan providers' and mass submitters' pre-approved plans. [17]

For the small-employer retirement plan start-up tax credit, see ¶2331.

¶ 4322   Employee contributions and employer matching contributions.

A plan may require an employee to contribute to the plan, as a condition to participation, or it may permit such contributions, if no discrimination results. [18]

Employee contributions and employer matching contributions under defined contribution plans (and those under a defined benefit plan treated as made under a defined contribution plan) must meet a nondiscrimination test that restricts the extent to which the actual contribution percentage (ACP) of eligible highly compensated employees can exceed the ACP for all other eligible employees. (Code Sec. 401(m), Code Sec. 414(k)(2)) The current year ACP for highly compensated employees is compared to the previous year's, or, electively, the current year's ACP for other employees. (Code Sec. 401(m)(2)) The ACP test can be satisfied using a safe-harbor. (Code Sec. 401(m)(11))[19] "SIMPLE" plans (¶4369) are deemed to satisfy the ACP test. (Code Sec. 401(m)(10))[20]

Qualified Nonelective Contributions (QNECs) and Qualified Matching Contributions (QMACs) are employer contributions, other than elective contributions or matching contributions, that meet certain nonforfeitability requirements and distribution limits. These contributions are designed to allow a 401(k) plan to pass ADP/ACP testing. Employer contributions to a 401(k) plan are treated as QMACs or QNECs when they are allocated to participants' accounts. (Reg § 1.401(k)-6)[21]

Defined contribution plans generally must allow participants to immediately diversify any employee contributions or elective deferrals invested in employer securities into at least 3 other investment options. For employer contributions, other than elective deferrals, invested in employer securities, the same diversification rights must be given to participants with at least 3 years of service, or each beneficiary of such participants or deceased participants. (Code Sec. 401(a)(35)) Individuals with diversification rights must be offered the opportunity to divest the employer securities and reinvest in another investment at least quarterly. [22]

An ESOP won't lose its exemption from the application of the diversification rules just because it receives rollover contributions of amounts from another plan that are held in a separate account. The exemption continues to apply even if those amounts were attributable to contributions that were subject to Code Sec. 401(k) or Code Sec. 401(m) in the other plan.[23]

---

14. ¶T-10500 *et seq.*; ¶4014.01
15. ¶T-10506 *et seq.*
16. ¶T-10631; ¶4014.01
17. ¶T-10630 *et seq.*
18. ¶H-6556.1 *et seq.*; ¶4014.21

19. ¶H-6565; ¶4014.21
20. ¶H-6565; ¶4014.21
21. ¶H-9071.15
22. ¶H-8071; ¶4014.12
23. ¶H-8072; ¶4014.12

¶ 4323   Ceiling on deductions for contributions to pension and annuity plans.

Subject to applicable limits (see following) an employer can deduct its timely paid (¶4326) contributions to a qualified plan. (Code Sec. 404(a); Reg § 1.404(a)-1(b))[24] However, the plan to which the contribution is made must be in existence by the end of the employer's tax year. [25]

The employer may choose one of three alternative special ceilings on annual deductions for contributions to a pension or annuity plan, to get the largest deduction: [26]

(1) The "level cost" ceiling permits a deduction equal to an amount necessary to provide for all participating employees the remaining unfunded cost of their past and current service credits, distributed as a level amount (or level percentage of compensation) over the entire future remaining service of each employee. If the remaining unfunded cost with respect to any three individuals is more than 50% of the total remaining unfunded cost, the unfunded cost attributable to those three must be distributed over at least five tax years. (Code Sec. 404(a)(1)(A)(ii))

(2) The "normal cost" ceiling permits the employer to deduct contributions equal to (a) the "normal cost" (cost of credits for current services determined as though past service credits had been properly funded), plus (b) an amount necessary to amortize the cost of past service or supplementary or annuity credits provided by the plan in equal annual payments (until fully amortized) over ten years. (Code Sec. 404(a)(1)(A)(iii))

(3) If the minimum funding standard (¶4319) exceeds the "level cost" or "normal cost" ceiling applicable to the plan, the employer can deduct the amount necessary to satisfy the minimum funding standard. (Code Sec. 404(a)(1)(A)(i))

The single-employer defined benefit plan contribution deduction limit for any tax year is the greater of: (i) the excess (if any) of (A) the sum of: the plan's funding target, the plan's target normal cost, and a cushion amount for a plan year, over (B) the value of plan assets (determined under Code Sec. 430(g)(3)) as of the valuation date for the plan year (Code Sec. 404(o)(2)(A)); over (ii) the minimum required contribution for the plan year. (Code Sec. 404(o))[27]

The maximum annual deduction under the above ceilings, however, cannot generally exceed the full funding limit for the year (Code Sec. 404(a)(1)(A)).[28] Money purchase and target benefit plans also are subject to the 25%-of-compensation deduction limit that applies to profit-sharing plans (¶4324). (Code Sec. 404(a)(3)(A)(v))[29]

Contributions in excess of the amount deductible (except contributions to SIMPLE plans (¶4369) for household workers (Code Sec. 4972(c)(6))) are subject to a nondeductible 10% excise tax in certain cases (Code Sec. 4972), but may be carried over and deducted in later years, subject to the above limitations. (Code Sec. 404(a)(1)(E))[30]

¶ 4324   Ceiling on deductions for contributions to profit-sharing and stock bonus plans.

The special ceiling on deductions for contributions under a profit-sharing, stock-bonus, or "SIMPLE" plan is 25% of the aggregate compensation (exclusive of qualified plan contributions) paid or accrued during the tax year for all employees participating in the plan. (Code Sec. 404(a)(3)(A); Code Sec. 404(m)(1); Reg § 1.404(a)-9(c)) Contributions in excess of this limit may be carried over and deducted in a later year to the extent that

---

24. ¶H-10001; ¶4044.01
25. ¶H-10021; ¶4044.02
26. ¶H-10102 *et seq.*; ¶4044.04
27. ¶H-10106; ¶4044.02

28. ¶H-10105 *et seq.*; ¶4044.04
29. ¶H-10102; ¶4044.07
30. ¶H-10125 *et seq.*; ¶4044.04

contributions for that later year are below the applicable percentage limit for that year. (Code Sec. 404(a)(3)(A)(ii))[31]

The percentage of compensation limit on deductible contributions to a stock bonus or profit-sharing plan for a self-employed individual (Keogh plan) is 25% of "earned income," which is 25% of net earnings from self-employment less the self-employment tax deduction and deductible qualified plan contributions. (Code Sec. 404(a)(8)(B))[32]

Elective deferrals (¶4306) are not subject to the deduction limits for stock bonus and profit sharing plans, combination defined contribution and defined benefit plans, or ESOPs. (Code Sec. 404(n))[33] Compensation includes elective deferral amounts, amounts deferred to a cafeteria plan, and certain pre-disability compensation. (Code Sec. 404(a)(12))[34]

¶ 4325   Deduction ceiling for combinations of qualified plans.

If there is a mixture of one or more defined contribution plans and one or more defined benefit plans, or any combination of two or more pension trusts, annuity plans, and stock bonus or profit-sharing trusts, an overall limit on deductible contributions applies. Under this limit, the total amount deductible for *all* plans is the greater of: (1) 25% of the compensation (exclusive of qualified plan contributions) paid or accrued during the tax year to the beneficiaries of the various trusts or plans, or (2) the total contributions to the trusts or plans to the extent those contributions don't exceed the amount necessary to satisfy the Code Sec. 412 minimum funding standards. The amount necessary to satisfy the Code Sec. 412 minimum funding standard must not be less than the plan's funding shortfall under Code Sec. 430. (Code Sec. 404(a)(7)(A))

The 25% limit does not apply if the only amounts contributed to the defined compensation plan are elective deferrals. (Code Sec. 404(a)(7)(C)(ii))[35] Further, the combined plan limit applies only to employer contributions to one or more defined contribution plans to the extent the contributions exceed 6% of the compensation otherwise paid or accrued to plan beneficiaries during the tax year. [36]

In determining the limit on deductions where there is a combination of one or more defined benefit and one or more defined contribution plans, any defined benefit plan guaranteed by the PBGC is not taken into account. (Code Sec. 404(a)(7)(C)(iv))

¶ 4326   Timely payment requirement.

A contribution actually must be paid to the trust or under the plan to be deductible. (Code Sec. 404(a))[37] However, payments (including those made to "SIMPLE" plans (¶4369) (Code Sec. 404(m)(2)(B)), made after the end of a year are considered paid on the last day of the year if paid by the employer no later than the due date of its tax return (including extensions). (Code Sec. 404(a)(6))[38] This applies to both cash and accrual employers, even if other accrual requirements are not met. (Reg § 1.404(a)-1(c))[39]

¶ 4327   How employees are taxed.

Apart from certain "lump-sum" payments qualifying for the preferential tax treatment (¶4328 *et seq.*), and "rollovers" (¶4348), distributions from a qualified plan (reported to recipients on Form 1099-R) generally are taxed to the employee under the annuity rules (¶1350 *et seq.*) in the year distributed or otherwise made available to the employee. (Code

---

31. ¶H-10202; ¶4044.06
32. ¶H-10204; ¶4044.08
33. ¶H-10202; ¶4044.08
34. ¶H-10203; ¶4044.08
35. ¶H-10120 *et seq.*; ¶4044.09

36. ¶H-10120
37. ¶H-10010; ¶4044.01
38. ¶H-10016; ¶4044.01
39. ¶H-10017; ¶4044.01

Sec. 402(a); Reg § 1.402(a)-1(a)) Thus, the excess of the distribution (cash or fair market value of property) over the amount of any after-tax plan contributions made by the employee, is ordinary income. (Code Sec. 402; Reg § 1.402(a)-1(a)(1)(i))[40]

Certain early (¶4333) distributions are subject to penalty.

For special income-averaging rules that apply to certain disaster-related distributions, see ¶4333.

¶ 4328   Preferential treatment for certain lump-sum distributions.

Distributions from a qualified plan to an employee or his beneficiaries, that are lump-sum distributions, are taxable as ordinary income, subject to special elections for pre-'74 capital gain treatment and/or ten-year forward averaging for those born before '36.

A lump-sum distribution eligible for preferential tax treatment is a distribution or payment from an exempt trust or annuity within one tax year of the recipient of the balance to the credit of the participant (excluding amounts payable to an alternate payee under a qualified domestic relations order (QDRO; see ¶4309), which separately can qualify for lump-sum treatment to the alternate payee): (1) on account of an employee's (other than a self-employed's) separation from service; or (2) after attaining age 59 ½ (regardless of his separation from service); or (3) on account of his death; or (4) on account of disability. (Code Sec. 402(e)(4)(D))[41]

¶ 4329   Lump-sum distributions of securities of employer corporation.

If a lump-sum distribution consists in part of securities of the employer, the net unrealized appreciation in value of the securities while held by the trust is not taxed to the recipient at the time of distribution. But the same amount also is excluded from the recipient's basis in the securities, so that it's taken into account for tax purposes if and when the securities are later disposed of in a taxable transaction. The distributee, however, has the right to elect, on the tax return on which a distribution is required to be included, to have this rule not apply, i.e., to include any net unrealized appreciation in income. (Code Sec. 402(e)(4)(B); Reg § 1.402(a)-1(b)(1))[42] Net unrealized appreciation that isn't included in income at the time of distribution is long-term capital gain when it's realized in a later taxable transaction. (Reg § 1.402(a)-1(b)(1)(i))[43]

¶ 4330   Tax on current payments for life insurance protection.

The cost of current life insurance protection under a life insurance contract purchased with employer contributions to a qualified plan (or earnings thereon) is income to the insured employee for the tax year of purchase, where the benefits are payable to him or his beneficiaries. (Code Sec. 72(m)(3); Reg § 1.72-16(b)) The taxable amount is generally determined under IRS's "Table 2001," carried at IRS Notice 2002-8. [44]

¶ 4331   Tax on failure to notify participants of benefit-accrual reduction.

Defined benefit plans and individual account plans subject to minimum funding standards are subject to an excise tax of $100 per day per participant, subject to an overall dollar limit, for failure to provide written notice to any participant, employee organization, or alternate payee under a qualified domestic relations order within a reasonable time when the plan is amended to provide for a significant reduction in the rate of future

---

40. ¶H-11006 *et seq.*; ¶4024
41. ¶H-11200 *et seq.*; ¶4024.03
42. ¶s H-11501, H-11503; ¶4024.02

43. ¶H-11510
44. ¶H-10507 *et seq.*; ¶724.24

benefit accrual. (Code Sec. 4980F(a); Reg § 54.4980F-1)[45] Plans with fewer than 100 participants or that offer participants the option to choose between a new benefit formula and the old one may be able to use a simplified notice form or be exempted by IRS from the notice requirements. (Code Sec. 4980F(e)(2)(A))[46]

¶ 4332   Loans from qualified plans.

A loan from a qualified plan isn't treated as a taxable distribution to the plan participant only if it must be repaid within five years (except for certain home loans), and doesn't exceed the *lesser* of: (1) $50,000, or (2) the greater of (a) ½ of the present value of the employee's nonforfeitable accrued benefit under the plan, or (b) $10,000. If a plan loan (when added to the employee's outstanding balance of all other plan loans at the time the loan is made and the highest outstanding loan balance during the year before the loan was made) exceeds these limits, the excess is treated (and taxed) as a plan distribution (¶4327). The entire amount of a plan loan that isn't required to be repaid within five years (except for certain home loans) is treated as a plan distribution. (Code Sec. 72(p))[47] The outstanding balance of a plan loan is treated as distributed if the borrower fails to make a scheduled loan repayment installment before any allowable grace period expires. (Reg § 1.72(p)-1, Q&A 10(b))[48] Loan repayment following a deemed distribution increases the participant's investment in the contract (basis). (Reg § 1.72(p)-1, Q&A 21)[49]

A plan loan must be amortized in substantially level payments, at least quarterly, over its term. (Code Sec. 72(p)(2)(C))[50] The level amortization requirement doesn't apply while the employee is on leave without pay for up to one year. (Reg § 1.72(p)-1, Q&A 9)[1]

For loans made in the period beginning Sept. 29, 2017 and ending Dec. 31, 2018, the Disaster Tax Relief and Airport and Airway Extension Act of 2017 temporarily increased the loan limit for qualified individuals, and delays certain plan loan repayment dates, increases the repayment term, and adjusts the due dates of subsequent repayments accordingly. Similar rules apply to "qualified 2016 disaster distributions" under the Tax Cuts and Jobs Act and retirement plan loans made to certain victims of California wildfires during the period beginning Feb. 9, 2018 and ending Dec. 31, 2018. [2]

¶ 4333   Penalty for early withdrawals—Form 5329.

Early withdrawals from a qualified retirement plan, SIMPLE plan, or IRA result in an additional tax (reported on Form 5329) equal to 10% of the amounts withdrawn that are includible in gross income. (Code Sec. 72(t)(1)) The additional tax applies to all withdrawals unless specifically excepted. Exceptions include distributions (i) made on or after age 59½; (ii) made to a beneficiary or estate on or after death; (iii) attributable to disability; (iv) from a qualified plan after an employee's separation from service in or after the year in which he attains age 55 (this rule does not apply to IRAs); (v) not in excess of the amount allowable as a medical expense deduction for the year, whether or not the distributee itemizes; (vi) that are part of a series of substantially equal periodic (annual or more frequent) payments (made after separation from service if from a qualified plan) for the life (or life expectancy) of the employee or the joint lives (or joint life expectancies) of the employee and his beneficiary; (vii) from an IRA not exceeding amounts paid for medical insurance by IRA owners who have received unemployment compensation for at least 12 weeks (or could have except for being self-employed); (viii) from an IRA for qualified higher education expenses; (ix) from an IRA for qualified "first-home" purchases, subject to $10,000 lifetime cap; (x) from a qualified plan to an alternate payee under a qualified

45. ¶H-7374
46. ¶H-7368
47. ¶H-11067 *et seq.*; ¶724.23
48. ¶H-11070; ¶724.23

49. ¶724.23
50. ¶H-11068; ¶724.23
1. ¶H-11068.1; ¶724.23
2. ¶H-11006.3

domestic relations order (QDRO ¶4309; this rule does not apply to IRAs); (xi) made on account of an IRS tax levy, and (xii) from a phased or composite retirement annuity under the Federal Phased Retirement Program. (Code Sec. 72(t)(2), Code Sec. 72(t)(3))[3]

For transfers of an IRA to a spouse (or former spouse) under a divorce or separation instrument, see ¶4346.

Taxpayers who used the annuitization or amortization methods to compute substantially equal payments can make a one-time switch to the required minimum distribution method, which generally requires smaller annual distributions, without triggering the 10% penalty.[4]

The additional tax is 25%, rather than 10% on amounts received from a SIMPLE retirement account (¶4369) during the employee's first two years of participation. (Code Sec. 72(t)(6))[5]

The tax applies to certain involuntary cash-outs and deemed distributions. It doesn't apply to amounts distributed from unfunded deferred compensation plans of tax-exempt employers or state and local government employees, i.e., Code Sec. 457 plans.[6]

The 10% early withdrawal tax does not apply to distributions from a governmental plan to a qualified public safety employee (e.g., State or local firefighter or policeman, and certain federal government employees, including federal law enforcement, custom and border patrol officers, firefighters and air traffic controllers,) who separates from service after age 50. (Code Sec. 72(t)(10))

The 10% additional tax also does not apply to any "qualified reservist distribution" made to individuals ordered or called to active duty for more than 179 days (or an indefinite period) after Sept. 11, 2001. (Code Sec. 72(t)(2)(G)(i))[7]

Under the Disaster Tax Relief and Airport and Airway Extension Act of 2017, which provides temporary tax relief to victims of Hurricanes Harvey, Irma, and Maria, up to $100,000 of "qualified hurricane distributions." Generally, a "qualified hurricane distribution" is one made to an individual whose principal place of abode was in the Hurricane Harvey, Irma, or Maria disaster areas and who sustained a hurricane-related economic loss, during the period after the date of the relevant hurricane and before Jan. 1, 2019. [8]

If a repayment of a qualified hurricane distribution from an eligible retirement plan or IRA is made within the three-year period beginning on the day after the date the distribution is received, then the taxpayer is treated, to the extent of the repayment contribution, as having received the qualified hurricane distribution in a rollover distribution, and as having transferred the repayment amount to the eligible retirement plan or IRA in a direct trustee-to-trustee transfer within 60 days of the distribution.

Similar rules to those above apply to "qualified 2016 disaster distributions" under the Tax Cuts and Jobs Act and to "qualified wildfire distributions" made to certain victims of California wildfires under the Bipartisan Budget Act of 2018 on or after Oct. 8, 2017 and before Jan. 1, 2019.[9]

The Disaster Tax Relief and Airport and Airway Extension Act of 2017 also provides similar recontribution rules for retirement plan or IRA withdrawals that were to be used to buy or build a principal residence in a Hurricane Harvey, Irma, or Maria disaster area, but where the home purchase or construction was cancelled on account of the hurricanes. Similar relief was provided to California wildfire victims. [10]

---

3. ¶H-11100 *et seq.*; ¶724.22
4. ¶H-11107
5. ¶H-12377
6. ¶H-11101; ¶724.22

7. ¶H-11116; ¶724.22
8. ¶H-11006.1
9. ¶H-11006.2
10. ¶H-11006.2

¶ 4334   Required minimum distributions (RMDs).

A qualified plan must provide that the employee's entire interest will be distributed, starting Apr. 1 of the calendar year following the later of the year in which he: (a) reaches age 70 ½ or (b) retires (except for 5% owners). Benefits to a participant can be paid all at once (in a lump sum), or no later than over (i) his life, (ii) his life and the life of a designated beneficiary, (iii) a period of not more than his life expectancy, or (iv) a period of not more than his life expectancy and that of a designated beneficiary. (Code Sec. 401(a)(9)(A), Code Sec. 401(a)(9)(C)) (Similar rules apply to IRAs, see ¶4346.) A qualified plan may provide that the required beginning date for all employees (including non-5% owners) is Apr. 1 of the calendar year following the calendar year in which the employee attained age 70 ½.[11]

Where distributions to a participant have begun, but he dies before his entire interest has been distributed, his remaining interest must be distributed at least as rapidly as under the method of distribution in effect at the date of his death. (Code Sec. 401(a)(9)(B)(i)) Where he dies before receiving any required plan distributions, his entire interest must be distributed within five years after his death, except where the employee's interest: (1) is distributed over the life of a designated beneficiary (or over a period not extending beyond the life expectancy of the beneficiary) and the distributions begin no later than one year after the date of the employee's death (Code Sec. 401(a)(9)(B)(ii), Code Sec. 401(a)(9)(B)(iii)), or (2) is distributed over the life of the surviving spouse (or over a period not extending beyond his life expectancy), and the distributions begin no later than the date on which the employee would have reached age 70½. If the surviving spouse dies before payments must begin, then the 5-year rule applies as if the surviving spouse were the employee. (Code Sec. 401(a)(9)(B)(iv))

Failure to make the required distributions is subject to an excise tax (report on Form 5329) equal to 50% of the minimum amount that should have been distributed over the amount actually distributed. (Code Sec. 4974(a))[12]

Lifetime distributions. The RMD for each year is found by dividing the account balance as of the end of the preceding year by the age-based factor from the table in Reg § 1.401(a)(9)-9, Q&A 2. Portions of this table are excerpted below (the full table goes to age 115).

Uniform Lifetime Table

Employee's Age	Distribution Period	Employee's Age	Distribution Period
70	27.4	83	16.3
71	26.5	84	15.5
72	25.6	85	14.8
73	24.7	86	14.1
74	23.8	87	13.4
75	22.9	88	12.7
76	22.0	89	12.0
77	21.2	90	11.4
78	20.3	91	10.8
79	19.5	92	10.2
80	18.7	93	9.6
81	17.9	94	9.1
82	17.1	95	8.6

11. ¶H-8275.1 *et seq.*; ¶4014.15   12. ¶H-8500 *et seq.*; ¶49,744

This table is used for lifetime distributions of the account owner regardless of the identity of the beneficiary or age differential between account owner and designated beneficiary, unless the account owner's spouse is the sole beneficiary and is more than 10 years younger than the account owner, in which case the distribution period may be measured by the joint life and last survivor life expectancy of the employee and spouse, using the life expectancies in the joint and last survivor table of Reg § 1.401(a)(9)-9, Q&A 3.[13]

Determination of designated beneficiary. The account owner's designated beneficiary is determined based on the beneficiaries designated as of the account owner's date of death who remain beneficiaries on Sept. 30 of the year following the year of the account owner's death. Any beneficiary eliminated by distribution of the benefit or through disclaimer (or otherwise) during the period between the account owner's death and Sept. 30 of the year following the year of death is disregarded in determining the designated beneficiary for purposes of calculating RMDs. (Reg § 1.401(a)(9)-4, Q&A 4(a)) Except for certain trusts (see below), only an individual may be a designated beneficiary for purposes of the RMD rules. (Reg § 1.401(a)(9)-4, Q&A 3)[14]

Trusts as beneficiaries. An underlying beneficiary of a trust may be treated as the account owner's designated beneficiary for RMD purposes when the trust is named as the beneficiary of a retirement plan or IRA, if certain requirements are met (e.g., documentation of the underlying beneficiaries of the trust must be provided timely to the plan administrator, and beneficiaries of the trust can be identified). (Reg § 1.401(a)(9)-4, Q&A 6(b), Reg § 1.401(a)(9)-4, Q&A 5)[15]

Post-death distributions. For non-annuity-type payouts after the death of the account owner:

. . . If the account has a designated beneficiary, and the account owner died before his required beginning date (generally, April 1 following the year in which the account owner attains age 70 ½), the remaining account balance may be paid out over the remaining life expectancy of the beneficiary, using the life expectancy of the beneficiary in the Single Life Table of Reg § 1.401(a)(9)-9, Q&A 1.

. . . If the account has a designated beneficiary, and the account owner died after the date he was required to begin receiving distributions, the remaining account balance may be paid out over the longer of the remaining life expectancy of the beneficiary or the remaining life expectancy of the account owner. In either instance, the life expectancy for post-death RMDs is determined using the Single Life Table of Reg § 1.401(a)(9)-9, Q&A 1.

. . . If the account does not have a designated beneficiary: (1) If the account owner dies after his required beginning date (generally, April 1 following the year in which the IRA owner attains age 70 ½), the remaining balance is paid out over the remaining life expectancy of the account owner, using the Single Life Table of Reg § 1.401(a)(9)-9, Q&A 1. (2) If the account owner dies before his required beginning date, the account balance must be paid out no later than 5 years after the year of the owner's death. (Reg § 1.401(a)(9)-3, Q&A 1, Reg § 1.401(a)(9)-5, Q&A 5)[16]

The 50% excise tax on failures to make RMDs is waived during the first five years after the year of the account owner's death before the required beginning date if the entire benefit is distributed by the end of the fifth year following the year of death. (Reg § 54.4974-2, Q&A 4)

Annuity type distributions. Separate rules apply to annuity type required distributions, namely defined-benefit (i.e., pension) plan RMDs, as well as annuity contracts purchased

---

13. ¶H-8279; ¶4014.153
14. ¶H-8278; ¶4014.153

15. ¶H-8278.4; ¶4014.153
16. ¶H-8279.8; ¶4014.153

from firms such as insurance companies to make RMDs from other qualified plans and IRAs. (Reg § 1.401(a)(9)-6) Under these rules, distributions of an employee's entire interest must be paid in the form of periodic annuity payments for the employee's or beneficiary's life (or the joint lives of the employee and beneficiary) or over a comparable period certain. The payments must be nonincreasing or only increase as provided in the regs. (Reg § 1.401(a)(9)-6, Q&A 1)[17]

¶ 4335 Excise tax on employer reversions—Form 5330.

An "employer reversion" from a qualified plan (except for certain exempt employers and government plans) is, in addition to being includible in the employer's gross income, also subject to a 50% excise tax (20% in certain cases). (Code Sec. 4980(a), Code Sec. 4980(b), Code Sec. 4980(c)(1), Code Sec. 4980(d)) Pay with Form 5330 filed no later than the last day of the month following the month in which the reversion occurred. [18]

¶ 4336 Excise tax on prohibited transactions—Form 5330.

An excise tax is imposed on a disqualified person who takes part in a prohibited transaction with a qualified plan, IRA, or medical savings account. The tax (report on Form 5330 each year for each transaction (Reg § 54.6011-1(b))) is 15% of the amount involved in the prohibited transaction for each tax year (or part of the year) in the taxable period. And if the prohibited transaction isn't timely corrected, the disqualified person must pay an additional tax of 100% of the amount involved. (Code Sec. 4975(a), Code Sec. 4975(b))[19] Neither level of tax is imposed on a fiduciary acting only as such. (Code Sec. 4975(a))[20]

Providing investment advice through an "eligible investment advice arrangement" to participants and beneficiaries of a defined contribution plan who direct the investment of their accounts under the plan and to beneficiaries of IRAs (as well as HSAs, Archer MSAs, and Coverdell education savings accounts) is exempt from the prohibited transaction rules. (Code Sec. 4975(d)(17))[21]

Other transactions also are exempt from the prohibited transaction rules, including certain transactions between plans and service providers, for adequate consideration (Code Sec. 4975(d)(20)), and certain otherwise prohibited transactions involving the sale or exchange of securities and commodities between the plan and a party in interest that are corrected within 14 days (Code Sec. 4975(d)(23)).

¶ 4337 Transfers to health benefits and applicable life insurance accounts before 2026.

Before Jan. 1, 2026, excess pension assets may be transferred to a retiree health benefit account without the transfer being treated as either a prohibited transaction or a reversion to the employer if certain conditions are met. Transfers of excess pension assets may also be made to buy retiree group-term life insurance (an "applicable life insurance account"). (Code Sec. 420(a))[22]

Single-employer plans can use excess pension assets to fund future retiree health or life insurance benefits by making qualified future transfers to retiree health benefit accounts or applicable life insurance accounts, if certain minimum cost requirements are maintained. Similar rules apply to "collectively bargained transfers" to fund collectively bargained retiree health liabilities or life insurance benefits. A qualified future transfer or

---

17. ¶H-8280; ¶4014.153
18. ¶H-8900 *et seq.*; ¶49,804
19. ¶H-12510

20. ¶H-12514 *et seq.*; ¶49,754
21. ¶H-12558.1; ¶49,754.01
22. ¶H-8163; ¶4204

collectively bargained transfer must meet the requirements applicable to qualified transfers, with certain modifications to the requirements, one of which is the minimum cost requirement. (Code Sec. 420(f))

For qualified future transfers, the minimum cost requirement is satisfied if, during the transfer period and the four subsequent years, the annual average amount of employer costs is not less than applicable employer cost determined for the transfer. For collectively bargained transfers, the minimum cost requirement is satisfied if each collectively bargained group health plan or group-term life insurance plan provides that the collectively bargained employer cost for each tax year in the collectively bargained cost maintenance period is not less than the amount specified by the collective bargaining agreement.

Qualified transfers may satisfy the minimum cost requirement by satisfying the minimum cost requirement that applies to a collectively bargained transfer. (Code Sec. 420(c)(3)(A))[23]

Multiemployer plans may transfer excess pension assets to retiree health accounts. (Code Sec. 420(a); Code Sec. 420(e)(5)) Assets transferred in a qualified transfer to a retiree health account or applicable life insurance account will not be treated as assets in the plan for purpose of the minimum contribution rules. (Code Sec. 430(l))[24]

Generally, only group-term life insurance not in excess of $50,000 may be purchased with excess pension assets. [25]

¶ 4338 Distributions from governmental retirement plans for health and long-term care insurance for public safety officers.

Public safety officers may exclude from income governmental retirement plan distributions that don't exceed accident, health or long-term care insurance premiums for themselves, their spouses, and dependents, if the distributions are paid directly to insurers. The exclusion is limited to $3,000 per year. (Code Sec. 402(l), Code Sec. 403(a), Code Sec. 403(b), Code Sec. 457(a))[26] The accident or health plan receiving the payments of qualified health insurance premiums may be a self-insured plan. [27]

¶ 4339 Plans that fail to qualify or that lose qualified status.

The following rules apply to a plan that fails to qualify or loses its qualified status:

Contributions to the trust by an employer are included in the gross income of the employee. (Code Sec. 402(b)) The employee must report the value of his interest in the employer's contributions the first time his interest isn't subject to substantial risk of forfeiture, or is transferable free of such risk, whichever occurs first. (Reg § 1.402(b)-1)[28]

An employer's contributions are deductible in the tax year in which an amount attributable to the contribution is includible in the gross income of employees participating in the plan (Code Sec. 404(a)(5)), even if the employer is an accrual basis taxpayer. [29]

The amount actually distributed or made available to the employee or other distributee (beneficiary, etc.) is taxable in the year distributed or made available under the regular annuity rules (¶1350 *et seq.*), with a minor exception for distribution of trust income before the annuity is to begin. (Code Sec. 402(b)(2))[30]

Premiums paid by an employer for an annuity contract not purchased under a qualified annuity plan (¶4304), are included in the employee's gross income. Amounts actually paid

23. ¶H-8173; ¶4204.01
24. ¶H-8164; ¶4304.01
25. ¶H-8167; ¶4204
26. ¶H-11089; ¶4024.02

27. ¶H-11091
28. ¶H-3200 *et seq.*; ¶4024.01
29. ¶H-3677 *et seq.*; ¶4044.16
30. ¶H-3246; ¶4024.01

or made available to any employee-beneficiary under the nonqualified annuity contract are taxed under regular annuity rules. (Code Sec. 403(c))[31]

¶ 4340 Retirement Savings Plans for Individuals (IRAs). ▬▬▬▬

Employees and self-employed individuals who aren't active participants in an employer-maintained retirement plan can deduct up to $5,500 for 2018 ($6,000 for 2019), plus an additional catch-up contribution for those 50 and over, for contributions to an individual retirement account (IRA), or for the purchase of individual retirement annuities or endowment contracts. An individual who is an active participant in an employer plan (or whose spouse is) can't make deductible IRA contributions unless his adjusted gross income is below specified levels (¶4341).

An individual retirement account (IRA) is a trust (or custodial account) created or organized in the U.S. with a written governing instrument. [32] The assets of the account must be invested in a trusteed or custodial account with a bank, savings and loan association, credit union or other qualified person. (Code Sec. 408(a)(2))[33]

IRAs may be set up by employers for employees and by unions for members if these employer- and association-sponsored IRAs separately account for the interest of each participant (or his spouse). (Code Sec. 408(c); Reg § 1.408-2(c))[34] Qualified retirement plans, tax-sheltered annuities, and government retirement plans may allow employees to make voluntary contributions to separate IRA or Roth IRA accounts or annuities. (Code Sec. 408(q))[35]

Individuals who turn age 50 before the close of the tax year may increase the maximum permitted annual contribution by $1,000; a "catch-up" contribution. (Code Sec. 219(b)(5)(B))[36]

Except for rollover contributions (¶4348) the maximum amount that may be contributed to IRAs for any individual for 2018 is $6,500; $5,500 + $1,000 catch-up contribution ($7,000 for 2019: $6,000 + $1,000). (Code Sec. 408(a)(1), Code Sec. 408(b)(4), Code Sec. 219(b)(1)(A), Code Sec. 219(b)(5)(A), Code Sec. 219(b)(5)(C))[37]

IRA funds can't be used to buy life insurance. (Code Sec. 408(a)(3))[38] IRA contributions may not be invested in "collectibles" (except for certain coins and bullion), the acquisition of which is treated as an includible distribution (and possibly subject to early distribution penalties). (Code Sec. 408(m))[39]

Individual retirement annuities are nontransferable flexible premium annuity or endowment contracts issued by an insurance company. (Code Sec. 408(b))[40]

No tax is paid on income earned on contributions until the retirement savings are distributed or retirement bonds are cashed, at which time the distributions or retirement bond proceeds are taxable (Code Sec. 408(d)(1))[41] though the tax-free "rollover" provisions (¶4348) may apply. Rules penalize excess contributions, early (before age 59 1/2) distributions (¶4333), and certain distributions deferred beyond age 70 1/2 (¶4346).

For deductible contributions, see ¶4341; for nondeductible contributions to traditional IRAs, see ¶4343.

For Roth IRAs, see ¶4356 *et seq.* For the saver's credit for lower-income taxpayers' contributions to IRAs, see ¶2363.

---

31. ¶H-3249; ¶4034.05
32. ¶H-12201; ¶4084.02
33. ¶H-12202 *et seq.*; ¶4084.02
34. ¶s H-12212, H-12213; ¶4084.02
35. ¶H-12280; ¶4084.07
36. ¶H-12215; ¶2194.01

37. ¶H-12215; ¶2194.01
38. ¶H-12201; ¶4084.02
39. ¶H-12259; ¶4084.03
40. ¶H-12208 *et seq.*; ¶4084.02
41. ¶H-12253; ¶4084.03;

¶ 4341   Deduction for IRA.

An individual who isn't an active participant in certain employer-sponsored retirement plans, and whose spouse isn't an active participant, can deduct, for a tax year, cash contributions to an IRA for that year, up to the lesser of: (1) $5,500 for 2018 ($6,000 for 2019), plus a $1,000 catch-up contribution, if eligible, see ¶4340, or (2) 100% of the compensation that's includible in his gross income for that year. (Code Sec. 219(b)(1))[42] For spousal IRAs, see ¶4344.

If the individual (or his spouse) is an active plan participant (for any part of a plan year in his tax year), and has adjusted gross income (AGI) that exceeds an "applicable dollar limit," the IRA deduction limit is reduced (but not below zero) by an amount (rounded to the next lowest multiple of $10) that bears the same ratio to the dollar limit on the deduction that his (and his spouse's if a joint return is filed) AGI (determined without regard to the IRA deduction and with certain other modifications), minus the applicable dollar limit, bears to $10,000 ($20,000 for joint return filers, except for non-active plan participants whose spouses are active plan participants). (Code Sec. 219(g)(1), Code Sec. 219(g)(2), Code Sec. 219(g)(3)(A), Code Sec. 219(g)(7)(B)) But the maximum IRA deduction can't be reduced below $200 unless the applicable dollar limit is reduced to zero. (Code Sec. 219(g)(2)(B))[43] The applicable dollar limit is higher than the usual limit for an individual who is not an active participant in an employer plan during any part of the year, but whose spouse is an active plan participant. The higher limit does not apply to the active-participant spouse. (Code Sec. 219(g)(7))[44]

The deduction phaseouts are as follows. For joint filers, the deduction phaseout for 2018 begins at modified AGI of $101,000 and is fully phased-out at modified AGI of $121,000 (for 2019, the deduction phaseout begins at modified AGI of $103,000 and is fully phased-out at modified AGI of $123,000). For single filers, or heads of households, the deduction phaseout for 2018 begins at modified AGI of $63,000 and is fully phased-out at modified AGI of $73,000 (for 2019, the deduction phaseout begins at modified AGI of $64,000 and is fully phased-out at modified AGI of $74,000). For marrieds filing separately, the deduction phaseout begins at modified AGI of zero, and is fully phased-out at modified AGI of $10,000 for 2018 and 2019. Finally, for a non-active participant whose spouse is an active participant, the deduction phaseout for 2018 begins at modified AGI of $189,000 and is fully phased-out at modified AGI of $199,000 (for 2019, the deduction phaseout begins at modified AGI of $193,000 and is fully phased-out at modified AGI of $203,000).

Spouses who file separate returns and live apart at all times during the year aren't treated as married for purposes of the IRA deduction phase-out. (Code Sec. 219(g)(4))[45]

"Compensation" means wages, salaries, commissions, tips, bonuses, professional fees and other amounts received for personal services. It doesn't include earnings from property, such as interest, rents and dividends, or pension and annuity payments or other deferred compensation. Only compensation includible in gross income is used. (Code Sec. 219(f)(1))[46] Compensation includes taxable alimony paid under a decree of divorce or separate maintenance. Compensation also includes any differential wage payments (¶3005). (Code Sec. 219(f)(1))[47]

The amount shown on Form W-2 as "Wages, tips, other compensation," less any amount shown as distributions from nonqualified plans can be used as "safe harbor" compensation.[48]

---

42. ¶H-12215; ¶2194
43. ¶H-12217; ¶2194.02
44. ¶H-12217.2; ¶2194.02
45. ¶H-12217; ¶2194.02

46. ¶H-12226; ¶2194.01
47. ¶H-12232; ¶2194.01
48. ¶H-12226

The "compensation" of a self-employed individual includes net earnings from self-employment reduced by any allowable deduction for contributions on his behalf to a tax-qualified plan, e.g., a Keogh plan. (Code Sec. 219(f)(1))[49] A self-employed individual's net earnings from self-employment are also reduced by the deduction allowed for one-half of the self-employment tax (¶1747). (Code Sec. 219(f)(1), Code Sec. 401(c)(2)(A)(vi))[50]

Combat pay excluded under Code Sec. 112 (¶1222) is treated as if it were includible compensation for IRA purposes. (Code Sec. 219(f)(7))[1]

No deduction is allowed for contributions for the benefit of an individual for the tax year he attains age 70 1/2 or any later year. (Code Sec. 219(d)(1))[2]

The IRA must be established no later than the due date (*not* including extensions) of the taxpayer's income tax return for the year the deduction is claimed. To be deductible for the preceding tax year, the contribution also must be made by that date. (Code Sec. 219(f)(3))[3]

No part of a premium (under an IRA endowment policy) that's used to buy life insurance is deductible. (Code Sec. 219(d)(3))[4]

No deduction is permitted for a rollover contribution (¶4348) (Code Sec. 219(d)(2))[5] or for any contribution to an "inherited" IRA —one acquired by other than the surviving spouse as a result of the death of the employee-participant. (Code Sec. 219(d)(4))[6] Further, inherited IRAs are not exempt from a debtor's bankruptcy estate. [7]

¶ 4342 Active participant defined.

An individual who (or whose spouse) is an active participant in a qualified pension, profit-sharing, stock bonus or annuity plan, government plan, tax-sheltered annuity plan, SEP, SIMPLE retirement plan, or certain other trusts can't make deductible IRA contributions unless his adjusted gross income falls with the dollar limits at ¶4341. (Code Sec. 219(g))[8]

An individual is an active participant for any tax year in which he's eligible to participate in a defined benefit plan, or any year in which employer or employee contributions or forfeitures are added to his account in a defined contribution plan. [9]

¶ 4343 Nondeductible IRA contributions—Form 8606.

An active participant in a qualified plan who may not be eligible to make deductible contributions either in whole or in part to an IRA (see ¶4342), can make (use Form 8606) designated nondeductible contributions (DNCs) to an IRA for a tax year (Code Sec. 408(o)(2)(C)(i)) up to the due date (*without* extensions) for the taxpayer's income tax return for that year. (Code Sec. 408(o)(3))[10]

The amount of any DNCs made in any tax year on behalf of an individual is limited to the excess of: (1) for 2018, the lesser of $5,500 ($6,000 for 2019), plus an additional $1,000 for those 50 and over, see ¶4340, or 100% of compensation (including the higher-earning spouse's compensation (¶4344)), over (2) the amount allowable as a deduction for IRA contributions by active participants. (Code Sec. 408(o)(2)(B)(i))[11]

A taxpayer can elect to treat an otherwise deductible contribution as a DNC, thereby increasing, to that extent, his DNC limit for that year. (Code Sec. 408(o)(2)(B)(ii))[12]

49. ¶H-12226
50. ¶s H-9514, H-12228
1. ¶H-12215.1 *et seq.*
2. ¶H-12234; ¶2194.01
3. ¶H-12233; ¶2194.01
4. ¶H-12236; ¶2194.01
5. ¶H-12235

6. ¶H-12237; ¶2194.01
7. ¶H-12207.1
8. ¶H-12217 *et seq.*; ¶2194.02
9. ¶H-12220 *et seq.*; ¶2194.02
10. ¶s H-12238, H-12240; ¶4084.01
11. ¶H-12239; ¶4084.01
12. ¶H-12240; ¶4084.01

DNCs and deductible contributions may be made to the same IRA. [13]

¶ 4344   Special IRA deduction rules for married taxpayers.

Married taxpayers can each make deductible contributions to separate IRAs, subject to the deduction phase-out rules at ¶4341 that apply if either or both are active participants in an employer retirement plan for any part of the tax year. [14]

For 2018, an individual who files a joint return and has less taxable compensation than his spouse may contribute to a spousal IRA and deduct the lesser of (1) $5,500 ($6,000 for 2019), plus an additional $1,000 for those 50 and over, see ¶4340, or (2) the sum of (a) that individual's includible compensation for the tax year, plus (b) the includible compensation of the individual's spouse reduced by the sum of the spouse's allowable IRA deduction, designated nondeductible IRA contribution, and Roth IRA contribution for that tax year. (Code Sec. 219(c))[15]

¶ 4345   Penalties for excess contributions—Form 5329.

An individual who contributes more to an IRA than he is entitled to deduct must pay (use Form 5329) a 6% excise tax on the excess *every year*. The tax for any particular year, however, can't exceed 6% of the value of the IRA (as of the close of the tax year). (Code Sec. 4973(a))

An excess contribution to an IRA is the sum of: (1) the excess of the amount contributed for the tax year (*other than* a contribution to a Roth IRA or a rollover contribution), over the amount allowable as a deduction for the contribution, plus (2) any excess contribution for the preceding tax year, *reduced by* the sum of taxable distributions for the tax year, distributions for the tax year of excess contributions after the due date of the return, and the excess (if any) of the maximum amount allowable as a deduction for the tax year, over the amount contributed to the IRA for the tax year (without regard to any deduction for a preceding year's excess contribution), *including* the amount contributed to a Roth IRA. (Code Sec. 4973(b))[16]

There's no 6% penalty for the year of the contribution (or any other year) if the taxpayer is allowed no IRA deduction for the excess *and* withdraws the excess (together with any net income earned on it) by the due date for filing his income tax return for the year the excess contribution was made. (Code Sec. 4973(b))[17]

For tax on excess contributions to Roth IRAs, see ¶4357.

¶ 4346   Distributions from IRAs and individual retirement annuities.

Payouts from an IRA can be made without penalty once the participant attains age 59 $1/2$ (or earlier in the case of death, disability, annuitized payments, certain medical-related distributions, higher education expenses, certain first-time homebuyer expenses, and IRS levies, see ¶4333). These distributions can be made in a lump-sum or in installments and are taxable as ordinary income under the annuity rules (see ¶1350 *et seq.*), when received, except that distributions are tax-free if reinvested (i.e., "rolled over," see ¶4348 *et seq.*) within 60 days into that or another IRA. (Code Sec. 408(d)(3)(A))[18] (If not reinvested, the distribution is taxable in the year received, not the year in which the 60-day rollover period ends.)[19] A distribution from a SIMPLE retirement plan (¶4369) can't be rolled over

---

13. ¶H-12238; ¶4084.01
14. ¶H-12217; ¶2194.02
15. ¶s H-12230, H-12231; ¶2194.01
16. ¶H-12242 *et seq.*; ¶49,734

17. ¶H-12247 *et seq.*; ¶49,734
18. ¶H-12253; ¶4084.03
19. ¶s H-11460, H-12253; ¶4084.03

tax-free except to another SIMPLE plan during the employee's first two years of participation in the plan. (Code Sec. 408(d)(3)(G))

Amounts distributed from an IRA are included in gross income under the Code Sec. 72 annuity rules. (Code Sec. 408(d)(1)) In applying the annuity rules, all IRAs (other than Roth IRAs) are treated as one contract, all distributions made during any tax year are treated as one distribution, and the value of the contract, income on the contract, and investment in it are determined at the end of the calendar year in which the tax year begins. (Code Sec. 408(d)(2))[20] Part of an individual's withdrawal from an IRA is excludible if he previously made nondeductible IRA contributions. The excludible part is (the amount withdrawn × [aggregate nondeductible IRA contributions ÷ aggregate balance on the last day of the tax year of all IRAs of the individual]). For purposes of the calculation, IRAs include all of the taxpayer's traditional IRAs, SEPs and SIMPLE IRAs. [21]

Up to $100,000 of taxable distributions from a traditional IRA (or Roth IRA, see ¶4356) can be excluded from a taxpayer's income each year if the distribution is made: (1) directly by the IRA trustee to a Code Sec. 170(b)(1)(A) charity, other than a Code Sec. 509(a)(3) organization (see ¶4127) or a Code Sec. 4966(d)(2) donor advised fund (see ¶4131); and (2) on or after the date the IRA owner attains age 70 ½. (Code Sec. 408(d)(8)(F))

Losses in an IRA are currently nondeductible due to the suspension of miscellaneous itemized deductions (¶3109).[22]

Distributions from an IRA are reported on Form 1099-R. Distribution recipients who at any time made nondeductible contributions to a IRA (¶4343), must file Form 8606.

The transfer of an interest in an IRA (but not the distribution of funds from an IRA) to a spouse under a divorce or separation instrument isn't taxable (the transferred IRA is treated as the spouse's). (Code Sec. 408(d)(6))[23] Roth IRAs (¶4356 *et seq.*) are treated separately. (Code Sec. 408A(d)(4))

For the tax on early distributions from an IRA, see ¶4333.

Distribution of a participant's entire interest in his IRA (other than a Roth IRA, see ¶4361) must be made under rules similar to the Code Sec. 401(a)(9) required distribution rules for qualified plans (¶4334), (Code Sec. 408(a)(6), Code Sec. 408(b)(3)) except that required distributions from an IRA can't be deferred beyond age 70- ½ due to the account owner's not being retired (Code Sec. 401(a)(9)(C)(ii)(II), see ¶4308). While the required minimum distribution must be separately calculated for each IRA an individual has, the amounts may then be totalled, and the total distribution taken from any one or more of the individual's IRAs. Failure to make the required distributions results in a nondeductible excise tax payable (on Form 5329) by the recipient. The tax is 50% of the excess of the minimum amount that should have been distributed over the amount actually distributed. (Code Sec. 4974(a))[24] IRS can waive the 50% tax if the shortfall in the amount distributed is due to "reasonable error" and reasonable corrective steps are taken. (Code Sec. 4974(d))[25]

IRAs can make hardship distributions to victims of Hurricanes Harvey, Irma, and Maria, see ¶4333.

---

20. ¶H-12253; ¶4084.03
21. ¶H-12253; ¶4084.03
22. ¶H-12255

23. ¶H-12261; ¶4084.03
24. ¶H-8501; ¶49,744
25. ¶H-8508; ¶49,744

¶ 4347   Exemption of IRA from tax.

Income earned by an IRA is tax-exempt until distribution. This tax exemption doesn't apply to the unrelated business income tax, see ¶4123. Engaging in a prohibited transaction causes loss of the exemption. (Code Sec. 408(e))[26] Certain nominal gifts, free banking services, and free group term life insurance offered by banks for opening and contributing to an IRA are exempted from the prohibited transaction rules. [27]

If the owner of an individual retirement annuity borrows any money under, or by use of, the annuity contract, the contract stops being an individual retirement annuity as of the first day of the tax year, and the owner must include in income for that year an amount equal to the fair market value of the contract on the first day of the year. (Code Sec. 408(e)(3))[28] If the individual for whom an IRA is established uses the account or any portion of it as security for a loan, that portion is treated as distributed to that individual. (Code Sec. 408(e)(4))[29]

¶ 4348   Tax-free rollovers from qualified plans.

A tax-free rollover from a qualified plan is any portion of the balance of an employee's credit in a qualified trust paid to the employee in an "eligible rollover distribution," any portion of which the employee then transfers to an "eligible retirement plan." (Code Sec. 402(c)(1))[30] A distribution must be rolled over within 60 days after receipt to be tax-free, but IRS may waive the 60-day rollover period for equitable reasons (Code Sec. 402(c)(3), Code Sec. 408(d)(3); Reg § 301.7508A-1(c)(1)), if certain conditions are met. [31]

IRS has established a program allowing taxpayers to self-certify that there was reasonable cause for their missing the 60-day IRA rollover window. A taxpayer typically will qualify for a waiver if one or more of 11 circumstances applies to him or her. (Rev Proc 2016-47, 2016-37 IRB)

An "eligible rollover distribution" is any distribution to an employee of all or any portion of the balance to the credit of the employee in a qualified trust. (Code Sec. 402(c)(4)) An "eligible rollover distribution" does *not* include:

(1) any distribution that's one of a series of substantially equal periodic payments made (at least annually) for (a) the life (or life expectancy) of the employee, or the joint lives (or joint life expectancies) of the employee and the employee's designated beneficiary, or (b) a specified period of ten years or more (Code Sec. 402(c)(4)(A));

(2) any distribution to the extent it is a required distribution under Code Sec. 401(a)(9); (Code Sec. 402(c)(4)(B); Reg § 1.402(c)-2) and

(3) any hardship distribution. (Code Sec. 402(c)(4)(C), Code Sec. 403(b)(8)(B))[32]

caution: An eligible rollover distribution from a qualified plan is subject to 20% withholding, unless there is a direct trustee-to-trustee transfer, see ¶3036.

Amounts transferred in a direct trustee-to-trustee transfer (¶4308) are excludable from income for the tax year of the transfer. (Code Sec. 402(e)(6))[33]

Certain payments can't be rolled over, e.g., corrective distributions of excess 401(k) contributions, loans treated as deemed distributions, and dividends paid on employer securities. (Reg § 1.402(c)-2, Q&A 4) However, where a plan loan offset amount is treated as a default, it is an eligible rollover distribution that may be rolled over tax −free to an IRA.

---

26. ¶H-12214; ¶4084.03
27. ¶H-12530
28. ¶H-12251; ¶4084.03
29. ¶H-12252; ¶4084.03

30. ¶H-11402; ¶4024.04
31. ¶H-11452; ¶H-11452.2; ¶4024.04
32. ¶H-11406; ¶4024.04
33. ¶H-11403; ¶4024.04

(Reg § 1.402(c)-2, Q&A 9)[34] For tax years beginning after 2017, the rollover period for certain "qualified plan loan offsets" is extended from 60 days to the tax return due date (including extensions). (Code Sec. 402(c)(3)(A))[35]

An "eligible retirement plan" is: (1) an individual retirement account (not a Roth IRA), (2) an individual retirement annuity (other than an endowment contract), (3) a qualified trust, (4) an annuity plan, (5) a Code Sec. 403(b) annuity, and (6) a governmental section 457 plan. If any portion of an eligible rollover distribution is attributable to payments or distributions from a designated Roth account (see ¶4363), then an eligible retirement plan with respect to that portion includes only (a) another designated Roth account, and (b) a Roth IRA. (Code Sec. 402(c)(8)(B))[36]

If noncash property (e.g., securities) is distributed, the employee can sell the property and roll over the proceeds. There's no gain or loss recognized on the sale if the full proceeds are rolled over. (Code Sec. 402(c)(6)(A))[37] If cash is distributed, it must be recontributed as cash.[38]

Plan administrators must inform recipients of potential rollovers in writing of the applicable rollover rules, no less than 30 days, and no more than 90 days before making an eligible rollover distribution (but the 30-day time period may be waived by a participant in certain cases, and a summary notice procedure also is available). (Code Sec. 402(f); Reg § 1.402(c)-2, Q&A 2, Reg § 1.402(f)-1, Q&A 2(b))[39]

Where a participant with a small accrued benefit (a nonforfeitable accrued benefit whose present value is $5,000 or less) is terminating his employment with the company sponsoring the plan, the plan may provide for the distribution of the employee's benefit without his consent, or the consent of his spouse (a "mandatory distribution" or an "involuntary cash-out distribution"). Such mandatory distributions must follow the automatic rollover rules. Under these rules, plans with mandatory distribution provisions must transfer the amount of the distribution to an IRA of a designated trustee or issuer where (i) the distribution of a nonforfeitable accrued benefit is more than $1,000, but no more than $5,000; and (ii) the plan participant (or beneficiary) receiving the distribution does not elect to have the distribution paid directly to another qualified plan or IRA (a direct rollover), and does not elect to receive the distribution himself. (Code Sec. 401(a)(31)(B))[40]

The plan administrator must also notify the distributee in writing that the distribution may be transferred without cost or penalty to another IRA.[41]

For the special recontribution rules that apply to "qualified hurricane distributions," and to withdrawals for home purchases or construction that were not used due to the hurricanes, see ¶4333.

For rollovers of after-tax contributions, see ¶4351.

¶ 4349   Other types of rollovers.

Permissible types of tax-free 60-day rollovers, besides those covered at ¶4348, include:

. . . Rollovers from one type of IRA (individual retirement account or individual retirement annuity) to the same or another type. But these rollovers may be made no more than once in a one-year period. (Code Sec. 408(d)(3))[42] Further, the one IRA rollover per year limit applies on an aggregate basis, not on an IRA-by-IRA basis; thus, taxpayers with multiple IRAs can make just one rollover per year for all their IRAs.[43] Qualified rollovers from an IRA to a Roth IRA are disregarded for purposes of the one-year rule.

34. ¶H-11415; ¶4014.27
35. ¶H-11452
36. ¶H-11440; ¶4024.04
37. ¶H-11448; ¶4024.04
38. ¶H-11402

39. ¶H-11458; ¶4024.04
40. ¶H-8251.3; ¶4014.27
41. ¶H-8251.6
42. ¶H-11460 *et seq.*; ¶4084.03
43. ¶H-11463.0; ¶4084.03

(Code Sec. 408A(e)) However, a distribution from a SIMPLE retirement plan (¶4369) can't be rolled over tax-free except to another SIMPLE plan during the employee's first two years of participation in the plan. (Code Sec. 408(d)(3)(G))

... From one type of IRA (individual retirement account or individual retirement annuity) to an eligible retirement plan (¶4348) (limited to amount which would otherwise be included in gross income). (Code Sec. 408(d)(3)(A)(ii))

... Eligible rollover distributions from a Code Sec. 403(b) plan to an eligible retirement plan (¶4348) and from an eligible retirement plan to a Code Sec. 403(b) plan. (Code Sec. 402(c)(8)(B), Code Sec. 403(b)(8)(A)(ii))

... Eligible rollover distributions from a Code Sec. 457 plan to an eligible retirement plan (¶4348) and from an eligible retirement plan to a Code Sec. 457 plan. (Code Sec. 402(c)(8)(B), Code Sec. 457(e)(16))

... Wrongfully levied retirement plan account or benefit returned after Dec. 31, 2017, and any interest on it, if the plan permits, or to an individual retirement plan eligible to receive a rollover distribution from the plan. The rollover must be made by the unextended return due date for the tax year in which the funds were returned, and the contribution is treated as made for that tax year. Any amount includible in income resulting from the distribution caused by the levy is to be refunded or credited. (Code Sec. 6343(f))[44]

For taxable rollovers to Roth IRAs, see ¶4352.

¶ 4350   Partial rollovers.

When an employee elects to roll over less than his entire distribution:

(1) the portion not rolled over is taxed under the regular rules for taxing ordinary income. Ten-year forward averaging and/or capital gains treatment, where applicable, for lump-sum distributions (¶4328) don't apply if any part of the lump-sum distribution is rolled over; (Code Sec. 402(c)(1), Code Sec. 402(d)(4)(K) before amend by Sec. 1401(a), PL 104-188, 8/20/96)

(2) the basis recovery rules of Code Sec. 72(e) apply to a distribution that's rolled over under Code Sec. 402(c); and

(3) any net unrealized appreciation in employer securities attributable to nondeductible employee contributions is subject to tax immediately. [45]

¶ 4351   Rollovers of after-tax contributions.

Generally, only otherwise taxable amounts of an eligible rollover distribution may be rolled over. However, the "nontaxable" portion of a eligible rollover distribution (attributable to after-tax employee contributions) may be rolled over to the extent that the "taxable" portion is rolled over to (1) an IRA, or (2) to a defined contribution plan or tax-sheltered Code Sec. 403(b) annuity that will account separately for the taxable and nontaxable portions. In such a case, the amount transferred is treated as consisting first of the portion of the distribution that would be includible in income were it not for the rollover. (Code Sec. 402(c)(2))[46]

---

44. ¶V-5141
45. ¶H-11405 *et seq.*; ¶4024.04

46. ¶H-11406.1; ¶4024.04

¶ 4352   Qualified plan to Roth IRA rollovers.

Distributions from qualified retirement plans, tax-sheltered Code Sec. 403(b) annuities, and governmental Code Sec. 457 plans may be rolled over directly into a Roth IRA, generally subject to the usual rules that apply to rollovers from a traditional IRA into a Roth IRA (see ¶4359). For example, a rollover from a qualified retirement plan into a Roth IRA is includible in gross income (except to the extent it represents a return of after-tax contributions), and the 10% early distribution tax does not apply. (Code Sec. 408A(e)) A rollover from a qualified plan, etc., to a Roth IRA doesn't count for purposes of the one-rollover-per-year rule. [47] The rollover also can be made through a distribution from the plan that's then contributed (rolled over) to the Roth IRA within 60 days. In either case, the amount rolled over must be an eligible rollover distribution.

For the tax treatment of amounts rolled into a Roth IRA from an eligible retirement plan that are later distributed within 5 years, see ¶4362.

¶ 4353   One-time IRA to HSA rollovers.

Taxpayers may make a one-time-only tax-free rollover, via direct trustee-to-trustee-transfer, from an IRA to a Health Savings Account (HSA) (¶1528). (Code Sec. 408(d)(9)) The rollover amount is nondeductible and is limited to the otherwise maximum deductible HSA contribution amount, computed on the basis of the type of coverage under the taxpayer's high deductible health plan (HDHP) at the time of the contribution. The rollover reduces the otherwise allowable HSA contribution amount.

Generally, only one rollover may be made during a taxpayer's lifetime, but if one is made during a month in which he has self only coverage as of the first day of the month, an additional rollover may be made during a subsequent month within the tax year in which he has family coverage. (Code Sec. 408(d)(9)(C)(ii))

If a taxpayer does not remain an eligible individual (except because of death or disability) during the testing period (begins with the month of the contribution and ends on the last day of the 12th month following that month), the amount of the IRA distribution that would otherwise have been includible is taxed to him and is subject to a 10% penalty tax. The amount is includible in income for the tax year of the first day during the testing period that the taxpayer is not an eligible individual. (Code Sec. 408(d)(9)(D))[48]

A qualified HSA funding distribution may be made from a traditional IRA or a Roth IRA, but not from an ongoing SIMPLE IRA or SEP IRA. Further, a qualified HSA funding distribution must not exceed the IRA or Roth IRA account owner's maximum annual HSA contribution.[49]

¶ 4354   Surviving spouse's rollover of distribution from decedent.

A surviving-spouse beneficiary may elect to treat the entire beneficiary interest in the decedent's IRA as the spouse-beneficiary's own IRA if he or she is the sole beneficiary of the IRA and has an unlimited right to withdraw amounts from it. However, this requirement is not satisfied if a trust is named beneficiary of the IRA even if the spouse is sole beneficiary of the trust. (Reg § 1.408-8, Q&A 5(a)) The election is made by the surviving spouse redesignating the account as an account in her name as IRA owner rather than as beneficiary. Alternatively, a surviving spouse is deemed to have made the election if, at any time, either of the following occurs: (1) any amount required to be distributed to the surviving spouse as beneficiary is not timely distributed, or (2) any additional amount is

47. ¶H-11463; ¶408A4
48. ¶H-12253.1A; ¶4084.03
49. ¶H-12253.1B; ¶4084.03

contributed to the IRA. (Reg § 1.408-8, Q&A 5(b)) If the election is made, the surviving spouse is considered the IRA owner for all purposes under the Code. (Reg § 1.408-8, Q&A 5(c))[50]

A surviving spouse may also roll a distribution from a qualified plan, annuity, or IRA over to any other qualified plan, annuity, or IRA in which the surviving spouse participates that accepts rollover contributions. (Code Sec. 402(c)(9), Code Sec. 408(d)(3)(C))[1]

¶ 4355   Rollover by beneficiary other than surviving spouse.

Distributions from qualified plans, tax-sheltered annuities (¶4375 *et seq.*), and Code Sec. 457 government plans may be rolled over (in a direct trustee –to–trustee transfer, see ¶4308) to a non-spouse beneficiary's IRA that's established for the purpose of receiving the distribution. This "recipient IRA" is treated as an inherited IRA, and so is subject to the required minimum distribution (RMD) rules that apply to inherited IRAs of nonspouse beneficiaries (¶4334). To the extent provided by IRS, the change applies to benefits payable to a trust maintained for a designated beneficiary to the same extent it applies to the beneficiary. (Code Sec. 402(c)(11), Code Sec. 403(a)(4)(B), Code Sec. 457(e)(16)(B))[2]

¶ 4356   Overview—Roth IRAs.

Taxpayers can make nondeductible contributions to Roth IRAs. A Roth IRA is an IRA that is designated as a Roth IRA when it's established (Code Sec. 408A(b)); it's treated as a traditional IRA (¶4340 *et seq.*) except to the extent that special rules apply to it. (Code Sec. 408A(a))

Contributions to a Roth IRA aren't deductible (Code Sec. 408A(c)(1)), and are limited based on modified adjusted gross income (¶4357). Qualified distributions from a Roth IRA aren't included in income (Code Sec. 408A(d)(1)) and other distributions are treated as a return of investment to the extent of contributions to Roth IRAs (¶4361). (Code Sec. 408A(d)(4)) Rollovers from traditional IRAs to Roth IRAs are taxable, but not subject to the 10% early distribution penalty tax. (Code Sec. 408A(d)(3))[3] (Reg § 1.408A-3, Reg § 1.408A-4, Reg § 1.408A-5)

Use Form 5305-R, Form 5305-RA, and Form 5305-RB to set up Roth trust, custodial, and annuity accounts, respectively, with financial institutions.

¶ 4357   Contributions to Roth IRAs.

For 2018, an individual can make annual nondeductible contributions to a Roth IRA in amounts up to $5,500 ($6,000 for 2019), plus an additional $1,000 for those 50 and older, or 100% of compensation, if less, reduced by the amount of contributions for the tax year made to all other IRAs (Code Sec. 408A(c)(1), Code Sec. 408A(c)(2) but not reduced by contributions to a SEP (¶4365) or SIMPLE plan (¶4369) (Code Sec. 408A(f)(2); Reg § 1.408A-3, Q&A 3(c))[4] The allowable contribution phases out ratably (in $10 increments) over the following levels of modified adjusted gross income (AGI):

- For joint filers, $189,000 to $199,000 for 2018 ($193,000 to $203,000 for 2019);
- For married persons filing separately, $0 to $10,000 for 2018 and 2019; and
- For single taxpayers and heads of household, $120,000 to $135,000 for 2018 ($122,000 to $137,000 for 2019).

However, a $200 contribution may be made if the phase-out lowers the contribution limit to under $200 but more than $0. (Code Sec. 408A(c)(3)(A), Code Sec. 408A(c)(3)(B);

---

50. ¶H-12264.7
1. ¶H-11467 *et seq.*; ¶4084.03
2. ¶H-11437; ¶H-11438

3. ¶H-12290 *et seq.*; ¶408A4
4. ¶H-12290.7; ¶408A4

Reg § 1.408A-3, Q&A 3(b))

AGI for purposes of the Roth IRA contribution phaseout is defined as it is for traditional IRA purposes (¶4341), except that it does not include income resulting from the conversion from a traditional IRA to a Roth IRA (¶4359). (Code Sec. 408A(c)(3)(B)(i); Reg § 1.408A-3, Q&A 5)[5]

observation: The modified AGI-based contribution limits for Roth IRAs apply whether or not the taxpayer is a participant in a qualified retirement plan.

Roth IRA contributions for a year must be made by the unextended tax return due date for the contribution year. (Code Sec. 408A(c)(7); Reg § 1.408A-3, Q&A 2(b))[6] Unlike traditional IRAs, contributions are permitted after age 70 1/2. (Code Sec. 408A(c)(4))[7] For rollover contributions, see ¶4359.

A 6% excise tax is imposed each year on excess contributions to an IRA (¶4345). Similar rules apply to a Roth IRA. (Code Sec. 4973(f))[8]

Any contribution distributed from a Roth IRA before the due date of the individual's tax return is treated as an amount not contributed. (Code Sec. 4973(f))[9]

For the saver's credit for lower-income taxpayers' contributions to Roth IRAs, see ¶2358.

A recipient of a military death gratuity or Servicemembers' Group Life Insurance (SGLI) proceeds can contribute the amounts received (reduced by any amounts contributed to a Coverdell education savings account, ¶2207) to a Roth IRA as qualified rollover contributions. The requirement that only one tax-free rollover contribution can be made to a Roth IRA during any one-year period (¶4349) doesn't apply. The rollover has to be made within one year of receipt of a payment. (Code Sec. 408A(e)(2))[10]

¶ 4358 Recharacterizing (changing the nature of) IRA contributions.

A taxpayer may elect to recharacterize an IRA *contribution,* that is, treat a contribution to one type of IRA (Roth IRA or traditional IRA) as made to a different type of IRA. (Code Sec. 408A(d)(6); Reg § 1.408A-5)

observation: The recharacterization election allows a contribution to a traditional IRA to be treated as made to a Roth IRA, or a contribution to a Roth IRA to be treated as made to a traditional IRA.

Before 2018, a taxpayer also could recharacterize a traditional-IRA-to-Roth-IRA conversion (i.e., treat the conversion as never having been made). Effective Jan. 1, 2018, under Code Sec. 408A(d)(6)(B), a traditional-IRA-to-Roth-IRA conversion cannot be recharacterized (i.e., converted back to a regular IRA). However, a regular-IRA-to-Roth-IRA conversion made in 2017 may be recharacterized as a contribution to a traditional IRA if the characterization is made by Oct. 15, 2018. [11]

To make the recharacterization election:

... The taxpayer must notify the trustees of the first (distributing) and second (receiving) IRAs of his election to recharacterize a contribution (regular or conversion), i.e., that he is electing for tax purposes to treat the contribution as having been made to the second IRA, instead of the first IRA. The taxpayer must provide the trustees with specified information (including the type and amount of the contribution being recharacterized) sufficient to effect the recharacterization transfer.

5. ¶H-12290.9; ¶408A4
6. ¶H-12290.14; ¶408A4
7. ¶H-12290.13; ¶408A4
8. ¶H-12242.1; ¶49,734

9. ¶H-12242.1; ¶49,734
10. ¶H-12290.19A
11. ¶H-12290.23

. . . The contribution (regular or conversion) originally made to first IRA, plus net income (if any) allocable to the contribution (Reg § 1.408A-10, Reg § 1.408A-5, Q&A 2(c)), must be transferred from the first IRA to the second IRA via a trustee-to-trustee transfer.

. . . The trustee-to-trustee transfer must be made on a timely basis. (Reg § 1.408A-5, Q&A-6)[12]

An IRA contribution for a tax year may be recharacterized as late as six months after the unextended due date for filing the return for that year. (Reg § 301.9100-2(b))[13]

A recharacterization election cannot be revoked after the transfer. (Reg § 1.408A-5, Q&A 6(b))

The contribution that is being recharacterized is treated as having been originally contributed to the second IRA on the same date and (in the case of a regular contribution) for the same tax year that the contribution was made to the first IRA. (Reg § 1.408A-5, Q&A 3)

caution: For the limit on *reconversion* to a Roth IRA following a recharacterization from a Roth IRA to a traditional IRA, see ¶4360.

¶ 4359   Conversions of traditional IRAs to Roth IRAs—Form 8606.

Taxpayers, including marrieds filing separately, may convert amounts in a traditional IRA to amounts in a Roth IRA without regard to their modified adjusted gross income (AGI) or filing status.[14] The conversion may be done in one of three ways:

(1) Rollover to a Roth IRA of a distribution from a traditional IRA within 60 days of the distribution.

(2) Trustee-to-trustee transfer from the trustee of the traditional IRA to the trustee of the Roth IRA.

(3) Transfer of an amount in a traditional IRA to a Roth IRA maintained by the same trustee. (Code Sec. 408A(d)(3)(C); Reg § 1.408A-4, Q&A 1(b))

Amounts from a SEP-IRA (¶4366) or a SIMPLE IRA (¶4346) also may be converted to a Roth IRA, but a conversion from a SIMPLE IRA may be made only after the 2-year period beginning on the date on which the taxpayer first participated in any SIMPLE IRA maintained by the taxpayer's employer. (Reg § 1.408A-4, Q&A 4)

The conversion is subject to tax (report on Form 8606) as if it were distributed from the traditional IRA and not recontributed to another IRA (¶4346) (Code Sec. 408A(d)(3)(A)(i)), but isn't subject to the 10% early distribution tax. (Code Sec. 408A(d)(3)(A)(ii); Reg § 1.408A-4, Q&A 7)[15]

When a traditional individual retirement annuity is converted to a Roth IRA, the amount treated as distributed is the FMV of the annuity contract on the date it is converted. Similarly, when a traditional IRA holding an annuity contract as an account asset is converted to a Roth IRA, the amount that is treated as distributed with respect to the annuity contract is the FMV of the annuity contract on the date the annuity contract is converted (i.e., distributed or treated as distributed from the traditional IRA). (Reg § 1.408A-4, Q&A 14(a))[16]

---

12. ¶H-12290.22; ¶408A4
13. ¶H-12290.23A
14. ¶H-12290.16A; ¶408A4

15. ¶H-12290.20; ¶408A4
16. ¶H-12290.20A; ¶408A4

¶ 4360   Reconversion to Roth IRA—before 2018.

Before 2018, a person who converted an amount from a traditional IRA to a Roth IRA (¶4359) could not only transfer the amount back to a traditional IRA (i.e., recharacterize it, see ¶4358) but later could reconvert that amount from a traditional IRA to a Roth IRA.

Before 2018, a reconversion made before the later of the beginning of the next tax year or the end of the 30-day period that began on the day of the recharacterization was treated as a failed conversion, subject to correction through a recharacterization back to a traditional IRA. A failed conversion results in a distribution from the traditional IRA that's subject to tax (and possibly penalty tax) followed by a regular contribution to the Roth IRA. To the extent it exceeded the annual contribution limit, the amount treated as a regular contribution to the Roth IRA was treated as an excess contribution subject to the excise tax under Code Sec. 4973. (Reg § 1.408A-4, Q&A 3(b), Reg § 1.408A-4, Q&A 1(d), Reg § 1.408A-5, Q&A 9(a)(1)) For purposes of the reconversion timing rules, above, a failed conversion resulting from not having satisfied the statutory requirements is treated as a conversion in determining when an IRA owner may make a reconversion. (Reg § 1.408A-5, Q&A 9(a)(2))[17]

Effective Jan. 1, 2018, under Code Sec. 408A(d)(6)(B), an IRA-to-Roth-IRA conversion cannot be recharacterized (i.e., converted back to a regular IRA), and therefore cannot be reconverted. However, a regular-IRA-to-Roth-IRA conversion made in 2017 may be recharacterized as a contribution to a traditional IRA if the characterization is made by Oct. 15, 2018.[18]

¶ 4361   Distributions from Roth IRAs—Form 8606.

Qualified distributions. Qualified distributions from Roth IRAs aren't included in income. (Code Sec. 408A(d)(1)) These are distributions made after the 5-tax-year period beginning with the first tax year for which the taxpayer or the taxpayer's spouse made a contribution to a Roth IRA established for the taxpayer, including a qualified rollover contribution from an IRA other than a Roth IRA (Code Sec. 408A(d)(2)(B)), and that are made:

(1) on or after attaining age 59 1/2,

(2) at or after death (to a beneficiary or estate),

(3) on account of disability, or

(4) for a first-time home purchase expense under Code Sec. 72(t)(2)(F). (Code Sec. 408A(d)(2)(A), Code Sec. 408A(d)(5); Reg § 1.408A-6, Q&A 1)[19]

The 5-year period for qualified distributions isn't recalculated when a Roth IRA owner dies. The 5-year period for a beneficiary's inherited Roth IRA is determined independently of the period for any other Roth IRA that the beneficiary may have, except that the 5-year period for a spousal beneficiary with both an inherited Roth IRA and his own Roth IRA ends with the earlier of the five-year periods. (Reg § 1.408A-5, Q&A 7)

Corrective distributions made by the return due date, plus extensions, for the tax year of the contribution aren't qualified distributions. (Code Sec. 408A(d)(2)(C); Reg § 1.408A-6, Q&A 2)[20]

Nonqualified distributions. Distributions that aren't qualified distributions are treated as made first from contributions to all of an individual's Roth IRAs and are nontaxable to

17. ¶H-12290.15 *et seq.*; ¶408A4
18. ¶H-12290.23

19. ¶H-12290.28; ¶408A4
20. ¶H-12290.30; ¶408A4

that extent; distributions in excess of contributions are taxable. (Code Sec. 408A(d)(4))[21]

Order of distributions. Distributions are treated as made from contributions to the Roth IRA to the extent that the distribution, when added to all previous distributions from the Roth IRA, doesn't exceed the total amount of all contributions. (Code Sec. 408A(d)(4)(B)(i)) Contributions are treated as withdrawn in the following order: first, contributions other than qualified rollover contributions (i.e., qualified conversions, see ¶4359); second, qualified rollover contributions (on a FIFO basis); third, a distribution allocable to a qualified rollover contribution is allocated first to the part of the contribution required to be included in gross income. (Code Sec. 408A(d)(4)(B)(ii); Reg § 1.408A-6, Q&A 8)[22] All of a taxpayer's Roth IRAs are treated as a single Roth IRA. (Code Sec. 408A(d)(4)(A), Code Sec. 408(d)(2))

Losses in a Roth IRA are currently nondeductible due to the suspension of miscellaneous itemized deductions (¶3109).[23]

Report Roth IRA distributions on Form 8606, Part III.

Roth IRAs aren't subject to the required minimum distribution rules of Code Sec. 401(a)(9)(A) or the incidental benefit requirements of Code Sec. 401(a) (¶4334). Instead, after the Roth IRA owner's death, the distribution rules in Reg § 1.408-8 apply as though the Roth IRA owner died before his required beginning date. Thus, the entire Roth IRA must generally be distributed within five years of the owner's death unless it is distributed over the life expectancy of a designated beneficiary, and distributions commence prior to the end of the calendar year following the year of the owner's death. Where the sole beneficiary of a Roth IRA is the Roth IRA owner's surviving spouse, the spouse may delay distributions until the Roth IRA owner would have reached age 70 $1/2$, or may treat the Roth IRA as his or her own. (Reg § 1.408A-6, Q&A 14(b)) (Code Sec. 408A(c)(5))[24]

For the 10% early distribution penalty tax, see ¶4362. For distributions from designated Roth accounts, see ¶4363.

¶ 4362   10% early distribution tax on Roth IRA distributions.

As with other IRAs (¶4333) the Code Sec. 72(t) 10% early withdrawal tax applies to the portion of an early withdrawal that is includible in income. In addition, however, a distribution from a Roth IRA is subject to the early withdrawal tax as if it *were* includible in income, if that distribution (or any portion of it): (1) is allocable (under rules at ¶4361) to a "qualified rollover contribution;" and (2) is made within the five-tax year period beginning with the tax year for which the contribution was made. However, the 10% tax applies only to the extent that the amount of the qualified rollover contribution was includible in income. (Code Sec. 408A(d)(3)(F))[25]

¶ 4363   Designated Roth (Roth 401(k)) Accounts. ▰

An employer's Code Sec. 401(k) plan, or Code Sec. 403(b) annuity (¶4375) may include a qualified Roth contribution program (i.e., a "Roth 401(k)") that allows participants to elect to have all or part of their elective deferrals treated as Roth contributions—that is to make "designated Roth contributions." (Code Sec. 402A) Designated Roth contributions, which are currently includible in income, aren't subject to the AGI-based phaseouts for regular Roth IRA contributions (¶4357). Qualified distributions are excludable from income. (Code Sec. 402A(d))[26]

Designated Roth contributions. These are elective contributions under a 401(k) plan that

---

21. ¶H-12290.34; ¶408A4
22. ¶H-12290.35; ¶408A4
23. ¶H-12255

24. ¶H-12290.42; ¶408A4
25. ¶H-12290.38; ¶408A4
26. ¶H-12295.1 *et seq.*; ¶402A4

are:

(1) designated irrevocably by the employee when he makes the cash or deferred arrangement (CODA) election as designated Roth contributions;

(2) treated by the employer as includible in the employee's income when he would have received the contribution in cash had he not made the CODA election (e.g., by treating the contributions as wages subject to applicable withholding requirements); and

(3) maintained by the plan in a separate account. (Code Sec. 402A(b)(2); Reg § 1.401(k)-1(f)(1), Reg § 1.401(k)-1(f)(2))[27]

A 401(k) plan can't provide for designated Roth contributions unless it also offers pre-tax elective contributions. (Reg § 1.401(k)-1(f)(1)(i))[28]

A designated Roth contribution must satisfy the requirements that apply to elective contributions made under a qualified CODA (i.e., a 401(k) plan), such as the nonforfeitability and distribution restrictions for elective contributions, and the Code Sec. 401(k) ADP (actual deferral percentage) test; see ¶4306. (Reg § 1.401(k)-1(f)(3))[29]

Governmental section 457 plans may also provide designated Roth accounts. (Code Sec. 402A(e)(1)(C))[30]

In-plan Roth rollovers. Employers may amend their Roth 401(k), 403(b), or 457 plans to allow participants to transfer an eligible rollover distribution (ERD) to their designated Roth account in the plan. (Code Sec. 402A(c)(4)) An ERD is a distribution (1) from a non-designated Roth account in the same plan, (2) because of an event that triggers an ERD from the plan; and (3) otherwise meets the rollover requirements. For transfers of amounts not otherwise distributable, a plan will not be treated as violating the distribution restrictions of (i) Code Sec. 401(k)(2)(B)(i), (ii) Code Sec. 403(b)(7)(A)(i), (iii) Code Sec. 403(b)(11), (iv) Code Sec. 457(d)(1)(A), or (v) 5 USC §8433, solely because of the transfer. (Code Sec. 402A(c)(4)(E))

Thus, for transfers to designated Roth accounts, IRS timing restrictions on distributions—such as age or severance from employment—need not be met.[31] However, once the ERD has been transferred in an in-plan Roth rollover, the ERD—plus any applicable earnings—is again subject to the distribution restrictions that applied before the transfer. (Notice 2013-74, 2013-52 IRB 819)[32]

The participant must include in gross income the amount that would be includible in gross income if it were not part of a qualified rollover distribution. (Code Sec. 402A(c)(4)(A)(i))[33]

Any distribution from an applicable retirement plan (other than from a designated Roth account) that is contributed in a qualified rollover contribution to the designated Roth account, is not taken into account as a designated Roth contribution. (Code Sec. 402A(c)(4)(C))[34]

Distributions from designated Roths. A qualified distribution from a designated Roth is excluded from income if it meets the requirements for qualified distributions from Roth IRAs (¶4361), with the following differences:

... A distribution for a first-time home purchase isn't excluded. (Code Sec. 402A(d)(2)(A))[35]

... The five-year period necessary for a distribution to be excluded begins on the first day of the employee's tax year for which he first had designated Roth contributions

27. ¶H-12295.5
28. ¶H-12295.5
29. ¶H-12295.3
30. ¶H-12295.2
31. ¶H-12295.5E

32. ¶H-12295.5E
33. ¶H-12295.5K
34. ¶H-12295.5A
35. ¶H-12295.6A

made to the plan. If a direct rollover is made from a designated Roth account under another plan, the five-year period begins on the first day for which the employee first had designated Roth contributions made to the other plan, if earlier. (Reg § 1.402A-1, Q&A 4)[36]

. . . Designated Roth accounts are subject to the lifetime required minimum distribution (RMD) rules of Code Sec. 401(a)(9)(A) and Code Sec. 401(a)(9)(B) (¶4334). (Reg § 1.401(k)-1(f)(4)(i)) By contrast, a regular Roth IRA is not subject to the Code Sec. 401(a)(9)(A) lifetime RMD rules (¶4361).

Where disbursements are made from a taxpayer's designated Roth account to the taxpayer and also to the taxpayer's Roth IRA or designated Roth account in a direct rollover, then pretax amounts will be allocated first to the direct rollover, rather than being allocated pro rata to each destination. Also, a taxpayer may direct the allocation of pretax and after-tax amounts that are included in disbursements from a designated Roth account that are directly rolled over to multiple destinations, applying the same allocation rules to distributions from designated Roth accounts that apply to distributions from other types of accounts. (Reg § 1.402A-1, Q&A-5)[37]

A distribution from a designated Roth account that is not a qualified distribution is taxable to the distributee under the Code Sec. 72 rules, *not* under the regular Roth IRA ordering rules (¶4361). (Reg § 1.402A-1, Q&A 3)

¶ 4364   Deemed IRAs. ▬▬▬▬▬▬▬▬▬▬▬▬▬▬

Qualified plans, Code Sec. 403(b) annuities (¶4375), and governmental Code Sec. 457 plans may include a deemed IRA, which is a separate account or annuity in a qualified employer plan to which plan participants may make voluntary IRA or Roth IRA contributions.

The qualified plan must elect to allow employees to make voluntary employee contributions (designated as such by the employees) to a separate account or annuity (meeting the requirements for a traditional IRA or Roth IRA) established under the plan. However, the general requirement that IRA assets not be commingled does not apply to deemed IRAs. (Code Sec. 408(q))[38]

SEPs (see ¶4365) and SIMPLE IRAs (¶4369) cannot be used as deemed IRAs. (Reg § 1.408(q)-1(b))[39]

Contributions to a deemed IRA are treated as contributions to an IRA, and not as contributions to the qualified employer plan. Thus, a deemed IRA contribution is in addition to the $18,500 maximum amount for 2018 ($19,000 for 2019) that can be contributed to a 401(k) plan (excluding catch-up contributions). (Code Sec. 408(q)(1))

The ceilings on modified adjusted gross income that limit a taxpayer's ability to make Roth IRA contributions (¶4357) or deductible contributions to a regular IRA (¶4341) also apply to voluntary contributions to a deemed IRA. (Code Sec. 408(q)(1)(B); Reg § 1.408(q)-1(f)(4))[40]

A deemed IRA isn't subject to the rules that apply to the qualified employer plan, so contributions to a deemed IRA are not taken into account in applying those rules to any other contributions under the plan. Thus, deemed IRA contributions don't count against the 100% of income or dollar limit on annual additions to defined contribution plans. (Reg § 1.408(q)-1(c))

36. ¶H-12295.6B *et seq.*
37. ¶H-12295.10 ¶402A4
38. ¶H-12280; ¶4084.07

39. ¶H-12280; ¶4084.07
40. ¶H-12284

¶ **4365**   **Simplified Employee Pensions (SEPs).** ▌▬▬▬▬▬▬▬▬▬▬▬▬▬▬

An employer can make deductible contributions on behalf of its employees to a simplified employee pension (SEP). These deductible employer contributions are excluded from the gross income of the employee.

¶ **4366**   **Simplified employee pension (SEP) defined.**

A SEP is an individual retirement account or individual retirement annuity (IRA, see ¶4340), established by an employer by filing Form 5305-SEP, in which:

(1) The employer contributions are made only under a definite written allocation formula that is executed within the time for making a deductible contribution (¶4367)[41] that specifies (a) the requirements that an employee must satisfy to share in an allocation, and (b) how the allocated amount is computed. (Code Sec. 408(k)(5))[42]

(2) Employer contributions for a year must be made to each SEP of each employee who has reached age 21, performed service for the employer during at least three of the immediately preceding five years and has received at least $600 in compensation for 2018 and 2019. (Code Sec. 408(k)(2))[43]

(3) The employer contributions don't discriminate in favor of highly compensated employees. (Code Sec. 408(k)(3)(A))[44]

(4) The employer contributions aren't conditional on the retention in the plan of any portion of the amounts contributed. (Code Sec. 408(k)(4))[45]

(5) The employer doesn't restrict employee withdrawals. (Code Sec. 408(k)(4)(B))[46]

(6) Elective deferrals made by each highly compensated employee under a salary reduction arrangement may not exceed the average of the deferral percentage of all other eligible employees multiplied by 1.25. (Code Sec. 408(k)(6)(A)(iii))[47]

Employer contributions are discriminatory unless they bear a uniform relationship to the first $275,000 for 2018 ($280,000 for 2019) of the compensation (including self-employed income) of each employee maintaining the SEP. (Code Sec. 408(k)(3)(C))[48]

Employees covered by a collective bargaining agreement and nonresident aliens may be excluded from participation in the plan and from the discrimination test under certain conditions. (Code Sec. 408(k)(3)(B))[49]

Maximum allowable contributions made by an employer to a SEP on behalf of an employee for any year cannot exceed the lesser of: (1) 25% of compensation (limited by the annual compensation limit, see ¶4308) from the employer includible in the employee's gross income for the year (determined without regard to the employer's contributions to the SEP), or (2) the dollar limitation for defined contribution plans ($55,000 for 2018; $56,000 for 2019; see ¶4317). (Special calculations are needed for self-employeds, like those for Keogh plans, see ¶4316.) Employee elective deferrals to a SEP do not count towards the limit. Where the SEP is integrated with social security, the dollar limitation in (2) is reduced by the amount taken into account above the integration level, in the case of a highly compensated employee. (Code Sec. 402(h)(2))[50]

---

41. ¶H-12303; ¶4084.05
42. ¶H-12310; ¶4084.05
43. ¶H-12305; ¶4084.05
44. ¶H-12306; ¶4084.05
45. ¶H-12309; ¶4084.05

46. ¶H-12309; ¶4084.05
47. ¶H-12321; ¶4084.05
48. ¶H-12307; ¶4084.05
49. ¶H-12306
50. ¶s H-12308, H-12311; ¶4084.05

¶ 4367   Employer's deduction for contributions to a SEP.

A contribution by an employer to a SEP is deductible for a tax year if made on account of that year and not later than the time prescribed for filing the return for that year plus extensions.[1] The deduction can't exceed 25% of the compensation paid to the employees during the calendar year, up to the defined contribution plan limit (¶4317). Contributions that exceed this limit can be carried over to, and deducted in, succeeding tax years in order of time. (Code Sec. 404(h))[2]

An employer may elect to use either the calendar year or, subject to such terms and conditions as IRS may prescribe, its own tax year as the computation period for purposes of determining contributions to a SEP. (Code Sec. 408(k)(7)) If the calendar year is used, contributions made for a year are deductible for the employer's tax year with which or within which the calendar year ends. If the employer's "regular" tax year is used, contributions are deductible for that tax year. For purposes of deductibility, contributions are treated as if they were made for a tax year if the contributions are made on account of the tax year and are made not later than the time prescribed by law for filing the return for the tax year, plus extensions. (Code Sec. 404(h)(1)(A), Code Sec. 404(h)(1)(B))[3] Special rules apply where the employer also contributes to other plans. (Code Sec. 404(h)(2), Code Sec. 404(h)(3))[4]

¶ 4368   Employee's treatment of SEP contributions and withdrawals.

Contributions made to a SEP by an employer on behalf of an employee are excluded from the employee's gross income, up to the deduction limits at ¶4367. (Code Sec. 402(h)(1)) Contributions in excess of those limits are taxed to the employee in the year made. (Code Sec. 402(h)(2))[5] Payments made from the SEP are taxed to the recipient under the IRA rules (¶4346). (Code Sec. 402(h)(3))[6]

¶ 4369   "SIMPLE" Retirement Plans.

An eligible employer (¶4370) that doesn't have a qualified plan can establish a "SIMPLE" (savings incentive match plan for employees) retirement plan (defined at ¶4372), without having to meet most requirements for qualified plans.

For qualified salary reduction arrangements under SIMPLE plans, see ¶4371. For contributions to SIMPLE plans, see ¶4373; for distributions, see ¶4374.

¶ 4370   Employers eligible to adopt SIMPLE retirement plans.

A "SIMPLE retirement plan" can be adopted (use Form 5305-SIMPLE, Form 5304-SIMPLE if there is no designated financial institution, or Form 5305-SA for a SIMPLE individual retirement custodial account) by an employer with 100 or fewer employees who received at least $5,000 of compensation from the employer for the preceding year (Code Sec. 408(p)(2)(C)(i)(I)) that doesn't have another employer-sponsored retirement plan (including a SEP or annuity plan), except for a collectively bargained plan covering employees ineligible to participate in the SIMPLE plan, to which contributions were made or benefits accrued for the year. (Code Sec. 408(p)(2)(D))[7] "Employee" includes a self-employed individual. (Code Sec. 408(p)(6)(B)) A qualifying employer that maintains a SIMPLE plan but later fails to qualify may continue to maintain the plan for two years after its last year of

---

1. ¶H-12312 *et seq.*; ¶4084.05
2. ¶H-12315; ¶4044.08
3. ¶H-12317; ¶4044.08
4. ¶H-12318 *et seq.*; ¶4084.05

5. ¶H-12311; ¶4084.05
6. ¶H-12319.3
7. ¶H-12351; ¶4084.06

eligibility, subject to certain restrictions for acquisitions, dispositions and similar transactions. (Code Sec. 408(p)(2)(C)(i)(II), Code Sec. 408(p)(10))[8]

¶ 4371 "Qualified salary reduction arrangements" under SIMPLE plans.

Employees designate contributions to be made to a SIMPLE plan under a "qualified salary reduction arrangement." This is a written arrangement under which an employee may elect to have the employer make elective employer contributions (expressed as a percentage of compensation, or, if the employer permits, a specific dollar amount) to a SIMPLE retirement account on behalf of the employee, or to the employee directly in cash. The amount that an employee may elect for any year can't exceed $12,500 for 2018 ($13,000 for 2019). (Code Sec. 408(p)(2)(A)(i), Code Sec. 408(p)(2)(A)(ii), Code Sec. 408(p)(2)(E))[9] SIMPLE 401(k) or SIMPLE IRA participants who are age 50 or over by the end of the plan year may make additional catch-up contributions of up to $3,000 for 2018 and 2019. (Code Sec. 414(v)(2)(B)(ii), Code Sec. 414(v)(2)(C))[10]

For the saver's credit for lower-income taxpayers' elective contributions to SIMPLE plans, see ¶2358.

The employer must make either:

(1) a matching contribution equal to the amount the employee contributes, up to 3% (Code Sec. 408(p)(2)(C)(ii)(I)) of the employee's compensation for the year, or, electively, as little as 1% in no more than two out of the previous five years, if the employer timely notifies the employees of the lower percentage (Code Sec. 408(p)(2)(C)(ii)(II))[11] ; or

(2) a nonelective contribution of 2% of compensation for each employee eligible to participate who has at least $5,000 of compensation from the employer for the year. (Code Sec. 408(p)(2)(D)(i))[12]

No other contributions may be made. (Code Sec. 408(p)(2)(A)(iv), Code Sec. 408(p)(8)) Elective employer contributions must be made no later than 30 days after the month for which the contributions are to be made. (Code Sec. 408(p)(5)(A)(i)) Matching contributions and nonelective contributions must be made by the deductible contribution due date for the year. (Code Sec. 408(p)(5)(A)(ii))[13]

"Compensation" is wages for income tax withholding purposes plus the amount of the employee's elective deferrals (Code Sec. 408(p)(6)(A)(i)) (for a self-employed person, net self-employment earnings (under Code Sec. 1402(a)) without regard to the SIMPLE retirement plan provisions. (Code Sec. 408(p)(6)(A)(ii)) For purposes of determining contributions to a SIMPLE plan, the definition of compensation includes wages paid to domestic workers, even though those amounts are not subject to income tax withholding. (Code Sec. 408(p)(6)(A)(i))

The compensation taken into account for purposes of determining the amount of the 2% nonelective contribution can't exceed the limit on compensation (under Code Sec. 401(a)(17), see ¶4308) that may be taken into account for the year. (Code Sec. 408(p)(2)(B)(ii))[14]

¶ 4372 SIMPLE retirement account defined.

A "SIMPLE retirement account" into which employer contributions under a SIMPLE retirement plan are made) is an individual retirement account or annuity (Code

---

8. ¶H-12352.1; ¶4084.06
9. ¶H-12357; ¶4084.06
10. ¶H-9244.1; ¶4144.26
11. ¶H-12359; ¶4084.06

12. ¶H-12360; ¶4084.06
13. ¶H-12364; ¶4084.06
14. ¶H-12358; ¶4084.06

Sec. 408(p)(1)): (1) that meets certain vesting, participation and administrative requirements (Code Sec. 408(p)(1)(A)); (2) for which, for contributions made before Dec. 19, 2015,
the only contributions allowed are contributions under a "qualified salary reduction arrangement" (former Code Sec. 408(p)(1)(B)) or rollovers or transfers from another SIMPLE
IRA and (3) for which, with respect to contributions made after Dec. 18, 2015, the only
contributions allowed are: a) contributions under a qualified salary reduction arrangement, and b) various rollovers, including rollovers from an IRA or from another SIMPLE
IRA, but only if made after the 2-year period beginning on the date that the employee first
participated in a qualified salary reduction arrangement maintained by the employee's
employer. (Code Sec. 408(p)(1)(B)).

Employees' rights to all SIMPLE account contributions must be nonforfeitable. (Code
Sec. 408(p)(3)) All employees (except those who can be excluded from a qualified plan (Code
Sec. 408(p)(4)(B)) who received at least $5,000 in compensation from the employer during
any two preceding years (Code Sec. 408(p)(4)(A)(i)), and are reasonably expected to receive
at least $5,000 in compensation during the current year (Code Sec. 408(p)(4)(A)(ii)) must
be eligible either to elect to make a salary reduction contribution or receive nonelective
contributions. (Code Sec. 408(p)(4)(A))[15]

¶ 4373   Contributions to SIMPLE retirement accounts.

Employer contributions to SIMPLE accounts are deductible in the employer's tax year
with which (or within which) the calendar year for which the contributions were made
ends. (Code Sec. 404(m)(1); Code Sec. 404(m)(2)(A)) Contributions are treated as made for
the tax year if they are made (a) on account of that year, and (b) not later than the time for
filing that year's tax return (including extensions). (Code Sec. 404(m)(2)(B))[16]

Contributions to simplified employee pensions are excluded from the employee's income
similar to the rules for SEPs under Code Sec. 402(h)(1) (¶4368). Employees aren't entitled
to a deduction for employer contributions made on their behalf to a SIMPLE retirement
account. (Code Sec. 219(b)(4)) Any elective contributions under a SIMPLE retirement plan
are included in the sum of elective deferrals, subject to an annual limit on the amount that
can be excluded from income. (Code Sec. 402(g)(3)(D))[17] Matching contributions on behalf
of self-employed persons aren't treated as employer elective contributions for this purpose.
(Code Sec. 408(p)(9))[18]

SIMPLE plans may also incorporate an automatic enrollment arrangement (ACA),
which permits an employer to make contributions to an employee's SIMPLE IRA without
the employee having made an affirmative election to participate in the plan. [19]

¶ 4374   SIMPLE retirement account distributions.

Rules similar to those for distributions from simplified employee pensions (SEPs), apply
to SIMPLE retirement accounts. (Code Sec. 402(k)) Thus, they are taxed under the rules
relating to IRAs in the year of distribution. (Code Sec. 402(h)(3))[20] For tax-free rollovers of
SIMPLE retirement account distributions, see ¶4346.[21] For early withdrawal penalties for
SIMPLE account distributions, see ¶4333.[22]

¶ 4375   Tax-Sheltered 403(b) Annuities. ▬▬▬▬▬▬▬▬▬▬▬

Employees of tax-exempt educational, charitable, religious, etc., organizations, or
public schools get special tax advantages from annuities bought for them by the

15. ¶H-12361; ¶4084.06
16. ¶H-12372; ¶4084.06
17. ¶H-12373
18. ¶H-12357; ¶4084.06

19. ¶H-12365.1
20. ¶H-12374; ¶4084.06
21. ¶H-12375
22. ¶H-12377

exempt employers.

Tax-sheltered annuities offer benefits similar to those under a qualified employee plan. The tax isn't imposed when the annuity is bought, but is deferred until payments are received. (Code Sec. 403(b); Reg § 1.403(b)-1)[23] These annuities may be bought only for common law employees of certain exempt educational, charitable, religious, etc., employers, and by or for certain self-employed ministers. (Code Sec. 403(b)(1)(A))[24] The annuity must be nonforfeitable (except for failure to pay premiums) and nontransferable. (Code Sec. 403(b)(1)(C); Reg § 1.401-9(b)(3))[25] Certain elective deferral limits must be met if the annuity is part of a salary reduction arrangement (¶4377). (Code Sec. 403(b)(1)(E))[26] Also, except for annuities bought by church employers, certain nondiscrimination tests must be met. (Code Sec. 403(b)(1)(D), Code Sec. 403(b)(12))[27] Tax-sheltered annuities are treated as defined contribution plans for purposes of the contribution limits (¶4317).[28]

¶ 4376 How tax-sheltered annuity arrangements work.

Employees of a qualifying employer can get a prescribed amount of their compensation in the form of a tax-sheltered annuity. The employee pays no immediate tax on the amount the employer pays for the annuity, but the employee is taxed under the regular annuity rules (¶1350 *et seq.*) when the annuity payments are made. (Code Sec. 403(b)(1))[29]

The tax deferral is denied for distributions attributable to contributions made under a salary reduction agreement (¶4377), unless the annuity provides that payments may be paid only: (1) when the employee attains age 59 1/2, separates from employment, dies, or becomes disabled, or (2) in the case of hardship. (Code Sec. 403(b)(11)) (The early distribution penalty applies, ¶4333). (Code Sec. 72(t)) The contract may not provide for the distribution of any income attributable to such contributions in the case of hardship. (Code Sec. 403(b)(11))[30] Tax-sheltered annuities are subject to the loan rules at ¶4332. (Code Sec. 72(p)(4)(A))[31]

403(b) plans can make hardship distributions available to victims of Hurricanes Harvey, Irma, and Maria. In addition, special rules apply to "qualified hurricane distributions" and "California wildfire distributions" from, and rollovers to, 403(b) plans, see ¶4333.[32]

For rollovers to and from Code Sec. 403(b) plans, see ¶4348 and ¶4349.

¶ 4377 Tax-sheltered annuity salary-reduction agreements.

An employee of a qualifying employer can agree to reduce his salary or forego an increase as a means of contributing to a 403(b) plan. The rules that apply to cash or deferred arrangements under Code Sec. 401(k) (¶4306) determine how often a salary reduction may be entered into, the compensation to which the agreement applies, and the ability to revoke the agreement. [33]

All of the employer's employees (except those covered by a CODA or an eligible Code Sec. 457 plan) must get a chance to elect to have the employer contribute more than $200 under the salary reduction agreement, on a nondiscriminatory basis, if *any* employee may so elect. (Code Sec. 403(b)(12)(A))[34] The employee's elective deferrals for a year can't exceed the CODA limits, including catch-up contributions for those age 50 or over (¶4306). (Code Sec. 403(b)(1)(E); Reg § 1.403(b)-4(c))[35]

23. ¶H-12450 *et seq.*; ¶4034.04
24. ¶H-12452, H-12453; ¶4034.04
25. ¶H-12454; ¶4034.04
26. ¶H-12454 *et seq.*; ¶4034.04
27. ¶H-12464; ¶4034.04
28. ¶H-12454 *et seq.*; ¶4034.04
29. ¶H-12451

30. ¶H-12479; ¶4034.04
31. ¶H-11066; ¶724.23
32. ¶H-11066.1 *et seq.*
33. ¶H-12465; ¶4034.04
34. ¶H-12465; ¶4034.04
35. ¶H-12454; ¶4034.04

A 403(b) plan can include a qualified Roth contribution program (see ¶4363).

The term "salary reduction agreement" includes a plan or arrangement whereby a payment will be made if the employee:

... elects to reduce compensation pursuant to a cash or deferred election as defined at Reg § 1.401(k)-1(a)(3);

... elects to reduce compensation pursuant to a one-time irrevocable election made at or before the time of initial eligibility to participate in the plan or arrangement (or pursuant to a similar arrangement involving a one-time irrevocable election); or

... agrees as a condition of employment (whether the condition is set by statute, contract, or otherwise) to make a contribution that reduces the employee's compensation. (Reg § 31.3121(a)(5)-2(a))[36]

For the saver's credit for lower-income taxpayers' contributions to 403(b) annuities, see ¶2358.

¶ 4378   Tax-sheltered annuity contribution limit.

If a qualifying employer buys a tax-sheltered annuity for an employee and the employee's rights are nonforfeitable, the premium paid is not taxable to the employee at that time, up to the applicable limit for a defined contribution plan under Code Sec. 415 (¶4317). (Code Sec. 403(b)(1), Code Sec. 415(c)(1), Code Sec. 415(k)(4); Reg § 1.403(b)-3(b)(3))[37]

Special limits apply for contributions by church plans. (Code Sec. 415(c)(7))

¶ 4379   "Includible compensation" and "years of service."

"Includible compensation" means the amount of compensation received by the employee from the qualified employer that is includible in his gross income (without regard to the exclusion for certain foreign source earned income) for the most recent period ending not later than the close of the employee's tax year that can be counted as one "year of service" and which precedes the tax year by no more than five years. Amounts contributed by the employer for tax-sheltered annuities are not included. Elective deferrals and any amount contributed or deferred by the employer at the employee's election that is excluded from income under Code Sec. 125 or Code Sec. 457 are included. (Code Sec. 403(b)(3))[38]

"Includible compensation" doesn't include any compensation *earned* when the employer wasn't a qualified employer. But it's immaterial whether the employer was qualified when the compensation is actually *received* by the employee.[39]

Similar rules apply to compensation received from "eligible employers." (Reg § 1.403(b)-2(b)(11)

The employee's "years of service," which can't be less than one, includes one year for each full year he was a full-time employee of the organization buying the annuity for him, plus a fraction of each year, as prescribed by regs, for each full year he was a part-time employee, or for each part of a year he was a full or part-time employee. (Code Sec. 403(b)(4))[40])

An employee's years of service equals the aggregate of the annual work periods during which he is employed by the eligible employer. (Reg § 1.403(b)-4(c))

---

36. ¶H-4650
37. ¶H-12467; ¶4034.04
38. ¶H-12468; ¶4034.04

39. ¶H-12468; ¶4034.04
40. ¶H-12469 *et seq.*; ¶4034.04

Chapter 22   Farmers

¶ 4500   Farmers. ▬▬▬▬▬▬▬▬▬▬▬▬▬▬▬▬▬▬▬▬▬▬▬

Farmers get tax breaks not generally available to others, including: 3-year income averaging (¶4502), a 2-year net operating loss carryback period (¶4503), favorable accounting (¶4505 *et seq.*) and inventory methods (¶4513 *et seq.*), income deferrals (¶4508), capital gain-ordinary loss treatment (¶4524, ¶4526), and the deduction of items normally capitalized (¶4516 *et seq.*).

For tax years after 2017 and before 2026, certain specified agricultural or horticultural cooperatives may also claim a deduction under Code Sec. 199A(g) for a percentage of the cooperative's qualified production activities income (¶1601).

¶ 4501   Farmers' income and expenses—Schedule F (Form 1040).

Farm income (and expenses) are reported on Form 1040, Schedule F. A farmer's gross income includes cash and the fair market value of goods received ("barter income") from crops, produce, poultry and livestock. (Reg § 1.61-4(c)) The value of produce consumed by the farmer's family isn't included, but expenses incurred in raising that produce can't be deducted.[1]

Farmers may deduct the ordinary and necessary expenses of operating a farm for profit—e.g., rent, labor, feed (¶4515), fertilizer (¶4516). (Reg § 1.162-12(a))[2] For required capitalization of certain expenses, see ¶4519.

¶ 4502   Three-year averaging for farming or fishing income—Schedule J.

An individual (including a partner in a partnership and a shareholder of an S corporation, but not including an estate or trust) engaged in a farming or fishing business may elect 3-year averaging of "elected farm income" (below) for regular income tax (but not for employment tax) purposes. If the election is made, the tax for the year is equal to the sum of (1) the tax computed on taxable income reduced by elected farm or fishing income, and (2) the increase in tax that would result if taxable income for the three prior tax years were increased by an amount equal to one-third of the elected farm or fishing income. Any adjustment under this provision for any tax year is taken into account in applying this provision for any later tax year. (Code Sec. 1301(a), Code Sec. 1301(b)(3); Reg § 1.1301-1(b)) Taxable income for prior years can be less than zero, but in that case any amount that may provide a benefit in another tax year (such as an NOL) is added back in determining base year taxable income. (Reg § 1.1301-1(d)(2))[3]

Elect by filing Form 1040, Schedule J with a return for the election year (including a late or amended return if the time for filing for a credit or refund has not expired). An individual may change or revoke a previous election, if the period of limitation on filing a claim for credit or refund has not expired for the election year. (Reg § 1.1301-1(c))

"Elected farm income" means the amount of taxable income for the tax year attributable to any farming or fishing business that's specified in the election to average farm or fishing income (Code Sec. 1301(b)(1)(A); Reg § 1.1301-1(e)(2)), including farm wages paid to an S shareholder (Reg § 1.1301-1(e)(1)), income of fishing-boat crew members compensated by a share of the boat's catch or a share of the catch proceeds (Reg § 1.1301-1(b)(3)), and certain crop-share income. (Reg § 1.1301-1(b)(2)) Gain from the sale or other disposition of property (other than land) regularly used by the taxpayer in a farming or fishing

---

1. ¶N-1151; ¶1624.340
2. ¶N-1301; ¶1624.340

3. ¶N-1515 *et seq.*

References beginning with a single letter are to paragraphs in Federal Tax Coordinator 2d and RIA's Analysis of Federal Taxes: Income. Those beginning with numbers are to paragraphs in United States Tax Reporter.

business for a substantial period is treated as attributable to that farming business. (Code Sec. 1301(b)(1)(B); Reg § 1.1301-1(e)(1)(ii)(A))[4] A landlord is engaged in a farming business for farm averaging purposes for rental income based on a share of production (not fixed rent) from a tenant's farming business determined under a written agreement entered into before the tenant begins significant activities on the land. Similar rules apply to fishing-boat lessors who share in the catch. (Reg § 1.1301-1(e)(2)) Tobacco quota payments don't qualify for income averaging.[5]

Electing income averaging does not cause the taxpayer's AMT to increase because regular tax liability for determining the AMT is computed as though the election had not been made, see ¶3201.

¶ 4503   Farming NOL carryback and carryover periods.

Although NOLs arising in tax years after 2017 can be carried forward indefinitely but generally cannot be carried back (¶1814), any part of an NOL that's a "farming loss" can be carried back to each of the two tax years preceding the tax year of the loss. (Code Sec. 172(b)(1)(B)(i))[6] A farming loss is the lesser of: (1) the amount that would be the NOL for the tax year if only income and deductions attributable to farming businesses are taken into account, or (2) the amount of the NOL for the tax year. (Code Sec. 172(b)(1)(B)(ii))[7] In determining the order in which NOLs are absorbed, a farming loss for any tax year is treated as a separate NOL for that tax year and is taken into account after the remaining part of that year's NOL. (Code Sec. 172(b)(1)(B)(iii))[8] Farmers may elect to forego the 2-year carryback. The election is made in the manner prescribed by IRS and must be made by the return due date (including extensions) for the tax year of the NOL. The election is irrevocable for the tax year for which it is made. (Code Sec. 172(b)(1)(B)(iv))[9]

observation: For post-2017 tax year losses, NOL deductions —including those of farmers—are generally limited to 80% of taxable income (¶1812 *et seq.*).

¶ 4504   Limitation on deduction of farm losses.

For tax years beginning after Dec. 31, 2017 and before Jan. 1, 2026, the excess farm loss disallowance rule under Code Sec. 461(j), which limited (except by C corporations) the amount of farming losses that could be claimed for any tax year in which certain subsidies were received, is suspended, and noncorporate taxpayers —including farmers—are, instead, subject to a broader "excess business loss" disallowance rule under Code Sec. 461(l) (see ¶1774).[10]

¶ 4505   Farmers' accounting methods.

Farmers (unless listed at ¶4510) may use the cash method (¶4506), the accrual method (¶4509), the crop method (¶4512), or a "hybrid" method combining any of these methods if it clearly reflects income (¶2817). (Reg § 1.61-4, Reg § 1.446-1(c), Reg § 1.471-6(a))[11]

Farmers are not required to use inventories (regardless of whether they satisfy the gross receipts test under Code Sec. 448(c); see ¶2818) unless they are subject to the uniform capitalization rules (¶4519). (Reg § 1.471-6(a))[12] But a farmer that does use inventories must use the accrual method at least for purchases and sales. [13]

4. ¶N-1515 *et seq.*
5. ¶N-1501 *et seq.*; ¶13,014
6. ¶M-4311; ¶1724.436
7. ¶M-4311
8. ¶M-4303; ¶1724.437

9. ¶M-4313; ¶1724.437
10. ¶N-1331
11. ¶N-1010 *et seq.*; ¶s 614.053, 4464.09
12. ¶N-1100 *et seq.*; ¶4714.73
13. ¶N-1017

¶ 4506   Cash method farmers.

Cash method farmers include income in the year actually or constructively received, whichever is earlier (¶2819). Gross income includes receipts of: (1) proceeds from sales of *raised* livestock or produce; (2) profits from the sale of any *purchased* property, including livestock, (3) breeding fees, (4) fees from renting teams, machinery or land, (5) taxable subsidy and conservation payments, (6) crop insurance proceeds, and (7) all other gross income. (Reg § 1.61-4(a))[14] For deferral of insurance proceeds and forced livestock sales, see ¶4508.

Expenses are ordinarily deductible in the year paid (other than the cost of animals and plants bought for resale, see ¶4507). (Reg § 1.61-4(a))[15] For feed expenses, see ¶4515, and for pre-paid expenses, see ¶4517. An option to accelerate the receipt of any payment under a production flexibility contract that is payable under the FAIR Act of 1996 as in effect on Dec. 17, '99 won't accelerate the recognition of income unless the option is exercised. (Sec. 525 of P.L. 106-170) The constructive receipt rules also don't apply to options to receive payments under the Farm Security and Rural Investment Act of 2002. [16]

¶ 4507   Cash method farmer's deduction of costs of purchased animals and plants—election to deduct in year bought or year sold.

Cash method farmers generally deduct the costs of animals and plants bought for resale in the year they are sold. (Reg § 1.61-4(a)) But for the following animals and plants, a farmer may elect to deduct the costs either for the year they are purchased or for the year they are sold, if the method chosen clearly reflects income:

. . . baby chicks and pullets bought for raising and resale;

. . . hens bought for commercial egg production;

. . . seeds and young plants (other than Christmas trees and timber) bought for further development and cultivation before sale. (Reg § 1.162-12)[17]

The farmer makes the election by deducting the cost for the first year in which the items are bought. Once the farmer elects this option, it must be used consistently until IRS consents to a change (¶2835).[18]

¶ 4508   One-year deferral elections for cash method farmers—"disaster" receipts.

A cash method farmer can elect to defer reporting certain insurance proceeds and federal disaster payments (including payments under Title II (but not Title I) of the '88 Disaster Assistance Act) until the tax year after the year of the destruction or damage to, or inability to plant, the crops, if the farmer shows that under his or her practice, the income from the crops would have been reported in a later year. To elect, check the box in Part I on Schedule F and attach a statement to the return (or amended return) for the year payments are received. (Code Sec. 451(f); Reg § 1.451-6)[19]

One-year deferral also may be elected for income from livestock sold on account of a drought, flood or other weather-related condition so severe that the sale had to take place in an earlier year than normal. Elect on a statement attached to the return for the sale year. (Code Sec. 451(g)(1); Reg § 1.451-7(g)) However, if the period for buying replacement property for such livestock under the involuntary conversion rules (¶2432) is extended to

---

14. ¶N-1013; ¶614.054
15. ¶614.054
16. ¶N-1152.1; ¶4514.039

17. ¶s N-1021, N-1022
18. ¶N-1022
19. ¶N-1024 *et seq.*; ¶s 614.054, 4514.171

four years from the end of the year of sale (see ¶2438), the election of one-year deferral is valid if made during that replacement period. (Code Sec. 451(g)(3))[20]

¶ 4509   Accrual method farmers.

Accrual farmers include farm income for the year earned, regardless of when payment is received, and deduct farm expenses for the year the "all events test" is met (¶2823 *et seq.*). Accrual farmers also must use inventories to determine gross income (¶4513). (Code Sec. 461(h); Reg § 1.61-4(b), Reg § 1.446-1(c))[21] For when the accrual method is mandatory, see ¶4510.

An accrual farmer's gross income for a tax year is the sum of: (1) the sales price of all livestock and other products held for sale that are sold during the year, (2) the inventory value of the livestock, etc. (i.e., the proceeds from the disposition of livestock, etc., during the year, plus the inventory value of livestock, etc., not sold at the end of the year, reduced by the inventory value of livestock, etc., on hand at the start of the year, and by the cost of any livestock, etc., bought during the year and included in inventory), (3) miscellaneous farm receipts, e.g., fees from breeding, (4) all subsidy and conservation payments includible that year, plus (5) gross income from all other sources. Crop shares are included in the year they are reduced to money or its equivalent. (Reg § 1.61-4(b))[22]

¶ 4510   When accrual accounting is mandatory for farmers.

For tax years beginning after 2017, the accrual method is *not* required, and the cash method may be used, by farming C corporations (and farming partnerships with a C corporation partner) that satisfy a $25 million gross receipts test —i.e., with annual average gross receipts for the three prior tax years that do not exceed $25 million for 2018 ($26 million for 2019, as calculated by Thomson Reuters using inflation data). (Code Sec. 447(c))[23]

Farming C corporations (and farming partnerships with a C corporation partner) that don't satisfy the gross receipts test must use the accrual method, unless they qualify under one of the limited exceptions below. The accrual method must also be used by tax shelters, including farm syndicates (¶4511), and by farmers that use inventories (¶4705).

S corporations (Code Sec. 447(c)(1), certain corporations (and partnerships having a corporate partner) described in Code Sec. 447(e),[24] and nurseries, sod farms, and raisers and harvesters of trees (other than fruit and nut trees) (Code Sec. 447(a))[25] aren't required to use the accrual method.

¶ 4511   Tax shelters and farming syndicates.

All tax shelters, including farming syndicates, must use the accrual method. (Code Sec. 448(a)(3))[26] For pre-paid expenses, see ¶4517. For uniform capitalization rules, see ¶4519. For tax shelter losses for AMT purposes, see ¶3211.

A farming syndicate is any partnership (or other noncorporate enterprise) or S corporation engaged in the business of farming if:

(1) at any time, interests in the partnership, etc., have been offered for sale in an offering required to be registered with any federal or state agency having authority to regulate the offering of securities for sale; (Code Sec. 461(k)(1)(A)or

(2) more than 35% of the losses during any periods are allocable to limited partners or

---

20. ¶N-1031 *et seq.*; ¶4514.176
21. ¶N-1017; ¶4614.15
22. ¶N-1014, N-1017; ¶614.051
23. ¶N-1037

24. ¶N-1049; ¶4474
25. ¶N-1036 *et seq.*; ¶4474
26. ¶G-2456; ¶4484

limited entrepreneurs (Code Sec. 461(k)(1)(B)); or

(3) it's a tax shelter. (Code Sec. 461(i)(3), Code Sec. 461(i)(4))[27]

The Court of Appeals for the Fifth Circuit has held that Code Sec. 461(j)(2), under which the interest of any individual who has actively participated in the management of any trade or business of farming would be treated as not held by a limited partner or limited entrepreneur for purposes of (2), above, could be met by an individual who actively participated and owned a super-majority interest in the farming partnership through her wholly owned S corporation, rather than in her individual name. IRS, on the other hand, believes that the active participation exception applies only to an interest held by an individual, and generally will not follow the Fifth Circuit's decision in cases involving taxpayers outside of the Fifth Circuit.[28]

¶ 4512   Crop method of accounting.

A farmer may, with IRS consent, use the crop method to report income from crops (other than timber) for which the process of planting, harvesting and sale isn't completed within the same tax year. (Reg § 1.61-4(c))[29] Under this method, all expenses of the crop (including expenses of seed or young plants) are charged, and all crop receipts are credited, to a crop account. Profit (or loss) is realized and included in (or deducted from) income only in the year the crop is harvested and disposed of. (Reg § 1.61-4(c), Reg § 1.162-12(a))[30]

¶ 4513   Farmers' inventories.

A farmer using inventories (¶4514) *must* inventory:

. . . all livestock and poultry, whether raised or purchased, held primarily for sale (Reg § 1.61-4(b));

. . . all harvested and purchased farm products held for sale, feed, or seed, such as grain, hay ensilage, concentrates, cotton, tobacco;

. . . supplies, unless only small amounts are on hand;

. . . if in the hatchery business, eggs in incubation and growing and pre-market chickens. (Inventories *may* be used for hens primarily held for egg production that are also held for sale after their egg-producing life.)[31]

Livestock held for dairy, breeding, sporting or draft purposes may be inventoried at the taxpayer's election. But raised livestock must be inventoried by farmers using the unit-livestock-price method. (Reg § 1.61-4(b), Reg § 1.471-6(f))[32]

¶ 4514   Inventory valuation methods for farmers.

Methods that farmers use to value inventory include:

. . . *Cost method* (¶2863). (Reg § 1.471-3)[33]

. . . *Lower-of-cost-or-market method* (¶2864). (Reg § 1.471-4)[34]

. . . *Farm price method.* Each item, raised or purchased, is valued at its market price less estimated direct cost of disposition. A farmer using this method must use it for all inventory, except that the unit-livestock-price method may be used for livestock at the farmer's election. (Reg § 1.471-6(d))[35]

. . . *Unit-livestock-price method.* Livestock is reasonably classified according to kind and

27. ¶G-2457.1; ¶4644
28. ¶G-2457.1; ¶4644
29. ¶N-1018 *et seq.*; ¶614.056
30. ¶N-1019; ¶614.056
31. ¶N-1102; ¶614.057

32. ¶s N-1109, N-1113; ¶s 614.057, 4714.73
33. ¶N-1106; ¶s 614.057, 4714.41, 4714.73
34. ¶N-1107; ¶s 614.057, 4714.51
35. ¶N-1112; ¶s 614.057, 4714.73

age. A standard unit price is used for each animal within a class. Unit prices must reflect costs capitalized under the uniform capitalization rules (¶4519). Once elected, the "unit-price" method is binding and cannot be changed without IRS's consent. Users of this method must annually reevaluate their unit prices and adjust them to reflect increases or decreases in the costs of raising livestock. (Reg § 1.471-6(f))[36]

¶ 4515   Feed expenses of farmers.

The cost of feed is a deductible business expense. (Reg § 1.162-12(a))[37] A cash method farmer may deduct, in the year paid, the cost of feed that the farmer's livestock will consume that year. Payments for feed to be used in the next tax year ("pre-paid feed") aren't deductible until the year of consumption, except the farmer may deduct pre-paid feed expenses in the payment year if: (1) the payment represents a purchase and not a deposit, (2) the advance payment is for a business purpose and not merely for tax avoidance, *and* (3) deduction in the payment year doesn't materially distort income. [38] For pre-paid farm expenses generally, see ¶4517.

¶ 4516   Fertilizer, lime, etc. expenses of farmers.

The cost of acquiring fertilizer, lime, marl, and other materials used to enrich, neutralize, or condition farmland, and the costs of applying them, are deductible in the year the costs are paid or incurred if the benefit doesn't last beyond one year. If the benefit lasts substantially more than a year the costs generally are capitalized but the farmer may elect to deduct them in the year paid or incurred (Code Sec. 180(a))[39] by deducting them on his or her return for that year. (Code Sec. 180(c); Reg § 1.180-2)[40] The election to deduct isn't allowable for costs of preparing land not previously used for farming by the taxpayer or by the farmer's tenant. (Code Sec. 180(b); Reg § 1.180-1(b))[41]

If fertilizer expenses are capitalized, the taxpayer may deduct a portion of the capitalized amounts for each year the benefits last. [42]

¶ 4517   Pre-paid farm expenses.

A cash method taxpayer's current deduction for pre-paid farm expenses (i.e., for farm supplies that won't be used until a later tax year) is limited to one-half of the other deductible farming expenses for the year (for a special rule for feed, see ¶4515). The "excess" part (i.e., over that one-half amount) isn't deductible until the year the supplies are used. (Code Sec. 464(a); Code Sec. 464(d))[43]

But this limit *doesn't apply* if the taxpayer's (or a family member's) principal home (within the meaning of Code Sec. 121, see ¶2442) is a farm or his or her principal business is farming, if: (1) for the three preceding tax years, the farmer's total pre-paid farm expenses are less than 50% of total other deductible farm expenses, or (2) for the current year, pre-paid farm expenses are more than 50% of other farm expenses because of a change in business operations attributable to extraordinary circumstances. (Code Sec. 464(d)(2))[44]

36. ¶N-1113; ¶s 614.057, 4714.73
37. ¶N-1311; ¶1624.340
38. ¶N-1312; ¶1624.340
39. ¶N-1306; ¶1804
40. ¶N-1307
41. ¶N-1306
42. ¶N-1306
43. ¶N-1319 *et seq.*; ¶4644
44. ¶N-1319; ¶4644

¶ 4518 Pre-productive period expenses of farmers.

The taxpayer has the option to either deduct or capitalize certain costs of developing and operating his or her farm and crops (e.g., taxes, interest, upkeep) during its pre-productive period (Reg § 1.162-12(a))[45] (subject to the uniform capitalization rules, see ¶4519). But capital expenditures aren't deductible.[46] The pre-productive period begins when the farmer first acquires the seed or plant, and ends when the plant produces marketable quantities, or is reasonably expected to be sold or otherwise disposed of. (Code Sec. 263A(e)(3))[47]

¶ 4519 Application of uniform capitalization rules to farmers and ranchers.

Farmers and ranchers are subject to the uniform capitalization rules for taxpayers generally (¶1640) with respect to the production, growing, or raising of property that: (i) is produced by a farmer required to use the accrual method (¶4510), (Code Sec. 263A(a), Code Sec. 263A(d)(1); Reg § 1.263A-4(a), Reg § 1.263A-4(b)) or (ii) has a pre-productive period (¶4518) of more than two years. (Code Sec. 263A(d)(1)(A)(ii))

For taxpayers not required to use the accrual method, the uniform capitalization rules *don't apply* to costs related to any animal, or plant with a pre-productive period of two years or less, which is produced by a taxpayer in a farming business. (Code Sec. 263A(d)(1)(A); Reg § 1.263A-4(a)(2))[48] The pre-productive period is the period before the first marketable crop or yield, for plants that have more than one crop or yield (e.g., the orange tree); the period before a crop or yield is disposed of, for the crop or yield of a plant that will have more than one crop or yield (e.g., the orange); or, for any other plant, the period before it is disposed of. (Reg § 1.263A-4(b)(2)) IRS Publication 225, Farmer's Tax Guide, contains a noninclusive list of plants with pre-productive periods in excess of 2 years.[49]

For exception for replanting because of casualties, see ¶4520. For election out of the uniform capitalization rules, see ¶4521.

¶ 4520 Exception to uniform capitalization rules for replanting because of casualty.

The uniform capitalization rules (¶4519) don't apply to costs incurred for the replanting, cultivation, maintenance and development of plants bearing an edible crop for human consumption (including citrus or almond) that were lost or damaged (while in the taxpayer's hands) by freezing temperatures, disease, drought, pests, or casualty. (Code Sec. 263A(d)(2)(A); Reg § 1.263A-4(e)(1), Reg § 1.263A-4(e)(4))[50]

This casualty exception generally applies to the costs of the person owning (owner) the plants at the time of the loss or damage. But costs paid or incurred by another person (payor) in any tax year also may qualify if in that year: (1) the owner has a more-than-50% equity interest in the plants, and (2) the payor owns any of the remaining equity interest in them *and* materially participates in their planting, maintenance, cultivation or development. (Code Sec. 263A(d)(2)(B); Reg § 1.263A-4(e)(2))[1]

For amounts paid or incurred for replanting, etc. after Dec. 22, 2017, and before Dec. 23, 2027 for citrus plants lost or damaged due to casualty, the costs may also be deducted by a person other than the taxpayer if (1) the taxpayer has an equity interest of not less than

45. ¶N-1302; ¶1624.349
46. ¶N-1303; ¶1624.349
47. ¶N-1074.1
48. ¶N-1071 et seq.; ¶263A4

49. ¶N-1071.1; ¶263A4.15
50. ¶N-1081; ¶1624.339
1. ¶N-1082; ¶263A4

50% in the replanted citrus plants at all times during the tax year in which the replanting costs are paid or incurred and such other person holds any part of the remaining equity interest, *or* (2) such other person acquires all of the taxpayer's equity interest in the land on which the lost or damaged citrus plants were located at the time of such loss or damage, and the replanting is on such land. (Code Sec. 263A(d)(2)(C)) This temporary allowance removes the material participation requirement to qualify for the exception. [2] IRS has provided automatic consent for farmers to change their method of accounting from applying Code Sec. 263A to citrus replanting costs to instead deducting those costs under Code Sec. 263A(d)(2)(C).[3]

¶ 4521   Farmers' election to have uniform capitalization rules not apply.

Except as noted below, a farmer may elect to have the uniform capitalization rules at ¶4519 *not* apply to any plant produced in his or her farm business (Code Sec. 263A(d)(3)(A)), so he or she may currently deduct all otherwise deductible preproductive costs.[4]

If the taxpayer or any related person (as specially defined) makes the election, Code Sec. 168(g)(2) alternative (i.e., straight-line) depreciation must be used for all of the taxpayer's property used predominantly in the farming business that was placed in service in any tax year during which the election is in effect (Code Sec. 263A(e)(2)(A); Reg § 1.263A-4(d)(4)(ii)), and other requirements in the regs must be followed. (Reg § 1.263A-4(d)(4))[5]

If the election is made, any plant for which amounts would have been capitalized *but for* the election is treated as Code Sec. 1245 property (if it's not otherwise Code Sec. 1245 property). (Code Sec. 263A(e)(1)(A)(i); Reg § 1.263A-4(d)(4)(i)) Deductible amounts that *but for* the election would have been capitalized are treated as depreciation deductions for Code Sec. 1245 purposes (Code Sec. 263A(e)(1)(A)(ii), Code Sec. 263A(e)(1)(B)) so that they are recaptured as ordinary income when the product is disposed of, see ¶2677.[6]

The election can't be made for any item attributable to the planting, cultivation, maintenance or development of any citrus or almond grove (or part of a grove) that's incurred before the close of the 4th tax year beginning with the tax year the trees were planted. For this purpose, the portion of a grove planted in one tax year must be treated separately from the portion planted in another tax year. (Code Sec. 263A(d)(3)(C); Reg § 1.263A-4(d)(2))[7]

A taxpayer makes the election by *not* applying the rules of Code Sec. 263A to determine the capitalized costs of plants produced in a farming business and by applying the rules of Reg § 1.263A-4(d)(4) on the original return for the first tax year capitalization of Code Sec. 263A costs is required. For partnerships or S corporations, the election is made by the partner, shareholder, or member. (Code Sec. 263A(d)(3)(D); Reg § 1.263A-4(d)(3)(i)) A taxpayer that does not make the automatic election described above must get IRS consent (¶2835) to change accounting methods. (Reg § 1.263A-4(d)(3)(ii))[8] The election can't be made by a corporation, partnership, or tax shelter that is required to use the accrual method of accounting, see ¶4510 and ¶4511. (Code Sec. 263A(d)(3)(B))[9]

¶ 4522   Soil and water conservation, anti-erosion, and endangered species recovery costs.

Farmers may deduct currently, as business expenses, certain outlays for soil and water conservation or erosion prevention that are incurred to maintain the farm and preserve its

---

2. ¶N-1082.2
3. ¶G-2203.62A
4. ¶N-1084; ¶263A4
5. ¶N-1090; ¶263A4

6. ¶N-1093; ¶263A4
7. ¶N-1089; ¶263A4
8. ¶N-1087; ¶263A4
9. ¶N-1085; ¶263A4

normal productivity, and not to increase its value or convert it to a new use. Costs that result in the acquisition of depreciable property must be capitalized. [10]

A farmer may elect to deduct certain nondepreciable expenditures for conservation, etc., of land he or she uses for farming (Code Sec. 175(a)) if the expenditures are consistent with a federal or state approved conservation plan. (Code Sec. 175(c)(3))[11] Qualifying expenditures include (1) costs of: treating or moving earth (e.g., leveling, terracing or restoring fertility); constructing and protecting diversion channels, drainage ditches, earthen dams; eradicating brush; planting windbreaks; producing vegetation primarily to conserve soil or water, or prevent soil erosion, and (2) expenses paid or incurred for endangered species recovery, including site-specific management actions under the Endangered Species Act of '73. (Code Sec. 175(c); Reg § 1.175-2(a), Reg § 1.175-2(b)(2)) Costs of draining or filling wetlands or for center pivot irrigation systems don't qualify. (Code Sec. 175(c)(3)(B)) Nor does the election apply to depreciable assets. (Reg § 1.175-2(b)(1))[12]

The amount of conservation, etc., expenses a farmer may deduct in any tax year under this election can't exceed 25% of the farmer's gross income from farming for the year. Any excess may be carried over to and deducted in the next tax year (subject to that year's 25% ceiling). (Code Sec. 175(b); Reg § 1.175-5(b))[13]

Elect by deducting the expenses on the return for the first tax year they are incurred. (Reg § 1.175-6(a))[14] IRS consent is needed to elect for a year other than that first year. (Code Sec. 175(d)(2))[15] Once the election is made, a farmer must continue to deduct all qualifying expenditures (subject to the 25% ceiling) unless IRS consents to a change. (Code Sec. 175(e))[16]

A farmer must recapture as ordinary income (use Form 4797) part of the conservation, etc., expenses if the farm land is disposed of after being held for less than 10 years. (Code Sec. 1252)[17]

¶ 4523 Depreciation for farm property—Form 4562.

A farmer may take depreciation deductions (on Form 4562) on property used in a farming business (Code Sec. 168(b)(2)(B)), including: buildings (except his or her dwelling); farm machinery; other physical property (not including land); orchards (trees and vines bearing fruits or nuts); and draft, breeding, sporting or dairy livestock (unless inventoried). (Reg § 1.167(a)-6(b))[18]

Farm property placed in service before 2018 generally was depreciated under MACRS using the 150% declining balance method, but straight line applied to nonresidential real property, and trees or vines bearing fruits or nuts. (Code Sec. 168(b)(1)(B), Code Sec. 168(b)(2)(B), Code Sec. 168(b)(3)(A), Code Sec. 168(b)(3)(B))[19] For property placed in service after 2017, most MACRS farming property (subject to certain exceptions; see below) may be depreciated under the 200% declining balance method (¶1924).[20]

⭐*observation:* Thus, farming property can be depreciated under the 200% declining balance method except for (1) buildings and trees or vines bearing fruits or nuts (to which the straight-line method applies), (2) property for which the taxpayer elects either the straight-line method or 150% declining balance method, (3) 15- or 20-year MACRS property that has to be depreciated under the 150% declining balance method, and (4)

---

10. ¶N-1401; ¶1754
11. ¶N-1402; ¶1754.02
12. ¶N-1407, N-1409; ¶1754.02
13. ¶N-1415; ¶1754.02
14. ¶N-1420
15. ¶N-1421; ¶1754

16. ¶N-1422
17. ¶N-1423; ¶12,524
18. ¶N-1304; ¶1674.035
19. ¶L-8912; ¶1684.01
20. ¶L-9402.2

property subject to the ADS. Land improvements other than buildings are 15-year property, and fences and grain bins have a 7-year recovery period, and single-purpose agricultural or horticultural structures (e.g., greenhouses, specialized housing for livestock) have a 10-year recovery period.

Machinery and equipment used in agriculture is included within the 5-year MACRS class (¶1915) for property placed in service after 2017 in a tax year that ends after 2017; for property placed in service in earlier tax years, it is included in the 7-year MACRS class (¶1916).[21] Certain MACRS property, however, must be depreciated under ADS (¶1930), including any MACRS property with a recovery period of 10 years or more that is held by an "electing farm business"; i.e., one that elects under Code Sec. 163(j)(7)(C) to not be subject to the post-2017 business interest deduction limitation (¶1710).[22]

⊘observation: If a farming business has average gross receipts of no more than $25 million for the three previous tax years and isn't a tax shelter, the business isn't subject to the business interest deduction limitations. Thus, the taxpayer that owns it doesn't have to decide whether or not to be make the election for that real property trade or business.

⊘recommendation: In deciding whether to make the Code Sec. 163(j)(7)(C) election, a taxpayer with a farming business should compare the overall effect on it of the business interest limitation (which will generally have the result of deferring deductions) to claiming depreciation deductions at a decelerated rate and over a longer period.

The cost of *purchased* dairy, etc., livestock may be recovered under MACRS. The cost of *raised* livestock may be either deducted (but costs so deducted can't be included in depreciable basis) (Reg § 1.61-4(a), Reg § 1.162-12(a)) or capitalized as the taxpayer chooses. [23] But accrual method farmers using inventories can't depreciate any purchased dairy, etc., livestock that's inventoried. (Reg § 1.167(a)-6)[24]

¶ 4524   Dispositions of unharvested crop with land.

Gain or loss on an unharvested crop sold, exchanged, or compulsorily or involuntarily converted with the underlying land qualifies under the capital gain-ordinary loss rule of Code Sec. 1231 (¶2669 *et seq.*), if: (1) the land was used in the taxpayer's trade or business and was held for the long-term capital gain holding period (¶2655), *and* (2) the land and crops are sold at the same time and to the same person. (Code Sec. 1231(b)(4)) It doesn't matter how long the crops were held, or their state of maturity. (Reg § 1.1231-1(f))[25]

¶ 4525   Dispositions of converted wetlands or highly erodible croplands.

Gain on the disposition of land used for farming that is converted wetland or highly erodible cropland is ordinary income. Loss is long-term capital loss. (Code Sec. 1257)[26]

¶ 4526   Dispositions of breeding, dairy, sporting, draft livestock.

Gains and losses from the sale, exchange, or involuntary conversion of animals held for draft, breeding, dairy, or sporting purposes qualify for capital gain-ordinary loss treatment under Code Sec. 1231 (¶2669 *et seq.*) as follows:

. . . cattle and horses held for 24 months or more from the date of acquisition;

---

21. ¶L-8205; ¶1684.01
22. ¶L-9402.2
23. ¶s N-1020, N-1350 *et seq.*; ¶1624.339

24. ¶N-1351; ¶1674.035
25. ¶N-1206; ¶12,314.13
26. ¶N-1431 *et seq.*; ¶12,574

. . . other livestock (except poultry) held for 12 months or more from the date of acquisition. (Code Sec. 1231(a), Code Sec. 1231(b)(3); Reg § 1.1231-2(a))[27]

Inventorying the livestock doesn't preclude Code Sec. 1231 treatment if the animal is held for the required purposes and relevant period and not for sale to customers. [28]

¶ 4527   Special farm payments.

Conservation programs. Unless the taxpayer elects out (Code Sec. 126(c)), gross income doesn't include the excludable part of payments received under certain cost-sharing conservation programs specified in Code Sec. 126(a)(1) to Code Sec. 126(a)(8). (Code Sec. 126(b))[29] Part or all of the cost-share payments made under the Forest Health Protection Program may qualify for the Code Sec. 126 exclusion.

Pledge of crops to secure CCC loan. Farmers who pledge part or all of their production to secure a Commodity Credit Corporation (CCC) loan can make a special election to treat the loan proceeds as income in the year received and obtain a basis in the commodity for the amount reported as income. Thus, instead of a loan, the money advanced to the farmer may be treated as the sales price of the commodity pledged for the loan. Elect by reporting the CCC loan proceeds as income on Schedule F, Form 1040 for the year the loan is received and attaching a statement to the return showing the details of the CCC loan. [30]

---

27. ¶s N-1209, N-1223; ¶s 12,314, 12,314.12
28. ¶N-1209

29. ¶N-1181; ¶1264
30. ¶N-1164; ¶774.03

Chapter 23 Foreign Income—Foreign Taxpayers—Foreign Currency Transactions

¶ 4600 Foreign Income of U.S. persons. ▄▄▄▄▄▄▄▄▄▄▄▄

U.S. persons are generally taxable on their worldwide income, subject to a participation exemption for certain corporate taxpayers (see ¶3315). For these purposes, a U.S. person is a U.S. citizen (¶4601), resident alien (¶4602), domestic corporation (¶4604), or other domestic entity (Code Sec. 7701(a)(3)) Individual U.S. persons who work or live abroad may be allowed certain exclusions, exceptions or credits (see ¶4605 *et seq.*). U.S. persons who conduct businesses through foreign corporations may be taxed on the corporations' undistributed income (see ¶4611 *et seq.*). A foreign tax credit is available to mitigate the risk of double taxation, see ¶2362 *et seq.* U.S. persons who give up U.S. citizenship or terminate long-term U.S. residency are subject to expatriation tax rules (¶4640).

¶ 4601 Taxation of U.S. citizens.

U.S. citizens, whether they reside in the U.S. or abroad, are generally subject to U.S. income tax on their income from sources within and without the U.S. (Reg § 1.1-1(b)) A U.S. citizen is every person born or naturalized in the U.S. and subject to its jurisdiction. (Reg § 1.1-1(c))[1]

¶ 4602 Taxation of resident aliens.

A resident alien individual generally is subject to U.S. tax in the same manner as a U.S. citizen (¶4601), with certain minor exceptions. (Reg § 1.1-1(b); Reg § 1.871-1(a))[2]

Resident alien. An alien individual is treated as a U.S. resident for any calendar year in which he (1) is a lawful permanent resident (the green card test), (2) meets a substantial presence test, or (3) makes the first year election. (Code Sec. 7701(b)(1)(A))[3]

Substantial presence test. Subject to certain exceptions, an individual meets the substantial presence test (i.e., is a U.S. resident) for any calendar (current) year if:

(1) he is present in the U.S. on at least 31 days during the year, *and*

(2) the sum of the number of days he was present in the U.S. during the current year and the two preceding calendar years, in each case multiplied by the applicable multiplier (1 for the current year, $\frac{1}{3}$ for the first preceding year, and $\frac{1}{6}$ for the second preceding year), is at least 183. (Code Sec. 7701(b)(3)(A))[4]

An individual isn't treated as present in the U.S. on any day on which he is an exempt individual (e.g., foreign official, teacher), or his medical condition prevents him from leaving the U.S. Form 8843 is used to claim the exemption. (Code Sec. 7701(b)(3)(D); Code Sec. 7701(b)(5)) Further, an individual who otherwise meets the substantial presence test can avoid being treated as a U.S. resident that year if he: (1) is present in the U.S. on fewer than 183 days during the year, and (2) files a "closer connection statement" on Form 8840 which establishes that for the year, he has a tax home (¶1541) in a foreign country to which he has a closer connection than to the U.S. (Code Sec. 7701(b)(3)(B))[5]

First year election to be taxed as a U.S. resident. A qualifying alien who arrives in the U.S. too late in a calendar year to meet the substantial presence test may under certain

---

1. ¶O-1001 *et seq.*
2. ¶O-1008 *et seq.*
3. ¶O-1051 *et seq.*; ¶8714

4. ¶O-1057; ¶8714
5. ¶O-1062 *et seq.*; ¶8714

References beginning with a single letter are to paragraphs in Federal Tax Coordinator 2d and RIA's Analysis of Federal Taxes: Income. Those beginning with numbers are to paragraphs in United States Tax Reporter.

circumstances elect (on a statement attached to the return) to be taxed as a U.S. resident for part of that first (election) year if he meets the substantial presence test in the *next* calendar year. (Code Sec. 7701(b)(4); Reg § 301.7701(b)-4(c)(3))[6]

¶ 4603   **Taxation of residents of U.S. possessions—Forms 1040-SS, 1040-PR, 4563.**

Puerto Rico. A nonresident alien individual (¶4625) who is a bona fide resident of Puerto Rico during the entire tax year is subject to taxation in the same manner as a resident alien individual (¶4602, except that income from Puerto Rico sources (except amounts received for services performed as an employee of the U.S.) is excluded (on Form 1040-PR) from gross income. The exclusion is available to all bona fide residents of Puerto Rico, regardless of U.S. citizenship/residence status. (Code Sec. 876; Code Sec. 933; Reg § 1.1-1(b))[7]

America Samoa. A nonresident alien individual who is a bona fide resident of American Samoa during the entire tax year is subject to taxation in the same manner as a resident alien individual, except that gross income for U.S. income tax purposes doesn't include income from sources within Guam, American Samoa, or the Northern Mariana Islands or income that is effectively connected with the individual's conduct of a trade or business within any of those possessions. The exclusion (which is available to all bona fide residents of American Samoa, regardless of U.S. citizenship/residence status) doesn't apply to amounts received for services performed as an employee of the U.S. Form 4563 is used for the exclusion of income for bona fide residents of American Samoa. (Code Sec. 876; Code Sec. 931; Reg § 1.1-1(b))[8]

Guam or the CNMI. Bona fide Guam or CNMI residents during the entire tax year, whether or not they are U.S. citizens or resident aliens, file their income tax returns with the possession of which they are bona fide residents, and are relieved from having to file a U.S. income tax return and pay any U.S. income tax liability, provided that they fully report and pay their taxes to the possession. (former Code Sec. 935) [9]

Virgin Islands. An individual who is a bona fide Virgin Islands resident for the entire tax year (or files a joint return with such a person) files a Virgin Islands return and pays Virgin Islands tax on his worldwide income for that year. If the individual properly files and reports all his or her income from all sources on a Virgin Islands tax return and pays the Virgin Islands tax, the individual is not subject to tax in the U.S. A U.S. citizen or resident, other than a bona fide resident of the Virgin Islands, who has Virgin Island source income, files an income tax return for the tax year with both the U.S. and the Virgin Islands, and pays Virgin Islands tax on the Virgin Islands source income. (Code Sec. 932)[10]

A bona fide resident of a possession is a person who is present for at least 183 days during the tax year in that possession, and who doesn't have a tax home (¶4608) outside the specified possession during the tax year and doesn't have a closer connection to the U.S. or a foreign country than to that specified possession. (Code Sec. 937(a)) IRS has stated that individuals won't lose their status as bona fide residents of Puerto Rico or the Virgin Islands due to a dislocation of up to 268 days (effective beginning Sept. 6, 2017, and ending May 31, 2018) caused by Hurricane Irma or Hurricane Maria. (Notice 2018-19) [11]

---

6. ¶O-1072 *et seq.*; ¶8714
7. ¶O-1450 *et seq.*; ¶9314.04
8. ¶O-1430 *et seq.*; ¶9314.02

9. ¶O-1400 *et seq.*; ¶9314.03
10. ¶O-1470 *et seq.*; ¶9314.05
11. ¶O-1085 *et seq.*; ¶9374.01

¶ 4604   Taxation of domestic corporations—Forms 1120, 4876-A.

A domestic corporation is generally subject to U.S. tax on its taxable income from whatever source derived. (Code Sec. 11; Code Sec. 61; Code Sec. 63) A domestic corporation is one created or organized in, or under the laws of, the U.S. or any state. (Code Sec. 7701(a)(4))[12]

A qualifying domestic corporation that elects on Form 4876-A to be a small interest-charge domestic international sales corporation (IC-DISC) is not subject to tax. Instead its shareholders are subject to tax on their pro rata share of IC-DISC income. However, an IC-DISC can retain the first $10 million of its qualified export receipts tax-free until it is actually distributed to shareholders, if it pays an interest charge on the accumulated untaxed income. (Code Sec. 991 *et seq.*)[13]

¶ 4605   Partial exclusion for foreign earned income—Form 2555.

A qualified individual (¶4608) may elect on Form 2555 to exclude from gross income his foreign earned income up to the inflation-adjusted exclusion amount (discussed below) and subject to limitations (¶4609). (Code Sec. 911(a)(1), Code Sec. 911(b)(2))[14] For a *separate* exclusion for foreign housing costs, see ¶4606.

An individual's foreign earned income is his earned income from foreign countries attributable to services he performed during the period he was a qualified individual, with certain exceptions. (Code Sec. 911(b)(1))[15] Earned income means wages and other amounts received as compensation (i.e., not as a distribution of profits) for personal services actually rendered, including the fair market value of compensation paid with property (Code Sec. 911(d)(2)(A); Reg § 1.911-3(b)(1)) and, where both personal services and capital are material income-producing factors in the taxpayer's noncorporate business, a reasonable allowance (up to 30% of his share of the net profits) as compensation for personal services. (Code Sec. 911(d)(2)(B))[16]

An individual's foreign earned income exclusion amount for a tax year can't exceed his foreign earned income for the year, as computed on a daily basis at an annual rate of $103,900 for 2018 ($105,900 in 2019, as calculated by Thomson Reuters using inflation data). (Code Sec. 911(b)(2)(A), Code Sec. 911(b)(2)(D))[17]

For married couples where both spouses are qualified individuals, each chooses whether to elect the exclusion. (Reg § 1.911-5(a)(1)) The amount of the exclusion is computed separately for each spouse based on the income attributable to that spouse's services. If the spouses file separate returns, each may exclude the amount of his foreign earned income attributable to his services, subject to the ceiling. If the spouses file a joint return, the sum of those separate amounts may be excluded. (Reg § 1.911-5(a)(2))[18] Employees of the U.S. government and agencies do not qualify for the Code Sec. 911 exclusion and deduction. For exclusions available to government employees abroad, see ¶4610.

¶ 4606   Partial exclusion for foreign housing costs—Form 2555.

A qualified individual (¶4608) may elect on Form 2555 to exclude from gross income his housing cost amount. (Code Sec. 911(a)(2))[19]

However, the exclusion amount is limited to the taxpayer's foreign earned income for the tax year attributable to employer-provided amounts. If both the housing cost amount exclusion and the foreign earned income exclusion (¶4605) are elected, the housing cost

---

12. ¶O-1006
13. ¶O-2020 *et seq.*; ¶9914 *et seq.*
14. ¶O-1100 *et seq.*, ¶O-1350 *et seq.*; ¶9114 *et seq.*
15. ¶O-1140 *et seq.*

16. ¶O-1117
17. ¶O-1102; ¶9114.12
18. ¶O-1115; ¶9114.09
19. ¶O-1160 *et seq.*, O-1350 *et seq.*; ¶9114.13

amount exclusion must be taken first. (Reg § 1.911-4(d)(1))[20]

The housing cost amount is the excess of: (1) the individual's housing expenses for the year (but not exceeding an amount equal to 30% of the taxpayer's foreign earned income exclusion (computed on a daily basis) (¶4605) multiplied by the number of qualifying days in the tax year), over (2) 16% of the taxpayer's foreign earned income exclusion (computed on a daily basis) multiplied by the number of qualifying days in the tax year. (Code Sec. 911(c)) A qualifying day is a day on which the taxpayer's tax home is in a foreign country and the taxpayer meets the bona fide residence or 330-day test (see ¶4608). For 2018, the maximum amount of the foreign housing cost exclusion is $14,546 ($103,900 × 30%) − ($103,900 × 16%) ($14,826 for 2019, as calculated by Thomson Reuters using inflation data). IRS provides a higher adjusted limitation on housing expenses in high-cost localities. (Code Sec. 911(c)(2)(B))[21]

Housing expenses are those reasonable expenses paid or incurred during the tax year by or on behalf of an individual for housing for the individual (and, if they reside with him, for his spouse and dependents) in a foreign country. (Code Sec. 911(c)(3)(A))[22] For a deduction for housing costs when the taxpayer has income from self-employment (i.e., non-employer provided amounts), see ¶4607.

For married couples where both spouses are qualified individuals, each chooses whether to elect the exclusion. (Reg § 1.911-5(a)(1)) The housing cost amount attributable to employer provided amounts is determined separately for each spouse. (Reg § 1.911-5(a)(3)(iii)) Where spouses reside together and file a joint return, they may compute their exclusion separately or jointly. If they reside together and file separate returns, they must make separate computations, but they may allocate the housing expenses between them. (Reg § 1.911-5(a)(3)(i)) Where spouses reside apart, they both may exclude (or deduct) their respective housing cost amounts if their tax homes (¶1541) aren't within reasonable commuting distance of each other and neither spouse's residence is within a reasonable commuting distance of the other spouse's tax home. If the spouses' tax homes or residences *are* within reasonable commuting distance, only one spouse may exclude (or deduct) his or her housing cost amount. (Reg § 1.911-5(a)(3)(ii))[23]

¶ 4607   Deduction for foreign housing expenses not provided by employer.

A qualified individual (¶4608) may deduct foreign housing expenses that are attributable to self-employment. (Code Sec. 911(c)(4)(A); Reg § 1.911-4(d)(3)) The deduction is limited to the individual's foreign earned income for the tax year which isn't otherwise excluded from gross income under either the foreign earned income (¶4605) or foreign housing costs (¶4606) exclusions. (Code Sec. 911(c)(4)(B)) Any unused housing expenses may be carried over and deducted in the next tax year, subject to that year's limits. (Code Sec. 911(c)(4)(C))[24] For the exclusion for housing costs where the taxpayer has employer provided income, see ¶4606.

¶ 4608   Qualification for the foreign earned income/housing cost exclusions.

Generally, a taxpayer qualifies for the foreign earned income (¶4605) and housing cost (¶4606) exclusions for a tax year if his "tax home" is in a foreign country *and* he is either:

. . . a U.S. citizen who can establish that he has been a bona fide resident of one or more foreign countries for an uninterrupted period which includes the entire tax year; (Code Sec. 911(d)(1)(A))[25] or

. . . a U.S. citizen or resident who, during any period of 12 consecutive months, is present

---

20. ¶O-1168
21. ¶O-1166; ¶9114.02
22. ¶O-1162; ¶9114.02

23. ¶s O-1174, O-1175
24. ¶O-1171, ¶O-1173
25. ¶O-1250 *et seq.*; ¶9114.04

in one or more foreign countries during at least 330 full days. (Code Sec. 911(d)(1)(B))[26]

An individual's "tax home" is his home for purposes of deducting away-from-home travel expenses (¶1541). He has no tax home in a foreign country for any period his abode is in the U.S. (unless the individual is serving in a designated combat zone). (Code Sec. 911(d)(3)) But the fact that an individual is temporarily present in the U.S. or maintains a U.S. dwelling (even if used by his spouse or dependents) doesn't necessarily mean his abode is in the U.S. (Reg § 1.911-2(b))[27] For married couples, qualification is determined separately. (Reg § 1.911-5(a)(1))

The residency requirements are waived for specified countries if taxpayers reasonably expected to meet the eligibility requirements for the foreign earned income and housing cost exclusions, but left the country due to adverse or dangerous conditions. (Code Sec. 911(d)(4))[28]

¶ 4609 Adjustments and disallowances made in determining tax liability.

Tax rate adjustment. A "stacking" rule limits the benefits of the earned income and housing cost exclusions by adding back the excluded amounts to taxable income solely for purposes of determining the applicable marginal tax rate. Special rules apply where the net capital gain exceeds the individual's taxable income for a tax year. (Code Sec. 911(f))[29]

Disallowance of deductions and credits allocable to excluded income. No deduction, exclusion or credit, including any credit or deduction for foreign taxes (see ¶2362 *et seq.*), is allowable to the extent the deduction, etc., is allocable to or chargeable against foreign income excluded from gross income under the foreign earned income (¶4605) or housing costs (¶4606) exclusions. (Code Sec. 911(d)(6); Reg § 1.911-6(a))[30]

¶ 4610 Exemption for certain U.S. government employees and Peace Corp volunteers abroad.

For civilian officers and U.S. government employees, gross income doesn't include certain allowances (other than amounts received as post differentials) (Code Sec. 912(1)), including cost-of-living allowances received by persons stationed outside the continental U.S. (except Alaska). (Code Sec. 912(2))[31] In addition, gross income doesn't include certain allowances to Peace Corps volunteers or volunteer leaders and family members, other than termination payments, leave allowances, allowances to members of the family of a volunteer leader who is training in the U.S., and the part of an allowance designated as basic compensation. (Code Sec. 912(3))[32]

¶ 4611 Taxation of U.S. shareholders of controlled foreign corporations (CFCs)—Form 5471.

If a foreign corporation is a CFC (¶4612) at any time during any tax year, every person who is a U.S. shareholder (¶4612) of the corporation, and who owns stock (directly or indirectly) in the corporation on the last day in that year on which the corporation is a CFC, includes in gross income for his tax year in which or with which the tax year of the corporation ends his pro rata share of:

. . . the corporation's "subpart F income" (¶4613) for that year; (Code Sec. 951(a)(1)(A))[33] and

. . . any increase during the tax year in the CFC's earnings invested in U.S. property (to

---

26. ¶O-1300 *et seq.*; ¶9114.05
27. ¶O-1202, ¶O-1203; ¶9114.03
28. ¶O-1273; ¶9114.03
29. ¶O-1101.1; ¶9114

30. ¶O-1112; ¶9114.11
31. ¶H-3133, H-3135; ¶9124.01
32. ¶H-3136; ¶9124.02
33. ¶O-2400 *et seq.*, ¶O-2470 *et seq.*; ¶9514 *et seq.*

the extent not included as subpart F income). (Code Sec. 951(a)(1)(B), Code Sec. 956)[34]

A U.S. shareholder of any CFC for any tax year of the U.S. shareholder must also include in gross income the shareholder's global intangible low-taxed income (GILTI) for the tax year, see ¶4615.

The U.S. shareholder reports theses amounts on Form 5471. [35]

Amounts included in a U.S. shareholder's gross income under the above rules (known as previously taxed income or PTI) are not included in income a second time when they are subsequently distributed. (Code Sec. 959)[36]

¶ 4612   Controlled foreign corporation (CFC) and U.S. shareholder defined.

A CFC is a foreign corporation more than 50% (25%, for certain insurance companies) of whose stock *by vote or value* is, on any day in the corporation's tax year, owned (directly, indirectly, or constructively) by U.S. shareholders. (Code Sec. 957(a), Code Sec. 957(b))

A U.S. shareholder is, with respect to any foreign corporation, a U.S. person (i.e., a U.S. citizen or resident, or a U.S. corporation, partnership, estate or trust), that owns (directly, indirectly or constructively) 10% or more of the combined voting power of all classes of stock of the corporation, or 10% or more of the total value of shares of all classes of stock of the corporation. (Code Sec. 951(b))[37]

¶ 4613   What is subpart F income?

A controlled foreign corporation's (CFC's) subpart F income consists of:

(1) Insurance income. (Code Sec. 952(a)(1), Code Sec. 953)[38]

(2) Foreign base company income (FBCI) (Code Sec. 952(a)(2), Code Sec. 954; Reg § 1.954-1), which is:

(a) Foreign personal holding company income (FPHCI), including investment income such as dividends, interest, rents, royalties and annuities; gains from certain property and commodities transactions; certain personal services income; and certain other passive type income. (Code Sec. 954(c); Reg § 1.954-2) Exceptions apply for certain income received from related parties or as part of an active business, as well as for qualified banking, financing and insurance income. In addition, look-through rules may apply. (Code Sec. 954(c))[39]

(b) Foreign base company sales and services income. (Code Sec. 954(d), Code Sec. 954(e), Code Sec. 954(g); Reg § 1.954-3, Reg § 1.954-4, Reg § 1.954-8)[40]

(3) Income attributable to operations that constitute participation in or cooperation with an unsanctioned international boycott. (Code Sec. 952(a)(3))[41]

(4) The amount of any illegal (under the U.S. Foreign Corrupt Practices Act) payment made (directly or indirectly) by or for the CFC to a government official, employee or agent. (Code Sec. 952(a)(4))[42] and

(5) Income from foreign countries with which the U.S. doesn't have diplomatic relations or that have been identified as sponsors of terrorism. (Code Sec. 952(a)(5))[43]

In any tax year where the sum of the CFC's FBCI and insurance income exceeds 70% of its gross income, *all* of the CFC's gross income is includible in its subpart F income.

34. ¶O-2760 *et seq.*; ¶9564 *et seq.*
35. ¶S-3586.1
36. ¶O-2430 *et seq.*; ¶9594 *et seq.*
37. ¶O-2302, ¶O-2303; ¶9514, 9574
38. ¶O-2500 *et seq.*; ¶9534.01

39. ¶O-2530 *et seq.*; ¶9544.02
40. ¶O-2620 *et seq.*, ¶O-2650 *et seq.*; ¶9544.03 *et seq.*
41. ¶O-2731; ¶9524.02
42. ¶O-2732; ¶9524.03
43. ¶O-2733; ¶9524.04

However, in any tax year where this sum is less than 5% of the CFC's gross income or $1 million (whichever is less), *none* of the CFC's income is FBCI or insurance income. (Code Sec. 954(b)(3); Reg § 1.954-1(b)) In addition, any item of FBCI or insurance income that is subject to an effective rate of foreign tax that is greater than 90% of the maximum U.S. corporate rate may, at the election of the CFC's controlling U.S. shareholders, be excluded from subpart F income. (Code Sec. 954(b)(4); Reg § 1.954-1(d))[44]

¶ 4614   U.S. shareholders of CFCs are taxed on global intangible low-taxed income (GILTI).

A U.S. shareholder (¶4612) of a CFC (¶4612) must include in gross income for a tax year its global intangible low-taxed income (GILTI) in a manner similar to a subpart F inclusion (see ¶4611 *et seq.*). The GILTI is then treated as subpart F income for certain purposes of the Code (such as the PTI rules, see ¶4611) but not others. (Code Sec. 951A(a), Code Sec. 951A(f)) For a limited foreign tax credit available for GILTI, see ¶2369.

GILTI is, with respect to any U.S. shareholder for the shareholder's tax year, the excess (if any) of the shareholder's net CFC tested income over the shareholder's net deemed tangible income return. (Code Sec. 951A(b)(1))

The net CFC tested income is, with respect to any U.S. shareholder, the excess of the aggregate of its pro rata share of the tested income of each CFC with respect to which it is a U.S. shareholder over the aggregate of its pro rata share of the tested loss of each CFC with respect to which it is a U.S. shareholder. (Code Sec. 951A(c)(1))

The shareholder's net deemed tangible income return is an amount equal to the excess of (i) 10% of the aggregate of the shareholder's pro rata share of the qualified business asset investment (QBAI) of each CFC with respect to which it is a U.S. shareholder; over (ii) the amount of interest expense taken into account under Code Sec. 951A(c)(2)(A)(ii) in determining the shareholder's net CFC tested income for the tax year to the extent the interest income attributable to the expense is not taken into account in determining the shareholder's net CFC tested income. (Code Sec. 951A(b)(2))

The tested income of a CFC is the excess of its gross income over the deductions (including taxes) properly allocable to gross income, but does not include effectively connected income, subpart F income, highly-taxed foreign income, foreign oil and gas extraction income, or certain related party payments. (Code Sec. 951(c)(2)(A)) A tested loss is the excess of those deductions over that gross income of the CFC. (Code Sec. 951(c)(2)(B))[45]

IRS has issued proposed regulations to implement the above rules, including reporting rules requiring the filing of Form 8992, U.S. Shareholder Calculation of Global Intangible Low-Taxed Income. (Prop Reg. § 1.951A-0 *et seq.*)

A U.S. shareholder that is a domestic corporation is taxed at an effective tax rate of 10.5% on GILTI. This effective tax rate is achieved by means of a 50% deduction on the GILTI amount (plus the attributable Code Sec. 78 gross-up) (see ¶3312). The deduction may be limited based on taxable income. (Code Sec. 250)[46]

¶ 4615   Pre-2018 deferred foreign income included in subpart F as part of transition to a participation exemption system.

In the last tax year of a deferred foreign income corporation that begins before Jan. 1, 2018 (the inclusion year), the subpart F income of the corporation is increased by the greater of the accumulated post-'86 deferred foreign income of the corporation measured as of Nov. 2, 2017, or Dec. 31, 2017. (Code Sec. 965(a)) The accumulated post-'86 deferred

---

44. ¶O-2670 *et seq.*; ¶9544.01
45. ¶O-2790 *et seq.*; ¶951A4

46. ¶O-3000 *et seq.*; ¶2504

foreign income is the post-'86 earnings and profits except for amounts that were subject to U.S. tax as income effectively connected with a U.S. trade or business or that would be treated as previously taxed income (¶4611). (Code Sec. 965(d)(2)) A deferred foreign income corporation is any specified foreign corporation with accumulated post-'86 deferred foreign income on either Nov. 2, 2017, or Dec. 31, 2017. (Code Sec. 965(d)(1)) A specified foreign corporation is any CFC (as defined pre-2018); or any foreign corporation (other than a PFIC that is not also a CFC) with respect to which one or more domestic corporations is a U.S. shareholder (the latter is treated as a CFC for purposes of taking this subpart F income into account). (Code Sec. 965(e)) A specified foreign corporation with a *deficit* in post-'86 earnings and profits on Nov. 2, 2017 is an E&P deficit foreign corporation. (Code Sec. 965(b)(3)(B))[47]

Any U.S. person who owns (directly, indirectly or constructively) 10% or more of the combined voting power of all classes of stock of a deferred foreign income corporation (hereafter a 10% U.S. shareholder) must include in gross income his pro rata share of this subpart F income, but such inclusions are netted against his pro rata share of the aggregate foreign E&P deficits attributable to his E&P deficit foreign corporations. (Code Sec. 965(b))[48]

A reduced effective rate of tax applies to the mandatory inclusion by means of a deduction in an amount that allows cash and cash equivalents to be subject to an effective rate of tax at 15.5%, and any remaining earnings to be subject to an effective rate of 8%. (Code Sec. 965(c)(1)) A 10% U.S. shareholder's aggregate foreign cash position is the higher of (1) his pro rata share of the cash position of each of his specified foreign corporations at the close of the inclusion year, or (2) the average of his pro rata share of the cash position of each of his specified foreign corporations for the last two tax years ending before Nov. 2, 2017. (Code Sec. 965(c)(3))[49] The foreign tax credit (¶2362) is disallowed for the portion of the taxes attributable to the amount deducted under this rule. (Code Sec. 965(g))[50]

A 10% U.S. shareholder of a deferred foreign income corporation may elect not to take pre-2018 accumulated deferred foreign income into account for net operating loss (NOL, ¶1815) purposes. (Code Sec. 965(n))[1]

The tax liability due to a 10% U.S. shareholder's inclusion of deferred pre-2018 foreign income is payable in installments over eight years. (Code Sec. 965(h))[2] Additional rules apply to S corporations and real estate investment trusts. (Code Sec. 965(i); Code Sec. 965(m))[3]

IRS has issued proposed regs (that would apply retroactively), further modified by Notice 2018-78, implementing, supplementing, and modifying prior guidance under Code Sec. 965. (Prop Reg. § 1.965-1 *et seq.*)[4]

¶ 4616   Gain from disposition of foreign corporation stock may be treated as a dividend.

If a U.S. person sells or exchanges stock in a foreign corporation, and that person owns (directly, indirectly, or constructively) 10% or more of the combined voting power of all classes of stock of the foreign corporation at any time during the 5-year period ending on the date of the sale when the corporation was a CFC (¶4612), then the gain recognized on the sale is included in the U.S. person's gross income as a dividend, to the extent of the foreign corporation's E&P attributable to that stock. (Code Sec. 1248(a))[5]

A sale or exchange includes a redemption of stock under Code Sec. 302(a) (¶3515 *et seq.*),

47. ¶O-2701; ¶9654.01
48. ¶O-2706 *et seq.*; ¶9654.04 *et seq.*
49. ¶O-2712; ¶9654.06
50. ¶O-2716; ¶9654.07
1. ¶O-2722; ¶9654.12

2. ¶O-2718; ¶9654.09
3. ¶O-2720 *et seq.*; ¶9654.10 *et seq.*
4. ¶O-2700 *et seq.*; ¶9654 *et seq.*
5. ¶O-2800 *et seq.*; ¶12,484 *et seq.*

a liquidation under Code Sec. 331(a) (¶3559), as well as amounts treated as gain from a sale of exchange under Code Sec. 301(c)(3). (Reg § 1.1248-1(b))[6]

Dividend treatment may also apply to certain distributions by, and dispositions of, a *domestic* corporation, e.g., where the corporation was formed or availed of principally for holding (directly or indirectly) stock of one or more foreign corporations. (Code Sec. 1248(e), Code Sec. 1248(f))[7]

Dividend treatment under this provision doesn't apply to redemptions to pay death tax under Code Sec. 303 or amounts treated as dividends, ordinary income, or short-term capital gains under other Code provisions. (Code Sec. 1248(g))[8]

If the shareholder is an individual, there is a limit on the amount of tax imposed on the dividend portion of his gain. (Code Sec. 1248(b))[9]

In addition, gain recognized by a CFC from the sale or exchange of stock in a foreign corporation is treated as a dividend to the same extent that it would have been so treated under Code Sec. 1248(a) if the CFC were a U.S. person. The foreign-source portion of dividend is treated as subpart F income of the selling CFC for which the deduction under the Code Sec. 245A DRD (¶3315) is available. [10]

¶ 4617   Sales of patents, etc., to a foreign corporation.

A U.S. person who sells (or exchanges) a patent, invention, model, or design (whether or not patented), a copyright, a secret formula or process or similar property right to a foreign corporation in which the seller owns (directly, indirectly or constructively) stock with over 50% of the combined voting power of all classes of stock must treat as *ordinary income* any gain recognized on that sale (or exchange). (Code Sec. 1249)[11]

¶ 4618   Passive foreign investment company (PFIC) defined.

A PFIC is any foreign corporation if: (1) at least 75% of its gross income for its tax year is passive, or (2) at least 50% of the assets it held during the year produce passive income or are held for the production of passive income. (Code Sec. 1297(a)) The passive assets test is generally applied based on the fair market value (FMV) of the corporation's assets, but assets are valued based on their adjusted basis where the corporation isn't publicly traded and either is a CFC or elects to use the adjusted basis instead of FMV. (Code Sec. 1297(e))[12]

How a U.S. person who is a PFIC shareholder is taxed depends on whether they have made a qualifying electing fund (QEF) election (¶4620), a mark-to-market election (¶4621), or no election (¶4619).

¶ 4619   Taxation of U.S. persons who are PFIC shareholders in the absence of an election—Form 8621.

A U.S. person who is a shareholder in a PFIC (¶4618) that has not made a qualifying electing fund (¶4620) or mark-to-market (¶4621) election can defer the U.S. tax with respect to that investment until he disposes of the PFIC stock or receives an excess distribution. At that time, the shareholder must pay U.S. tax, plus interest based on the value of the tax deferral, at ordinary income rates, and report the amounts on Form 8621. (Code Sec. 1291(a), Code Sec. 1298(f))[13]

An excess distribution is a current year distribution received by a shareholder on PFIC

---

6. ¶O-2801; ¶12,484
7. ¶O-2804 *et seq.*; ¶12,484.01 *et seq.*
8. ¶O-2803; ¶12,484.01
9. ¶O-2811; ¶12,484.04

10. ¶O-2800.2; ¶9644.05
11. ¶O-2900 *et seq.*; ¶12,494 *et seq.*
12. ¶O-2201 *et seq.*; ¶12,974
13. ¶O-2221 *et seq.*, ¶O-2258; ¶12,914.01, 12,984

stock, to the extent the distribution exceeds its ratable portion of 125% of the average amount received with respect to the stock during the three preceding years (or, if shorter, the shareholder's holding period prior to the tax year). (Code Sec. 1291(b))[14] Portions of distributions that aren't excess distributions are taxed under the normal rules for corporate distributions, see ¶1283 *et seq.*[15]

A U.S. person holding stock in a PFIC is generally not subject to the PFIC rules if the PFIC is also a CFC (¶4612) and the U.S. person is a U.S. Shareholder (¶4612). (Code Sec. 1297(d))[16]

¶ 4620 Electing qualified electing fund (QEF) treatment for passive foreign investment company (PFIC) stock—Form 8621.

A PFIC (¶4618) is treated as a QEF with respect to a particular shareholder if the shareholder so elects and the PFIC complies with the requirements for determining its ordinary earnings and net capital gain and otherwise carrying out the purposes of the election. (Code Sec. 1295)[17]

A U.S. investor in a PFIC makes the QEF election by attaching a completed Form 8621 to his or her timely filed income tax return (original or amended, by the due date (as extended) for the original return) for that year, reflecting the information provided by the PFIC in its annual information statement. (Code Sec. 1295(b)(2); Reg § 1.1295-1(e), Reg § 1.1295-1(f)(1))[18]

If the election is made, the electing shareholder is not subject to the deferred tax and interest charge (¶4619). (Code Sec. 1291(d)(1)) Instead, the electing shareholder must currently include in income his or her share of the PFIC's earnings and profits (with appropriate basis adjustments for amounts not distributed and previously taxed distributions). The fund's ordinary income and net capital gain are passed through to the shareholder as ordinary income and long-term capital gain. (Code Sec. 1293)[19] For the availability of the foreign tax credit as to QEF inclusions, see ¶2369.

If a PFIC is also a controlled foreign corporation (CFC), (¶4612), amounts includible in gross income under the CFC rules (¶4611) are not included under the QEF rules. (Code Sec. 951(c))[20]

¶ 4621 Electing mark-to-market treatment for passive foreign investment company (PFIC) stock—Form 8621.

A U.S. person who is a shareholder in a PFIC may make a mark-to-market election with respect to marketable (i.e., regularly traded) PFIC stock and avoid the otherwise applicable PFIC rules (¶4619). (Code Sec. 1296, Code Sec. 1291(d))[21] The election is made by filing Form 8621 with the return. (Reg § 1.1296-1(b), Reg § 1.1296-1(h)(1))[22]

A shareholder of a PFIC that makes a mark-to-market election with respect to marketable PFIC stock must report as ordinary income each year the amount by which the fair market value (FMV) of the PFIC stock at the close of the tax year exceeds the shareholder's adjusted basis in the stock. If the stock's basis exceeds the FMV at the end of the year, the shareholder has an ordinary loss deduction to the extent of the lesser of the amount of that excess, or the unreversed inclusions with respect to the PFIC stock. (Code Sec. 1296(a), Code Sec. 1296(c)) The amount of unreversed inclusions equals the sum of all income inclusions in past years, reduced by any deductions allowed in past years. (Code

---

14. ¶O-2227; ¶12,914.01
15. ¶O-2225
16. ¶O-2250; ¶12,974
17. ¶O-2260 *et seq.*; ¶12,954
18. ¶O-2270; ¶12,954, 12,954.01

19. ¶O-2261 *et seq.*; ¶12,934, ¶12,954
20. ¶O-2266; ¶9514.03
21. ¶O-2290 *et seq.*; ¶12,964
22. ¶O-2297; ¶12,964

Sec. 1296(d)) Any gain or loss on the actual sale or disposition of the PFIC stock is treated as ordinary income or loss. (Code Sec. 1296(c))[23]

¶ 4622 U.S. beneficiaries of foreign trusts—Form 3520, Form 4970.

A U.S. beneficiary is taxed on a foreign trust's foreign and U.S. source income at the time it becomes distributable. (Code Sec. 652; Code Sec. 662)[24] Distributions are reported on Form 3520. Distributions to the U.S. beneficiary of accumulated trust income are subject to special trust throwback rules (¶3952 *et seq.*)[25] and a nondeductible interest charge. (Code Sec. 668) The beneficiary uses Form 4970 to compute the tax on accumulation distributions.[26]

¶ 4623 Recognition of gain on transfers to foreign estates or foreign non-grantor trusts.

Gain is recognized upon a transfer of appreciated property by a U.S. person to a foreign estate or trust to the extent its fair market value (FMV) exceeds its basis in the hands of the transferor. (Code Sec. 684) Similarly, if a domestic trust becomes a foreign trust, the trust is treated as having transferred, immediately before becoming a foreign trust, all of its assets to a foreign trust, and must recognize gain on any appreciated assets transferred. (Reg § 1.684-4)

Gain is not recognized on transfers of property by a U.S. person:

. . . to foreign grantor trusts,

. . . to exempt charitable trusts,

. . . by reason of death of the U.S. transferor,

. . . to unrelated foreign trusts for FMV, under Code Sec. 1032, and

. . . with respect to certain distributions to a trust on an interest held by the trust in certain investment trusts, liquidating trusts, or environmental remediation trusts (Reg § 1.684-3)[27]

For gain recognition on transfers to a foreign corporation, see ¶3568. For gain recognition on transfers to foreign partnerships, see ¶3708.

¶ 4624 Tax sanctions for international boycott activities— Form 5713.

If a taxpayer participates in or cooperates with an unsanctioned international boycott or has operations in or related to a country carrying out such a boycott, he is denied certain tax benefits, including the foreign tax credit (¶2362), reduced deferral under IC-DISC rules (¶4604) and income deferral under subpart F (¶4613). Taxpayers that have operations in a country on the IRS's boycott list or in a country that requires participation or cooperation with an international boycott, namely, Iraq, Kuwait, Lebanon, Libya, Qatar, Saudi Arabia, Syria, United Arab Emirates, and Yemen, must make a report to IRS on Form 5713. (Code Sec. 908(a), Code Sec. 952(a)(3), Code Sec. 995(b)(1)(F)(ii), Code Sec. 999)[28]

¶ 4625 Taxation of Nonresident Aliens and Foreign Corporations.

A nonresident alien or foreign corporation (below) is generally only taxed on (i) investment income from U.S. sources (at a 30% or lower treaty rate), and (ii) if engaged in a U.S. trade or business, net income effectively connected with that business (ECI) (at regular U.S. rates). Tax on ECI may be eliminated or reduced

23. ¶O-2290 *et seq.*; ¶12,964
24. ¶C-3021
25. ¶C-4003; ¶s 6664, 6684
26. ¶C-4107 *et seq.*; ¶6684
27. ¶C-1020 *et seq.*; ¶6844
28. ¶O-3500 *et seq.*; ¶9994 *et seq.*

under a treaty, which usually conditions U.S. taxation on the presence of a permanent establishment (or sometimes, a fixed base). Income from U.S. real estate investments may be taxed as ECI (¶4636 *et seq.*). A foreign taxpayer also may be subject to the accumulated earnings tax (¶3317 *et seq.*), a branch profits tax (¶4634), and/or a transportation tax (¶4638). A nonresident alien may exclude from income compensation received for services as an employee of a foreign government or international organization if certain conditions are met (Code Sec. 893)[29]

A *nonresident alien individual* is an individual who isn't a U.S. citizen or resident (¶4601, ¶4602). (Code Sec. 7701(b)(1)(B))[30]

A *foreign corporation* is one that's created or organized outside the U.S. or under any law other than that of the U.S., a state, or the District of Columbia. (Code Sec. 7701(a)(5))[31]

Corporations organized in a possession are not treated as foreign corporations under certain circumstances and for certain purposes. (Code Sec. 881(b); Reg § 1.881-5)[32]

¶ 4626   Tax treaties—Form 8833.

The U.S. has income tax treaties with a number of foreign countries under which residents or citizens of those countries are taxed at a reduced rate or are exempt from U.S. income tax on certain U.S. source income. (Code Sec. 894)[33] With limited exceptions, a taxpayer who takes a return position that a treaty overrules or otherwise modifies, and reduces any U.S. tax incurred at any time, must disclose that return position on Form 8833 attached to the return. (Code Sec. 6114(a); Reg § 301.6114-1)[34]

¶ 4627   Determining whether income is U.S. or foreign source.

Specific rules are used to determine the source of the following types of income:

Compensation generally is sourced where the services were performed, except in the case of nonresident aliens temporarily present in the U.S. (Code Sec. 861(a)(3), Code Sec. 862(a)(3); Reg § 1.861-4)[35]

Rents and royalties are sourced where the leased or licensed property is located or used. (Code Sec. 861(a)(4), Code Sec. 862(a)(4))[36]

Income from the sale of intangible property, when payment is contingent on the use or productivity of the property, is sourced as royalty income (i.e., sourced at the place of use). (Code Sec. 865(d))[37]

Proceeds from the sale of personal property generally are sourced where the seller resides. (Code Sec. 865(a))[38]

Proceeds from the sale of inventory, generally are sourced on the basis of place of sale for purchased inventory, and on the basis of production activities for produced inventory. (Code Sec. 863(b), Code Sec. 865(b))[39]

Proceeds from sales of real property are sourced at the location of the property. (Code Sec. 861(a)(5), Code Sec. 862(a)(5))[40]

Dividends generally are sourced where the corporation is incorporated. However, dividends received from a foreign corporation are treated in part as from U.S. sources if 25% or more of the corporation's gross income was effectively connected with the conduct of a U.S.

29. ¶O-10100 *et seq.*, O-10300 *et seq.*, O-11829; ¶8714 *et seq.*, 8814 *et seq.*, 8934
30. ¶O-1086; ¶8714
31. ¶O-10360; ¶8814.01
32. ¶O-10361; ¶s 8814.01, 8814.02
33. ¶O-15000 *et seq.*; ¶8944
34. ¶O-15010 *et seq.*; ¶61,144

35. ¶O-10931.1, O-10934; ¶8614.15 *et seq.*
36. ¶O-10936; ¶8614.22
37. ¶O-10954; ¶8614.22
38. ¶O-10948; ¶8654 *et seq.*
39. ¶O-10957 *et seq.*; ¶8634.02
40. ¶O-10945, O-10946; ¶8614.24

business for the 3-year period (or shorter period of its existence) ending with the close of its tax year preceding the declaration of the dividends. (Code Sec. 861(a)(2), Code Sec. 862(a)(2))[41]

Dividend equivalents determined by reference to the payment of a U.S. source dividend are treated as U.S.-source dividends. (Code Sec. 871(m))[42]

Interest generally is sourced where the debtor is located. (Code Sec. 861(a)(1), Code Sec. 862(a)(1))[43]

Amounts received for the provision of a guarantee are from U.S. sources if paid by: (1) a noncorporate U.S. resident or a U.S. corporation for the provision of a guarantee of the resident or corporation; or (2) any foreign person for the provision of a guarantee if the payment is connected with income that is effectively connected, or treated as effectively connected, with the conduct of a U.S. trade or business. (Code Sec. 861(a)(9))[44]

Insurance income from insuring U.S. risks is U.S.-source. (Code Sec. 861(a)(7))[45]

International communications income derived by a U.S. person from the transmission of communications or data between the U.S. and a foreign country or U.S. possession is half foreign-source and half U.S.-source. A foreign person's international communications income is foreign-source, except where it is attributable to an office or fixed place of business in the U.S. (Code Sec. 863(e)(1))[46]

Space and ocean activity income of a U.S. person is U.S.-source (while that of a foreign person is foreign-source). (Code Sec. 863(d)(1))[47]

Transportation income derived from the use and performance of services directly related to the use of a vessel or aircraft from transportation that either begins or ends in the U.S. is half foreign-source and half U.S.-source. (Code Sec. 863(c))[48]

¶ 4628 Allocating deductions between U.S.- and foreign-source income.

Generally, in determining U.S.-source and foreign-source income, the taxpayer must allocate all deductions to particular classes of gross income and then apportion those deductions among various groups within the class. A deduction that isn't definitely related to any gross income (e.g., charitable contributions) must be apportioned ratably based on gross income. (Reg § 1.861-8(a)(2))[49]

However, allocations and apportionments of interest expense must be determined using the adjusted bases of the assets rather than gross income. (Code Sec. 864(e)(2)),Reg § 1.861-9T)[50]

¶ 4629 U.S.-source income not effectively connected with a U.S. business taxed at 30% rate.

Nonresident aliens and foreign corporations are taxed at a flat 30% (or lower treaty rate) on the following types of U.S.-source income that is not "effectively connected" with a U.S. business:

... subject to exceptions discussed below, interest (other than original issue discount, or OID), dividends, rents, salaries, wages, premiums, annuities, compensations, remunerations, emoluments and other fixed or determinable annual or periodical gains, profits and income. (Code Sec. 871(a)(1)(A), Code Sec. 881(a)(1))

... gain on the disposition of certain timber, coal, and iron ore mined in the U.S. (Code

41. ¶O-10926, ¶O-10928; ¶8614.09 *et seq.*
42. ¶O-10930.1; ¶8714.02
43. ¶O-10906 *et seq.*; ¶8614.01
44. ¶O-10923; ¶8614.14
45. ¶O-10985; ¶8614.27

46. ¶O-10984; ¶8634.045
47. ¶O-10976; ¶8634.04
48. ¶O-10941; ¶8634.03
49. ¶O-11000 *et seq.*; ¶8614.29
50. ¶O-11108 *et seq.*; ¶8614.29

Sec. 871(a)(1)(B), Code Sec. 881(a)(2))

. . . payments on OID obligations, and gain on the sale of certain OID obligations (¶1310 *et seq.*). (Code Sec. 871(a)(1)(C), Code Sec. 881(a)(3))

. . . gain from the disposition of patents, copyrights, goodwill, etc. to the extent the gain is from payments contingent on the productivity, use, or disposition of that property (Code Sec. 871(a)(1)(D), Code Sec. 881(a)(4))

. . . amounts included in income from holding a residual interest in a real estate mortgage investment conduit (REMIC). (Code Sec. 860G(b)(1), Reg § 1.860G-3)[1]

. . . certain U.S. source capital gain if the nonresident alien is in the U.S. for at least 183 days during the tax year. (Code Sec. 871(a)(2))

. . . 85% of any social security benefits received. (Code Sec. 871(a)(3))[2]

The following types of income are exempt from the 30% tax otherwise applicable under the rules above:

. . . certain dividends including (i) dividends paid by a foreign corporation with less than 25% effectively connected income that is treated as U.S. source income under Code Sec. 861(a)(2)(B), (Code Sec. 871(i)(2)(D)) (ii) dividends paid by an existing 80/20 company, (Code Sec. 871(i)(2)(B)(i)) and (iii) interest-related dividends and short-term capital gains dividends from a regulated investment company (RIC). (Code Sec. 871(k), Code Sec. 881(e))[3]

. . . certain interest including (i) portfolio interest, (Code Sec. 871(h), Code Sec. 881(c)) (ii) interest earned on bank account deposits, (Code Sec. 871(i)(2)(A)) and (iii) interest paid by an existing 80/20 company. (Code Sec. 871(i)(2)(B)(ii)[4]

. . . certain gambling winnings. (Code Sec. 871(j))[5]

For the withholding regime that applies to non-effectively connected income, see ¶4649 *et seq.*

¶ 4630 Election to treat real property income as income connected with a U.S. business.

A nonresident alien individual or foreign corporation may elect to treat certain income from U.S. real property held for investment as effectively connected with the conduct of a U.S. business (¶4631). (Code Sec. 871(d), Code Sec. 882(d)) The electing foreign taxpayer is then taxed at regular U.S. rates (not 30%) on net rather than gross income, and may take depreciation deductions, etc.[6] The election is made on a statement attached to the income tax return for the election year. (Reg § 1.871-10(d)(1)(ii))[7]

¶ 4631 Income "effectively connected" with a U.S. business (ECI).

A foreign corporation or nonresident alien engaged in a U.S. business (¶4632) at any time in the tax year is taxed at regular U.S. rates on ECI, i.e., gross income effectively connected with the U.S. business, less allowable deductions (¶4633). (Code Sec. 871(b), Code Sec. 882(a))[8] U.S. source investment income (generally Code Sec. 871(a) income and U.S. source capital gains) is effectively connected to a U.S. trade or business only if the activities of the U.S. trade or business were a material factor in the realization of that income, or the income, gain, or loss is derived from assets used in or held for use in the conduct of a U.S. trade or business. Other U.S. source income is generally treated as ECI.

---

1. ¶O-10102
2. ¶O-10201 *et seq.*; ¶s 8714.02, 8814.02
3. ¶O-10228 *et seq.*; ¶8714.05 *et seq.*
4. ¶O-10204, O-10220, O-10405, O-10912.1; ¶8714.05, 8814.02

5. ¶O-10240; ¶8714.06
6. ¶O-10615; ¶8714.04, 8824
7. ¶O-10619
8. ¶O-10500 *et seq.*, O-10600 *et seq.*; ¶8644.02 *et seq.*, 8714.03

(Code Sec. 864(c)(2), Code Sec. 864(c)(3))[9]

Foreign-source income treated as effectively connected to a U.S. trade or business is limited to the items below and only to the extent the item is attributable to an office or other fixed place of business in the U.S.:

... Rents or royalties from intangible property derived from an active licensing business.

... Dividends, interest, or guarantee fees derived from an active banking, financing or trading business.

... Certain inventory sales attributable to a U.S. sales office.

... Income or gain that is equivalent to the above items.

... Foreign source income of a foreign insurance company attributable to its U.S. business. (Code Sec. 864(c)(4))[10]

Notwithstanding any other tax rules, if a nonresident alien individual or foreign corporation owns, directly or indirectly, an interest in a partnership that is engaged in any trade or business in the U.S., gain or loss on the sale or exchange of all (or any portion of) the interest is treated as effectively connected with the conduct of the trade or business to the extent it does not exceed the selling partner's distributive share of partnership gain or loss that would have been effectively connected with the trade or business had the partnership sold all of its assets in a taxable transaction. (Code Sec. 864(c)(8))[11]

¶ 4632 What is "engaging in a U.S. business"?

A foreign corporation is engaged in a U.S. trade or business if it carries on continuous and regular business activities in the U.S. [12]

The *performance of personal services* in the U.S. constitutes engaging in a U.S. trade or business unless the performer of services is a nonresident alien individual (i) whose compensation for those services is $3,000 or less, (ii) who is in the U.S. for 90 days or less, and (iii) who works either for a foreign person not engaged in business in the U.S., or for a foreign office of a U.S. person. (Code Sec. 864(b)(1))[13]

The *trading of securities* through a resident broker, commission agent, custodian, or other independent agent doesn't constitute engaging in a trade or business as long as the taxpayer doesn't have a U.S. office through which the trading transactions are effected. The trading of securities and commodities for one's own account isn't engaging in a U.S. trade or business, however effected. These two exceptions apply to certain commodity trading as well. (Code Sec. 864(b)(2))[14]

If a *partnership, estate or trust* is engaged in a U.S. business, the entity's foreign partners or beneficiaries are considered so engaged. (Code Sec. 875)[15]

Alien students and exchange visitors may be treated as engaging in the U.S. trade or business, and may be subject to tax on their scholarship or fellowship grants. (Code Sec. 871(c))[16]

¶ 4633 Deductions and credits of foreign corporations and nonresident aliens engaged in a U.S. trade or business.

A nonresident alien individual and a foreign corporation are allowed deductions only against income effectively connected with the conduct of a U.S. trade or business (¶4631) and only for expenses connected with that income. (Code Sec. 873(a), Code

---

9. ¶O-10604 *et seq.*; ¶8644.03
10. ¶O-10622; ¶8644.04
11. ¶O-10610
12. ¶O-10500 *et seq.*

13. ¶O-10502; ¶8644.01
14. ¶O-10510 *et seq.*; ¶8644.01
15. ¶O-10504, O-10505; ¶8754
16. ¶O-10503; ¶8714.03

Sec. 882(c)(1)(A); Reg § 1.882-5)[17] A deduction for charitable contributions, however, is allowed whether or not connected with a U.S. business. In addition, individual nonresident aliens are allowed a deduction for nonbusiness casualty and theft losses. (Code Sec. 873(b), Code Sec. 882(c)(1)(B))[18]

A nonresident alien individual or foreign corporation engaged in a U.S. trade or business is entitled to the foreign tax credit for taxes imposed by foreign countries other than the taxpayer's home country, as well as other credits beyond those available to other foreign taxpayers. (Code Sec. 882(c)(3), Code Sec. 906; Reg § 1.871-8)[19] Generally, a true and accurate return (¶4642 *et seq.*) must be filed in order to get the benefit of an otherwise allowable deduction or credit. (Code Sec. 874(a), Code Sec. 882(c)(2))[20]

¶ 4634   Branch profits tax on foreign corporations—Form 8848.

A foreign corporation engaged in a U.S. trade or business through a branch office is liable for a branch profits tax (in addition to regular income tax on ECI) equal to 30% of the tax year's dividend equivalent amount. (Code Sec. 884(a)) The dividend equivalent amount is the corporation's effectively connected earnings and profits (E&P), *reduced* (not below zero) by any increase for the year in its U.S. net equity (i.e., amounts reinvested in the U.S. business), and *increased* (within limits) by any decrease for the year in its U.S. net equity. (Code Sec. 884(b))[21]

If a foreign corporation is subject to the branch profits tax for any tax year (whether any branch profits tax is actually due), the 30% tax on U.S. source non-ECI (¶4629) and the related withholding (¶4648 *et seq.*) do not apply to any dividends it pays out of its E&P for that year. (Code Sec. 884(e)(3))[22]

The branch profits tax isn't imposed on a foreign corporation for the year it completely terminates its U.S. trade or business, except where there is a Code Sec. 381(a) corporate liquidation or reorganization, or a Code Sec. 351 incorporation. In order to completely terminate, a corporation must waive the statute of limitations for the year on Form 8848 attached to the income tax return. (Reg § 1.884-2T(a), Reg § 1.884-2T(c), Reg § 1.884-2)[23]

The branch profits tax may be reduced or eliminated by an income tax treaty if the taxpayer is a qualified resident of the treaty country. (Code Sec. 884(e))[24]

¶ 4635   Branch-level interest tax.

If a foreign corporation is engaged in a U.S. trade or business or has gross income treated as ECI (¶4631), interest paid by the corporation's U.S. trade or business (i.e., its U.S. branch) is treated as if it were paid by a U.S. corporation. (Code Sec. 884(f)(1)(A)) In addition, if the interest allocable to the branch exceeds the interest actually paid by the branch, the difference is treated as interest paid by a U.S. subsidiary to its foreign parent and the foreign parent is subject to the 30% tax on that amount. (Code Sec. 884(f)(1)(B)) The branch-level interest tax may be reduced or eliminated by treaty. (Code Sec. 884(f)(3))[25]

¶ 4636   The Foreign Investment in Real Property Tax Act (FIRPTA).

Under FIRPTA, gain or loss of a nonresident alien or foreign corporation from the disposition of a U.S. Real Property Interest (USRPI) is treated as effectively connected with a U.S. trade or business (Code Sec. 897(a)(1)) and is subject to tax and related

17. ¶O-10641, O-10648, O-10649; ¶8734, 8824, 8824.01
18. ¶O-10641, O-10648; ¶8734, 8824
19. ¶O-4102, O-10643, O-10675; ¶9064.01
20. ¶O-10644, O-10676; ¶8824
21. ¶O-11300 *et seq.*; ¶8844

22. ¶O-11315; ¶8844
23. ¶O-11316 *et seq.*; ¶8844
24. ¶O-11314, O-11334 *et seq.*; ¶8844
25. ¶O-11326 *et seq.*; ¶8844

reporting as well as withholding requirements (see ¶4647 and ¶4660) under the FIRPTA rules.[26]

A USRPI includes: (1) an interest in real property located in the U.S. or the Virgin Islands, and (2) any interest (other than solely as a creditor) in any U.S. corporation unless the corporation is shown *not* to have been a U.S. real property holding corporation (USRPHC) during the 5-year period ending on the date of disposition (or, if shorter, the period held by the taxpayer). (Code Sec. 897(c)(1)(A))[27]

A USRPI does *not* include an interest in a domestically controlled real estate investment trust (REIT) or regulated investment company (RIC). (Code Sec. 897(h)(2))[28] Special rules apply to foreign taxpayers that receive distributions from RICs and REITs. (Code Sec. 897(h))[29]

Foreign taxpayers that hold USRPIs indirectly through an interest in a corporation, partnership, estate or trust are subject to U.S. tax on any gain attributable to the entity's USRPIs upon the disposition of their interest in the entity. (Code Sec. 897(g))[30]

¶ 4637   Election to be treated as a U.S. corporation for FIRPTA purposes.

A foreign corporation may elect to be treated as a U.S. corporation on the disposition of a U.S. real property interest (USRPI) (¶4636) for purposes of the FIRPTA rules, including reporting and withholding (¶4647 and ¶4660), if the corporation: (i) is entitled to nondiscriminatory treatment under an income tax treaty, (ii) qualifies as a U.S. real property holding corporation under Reg § 1.897-2(b)(1), (iii) holds a USRPI at the time of the election; and (iv) makes a timely and proper election. (Code Sec. 897(i); Reg § 1.897-3(b), Reg § 1.897-8T(b))[31]

¶ 4638   4% tax on transportation income.

A 4% tax is imposed on the U.S.-source gross transportation income of foreign corporations and nonresident aliens. (Code Sec. 887) Income subject to this 4% gross-basis tax isn't subject to the 30% tax on non-effectively connected income (¶4629) or the regular U.S. tax on effectively connected income (¶4631). (Code Sec. 887(c))[32]

¶ 4639   Excise tax on foreign procurement payments.

A 2% excise tax applies to specified Federal procurement payments to foreign persons, i.e., payments made under a contract with the U.S. for the provision of goods manufactured or produced, or services provided, in any country which is not a party to an international procurement agreement with the U.S. The excise tax is enforced by withholding. (Code Sec. 5000C)[33] Certain foreign vendors (e.g., vendors protected under a nondiscrimination clause of a treaty) and certain transactions (e.g., small purchases under $150,000) are exempt. (Reg § 1.5000C-1, Reg § 1.5000C-2, and Reg § 1.5000C-3)[34]

¶ 4640   Giving up U.S. citizenship or terminating long-term residency— Form 8854.

A covered expatriate (defined below) is subject to a mark-to-market rule under which his property is generally treated as sold on the day before the expatriation date for fair market value (FMV). (Code Sec. 877A)[35]

The gain from the deemed sale is taken into account at that time without regard to other

26. ¶O-10700 *et seq.*; ¶8974 *et seq.*
27. ¶O-10735 *et seq.*; ¶8974
28. ¶O-10753; ¶8974
29. ¶O-10734 *et seq.*; ¶8974.02
30. ¶O-10733; ¶8974

31. ¶O-10810 *et seq.*; ¶8974.01
32. ¶O-11500 *et seq.*; ¶8874
33. ¶O-13351 *et seq.*; ¶50,00C4 *et seq.*
34. ¶O-13352 *et seq.*; ¶50,00C4.01
35. ¶O-11650 *et seq.*; ¶877A4

Code provisions, and any loss generally is taken into account to the extent otherwise provided in the Code, except that the wash sale rules of Code Sec. 1091 don't apply. (Code Sec. 877A(a)(2)) However, any net gain on the deemed sale is taxed only to the extent it exceeds an inflation adjusted amount that is $711,000 for 2018 ($725,000 in 2019, as calculated by Thomson Reuters using inflation data). (Code Sec. 877A(a)(3)) Subsequent gains or losses that are realized are adjusted for the gains and losses taken into account under the deemed sale rules without regard to this exemption. (Code Sec. 877A(a)(2))[36]

The mark-to-market deemed sale rule does not apply to deferred compensation items, interests in nongrantor trusts, and specified tax deferred accounts. (Code Sec. 877A(c))[37]

Covered expatriates are U.S. citizens who relinquish citizenship and long-term residents who terminate U.S. residency, if they meet any of the following tests:

(1) the individual's average annual net income tax for the period of five tax years ending before the date of the loss of U.S. citizenship was greater than an inflation adjusted amount that is $165,000 for losses of citizenship in 2018 ($168,000 in 2019, as calculated by Thomson Reuters using inflation data) (the "average annual net income tax" test);

(2) the individual's net worth as of that date was $2 million or more (the "net worth" test); or

(3) the individual: (i) fails to certify under penalty of perjury that he has met the requirements of the Code for the five preceding tax years, or (ii) fails to submit evidence of his compliance as IRS may require. The certification is made on Form 8854. (Code Sec. 877(a)(2), Code Sec. 877A(g)(1)(A))

However, an individual will not be treated as a covered expatriate under the average annual net income tax or net worth tests if he: (1) became at birth a citizen of the U.S. and a citizen of another country and, as of the expatriation date, continues to be a citizen of, and is taxed as a resident of, the other country, and has been a U.S. resident (under the substantial presence test) for not more than 10 tax years during the 15 tax-year period ending with the tax year in which the expatriation date occurs; or (2) gives up his U.S. citizenship before becoming 18½ years old and was a U.S. resident for not more than 10 tax years before the relinquishment date. (Code Sec. 877A(g)(1)(B))[38]

Election to defer tax on expatriation. An individual may irrevocably elect, on a property-by-property basis, to defer payment of the mark-to-market tax imposed on the deemed sale of property. Interest is charged for the period the tax is deferred. The deferred tax generally is due when the return is due for the tax year in which the property is disposed of. (Code Sec. 877A(b))[39]

¶ 4641   Corporate and partnership inversions.

If (i) a foreign corporation (surrogate foreign corporation) directly or indirectly acquires substantially all of the properties held by a domestic corporation or substantially all of the properties constituting a trade or business of a domestic partnership (each an expatriated entity), and (ii) the expanded affiliated group (EAG) that includes the surrogate foreign corporation doesn't have substantial business activities in the country in which the surrogate foreign corporation was created or organized, then, after the transaction, if the former owners of the expatriated entity own:

...80% or more of the interests in the surrogate foreign corporation, the surrogate foreign corporation is taxed as a domestic entity.

...60% or more of the interests the surrogate foreign corporation, the expatriated entity's inversion gain (defined below) is taxed at the maximum corporate rate. (Code

---

36. ¶O-11651.1, ¶O-11652; ¶877A4   38. ¶O-11659; ¶877A4
37. ¶O-11654; ¶877A4   39. ¶O-11653; ¶877A4

Sec. 7874)[40]

Inversion gain is any income or gain recognized by reason of the expatriated entity's transfer during a 10-year period after the inversion of stock or other properties, and any income received or accrued during that period by reason of a license of any property by an expatriated entity as part of the inversion or after the inversion, if the transfer or license is to a foreign related person. Inversion gain cannot be offset by a net operating loss or the foreign tax credit. (Code Sec. 7874(d)(2), Code Sec. 7874(e))[41]

An EAG has *substantial business activities* in the foreign country only if at least 25% of the group employees and their compensation are based, the value of the group's total assets are located, and the group's income is derived, in the relevant country. However, an EAG cannot have substantial business activities in the foreign country unless the foreign acquiring corporation is liable to tax as a resident of the foreign country. (Reg § 1.7874-3)[42]

Special rules address transactions that are structured to avoid the purposes of the inversion rules. Thus, in determining stock ownership, disqualified stock (Reg § 1.7874-4), certain transferred stock (Reg § 1.7874-5 and Reg § 1.7874-6), stock attributable to passive assets (Reg § 1.7874-7), stock attributable to multiple domestic entity acquisitions (Reg § 1.7874-8), certain third-country transactions (Reg § 1.7874-10) and non-ordinary course distributions (Reg § 1.7874-10) are disregarded. [43]

¶ 4642   Returns Relating to Foreign Taxpayers.

U.S. income tax returns must be filed by nonresident alien individuals (¶4643) and foreign corporations engaged in a U.S. business (¶4645). An income tax return is also required for a partnership with gross income from U.S. sources or that is effectively connected with the conduct of a U.S. trade or business (¶4646). Information returns are required for certain foreign transactions (¶4647).

¶ 4643   Return of nonresident alien individual—Forms 1040NR and 1040NR-EZ.

A nonresident alien individual must file a U.S. tax return (Form 1040NR, or, for certain nonresident aliens with no dependents, Form 1040NR-EZ) for any tax year he was engaged in business in the U.S. (¶4632) or deemed to be so engaged, even where he has no income effectively connected to the business (¶4631), no other U.S.-source income, or his income is tax-exempt (by treaty or otherwise). (Reg § 1.6012-1(b)(1)) However, if the individual is at no time during the year engaged in a U.S. trade or business, he is not required to file a return if his tax liability is fully satisfied by withholding. (Reg § 1.6012-1(b)(2))[44] In general, the individual won't get the benefit of otherwise allowable deductions and credits if he does not file a true and accurate return. (Code Sec. 874(a); Reg § 1.874-1(a))[45]

Form 1040NR and Form 1040NR-EZ are due by the 15th day of the sixth month (i.e., June 15), or fourth month (April 15) if the alien had wages subject to wage withholding, after the close of the tax year. (Reg § 1.6072-1(c))[46]

¶ 4644   Departing alien–certificate of compliance— Forms 1040C, 2063.

An alien (resident or nonresident) cannot leave the U.S. without obtaining a certificate of compliance with income tax law (sailing or departure permit), except most tourists, students, trainees, and foreign government personnel and their family members aren't required to get a certificate of compliance. (Code Sec. 6851(d)(1), Reg § 1.6851-2(a)(2)) The alien files either Form 1040C (if he has income subject to U.S. tax) or Form 2063 (if he has

---

40. ¶F-5700 *et seq.*; ¶78,744 *et seq.*
41. ¶F-5724, F-5725; ¶78,744.03
42. ¶F-5706; ¶78,744.01
43. ¶F-5711 *et seq.*; ¶78,744.04 *et seq.*

44. ¶S-1750 *et seq.*; ¶60,124.02
45. ¶O-10644; ¶8744
46. ¶S-4703; ¶60,724

no such income) in order to receive the certificate. (Reg § 1.6851-2(b))[47]

¶ 4645   Return of foreign corporation—Form 1120F.

A foreign corporation must file a U.S. income tax return (Form 1120F) if it was engaged in business in the U.S. (¶4632) during the tax year (or deemed to be so engaged), even if (i) the corporation has no income effectively connected to such business (¶4631) or other U.S.-source income, or (ii) its income is tax-exempt (by treaty or otherwise). However, if the foreign corporation has no gross income for the tax year, it is not required to complete the return schedules. (Reg § 1.6012-2(g))[48] In general, the foreign corporation won't get the benefit of otherwise allowable deductions and credits if it does not file a true and accurate return. (Code Sec. 882(c)(2))[49]

Foreign corporations that have no U.S. office or place of business must file their return by the 15th day of June following the close of the tax year (in the case of a fiscal year-based return, on or before the 15th day of the sixth month following the end of the fiscal year). (Code Sec. 6072(c))[50]

¶ 4646   Return of foreign partnership—Form 1065.

A foreign partnership isn't required to file a partnership return (Form 1065), unless it has gross income that is (or is treated as) effectively connected with the conduct of a trade or business within the U.S. (ECI) or has gross income from sources within the U.S. (U.S.-source income). (Code Sec. 6031(e)) A foreign partnership, other than a withholding foreign partnership, that has $20,000 or less of U.S.-source income and has no ECI during its tax year need not file a partnership return if, at no time during the partnership tax year, 1% or more of any item of partnership income, gain, loss, deduction, or credit is allocable in the aggregate to direct U.S. partners. The U.S. partners must directly report their shares of the allocable items of partnership income, gain, loss, deduction, and credit. (Reg § 1.6031(a)-1(b)(2))

A foreign partnership (other than a withholding foreign partnership) for which one or more withholding agents file the required Form 1042 and Form 1042-S and pay the associated withholding tax, and that has U.S.-source income but no ECI and no U.S. partners, is not required to file a partnership return. If the partnership does have U.S. partners, it must file a partnership return, but it need only file Schedules K-1 for its direct U.S. partners and for its pass-through partners through which U.S. partners hold an interest in the foreign partnership. (Reg § 1.6031(a)-1(b)(3))[1]

¶ 4647   Information returns—Forms 926, 5471, 5472, 8865, 8938, 8975.

A U.S. person who controls a foreign corporation for at least 30 consecutive days in his or her tax year must furnish IRS with certain information concerning the foreign corporation on Form 5471. (Code Sec. 6038; Reg § 1.6038-2(a)) Control means more than 50% ownership (by vote or value) of the corporation's stock. (Code Sec. 6038(e)(2))[2] Similarly, a U.S. partner that controls a foreign partnership must also furnish IRS with information on Form 8865. (Code Sec. 6038; Reg § 1.6038-3(a)(1)) A person controls a partnership if the person owns, directly or indirectly, more than a 50% interest in the partnership. (Code Sec. 6038(e)(3))[3]

The organization or reorganization of, or acquisition of stock in, a foreign corporation must be reported on Form 5471 by certain U.S. shareholders, officers and directors. (Code Sec. 6046)[4] The acquisition, disposition or substantial change in size of an interest in a

47. ¶S-1760 *et seq.*; ¶68,514.04
48. ¶S-1910 *et seq.*; ¶60,124.03
49. ¶O-10676; ¶8824
50. ¶S-4704; ¶60,724

1. ¶S-2717.1 *et seq.*; ¶60,314.01
2. ¶S-3586 *et seq.*; ¶60,384
3. ¶S-3585 *et seq.*; ¶60,384
4. ¶S-3602 *et seq.*; ¶60,464

foreign partnership must be reported on Form 8865 by a U.S. person if he or she holds a 10% or greater interest in the partnership either before or after the acquisition/disposition or if the change in size of the interest is at least 10%. (Code Sec. 6046A)[5]

A U.S. corporation at least 25% of which is owned by one foreign person, or a foreign corporation engaged in a U.S. trade or business must maintain records and furnish IRS with certain information on Form 5472 regarding transactions with related parties during the tax year. A U.S. disregarded entity wholly owned by a foreign person is treated as a U.S. corporation separate from its owner for these purposes. (Code Sec. 6038A(a), Code Sec. 6038C; Reg § 1.6038A-1(c)(1), Reg § 1.6038A-2(a)(1) *et seq.*)[6]

Each U.S. person (i) transferring property to a foreign corporation (or a partnership under certain conditions) in specified tax-free exchanges, or (ii) distributing property in complete liquidation to a non-U.S. person, must report the transfer to IRS on Form 926 for corporations, Form 8865 for partnerships. (Code Sec. 6038B)[7]

Any individual who, during the tax year, holds any interest in a specified foreign financial asset as defined in Reg § 1.6038D-3, must attach to his or her income tax return for that tax year required information on Form 8938 for each specified foreign financial asset if the aggregate value of all the individual's specified foreign financial assets exceeds $50,000 (higher thresholds apply in certain cases under the regs). These same rules apply to any domestic entity formed or availed of for purposes of holding specified foreign financial assets. (Code Sec. 6038D; Reg § 1.6038D-1, Reg § 1.6038D-2)[8]

To the extent provided in regs, foreign investors in U.S. real property will be required to report their direct ownership interests to IRS. (Code Sec. 6039C)[9]

Except for certain corporations with annual revenues of less than $850 million, every U.S. person that is the ultimate parent entity of a U.S. multinational enterprise (MNE) group must make an annual return on Form 8975 (Country-by-Country Report or CbCR) setting forth the required information. (Reg § 1.6038-4)[10]

¶ 4648　Tax Withholding on Payments to Foreign Taxpayers. ▬▬▬

Several withholding regimes enforce the imposition of tax and/or reporting requirements on foreign taxpayers. These include (i) withholding at a 30% or lower rate on the gross amount of U.S. source fixed and determinable income items (chapter 3 or "FDAP" withholding, see ¶4649 *et seq.*), (ii) 30% withholding on certain withholdable payments under the Foreign Account Tax Compliance Act if the payee doesn't provide the required documentation (FATCA withholding, see ¶4654 *et seq.*), (iii) wage withholding (¶4657), (iv) withholding on effectively connected income of foreign partners in a partnership (¶4658), and (v) withholding on the disposition of U.S. real property interests (¶4660).

¶ 4649　Which taxpayers are subject to FDAP withholding?

Nonresident alien individuals and foreign partnerships are subject to FDAP (¶4648) withholding (Code Sec. 1441(a)), as are foreign corporations (Code Sec. 1442(a)), foreign trusts, foreign estates, foreign branches of U.S. financial institutions for which a QI agreement (¶4652) is in effect (but only for withholding purposes), and any other person that is not a U.S. person. (Reg § 1.1441-1(c)(2), Reg § 1.1441-1(c)(12)) However, an alien individual who made an election to be treated as a resident of the U.S. is nevertheless treated as a nonresident alien individual for withholding purposes. (Reg § 1.1441-1(c)(3)(ii)) A corporation organized in the Virgin Islands, American Samoa, Guam, or the Commonwealth of the Northern Mariana Islands is not a foreign corporation for withholding purposes if

5. ¶S-3643 *et seq.*; ¶60,46A4
6. ¶D-1165.1, ¶S-3485 *et seq.*, ¶S-3510 *et seq.*; ¶60,38A4, 60,38C4
7. ¶S-3629 *et seq.*; ¶60,38B4

8. ¶S-3650.1 *et seq.*, ¶60,38D4
9. ¶S-3481 *et seq.*; ¶60,39C4
10. ¶S-3490 *et seq.*, ¶60,384.02

certain tests are met. (Code Sec. 1442(c))[11]

¶ 4650   What income is subject to FDAP withholding?

The amounts subject to FDAP withholding (¶4648) are U.S. source amounts that are either fixed or determinable annual or periodical income (FDAP income) or certain gains from the disposition of timber, coal or domestic iron ore, and from contingent price sales of intangible property. (Reg § 1.1441-2(a), Reg § 1.1441-2(c)) FDAP income includes all gross income except for gains derived from the sale of property (including market discount and option premiums, but not including original issue discount (OID)), namely interest (other than OID), dividends, rent, salaries, wages, premiums, annuities, compensations, remunerations, emoluments, payments on and gain on sale of OID obligations, social security benefits to the extent of 85% of those benefits, excess inclusions of holders of real estate mortgage investment conduit (REMIC) residual interests, dividend equivalents, patronage dividends, and alimony payments. (Code Sec. 1441(b), Code Sec. 1441(g), Code Sec. 860G(b)(1); Reg § 1.1441-2(b))[12]

Items exempt from FDAP withholding include (but are not limited to):

. . . income (other than compensation for personal services) which is effectively connected with the conduct of a U.S. business and taxed at regular U.S. tax rates. (Code Sec. 1441(c)(1))

. . . portfolio interest, substitute interest payments, certain kinds of deposit interest, interest and OID on short-term obligations. (Code Sec. 1441(c); Reg § 1.1441-1(b)(4))

. . . compensation for personal services of a nonresident alien individual if such compensation is effectively connected with the conduct of a trade or business within the U.S. *and* it: (i) is subject to the wage withholding regime (see ¶4657), (ii) would be subject to the wage withholding regime, except that it is specifically exempted from the definition of wages for these purposes, (iii) is for services performed by Canadian or Mexican residents who enter or leave the U.S. at frequent intervals, (iv) is exempt from tax by law or treaty, (v) is paid as a commission or rebate by a ship supplier under certain circumstances; or (vi) is exempt from withholding under a statutory "all-or-nothing" rule if the employee and employer enter into a voluntary nonwage withholding agreement. (Code Sec. 1441(c)(4); Reg § 1.1441-4(b))

. . . regulated investment company (RIC) dividends that are paid out of interest that would not be subject to withholding, and certain short-term capital gains under Code Sec. 871(k). (Code Sec. 1441(c)(12))[13]

¶ 4651   Rate of FDAP withholding.

The amount of tax to be withheld on an item of FDAP income (¶4650) is generally 30%, except that the rate is reduced to 14% on certain scholarship or fellowship amounts received by a nonresident alien individual temporarily present in the U.S. (Code Sec. 1441(a), Code Sec. 1441(b))[14]

The rate of withholding on non-compensation income may be reduced to the extent provided under an income tax treaty in effect between the U.S. and a foreign country (see ¶4652 for required documentation). (Reg § 1.1441-6(a))[15]

---

11. ¶O-11900 *et seq.*; ¶14,414 *et seq.*
12. ¶O-11902 *et seq.*; ¶14,414 *et seq.*
13. ¶O-11960 *et seq.*; ¶14,414.02, ¶14,414.06

14. ¶O-11901, ¶O-11998; ¶14,414
15. ¶O-12032

¶ **4652** **Documentation to be provided to the FDAP withholding agent—Forms W-9, W-8, 8233.**

The withholding agent. Any person having the control, receipt, custody, disposal, or payment of an item of a U.S. source FDAP income (¶4650) of a foreign person (¶4649) is a FDAP withholding agent. (Code Sec. 1442(a), Code Sec. 1441(a); Reg § 1.1441-7(a)) The withholding agent must withhold at a 30% rate on that income unless it can reliably associate the payment with documentation upon which it can rely to treat the payment as made to a payee that is a U.S. person or as made to a foreign beneficial owner entitled to a reduced rate of withholding (see below). However, a withholding agent need not withhold if the foreign person assumes responsibility for withholding (i) as a qualified intermediary (QI, ¶4656), (ii) as a U.S. branch of a foreign person, or (iii) as a withholding foreign partnership or withholding foreign trust (¶4656). FDAP withholding is also not required if FATCA withholding (¶4654) was applied to the payment. (Reg § 1.1441-1(b)(1))[16]

A U.S. partnership is required to withhold as a FDAP withholding agent on an amount subject to withholding that is includible in the gross income of a partner that is a foreign person. Similarly, a U.S. trust is required to withhold as a FDAP withholding agent on the distributable net income (DNI) includible in the gross income of a foreign beneficiary to the extent the DNI is an amount subject to withholding. (Reg § 1.1441-5(b))[17]

Documentation of U.S. status of beneficial owner or payee. Absent actual knowledge or reason to know otherwise, a withholding agent may treat a payee as a U.S. person if (i) the payee is required to furnish a Form W-9 and furnishes it under the backup withholding rules, and it includes the payee's taxpayer identification number (TIN) or (ii) the payee is not required to furnish the Form W-9 but provides the withholding agent with a Form W-9 (or a substitute form) that contains the payee's name, address, and TIN. The form must be signed under penalties of perjury. (Reg § 1.1441-1(d)) A withholding agent that makes a payment to an intermediary, flow-through entity, or U.S. branch or territory financial institution may treat the payment as made to a U.S. payee to the extent that, prior to the payment, the withholding agent can reliably associate the payment with: (a) a Form W-9 attached to a valid intermediary, flow-through, or U.S. branch withholding certificate; or (b) a Form W-8 that evidences an agreement to treat a U.S. branch as a U.S. person. (Reg § 1.1441-1(d)(4))[18]

Documentation of entitlement to reduced rate of withholding under tax treaty. Absent actual knowledge or reason to know otherwise, a withholding agent may rely on a claim that a beneficial owner is entitled to a reduced rate of withholding under a treaty if, before the payment, the withholding agent can reliably associate the payment with a Form W-8BEN beneficial owner withholding certificate that includes the required information, representations and certifications. (Reg § 1.1441-6)[19]

In the case of compensation income, the form used is Form 8233 containing the required information. (Reg § 1.1441-4(b)(2))[20]

Documentation that income is effectively connected. Absent actual knowledge or reason to know otherwise, a withholding agent may rely on a claim of exemption from withholding for income effectively connected with a U.S. trade or business if, prior to the payment to the foreign person, the withholding agent can reliably associate the payment with a valid Form W-8ECI. To be valid, in addition to other applicable requirements, the form must include the TIN and represent, under penalties of perjury, that the amounts for which the certificate is furnished are effectively connected with the conduct of a trade or business in the U.S. and includable in the beneficial owner's gross income for the tax year.

16. ¶O-11901, ¶O-11914 *et seq.*; ¶14,414 *et seq.*
17. ¶O-12005.1, ¶O-12010; ¶14,414.07, ¶14,414.09
18. ¶O-11929.6

19. ¶O-12030 *et seq.*; ¶14,414.025
20. ¶O-11991.1; ¶14,414.06

(Reg § 1.1441-4(a)(2)(i))[21]

¶ 4653 Reporting FDAP withholding amounts—Forms 1042, 1042-S.

A withholding agent must file an annual income tax return on Form 1042 for income paid during the preceding calendar year that the withholding agent is required to report on an information return on Form 1042-S (see below). The income tax return must be filed with IRS on or before Mar. 15 of the calendar year following the year in which the income was paid, even if no tax was required to be withheld during the preceding calendar year. A single Form 1042 may be filed by a withholding agent to report FDAP and FATCA (¶4654) amounts, including tax withheld. (Reg § 1.1461-1(b)(1))[22]

A withholding agent must also make an information return on Form 1042-S to report the amounts subject to reporting that were paid during the preceding calendar year. An individual who is not acting in the course of a trade or business does not have to file a return for reportable amounts unless that person actually withholds or is required to withhold. A Form 1042-S must be prepared for each recipient of an amount subject to reporting and for each single type of income payment. One copy of the form must be filed with IRS on or before Mar. 15 of the calendar year following the year in which the amount subject to reporting was paid, another copy must be furnished to the recipient for whom the form is prepared on or before the same date, and a third copy must be retained by the withholding agent. (Reg § 1.1461-1(c)(1))[23]

Amounts subject to reporting. Subject to certain exceptions, the amounts subject to reporting are the amounts subject to withholding (as described in ¶4650) paid to a foreign payee, even if no amount is withheld from the payment because of a treaty or Code exception to taxation, or because an amount withheld was reimbursed to the payee under certain adjustment procedures. In addition, amounts subject to reporting include any amounts paid to a foreign payee on which a withholding agent actually withheld (either under the FDAP provisions or the backup withholding provisions (see ¶3044 *et seq.*)), whether or not the amount is subject to withholding. (Reg § 1.1461-1(c)(2))[24]

¶ 4654 FATCA withholding—Forms 8966, 8957.

In order to induce reporting on certain U.S.-owned foreign accounts, the Foreign Account Tax Compliance Act (FATCA) requires a withholding agent to withhold at a 30% rate on "withholdable payments" to (i) foreign financial institutions (FFIs; as defined in Reg § 1.1471-5(e)) that do not agree to report the required information to IRS regarding their U.S. accounts ("nonparticipating FFIs"), and (ii) nonfinancial foreign entities (NFFEs) that do not provide information on their substantial U.S. owners to the withholding agent. (Code Sec. 1471 through Code Sec. 1474)[25]

Withholding on payments to FFIs. An FFI isn't subject to withholding if it: (i) enters into an FFI agreement with IRS under which it assumes specific compliance and reporting (on Form 8966) obligations (a "participating FFI"), or (ii) is deemed to comply with the compliance and reporting requirements (a "deemed-compliant FFI"). An FFI may satisfy the compliance and reporting requirements but elect to be withheld upon rather than to withhold. An FFI registers on Form 8957 via an online FATCA registration system in order to enter into its FFI agreement. (Code Sec. 1471; Reg § 1.1471-2(a))[26]

Withholding on payments to NFFEs. An NFFE isn't subject to withholding if (i) the payee or the beneficial owner provides the withholding agent with either a certification that the foreign entity does not have a substantial U.S. owner or the name, address and

21. ¶O-11968; ¶14,414.02
22. ¶S-3471; ¶14,614.01
23. ¶S-3471.2; ¶14,614.01

24. ¶S-3477; ¶14,614.01
25. ¶O-13070 *et seq.*; ¶14,714 *et seq.*
26. ¶O-13072 *et seq.*; ¶14,714.1 *et seq.*

taxpayer identification number (TIN) of each substantial U.S. owner; and (ii) certain reporting requirements are met. Withholding also does not apply to excepted NFFEs. (Code Sec. 1472; Reg § 1.1472-1)[27]

Withholding agent. A withholding agent for purposes of the FATCA provisions is any person, U.S. or foreign, in whatever capacity acting, that has the control, receipt, custody, disposal, or payment of a withholdable payment or foreign passthru payment. (Code Sec. 1473(4); Reg § 1.1473-1(d))[28]

Withholdable payments. Withholdable payments are non-effectively connected (i) payments of U.S. source interest (including any original issue discount), dividends, rents, salaries, wages, premiums, annuities, compensations, remunerations, emoluments, and other fixed or determinable annual or periodical gains, profits; and (ii) for sales or other dispositions after 2018, gross proceeds from the sale or other disposition of any property of a type that can produce U.S. source interest or dividends. However, payments on certain obligations outstanding on July 1, 2014 (grandfathered obligations) are exempt from withholding tax altogether. (Code Sec. 1473(1); Reg § 1.1471-2(b), Reg § 1.1473-1(a))[29]

¶ 4655 Reporting FATCA withholding—Forms 1042, 1042-S.

Every FATCA withholding agent (¶4654) must file an income tax return on Form 1042 to report reportable amounts (generally, withholdable payments (¶4654) including those reportable under the FDAP provisions (see ¶4653)). This income tax return is filed on the same income tax return used to report amounts subject to withholding under the FDAP withholding provisions (¶4653). A Form 1042 must be filed even if no tax was required to be withheld under the FATCA provisions during the preceding calendar year. (Reg § 1.1474-1(c), Reg § 1.1474-1(d)(2))[30]

Every FATCA withholding agent must file an information return on Form 1042-S to report to IRS reportable amounts that were paid to a recipient during the preceding calendar year. Except as otherwise provided in the regs, a separate Form 1042-S must be filed with IRS for each recipient of an amount subject to reporting and for each separate type of payment made to a single recipient. One copy of the form must be filed with IRS on or before Mar. 15 of the calendar year following the year in which the amount subject to reporting was paid, another copy must be furnished to the recipient (and certain intermediaries) on or before the same date, and the withholding agent must retain a third copy. (Reg § 1.1474-1(d)(1))[31]

¶ 4656 Qualified intermediary (QI), withholding foreign partnership (WFP), and withholding foreign trust (WFT) agreements.

QIs. A QI is a foreign entity (typically, a financial institution) that enters into an agreement with IRS under which it acts as an agent on behalf of persons for whom it receives payment and subjects itself to the withholding and reporting provisions applicable to withholding agents under the FDAP (¶4649 *et seq.*) and FATCA (¶4650 *et seq.*) provisions, and to payors under the backup withholding (¶3044 *et seq.*) and information reporting (¶4737 *et seq.*) rules, in addition to other withholding rules, except to the extent provided under the agreement. The QI furnishes a QI withholding certificate instead of transmitting to the withholding agent the withholding certificates or other documentation it has obtained from the payees. A QI may assume the primary obligation to withhold, deposit, and report amounts under the FATCA and FDAP provisions and/or under the backup withholding and information reporting provisions if it meets the relevant requirements. A QI that assumes primary withholding responsibility for payments made to an

---

27. ¶O-13074, O-13093; ¶14,724, 14,724.1
28. ¶O-13077; ¶14,734.2
29. ¶O-13078 *et seq.*; ¶14,714.4, ¶14,734.1

30. ¶S-3471.1, ¶S-3478.1; ¶14,744, ¶14,744.2
31. ¶S-3471.2; ¶14,744.2

account under the FDAP provisions is also required to assume primary withholding responsibility under the FATCA provisions. If the QI has assumed primary withholding responsibility for the payment, the withholding agent is not required to withhold on the payment and is not required to determine that the QI actually performs its primary withholding responsibilities. (Reg § 1.1441-1(e)(5))[32]

WFPs and WFTs. Foreign trusts and partnerships may similarly enter into agreements with IRS under which they may act as withholding agents. (Reg § 1.1441-5(c)(2), Reg § 1.1441-5(e)(5)(v))[33]

¶ 4657 Withholding on effectively connected wages of a nonresident alien individual.

Compensation paid for personal services performed by a nonresident alien individual which meets the definition of "wages" (¶3005), and which is effectively connected with a U.S. trade or business, is subject to regular graduated income tax withholding with certain adjustments under Code Sec. 3402. (Reg § 31.3401(a)(6)-1(a))[34]

The following aren't wages subject to the wage withholding regime:

(1) Wages paid for services performed outside the U.S. by a nonresident alien individual other than a resident of Puerto Rico (PR). (Reg § 31.3401(a)(6)-1(b))

(2) Remuneration paid to Canadian and Mexican residents who enter or leave the U.S. at frequent intervals and are engaged in transportation service or in service on international projects. (Reg § 31.3401(a)(6)-1(c))

(3) Wages paid (i) to PR residents for services performed in PR for an employer other than the U.S. government, (ii) for services performed outside the U.S., but not in PR, by a PR resident for an employer other than the U.S. government if the individual does not expect to be a PR resident during the entire tax year, or (iii) for services performed outside the U.S. by a nonresident alien individual who is a PR resident as an employee of the U.S. government, if the individual does not expect to be a PR resident during the entire tax year. (Reg § 31.3401(a)(6)-1(d))

(4) Wages exempt from tax by law or treaty. (Reg § 31.3401(a)(6)-1(f))[35]

⚫*observation:* Compensation paid to self-employed individuals would not meet the definition of wages for purposes of the above, but will generally be subject to withholding under the FDAP provisions (¶4648 *et seq.*) unless an exception (¶4650) applies.

¶ 4658 Withholding by partnerships with respect to foreign partners— Forms 8813, 8804, 8805.

A partnership must pay a withholding tax if it has "effectively connected taxable income" for the tax year (whether or not the income is distributed), any part of which is allocable to a foreign partner. (Code Sec. 1446(a)) Unless the partner can show that the tax should be lower, the partnership must withhold at the highest rate of U.S. (corporate or individual, as applicable) tax to which the foreign partner would be subject on that allocable income. (Code Sec. 1446(b); Reg § 1.1446-3, Reg § 1.1446-6) The partnership must determine the status of its partners based on the Form W-8 or Form W-9 filed by the partners. In the absence of documentation of a partner's status, the partnership must follow the presumptions in the regs. (Reg § 1.1446-1) Special rules apply to publicly traded partnerships and tiered partnerships. (Reg § 1.1446-4, Reg § 1.1446-5)[36]

---

32. ¶O-12700 *et seq.*; ¶14,414.01
33. ¶O-12770 *et seq.*; ¶14,414.07, ¶14,414.09
34. ¶H-4436; ¶34,014.22

35. ¶H-4436.1; ¶34,014.22
36. ¶O-12100 *et seq.*; ¶14,464

The partnership must pay the withheld amount in installments together with a Form 8813, report the partnership's total withholding liability for its year on Form 8804, and notify each foreign partner of his share thereof on Form 8805. (Reg § 1.1446-3)[37]

¶ 4659 Withholding on amounts realized on dispositions of partnership interests—Forms 8288, 8288-A.

If any portion of the gain on the disposition of a partnership interest would be treated as effectively connected with the conduct of a U.S. trade or business (see ¶4631), the transferee must withhold 10% of the amount realized on the disposition. (Code Sec. 1446(f)(1)) However, no withholding is required if the transferor provides a nonforeign affidavit. (Code Sec. 1446(f)(2)) IRS intends to issue regulations implementing these rules and has announced that until then, taxpayers must use the principles applicable to withholding on U.S. real property interests (see ¶4660), including the use of Form 8288 and Form 8288-A. De minimis exceptions to the withholding requirement will also apply. (Notice 2018-29). [38]

¶ 4660 Withholding on U.S. real property interest (USRPI) dispositions—Forms 8288, 8288-A.

Any person who acquires a USRPI from a foreign person must generally withhold a tax of 15% on the amount realized by the transferor foreign person (see ¶4636). (Code Sec. 1445(a); Reg § 1.1445-1(a); Reg § 1.1445-1(b)) The amount realized is the sum of cash received, the fair market value of any other property received, and any liability assumed by the transferee (e.g., buyer) or to which the USRPI was subject. (Reg § 1.1445-1(g)(5)) The amount required to be withheld can't exceed the transferor's maximum tax liability with respect to the transfer (i.e., the maximum amount of U.S. income tax that could be imposed with respect to the disposition, plus any unsatisfied withholding liability of the transferor with respect to USRPI). (Code Sec. 1445(c))[39]

The transferee of a partnership interest or of a beneficial interest in a trust or estate is required to deduct and withhold 15% of the amount realized on a disposition where the entity directly or indirectly owns a USRPI. (Code Sec. 1445(e)(5); Reg § 1.1445-11T(b))[40]

Withholding is not required where the transferor gives the transferee a sworn "nonforeign affidavit" which includes his U.S. TIN, a sworn "non-USRPHC affidavit" (¶4636) stating the interest in not a USRPI, or a statement from IRS that withholding is not required. Withholding also does not apply if the USRPI is acquired by the transferee as his residence, and the amount realized doesn't exceed $300,000; where the amount exceeds $300,000 but is not more than $1 million, a 10% withholding rate applies. (Code Sec. 1445(b); Reg § 1.1445-1(b))[41]

The transferee of the USRPI acquired from a foreign person must report on Form 8288 and Form 8288-A, and pay over to IRS the amounts withheld by the 20th day after transfer. (Reg § 1.1445-1(c), Reg § 1.1445-1(d))[42]

¶ 4661 Foreign Currency Rules. ▄▄▄▄▄▄▄▄▄▄▄

U.S. taxpayers are generally required to make all federal income tax determinations, including those stemming from transactions involving foreign currency, in their "functional currency." (Code Sec. 985(a))[43]

A U.S. taxpayer's functional currency is generally the U.S. dollar (Code Sec. 985(b)(1)(A)), except in the case of a "qualified business unit" (QBU) that uses the

---

37. ¶S-2718 *et seq.*
38. ¶O-12116 *et seq.*; ¶14,464
39. ¶O-13001 *et seq.*; ¶14,454 *et seq.*
40. ¶O-13037; ¶14,454.02

41. ¶O-13010 *et seq.*; ¶14,454
42. ¶O-13002.1; ¶14,454
43. ¶G-6900 *et seq.*; ¶9854 *et seq.*

currency of the economic environment in which a significant part of its activities are conducted and which is used to keep its books and records. (Code Sec. 985(b)(1)(B)). A QBU may elect to use the U.S. dollar instead if it meets certain requirements. (Code Sec. 985(b)(3))[44]

A QBU is any separate and clearly identified unit (or activity) of a trade or business of a taxpayer which maintains separate books and records. (Code Sec. 989(a)) A corporation is a QBU and a partnership, trust or estate is a QBU of a partner or beneficiary. An individual is not a QBU. (Reg § 1.989(a)-1(b)(2)(i))[45] If a U.S. taxpayer has one or more QBUs with non-dollar functional currencies, profits and losses are computed separately for each unit in its functional currency and then translated into dollars at the appropriate exchange rate. (Code Sec. 987)[46]

¶ 4662   Foreign currency gains and losses; section 988 transactions.

Foreign currency gain or loss attributable to a "section 988 transaction" must generally be computed separately for each transaction and treated as ordinary income or expense, as the case may be. (Code Sec. 988(a)(1)(A)) However, a taxpayer may elect to treat the foreign currency gain or loss attributable to certain forward contracts, futures contracts, or options as capital gain or loss. (Code Sec. 988(a)(1)(B))[47] A section 988 transaction is (i) the acquisition of a debt instrument or becoming the obligor under a debt instrument, (ii) the accruing (or otherwise taking into account) of an item of expense or gross income or receipts which is to be paid or received after the accrual date, or (iii) the entering into or acquiring of a forward contract, futures contract, option, or similar financial instrument, if the amount the taxpayer is entitled to receive, or is required to pay, by reason of such transaction is either: (1) denominated in terms of a nonfunctional currency; or (2) determined by reference to the value of one or more nonfunctional currencies. (Code Sec. 988(c)(1))[48]

The source of currency gains and losses is determined by reference to the residence of the taxpayer or qualified business unit (QBU) on whose books the relevant asset, liability, or item of income or expense is properly reflected. A special source rule applies for certain related party loans. (Code Sec. 988(a)(3))[49]

Two or more separate transactions may be integrated into a single "section 988 hedging transaction" which is taxed in accordance with its economic substance. (Code Sec. 988(d); Reg § 1.988-5)[50]

The Code Sec. 988 rules do not apply to a personal transaction (any transaction entered into by an individual unless the expenses properly allocable to it qualify as deductible business or investment expenses), unless the gain that would otherwise be recognized exceeds $200. An individual recognizes no gain from the fluctuations in exchange rates upon the disposition of foreign currency in a personal transaction. (Code Sec. 988(e))[1]

---

44. ¶G-6901, G-6906, G-6918; ¶9854
45. ¶G-6912
46. ¶G-6978 *et seq.*; ¶9874
47. ¶G-7001, G-7024

48. ¶G-6988 *et seq.*; ¶9884 *et seq.*
49. ¶G-7029; ¶9884.01
50. ¶G-7037; ¶9884.02
1. ¶G-7047, ¶G-7048; ¶9884.01

Chapter 24   Returns and Payment of Tax

¶ 4700   **Returns and Payment of Tax.** ▬▬▬▬▬▬▬▬▬▬▬

An individual taxpayer must file an income tax return if his or her gross income equals or exceeds a specified amount (¶4701). Married taxpayers may file a joint return (¶4704). Corporations (¶4724 *et seq.*), trusts and estates (¶4732 *et seq.*) also file income tax returns. A partnership files an information return (¶4731). Payors and others must file information returns to report specified payments, sales, etc. (¶4737 *et seq.*).

¶ 4701   **Who must file individual income tax returns?**

For tax years beginning after Dec. 31, 2017 and before Jan. 1, 2026, the filing requirement rules of Code Sec. 6012(a) (based on exemption amount and standard deduction) don't apply. Instead, every individual who has gross income for the tax year must file an income tax return, except:

(1)   an unmarried individual (as determined under Code Sec. 7703), who has gross income for the tax year that doesn't exceed the standard deduction for that individual for that tax year (for post-2017 standard deductions, see ¶3110) (Code Sec. 6012(f)(1)); or

(2)   an individual entitled to file jointly if: (i) the individual's gross income, when combined with the spouse's gross income, doesn't exceed, for the tax year, the standard deduction that would apply to the taxpayer for the tax year if the individual and spouse filed jointly (see ¶3110); (ii) the individual and spouse have the same household as their home at the end of the tax year; (iii) the spouse doesn't file separately; and (iv) neither the individual nor spouse is an individual for whom a dependency deduction may be claimed by another taxpayer, who has income (other than earned income) in excess of the limited deduction allowed for dependents (Code Sec. 6012(f)(2)) ($1,050 for 2018 and $1,100 for 2019, as calculated by Thomson Reuters using inflation data). [1]

Other filing requirements. The following may have to file an income tax return even though they have gross income below the levels listed above: individuals receiving tips from which social security tax wasn't withheld; [2] individuals owing AMT; [3] employees who receive more than $108.28 of wages from a church or church-controlled organization that is exempt from payroll taxes; [4] individuals receiving income from U.S. possessions; [5] nonresident aliens (NRAs) [6] but not NRAs who earn less than the personal exemption; [7] individuals who change their citizenship or country of residence during the year; [8] individuals who must pay a tax with respect to an IRA or other tax-favored account (if filing only for this reason, use Form 5329 by itself); [9] individuals who owe uncollected payroll tax on group-term life insurance; [10] individuals who owe recapture tax on certain credits; [11] individuals receiving advance payment of the premium tax credit (PTC or "premium assistance credit");[12] and certain self-employed individuals (¶4713).

The individual filing thresholds for a decedent's final return aren't reduced or prorated. [13]

Guardians or fiduciaries should file returns for minors and others who are incapable of

---

1. ¶A-2804; ¶634
2. ¶S-1709; ¶60,124
3. ¶S-1716; ¶60,124
4. ¶S-1718; ¶60,124
5. ¶S-1704.3; ¶60,124.02
6. ¶S-1750 *et seq.*; ¶60,124.02
7. ¶S-1755

8. ¶S-1758
9. ¶S-1708.1; ¶60,124
10. ¶S-1708.1; ¶60,124
11. ¶S-1708.1; ¶60,124
12. ¶S-1708.1; ¶60,124
13. ¶C-9602, ¶C-9603; ¶60,124.04

References beginning with a single letter are to paragraphs in Federal Tax Coordinator 2d and RIA's Analysis of Federal Taxes: Income. Those beginning with numbers are to paragraphs in United States Tax Reporter.

filing their own returns. A minor may make his own return. (Reg §   1.6012-3(b)(3))[14] For the election to claim a child's income on a parent's return, see ¶3132.

¶ 4702   Individual income tax returns.

U.S. citizens and residents use Form 1040 (Reg §   1.6012-1(a)(6)), Form 1040A (Reg § 1.6012-1(a)(7)(i)), or Form 1040EZ.

observation: IRS has issued a draft of a shorter, simpler Form 1040 for the 2019 tax season which would replace the current Form 1040, as well as the Form 1040A and the Form 1040EZ. All taxpayers will use the same form. The new Form 1040 uses a "building block" approach, in which the tax return is reduced to a simple form. That form can be supplemented with additional schedules if needed. Taxpayers with straightforward tax situations would only need to file this new Form 1040 with no additional schedules.

Form 1040A may be used by a taxpayer in any filing status who: (1) has income only from wages, salaries, tips (that are reported on Form W-2), interest, ordinary dividends, capital gain distributions, taxable scholarships and fellowship grants, pensions, annuities, IRAs, unemployment compensation, taxable social security and railroad retirement benefits, and AK Permanent Fund dividends; (2) can only claim certain adjustments to gross income (deductions for educator expenses, IRA contributions, student loan interest, and tuition and fees); (3) doesn't itemize deductions; (4) has taxable income less than $100,000; and (5) has only certain tax credits. A taxpayer may generally use Form 1040A even if he owes AMT.[15]

Single or married filing jointly taxpayers under 65 who aren't blind can use Form 1040EZ if they claim no dependents, have income only from wages, salaries, tips, taxable scholarships or fellowships, unemployment compensation, AK Permanent Fund dividends, and interest (of $1,500 or less), no adjustments to gross income, no itemized deductions, taxable income less than $100,000 and no tax credits other than the earned income credit (EIC).[16]

For tax years beginning after Feb. 9, 2018, persons age 65 and older at the end of the tax year can use Form 1040SR, which will be similar to Form 1040EZ, but not restricted based on income, and can include social security benefits, distributions from retirement plans, annuities and other deferred pay arrangements, interest and dividends, and adjusted net capital gain. [17]

¶ 4703   E-filing individual returns.

Tax preparers can e-file current year returns (but not after Oct. 15 even with a filing extension) and Form 4868 automatic filing extensions for individual taxpayers, [18] including returns that show a balance due. [19] But, e-filing isn't allowed for returns for years other than the current tax year, amended returns, fiscal year returns, or in certain other situations.[20] Preparers reasonably expected to file more than 10 individual tax returns will have to file those returns on magnetic media, i.e. electronically (see ¶S-1601.1).

An electronic return may be a composite return consisting of electronically transmitted data and of paper documents (filed later) that can't be electronically transmitted, or it may be completely paperless. [21] There are procedures for accepting digital or electronic signatures. (Code Sec. 6061(b))[22] All taxpayers who e-file their returns have to use electronic signatures under 1 of 2 methods: either a self-select Personal Identification Number (PIN)

14. ¶S-1704.1; ¶s 60,124, 60,124.04
15. ¶S-1715; ¶60,114.01
16. ¶S-1715; ¶60,114.01
17. ¶S-1704.4A; ¶60,114.01
18. ¶S-1600.1; ¶60,114.08

19. ¶S-1617; ¶60,114.08
20. ¶S-1604
21. ¶S-1608 *et seq.*; ¶60,114.08
22. ¶S-4518; ¶60,614

or a practitioner PIN. Practitioner PINs require the use of Form 8879, which is retained by the practitioner.[23] For submitting payments, see ¶4720.

¶ 4704 Spouses—joint or separate returns.

Married persons (¶4705) can choose to file a joint return (reporting their combined taxable income) (Code Sec. 6013(a))[24] or a separate return. (Code Sec. 1(d))[25]

Neither a return prepared and executed by IRS nor a Form 870 waiver is a valid election to file a joint return.[26]

observation: Filing separately may save taxes due to the floors on some deductions (e.g., medical expenses). Each floor is measured against AGI, so if either spouse has high amounts of these expenses, measuring them against a separate AGI can produce a larger deduction than if measured against joint AGI. But, any advantages may be offset by many restrictive rules for separate filers.

Separate returns. Each spouse is liable only for his own tax and penalties. [27]

Joint returns. Except as noted at ¶4709 to ¶4711, each spouse is jointly and severally liable for the full amount of the tax, penalties (other than civil fraud (¶4884)), and interest arising out of their joint return, regardless of the amount of his separate taxable income. (Code Sec. 6013(d)(3)) Only the spouse committing fraud can be subjected to fraud penalties.[28]

¶ 4705 Married defined for joint return purposes.

To file a joint return (¶4704), individuals must be legally married as of the *end* of the tax year or at the time of death of a spouse who dies before the close of the tax year. (Code Sec. 6013(d))[29] If the spouses filed a joint return during their "marriage" and later get an annulment, they must refile as separate unmarried persons. [30]

The terms "spouse," "husband," and "wife" mean an individual lawfully married to another individual. The term "husband and wife" means two individuals lawfully married to each other. IRS recognizes a marriage of two individuals if the marriage is recognized by the state, possession, or territory of the U.S. in which the marriage was entered into, regardless of domicile. Marriage does *not* include a registered domestic partnership, civil union, or other similar formal relationship recognized under state law that is not denominated as a marriage. [31]

¶ 4706 Qualifying for joint returns.

Spouses can file a joint return even if only one has income (Code Sec. 6013(a))[32] and even if they have different accounting *methods.*

A joint return *can't* be filed if: (a) *either spouse was a nonresident alien* (NRA) at any time during the tax year (Code Sec. 6013(a)(1)),[33] but where 1 spouse is an NRA for the entire year (Code Sec. 6013(g)) or where an NRA spouse becomes a U.S. resident during the tax year (Code Sec. 6013(h)), spouses can file jointly if they agree to subject their worldwide income to U.S. tax; [34] or (b) *the spouses have different tax years,* except when 1 spouse dies, see ¶4708.

23. ¶S-1617.3
24. ¶S-1801; ¶60,134 *et seq.*
25. ¶A-1502; ¶14.01
26. ¶S-1832
27. ¶V-8501.1
28. ¶V-8502; ¶s 60,134.05, 66,534.11

29. ¶S-1803; ¶60,134.03
30. ¶A-1609; ¶60,134.03
31. ¶A-1603; A-1603.1; ¶K-2141.5
32. ¶S-1801; ¶60,134
33. ¶S-1802; ¶60,134
34. ¶A-1800 *et seq.*; ¶60,134.01

¶ 4707   Changing from joint to other filing status and vice versa.

Once a joint return has been filed, spouses can revoke it by filing separate returns up until the return's due date. After the due date, they can't switch. (Reg § 1.6013-1(a))[35]

🅁🄸🄰*observation:* A couple may file jointly in one year and separately in another.

A married couple who filed separate returns can switch to a joint return after the due date if: (a) the joint return is filed within 3 years from the original due date (without extension), and (b) neither spouse has, with respect to his previously filed separate return, petitioned the Tax Court, filed a suit for refund, or entered into a closing agreement or final compromise. (Code Sec. 6013(b); Reg § 1.6013-2(b))[36]

¶ 4708   Joint return for year spouse(s) dies.

A joint return may be filed for spouses where their tax years start on the same day and end on different days because of the death of either or both (unless the surviving spouse (SS) remarries before the end of his tax year). The joint return must be made for the tax year of each. (Code Sec. 6013(a)(2))[37] For when to file, see ¶4716.

🅁🄸🄰*recommendation:* File a joint return to get the benefits of the joint return rates, and to use up decedent's (DS's) net operating loss, capital loss, charitable contribution carryforwards, or other expiring deductions or credits, if SS has income or can generate income before the end of SS's tax year.

SS may file a joint return if: DS hasn't already filed a return for the tax year; an executor wasn't appointed when the joint return is made; and an executor hasn't been appointed before the extended due date for filing SS's return. (Code Sec. 6013(a)(3))[38]

🅁🄸🄰*observation:* The return for the year before the year of death also is subject to these rules if DS died before filing a return for that year.

If an executor or administrator is appointed by the filing due date, SS *can't* file a joint return for DS. Only the fiduciary can act for DS, so both the fiduciary and SS must sign the joint return. Even if SS properly filed a joint return (because no fiduciary had been appointed by the due date), the fiduciary may disaffirm (revoke) the joint return by filing a *separate* return for DS within 1 year after the extended due date. Any joint return improperly filed by SS or disaffirmed by the fiduciary is treated as SS's *separate* return. (Code Sec. 6013(a)(3))[39] For when SS can use joint return rates, see ¶3125.

¶ 4709   Elective relief from joint tax liability (innocent spouse rule)—Form 8857.

Unless an exception (¶4712) applies, an individual who has filed a joint return may elect relief from joint and several liability (¶4704) under innocent spouse rules. (Code Sec. 6015(a)(1)) An individual is relieved of liability for tax, interest, penalties, etc. for a tax year to the extent the liability is due to an understatement if: (a) a joint return was filed for the tax year; (b) there's an understatement of tax on the return due to the other spouse's erroneous items; (c) the individual shows that, in signing the return, he didn't know or have reason to know of the understatement; (d) under the facts and circumstances, it would be inequitable to hold the individual liable for the deficiency; and (e) the individual elects the benefits of the innocent spouse rules, by filing Form 8857 (separately from the tax return) and the required attached statement, no later than 2 years after IRS

---

35. ¶S-1831; ¶60,134.01
36. ¶S-1829; ¶S-1830; ¶60,134.01
37. ¶S-1805; ¶60,134

38. ¶S-1806; ¶60,134
39. ¶S-1806; ¶60,134

has begun collection activities against the individual. (Code Sec. 6015(b)(1))[40]

❂observation: Innocent spouse relief isn't available for unpaid liabilities that were properly reported on a joint return, because in that situation there's no understatement of tax. However, equitable relief (¶4711) may be available.

A spouse who knew or had reason to know of the understatement, but shows that he didn't know or have reason to know of its *extent*, can be relieved of liability to the extent of the understatement of which he didn't know or have reason to know. (Code Sec. 6015(b)(2))[41]

Special innocent spouse relief applies to a spouse of a partner in a partnership subject to unified partnership audit procedures (¶4839).

Any determination of innocent spouse relief is made without regard to community property laws. (Reg § 1.6015-1(f)(1))[42] For a spouse's separate liability election, see ¶4710.

Upon receipt of a request for relief (¶4710; ¶4711), IRS must send a notice to the nonrequesting spouse's last known address informing that spouse of the requesting spouse's claim for relief. (Reg § 1.6015-6(a)(1)) The nonrequesting spouse may file a protest and receive an IRS appeals conference regarding a determination. [43] IRS's procedures protect domestic abuse victims who fear retaliation for applying for innocent spouse relief.[44] The nonrequesting spouse may also intervene to support the requesting spouse's innocent spouse claim. [45]

¶ 4710   Separate liability ("allocation of liability") election—Form 8857.

An individual who files a joint return and meets the eligibility requirements can elect to limit his liability for a deficiency. The separate liability election may be made in addition to the innocent spouse election (¶4709). (Code Sec. 6015(a)(2))[46] The relief is available only for unpaid liabilities from understatements; refunds aren't allowed. (Reg § 1.6015-3(c)(1))[47]

An individual can elect only if, when the election is filed, he's no longer married to, or is legally separated from, the spouse with whom the joint return was filed, or wasn't a member of the same household as that spouse at any time during the previous 12-month period. If IRS shows that assets were transferred between spouses in a fraudulent scheme joined in by both spouses, a separate liability election by either spouse is invalid. (Code Sec. 6015(c)(3)(A))[48]

To elect, file Form 8857 (separately from the return) with specified attachments no later than 2 years after IRS begins collection activity against the electing spouse. (Code Sec. 6015(c)(3)(B); Reg § 1.6015-5)[49] For equitable claims, see ¶4711.

Except as provided below, an electing spouse's liability for a deficiency that IRS assesses won't exceed the portion of the deficiency properly allocable to that spouse. (Code Sec. 6015(c)(1), Code Sec. 6015(d)(3)(A))[50] The liability is generally allocated between the spouses in proportion to the net items taken into account in determining the deficiency as if separate returns were filed. (Code Sec. 6015(d)(1))[1] But, the limitation on an electing spouse's tax liability is increased by the value of property transferred to that spouse by the nonelecting spouse principally to avoid tax, which is rebuttably presumed (except for divorce or separate maintenance transfers) to be the case for transfers made anytime after

40. ¶V-8506 *et seq.*; ¶60,154.01
41. ¶V-8510.1; ¶60,154.01
42. ¶V-8504
43. ¶V-8506.3 *et seq.*
44. ¶V-8506.2
45. ¶U-2152

46. ¶V-8533; ¶60,154.02
47. ¶T-5513
48. ¶V-8534; ¶60,154.02
49. ¶V-8536; ¶60,154.02
50. ¶V-8537; ¶60,154.02
1. ¶V-8539; ¶60,154.02

1 year before the first letter of proposed deficiency is sent. (Code Sec. 6015(c)(4))[2] Also, except where a joint return was signed under duress, the election doesn't apply to the extent that IRS has evidence that the electing spouse had *actual* knowledge of an item giving rise to all or part of a deficiency allocable to the other spouse. (Code Sec. 6015(c)(3)(C))[3]

¶ 4711   Equitable relief for spouses—Form 8857.

If under all the facts and circumstances it's inequitable to hold a spouse liable for any portion of any unpaid tax or deficiency, and relief isn't available under the innocent spouse (¶4709) or separate liability election (¶4710) rules, IRS may relieve that spouse of liability for that unpaid tax or deficiency (Code Sec. 6015(f); Reg § 1.6015-4) and in limited cases may issue a refund. To request equitable relief, file Form 8857 (separately from the tax return) with specified attached statement. (Reg § 1.6015-5(a))

These threshold conditions must be met for equitable relief:

(1) The requesting spouse filed a joint return for the tax year for which relief is sought.

(2) Relief isn't available under Code Sec. 6015(b) or Code Sec. 6015(c).

(3) The relief claim must be timely filed. Requests must be made before the collection statute expiration date (CSED) under Code Sec. 6502 or within the limitations period on credits or refunds in Code Sec. 6511.

(4) No assets were transferred between the spouses as part of a fraudulent scheme.

(5) The nonrequesting spouse didn't transfer disqualified assets to the requesting spouse. If there were transfers, relief is limited to the extent the liability exceeds the assets' value.

(6) The requesting spouse didn't knowingly file a fraudulent joint return.

(7) The liability is attributable (in full or partially) to an item of the nonrequesting spouse or an underpayment from the nonrequesting spouse's income. [4]

IRS will make a streamlined determination where a requesting spouse establishes that the requesting spouse: (a) is no longer married to the nonrequesting spouse; (b) would suffer economic hardship if relief isn't granted; and (c) did not know or have reason to know of the understatement or deficiency. If a requesting spouse doesn't qualify for a streamlined determination, IRS considers these factors (a nonexclusive list): marital status; economic hardship (based on federal poverty guidelines) if relief isn't granted; knowledge or reason to know of the item giving rise to the understatement or underpayment; abuse by the nonrequesting spouse; whether either spouse had a legal obligation to pay the liability; whether the requesting spouse significantly benefitted; whether the requesting spouse has made a good faith effort to comply with the tax law in tax years after the year for which the request is made; and whether the requesting spouse was in poor physical or mental health. [5]

If the nonrequesting spouse abused the requesting spouse or maintained control over the household finances by restricting the requesting spouse's access to financial information, IRS may: (i) consider certain threshold conditions and the conditions for streamlined determinations met, or (ii) weigh certain factors in favor of relief.

The Tax Court reviews denied claims under a de novo standard. [6]

2. ¶V-8538; ¶60,154.02
3. ¶V-8549.1; ¶60,154.02
4. ¶V-8553; ¶V-8554; ¶60,154.04

5. ¶V-8556; ¶60,154.04
6. ¶U-2148; ¶60,154.03

¶ 4712   Exceptions to innocent spouse relief.

Innocent spouse relief (¶4709, ¶4710, ¶4711) isn't available: (1) for liabilities other than income taxes, (e.g. "nanny" taxes, see ¶3031), that are reported on a joint federal income tax return (Reg § 1.6015-1(a)(3));[7] (2) for a tax year for which the spouse seeking relief has entered into an offer in compromise or a closing agreement with IRS that disposes of the liability (Reg § 1.6015-1(c));[8] or (3) if a spouse transferred assets to the other spouse as part of a fraudulent scheme to defraud IRS or another third party. (Reg § 1.6015-1(d))[9]

¶ 4713   Self-employed individuals' tax returns—Form 1040 and Schedule SE.

Individuals (except nonresident aliens) who have $400 or more net earnings from self-employment (¶3135) have to file Form 1040 (including Form 1040, Schedule SE) even if the individual's gross income is less than the filing thresholds (¶4701). (Code Sec. 6017) Report self-employment tax (¶3133) on Form 1040.[10]

¶ 4714   Decedent's final return.

A final income tax return is filed for a decedent who would be required to file if alive, for the part of the year up to the date of death. A decedent's final return is filed by the person entrusted with his property (e.g., the estate's executor). (Code Sec. 6012(b)(1))[11] For refunds, see ¶4850.[12] For a surviving spouse's joint return, see ¶4708. For standard deduction on a decedent's final return, see ¶3110.[13] For due date, see ¶4716. For the income and deductions reportable on the return, see ¶3963.

recommendation: Even though a final return may not otherwise be required, file one to claim any refund due for tax withheld from salary or for estimated tax paid.

¶ 4715   U.S. military and civilian employees dying in combat/terrorist attacks.

If a U.S. military or civilian employee dies as a result of wounds or injury sustained in a terrorist or military action, income tax won't apply for the year of death and any earlier year beginning with the last year ending before the year in which the wounds or injury were sustained. (Code Sec. 692(c)(1)) IRS has outlined procedures for determining whether a terrorist or military action has occurred. Refund of withheld or estimated taxes may be claimed by filing Form 1040, or, on an amended return (Form 1040X). On joint returns, the tax liability is allocated between the deceased and surviving spouses. [14]

¶ 4716   When and where to file individual returns.

Income tax returns (including self-employment tax returns and a decedent's final return) of U.S. citizens and resident aliens must be filed by the 15th day of the 4th month following the end of the tax year (Apr. 15 for calendar year taxpayers) at the address specified on the form or in the instructions. (Code Sec. 6072(a); Reg § 1.6072-1(a)(1), Reg § 1.6072-1(b))[15] However, calendar year taxpayers in Maine and Massachusetts have until Apr. 17, 2019 to file their 2018 returns because of the Patriots' Day holiday in those states and the Emancipation Day holiday in the District of Columbia. For a nonresident alien's return, see ¶4643.

A "short period return" must be filed by the 15th day of the 4th month following the end

---

7. ¶V-8501; ¶60,154
8. ¶V-8505; ¶60,154
9. ¶V-8535; ¶60,154
10. ¶S-1717; ¶14,024; ¶60,174
11. ¶C-9601, S-1704.2; ¶60,124.04

12. ¶T-5710; ¶60,124.04
13. ¶C-9602 *et seq.*
14. ¶C-9660 *et seq.*; ¶6924
15. ¶S-4701 *et seq.*; ¶S-5100 *et seq.*; ¶60,724; ¶60,914

of the short period. (Reg § 1.6071-1(b))[16]

¶ 4717   Extensions of time for filing individual returns—Form 4868.

File Form 4868 to get an automatic 6-month filing extension (until Oct. 15 for a calendar year taxpayer). (Reg § 1.6081-4)[17] The form must show the full amount properly estimated as tax for the year but it doesn't have to include payment of the balance of the tax estimated to be due. (Reg § 1.6081-4(b))[18] Failure to include the balance due won't affect the extension, but interest and penalties apply. [19] Extension requests may be e-filed.[20] For payment extensions, see ¶4721. IRS can terminate extensions on 10 days' notice. (Reg § 1.6081-4(d))[21]

Extensions can't exceed 6 months unless the taxpayer is abroad. (Code Sec. 6081(a))[22]

¶ 4718   Extension for citizen or resident with non-U.S. tax home—Forms 4868, 2350.

A U.S. citizen or resident whose tax home and abode is outside the U.S. and Puerto Rico (Reg § 1.6081-5(a)(5)) and a U.S. citizen or resident in military or naval service on duty outside the U.S. and Puerto Rico (Reg § 1.6081-5(a)(6)) get automatic extensions until the 15th day of the sixth month after the end of the tax year. A statement must be attached to the return which shows that the taxpayer qualified for the extension. (Reg § 1.6081-5(b))[23] The automatic 6-month extension for individuals (¶4717) runs concurrently with the 2-month extension of time to file. (Reg § 1.6081-4(a))[24]

⊘Illustration: On Apr. 15, T, a U.S. citizen using the calendar year, has a tax home outside the U.S. and Puerto Rico. T's tax return and tax payment are due on June 15. If T files Form 4868 by June 15 and pays any estimated unpaid tax, T has until Oct. 15 to file.

U.S. citizens and resident aliens who expect to qualify for the foreign earned income exclusion (¶4605) (and owe no tax), can request an extension of up to 2 months on Form 2350 by that due date. (Reg § 1.911-7(c)(2))[25].

¶ 4719   Combat zone, declared disaster, terrorist or military action extensions.

Individuals serving in the U.S. armed forces in a Presidentially-designated area as a "combat zone" (¶1222) or in a 10 USC §101(a)(13) "contingency operation" can suspend the period of time to perform various tax actions (e.g., tax return filing). (Code Sec. 7508) The suspension also applies to individuals serving in support of the Armed Forces in a combat zone, or acting under the Armed Forces' direction. These individuals get extra time to perform tax acts (e.g., filing of a return, or filing a refund claim, etc.) and the period is extended for the determination and assessment of their federal tax liability. (Code Sec. 7508(a)(1)) Generally, the suspension includes (1) any period of continuous hospitalization as a result of injury received while serving in the combat zone, (2) time missing in action status plus (3) a 180-day period after the termination of service or hospitalization. However, with respect to tax collection by IRS there is *no* suspension for the period of hospitalization or the 180 days thereafter. [26]

IRS may allow taxpayers affected by a Code Sec. 165(i)(5) "federally-declared" disaster

---

16. ¶S-4710; ¶60,724
17. ¶S-5011; ¶60,814.03
18. ¶S-5013; ¶60,814.03
19. ¶s S-5010, S-5011; ¶60,814.03
20. ¶S-1606; ¶60,814.03
21. ¶S-5009; ¶60,814.03

22. ¶S-5003; ¶60,814.01
23. ¶S-5064; ¶60,814.01
24. ¶S-5065; ¶60,814.03
25. ¶S-5020; ¶9114.13
26. ¶S-8011; ¶75,084

or a Code Sec. 692(c)(2) terrorist or military action to extend for up to 1 year (1) the timely performance of acts under Code Sec. 7508(a)(1) (including filing a return); (2) the amount of any interest, penalty, additional amount, or addition to tax due for periods after the disaster date; and (3) the amount of any tax credit or refund. [27] (Code Sec. 7508A) IRS has specified acts subject to postponement, [28] (Reg § 301.7508A-1) including disasters occurring in 2018. [29]

On notice to IRS, the collection of a service member's income tax falling due before or during his military service is deferred up to 180 days after termination of the taxpayer's service (or his release from it), if his ability to pay the tax is materially affected by the military service. No interest or penalty accrues for the deferment period because of the nonpayment of any deferred amount. Also, the running of the statute of limitations against the collection of any deferred amount, by seizure or otherwise, is suspended for the period of service plus 270 days. [30] For tax relief for U.S. military and civilian employees dying in combat or terrorist attacks, see ¶4715.

¶ 4720 Payment of taxes due—Form 1040-V.

The tax is due on the original due date for filing the return despite any extensions of time for *filing* the return. (Code Sec. 6151(a); Reg § 1.6151-1(a))[31] If IRS computes the tax, the tax due date is the later of the thirtieth day after the date IRS mails the tax bill or the tax return due date. (Reg § 1.6151-1(b))[32] The automatic filing extension for taxpayers with a tax home and abode, or in military service, outside the U.S. (¶4718), also extends the time for payment. (Reg § 1.6081-5(a))[33] For treatment of extension requests without full payment, see ¶4717.

Taxpayers with a balance due on a return use Form 1040-V to make their payments, make a credit card payment by phone or online, or make a payment using the electronic federal tax payment system (EFTPS). Taxpayers may pay their taxes in cash at participating 7-Eleven stores after following IRS procedures. [34] Make tax payments by check or money order payable to the U.S. Treasury. Receipt of the check is payment, if the check is honored. IRS will accept personal checks or money orders drawn on any U.S. financial institution if the check or money order is collectible in U.S. currency. Express, telegraphic, and similar money orders are also acceptable. (Reg § 301.6311-1)[35]

Taxes (including interest and penalties) can be paid by any commercially acceptable means that IRS deems appropriate by regs, including approved credit or debit cards as provided in IRS forms, etc. (Code Sec. 6311(a), Code Sec. 6311(d)(1); Reg § 301.6311-2) Taxpayers can: (1) authorize IRS to debit a bank account for the unpaid balance, or (2) make credit or debit card payments through tax software, by phone, or on-line. IRS doesn't set or collect any fees for credit or debit card payments, but convenience fees may be charged by these service providers: WorldPay US, Inc (844-729-8298; PayUSAtax.com); Link2Gov Corp. (888-729-1040; Pay1040.com); and Official Payments Corp. (888-872-9829; OfficialPayments.com/fed). Paper and e-filers may use this system to charge taxes to credit or debit cards. The option to pay taxes by credit or debit card also applies to payments with automatic extensions and to estimated tax payments. Taxpayers who charge a payment with an automatic extension request or who charge an estimated tax payment don't need to file paper Form 4868 or Form 1040-ES. [36]

Tax payment by credit or debit card is deemed made when the issuer properly authorizes the transaction, provided payment is actually received by IRS in the ordinary course of

27. ¶S-8502; ¶75,08A4
28. ¶S-8012; ¶75,08A4
29. ¶S-8501.09
30. ¶S-8001; ¶63,014.04
31. ¶S-5451; ¶61,514

32. ¶S-5454; ¶61,514
33. ¶S-5064; ¶60,814
34. ¶S-5454.1
35. ¶S-5752; ¶63,114
36. ¶S-5756.1A *et seq.*, ¶S-1629.1; ¶63,114

785

business and isn't returned due to error resolution processing. (Reg § 301.6311-2(b))[37]

Where quarterly estimated tax payments (¶3145) aren't necessary, payments are generally made with the individual's return (¶4716).[38]

¶ 4721   Extension of time for paying individual income tax—Form 1127.

Apply on Form 1127 for a reasonable extension of time (not to exceed 6 months, unless taxpayer is abroad) to pay the tax. (Code Sec. 6161(a)(1)) File by the due date for payment of the tax. (Reg § 1.6161-1(c)) IRS grants extensions, generally within 30 days, only on a satisfactory showing that payment on the due date will result in undue hardship (more than an inconvenience), e.g., that taxpayer would have to sell property at a great financial sacrifice (i.e., below fair market value) to pay the tax. (Reg § 1.6161-1(b))[39]

¶ 4722   Installment payments of individual income tax—Forms 9465, 433-A, 433-F.

To request an installment agreement, attach Form 9465 to the front of a balance-due return or submit an on-line payment application. A fee of $225 for a regular installment agreement ($107 for a direct debit agreement; $149 for an online payment agreement; $31 for a direct debit online payment agreement; $89 for restructured or reinstated installment agreements; and $43 for low-income taxpayers to enter any type of agreement except direct debit online, for which the lower $31 rate applies), (Reg § 300.1(b)),[40] interest, and a late-payment penalty (see ¶4876) apply.

IRS must enter into an installment agreement (guaranteed installment agreement) requested by an *individual* whose aggregate tax liability (without interest, penalties, additions to tax, and additional amounts) isn't more than $10,000; and who (or whose spouse for joint return liability) hasn't failed to file or to pay income tax, or entered into another installment agreement, during any of the preceding 5 tax years, if IRS determines that the taxpayer is financially unable to pay the liability in full when due (and the taxpayer submits information that IRS may require to make this determination). The agreement must require full payment within 3 years, and the taxpayer must agree to comply with all Code provisions while it's in effect. (Code Sec. 6159(c); Reg § 301.6159-1(c)) IRS grants streamlined installment agreement requests to taxpayers who agree to pay a balance due of $50,000 or less within a 6-year period, without requiring a collection manager's approval. Taxpayers seeking installment agreements exceeding $50,000 have to supply IRS with Form 433-A or Form 433-F. Under a "test" program scheduled to run through Sept. 30, 2018, IRS expanded the criteria for streamlined processing to also apply to individual taxpayers who agree to pay a balance due of between $50,000 and $100,000 within a 7-year period.[41]

IRS may (but isn't required to, except as noted above) enter into an installment agreement if it determines that the agreement will facilitate full or partial collection of the tax. (Code Sec. 6159(a); Reg § 301.6159-1(a)) IRS may disregard frivolous submissions of installment payment applications. (Code Sec. 7122(f))[42]

An individual who had an automatic 6-month extension of time to file without paying the tax estimated to be due (¶4717), but can't pay by the extended due date, should use Form 9465 to arrange an installment agreement. [43]

---

37. ¶S-5756.4
38. ¶S-5200 *et seq.*
39. ¶S-5851; ¶61,614
40. ¶T-10021, T-10022; ¶61,594

41. ¶V-5010 *et seq.*; ¶61,594
42. ¶T-9612; ¶61,594
43. ¶s S-5020, V-5010 *et seq.*; ¶61,594

¶ 4723 Amended income tax returns—Form 1040X.

Amended income tax returns (on Form 1040X) may be filed to claim a refund (¶4852) after an original return has been filed if the period of limitations is open. (Reg § 301.6402-3(a)(2))[44] Amended returns can't be e-filed. [45]

¶ 4724 Corporate returns.

Every corporation that is subject to income tax, and that's in existence during any portion of a tax year, must file an income tax return for that year (or portion), regardless of the amount of its gross income or whether it has taxable income. (Code Sec. 6012(a)(2); Reg § 1.6012-2(a))[46] A corporation that has merely received a charter doesn't have to file if it furnishes a statement to IRS that it hasn't perfected its organization, transacted any business, or received income from any source. (Reg § 1.6012-2(a)(2))[47]

After a corporation ceases business and dissolves, retaining no assets, it must file a return for that part of the year during which it was in existence. But retention of even a small amount of cash keeps the corporation alive for filing purposes until the cash is distributed or paid. (Reg § 1.6012-2(a)(2))[48] A receiver, bankruptcy trustee, etc. that has control and custody of all (or substantially all) of a corporation's business or property must make the return in the same manner as the corporation would. (Code Sec. 6012(b)(3))[49]

If a corporation doesn't file a required return, IRS may make its return. (Code Sec. 6020)[50]

¶ 4725 Who signs corporate returns.

The return and all related documents requiring a signature on a corporation's behalf, must be signed by the president, vice-president, treasurer, assistant treasurer, chief accounting officer (controller) or any other officer duly authorized to sign. If an LLC treated as a corporation doesn't have any of the specific officers listed above, the managing member or another individual authorized to act for the company can sign the return. If a return is made for the corporation by a trustee, receiver, etc., that fiduciary must sign. (Code Sec. 6062)[1]

¶ 4726 Corporate income tax forms—Form 1120.

Most domestic corporations file Form 1120 as their income tax return. (Reg § 1.6012-2(a)) Form 1120, Schedule PH must be attached if the corporation is a personal holding company (¶3321 *et seq.*). (Reg § 1.6012-2(b))[2] (For foreign corporation returns, see ¶4645.)

A regulated investment company (mutual fund) uses Form 1120-RIC, [3] a real estate investment trust, Form 1120-REIT, [4] a political organization, Form 1120-POL, a homeowners association, Form 1120-H, [5] and a designated settlement fund,Form 1120-SF. [6] Insurance companies use Form 1120L (life) or Form 1120-PC (property and casualty). [7]

S corporations use Form 1120S, which must show information on actual and constructive distributions to shareholders. (Code Sec. 6037(a); Reg § 1.6012-2(h)) The corporation

44. ¶S-5151.5; ¶s 60,114.01, 64,024.15
45. ¶S-1604
46. ¶S-1900, S-1901, S-1908; ¶60,124.03
47. ¶S-1908; ¶60,124.03
48. ¶S-1909; ¶60,124.03
49. ¶S-2014; ¶60,124.04
50. ¶S-1004; ¶60,204

1. ¶S-4508; ¶60,614
2. ¶S-1902, S-1903; ¶60,124.03
3. ¶S-1920; ¶8514.09
4. ¶S-1919; ¶8564.10
5. ¶S-1921, ¶S-1922; ¶5284, ¶60,124
6. ¶S-1925; ¶468B4
7. ¶S-1904; ¶60,124.03; ¶8314

must, by the date it files the return, furnish this information to anyone who was a shareholder during the tax year. (Code Sec. 6037(b))[8]

Small corporations (less than $250,000 in gross receipts and less than $250,000 in assets) don't have to complete Schedules L, M-1, and M-2 of Form 1120; or Schedules L and M-1 of Form 1120S.[9] Large corporations (reporting total assets of $10 million or more on Form 1120, Schedule L) and large partnerships (¶4731) must file the more detailed Schedule M-3 instead of M-1. On the M-3, research and development costs have to be separately stated but no supporting attachment is required. M-3 filers must file Schedule B reporting information about allocations, transfers of interest, cost sharing arrangements, and changes in methods of accounting. Corporations and partnerships with at least $10 million but less than $50 million in total assets at year end can file Schedule M-1 in place of Schedule M-3, Parts II and III, but they must file Schedule M-3, Part I. Corporations and partnerships filing Forms 1120, 1120-C, 1120-F, 1120S, 1065, and 1065B with $10 million to $50 million in total assets will not be required to file Form 1120, Schedule B, Form 1065, Schedule C, or Form 8916-A.[10]

Corporations (filing Form 1120), insurance companies (filing Form 1120L or Form 1120PC), and foreign corporations (filing Form 1120F) with both uncertain tax positions and at least $10 million of assets have to file Schedule UTP if they or a related party issued audited financial statements. (Reg § 1.6012-2(a)(4)) Schedule UTP requires a concise description of each uncertain *federal* tax position for which the taxpayer or a related entity recorded a reserve on financial statements (or which no reserve was recorded because of an expectation to litigate). The description shouldn't exceed a few sentences; but, it must contain relevant facts affecting the tax treatment of the position and information that reasonably can be expected to apprise IRS of the tax position's identity and nature. Tax positions are ranked by size (i.e., the amount of the reserve) but the size of a tax position isn't reported. Positions have to be designated as major tax positions if the reserve for that position exceeds 10% of the reserves for all tax positions reported. Tax positions taken *before 2010* do not have to be reported. The requirement to report the tax position exists even if IRS identifies the tax position for examination before the recording of the reserve. A separate Form 8275 need not be filed to avoid accuracy-related penalties with respect to the tax position other than a reportable transaction. IRS has announced rules under which it will seek workpapers that document the completion of Schedule UTP.[11]

If the corporation deducts: (a) the cost of goods sold, it must file Form 1125-A or (b) officer compensation and has $500,000 of receipts, it must file Form 1125-E.[12] A corporation uses Form 8822-B to notify IRS of a new business address or location.

E-filing. A corporation that files at least 250 returns of any kind in the aggregate, including information returns, during the calendar year ending with or within its tax year must e-file its income tax return (i.e., the Form 1120 and Form 1120S series) if it has assets of $10 million or more. Exemptions apply for forms that can't be e-filed and where IRS waives the requirement for undue hardship. A corporation can request a written request for a waiver. All members of a controlled group must e-file if the controlled group in the aggregate files at least 250 returns (including information returns). Failure to e-file when required to do so is deemed to be a failure to file a return. (Reg § 301.6011-5) IRS allows a filer 10 calendar days from the date of first transmission to perfect a rejected e-file return for resubmission. For returns that can't be accepted for processing electronically, the filer generally has 10 days to file a paper return.[13]

---

8. ¶S-1905, S-1906; ¶60,374
9. ¶S-1902
10. ¶S-1902.1

11. ¶S-4460.1, ¶S-4460.4 *et seq.*
12. ¶S-1902
13. ¶S-1941; ¶60,114.022

¶ 4727   When and where to file corporate income tax returns.

Domestic corporations (including RICs, REITs, but not S corporations; see below) generally must file their returns by the 15th day of the *4th* month after the end of the tax year (Apr. 15 for a calendar year corporation). However, under a special rule, C corporations with fiscal years ending on June 30 file by the 15th day of the *3rd* month after the end of the tax year until their first tax year beginning after Dec. 31, 2025, at which point they must file by the 15th day of the fourth month following the end of the tax year. [14]

S corporations must file their returns by the 15th day of the *3rd* month after the end of the tax year (Mar. 15 for a calendar year S corporation). (Code Sec. 6072(a), Code Sec. 6072(b); Reg § 1.6037-1(b); Reg § 1.6072-2T)[15]

"Short period" returns must be filed by the 15th day of the 4th month (3rd month for S corporations and C corporations with fiscal years ending on June 30) after the end of the short period. [16]

File as directed on the form's instructions. (Code Sec. 6091(b)(2)(A); Reg § 1.6091-2(c)) Hand-carried returns may be filed with any person assigned the responsibility to receive hand-carried returns in the local IRS office (i.e., the office in which the corporation has its principal place of business). (Code Sec. 6091(b)(4); Reg § 1.6091-2(d)(2))[17]

For extensions, see ¶4728.

¶ 4728   Extensions for filing corporate returns—Form 7004.

Automatic extensions —Form 7004. Except as otherwise provided, a corporation (including an S corporation, an affiliated group planning to file a consolidated return (¶3339), and a foreign corporation with a U.S. office) can get an automatic 6-month extension by filing Form 7004 that shows its estimated tax liability by the original due date. For any return for a tax year of a C corporation which ends on June 30 and begins after Dec. 31, 2015 and before Jan. 1, 2026, the automatic extension period is 7 months (not 6 months). (Code Sec. 6081(b); Reg § 1.6081-3T)[18]

A filing extension won't extend the time for *paying* the tax, see ¶4729. (Reg § 1.6081-3(c))[19] IRS can terminate an extension on 10 days' notice. (Code Sec. 6081(b); Reg § 1.6081-3(d))[20]

Blanket extensions. A domestic corporation that does business and keeps its records outside the U.S. or Puerto Rico, or whose principal income is from sources within U.S. possessions, and a resident foreign corporation, may file its return up to the 15th day of the sixth month after the end of the tax year. A statement setting forth the qualifying facts must be attached to the return. (Reg § 1.6081-5(a)(2), Reg § 1.6081-5(a)(4), Reg § 1.6081-5(b))[21]

¶ 4729   Payment of corporate tax; extensions—Forms 1127, 1138.

Pay in full by the due date (without extension) for filing the return (¶4727). (Code Sec. 6151(a))[22] For corporate estimated tax, see ¶3344 *et seq.*

Six-month extension for undue hardship —Form 1127. IRS may grant an extension (up to 6 months) for paying corporate income tax at the taxpayer's request (on Form 1127) by

---

14. ¶S-4704; ¶60,724
15. ¶S-4923; ¶s 60,374, 60,724
16. ¶S-4710; ¶60,724
17. ¶S-5104; ¶60,914
18. ¶S-5024 *et seq.*; ¶60,814.02

19. ¶S-5027; ¶60,814.02
20. ¶S-5009; ¶60,814.02
21. ¶S-5064; ¶60,814.01
22. ¶S-5451; ¶61,514

the payment due date if undue hardship is shown (¶4721). Late applications won't be considered. (Code Sec. 6161(a); Reg § 1.6161-1)[23]

Loss carryback expected —Form 1138. A corporation that expects a net operating loss in a current year can get an extension for paying the *preceding* year's tax based on the expected carryback (Code Sec. 6164(a)), by filing Form 1138. (Reg § 1.6164-1) The extension expires the last day of the month for filing the current year return or, if an application for a tentative carryback refund (Form 1139, see ¶4853) is filed before that date, on the date IRS sends notice that the refund is allowed or disallowed. (Code Sec. 6164(d))[24]

¶ 4730   Tax deposits.

Unless an exemption applies, a corporation must make electronic deposits of all depository taxes using the Electronic Federal Tax Payment System (EFTPS). (Reg § 31.6302-1(h)(2)(iii)) For how taxpayers make tax deposits by Automated Clearing House (ACH) payments or by telephone, see ¶3029. Also, if corporations are unwilling or unable to use EFTPS, it can arrange for a tax professional, financial institution, payroll service, etc. to make a deposit on its behalf using a master account. It can also arrange for its financial institution to initiate a same-day tax wire payment on its behalf. [25]

Corporations make their income and estimated tax payments by depositing them by the return due date (¶4727) (Code Sec. 6302; Reg § 1.6302-1(a))[26] and reporting the deposits on the return.[27] For de minimis rule for deposits of employment taxes, see ¶3028.

¶ 4731   Partnership income tax return—Form 1065, Schedule K-1; Form 7004.

Partnerships (except foreign partnerships with no or de minimis U.S. source gross income and no gross income effectively connected with a U.S. trade or business) (Reg § 1.6031(a)-1(b)) must file Form 1065 (Form 1065-B for electing large partnerships) to report their income and deductions. (Code Sec. 6031(a), Code Sec. 6031(e); Reg § 1.6031(a)-1(a))[28] Certain tax-exempt bond partnerships are exempt from filing. [29] (Reg § 1.6031(a)-1(a)(3)(ii)) A foreign partnership that is otherwise exempt from filing must file a return to make an election, (Reg § 1.6031(a)-1(b)) and a foreign or domestic partnership must file to elect out of the Code's partnership rules. (Reg § 1.6031(a)-1(c))

A partnership needn't file a partnership return for any period before it has taxable income or incurs deductible expenses. (Reg § 1.6031(a)-1(a)(3))[30] Nor does it file if it doesn't have any gross income that is effectively connected with the conduct of a U.S. trade or business, or any U.S. source gross income. (Reg § 1.6031(a)-1(b)(1))[31]

Form 1065 is due on the 15th day of the 3rd month after the end of the partnership's tax year (Mar. 15 for a calendar year partnership). (Code Sec. 6072(b));[32] and regs provide an automatic extension of 6 months (to Sept. 15 for a calendar year partnership). (Reg § 1.6081-2T).[33]

Every partnership required to file a return must furnish (by the extended return due date) Form 1065, Schedule K-1, containing information from the return to every person who was a partner (or who held a partnership interest as a nominee for another person) at any time during the partnership's tax year. Form 1065, Schedule K-1 must indicate whether a partner contributed built-in gain or loss property during the tax year. An "electing large partnership" (¶3701) must provide the information by Mar. 15th following

23. ¶S-5850 *et seq.*, ¶S-5862 *et seq.*; ¶61,614
24. ¶S-5865 *et seq.*; ¶61,644
25. ¶S-5623, S-5628; ¶63,014
26. ¶S-5601, S-5604, S-5607; ¶63,014
27. ¶S-5601
28. ¶S-2701; ¶60,314

29. ¶S-2708
30. ¶S-2701; ¶60,314
31. ¶S-2717.1; ¶60,314
32. ¶S-4923; ¶60,724
33. ¶S-5030; ¶60,814

the end of its tax year. (Code Sec. 6031(b); Reg § 1.6031(b)-1T(a))[34] (The nominee must in turn give the information it gets to the other person (Code Sec. 6031(c)(2); Reg § 1.6031(c)-1T(h)) and furnish the partnership with specified information about that person.) (Code Sec. 6031(c)(1); Reg § 1.6031(c)-1T(a))[35] If a partnership deducts the cost of goods sold, it must file Form 1125-A.[36] For large partnerships that have to file Schedule M-3, see ¶4727.

E-filing. Partnerships with more than 100 partners must e-file Form 1065 and Form 1065, Schedule K-1, unless IRS excludes them from e-filing. Hardship waivers are available. (Reg § 301.6011-3)[37] Partnerships can furnish Form 1065, Schedule K-1 electronically to partners if the recipient affirmatively consents to that format.[38]

¶ 4732 Income tax returns of trusts and estates—Forms 1041, K-1, 7004, 8453-FE, etc.

Trusts (¶4733) and estates (¶4734) must file income tax and information returns.[39]

If there are *joint* fiduciaries, a return by one will suffice if he states in the return that he has sufficient knowledge of the facts to make the return and that it is true to the best of his knowledge and belief. (Reg § 1.6012-3(c))[40]

A fiduciary who prepares the trust's or estate's return must furnish to beneficiaries (or their nominees) receiving distributions, or to whom an income item is allocated, a Form 1041, Schedule K-1 or a substitute containing the same information. This must be furnished on or before a return is filed, and a copy must be filed with Form 1041. (Code Sec. 6034A(a)) If a nominee is given the information, he must furnish it to his beneficiary, and he must furnish to the estate or trust specified information about the beneficiary. (Code Sec. 6034A(b))[41]

Income tax returns that must be filed by estates and domestic trusts, and foreign trusts having a U.S. office or place of business, are due by the 15th day of the 4th month following the end of the tax year. (Reg § 1.6072-1(a)(1)) Foreign trusts and estates of nonresident aliens that don't have an office or place of business in the U.S. must file by the 15th day of the 6th month following the end of the tax year. (Reg § 1.6072-1(c))[42] Fiduciaries use Form 8453-F to e-file Form 1041.[43]

Under regs, non-bankruptcy estates and trusts get an automatic 5 $1/2$-month extension to file Form 1041 by filing Form 7004 showing the full amount properly estimated as tax by the return's due date. (Reg § 1.6081-6T)[44] IRS can terminate an automatic extension on 10 days' notice. (Reg § 1.6081-6(e))[45] For *payment* extensions, see ¶4721.

¶ 4733 Income tax returns of trusts—Forms 1041; 5227.

A trustee files Form 1041 if the trust isn't tax-exempt and if the trust has: (a) any taxable income for the year; (b) gross income of $600 or more; or (c) any beneficiary who is a nonresident alien. (Code Sec. 6012(a)(4), Code Sec. 6012(a)(5))[46]

Trust income taxable to the grantor or other "owner" is reported on a separate attachment to Form 1041, except that alternative reporting methods are available. The alternatives available depend on whether the trust is treated as owned by 1 grantor, or by 2 or more grantors (which in the latter case may require a trustee to provide Form 1099 and a statement showing trust income items, deductions and credits). (Reg § 1.671-4(b))[47]

34. ¶S-2710; ¶60,314
35. ¶S-2740; ¶60,314
36. ¶S-2701
37. ¶S-1350 *et seq.*; ¶60,114.065
38. ¶S-2710.1
39. ¶S-2004, S-2007; ¶60,124.04
40. ¶S-2002; ¶60,124.04
41. ¶S-2019, S-2020; ¶60,34A4
42. ¶S-4707; ¶60,724
43. ¶S-1632
44. ¶S-5032; ¶60,814.05
45. ¶S-5009; ¶60,814.05
46. ¶S-2007; ¶60,124.04
47. ¶S-2009 *et seq.*; ¶6714

Split-interest trusts file Form 5227 even if they must currently distribute all net income. (Code Sec. 6034(a))[48]

¶ 4734　Income tax returns of estates—Form 1041.

The executor or administrator must file Form 1041 if gross income for the estate's tax year is $600 or more (Code Sec. 6012(a)(3)) *or* if any beneficiary is a nonresident alien. (Code Sec. 6012(a); Reg § 1.6012-3(a)(1)(iii))[49] A fiduciary doesn't have to file a copy of the will for income tax purposes unless IRS *requests* a copy. (Reg § 1.6012-3(a)(2))[50]

The executor who probates the entire will (in the state the decedent was domiciled) files Form 1041 reporting all the income. Any out-of-state (i.e., ancillary) executor *also* files a Form 1041, but it shows only the gross income received by the ancillary fiduciary and the deductions attributable to that income. (Reg § 1.6012-3(a)(3))[1]

¶ 4735　Extension for making elections.

Two automatic extensions are available for taxpayer elections, if the taxpayer takes corrective action within the extension period:

(1) An automatic *12-month extension* for certain regulatory elections specified in Reg § 301.9100-2(a)(2). The more widely applicable ones are: the election to use a tax year other than the required tax year (¶2813); the election to use the LIFO inventory method (¶2868); and the election to adjust basis on partnership transfers and distributions (¶3772). The extension is available regardless of whether the taxpayer timely filed its return for the year the election should have been made. (Reg § 301.9100-2(a)(1))[2]

(2) An automatic *6-month extension* for regulatory elections and statutory elections which are required to be made by the due date of the return or the due date of the return *including extensions,* for taxpayers who timely filed the return for the year in which the election should have been made. (Reg § 301.9100-2(b))[3]

Nonautomatic extensions of time are available for regulatory elections that don't qualify for an automatic extension, if the taxpayer shows IRS that he acted reasonably and in good faith, and that granting relief won't prejudice IRS's interests. (Reg § 301.9100-3(a)) A request for a nonautomatic extension is generally a request for a letter ruling, and is submitted under those procedures, with the applicable user fee. (Reg § 301.9100-3(e)(5))[4]

The grant of an extension of time to make an election isn't a determination that the taxpayer is otherwise eligible to make the election. (Reg § 301.9100-1(a))[5]

¶ 4736　Income tax returns of individual bankruptcy estates—Forms 1041, 7004.

The debtor-in-possession or trustee, if one is appointed, for a bankruptcy estate for an individual under Chapter 7 or 11 must file an income tax return (Form 1041) if the estate's gross income equals at least the sum of the exemption amount plus the basic standard deduction for unmarried taxpayers who weren't surviving spouses or heads of household. (Code Sec. 6012(a)(8)) This amount is $12,000 for 2018 ($12,200 for 2019, as calculated by Thomson Reuters using inflation data).[6] File Form 7004 for an automatic 6-month extension. (Reg § 1.6081-6(a)(2))[7]

---

48. ¶S-2806; ¶60,344
49. ¶S-2004; ¶60,124.04
50. ¶S-2006; ¶60,124.04
1. ¶S-2005; ¶60,124.04
2. ¶S-4819; ¶78,054.02

3. ¶S-4821; ¶78,054.02
4. ¶S-4823; ¶78,054.02
5. ¶S-4815.1; ¶78,054.02
6. ¶C-9700 *et seq.*, S-2016; ¶60,124
7. ¶S-5032; ¶60,814.05

¶ 4737   Information returns—Form 1099, etc. and filing dates.

Taxpayers report certain activities with third parties on information returns and statements. These are filed with IRS and in some cases furnished to third parties (¶4742).[8] For e-filing, see ¶4753. Payors (including nominees, see ¶4738) report their payments for a calendar year by filing an appropriate Form 1099 (or permitted substitute form) for payee (with a Form 1096 transmittal statement) after Sept. 30 of the calendar year of the payment (but not before the payor's final payments for the year) and by the next Feb. 28. (Reg § 1.6042-2(c), Reg § 1.6044-2(d), Reg § 1.6049-1(c)), except for nonemployee compensation returns for which the due date is Jan. 31. (Code Sec. 6071(c)[9] And returns filed electronically, other than nonemployee compensation returns, aren't due until Mar. 31 after the end of the calendar year to which they relate. (Code Sec. 6071(b))[10] For extensions, see ¶4747.

¶ 4738   Nominees and middleman information returns—Forms 1099, 1099-DIV.

If reportable interest or dividends are paid to any person who, as middleman or nominee, then pays them over to the actual (or beneficial) owner, the original payor (corporation, bank, etc.) must file an information return (Form 1099 or Form 1099-DIV for dividends) with respect to the nominee, who must file anotherForm 1099 (or Form 1099-DIV) with respect to the actual or beneficial owner. (Code Sec. 6042(a)(1)(B), Code Sec. 6049(a)(2); Reg § 1.6042-2(a)(1)(iii), Reg § 1.6049-4(b)(3))[11]

A nominee is a payee who isn't the actual owner of the dividend or interest, but who would be required to furnish his TIN (¶4752) to the payor for inclusion on the *payor's* return. Nominees include banks, etc., and, for dividends, dealers and brokers. (Reg § 1.6042-2(a)(2), Reg § 1.6049-1(a)(2))[12] Special reporting rules apply to payments to joint payees (Reg § 1.6041-1(c)); and payments on behalf of another. (Reg § 1.6041-1(e))

¶ 4739   Dividend reporting—Forms 1099-DIV, 5452, 1099-PATR.

A payor (including nominees, see ¶4738) must file a Form 1099-DIV for each person to whom it pays "reportable" dividends aggregating $10 or more during the calendar year. (Code Sec. 6042(a), Reg § 1.6042-2(a)(1)) Dividends qualifying for preferential tax rates must be differentiated from nonqualified dividends. [13] For payee statements, see ¶4742.

Reportable dividends are corporate "dividends" (¶1283 *et seq.*) and substitute dividends (e.g., payments in lieu of dividends that brokers pay on short sales). (Code Sec. 6042(b)(1))[14] Nontaxable dividends are reported on Form 5452. [15]

Cooperatives (¶4206) report *patronage dividends* aggregating $10 or more to any payee in a calendar year on Form 1099-PATR. (Code Sec. 6044(a)(1); Reg § 1.6044-2(b))[16]

¶ 4740   Interest reporting—Forms 1099-INT; 1042-S.

Every person (including nominees, see ¶4738) who pays $10 or more of reportable interest to any person (except certain payees) in a calendar year reports the payments (Code Sec. 6049(a)(1), Code Sec. 6049(d)) on Form 1099-INT.[17] For payee statements, see ¶4742.

Reportable interest is interest on: (a) obligations issued publicly or in registered form

---

8. ¶S-2900 *et seq.*, S-4930
9. ¶S-4930; ¶s 60,424, 60,494
10. ¶S-1305; ¶S-4930; ¶60,414.06
11. ¶S-2904 *et seq.*; ¶s 60,424, 60,494
12. ¶s S-2904 *et seq.*, S-3003 *et seq.*; ¶60,424, 60,494

13. ¶S-2901, ¶S-2910; ¶60,424
14. ¶S-2910, S-3724; ¶60,424
15. ¶S-2914; ¶60,424
16. ¶S-2951; ¶60,444
17. ¶S-3001 *et seq.*; ¶60,494

(other than a short-term obligation held by a corporation), (b) deposits with banks or brokers, and (c) amounts held by insurance or investment companies. (Code Sec. 6049(b)(1))[18] Reportable interest also includes original issue discount (¶4741); amounts includible in gross income with respect to regular real estate mortgage investment conduits interests (¶4204) (Code Sec. 6049(d)(6)(A)(i), Code Sec. 6049(d)(7)(A));[19] and interest paid on tax-exempt bonds. But interest on obligations issued by a natural person isn't "reportable." (Code Sec. 6049(b)(2))[20]

A payor reports on Form 1042-S interest aggregating $10 or more that is paid to a nonresident alien individual (NRA) on deposits maintained at U.S. offices of financial institutions if the NRA lives in a country with which the U.S. has in effect an information exchange agreement. A payor can elect to report all interest paid to all NRAs. (Reg § 1.6049-4(b)(5), Reg § 1.6049-8)[21]

¶ 4741   Reporting original issue discount (OID)—Forms 1099-OID, 8281.

An issuer (or nominee, see ¶4738) reports OID of at least $10 on any obligation as an interest payment. (Code Sec. 6049(d)(6)) Form 1099-OID is used to report the OID and any interest actually paid on the obligation. [22] Form 8281 must be filed by certain issuers of publicly-offered debt instruments having OID within 30 days after issuance. (Code Sec. 1275(c)(2); Reg § 1.1275-3(c))[23]

observation: The one-time reporting requirement on Form 8281 is in addition to the annual information reporting on Form 1099-OID.

If a broker has to file a statement for a debt instrument (statements to recipients of interest payments and holders of obligations for attributed OID), the broker generally reports any bond premium (under Reg § 1.171-1(d), see ¶2165) or acquisition premium (under Reg § 1.1272-2(b)(3), see ¶2621) for the calendar year. [24]

For tax-exempt obligations acquired after 2016, a payer must report the daily portions of OID on a tax-exempt obligation. (Reg § 1.6049-10)[25]

¶ 4742   Payee statements—Form 1099.

Payors of reportable dividends (and payments in lieu of dividends) and interest (including OID) must furnish payees with specified written statements of the amount reported to IRS (i.e., Copy B of Form 1099 sent to IRS). This generally must be done, either in person or in a "statement mailing," by Jan. 31 of the year following the calendar year for which the payor's Form 1099 was required. (Reg § 1.6042-4(d)(1), Reg § 1.6044-5(b), Reg § 1.6049-3(c)(1)) Payees can consent to receiving Form 1099 statements electronically. [26]

¶ 4743   Business payments of $600 or more—Form 1099-MISC.

With limited exceptions, every person, corporate or otherwise, engaged in a trade or business who, in the course of that business, makes payments aggregating $600 or more to another person (e.g., an independent contractor) in a calendar year must file Form 1099-MISC setting forth the payee's name and address and the amount paid, and furnish a statement to the payee. Any return or statement reporting nonemployee compensation must be filed by Jan. 31 of the year following the calendar year to which the returns

---

18. ¶S-3011 *et seq.*, ¶S-3023 *et seq.*; ¶60,494
19. ¶s S-3073, S-3087; ¶60,494
20. ¶S-3038, S-3040, S-3042; ¶60,494
21. ¶S-3012.1; ¶S-3012.1A; ¶60,494.05
22. ¶S-3073, S-3074; ¶60,494

23. ¶S-3080 *et seq.*; ¶12,714.06
24. ¶S-3078.1; ¶60,494.01
25. ¶S-3040; ¶60,494.01
26. ¶S-2927 *et seq.*; ¶60,424, 60,444, 60,494

relate.[27] Reportable payments are: rent, salaries, wages, premiums, annuities, compensations, remunerations, emoluments, prizes or awards (that aren't for services rendered), or other fixed or determinable gains, profits and income. (Code Sec. 6041; Reg § 1.6041-1)[28] This rule doesn't apply to transactions covered by other information return rules (e.g., dividends, see ¶4739), or most payments to corporations (including LLCs that elect to be treated as corporations, ¶3702). Payments of bills for merchandise, telegrams, telephone, freight, storage, and similar charges are exempt from the return requirement. (Reg § 1.6041-3(c)) But, a taxpayer has to report certain payments to doctors or corporations engaged in providing medical care (including veterinary care) if the payment is made in the course of the taxpayer's trade or business. (Reg § 1.6041-3) Also, persons who, in the course of a trade or business it's engaged in, pay reportable gambling winnings must make an information return with respect to those payments (for winnings of $1,200 and above for bingo and slot machines; $1,500 and above for keno). A separate information return is required for each payment. (Reg § 1.6041-10)[29] IRS has issued guidance on how reporting applies to payments made with credit or debit cards. [30]

¶ 4744 Mortgage interest (and points) received—Form 1098.

A person ("interest recipient") who receives interest, or reimburses interest overpayments, aggregating $600 or more for a calendar year on a mortgage must report (on Form 1098) those receipts or reimbursements, even if the interest is received on behalf of another. This applies to any person (including cooperative housing corporations) who, in the course of his trade or business (except governmental recipients), receives interest on a mortgage secured all or in part by real property, where the payor of record is an individual. (Code Sec. 6050H; Reg § 1.6050H-1, Reg § 1.6050H-2(a))[31] The return must also include any points received in the year that were paid directly by the buyer (including certain points paid by or charged to the seller). (Code Sec. 6050H(b)(2)(C); Reg § 1.6050H-1(f))[32] For 2011-2021, HUD and state housing finance authorities (State HFAs) can report payments made to or on behalf of financially distressed homeowners under programs such as Emergency-Homeowners' Loan Program (EHLP) or similar programs designed by State HFAs on Form 1098-MA or on a statement containing the required information. [33]

¶ 4745 Reporting qualified residence interest on seller-provided financing.

A return on which taxpayer claims a deduction for qualified residence interest (¶1729) on seller-provided financing must show the name, address and TIN of the person (the seller) to whom the interest is paid or accrued on Form 1040, Schedule A. Any person who receives or accrues interest from seller-provided financing must include on Form 1040, Schedule B for the tax year in which the interest is so received or accrued the name, address and TIN of the person liable for the interest. (Code Sec. 6109(h))[34]

¶ 4746 Other information returns.

. . . *Abandonment or foreclosure of property held as security* for a business loan must be reported by the lender on Form 1099-A (Code Sec. 6050J; Reg § 1.6050J-1T) (unless related to a discharge of debt reported on Form 1099-C, below). [35]

. . . *Accelerated death benefits* paid to any individual must be reported by the payor (Code Sec. 6050Q) on Form 1099-LTC.[36]

---

27. ¶S-3658; ¶60,714
28. ¶S-3655 *et seq.*, ¶S-3658; ¶s 60,414, 60,414.06
29. ¶S-3676, S-3667, S-3697.1; ¶60,414.06
30. ¶S-3699.18; ¶34,064
31. ¶S-3901 *et seq.*; ¶60,50H4

32. ¶S-3907 *et seq.*
33. ¶V-1810.4 *et seq.*
34. ¶S-1524 *et seq.*; ¶61,094
35. ¶S-4200 *et seq.*; ¶60,50J4
36. ¶S-3440; ¶60,50Q4

. . . *Acquiring corporation in taxable acquisition* must file information returns with IRS and furnish statements to shareholders if a shareholder of the acquired corporation recognizes gain or loss in whole or in part due to the acquisition. (Code Sec. 6043A(a))[37]

. . . *Alcohol and biodiesel fuel tax benefits, Code Sec. 34 credit for farming, off-highway and certain other nontaxable uses of fuel* —information return required by persons claiming alcohol or biodiesel fuel tax benefits or a Code Sec. 34 credit, providing information on the benefits or credit. (Code Sec. 4104(a))[38]

. . . *Attorney's fees* paid in the course of a trade or business that aren't reportable as wages or under Code Sec. 6041 (or would have to be reported under Code Sec. 6041 but for the $600 limitation, see ¶4743), whether or not the services are performed for the payor (Code Sec. 6045(f); Reg § 1.6045-5) and whether or not the attorney is the exclusive payee, on Form 1099-MISC. (Reg § 1.6045-5)[39]

. . . *Applicable large employers* (ALEs) must offer their full-time employees and their dependents the opportunity to enroll in minimum essential coverage (MEC, ¶4898) under an eligible employer-sponsored plan have to report insurance coverage (including health reimbursement accounts) on Form 1094-C and Form 1095-C. Use Form 8809 to request an extension. (Code Sec. 6056; Reg § 301.6056-1)[40]

. . . *Banks and on-line payment networks* (payment settlement entities (PSEs) or third party settlement organizations (TPSOs)) have to report credit card sales to IRS and "participating payees" on Form 1099-K. TPSOs have to report payments made in settlement of third party network transactions only if the amount to be reported exceeds $20,000 and the aggregate number of transactions exceeds 200 for any payee within a calendar year. (Code Sec. 6050W; Reg § 1.6050W-1)[41]

. . . *Barter exchanges* having at least 100 exchanges of property or services are made in the calendar year are reported on Form 1099-B. (Code Sec. 6045; Reg § 1.6045-1(e))[42]

. . . *Basis information, regarding property acquired from decedents,* must be provided by executors and/or certain beneficiaries to persons who acquire property from a decedent. (Code Sec. 6035(a))[43]

. . . *Brokers* must report each sale of securities, commodities, regulated futures contracts, foreign currency contracts, forward contracts, and debt instruments the broker effects for its customers, on Form 1099-B. (Code Sec. 6045; Reg § 1.6045-1(c), Reg § 1.6045-2)[44] Brokers also must report customer's adjusted basis (determined under Reg § 1.6045-1(n)(6)) and character of gain or loss for sales of "covered securities" (as defined in Code Sec. 6045(g)(3) and Reg § 1.6045-1(a)(15). Brokers can treat all securities as covered securities to simplify reporting. For a debt instrument acquired after 2014, brokers can't take into account an election under Reg § 1.1272-3 when computing basis, but can assume that a customer elected to determine accrued market discount using a constant yield method (unless the customer notifies the broker otherwise). (Code Sec. 6045(g); Reg § 1.6045-1(d)(6); Reg § 1.6045-1(n))[45] Also, brokers that transfer covered securities to other brokers have to provide statements to other brokers. (Code Sec. 6045A; Reg § 1.6045A-1)[46]

. . . *Cash of more than $10,000,* including certain cash equivalents (e.g., cashier's checks, foreign currency) received in connection with a trade or business must be reported by the recipient (Code Sec. 6050I(a), Code Sec. 6050I(d); Reg § 1.6050I-1(a)(1), Reg § 1.6050I-1(c)(1)) within 15 days after receipt. Use Form 8300 (Reg § 1.6050I-1(e)), except that banks file Financial Crimes Enforcement Network (FinCEN) Form 104 and casinos, under special rules (Reg § 1.6050I-1(d)(2)), file FinCEN Form 103 (certain Nevada

37. ¶S-4317; ¶6043A4
38. ¶S-4466; ¶41,044
39. ¶S-3851; ¶60,454.06
40. ¶S-3331; ¶60,564
41. ¶S-3699.19; ¶60,50W4

42. ¶S-3731 *et seq.*; ¶60,454
43. ¶S-2309; ¶60,354
44. ¶S-3700 *et seq.*; ¶60,454
45. ¶S-3741 *et seq.*; ¶60,454.08
46. ¶S-3761 *et seq.*; ¶60,45A4

casinos file Form 8852) to report cash from gaming activities. [47] Recipients in U.S. territories must report. [48] Special rules apply for cash installment payments. (Reg § 1.6050I-1(b)) [49]

. . . *Change in control or recapitalization of a corporation* generally must be reported on Form 8806 showing the parties to the transaction, the fees involved, the changes in capital structure and any other information IRS requires. (Code Sec. 6043(c); Reg § 1.6043-4) [50]

. . . *Charitable organization required to acknowledge gift of auto, plane, or boat* (¶2138) must provide the information required on Form 1098-C to IRS. (Code Sec. 170(f)(12)(D)) [1]

. . . *Charitable property disposition* by the donee within 3 years of contribution must be reported on Form 8282 by the charity, if the deduction claimed for the property exceeds $5,000 (but disposition of items appraised for $500 or less doesn't have to be reported). (Code Sec. 6050L; Reg § 1.6050L-1) [2]

. . . *Commodity Credit Corporation (CCC)* must report market gain associated with the repayment of a CCC loan, regardless of whether the taxpayer repays the loan with cash or uses CCC certificates in repayment of the loan, on Form 1099-G. (Code Sec. 6039J) [3]

. . . *Direct sales of consumer goods* of $5,000 or more to any 1 buyer in a calendar year must be reported by the seller (Code Sec. 6041A) on Form 1099-MISC. [4]

. . . *Discharge of debt (including student loans) by banks, and other financial entities and organizations having a significant lending trade or business* of $600 or more is reported to IRS, on Form 1099-C. (Code Sec. 6050P; Reg § 1.6050P-1, Reg § 1.6050P-2) [5]

. . . *Donee of qualified intellectual property* (¶2106) must file annual information return (Form 8899) of net income from property for each specified tax year of the donee. (Code Sec. 6050L(b)(1); Reg § 1.6050L-2) [6]

. . . *Education-related payments* received (or billed) by higher education institutions for qualified tuition and related expenses; qualified tuition refunds (Form 1098-T) (Reg § 1.6050S-1); and interest of $600 or more received from an individual for a calendar year on an educational loan (Form 1098-E) are reported. (Code Sec. 6050S; Reg § 1.6050S-3) [7] For educational loans, lenders report amounts (in addition to all other interest paid) attributable to capitalized interest and loan origination fees. [8] Certain statements to students and borrowers may be provided electronically. (Reg § 1.6050S-2(a)(1), Reg § 1.6050S-4(a)) [9]

. . . *Education savings distributions* (certain) from Coverdell ESAs [10] and qualified tuition programs or 529 plans are reported on Form 1099-Q. [11]

. . . *Employer-owned life insurance contracts* issued after Aug. 17, 2006, must be reported on Form 8925 by applicable policyholders. (Code Sec. 6039I; Reg § 1.6039I-1) [12]

. . . *Fishing boat operators* report crew payments on Form 1099-MISC. (Code Sec. 6050A; Reg § 1.6050A-1) [13]

. . . *Fish bought for resale* for cash (of $600 or more) are reported on Form 1099-MISC for each seller by persons engaged in the trade or business of buying fish for resale. (Code Sec. 6050R) [14]

. . . *Foreign financial accounts* (including on-line poker accounts) are reported on Financial Crimes Enforcement Network (FinCEN) Form 114 (FBAR) by any person (including

---

47. ¶S-4000 *et seq.*; ¶60,50I4 *et seq.*
48. ¶S-4012
49. ¶S-4019 *et seq.*; ¶60,50I4.02
50. ¶S-4308; ¶60,434
1. ¶K-3948.1; ¶S-2872.1
2. ¶S-2873; ¶60,50L4
3. ¶N-1171.1; ¶60,39J4
4. ¶S-3677; ¶60,41A4
5. ¶S-4251 *et seq.*; ¶60,50P4

6. ¶S-2882.1; ¶60,50L4
7. ¶S-3430 *et seq.*; ¶60,50S4
8. ¶S-3432.11; ¶60,50S4.01
9. ¶S-1370; ¶60,50S4.01
10. ¶S-3428
11. ¶S-3422
12. ¶S-3231; ¶60,39I4
13. ¶S-3695; ¶60,50A4
14. ¶S-3695.1; ¶60,50R4

a person acting as an agent) with a financial interest in or signature authority over the account, if the aggregate value of these accounts exceeds $10,000 at any time during the calendar year. FBAR is due by Apr. 15 of the year following the year that the account holder meets the $10,000 threshold, but is eligible for an automatic 6-month extension. [15]

... *Individuals and specified domestic entities holding any interest in specified foreign financial assets* have to attach the information required on Form 8938 to their income tax returns if the aggregate value of those assets exceed $50,000 ($100,000 for certain married individuals) or a higher amount prescribed by IRS. Specified foreign financial assets include stock, securities, financial instruments, and contracts that are held for investment, are not held in an account maintained by a financial institution, and are issued by a person organized under the laws of a U.S. possession. The maximum fair market value for a specified foreign financial asset with no positive value during the year is treated as zero. (Code Sec. 6038D; Reg § 1.6038D-1; Reg § 1.6038D-2; Reg § 1.6038D-3; Reg § 1.6038D-5) [16]

... *Insurers* (including self-insured employers) that provide minimal essential coverage (MEC, ¶4898) to any individual during a calendar year report health insurance coverage information for coverage on Form 1095-B. Proposed reliance regs provide guidance under Code Sec. 6055 relating to Form 1095-B. (Code Sec. 6055; Reg § 1.6055-1; Prop Reg. § 1.6055-1 ("Taxpayers may rely")) [17]

... *IRA (and Roth IRA) contributions and withdrawals* must be reported by the IRA trustees or issuer (Code Sec. 408(i), Code Sec. 408A(d)(3)(D)), on Form 5498. [18] The trustee also reports on Form 5498 that a required minimum distribution (but not the amount) is required for an IRA for a calendar year. (Reg § 1.408-8, Q&10) [19] For required distributions, information is provided to the IRA owner by Jan. 31 of the required distribution year. [20]

... *Issuers* of specified securities (i.e., stocks, bonds, commodity contracts, etc.) report organizational actions (e.g., stock splits, mergers, acquisitions, etc.) affecting basis on Form 8937. It is due within 45 days of the action or, if earlier, by Jan. 15 of the next calendar year. But, the issuer can post the form on its primary public website in a readily accessible format by the due date (instead of filing). (Code Sec. 6045B; Reg § 1.6045B-1) [21]

... *Life insurance contracts:* Reporting requirements apply to the acquirer of an existing life insurance contract or interest therein in a reportable policy sale after 2017 (and to the issuer of the contract) and to the payor of reportable death benefits after 2017. (Code Sec. 6050Y) IRS says reporting will not be required until after final regs are issued, and has issued draft 2018 Form 1099-LS, which is to be used by acquirers of a life insurance contract. [22]

... *Liquidating corporations* report the adoption of the plan of liquidation on Form 966, [23] and liquidating distributions (Code Sec. 6043(a)) on Form 1099-DIV. [24]

... *Long-term care payments* made under a long-term care insurance contract to any individual must be reported by the payor (Code Sec. 6050Q) on Form 1099-LTC. [25]

... *Medical savings account and health savings account contributions and distributions* are reported by a trustee on Form 5498-SA and Form 1099-SA. (Code Sec. 220(h)) [26]

... *Mortgage credit certificate* (MCC) information is reported (on Form 8329) by each person who makes a "certified indebtedness" loan under an MCC program. (Reg § 1.25-

---

15. ¶S-3650; ¶60,114.06
16. ¶S-3650.1; S-3650.2; ¶60,38D4
17. ¶S-3321; ¶60,554
18. ¶S-3391; ¶4084.04
19. ¶S-3392.1; ¶4084.04
20. ¶S-3392.2; ¶4084.04

21. ¶S-3781, S-3786; ¶60,45B4
22. ¶S-3240 *et seq.*
23. ¶S-4314; ¶60,434
24. ¶S-4315; ¶60,434
25. ¶S-3435.1 *et seq.*; ¶60,50Q4
26. ¶H-1328.1; ¶2204.01

8T(a))[27] Each state or political subdivision with MCC programs reports (on Form 8330) the amount of MCCs issued each quarter. (Code Sec. 25(g); Reg § 1.25-4T)[28]

. . . *Mortgage insurance premiums* aggregating $600 or more for any calendar year must be reported on Form 1098 by any person who, in the course of a trade or business, received the premiums. (Code Sec. 6050H(h)(1), Reg § 1.6050H-3)[29]

. . . *Outbound Code Sec. 355 distributions* (¶3545) and outbound Code Sec. 332 corporate liquidations (Reg § 1.6038B-1(e))[30] are reported on Form 926.[31]

. . . *Parent tax-exempt organizations* that are controlling organizations (Code Sec. 512(b)(3)) report transactions with controlled entities on Form 990-T. (Code Sec. 6033(h))[32]

. . . *Partnership interest sales or exchanges* due to unrealized receivables, inventory, collectibles, or Code Sec. 1250 gain are reported by partnerships on Form 8308. (Code Sec. 6050K; Reg § 1.6050K-1(a)(1))[33] A partnership doesn't have to file until it's notified of the exchange (Code Sec. 6050K(c)(2)), i.e., when it receives written notification required from the transferor, or has knowledge of it. (Reg § 1.6050K-1)[34]

. . . *Pension, profit-sharing plans* file annual return/report forms in the Form 5500 series (Code Sec. 6058(a)),[35] file Form 5310A to notify IRS of plan mergers, consolidations, or divisions, (Code Sec. 6057(b)(4))[36] and make returns and reports of designated Roth contributions. (Code Sec. 6047(f)) Form 5500 series is due no later than the last day of the 7th month after the plan year ends (July 31 for calendar year plans). There is an automatic 2 1/2 month extension to file certain Form 5500.[37] Form 8955-SSA is used to report information about separated participants with deferred vested benefits.[38] A short Form 5500-SF may be filed by plans: covering fewer than 100 participants at the beginning of the plan year; not holding employer securities; investing 100% in certain secure, easy to value assets; eligible for a waiver under DOL annual examination and report rules; and not multiemployer plans.[39] 1-participant plan with total assets of $250,000 or less are exempt from filing the annual return. If that plan must file a return, it can file a paper Form 5500-EZ (or Form 5500-SF e-file).[40] All other annual reports — including any statements and schedules — are filed electronically with DOL using EFAST2.[41] Use Form 5558 to request extensions for filing Form 5500 and Form 8955-SSA.[42]

. . . *Political organizations* except for certain state and local committees under Code Sec. 527 must file an initial notice of status (Form 8871) (Code Sec. 527(i)),[43] and periodic reports of contributions and expenditures (Form 8872) (Code Sec. 527(j)(2)), which can be filed on-line with an IRS-supplied user ID and password.[44]

. . . *Premium and advance payment* information is reported by an Exchange on Form 1095-A, see ¶2344. IRS announced that Exchanges may, but aren't required to, report information relating to catastrophic health plan coverage enrolled in through an Exchange for coverage years after 2017. (Code Sec. 6055)[45]

. . . *Real estate* reporting persons (as defined in Code Sec. 6045(e)(2)) must report real estate transactions on Form 1099-S, including the sale of a condominium unit or stock in a cooperative housing unit. For a residential transactions, the return includes any portion of real property tax treated as imposed on the buyer. Reporting isn't required for sales of principal residences for $250,000 or less ($500,000 or less for married sellers)

27. ¶S-4206; ¶254.02
28. ¶S-4207; ¶254.02
29. ¶S-3923; ¶60,50H4
30. ¶S-3640.1; ¶S-3640.1A
31. ¶S-3630; ¶60,38B4
32. ¶S-2862.2; ¶60,334
33. ¶S-2725 *et seq.*; ¶60,50K4
34. ¶S-2734 *et seq.*; ¶60,50K4
35. ¶S-3351; ¶4014.01, 60,584
36. ¶S-3383, S-3384; ¶4014.01, 60,574

37. ¶S-3400.1; S-3366.1
38. ¶S-3369
39. ¶S-3355.1
40. ¶S-3357
41. ¶S-3351
42. ¶S-5057¶60,814.11
43. ¶S-2858.7
44. ¶S-2858.9
45. ¶S-3321

(regs can permit higher amounts) if the reporting person receives specified written assurances (on IRS's certification form) from the seller by Jan. 31 following the year of sale. (Code Sec. 6045(e); Reg § 1.6045-4)[46] Reportable real estate transactions also include sales or exchanges of standing timber for lump-sum payments. (Reg § 1.6045-4(b)(2)(i)(E), Reg § 1.6045-4(s))[47]

. . . *Receipt of fines, penalties, etc. by government and other agencies of $600 or more for law violations.* Government agencies (or entities treated as such agencies) that are complainants or investigators with respect to a violation or potential violation of any law must report to IRS and to the taxpayer the amount of each settlement agreement or order entered into where the aggregate amount required to be paid or incurred to or at the direction of the government is at least $600 (or such other amount as may be specified by IRS). (Code Sec. 6050X) IRS transitional guidance says reporting will not be required until the date specified in proposed regulations, which will not be earlier than Jan. 1, 2019. [48]

. . . *Refunds of state and local income tax* of $10 or more must be reported by the state or local tax authority/payor on Form 1099-G. (Code Sec. 6050E; Reg § 1.6050E-1)[49]

. . . *Royalty payments* of $10 or more per year per payee (including nominees) must be reported unless the payee is a corporation, exempt organization or government (Code Sec. 6050N), on Form 1099-MISC. Where a publisher pays royalties to an author's agent and the agent subtracts his commission and expenses, both parties report the gross royalties on Form 1099-MISC, unreduced by the subtracted amounts. [50]

. . . *Transfers under incentive stock options (ISOs) and employee stock purchase plans (ESPPs)* are reported by corporations on Form 3921 and Form 3922. (Code Sec. 6039(a); Reg § 1.6039-1)[1]

. . . *Sick pay* (nonwage) paid by a third party to an employee must be reported by the third party to the employee's employer. An employer or third party files Form 8922 if the employer is including the employer FICA tax on sick pay wages on the employer's Form 941 but the third party is including the employee FICA tax on the same sick pay wages on the third party's Form 941 (split liability). Whether the employer or the third party is required to file the Form 8922 depends on which entity is filing Form W-2 for the sick pay. (Code Sec. 6051(f)(1); Reg § 31.6051-3(a))[2]

. . . *Simplified employee pension (SEP) contributions* are reported by the SEP trustee or issuer of a SEP endowment contract (Code Sec. 408(l); Reg § 1.408-7) on Form 5498.[3]

. . . *Sponsoring organizations* (under Code Sec. 4966(d)(1), ¶4131), on their annual information returns (Form 990-T), must include information relating to donor advised funds (DAFs, ¶4127) owned by an organization at the end of the tax year. (Code Sec. 6033(k))[4]

. . . *Supporting organizations* (Code Sec. 509(a)(3)) must file annual information returns listing supported organizations, the type of supporting organization, certify that the organization isn't controlled by 1 or more disqualified persons. (Code Sec. 6033(l))[5]

. . . *Tips* must be reported by employees to employers on Form 4070. (Code Sec. 6053(a); Reg § 31.6053-1(b)(2))[6] Large food and beverage establishments (more than 10 employees on a typical business day) must report to IRS (on Form 8027) and to employees tips reported by the employees to the employer plus the excess (as specially allocated) of 8% of the establishment's gross receipts (as specially defined) over the amount of tips reported by the employees. The 8% can be reduced to not below 2%, on application to IRS. (Code Sec. 6053(c)(3); Reg § 31.6053-3)[7] An employer doesn't have to report tips that

46. ¶S-3800 *et seq.*; ¶60,454.04; *et seq.*
47. ¶S-3813; ¶60,454.04
48. ¶S-4271; ¶60,50X4
49. ¶S-3690; ¶60,50E4
50. ¶S-3684 *et seq.*; ¶60,50N4
1. ¶S-3206.1 *et seq.*; ¶60,394

2. ¶S-3173; ¶60,514
3. ¶S-3399 *et seq.*; ¶4084.05
4. ¶S-2862.3; ¶60,334
5. ¶S-2823.1; ¶60,334
6. ¶H-4344; ¶60,534
7. ¶S-3250 *et seq.*; ¶S-3303; ¶60,534

aren't reported to the employer until it receives a Code Sec. 3121(q) Notice and Demand. Then, the employer reports them on its next Form 941.[8]

. . . *Unemployment insurance benefit* payments of $10 or more must be reported by the payor on Form 1099-G. (Code Sec. 6050B; Reg § 1.6050B-1)[9]

¶ 4747 Extension of time for information returns—Form 8809.

Use Form 8809 to request a 30-day extension to file the following forms: W-2G, 1042-S, 1094-C, 1095-B, 1095-C, 3921, 3922, 8027, 1097 series, 1098 series, 1099 series (except forms reporting nonemployee compensation) and 5498 series. Approval is automatic for 30-day extension requests (no signature or explanation needed). Detailed explanation and signature are required for requests beyond the original 30-day extension. For returns due after Dec. 31, 2018, anyone required to file Form W-2 series returns (except Form W-2G) or a form reporting nonemployee compensation will only be allowed to request a single 30-day "non-automatic" extension. (Reg § 1.6081-8)[10] "Non-automatic" extensions are also available to file Social Security Administration's copy of Forms W-2 and W-3. (Reg § 31.6081(a)-1) Make a written application (don't use Form 8809) to request an extension of up to 30 days for furnishing the payee statement, see ¶4742.[11]

¶ 4748 Material advisors must disclose reportable transactions and maintain lists—Forms 8918, 13976.

Each material advisor with respect to any reportable transaction (Code Sec. 6707A(c), ¶4893) files Form 8918 setting out: information identifying and describing a transaction and its expected tax benefits, and any other information that IRS requests. (Code Sec. 6111(a); Reg § 301.6111-3(a)) It is due by the last day of the month following the calendar quarter in which a person becomes a material adviser.[12] For penalties, see ¶4895.

A material advisor is any person who provides any material aid, assistance, or advice with respect to organizing, managing, promoting, selling, implementing, insuring, or carrying out any reportable transaction, and who directly or indirectly derives gross income in excess of a threshold amount (or such other amount prescribed by IRS) for that assistance or advice. (Code Sec. 6111(b)(1)(A); Reg § 301.6111-3(b)) A person becomes a material adviser when (1) he makes a tax statement, (2) he receives (or expects to receive) the minimum fees, and (3) the transaction is entered into by the taxpayer.[13]

The threshold amount is $50,000 for a reportable transaction substantially all of the tax benefits from which are provided to natural persons, and $250,000 in any other case. (Code Sec. 6111(b)(1)(B); Reg § 301.6111-3(b)(3))[14]

Each material advisor must maintain a list with respect to any reportable transaction. The list must identify each person for whom the advisor acted as a material advisor for the transaction and contain any other information as IRS regs may require. The list may (but is not required to) be kept on Form 13976. (Code Sec. 6112(a); Reg § 301.6112-1)[15]

¶ 4749 Participation in confidential tax avoidance transactions—Form 8886.

Taxpayers must disclose (on Form 8886 due with an original or amended return reporting participation) their participation in "reportable transactions," by attaching an information statement to their income tax returns, including: (a) listed transactions (i.e., transactions that have been specifically identified by IRS as tax avoidance transactions such as

8. ¶H-4714.1
9. ¶S-3694; ¶60,50B4
10. ¶S-5049; ¶60,814.07
11. ¶S-5051, S-5054; ¶60,814.07

12. ¶S-4401, ¶S-4413; ¶61,114
13. ¶S-4402; ¶61,114
14. ¶S-4406; ¶61,114
15. ¶S-4414; ¶61,124

"sale in/lease-out" (SILO) or "lease-in-lease-out" (LILO) transactions, certain offsetting currency transactions solely used to import losses but not gains, basket option contracts, and certain syndicated conservation easement transactions); (b) confidential transactions offered under conditions of confidentiality and for which the taxpayer has paid an advisor a minimum fee; (c) transactions with contractual protection; (d) loss transactions resulting in a taxpayer claiming a tax loss exceeding specified amounts; and (e) transactions of interest (i.e., transactions that are the same or substantially similar to transactions identified by IRS). (Reg § 1.6011-4) *Transactions of interest* include certain charitable contributions of real property interests ("successor member interests") that involve inflated valuations, "toggling" grantor trust transactions where grantor trusts are purportedly terminated and recreated to generate large losses, certain sales of interests in charitable remainder trusts that result in the grantor or other non-charitable recipient receiving the value of the trust while claiming to recognize little or no taxable gain, certain transactions involving blocker partnerships to avoid the inclusion of income of lower-tier controlled foreign corporations, basket contracts, and micro-captive transactions. [16]

A copy of Form 8886 must be sent to the IRS Office of Tax Shelter Analysis (OTSA). For penalties, see ¶4893. Taxpayers also must disclose participation in listed transactions involving estate tax (Reg § 20.6011-4), gift tax (Reg § 25.6011-4), employment tax (Reg § 31.6011-4), excise tax related to private foundations and certain other tax exempts (Reg § 53.6011-4), excise taxes relating to qualified pension and other plans under Code Sec. 4971 through Code Sec. 4980F (Reg § 54.6011-4), and excise taxes relating to public charities. (Reg § 56.6011-4) Disclosure requires, among other things, the expected tax treatment of and all potential tax benefits expected from the transaction, a sufficiently detailed description of the transaction, and the identity of all parties involved in the transaction. Confidential corporate tax shelters also are subject to the tax shelter registration rules of Code Sec. 6111. Affected transactions are listed transactions and other tax-structured transactions as specially defined. (Reg § 301.6111-2) [17]

¶ 4750   Preparer's duty in preparation of returns.

A tax return preparer (¶4751) must:

. . . *sign the return* as prescribed by IRS in forms, instructions, etc. (Code Sec. 6695(b)) If the return isn't signed electronically, he must sign a completed return before it is presented to a taxpayer for signature. If the preparer is unavailable for signature, another preparer must review the entire return and sign it. (Reg § 1.6695-1(b)(1)) Preparers may sign original or amended returns, or extension requests, as a return preparer with a stamp, mechanical device, or computer software program. The method used must contain either a facsimile of the preparer's signature or his printed name. [18]

. . . *enter a preparer tax ID number (PTIN)*. (Code Sec. 6109(a)(4)) All compensated preparers (including those who already have PTINs) must register on the on-line registration system (on the Tax Professionals page at irs.gov) or submit a paper Form W-12 (4 to 6 weeks of response time). Preparers must renew PTINs annually. IRS isn't currently requiring preparers to pay user fees for PTINs. IRS established a voluntary education program (Annual Filing Season Program, or AFSP) for return preparers (other than attorneys, CPAs, EAs, etc.). Applicants apply for AFSP in the same manner as applying for a PTIN. IRS has published an on-line directory of preparers who have satisfied the requirements for AFSP or who have recognized credentials (e.g., an attorney, CPA, enrolled agents) at IRS.gov/chooseataxpro. (Reg § 1.6109-2) [19] An enrolled retirement plan agent (ERPA) needs a PTIN if, for compensation, he prepares, or assists in the preparation of, all or substantially all of any tax return or claim for refund that is not an

---

16. ¶S-4429; ¶61,114
17. ¶S-4434; ¶61,114

18. ¶S-4603, ¶S-4604; ¶66,954
19. ¶S-1522 *et seq.*, ¶T-10906.1; ¶61,094

exempt form (e.g., Form 5300 and Form 5500 are exempt forms). [20]

...*enter an address where the return was prepared* on any return he prepares; if there's a partnership or employment arrangement between 2 or more preparers, the identifying number of the partnership or employer must also appear on the return or claim for refund. The identifying number of a preparer (whether an individual, corporation, or partnership) who employs or engages 1 or more persons to prepare returns or refund claims is that preparer's employer identification number (EIN). (Reg § 1.6109-2(a))[21]

...*furnish the taxpayer with a completed copy of any tax return* no later than when the return is presented for signature. (Code Sec. 6107(a)) The same rule applies to a return prepared for a nontaxable entity (i.e., partnership or S corporation). (Reg § 1.6107-1(a))[22]

...*retain for 3 years a completed copy of each return* or a list of the name and TIN of each taxpayer for whom a return was prepared (Code Sec. 6107(b));[23]

...*retain a record of the name, TIN, and principal place of work of each income tax return preparer* employed or engaged by the preparer/employer during each July 1-June 30 period. (Reg § 1.6060-1(a)(1))[24]

...*e-file* individual income tax returns (and estate and trust returns), unless the preparer neither files nor reasonably expects to file 10 or more individual income tax returns in a calendar year. (Code Sec. 6011(e); Reg § 301.6011-7) E-filing is mandatory for preparers anticipating filing 11 or more federal individual or trust tax returns. Firms have to compute the number of returns in the aggregate that they reasonably expect to file as a firm. Clients can independently choose to file paper returns. Preparers should document each client's choice to file a paper return and keep a copy of the signed statement on file. Use Form 8944 to request hardship waivers from e-filing. [25]

For penalties on return preparers, see ¶4890.

¶ 4751 Tax return preparer defined.

A tax return preparer is any person, including a partnership or corporation, who, in return for compensation, prepares, or employs or engages another to prepare, all or a substantial portion of any federal tax return or refund claim. (Code Sec. 7701(a)(36)(A)) A *signing* tax return preparer is the individual tax return preparer who has the primary responsibility for the overall substantive accuracy of the preparation of the return or refund claim. (Reg § 301.7701-15(b)(1))

A *nonsigning* tax return preparer is any tax return preparer who is not a signing tax return preparer but who prepares all or a substantial portion of a return or claim for refund for events that have occurred at the time the advice is rendered. Time spent on advice that is given after events have occurred that represents less than 5% of the individual's aggregate time with respect to the position giving rise to the understatement is not taken into account. Examples of nonsigning tax return preparers are preparers who provide advice to a taxpayer or another preparer when that advice leads to a position or entry that is a substantial portion of the return. (Reg § 301.7701-15(b)(2)(i))[26]

A person may also be a "preparer" of a related return if an entry on a return he actually prepared (e.g., partnership or S corporation return) is directly reflected on the related return (e.g., partner's or shareholder's return), and the entry is a substantial portion of the related return. (Reg § 301.7701-15(b)(3)(iii))[27]

---

20. ¶S-1522.1
21. ¶S-1522; ¶61,094
22. ¶S-1102; ¶61,074
23. ¶V-2675; ¶61,074

24. ¶S-1106, V-2676; ¶60,604
25. ¶S-1601; ¶60,114.075
26. ¶S-1107; ¶77,014.24
27. ¶S-1117

A portion of a return prepared by a nonsigning tax return preparer won't be "substantial" if, aggregating all schedules, etc., he prepared, that portion involves amounts of gross income, deductions, or amounts on which credits are based that are: (1) less than $10,000, or (2) less than $400,000 *and* less than 20% of the gross income (AGI, for individuals) as shown on the return. (Reg § 301.7701-15(b)(3)(ii)(A))[28]

A tax consultant is a "preparer" even though he may do no more than review a return already prepared by the taxpayer. [29] A person is a "preparer" if he supplies enough information and advice so that completion of a return is a mere mechanical or clerical matter (Reg § 301.7701-15(c))[30] but not if he merely furnishes typing, reproducing or other mechanical assistance with respect to preparing a return. (Code Sec. 7701(a)(36)(B)(i); Reg § 301.7701-15(f)(1)(viii)) A person who provides a computerized return preparation service is a preparer if his computer programs provide substantive tax determinations, but not if his services are limited to mechanical calculations and processing. [31]

¶ 4752 Taxpayer identification number (TIN)—Forms SS-5; W-7.

Any person who files a return, statement, or other document must include his own TIN (Code Sec. 6109(a)(1))[32] and the TIN of any other person, as required by the form or instructions to the form. (Code Sec. 6109(a)(3); Reg § 301.6109-1(c))[33] Thus, for divorce or separation instruments executed before Jan. 1, 2019, an alimony payor's return must include the payee's TIN. (Use Form W-9 to request another person's TIN.) [34] A child to whom the kiddie tax rules (¶3128 *et seq.*) apply for any tax year must provide his parent's TIN on his or her (i.e., the child's) tax return for that year (Form 8615). (Code Sec. 1(g)(6))[35] For the requirement to include a Social Security number (SSN) for each qualifying child for whom a child tax credit is claimed from 2018 to 2025, see ¶2350.

SSNs are used to identify individuals, sole proprietors not otherwise required to use employer identification numbers (EINs), and grantor trusts. (Code Sec. 6109(d); Reg § 301.6109-1(a))[36] To get an SSN, file Form SS-5. (Reg § 301.6109-1(d)(1))[37] Information return filers can use a truncated TIN (TTIN) on paper and electronic payee statements (e.g., Form 1098, Form 1099, Form 5498). (Reg § 301.6109-4)[38]

Aliens who aren't eligible for SSNs use IRS individual taxpayer identification numbers (ITINs) requested on Form W-7 in accordance with IRS procedures. (Reg § 301.6109-1(a))[39] Prospective adoptive parents who have had a child placed lawfully with them for legal adoption may apply (use Form W-7A) for a temporary (2-year) adoption taxpayer identification number (ATIN) for the child (unless the child is an alien eligible to get an ITIN) to satisfy filing requirements (but not for earned income credit purposes (¶2338)). (Reg § 301.6109-3)[40]

Other entities use EINs. (Reg § 301.6109-1(a)) Taxpayers can request an EIN instantly on-line by entering the required information or by phone, mail, or fax. Persons issued an EIN must provide IRS with any updated application information that IRS requires. (Reg § 301.6109-1(d))[41] All employers (corporations, partnerships or sole proprietors) must use EINs for reporting employment and excise taxes. [42] Large food and beverage establishments use an identifying number for tip reporting. (Reg § 31.6053-3(a)(5))[43]

Buildings that have been or will be allocated a low-income housing credit must be

---

28. ¶S-1116
29. ¶S-1109
30. ¶S-1109; ¶61,074
31. ¶S-1110; ¶61,075
32. ¶S-1502; ¶61,094
33. ¶S-1531; ¶61,094
34. ¶S-1535; ¶2158.40
35. ¶S-1544

36. ¶S-1505; ¶61,094
37. ¶S-1581; ¶61,094
38. ¶S-1501A
39. ¶S-1508.1; S-1582.1 et seq.; ¶61,094
40. ¶S-1504.6 *et seq.*; ¶61,094.01
41. ¶S-1582 *et seq.*; ¶61,094
42. ¶S-1505; ¶61,094
43. ¶S-3289

assigned a building identification number (BIN) by the applicable state housing credit agency.[44]

Foreign transferors of U.S. real property interests (and transferees where applicable) must provide their TINs on withholding tax returns, applications for withholding certificates, etc. Foreign persons must have TINs for placement on any return, statement, or other document required by the regs under Code Sec. 897 or Code Sec. 1445. (Reg § 301.6109-1(b)(2)(vi))[45]

¶ 4753   Magnetic media and electronic filing—Form 4419.

Certain information returns (including statements, returns, and reports relating to health insurance coverage, pension plans, retirement benefits, and deferred compensation plans under Code Sec. 6055, Code Sec. 6056, Code Sec. 6057, Code Sec. 6058, and Code Sec. 6059) *must* be filed on magnetic media. (Code Sec. 6011(e)(2)(A); Reg § 301.6057-3; Reg § 301.6058-2; Reg § 301.6059-2)[46]

There are exceptions for low-volume filers (fewer than 250 returns), but partnerships with more than 100 partners (counting any person who is a partner at any time during its tax year) must file on magnetic media. (Reg § 301.6011-3)[47] E-filing satisfies the magnetic media requirement. Hardship waivers (request on Form 8508) are available. Filers request waivers by submitting written requests 45 days before the due date. (Code Sec. 6011(e)(2)(B))[48] All annual reports —including any statements and schedules —for employee benefit plans must be filed electronically under the EFAST2 program (¶4746).[49]

The 250–or-more-return rule doesn't apply to any return filed by a financial institution for tax for which the institution is liable as a withholding agent under Code Sec. 1461 or Code Sec. 1474(a)). (Code Sec. 6011(e)(4))[50]

Submit Form 4419 at least 45 days before the return due date to apply to transmit information returns electronically/magnetically. [1] The due dates for filing paper information returns also apply to magnetic media filings, but not to e-filing. For magnetic media, Form 1098, forms in the Form 1099 series, and Form W-2G must be postmarked by Feb. 28. For e-filing, the due date for information returns is Mar. 31; however, for W-2, W-3 and nonemployee compensation returns and statements, the due date is Jan. 31. [2] A transmittal statement on Form 4804 must accompany magnetic media; Form 4804 isn't required for e-filers.[3]

Authorized IRS e-file providers include their e-filing identification numbers (EFINs) with all electronic return data transmitted to IRS. IRS can expel authorized IRS e-file providers who use a stolen identity to apply for an EFIN or e-file fraudulent returns. [4]

Individuals and organizations with 25 or more trucks, tractors or other heavy vehicles used on highways have to file excise tax Form 2290 electronically. [5]

¶ 4754   Timely mailing as timely filing and paying.

A return, claim, statement, document or payment (except a tax deposit) that must be filed or made by a certain date generally is considered timely filed or made if it has a timely postmark. (Code Sec. 7502(c)(1))[6] This also applies to claims for credit or refund made on a late-filed original return but doesn't apply to an amended return showing

---

44. ¶S-1521; ¶424.70
45. ¶S-1508
46. ¶S-1301; ¶60,114.07
47. ¶S-1350; ¶60,114.065
48. ¶S-1314; ¶60,114.07
49. ¶S-3351; ¶S-3353
50. ¶S-1302; ¶60,114.07

1. ¶S-1311
2. ¶S-1305
3. ¶S-1308
4. ¶S-1601.3
5. ¶W-6456
6. ¶T-10751; ¶75,024

additional tax. (Reg § 301.7502-1(f))[7] For the timely mailing rule to apply, the return, etc., must be: (1) deposited in the U.S. mail in a properly addressed envelope or wrapper with sufficient postage; (Code Sec. 7502(a)(2)(B)) (2) postmarked by the prescribed filing or payment date (Code Sec. 7502(a)(2)(A)) (returns postmarked after the due date are considered filed when received by IRS); and (3) actually delivered by U.S. mail to the proper place. (Code Sec. 7502(a)(1))[8] A Tax Court petition mailed in a foreign country was timely even though it lacked a U.S. postmark where it was shown by the U.S. mail tracking system to have entered the U.S. domestic mail service within the required time period. But other courts have held the U.S. tracking system entry isn't relevant under timely filing rules.[9] Some courts permit delivery to be proven by a common-law "mailbox rule" (i.e., when mail is properly addressed and deposited in the U.S. mail, with prepaid postage, there is a rebuttable presumption that the addressee received it in the ordinary course of the mail).[10]

The timely-mailing rule applies to private delivery services (PDSs) such as: *DHL Express:* DHL Express 9:00; DHL Express 10:30; DHL Express 12:00; DHL Express Worldwide; DHL Express Envelope; DHL Import Express 10:30; DHL Import Express 12:00; and DHL Import Express Worldwide; *FedEx:* First Overnight; FedEx Priority Overnight; FedEx Standard Overnight; FedEx 2 Day; FedEx International Next Flight Out; FedEx International Priority; FedEx International First; and FedEx International Economy; *UPS* Next Day Air Early AM; UPS Next Day Air; UPS Next Day Air Saver; UPS 2nd Day Air; UPS 2nd Day Air A.M.; UPS Worldwide Express Plus; and UPS Worldwide Express. (Code Sec. 7502(f); Reg § 301.7502-1(c)(3))[11]

The postmark stamp date on the mailing envelope overrides the postmark stamp date on a Certificate of Mailing (P.S. Form 3817).[12] If a private postage meter is used (including a Stamps.com postage label), the postmark isn't enough. The document must actually be received by the proper office or officer not later than the time the postmark indicates it ordinarily would be received. If it is actually received later, taxpayer can prove timely mailing only by showing: (1) that the document was deposited in the mail before the last collection that was postmarked (by the U.S. Post Office) on the last day for filing; and (2) that the delay in receiving the document was due to delay in transmission of the mail; and (3) the cause of the delay. (Reg § 301.7502-1(c)(1)(iii)(B))[13]

An e-filed tax return (¶4703) isn't considered filed until IRS acknowledges the electronic portion of the return as accepted and a signature has been received either electronically or on Form 8453 (used to transmit paper schedules or forms that can't be e-filed).[14]

¶ 4755   Effect of registered or certified mail.

The date of registration is considered to be the postmark date, (Code Sec. 7502(c)(1)(B)) and registration is prima facie evidence the return, etc., was delivered to the agency, officer or office to which addressed. (Code Sec. 7502(c)(1)(A))[15] The U.S. postmark date on the sender's receipt is treated as the postmark date of a document sent by certified mail (Reg § 301.7502-1(c)(2)), and proof that a properly postmarked certified mail sender's receipt was properly issued and that the envelope or wrapper was properly addressed is prima facie evidence that the document was properly delivered. (Reg § 301.7502-1(e)(2))[16]

---

7. ¶T-10752; ¶T-10752.1; ¶75,024
8. ¶T-10751; ¶75,024
9. ¶T-10751 *et seq.*; ¶75,024
10. ¶T-10774 *et seq.*
11. ¶T-10781, ¶T-10787; ¶75,024

12. ¶T-10762
13. ¶T-10763
14. ¶S-1609, ¶S-1617.3; ¶60,114.08
15. ¶T-10762.3; ¶75,024
16. ¶T-10776.1

¶ 4756   Due date on Saturday, Sunday or holiday.

If a due date falls on Sat., Sun. or legal holiday, there is an automatic extension of time to the next succeeding day that isn't a Sat., Sun. or legal holiday. The rule applies to *all acts* required to be performed under the Code both by the *taxpayer* and IRS. "Legal holiday" includes: (1) the legal holidays throughout the state or possession where the office at which the act to be performed is located even if not a legal holiday in the state or possession where the taxpayer resides, and (2) all legal holidays in the District of Columbia (D.C.) (Code Sec. 7503), i.e.: New Year's Day (Jan. 1); Inauguration Day (Jan. 20, every 4th year); Martin Luther King, Jr.'s birthday (3rd Mon. in Jan.); Washington's birthday (3rd Mon. in Feb.); Emancipation Day (Apr. 16); Memorial Day (last Mon. in May); Independence Day; Labor Day (first Mon. in Sept.); Columbus Day (second Mon. in Oct.); Veterans Day (Nov. 11); Thanksgiving Day (4th Thurs. in Nov.); and Christmas Day (Dec. 25). If a holiday in D.C. falls on Sunday, the next day is a holiday in D.C. If a legal holiday in D.C. (other than Inauguration Day) falls on a Sat., it's treated as falling on the preceding Fri.[17]

¶ 4757   How to get a copy of a tax return— Forms 4506, 4506-T, 4506T-EZ.

Use Form 4506.[18] IRS charges $50 for each return requested. Use Form 4506-T to request free tax return transcripts, tax account transcripts, W-2 information, 1099 information, verification of non-filing, or a record of account.[19] For a free Form 1040 series tax return transcript, use Form 4506T-EZ or IRS's telephone automated system to order. Transcripts requested under the automated system can't be mailed to a third party.

17. ¶T-10790 *et seq.*; ¶75,034
18. ¶S-6407; ¶s 61,034, 61,034.09

19. ¶S-6409; ¶61,034

Chapter 25 Deficiencies—Refunds—Penalties

¶ 4800   **Tax Audits, Deficiencies and Assessments.** ▪▪▪▪▪▪▪▪▪▪

IRS preliminarily checks every return filed (¶4801 *et seq.*) and selects returns for audit based on various criteria (¶4803). Once IRS finishes an audit, a taxpayer has various alternatives (¶4813 *et seq.*) for resolving any disputed items.

¶ 4801   **Mathematical, etc., check of returns.**

IRS checks every return for math errors and computes tax using the amounts on the return. If the taxpayer made a computational error resulting in a tax underpayment, IRS sends a corrected computation and a notice and demand for payment of any balance due (which doesn't entitle the taxpayer to petition the Tax Court) (Code Sec. 6213(b)(1)) or reduces any refund. (Reg § 601.105(a))

Examples of math errors are: failure to include a correct taxpayer identification number (TIN) on the return, as required under Code Sec. 21(child care credit), Code Sec. 24 (child credit), Code Sec. 25A (higher education credit), and Code Sec. 32 (earned income credit (EIC)). (Code Sec. 6312(g)(2))[1]

A taxpayer has 60 days from the date the notice is sent to file a request for an abatement of the summary assessment. IRS can't collect on the assessment until the taxpayer agrees or the 60-day period expires. After the abatement period has expired, IRS can reassess the tax by following the regular deficiency procedures and issuing a 90-day letter (¶4823). (Code Sec. 6213(b)(2))[2]

Adjustments to make an S corporation shareholder's return consistent with the corporation's return are treated as resulting from math or clerical error. (Code Sec. 6037(c)(3))[3] Similar rules apply to estate and trust beneficiary returns. (Code Sec. 6034A(c)(3))[4]

A taxpayer's federal income and estate tax returns may also be checked against his state or foreign tax returns.[5]

¶ 4802   **Check against information returns.**

IRS compares the taxpayers' income tax returns against information returns under a document matching program (Information Returns Program). If there is a mismatch, IRS sends the taxpayer a computer-generated notice (CP-2000), which must describe the basis for, and identify, any amounts of taxes, additions, interest or penalties claimed to be due. (Code Sec. 7522) The notice, which isn't a demand for payment, can be challenged by the taxpayer, who has the burden of proof. IRS also matches information filed by pass-through entities (partnerships, S corporations, and trusts) to what the partners, shareholders, and beneficiaries report on their own returns.[6]

¶ 4803   **Returns selected for examination.**

IRS selects returns for examination, e.g., based on discrepancy with information returns (¶4802), the filing of frivolous returns, random sampling (National Research Program (NRP)), etc. IRS attempts to select tax returns for audit that have the greatest audit potential.[7]

---

1. ¶T-3628; ¶62,134.02
2. ¶T-3902.1; ¶62,134.02
3. ¶D-1801; ¶60,374
4. ¶C-3081; ¶C-9081; ¶60,34A4

5. ¶T-1005; ¶T-1006
6. ¶s T-1003, T-1004; ¶75,224
7. ¶T-1023, T-1060 *et seq.*

References beginning with a single letter are to paragraphs in Federal Tax Coordinator 2d and RIA's Analysis of Federal Taxes: Income. Those beginning with numbers are to paragraphs in United States Tax Reporter.

¶ 4804   Settlement initiatives.

IRS allows qualifying taxpayers that have failed to comply with U.S. tax and information return obligations to settle on terms that would be more favorable than would result from litigation. IRS considers voluntary taxpayer disclosures in determining whether cases will be criminally prosecuted.

"Streamlined procedures" apply to persons that certify that failures to report and pay tax due in respect of foreign financial assets were not due to willful conduct. Individual taxpayers (including estates of individual taxpayers) who qualify for the streamlined procedures pay no penalty or a small penalty. [8]

IRS's offshore voluntary disclosure program (OVDP) closed on Sept. 28, 2018. [9]

¶ 4805   Types of examinations (audits); time and place.

IRS fixes the time and method of examination, which must be reasonable under the circumstances. (Code Sec. 7605(a); Reg § 301.7605-1(a)) An examination may be at: (1) an IRS office, with the taxpayer bringing (office audit) or mailing (correspondence audit) his records (Reg § 601.105(b)(2)(ii)), or (2) the office of the taxpayer (or his representative) (field audit). Taxpayers or their representatives may make written requests to change the place that IRS has set for an examination. (Reg § 301.7605-1(e)(1); Reg § 601.105(b)(3))[10]

In a regular income tax audit, an IRS agent examines the taxpayer's books, papers, records, or other data to determine whether the records support the income reported and the deductions taken by the taxpayer. (Code Sec. 7602)[11]

IRS is limited in its ability to conduct a "financial status" examination or an "economic reality" examination, to determine the existence of unreported income. (Code Sec. 7602(e)) Financial status or economic reality audit techniques are IRS indirect methods of examination, such as the bank deposits method (¶2852).[12]

¶ 4806   Taxpayer's rights in an examination.

Before or at an initial in-person interview (other than criminal investigations), IRS must give the taxpayer an explanation (written or oral) of the audit process (and assessment and collection) and his rights under that process. (Code Sec. 7521(b)(1))[13] A taxpayer has the right to: be represented by an advisor (¶4807); make certain audio (but generally not videotape) recordings of meetings (on advance notice) with the IRS agent (Code Sec. 7521(a)(1)); claim additional deductions not claimed on the return; ask that a particular technical question raised in the examination be referred to IRS's National Office for technical advice; not be subjected to unnecessary examinations (¶4809); and claim constitutional rights if questioned about possible criminal violations. [14]

¶ 4807   Who can represent the taxpayer?

The taxpayer's representative may be an attorney, CPA, enrolled agent, enrolled actuary or any other person permitted (under Treas Dept Circ No. 230, Sec. 10.3) to represent taxpayers before IRS, who isn't disbarred or suspended from practice before IRS, and who has a written power of attorney (on Form 2848) executed by the taxpayer. Absent a summons, IRS can't require the taxpayer to accompany the representative. (Code Sec. 7521(c))[15] IRS must suspend an interview if the taxpayer clearly states a desire to

---

8. ¶V-3867 *et seq.*; ¶72,014.15
9. ¶V-3850 *et seq.*; ¶72,014.15
10. ¶T-1090 *et seq.*, ¶T-1102; ¶76,054
11. ¶T-1181*et seq.*; ¶76,024

12. ¶T-1076; ¶76,024
13. ¶T-1122 *et seq.*; ¶75,214
14. ¶s T-1120 *et seq.*, T-1129 *et seq.*; ¶76,024.10
15. ¶s T-1124, T-1127; ¶75,214

consult with a representative. (Code Sec. 7521(b)(2))[16]

Attorney-client privilege extends to attorney-client communications made in confidence by the client that encompass legal advice from an attorney in that capacity unless the client waives the protection. [17] With respect to non-criminal tax matters and proceedings, the attorney-client privilege also applies to communications between a taxpayer and any federally authorized tax practitioners for tax advice (except for tax shelters) to the extent the communication would be privileged were it between a taxpayer and an attorney. (Code Sec. 7525)[18] The work product privilege applies to materials prepared by an attorney and an attorney's agents and representatives for the purpose of anticipated litigation. A strong showing of necessity and inability to get equivalent information without undue hardship is required to overcome the privilege. [19]

¶ 4808   IRS's power to summon persons and records.

Where there is a legitimate purpose for an investigation, IRS can issue a summons for testimony, books, records, or other data (Code Sec. 7602(a)) that are potentially relevant to a particular tax inquiry. [20] The summons (Form 2039) must describe with reasonable certainty the records sought (Code Sec. 7603). It also must set the time for appearance before IRS, which must be not less than ten days from summons date. (Code Sec. 7605(a))[21] If the taxpayer intentionally disregards the summons, IRS can apply to the district court (or a U.S. Commissioner) for an order directing compliance. (Code Sec. 7604(b))[22]

IRS may enforce a summons ("third-party summons") on a person other than the taxpayer for testimony and records. (Certain communications (see ¶4807) are privileged.) IRS must send a notice of the summons, including a copy and an explanation of the taxpayer's right to institute a suit to quash the summons to any person identified in the summons other than the summoned party. (Code Sec. 7609(a)(1); Reg § 301.7609-1)

Taxpayer intervention in a proceeding to enforce the summons or a taxpayer proceeding to quash a summons will result in a suspension of the assessment period. (Code Sec. 7609(e)(1); Reg § 301.7609-5(b))[23]

IRS may only issue, or begin an action to enforce, a summons for tax-related computer software source code under certain circumstances. (Code Sec. 7612)[24]

¶ 4809   One examination rule—unnecessary examinations.

IRS can't conduct unnecessary examinations of a taxpayer and can make only one inspection of a taxpayer's books and records a tax year unless the taxpayer requests otherwise, IRS gives notice *in writing* that an additional inspection (i.e., reexamination) is necessary (Code Sec. 7605(b))[25] , or IRS suspects fraud. [26]

¶ 4810   National Taxpayer Advocate (NTA)—Taxpayer Assistance Orders (TAOs).

The Office of the Taxpayer Advocate is headed by the NTA, who reports directly to the Commissioner. (Code Sec. 7803(c)(1)) Its functions are to assist taxpayers in resolving problems with IRS, identify areas where taxpayers have problems dealing with IRS, propose changes in IRS administrative practices to mitigate these identified problems, and identify potential legislative changes that may do so. (Code Sec. 7803(c)(2)(A)) A taxpayer

16. ¶T-1127; ¶75,214
17. ¶T-1314
18. ¶T-1334; ¶75,254
19. ¶T-1330; ¶T-1334.1; ¶76,024.07
20. ¶T-1201, T-1212; ¶76,024
21. ¶T-1354; ¶T-1099; ¶76,024.04

22. ¶T-1357; ¶76,044
23. ¶T-1250 *et seq.*; ¶V-3714; ¶76,094
24. ¶T-1290 *et seq.*; ¶76,124
25. ¶T-1425 *et seq.*; ¶76,054
26. ¶T-1443 *et seq.*; ¶76,024.09

can make, in a manner prescribed by the regs, an application to request the NTA issue a TAO in cases involving significant hardship because of IRS's administration of the tax laws. (Code Sec. 7811(a)(1); Reg § 301.7811-1(b))[27]

¶ 4811   User fees for IRS rulings or determinations.

IRS charges taxpayers a separate user fee for each request for a ruling, opinion letter, determination letter, or other similar request. (Code Sec. 7528(a)) User fees must be paid electronically.[28]

¶ 4812   Proposed deficiencies—revenue agent's report (RAR).

An IRS examiner may propose adjustments to a taxpayer's return before determining a deficiency (¶4822).[29] The taxpayer can agree to the adjustments or argue they should be modified before the examiner submits the RAR. Once the RAR is submitted, along with a proposed deficiency letter (the "30-day letter," see ¶4813), the taxpayer has 30 days to (1) accept the findings and limit his appeal to a claim or suit for refund, (2) request an Appeals Office conference (¶4815), or (3) do nothing, in which case IRS sends a statutory notice of deficiency (i.e., a 90-day letter, see ¶4823). (Reg § 601.105(d)(1))[30]

¶ 4813   The 30-day letter.

The revenue agent's report (RAR) (¶4812) that IRS sends, along with a ("30-day letter") to a taxpayer who rejects the examiner's findings from a field or office audit, must show the basis for and amount of any proposed adjustments. (Code Sec. 7522(a), Code Sec. 7522(b)(3)) The letter also explains appeal procedures and asks a taxpayer to indicate within 30 days whether he will: accept the findings and sign a waiver of restrictions on assessment (Form 870, which allows IRS to collect the deficiency without issuing a 90-day letter (¶4823), and limits the taxpayer's appeal to a claim or suit for refund (no Tax Court petition)); request an Appeals Office conference (¶4815); or do nothing and IRS will send a 90-day letter. (Reg § 601.105(d)(1)) IRS must include an explanation of the entire process from examination through collection as to a proposed deficiency with any first letter of proposed deficiency that allows the taxpayer an opportunity for administrative review in the IRS Office of Appeals.[31]

¶ 4814   Early referral to Appeals.

Any taxpayer may request early referral of one or more unresolved issues, from either the examination or collection division, to the IRS Office of Appeals. (Code Sec. 7123(a))[32]

¶ 4815   Appeals Office conference.

The taxpayer can get an Appeals Office conference by sending a written request (in response to a 30-day letter, see ¶4813) and any required protest (¶4816) to IRS.[33] An Appeals Office proceeding is informal, and testimony isn't under oath, although the taxpayer may be asked to submit affidavits. (Reg § 601.106(c))[34] An Appeals Office conference is available to a taxpayer even after IRS has issued a 90-day letter (¶4823). (Reg § 601.106(b))[35]

---

27. ¶T-10205 *et seq.*; ¶78,114 *et seq.*
28. ¶T-10000 *et seq.*; ¶75,284
29. ¶T-1550 *et seq.*
30. ¶T-1600 *et seq.*
31. ¶T-1601 *et seq.*; ¶75,224

32. ¶T-1709 *et seq.*; ¶71,234
33. ¶T-1711
34. ¶T-1720
35. ¶T-1702 *et seq.*

¶ 4816   Protest.

An oral request is enough to get Appeals consideration in all office or correspondence audit cases. In a field audit case, a written protest is: required if the total amount of the proposed increase in tax (including penalties), proposed overassessment or claimed refund, or compromise offer exceeds $10,000 for any tax period; optional (but a statement of issues is required) if that total amount is between $2,500 and $10,000; and not required if it is less than $2,500. (Reg § 601.106(a)(1)(iii)(a))[36] The 30-day letter (¶4813) contains instructions for the protest (Reg § 601.105(d)(2)) and spells out the required information. [37]

¶ 4817   Appeals Office settlement authority; nonbinding mediation and arbitration.

The Appeals Office has authority to settle all factual and legal issues raised by the examiner's report (RAR, see ¶4812) or the taxpayer's protest (¶4816) (Reg § 601.106(f)(2))[38] as long as the case isn't docketed in the Tax Court. (Reg § 601.106(a)(2))[39] If no settlement is reached, IRS will prepare a 90-day letter (¶4823).[40] Under procedures prescribed by IRS, either the taxpayer or IRS Office of Appeals can request nonbinding mediation on any issue that is still unresolved after the conclusion of appeals procedures, or unsuccessful attempts to enter into a closing agreement or a compromise. (Code Sec. 7123(b)(1))[41] In addition, a taxpayer and IRS can jointly request binding arbitration of factual issues unresolved after the conclusion of appeals procedures or after unsuccessful attempts to enter into a closing agreement or a compromise. (Code Sec. 7123(b)(2))[42]

¶ 4818   Execution of Appeals Office settlement—Forms 870, 890.

If the taxpayer accepts IRS's position in full, with no concessions, he signs a Form 870 (Form 890, in gift, estate or generation-skipping transfer tax cases), waiving restrictions on assessment (¶4829). (Reg § 601.106(d)(2))[43] For concessions, see ¶4819.

¶ 4819   Settlement with concessions—Forms 870-AD, 890-AD.

If the Appeals Office makes any concessions, a Form 870-AD (Form 890-AD, in estate tax cases) is executed stating that: the settlement is subject to acceptance by IRS; on acceptance, it won't be reopened by IRS absent fraud, malfeasance, concealment or misrepresentation of a material fact, an important mathematical mistake, or an excessive tentative net operating loss (NOL) carryback; *and* the taxpayer waives his right to file a claim for refund (other than from an NOL carryback) for any years covered by the agreement. [44]

¶ 4820   Final closing agreements—Forms 866, 906.

The taxpayer and IRS may conclusively settle a tax dispute by entering into a final agreement to close either a tax year that has ended (use Form 866) (Code Sec. 7121(a); Reg § 301.7121-1(b)(2), Reg § 601.202(a)(2))[45] or a specific transaction, past or future (use Form 906). (Reg § 601.202(b))[46] The agreement is irrevocable (except for fraud, malfeasance or misrepresentation of a material fact) and binds both parties. (Code Sec. 7121(b)) User fees (¶4811) apply. [47]

---

36. ¶T-1713
37. ¶T-1717
38. ¶T-1721
39. ¶T-1725
40. ¶T-1732
41. ¶T-1733; ¶71,234

42. ¶T-1756
43. ¶T-1731
44. ¶T-3402; ¶62,134.03
45. ¶T-9500; ¶71,214.02
46. ¶T-9521; ¶71,214.02 *et seq.*
47. ¶T-9507; ¶s 71,214.07, 71,214.08

¶ 4821   Offer in compromise (OIC)—Forms 656, 433-A, 433-B.

Civil or criminal tax cases can be compromised by IRS, after assessment, before referral to the Department of Justice (after referral, compromise can be only by the Attorney General). (Code Sec. 7122(a))[48] IRS may compromise tax liabilities on any of these grounds: (1) doubt as to collectibility, (2) doubt as to liability, (3) to promote effective tax administration because either (a) collection of the full amount would cause economic hardship for the taxpayer, or (b) compelling public policy or equity considerations justify compromise. (Reg § 301.7122-1(b)) To make an offer, file Form 656 and, except for offers based solely on doubt as to liability, Form 433-A (individuals) or Form 433-B (businesses) (sole proprietors file must file both of the latter forms) and pay the $186 processing fee. (Reg § 301.7122-1(d)(1))[49] IRS may disregard frivolous offer submissions. (Code Sec. 7122(f))[50]

¶ 4822   Deficiency defined.

A deficiency is the amount by which a taxpayer's correct tax liability is more than the excess of: (1) the tax shown on the return (except that math and clerical errors are corrected), plus (2) the amounts previously assessed (or collected without assessment) as a deficiency, over (3) the amount of any rebates (credits, refunds, or other repayments). (Code Sec. 6211(a), Code Sec. 6213(b))

In determining a deficiency, any excess of certain specified credits over the tax imposed by subtitle A (without taking into account those credits) and any excess of those credits shown by the taxpayer on the return over the amount shown as tax on the return (without taking into account those credits) is taken into account as a negative amount of tax. (Code Sec. 6211(b)(4))[1]

If no return was filed, or if a return doesn't show any tax, the deficiency equals the entire amount of the correct tax. (Reg § 301.6211-1(a))[2]

¶ 4823   Notice of deficiency—"90-day letter."

A statutory notice of deficiency ("90-day letter"), which must be sent by certified or registered mail to the taxpayer's last known address, tells the taxpayer that IRS has determined a deficiency (in income, estate or gift tax, or excise tax on private foundations or pension plans). (Code Sec. 6212(a))[3] The letter must describe the basis for and identify the amounts (if any) of tax, interest, additional amounts, additions to tax and assessable penalties. (Code Sec. 7522(a))[4] After receiving the letter, the taxpayer can: pay the deficiency, not pay and seek to rescind it, pay and file a refund claim (¶4852), take no action (let tax be assessed) and then file a compromise offer (¶4821), or file a Tax Court petition (¶4862).[5]

¶ 4824   Time for making assessments.

Unless the taxpayer and IRS sign a closing agreement (¶4820), or the taxpayer voluntarily pays the deficiency or signs a Form 870 (¶4813), or IRS determines collection is in jeopardy (¶4827), or in the case of court ordered restitution (¶4826), IRS can't assess deficiencies in income, estate, and gift taxes, and the excise taxes on private foundations and qualified pension, etc., plans until after the taxpayer has had an opportunity to make

48. ¶T-9600; T-9649; ¶71,224 *et seq.*
49. ¶T-10024; ¶71,224.03
50. ¶T-9612; ¶71,224.03
1. ¶T-1501*et seq.*; ¶62,114

2. ¶T-1506*et seq.*; ¶62,114.01
3. ¶T-2700 *et seq.*; ¶62,124*et seq.*
4. ¶T-2714 *et seq.*; ¶75,224
5. ¶T-2738

a Tax Court appeal. (Code Sec. 6213(a))[6]

¶ 4825 Assessment of interest and penalties.

Interest may be assessed when the underlying tax is collectible. (Code Sec. 6601(g))[7]

For income, estate, gift and certain excise taxes, the negligence and fraud penalties are assessed like deficiencies (¶4824). So are the delinquency penalties (¶4875, ¶4876), but only if attributable to a deficiency and not if measured by the tax shown on the return. (Code Sec. 6665(b))[8] The penalty for estimated tax underpayments (¶ 3348) is assessed as a deficiency only if no return is filed.(Code Sec. 6665(a))

The normal assessment and collection rules don't apply to the penalties for promoting an abusive tax shelter (¶4891), aiding and abetting a tax understatement (¶4887), filing a frivolous return (¶4900). A taxpayer may delay collection of these penalties by paying at least 15% of the penalty and filing a claim for refund of it, within 30 days of notice and demand for payment. If IRS denies the claim, the taxpayer has 30 days to sue for refund in a district court (where IRS may counterclaim for the unpaid penalty amount). (Code Sec. 6703(b), Code Sec. 6703(c))[9]

¶ 4826 Assessment of restitution payments.

IRS can assess and collect restitution for unpaid taxes owed by defendants in criminal tax cases as if it were a tax. (Code Sec. 6201(a)(4))[10] Court-ordered restitution can be assessed, or a court proceeding for the amount can be begun without assessment, at any time. (Code Sec. 6501(c)(11))[11] A tax liability ordered pursuant to a restitution order is not subject to the deficiency procedures (¶4823). (Code Sec. 6201(a)(4)(C))

IRS may not collect criminal restitution and a civil tax liability for the same period. Where a taxpayer makes payments to satisfy a restitution-based assessment, IRS must also apply the payment to satisfy the civil tax liability for the same tax period. [12]

¶ 4827 Jeopardy assessment and termination of a tax year.

If IRS believes assessment or collection of a deficiency will be jeopardized by delay, it can immediately assess the deficiency (plus interest and penalties) and demand payment. (Code Sec. 6861(a); Reg § 301.6861-1(a)) But, within 60 days after the assessment, IRS must issue the taxpayer a 90-day letter (¶4823). (Code Sec. 6861(b))[13] IRS Chief Counsel must pre-approve these "jeopardy assessments." (Code Sec. 7429(a)(1)(A))[14] Collection is in jeopardy if (1) the taxpayer is or appears to be designing quickly to leave the U.S. or conceal themselves and/or place property beyond IRS's reach, (2) the taxpayer's financial solvency is or appears to be imperiled. (Code Sec. 6861; Reg § 301.6861-1(a); Reg § 1.6851-1(a))[15]

IRS can also terminate a tax year and demand immediate payment of income taxes for the current and preceding year, if it finds that a taxpayer plans to leave or remove his property from the U.S., conceal himself or his property in the U.S., or do anything that would impair the collection of those taxes ("termination assessment"). Within 60 days, IRS must issue a 90-day letter for the full year. (Code Sec. 6851(a), Code Sec. 6852(a))[16]

There are procedures for administrative and judicial review of jeopardy and termination

---

6. ¶T-3602; ¶62,134
7. ¶T-3646; ¶66,014.01
8. ¶T-3638 *et seq.*; ¶66,654
9. ¶V-5650; ¶67,034
10. ¶T-3639; ¶62,014
11. ¶T-4172; ¶65,014.149

12. ¶T-3639; ¶62,014
13. ¶T-3700 *et seq.*; ¶68,614 *et seq.*
14. ¶T-3733.1; ¶74,294
15. ¶T-3701 *et seq.*; ¶68,614
16. ¶T-3717 *et seq.*; ¶68,514

assessments (Code Sec. 7429)[17] and for stay of collection. (Code Sec. 6863)[18]

Ⓡⁱᴬ *observation:* A jeopardy assessment is used only where IRS makes its determination *after* the end of the tax year to which it relates. In a termination assessment, the determination is made *before* the related tax year ends or *before* the due date to file a return and pay the tax.

¶ 4828　Assessments in bankruptcy or receivership proceedings.

IRS may make an immediate assessment of any deficiency whether or not a 90-day letter (see ¶4823) has been issued: (1) on the debtor's estate in a Title 11 bankruptcy case; (2) on the debtor, but only if liability for the tax becomes res judicata under a determination in a Title 11 bankruptcy case; or (3) on the appointment of a receiver for the taxpayer in any receivership proceeding. (Code Sec. 6871(a), Code Sec. 6871(b))[19]

¶ 4829　General three-year statute of limitations on assessments.

Generally (for exceptions, see ¶4831, ¶4834), all taxes must be assessed: (1) within three years after the date the return was filed (below), or (2) if the tax is payable by stamp, within three years after the date any part of the tax was paid. (Code Sec. 6501(a))[20] A return filed before the deadline is considered filed on the due date. (Code Sec. 6501(b)(1))[21] But a return of tax withheld (from wages or at source) for any period ending with or within a calendar year is, if filed before Apr. 15 of the next calendar year, considered filed *on* Apr. 15. (Code Sec. 6501(b)(2); Reg § 301.6501(b)-1(b))[22] The assessment period for a late-filed return starts on the day after actual filing. (Code Sec. 6501(a))[23] If within 60 days before the limitations period expires, IRS receives an amended return that shows an increase in tax liability, IRS has 60 days from the receipt to assess the additional tax. (Code Sec. 6501(c)(7))[24]

The assessment period for items of a partnership, S corporation, trust or estate that are passed through to and reported by the partners, shareholders or beneficiaries, is based on their returns (not the partnership's, etc.). (Code Sec. 6501(a)).[25]

¶ 4830　Expiration of the limitations period as a bar to assessment.

A taxpayer who claims that the assessment of a tax is barred by the expiration of the limitations period (¶4829) must raise the issue and has the burden of proof. [26]

¶ 4831　Six-year assessment period.

Over-25% omissions. The assessment period is six years for taxpayers that omit from gross income (or an estate omits items includible in the gross estate) in an amount that exceeds 25% of the amount of gross income stated on the return. For this purpose, "omissions" don't include amounts for which adequate information is given on the return or attached statements. (Code Sec. 6501(e))[27]

Personal holding company tax on a personal holding company (PHC) that didn't file a PHC schedule with its income tax return may be assessed within six years after the income tax return was filed. (Code Sec. 6501(f))[28]

17. ¶T-3735 *et seq.*; ¶74,294
18. ¶T-3757 *et seq.*; ¶68,634 *et seq.*
19. ¶T-3802; ¶68,714
20. ¶T-4001; ¶65,014
21. ¶T-4002; ¶65,014.09
22. ¶T-4010; ¶65,014.09

23. ¶T-4003; ¶s 65,014.01, 65,014.02
24. ¶T-4209.1; ¶65,014.28
25. ¶T-4020 *et seq.*; ¶65,014.04
26. ¶T-4030; ¶65,014.01
27. ¶T-4201 *et seq.*; ¶65,014.15
28. ¶T-4218; ¶65,014.29

Understatements due to foreign financial assets. A 6-year limitations period applies for assessment of tax on understatements of income attributable to foreign financial assets if there is an omission of gross income in excess of $5,000 attributable to an asset for which information reports are required under Code Sec. 6038D or would be required if certain Code Sec. 6038D exceptions didn't apply. (Code Sec. 6501(e)(1)(A)(ii))[29]

Net tax liability due to pre-2018 accumulated deferred foreign income. A 6-year assessment period applies for the assessment of the net tax liability due to pre-2018 accumulated foreign income (¶4615). (Code Sec. 965(k))[30]

¶ 4832   Assessment period for carrybacks and carryovers.

A deficiency attributable to a taxpayer's carryback of a net operating loss (NOL), capital loss, or business credit may be assessed at any time before expiration of the period applicable to the year the loss was sustained or the credit earned. (Code Sec. 6501(h), Code Sec. 6501(j))[31] A deficiency attributable to a foreign tax credit carryback may be assessed up to one year after the credit year's assessment period expires. (Code Sec. 6501(i))[32]

¶ 4833   Assessment period for unreported listed transactions.

If a taxpayer fails to include on a return or statement for a tax year information about a listed transaction (¶4893) that is required under Code Sec. 6011, the time for assessment of tax with respect to such transaction won't expire before one year after the earlier of: (1) the date the required information is furnished to IRS, or (2) the date a material advisor meets the list-maintenance requirements with respect to a request by IRS under Code Sec. 6112(b) related to that transaction. (Code Sec. 6501(c)(10); Reg § 301.6501(c)-1(g))[33]

¶ 4834   When the assessment period remains open.

The assessment period is open indefinitely in a number of situations, including where a taxpayer:

... fails to file a required return (Code Sec. 6501(c)(3)), but the assessment period starts to run if a trust or partnership return is filed by a taxpayer later held to be a corporation (Code Sec. 6501(g)(1)) or an exempt organization return is filed by an organization later held to be taxable (Code Sec. 6501(g)(2));[34]

... files a false or fraudulent income, gift or estate tax return with intent to evade tax. (Code Sec. 6501(c)(1)) The courts disagree as to whether, to keep the assessment period open, the taxpayer must have the fraudulent intent (Tax Court and the Federal Circuit) or whether the fraudulent intent of another party — e.g., income tax preparer, accountant, tax shelter promoter — may suffice (2nd Circuit). [35]

... willfully attempts in any manner to defeat and evade taxes (Code Sec. 6501(c)(2));[36]

... fails to pay any part of a tax required to be paid by stamp (Code Sec. 6501(a); Reg § 301.6501(a)-1);[37]

... for gift tax, fails to show or adequately disclose (1) any gift of property (or increase in taxable gifts) whose value is determined under the special valuation rules or (2) any post-Aug. 5, '97 gift. (Code Sec. 6501(c)(9); Reg § 301.6501(c)-1(e), Reg § 301.6501(c)-1(f))[38] Filing an amended return with required information will get the limitation period running for a prior gift that wasn't adequately disclosed. [39]

---

29. ¶T-4210.1; ¶65,014.155
30. ¶O-2723
31. ¶T-4034; ¶65,014.28
32. ¶T-4042; ¶65,014.28
33. ¶T-4163; ¶65,014.147
34. ¶T-4101 *et seq.*; ¶s 65,014.05, 65,014.06, 65,014.14

35. ¶T-4127; ¶65,014.13
36. ¶T-4141; ¶65,014.13
37. ¶T-4122
38. ¶T-4147; ¶65,014.28
39. ¶T-4162

. . . is subject to the tax for termination of private foundation status, see ¶4130.[40]

. . . fails to notify IRS of an election not to take, or to revoke, certain credits, in which case the assessment of a deficiency attributable to such an election remains open until one year after IRS is notified of the election or revocation. (Code Sec. 6501(m))[41]

IRS says that a responsible person liable for the trust fund recovery penalty is subject to an unlimited assessment period where the employer has committed fraud, willfully attempted to evade tax, or failed to file an employment tax return. [42] The penalties for promoting abusive tax shelters, or for aiding and abetting an understatement, can be assessed at any time, [43] as can the penalty (but not the tax) imposed on a return preparer for willful tax understatements, [44] and certain restitution in criminal tax cases (¶4826).[45]

For information required under certain provisions, the assessment period for tax as to any tax return, event or period to which the information relates won't expire before the date that is 3 years after the information is given to IRS. The provisions include Code Sec. 1295(b), Code Sec. 1298(f), Code Sec. 6038, Code Sec. 6038A, Code Sec. 6038B, Code Sec. 6038D, Code Sec. 6046, Code Sec. 6046A, and Code Sec. 6048. However, if the failure to furnish the information required under these Code sections is due to reasonable cause and not willful neglect, the suspension of the assessment limitations period will apply only to the items related to that failure. (Code Sec. 6501(c)(8)[46]

¶ 4835　Voluntary extension of the assessment period—Form 872.

At any time *before* expiration of the assessment period (¶4829), a taxpayer and IRS can agree in writing (usually on a form in the Form 872 series) to extend the assessment period (except for estate taxes). They can also enter into successive agreements further extending the period. (Code Sec. 6501(c)(4))[47]

observation: Form 872 is generally referred to by IRS as a *"consent."* Tax practitioners sometimes refer to it as a *"waiver,"* which technically means a Form 870 (¶4818).

Restricted consent. A restricted consent postpones the close of the tax year with respect to an unsettled issue. It is used where some issues are resolved, but settlement of others must await the establishment of an IRS position through a court decision, etc., or where other equally meritorious circumstances exist. [48]

Indefinite consent—Form 872-A. A taxpayer whose case is before the Appeals Office (¶4815) can execute Form 872-A, which is an indefinite extension. [49] It expires 90 days after: (1) Appeals receives notice (on Form 872-T) of the taxpayer's desire to terminate the extension, (2) IRS mails Form 872-T to the taxpayer, or (3) IRS mails a 90-day letter. [50]

IRS must notify the taxpayer of his right to refuse to extend the assessment limitations period, or to limit the extension to particular issues or a particular time period, on each occasion the taxpayer is requested to provide consent. (Code Sec. 6501(c)(4)(B))[1]

¶ 4836　Suspension of the assessment period.

A 90-day letter (¶4823) suspends the assessment period. The assessment period stops running on the date IRS mails the letter, and doesn't resume until 60 days after: (1) the 90-day period (150 days if the letter is addressed to a person outside the U.S.) if no petition is filed, or (2) the Tax Court's decision becomes final if a petition is filed. (Code

---

40. ¶T-4143
41. ¶T-4014.1; ¶65,014.28
42. ¶T-4029.1
43. ¶s T-4125, T-4126; ¶67,034
44. ¶T-4145; ¶66,964
45. ¶T-4172; ¶65,014.149

46. ¶T-4146; ¶65,014.28
47. ¶T-4400 *et seq.*; ¶S-4518; ¶65,014.17 *et seq.*
48. ¶T-4445
49. ¶T-4402
50. ¶T-4457 *et seq.*
1. ¶T-4403; ¶65,014

Sec. 6503(a))[2] A taxpayer's application for a Taxpayer Assistance Order (¶4810) also suspends the assessment period, up to the date the National Taxpayer Advocate makes a decision. (Code Sec. 7811(d))[3]

The assessment period is suspended in Tax Court employment tax determinations. (Code Sec. 7436(d)(1))[4]

For returns of corporations being examined under the coordinated examination program or a successor program, the issuance of a "designated summons" or a related summons also suspends the assessment period, pending final resolution of its enforcement. (Code Sec. 6503(j); Reg § 301.6503(j)-1)[5]

¶ 4837 Request for prompt assessment—Form 4810.

The normal three-year assessment period can be cut to 18 months *at the taxpayer's request* (use Form 4810) for an income tax return of a decedent or an estate, or for a return of a dissolved or dissolving corporation. (Code Sec. 6501(d))[6]

¶ 4838 Statutory (mitigation) and judicial relief for barred years.

After the period for assessment or refund has run, IRS generally can't make an assessment, and a taxpayer generally can't get a refund. But an otherwise closed year may be reopened under the Code's "mitigation" provisions. (Code Sec. 1311, Code Sec. 1312, Code Sec. 1313)[7]

In addition, relief from the limitation periods may be available, even if the statutory mitigation conditions aren't met, under the doctrines of equitable recoupment , [8] estoppel,[9] or election.[10]

¶ 4839 Unified Audit and Review for Partnerships—Tax Years Beginning Before 2018.

Under the pre-2018 partnership audit rules, IRS generally can't adjust partnership items on a partner's return except by a unified entity-level proceeding (i.e., a "TEFRA proceeding," as enacted by the Tax Equity and Fiscal Responsibility Act; (TEFRA) in ¶4840). A decision in the unified proceeding binds all partners and permits IRS to make the necessary corresponding adjustments on their individual returns. Simplified procedures apply for electing large partnerships (¶4844).

✔/caution: The unified partnership audit procedures described at ¶4840 through ¶4845 have been replaced with the partnership audit rules described at ¶4846 *et seq.* effective for returns filed for partnership tax years beginning *after Dec. 31, 2017,* but taxpayers can elect to apply them sooner.

¶ 4840 Unified audit and review procedure for partnerships and partners—tax years beginning before 2018.

The tax treatment of any partnership item (¶4841), and the applicability of any penalty, addition to tax or additional amount which relates to an adjustment to a partnership item, is generally determined at the partnership level, in one unified proceeding. (former Code Sec. 6221); Reg § 301.6221-1(c) No assessment of a deficiency attributable to any partnership item may be made before the end of the 150th day after IRS issues a notice of final

---

2. ¶T-4300 *et seq.*; ¶65,034.01
3. ¶T-4325; ¶78,114.01
4. ¶T-4301.2; ¶74,364
5. ¶T-4333 *et seq.*; ¶65,034.04
6. ¶T-4500 *et seq.*; ¶65,014.16

7. ¶T-5000 *et seq.*; ¶13,134
8. ¶T-5200 *et seq.*; ¶65,144
9. ¶T-5300 *et seq.*; ¶74,338.400
10. ¶T-5400 *et seq.*; ¶74,338.424

partnership administrative adjustment (FPAA, see ¶4843) to the tax matters partner (TMP, see ¶4842) or, if the TMP files a Tax Court petition in that 150-day period, before the Tax Court decision becomes final. (former Code Sec. 6225(a)) [11] However, IRS can make an earlier assessment in certain abusive tax shelter situations. (Reg § 301.6231(c)-1)[12]

These rules apply to any partnership (except electing large partnerships, see ¶4844, and certain small partnerships, see ¶4845) required to file a partnership return (Form 1065), and to any entity that, for the year it filed a partnership return, either wasn't a partnership or didn't exist for the full year. (former Code Sec. 6231(a)(1), former Code Sec. 6233; Reg § 301.6233-1)[13] A real estate mortgage investment conduit (¶4204) is treated as a partnership for these purposes. (Code Sec. 860F(e))[14]

¶ 4841 Definition of "partnership items"—tax years beginning before 2018.

A "partnership item" is any item that must be taken into account for the partnership's tax year, to the extent regs provide the item is more appropriately determined at the partnership level than at the partner level (former Code Sec. 6231(a)(3)) [15] The regs provide a broad list of categories which are required to be taken into account for a partnership's tax year at the partnership level. (Reg § 301.6231(a)(3)-1(a))[16]

¶ 4842 Tax matters partner (TMP)—tax years beginning before 2018.

The TMP acts on behalf of the partners in unified partnership proceedings. The TMP is: (a) the general partner the partnership designates as such on its return (Form 1065) (Form 1066, for a real estate mortgage investment conduit (Reg § 1.860F-4(d))); or (b) if no designation is made, the general partner with the largest profits interest in the partnership at the end of the tax year. (former Code Sec. 6231(a)(7))

¶ 4843 Final partnership administrative adjustment (FPAA)—tax years beginning before 2018.

If after auditing the partnership IRS concludes that adjustments to the return are needed, it will issue a FPAA, which must be sent to the tax matters partner (TMP) and to "notice partners" IRS knows are eligible to receive notice. (former Code Sec. 6223(a)) [17] The TMP has 90 days from when the FPAA was mailed to file a petition for judicial review of it. (former Code Sec. 6226(a)) If the TMP doesn't file in that time, any notice partner can file the partnership petition within the next 60 days. (former Code Sec. 6226(b)(1)) Detailed procedures govern the conduct of the partnership-level proceeding (former Code Sec. 6224; Reg § 301.6224(a)-1, Reg § 301.6224(c)-3),[18] assessments (former Code Sec. 6225, former Code Sec. 6224), judicial review of FPAAs (former Code Sec. 6226, former Code Sec. 6229; Reg § 301.6226(f)-1), and other matters. [19]

¶ 4844 Unified audit procedure for electing large partnerships—tax years beginning before 2018.

For partnerships with 100 or more partners that elect to be treated as electing large partnerships (¶3701), IRS adjustments at the partnership level flow through to the partners for the year in which the adjustment takes effect. Adjustments generally will not affect prior-year returns of any partners (except in the case of changes to any partner's distributive shares). A partner in an electing large partnership isn't allowed to treat

---

11. ¶T-4015; ¶62,254
12. ¶T-6517; ¶62,214
13. ¶T-2103; ¶62,214.11
14. ¶E-6927; ¶860A4
15. ¶T-2110 *et seq.*; ¶62,214

16. ¶T-2110 *et seq.*; ¶62,214
17. ¶T-2215 *et seq.*
18. ¶T-2156 *et seq.*; ¶62,214
19. ¶T-2215 *et seq.*

820

partnership items on his return inconsistently with the partnership return. Only the partnership can request a refund, and the partners of an electing large partnership do not have the right to participate in partnership-level administrative proceedings. IRS need not give notice to individual partners of the beginning of an administrative proceeding or of a final adjustment. (former Code Sec. 6240 through former Code Sec. 6255) [20]

¶ 4845   Exception for certain small partnerships—tax years beginning before 2018.

The unified audit rules at ¶4839 *et seq.* don't apply to a "small" partnership (unless it elects them under procedures set forth by regs). (Reg § 301.6231(a)(1)-1(b)(2)) A partnership is "small" for a tax year if it has ten or fewer partners, each of whom is an individual (other than a nonresident alien), a C corporation, or an estate of a deceased partner. A partnership doesn't qualify for the small partnership exception if any of its partners is a "pass-thru partner." (former Code Sec. 6231(a)(1)(B)(i); Reg § 301.6231(a)(1)-1(a)(1), Reg § 301.6231(a)(1)-1(a)(2), Reg § 301.6231(a)(1)-1(a)(3))[21]

¶ 4846   Unified Audit and Review for Partnerships—Tax Years Beginning After 2017.

Under the post-2017 partnership audit rules, in general, any adjustment to a "partnership-related item" (¶4847) is determined, and any tax attributable assessed and collected, and the applicability of any penalty, addition to tax, or additional amount which relates to an adjustment to any such item determined, at the partnership level. (Code Sec. 6221(a))

caution: The following rules at ¶4847 *et seq.* apply for tax returns filed for partnership tax years beginning after 2017, except that an election may be made to apply them for any partnership return filed for a tax year beginning after Nov. 2, 2015. For the partnership audit rules generally applicable for tax returns filed for partnership tax years beginning before 2018, see ¶4839 *et seq.*

¶ 4847   Partnership audit procedures for post-2017 partnership returns—scope and applicability.

In general, any adjustment to a "partnership-related item" (below) is determined, any tax attributable thereto will be assessed and collected, and any penalty, addition to tax, or additional amount relating to an adjustment to any such item will be determined, at the partnership level. (Code Sec. 6221(a) Code Sec. 6223)[22]

A "partnership-related item" means any item or amount with respect to the partnership that is relevant in determining the income tax liability of any person, without regard to whether the item or amount appears on the partnership's return and including an imputed underpayment and an item or amount relating to any transaction with, basis in, or liability of, the partnership. (Code Sec. 6241(2)(B))

These rules generally apply to any partnership required to file a partnership return (Form 1065) and, to the extent to be provided in regs, where a partnership return is filed by an entity for a tax year but it is determined that the entity is not a partnership (or that there is no entity) for such year. (Code Sec. 6241(1); Code Sec. 6241(8))[23]

A partnership will designate a partnership representative who will have the power to

---

20. ¶T-2300 *et seq.*; ¶62,404
21. ¶T-2104, T-2109; ¶62,214.10
22. ¶T-2401; ¶62,214.12
23. ¶T-2403; ¶62,214.12

bind the partnership, or if none is appointed, IRS will appoint a partnership representative. (Code Sec. 6223)[24]

Partnerships required to furnish 100 or fewer statements to partners or nominees under Code Sec. 6031(b) and whose partners are individuals, C corporations (including RICs and REITs) , foreign entities that would be treated as C corporations if they were domestic, S corporations, or estates of deceased partners can elect out of partnership audit procedure rules for post-2017 partnership returns. All partners (and shareholders of S corporation partners) must be notified of the election. (Code Sec. 6221(b); Reg § 301.6221(b)-1(b))[25]

¶ 4848   Partnership-level adjustments for post-2017 partnership returns.

If IRS adjusts any partnership-related items (referred to as a partnership adjustment) (Code Sec. 6241(2)(A)), the partnership, rather than the partners, is subject to the liability for any imputed underpayment and will take any other adjustments into account in the adjustment year. (Code Sec. 6225(a)) The imputed underpayment is determined by netting, in the manner described in Code Sec. 6225(b), all partnership adjustments with respect to the reviewed year and applying the highest rate of tax in effect for that year under Code Sec. 1 or Code Sec. 11. Items of different character (e.g., capital or ordinary) are not netted together in determining the amount of an imputed underpayment, and certain limitations apply on adjustments that may be taken into account. [26]

IRS will establish procedures under which adjustments may be modified to reflect a lower level of tax due because of (i) payment of the tax by the partners either through amended returns or by the use of a "pull-in" procedure in which the partners otherwise take the adjustment into account, (ii) tax-exempt partners, (iii) lower rates applying to the partners, (iv) special rules relating to specified passive losses of publicly traded partnerships (as defined in Code Sec. 469(k)(2)), or (v) as otherwise specified by IRS regs or other guidance. (Code Sec. 6225(c))[27]

As an alternative to taking IRS audit adjustments into account at the partnership level, a partnership can elect out of those rules (in a manner to be specified by IRS, and revocable only with IRS's consent) not later than 45 days after the date of the notice of final partnership adjustment, provided that it furnishes (in a manner to be specified by IRS), to each partner of the partnership for the reviewed year and to IRS, a statement of the partner's share of any adjustment to any partnership-related items (as determined in the notice of final partnership adjustment). The partners would then take the adjustments into account. Where the adjustments result in an imputed underpayment, interest and penalties are imposed, with interest imposed at the Code Sec. 6621(a)(2) underpayment rate determined by adding five percentage points (instead of three percentage points) to the federal short-term rate. (Code Sec. 6226)[28]

¶ 4849   Partnership-level assessment and review procedures for post-2017 partnership returns.

For post-2017 partnership returns, IRS may mail to the partnership and the partnership representative: (i) notice of any administrative proceeding initiated at the partnership level, (ii) notice of any proposed partnership adjustment, and (iii) notice of any final partnership adjustment. A notice of administrative proceeding will prevent the partnership from filing a request for administrative adjustments on its own. A notice of a final partnership adjustment will not be mailed earlier than 270 days (the number of days a partnership has to request a modification of a proposed partnership adjustment) after the

24. ¶T-2402; ¶62,214.12
25. ¶T-2404; ¶62,214.13
26. ¶T-2405; ¶62,214.14

27. ¶T-2405.1; ¶62,214.14
28. ¶T-2407; ¶62,214.15

date on which the notice of the proposed partnership adjustment is mailed or after the partnership filed an administrative adjustment request. Exceptions are provided for mathematical or clerical errors (including violations of the Code Sec. 6222 consistency rules relating to an interest in a lower tier partnership), or where the partnership waives the restrictions on assessment. Special limitation periods apply for partnership assessments. (Code Sec. 6231(a), Code Sec. 6235(a))[29]

Where an imputed underpayment under Code Sec. 6225 or any specified similar amount attributable to a partnership or an S corporation that is a partner in a partnership that makes a Code Sec. 6226 election to take adjustments into account at the partner level (see ¶4848) (or any interest or penalties relating to any such amount) is not paid within 10 days after the date on which IRS provides notice and demand for payment, (i) the amount is subject to an increased interest rate. and (ii) IRS may assess on each partner (or former partner) of the partnership a tax equal to the partner's proportionate share of that amount. (Code Sec. 6232(f))[30]

Interest on imputed underpayments will be calculated under the applicable interest rules for the period beginning on the date for filing the partnership return for the reviewed year and ending on the return due date for the adjustment year (or, if earlier, the date payment of the imputed underpayment is made). Similarly, penalties will be determined as if the partnership had been an individual subject to income tax for the reviewed year and the imputed underpayment was an actual underpayment (or understatement) for the year. (Code Sec. 6233)[31]

A partnership will have 90 days from when the notice of a final partnership adjustment to file a petition for a readjustment for the tax year with (i) the Tax Court, (ii) the U.S. district court for the district in which the partnership's principal place of business is located, or (iii) the Court of Federal Claims. However, if the partnership adjustment was made as provided by the notice of final partnership adjustment, a petition in a U.S. district court or the Court of Federal Claims may be filed only if the partnership deposits with IRS the amount of the imputed underpayment (as of the date of filing of the petition). (Code Sec. 6234)[32]

¶ 4850   Recovering Overpayments by Refund or Credit; Tax Litigation.

A taxpayer can recover an overpayment as a credit or a refund by properly filing a claim (¶4852) and, if the claim is denied, bringing suit (¶4861 *et seq.*). A taxpayer who has been issued a 90-day letter (¶4823) can go to Tax Court without first paying the disputed tax.

An overpayment is the excess of the amount paid (or withheld) as tax over the taxpayer's correct tax liability. It includes the part of a correct tax paid after the applicable assessment period has run. (Code Sec. 6401)[33] An overpayment can be recovered as a refund or credit, generally only by the taxpayer who paid the tax, but IRS may first credit the overpayment (including interest) against *any* of the taxpayer's past due tax liability (including interest, additions, penalties). (Code Sec. 6402(a); Reg § 301.6402-3(a)(5)) For offset against nontax debts, see ¶4851.

No credit or refund for an overpayment will be made to a taxpayer before the 15th day of the second month following the close of that tax year, if the taxpayer claimed the earned income tax credit or additional child tax credit on the tax return. (Code Sec. 6402(m))[34]

Electronic filers may elect (on Form 8453) to have their refunds deposited directly into their bank accounts. Paper filers elect direct deposit by filling in the appropriate blanks on

---

29. ¶T-2408; ¶T-2409; ¶T-2410; ¶62,214.16; ¶62,214.17
30. ¶T-2409; ¶62,214.16
31. ¶T-2406; ¶62,214.14

32. ¶T-2411; ¶62,214.19
33. ¶T-5500 *et seq.*; ¶64,014
34. ¶T-5600 *et seq.*, T-5700 *et seq.*; ¶64,024

the "Refund" lines of Form 1040. In either case, use Form 8888 to direct deposit a refund into two or three accounts including IRAs. [35]

A refund may be claimed for a deceased taxpayer. Attach Form 1310 (not needed for surviving spouse filing jointly with decedent) to the decedent's final return (¶4714).[36]

¶ 4851   Overpayments applied to child support and other nontax debts.

If a state notifies the Treasury that a taxpayer owes any child support payments, it must first apply the taxpayer's overpayment (including earned income amounts) to those past-due obligations, before making any refund or credit. (Code Sec. 6402(c))[37] If a federal agency notifies the Treasury of any past-due, legally enforceable non-tax debt a taxpayer owes the agency, IRS must apply the balance (i.e., after the child support offset) of the taxpayer's overpayment to that non-tax debt. (Code Sec. 6402(d))[38] After these reductions, refunds can be reduced by state income tax debts, (Code Sec. 6402(e))[39] or reduced to recover debts to states for certain overpayments of unemployment compensation. (Code Sec. 6402(f))[40]

¶ 4852   Refund claim.

To get a refund, a taxpayer must file a timely (¶4857) written claim. For income, gift and federal unemployment taxes, a separate claim must be made for each tax year or period. (Reg § 301.6402-2(a), Reg § 301.6402-2(d)) To claim their refund, individuals who have filed Form 1040 or Form 1040A must use Form 1040X, and corporations who have filed Form 1120 must use Form 1120X. Where a form other than Form 1040, Form 1040A, or Form 1120 was filed, a refund claim must be made on the appropriate amended income tax return. (Reg § 301.6402-3(a)) Form 843 is used for refunds of most non-income taxes other than certain excise taxes. (Reg § 601.105(e)(1))[41]

IRS must provide the taxpayer with an explanation for the disallowance of a refund claim. (Code Sec. 6402(l))[42]

¶ 4853   Quick refund for carrybacks and claim of right—Forms 1045, 1139.

A taxpayer who reports a carryback of a capital loss, business credit, or capital loss from a Code Sec. 1256 contract under Code Sec. 1212(c) on his return, or a farmer who reports a net operating loss carryback, can quickly recover a refund based on the carryback by filing Form 1045 (individuals) or Form 1139 (corporations) on or after the date the return for the loss or credit year is filed, and within 12 months after the end of the tax year from which the carryback is made. (Code Sec. 6411(a); Reg § 1.6411-1(b)(1))[43] This procedure also applies to overpayments attributable to a "claim of right" adjustment (¶2856), where the amount of repayment in any one year exceeds $3,000. (Code Sec. 6411(d))[44] IRS has 90 days from the later of the date the claim is filed or the last day of the month the loss year return is due (with extensions), to make any credit or refund. (Code Sec. 6411(b); Reg § 1.6411-3)[45] IRS's determination is tentative. If the claim is rejected, the taxpayer can't sue but must first file a standard refund claim. (Code Sec. 6411(b); Reg § 1.6411-3(c)) Even if IRS grants the refund, it can later examine the loss year return and the refund application. IRS may assess any part of the refund it finds excessive, without issuing a 90-day letter. (Code Sec. 6213(b)(3))[46]

35. ¶T-5610 *et seq.*
36. ¶T-5710
37. ¶T-6013 *et seq.*; ¶64,024.26
38. ¶T-6023 *et seq.*; ¶64,024.23
39. ¶T-6038; ¶64,024
40. ¶T-6045.1

41. ¶T-6700 *et seq.*; ¶64,024, ¶64,024.08
42. ¶T-5618.1
43. ¶T-6501 *et seq.*; ¶64,114
44. ¶T-6522; ¶64,114
45. ¶T-6509; ¶64,114
46. ¶T-3633; ¶62,134.02

¶ 4854   Quick refunds of corporate estimated tax overpayments—Form 4466.

A corporation that overpaid estimated tax (¶3344 *et seq.*) can get a refund within 45 days after filing Form 4466. (Code Sec. 6425(b)(1), Code Sec. 6425(b)(2); Reg § 1.6425-1(b)) The form must be filed *after* the corporation's tax year ends and *on or before* the 15th day of the fourth month after the year ends (or before the corporation first files its income tax return for that year, if earlier); but for C corporations with a tax year ending on June 30, for tax years beginning before Jan. 1, 2026, the deadline is the 15th day of the *third* month. (Code Sec. 6425(a)(1)) The corporation's estimated tax overpayment must be at least 10% of its revised expected annual tax, *and* at least $500. (Code Sec. 6425(b)(3)) If a corporate estimated tax overpayment refund is excessive, an addition to tax equal to the underpayment interest rate (¶4868), times the excessive amount is imposed. (Code Sec. 6655(h))[47]

¶ 4855   Protective refund claims.

A protective refund claim is a regular refund claim (see ¶4852) filed merely to keep a particular claim alive. It is generally used where IRS has a settled view adverse to a taxpayer on an issue being litigated by other taxpayers. A protective refund claim is usually filed just before the refund claim period expires. It will keep the taxpayer's claim alive (i.e., protect his right to sue) for the additional period from the date of filing to the date of rejection plus the refund suit period. [48]

¶ 4856   Interest on overpayments.

IRS pays interest on overpayments. (Code Sec. 6611(a)) The interest (compounded daily) runs from the date of the overpayment (below) to a date not more than 30 days before the refund is made (or to the (unextended) return due date for the amount against which the overpayment is credited). (Code Sec. 6611(b))[49] But no interest is payable on a refund arising from an original income, employment, excise, estate or gift tax return made within 45 days after the later of the return due date (without extensions) or the date it was filed. (Code Sec. 6611(e)(1); Reg § 301.6611-1(j))[50] If a refund arising from an amended return or refund claim is issued within 45 days, no interest is payable for that up-to-45-day period. (Code Sec. 6611(e)(2))[1] For refunds or credits arising from an adjustment initiated by IRS, the interest period is reduced by 45 days. (Code Sec. 6611(e)(3))[2] The grace period during which the government isn't required to pay interest on overpayments is increased from 45 days to 180 days for overpayments resulting from excess amounts deducted and withheld under chapter 3 of the Code (Code Sec. 1441 through Code Sec. 1464 (withholding on nonresident aliens and foreign corporations)) or chapter 4 of the Code (Code Sec. 1471 through Code Sec. 1474). (Code Sec. 6611(e)) For returns filed after the due date (with extensions), no interest is payable for the period preceding the actual filing date. (Code Sec. 6611(b)(3))[3] And, no interest is payable on an estate's overpayment unless it shows that the interest (and refund) won't escheat to the state. (Code Sec. 6408)[4] IRS also won't pay interest when it refunds a conditional or advance payment of taxes. [5]

The overpayment rate for individuals is the short-term applicable federal rate (AFR) plus 3 percentage points (same as the underpayment rate, see ¶4868). The overpayment rate for corporations (including non-profit corporations) is generally the short-term AFR plus 2 percentage points. However, the rate for C corporations is reduced to the short-term

---

47. ¶T-6600 *et seq.*; ¶s 64,254, 66,554
48. ¶T-6742; ¶64,024.17
49. ¶s T-8008, T-8031, T-8034; ¶66,114
50. ¶T-8024; ¶66,114
1. ¶T-8027; ¶66,114

2. ¶T-8028; ¶66,114
3. ¶T-8008; ¶66,114
4. ¶s T-8063, T-8065; ¶64,084
5. ¶T-8046

AFR plus 0.5 percentage points, to the extent the overpayment for any period exceeds $10,000. (Code Sec. 6621(a)(1))[6] For the period from Jan. 1, 2017 to Mar. 31, 2018, the actual overpayment rate for individuals is 4% and for corporations is 3% (1.5% if the overpayment is by a C corporation and exceeds $10,000). For the period from Apr. 1, 2018 to Dec. 31, 2018, the actual overpayment rate for individuals is 5% and for corporations is 4% (2.5% if the overpayment is by a C corporation and exceeds $10,000). [7]

A deposit that is returned to a taxpayer is treated as a payment of tax for any period to the extent (and only to the extent) attributable to a disputable tax for that period. (Code Sec. 6603(d)(1)) However, the interest on the return of such a deposit is payable only at the short-term AFR rate compounded daily. (Code Sec. 6603(d)(4))[8] The overpayment date for taxes withheld or paid as estimated taxes is the unextended due date of the return. (Code Sec. 6513(b))[9] Overpayments resulting from the carryback of an NOL, net capital loss, business credit, or foreign tax credit, are considered not to have been made before the "filing date" for the tax year in which the loss or credit arose or the foreign tax was in fact paid or accrued. (Code Sec. 6611(f))[10] Similarly, where a business credit carryback is attributable to an NOL, etc., carryback from a later year, the overpayment is considered not to have been made before the filing date for that later year. (Code Sec. 6611(f)(3))[11]

¶ 4857   Deadline for refund claims.

A claim for credit or refund of a tax paid by *return* must be filed within the later of: (1) three years from the date the return was timely or untimely filed (or the due date if filed earlier), or (2) two years from the date the tax was paid. If the required return wasn't filed, the claim must be filed within two years from when the tax was paid. (Code Sec. 6511(a))[12] For the prohibited transaction excise tax (¶4336), the relevant return is the plan's annual Form 5500, not Form 5330 on which the tax is reported. [13]

A longer refund claim period applies in these cases:

. . . If a taxpayer and IRS execute one of the Form 872 series extending the assessment period (see ¶4835), the claim can be filed within six months after the expiration of the extended assessment period. (Code Sec. 6511(c)(1))[14]

. . . For an overpayment resulting from carryback of an NOL, net capital loss, or business credit, the period expires three years after the time the return is due (including extensions) for the year the loss or credit arose, not the year to which it's carried back. (Code Sec. 6511(d)(2), Code Sec. 6511(d)(4))[15] If the overpayment is attributable to a carryback from a later year, the period expires three years after the time for filing the return (including extensions) for that later year. (Code Sec. 6511(d)(4))[16]

. . . For an overpayment resulting from the payment or accrual of foreign taxes for which a foreign tax credit is allowed, the claim period is ten years. (Code Sec. 6511(d)(3))[17]

. . . For an overpayment resulting from a bad debt or from worthless securities, the claim period is seven years. (Code Sec. 6511(d)(1))[18]

. . . For self-employment tax claims attributable to Tax Court employment status proceedings, the claim period is two years after the calendar year the Tax Court determination becomes final. (Code Sec. 6511(d)(7))[19]

. . . For credit or refund claims for retired military personnel who receive disability determinations from the Dept. of Veterans Affairs (VA), the refund claim filing period is

6. ¶T-8002, ¶T-8002.1; ¶66,214
7. ¶T-8002 *et seq.*; ¶66,214
8. ¶S-5804.3; ¶66,034.01
9. ¶T-7530; ¶s 66,114, 65,134
10. ¶T-8049 *et seq.*; ¶66,114
11. ¶T-8051; ¶66,114
12. ¶T-7501 *et seq.*; ¶65,114

13. ¶T-7524; ¶65,114.04
14. ¶T-7574; ¶65,114.09
15. ¶T-7554; ¶s 65,114.11, 65,114.13
16. ¶T-7563; ¶65,114.13
17. ¶T-7569; ¶65,114.12
18. ¶T-7552; ¶65,114.10
19. ¶T-7573.1; ¶65,114.155

extended for one year after the date of a disability determination from the VA (if later than the time allowed under the general refund limitations period). The extended time period doesn't apply for any tax year beginning more than five years before the date of the disability determination. (Code Sec. 6511(d)(8))[20]

... For a refund claim for overpayment of taxes on wrongful incarceration damages that were retroactively made excludible under Code Sec. 139F (see ¶1376), the claim must be filed *before* Dec. 18, 2018.[21]

and

And, if certain requirements are met, the limitations period may be suspended during any period an individual is unable to manage his financial affairs by reason of a medically-determinable physical or mental impairment. (Code Sec. 6511(h))[22]

¶ 4858   Refund suit period.

A taxpayer *must* file a refund claim with IRS before starting a suit for refund (or credit). (Code Sec. 7422(a))[23] The refund suit can't be started *before* six months from filing the claim (unless IRS acts on the claim in that period), or *after* two years from the date IRS mails a notice of disallowance. (Code Sec. 6532(a)(1)) The taxpayer can waive (on Form 2297) issuance of this notice, and the 2-year period will start on the date the waiver is filed. (Code Sec. 6532(a)(3)) Also, the taxpayer and IRS can execute a Form 907 extending the 2-year period. (Code Sec. 6532(a)(2))[24]

¶ 4859   Limits on amount of refund or credit.

If a claim is filed within three years from the time the return was filed, the refund or credit is limited to the portion of tax paid during the three years (plus the period of any filing extension) immediately preceding the filing of the claim. (Code Sec. 6511(b)(2)(A))[25] If the claim wasn't filed within the three-year period, the refund or credit is limited to the portion of the tax paid during the two years immediately preceding the filing of the claim. (Code Sec. 6511(b)(2)(B)) This two-year limitation also applies if a claim, but no return, was filed. (Reg § 301.6511(b)-1(b)(1)(iii))[26] Where no claim is filed and a refund or credit is allowed within three years from the time the return was filed, the refund or credit is limited to the portion of the tax paid during the three years immediately before the allowance. If the refund or credit is not allowed within that three-year period, it's limited to the portion of the tax paid during the two years immediately before the allowance. (Code Sec. 6511(b)(2)(C))[27] For purposes of determining the amount of an individual taxpayer's refund or credit under these rules, the refund claim periods described above are suspended during any period when the individual is unable to manage his financial affairs (see ¶4857). (Code Sec. 6511(h))[28]

¶ 4860   Refunds of refundable credits.

Any refund or advance payment of a refundable credit made to an individual isn't taken into account as income, and isn't taken into account as resources for a period of 12 months from receipt, in determining the eligibility of the recipient or any other individual for benefits or assistance, or the amount or extent of benefits or assistance, under any federal program or any state or local program financed in whole or part with federal funds. (Code Sec. 6409)

---

20. ¶T-7573.2; ¶65,114.16
21. ¶J-5853
22. ¶T-7506; ¶65,114.04
23. ¶T-6701; ¶74,224
24. ¶T-9034; ¶65,324.01

25. ¶T-7537; ¶65,114.07
26. ¶s T-7546, T-7547; ¶65,114.07
27. ¶T-7548; ¶65,114.07
28. ¶T-7506; ¶65,114.04

¶ 4861　　Tax litigation: available forums and burden of proof.

A taxpayer may go to:

. . . the Tax Court: to set aside a deficiency determined by IRS (¶4862) (Code Sec. 6214(a));[29] to review appeals of Collection Due Process hearings (¶4907 *et seq.*) (Code Sec. 6330(d)(1));[30] to determine worker classification in certain cases and, according to Tax Court, the correct amount of employment taxes that relate to such determinations (Code Sec. 7436);[31] to review IRS's failure to abate interest to taxpayers within certain net worth limits who bring an action within 180 days of IRS's final adverse determination, and to order abatement if IRS abused its discretion (Code Sec. 6404(h));[32] for a declaratory judgment on retirement plan qualification (Code Sec. 7476(a));[33] for eligibility for deferral of estate tax on a closely held business interest (Code Sec. 7479);[34] for the value of certain gifts made (Code Sec. 7477; Reg § 301.7477-1);[35] to redetermine transferee liability (¶4916) (Code Sec. 6901);[36] to adjust partnership items (Code Sec. 6221);[37] over actions for administrative costs (Code Sec. 7430);[38] to determine innocent spouse relief when a deficiency has been issued and the taxpayer elects regular or separate innocent spouse relief or requests equitable relief (but the Tax Court can't rule on the timeliness of an assessment in reviewing a denial of innocent spouse relief) (Code Sec. 6015(e));[39] to review awards to whistleblowers (Code Sec. 7623(b)(4));[40] and for other matters;

. . . a U.S. district court to enjoin IRS from assessing and collecting a tax in certain cases (¶4912), or to get damages for IRS's unauthorized collection activities or failure to release a lien; (Code Sec. 7432, Code Sec. 7433)[41]

. . . a bankruptcy court to sue for up to $1 million in damages for willful IRS violations of automatic stay or discharge in bankruptcy. (Code Sec. 7433(e))[42]

. . . a U.S. district court or the U.S. Court of Federal Claims: to recover an overpayment of taxes (after filing a refund claim); (Code Sec. 6532(a))[43] or to determine the correct amount of (or for a refund of) the estate's estate tax liability, even if it wasn't fully paid due to a Code Sec. 6166 election; (Code Sec. 7422(j)(1))[44]

. . . the Tax Court, the district court for the DC Circuit, or the U.S. Court of Federal Claims for a declaratory judgment on the tax status of exempt organizations and foundations. (Code Sec. 7428(a))[45]

For taxpayers other than certain large partnerships, corporations, and trusts, IRS has the burden of proof in any court proceeding with respect to any factual issue relevant to ascertaining a taxpayer's liability for any tax imposed by subtitle A or B of the Code, e.g., income and self-employment, gift, estate, and generation-skipping transfer taxes, if the taxpayer: introduces credible evidence with respect to the issue; has complied with the substantiation requirements; has maintained all required records; and has cooperated with reasonable IRS requests. (Code Sec. 7491(a))[46] IRS has the burden of production (i.e., to come forward initially with evidence) in any court proceeding with respect to the liability of any individual for any penalty imposed by the Code. (Code Sec. 7491(c))[47]

---

29. ¶U-2100 *et seq.*; ¶62,144, ¶74,414
30. ¶V-5272, ¶V-6015; ¶63,304
31. ¶U-2143; ¶74,364
32. ¶U-2129.1; ¶64,044
33. ¶U-3700 *et seq.*; ¶74,764
34. ¶U-3851 *et seq.*¶74,217.02
35. ¶U-3880;¶74,217.02
36. ¶V-9200; ¶69,014
37. ¶T-2100 *et seq.*; ¶62,214
38. ¶U-1242; ¶74,304

39. ¶U-2148
40. ¶U-2154; ¶76,234
41. ¶s V-5801, V-6113; ¶s 74,324, 74,334
42. ¶V-5820 *et seq.*; ¶74,334
43. ¶s U-4000 *et seq.*, U-6000 *et seq.*; ¶74,224
44. ¶T-9007.1; ¶74,224
45. ¶s U-3800 *et seq.*, U-4116, U-6005; ¶74,284
46. ¶U-1351; ¶74,914
47. ¶U-1331; ¶74,914

¶ 4862 The Tax Court.

To get Tax Court review of a deficiency, a taxpayer must file a petition with the Tax Court at Washington, D.C., in response to a 90-day letter (see ¶4823) from IRS, within 90 days (150 days if the letter is addressed to a person outside the U.S.) after the letter is mailed (i.e., postmarked). A petition is timely if it's filed with the Tax Court on or before the last date specified by IRS in the 90-day letter for filing it. (Code Sec. 6213(a))[48] For the types of matters within the Tax Court's jurisdiction, see ¶4861.

The Tax Court's jurisdiction is generally limited to the review (without a jury) of deficiencies asserted by IRS (and not paid when the 90-day letter is issued). It can order payment of a refund if it determines the taxpayer overpaid. (Code Sec. 6512(b)) But it can't grant equitable relief. The Tax Court has jurisdiction to order a refund of any amount collected while IRS was prohibited from collecting a deficiency by levy or court proceeding but only if a timely petition for a redetermination of the deficiency has been filed and only with respect to the deficiency at issue. (Code Sec. 6213(a))[49] The Tax Court is generally barred from determining whether the tax for any period not before it has been overpaid or underpaid. However, it may apply the doctrine of equitable recoupment. (Code Sec. 6214(b))[50]

¶ 4863 Settlement after Tax Court petition is filed.

IRS District Counsel will refer all docketed Tax Court cases to the Appeals Office for consideration of settlement (unless Appeals issued the deficiency notice, in which case there will be no referral if there is little likelihood that all or part of the case can be settled in a reasonable period of time). Counsel and Appeals can agree otherwise, work together, or transfer the case back and forth to promote efficient disposition of the case. The taxpayer-petitioner and/or his representative will be notified as to who has the case and the settlement authority.[1] If the taxpayer and IRS agree on a settlement, they enter into a written agreement stipulating the amount of any deficiency or overpayment. This stipulation is filed with the Tax Court which will enter a decision in accordance with it. (Reg § 601.106(d)(3)(i))[2]

¶ 4864 Small tax claims in Tax Court.

Special informal procedures apply, at a taxpayer's election and with the Tax Court's concurrence, to any Tax Court case where neither the amount (including any additions to tax, additional amounts and penalties) of the deficiency disputed nor of any claimed overpayment exceeds $50,000 (the Tax Court has held that the limit includes tax, interest and penalties and applies to the total owed for all years in a single proceeding). The taxpayer thus gets the Court's decision faster and more easily, but gives up the right to appeal. (Code Sec. 7463)[3]

¶ 4865 Appeals from Tax Court, district court and U.S. Court of Federal Claims.

Decisions of the Tax Court and U.S. district courts are appealable to the U.S. Court of Appeals.[4] The appeal is made in the circuit where the taxpayer's legal residence (for appeals from Tax Court)[5] or the trial court (for appeals from district courts) is located.[6] U.S. Court of Federal Claims decisions may be appealed to the Court of Appeals for the

---

48. ¶U-2300 *et seq.*; ¶62,134 *et seq.*
49. ¶U-2134.1; ¶s 65,124, 74,424
50. ¶U-2138; ¶62,144.02
1. ¶T-1902 *et seq.*
2. ¶T-1909

3. ¶U-3600 *et seq.*; ¶74,536.1704
4. ¶s U-3417, U-5000 *et seq.*; ¶s 74,336.12, 74,824
5. ¶U-5202; ¶74,824
6. ¶U-5401

Federal Circuit. [7] Appeals from U.S. Courts of Appeals are to the U.S. Supreme Court. [8]

¶ 4866   Recovery of attorneys' fees and costs.

Taxpayers whose net worth doesn't exceed specified limits, who meet other requirements, and who prevail against the U.S. in court (or at the administrative level) may be awarded reasonable litigation and administrative costs (including the costs of recovering the award). (Code Sec. 7430) The limit on attorney fee recoveries is $200 per hour for 2018 (and 2019, as calculated by Thomson Reuters based on inflation data). (Code Sec. 7430(c)(1))[9] To avoid an award of fees, IRS must show its position was substantially justified. (Code Sec. 7430(c)(4)(B)) Administrative costs can be awarded from the date IRS sends the "30-day letter." (Code Sec. 7430(c)(2)) When an individual is representing a taxpayer on a pro bono basis, the fees recoverable may exceed the amounts that the taxpayer paid or incurred. (Code Sec. 7430(c)(3)(B)) IRS losses on similar issues in other circuits are taken into account in determining whether its position was substantially justified (Code Sec. 7430(c)(4)(B)(iii)), and costs can be awarded where IRS rejects a taxpayer's offer and later gets a judgment not exceeding the offer. (Code Sec. 7430(c)(4)(E)(i); Reg § 301.7430-7)[10]

¶ 4867   Interest and Penalties.

Interest is charged on underpayments of tax (¶4869 *et seq.*). Various civil and criminal penalties are imposed on taxpayers (and/or return preparers) who violate the tax law (¶4875 *et seq.*).

¶ 4868   Interest on underpayments.

Interest is generally payable whenever any tax or civil penalty isn't paid when due (Code Sec. 6601(a)), even if the taxpayer has been granted an extension of time to pay the tax. (Code Sec. 6601(b)(1); Reg § 301.6601-1(a)) There's no interest on late payments of estimated tax (Code Sec. 6601(h)) (but for comparable penalty computations, see ¶3154 (individuals) and ¶3349 (corporations)) or unemployment tax. (Code Sec. 6601(i))[11] Interest is payable on an erroneous refund or credit. (Code Sec. 6602)[12]

The rate of interest on tax underpayments and penalties is the short-term applicable federal rate (AFR) plus 3 percentage points. (Code Sec. 6621(a)(2))[13] For the period from Jan. 1, 2017 to Mar. 31, 2018, the actual interest rate on underpayments is 4%. For the period from Apr. 1, 2018 to Dec. 31, 2018, the actual interest rate on underpayments is 5%.[14] However, if a C corporation's tax underpayment for any tax period exceeds $100,000, a higher interest rate applies for the period after the 30th day after a notice (or proposed notice) of deficiency. For the period from Apr. 1, 2018 to Dec. 31, 2018, the rate is 7%. (Code Sec. 6621(c); Reg § 301.6621-3)[15] A net interest rate of zero applies to equivalent amounts of underpayments and overpayments by the same taxpayer. (Code Sec. 6621(d)) Taxpayers request interest netting on Form 843. [16]

¶ 4869   Interest accrual period.

Interest on unpaid tax liabilities runs from the last day prescribed by the Code for payment (disregarding extensions or any installment payment agreement) (Code Sec. 6601(b)(1)), to the date paid. (Code Sec. 6601(a)) However, where the tax is paid within 21 days after notice and demand (10 business days if the amount is $100,000 or

---

7. ¶U-6001; ¶74,336.10
8. ¶s U-5700 *et seq.*, U-7000 *et seq.*; ¶74,336.15
9. ¶U-1262 *et seq.*; ¶74,304
10. ¶U-1240 *et seq.*; ¶74,304
11. ¶V-1000 *et seq.*; ¶66,014

12. ¶T-9108; ¶66,024
13. ¶V-1100 *et seq.*; ¶66,214
14. ¶V-1102; ¶66,214
15. ¶V-1106 *et seq.*; ¶66,214
16. ¶V-1303 *et seq.*; ¶66,014

more), interest stops on the date of the notice and demand. (Code Sec. 6601(e)(3))[17] (For payments to stop interest, see ¶4870.) Also, where a taxpayer consents to immediate assessment (by signing one of the Form 870 waiver of assessment series, see ¶4818) and IRS doesn't make notice and demand for payment within 30 days of the filing of that consent, interest stops running during the period beginning immediately after that 30th day and ending with the date of the notice and demand. (Code Sec. 6601(c))[18]

Interest on civil penalties runs from the date of notice and demand if not paid within 21 days after that date (10 business days for amounts of $100,000 or more). (Code Sec. 6601(e)(2)(A)) But for the penalties for failure to file, valuation misstatement (income tax) or understatement (estate or gift tax), substantial understatement, negligence, and fraud, the interest period begins on the *return* due date (with extensions). In either case, the interest stops on the date the penalty is paid. (Code Sec. 6601(e)(2)(B))[19]

¶ 4870 Deposits to prepay and/or stop the running of interest.

A cash deposit made in conformity with IRS rules may be used to pay income, gift, estate, or generation-skipping tax or certain excise taxes that have not yet been assessed at the time of the deposit. (Code Sec. 6603(a)) The amount of the deposit that is later used by IRS to pay tax is treated as a tax payment at the time of the deposit, for purposes of determining whether the taxpayer owes interest on an underpayment of tax. (Code Sec. 6603(b)) Interest may be allowed on the return of all or part of such a deposit, see ¶4856.[20]

¶ 4871 How other year's tax payments affect interest.

Interest on a deficiency isn't eliminated when the deficiency is eliminated by a net operating loss (NOL), net capital loss, foreign tax credit or business credit carryback. It accrues from its original due date to the filing date for the tax year in which the carryback arose (or, with respect to any portion of a credit carryback attributable to a carryback from a later year, to the filing date for that later year). (Code Sec. 6601(d))[21]

An underpayment of tax in one year may be paid by crediting against it an overpayment of tax in another year. (Code Sec. 6402(a)) No interest accrues on any portion of the underpayment so paid for any period after the return due date (without extension) for the overpayment year or, if later, when the offsetting return is filed. This rule doesn't apply to the extent the zero rate (¶4868) applies. (Code Sec. 6601(f))[22] When a taxpayer elects to apply an overpayment to the following year's estimated taxes, the overpayment will be applied to unpaid installments of estimated tax due on or after the date(s) the overpayment arose, in the order in which they are required to be paid to avoid an estimated tax penalty. IRS will assess interest on a later determined deficiency for the overpayment year only from the date(s) that the overpayment is applied to the following year's estimated taxes.[23]

¶ 4872 Abatement of interest, penalties and additions to tax—Form 843.

IRS has discretion to abate interest assessed because of a deficiency attributable to any unreasonable error or delay by an IRS employee in performing a managerial or ministerial act. (Code Sec. 6404(e)(1); Reg § 301.6404-2)[24] .

IRS must abate any portion of any penalty or addition to tax attributable to erroneous written advice (as defined in Reg § 301.6404-3(c)(1)) that the taxpayer reasonably relied

---

17. ¶V-1200 *et seq.*, ¶V-1300; ¶66,014.02
18. ¶V-1307; ¶66,014.02
19. ¶V-1218; ¶66,014.02
20. ¶S-5804 *et seq.*; ¶66,034

21. ¶V-1302; ¶66,014.03
22. ¶V-1301; ¶66,014.03
23. ¶V-1210
24. ¶T-3951 *et seq.*; ¶64,044

on that was furnished to the taxpayer by an IRS employee in response to a specific written request. (Code Sec. 6404(f)(1), Code Sec. 6404(f)(2)(A)), (Code Sec. 6404(f)(2)(B))[25] To obtain such an abatement, a taxpayer must make an abatement request on Form 843 (with certain required attachments). (Reg § 301.6404-3(d))[26]

For taxpayers affected by a federally declared disaster or a terroristic or military action, IRS may postpone the deadlines for performing various tax acts for a period of up to one year. (Code Sec. 7508A(a)(2))[27]

¶ 4873   Interest and penalty suspension for failing to notify individual of liability.

Where an individual taxpayer files an income tax return on or before the return due date (including extensions), IRS must generally suspend the imposition of interest and penalty with respect to any taxpayer failure relating to that return if IRS doesn't —during the 36-month period beginning on the date the return is filed or, if later, the date it's due (without extensions)—provide a notice to the taxpayer specifically stating his liability and the basis for the liability. There are several exceptions to this rule, including for any interest or penalty in a case involving fraud or with respect to any (i) tax liability shown on a return, (ii) gross misstatement, (iii) reportable transaction not meeting the applicable disclosure requirements, or (iv) listed transaction.

The suspension period begins on the day after the end of the 36-month period and ends on the date that's 21 days after IRS provides the notice. Where a taxpayer files an amended return (or other written document) showing additional tax liability, the 36-month period for IRS to issue the required notice of liability (and avoid interest or penalty suspension) is restarted. (Code Sec. 6404(g); Reg § 301.6404-4)[28]

¶ 4874   When reasonable cause excuses civil penalties.

Certain civil penalties won't be imposed if the taxpayer's failure to perform the required act was due to reasonable cause —e.g., reliance on tax expert or IRS advice, irregularities in mail delivery, death or serious illness, unavoidable absence, casualty, disaster. The taxpayer generally has the burden of showing that the failure was due to reasonable cause and not willful neglect. [29]

No accuracy-related (¶4877 *et seq.*) or fraud (¶4884) penalty applies to any portion of an underpayment for which the taxpayer shows reasonable cause and good faith. (Code Sec. 6664(c)(1); Reg § 1.6664-4) The failure to disclose a reportable transaction (¶4749) is a strong indication of failure to act in good faith. (Reg § 1.6664-4(d))[30]

¶ 4875   Failure to file income, estate or gift tax returns when due.

The failure to file penalty is 5% of the amount of tax required to be shown on the return (less any earlier payments and credits) for the first month (Code Sec. 6651(b)(1)), plus an additional 5% for each month (or fraction of a month) the failure continues without reasonable cause (¶4874), but not more than 25%. (Code Sec. 6651(a)(1))[31] The minimum penalty for failure to file any income tax return within 60 days of the due date (including extensions) is the lesser of $210 in 2018 ($215 for 2019, as calculated by Thomson Reuters based on inflation data), or the amount of tax required to be shown on the return. (Code Sec. 6651(a))[32]

The penalty is reduced (but not below the above minimum) by the amount of any failure-

---

25. ¶T-3908 *et seq.*; ¶64,044
26. ¶T-3914 *et seq.*; ¶64,044
27. ¶S-8502; ¶75,08A4
28. ¶V-1401, ¶V-1601.2; ¶64,044

29. ¶V-1776 *et seq.*, ¶V-2750 *et seq.*; ¶66,644
30. ¶V-2060
31. ¶V-1750 *et seq.*; ¶66,514.01
32. ¶V-1752; ¶66,514.01

to-pay penalty (0.5%, see ¶4876) for that month. (Code Sec. 6651(c)(1)) The 25% ceiling is applied to each penalty before making this reduction. [33] If the failure to file is fraudulent, the penalty is increased to 15% per month (or fraction of a month), up to a 75% cap. (Code Sec. 6651(f))[34]

¶ 4876   Failure to pay tax.

A penalty is imposed on a taxpayer who, without reasonable cause (¶4874) fails to pay the tax shown on a return or an assessed deficiency of that tax by the prescribed date. The penalty is 0.5% of tax shown (or assessed) for each month (or fraction of a month) that it isn't paid (but not more than 25%). (Code Sec. 6651(a)(2), Code Sec. 6651(a)(3))[35] A substitute return prepared by IRS is a return. (Code Sec. 6651(g)(2); Reg § 301.6020-1(b)(3))[36] The penalty is increased to 1% per month (or fraction of a month), up to 25% penalty maximum, if the tax isn't paid within ten days after IRS serves notice of levy. (Code Sec. 6651(d))[37] The penalty is reduced to 0.25% per month for individuals paying in installments. (Code Sec. 6651(h))[38] An individual who gets an automatic extension of time for *filing* is subject to the penalty (absent reasonable cause) if any additional payment due with the extended return *either*: (1) exceeds 10% of the total shown on Form 1040, *or* (2) isn't paid by the extended filing date. (Reg § 301.6651-1(c)(3))[39] If a subsequent event results in a decrease in the amount required to be shown on a return, the penalty will be computed using this lesser amount. [40]

¶ 4877   Accuracy-related penalty.

An "accuracy-related" civil penalty applies if any portion of an understatement of tax on a tax return is due (absent reasonable cause, see ¶4874) to: negligence (¶4878), substantial income tax valuation misstatements (¶4879), income tax understatements (¶4880), estate or gift tax valuation understatements (¶4882), pension liability overstatements (¶4883), disallowance of benefits due to lack of economic substance (¶4897), or undisclosed foreign financial asset understatements (¶4881). (Code Sec. 6662(a), Code Sec. 6662(b), Code Sec. 6664(c)(1); Reg § 1.6662-2(a))[41] The accuracy-related penalty doesn't apply to any portion of an underpayment for which the fraud penalty (¶4884) is imposed or to the portion of any underpayment which is attributable to a reportable transaction understatement on which the Code Sec. 6662A reportable transaction understatement penalty is imposed, except: (i) for purposes of determining whether an underpayment is substantial or (ii) where the 40% gross valuation misstatement penalty applies. (Code Sec. 6662(b))[42] Also, it only applies if a return is filed by the taxpayer (not by IRS). (Code Sec. 6664(b); Reg § 1.6662-2(a))[43]

¶ 4878   Negligence.

The "accuracy-related" penalty is imposed if any part of an underpayment of tax is due either to negligence or to disregard of rules or regs but without intent to defraud. The penalty is 20% of the portion of the underpayment attributable to the negligence, etc. (Code Sec. 6662(a), Code Sec. 6662(b)(1)) For rules common to all accuracy-related penalties, see ¶4877. "Negligence" includes any failure to make a reasonable attempt to comply with the law or to exercise ordinary and reasonable care in preparing a tax return, as well

33. ¶V-1791; ¶66,514.01
34. ¶V-1753; ¶66,514.01
35. ¶V-1671 *et seq.*; ¶66,514.01
36. ¶V-1685; ¶60,204
37. ¶V-1683; ¶66,514.01
38. ¶V-1684; ¶66,514

39. ¶V-1681; ¶66,514.06
40. ¶V-1672
41. ¶V-2000 *et seq.*; ¶66,624
42. ¶V-2002; ¶66,624
43. ¶V-2051; ¶66,624

as failure to keep adequate books and records or to substantiate items properly. "Disregard" includes any careless, reckless or intentional disregard. (Code Sec. 6662(c); Reg § 1.6662-3(b))[44] The penalties are not imposed for a position with respect to an item (other than a reportable transaction) that is contrary to a revenue ruling or a notice (other than a proposed rulemaking) published in the IRB, if the position has a realistic possibility of being sustained on its merits. (Reg § 1.6662-3(a)) The penalty for disregard of rules or regs isn't imposed where a position is contrary to a rule or reg if the position is disclosed and has a reasonable basis, the taxpayer keeps adequate books and records and substantiates items properly; and, in the case of a position contrary to a reg, the position represents a good faith challenge to the reg. (Reg § 1.6662-3(c), Reg § 1.6662-7(c))[45]

¶ 4879   Misstating value or basis of property on income tax return.

The accuracy-related penalty is imposed on a taxpayer who makes any of these "substantial valuation misstatements": (Code Sec. 6662(a), Code Sec. 6662(b)(3), Code Sec. 6662(e))

. . . any value (or adjusted basis) claimed on an income tax return that is 150% or more of the correct figure (Code Sec. 6662(e)(1)(A));

. . . Code Sec. 482 transfer price adjustments where the price for any property (or its use) or services on an income tax return is 200% or more, or 50% or less, of the correct figure—transactional penalty (Code Sec. 6662(e)(1)(B)(i); Reg § 1.6662-6(b));

. . . a net increase in taxable income for a tax year (without regard to carryovers) resulting from all Code Sec. 482 adjustments in the transfer price of any property (or its use) or services, that (with certain adjustments) exceeds the lesser of $5 million or 10% of the taxpayer's gross receipts —net adjustment penalty. (Code Sec. 6662(e)(1)(B)(ii), Code Sec. 6662(e)(3); Reg § 1.6662-6(c))[46]

The penalty equals 20% of the portion of any income tax underpayment that results from the misstatement (except to the extent the fraud penalty is imposed) (Code Sec. 6662(a), Code Sec. 6662(b))—40% if the misstatement is gross (the above 200%, 150%, 50% and $5 million/10% figures are, respectively, 400%, 200%, 25% or $20 million/20%, or the correct value or basis is zero). (Code Sec. 6662(h); Reg § 1.6662-5(g))[47] The penalty doesn't apply unless the amount of the underpayment for the tax year attributable to all these misstatements for the year exceeds $5,000 ($10,000 for corporations other than S corporations or personal holding companies). (Code Sec. 6662(e)(2))[48] Reasonable cause (¶4874) excuses the penalty. There's no disclosure exception. (Code Sec. 6664(c)(1); Reg § 1.6662-5(a))[49] Strict appraisal requirements apply to overvalued charitable gifts. (Code Sec. 6664(c)(3))[50]

¶ 4880   Penalty on substantial understatements of income tax.

The 20% accuracy-related penalty is imposed on any portion of an underpayment of tax that (absent reasonable cause, see ¶4874) is attributable to any substantial understatement of income tax (or self-employment tax, see ¶3133 *et seq.*). (Code Sec. 6662(a), Code Sec. 6662(b)(2))[1] For rules common to all accuracy-related penalties, see ¶4877. For corporate taxpayers (other than S corporations and personal holding companies), an understatement is substantial if the amount of the understatement exceeds the lesser of (1) 10% of the tax required to be shown on the return for that tax year (or $10,000, if that is greater), or (2) $10 million. For other taxpayers, an understatement is substantial if it exceeds the greater of $5,000 or 10% of the tax required to be shown on the return (5% if the deduction

---

44. ¶V-2105; ¶66,624.01
45. ¶V-2106 *et seq.*; ¶66,624.02
46. ¶V-2200 *et seq.*; ¶66,624
47. ¶V-2206 *et seq.*; ¶66,624

48. ¶V-2205; ¶66,624
49. ¶V-2234; ¶66,644
50. ¶V-2237; ¶66,644
1. ¶V-2150 *et seq.*; ¶66,624.03

under Code Sec. 199A for qualified business income (¶1595 *et seq.*) is claimed). (Code Sec. 6662(d)(1); Reg § 1.6662-4(b)(1))[2] An understatement is the excess of (a) the tax amount required to be shown on the return, over (b) the tax amount that's shown (or withheld) reduced by any rebate. (Code Sec. 6662(d)(2)(A); Reg § 1.6662-4(b)(2), Reg § 1.6662-4(b)(3))[3] The understatement is reduced to the extent attributable to an item (other than tax shelter items, see below) for which:

. . . there is or was substantial authority for how the taxpayer treated it (Code Sec. 6662(d)(2)(B)(i)), or

. . . the relevant facts affecting the item's tax treatment are adequately disclosed on the return (IRS lists which items on the return qualify) or on a Form 8275 (Form 8275-R if the taxpayer's position is contrary to a reg) attached to the return *and* there's a reasonable basis (¶4878) for the taxpayer's treatment of the item. (Code Sec. 6662(d)(2)(B)(ii); Reg § 1.6662-4(f))[4]

"Substantial authority" exists for the tax treatment of an item only if the weight of the authorities supporting the treatment is substantial in relation to the weight of authorities supporting contrary positions. (Reg § 1.6662-4(d)(3)(i))[5]

¶ 4881 Penalty on undisclosed foreign financial assets understatement.

A 40% penalty is imposed on any understatement attributable to an undisclosed foreign financial asset. (Code Sec. 6662(j)(3)) The term "undisclosed foreign financial asset" includes all assets subject to information reporting requirements under Code Sec. 6038 (return of U.S. person who controls a foreign corporation or partnership), Code Sec. 6038B (return of U.S. person making "outbound" transfers to foreign entities), Code Sec. 6038D (self-reporting required for "specified foreign financial assets"), Code Sec. 6046A (return of U.S. person who acquires, disposes of, or has substantial changes in, foreign partnership interests), or Code Sec. 6048 (information reporting as to foreign trusts) for which the required information wasn't provided by the taxpayer as required under the applicable reporting provisions. (Code Sec. 6662(j)(2)) An understatement is attributable to an undisclosed foreign financial asset if it is attributable to any transaction involving the asset. (Code Sec. 6662(j)(1))[6]

¶ 4882 Penalty for understating value of property on gift or estate tax return.

If the value of any property claimed on any gift or estate tax return is 65% or less of the correct value, the 20% accuracy-related penalty (¶4877) is imposed on an underpayment of tax that's attributable to that understatement. (Code Sec. 6662(a), Code Sec. 6662(b)(5), Code Sec. 6662(g)(1)) The penalty is increased to 40% for gross misstatements —i.e., the claimed value is 40% or less of the correct figure. (Code Sec. 6662(h)(1), Code Sec. 6662(h)(2)(C))[7] The penalty applies only if the portion of the underpayment attributable to all these undervaluations for the tax period exceeds $5,000. (Code Sec. 6662(g)(2))[8]

¶ 4883 Overstatement of pension liabilities.

A taxpayer who (absent reasonable cause, see ¶4874) substantially overstates pension liabilities for a tax year is subject to the accuracy-related penalty (¶4877) if the overstatement results in an income tax underpayment of $1,000 or more. (Code Sec. 6662(a), Code Sec. 6662(b)(4), Code Sec. 6662(f)(2))[9] The penalty equals 20% of the underpayment (40%

---

2. ¶V-2159; ¶66,624.03
3. ¶V-2154; ¶66,624.03
4. ¶s V-2154, V-2167 et seq.; ¶66,624.04
5. ¶V-2161, ¶V-2163; ¶66,624.04

6. ¶V-2276; ¶66,624.13
7. ¶s V-2251, V-2252; ¶66,624, ¶66,624.10
8. ¶V-2251; ¶66,624, ¶66,624.10
9. ¶V-2260 *et seq.*; ¶66,624.09

for "gross" overstatements). (Code Sec. 6662(a), Code Sec. 6662(h)(1))[10] Pension liabilities are substantially overstated if the actuarial determination of the liabilities taken into account in computing the contribution deduction (¶4323) is at least 200% of the correct amount. (Code Sec. 6662(f)(1)) The overstatement is "gross" if it's 400% or more of the correct figure. (Code Sec. 6662(h)(2)(B))[11]

¶ 4884   Fraud.

Fraudulent underpayment of tax required to be shown on a return results in a civil penalty of 75% of the portion of the underpayment attributable to fraud. (Code Sec. 6663(a))[12] The fraud penalty can be imposed only if a return is filed (not by IRS). (Code Sec. 6664(b))[13] It won't be imposed where the taxpayer shows reasonable cause (¶4874) and good faith. (Code Sec. 6664(c)(1))[14] Imposition of the fraud penalty on any part of an underpayment precludes imposition of any of the accuracy-related penalties (¶4877) on that same part. (Code Sec. 6662(b))[15] If IRS establishes that any part of an underpayment is attributable to fraud, the entire underpayment is treated as attributable to fraud, except for any part the taxpayer establishes (by a preponderance of the evidence) isn't so attributable. (Code Sec. 6663(b))[16]

¶ 4885   Trust fund recovery penalty for responsible persons.

Willful failure to collect or account for and pay over a tax or willful attempt to evade or defeat a tax, by a "responsible person" required to collect, account for, and pay over the tax carries a civil "trust fund recovery penalty" equal to 100% of the total tax evaded or not accounted for and paid over. (Code Sec. 6672) IRS can't assess the penalty without notifying a responsible person of its intent to do so at least 60 days before making notice and demand for the penalty (unless collection is in jeopardy). (Code Sec. 6672(b)) A "responsible person" is an officer or employee of the corporation, or a partner or employee of a partnership, who is under a duty to perform the act at issue. (Code Sec. 6671(b))[17] A responsible person also includes any person who is connected or associated with an employer in such a manner that he has the power to see that the taxes are paid. [18] Unpaid volunteer board members of exempt organizations who aren't involved in day-to-day financial activities and don't know about the penalized failure are exempt from the penalty, unless that results in no one being liable for it. (Code Sec. 6672(e))[19] IRS must disclose, at the written request of a responsible person, the names of other responsible persons and the collection activities related to them. (Code Sec. 6103(e)(9))[20] Responsible persons who pay more than their proportionate share of tax have the right to recover the excess from other responsible persons. (Code Sec. 6672(d))[21]

¶ 4886   Penalty for filing erroneous refund claim.

If a claim for refund or credit of income tax is made for an "excessive amount," the person making the claim is liable for a penalty equal to 20% of the excessive amount. (Code Sec. 6676(a)) An "excessive amount" is the amount by which the claimed refund or credit exceeds the allowable amount. (Code Sec. 6676(b)) The penalty doesn't apply if it is shown that the claim for the excessive amount is due to a reasonable cause. (Code Sec. 6676(a))

---

10. ¶V-2262; ¶66,624.09
11. ¶V-2263; ¶s 66,624, 66,624.09
12. ¶V-2300 *et seq.*; ¶s 66,634, 66,534
13. ¶V-2051; ¶66,634
14. ¶V-2060; ¶66,644
15. ¶V-2002; ¶66,624

16. ¶V-2302; ¶66,634
17. ¶V-1700 *et seq.*; ¶66,724
18. ¶V-1704; ¶66,724
19. ¶V-1703.1
20. ¶S-6313.1
21. ¶V-1730

But the reasonable cause exception doesn't apply to transactions that lack economic substance (¶4897). (Code Sec. 6676(c)) The penalty doesn't apply to any portion of the excessive amount that's subject to an accuracy-related penalty imposed under Code Sec. 6662 (¶4877) or Code Sec. 6662A (¶4894) or a fraud penalty under Code Sec. 6663 (¶4884). (Code Sec. 6676(c))[22]

¶ 4887 Penalty for aiding and abetting understatement of tax liability.

A penalty of $1,000 ($10,000 for a corporation) (Code Sec. 6701(b))[23] is imposed on any person who aids or assists, procures or advises with respect to the preparation or presentation of any portion of a return, affidavit, claim or other document connected with any matter arising under the internal revenue laws, and who knows (or has reason to believe) that the portion will be used in connection with any material matter arising under those laws, and knows that an understatement of another person's tax would result from that use (Code Sec. 6701(a)), even if there is no actual understatement. [24] The penalty applies whether or not the taxpayer knew of or gave consent to the understatement. (Code Sec. 6701(d))[25] The term "advises" includes the actions of lawyers and accountants who counsel a particular course of action [26] and appraisers who falsely or fraudulently overstate the value of property in a qualified appraisal (of property for which a charitable contribution is claimed, see ¶2137). (Reg § 1.170A-13(c)(3)(iii))[27]

observation: Unlike the return preparer penalties, which apply only to "paid" preparers (¶4888), the aiding and abetting penalty applies regardless of whether a fee is charged.

¶ 4888 Return preparer understatement penalties.

If a tax return preparer prepares returns or refund claims for which any part of a tax liability understatement is due to an "unreasonable position" and the preparer knew or should have known of the position, the preparer must pay a penalty for each return or claim equal to the greater of $1,000 or 50% of the income derived (or to be derived) by the preparer with respect to the return or claim. (Code Sec. 6694(a)(1)) If the position is with respect to a reportable transaction (to which Code Sec. 6662A applies, ¶4894) or is with respect to a tax shelter, a position is unreasonable if it wasn't reasonable to believe that the position would more likely than not be sustained on its merits. In other cases, a position is unreasonable if (1) there wasn't substantial authority for it or (2) for a position that was disclosed in the return or in a statement attached to the return (under Code Sec. 6662(d)(2)(B)(ii)(I)), there was no reasonable basis for it. (Code Sec. 6694(a)(2); Reg § 1.6694-2(a)(1)) However, there's no penalty if it is shown that there was reasonable cause for the understatement and the preparer acted in good faith. (Code Sec. 6694(a)(3); Reg § 1.6694-2(e))

"Tax return preparer" means any person who is a tax return preparer under the rules at ¶4751. An individual is a tax return preparer if he is primarily responsible for the position on the return or claim for refund giving rise to an understatement. There is only one individual within a firm primarily responsible for each position on the return or refund claim giving rise to an understatement. If there is a signing tax return preparer under the rules at ¶4751, he will generally be considered the person primarily responsible for the positions on the return or refund claim unless it's concluded that the signing tax return preparer isn't primarily responsible for the position. (Reg § 1.6694-1(b))[28]

22. ¶V-2291; ¶66,764
23. ¶V-2352; ¶67,104
24. ¶V-2351 *et seq.*; ¶67,014
25. ¶V-2354; ¶67,014

26. ¶V-2353; ¶67,014
27. ¶V-2351
28. ¶V-2632 *et seq.*; ¶66,944

A tax return preparer who prepares returns or refund claims for which any part of a tax liability understatement is due to willful or reckless conduct must pay a penalty for each return or claim equal to the greater of (1) $5,000; or (2) 75% of the income derived (or to be derived) by the tax return preparer for preparing the return or claim. (Code Sec. 6694(b); Reg § 1.6694-3(a)) "Willful or reckless conduct" is conduct by the tax return preparer which is a willful attempt to understate the tax liability on the return or claim, or a reckless or intentional disregard of rules or regulations. (Code Sec. 6694(b)(2); Reg § 1.6694-3(b), Reg § 1.6694-3(c)) A penalty payable by a person due to willful or reckless conduct in connection with a return or refund claim is reduced by the penalty paid by that person due to an unreasonable position. (Code Sec. 6694(b)(3); Reg § 1.6694-3(f))[29]

IRS has provided lists of the documents covered by the above penalties. [30]

¶ 4889   Penalty for valuation misstatements attributable to incorrect appraisals.

A penalty is imposed on any person who: (A) prepares a property appraisal and knows, or reasonably should have known, that the appraisal would be used in connection with a return or a refund claim, and (B) the claimed property value on the return or refund claim that is based on the appraisal results in a substantial valuation misstatement under Code Sec. 6662(e), a gross valuation misstatement under Code Sec. 6662(h) (¶4879), or a substantial estate or gift tax valuation understatement under Code Sec. 6662(g). (Code Sec. 6695A(a))[31]

¶ 4890   Other penalties on tax return preparers.

A tax return preparer may be subject to inflation-adjusted civil penalties as follows (2019 amounts calculated by Thomson Reuters based on inflation data):

... For 2018 and 2019, $50 for each failure to furnish completed copy of return to the taxpayer (maximum penalty $26,000 in 2018 and $26,500 in 2019). (Code Sec. 6695(a))[32]

... For 2018 and 2019, $50 for each failure to sign a return as required (maximum penalty $26,000 in 2018 and $26,500 in 2019). (Code Sec. 6695(b))[33]

... For 2018 and 2019, $50 for each failure to show his taxpayer ID number or preparer tax identification number as required (maximum penalty $26,000 in 2018 and $26,500 in 2019). (Code Sec. 6695(c))[34]

... For 2018 and 2019, $50 for each failure to retain a copy of a prepared return or to include it on a list of prepared returns (maximum penalty $26,000 in 2018 and $26,500 in 2019). (Code Sec. 6695(d))[35]

... For 2018 and 2019, $50 for each failure to file, or include a required item on, an information return mandated by Code Sec. 6060 (which requires that a record be made and maintained of the preparers employed or engaged during a return period) (maximum penalty $26,000 in 2018 and $26,500 in 2019). (Code Sec. 6695(e))[36]

... For 2018, $520 (and for 2019, $530), with no maximum, for each check with respect to taxes issued to a taxpayer that the preparer endorses or otherwise negotiates, except where the preparer is a bank and deposits the check to the taxpayer's account in the bank. (Code Sec. 6695(f))[37]

... For 2018, $520 (and for 2019, $530), with no maximum, for each failure to follow regulatory due diligence requirements in claiming the earned income credit, child tax credit, Hope Scholarship Credit, and eligibility for head-of-household filing status. To

29. ¶V-2630; ¶66,944
30. ¶V-2631.3; ¶66,944
31. ¶V-2691; ¶66,95A4
32. ¶V-2674; ¶66,954
33. ¶V-2673; ¶66,954

34. ¶V-2677; ¶66,954
35. ¶V-2675; ¶66,954
36. ¶V-2676; ¶66,954
37. ¶V-2671; ¶66,954

avoid the penalty, Form 8867 must be submitted with the return or refund claim claiming the credit. (Code Sec. 6695(g); Reg § 1.6695-2)[38]

Improper disclosure or use of information by return preparers is subject to a civil penalty of $250 for each improper disclosure or use ($10,000 maximum per calendar year), (Code Sec. 6713(a))[39] as well as a criminal penalty if the disclosure is done knowingly or recklessly. (Code Sec. 7216)[40] Regs provide exceptions to these penalties (Reg § 301.7216-1(a), Reg § 301.7216-2)[41] and additional exceptions where the taxpayer consents.

IRS may get a district court to enjoin a preparer from engaging in specific misconduct, but only if an injunction is appropriate to prevent recurrence of the misconduct. If the court finds that the preparer has continually or repeatedly engaged in this misconduct and an injunction isn't sufficient to prevent the preparer's interference with proper tax administration, it can enjoin him from practicing. (Code Sec. 7407)[42]

¶ 4891   Abusive tax shelters and conduct.

A person who promotes an abusive tax shelter is subject to a penalty equal to the lesser of $1,000 or 100% of the gross income derived or to be derived from the activity. However, if an activity on which the penalty is imposed involves a false or fraudulent statement, the penalty equals 50% of the gross income derived or to be derived by that person from the activity. (Code Sec. 6700(a))[43] IRS may seek an injunction to stop any action or failure to take action:

(1) that is subject to penalty under Code Sec. 6700, Code Sec. 6701 (aiding or abetting an understatement, see ¶4887), Code Sec. 6707 (failure to furnish information regarding reportable transactions, see ¶4895), and Code Sec. 6708 (failure to provide list of advisees with respect to reportable transactions, see ¶4892) or

(2) in violation of any requirement imposed by regs issued under Section 330 of Title 31 of the U.S. Code (rules regulating the practice of taxpayer representatives before the Department of the Treasury), i.e., the Circular 230 rules. (Code Sec. 7408)[44]

¶ 4892   Penalty for failure to provide reportable transaction advisee list.

Any person required under Code Sec. 6112 to maintain a list of advisees with respect to reportable transactions (see ¶4748) who fails to make that list available to IRS on its written request within 20 business days is liable for a $10,000 per day penalty each day of that failure after the 20th day. This penalty isn't imposed, however, for any day that the failure to provide the list is due to reasonable cause. In certain circumstances, IRS has the discretion to extend the 20-day production period. (Reg § 301.6708-1) (Code Sec. 6708(a))[45]

¶ 4893   Penalty imposed for failure to report reportable transactions.

A penalty is imposed on any person who fails to include on any return or statement any information that's required to be disclosed under Code Sec. 6011 (see ¶4749) with respect to a reportable transaction. (Code Sec. 6707A(a); Reg § 301.6707A-1(a)) The penalty is 75% of the decrease in tax shown on the return resulting from the transaction (or which would have resulted if the transaction were respected) subject to a maximum of $10,000 for natural persons and $50,000 for others (increased to $100,000 and $200,000 respectively if a listed transaction is involved). The minimum penalty per transaction is $5,000 for natural persons and $10,000 for others. (Code Sec. 6707A(b)) The status of transactions as

38. ¶V-2677.1; ¶S-1106.1; ¶66,954.01
39. ¶V-2678; ¶67,134
40. ¶V-3308; ¶72,164
41. ¶V-2678; ¶V-3309 *et seq.*; ¶72,164

42. ¶V-2680 *et seq.*; ¶74,074
43. ¶V-2403; ¶67,004
44. ¶V-2451; ¶74,084
45. ¶V-2503; ¶67,084

reportable transactions and listed transactions is determined under regs under Code Sec. 6011. (Code Sec. 6707A(c); Reg § 1.6011-4(b))

IRS can rescind all or a portion of a Code Sec. 6707A penalty if (a) the violation relates to a reportable transaction that isn't a listed transaction and (b) rescission would promote compliance with the Code and effective tax administration. (Code Sec. 6707A(d)) Regs list factors considered in determining whether to grant rescission requests. (Reg § 301.6707A-1(d)) IRS procedures establish how to request rescission. [46]

¶ 4894   Penalty for understatements regarding reportable transactions.

A 20% accuracy-related penalty applies for reportable transaction understatements. (Code Sec. 6662A(a)) The penalty is 30% for any portion of any reportable transaction understatement for which specified disclosure rules are not met. (Code Sec. 6662A(c)) A reportable transaction understatement is the sum of (1) the increase in taxable income resulting from a difference between (a) the proper tax treatment of an item subject to the penalty rules and (b) the taxpayer's treatment of the item (on the taxpayer's tax return), multiplied by the highest noncorporate rate (or corporate tax rate, in the case of a corporation), and (2) the amount of the decrease (if any) in the total amount of income tax credits which results from a difference between (a) the taxpayer's treatment of an item subject to the penalty rules (on the taxpayer's tax return) and (b) the proper tax treatment of the item. (Code Sec. 6662A(b)(1)) The penalty doesn't apply to any part of an understatement on which the 40% penalty for transactions that lack economic substance (¶4897) is imposed. (Code Sec. 6662A(e)(2)(B))[47] For this purpose, any reduction in the excess of deductions allowed in the tax year over gross income for the year, and any reduction in the amount of capital losses which would (without regard to the capital loss carryover rules) be allowed for the year, is treated as an increase in taxable income. (Code Sec. 6662A(b)(1))

An item is subject to the penalty rules if the item is attributable to any listed transaction and any reportable transaction (other than a listed transaction) if a significant purpose of the transaction is federal income tax avoidance or evasion. (Code Sec. 6662A(b)(2)(B)) Listed and reportable transactions are defined under the Code Sec. 6707A penalty rules for reportable transactions for which disclosure is required (see ¶4893) (Code Sec. 6662A(d)) A limited reasonable cause exception applies if certain disclosure, substantial authority and reasonable belief requirements are met. (Code Sec. 6662A(d))[48] But this exception doesn't apply to any part of a reportable transaction understatement which is attributable to a transaction that lacks economic substance under Code Sec. 7701(o) or fails to meet the requirements of any similar rule of law (¶4897). (Code Sec. 6664(d)(2))[49]

¶ 4895   Material advisor's penalty for not reporting reportable transactions.

A material advisor who fails to file a timely information return required under Code Sec. 6111(a) (¶4748), or who files a false or incomplete information return, for a reportable transaction (including a listed transaction) is subject to a penalty of $50,000 for each failure. But, if the failure relates to a listed transaction, the penalty increases to the greater of: (1) $200,000, or (2) 50% of the gross income received by the advisor that is attributable to aid, assistance, or advice provided for the listed transaction before the date the advisor files an information return including the transaction. If the reporting failure is intentional, the 50% of gross income penalty amount (item 2 above) is increased to 75% of gross income. (Code Sec. 6707(a), Code Sec. 6707(b)) Reportable and listed transactions are defined under Code Sec. 6707A(c) (see ¶4893). (Code Sec. 6707(d))

IRS can rescind all or a portion of a Code Sec. 6707 penalty under rules that are similar

---

46. ¶V-2531 *et seq.*; ¶67,07A4
47. ¶V-2281; ¶66,62A4

48. ¶V-2284; ¶66,62A4
49. ¶V-2284; ¶66,644.01

to the rescission rules that apply to taxpayers under Code Sec. 6707A (see ¶4893). (Code Sec. 6707(c); Reg § 301.6707-1)[50]

¶ 4896 Penalties for tax-exempts acting as tax shelter accommodation parties.

With limited exceptions, a tax-exempt entity that is a party to a prohibited tax shelter transaction (see ¶4115) must disclose to IRS: (a) that the entity is a party to the prohibited tax shelter transaction; and (b) the identity of any other party to the transaction which is known to such tax-exempt entity The penalty for failing to comply is $100 for each day during which such failure continues, not to exceed $50,000 with respect to any one disclosure.(Code Sec. 6033(a)(2), Code Sec. 6652(c)(3))[1]

¶ 4897 Penalty for transaction lacking economic substance.

A 20% penalty applies to an underpayment attributable to any disallowance of claimed tax benefits because of a transaction lacking economic substance (as defined in Code Sec. 7701(o), see below), or failing to meet the requirements of any similar rule. (Code Sec. 6662(b)(6)) The penalty rate is increased to 40% if the taxpayer doesn't adequately disclose the relevant facts affecting the tax treatment. (Code Sec. 6662(i)(1)) An amended return or supplement to a return is not taken into account if filed after the taxpayer has been contacted for audit or such other date as IRS specifies. (Code Sec. 6662(i)(3)) No reasonable cause and good faith exception applies. (Code Sec. 6664(c)(2)) This provision doesn't apply to personal transactions of individuals, only to transactions entered into in connection with a trade or business or an activity engaged in for the production of income. (Code Sec. 7701(o)(5)(B)) The penalty also doesn't apply to any portion of an underpayment on which a fraud penalty is imposed (¶4884).[2]

Economic substance. A transaction is treated as having economic substance only if (apart from Federal income tax effects): (1) the transaction changes in a meaningful way the taxpayer's economic position, and (2) the taxpayer has a substantial purpose for entering into the transaction. (Code Sec. 7701(o)(1)) Any State or local income tax effect related to a Federal income tax effect is treated in the same manner as a Federal income tax effect. (Code Sec. 7701(o)(3)) A taxpayer may rely on factors other than profit potential to show that a transaction results in a meaningful change in the taxpayer's economic position or that the taxpayer has a substantial non-Federal-income-tax purpose for entering the transaction. Code Sec. 7701(o) doesn't require a minimum return that will meet the profit potential test. But, if a taxpayer relies on profit potential, the present value of the reasonably expected pre-tax profit must be substantial in relation to the present value of the expected net tax benefits that would be allowed if the transaction were respected ("the pre-tax profit to tax benefit ratio test"). (Code Sec. 7701(o)(2)(A)) IRS will continue to rely on relevant case law under the common-law economic substance doctrine in applying the two-prong conjunctive test at items (1) and (2) above.[3]

¶ 4898 Health-care-related penalties.

Individual mandate. Nonexempt U.S. citizens and legal residents must maintain monthly "minimum essential health coverage" for themselves and dependent family members or pay a shared responsibility payment with their federal tax return. This requirement is commonly referred to as the "individual mandate." (Code Sec. 5000A) Minimum essential coverage includes government-sponsored programs, eligible employer-sponsored plans, plans in the individual market, certain grandfathered group health plans, and other

---

50. ¶V-2500 *et seq.*; ¶67,074
1. ¶V-2538; ¶66,524.01

2. ¶V-2271; ¶66,624.12
3. ¶M-5901; ¶77,014.35

specified coverage. (Code Sec. 5000A(f)(1); Reg § 1.5000A-2)[4]

The amount of the shared responsibility payment is the lesser of (i) the sum of the monthly penalty amounts for months in the tax year during which one or more failures occurs, or (ii) the sum of the monthly national average bronze plan premiums for the plan. The monthly penalty amount is equal to 1/12 of the greater of: (i) a flat dollar amount per family member up to a ceiling of three times the flat dollar amount, or (ii) 2.5% of the amount by which the taxpayer's household income exceeds the filing threshold. (Code Sec. 5000A(c))[5]

For 2018: a) the flat dollar amount per family member is $695; b) the monthly national average bronze plan premium is $283 per individual and $1,415 for a shared responsibility family with five or more members. [6]

For months beginning after Dec. 31, 2018, the percentage by which the excess of the taxpayer's household income over the taxpayer's applicable filing threshold is multiplied is zero; and the flat dollar amount is zero. As a result, there is no shared responsibility penalty payment nor is there any penalty imposed for failing to maintain minimum essential coverage. (Code Sec. 5000A(c)(2); Code Sec. 5000A(c)(3))[7]

Employer mandate. An applicable large employer (i.e., one with at least 50 full-time, including full-time equivalent employees) must pay an assessable payment (the "employer shared responsibility payment"; "employer mandate") if at least one full-time employee has been certified to the employer as having purchased health insurance through a state exchange for which an applicable premium tax credit or cost-sharing reduction is allowed or paid to the employee, and the employer either (1) doesn't offer health care coverage for its full-time employees, or (2) offers minimum essential coverage that is unaffordable or does not provide minimum value. (Code Sec. 4980H)

Employers (including applicable large employers) are subject to the Code Sec. 4980D excise tax if they maintain group health plans that don't satisfy detailed requirements. [8] However, "small employer health reimbursement arrangements" are exempt. (Code Sec. 9831(d)(1), Code Sec. 9831(d)(2))[9]

"Cadillac tax." For tax years beginning after Dec. 31, 2021, a 40% excise tax will be levied on insurance companies and plan administrators for employer-sponsored health coverage to the extent that annual premiums exceed an inflation-adjusted threshold amount (a so-called "Cadillac tax"). (Code Sec. 4980I) An additional threshold amount will apply for retired individuals age 55 and older and for plans that cover employees engaged in high risk professions. [10]

¶ 4899   Failure to file information returns and provide payee statements penalties.

Subject to several exceptions including a reasonable cause exception, a payor who fails to timely file a required information return, furnish a payee statement (¶4336), or include all required information, or who provides incorrect information, is subject to penalties. The amount of the penalty depends on the time frame within which the failure is remedied. Where the taxpayer's average gross receipts for the most recent 3 tax years before the calendar year of the failure do not exceed $5 million, the annual maximum amount of penalty is less than it is for other taxpayers.

For returns and statements required to be filed in 2018, the inflation-adjusted penalty

---

4. ¶A-6400 *et seq.*; ¶50,00A4 *et seq.*
5. ¶V-3900; ¶V-3901; ¶V-3905; ¶V-3906; ¶V-3907; ¶50,00A4
6. ¶V-3905 *et seq.*; ¶50,00A4.2 *et seq.*
7. ¶V-3900; ¶V-3901; ¶V-3905; ¶V-3906; ¶V-3907; ¶50,00A4 *et seq.*

8. ¶H-1325.34, ¶49,80D4
9. ¶H-1349.18 *et seq.*, ¶98,314
10. ¶H-1226 *et seq.*; ¶49,80I4 *et seq.*

amounts are: (1) $50 per return or statement ($545,500 calendar year maximum — $191,000 if the gross receipts test is met) if corrected within 30 days from the required filing date (Code Sec. 6721(b)(1), Code Sec. 6721(d)(1)(B), Code Sec. 6722(b)(1)(A), Code Sec. 6722(d)(1)(B)); (2) $100 per return or statement ($1,637,500 calendar year maximum—$545,500 if the gross receipts test is met) if corrected on or before Aug. 1 of the calendar year of the required filing date (Code Sec. 6721(b)(2), Code Sec. 6721(d)(1)(C), Code Sec. 6722(b)(2)(A), Code Sec. 6722(d)(1)(C)); and (3) $270 penalty per return or statement ($3,275,500 calendar year maximum —$1,091,500 if the gross receipts test is met). (Code Sec. 6721(a), Code Sec. 6721(d)(1)(A), Code Sec. 6722(a), Code Sec. 6722(d)(1)(A), Code Sec. 6724(a))[11]

For returns and statements required to be filed in 2019, as calculated by Thomson Reuters based on inflation data, the inflation-adjusted penalty amounts are: (1) $50 per return or statement ($552,000 calendar year maximum —$193,000 if the gross receipts test is met) if corrected within 30 days from the required filing date (Code Sec. 6721(b)(1), Code Sec. 6721(d)(1)(B), Code Sec. 6722(b)(1)(A), Code Sec. 6722(d)(1)(B)); (2) $110 per return or statement ($1,656,500 calendar year maximum —$552,000 if the gross receipts test is met) if corrected on or before Aug. 1 of the calendar year of the required filing date (Code Sec. 6721(b)(2), Code Sec. 6721(d)(1)(C), Code Sec. 6722(b)(2)(A), Code Sec. 6722(d)(1)(C)); and (3) $270 penalty per return or statement ($3,313,000 calendar year maximum — $1,104,000 if the gross receipts test is met). (Code Sec. 6721(a), Code Sec. 6721(d)(1)(A), Code Sec. 6722(a), Code Sec. 6722(d)(1)(A), Code Sec. 6724(a))[12]

Subject to exceptions, where a failure described above is due to intentional disregard, higher penalty amounts apply, and there is no calendar year maximum. For returns and statements required to be filed in 2018, the intentional disregard inflation-adjusted penalty is the greater of: (i) $540 per return ($550 for 2019, as calculated by Thomson Reuters based on inflation data), or (ii) a percentage of the aggregate amount of items required to be reported correctly (5% for returns and statements required under Code Sec. 6045, Code Sec. 6050K, or Code Sec. 6050L; 10% for return or statements *other than* those required under Code Sec. 6041A, Code Sec. 6050H, or Code Sec. 6050J). For returns required under Code Sec. 6050I(a), the penalty for 2018 is the greater of (i) $27,350 or (ii) the amount of cash received up to $109,000; and for returns required to be filed under Code Sec. 6050V, the penalty is the greater of (i) $540 per return or (ii) 10% of the value of the benefit of any contract with respect to which information is required to be included on the return. The corresponding amounts for 2019, as calculated by Thomson Reuters based on inflation data, are $27,600, $110,000, and $550, respectively. (Code Sec. 6721(e), Code Sec. 6722(e))[13]

Definition of information return. The term "information return" means:

... any statement of the amount of payments to another person required by:

   ... Code Sec. 6041(a) (payments of $600 or more).

   ... Code Sec. 6041(b) (certain foreign payments of interest and dividends).

   ... Code Sec. 6042(a)(1) (corporate dividends).

   ... Code Sec. 6044(a)(1) (patronage dividends).

   ... Code Sec. 6049(a) (payments of interest).

   ... Code Sec. 6050A(a) (payments made by certain fishing boat operators).

   ... Code Sec. 6050N(a) (payments of royalties).

   ... Code Sec. 6051(d) (tax withheld).

   ... Code Sec. 6050R (cash payments by purchasers of fish for resale).

---

11. ¶V-1803 *et seq.*; ¶67,214, 67,244 *et seq.*
12. ¶V-1803 *et seq.*; ¶67,214, 67,244 *et seq.*

13. ¶V-1811 *et seq.*, V-1816 *et seq.*; ¶67,214, 67,224

... Code Sec. 110(d) (qualified lease construction allowances for short-term leases).

... any return required by:

... Code Sec. 6041A(a) (payments by recipients of services) or Code Sec. 6041A(b) (returns of direct sellers).

... Code Sec. 6043A(a) (taxable mergers and acquisitions).

... Code Sec. 6045(a) (transactions, including realty transactions, reportable by brokers).

... Code Sec. 6045(d) (certain "substitute payments" made to brokers on behalf of customers in connection with short sales).

... Code Sec. 6045B (organizational actions affecting the basis of a "specified security").

... Code Sec. 6050H(a) (payments of $600 or more in a calendar year of mortgage interest that is received in the course of a trade or business).

... Code Sec. 6050I(a) (receipts of more than $10,000 in cash in one transaction (or two or more related transactions) that are received in the course of a trade or business).

... Code Sec. 6050I(g)(1) (receipt of more than $10,000 in cash by court clerks as bail).

... Code Sec. 6050J(a) (foreclosures and abandonments of property held as security for business loans).

... Code Sec. 6050K(a) (certain exchanges of partnership interests).

... Code Sec. 6050L(a) (certain dispositions of donated property).

... Code Sec. 6050P (discharges of debt by certain financial and government entities).

... Code Sec. 6050Q (relating to certain long-term care benefits).

... Code Sec. 6050S (payments for qualified tuition and related expenses and deductible payments of interest on qualified education loans).

... Code Sec. 6050T (credit for health insurance costs of eligible individuals).

... Code Sec. 6052(a) (wages paid in the form of group-term life insurance).

... Code Sec. 6050V (applicable insurance contracts in which certain exempt organizations hold interests).

... Code Sec. 6050Y (reportable death benefits).

... Code Sec. 6053(c)(1) (certain tips from "large food or beverage establishments").

... Code Sec. 1060(b) or Code Sec. 1060(e) (information required of transferors and transferees with respect to applicable asset acquisitions).

... Code Sec. 4101(d) (relating to fuels taxes).

... Code Sec. 338(h)(10)(C) (relating to elective recognition of gain or loss).

... Code Sec. 264(f)(5)(A)(iv) (natural-person-as-holder exception to the disallowance of the deduction of interest buildup on certain life insurance and annuity contracts).

... Code Sec. 6050U (for charges or payments for qualified long-term care insurance contracts, under combined arrangements).

... Code Sec. 6039(a) (transfers of stock from exercises of incentive stock options and certain purchases from employee stock purchase plans).

... Code Sec. 6050W (for returns relating to payment card transactions and third party network transactions).

... Code Sec. 6055 (relating to minimum health coverage).

... Code Sec. 6056 (relating to health care coverage by applicable large employers).

... any statement of the amount of payments to another person required to be made to IRS under:

... Code Sec. 408(i) (individual retirement accounts (IRAs) or annuities).

... Code Sec. 6047(d) (employers, plan administrators, etc.).

... and any statement required to be filed with IRS under Code Sec. 6035 (relating primarily to furnishing estate tax values of properties to IRS and the property recipients for basis determination purposes). (Code Sec. 6724(d)(1))[14]

Definition of payee statement. The term "payee statement" means any statement required to be furnished under a list of enumerated provisions. (Code Sec. 6724(d)(2))[15]

¶ 4900 Other civil penalties relating to information reporting and other items.

Other civil penalties are provided for:

... failure to file information returns for dividend payments under $10 (Code Sec. 6652(a));

... failure to file actuarial report of pension plan (¶4746) (Code Sec. 6652(e));[16]

... failure to file annual return for a pension plan (¶4746) (Code Sec. 6652(c));[17]

... failure to file annual return for an exempt organization or private foundation (¶4126) (Code Sec. 6652(c));[18]

... failure by split-interest trust to file an information return (Code Sec. 6652(c)(2)(C));[19]

... failure by an exempt organization to report excise tax on personal benefit contracts (Code Sec. 170(f)(10)(F)(iii));

... failure by any person, under a duty to comply with Code Sec. 6104(d) requirements relating to public inspection of, and provision of copies of, exempt organization annual returns or exempt status application materials (Code Sec. 6652(c)(1)(C), Code Sec. 6652(c)(1)(D));[20]

... failure to file fringe benefit plan return (Code Sec. 6652(e));[21]

... failure to provide a written explanation to the recipient of a qualified rollover distribution (Code Sec. 6652(i));[22]

... failure to file notification of change of status of pension plan (Code Sec. 6652(d)(2));[23]

... failure to file registration statement of pension plan (¶4746) (Code Sec. 6652(d)(1)),[24] or to give a plan participant a statement of the information in the statement (Code Sec. 6690);[25]

... failure to provide notice of a transfer of qualified stock to a qualified employee as required by Code Sec. 83(i)(6) (Code Sec. 6652(i));[26]

... failure to file individual retirement account, simple retirement account reports, Archer MSA, HSA, CESA, and qualified tuition program, reports (Code Sec. 6693);[27]

... overstatement reported on return by IRA participant of the amount of designated nondeductible contributions (Code Sec. 6693(b));[28]

... failure to keep records for reporting on pension, annuity, etc., payments subject to withholding (Code Sec. 6704(a));[29]

... failure to notify recipients of plan distributions of their option to elect out of withholding (Code Sec. 6652(i));

---

14. ¶V-1804; ¶67,214
15. ¶V-1815; ¶67,224
16. ¶V-1971; ¶66,924
17. ¶V-1971
18. ¶V-2714; ¶66,524
19. ¶V-2717; ¶66,524
20. ¶V-2718; ¶s 66,524, 66,854
21. ¶V-1973

22. ¶V-1984; ¶66,524
23. ¶V-1971; ¶66,524
24. ¶V-1971
25. ¶V-1972; ¶66,904
26. ¶V-1989
27. ¶V-1974 *et seq.*; ¶66,934
28. ¶V-1981; ¶66,934
29. ¶V-1986; ¶67,044

... failure by a corporation that issues qualified small business stock to make prescribed reports to IRS (Code Sec. 6652(k));[30]

... failure to provide notice to eligible employees with respect to small employer health reimbursement arrangements (Code Sec. 6652(o));[31]

... failure to file certain returns for foreign corporations, partnerships (Code Sec. 6679),[32] and trusts (Code Sec. 6677);[33]

... failure to file information returns in connection with foreign corporations and partnerships (¶4647) (Code Sec. 6038(b), Code Sec. 6038(c), Code Sec. 6038A(d), Code Sec. 6038B(c), Code Sec. 6038C(c);[34]

... failure to include tax information with passport or green card applications (Code Sec. 6039E(c));[35]

... failure to keep records, furnish information, or file domestic international sales corporation (DISC) returns (¶4604) (Code Sec. 6686);[36]

... failure to keep records, furnish information or file returns for a former foreign sales corporation (FSC) (Code Sec. 6686);[37]

... failure to meet FIRPTA reporting requirements (Code Sec. 6652(f));[38]

... failure to file notice of redetermination of certain foreign taxes (Code Sec. 6689);[39]

... failure to withhold tax on U.S. income of certain foreign persons (Code Sec. 1463);[40]

... failure to disclose a treaty-based position taken on a return that overrules or otherwise modifies the tax law (¶4626) (Code Sec. 6712);[41]

... failure by individual who loses U.S. citizenship or terminates U.S. residency (¶4640) to file expatriate information statement (Code Sec. 6039G(a));

... failure by an exempt organization to disclose that information it is offering to sell or soliciting money for is available free from the federal government (Code Sec. 6711);[42]

... failure by an exempt organization to disclose that fund-raising solicitations are nondeductible as charitable contributions (¶4121) (Code Sec. 6710);[43]

... failure by an exempt organization to make the required disclosure for quid pro quo contributions of $75 or more (¶4121) (Code Sec. 6714);[44]

... willful failure to make available for inspection or provide copies of, a return or application for exemption of certain exempt organizations (Code Sec. 6685);[45]

... any repeated or willful and flagrant act or failure to act by any person who becomes liable for any excise tax on a private foundation by reason of the act or failure to act (Code Sec. 6684);[46]

... making a negligent or fraudulent misstatement in connection with the issuance of a mortgage credit certificate or failing to file the required report (¶4746) (Code Sec. 6709);[47]

... failure to file a partnership return (¶4731) (Code Sec. 6698);[48]

... failure to file an S corporation return (Code Sec. 6699);[49]

... failure to file returns with respect to qualified rental housing projects (Code Sec. 42(l)(2), Code Sec. 6652(j));[50]

---

30. ¶V-1843
31. ¶V-1988
32. ¶V-1903; ¶66,794
33. ¶V-1901; ¶66,774
34. ¶V-1903; V-1931; V-1951; V-1961 *et seq.*
35. ¶V-1910
36. ¶V-1912; ¶66,864
37. ¶V-1912; ¶66,864
38. ¶V-1909
39. ¶V-1983; ¶66,894
40. ¶O-11911; ¶14,614.01

41. ¶V-1908; ¶67,124
42. ¶V-2705; ¶67,114
43. ¶V-2701; ¶67,104
44. ¶V-2703; ¶67,144
45. ¶V-2718; ¶66,854
46. ¶V-2721; ¶66,844
47. ¶V-1998; ¶67,094
48. ¶V-1762 *et seq.*; ¶66,984
49. ¶V-1763.3; ¶66,994
50. ¶V-1996; ¶66,524

... failure to deposit taxes (an IRS procedure explains how IRS applies deposits in determining the penalty when there is a shortfall) (Code Sec. 6656(a))[1] (including deposits required to be made by electronic funds transfer (EFT, see ¶3029);[2]

... use of any commercially acceptable instrument to pay taxes, if the amount isn't duly paid (Code Sec. 6657);[3]

... failure to pay stamp taxes (Code Sec. 6653);[4]

... claiming excessive gasoline tax rebates (Code Sec. 6675);[5]

... filing a frivolous income tax return or submitting a position identified as frivolous on IRS's list of frivolous positions (Code Sec. 6702);[6]

... use of Tax Court primarily for delay or where taxpayer's position is frivolous or groundless, he hasn't exhausted administrative remedies or he has instituted a frivolous or groundless claim for damages against the U.S. (Code Sec. 6673);[7]

... failure to comply with a specified information reporting requirement, including providing taxpayer identification numbers (Code Sec. 6723; Reg § 301.6723-1(a));[8]

... failure to report tips (¶4746) (Code Sec. 6652(h));[9]

... failure by broker to provide back-up withholding notice (Code Sec. 6705);[10]

... failure to file information return for change in control or recapitalization of corporation (¶4746) (Code Sec. 6652(l));[11] and

... making a false statement that results in reduced amounts of withholding (Code Sec. 6682),[12] or relates to the applicability of backup withholding. (Code Sec. 6682)[13]

¶ 4901   Damages for filing fraudulent information return.

If any person willfully files a fraudulent information return as to payments purported to be made to any other person, that other person may sue the filer for damages for the greater of (1) $5,000, or (2) actual damages plus costs, and, in the court's discretion, reasonable attorney's fees. (Code Sec. 7434)[14]

¶ 4902   Criminal tax evasion.

Tax evasion is a felony punishable by a fine of up to $100,000 ($500,000 for a corporation) and/or up to five years' imprisonment, plus costs of prosecution. (Code Sec. 7201) The elements of the crime are willfulness, an attempt to evade tax and additional tax due. [15]

¶ 4903   Other criminal penalties.

Any person who willfully aids or assists in, or procures, counsels or advises the preparation or presentation of a materially false or fraudulent return, affidavit, claim or other document, is subject to a criminal penalty of up to $100,000 ($500,000 for a corporation) and/or up to three years' imprisonment, plus costs of prosecution. (Code Sec. 7206(2))[16] Other criminal penalties (fines and/or imprisonment) are imposed for willful failure to: (1) file a return (Code Sec. 7203);[17] (2) pay a tax (Code Sec. 7203);[18] (3) collect or pay over a tax as required (Code Sec. 7202);[19] (4) keep proper records (Code Sec. 7203);[20] (5) supply

1. ¶V-1652; ¶66,564
2. ¶V-1658
3. ¶V-1687; ¶66,574
4. ¶V-2722
5. ¶V-2726
6. ¶V-2551; ¶V-2571; ¶67,024
7. ¶V-2601 *et seq.*; ¶66,734
8. ¶V-1821 *et seq.*; ¶67,234
9. ¶V-1745; ¶66,524
10. ¶V-1842; ¶67,054

11. ¶V-1845; ¶66,524
12. ¶V-1741; ¶66,824
13. ¶V-1743; ¶66,824
14. ¶S-4470 *et seq.*
15. ¶V-4100 *et seq.*; ¶72,014
16. ¶V-3113; ¶72,064
17. ¶V-3002; ¶72,034
18. ¶V-3001; ¶72,034
19. ¶V-3017; ¶72,024
20. ¶V-3007; ¶72,034

tax information (Code Sec. 7203);[21] or (6) furnish a W-2 to employees in the manner, at the time or with the information required, or willful filing of a false or fraudulent W-2. (Code Sec. 7204)[22] Criminal penalties are also imposed for: willful filing of a false or fraudulent return (Code Sec. 7207);[23] failure to obey a summons (Code Sec. 7210);[24] and various other offenses relating to returns, statements, stamp taxes, etc. [25]

¶ 4904   Revocation or denial of passport.

If an individual has a seriously delinquent federal tax debt (i.e., a tax liability, including interest and penalties, in excess of $51,000 for 2018 ($52,000 for 2019, as calculated by Thomson Reuters based on inflation data) for which a notice of lien (for which administrative rights have been exhausted or lapsed) or levy has been filed, IRS will transmit a certification to the State Department for action to deny, revoke or limit the individual's passport. A seriously delinquent federal tax debt doesn't include a debt that is being paid in a timely manner under an installment agreement or offer-in-compromise, or for which a collection action is suspended because a collection due process hearing has been requested or is pending or innocent spouse relief has been requested. (Code Sec. 7345)[26]

¶ 4905   Tax Collection.

IRS has broad tax collection powers, including seizure and sale of a taxpayer's property (i.e., levy and distraint; ¶4907) and liens (¶4913).

Before IRS can start administrative collection proceedings, it must, within 60 days after a tax has been assessed, send the taxpayer a notice of the amount assessed and a demand for payment. (Code Sec. 6303(a), Code Sec. 6331(a))[27] The taxpayer usually gets at least ten days from a date stated in the notice and demand, to pay the tax, unless IRS finds that collection is in jeopardy. (Code Sec. 6331(a); Reg § 301.6331-1(a)(3))[28] Taxpayers suffering undue hardship can get an extension of time for paying the assessed taxes. [29] IRS must send delinquent taxpayers a written notice of the amount of the delinquency at least annually. (Code Sec. 7524)[30]

For installment agreements, see ¶4906.

¶ 4906   Agreements for installment payments of tax—Form 9465.

IRS may enter into a written agreement with a taxpayer to satisfy liability for *any tax* in installment payments. (Code Sec. 6159(a); Reg § 301.6159-1(a))[31] An individual who owes $10,000 or less and meets other conditions can force IRS to enter into an installment agreement. (Code Sec. 6159(c))[32] A taxpayer uses Form 9465 (attached to his balance due return) to request an installment agreement. [33] IRS may require the taxpayer to agree to certain terms and conditions. (Reg § 301.6159-1(b)(1))[34] Individuals can also apply online. A user fee of $225 (reduced in the case of certain online payment agreements or direct debit payments, and waived or refunded for certain low-income taxpayers) is imposed. (Code Sec. 6343(f); Reg § 300.0, Reg § 300.1, Reg § 300.2)[35]

For additional information regarding installment agreements, see ¶4722.

---

21. ¶V-3008; ¶72,034
22. ¶V-3013; ¶72,044
23. ¶V-3122
24. ¶V-3503; ¶72,104
25. ¶V-3500 *et seq.*
26. ¶V-3507
27. ¶s V-5003, V-5004; ¶s 63,014.03, 63,314.01
28. ¶V-5007; ¶63,314.01
29. ¶V-5009
30. ¶V-5009.2
31. ¶V-5010; ¶61,594
32. ¶V-5012; ¶61,594
33. ¶V-5010; ¶61,594
34. ¶V-5011; ¶61,594
35. ¶T-10020 *et seq.*; ¶61,594

¶ 4907   Seizure and sale of a delinquent taxpayer's property—levy and distraint.

IRS has power to seize any property, other than specified exempt property, of a delinquent taxpayer, sell it, and apply the proceeds to pay the unpaid taxes. [36] The property seized may be real, personal, tangible, or intangible, including receivables, evidences of debt, securities (Code Sec. 6331(a)) and, to the extent they exceed a specified amount, present and future wages. (Reg § 301.6331-2(c)) There are exemptions for certain kinds of income (Code Sec. 6334(d)) and property (e.g., clothing, tools) (Code Sec. 6334(a)), and a complete exemption for a taxpayer's principal residence unless a judge or magistrate approves the levy in writing. (Code Sec. 6334(a)(13)(B)) Levy is prohibited where an installment agreement is pending or in effect. (Code Sec. 6331(k); Reg § 301.6331-4) Regs enumerate various categories of exemptions. (Reg § 301.6334-1)[37][38]

A penalty (plus costs and interest) applies if the person fails or refuses to surrender the property. (Code Sec. 6332(d))[39]

Salary and wages and certain other payments are subject to continuous levy. (Code Sec. 6331(e); Code Sec. 6331(h)(1))[40] However, in an internal memo, IRS stated that it will exclude from such levies Social Security disability insurance payments. [41]

Collection Due Process hearing. Subject to exceptions, IRS may not levy against a person's property or right to property unless it gives the person a notification in writing of his right to, and the opportunity for, a pre-levy Collection Due Process hearing with IRS. (Code Sec. 6330(a)(1); Reg § 301.6330-1(a)(1)) The exceptions relate to jeopardy levies (¶4827), levies to collect from state tax refunds, federal contractor levies, and persons subject to employment tax levies who made a previous recent hearing request as to unpaid employment taxes. (Code Sec. 6330(f)) The notice—the Collection Due Process Hearing Notice (CDP Notice)—must be given at least 30 days before the day of the first levy with respect to the unpaid tax for the tax period. (Code Sec. 6330(a)(2)) A person who receives a CDP Notice may request a hearing (use Form 12153) with the IRS Office of Appeals within the 30-day period beginning on the day after the date of the CDP Notice. (Code Sec. 6330(b)(1); Reg § 301.6330-1(b)(1), Reg § 301.6330-1(c)(1)) A person who requests a CDP hearing can, within 30 days of the date it was made, appeal the determination reached at the hearing. (Code Sec. 6330(d); Reg § 301.6330-1(f)) The Tax Court has sole jurisdiction over all CDP appeals. (Code Sec. 6330(d)(1)) IRS can disregard frivolous requests for a hearing before a levy is made. (Code Sec. 6330(g))[42]

¶ 4908   Wrongful seizures.

If IRS wrongfully levies on property, it may, on written request, return the specific property seized (or the proceeds from its sale) or the amount of money levied on (Code Sec. 6343(b)), with interest (Code Sec. 6343(c)). IRS may also return (without interest) property, including money deposited in the Treasury, that has been levied on if IRS determines that: (1) the levy was premature or otherwise not in accordance with its administrative procedures (Code Sec. 6343(d)(2)(A)); (2) the taxpayer has agreed to pay off the underlying tax liability in installments, unless the agreement provides otherwise (Code Sec. 6343(d)(2)(B)); (3) the return of the property will make collection of the underlying tax liability easier (Code Sec. 6343(d)(2)(C)); or (4) the return of the property is in the taxpayer's best interests, as determined by the National Taxpayer Advocate (¶4810), and IRS, and the taxpayer or the National Taxpayer Advocate consent. (Code Sec. 6343(d)(2)(D);

---

36. ¶V-5100 *et seq.*; ¶63,314

37. ¶V-5200 *et seq.*; ¶s 63,314.03, 63,314.05

38. ¶V-5253 *et seq.*; ¶63,314.01

39. ¶V-5116; ¶63,314.04

40. ¶V-5214, ¶V-5216; ¶63,314.01

41. ¶V-5217

42. ¶V-5271 *et seq.*; ¶63,304

Reg § 301.6343-3)[43]

For levies made after Dec. 22, 2017 (and those for which the prior-law 9-month period of limitations remained open), an amount equal to the money levied upon or the money received from a sale of the property may be returned within two years from the date of the levy. For levies made before Dec. 23, 2017, a 9-month period was in effect. (Code Sec. 6343(b))[44]

For treatment of returned wrongfully levied retirement plan assets, see ¶4349.

¶ 4909   Third-party remedies for wrongful IRS seizures.

If IRS wrongfully seizes property of a person other than the taxpayer, the third party may sue for its return (or the sale proceeds, if it has been sold) (Code Sec. 7426), but must start the suit within nine months of the levy (for levies made after Dec. 22, 2017 and pre-Dec. 23, 2017 levies for which the 9-month period had not expired as of Dec. 22, 2017, this time limit is extended to two years from the date of the levy). (Code Sec. 6532(c)(1)) The Supreme Court held that Code Sec. 7426(a)(1) is the exclusive remedy for third-party levy claims.[45] The third party may also recover damages (subject to limits, see ¶4910) if the action results in a finding that any IRS officer or employee recklessly, intentionally, or negligently disregarded any Code or reg provision. (Code Sec. 7426(h)) Regs spell out procedures for claiming damages. (Reg § 301.7426-2)[46] The owner (or his heirs, etc.) of any realty sold to satisfy a tax liability can redeem the property at any time within 180 days after the sale. (Code Sec. 6337(b)(1))[47]

¶ 4910   Damages for unauthorized IRS collection actions.

If any IRS officer or employee recklessly, intentionally or negligently disregards a Code or reg section in connection with collection of tax, the taxpayer may bring a civil suit for damages against the U.S. in a district court. Damages are limited to the lesser of (1) $1 million ($100,000 for negligence) or (2) the actual, direct economic damages thus sustained plus the costs of the action. (Code Sec. 7433(b); Reg § 301.7433-1)[48] A taxpayer may petition a bankruptcy court for damages (subject to the above limits) if, in connection with any collection of tax, an IRS officer or employee willfully violates any provision of 11 USC 362 (relating to the automatic stay arising when a debtor files for bankruptcy) or 11 USC 524 (relating to the effect of a bankruptcy discharge, which operates as an injunction against commencement or continuation of actions to collect a discharged debt as a personal liability of the debtor). (Code Sec. 7433(e); Reg § 301.7433-2)[49]

¶ 4911   Collection period.

IRS must generally start distraint or court proceedings within ten years after assessment (Code Sec. 6502(a)). But if no return is filed, a collection suit may be brought at any time, without assessment. (Code Sec. 6501(c)(3))[50] The collection period may be extended in connection with installment agreements (Code Sec. 6502(a); Reg § 301.6502-1)[1] or suspended under various circumstances. (Code Sec. 6330(e)(1); Reg § 301.6330-1(g))[2]

¶ 4912   Injunctions against tax collection.

Injunctions against collection of taxes are generally barred. But exceptions apply during the period allowed to file a Tax Court petition or, where a petition has been filed, before

---

43. ¶V-5136, ¶V-5137
44. ¶V-5127
45. ¶V-5120, ¶V-5126; ¶s 65,324.04, 74,264
46. ¶V-5135; ¶74,264
47. ¶V-5424; ¶63,354.03

48. ¶V-5800 *et seq.*; ¶74,334
49. ¶V-5820; ¶74,334
50. ¶V-5600 *et seq.*; ¶65,024
1. ¶V-5604 *et seq.*; ¶65,024
2. ¶V-5277; ¶63,304

the Tax Court's decision becomes final, and where an individual other than the taxpayer sues to recover property wrongfully seized and in other cases. (Code Sec. 7421(a))[3]

¶ 4913   Federal tax liens.

Federal tax liens are claims against a taxpayer's property for payment of delinquent taxes (including any interest, additional amounts, additions to tax, assessable penalties, or accrued costs).[4] There are various federal tax liens, including:

. . . general tax lien, which applies to all property, both real and personal, tangible and intangible including a tenancy by the entirety and an heir's interest in an estate even though he later attempts to disclaim it (Code Sec. 6321; Reg § 301.6321-1);[5]

. . . gift tax lien (Code Sec. 6324(b); Reg § 301.6324-1(b));[6]

. . . estate tax lien (Code Sec. 6324(a); Reg § 301.6324-1(a));[7]

. . . special lien for deferred estate tax attributable to a farm or other closely held business (Code Sec. 6324A; Reg § 20.6324A-1, Reg § 301.6324A-1);[8]

. . . special lien for recapture of estate tax attributable to special use valuation of a farm or closely held business (Code Sec. 6324B; Reg § 20.6324B-1);[9]

. . . generation-skipping transfer tax lien. (Code Sec. 2661; Reg § 26.2662-1(f))[10]

IRS must give written notice of its filing of a notice of lien (NFTL), to the person whose property is to be subject to the lien, not more than five days after it files the notice of lien (Code Sec. 6320(a); Reg § 301.6320-1(a))[11] IRS must hold a Collection Due Process hearing with respect to the filing if the taxpayer timely requests one (use Form 12153). (Code Sec. 6320(b)(1); Reg § 301.6320-1(b)) But IRS can disregard frivolous requests for a hearing before a lien is filed. (Code Sec. 6320(c))[12] Regs explain how a request for a withdrawal of a federal tax lien is made. (Reg § 301.6323(j)-1)[13]

¶ 4914   Priority of tax liens.

Priority of tax liens is governed by federal, not state, law.[14] The general rule is that a lien first in time is first in right.[15] But a tax lien is subordinated to certain later liens that arise before notice of the tax lien (Form 668) is filed. This protects judgment lien creditors, mechanic's lienors, and certain qualifying purchasers and holders of security interests. (Code Sec. 6323(a); Reg § 301.6323(a)-1[16] Another exception protects certain interests arising even after the notice of the tax lien was filed, e.g., attorney's liens and certain security interests. (Code Sec. 6323(b); Reg § 301.6323(b)-1)[17]

The special gift and estate tax liens don't have to be filed to be superior to claims arising after the special lien arises. But certain later purchasers and creditors are protected. (Code Sec. 6324A(d)(3), Code Sec. 6324B(c)(1))[18]

IRS may withdraw a notice of lien if it was filed prematurely or otherwise not in accordance with its administrative procedures, and for certain other reasons. (Code Sec. 6323(j)(1)) At the taxpayer's request, IRS must make reasonable efforts to notify credit reporting agencies and creditors specified by the taxpayer of the withdrawal of the notice. (Code Sec. 6323(j)(2))[19]

3. ¶V-5701; ¶74,214
4. ¶V-5900 *et seq.*
5. ¶V-5902 *et seq.*; ¶63,214
6. ¶V-6042; ¶63,244 (Estate & Gift)
7. ¶V-6044; ¶63,244 (Estate & Gift)
8. ¶V-6046; ¶63,24A4 (Estate & Gift)
9. ¶V-6051; ¶63,24B4 (Estate & Gift)
10. ¶V-6053
11. ¶V-6001; ¶63,204

12. ¶V-6005; ¶63,204
13. ¶V-6134; ¶63,234.18
14. ¶V-6324; ¶63,234
15. ¶V-6301; ¶63,214.04
16. ¶V-6400 *et seq.*; ¶63,234
17. ¶V-6426; ¶63,234
18. ¶s V-6455, V-6456
19. ¶V-6134

¶ 4915   Taxes in bankruptcy or receivership proceedings.

A receiver in a receivership proceeding must give IRS notice of the receivership. (Code Sec. 6036) (Use Form 56) But a bankruptcy trustee, debtor-in-possession, or other like fiduciary in a bankruptcy proceeding needn't give notice (Reg § 301.6036-1(a)(1)(i)) because notice under the Bankruptcy Rules is sufficient. [20] The filing of a federal bankruptcy petition (but not the start of a state receivership proceeding) automatically stays any tax proceedings against the taxpayer-debtor. [21] The running of the assessment period is suspended from the date a bankruptcy or receivership proceeding is instituted until 30 days after IRS has received notice of the proceeding, but the suspension may not exceed two years. (Code Sec. 6872; Reg § 301.6872-1)[22]

Although a taxpayer's bankruptcy triggers an immediate assessment (¶4828) collection of the tax is stayed while the taxpayer-debtor's assets are under the control of a court in bankruptcy or receivership proceedings. [23] There is no general bar to discharge of taxes in bankruptcy, but there are broad rules barring discharge of taxes in certain circumstances. [24]

¶ 4916   Transferee's liability for transferor's unpaid taxes.

A transferee is liable for a taxpayer-transferor's unpaid taxes (and interest and penalties) where: (1) the transfer is void or voidable under rules of equity, [25] (2) transferee liability is imposed by statute, [26] or (3) transferee liability arises under contract. [27] Transferees include a donee, heir, legatee, devisee or distributee of a decedent's estate, a shareholder of a dissolved corporation, the assignee or donee of an insolvent person, certain fiduciaries, a successor in a tax-free corporate reorganization, and various other classes of distributees. (Code Sec. 6901(h); Reg § 301.6901-1(b))[28] IRS must assess the (first) transferee within one year after the limitations period against the transferor has run. (Code Sec. 6901(c)(1))[29]

¶ 4917   Early discharge of executor's personal liability.

An executor or administrator can be discharged from personal liability for estate tax as early as nine months after the estate tax return is due (or filed, if later) if he makes a written request to IRS to determine the estate tax liability, and any tax determined to be due is paid (or a bond is posted if the payment period was extended). (Code Sec. 2204(a))[30] A trustee or other fiduciary can get a similar discharge. (Code Sec. 2204(b))[31] An executor or administrator can also request (on Form 5495) early discharge from personal liability for a decedent's income and gift taxes. (Code Sec. 6905(a))[32]

---

20. ¶S-4103; ¶60,364
21. ¶U-1220; ¶68,714
22. ¶T-4323.1; ¶68,724
23. ¶V-7301 *et seq.*; ¶68,714
24. ¶V-7360 *et seq.*; ¶68,734.01
25. ¶s V-9100 *et seq.*, V-9200 *et seq.*; ¶69,014
26. ¶V-9300 *et seq.*; ¶69,014

27. ¶V-9400 *et seq.*; ¶69,014.02
28. ¶V-9001; ¶69,014.01
29. ¶V-9801; ¶69,014.10
30. ¶s T-4511, T-4512; ¶22,044 (Estate & Gift)
31. ¶T-4513; ¶22,044 (Estate & Gift)
32. ¶T-4518; ¶69,054

Chapter 26 Estate, Gift and Generation-Skipping Transfer Taxes

¶ 5000   **Estate Tax.** ▬▬▬▬▬▬▬▬▬▬▬▬▬▬▬▬▬▬▬▬▬▬▬▬▬▬▬▬▬▬▬▬

The federal estate tax is imposed on the transfer of an individual's property at death and on other transfers considered to be the equivalent of transfers at death. The tax is imposed on the "taxable estate" (¶5018), which is the value of the total property transferred or considered transferred at death (the "gross estate"), reduced by various deductions. The tax is computed under a unified rate schedule under which lifetime taxable gifts and transfers at death are taxed on a cumulative basis.

For decedents dying and gifts made in 2018 and 2019, the maximum estate and gift tax rate, and, the generation-skipping transfer (GST) tax rate, is 40%. (Code Sec. 2001(c); ¶1114) For estates of decedents dying and gifts made after 2017 and before 2026, the basic exclusion amount is $10 million, as indexed for inflation occurring after 2011. (Code Sec. 2010(c)(3)) The basic exclusion amount for gifts and estates, and the exemption amount for generation-skipping transfers, is $11,180,000 for 2018 ($11,400,000 for 2019, as calculated by Thomson Reuters based on inflation data, see ¶5028).

In determining the tax on estates of individuals who at death were citizens or residents of the U.S., the entire estate is considered. (Code Sec. 2033; Reg § 20.0-2(b)(1))[1] For nonresident aliens, see ¶5040.

¶ 5001   **Property owned by the decedent.**

The gross estate of a decedent, who was a U.S. citizen or resident at the time of death, includes the value of all property in which the decedent had an interest at the time of death, to the extent of the interest beneficially owned by the decedent. (Code Sec. 2033; Reg § 20.2033-1(a))[2]

The gross estate of a nonresident alien includes property "situated in the U.S." (see ¶5040).

¶ 5002   **Gifts within three years of death—Form 706, Schedule G.**

An individual who transferred an interest in, or relinquished a power over, any property within three years of death must include the value of the property in the gross estate (on Form 706, Schedule G) to the extent it would have been included in the gross estate under Code Sec. 2036 (transfers with retained life estate, etc., ¶5004), Code Sec. 2037 (transfers taking effect at death, ¶5006), Code Sec. 2038 (revocable transfers, ¶5007), or Code Sec. 2042 (life insurance proceeds, ¶5014), if the interest or relinquished power had been retained. (Code Sec. 2035(a))[3] This rule doesn't apply to any bona fide sale for full and adequate consideration. (Code Sec. 2035(d))

¶ 5003   **Gift tax "gross-up"—Form 706, Schedule G.**

Gift tax paid by the decedent, the decedent's estate or the decedent's donees, on gifts made by decedent or his or her spouse within three years of decedent's death —including, according to the Ninth Circuit and Tax Court, deemed gifts under Code Sec. 2519 (¶5051)—is included in the gross estate (on Form 706, Schedule G). But, gift tax paid by

---

1. ¶R-1010 *et seq.*, ¶R-2000 *et seq.*; ¶20,314 *et seq.*, ¶20,334 *et seq.*   3. ¶R-2201 *et seq.*; ¶20,354
2. ¶R-2001; ¶20,334

References beginning with a single letter are to paragraphs in Federal Tax Coordinator 2d and RIA's Analysis of Federal Taxes: Income. Those beginning with numbers are to paragraphs in United States Tax Reporter.

the spouse on the spouse's share of decedent's gifts under the gift-splitting rules isn't included. (Code Sec. 2035(b))[4] The gift tax gross-up rule does not apply to the payment of a gift tax by a nonresident alien within three years of death. [5]

¶ 5004 Retained life estate—Form 706, Schedule G.

A decedent's gross estate includes transfers under which he or she retained the possession or enjoyment of, or the right to the income from, the transferred property (on Form 706, Schedule G). (Code Sec. 2036(a)(1); Reg § 20.2036-1)[6]

The decedent's gross estate also includes transfers where he or she retained the right to designate the person(s) to possess or enjoy the transferred property or its income. (Code Sec. 2036(a)(2))[7]

These rules don't apply to any bona fide sale for full and adequate consideration. (Code Sec. 2036(a))

A decedent who transfers property during life to a trust and retains the right to an annuity, unitrust, or other income payment from, or retains the use of an asset in, the trust has retained the right to income from all or a specific portion of the property transferred. The includible amount is that portion of the trust corpus, valued as of the decedent's death (or the alternate valuation date, if applicable) necessary to yield that annual payment (or use) applying the appropriate Code Sec. 7520 interest rate in effect on the date of death (or alternate valuation date). The regs also provide guidance on the portion of trust property includible in the grantor's gross estate where the grantor has a "graduated retained interest." (Reg § 20.2036-1(c)(2))[8]

Where a decedent had funded the purchase of life insurance policies using three separate split-dollar agreements, the Tax Court denied summary judgment to the estate, finding that Code Sec. 2036 (among other Code sections) did apply in determining whether the cash values of the policies were includible in the decedent's gross estate as (a) a lifetime transfer over which the decedent had retained the right to receive income, or (b) a right, either alone or in conjunction with another person, to designate who could possess or enjoy the property or income therefrom.[9]

¶ 5005 Retention of voting rights in stock of a controlled corporation—Form 706, Schedule G.

Retention of voting rights in stock of a controlled corporation is a retention of the enjoyment of the transferred stock. The value of the transferred stock is included in the decedent's gross estate (on Form 706, Schedule G). (Code Sec. 2036(b))[10]

¶ 5006 Transfers taking effect at death—Form 706, Schedule G.

If a decedent transfers property during life, but the transferee can't possess or enjoy the property except by surviving the decedent, and the decedent retained a significant reversionary interest (exceeding 5% of the value of the transferred property immediately before the decedent's death), then the property is includible in decedent's gross estate (on Form 706, Schedule G). This rule doesn't apply to bona fide sales for full and adequate consideration. (Code Sec. 2037)[11]

---

4. ¶R-2210 *et seq.*; ¶20,354
5. ¶R-8006
6. ¶R-2400 *et seq.*; ¶20,364
7. ¶R-2450; ¶20,364
8. ¶R-2408.1; ¶20,364
9. ¶R-2402
10. ¶R-2436; ¶20,364
11. ¶R-2500 *et seq.*; ¶20,374

¶ 5007   Revocable transfers—Form 706, Schedule G.

The decedent's gross estate includes (on Form 706, Schedule G) lifetime transfers if the enjoyment of the transferred property was subject at death to any change through the exercise by the decedent of a power to alter, amend, revoke or terminate. This includes any power affecting the time or manner of enjoyment of property or its income. (Code Sec. 2038(a)(1)) This rule doesn't apply to any bona fide sale for full and adequate consideration.[12]

Includible revocable transfers include savings bank (Totten) trusts that are revocable in form,[13] and custodial accounts where the donor is custodian.[14]

Under IRS guidance, trust assets are not includible in the gross estate under Code Sec. 2038 on account of the grantor having retained the power, exercisable in a nonfiduciary capacity, to acquire property held by the trust by substituting other property of equivalent value.[15]

¶ 5008   Qualified terminable interest property (QTIP).

Qualified terminable interest property (QTIP) for which the estate tax (¶5023) or gift tax (¶5051) marital deduction was elected is includible in the estate of the donee spouse at its then fair market value unless the donee disposed of any part of the qualifying income interest for life. (Code Sec. 2044) The property is treated as passing from the surviving spouse. (Code Sec. 2044(c))

The surviving spouse's executor may recover the estate taxes caused by the inclusion from the persons to whom the property passes at the surviving spouse's death, unless the surviving spouse's will specifically indicates an intent to waive the right of recovery. (Code Sec. 2207A(a))[16]

¶ 5009   Powers of appointment—Form 706, Schedule H.

If the decedent possessed a general power of appointment (created after Oct. 21, '42) at the time of death, the property subject to the power is included in the gross estate (on Form 706, Schedule H). (Code Sec. 2041(a))[17] A "general" power is one exercisable in favor of the decedent, the decedent's estate, the decedent's creditors, or the creditors of the decedent's estate. (Code Sec. 2041(b)(1))[18]

¶ 5010   Jointly-held property—Form 706, Schedule E.

Joint ownership acquired through gift, bequest, devise, or inheritance from another. The decedent's fractional share of the property is included in the gross estate (on Form 706, Schedule E). (Reg § 20.2040-1(a)(1))[19]

Joint ownership created by co-owners. Except for spouse tenancies (¶5011), the *entire* value of the property is included in the co-owner's gross estate except the part, if any, attributable to the consideration in money or money's worth furnished by the other joint owner(s). Consideration furnished by the surviving joint owner(s) doesn't include money or property acquired from the decedent for less than full and adequate consideration in money or money's worth. (Reg § 20.2040-1(a)(2))[20]

---

12. ¶R-2600 *et seq.*; ¶20,384
13. ¶R-2621
14. ¶R-2620; ¶20,384.03
15. ¶R-2612.1
16. ¶R-6439 *et seq.*; ¶s 20,444, 20,564.08, 22,07A4, 25,194

17. ¶R-3000 *et seq.*; ¶20,414
18. ¶R-3006; ¶20,414
19. ¶s R-2705, R-2709; ¶20,404
20. ¶R-2700 *et seq.*; ¶20,404

Tenancy in common. Only the value of decedent's undivided share of the property is included in the gross estate. [21]

¶ 5011   Spouses' jointly-held property—Form 706, Schedule E.

If an interest in property created after '76 is held by a decedent and his or her spouse as tenants by the entirety or as joint tenants with right of survivorship (if the decedent and spouse are the only joint tenants), one-half of the value of the jointly owned interest will be included in the estate of the decedent spouse regardless of which spouse furnished the original consideration (on Form 706, Schedule E). (Code Sec. 2040(b)) Where the surviving spouse isn't a U.S. citizen, this rule applies only if the property passes in a qualified domestic trust (QDOT, ¶5026). (Code Sec. 2056(d)(1)(B), Code Sec. 2056(d)(2))[22]

¶ 5012   Community property.

The value of the interest in community property vested in the decedent by state law — ordinarily, half of the community property — is included in the decedent spouse's estate. [23]

¶ 5013   Annuities—Form 706, Schedule I.

The value of an annuity or other payment receivable by a beneficiary is included in the decedent's gross estate (on Form 706, Schedule I) if, under the contract or agreement, either:

(1) an annuity or other payment was payable to decedent, either alone or with another person(s), for decedent's life or for any period not ascertainable without reference to the decedent's death or for any period that doesn't in fact end before death; or

(2) the decedent possessed, for one of the periods in (1), above, the right to receive such an annuity or other payment, either alone or with another. (Code Sec. 2039(a))

The amount included is an amount proportionate to the part of the purchase price contributed by the decedent. Contributions made by an employer are considered made by the employee if made by reason of employment. (Code Sec. 2039(b))[24]

¶ 5014   Life insurance—Form 706, Schedule D.

Proceeds of insurance on the decedent's life receivable by the executor or administrator, or payable to the decedent's estate, are includible in the gross estate (on Form 706, Schedule D). (Code Sec. 2042(1)) The estate needn't be specifically named as the beneficiary. (Reg § 20.2042-1(b)(1))[25]

Proceeds of insurance on the decedent's life not receivable by or for the benefit of the estate are includible if the decedent possessed at death or transferred within three years of death any incidents of ownership in the policy, exercisable either alone or with any other person. (Code Sec. 2042(2)) "Incidents of ownership" include the power to change the beneficiary, to revoke an assignment, to pledge the policy for a loan, etc. (Reg § 20.2042-1(c)(2)), and certain reversionary interests. (Reg § 20.2042-1(c)(3))[26]

¶ 5015   Group term life insurance—Form 706, Schedule D.

An employee can prevent inclusion in his or her estate (under the rule at ¶5014, on Form 706, Schedule D) of the proceeds of group term life insurance furnished by the

---

21. ¶R-2707; ¶20,334.15
22. ¶R-2724 *et seq.*; ¶20,404
23. ¶R-2800 *et seq.*; ¶s 20,334.16, 20,334.17

24. ¶R-4401 *et seq.*; ¶20,394
25. ¶R-4002 *et seq.*; ¶20,424.01
26. ¶R-4006 *et seq.*; ¶20,424

employer by transferring the insurance before death, if:

(1) the group policy and applicable state law permit the employee to make an absolute assignment of all the employee's incidents of ownership, and

(2) the employee irrevocably assigns all policy rights. [27]

¶ 5016 Value of property included in the gross estate.

The value of property included in the gross estate is the fair market value (FMV) of the property at the date of the decedent's death (or at the alternate valuation date, see below). (Code Sec. 2031; Reg § 20.2031-1) [28]

Regs provide rules for valuing specific types of properties including: stocks and bonds (Reg § 20.2031-2); business interests (Reg § 20.2031-3); notes (Reg § 20.2031-4); household and personal effects (Reg § 20.2031-6); and life insurance and annuity contracts. (Reg § 20.2031-8)

An executor may elect (on Form 706, Schedule U) to exclude from the gross estate up to 40% of the value of land subject to a qualified conservation easement meeting certain requirements and subject to a dollar cap of $500,000. (Code Sec. 2031(c)) [29]

The FMV of annuities (other than commercial annuities), life estates, term of years, remainders, and reversions is determined under IRS tables, which include an interest rate component and, if applicable, a mortality component. The interest rate component changes monthly and this can affect planning strategies (e.g., lower interest rates favor private annuities and GRATs, ¶5057).

A district court found that a GRAT was includible in a decedent's estate, where the decedent had died before the termination of the GRAT, because the annuity comprised some possession, enjoyment, or right to income from the transferred property. [30]

The executor can elect (irrevocably, on Form 706) to use an alternate valuation date rather than the decedent's date of death to value the property included in the gross estate. This alternate date is generally six months after decedent's death or earlier date of sale or distribution. (Code Sec. 2032(a)) [31] Alternate valuation can be elected only if its use decreases both the value of the gross estate and the combined estate and GST tax liability. (Code Sec. 2032(c); Reg § 20.2032-1(b)(1)) [32]

observation: The executor can't elect alternate valuation to step up the basis of assets that increase in value after death (for example, where there would otherwise be no estate tax cost to the increased valuation because the marital deduction eliminates any tax).

¶ 5017 Special-use valuation of farm or other business real property—Form 706, Schedule A-1.

If certain conditions are met, an executor may elect (irrevocably, on Form 706, Schedule A-1) to value qualified real property used for farming purposes or in a trade or business on the basis of the property's value for its actual use, rather than on its highest and best use. The total decrease in the value of all real property under this election may not exceed $1,140,000 for individuals dying in 2018 ($1,160,000 for individuals dying in 2019, as calculated by Thomson Reuters based on inflation data). (Code Sec. 2032A) [33]

One condition for electing special use valuation is that at least 25% of the adjusted value

27. ¶R-4033
28. ¶R-1006; ¶20,314
29. ¶R-4700 *et seq.*; ¶20,314.13
30. ¶R-2408.1
31. ¶R-5002; ¶20,324
32. ¶R-5001; ¶20,324
33. ¶R-5200 *et seq.*; ¶20,32A4

of the gross estate must consist of the adjusted value of real property which meets certain requirements. Under Reg § 20.2032A-8(a)(2), special use valuation may be elected for less than all of an estate's qualified real property, if the partial election covers sufficient property to satisfy the threshold requirements of at least 25% of the adjusted value of the gross estate. But a district court has held that this reg is invalid to the extent that it bars a partial special use valuation election covering less than 25% of the adjusted value of the gross estate. [34]

The resulting estate tax savings from special use valuation may be recaptured (use Form 706-A) under certain conditions. (Code Sec. 2032A(c))[35]

¶ 5018   Computing the taxable estate.

To get the taxable estate, deduct the following from the gross estate (¶5000):[36]

... Funeral expenses. (Code Sec. 2053(a)(1))

... Administration expenses, such as executors' and administrators' commissions, attorneys', accountants' and appraisers' fees, and court costs. (Code Sec. 2053(a)(2); Reg § 20.2053-3)

... Claims against the estate, including property taxes accrued before the decedent's death, unpaid income and gift taxes, and medical expenses of the decedent paid by the estate after death (to the extent not claimed as an income tax deduction, see ¶2143). (Code Sec. 2053(a)(3); Reg § 20.2053-6)

... Transfers in satisfaction of claims by the decedent's former spouse. (Code Sec. 2043(b)(2))

... Indebtedness on property if the total value of the property is included in the gross estate. (Code Sec. 2053(a)(4))

... Casualty and theft losses. (Code Sec. 2054)

... Transfers to charitable and similar organizations (Code Sec. 2055), see ¶5020.

... Transfers to surviving spouse (marital deduction) (Code Sec. 2056), see ¶5021.

... State death taxes (Code Sec. 2058), see ¶5027.

For an item to be deductible as a debt, claim, or expense, it must also be allowable by the jurisdiction under which the estate is being administered. (Code Sec. 2053(a))[37] Post-death events are taken into account in determining the deductible amount of a claim or other expense under Code Sec. 2053, and deductions generally are limited to amounts actually paid by the estate in satisfaction of deductible claims and expenses. Exceptions apply for claims against the estate with respect to which there is an asset or claim includible in the gross estate that is substantially related to the claim against the estate, and for claims against the estate that, collectively, do not exceed $500,000 (not including those deductible as ascertainable amounts). However, in each case, the amount of the deduction is subject to adjustment to reflect post-death events. (Reg § 20.2053-1, Reg § 20.2053-4)

Form 706 has a Schedule PC – Protective Claim for Refund, which an estate can file to preserve its right to a refund of estate taxes paid when a claim or expense which is the subject of unresolved controversy at the time of filing the return later becomes deductible. [38]

---

34. ¶R-5256
35. ¶R-5301; ¶20,32A4
36. ¶R-5400 *et seq.*; ¶s 20,514, 20,534, 20,544, 20,554, 20,564

37. ¶R-5404; ¶20,534 *et seq.*
38. ¶R-5403

¶ 5019   Income vs. estate tax deduction.

Many estate administration expenses can qualify as an estate tax deduction on the estate tax return and as an income tax deduction, or an offset against the sales price of property in determining gain or loss, on the estate's income tax return. But the estate is entitled to an income tax deduction or offset only if an estate tax deduction for the item is waived. (Code Sec. 642(g))[39] For the election to take an income tax or estate tax deduction, see ¶3923.

¶ 5020   Deductions for charitable bequests—Form 706, Schedule O.

Deductions are allowed (on Form 706, Schedule O) for the value of property included in the gross estate and transferred by a decedent during life or by will to or for the use of the U.S., any state, political subdivision thereof, or the District of Columbia, and to various types of charitable organizations (Code Sec. 2055(a)), including foreign ones.[40]

Strict requirements apply where the charitable bequest is of an income interest or a remainder interest. (Code Sec. 2055(e))[41]

¶ 5021   Marital deduction—Form 706, Schedule M.

A marital deduction is allowed (on Form 706, Schedule M) for the value of all property included in the gross estate that passes to the decedent's surviving spouse in a manner qualifying for the deduction. (Code Sec. 2056(a))[42]

A surviving spouse's dower or curtesy interest (or statutory interest in lieu thereof) is treated as passing from the decedent to the surviving spouse for purposes of the marital deduction. (Code Sec. 2056(c)(3), Reg § 20.2056(c)-1(a)(3))[43]

For terminable interests, see ¶5022. For where the surviving spouse isn't a U.S. citizen, see ¶5026.

¶ 5022   Terminable interests and the marital deduction—Form 706, Schedule M.

With certain exceptions (see, e.g., ¶5023), a terminable interest does not qualify for the marital deduction (on Form 706, Schedule M) if another interest in the same property passed from the decedent to some other person for less than adequate and full consideration in money or money's worth and, by reason of its passing, that other person or his or her heirs may enjoy part of the property after the termination of the interest of the surviving spouse. (Code Sec. 2056(b)(1); Reg § 20.2056(b)-1(c)) A terminable interest is one that will terminate or fail after a certain period of time, the happening of some contingency, or the failure of some event to occur. (Reg § 20.2056(b)-1(b))[44]

¶ 5023   Qualified terminable interest property (QTIP) election—Form 706, Schedule M.

Property in which a spouse is given only a life estate may qualify for the marital deduction as an exception to the terminable interest rule (¶5022) if the executor elects (by listing the property on Form 706, Schedule M and deducting its value) to have all or part of the property so qualify and the surviving spouse has a "qualifying income interest for life." A surviving spouse has such an interest if:

---

39. ¶R-5507; ¶20,534
40. ¶R-5700 *et seq.*; ¶20,424
41. ¶R-5735 *et seq.*; ¶s 20,554, 20,554.14, 20,554.16

42. ¶R-6005
43. ¶R-6017
44. ¶R-6300 *et seq.*; ¶20,564

(1) the surviving spouse is entitled for life to all the income from the property, payable at least annually, or the spouse has a usufruct interest for life in the property; and

(2) no person (including the spouse) has a power to appoint any part of the property to any person other than the surviving spouse during the surviving spouse's life. (Code Sec. 2056(b)(7))[45]

A surviving spouse's interest can meet the "all income" requirement if the spouse is entitled to income as determined by applicable local law that provides for a reasonable apportionment between the income and remainder beneficiaries of the trust's total return. (Reg § 20.2056(b)-5(f)(1), Reg § 20.2056(b)-7(d)(2))[46]

QTIP treatment isn't defeated merely because the spouse's income interest is contingent on the executor making a QTIP election. (Reg § 20.2056(b)-7(d)(3))[47]

An annuity, including one arising under community property law, where only the surviving spouse has the right to receive payments before the death of that surviving spouse, is a qualifying income interest for life, and the QTIP election is treated as made with respect to that interest unless the executor otherwise elects. (Code Sec. 2056(b)(7)(C))[48]

Certain individual retirement accounts (IRAs) qualify. (Reg § 20.2056(b)-7(h), Ex 10)[49]

Partial QTIP elections that relate to a fractional or percentage share of the property are allowed. (Reg § 20.2056(b)-7(b)(2))[50] Protective QTIP elections are possible. (Reg § 20.2056(b)-7(c))[1]

For inclusion of the QTIP in the surviving spouse's estate, see ¶5008.

¶ 5024   Effect of death taxes on amount of marital deduction.

Federal estate or other death taxes payable out of the marital share reduce the amount of the bequest that qualifies for the marital deduction. (Code Sec. 2056(b)(4)(A))

The surviving spouse's interest can be completely absolved from the burden of the tax by a provision in decedent's will that is effective under local law. In such a case, death taxes won't affect the amount of the deduction.[2]

¶ 5025   Effect of administration expenses on amount of marital deduction.

The marital deduction is reduced by estate transmission expenses paid from the marital share (Reg § 20.2056(b)-4(d)(2)), but not by estate management expenses attributable to and paid from the marital share unless those expenses are deducted on the estate tax return under Code Sec. 2053. (Reg § 20.2056(b)-4(d)(3)) The marital deduction is reduced to the extent estate management expenses are paid from the marital share and are attributable to other property. (Reg § 20.2056(b)-4(d)(4)) Estate transmission expenses are expenses that wouldn't have been incurred but for the necessity of collecting the decedent's assets, paying any debts and death taxes, and distributing the decedent's property. They include any administration expense that is not a management expense. (Reg § 20.2056(b)-4(d)(1)(ii)) Management expenses are those incurred in connection with the investment of estate assets or with their preservation or maintenance during a reasonable period of administration. (Reg § 20.2056(b)-4(d)(1)(i))[3]

---

45. ¶R-6393; ¶20,564.08
46. ¶R-6355
47. ¶R-6400; ¶20,564.08
48. ¶R-6413 *et seq.*; ¶20,564.08
49. ¶R-6421

50. ¶R-6431; ¶20,564.08
1. ¶R-6430
2. ¶R-6612 *et seq.*; ¶20,564.17
3. ¶R-6608; ¶20,564.05

¶ 5026   Marital deduction where surviving spouse isn't a U.S. citizen—qualified domestic trust (QDOT) requirement.

No marital deduction is allowed if the surviving spouse isn't a U.S. citizen (Code Sec. 2056(d)(1)(A); Reg § 20.2056A-1(a)), unless the property passes (or is treated as passing) to the spouse in a QDOT (Code Sec. 2056(d)(2))—a trust that satisfies certain requirements (Code Sec. 2056A; Reg § 20.2056A-2)—or the spouse timely becomes a citizen. (Code Sec. 2056(d)(4); Reg § 20.2056A-1(b))[4]

An estate tax is imposed (use Form 706-QDT) on any distribution (other than an income or a hardship distribution (Reg § 20.2056A-5(c))) from the trust before the date of the surviving spouse's death and on the value of the property remaining in the trust on the date of death of the surviving spouse (Code Sec. 2056A(b)(1)) (or the date the trust ceases to qualify). (Code Sec. 2056A(b)(3))[5]

¶ 5027   Deduction for state death taxes.

The value of the taxable estate is determined by deducting from the gross estate any estate, inheritance, legacy, or succession taxes actually paid to any state or the District of Columbia for any property included in the gross estate, but not including any taxes paid for the estate of a person other than the decedent. (Code Sec. 2058)[6]

¶ 5028   Applicable exclusion amount and applicable credit amount.

The applicable exclusion amount equals the decedent's basic exclusion and, in the case of a surviving spouse, the deceased spousal unused exclusion (DSUE) amount (see ¶5029), if any. (Code Sec. 2010(c)(2))

For decedents dying in 2018, the basic exclusion amount is \$11,180,000. The basic exclusion amount is adjusted annually for inflation. For decedents dying in 2019, as calculated by Thomson Reuters based on inflation data, the basic exclusion amount is \$11,400,000. (Code Sec. 2010(c)(3))

The applicable credit amount equals the amount of the tentative tax that would be owed under the rate schedule set forth at ¶1114 on an amount equal to the applicable exclusion amount. (Code Sec. 2010(c)(1)) For 2018, the applicable credit amount is \$4,417,800, which is the tax that would otherwise be imposed on \$11,180,000. For 2019, as calculated by Thomson Reuters based on inflation data, the applicable credit amount is \$4,505,800, which is the tax that would otherwise be imposed on \$11,400,000.

¶ 5029   Deceased spousal unused exclusion (DSUE) amount allows "portability" of unused part of exclusion of first spouse to die—Form 706, Part 6.

For a surviving spouse of a deceased spouse, the DSUE amount, used in computing the applicable credit amount against estate tax, see ¶5028, is the lesser of (1) the basic exclusion amount (see ¶5028), or (2) the excess of (a) the applicable exclusion amount of the last deceased spouse of the surviving spouse (below), over (b) the amount on which the tentative tax on the estate of the deceased spouse is determined. (Code Sec. 2010(c)(4))[7]

A DSUE amount may not be taken into account by a surviving spouse unless the fiduciary of the estate of the deceased spouse files an estate tax return on which the amount is computed, and makes an election on the return that the amount may be taken into account by the surviving spouse. The election, once made, is irrevocable. No election

---

4. ¶R-6201 *et seq.*; ¶s 20,564, 20,56A4
5. ¶R-7081 *et seq.*; ¶20,56A4.02

6. ¶R-6901; ¶20,584
7. ¶R-7107 *et seq.*; ¶20,104.01

may be made if the estate tax return of the deceased spouse is filed after the due date (including extensions) for filing the return. (Code Sec. 2010(c)(5)(A))[8]

The only action required to elect portability of the DSUE amount, if any, is to file a timely and complete Form 706. Executors who are not required to file Form 706 but who are filing to elect portability of the DSUE amount to the surviving spouse aren't required to report the value of certain property eligible for the marital deduction or the charitable deduction, but the value of those assets must be estimated and included in the total value of the gross estate. Taxpayers can opt out of electing to transfer any DSUE amount to a surviving spouse by checking the box on Section A of Part 6 of Form 706. (Reg § 20.2010-2(a))[9]

If the executor elects transfer or portability of the DSUE amount, the surviving spouse can apply the DSUE amount received from the estate of his or her last deceased spouse (see ¶5030) against any tax liability arising from subsequent lifetime gifts (by completing Schedule C of Form 709) and transfers at death. (Code Sec. 2010(c)(4), Reg § 20.2010-3)[10]

Applicable regs relating to Code Sec. 2010 don't prohibit IRS from examining the return of a predeceased spouse who elected portability when the second spouse dies. Further, IRS may adjust the DSUE amount by gifts made before Dec. 31, 2010, when the DSUE amount affects an estate tax return for a decedent dying after Dec. 31, 2010. [11]

¶ 5030 Last deceased spouse for purposes of the deceased spousal unused exclusion (DSUE) amount.

For purposes of determining the DSUE amount (¶5029), the "last deceased spouse" is the most recently deceased individual who, at that individual's death after Dec. 31, 2010, was married to the surviving spouse. (Reg § 20.2010-1(d)(5)) Later remarriage or divorce does not change the identity of the last deceased spouse. (Reg § 20.2010-3(a))[12]

¶ 5031 Deceased spousal unused exclusion (DSUE) amount for a non-citizen surviving spouse.

If a surviving spouse is not a U.S. citizen on the date of the last deceased spouse's (¶5030) death, but the surviving spouse becomes a U.S. citizen after the death of the last deceased spouse, then the DSUE amount of the surviving spouse's last deceased spouse is available to the surviving spouse on the date the surviving spouse becomes a U.S. citizen. This rule applies when the property of the last deceased spouse does not pass to the surviving spouse in a qualified domestic trust (QDOT, see ¶5026). Reg § 20.2010-3(c)(2)[13]

When property passes from a decedent for the benefit of a non-citizen surviving spouse in a QDOT, and portability is elected, the DSUE amount must be redetermined upon the occurrence of the final distribution or other event (generally the death of the surviving spouse or the earlier termination of all QDOTs for that surviving spouse) on which estate tax is imposed. Reg § 20.2010-2(c)(4)(i)[14]

Where a QDOT has been validly established, if the non-citizen surviving spouse beneficiary becomes a citizen of the U.S. after the death of the last deceased spouse, then the DSUE amount will become available to the surviving spouse (without redetermination, as described above) as of the date the surviving spouse becomes a U.S. citizen. (Reg § 20.2010-3(c)(3))[15]

---

8. ¶R-7110; ¶20,104.01
9. ¶R-7111; ¶20,104.01
10. ¶R-7109; ¶20,104.01
11. ¶R-7113

12. ¶R-7109; ¶20,104.01
13. ¶R-7112; ¶20,104.01
14. ¶R-7108; ¶20,104.01
15. ¶R-7112; ¶20,104.01

¶ 5032   Credit for tax on prior transfers—Form 706, Schedule Q.

Credit is allowed (on Form 706, Schedule Q) against the estate tax, for federal estate tax paid by the estate of another decedent (the transferor) on the transfer of property to the present decedent, where the transferor died within ten years before, or within two years after, the present decedent's death. (Code Sec. 2013)[16]

Where a transferor decedent was denied a marital deduction because the surviving spouse wasn't a U.S. citizen or where the estate tax on qualified domestic trust distributions applied (see ¶5026), the surviving spouse decedent is allowed a credit for the estate tax paid by the transferor decedent, or by the trust, without regard to when the transferor decedent died. (Code Sec. 2056(d)(3))[17]

¶ 5033   Credit for gift taxes paid on pre-'77 gifts.

Credit for gift taxes paid on pre-'77 gifts is allowed against the estate tax where gifts were made by a decedent before '77 of property included in the gross estate. (Code Sec. 2012(a))[18]

¶ 5034   Credit for foreign death taxes—Form 706, Schedule P.

Credit is allowed (on Form 706, Schedule P), subject to certain limits, against the estate tax for estate, inheritance, legacy, or succession taxes actually paid to any foreign country or U.S. possession. (Code Sec. 2014)[19]

¶ 5035   Computation of estate tax—Form 706.

First, compute a tentative tax under the unified rate schedule at ¶1114 (which applies a maximum tax rate of 40% for 2018 and 2019 transfers) on the total of: (1) the amount of the taxable estate (¶5018), and (2) the total amount of adjusted taxable gifts made by the decedent after '76 that aren't includible in the gross estate. (Code Sec. 2001(b)(1)) Then reduce this amount by the amount of gift tax payable on the decedent's post-'76 gifts to get the gross estate tax payable (before credits). The gift tax payable is the gift tax that would have been paid if the rates in effect at the time of the decedent's death had applied, and not the amount actually paid based on the rates in effect at the time of the gift. IRS is directed to issue regs to make any adjustments needed by changes in the basic exclusion amount at the time of a decedent's death and the exclusion amount that applies to any gifts made by the decedent. (Code Sec. 2001(b)(2); Code Sec. 2001(g))

The net estate tax payable is the gross estate tax minus the applicable credit amount (¶5028, previously called the unified credit) and allowable credits for gift taxes on pre-'77 gifts, estate taxes on earlier transfers, and foreign death taxes (¶5028 *et seq.*). (Code Sec. 2010, Code Sec. 2011, Code Sec. 2012, Code Sec. 2013, Code Sec. 2014)[20]

The estate of a "qualified decedent" who was an armed forces member, victim of terrorism, or an astronaut who died in the line of duty, is entitled to compute its estate tax liability under a special estate tax rate schedule containing lower rates. (Code Sec. 2201)[21]

¶ 5036   Return requirements—Form 706.

An executor must file an estate tax return Form 706 if the decedent's gross estate at death exceeds the basic exclusion amount for the calendar year of death ($11,180,000 for

---

16. ¶R-7300 *et seq.*; ¶20,134
17. ¶R-7301; ¶20,564
18. ¶R-7501; ¶20,124

19. ¶R-7400 *et seq.*; ¶20,144
20. ¶R-7001 *et seq.*; ¶20,014.02
21. ¶R-7011; ¶22,014

estates of individuals dying in 2018; $11,400,000 for 2019, as calculated by Thomson Reuters based on inflation data, see ¶5028). This dollar amount is reduced by certain gifts made by the decedent. (Code Sec. 6018(a)(1), Code Sec. 6018(a)(3))[22]

¶ 5037   When to file estate tax return.

Generally, an estate should file an estate tax return within nine months after the date of death. (Code Sec. 6075(a))[23]

IRS will grant an automatic 6-month extension to file Form 706 and may grant a 6-month discretionary filing extension (1) for estates that didn't seek an automatic extension, (2) to file Form 706-NA for the estates of nonresident alien, and (3) to file specialized estate tax forms for various recapture estate taxes (e.g., Form 706-A for recapture of special use valuation). (use Form 4768 for all extensions). An executor who is abroad can request a longer discretionary extension. (Reg § 20.6081-1)[24]

¶ 5038   When to pay tax.

The estate tax must be paid at the time for filing the return (see ¶5037). Filing extensions don't extend the time for payment (Reg § 20.6151-1),[25] but extensions of time to pay can be granted (use Form 4768) for reasonable cause. (Code Sec. 6161(a)(1))[26]

Special extensions (elected on Form 706) are available where a future interest is included in the estate (Code Sec. 6163)[27] or where the estate consists largely of a closely held business. (Code Sec. 6166)

Tax deferred under Code Sec. 6166 can be accelerated upon the happening of certain events, but IRS privately ruled that a change in the form of doing business will not result in such an acceleration.[28]

The estate tax on distributions made from qualified domestic trusts (QDOTs, see ¶5026), before the surviving spouse's death is due on Apr. 15 of the year following the calendar year the taxable event occurs. (Code Sec. 2056A(b)(5))[29]

¶ 5039   Estate tax closing letters.

Estate tax closing letters are issued only upon request by the taxpayer. Authorized representatives may request a hardcopy account transcript, which is an acceptable substitute for an estate tax closing letter, by submitting Form 4506-T. Also, the Transcript Delivery Service (TDS) may be used by registered tax professionals to request an online transcript.[30]

¶ 5040   Estates of nonresident aliens—Form 706-NA.

Decedents who were neither U.S. citizens nor U.S. residents are taxed only on the transfer of property situated within the U.S. (on Form 706-NA). With that exception, the make-up of the gross estate is the same as that for a U.S. citizen or resident. (Code Sec. 2103)

The same rate schedule that applies to the estates of U.S. citizens (¶1114) applies to the estates of nonresident aliens. (Code Sec. 2101(b))

A marital deduction is allowed under the principles of the regular marital deduction

22. ¶S-2300 *et seq.*; ¶60,184
23. ¶S-4902; ¶60,754
24. ¶S-5035.1; ¶60,814
25. ¶S-5851; ¶61,514
26. ¶S-5900 *et seq.*; ¶61,614

27. ¶S-5910; ¶61,634
28. ¶S-6000 *et seq.*; ¶61,664
29. ¶R-7085 *et seq.*; ¶20,56A4.02
30. ¶T-4511

rules (¶5021 *et seq.*), with respect to U.S. property. (Code Sec. 2106(a)(3)) Estates of non-resident aliens may deduct a portion of certain expenses and losses, such as funeral and administration expenses and debts with respect to property included in the gross estate. The portion is determined by the proportion of the value of the gross estate situated in the U.S. to the value of all estate property, wherever situated. (Code Sec. 2106)

An applicable credit of $13,000 is allowed against the estate tax of nonresident aliens, with an alternative credit computation for estates of certain residents of U.S. possessions (Code Sec. 2102(b)(1), Code Sec. 2102(b)(2)), and to the extent required under certain treaty obligations of the U.S. (Code Sec. 2102(b)(3)(A)) The $13,000 is reduced by any gift tax applicable credit allowed. (Code Sec. 2102(b)(3)(B))

Credits are also allowed for estate tax on prior transfers and gift tax on certain pre-'77 gifts. (Code Sec. 2102(b)(5))[31]

An estate tax return on Form 706-NA must be filed for the estate of every nonresident not a U.S. citizen if the value of the part of the estate in the U.S. exceeds $60,000 (Code Sec. 6018(a)(2)), reduced by: (1) the amount of adjusted taxable gifts made by the decedent after '76, and (2) the amount of any pre-'77 specific exemption allowed for gifts made by the decedent after Sept. 8, '76. (Code Sec. 6018(a)(3))[32] The time for filing the return is the same as for U.S. citizens or residents, see ¶5037.

Expatriates and former long-term residents who gave up citizenship or terminated residency before June 17, 2008. A tougher expatriate estate tax is imposed on the transfer of a taxable estate of a decedent nonresident non-U.S. citizen who dies during the 10-year period that he or she is subject to the expatriate alternative tax described at ¶4645. (Code Sec. 2107(a))[33]

Expatriates and former long-term residents who gave up citizenship or terminated residency after June 16, 2008. A special transfer tax (the Code Sec. 2801 tax) is imposed on any U.S. citizen or resident who receives any "covered gift or bequest" from a "covered expatriate," see ¶4640. (Code Sec. 2801(a)) The tax applies to any covered gift or bequest valued in excess of the annual exclusion amount in effect for gift tax purposes in the year of the transfer. (Code Sec. 2801(c)) The amount of the Code Sec. 2801 tax is determined by multiplying the value of the covered gift or bequest by the greater of (i) the highest estate tax rate listed in the Code Sec. 2001(c) rate table in effect on the date the transferee receives the covered gift or bequest, or (ii) the highest gift tax rate listed in the Code Sec. 2502(a) rate table in effect on that date. (Code Sec. 2801(a))[34]

¶ 5041 Gift Tax.

The gift tax is integrated with the estate tax under a "unified" rate schedule (¶1114) that imposes a single tax on transfers during life and at death (see ¶5000) which effectively imposes no tax on gifts unless the total amount of taxable gifts for the year and all prior years exceeds $11,180,000 for 2018 ($11,400,000 for 2019, as calculated by Thomson Reuters based on inflation data).

The tax is imposed on the transfer, not on the property transferred. It applies even though the property transferred may be exempt from income or other taxes. (Code Sec. 2501(a); Reg § 25.2501-1, Reg § 25.2511-1(a), Reg § 25.2511-2)[35]

For who must pay the gift tax, see ¶5042; what a gift is, ¶5043 *et seq.*; allowable exclusions and deductions, ¶5049 *et seq.*; credits against the tax, ¶5053; how the tax is computed, ¶5054 *et seq.*; and return requirements, ¶5058.

---

31. ¶R-8000 *et seq.*; ¶21,014.02
32. ¶S-2302; ¶60,184
33. ¶R-8033; ¶21,074

34. ¶R-8101
35. ¶Q-1000 *et seq.*; ¶s 25,009, 25,014

¶ 5042   Who must pay gift tax?

The gift tax must be paid by the person (the donor) who makes the gift. (Code Sec. 2501(a); Reg § 25.2511-2(f)) It applies only to donors who are individuals (Reg § 25.2501-1(b)), but a gift by a corporation may be treated as a gift by the shareholders. (Reg § 25.2511-1(h)(1))[36]

If the donor fails to pay the tax when due, the donee is also liable for the tax to the extent of the value of the gift (Code Sec. 6324(b); Reg § 25.2502-2, Reg § 301.6324-1(b)), and potentially for interest on that amount. [37]

These rules apply to a U.S. citizen or resident no matter where the gift property (tangible or intangible) is situated. (Code Sec. 2501(a); Reg § 25.2501-1(a), Reg § 25.2511-3(a))[38]

A nonresident who's not a U.S. citizen is subject to gift tax only if the gift property is real estate or tangible personal property and is situated in the U.S. at the time of the gift. (Code Sec. 2501(a), Code Sec. 2511(a); Reg § 25.2511-1(b), Reg § 25.2511-3(a)) A nonresident generally isn't subject to tax on a gift of intangible property. (Code Sec. 2501(a)(2))

For a special transfer tax for recipients of gifts and bequests from expatriates and former long-term residents who gave up citizenship or terminated residency after June 16, 2008, see ¶5040.

¶ 5043   What is a gift?

All transactions whereby property or property rights are gratuitously bestowed on another are gifts. (Reg § 25.2511-1(c))

A gift isn't complete until the donor parts with dominion or control over the transferred property or property interest. The donor must be left without power to change the disposition of the property either for the donor's own benefit or for that of others. (Reg § 25.2511-2(b))[39]

A transfer of property by a shareholder to a corporation for less than adequate consideration represents gifts to the other individual shareholders of the corporation to the extent of their proportionate interests. (Reg § 25.2511-1(h)(1))

There's no gift tax on a transfer to a political organization. (Code Sec. 2501(a)(4))[40] Also, there is no gift tax on contributions to certain tax-exempt organizations, including: non-profit civic organizations operated exclusively for social welfare and local employees' associations whose net earnings are used solely for charitable, educational or recreational purposes that are exempt under Code Sec. 501(c)(4); labor, agricultural or horticultural organizations that are exempt under Code Sec. 501(c)(5); and chambers of commerce, business leagues, real estate boards, boards of trade or professional football leagues not organized for profit or private benefit that are exempt under Code Sec. 501(c)(6). (Code Sec. 2501(a)(6))[41]

¶ 5044   Below-market loans.

If a below-market (or interest-free) loan is a "gift loan" (that is, a below-market loan where the forgoing of interest is in the nature of a gift), it's treated as: (1) a loan to the borrower/donee in exchange for an interest-paying note, and (2) a gift to the borrower of the funds to pay the interest. The amount of the gift equals:

. . . the forgone interest—excess of interest payable at the applicable federal rate (AFR,

---

36. ¶s Q-1000 *et seq.*, Q-2400 *et seq.*; ¶s 25,014, 25,114
37. ¶V-9301; ¶63,244
38. ¶Q-1016; ¶25,014, 25,114

39. ¶Q-3004; ¶25,114.01
40. ¶Q-3201; ¶25,014
41. ¶Q-3203; ¶25,014

¶1118) over actual interest payable —if the loan is a demand loan; or

. . . the excess of the amount loaned over the present value (using a discount rate equal to the AFR) of all payments required under the terms of the loan, if the gift loan is a term loan. (Code Sec. 7872)[42]

For demand loans, the gift is treated as made on the last day of the calendar year. (Code Sec. 7872(a)) For term loans, the gift is treated as made on the date the loan was made. (Code Sec. 7872(b))[43]

These rules don't apply to certain gift loans between individuals that don't exceed $10,000. (Code Sec. 7872(c)(2))[44]

If the outstanding balance of a gift loan made between individuals is $100,000 or less, the amount of interest treated as retransferred by the borrower to the lender each year doesn't exceed the borrower's net investment income for that year. If the net investment income is $1,000 or less, the amount treated as retransferred is zero. (Code Sec. 7872(d)(1))[45]

¶ 5045   Joint ownership of property.

A gift may result where property is placed in joint ownership with someone other than a spouse or where joint ownership with someone other than a spouse ends. [46]

If an individual buys property with her own funds and has the title conveyed to herself and others as joint tenants with rights of survivorship, but these rights may be defeated by any joint tenant severing their interest, there is an immediate gift to the other joint tenants of equal shares of the property. (Reg § 25.2511-1(h)(5))[47]

An individual doesn't make a gift by merely opening a joint bank account with his own funds for himself and another person from which he can regain the entire funds without the other's consent; rather, a gift is made only when the other person withdraws money for that other person's own benefit. [48]

¶ 5046   Qualified disclaimers.

A qualified disclaimer (an irrevocable and unqualified refusal to accept ownership, made in writing by a specified deadline) with respect to any interest in property has the effect of treating that interest, for gift (and estate and generation-skipping transfer tax) purposes, as if it had never been transferred to the disclaimant. (Code Sec. 2518) And the disclaimant isn't treated as having made a gift to the person to whom the interest passes by reason of the disclaimer. (Reg § 25.2518-1(b))[49]

¶ 5047   Amount of the gift.

The amount of the gift is the money given or, if property is given, the property's value as of the date of the gift, less any consideration received. (Code Sec. 2512(a))[50] For a "net gift," i.e., a gift conditioned on the gift tax being paid by the donee, the value of the gift is reduced by the gift tax amount. The Tax Court has held that a donee's agreement to pay the potential estate tax liability under Code Sec. 2035(b) (¶5003) reduces the value of the gift.[1]

The market value of annuities (other than commercial annuities), unitrust interests, life

---

42. ¶Q-2150 et seq.; ¶78,724
43. ¶Q-2150; ¶78,724
44. ¶Q-2165; ¶78,724
45. ¶J-2905; ¶78,724
46. ¶Q-2900 et seq.; ¶25,114

47. ¶Q-2906; ¶25,114
48. ¶Q-2921 et seq.
49. ¶Q-2350 et seq.; ¶25,184
50. ¶Q-1200; ¶25,124
1. ¶Q-1400

estates, term of years, remainders, and reversions transferred by gift is determined by use of standard or special Code Sec. 7520 actuarial factors. (Reg § 25.2512-5(a), Reg § 25.7520-1(a)) These factors are derived by using the appropriate Code Sec. 7520 interest rate[2] and, if applicable, the mortality component for the valuation date of the interest that's being valued. These factors appear in IRS issued tables. (Reg § 25.2512-5(d)(1))[3]

A taxable gift can also occur under Code Sec. 2701 (certain transfers of partnership or corporation interests), even though there may not be a taxable gift under normal tax rules. The amount of the gift is determined under the valuation rules of that Code section. [4]

¶ 5048   Taxable gifts.

Taxable gifts are the gifts made during the calendar year after the annual exclusion (¶5049), and reduced by allowable deductions (¶5051, ¶5052). (Code Sec. 2503(a), Code Sec. 2503(b))[5]

¶ 5049   Annual exclusion.

For 2018 (and 2019, as calculated by Thomson Reuters based on inflation data), the first $15,000 of gifts of a present interest made by a donor *to each donee* is excluded from the amount of the donor's taxable gifts. (Code Sec. 2503(b))[6] For 2018, the first $152,000 of gifts made by a donor to a spouse who isn't a U.S. citizen is excluded ($155,000 for 2019, as calculated by Thomson Reuters based on inflation data). (Code Sec. 2523(i)(2))[7]

No annual exclusion is allowed for gifts of future interests (Code Sec. 2503(b); Reg § 25.2503-2), e.g., reversions or remainders. (Reg § 25.2503-3)[8]

A "Crummey" power (in general, a trust beneficiary's noncumulative right to withdraw a specified amount of trust principal within a limited period) makes a transfer to the trust a gift of a present interest, but not if the Crummey power is unenforceable in a state court.[9]

A transfer for the benefit of a *minor* isn't considered a gift of a future interest if the property and its income:

(1) may be expended by or for the benefit of the minor before the minor reaches 21, and

(2) any balance not so expended *will pass to the minor* when the minor reaches 21, or if the minor dies before 21 will go either to the minor's *estate* or as the minor may appoint under a general power of appointment. (Code Sec. 2503(c); Reg § 25.2503-4(a))[10]

Gifts to minors made through custodians designated under Uniform Acts for gifts or transfers to minors qualify for the annual exclusion. [11]

¶ 5050   Educational or medical payment exclusion.

The gift tax doesn't apply to amounts paid by one individual:

(1) on behalf of another individual directly to a qualifying educational organization as tuition for that other individual. (Code Sec. 2503(e); Reg § 25.2503-6(b)(2))

(2) on behalf of another individual directly to a provider of medical care as payment for that medical care. (Code Sec. 2503(e); Reg § 25.2503-6(b)(3)) Payments for medical insurance qualify for this exclusion. (Reg § 25.2503-6(b)(3))

2. ¶P-6619
3. ¶P-6615; ¶25,124
4. ¶Q-3402
5. ¶Q-1000; ¶25,034
6. ¶Q-5000 *et seq.*; ¶25,034

7. ¶Q-5003; ¶25,034
8. ¶Q-5100 *et seq.*; ¶25,034
9. ¶Q-5112; ¶25,034
10. ¶Q-5201 *et seq.*; ¶25,034
11. ¶Q-5212; ¶25,034

These exclusions are available in addition to the annual gift tax exclusion (¶5049). (Reg § 25.2503-6(a))[12] No gift tax return is required. (Code Sec. 6019)[13]

Contributions to qualified tuition programs (QTPs, ¶2209 *et seq.*) and Coverdell Education Savings Accounts (CESAs, ¶2205 *et seq.*) don't qualify for the Code Sec. 2503(e) tuition exclusion, but are instead treated as present gifts that can qualify for the gift tax annual exclusion including by electively spreading contributions in a single year over a five-year period. A contributor isn't subject to gift tax on distributions from QTPs and CESAs. (Code Sec. 529(c), Code Sec. 530(d)(3)) A transfer by reason of a change in the designated beneficiary under a QTP, or a rollover to the account of a new beneficiary, is subject to gift and generation-skipping transfer taxes unless the new beneficiary is: (1) assigned to the same generation as, or a higher generation than, the old beneficiary; and (2) a member of the old beneficiary's family. (Code Sec. 529(c)(5)(B))

¶ 5051 Marital deduction.

A marital deduction is allowed for the value of all qualifying gifts made by one spouse to the other if the donee spouse is a U.S. citizen (with some exceptions) and the gift isn't a nondeductible "terminable interest." (Code Sec. 2523)[14]

Qualified terminable interest property (QTIP) qualifies for the deduction if the donee spouse receives income payments for life and no person has a power to appoint any part of the property to anyone other than the donee spouse during that spouse's life. (Code Sec. 2523(f))[15]

For an increased exclusion for transfers to noncitizen spouses, see ¶5049.

If an estate (¶5023) or gift tax QTIP marital deduction is taken, the QTIP property is included in the spouse's estate on death (¶5008). However, transfer tax is accelerated if the spouse makes a gift of the income interest. Under Code Sec. 2519, if a spouse makes a gift of any portion of the qualifying income interest in the QTIP trust, the spouse is deemed to make a transfer of the entire value of the remainder. [16]

¶ 5052 Charitable gifts.

Charitable gifts and certain similar gifts are deducted in arriving at taxable gifts for the calendar year. (Code Sec. 2522)[17] A number of Courts of Appeal have upheld the use of defined value formula clauses to limit the gift tax liability resulting from transfers of hard-to-value assets (e.g., closely held stock or family limited partnership interests), by reallocating the transferred assets among charitable and noncharitable donees when the value of the assets is increased on audit of the gift tax return. [18]

¶ 5053 Credit against gift tax.

For gifts made in 2018, the credit will be $4,417,800 (the amount that exempts the $11,180,000 basic exclusion amount for 2018 from gift tax). For gifts made in 2019, as calculated by Thomson Reuters based on inflation data, the credit will be $4,505,800 (the amount that exempts the $11,400,000 basic exclusion amount for 2019 from gift tax). See ¶5028.

The credit against tax on gifts in a calendar year is reduced by the sum of all amounts allowable as a credit in preceding calendar periods. In determining this reduction, the gift tax rates that are in effect for the calendar year of the gift (instead of the rates in effect for

12. ¶Q-5250 *et seq.*; ¶25,034
13. ¶S-2201; ¶25,014
14. ¶Q-6100 *et seq.*; ¶25,234
15. ¶Q-6300 *et seq.*; ¶25,234

16. ¶Q-6315; ¶25,194
17. ¶Q-6000 *et seq.*; ¶25,224
18. ¶Q-1983.2

the preceding calendar periods) are used in determining the amounts allowable as a credit for all preceding calendar periods. (Code Sec. 2505)[19] The instructions to Form 709 contain a worksheet that is used to determine the amount of the applicable credit amount used for post-'76 gifts where prior gifts total more than $500,000.

¶ 5054   How to compute gift tax if no gifts made before current year.

If a person has *not* made any taxable gifts (in excess of annual exclusions and deductions and the pre-'77 specific lifetime exemption) before the calendar year for which the tax is being computed, the gift tax is computed as follows: [20]

(1) Determine the aggregate value of the total gifts made during the calendar year for which the tax is being computed. If the donor is married, and the donor and the donor's spouse have consented to split their gifts to third parties, only half of the gifts the donor made to third parties plus half of the gifts, if any, the donor's spouse made to third parties are included in computing the donor's total gifts. (A separate gift tax computation is made for the spouse, and the other half of the donor's gifts to third parties plus the other half of the spouse's gifts to third parties are included in computing the spouse's total gifts.)

(2) Deduct from the amount in (1), above, any amounts qualifying for the year's annual exclusion (¶5049).

(3) From the excess of (1) over (2), above, subtract the amount of charitable (¶5052) and marital (¶5051) gifts.

(4) Compute a gift tax on the excess of (1) over the sum of (2) and (3); for gifts made during 2018 or 2019, use the rate schedule at ¶1114.

(5) Subtract from the gift tax computed in (4) the allowable unified credit (now called the applicable credit amount).

¶ 5055   Cumulative computation where gifts were made before current year.

Previous taxable gifts affect the amount of gift tax imposed on gifts made in the current year. These taxable gifts are taken into account whether they were made before '77 or after '76. (Code Sec. 2502) In general, the gift tax (before the applicable credit amount) is the excess of: (1) a tentative tax computed under the unified rate schedules on the aggregate sum of taxable gifts for the current calendar year for which the tax is being computed *and* taxable gifts for all preceding years, over (2) a tentative tax (determined on the basis of the gift tax rates in effect for the current year, see ¶5053) on the aggregate sum of the taxable gifts for all of the years preceding the current calendar year for which the tax is being computed. (Code Sec. 2502(a)) The gift tax payable is the excess of the tentative tax in (1) over the tentative tax in (2), reduced by the applicable credit amount allowable. [21]

¶ 5056   Split gifts to third parties by married donors.

Spouses may consent to have their gifts to others treated as if made one-half by each (Code Sec. 2513(a); Reg § 25.2513-1) if:

. . . both spouses are U.S. citizens or residents on the date of the gift (Code Sec. 2513(a));

. . . both spouses consent (on Form 709) to have all gifts made to others in the calendar year treated as split gifts (Code Sec. 2513(a), Code Sec. 2513(b), Code Sec. 2513(c); Reg § 25.2513-1(b)(5)); and

. . . the consenting spouses are married to each other on the date of the gift and don't

19. ¶Q-8005; ¶25,054
20. ¶Q-8010 *et seq.*; ¶25,009

21. ¶Q-8011; ¶25,024

remarry during the remainder of the calendar year. (Code Sec. 2513(a))[22]

Each spouse is liable, jointly and severally, for the *entire* gift tax for the period in which he or she consents to split gifts. (Code Sec. 2513(d); Reg § 25.2513-4)[23]

Gifts of community property to a third party are generally considered to have been made one half by each spouse. [24]

¶ 5057 Gift tax on "estate freeze" transfers (Chapter 14 rules).

For gift tax valuation purposes, certain interests retained by the transferor after a transfer to a family member are disregarded. These Chapter 14 (of the Code) rules apply to:[25]

. . . transfers of interests in corporations and partnerships;

. . . transfers of interests in trusts (other than certain trusts known as GRATs, GRUTs, and qualified personal residence trusts, see below);

. . . buy-sell agreements and options; and

. . . lapsing rights.

An individual can save transfer tax by setting up a GRAT (grantor retained annuity trust). The individual retains an annuity interest for a specified term at the expiration of which the trust property goes to a child or other individual named at the outset. Gift tax is payable but only on the present value of the remainder interest. Some GRATs are structured so that the present value of the individual's annuity equals virtually 100% of what the individual puts into the trust. Such a so-called "zeroed-out GRAT" eliminates gift tax on the transfer and allows wealth to be transferred free of any gift or estate tax if the property appreciates and the grantor survives the term.

A GRIT (grantor retained income trust) is like a GRAT, except that the grantor retains an income interest instead of an annuity interest. Code Sec. 2702 generally treats the grantor as making a gift of the full value of the property. However, the value of the gift of the remainder is determined under the valuation tables where the trust is funded with a personal residence of the grantor or the remainder goes to someone falling outside of the definition of a family member.

A GRUT is a grantor retained unitrust.

¶ 5058 Gift tax returns—Form 709.

Any individual who makes gifts to any one donee during a calendar year that aren't fully excluded under the annual exclusion (see ¶5049) must file a gift tax return (Form 709). A return must be filed even if no tax is payable. (Reg § 25.6019-1(f)) But, no return is required to report a qualified transfer for educational or medical costs (¶5050), most charitable transfers, or a transfer that qualifies for the marital deduction (¶5051) (Code Sec. 6019), except that a return must be filed to make a QTIP (¶5051) election. (Reg § 25.6019-1(a))[26] The return is due on Apr. 15 of the year following the year the gifts were made. (Code Sec. 6075) A different rule applies if the donor has died. [27] An extension for filing the income tax return automatically extends the time for filing the gift tax return for the same calendar year. (Code Sec. 6075(b)(2)) Use Form 8892 to request an extension of time to file Form 709 when not applying for an extension to file an income tax return or to make a payment of gift (or GST) tax when applying for an extension of time to file Form

---

22. ¶Q-7000 *et seq.*; ¶25,134
23. ¶V-8505 *et seq.*; ¶25,134
24. ¶Q-2929 *et seq.*; ¶25,134.01

25. ¶Q-3350; ¶s 27,014, 27,024, 27,034, 27,044
26. ¶S-2200 *et seq.*; ¶s 25,014, 60,194
27. ¶S-4901; ¶60,754

709. (Reg § 25.6081-1)[28]

¶ 5059   Generation-Skipping Transfer (GST) Tax. ▆▆▆▆▆▆▆▆▆▆

A GST tax is imposed on transfers outright or in trust to beneficiaries more than one generation below the transferor's generation at a rate equal to the maximum gift and estate tax rate, which is 40% (Code Sec. 2001(c)), multiplied by the "inclusion ratio." (Code Sec. 2641)[29]

The GST tax generally applies to GSTs made after Oct. 22, '86. (Tax Reform Act of '86 (TRA '86) § 1431(a)) However, it doesn't apply to any GST from a "grandfathered" trust that was irrevocable on Sept. 25, '85, unless the transfer is made out of corpus added to the trust after Sept. 25, '85. (TRA '86 § 1433(b)(2)(A))

A GST is any one of three taxable events: (1) a *taxable termination* of an interest in a trust if, after the termination, all interests in the trust are held by or for the benefit of persons two or more generations below that of the transferor (trustee pays the GST tax on taxable terminations on Form 706GS(T)), (2) a *taxable distribution* of income or principal from a trust to or for the benefit of a person two or more generations below that of the transferor (transferee pays the tax on Form 706GS(D), the trustee must file Form 706GS(D-1)), and (3) a *direct skip,* which is a transfer of an interest in property to or for the benefit of a person two or more generations below that of the transferor (transferor pays tax with Form 709 for lifetime direct skips, executor pays with Form 706 and attached Form 706, Schedule R or Form 706, Schedule R-1, for direct skips occurring at death). (Code Sec. 2611(a), Code Sec. 2612) (Use Form 8892 to request an extension of time to file Form 709 when not applying for an extension to file an income tax return or to make a payment of GST tax when applying for an extension of time to file Form 709.) In determining whether there is a GST, a special rule "steps up" the generation of an individual (or the descendants of an individual) with a deceased parent that's a descendant of the transferor's parent. (Code Sec. 2651(e)(1); Reg § 26.2651-1)[30]

¶ 5060   Exemptions from tax.

Every individual is allowed an exemption equal to the estate tax basic exclusion ($11,180,000 for 2018, $11,400,000 for 2019, as calculated by Thomson Reuters based on inflation data; see ¶5028), which may be allocated to any property transferred. (Code Sec. 2631) Married couples may treat transfers as made one-half by each spouse, in effect giving them a combined $22,360,000 exemption for transfers in 2018 ($22,800,000 in 2019, as calculated by Thomson Reuters based on inflation data). (Code Sec. 2652(a)(2))[31] Once a transfer is designated as exempt, all later appreciation in the value of the exempt property is also exempt.[32] The tax doesn't apply to lifetime transfers (except for certain transfers in trust) that are exempt from gift tax because of the annual exclusion (¶5049) or the exclusion for certain tuition and medical expense payments (¶5050). (Code Sec. 2642(c)(3)) For lifetime transfers, the available GST exemption is automatically allocated to a direct skip under Code Sec. 2632(b), and to indirect skips made after Dec. 31, 2000 under Code Sec. 2632(c), unless the individual elects out of the automatic allocation under Code Sec. 2632(b)(3) and Code Sec. 2632(c)(5), respectively. The automatic allocation under Code Sec. 2632(c) also applies to an indirect skip occurring upon the post-2000 termination of an estate tax inclusion period. (Code Sec. 2632(c)(4)) Regs provide details about these elections. (Reg § 26.2632-1)[33]

---

28. ¶S-5035; ¶s 60,754, 60,814

29. ¶R-9575; ¶26,414

30. ¶R-9500 *et seq.*; ¶26,014, 26,114, 26,124

31. ¶R-9551; ¶s 26,014, 26,314

32. ¶R-9557; ¶26,324

33. ¶R-9501 *et seq.*; ¶26,424

¶ 5061　　Computation of GST tax—Form 706, Schedule R.

The amount of GST tax imposed on any GST is the "taxable amount" multiplied by the "applicable rate." (Code Sec. 2602) The calculation of the GST tax is made on Form 706, Schedule R.

The "taxable amount" is the value of the property subject to GST tax and depends on what type of GST is involved (see ¶5059).[34]

The "applicable rate" is the product of the maximum federal estate tax rate (40%) and the "inclusion ratio," which is determined according to the amount of the GST exemption allocated to the trust (or allocated to the property transferred in the skip in cases of a direct skip).[35]

---

34. ¶R-9571 *et seq.*; ¶26,014　　　　　　　35. ¶R-9575*et seq.*; ¶26,014

INDEX

References are to paragraph [¶] numbers.

A

Abandonment
. deductible loss 1776
. depreciable property 1906; 1909
. mortgaged property, loss on 1780
. oil and gas properties 1965
. passive activity losses 1801
. reorganizations 3544
. reporting of, for secured property 4746
Abatement of interest 4861; 4872
ABLE accounts for the disabled or blind . . . 2226; 2358
Abortion, as medical expense 2144
**Above-the-line deductions (adjustments
    to income)**
    generally 3102
. Archer medical savings account (MSA)
    contributions 1527
. business-related expenses of statutory em-
    ployees . . . . 3103 et seq.
. educators' professional development and
    classroom expenses 2224
. health savings account (HSA) contributions . . . 1528
. higher education expenses 2225
. IRA contributions 4340; 4341
. military reservists, overnight travel ex-
    penses 1548
. student loan interest 2220; 2221
. taxes 1749
Abusive tax shelters
. debt instruments issued in connection with 1314
. penalties 4834; 4891
Accident and health insurance plans *See
    "Health and accident insurance plans"*
Accountants
. audits by IRS, representing taxpayer at 4807
. expenses of 1617
. fees for 1586; 5018
Accounting income 3936
Accounting methods *See also "Accrual ba-
    sis"; "Cash basis"*
    generally . . . . 2816 et seq.
. advance trade discount method 2824
. carryover by successor corporation 3550
. changes of
    generally . . . . 2818; 2834 et
                                                    seq.
. . adjustments required . . . . 2838 et seq.
. . application for 2837
. . automatic consent procedure 2837; 2842;
                                                    4520
. . definition 2836
. . depreciation, accounting for 1901; 2836
. . four-year/one-year rule, adjustment inclu-
    sion periods 2840
. . high-impact adjustments, relief for 2841
. . inventories 2862; 2875
. . IRS permission to change 2835
. establishing method 2817
. farmers . . . . 4505 et seq.
. limits on choice of 2818

Accounting methods *See also "Accrual basis"; "Cash basis"*
    — Cont'd
. long-term contracts . . . . 2844 et seq.
. nonaccrual experience method 2823
Accounting period . . . . 2800 et seq.
                                        *See also "Tax-
                                         able year"*
Accounting reserves, deductibility 2843
Accounts receivable
. amortization 1968
. basis of 2470
. capital assets, as 2612
Accrual basis
. advance payments . . . . 2827 et seq.
. charitable deductions, corporate 2133
. compensation for personal services
. . time for deduction . . . . 1536 et seq.
. . time to report 1271
. contested liability 1760; 2832
. contingent rights to income 2824
. dealers' reserves 2826
. decedents 3963
. deductions . . . . 2830 et seq.
. disputed liability for goods, income accrual
    for 2825
. economic performance 2831
. farmers . . . . 4509 et seq.
. gain or loss on sale or exchange 2407
. income recognition . . . . 2823 et seq.
. insurance premiums, deduction of 1590
. interest income, time to report 1332; 1334
. interest paid, time to deduct 1741
. payroll tax liability 1537
. previously reported income, repayments of,
    time for deduction 2855
. real property tax
. . apportioned between buyer and seller 1762
. . election to accrue ratably 1761
. . time for deduction 1763
. recurring item exception 2831
. related cash basis taxpayer, payments to 2833
. rental income, time to report 1336
. royalties 1342
. small taxpayer exceptions 2818
. taxes, time for deduction . . . . 1759 et seq.
Accrued market discount . . . . 1321 et seq.
Accumulated adjustments account 3372; 3374
Accumulated earnings tax
    generally 3317
. accumulated taxable income 3319
. controlled group 3338
. credit, accumulated earnings 3320
. dividends-paid deduction . . . . 3331 et seq.
. reasonable needs of business, accumula-
    tions for 3318; 3320
Accumulation distributions 3952; 3953
Achievement awards, employee *See "Em-
    ployee achievement awards"*
Acquisition indebtedness
. corporate, interest on 1725
. exempt organizations 4125

References are to paragraph [¶] numbers.

References are to paragraph [¶] numbers.

References are to paragraph [¶] numbers.

References are to paragraph [¶] numbers.

References are to paragraph [¶] numbers.

MARGIN INDEX
To use, bend book in half and follow margin index to page with black edge marker.

The left index column refers to the left bank of markers; the right index column
to the right bank of markers.